Weiss Ratings' Guide to Health Insurers

Weiss Ratings' Guide to Health Insurers

A Quarterly Compilation of Health Insurance Company Ratings and Analyses

Winter 2019-20

GREY HOUSE PUBLISHING

Weiss Ratings
4400 Northcorp Parkway
Palm Beach Gardens, FL 33410
561-627-3300

WeissRatings
Independent. Unbiased. Accurate. Trusted.

Published by Grey House Publishing, Inc., located at 4919 Route 22, Amenia, NY 12501; telephone 518-789-8700. Grey House Publishing neither guarantees the accuracy of the data contained herein nor assumes any responsibility for errors, omissions or discrepancies. Grey House Publishing accepts no payment for listing; inclusion in the publication of any organization, agency, institution, publication, service or individual does not imply endorsement of the publisher.

Grey House Publishing
4919 Route 22
PO Box 56
Amenia, NY 12501-0056

Edition No. 99, Winter 2019-20

ISBN: 978-1-64265-559-9
ISSN: 2158-5938

Contents

Terms and Conditions

This document is prepared strictly for the confidential use of our customer(s). It has been provided to you at your specific request. It is not directed to, or intended for distribution to or use by, any person or entity who is a citizen or resident of or located in any locality, state, country or other jurisdiction where such distribution, publication, availability or use would be contrary to law or regulation or which would subject Weiss Ratings or its affiliates to any registration or licensing requirement within such jurisdiction.

No part of the analysts' compensation was, is, or will be, directly or indirectly, related to the specific recommendations or views expressed in this research report.

This document is not intended for the direct or indirect solicitation of business. Weiss Ratings, LLC and its affiliates disclaims any and all liability to any person or entity for any loss or damage caused, in whole or in part, by any error (negligent or otherwise) or other circumstances involved in, resulting from or relating to the procurement, compilation, analysis, interpretation, editing, transcribing, publishing and/or dissemination or transmittal of any information contained herein.

Weiss Ratings has not taken any steps to ensure that the securities or investment vehicle referred to in this report are suitable for any particular investor. The investment or services contained or referred to in this report may not be suitable for you and it is recommended that you consult an independent investment advisor if you are in doubt about such investments or investment services. Nothing in this report constitutes investment, legal, accounting or tax advice or a representation that any investment or strategy is suitable or appropriate to your individual circumstances or otherwise constitutes a personal recommendation to you.

The ratings and other opinions contained in this document must be construed solely as statements of opinion from Weiss Ratings, LLC, and not statements of fact. Each rating or opinion must be weighed solely as a factor in your choice of an institution and should not be construed as a recommendation to buy, sell or otherwise act with respect to the particular product or company involved.

Past performance should not be taken as an indication or guarantee of future performance, and no representation or warranty, expressed or implied, is made regarding future performance. Information, opinions and estimates contained in this report reflect a judgment at its original date of publication and are subject to change without notice. Weiss Ratings offers a notification service for rating changes on companies you specify. For more information visit WeissRatings.com or call 1-877-934-7778. The price, value and income from any of the securities or financial instruments mentioned in this report can fall as well as rise.

Message To Insurers

All data on insurers filing a Health financial statement received on or before August 15, 2019 has been considered or incorporated into this edition of the Directory. If there are particular circumstances which you believe could affect your rating, please use the online survey (http://weissratings.com/survey/) or e-mail Weiss Ratings (insurancesurvey@weissinc.com) with documentation to support your request. If warranted, we will make every effort to incorporate the changes in our next edition.

Welcome to Weiss Ratings'
Guide to Health Insurers

Most people automatically assume their insurance company will survive, year after year. However, prudent consumers and professionals realize that in this world of shifting risks, the solvency of insurance companies can't be taken for granted.

If you are looking for accurate, unbiased ratings and data to help you choose health insurance for yourself, your family, your company, or your clients, *Weiss Ratings Guide to Health Insurers* gives you precisely what you need.

In fact, it's the only source that currently provides ratings and analyses on over 1,000 health insurers.

Weiss Ratings' Mission Statement

Weiss Ratings' mission is to empower consumers, professionals, and institutions with high quality advisory information for selecting or monitoring a financial services company or financial investment.

In doing so, Weiss Ratings will adhere to the highest ethical standards by maintaining our independent, unbiased outlook and approach to advising our customers.

Why rely on Weiss Ratings?

Weiss Ratings provides fair, objective ratings to help professionals and consumers alike make educated purchasing decisions.

At Weiss Ratings, integrity is number one. Weiss Ratings never takes a penny from insurance companies for its ratings. And, we publish Weiss Safety Ratings without regard for insurers' preferences. However, other rating agencies like A.M. Best, Fitch, Moody's, and Standard & Poor's are paid by insurance companies for their ratings and may even suppress unfavorable ratings at an insurer's request.

Our ratings are more frequently reviewed and updated than any other ratings. You can be sure that the information you receive is accurate and current – providing you with advance warning of financial vulnerability early enough to do something about it.

Other rating agencies focus primarily on a company's current claims paying ability and consider only mild economic adversity. Weiss Ratings also considers these issues, but in addition, our analysis covers a company's ability to deal with severe economic adversity and a sharp increase in claims.

Our use of more rigorous standards stems from the viewpoint that an insurance company's obligations to its policyholders should not depend on favorable business conditions. An insurer must be able to honor its policy commitments in bad times as well as good.

Our rating scale, from A to F, is easy to understand. Only a few outstanding companies receive an A (Excellent) rating, although there are many to choose from within the B (Good) category. An even larger group falls into the broad average range which receives C (Fair) ratings. Companies that demonstrate marked vulnerabilities receive either D (Weak) or E (Very Weak) ratings.

How to Use This Guide

The purpose of the *Guide to Health Insurers* is to provide policyholders and prospective policy purchasers with a reliable source of insurance company ratings and analyses on a timely basis. We realize that the financial strength of an insurer is an important factor to consider when making the decision to purchase a policy or change companies. The ratings and analyses in this Guide can make that evaluation easier when you are considering:

- Medical reimbursement insurance
- Managed health care (PPOs and HMOs)
- Disability income
- Long-term care (nursing home) insurance

This Guide includes ratings for health insurers such as commercial for-profit insurers, mutual insurers, Blue Cross/Blue Shield plans, and for-profit and not-for-profit insurers. This is the only source of ratings on many of these companies.

In addition, many companies that offer health insurance also offer life, property or liability insurance. If you are shopping for any of those types of coverage, please refer to either our *Guide to Life and Annuity Insurers* or our *Guide to Property and Casualty Insurers.*

The rating for a particular company indicates our opinion regarding that company's ability to meet its commitments to the policyholder – not only under current economic conditions, but also during a declining economy or in the event of a sharp increase in claims. Such an increase in claims and related expenses may be triggered by any number of occurrences including rising medical costs, malpractice lawsuits, out-of-control administrative expenses, or the unexpected spread of a disease such as AIDS. The safest companies, however, should be prepared to deal with harsh and unforeseen circumstances.

To use this Guide most effectively, we recommend you follow the steps outlined below:

Step 1 To ensure you evaluate the correct company, verify the company's exact name and state of domicile as it was given to you or appears on your policy. Many companies have similar names but are not related to one another, so you want to make sure the company you look up is really the one you are interested in evaluating.

Step 2 Turn to Section I, the Index of Companies, and locate the company you are evaluating. This section contains all health insurance companies analyzed by Weiss Ratings including those that did not receive a Safety Rating. It is sorted alphabetically by the name of the company and shows the state of domicile following the name for additional verification.

Step 3 Once you have located your specific company, the first column after the state of domicile shows its Weiss Safety Rating. See *About Weiss Safety Ratings* for information about what this rating means. If the rating has changed since the last issue of this Guide, a downgrade will be indicated with a down triangle ▼ to the left of the company name; an upgrade will be indicated with an up triangle ▲.

Step 4 Following Weiss Safety Rating is some additional information about the company such as its type, size and capital level. Refer to the introduction of Section I, to see what each of these factors measures.

Step 5 Some insurers have a bullet • following the domicile state in Section I. This means that more detailed information about the company is available in Section II.

If the company you are evaluating is identified with a bullet, turn to Section II, the Analysis of Largest Companies , and locate it there (otherwise skip to step 9). Section II contains all health insurers and Blue Cross/Blue Shield plans plus the largest property & casualty and life & annutiy insurers offering health insurance rated by Weiss, regardless of rating. It too is sorted alphabetically by the name of the company.

Step 6 Once you have identified your company in Section II, you will find its Safety Rating and a description of the rating immediately to the right of the company name. Then, below the company name is a description of the various rating factors that were considered in assigning the company's rating. These factors and the information below them are designed to give you a better feel for the company and its strengths and weaknesses. Refer to the introduction of Section II to get a better understanding of what each of these factors means.

Step 7 To the right, you will find a five-year summary of the company's Safety Rating, capitalization and income. Look for positive or negative trends in these data. Below the five-year summary, we have included a graphic illustration of the most crucial factor or factors impacting the company's rating. Again, the Section II introduction provides an overview of the content of each graph or table.

Step 8 If the company you are evaluating is a Medicare HMO, you can also look it up in Section VII to get some idea of the quality of service being offered. Here you can see the number of complaints against a company that have reached the federal review level based on the most recent data available.

Step 9 If you are interested in long-term care insurance, you can turn to Section V and get a listing of long-term care insurers. To compare long-term care policies see the Long-Term Care Insurance Planner within the Appendix.

Step 10 If the company you are evaluating is not highly rated and you want to find an insurer with a higher rating, turn to the page in Section IV that has your state's name at the top. This section contains those Recommended Companies (rating of A+, A, A- or B+) that are licensed to underwrite health insurance in your state, sorted by rating. From here you can select a company and then refer back to Sections I and II to analyze it.

Step 11 If you decide that you would like to contact one of Weiss Recommended Companies about obtaining a policy or for additional information, refer to Section III where you will find all of Weiss recommended companies listed alphabetically by name. Following each company's name is its address and phone number to assist you in making contact.

Step 12 Many consumers have reported to us the difficulties they have encountered in finding a Recommended Company that offers the best pricing and benefits. Therefore, when considering medical reimbursement or managed care coverage, you may want to consider other companies that have received a good (B or B-) rating even though they did not make Weiss Recommended List. However, for long-term policies such as nursing home care or disability income, we recommend sticking to companies with a rating of B+ or higher.

Step 13 In order to use Weiss Safety Ratings most effectively, we strongly recommend you consult the Important Warnings and Cautions. These are more than just "standard disclaimers." They are very important factors you should be aware of before using this Guide. If you have any questions regarding the precise meaning of specific terms used in the Guide, refer to the Glossary.

Step 14 Make sure you stay up to date with the latest information available since the publication of this Guide. For information on how to set up a rating change notification service, acquire follow-up reports, or receive a more in-depth analysis of an individual company, visit www.weissratings.com or call 1-877-934-7778.

Data Sources: Annual and quarterly statutory statements filed with state insurance commissioners and data provided by the insurance companies being rated. Medicare HMO complaint data were provided by the Centers for Medicare and Medicaid Services: The Center for Health Dispute Resolution, (formerly known as Health Care Financing Administration), and is reprinted here. The National Association of Insurance Commissioners has provided some of the raw data. Any analyses or conclusions are not provided or endorsed by the NAIC.

Date of data analyzed: March 31, 2019 unless otherwise noted

About Weiss Safety Ratings

The Weiss Ratings of insurers are based upon the annual and quarterly financial statements filed with state insurance commissioners. This data may be supplemented by information that we request from the insurance companies themselves. However, if a company chooses not to provide supplemental data, we reserve the right to rate the company based exclusively on publicly available data.

The Weiss Ratings are based on a complex analysis of hundreds of factors that are synthesized into a series of indexes: capitalization, investment safety (life, health and annuity companies only), reserve adequacy (property and casualty companies only), profitability, liquidity, and stability. These indexes are then used to arrive at a letter grade rating. A weak score on any one index can result in a low rating, as financial problems can be caused by any one of a number of factors, such as inadequate capital, unpredictable claims experience, poor liquidity, speculative investments, inadequate reserving, or consistent operating losses.

Our **Capital Index** gauges capital adequacy in terms of each insurer's ability to handle a variety of business and economic scenarios as they may impact investment performance, claims experience, persistency, and market position. The index combines two Risk-Adjusted Capital ratios as well as a leverage test that examines pricing risk.

Our **Investment Safety Index** measures the exposure of the company's investment portfolio to loss of principal and/or income due to default and market risks. Each investment area is rated by a factor that takes into consideration both quality and liquidity. (This factor is measured as a separate index only for life, health, and annuity insurers.)

Our **Reserve Adequacy Index** measures the adequacy of the company's reserves and its ability to accurately anticipate the level of claims it will receive. (This factor is measured as a separate index only for property and casualty insurers.)

Our **Profitability Index** measures the soundness of the company's operations and the contribution of profits to the company's financial strength. The profitability index is a composite of five sub-factors: 1) gain or loss on operations; 2) consistency of operating results; 3) impact of operating results on surplus; 4) adequacy of investment income as compared to the needs of policy reserves (life, health and annuity companies only); and 5) expenses in relation to industry norms for the types of policies that the company offers.

Our **Liquidity Index** evaluates a company's ability to raise the necessary cash to settle claims and honor cash withdrawal obligations. We model various cash flow scenarios, applying liquidity tests to determine how the company might fare in the event of an unexpected spike in claims and/or a run on policy surrenders.

Our **Stability Index** integrates a number of sub-factors that affect consistency (or lack thereof) in maintaining financial strength over time. These sub-factors will vary depending on the type of insurance company being evaluated but may include such things as 1) risk diversification in terms of company size, group size, number of policies in force, types of policies written, and use of reinsurance; 2) deterioration of operations as reported in critical asset, liability, income and expense items, such as surrender rates and premium volume; 3) years in operation; 4) former problem areas where, despite recent improvement, the company has yet to establish a record of stable performance over a suitable period of time; 5) a substantial shift in the company's operations; 6) potential instabilities such as reinsurance quality, asset/liability matching, and sources of capital; and 7) relationships with holding companies and affiliates.

In order to help guarantee our objectivity, we reserve the right to publish ratings expressing our opinion of a company's financial stability based exclusively on publicly available data and our own proprietary standards for safety.

Each of these indexes is measured according to the following range of values.

Critical Ranges In Our Indexes

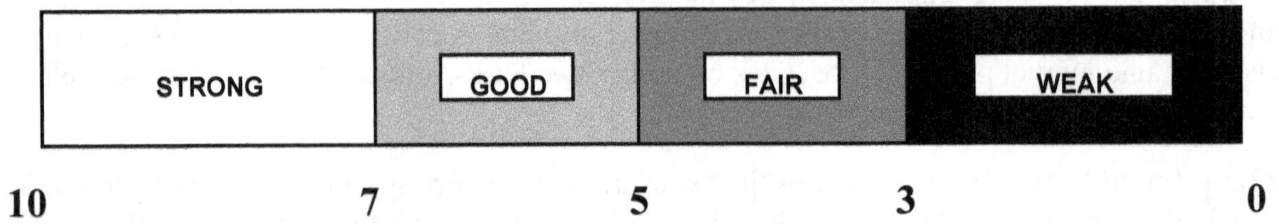

What Our Ratings Mean

A **Excellent.** The company offers excellent financial security. It has maintained a conservative stance in its investment strategies, business operations and underwriting commitments. While the financial position of any company is subject to change, we believe that this company has the resources necessary to deal with severe economic conditions.

B **Good.** The company offers good financial security and has the resources to deal with a variety of adverse economic conditions. It comfortably exceeds the minimum levels for all of our rating criteria, and is likely to remain healthy for the near future. However, in the event of a severe recession or major financial crisis, we feel that this assessment should be reviewed to make sure that the firm is still maintaining adequate financial strength.

C **Fair.** The company offers fair financial security and is currently stable. But during an economic downturn or other financial pressures, we feel it may encounter difficulties in maintaining its financial stability.

D **Weak.** The company currently demonstrates what, in our opinion, we consider to be significant weaknesses which could negatively impact policyholders. In an unfavorable economic environment, these weaknesses could be magnified.

E **Very Weak.** The company currently demonstrates what we consider to be significant weaknesses and has also failed some of the basic tests that we use to identify fiscal stability. Therefore, even in a favorable economic environment, it is our opinion that policyholders could incur significant risks.

F **Failed.** The company is deemed failed if it is either 1) under supervision of an insurance regulatory authority; 2) in the process of rehabilitation; 3) in the process of liquidation; or 4) voluntarily dissolved after disciplinary or other regulatory action by an insurance regulatory authority.

\+ The **plus sign** is an indication that the company is in the upper third of the letter grade.

\- The **minus sign** is an indication that the company is in the lower third of the letter grade.

U **Unrated.** The company is unrated for one or more of the following reasons: (1) total assets are less than $1 million; (2) premium income for the current year was less than $100,000; (3) the company functions almost exclusively as a holding company rather than as an underwriter; (4) in our opinion, we do not have enough information to reliably issue a rating.

How Our Ratings Differ From Those of Other Services

Weiss Safety Ratings are conservative and consumer oriented. We use tougher standards than other rating agencies because our system is specifically designed to inform risk-averse consumers about the financial strength of health insurers.

Our rating scale (A to F) is easy to understand by the general public. Users can intuitively understand that an A+ rating is at the top of the scale rather than in the middle like some of the other rating agencies.

Other rating agencies give top ratings more generously so that most companies receive excellent ratings.

More importantly, other rating agencies focus primarily on a company's *current* claims paying ability or consider only relatively mild economic adversity. We also consider these scenarios but extend our analysis to cover a company's ability to deal with severe economic adversity and potential liquidity problems. This stems from the viewpoint that an insurance company's obligations to its policyholders should not be contingent upon a healthy economy. The company must be capable of honoring its policy commitments in bad times as well.

Looking at the insurance industry as a whole, we note that several major rating firms have poor historical track records in identifying troubled companies. The 1980s saw a persistent decline in capital ratios, increased holdings of risky investments in the life and health industry as well as recurring long-term claims liabilities in the property and casualty industry. The insurance industry experienced similar issues before and during the Great Recession of 2007-2009. Despite these clear signs that insolvency risk was rising, other rating firms failed to downgrade at-risk insurance companies. Instead, they often rated companies by shades of excellence, understating the gravity of potential problems.

Other ratings agencies have not issued clear warnings that the ordinary consumer can understand. Few, if any, companies receive "weak" or "poor" ratings. Surely, weak companies do exist. However, the other rating agencies apparently do not view themselves as consumer advocates with the responsibility of warning the public about the risks involved in doing business with such companies.

Additionally, these firms will at times agree *not* to issue a rating if a company denies them permission to do so. In short, too often insurance rating agencies work hand-in-glove with the companies they rate.

At Weiss Ratings, although we seek to maintain good relationships with the firms, we owe our primary obligation to the consumer, not the industry. We reserve the right to rate companies based on publicly-available data and make the necessary conservative assumptions when companies choose not to provide additional data we might request.

Comparison of Insurance Company Rating Agency Scales

Weiss Ratings [a]	Best [a]	S&P	Moody's	Fitch
A+, A, A-	A++, A+	AAA	Aaa	AAA
B+, B, B-	A, A-	AA+, AA AA-	Aa1, Aa2, Aa3	AA+, AA, AA-
C+, C, C-	B++, B+,	A+, A, A-, BBB+, BBB, BBB-	A1, A2, A3, Baa1, Baa2, Baa3	A+, A, A-, BBB+, BBB, BBB-
D+, D, D-	B, B- C++, C+, C, C-	BB+, BB, BB-, B+, B, B-	Ba1, Ba2, Ba3, B1, B2, B3	BB+, BB, BB-, B+, B, B-
E+, E, E- F	D E, F	CCC R	Caa, Ca, C	CCC+, CCC, CCC- DD

[a] Weiss Ratings and Best use additional symbols to designate that they recognize an insurer's existence but do not provide a rating. These symbols are not included in this table.

Rate of Insurance Company Failures

Weiss Ratings provides quarterly safety ratings for thousands of insurance companies each year. Weiss Ratings strives for fairness and objectivity in its ratings and analyses, ensuring that each company receives the rating that most accurately depicts its current financial status, and more importantly, its ability to deal with severe economic adversity and a sharp increase in claims. Weiss Ratings has every confidence that its safety ratings provide an accurate representation of a company's stability.

In order for these ratings to be of any true value, it is important that they prove accurate over time. One way to determine the accuracy of a rating is to examine those insurance companies that have failed, and their respective Safety Ratings. A high percentage of failed companies with "A" ratings would indicate that Weiss Ratings is not being conservative enough with its "secure" ratings, while conversely, a low percentage of failures with "vulnerable" ratings would show that Weiss Ratings is overly conservative.

Over the past 29 years (1989–2018) Weiss Ratings has rated 645 insurance companies, for all industries, that subsequently failed. The chart below shows the number of failed companies in each rating category, the average number of companies rated in each category per year, and the percentage of annual failures for each letter grade.

	Safety Rating	Number of Failed Companies	Average Number of Companies Rated per year	Percentage of Failed companies per year (by ratings category)*
Secure	A	1	152	0.02%
	B	8	1,115	0.02%
	C	73	1,610	0.15%
Vulnerable	D	278	737	1.26%
	E	285	216	4.41%

A=Excellent, B=Good, C=Fair, D=Weak, E=Very Weak

On average, only 0.10% of the companies Weiss rates as "secure" fail each year. On the other hand, an average of 1.97% of the companies Weiss rates as "vulnerable" fail annually. That means that a company rated by Weiss Ratings as "Vulnerable" is almost 20.7 times more likely to fail than a company rated as "Secure".

When considering a Weiss Safety Rating, one can be sure that they are getting the most fair, objective, and accurate financial rating available anywhere.

*Percentage of Failed companies per year = (Number of Failed Companies) / [(Average Number of Companies Rated per year) x (years in study)]

Data as of December 31, 2018 for Life and Annuity Insurers, Property & Casualty Insurers, and Health Insurers.

What Does Average Mean?

At Weiss Ratings, we consider the words average and fair to mean just that – average and fair. So when we assign our ratings to insurers, a large percentage of companies receive an average C rating. That way, you can be sure that a company receiving Weiss B or A rating is truly above average. Likewise, you can feel confident that companies with D or E ratings are truly below average.

Current Weiss Ratings Distribution for Health Insurers

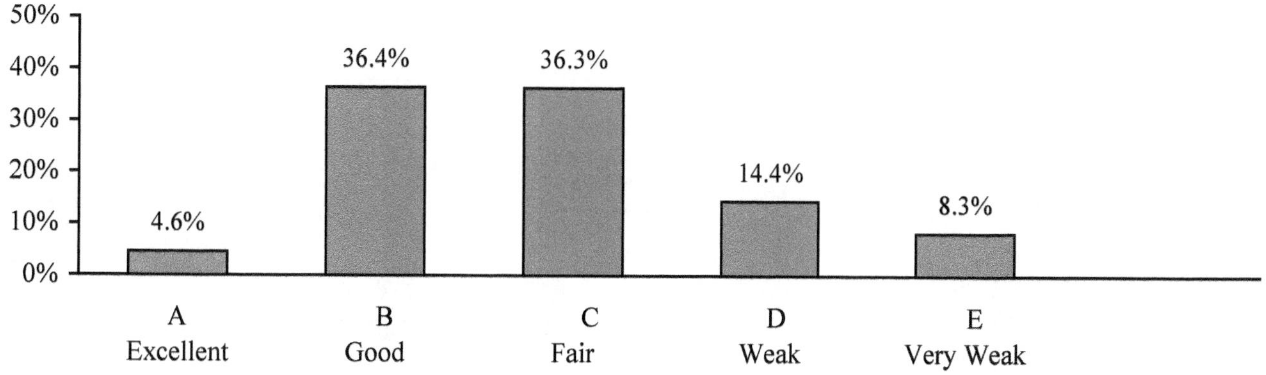

Important Warnings and Cautions

1. A rating alone cannot tell the whole story. Please read the explanatory information contained in this publication. It is provided in order to give you an understanding of our rating philosophy, as well as paint a more complete picture of how we arrive at our opinion of a company's strengths and weaknesses.

2. Weiss Safety Ratings represent our opinion of a company's insolvency risk. As such, a high rating means we feel that the company has less chance of running into financial difficulties. A high rating is not a guarantee of solvency nor is a low rating a prediction of insolvency. Weiss Safety Ratings are not deemed to be a recommendation concerning the purchase or sale of the securities of any insurance company that is publicly owned.

3. Company performance is only one factor in determining a rating. Conditions in the marketplace and overall economic conditions are additional factors that may affect the company's financial strength. Therefore, a rating upgrade or downgrade does not necessarily reflect changes in the company's profits, capital or other financial measures, but may be due to external factors. Likewise, changes in Weiss indexes may reflect changes in our risk assessment of business or economic conditions as well as changes in company performance.

4. All firms that have the same Safety Rating should be considered to be essentially equal in strength. This is true regardless of any differences in the underlying numbers which might appear to indicate greater strengths. Weiss Safety Rating already takes into account a number of lesser factors which, due to space limitations, cannot be included in this publication.

5. A good rating requires consistency. If a company is excellent on four indicators and fair on one, the company may receive a fair rating. This requirement is necessary due to the fact that fiscal problems can arise from any *one* of several causes including speculative investments, inadequate capital resources or operating losses.

6. We are an independent rating agency and do not depend on the cooperation of the companies we rate. Our data are derived from annual and quarterly financial statements that we obtain from federal regulators and filings with state insurance commissioners. The latter may be supplemented by information insurance companies voluntarily provide upon request. Although we seek to maintain an open line of communication with the companies, we do not grant them the right to stop or influence publication of the ratings. This policy stems from the fact that this publication is designed for the protection of the consumer.

7. Affiliated companies do not automatically receive the same rating. We recognize that a troubled company may expect financial support from its parent or affiliates. Weiss Safety Ratings reflect our opinion of the measure of support that may become available to a subsidiary , if the subsidiary were to experience serious financial difficulties. In the case of a strong parent and a weaker subsidiary, the affiliate relationship will generally result in a higher rating for the subsidiary than it would have on a stand-alone basis. Seldom, however, would the rating be brought up to the level of the parent. This treatment is appropriate because we do not assume the parent would have either the resources or the will to "bail out" a troubled subsidiary during a severe economic crisis. Even when there is a binding legal obligation for a parent corporation to honor the policy obligations of its subsidiaries, the possibility exists that the subsidiary could be sold and lose its parental support. Therefore, it is quite common for one affiliate to have a higher rating than another. This is another reason why it is especially important that you have the precise name of the company you are evaluating.

Section I

Index of Companies

An analysis of over 1,528 rated and unrated

U.S. Health Insurers

Companies are listed in alphabetical order.

Section I Contents

This section contains the information about company type, size and capital level for all rated and unrated health insurers analyzed by Weiss Ratings.

1. **Insurance Company Name** The legally-registered name, which can sometimes differ from the name that the company uses for advertising. If you cannot find the company you are interested in, or if you have any doubts regarding the precise name, verify the information with the company before looking the name up in this Guide. Also, determine the domicile state for confirmation. (See column 2.)

2. **Domicile State** The state which has primary regulatory responsibility for the company. It may differ from the location of the company's corporate headquarters. You do not have to be living in the domicile state to purchase insurance from this firm, provided it is licensed to do business in your state.

   Also use this column to confirm that you have located the correct company. It is possible for two unrelated companies to have the same name if they are domiciled in different states.

3. **Safety Rating** Our rating is measured on a scale from A to F and considers a wide range of factors. Please see *What Our Ratings Mean* for specific descriptions of each letter grade and the following pages for information on how our ratings differ from those of other rating agencies. Most important, when using this rating, please be sure to consider the Important Warnings and Cautions regarding the ratings' limitations and the underlying assumptions.

4. **Data Date** The latest quarter-end for which we have received the company's financial statement.

5. **Total Assets** All assets admitted by state insurance regulators in millions of dollars as of the most recent quarter end. This includes investments and current business assets such as receivables from agents, reinsurers and subscribers.

   The overall size is an important factor which affects the ability of a company to manage risk. Mortality, morbidity (sickness) and investment risks can be more effectively diversified by large companies. Because the insurance business is based on probability, the number of policies must be large enough so that actuarial statistics are valid. The larger the number of policyholders, the more reliable the actuarial projections will be. A large company with a correspondingly large policy base can spread its risk and minimize the effects of claims experience that exceeds actuarial expectations.

6. **Total Premiums** The amount of insurance premiums received from policyholders as of the most recent year end. If the company issues life insurance or property insurance, those premiums are included in this figure as well.

   Generally speaking, companies with large premium volume generally have more predictable claims experience.

7. **Health** The amount of insurance premiums received from policyholders for health

Premiums policies only as of the most recent year end.

Compare this figure with Total Premiums in the previous column to see how much of the company's business relates to health coverage.

8. Capital and Surplus The company's statutory net worth in millions of dollars as of the most recent quarter end. Consumers may wish to limit the size of any policy so that the policyholder's maximum benefits do not exceed approximately 1% of the company's capital and surplus. For example, when buying a policy from a company with capital and surplus of $10,000,000, the 1% limit would be $100,000. (When performing this calculation, do not forget that figures in this column are expressed in millions of dollars.)

Critical Ranges In Our Ratios

Indicators	*Strong*	*Good*	*Fair*	*Weak*
Risk-Adjusted Capital Ratio #1	—	1.0 or more	0.75 - 0.99	0.74 or less
Risk-Adjusted Capital Ratio #2	1.0 or more	0.75 - 0.99	0.5 - 0.74	0.49 or less

9. Risk-Adjusted Capital Ratio #1 This ratio examines the adequacy of the company's capital base and whether the company has sufficient capital resources to cover potential losses which might occur in an average recession or other moderate loss scenario. Specifically, the figure cited in this column answers the question: For every dollar of capital that we feel would be needed, how many dollars in capital resources does the company actually have? (See the table above for the levels which we believe are critical.) You may find that some companies have unusually high levels of capital. This often reflects special circumstances related to the small size or unusual operations of the company.

10. Risk-Adjusted Capital Ratio #2 This is similar to item 9. But in this case, the question relates to whether the company has enough capital cushion to withstand a *severe* recession or other severe loss scenario. For more details on risk-adjusted capital, see the Appendix.

INSURANCE COMPANY NAME	DOM. STATE	RATING	DATA DATE	TOTAL ASSETS ($MIL)	TOTAL PREMIUMS ($MIL)	HEALTH PREMIUMS ($MIL)	CAPITAL & SURPLUS ($MIL)	RISK ADJUSTED CAPITAL RATIO 1	RISK ADJUSTED CAPITAL RATIO 2
21ST CENTURY CENTENNIAL INS CO	PA	B	1q 2019	615.2	70.3	0.0	615.0	1.87	1.87
21ST CENTURY PREMIER INS CO	PA	• B-	1q 2019	296.4	0.5	0.2	296.4	4.59	4.54
4 EVER LIFE INS CO	IL	• B	1q 2019	171.1	161.3	154.1	82.8	7.17	4.74
AAA LIFE INS CO	MI	B	1q 2019	676.9	912.8	72.5	176.9	3.40	1.92
ABILITY INS CO	NE	D	1q 2019	744.7	65.7	65.3	23.8	0.54	0.37
ABSOLUTE TOTAL CARE INC	SC	• C+	1q 2019	143.7	544.8	544.8	72.6	2.54	2.12
ACCENDO INS CO	UT	U		--	--	--	--	--	--
ACCESS INS CO	TX	F	3q 2017	214.1	311.3	0.0	30.6	0.90	0.78
ACCESS SENIOR HEALTHCARE INC	CA	• E-	1q 2019	5.3	28.8	28.8	1.5	0.30	0.19
ACCESSCARE GENERAL WI INS INC	WI	U		--	--	--	--	--	--
ACE AMERICAN INS CO	PA	C	1q 2019	23,923.6	4,965.6	561.8	5,615.8	2.18	1.50
ADVANCE INS CO OF KANSAS	KS	• B+	1q 2019	61.2	11.7	4.0	51.7	3.93	2.57
ADVENTIST HEALTH PLAN INC	CA	• D	1q 2019	7.1	30.1	30.1	3.1	0.93	0.59
ADVICARE CORP	SC	U		--	--	--	--	--	--
AEGIS SECURITY INS CO	PA	D+	1q 2019	195.6	197.1	12.4	63.9	0.46	0.34
AETNA BETTER HEALTH (AN OHIO CORP)	OH	• B	1q 2019	371.6	960.8	960.8	206.6	4.34	3.62
AETNA BETTER HEALTH INC	IL	• C	1q 2019	116.3	197.3	197.3	61.5	4.99	4.16
AETNA BETTER HEALTH INC (A CT CORP)	CT	U		--	--	--	--	--	--
AETNA BETTER HEALTH INC (A LA CORP)	LA	• C	1q 2019	198.0	634.7	634.7	57.3	2.62	2.19
AETNA BETTER HEALTH INC (A NJ CORP)	NJ	• B	1q 2019	141.5	364.1	364.1	43.5	2.38	1.98
AETNA BETTER HEALTH INC (A PA CORP)	PA	• C	1q 2019	380.2	1,013.9	1,013.9	134.5	3.02	2.52
AETNA BETTER HEALTH OF CA INC	DE	• D+	1q 2019	30.9	21.2	21.2	17.1	6.28	3.87
AETNA BETTER HEALTH OF KS INC	KS	U		--	--	--	--	--	--
AETNA BETTER HEALTH OF MICHIGAN INC	MI	• B	1q 2019	130.7	293.6	293.6	50.8	3.48	2.90
AETNA BETTER HEALTH OF MISSOURI LLC	MO	• C	1q 2019	41.4	1.0	1.0	41.1	38.20	31.83
AETNA BETTER HEALTH OF NV INC	NV	U		--	--	--	--	--	--
AETNA BETTER HEALTH OF TEXAS INC	TX	• B	1q 2019	99.4	314.5	314.5	47.9	3.23	2.69
AETNA BETTER HLTH OF KY INS CO	KY	• B+	1q 2019	524.3	1,121.8	1,121.8	337.4	5.84	4.87
AETNA BETTER HLTH OF WA INC	WA	U		--	--	--	--	--	--
AETNA HEALTH & LIFE INS CO	CT	• C	1q 2019	159.3	374.0	374.0	84.4	1.55	1.16
AETNA HEALTH INC (A CT CORP)	CT	• C	1q 2019	71.8	156.1	156.1	47.2	4.75	3.96
AETNA HEALTH INC (A FLORIDA CORP)	FL	• B-	1q 2019	434.2	1,673.8	1,673.8	199.7	2.31	1.92
AETNA HEALTH INC (A GEORGIA CORP)	GA	• C	1q 2019	188.6	255.1	255.1	68.7	4.99	4.16
AETNA HEALTH INC (A MAINE CORP)	ME	• B	1q 2019	34.8	66.8	66.8	23.6	5.86	4.88
AETNA HEALTH INC (A NEW JERSEY CORP)	NJ	• B	1q 2019	283.8	699.4	699.4	167.0	4.35	3.63
AETNA HEALTH INC (A NEW YORK CORP)	NY	• B	1q 2019	288.1	117.4	117.4	226.4	17.65	14.71
AETNA HEALTH INC (A PA CORP)	PA	• B	1q 2019	1,104.1	3,153.5	3,153.5	555.3	4.00	3.34
AETNA HEALTH INC (A TEXAS CORP)	TX	• C	1q 2019	138.5	472.3	472.3	59.8	1.98	1.65
AETNA HEALTH INC (LA)	LA	• B-	1q 2019	36.7	95.5	95.5	26.8	4.68	3.90
AETNA HEALTH INS CO	PA	• C	1q 2019	20.5	29.3	29.3	13.3	5.86	4.88
AETNA HEALTH INS CO OF NY	NY	U		--	--	--	--	--	--
AETNA HEALTH OF CALIFORNIA INC	CA	• B	1q 2019	440.5	1,389.2	1,389.2	195.1	2.09	1.41
AETNA HEALTH OF IOWA INC	IA	• C+	1q 2019	53.6	31.8	31.8	41.6	21.53	17.94
AETNA HEALTH OF UTAH INC	UT	• C	1q 2019	83.3	224.3	224.3	41.7	5.22	4.35
AETNA HEALTHASSURANCE PA INC	PA	• D	1q 2019	89.0	299.2	299.2	55.5	3.09	2.57
AETNA LIFE INS CO	CT	• B	1q 2019	22,067.5	31,772.8	30,754.2	4,433.3	1.46	1.11
AF&L INS CO	PA	D	1q 2019	116.1	14.4	14.4	4.0	0.22	0.15
AHF MCO OF GEORGIA INC	GA	• D+	1q 2019	4.3	0.2	0.2	4.1	152.49	127.07
AIDS HEALTHCARE FOUNDATION MCO OF FL	FL	• E+	1q 2019	29.6	138.9	138.9	12.0	0.61	0.51
AIG INS CO - PR	PR	B	1q 2019	163.2	90.6	0.2	94.7	4.81	3.30
AIG SPECIALTY INS CO	IL	C+	1q 2019	125.7	662.3	1.2	84.6	14.60	13.14
ALAMEDA ALLIANCE FOR HEALTH	CA	F	1q 2019	564.6	894.9	894.9	188.4	2.88	1.76

INSURANCE COMPANY NAME	DOM. STATE	RATING	DATA DATE	TOTAL ASSETS ($MIL)	TOTAL PREMIUMS ($MIL)	HEALTH PREMIUMS ($MIL)	CAPITAL & SURPLUS ($MIL)	RISK ADJUSTED CAPITAL RATIO 1	RISK ADJUSTED CAPITAL RATIO 2
ALFA LIFE INS CORP	AL	B-	3q 2018	1,479.5	159.4	0.6	272.2	2.72	1.53
ALIGNMENT HEALTH PLAN	CA	• E	1q 2019	96.9	449.2	449.2	14.7	0.02	0.01
ALIGNMENT HLTH PLAN OF IL INC	IL	U		--	--	--	--	--	--
ALL SAVERS INS CO	IN	• C	1q 2019	632.7	493.8	493.8	452.0	6.76	5.13
ALLCARE HEALTH PLAN INC	OR	• E	1q 2019	12.2	33.1	33.1	7.2	0.96	0.80
ALLEGIAN INS CO	TX	• C-	1q 2019	5.8	0.3	0.3	5.5	2.58	2.15
ALLEGIANCE L&H INS CO	MT	• C+	1q 2019	16.9	14.4	14.4	14.1	9.54	7.95
ALLIANCE HEALTH & LIFE INS CO	MI	• C	1q 2019	143.1	347.5	347.5	54.7	1.98	1.65
ALLIANT HEALTH PLANS INC	GA	• D-	1q 2019	157.0	481.8	481.8	75.6	2.00	1.66
ALLIANZ GLOBAL RISKS US INS CO	IL	C+	1q 2019	8,049.5	1,431.7	13.4	1,960.0	1.08	0.86
▲ ALLIANZ LIFE INS CO OF NORTH AMERICA	MN	B-	1q 2019	147,009.1	12,389.8	176.5	7,521.5	3.21	1.77
ALLIANZ LIFE INS CO OF NY	NY	B+	1q 2019	3,530.0	302.9	3.4	205.7	5.57	3.82
ALLINA HLTH & AETNA INS CO	MN	• C	1q 2019	15.1	0.2	0.2	4.6	2.57	2.14
ALLSTATE LIFE INS CO	IL	B	1q 2019	30,361.7	458.9	18.7	3,603.6	2.09	1.25
ALLSTATE LIFE INS CO OF NEW YORK	NY	B-	1q 2019	6,172.0	217.1	45.1	645.4	2.66	1.40
ALOHACARE	HI	• B-	1q 2019	157.0	372.3	372.3	88.8	2.80	2.33
AMALGAMATED CASUALTY INS CO	DC	C	1q 2019	58.3	12.2	0.0	35.7	2.79	2.38
AMALGAMATED LIFE & HEALTH INS CO	IL	C	1q 2019	5.0	3.4	3.4	4.0	2.58	2.33
AMALGAMATED LIFE INS CO	NY	• A	1q 2019	148.4	74.3	37.7	66.9	4.07	3.10
AMBETTER OF MAGNOLIA INC	MS	• B-	1q 2019	177.3	493.8	493.8	71.3	5.89	4.91
AMBETTER OF NORTH CAROLINA INC	NC	U		--	--	--	--	--	--
AMBETTER OF PEACH STATE INC	GA	• B-	1q 2019	421.1	1,136.9	1,136.9	161.2	4.24	3.53
AMERICAN ALTERNATIVE INS CORP	DE	C	1q 2019	574.4	1,015.1	178.3	181.5	15.60	9.33
AMERICAN BANKERS INS CO OF FL	FL	B	1q 2019	2,361.9	4,448.1	153.8	630.4	2.80	1.90
AMERICAN BANKERS LIFE ASR CO OF FL	FL	• C+	1q 2019	328.9	302.7	148.3	51.9	4.78	2.74
AMERICAN BENEFIT LIFE INS CO	OK	C	1q 2019	191.8	8.3	0.0	25.3	3.10	1.79
AMERICAN CASUALTY CO OF READING	PA	C	1q 2019	133.5	558.9	0.0	133.5	1.98	1.94
AMERICAN CONTINENTAL INS CO	TN	• C	1q 2019	306.9	499.4	454.4	110.5	1.74	1.30
AMERICAN FAMILY INS CO	WI	B	1q 2019	410.2	1,858.1	0.4	25.6	2.21	1.99
AMERICAN FAMILY LIFE ASR CO OF NY	NY	• A-	1q 2019	978.2	335.5	322.6	334.3	6.09	4.11
AMERICAN FAMILY MUTL INS CO SI	WI	B+	1q 2019	18,119.9	4,709.9	28.3	6,658.8	2.24	1.72
AMERICAN FEDERATED LIFE INS CO	MS	B	1q 2019	26.0	17.5	8.5	9.9	2.31	2.08
AMERICAN FIDELITY ASR CO	OK	• B+	1q 2019	6,256.2	1,246.6	848.6	526.5	2.09	1.20
AMERICAN FINANCIAL SECURITY L I C	MO	D	1q 2019	18.3	9.5	9.5	8.2	2.06	1.63
AMERICAN GENERAL LIFE INS CO	TX	B	1q 2019	183,293.0	15,071.4	112.0	6,209.2	2.43	1.15
AMERICAN HEALTH & LIFE INS CO	TX	• A-	1q 2019	1,083.3	353.8	166.2	148.4	2.38	1.51
AMERICAN HEALTH PLAN INC	TN	U		--	--	--	--	--	--
AMERICAN HERITAGE LIFE INS CO	FL	• B	1q 2019	2,056.9	1,098.7	938.4	339.0	1.24	0.95
AMERICAN HOME ASR CO	NY	C	1q 2019	24,113.1	482.4	17.9	5,532.9	2.02	1.31
AMERICAN HOME LIFE INS CO	KS	C-	1q 2019	264.2	26.0	0.0	22.1	2.13	1.16
AMERICAN INCOME LIFE INS CO	IN	B-	1q 2019	4,211.9	1,050.4	86.7	322.5	1.51	0.89
AMERICAN INTEGRITY LIFE INS CO	AR	C-	1q 2019	1.6	0.3	0.1	1.1	1.94	1.75
AMERICAN LABOR LIFE INS CO	AZ	D	1q 2019	10.4	1.1	1.1	8.3	3.42	3.08
▲ AMERICAN LIFE & SECURITY CORP	NE	E+	1q 2019	30.7	5.9	0.0	18.9	5.05	4.55
AMERICAN LIFE INS CO	DE	• C	1q 2019	11,181.3	1,546.9	471.0	4,836.4	1.05	1.00
AMERICAN MEMORIAL LIFE INS CO	SD	B-	1q 2019	3,403.2	562.3	0.0	150.0	1.42	0.74
AMERICAN MODERN HOME INS CO	OH	C+	1q 2019	934.3	460.3	0.0	366.8	1.80	1.53
AMERICAN NATIONAL INS CO	TX	B	1q 2019	21,150.4	2,041.8	38.9	3,348.3	1.17	0.97
AMERICAN NATIONAL LIFE INS CO OF TX	TX	• B-	1q 2019	127.1	68.2	64.2	32.9	3.48	2.32
AMERICAN PROGRESSIVE L&H I C OF NY	NY	• C	1q 2019	285.3	625.5	616.2	124.2	1.10	0.89
AMERICAN PUBLIC LIFE INS CO	OK	• B	1q 2019	103.0	95.7	94.4	36.7	2.43	1.84
AMERICAN REPUBLIC CORP INS CO	IA	C	1q 2019	21.0	48.7	48.5	7.7	2.10	1.89

INSURANCE COMPANY NAME	DOM. STATE	RATING	DATA DATE	TOTAL ASSETS ($MIL)	TOTAL PREMIUMS ($MIL)	HEALTH PREMIUMS ($MIL)	CAPITAL & SURPLUS ($MIL)	RISK ADJUSTED CAPITAL RATIO 1	RATIO 2
AMERICAN REPUBLIC INS CO	IA	• B-	1q 2019	1,095.7	126.2	114.0	487.3	5.95	3.69
AMERICAN RETIREMENT LIFE INS CO	OH	• C+	1q 2019	141.6	401.3	401.0	78.9	1.46	1.12
AMERICAN SECURITY INS CO	DE	B	1q 2019	1,408.1	948.7	0.9	541.9	1.83	1.43
AMERICAN SENTINEL INS CO	PA	C	1q 2019	31.8	41.6	0.2	12.0	0.70	0.58
AMERICAN SPECIALTY HEALTH INS CO	IN	• B	1q 2019	9.8	1.1	1.1	8.8	46.48	38.74
AMERICAN SPECIALTY HEALTH ODS OF NJ	NJ	• B	4q 2018	3.5	11.4	11.4	2.2	1.14	0.95
AMERICAN STATES INS CO	IN	B-	1q 2019	147.2	329.6	0.1	135.8	52.74	47.46
AMERICAN UNITED LIFE INS CO	IN	B+	1q 2019	29,538.7	3,977.8	136.0	1,053.5	2.44	1.22
AMERICAS 1ST CHOICE HEALTH PLANS INC	SC	U		--	--	--	--	--	--
AMERICAS 1ST CHOICE SOUTH CAROLINA	SC	• C+	1q 2019	4.8	7.3	7.3	2.0	2.33	1.94
AMERICASHEALTH PLAN INC	CA	• D	1q 2019	5.2	6.4	6.4	2.0	3.77	2.66
AMERICHOICE OF NEW JERSEY INC	NJ	• B	1q 2019	568.7	2,714.5	2,714.5	256.7	1.55	1.29
AMERICO FINANCIAL LIFE & ANNUITY INS	TX	B-	1q 2019	4,725.8	530.8	19.0	534.0	2.05	1.19
AMERIGROUP COMMUNITY CARE NM	NM	• B	1q 2019	74.4	15.6	15.6	70.0	48.09	40.08
AMERIGROUP DISTRICT	DC	• B-	1q 2019	124.9	220.1	220.1	89.4	11.15	9.29
AMERIGROUP INS CO	TX	• B	1q 2019	289.2	1,014.4	1,014.4	153.2	2.82	2.35
AMERIGROUP IOWA INC	IA	• C	1q 2019	326.9	1,445.4	1,445.4	171.4	1.97	1.65
AMERIGROUP KANSAS INC	KS	• B-	1q 2019	206.8	1,078.9	1,078.9	177.8	2.83	2.36
AMERIGROUP MARYLAND INC	MD	• B-	1q 2019	486.2	1,113.1	1,113.1	188.4	3.08	2.57
AMERIGROUP MICHIGAN INC	MI	U		--	--	--	--	--	--
AMERIGROUP MISSISSIPPI INC	MS	U		--	--	--	--	--	--
AMERIGROUP NEW JERSEY INC	NJ	• A-	1q 2019	324.9	1,381.2	1,381.2	167.0	2.15	1.79
AMERIGROUP OHIO INC	OH	U		--	--	--	--	--	--
AMERIGROUP OKLAHOMA INC	OK	U		--	--	--	--	--	--
AMERIGROUP PENNSYLVANIA INC	PA	U		--	--	--	--	--	--
AMERIGROUP TENNESSEE INC	TN	• B-	1q 2019	508.1	1,739.0	1,739.0	191.9	2.09	1.74
AMERIGROUP TEXAS INC	TX	• A-	1q 2019	1,025.7	4,245.1	4,245.1	456.8	2.02	1.68
AMERIGROUP WASHINGTON INC	WA	• A-	1q 2019	302.8	491.1	491.1	161.6	5.92	4.93
AMERIHEALTH CARITAS IOWA INC	IA	• C	1q 2019	138.4	2.8	2.8	133.6	106.01	88.34
AMERIHEALTH CARITAS NH INC	NH	U		--	--	--	--	--	--
AMERIHEALTH CARITAS NM INC	NM	U		--	--	--	--	--	--
AMERIHEALTH CARITAS OF LOUISIANA INC	LA	• B	1q 2019	249.0	1,100.2	1,100.2	83.9	2.00	1.67
AMERIHEALTH CARITAS TEXAS INC	TX	U		--	--	--	--	--	--
AMERIHEALTH DISTRICT OF COLUMBIA INC	DC	• C+	1q 2019	118.2	563.5	563.5	40.0	1.47	1.23
AMERIHEALTH HMO INC	PA	• C+	1q 2019	114.4	7.7	7.7	23.7	13.93	11.61
AMERIHEALTH INSURANCE CO OF NJ	NJ	• C	4q 2018	551.5	1,095.4	1,095.4	209.6	3.68	3.07
AMERIHEALTH MICHIGAN INC	MI	• C	1q 2019	22.8	75.4	75.4	8.9	1.94	1.62
AMERIHEALTH NEBRASKA INC	NE	U		--	--	--	--	--	--
AMERITAS LIFE INS CORP	NE	• B	1q 2019	22,844.0	2,890.9	906.5	1,544.4	2.28	1.33
AMERITAS LIFE INS CORP OF NY	NY	• B-	1q 2019	1,680.9	167.8	42.4	92.5	1.79	0.95
AMEX ASSURANCE CO	IL	• B-	1q 2019	259.2	188.2	59.8	208.9	9.75	5.73
AMFIRST INS CO	OK	• B	1q 2019	69.5	73.1	73.1	60.0	3.22	2.68
AMGP GEORGIA MANAGED CARE CO INC	GA	• A-	1q 2019	310.5	1,233.6	1,233.6	148.9	2.31	1.92
AMGUARD INS CO	PA	C	1q 2019	1,218.8	905.6	12.8	202.0	1.36	0.90
ANTHEM BLUE CROSS LIFE & HEALTH INS	CA	• B-	1q 2019	2,445.3	1,817.7	1,817.7	1,320.7	8.12	6.77
ANTHEM HEALTH PLANS INC	CT	• B	1q 2019	749.1	1,996.1	1,996.1	370.8	2.86	2.39
ANTHEM HEALTH PLANS OF KENTUCKY INC	KY	• B	1q 2019	919.1	2,036.8	2,036.8	380.1	3.83	3.19
ANTHEM HEALTH PLANS OF MAINE INC	ME	• B	1q 2019	489.8	991.7	991.7	143.7	4.03	3.36
ANTHEM HEALTH PLANS OF NEW HAMPSHIRE	NH	• B	1q 2019	448.7	738.6	738.6	226.4	3.36	2.80
ANTHEM HEALTH PLANS OF VIRGINIA	VA	• B	1q 2019	1,779.7	3,210.7	3,210.7	753.8	4.35	3.63
ANTHEM INS COMPANIES INC	IN	• B-	1q 2019	3,987.7	7,116.0	7,116.0	1,396.8	3.01	2.51
ANTHEM KENTUCKY MANAGED CARE PLAN	KY	• A-	1q 2019	243.4	746.4	746.4	158.6	3.67	3.06

INSURANCE COMPANY NAME	DOM. STATE	RATING	DATA DATE	TOTAL ASSETS ($MIL)	TOTAL PREMIUMS ($MIL)	HEALTH PREMIUMS ($MIL)	CAPITAL & SURPLUS ($MIL)	RISK ADJUSTED CAPITAL RATIO 1	RISK ADJUSTED CAPITAL RATIO 2
ANTHEM LIFE & DISABILITY INS CO	NY	B	1q 2019	27.0	9.0	3.7	18.5	3.09	2.30
▲ ANTHEM LIFE INS CO	IN	• B+	1q 2019	759.7	225.2	98.7	161.6	2.44	1.68
APC PASSE LLC	AR	U		--	--	--	--	--	--
APEX HEALTH INC	NC	U		--	--	--	--	--	--
AR HEALTH & WELLNESS HLTH PLAN	AR	• C-	1q 2019	38.5	42.6	42.6	15.5	3.69	3.08
ARCADIAN HEALTH PLAN INC	WA	• B-	1q 2019	1,073.7	3,417.7	3,417.7	613.3	4.10	3.42
ARCH INS CO	MO	C	1q 2019	3,950.0	2,028.4	59.5	917.7	0.94	0.76
ARKANSAS ADVANCED CARE INC	AR	U		--	--	--	--	--	--
ARKANSAS BANKERS LIFE INS CO	AR	D	1q 2019	2.6	0.8	0.1	1.6	1.82	1.64
ARKANSAS SUPERIOR SELECT INC	AR	• E	1q 2019	13.6	27.9	27.9	5.1	0.93	0.77
ARKANSAS TOTAL CARE INC	AR	U		--	--	--	--	--	--
ARROWOOD INDEMNITY CO	DE	D	1q 2019	1,037.4	-0.3	0.0	173.2	0.36	0.21
ASPEN AMERICAN INS CO	TX	C+	1q 2019	895.0	456.8	0.6	525.6	2.04	1.64
ASPIRE HEALTH PLAN	CA	• E-	1q 2019	6.0	34.1	34.1	-34.8	0.00	0.00
ASPIRUS ARISE HEALTH PLAN OF WISCONS	WI	• C	1q 2019	49.3	92.5	92.5	16.3	1.37	1.14
ASSN HEALTH CARE MGMT INC	CA	• D	1q 2019	1.8	10.8	10.8	0.5	0.47	0.47
ASSURANCEAMERICA INS CO	NE	D+	1q 2019	111.0	168.0	1.6	21.2	0.82	0.73
ASSURITY LIFE INS CO	NE	• B+	1q 2019	2,750.1	271.4	116.9	337.1	2.49	1.45
ASSURITY LIFE INS CO OF NY	NY	B	1q 2019	8.3	0.3	0.2	7.3	3.40	3.06
ASURIS NORTHWEST HEALTH	WA	• B	1q 2019	121.4	168.7	168.7	85.7	8.47	7.06
ATHENE ANNUITY & LIFE ASR CO	DE	C	1q 2019	23,546.1	116.2	15.1	1,558.0	0.87	0.61
ATHENE ANNUITY & LIFE ASR CO OF NY	NY	C+	1q 2019	3,143.2	167.5	0.2	293.5	2.05	1.15
ATHENE ANNUITY & LIFE CO	IA	C	1q 2019	60,545.1	10,302.0	1.9	1,248.0	0.97	0.51
ATHENE LIFE INS CO OF NEW YORK	NY	C	1q 2019	943.6	46.0	0.6	78.4	2.47	1.19
ATLANTA LIFE INS CO	GA	D+	1q 2019	21.4	1.1	0.1	8.2	1.18	0.77
▼ ATLANTIC COAST LIFE INS CO	SC	C-	1q 2019	229.4	135.4	0.1	30.7	2.08	1.15
ATLANTIC SPECIALTY INS CO	NY	C	1q 2019	2,462.5	985.7	134.5	692.4	1.31	0.93
ATRIO HEALTH PLANS INC	OR	• D	1q 2019	63.4	203.9	203.9	20.3	1.11	0.92
AULTCARE HEALTH INSURING CORP	OH	• B	1q 2019	109.1	242.6	242.6	92.2	2.02	1.69
AULTCARE INS CO	OH	• B	1q 2019	93.2	277.1	277.1	50.9	2.00	1.67
AUTO CLUB LIFE INS CO	MI	C	1q 2019	852.4	7.3	0.6	90.8	1.06	0.76
AUTO-OWNERS LIFE INS CO	MI	B	1q 2019	4,057.5	364.4	17.9	495.9	3.32	1.74
AUXILIO PLATINO INC	PR	U		--	--	--	--	--	--
AVALON INS CO	PA	• D+	1q 2019	39.4	63.7	63.7	16.4	1.98	1.65
▼ AVEMCO INS CO	MD	C	1q 2019	113.6	25.8	0.0	78.0	4.23	3.98
AVERA HEALTH PLANS INC	SD	• B	1q 2019	89.5	241.1	241.1	49.2	1.78	1.49
AVMED INC	FL	• C	1q 2019	264.8	922.8	922.8	98.9	1.11	0.92
AXA EQUITABLE LIFE INS CO	NY	B+	1q 2019	201,023.4	13,640.5	51.1	7,165.7	3.37	1.76
▼ AXIS INS CO	IL	C+	1q 2019	1,812.6	911.9	122.3	546.6	1.91	1.31
AXIS REINS CO	NY	C+	1q 2019	3,872.9	78.8	0.2	989.6	2.05	1.22
BALTIMORE LIFE INS CO	MD	B	1q 2019	1,308.4	124.1	0.7	83.3	1.71	0.89
BANKERS CONSECO LIFE INS CO	NY	D	1q 2019	498.4	61.0	12.5	60.1	3.39	1.72
BANKERS FIDELITY ASR CO	GA	C+	1q 2019	10.8	37.8	37.8	9.1	3.57	2.76
BANKERS FIDELITY LIFE INS CO	GA	• C	1q 2019	151.8	143.0	134.2	33.2	1.04	0.82
BANKERS LIFE & CAS CO	IL	• D+	1q 2019	15,753.0	2,375.6	759.6	1,168.3	1.71	0.96
BANKERS LIFE OF LOUISIANA	LA	C	1q 2019	17.7	34.3	22.5	6.6	1.99	1.79
BANKERS RESERVE LIFE INS CO OF WI	WI	• C-	1q 2019	448.3	2,110.2	2,110.2	233.5	2.08	1.73
BANNER HEALTH & AETNA HLTH INS	AZ	• C	1q 2019	136.3	233.3	233.3	67.5	4.45	3.71
▲ BANNER HLTH & AETNA HLTH PLAN	AZ	• B-	1q 2019	22.1	27.5	27.5	12.9	5.35	4.46
BANNER LIFE INS CO	MD	C	1q 2019	4,375.9	1,935.8	2.0	530.6	2.30	1.48
▲ BAPTIST HEALTH PLAN INC	KY	• D	1q 2019	15.5	16.4	16.4	9.6	1.37	1.14
▲ BAY AREA ACCOUNTABLE CARE	CA	• D	1q 2019	46.4	126.7	126.7	12.7	0.68	0.42

INSURANCE COMPANY NAME	DOM. STATE	RATING	DATA DATE	TOTAL ASSETS ($MIL)	TOTAL PREMIUMS ($MIL)	HEALTH PREMIUMS ($MIL)	CAPITAL & SURPLUS ($MIL)	RISK ADJUSTED CAPITAL RATIO 1	RISK ADJUSTED CAPITAL RATIO 2
BAYCARE SELECT HEALTH PLANS	FL	U		--	--	--	--	--	--
BC&BS OF NEW MEXICO INS CO	NM	U		--	--	--	--	--	--
BCBSIL GP HMO NFP	IL	U		--	--	--	--	--	--
BCS INS CO	OH	• B-	1q 2019	343.2	367.1	173.1	155.3	10.74	6.12
BEACON HEALTH OPTIONS OF PA	PA	• E+	1q 2019	28.2	12.5	12.5	17.1	7.75	6.45
BEAZLEY INS CO	CT	B-	1q 2019	633.5	337.1	10.0	171.7	1.71	1.15
BEHEALTHY FLORIDA INC	FL	• C-	1q 2019	40.4	108.2	108.2	22.3	4.26	3.55
BENCHMARK INS CO	KS	C+	1q 2019	443.1	330.5	22.4	116.1	3.57	2.71
BENEFICIAL LIFE INS CO	UT	B	1q 2019	2,133.0	59.1	0.0	189.2	2.91	1.52
BERKLEY INS CO	DE	B	1q 2019	18,715.4	555.3	30.7	5,403.8	1.34	1.11
BERKLEY LIFE & HEALTH INS CO	IA	• A	1q 2019	336.2	391.7	391.6	174.8	4.83	3.53
BERKSHIRE HATHAWAY SPECIALTY INS CO	NE	C	1q 2019	4,864.2	890.9	145.4	3,647.6	6.90	4.04
BERKSHIRE LIFE INS CO OF AMERICA	MA	• B	1q 2019	3,988.4	604.0	594.1	191.5	2.27	1.08
BEST LIFE & HEALTH INS CO	TX	B+	1q 2019	23.7	42.8	42.1	17.6	1.74	1.41
BEST MERIDIAN INS CO	FL	B-	1q 2019	356.9	54.9	9.9	61.4	1.78	1.16
BLUE ADVANTAGE PLUS OF KANSAS CITY	MO	• C	1q 2019	49.7	100.6	100.6	16.6	1.06	0.89
BLUE CARE NETWORK OF MICHIGAN	MI	• B	1q 2019	2,607.1	4,239.2	4,239.2	1,680.2	7.12	5.94
BLUE CROSS & BLUE SHIELD MA HMO BLUE	MA	• B+	1q 2019	2,326.3	5,096.3	5,096.3	1,509.9	3.97	3.31
BLUE CROSS & BLUE SHIELD OF FLORIDA	FL	• B	1q 2019	6,126.3	10,866.0	10,866.0	1,952.0	3.85	3.20
BLUE CROSS BLUE SHIELD HEALTHCARE GA	GA	• A-	1q 2019	2,584.7	3,747.9	3,747.9	1,132.8	6.71	5.59
BLUE CROSS BLUE SHIELD OF ALABAMA	AL	• B+	1q 2019	4,116.3	6,026.5	6,026.5	2,127.9	6.21	5.18
BLUE CROSS BLUE SHIELD OF ARIZONA	AZ	• A+	1q 2019	2,403.3	2,207.4	2,207.4	1,626.8	7.77	6.48
BLUE CROSS BLUE SHIELD OF KANSAS INC	KS	• B	1q 2019	1,917.1	2,288.9	2,288.9	925.7	2.02	1.53
BLUE CROSS BLUE SHIELD OF KC	MO	• C+	1q 2019	1,337.2	1,590.0	1,590.0	786.3	5.96	4.97
BLUE CROSS BLUE SHIELD OF MA	MA	• C+	1q 2019	2,471.4	2,899.7	2,899.7	823.0	2.96	2.47
BLUE CROSS BLUE SHIELD OF MICHIGAN	MI	• B-	1q 2019	9,399.2	9,086.6	9,086.6	5,322.4	4.24	3.54
BLUE CROSS BLUE SHIELD OF MINNESOTA	MN	• C	1q 2019	2,784.9	3,956.2	3,956.2	1,061.2	3.56	2.96
BLUE CROSS BLUE SHIELD OF MS, MUTUAL	MS	• A	1q 2019	1,042.9	1,374.7	1,374.7	687.3	8.26	6.88
BLUE CROSS BLUE SHIELD OF NC	NC	• B+	1q 2019	6,006.9	9,118.0	9,118.0	3,759.6	6.60	5.50
BLUE CROSS BLUE SHIELD OF ND	ND	• B	1q 2019	777.4	1,185.0	1,185.0	476.9	3.64	3.03
BLUE CROSS BLUE SHIELD OF NEBRASKA	NE	• C	1q 2019	919.5	1,601.0	1,601.0	413.4	4.90	4.09
BLUE CROSS BLUE SHIELD OF RI	RI	• C	1q 2019	654.0	1,708.9	1,708.9	328.5	2.62	2.19
BLUE CROSS BLUE SHIELD OF SC INC	SC	• B+	1q 2019	4,742.7	3,804.2	3,804.2	3,075.1	6.16	5.14
BLUE CROSS BLUE SHIELD OF VERMONT	VT	• C+	1q 2019	252.3	517.4	517.4	110.7	2.13	1.77
BLUE CROSS BLUE SHIELD OF WISCONSIN	WI	• B-	1q 2019	608.3	726.9	726.9	347.5	3.97	3.31
BLUE CROSS BLUE SHIELD OF WYOMING	WY	• B-	1q 2019	625.1	612.2	612.2	368.4	5.87	4.89
BLUE CROSS COMPLETE OF MICHIGAN	MI	• B	1q 2019	294.3	755.9	755.9	116.6	2.98	2.48
BLUE CROSS OF CALIFORNIA	CA	• A+	1q 2019	7,997.8	15,774.6	15,774.6	3,429.6	3.91	2.49
BLUE CROSS OF IDAHO CARE PLUS INC	ID	• C+	1q 2019	165.0	349.5	349.5	79.8	2.23	1.86
BLUE CROSS OF IDAHO HEALTH SERVICE	ID	• B	1q 2019	980.3	1,243.6	1,243.6	653.5	6.60	5.50
BLUE RIDGE INDEMNITY CO	DE	C	1q 2019	18.7	2.0	0.0	15.8	16.49	10.33
BLUE SHIELD OF CALIFORNIA L&H INS CO	CA	• B	1q 2019	318.1	248.0	238.2	202.1	5.33	3.93
BLUEBONNET LIFE INS CO	MS	A-	1q 2019	65.0	5.0	0.0	61.5	8.35	7.52
BLUECHOICE HEALTHPLAN OF SC INC	SC	• B	1q 2019	386.7	609.8	609.8	258.6	7.51	6.26
BLUECROSS BLUESHIELD KANSAS SOLUTION	KS	• C+	1q 2019	60.1	3.9	3.9	56.7	24.52	20.43
BLUECROSS BLUESHIELD OF TENNESSEE	TN	• B+	1q 2019	4,339.8	5,411.3	5,411.3	3,436.7	7.15	5.96
BOSTON MEDICAL CENTER HEALTH PLAN	MA	• C	1q 2019	524.9	2,297.2	2,297.2	227.6	1.16	0.97
BOSTON MUTUAL LIFE INS CO	MA	• B+	1q 2019	1,484.3	244.0	64.1	225.4	2.06	1.36
BRAVO HEALTH MID-ATLANTIC INC	MD	• C	1q 2019	84.4	259.1	259.1	37.2	2.44	2.04
BRAVO HEALTH PENNSYLVANIA INC	PA	• C+	1q 2019	201.7	622.9	622.9	112.8	3.62	3.02
BRIDGESPAN HEALTH CO	UT	• B	1q 2019	45.3	16.2	16.2	38.3	28.05	23.38
BRIDGEWAY HEALTH SOL OF AZ	AZ	• C	1q 2019	32.1	13.8	13.8	10.9	12.49	10.41

INSURANCE COMPANY NAME	DOM. STATE	RATING	DATA DATE	TOTAL ASSETS ($MIL)	TOTAL PREMIUMS ($MIL)	HEALTH PREMIUMS ($MIL)	CAPITAL & SURPLUS ($MIL)	RISK ADJUSTED CAPITAL RATIO 1	RISK ADJUSTED CAPITAL RATIO 2
BRIGHT HEALTH CO OF ARIZONA	AZ	• D	1q 2019	28.3	10.8	10.8	13.3	5.07	4.23
▲ BRIGHT HEALTH INS CO	CO	• E+	1q 2019	85.0	108.7	108.7	23.3	2.17	1.81
BRIGHT HLTH INS CO OF AL INC	AL	• D	1q 2019	13.1	4.6	4.6	6.5	5.63	4.69
BRIGHT HLTH INS CO OF NEW YORK	NY	U		--	--	--	--	--	--
BRIGHT HLTH INS CO OH	OH	U		--	--	--	--	--	--
BRIGHT HLTH INS CO TN	TN	U		--	--	--	--	--	--
BRIGHTHOUSE LIFE INSURANCE CO	DE	B	1q 2019	169,664.8	6,870.0	224.2	5,736.1	2.79	1.45
▲ BROWN & TOLAND HEALTH SERVICES	CA	• E+	1q 2019	35.3	99.2	99.2	6.5	0.72	0.44
BUCKEYE COMMUNITY HEALTH PLAN INC	OH	• B	1q 2019	611.8	2,555.2	2,555.2	290.5	2.34	1.95
BUCKEYE HEALTH PLAN COMMUNITY	OH	• C-	1q 2019	8.2	9.2	9.2	3.3	2.45	2.05
BUPA INS CO	FL	• B	1q 2019	313.8	260.9	260.9	140.3	3.40	2.84
CALIFORNIA HEALTH & WELLNESS PLAN	CA	• D+	1q 2019	296.6	656.8	656.8	50.5	0.64	0.44
CALIFORNIA PHYSICIANS SERVICE	CA	• A+	1q 2019	9,021.3	17,113.1	17,113.1	5,445.4	3.15	2.13
CANADA LIFE ASSURANCE CO-US BRANCH	MI	C	1q 2019	4,666.5	90.2	2.2	194.0	1.41	0.74
CAPITAL ADVANTAGE ASR CO	PA	• C	1q 2019	697.0	1,380.5	1,380.5	357.7	4.36	3.63
CAPITAL ADVANTAGE INS CO	PA	• C	1q 2019	674.3	244.6	244.6	429.6	3.34	2.78
CAPITAL BLUE CROSS	PA	• B-	1q 2019	1,168.7	318.7	318.7	722.2	4.17	3.48
CAPITAL DISTRICT PHYSICIANS HEALTH P	NY	• A	1q 2019	621.6	1,511.9	1,511.9	395.2	3.02	2.52
CAPITAL HEALTH PLAN INC	FL	• B+	1q 2019	575.1	865.0	865.0	443.8	7.67	6.39
CAPITOL INDEMNITY CORP	WI	C	1q 2019	660.9	68.0	0.2	283.5	1.87	1.40
CARE 1ST HEALTH PLAN INC	CA	• A+	1q 2019	1,214.3	2,348.5	2,348.5	559.3	4.48	3.73
CARE IMPROVEMENT PLUS OF TEXAS INS	TX	• B	1q 2019	607.9	1,701.8	1,701.8	248.0	2.38	1.98
CARE IMPROVEMENT PLUS SOUTH CENTRAL	AR	• B-	1q 2019	778.0	1,673.8	1,673.8	525.6	6.32	5.27
CARE IMPROVEMENT PLUS WI INS	WI	• B	1q 2019	96.6	242.8	242.8	57.4	4.13	3.45
CARE N CARE INS CO	TX	• C	1q 2019	42.7	108.7	108.7	18.9	1.60	1.33
▼ CARE N CARE INS CO OF NORTH CAROLINA	NC	• E-	1q 2019	34.9	128.7	128.7	10.5	0.35	0.29
CARE WISCONSIN HEALTH PLAN INC	WI	• B+	1q 2019	61.5	150.3	150.3	36.6	2.17	1.81
CAREAMERICA LIFE INS CO	CA	U		--	--	--	--	--	--
CARECENTRIX OF NEW JERSEY INC	NJ	• D	4q 2018	10.8	24.0	24.0	4.6	0.84	0.70
CARECONNECT INS CO	NY	• E-	1q 2019	91.6	44.2	44.2	43.2	3.88	3.23
CARECORE NJ LLC	NJ	• D	4q 2018	30.4	147.2	147.2	7.9	3.76	3.13
CAREFIRST BLUECHOICE INC	DC	• C+	1q 2019	1,272.7	3,620.5	3,620.5	741.3	3.82	3.18
CAREFIRST OF MARYLAND INC	MD	• C+	1q 2019	1,810.5	1,966.4	1,966.4	766.5	4.01	3.34
CAREMORE HEALTH PLAN	CA	• B-	1q 2019	289.6	910.4	910.4	66.5	1.81	1.13
CAREMORE HEALTH PLAN OF ARIZONA INC	AZ	• B	1q 2019	61.5	166.4	166.4	38.6	5.36	4.46
CAREMORE HEALTH PLAN OF NEVADA	NV	• B-	1q 2019	31.4	96.6	96.6	19.6	3.50	2.92
CAREPARTNERS OF CT INC	CT	U		--	--	--	--	--	--
CAREPLUS HEALTH PLANS INC	FL	• B	1q 2019	538.2	1,771.3	1,771.3	173.1	3.63	3.02
CARESOURCE	OH	• B-	1q 2019	1,651.2	8,334.8	8,334.8	736.8	1.50	1.25
▲ CARESOURCE GEORGIA CO	GA	• C	1q 2019	172.9	659.7	659.7	83.0	1.14	0.95
CARESOURCE INDIANA INC	IN	• D+	1q 2019	335.2	782.1	782.1	78.8	1.31	1.09
CARESOURCE KENTUCKY CO	KY	• C	1q 2019	81.6	281.3	281.3	43.1	2.00	1.67
CARESOURCE WEST VIRGINIA CO	WV	• C	1q 2019	35.6	49.4	49.4	12.1	1.59	1.33
CARIBBEAN AMERICAN LIFE ASR CO	PR	B	1q 2019	37.8	25.9	11.2	10.2	2.02	1.74
CARIBBEAN AMERICAN PROPERTY INS CO	PR	C	1q 2019	45.6	54.8	0.0	22.8	0.76	0.50
CARILION CLINIC MEDICARE RESOURCES	VA	U		--	--	--	--	--	--
CARITEN HEALTH PLAN INC	TN	• B	1q 2019	504.0	1,403.1	1,403.1	242.0	4.00	3.34
CAROLINA COMPLETE HEALTH INC	NC	U		--	--	--	--	--	--
CATHOLIC SPECIAL NEEDS PLAN LLC	NY	• C	1q 2019	15.3	47.3	47.3	5.9	0.70	0.58
CATLIN INS CO	TX	• C+	1q 2019	169.1	70.5	30.4	53.5	1.53	0.97
CBHNP SERVICES INC	PA	U		--	--	--	--	--	--
CCHA LLC	CO	U		--	--	--	--	--	--

INSURANCE COMPANY NAME	DOM. STATE	RATING	DATA DATE	TOTAL ASSETS ($MIL)	TOTAL PREMIUMS ($MIL)	HEALTH PREMIUMS ($MIL)	CAPITAL & SURPLUS ($MIL)	RISK ADJUSTED CAPITAL RATIO 1	RISK ADJUSTED CAPITAL RATIO 2
CDI GROUP INC	CA	• E-	1q 2019	2.9	14.8	14.8	1.7	1.00	0.97
CDPHP UNIVERSAL BENEFITS INC	NY	• B	1q 2019	206.5	567.2	567.2	140.1	3.84	3.20
CELTIC INS CO	IL	• B-	1q 2019	2,461.8	2,425.9	2,425.9	441.3	2.91	2.42
CELTICARE HEALTH PLAN OF MA INC	MA	• C-	1q 2019	24.6	29.6	29.6	13.9	7.99	6.66
CENPATICO OF ARIZONA INC	AZ	U		--	--	--	--	--	--
CENTENE VENTURE CO FLORIDA	FL	U		--	--	--	--	--	--
CENTENE VENTURE CO ILLINOIS	IL	U		--	--	--	--	--	--
CENTENE VENTURE CO KANSAS	KS	U		--	--	--	--	--	--
CENTENNIAL CASUALTY CO	AL	C+	1q 2019	125.3	19.1	2.8	85.2	3.31	1.95
CENTRAL HEALTH PLAN OF CALIFORNIA	CA	• E+	1q 2019	60.2	408.2	408.2	12.6	0.37	0.23
CENTRAL SECURITY LIFE INS CO	TX	D+	1q 2019	86.1	2.7	0.1	5.7	0.66	0.59
CENTRAL STATES H & L CO OF OMAHA	NE	• B	1q 2019	382.3	62.8	28.5	142.3	3.53	2.63
CENTRAL STATES INDEMNITY CO OF OMAHA	NE	• C+	1q 2019	556.6	132.5	84.5	492.2	4.33	2.75
CENTRE LIFE INS CO	MA	• B-	1q 2019	1,655.3	16.5	16.5	94.6	4.24	2.55
CENTURION LIFE INS CO	IA	• C	1q 2019	501.7	0.1	0.0	315.9	24.64	11.06
CENTURY INS CO GUAM LTD	GU	C	1q 2019	28.4	11.9	0.0	18.3	4.34	2.50
CHA HMO INC	KY	• C+	1q 2019	495.0	190.2	190.2	162.2	16.78	13.99
CHEROKEE INS CO	MI	B-	1q 2019	605.0	218.0	54.3	202.9	2.80	1.67
CHESAPEAKE LIFE INS CO	OK	• A+	1q 2019	213.1	247.5	206.0	134.0	3.24	2.57
CHILDRENS COMMUNITY HEALTH PLAN INC	WI	• B+	1q 2019	161.7	434.4	434.4	81.5	2.22	1.85
CHILDRENS MEDICAL CENTER HEALTH PLAN	TX	• E-	1q 2019	89.4	264.6	264.6	47.0	1.42	1.18
CHINESE COMMUNITY HEALTH PLAN	CA	• E-	1q 2019	62.4	133.7	133.7	6.7	0.38	0.25
CHOICE PHYSICIANS NETWORK	CA	• E	1q 2019	28.8	130.6	130.6	5.7	0.41	0.25
CHRISTIAN FIDELITY LIFE INS CO	TX	• A-	1q 2019	59.8	27.0	25.5	28.9	3.51	2.56
CHRISTUS HEALTH PLAN	TX	• C-	1q 2019	91.2	166.9	166.9	41.6	2.38	1.98
CHUBB CUSTOM INS CO	NJ	B-	1q 2019	278.0	182.3	0.0	230.5	35.90	32.31
CHUBB NATIONAL INS CO	IN	B	1q 2019	266.7	588.9	0.0	177.5	21.09	18.98
CICA LIFE INS CO OF AMERICA	CO	C	1q 2019	161.3	64.5	0.6	49.1	1.97	1.72
CIGNA HEALTH & LIFE INS CO	CT	• B	1q 2019	10,443.5	17,189.7	17,189.3	4,820.7	2.10	1.60
CIGNA HEALTHCARE OF ARIZONA INC	AZ	• C	1q 2019	145.9	571.2	571.2	73.8	2.27	1.89
CIGNA HEALTHCARE OF CALIFORNIA INC	CA	• C	1q 2019	136.0	887.5	887.5	48.5	1.26	0.78
CIGNA HEALTHCARE OF COLORADO INC	CO	• C	1q 2019	3.3	2.6	2.6	3.1	6.30	5.25
CIGNA HEALTHCARE OF FLORIDA INC	FL	• C	1q 2019	3.0	1.1	1.1	2.6	4.60	3.83
CIGNA HEALTHCARE OF GEORGIA INC	GA	• C	1q 2019	79.0	254.0	254.0	42.5	2.58	2.15
CIGNA HEALTHCARE OF ILLINOIS INC	IL	• C	1q 2019	102.0	81.0	81.0	18.8	4.38	3.65
CIGNA HEALTHCARE OF INDIANA INC	IN	U		--	--	--	--	--	--
CIGNA HEALTHCARE OF NEW JERSEY INC	NJ	• E	1q 2019	13.5	4.8	4.8	11.5	13.32	11.10
CIGNA HEALTHCARE OF NORTH CAROLINA	NC	• D	1q 2019	76.5	170.7	170.7	37.8	3.74	3.12
CIGNA HEALTHCARE OF SOUTH CAROLINA	SC	• C	1q 2019	28.8	56.1	56.1	21.6	4.94	4.11
CIGNA HEALTHCARE OF ST LOUIS	MO	• C	1q 2019	14.3	19.8	19.8	9.5	5.19	4.33
CIGNA HEALTHCARE OF TENNESSEE INC	TN	• C-	1q 2019	8.5	21.3	21.3	6.1	3.33	2.77
CIGNA HEALTHCARE OF TEXAS INC	TX	• C-	1q 2019	34.1	76.4	76.4	25.1	5.83	4.86
CIGNA LIFE INS CO OF NEW YORK	NY	• A-	1q 2019	419.6	204.2	146.3	111.7	2.56	1.69
CIGNA NATIONAL HEALTH INS CO	OH	B-	1q 2019	15.4	4.6	4.0	14.6	1.60	1.55
CIGNA WORLDWIDE INS CO	DE	B-	1q 2019	53.3	9.6	0.0	12.1	1.67	1.50
CINCINNATI EQUITABLE LIFE INS CO	OH	D	1q 2019	161.0	38.0	0.0	8.8	1.07	0.76
CINCINNATI LIFE INS CO	OH	B-	1q 2019	4,558.2	363.1	6.9	186.8	1.23	0.66
CITIZENS FIDELITY INS CO	AR	C+	1q 2019	70.9	3.0	0.0	13.8	2.03	1.36
CITIZENS NATIONAL LIFE INS CO	TX	C	1q 2019	11.8	0.9	0.0	1.7	2.95	2.66
CITIZENS SECURITY LIFE INS CO	KY	C	1q 2019	29.8	77.3	72.2	16.3	0.76	0.67
CLAREMONT BEHAVIORAL SVCS		• C-	1q 2019	1.6	5.1	5.1	1.2	2.30	1.86
CLEAR SPRING HEALTH OF IL INC	IL	U		--	--	--	--	--	--

	INSURANCE COMPANY NAME	DOM. STATE	RATING	DATA DATE	TOTAL ASSETS ($MIL)	TOTAL PREMIUMS ($MIL)	HEALTH PREMIUMS ($MIL)	CAPITAL & SURPLUS ($MIL)	RISK ADJUSTED CAPITAL RATIO 1	RISK ADJUSTED CAPITAL RATIO 2
	CLEARRIVER HEALTH	TN	U		--	--	--	--	--	--
	CLOISTER MUTL CAS INS CO	PA	C	1q 2019	10.0	0.0	0.0	10.0	15.03	6.68
	CLOVER HMO NEW JERSEY INC	NJ	U		--	--	--	--	--	--
	CLOVER INSURANCE COMPANY	NJ	• C	1q 2019	115.3	290.1	290.1	34.0	0.44	0.37
	CMFG LIFE INS CO	IA	B-	1q 2019	18,869.5	2,654.8	571.3	2,180.4	1.58	1.23
	CMNTY CARE HLTH PLAN INC (WI)	WI	• B-	1q 2019	22.8	94.8	94.8	14.6	1.44	1.20
	CMNTY CARE HLTH PLAN OF LA INC	LA	• B-	1q 2019	385.7	1,138.8	1,138.8	170.9	2.72	2.27
	CMNTY CARE HLTH PLAN OF NV INC	NV	• B	1q 2019	174.8	652.4	652.4	83.8	2.37	1.98
	COLONIAL LIFE & ACCIDENT INS CO	SC	• C+	1q 2019	3,463.5	1,595.5	1,233.5	576.3	2.37	1.51
	COLONIAL LIFE INS CO OF TX	TX	C-	1q 2019	19.9	1.0	0.3	14.6	4.49	2.83
	COLONIAL PENN LIFE INS CO	PA	• D+	1q 2019	872.3	753.6	476.8	93.9	1.20	0.71
	COLORADO ACCESS	CO	• D	1q 2019	57.8	295.9	295.9	22.0	N/A	N/A
	COLUMBIAN LIFE INS CO	IL	C	1q 2019	335.0	243.4	0.0	26.9	1.95	1.08
	COLUMBIAN MUTUAL LIFE INS CO	NY	B	1q 2019	1,442.7	68.3	1.8	84.2	1.27	0.84
	COLUMBUS LIFE INS CO	OH	C+	1q 2019	4,179.2	367.2	0.0	280.0	1.90	0.98
	COMBINED INS CO OF AMERICA	IL	• C	1q 2019	2,328.5	1,056.9	947.9	182.0	1.02	0.73
	COMBINED LIFE INS CO OF NEW YORK	NY	• C+	1q 2019	486.9	156.6	135.1	55.7	1.47	1.04
	COMM TRAVELERS LIFE INS CO	NY	B-	1q 2019	27.7	6.9	6.9	14.0	2.92	2.63
▲	COMMENCEMENT BAY RISK MGMT INS	WA	• B	1q 2019	43.8	1.6	1.6	36.5	7.60	6.84
	COMMON GROUND HEALTHCARE COOPERATIVE	WI	• D	1q 2019	260.2	557.5	557.5	185.2	3.39	2.82
	COMMONWEALTH ANNUITY & LIFE INS CO	MA	B-	1q 2019	20,694.8	93.0	0.3	2,690.9	0.85	0.71
	COMMUNITY CARE ALLIANCE OF ILLINOIS	IL	• E-	1q 2019	10.0	34.1	34.1	-11.3	0.00	0.00
	COMMUNITY CARE BEHAVIORAL HEALTH	PA	• B+	1q 2019	386.8	970.0	970.0	249.2	4.39	3.66
▲	COMMUNITY CARE HEALTH PLAN	CA	• C+	1q 2019	13.6	46.4	46.4	9.4	1.84	1.15
	COMMUNITY FIRST GROUP HOSPITAL SERVI	TX	U		--	--	--	--	--	--
	COMMUNITY FIRST HEALTH PLANS INC	TX	• B-	1q 2019	126.0	537.4	537.4	66.8	1.32	1.10
	COMMUNITY HEALTH CHOICE INC	TX	• C	1q 2019	179.9	706.2	706.2	55.2	0.95	0.79
▲	COMMUNITY HEALTH CHOICE TX INC	TX	• C	1q 2019	175.8	957.6	957.6	96.0	1.22	1.02
	COMMUNITY HEALTH GROUP	CA	• B-	1q 2019	895.6	950.4	950.4	482.1	6.99	4.25
	COMMUNITY HEALTH PLAN OF WASHINGTON	WA	• B	1q 2019	483.7	864.0	864.0	179.1	2.55	2.12
	COMMUNITY INS CO	OH	• B-	1q 2019	2,141.0	5,398.4	5,398.4	950.8	3.12	2.60
	COMMUNITYCARE GOVERNMENT PROGRAMS	OK	• D	1q 2019	10.2	26.3	26.3	4.3	1.24	1.03
	COMMUNITYCARE HMO INC	OK	• B	1q 2019	199.9	589.5	589.5	107.1	2.98	2.48
	COMMUNITYCARE L&H INS CO	OK	• C	1q 2019	17.5	56.2	56.2	6.7	1.22	1.02
	COMPANION LIFE INS CO	NY	B-	1q 2019	1,183.4	137.5	0.0	58.5	1.62	0.86
	COMPANION LIFE INS CO	SC	• B+	1q 2019	420.6	813.9	781.5	235.4	2.86	2.20
	COMPANION LIFE INS CO OF CA	CA	B	1q 2019	26.7	23.8	23.8	11.5	2.92	2.63
	COMPCARE HEALTH SERVICES INS CORP	WI	• A-	1q 2019	376.3	914.3	914.3	186.1	3.63	3.03
	COMPREHENSIVE MOBILE INS CO	AZ	• B	1q 2019	2.6	4.4	4.4	2.5	4.38	3.65
	COMPREHENSIVE MOBILE PLAN UTAH INC	UT	• C+	1q 2019	1.1	1.3	1.3	1.0	6.13	5.10
	CONNECTICARE BENEFITS INC	CT	• C	1q 2019	207.7	566.4	566.4	63.0	2.21	1.84
	CONNECTICARE INC	CT	• C-	1q 2019	249.0	679.9	679.9	73.4	1.84	1.53
	CONNECTICARE INS CO	CT	• C	1q 2019	247.9	591.2	591.2	126.6	2.01	1.67
	CONNECTICARE OF MASSACHUSETTS INC	MA	• C	1q 2019	3.6	3.2	3.2	3.0	2.26	1.88
	CONNECTICUT DENTAL PRACTICE	CT	U		--	--	--	--	--	--
	CONNECTICUT GENERAL LIFE INS CO	CT	• B-	1q 2019	19,081.8	646.6	181.1	5,521.9	1.23	1.15
	CONSTELLATION HEALTH LLC	PR	U		--	--	--	--	--	--
	CONSTITUTION LIFE INS CO	TX	• D	1q 2019	388.3	83.1	71.8	40.6	2.64	1.40
	CONTINENTAL AMERICAN INS CO	SC	• B	1q 2019	711.8	575.8	555.1	160.3	1.89	1.42
	CONTINENTAL CASUALTY CO	IL	B-	1q 2019	42,945.5	6,767.2	474.1	10,202.2	1.93	1.46
	CONTINENTAL GENERAL INS CO	OH	• C+	1q 2019	4,240.2	306.6	277.1	274.2	1.86	1.01
▲	CONTINENTAL LIFE INS CO	PA	C	1q 2019	1.7	3.1	0.0	1.7	2.64	2.38

INSURANCE COMPANY NAME	DOM. STATE	RATING	DATA DATE	TOTAL ASSETS ($MIL)	TOTAL PREMIUMS ($MIL)	HEALTH PREMIUMS ($MIL)	CAPITAL & SURPLUS ($MIL)	RISK ADJUSTED CAPITAL RATIO 1	RISK ADJUSTED CAPITAL RATIO 2
CONTINENTAL LIFE INS CO OF BRENTWOOD	TN	• C+	1q 2019	364.4	509.1	505.3	160.0	0.86	0.77
CONTRA COSTA HEALTH PLAN	CA	• B	1q 2019	364.1	773.8	773.8	79.2	1.75	1.11
COOK CHILDRENS HEALTH PLAN	TX	• E+	1q 2019	154.6	549.9	549.9	86.0	1.74	1.45
COORDINATED CARE CORP	IN	• C+	1q 2019	574.7	1,723.8	1,723.8	237.0	3.15	2.62
COORDINATED CARE OF WASHINGTON INC	WA	• C-	1q 2019	239.6	596.6	596.6	81.1	2.42	2.02
COPIC INS CO	CO	B-	1q 2019	579.0	88.4	0.8	297.1	4.76	3.20
CORVESTA LIFE INS CO	AZ	U		--	--	--	--	--	--
COUNTRY LIFE INS CO	IL	A+	1q 2019	9,777.7	521.4	107.2	1,223.6	2.08	1.37
COUNTRYWAY INS CO	NY	C	1q 2019	30.5	40.2	0.0	25.4	16.35	14.72
COUNTY OF LOS ANGELES DEPT HEALTH	CA	U		--	--	--	--	--	--
COVENTRY HEALTH & LIFE INS CO	MO	• B-	1q 2019	1,333.5	1,728.0	1,728.0	1,010.5	6.89	5.74
COVENTRY HEALTH CARE OF FLORIDA INC	FL	• D	1q 2019	384.4	493.7	493.7	127.2	2.99	2.49
COVENTRY HEALTH CARE OF ILLINOIS INC	IL	• C	1q 2019	159.6	321.6	321.6	81.6	4.23	3.53
COVENTRY HEALTH CARE OF KANSAS INC	KS	• C	1q 2019	20.8	6.0	6.0	15.0	18.23	15.19
COVENTRY HEALTH CARE OF MISSOURI INC	MO	• C+	1q 2019	281.1	808.3	808.3	139.0	3.45	2.88
COVENTRY HEALTH CARE OF NEBRASKA INC	NE	• C	1q 2019	23.7	9.8	9.8	23.0	22.06	18.38
COVENTRY HEALTH CARE OF VIRGINIA INC	VA	• B-	1q 2019	266.4	731.9	731.9	69.7	1.55	1.29
COVENTRY HEALTH CARE OF WEST VA INC	WV	• B	1q 2019	211.2	632.8	632.8	91.3	3.19	2.65
COVENTRY HEALTH PLAN OF FLORIDA INC	FL	U		--	--	--	--	--	--
COX HEALTH SYSTEMS HMO INC	MO	U		--	--	--	--	--	--
COX HEALTH SYSTEMS INS CO	MO	• D+	1q 2019	51.9	153.5	153.5	18.8	0.75	0.63
CRESTPOINT HEALTH INS CO	TN	U		--	--	--	--	--	--
CRYSTAL RUN HEALTH INS CO INC	NY	• E	1q 2019	13.0	12.7	12.7	2.5	0.64	0.54
CRYSTAL RUN HEALTH PLAN LLC	NY	• E-	1q 2019	12.4	17.3	17.3	0.5	0.34	0.28
CSI LIFE INS CO	NE	B-	1q 2019	25.0	36.2	36.1	17.9	4.52	4.07
DAILY UNDERWRITERS OF AMERICA	PA	C+	1q 2019	51.6	16.8	0.0	36.3	2.94	2.21
DAKOTA CAPITAL LIFE INS CO	ND	D	1q 2019	8.1	1.6	0.1	1.5	0.77	0.69
DAVITA HEALTHCARE PARTNERS PLAN INC	CA	• E+	1q 2019	236.3	2,125.6	2,125.6	53.7	0.34	0.21
DB INS CO LTD US GUAM BRANCH	GU	C	1q 2019	75.0	39.5	0.0	38.9	7.26	4.47
DC CHARTERED HEALTH PLAN INC	DC	F	4q 2018	5.2	0.0	0.0	-15.5	0.00	0.00
DEAN HEALTH INS INC	WI	U		--	--	--	--	--	--
DEAN HEALTH PLAN INC	WI	• A	1q 2019	305.3	1,373.4	1,373.4	160.8	2.39	1.99
DEARBORN NATIONAL LIFE INS CO	IL	• B+	1q 2019	1,669.0	495.2	173.2	455.9	3.34	2.08
DEARBORN NATIONAL LIFE INS CO OF NY	NY	B+	1q 2019	21.1	0.5	0.2	11.0	2.99	2.69
DELAWARE AMERICAN LIFE INS CO	DE	• B+	1q 2019	119.0	77.1	65.0	65.8	4.19	3.13
DELAWARE LIFE INS CO OF NEW YORK	NY	B-	1q 2019	2,284.8	30.1	0.0	379.2	9.58	4.62
DELSURE HEALTH INSURANCE INC	DE	U		--	--	--	--	--	--
DELTA LIFE INS CO	GA	E+	1q 2019	65.3	14.7	1.0	5.0	0.35	0.21
DENTAL NETWORK INC	MD	U		--	--	--	--	--	--
DENVER HEALTH MEDICAL PLAN INC	CO	• B-	1q 2019	70.6	244.4	244.4	30.2	1.13	0.94
DESERET MUTUAL INS CO	UT	B	1q 2019	30.2	8.6	8.1	6.8	2.02	1.82
DEVOTED HEALTH INSURANCE CO	FL	U		--	--	--	--	--	--
DEVOTED HEALTH PLAN OF FL INC	FL	U		--	--	--	--	--	--
DEVOTED HLTH PLAN OF TX INC	TX	U		--	--	--	--	--	--
DIGNITY HEALTH PROVIDER RESOURCES	CA	• E	1q 2019	5.0	152.9	152.9	4.0	0.31	0.19
DOCTORS HEALTHCARE PLANS INC	FL	U		--	--	--	--	--	--
DOMINION NATIONAL INSURANCE CO	NJ	U		--	--	--	--	--	--
DRISCOLL CHILDRENS HEALTH PLAN	TX	• C-	1q 2019	127.9	664.1	664.1	52.1	0.76	0.64
EASY CHOICE HEALTH PLAN	CA	• C	1q 2019	118.0	388.9	388.9	31.6	1.11	0.71
EL PASO FIRST HEALTH PLANS INC	TX	• B+	1q 2019	58.8	194.9	194.9	42.4	2.25	1.87
ELAN INSURANCE USVI INC	VI	• E+	1q 2019	4.4	6.7	6.7	2.9	2.40	2.00
ELDERPLAN INC	NY	• C	1q 2019	271.8	1,081.6	1,081.6	104.5	1.14	0.95

INSURANCE COMPANY NAME	DOM. STATE	RATING	DATA DATE	TOTAL ASSETS ($MIL)	TOTAL PREMIUMS ($MIL)	HEALTH PREMIUMS ($MIL)	CAPITAL & SURPLUS ($MIL)	RISK ADJUSTED CAPITAL RATIO 1	RISK ADJUSTED CAPITAL RATIO 2
ELIPS LIFE INS CO	MO	• C	1q 2019	36.3	0.3	0.1	34.6	6.06	5.45
EMC NATIONAL LIFE CO	IA	B	1q 2019	907.8	69.7	1.7	117.5	2.99	1.69
EMI HEALTH	UT	• A	1q 2019	158.9	74.5	74.5	102.2	3.08	2.57
EMPATHIA PACIFIC INC	CA	• C-	1q 2019	3.1	1.5	1.5	2.6	22.27	15.61
EMPHESYS INS CO	TX	U		--	--	--	--	--	--
EMPIRE FIRE & MARINE INS CO	NE	C+	1q 2019	83.7	358.9	13.3	38.8	6.26	5.63
EMPIRE HEALTHCHOICE ASSURANCE INC	NY	• B-	1q 2019	2,201.6	2,634.3	2,634.3	898.5	4.78	3.99
EMPIRE HEALTHCHOICE HMO INC	NY	• B-	1q 2019	449.6	992.1	992.1	202.0	3.63	3.02
EMPOWER HLTHCR SOLUTIONS LLC	AR	U		--	--	--	--	--	--
ENTERPRISE LIFE INS CO	TX	• B	1q 2019	85.5	0.7	0.7	60.6	1.03	0.92
ENVISION INS CO	OH	• C	1q 2019	514.8	393.7	393.7	48.0	1.79	1.49
ENVOLVE DENTAL OF TEXAS INC	TX	U		--	--	--	--	--	--
EON HEALTH INC (GA)	GA	• C-	1q 2019	9.2	4.8	4.8	3.4	3.43	2.86
EPIC HEALTH PLAN	CA	• D-	1q 2019	73.3	477.3	477.3	31.0	0.35	0.21
EPIC LIFE INSURANCE CO	WI	C+	1q 2019	29.9	28.5	21.6	18.0	2.34	1.64
EQUITABLE LIFE & CASUALTY INS CO	UT	• C	1q 2019	647.2	302.8	177.2	59.1	0.99	0.70
▼ EQUITABLE NATIONAL LIFE INS CO	CT	C	1q 2019	11.7	4.5	4.5	8.6	3.51	3.16
▼ ERIE FAMILY LIFE INS CO	PA	B	1q 2019	2,501.1	222.0	0.2	313.6	3.10	1.70
ESSENCE HEALTHCARE INC	MO	• A-	1q 2019	223.8	738.8	738.8	93.5	1.57	1.31
EVANSTON INS CO	IL	C+	1q 2019	4,411.1	1,359.0	0.1	1,326.4	1.93	1.30
EVEREST REINS CO	DE	C	1q 2019	12,120.8	313.9	65.8	3,890.4	1.08	0.77
EXCELLUS HEALTH PLAN INC	NY	• B	1q 2019	3,365.7	5,746.6	5,746.6	1,312.3	3.48	2.90
EXPERIENCE HEALTH INC	NC	U		--	--	--	--	--	--
EYEMED INSURANCE CO	AZ	U		--	--	--	--	--	--
FAIR AMERICAN INS & REINS CO	NY	• B	1q 2019	229.2	78.8	35.7	201.2	46.10	34.44
FALLON COMMUNITY HEALTH PLAN	MA	• B-	1q 2019	407.3	1,514.4	1,514.4	172.8	1.49	1.24
FALLON HEALTH & LIFE ASR CO	MA	• C	1q 2019	16.3	23.6	23.6	6.1	1.41	1.18
▼ FAMILY BENEFIT LIFE INS CO	MO	D+	1q 2019	210.9	25.4	0.0	6.0	0.72	0.47
FAMILY HEALTH NETWORK INC	IL	• D-	1q 2018	69.4	419.3	419.3	27.3	0.14	0.11
FAMILY HERITAGE LIFE INS CO OF AMER	OH	• B-	1q 2019	1,231.3	282.3	278.6	119.5	1.69	1.04
FAMILY LIFE INS CO	TX	• C	1q 2019	143.7	68.7	46.1	28.4	3.07	2.42
FAMILYCARE HEALTH PLANS INC	OR	• E-	1q 2019	19.0	20.3	20.3	18.7	4.62	3.85
FARM BUREAU LIFE INS CO	IA	B+	1q 2019	9,174.1	659.0	6.0	606.9	2.06	1.09
FARM BUREAU LIFE INS CO OF MISSOURI	MO	A-	1q 2019	615.1	47.3	0.3	72.4	1.60	1.07
▼ FARM BUREAU MUTUAL INS CO OF AR	AR	B-	1q 2019	422.2	241.7	0.1	259.3	6.34	5.42
FARM BUREAU MUTUAL INS CO OF MI	MI	B	1q 2019	805.2	169.7	0.1	412.3	4.77	3.19
FARM FAMILY LIFE INS CO	NY	B-	1q 2019	2,607.1	268.6	5.4	234.1	2.27	1.20
FARMERS MUTUAL HAIL INS CO OF IA	IA	B-	1q 2019	669.3	593.8	0.0	444.2	2.52	2.02
FARMERS NEW WORLD LIFE INS CO	WA	B-	1q 2019	5,205.6	1,044.8	19.4	491.0	2.46	1.30
FEDERAL INS CO	IN	C+	1q 2019	15,562.0	5,735.2	291.2	4,988.8	2.44	1.71
FEDERAL LIFE INS CO	IL	C-	1q 2019	250.4	21.4	0.1	24.3	2.74	1.48
FEDERATED LIFE INS CO	MN	A	1q 2019	2,039.8	212.6	29.8	433.6	4.83	2.58
FEDERATED MUTUAL INS CO	MN	B	1q 2019	6,322.3	1,132.2	1.7	3,587.8	3.11	2.54
FIDELITY LIFE ASSN A LEGAL RESERVE	IL	C+	1q 2019	404.1	142.8	1.1	112.3	5.33	2.88
FIDELITY SECURITY LIFE INS CO	MO	• A-	1q 2019	970.0	966.0	926.5	249.8	4.71	2.88
▲ FIDELITY SECURITY LIFE INS CO OF NY	NY	B+	1q 2019	39.6	36.9	36.9	12.1	2.26	2.02
FINANCIAL AMERICAN LIFE INS CO	KS	D-	1q 2019	3.3	0.0	0.0	2.0	1.73	1.56
FIRST ALLMERICA FINANCIAL LIFE INS	MA	B	1q 2019	3,298.5	61.6	0.1	239.7	5.02	2.35
FIRST ASR LIFE OF AMERICA	LA	B	1q 2019	41.6	7.6	1.1	37.1	3.32	3.11
▼ FIRST CARE INC	MD	• D	1q 2019	13.9	15.2	15.2	10.3	8.57	7.14
FIRST COMMUNITY HEALTH PLAN INC	AL	• B	3q 2018	8.7	7.9	7.9	7.4	10.66	8.89
FIRST CONTINENTAL LIFE & ACC INS CO	TX	D-	1q 2019	4.7	20.4	20.4	2.3	1.03	0.85

INSURANCE COMPANY NAME	DOM. STATE	RATING	DATA DATE	TOTAL ASSETS ($MIL)	TOTAL PREMIUMS ($MIL)	HEALTH PREMIUMS ($MIL)	CAPITAL & SURPLUS ($MIL)	RISK ADJUSTED CAPITAL RATIO 1	RISK ADJUSTED CAPITAL RATIO 2
FIRST HEALTH LIFE & HEALTH INS CO	TX	• C+	1q 2019	422.3	553.2	552.6	171.2	1.89	1.55
FIRST INS CO OF HI LTD	HI	C	1q 2019	674.6	92.7	1.0	285.4	4.77	3.27
FIRST MEDICAL HEALTH PLAN INC	PR	• D	1q 2019	232.6	1,080.5	1,080.5	61.2	0.65	0.54
FIRST NATIONAL LIFE INS CO	NE	C	1q 2019	6.4	0.6	0.3	2.5	1.04	0.65
FIRST PENN-PACIFIC LIFE INS CO	IN	B	1q 2019	1,406.1	110.6	0.0	161.8	2.56	1.37
FIRST PRIORITY LIFE INS CO	PA	U		--	--	--	--	--	--
FIRST RELIANCE STANDARD LIFE INS CO	NY	• A-	1q 2019	218.0	93.6	61.5	62.3	4.82	3.21
FIRST SYMETRA NATL LIFE INS CO OF NY	NY	B	1q 2019	2,464.7	557.3	30.3	134.3	1.66	0.85
FIRST UNUM LIFE INS CO	NY	• C+	1q 2019	3,843.8	504.1	381.5	273.0	2.27	1.17
FIRSTCAROLINACARE INS CO	NC	• D	1q 2019	25.1	132.2	132.2	12.6	0.80	0.67
FIVE STAR LIFE INS CO	NE	C	1q 2019	304.1	146.5	0.2	27.9	1.96	1.22
FLORIDA BLUE MEDICARE INC	FL	U		--	--	--	--	--	--
FLORIDA COMBINED LIFE INS CO INC	FL	B-	1q 2019	20.7	133.5	113.8	4.1	1.16	1.04
FLORIDA HEALTH CARE PLAN INC	FL	• A-	1q 2019	213.3	611.9	611.9	115.7	3.66	3.05
FLORIDA MHS INC	FL	• D	1q 2019	86.1	618.1	618.1	28.0	0.77	0.64
FLORIDA TRUE HEALTH INC	FL	• D	1q 2019	86.9	1,207.9	1,207.9	31.4	0.61	0.51
FORESTERS LIFE INS & ANNUITY CO	NY	C+	1q 2019	2,634.4	285.6	0.0	73.9	1.53	0.83
FORETHOUGHT LIFE INS CO	IN	B	1q 2019	32,729.9	8,538.7	71.6	1,722.6	1.82	0.87
FOREVERCARE INC	AR	U		--	--	--	--	--	--
FOUNDATION LIFE INS CO OF AR	AR	D	1q 2019	5.5	1.5	0.2	1.4	1.11	1.00
FREEDOM HEALTH INC	FL	• B	1q 2019	260.8	1,093.3	1,093.3	76.0	1.51	1.26
FREEDOM LIFE INS CO OF AMERICA	TX	• B+	1q 2019	247.5	583.9	522.1	153.2	1.40	1.20
FREELANCERS INS CO	NY	U		--	--	--	--	--	--
FRESNO-KINGS-MADERA REGIONAL HEALTH	CA	• C+	1q 2019	462.6	1,178.2	1,178.2	66.8	1.07	0.65
FRIDAY HEALTH PLANS OF CO INC	CO	• E	1q 2019	20.6	82.2	82.2	7.3	0.80	0.67
GA CHAMBER FEDN BENEFIT PLAN	GA	U		--	--	--	--	--	--
GARDEN STATE LIFE INS CO	TX	A	1q 2019	138.9	23.7	0.0	83.9	9.13	8.22
GATEWAY HEALTH PLAN INC	PA	• B-	1q 2019	754.8	2,357.3	2,357.3	444.4	3.61	3.01
GATEWAY HEALTH PLAN OF OHIO INC	OH	• C	1q 2019	19.0	109.2	109.2	11.7	1.83	1.53
GEISINGER HEALTH PLAN	PA	• B+	1q 2019	663.7	2,671.9	2,671.9	324.8	1.62	1.35
GEISINGER INDEMNITY INS CO	PA	• B-	1q 2019	86.0	241.3	241.3	30.6	1.11	0.93
GEISINGER QUALITY OPTIONS INC	PA	• B-	1q 2019	75.6	264.1	264.1	39.5	1.72	1.43
GENESIS INS CO	DE	C	1q 2019	182.2	19.9	0.2	120.5	4.69	3.19
GENWORTH LIFE & ANNUITY INS CO	VA	C-	1q 2019	21,430.3	1,226.6	45.3	1,219.6	1.74	0.99
GENWORTH LIFE INS CO	DE	• C	1q 2019	40,255.7	2,777.5	2,484.9	1,876.9	0.93	0.64
GENWORTH LIFE INS CO OF NEW YORK	NY	• C	1q 2019	7,727.9	309.8	245.0	247.6	1.32	0.68
GERBER LIFE INS CO	NY	• B+	1q 2019	4,180.6	1,011.4	521.9	398.9	2.40	1.39
GERMANIA LIFE INS CO	TX	C+	1q 2019	97.5	10.7	0.0	10.3	1.22	1.08
GHS HEALTH MAINTENANCE ORGANIZATION	OK	• B-	1q 2019	56.9	36.7	36.7	26.4	8.38	6.98
GHS INS CO	OK	• E-	1q 2019	34.8	52.9	52.9	12.1	2.98	2.48
GHS MANAGED HEALTH CARE PLANS INC	OK	U		--	--	--	--	--	--
GLOBALHEALTH INC	OK	• D	1q 2019	57.1	329.4	329.4	9.1	0.41	0.34
GLOBE LIFE & ACCIDENT INS CO	NE	C+	1q 2019	4,744.4	857.9	37.5	315.6	1.02	0.66
GLOBE LIFE INSURANCE CO OF NY	NY	B-	1q 2019	249.5	70.3	40.8	22.6	1.38	0.86
GOLDEN RULE INS CO	IN	• B	1q 2019	593.8	1,289.8	1,261.9	307.6	1.76	1.37
GOLDEN SECURITY INS CO	TN	• B	1q 2019	58.0	67.9	67.9	38.8	2.24	1.86
GOLDEN STATE MEDICARE HEALTH PLAN	CA	• D-	1q 2019	22.8	81.7	81.7	6.3	0.56	0.34
GOOD HEALTH HMO INC	MO	• C	1q 2019	79.4	163.5	163.5	58.3	5.33	4.44
GOOD SAMARITAN INS PLAN OF ND	ND	• D	1q 2019	1.8	1.2	1.2	1.0	1.33	1.11
GOOD SAMARITAN INS PLAN OF NE	NE	• D	1q 2019	3.1	3.1	3.1	1.0	1.28	1.07
GOOD SAMARITAN INS PLAN OF SD	SD	• D	1q 2019	2.4	1.6	1.6	0.8	1.12	0.93
GOVERNMENT EMPLOYEES INS CO	MD	B	1q 2019	35,329.6	6,421.2	0.0	22,031.6	3.82	2.37

	INSURANCE COMPANY NAME	DOM. STATE	RATING	DATA DATE	TOTAL ASSETS ($MIL)	TOTAL PREMIUMS ($MIL)	HEALTH PREMIUMS ($MIL)	CAPITAL & SURPLUS ($MIL)	RISK ADJUSTED CAPITAL RATIO 1	RISK ADJUSTED CAPITAL RATIO 2
	GOVERNMENT PERSONNEL MUTUAL L I C	TX	• B	1q 2019	819.5	82.1	27.9	111.2	2.59	1.65
	GPM HEALTH & LIFE INS CO	WA	B	1q 2019	142.6	36.0	32.2	14.6	1.64	1.39
	GRANGE LIFE INS CO	OH	C	1q 2019	455.3	97.0	0.2	37.8	2.02	1.20
	GRANITE STATE HEALTH PLAN INC	NH	• C-	1q 2019	67.5	289.5	289.5	24.9	1.94	1.62
▼	GREAT AMERICAN INS CO	OH	B-	1q 2019	8,099.1	2,223.5	53.0	2,062.1	1.90	1.36
	GREAT AMERICAN LIFE INS CO	OH	B-	1q 2019	37,497.9	5,239.0	6.5	2,651.0	1.79	1.00
	GREAT AMERICAN SPIRIT INS CO	OH	C	1q 2019	17.4	60.3	0.3	17.4	221.00	110.50
	GREAT CENTRAL LIFE INS CO	LA	C+	4q 2018	24.8	2.2	0.2	9.1	1.34	0.87
	GREAT MIDWEST INS CO	TX	• B-	1q 2019	216.4	153.6	82.5	129.8	2.70	1.88
	GREAT NORTHERN INS CO	IN	B	1q 2019	549.2	1,327.2	0.9	387.3	42.25	35.00
	GREAT PLAINS CASUALTY INC	IA	C	1q 2019	25.2	4.8	0.0	23.3	6.30	3.72
	GREAT SOUTHERN LIFE INS CO	TX	A-	1q 2019	209.9	49.2	1.3	53.8	5.81	4.33
	GREAT WEST LIFE ASR CO	MI	C+	1q 2019	76.7	10.9	1.1	27.7	3.60	3.09
	GREAT-WEST LIFE & ANNUITY INS CO	CO	B-	1q 2019	57,052.8	5,489.7	43.0	1,378.4	1.38	0.74
	GREAT-WEST LIFE & ANNUITY INS OF NY	NY	B-	1q 2019	2,285.5	276.9	0.0	91.4	2.16	1.15
	GREATER GEORGIA LIFE INS CO	GA	B	1q 2019	68.4	36.9	16.4	24.1	1.33	0.99
	GREENHOUSE LIFE INSURANCE CO	AZ	U		--	--	--	--	--	--
	GREENVILLE CASUALTY INS CO INC	SC	C	1q 2019	11.5	9.6	1.3	7.5	2.67	2.47
▼	GREENWICH INS CO	DE	C-	1q 2019	1,432.1	693.9	57.7	450.7	1.64	1.35
	GROUP HEALTH COOP OF EAU CLAIRE	WI	• E+	1q 2019	50.7	163.7	163.7	24.7	1.40	1.17
	GROUP HEALTH COOP OF S CENTRAL WI	WI	• C	1q 2019	96.3	395.7	395.7	44.9	1.36	1.13
	GROUP HEALTH INCORPORATED	NY	• D+	1q 2019	694.1	808.1	808.1	348.0	4.62	3.85
	GROUP HEALTH PLAN INC	MN	• B	1q 2019	851.7	1,554.9	1,554.9	91.3	1.25	1.04
	GROUP HOSP & MEDICAL SERVICES INC	DC	• B	1q 2019	2,755.1	3,451.7	3,451.7	1,252.3	5.53	4.61
	GUARANTEE TRUST LIFE INS CO	IL	• B	1q 2019	648.1	258.3	242.0	98.6	2.11	1.37
	GUARANTY ASSURANCE CO	LA	• E+	1q 2019	2.3	7.8	7.8	1.1	1.03	0.86
	GUARANTY INCOME LIFE INS CO	LA	B	1q 2019	1,004.7	235.9	3.5	72.1	3.06	1.30
	GUARDIAN INS CO	VI	C-	1q 2019	36.7	28.6	0.0	11.3	1.40	1.09
	GUARDIAN LIFE INS CO OF AMERICA	NY	• A	1q 2019	59,690.7	8,310.7	3,351.4	7,209.7	2.72	1.75
	GUGGENHEIM LIFE & ANNUITY CO	DE	B-	1q 2019	13,761.1	638.2	0.0	631.0	1.72	0.91
	GULF GUARANTY LIFE INS CO	MS	C+	4q 2018	19.6	11.3	8.1	10.6	1.45	1.10
	GUNDERSEN HEALTH PLAN INC	WI	• C-	1q 2019	54.6	215.2	215.2	20.9	1.92	1.60
	GUNDERSEN HLTH PLAN MN INC	MN	• C	1q 2019	6.2	8.8	8.8	2.8	1.47	1.23
	HALLMARK LIFE INSURANCE CO	AZ	• D	1q 2019	403.5	658.4	658.4	105.9	1.76	1.46
	HAP MIDWEST HEALTH PLAN INC	MI	• C-	1q 2019	49.0	115.6	115.6	20.3	2.54	2.12
	HARKEN HEALTH INS CO	WI	U		--	--	--	--	--	--
	HARLEYSVILLE LIFE INS CO	OH	B	1q 2019	398.5	29.4	0.0	51.6	3.32	1.76
	HARMONY HEALTH PLAN INC	IL	• C	1q 2019	536.4	1,654.1	1,654.1	189.9	2.37	1.97
	HARTFORD FIRE INS CO	CT	C+	1q 2019	22,505.1	1,793.7	1.3	9,304.2	1.73	1.51
	HARTFORD LIFE & ACCIDENT INS CO	CT	• C	1q 2019	12,747.8	3,382.7	2,013.0	2,494.4	3.85	2.48
	HARVARD PILGRIM HC OF NEW ENGLAND	MA	• C	1q 2019	148.0	552.2	552.2	61.1	2.51	2.09
	HARVARD PILGRIM HEALTH CARE INC	MA	• C+	1q 2019	971.2	1,822.8	1,822.8	588.7	2.97	2.47
	HARVARD PILGRIM HEALTH CARE OF CT	CT	• D+	1q 2019	19.4	12.1	12.1	14.4	9.56	7.97
	HARVESTPLAINS HEALTH OF IOWA	IA	U		--	--	--	--	--	--
	HAWAII MANAGEMENT ALLIANCE ASSOC	HI	• C	1q 2019	48.5	161.1	161.1	20.7	0.92	0.77
▲	HAWAII MEDICAL SERVICE ASSOCIATION	HI	• B	1q 2019	1,353.3	3,539.8	3,539.8	598.0	2.59	2.16
	HCC LIFE INS CO	IN	• B	1q 2019	1,059.6	1,278.5	1,275.9	587.2	3.63	2.78
	HCSC INS SERVICES CO	IL	• D-	1q 2019	1,022.8	1,523.2	1,523.2	216.8	1.86	1.55
	HEALTH ALLIANCE CONNECT INC	IL	• C	1q 2019	55.7	227.5	227.5	24.0	1.76	1.46
	HEALTH ALLIANCE MEDICAL PLANS	IL	• B-	1q 2019	511.1	1,226.3	1,226.3	239.3	2.84	2.37
	HEALTH ALLIANCE NORTHWEST HEALTH PL	WA	• B	1q 2019	14.9	64.7	64.7	10.0	2.27	1.89
	HEALTH ALLIANCE PLAN OF MICHIGAN	MI	• C-	1q 2019	518.4	1,468.0	1,468.0	266.0	1.87	1.56

INSURANCE COMPANY NAME	DOM. STATE	RATING	DATA DATE	TOTAL ASSETS ($MIL)	TOTAL PREMIUMS ($MIL)	HEALTH PREMIUMS ($MIL)	CAPITAL & SURPLUS ($MIL)	RISK ADJUSTED CAPITAL RATIO 1	RISK ADJUSTED CAPITAL RATIO 2
HEALTH ALLIANCE-MIDWEST INC	IL	U		--	--	--	--	--	--
HEALTH CARE SVC CORP A MUT LEG RES	IL	• B	1q 2019	28,520.6	35,927.2	35,927.2	18,649.0	8.25	6.88
HEALTH COLORADO INC	CO	• C	1q 2019	9.2	44.1	44.1	4.8	0.69	0.58
HEALTH FIRST COMM PLANS INC	FL	• C+	1q 2019	95.9	259.8	259.8	49.9	2.36	1.97
HEALTH FIRST HEALTH PLANS INC	FL	• B	1q 2019	156.7	408.1	408.1	98.4	2.82	2.35
HEALTH FIRST INS INC	FL	• C	1q 2019	5.2	1.4	1.4	4.9	3.84	3.20
HEALTH INS CO OF AM INC	NY	U		--	--	--	--	--	--
HEALTH INSURANCE PLAN OF GREATER NY	NY	• C-	1q 2019	1,215.2	5,008.6	5,008.6	361.3	0.87	0.73
HEALTH NET COMMUNITY SOLUTIONS INC	CA	• B	1q 2019	2,833.4	6,244.4	6,244.4	1,233.5	2.91	1.96
HEALTH NET COMMUNITY SOLUTIONS OF AR	AZ	• C-	1q 2019	15.3	32.0	32.0	6.5	3.06	2.55
HEALTH NET HEALTH PLAN OF OREGON INC	OR	• D	1q 2019	157.2	499.0	499.0	62.4	1.97	1.64
HEALTH NET LIFE INS CO	CA	• C	1q 2019	685.2	1,376.6	1,375.4	353.0	2.94	2.33
HEALTH NET OF ARIZONA INC	AZ	• C	1q 2019	442.0	932.6	932.6	203.0	9.16	7.64
HEALTH NET OF CALIFORNIA INC	CA	• C	1q 2019	2,891.9	8,784.6	8,784.6	1,338.9	2.27	1.55
HEALTH NEW ENGLAND INC	MA	• B	1q 2019	202.7	771.1	771.1	91.7	1.21	1.01
HEALTH OPTIONS INC	FL	• A-	1q 2019	2,415.5	5,477.0	5,477.0	1,115.3	4.01	3.34
HEALTH PARTNERS PLANS INC	PA	• B	1q 2019	614.7	1,956.2	1,956.2	153.9	0.99	0.83
HEALTH PLAN OF CAREOREGON INC	OR	• C	1q 2019	72.1	187.4	187.4	36.1	1.74	1.45
HEALTH PLAN OF NEVADA INC	NV	• B+	1q 2019	708.2	2,943.4	2,943.4	392.2	2.99	2.49
HEALTH PLAN OF WV INC	WV	• C	1q 2019	240.3	574.8	574.8	131.3	1.85	1.54
HEALTH POINTE OF NEW YORK LLC	NY	U		--	--	--	--	--	--
HEALTH TRADITION HEALTH PLAN	WI	• C-	1q 2019	16.3	33.2	33.2	9.1	1.70	1.42
HEALTHASSURANCE PENNSYLVANIA INC	PA	• C	1q 2019	237.0	792.4	792.4	109.2	2.86	2.38
HEALTHFIRST HEALTH PLAN INC	NY	• B	1q 2019	888.6	2,620.6	2,620.6	358.8	1.75	1.46
HEALTHFIRST HEALTH PLAN NEW JERSEY	NJ	U		--	--	--	--	--	--
HEALTHFIRST INSURANCE CO	NY	• C+	1q 2019	46.1	34.2	34.2	14.3	3.52	2.93
HEALTHKEEPERS INC	VA	• B	1q 2019	1,568.7	3,484.9	3,484.9	665.7	2.98	2.48
HEALTHLINK HMO INC	MO	U		--	--	--	--	--	--
HEALTHNOW NY INC	NY	• B	1q 2019	1,194.8	2,647.1	2,647.1	696.1	4.23	3.53
HEALTHPARTNERS	MN	• B+	1q 2019	1,327.1	1,950.3	1,950.3	982.4	3.55	2.96
HEALTHPARTNERS INS CO	MN	• B+	1q 2019	416.8	992.7	992.7	258.2	3.74	3.11
HEALTHPARTNERS UNITYPOINT HLTH	IA	• D-	1q 2019	30.2	33.3	33.3	12.1	1.91	1.59
HEALTHPLEX OF NJ INC	NJ	U		--	--	--	--	--	--
HEALTHPLUS INS CO TRUST	MI	U		--	--	--	--	--	--
HEALTHSPAN INC	OH	U		--	--	--	--	--	--
HEALTHSPRING L&H INS CO	TX	• B-	1q 2019	1,154.9	4,142.2	4,142.2	610.3	2.77	2.31
HEALTHSPRING OF FLORIDA INC	FL	• B	1q 2019	150.0	826.4	826.4	82.7	2.23	1.86
HEALTHSUN HEALTH PLANS INC	FL	• B-	1q 2019	214.7	897.0	897.0	94.8	2.96	2.46
HEALTHY ALLIANCE LIFE INS CO	MO	• B	1q 2019	1,044.1	2,303.2	2,303.2	439.4	4.00	3.33
HEALTHY PALM BEACHES INC	FL	U		--	--	--	--	--	--
HEARTLAND NATIONAL LIFE INS CO	IN	C+	1q 2019	10.2	26.8	26.7	4.7	1.93	1.73
HEARTLANDPLAINS HEALTH	NE	• E	1q 2019	4.1	5.0	5.0	3.5	4.81	4.00
HENNEPIN HEALTH	MN	• B	1q 2019	81.1	235.0	235.0	47.7	2.04	1.70
HERITAGE PROVIDER NETWORK INC	CA	• D	1q 2019	618.9	2,866.4	2,866.4	160.3	0.72	0.45
HIGHMARK BCBSD INC	DE	• B	1q 2019	619.6	724.5	724.5	345.3	8.31	6.93
HIGHMARK BENEFITS GROUP INC	PA	U		--	--	--	--	--	--
HIGHMARK CASUALTY INS CO	PA	• C	1q 2019	317.9	4.1	4.1	194.9	5.22	3.03
HIGHMARK CHOICE CO	PA	U		--	--	--	--	--	--
HIGHMARK COVERAGE ADVANTAGE INC	PA	U		--	--	--	--	--	--
HIGHMARK INC	PA	• C	1q 2019	7,290.6	7,988.7	7,988.7	3,872.0	4.08	3.40
HIGHMARK SELECT RESOURCES INC	PA	U		--	--	--	--	--	--
HIGHMARK SENIOR HEALTH CO	PA	U		--	--	--	--	--	--

INSURANCE COMPANY NAME	DOM. STATE	RATING	DATA DATE	TOTAL ASSETS ($MIL)	TOTAL PREMIUMS ($MIL)	HEALTH PREMIUMS ($MIL)	CAPITAL & SURPLUS ($MIL)	RISK ADJUSTED CAPITAL RATIO 1	RISK ADJUSTED CAPITAL RATIO 2
HIGHMARK SENIOR SOLUTIONS CO	WV	U		--	--	--	--	--	--
HIGHMARK WEST VIRGINIA INC	WV	• B	1q 2019	912.7	1,197.8	1,197.8	517.6	6.74	5.62
HIP INS CO OF NEW YORK	NY	• D	1q 2019	45.6	8.4	8.4	41.6	32.32	26.93
HM HEALTH INS CO	PA	U		--	--	--	--	--	--
HM LIFE INS CO	PA	• B	1q 2019	741.1	835.2	835.2	405.9	4.44	2.92
HM LIFE INS CO OF NEW YORK	NY	• B	1q 2019	62.5	60.6	60.6	41.2	5.37	3.70
HMO COLORADO	CO	• B	1q 2019	357.3	820.6	820.6	196.8	4.98	4.15
HMO LOUISIANA INC	LA	• A+	1q 2019	801.6	1,141.4	1,141.4	454.1	6.82	5.69
HMO MINNESOTA	MN	• C+	1q 2019	1,105.9	2,445.3	2,445.3	614.6	4.14	3.45
HMO MISSOURI INC	MO	• B	1q 2019	86.1	207.1	207.1	36.8	3.73	3.11
HMO OF NORTHEASTERN PENNSYLVANIA INC	PA	U		--	--	--	--	--	--
HMO PARTNERS INC	AR	• A+	1q 2019	127.5	226.8	226.8	71.0	4.83	4.03
HN1 THERAPY NETWORK NEW JERSEY LLC	NJ	• C	4q 2018	2.6	2.7	2.7	2.3	0.83	0.69
▲ HNE INS CO	MA	• B	1q 2019	5.5	1.4	1.4	5.1	29.20	24.33
HNE OF CONNECTICUT INC	CT	U		--	--	--	--	--	--
HOME STATE HEALTH PLAN INC	MO	• C-	1q 2019	216.5	914.1	914.1	104.7	2.59	2.16
HOMELAND INS CO OF NY	NY	C+	1q 2019	118.7	160.5	3.1	117.4	118.00	57.10
HOMETOWN HEALTH PLAN INC	NV	• D	1q 2019	97.4	259.5	259.5	36.2	1.15	0.96
HOMETOWN HEALTH PROVIDERS INS CO	NV	• C+	1q 2019	75.6	180.5	180.5	34.6	1.80	1.50
HOOSIER MOTOR MUTUAL INS CO	IN	• C+	1q 2019	11.0	0.6	0.6	10.5	8.34	6.95
HOPKINS HEALTH ADV INC	MD	• E+	1q 2019	66.6	137.8	137.8	13.4	0.68	0.57
HORACE MANN INS CO	IL	B	1q 2019	534.1	248.4	0.0	182.1	2.87	1.93
HORACE MANN LIFE INS CO	IL	B	1q 2019	9,635.7	560.3	2.6	445.2	1.74	0.89
HORIZON HEALTHCARE OF NEW JERSEY INC	NJ	• C+	1q 2019	1,226.7	539.7	539.7	1,059.5	26.36	21.96
HORIZON HEALTHCARE SERVICES INC	NJ	• B	4q 2018	5,527.8	12,456.5	12,456.5	2,985.3	3.79	3.16
HORIZON INS CO	NJ	• C+	4q 2018	155.7	149.5	149.5	29.9	3.03	2.52
HOUSTON CASUALTY CO	TX	B-	1q 2019	3,607.3	451.1	21.2	2,080.0	1.68	1.43
HPHC INS CO	MA	• D+	1q 2019	250.0	752.7	752.7	106.2	2.38	1.98
HUDSON INS CO	DE	C-	1q 2019	1,281.0	1,083.5	1.5	443.6	2.03	1.75
HUMANA BENEFIT PLAN OF ILLINOIS	IL	• B+	1q 2019	693.4	1,906.1	1,906.1	339.9	3.79	3.16
HUMANA EAP & WORK-LIFE SVCS	CA	U		--	--	--	--	--	--
HUMANA EMPLOYERS HEALTH PLAN OF GA	GA	• C+	1q 2019	577.8	1,323.8	1,323.8	377.8	5.30	4.42
HUMANA HEALTH BENEFIT PLAN LA	LA	• C+	1q 2019	538.6	2,000.0	2,000.0	268.8	2.81	2.34
HUMANA HEALTH CO OF NEW YORK INC	NY	• C+	1q 2019	99.3	197.4	197.4	30.8	2.39	1.99
HUMANA HEALTH INS CO OF FL INC	FL	• B-	1q 2019	199.0	41.0	41.0	122.2	24.12	20.10
HUMANA HEALTH PLAN INC	KY	• C+	1q 2019	1,381.4	3,931.9	3,931.9	804.6	4.15	3.46
HUMANA HEALTH PLAN OF CA INC	CA	U		--	--	--	--	--	--
HUMANA HEALTH PLAN OF OHIO INC	OH	• C+	1q 2019	97.7	225.3	225.3	62.3	4.63	3.86
HUMANA HEALTH PLAN OF TEXAS INC	TX	• C+	1q 2019	211.2	749.9	749.9	105.0	2.73	2.27
HUMANA HEALTH PLANS OF PUERTO RICO	PR	• D	1q 2019	137.8	324.6	324.6	18.9	0.86	0.72
HUMANA INS CO (WI)	WI	• B	1q 2019	8,213.3	24,820.0	24,820.0	3,903.8	2.54	2.11
HUMANA INS CO OF KENTUCKY	KY	• B+	1q 2019	222.0	58.5	46.2	189.6	6.61	4.87
HUMANA INS CO OF NY	NY	• B-	1q 2019	153.1	270.9	270.9	77.9	5.72	4.77
HUMANA INS CO OF PUERTO RICO INC	PR	• C+	1q 2019	78.6	133.2	132.7	45.6	1.98	1.52
▲ HUMANA MEDICAL PLAN INC	FL	• A-	1q 2019	2,319.2	8,928.2	8,928.2	921.7	2.76	2.30
HUMANA MEDICAL PLAN OF MICHIGAN INC	MI	• C+	1q 2019	51.6	88.7	88.7	32.4	6.06	5.05
HUMANA MEDICAL PLAN OF PENNSYLVANIA	PA	U		--	--	--	--	--	--
HUMANA MEDICAL PLAN OF UTAH INC	UT	• C+	1q 2019	18.5	29.8	29.8	12.7	7.13	5.94
HUMANA REGIONAL HEALTH PLAN INC	AR	U		--	--	--	--	--	--
HUMANA WISCONSIN HEALTH ORGANIZATION	WI	• B	1q 2019	818.9	2,572.1	2,572.1	313.2	2.82	2.35
IA AMERICAN LIFE INS CO	TX	C	1q 2019	160.0	16.2	0.4	62.3	0.97	0.90
IDEALIFE INS CO	CT	B-	1q 2019	21.4	1.5	0.6	15.6	4.24	3.81

Arrows denote recent upgrades ▲ or downgrades▼

• Bullets denote a more detailed analysis is available in Section II.

INSURANCE COMPANY NAME	DOM. STATE	RATING	DATA DATE	TOTAL ASSETS ($MIL)	TOTAL PREMIUMS ($MIL)	HEALTH PREMIUMS ($MIL)	CAPITAL & SURPLUS ($MIL)	RISK ADJUSTED CAPITAL RATIO 1	RISK ADJUSTED CAPITAL RATIO 2
ILLINICARE HEALTH PLAN INC	IL	• C-	1q 2019	473.1	1,830.8	1,830.8	184.7	2.02	1.68
ILLINOIS MUTUAL LIFE INS CO	IL	• B+	1q 2019	1,507.2	115.6	57.3	241.5	3.69	2.06
ILLINOIS UNION INS CO	IL	C	1q 2019	394.4	638.4	0.7	138.0	13.26	11.93
IMPERIAL HEALTH PLAN OF CALIFORNIA	CA	• C-	1q 2019	12.8	24.9	24.9	4.1	1.07	0.71
IN UNIVERSITY HLTH PLANS INS	IN	U		--	--	--	--	--	--
INDEMNITY INS CO OF NORTH AMERICA	PA	C	1q 2019	317.6	1,329.9	1.1	154.4	16.16	14.55
INDEPENDENCE AMERICAN INS CO	DE	• B-	1q 2019	135.2	129.1	86.9	88.1	2.15	1.65
INDEPENDENCE ASSURANCE CO	PA	U		--	--	--	--	--	--
INDEPENDENCE BLUE CROSS	PA	• C+	1q 2019	269.1	351.4	351.4	33.1	3.34	2.78
INDEPENDENT CARE HEALTH PLAN	WI	• B+	1q 2019	86.5	285.1	285.1	32.1	2.59	2.16
INDEPENDENT HEALTH ASSOC INC	NY	• B-	1q 2019	711.8	1,403.3	1,403.3	404.9	3.82	3.19
INDEPENDENT HEALTH BENEFITS CORP	NY	• C	1q 2019	256.6	632.6	632.6	101.0	2.04	1.70
INDIANA UNIVERSITY HEALTH PLANS INC	IN	• E-	1q 2019	14.8	39.3	39.3	3.5	1.18	0.98
INDIANA UNIVERSITY HEALTH PLANS NFP	IN	• D	1q 2019	38.2	157.1	157.1	10.9	0.72	0.60
INDIVIDUAL ASR CO LIFE HEALTH & ACC	OK	D+	4q 2018	28.2	100.3	84.3	9.7	1.40	1.05
INLAND EMPIRE HEALTH PLAN	CA	• A	1q 2019	1,855.4	4,845.7	4,845.7	894.2	3.49	2.23
INNOVATION HEALTH INS CO	VA	• C-	1q 2019	131.9	163.2	163.2	91.2	5.73	4.78
INNOVATION HEALTH PLAN INC	VA	• C-	1q 2019	56.7	112.2	112.2	27.7	3.92	3.27
INS CO OF NORTH AMERICA	PA	• C	1q 2019	362.9	156.4	56.5	343.0	82.17	30.07
INS CO OF SCOTT & WHITE	TX	• D	1q 2019	30.4	87.1	87.1	16.7	1.55	1.29
INS CO OF THE SOUTH	GA	D+	1q 2019	56.6	115.1	1.5	14.9	0.44	0.38
INS CO OF THE STATE OF PA	IL	C-	1q 2019	201.7	875.1	7.2	60.9	6.50	5.85
INSTIL HEALTH INS CO	SC	U		--	--	--	--	--	--
INTEGON INDEMNITY CORP	NC	C	1q 2019	238.7	457.4	45.8	30.6	1.57	1.42
INTEGON NATIONAL INS CO	NC	B-	1q 2019	4,220.4	1,386.7	19.9	1,054.6	2.15	1.65
INTEGRAND ASR CO	PR	D+	1q 2019	94.2	62.3	1.0	28.6	0.67	0.43
INTER-COUNTY HEALTH PLAN INC	PA	U		--	--	--	--	--	--
INTER-COUNTY HOSPITALIZATION PLAN	PA	U		--	--	--	--	--	--
INTERBORO INS CO	NY	C	1q 2019	89.5	29.6	0.1	32.7	1.27	1.17
INTERVALLEY HEALTH PLAN	CA	• D	1q 2019	35.0	293.7	293.7	18.6	0.68	0.43
INTRAMERICA LIFE INS CO	NY	B	1q 2019	32.8	0.3	0.0	10.3	2.21	1.99
INVESTORS HERITAGE LIFE INS CO	KY	C-	1q 2019	793.2	105.2	1.7	31.7	1.55	0.78
INVESTORS LIFE INS CO NORTH AMERICA	TX	B	1q 2019	576.0	17.0	0.0	59.3	3.22	1.78
IRONSHORE INDEMNITY INC	MN	B-	1q 2019	279.2	253.8	54.8	89.5	9.24	8.31
ISLAND HOME INS CO	GU	C-	1q 2019	21.2	38.0	36.3	10.0	2.15	1.18
JACKSON NATIONAL LIFE INS CO	MI	B	1q 2019	239,575.1	17,080.2	43.9	5,006.7	1.88	1.04
JEFFERSON INS CO	NY	C-	1q 2019	545.0	698.4	19.9	365.9	1.54	1.33
JEFFERSON LIFE INS CO	TX	D	1q 2019	2.3	0.3	0.3	1.6	2.09	1.88
JEFFERSON NATIONAL LIFE INS CO	TX	C	1q 2019	6,696.3	1,164.0	1.6	45.0	0.95	0.57
JOHN ALDEN LIFE INS CO	WI	B-	1q 2019	207.8	17.5	9.9	17.9	4.42	3.94
JOHN HANCOCK LIFE & HEALTH INS CO	MA	• B	1q 2019	14,564.1	727.5	726.8	1,009.2	3.88	2.10
JOHN HANCOCK LIFE INS CO (USA)	MI	B-	1q 2019	230,681.7	20,066.8	1,500.4	9,203.3	1.69	1.06
JOHN HANCOCK LIFE INS CO OF NY	NY	B	1q 2019	16,668.3	1,077.3	2.5	1,664.5	4.45	2.30
K S PLAN ADMINISTRATORS LLC	TX	• B+	1q 2019	113.3	375.6	375.6	68.8	1.95	1.63
KAISER FNDTN HLTH PLAN OF WA	WA	• B	1q 2019	1,690.2	2,925.3	2,925.3	861.1	3.63	3.03
KAISER FNDTN HLTH PLAN WA OPTN	WA	• B	1q 2019	317.5	935.6	935.6	131.2	2.76	2.30
KAISER FOUNDATION HEALTH PLAN INC	CA	• A	1q 2019	80,034.0	75,176.3	75,176.3	35,872.8	4.00	2.88
KAISER FOUNDATION HP INC HI	HI	• B	1q 2019	571.1	1,582.2	1,582.2	138.6	2.86	2.38
KAISER FOUNDATION HP MID-ATL STATES	MD	• B	1q 2019	1,677.7	4,196.9	4,196.9	500.8	1.76	1.47
KAISER FOUNDATION HP NORTHWEST	OR	• B	1q 2019	1,301.7	4,027.1	4,027.1	516.2	3.95	3.29
KAISER FOUNDATION HP OF CO	CO	• B	1q 2019	1,609.3	3,858.4	3,858.4	473.6	2.89	2.41
KAISER FOUNDATION HP OF GA	GA	• B	1q 2019	665.2	2,065.2	2,065.2	149.7	0.93	0.78

INSURANCE COMPANY NAME	DOM. STATE	RATING	DATA DATE	TOTAL ASSETS ($MIL)	TOTAL PREMIUMS ($MIL)	HEALTH PREMIUMS ($MIL)	CAPITAL & SURPLUS ($MIL)	RISK ADJUSTED CAPITAL RATIO 1	RISK ADJUSTED CAPITAL RATIO 2
KAISER PERMANENTE INS CO	CA	• A-	1q 2019	197.7	118.2	118.2	120.2	12.21	10.17
KANSAS CITY LIFE INS CO	MO	B	1q 2019	3,375.2	308.9	58.7	277.4	1.48	0.91
KANSAS SUPERIOR SELECT INC	KS	• D+	1q 2019	3.0	3.3	3.3	1.2	0.87	0.73
KELSEYCARE ADMINISTRATORS LLC	TX	U		--	--	--	--	--	--
KENTUCKY HOME LIFE INS CO	KY	C-	1q 2019	5.2	1.8	0.6	3.4	3.07	2.76
KENTUCKY SPIRIT HEALTH PLAN INC	KY	U		--	--	--	--	--	--
▲ KERN HEALTH SYSTEMS	CA	• B+	1q 2019	467.7	767.9	767.9	204.1	4.34	2.65
KEYSTONE HEALTH PLAN CENTRAL INC	PA	• C-	1q 2019	82.5	250.6	250.6	39.4	2.78	2.32
KEYSTONE HEALTH PLAN EAST INC	PA	• B	1q 2019	1,299.0	3,274.5	3,274.5	537.7	3.44	2.86
KILPATRICK LIFE INS CO	LA	E+	1q 2019	194.3	15.8	0.2	6.2	0.56	0.33
LA HEALTH SERVICE & INDEMNITY CO	LA	• B	1q 2019	2,178.7	2,402.6	2,402.6	1,488.7	6.61	5.51
LAFAYETTE LIFE INS CO	OH	B	1q 2019	5,575.8	614.6	0.3	343.4	1.83	0.91
LAMORAK INS CO	PA	C+	1q 2019	26.6	0.5	0.0	25.4	9.11	5.27
LANDCAR LIFE INS CO	UT	U		--	--	--	--	--	--
LANGHORNE REINSURANCE AZ LTD	AZ	C	1q 2019	9.7	0.0	0.0	8.4	3.69	3.32
LASSO HEALTHCARE INSURANCE CO	TX	U		--	--	--	--	--	--
LEADERS LIFE INS CO	OK	B	1q 2019	7.7	11.2	0.9	3.7	1.82	1.64
LEGAL SERVICE PLANS OF VIRGINIA INC	VA	• B	1q 2019	1.4	9.5	9.5	0.9	1.55	1.29
LIBERTY ADVANTAGE LLC	NC	• D	1q 2019	5.5	15.4	15.4	1.8	0.67	0.56
LIBERTY BANKERS LIFE INS CO	OK	C	1q 2019	1,965.4	323.7	11.4	230.3	1.12	0.76
LIBERTY INS UNDERWRITERS INC	IL	C	1q 2019	294.4	3,381.1	88.0	137.5	14.45	13.01
LIBERTY LIFE ASR CO OF BOSTON	NH	• B-	1q 2019	4,142.3	2,886.7	1,347.4	537.5	4.92	2.25
▼ LIBERTY MUTUAL INS CO	MA	C+	1q 2019	50,287.4	2,088.7	9.8	17,037.0	1.09	1.00
LIBERTY NATIONAL LIFE INS CO	NE	B	1q 2019	7,892.5	569.9	139.6	559.1	1.95	1.03
LIBERTY UNION LIFE ASR CO	MI	• C+	1q 2019	14.2	16.1	16.1	8.3	9.58	7.99
LIFE ASSURANCE CO INC	OK	C-	1q 2019	4.6	1.9	0.4	2.7	1.97	1.77
LIFE INS CO OF ALABAMA	AL	• B	1q 2019	124.6	37.9	30.1	40.4	3.94	2.63
LIFE INS CO OF BOSTON & NEW YORK	NY	• A-	1q 2019	163.1	28.8	10.7	33.2	3.64	2.18
LIFE INS CO OF LOUISIANA	LA	D	4q 2018	10.1	0.3	0.1	4.4	2.05	1.59
LIFE INS CO OF NORTH AMERICA	PA	• B	1q 2019	8,795.5	3,679.9	2,216.4	1,761.5	2.57	1.66
LIFE INS CO OF THE SOUTHWEST	TX	B	1q 2019	20,773.0	2,468.3	0.1	1,335.1	2.08	1.02
LIFE OF AMERICA INS CO	TX	C	1q 2019	11.7	0.1	0.1	2.5	0.76	0.58
LIFE OF THE SOUTH INS CO	GA	C	1q 2019	105.3	143.9	92.1	20.6	0.72	0.58
LIFEMAP ASR CO	OR	• B-	1q 2019	95.8	113.4	81.8	50.9	2.02	1.47
LIFESECURE INS CO	MI	• D	1q 2019	429.5	60.1	54.9	46.3	2.42	1.57
LIFESHIELD NATIONAL INS CO	OK	• B-	1q 2019	92.3	89.9	81.6	31.8	2.04	1.43
LIFEWISE ASR CO	WA	• A	1q 2019	215.9	150.0	149.9	162.1	7.73	5.69
LIFEWISE HEALTH PLAN OF OREGON	OR	U		--	--	--	--	--	--
LIFEWISE HEALTH PLAN OF WASHINGTON	WA	• B-	1q 2019	115.7	139.8	139.8	87.6	11.75	9.79
LIFEWORKS ADVANTAGE, LLC	VA	• D+	1q 2019	4.6	17.8	17.8	1.9	0.56	0.47
LINCOLN BENEFIT LIFE CO	NE	C+	1q 2019	10,579.4	1,304.6	57.2	393.6	1.29	0.65
LINCOLN HERITAGE LIFE INS CO	IL	B-	1q 2019	1,049.6	547.2	2.9	90.0	2.19	1.18
LINCOLN LIFE & ANNUITY CO OF NY	NY	B	1q 2019	14,960.2	1,174.7	57.6	1,083.8	4.09	2.07
LINCOLN NATIONAL LIFE INS CO	IN	B	1q 2019	250,789.0	24,436.9	1,353.3	8,083.0	1.07	0.79
LOCAL INITIATIVE HEALTH AUTH LA	CA	• C	1q 2019	4,858.2	7,595.6	7,595.6	1,017.0	1.82	1.11
LONDON LIFE REINSURANCE CO	PA	• C+	1q 2019	154.4	0.0	0.0	63.7	6.98	6.28
LONGEVITY HLTH PLAN IL INC	IL	U		--	--	--	--	--	--
LONGEVITY HLTH PLAN NEW JERSEY	NJ	U		--	--	--	--	--	--
LONGEVITY HLTH PLAN NY INC	NY	U		--	--	--	--	--	--
LONGEVITY INS CO	TX	B	1q 2019	7.7	0.3	0.1	7.7	3.79	3.41
▼ LOUISIANA FARM BUREAU MUTUAL INS CO	LA	C+	1q 2019	247.5	143.8	0.1	166.5	6.72	6.03
LOUISIANA HEALTHCARE CONNECTIONS INC	LA	• E	1q 2019	562.2	2,279.9	2,279.9	125.1	2.47	2.06

INSURANCE COMPANY NAME	DOM. STATE	RATING	DATA DATE	TOTAL ASSETS ($MIL)	TOTAL PREMIUMS ($MIL)	HEALTH PREMIUMS ($MIL)	CAPITAL & SURPLUS ($MIL)	RISK ADJUSTED CAPITAL RATIO 1	RATIO 2
LOYAL AMERICAN LIFE INS CO	OH	• B-	1q 2019	354.6	275.7	268.1	135.0	1.17	0.99
LUMICO LIFE INSURANCE CO	MO	C	1q 2019	65.3	20.4	0.9	49.6	6.90	6.21
LYNDON SOUTHERN INS CO	DE	C+	1q 2019	239.9	475.7	2.1	55.6	2.59	1.74
MA DELIVERY INNOVATIONS INC	IL	U		--	--	--	--	--	--
MADISON NATIONAL LIFE INS CO INC	WI	• A-	1q 2019	337.4	147.7	94.8	199.8	1.46	1.39
MAGELLAN BEHAVIORAL HEALTH OF NE	NE	U		--	--	--	--	--	--
MAGELLAN BEHAVIORAL HEALTH OF NJ LLC	NJ	U		--	--	--	--	--	--
MAGELLAN BEHAVIORAL HEALTH OF PA INC	PA	• C+	1q 2019	125.9	543.4	543.4	66.5	1.48	1.23
MAGELLAN COMPLETE CARE OF ARIZONA	AZ	• D+	1q 2019	19.1	5.7	5.7	7.4	3.37	2.81
MAGELLAN COMPLETE CARE OF LOUISIANA	LA	• C	1q 2019	17.2	12.4	12.4	4.7	2.22	1.85
MAGELLAN COMPLETE CARE OF VA	VA	• D+	1q 2019	191.7	473.2	473.2	68.3	1.66	1.39
MAGELLAN LIFE INS CO	DE	• B-	1q 2019	11.1	11.7	11.7	10.3	6.71	5.59
MAGNA INS CO	MS	• D-	1q 2019	5.1	12.6	12.6	2.5	0.46	0.38
MAGNOLIA GUARANTY LIFE INS CO	MS	C	1q 2019	10.8	1.7	0.0	1.8	0.75	0.67
MAGNOLIA HEALTH PLAN INC	MS	• D+	1q 2019	222.1	1,280.6	1,280.6	90.9	1.23	1.02
MAINE COMMUNITY HEALTH OPTIONS	ME	• D+	1q 2019	185.7	380.3	380.3	62.2	0.89	0.74
MAMSI L&H INS CO	MD	• C+	1q 2019	47.9	131.4	131.4	20.8	3.03	2.53
MANHATTAN LIFE INS CO	NY	• B	1q 2019	631.6	220.8	163.8	61.9	1.45	1.02
MANHATTAN NATIONAL LIFE INS CO	OH	B-	1q 2019	148.1	14.4	0.1	8.9	1.10	0.99
MANHATTANLIFE ASSR CO OF AM	AR	• C	1q 2019	705.3	151.0	143.8	163.7	0.87	0.77
MAPFRE PAN AMERICAN INS CO	PR	C	1q 2019	45.4	55.4	0.0	27.8	1.84	1.28
MAPFRE PRAICO INS CO	PR	B-	1q 2019	453.6	313.7	0.0	166.8	1.28	0.89
MARKEL INS CO	IL	C+	1q 2019	2,566.3	616.3	17.9	1,272.8	1.46	1.27
MARQUETTE INDEMNITY & LIFE INS CO	AZ	D+	1q 2019	5.8	1.0	0.6	2.3	1.40	1.26
MARQUIS ADVANTAGE, INC.	OR	• D+	1q 2019	5.3	9.5	9.5	2.9	0.87	0.72
MARTINS POINT GENERATIONS ADVANTAGE	ME	• B	1q 2019	131.1	401.3	401.3	77.7	2.18	1.82
MARTINS POINT GENERATIONS LLC	ME	U		--	--	--	--	--	--
MASSACHUSETTS MUTUAL LIFE INS CO	MA	A-	1q 2019	249,945.6	23,269.1	748.3	15,699.4	1.67	1.17
MATTHEW THORNTON HEALTH PLAN	NH	• B	1q 2019	310.5	712.8	712.8	157.9	4.43	3.69
MCLAREN HEALTH PLAN COMMUNITY	MI	• B-	1q 2019	39.1	143.8	143.8	18.0	1.43	1.19
MCLAREN HEALTH PLAN INC	MI	• B-	1q 2019	241.5	729.6	729.6	122.7	2.02	1.69
MCNA INS CO	TX	• C-	1q 2019	194.7	726.5	726.5	125.5	1.85	1.54
MCS ADVANTAGE INC	PR	• D	1q 2019	378.2	1,907.8	1,907.8	188.0	1.46	1.22
MCS LIFE INS CO	PR	• D-	3q 2018	92.7	311.4	309.0	45.0	0.96	0.79
MD INDIVIDUAL PRACTICE ASSOC INC	MD	• C	1q 2019	86.0	281.8	281.8	59.1	11.09	9.24
MDWISE INC	IN	• B+	1q 2019	542.8	1,264.2	1,264.2	115.8	1.82	1.52
MDWISE MARKETPLACE INC	IN	U		--	--	--	--	--	--
MEDAMERICA INS CO	PA	• C	1q 2019	1,218.5	85.0	85.0	29.6	0.68	0.39
MEDAMERICA INS CO OF FL	FL	B	1q 2019	51.5	3.8	3.8	6.6	1.00	0.90
MEDAMERICA INS CO OF NEW YORK	NY	C	1q 2019	951.1	46.2	46.2	18.8	0.70	0.41
MEDCO CONTAINMENT INS CO OF NY	NY	• C	1q 2019	111.2	138.6	138.6	46.8	5.68	4.73
MEDCO CONTAINMENT LIFE INS CO	PA	• C	1q 2019	762.4	896.1	896.1	367.8	5.33	4.44
MEDICA HEALTH PLANS	MN	• C+	1q 2019	547.8	732.6	732.6	308.9	5.95	4.96
MEDICA HEALTH PLANS OF FLORIDA INC	FL	U		--	--	--	--	--	--
MEDICA HEALTH PLANS OF WI	WI	• C+	1q 2019	140.6	83.0	83.0	97.3	16.92	14.10
MEDICA HEALTHCARE PLANS INC	FL	• B	1q 2019	179.8	661.7	661.7	54.8	1.63	1.36
MEDICA INS CO	MN	• B	1q 2019	1,536.7	3,536.4	3,536.4	863.9	4.73	3.94
MEDICAL ASSOC CLINIC HEALTH PLAN	WI	• B-	1q 2019	4.2	26.1	26.1	3.2	1.35	1.13
MEDICAL ASSOCIATES HEALTH PLAN INC	IA	• B-	1q 2019	40.5	89.1	89.1	21.7	2.60	2.17
MEDICAL BENEFITS MUTUAL LIFE INS CO	OH	D	1q 2019	14.9	1.1	0.9	10.9	2.52	1.85
MEDICAL HEALTH INS CORP OF OHIO	OH	• B	1q 2019	266.2	497.7	497.7	100.3	4.16	3.47
MEDICAL MUTUAL OF OHIO	OH	• A	1q 2019	2,490.1	2,636.1	2,636.1	1,879.3	7.42	6.18

INSURANCE COMPANY NAME	DOM. STATE	RATING	DATA DATE	TOTAL ASSETS ($MIL)	TOTAL PREMIUMS ($MIL)	HEALTH PREMIUMS ($MIL)	CAPITAL & SURPLUS ($MIL)	RISK ADJUSTED CAPITAL RATIO 1	RISK ADJUSTED CAPITAL RATIO 2
MEDICO CORP LIFE INS CO	NE	B-	1q 2019	73.0	155.5	155.5	25.3	3.26	2.93
MEDICO INS CO	NE	• B-	1q 2019	83.1	142.9	141.5	38.3	4.66	4.20
MEDICO LIFE & HEALTH INS CO	IA	C	1q 2019	16.3	5.0	4.4	14.2	4.62	4.16
MEDIEXCEL HEALTH PLAN	CA	• C-	1q 2019	4.8	17.6	17.6	1.8	0.87	0.58
MEDISUN INC	AZ	• B	1q 2019	102.4	552.0	552.0	60.5	1.57	1.31
MEDMUTUAL LIFE INS CO	OH	B	1q 2019	46.3	32.1	6.7	33.0	2.72	2.08
MEDSTAR FAMILY CHOICE INC	MD	• C-	1q 2019	188.5	555.0	555.0	76.3	1.44	1.20
MEMBERS HEALTH INS CO	AZ	• C-	1q 2019	38.8	10.9	10.9	32.8	15.26	12.72
▲ MEMBERS LIFE INS CO	IA	B	1q 2019	190.3	829.1	0.0	39.0	4.07	3.66
MEMORIAL HERMANN COMM HEALTH	TX	U		--	--	--	--	--	--
MEMORIAL HERMANN HEALTH INS CO	TX	• C-	1q 2019	26.1	38.4	38.4	19.0	3.28	2.73
MEMORIAL HERMANN HEALTH PLAN INC	TX	• C-	1q 2019	47.8	78.9	78.9	15.8	1.65	1.38
MERCHANTS MUTUAL INS CO	NY	B-	1q 2019	567.1	230.2	0.0	231.6	2.74	2.28
MERCY MARICOPA INTEGRATED CARE	AZ	U		--	--	--	--	--	--
MERCYCARE HMO	WI	• C	1q 2019	42.9	106.8	106.8	14.3	1.14	0.95
MERCYCARE INS CO	WI	• D+	1q 2019	12.8	0.4	0.4	12.4	1.47	1.22
MERIDIAN HEALTH PLAN OF ILLINOIS INC	IL	• C	1q 2019	804.7	2,421.4	2,421.4	315.9	1.84	1.53
MERIDIAN HEALTH PLAN OF MICHIGAN INC	MI	• C	1q 2019	383.1	1,988.4	1,988.4	143.2	1.16	0.97
MERIT HEALTH INS CO	IL	• C+	1q 2019	129.9	103.7	103.7	52.0	9.74	8.11
MERIT LIFE INS CO	IN	B	1q 2019	343.1	-20.6	0.0	101.4	9.21	5.52
METROPOLITAN LIFE INS CO	NY	B-	1q 2019	385,428.6	35,131.2	7,936.4	9,155.1	1.86	0.95
METROPOLITAN P&C INS CO	RI	B-	1q 2019	7,112.8	1,504.1	26.6	2,419.0	2.02	1.61
METROPOLITAN TOWER LIFE INS CO	NE	B-	1q 2019	21,009.0	1,696.3	4.4	1,566.8	2.67	1.31
MG INSURANCE CO	AZ	• C-	1q 2019	29.9	16.4	16.4	29.4	N/A	N/A
MHNET L&H INS CO	TX	U		--	--	--	--	--	--
MHS HEALTH WISCONSIN	WI	• B-	1q 2019	89.2	210.3	210.3	56.3	4.67	3.89
MICHIGAN COMPLETE HEALTH INC	MO	• C-	1q 2019	15.8	63.7	63.7	7.4	2.16	1.80
▲ MID-WEST NATIONAL LIFE INS CO OF TN	TX	• B	1q 2019	62.2	16.7	6.8	28.9	4.00	3.60
MIDLAND NATIONAL LIFE INS CO	IA	B+	1q 2019	58,679.0	4,176.7	0.0	3,605.5	2.08	1.05
MII LIFE INSURANCE INC	MN	• C	1q 2019	1,321.8	13.7	13.7	41.0	2.43	2.03
MINNESOTA LIFE INS CO	MN	B+	1q 2019	50,012.0	7,617.4	376.8	2,985.8	2.21	1.38
MISSISSIPPI TRUE	MS	U		--	--	--	--	--	--
▲ MISSOURI CARE INC	MO	• C-	1q 2019	221.9	767.3	767.3	102.3	2.62	2.19
▲ MISSOURI CHAMBER FEDN BENEFIT	MO	• C	1q 2019	18.6	2.5	2.5	1.5	3.10	2.58
MISSOURI MEDICARE SELECT LLC	MO	• D+	1q 2019	2.1	2.0	2.0	1.5	1.15	0.96
MISSOURI VALLEY L&H INS CO	MO	• C-	1q 2019	36.4	47.4	47.4	19.8	0.97	0.81
MMM FLORIDA INC	FL	U		--	--	--	--	--	--
MMM HEALTHCARE LLC	PR	• E-	1q 2019	493.5	2,039.8	2,039.8	147.8	1.02	0.85
MMM MULTI HEALTH LLC	PR	• D	1q 2019	136.1	570.7	570.7	51.9	0.84	0.70
MODA HEALTH PLAN INC	OR	• E	1q 2019	310.0	437.4	437.4	126.2	1.36	1.13
MOLINA HEALTHCARE OF CALIFORNIA	CA	• C-	1q 2019	924.0	2,280.8	2,280.8	110.6	0.98	0.61
MOLINA HEALTHCARE OF FLORIDA INC	FL	• C	1q 2019	552.3	1,845.7	1,845.7	373.3	4.07	3.39
MOLINA HEALTHCARE OF ILLINOIS INC	IL	• C	1q 2019	269.9	1,009.0	1,009.0	131.5	3.10	2.58
MOLINA HEALTHCARE OF MICHIGAN INC	MI	• B	1q 2019	466.0	1,789.7	1,789.7	202.5	2.39	2.00
▼ MOLINA HEALTHCARE OF MS INC	MS	• D	1q 2019	55.9	22.8	22.8	18.4	6.90	5.75
MOLINA HEALTHCARE OF NEW MEXICO	NM	• C	1q 2019	332.8	1,428.8	1,428.8	197.6	2.51	2.09
MOLINA HEALTHCARE OF OHIO INC	OH	• B	1q 2019	585.3	2,593.0	2,593.0	252.8	2.09	1.74
▲ MOLINA HEALTHCARE OF PUERTO RICO INC	PR	• C+	1q 2019	198.5	710.8	710.8	112.6	2.82	2.35
▲ MOLINA HEALTHCARE OF SOUTH CAROLINA	SC	• B	1q 2019	166.1	525.2	525.2	79.6	2.98	2.49
MOLINA HEALTHCARE OF TEXAS INC	TX	• B	1q 2019	1,007.6	3,325.0	3,325.0	346.4	1.97	1.64
MOLINA HEALTHCARE OF TEXAS INS CO	TX	C+	1q 2019	9.0	37.3	37.3	8.9	3.98	3.26
MOLINA HEALTHCARE OF UTAH INC	UT	• C+	1q 2019	171.2	384.1	384.1	74.9	3.95	3.29

INSURANCE COMPANY NAME	DOM. STATE	RATING	DATA DATE	TOTAL ASSETS ($MIL)	TOTAL PREMIUMS ($MIL)	HEALTH PREMIUMS ($MIL)	CAPITAL & SURPLUS ($MIL)	RISK ADJUSTED CAPITAL RATIO 1	RATIO 2
MOLINA HEALTHCARE OF WASHINGTON INC	WA	• B	1q 2019	920.4	2,466.1	2,466.1	333.4	2.27	1.90
MOLINA HEALTHCARE OF WISCONSIN INC	WI	• C	1q 2019	65.8	157.4	157.4	35.2	5.27	4.39
MONARCH HEALTH PLAN	CA	• E+	1q 2019	186.4	692.1	692.1	83.8	1.12	0.67
MONARCH LIFE INS CO	MA	F	4q 2018	622.1	10.3	9.4	4.3	0.40	0.23
MONITOR LIFE INS CO OF NEW YORK	NY	B	1q 2019	19.3	6.0	5.4	11.9	3.39	3.05
MONTANA HEALTH COOPERATIVE	MT	• D	1q 2019	135.3	258.0	258.0	52.1	1.07	0.89
MONY LIFE INS CO	NY	B-	1q 2019	7,033.8	257.2	23.8	419.6	2.33	1.22
MONY LIFE INS CO OF AMERICA	AZ	B	1q 2019	4,029.3	719.1	27.4	254.6	1.73	1.18
MOTIVHEALTH INSURANCE CO	UT	• D	1q 2019	9.5	10.4	10.4	1.8	1.08	0.90
MOTORISTS COMMERCIAL MUTUAL INS CO	OH	B-	1q 2019	503.5	79.7	0.0	160.4	2.74	1.88
MOUNT CARMEL HEALTH INS CO	OH	• B-	1q 2019	7.4	8.7	8.7	6.0	4.98	4.15
MOUNT CARMEL HEALTH PLAN INC	OH	• B	1q 2019	347.1	582.5	582.5	252.7	5.17	4.31
MOUNT CARMEL HLTH PLAN OF ID	ID	U		--	--	--	--	--	--
MOUNTAIN LIFE INS CO	TN	C-	1q 2019	5.8	2.9	0.7	3.7	2.15	1.94
MULTINATIONAL LIFE INS CO	PR	C-	1q 2019	121.4	56.9	34.4	24.1	2.47	1.37
MUTL OF OMAHA MEDICARE	NE	U		--	--	--	--	--	--
MUTUAL BENEFIT ASSN OF HAWAII	HI	U		--	--	--	--	--	--
MUTUAL OF AMERICA LIFE INS CO	NY	B+	1q 2019	21,688.9	2,598.4	3.0	894.3	2.52	1.21
MUTUAL OF OMAHA INS CO	NE	• B-	1q 2019	8,332.2	1,471.9	1,471.9	3,209.7	0.98	0.91
MUTUAL SAVINGS LIFE INS CO	AL	B	1q 2019	475.6	37.5	4.1	53.4	2.92	1.78
MUTUAL TRUST LIFE INS CO	IL	B	1q 2019	2,050.5	198.2	0.2	154.8	2.22	1.11
MVP HEALTH INS CO	NY	• D-	1q 2019	5.4	19.8	19.8	3.9	2.24	1.87
MVP HEALTH PLAN INC	NY	• B	1q 2019	711.3	2,649.0	2,649.0	406.6	2.13	1.78
MVP HEALTH SERVICES CORP	NY	• C	1q 2019	166.5	734.1	734.1	88.9	0.90	0.75
NASSAU LIFE INS CO OF KS	KS	D	1q 2019	72.0	19.3	15.4	17.0	2.31	1.94
NASSAU LIFE INSURANCE CO	NY	D-	1q 2019	11,970.5	361.3	0.7	513.5	1.71	0.86
NATIONAL BENEFIT LIFE INS CO	NY	A-	1q 2019	585.5	173.5	0.8	157.4	6.55	3.52
NATIONAL CASUALTY CO	OH	B+	1q 2019	493.4	1,034.8	2.4	143.7	12.77	11.50
NATIONAL FAMILY CARE LIFE INS CO	TX	C	1q 2019	15.8	6.3	5.2	9.2	3.01	2.71
NATIONAL FIRE & MARINE INS CO	NE	C	1q 2019	11,472.6	1,799.5	0.0	7,009.3	2.42	1.55
NATIONAL FOUNDATION LIFE INS CO	TX	• B+	1q 2019	59.6	76.5	70.8	36.3	1.76	1.37
NATIONAL GUARDIAN LIFE INS CO	WI	• B-	1q 2019	4,139.1	909.6	379.8	353.4	1.59	1.02
NATIONAL HEALTH INS CO	TX	C	1q 2019	71.6	380.5	380.2	19.1	1.89	0.80
NATIONAL INCOME LIFE INS CO	NY	B+	1q 2019	280.7	85.8	6.7	36.1	2.45	1.45
NATIONAL INDEMNITY CO	NE	C+	1q 2019	239,968.7	265.4	0.0	132,317.6	1.80	1.47
NATIONAL INS CO OF WI INC	WI	C	1q 2019	15.1	0.4	0.4	11.6	9.69	7.60
NATIONAL INTEGRITY LIFE INS CO	NY	B	1q 2019	4,509.2	250.1	0.0	354.6	3.83	1.84
NATIONAL INTERSTATE INS CO	OH	C+	1q 2019	1,292.7	495.3	0.0	260.8	1.22	0.97
NATIONAL LIABILITY & FIRE INS CO	CT	C+	1q 2019	2,874.0	661.2	0.0	1,260.9	3.26	2.04
NATIONAL LIFE INS CO	VT	B-	1q 2019	9,660.1	566.3	18.8	2,249.9	1.43	1.22
NATIONAL LLOYDS INS CO	TX	C+	1q 2019	145.7	105.2	0.1	62.1	2.54	2.14
NATIONAL PROSPERITY L&H INS CO	TX	U		--	--	--	--	--	--
NATIONAL SECURITY INS CO	AL	B	1q 2019	57.5	6.1	1.8	15.5	2.30	1.85
NATIONAL TEACHERS ASSOCIATES L I C	TX	• B	1q 2019	596.1	130.5	127.3	146.7	3.56	2.33
NATIONAL UNION FIRE INS CO	PA	C	1q 2019	23,691.2	5,132.8	619.3	5,628.6	2.03	1.31
NATIONAL WESTERN LIFE INS CO	CO	B-	1q 2019	10,926.5	708.7	3.0	1,443.6	4.01	2.11
NATIONWIDE LIFE & ANNUITY INS CO	OH	C	1q 2019	27,580.5	6,544.4	0.0	1,727.6	2.83	1.37
NATIONWIDE LIFE INS CO	OH	B-	1q 2019	147,048.2	10,739.0	289.0	7,067.7	2.39	1.59
NATIONWIDE MUTUAL INS CO	OH	B	1q 2019	34,653.1	2,411.3	22.9	12,790.2	1.44	1.28
NATL PREVENTIVE SOLUTIONS CORP	IL	U		--	--	--	--	--	--
NAVICENT HEALTHPLAN INC	GA	U		--	--	--	--	--	--
NEBRASKA TOTAL CARE INC	NE	• C-	1q 2019	101.8	444.8	444.8	36.9	1.67	1.39

INSURANCE COMPANY NAME	DOM. STATE	RATING	DATA DATE	TOTAL ASSETS ($MIL)	TOTAL PREMIUMS ($MIL)	HEALTH PREMIUMS ($MIL)	CAPITAL & SURPLUS ($MIL)	RISK ADJUSTED CAPITAL RATIO 1	RISK ADJUSTED CAPITAL RATIO 2
NEIGHBORHOOD HEALTH PARTNERSHIP INC	FL	• C	1q 2019	184.9	714.4	714.4	52.6	1.22	1.01
NEIGHBORHOOD HEALTH PLAN	MA	• D	1q 2019	393.9	1,045.3	1,045.3	279.9	3.17	2.64
NEIGHBORHOOD HEALTH PLAN OF RI INC	RI	• C+	1q 2019	329.5	1,377.7	1,377.7	103.5	0.89	0.75
NETWORK HEALTH INS CORP	WI	• C	1q 2019	185.3	590.1	590.1	79.0	1.46	1.22
NETWORK HEALTH PLAN	WI	• B-	1q 2019	111.7	401.0	401.0	65.2	2.20	1.84
NEW ENGLAND LIFE INS CO	MA	B	1q 2019	9,080.0	204.6	6.3	220.4	2.13	1.10
NEW ERA LIFE INS CO	TX	• C	1q 2019	546.2	152.6	98.0	93.8	0.99	0.78
NEW ERA LIFE INS CO OF THE MIDWEST	TX	C+	1q 2019	141.6	63.9	48.5	14.5	1.28	0.82
NEW HAMPSHIRE INS CO	IL	C+	1q 2019	83.7	1,120.6	4.8	66.3	20.55	18.49
NEW HEALTH VENTURES INC	CO	U		--	--	--	--	--	--
NEW MEXICO HEALTH CONNECTIONS	NM	• E-	1q 2019	49.8	46.0	46.0	1.5	0.06	0.05
NEW WEST HEALTH SERVICES	MT	U		--	--	--	--	--	--
NEW YORK LIFE INS CO	NY	A-	1q 2019	181,647.2	16,545.2	524.7	20,914.5	1.78	1.33
▲ NEXTLEVEL HEALTH PARTNERS INC	IL	• C	1q 2019	77.4	261.5	261.5	23.8	0.88	0.73
NHC ADVANTAGE LLC	MO	• C-	1q 2019	6.4	2.7	2.7	1.7	1.91	1.60
NIAGARA LIFE & HEALTH INS CO	NY	B	1q 2019	18.5	33.8	32.2	9.9	3.00	2.39
NIPPON LIFE INS CO OF AMERICA	IA	• A-	1q 2019	229.2	352.0	349.6	142.7	3.25	2.57
NORTH AMERICAN CO FOR LIFE & H INS	IA	B	1q 2019	27,910.5	3,090.7	0.0	1,445.6	1.80	0.85
NORTH AMERICAN INS CO	WI	B+	1q 2019	18.5	11.7	11.7	13.0	3.43	2.58
NORTH CAROLINA FARM BU MUTUAL INS CO	NC	B	1q 2019	2,115.4	1,146.4	0.1	1,255.9	6.44	4.25
NORTH RIVER INS CO	NJ	C-	1q 2019	1,069.1	269.0	2.2	293.4	1.13	0.85
NORTHWEST DENTAL BENEFITS LLC	ID	U		--	--	--	--	--	--
NORTHWESTERN LONG TERM CARE INS CO	WI	• B	1q 2019	245.4	710.5	710.5	143.5	9.08	3.66
NORTHWESTERN MUTUAL LIFE INS CO	WI	B+	1q 2019	278,047.4	18,018.1	1,350.1	22,722.3	3.34	1.69
NORTHWESTERN NATL INS CO SEG ACCNT	WI	E-	4q 2018	17.3	0.3	0.3	-0.4	-0.04	-0.03
NOVA CASUALTY CO	NY	B-	1q 2019	98.7	238.5	0.0	91.1	1.94	1.90
NTA LIFE INS CO OF NEW YORK	NY	B	1q 2019	8.0	1.4	1.4	6.9	3.37	3.03
▼ OBI NATIONAL INS CO	PA	C	1q 2019	13.5	48.6	0.0	13.5	179.20	89.61
OCCIDENTAL LIFE INS CO OF NC	TX	C	1q 2019	252.5	45.9	0.1	27.2	2.73	1.58
OHIO CASUALTY INS CO	NH	C	1q 2019	6,852.3	993.9	0.0	1,909.1	2.74	1.90
▼ OHIO NATIONAL LIFE ASR CORP	OH	B	1q 2019	4,084.4	426.9	28.7	298.3	2.11	1.11
OHIO NATIONAL LIFE INS CO	OH	B-	1q 2019	29,436.1	2,319.0	12.2	902.9	1.15	0.75
OHIO STATE LIFE INS CO	TX	B-	1q 2019	12.8	28.7	0.0	10.5	18.77	12.00
OKLAHOMA FARM BUREAU MUTUAL INS CO	OK	B-	1q 2019	327.1	213.9	0.0	137.5	2.72	2.09
OKLAHOMA SUPERIOR SELECT INC	OK	• E+	1q 2019	3.2	5.4	5.4	1.8	1.40	1.16
OLD AMERICAN INS CO	MO	B-	1q 2019	270.5	91.0	0.4	19.8	2.06	1.16
OLD REPUBLIC LIFE INS CO	IL	• B-	1q 2019	109.4	24.7	15.8	35.1	4.09	2.50
OLD SPARTAN LIFE INS CO INC	SC	C	1q 2019	24.1	4.7	3.8	16.4	2.20	1.36
OLD SURETY LIFE INS CO	OK	C	1q 2019	30.8	57.4	57.3	13.5	0.73	0.57
OLD UNITED LIFE INS CO	AZ	• B	1q 2019	85.7	6.0	3.0	55.8	6.88	4.17
OMAHA HEALTH INSURANCE CO	NE	U		--	--	--	--	--	--
OMAHA INS CO	NE	• B-	1q 2019	95.8	655.2	655.2	48.6	1.76	0.92
ON LOK SENIOR HEALTH SERVICES	CA	• B	1q 2019	170.3	157.5	157.5	132.9	3.91	2.85
OPTILEGRA INC	SD	U		--	--	--	--	--	--
OPTIMA HEALTH INS CO	VA	• C	1q 2019	29.5	44.3	44.3	13.7	2.96	2.47
OPTIMA HEALTH PLAN	VA	• A	1q 2019	795.0	2,376.0	2,376.0	352.8	1.99	1.66
OPTIMUM CHOICE INC	MD	• B	1q 2019	114.2	272.3	272.3	37.8	6.31	5.25
▲ OPTIMUM HEALTHCARE INC	FL	• B	1q 2019	189.0	722.1	722.1	66.1	2.19	1.82
OPTUM INS OF OH INC	OH	B	1q 2019	375.1	0.7	0.0	77.3	6.89	6.20
ORISKA INS CO	NY	E	1q 2019	37.7	11.8	0.1	10.4	0.15	0.12
ORTHONET OF THE MID-ATLANTIC	NJ	U		--	--	--	--	--	--
OSCAR BUCKEYE STATE INS CORP	OH	U		--	--	--	--	--	--

Arrows denote recent upgrades ▲ or downgrades ▼

• Bullets denote a more detailed analysis is available in Section II.

INSURANCE COMPANY NAME	DOM. STATE	RATING	DATA DATE	TOTAL ASSETS ($MIL)	TOTAL PREMIUMS ($MIL)	HEALTH PREMIUMS ($MIL)	CAPITAL & SURPLUS ($MIL)	RISK ADJUSTED CAPITAL RATIO 1	RISK ADJUSTED CAPITAL RATIO 2
OSCAR GARDEN STATE INSURANCE	NJ	• D	1q 2019	49.6	20.9	20.9	7.3	1.74	1.45
OSCAR HEALTH PLAN INC	AZ	U		--	--	--	--	--	--
OSCAR HEALTH PLAN OF CALIFORNIA	CA	• E-	1q 2019	157.0	76.4	76.4	-67.7	0.00	0.00
OSCAR INS CORP	NY	• E-	1q 2019	225.8	180.4	180.4	32.8	2.86	2.39
OSCAR INS CORP OF NEW JERSEY	NJ	• D	4q 2018	5.4	0.3	0.3	5.4	3.79	3.15
OSCAR INSURANCE CO FLORIDA	FL	U		--	--	--	--	--	--
OSCAR INSURANCE COMPANY	TX	• D-	1q 2019	333.4	359.8	359.8	49.8	1.48	1.23
OSCAR INSURANCE CORP OF OHIO	OH	• D	1q 2019	41.0	86.3	86.3	27.8	2.36	1.97
OXFORD HEALTH INS INC	NY	• B	1q 2019	2,945.6	8,182.0	8,182.0	1,477.0	3.35	2.79
OXFORD HEALTH PLANS (CT) INC	CT	• B	1q 2019	584.4	1,661.7	1,661.7	219.3	2.61	2.17
OXFORD HEALTH PLANS (NJ) INC	NJ	• B	1q 2019	279.6	576.3	576.3	166.7	7.55	6.29
OXFORD HEALTH PLANS (NY) INC	NY	• B	1q 2019	449.9	871.1	871.1	253.9	4.76	3.97
OXFORD LIFE INS CO	AZ	B+	1q 2019	2,251.8	460.0	39.8	208.4	2.03	1.26
OZARK NATIONAL LIFE INS CO	MO	D+	1q 2019	751.8	84.4	0.2	47.1	1.83	1.04
PA HEALTH & WELLNESS INC	PA	• C	1q 2019	267.5	483.4	483.4	95.3	2.91	2.43
PACIFIC CENTURY LIFE INS CORP	AZ	• C-	1q 2019	368.7	0.0	0.0	366.5	32.29	19.54
PACIFIC GUARDIAN LIFE INS CO LTD	HI	• A-	1q 2019	568.1	85.1	44.3	86.7	3.06	1.78
PACIFIC INDEMNITY CO	WI	C+	1q 2019	10,957.0	669.7	0.0	3,357.6	2.23	1.36
PACIFICARE LIFE & HEALTH INS CO	IN	• B	1q 2019	188.5	12.8	12.8	183.5	18.81	16.93
PACIFICARE LIFE ASR CO	CO	U		--	--	--	--	--	--
PACIFICARE OF ARIZONA INC	AZ	• E	1q 2019	33.2	2.8	2.8	12.9	8.49	7.07
PACIFICARE OF COLORADO INC	CO	• B	1q 2019	827.7	3,243.6	3,243.6	450.9	3.10	2.58
PACIFICARE OF NEVADA INC	NV	• C	1q 2019	6.5	0.7	0.7	5.4	3.99	3.32
PACIFICSOURCE COMMUNITY HEALTH PLANS	OR	• B	1q 2019	139.6	309.2	309.2	93.4	2.89	2.41
PACIFICSOURCE HEALTH PLANS	OR	• C+	1q 2019	355.1	800.7	800.7	237.7	2.41	2.01
PAN AMERICAN LIFE INS CO OF PR	PR	B	1q 2019	9.8	17.5	17.2	5.6	1.80	1.39
PAN-AMERICAN LIFE INS CO	LA	• B	1q 2019	1,280.0	274.9	234.9	247.7	2.29	1.52
PARAMOUNT ADVANTAGE	OH	• B	1q 2019	258.9	1,341.1	1,341.1	106.6	1.05	0.88
PARAMOUNT CARE OF MI INC	MI	• B	1q 2019	15.9	22.9	22.9	13.2	4.26	3.55
PARAMOUNT HEALTH CARE	OH	• B	1q 2019	98.9	170.9	170.9	66.3	4.15	3.46
PARAMOUNT INS CO (OH)	OH	• A-	1q 2019	87.0	184.1	184.1	45.2	2.80	2.33
PARKLAND COMMUNITY HEALTH PLAN INC	TX	• B-	1q 2019	131.2	574.7	574.7	73.2	1.49	1.24
PARTNERRE AMERICA INS CO	DE	• C+	1q 2019	353.7	107.5	53.4	109.2	0.89	0.66
PARTNERSHIP HEALTHPLAN OF CALIFORNIA	CA	• C+	1q 2019	1,412.7	2,595.1	2,595.1	585.2	5.10	3.12
PATRIOT INS CO	ME	C	1q 2019	140.9	52.5	0.0	55.4	5.25	3.74
PAUL REVERE LIFE INS CO	MA	• C+	1q 2019	3,369.3	235.2	220.7	194.1	1.56	0.95
PAVONIA LIFE INS CO OF MICHIGAN	MI	C	1q 2019	1,097.1	29.1	3.1	76.3	1.79	0.99
PAVONIA LIFE INS CO OF NEW YORK	NY	C	1q 2019	29.9	3.7	0.0	9.6	2.16	1.94
PEACH STATE HEALTH PLAN INC	GA	• B-	1q 2019	360.0	1,090.1	1,090.1	236.0	4.39	3.66
PEKIN LIFE INS CO	IL	B	1q 2019	1,527.3	194.0	41.2	129.1	2.06	1.21
PENN MUTUAL LIFE INS CO	PA	B	1q 2019	21,835.8	1,874.0	8.0	1,778.9	1.69	1.14
PENNSYLVANIA LIFE INS CO	PA	U		--	--	--	--	--	--
PEOPLES HEALTH INC	LA	• C	1q 2019	73.3	843.7	843.7	45.7	1.30	1.08
PHILADELPHIA AMERICAN LIFE INS CO	TX	• B	1q 2019	304.4	254.6	235.3	49.2	1.66	1.13
PHILADELPHIA INDEMNITY INS CO	PA	B-	1q 2019	9,188.8	3,364.2	20.3	2,468.6	2.39	1.80
PHOENIX HEALTH PLANS INC	AZ	U		--	--	--	--	--	--
PHP INS CO	MI	• C	1q 2019	16.5	26.9	26.9	13.0	3.29	2.74
PHP INS CO OF IN INC	IN	• C+	1q 2019	3.4	0.6	0.6	2.4	7.69	6.41
PHYSICIANS BENEFITS TRUST LIFE INS	IL	C+	1q 2019	6.0	0.2	0.2	5.8	3.38	3.05
PHYSICIANS HEALTH CHOICE OF TEXAS	TX	• C	1q 2019	188.6	983.0	983.0	70.9	1.58	1.32
PHYSICIANS HEALTH PLAN OF NO IN	IN	• B	1q 2019	101.2	172.9	172.9	63.7	3.17	2.65
PHYSICIANS HP OF MID-MICHIGAN	MI	• C	1q 2019	88.3	199.6	199.6	51.9	1.93	1.61

	INSURANCE COMPANY NAME	DOM. STATE	RATING	DATA DATE	TOTAL ASSETS ($MIL)	TOTAL PREMIUMS ($MIL)	HEALTH PREMIUMS ($MIL)	CAPITAL & SURPLUS ($MIL)	RISK ADJUSTED CAPITAL RATIO 1	RISK ADJUSTED CAPITAL RATIO 2
	PHYSICIANS LIFE INS CO	NE	A-	1q 2019	1,685.6	334.9	66.3	155.1	2.81	1.43
	PHYSICIANS MUTUAL INS CO	NE	• A+	1q 2019	2,391.2	404.4	404.4	1,015.5	3.49	2.61
	PHYSICIANS PLUS INS CORP	WI	• C-	1q 2019	127.1	193.0	193.0	106.3	1.47	1.23
	PICA HEALTH INC	PR	U		--	--	--	--	--	--
	PIEDMONT COMMUNITY HEALTHCARE	VA	• D+	1q 2019	26.0	77.5	77.5	11.0	0.91	0.76
	PIEDMONT COMMUNITY HEALTHCARE HMO	VA	• C-	1q 2019	25.0	176.2	176.2	15.0	0.75	0.63
	PIEDMONT WELLSTAR HEALTHPLANS INC	GA	U		--	--	--	--	--	--
	PIONEER EDUCATORS HEALTH TRUST	OR	• E+	1q 2019	2.8	12.5	12.5	1.8	N/A	N/A
	PIONEER MUTUAL LIFE INS CO	ND	B	1q 2019	510.1	20.0	0.0	49.3	3.39	1.84
▲	PL MEDICO SERV DE SALUD BELLA VISTA	PR	• C+	1q 2019	3.3	6.5	6.5	1.4	0.96	0.80
	PLAN DE SALUD MENONITA	PR	U		--	--	--	--	--	--
	PLATEAU INS CO	TN	C	1q 2019	27.5	46.8	25.5	15.6	3.50	2.74
	PMC MEDICARE CHOICE LLC	PR	U		--	--	--	--	--	--
	PREFERRED CARE PARTNERS INC	FL	• B	1q 2019	559.2	2,261.0	2,261.0	169.9	1.64	1.37
	PREFERREDONE COMMUNITY HEALTH PLAN	MN	• D+	1q 2019	3.8	2.6	2.6	2.7	3.48	2.90
	PREFERREDONE INS CO	MN	• C-	1q 2019	95.6	230.3	230.3	42.3	1.19	0.99
	PREMERA BLUE CROSS	WA	• B	1q 2019	3,465.4	3,571.1	3,571.1	2,289.7	8.11	6.76
	PREMIER CHOICE DENTAL INC	AZ	U		--	--	--	--	--	--
	PREMIER HEALTH INSURING CORP	OH	• E	1q 2019	10.2	21.7	21.7	7.7	2.00	1.67
	PREMIER HEALTH PLAN INC	OH	• D-	1q 2019	6.4	3.8	3.8	5.9	2.54	2.12
	PREMIER HEALTH PLAN SERVICES INC	CA	• D	1q 2019	32.7	87.0	87.0	15.9	1.93	1.24
	PRESBYTERIAN HEALTH PLAN INC	NM	• B	1q 2019	633.7	2,149.4	2,149.4	192.4	1.34	1.12
▼	PRESBYTERIAN INS CO	NM	• C+	1q 2019	48.9	136.3	136.3	32.3	1.78	1.48
	PRESIDENTIAL LIFE INS CO	TX	C	1q 2019	4.4	0.1	0.0	3.0	2.52	2.27
	PRIMECARE MEDICAL NETWORK INC	CA	• B-	1q 2019	277.5	1,005.4	1,005.4	78.7	2.16	1.34
	PRIMERICA LIFE INS CO	TN	B	1q 2019	1,610.1	2,253.4	0.4	693.4	1.45	1.24
	PRINCIPAL LIFE INS CO	IA	B+	1q 2019	196,332.3	9,957.4	1,868.1	5,453.9	2.14	1.21
	PRIORITY HEALTH	MI	• A	1q 2019	1,388.7	3,180.0	3,180.0	843.4	3.74	3.11
	PRIORITY HEALTH CHOICE INC	MI	• A-	1q 2019	143.1	396.5	396.5	86.3	3.74	3.12
	PRIORITY HEALTH INS CO	MI	• B	1q 2019	135.2	245.3	245.3	62.2	3.52	2.93
	PROCARE ADVANTAGE LLC	TX	U		--	--	--	--	--	--
	PROFESSIONAL INS CO	TX	• D+	1q 2019	111.9	19.2	17.9	51.5	5.73	5.16
	PROMINENCE HEALTHFIRST	NV	• D	1q 2019	100.6	116.8	116.8	61.9	4.66	3.88
	PROMINENCE HEALTHFIRST OF TEXAS INC	TX	• D+	1q 2019	22.3	12.7	12.7	19.4	17.00	14.17
	PROMINENCE PREFERRED HEALTH INS CO	NV	• D-	1q 2019	38.2	12.5	12.5	33.9	21.39	17.83
	PROSPECT HEALTH PLAN	CA	• E+	1q 2019	22.6	243.0	243.0	7.5	0.36	0.22
	PROTEC INS CO	IL	C+	1q 2019	5.4	5.1	0.1	5.1	3.17	2.85
	PROTECTIVE INS CO	IN	B	1q 2019	990.5	516.7	23.5	384.1	1.48	1.13
	PROTECTIVE LIFE & ANNUITY INS CO	AL	C+	1q 2019	5,178.2	447.4	0.1	303.9	1.81	0.94
	PROTECTIVE LIFE INS CO	TN	B	1q 2019	58,633.9	3,791.5	19.4	4,450.1	1.53	1.06
	PROVIDENCE HEALTH ASR	OR	• A-	1q 2019	457.3	824.8	824.8	288.7	5.00	4.17
	PROVIDENCE HEALTH NETWORK	CA	• E-	1q 2019	13.2	135.9	135.9	0.1	0.13	0.08
	PROVIDENCE HEALTH PLAN	OR	• B	1q 2019	933.4	1,377.6	1,377.6	575.9	4.05	3.37
	PROVIDENT AMER LIFE & HEALTH INS CO	OH	B	1q 2019	9.3	7.5	6.9	8.2	1.67	1.52
	PROVIDENT AMERICAN INS CO	TX	C	1q 2019	18.6	0.8	0.5	12.3	0.82	0.73
	PROVIDENT LIFE & ACCIDENT INS CO	TN	• C+	1q 2019	7,975.2	1,036.0	718.0	627.6	2.49	1.26
	PROVIDENT LIFE & CAS INS CO	TN	• B-	1q 2019	734.2	93.7	91.9	128.4	4.10	2.37
▲	PROVIDER PARTNERS HEALTH PLAN INC	MD	• E	1q 2019	3.9	8.0	8.0	1.5	0.59	0.49
	PROVIDER PARTNERS HEALTH PLAN OF PA	PA	• E-	1q 2019	3.6	12.9	12.9	0.7	0.19	0.16
	PRUDENTIAL INS CO OF AMERICA	NJ	B	1q 2019	274,754.9	26,870.2	1,529.0	11,652.9	1.62	1.15
	PRUITTHEALTH PREMIER INC	GA	• D+	1q 2019	10.3	39.9	39.9	3.3	0.59	0.49
	PRUITTHEALTH PREMIER NC LLC	NC	U		--	--	--	--	--	--

INSURANCE COMPANY NAME	DOM. STATE	RATING	DATA DATE	TOTAL ASSETS ($MIL)	TOTAL PREMIUMS ($MIL)	HEALTH PREMIUMS ($MIL)	CAPITAL & SURPLUS ($MIL)	RISK ADJUSTED CAPITAL RATIO 1	RISK ADJUSTED CAPITAL RATIO 2
PRVDR PTNRS HLTH PLAN OH INC	OH	U		--	--	--	--	--	--
PUBLIC SERVICE INS CO	IL	F	4q 2016	295.1	53.0	0.0	28.3	0.13	0.07
PUPIL BENEFITS PLAN INC	NY	• C-	1q 2019	13.4	8.5	8.5	8.1	6.26	5.22
PURITAN LIFE INS CO OF AMERICA	TX	C	1q 2019	142.9	49.7	20.1	22.2	1.83	1.33
QBE INS CORP	PA	• B	1q 2019	2,551.2	1,133.8	320.0	785.6	2.00	1.34
QBE SEGUROS	PR	D	1q 2019	90.1	53.8	0.4	30.1	2.68	1.53
QBE SPECIALTY INS CO	ND	C	1q 2019	439.8	735.1	4.9	131.3	2.15	1.40
QCA HEALTH PLAN INC	AR	• C	1q 2019	103.9	206.4	206.4	61.7	3.91	3.26
QCC INS CO	PA	• B-	1q 2019	1,265.6	2,102.1	2,102.1	608.3	4.63	3.86
QUALCHOICE ADVANTAGE INC	AR	• C-	1q 2019	4.7	9.4	9.4	2.7	1.80	1.50
QUALCHOICE L&H INS CO	AR	• C	1q 2019	75.4	126.7	126.7	49.8	5.38	4.49
REGAL LIFE OF AMERICA INS CO	TX	D-	1q 2019	7.8	0.9	0.7	5.4	1.10	1.08
REGENCE BL CROSS BL SHIELD OREGON	OR	• A-	1q 2019	1,319.0	1,965.5	1,965.5	835.2	7.27	6.06
REGENCE BLUE CROSS BLUE SHIELD OF UT	UT	• B+	1q 2019	739.4	1,030.5	1,030.5	443.0	9.33	7.77
REGENCE BLUESHIELD	WA	• B	1q 2019	1,694.5	1,755.0	1,755.0	1,254.3	9.42	7.85
REGENCE BLUESHIELD OF IDAHO INC	ID	• B+	1q 2019	340.7	448.2	448.2	223.8	8.48	7.07
RELIABLE LIFE INS CO	MO	B-	1q 2019	19.8	114.7	8.9	12.0	2.00	0.99
RELIANCE STANDARD LIFE INS CO	IL	C+	1q 2019	14,367.6	3,419.5	818.1	1,330.0	1.94	1.03
RELIASTAR LIFE INS CO	MN	• B-	1q 2019	20,397.1	2,950.2	1,219.2	1,694.2	2.08	1.23
RELIASTAR LIFE INS CO OF NEW YORK	NY	B	1q 2019	2,874.4	268.1	59.0	286.9	3.31	1.79
RENAISSANCE L&H INS CO OF NY	NY	D	1q 2019	11.4	4.3	4.3	8.2	1.58	1.24
RESERVE NATIONAL INS CO	OK	• B-	1q 2019	142.2	159.4	144.6	33.5	1.28	0.97
RESPONSE INDEMNITY CO OF CA	CA	C-	1q 2019	24.7	26.1	0.0	5.5	1.59	1.43
RETAILERS INS CO	MI	C	1q 2019	24.1	10.0	0.5	10.7	1.73	1.40
RGA REINSURANCE CO	MO	• B-	1q 2019	36,492.4	33.6	12.5	2,131.1	1.80	0.97
RIVERLINK HEALTH	OH	• D	1q 2019	6.0	8.8	8.8	5.4	5.12	4.27
RIVERLINK HEALTH OF KENTUCKY INC	KY	• D+	1q 2019	5.4	8.7	8.7	5.0	3.98	3.32
RIVERSOURCE LIFE INS CO	MN	C+	1q 2019	101,688.4	5,573.7	333.2	3,024.4	1.75	1.08
RIVERSOURCE LIFE INS CO OF NY	NY	C	1q 2019	6,788.1	386.3	17.1	283.3	2.96	1.49
ROCKY MOUNTAIN HEALTH MAINT ORG	CO	• B-	1q 2019	156.7	403.7	403.7	75.3	3.55	2.96
ROCKY MOUNTAIN HOSPITAL & MEDICAL	CO	• B	1q 2019	1,046.8	1,748.7	1,748.7	537.6	3.11	2.59
ROYAL STATE NATIONAL INS CO LTD	HI	• C	1q 2018	39.7	5.4	2.9	30.3	5.02	3.72
ROYALTY CAPITAL LIFE INS CO	MO	D	1q 2019	3.6	0.1	0.0	3.5	3.09	2.78
RURAL MUTUAL INS CO	WI	B-	1q 2019	534.5	207.3	0.7	294.6	7.21	4.81
RYDER HEALTH PLAN INC	PR	• B	1q 2019	1.4	2.0	2.0	0.6	1.44	1.20
S USA LIFE INS CO INC	AZ	B-	1q 2019	27.0	23.4	9.6	15.1	3.41	3.07
SAGICOR LIFE INS CO	TX	C-	1q 2019	1,763.3	413.8	0.1	89.0	0.83	0.42
SAMARITAN HEALTH PLANS INC	OR	• C+	1q 2019	24.6	89.1	89.1	11.0	0.85	0.71
SAN FRANCISCO HEALTH AUTHORITY	CA	• B-	1q 2019	662.6	600.1	600.1	108.9	2.67	1.69
SAN JOAQUIN CNTY HEALTH	CA	• B+	1q 2019	660.0	1,050.0	1,050.0	344.7	5.63	3.42
SAN MATEO HEALTH COMMISSION	CA	• B	1q 2019	628.3	770.9	770.9	343.0	6.39	3.93
SANFORD HEALTH PLAN	SD	• C	1q 2019	285.2	908.5	908.5	141.3	1.60	1.33
SANFORD HEALTH PLAN OF MINNESOTA	MN	• D+	1q 2019	3.2	3.6	3.6	1.3	1.76	1.47
SANFORD HEART OF AMERICA HEALTH PLAN	ND	• C-	1q 2019	2.4	3.0	3.0	2.1	2.14	1.78
SANTA BARBARA SAN LUIS OBISPO REGION	CA	• B-	1q 2019	529.0	770.0	770.0	232.7	4.04	2.47
SANTA CLARA COUNTY HEALTH AUTHORITY	CA	• C	1q 2019	920.5	1,332.5	1,332.5	190.5	2.90	1.77
SANTA CLARA VALLEY	CA	• D+	1q 2019	192.6	544.4	544.4	36.8	0.75	0.47
SANTA CRUZ-MONTEREY-MERCED MGD MED	CA	• B-	1q 2019	851.6	1,145.9	1,145.9	501.9	8.24	5.11
SAPPHIRE EDGE INC	NE	U		--	--	--	--	--	--
SATELLITE HEALTH PLAN INC	CA	U		--	--	--	--	--	--
SBLI USA MUT LIFE INS CO INC	NY	B-	1q 2019	1,589.3	177.5	4.9	88.5	1.28	0.78
SC FARM BUREAU MUTUAL INS CO	SC	B-	1q 2019	134.0	78.7	0.1	77.5	3.82	3.39

INSURANCE COMPANY NAME	DOM. STATE	RATING	DATA DATE	TOTAL ASSETS ($MIL)	TOTAL PREMIUMS ($MIL)	HEALTH PREMIUMS ($MIL)	CAPITAL & SURPLUS ($MIL)	RISK ADJUSTED CAPITAL RATIO 1	RISK ADJUSTED CAPITAL RATIO 2
SCAN HEALTH PLAN	CA	• B	1q 2019	691.6	2,717.8	2,717.8	409.4	3.14	1.94
SCOTT & WHITE CARE PLANS	TX	U		--	--	--	--	--	--
SCOTT & WHITE HEALTH PLAN	TX	• C	1q 2019	434.5	716.1	716.1	223.6	2.49	2.07
▲ SCRIPPS HEALTH PLAN SERVICES INC	CA	• C-	1q 2019	130.9	674.1	674.1	41.1	0.86	0.52
SD STATE MEDICAL HOLDING CO	SD	• D	1q 2019	21.5	36.6	36.6	8.2	1.40	1.16
SEASIDE HEALTH PLAN	CA	• D-	1q 2019	13.0	42.7	42.7	8.3	0.29	0.19
SECURIAN LIFE INS CO	MN	B	1q 2019	1,218.5	1,334.6	84.4	354.4	5.26	3.33
SECURITY HEALTH PLAN OF WI INC	WI	• B+	1q 2019	445.1	1,340.1	1,340.1	183.0	1.82	1.52
SECURITY LIFE OF DENVER INS CO	CO	B-	1q 2019	14,705.7	927.0	0.0	812.2	1.31	0.75
SECURITY MUTUAL LIFE INS CO OF NY	NY	C	1q 2019	2,777.8	390.8	17.7	165.9	1.71	0.91
SECURITY NATIONAL LIFE INS CO	UT	D	1q 2019	673.1	84.4	0.1	47.6	1.06	0.63
SECURITY PLAN LIFE INS CO	LA	C-	1q 2019	308.5	42.4	0.6	15.2	0.81	0.55
SECURITYCARE OF TENNESSEE INC	TN	U		--	--	--	--	--	--
SELECT HEALTH OF SOUTH CAROLINA INC	SC	• B	1q 2019	332.4	1,465.7	1,465.7	151.7	2.00	1.67
▲ SELECTCARE HEALTH PLANS INC	TX	• B-	1q 2019	12.4	22.8	22.8	7.2	3.57	2.97
SELECTCARE OF TEXAS INC	TX	• B	1q 2019	240.2	870.9	870.9	80.9	2.10	1.75
SELECTHEALTH BENEFIT ASR CO INC	UT	• C+	1q 2019	26.7	31.9	31.9	18.5	3.60	3.00
SELECTHEALTH INC	UT	• C	1q 2019	1,428.1	3,109.3	3,109.3	613.9	2.76	2.30
SELECTIVE INS CO OF AM	NJ	B	1q 2019	2,582.6	583.3	0.0	648.6	2.81	1.85
SENDERO HEALTH PLANS INC	TX	• E	1q 2019	57.3	124.3	124.3	13.0	0.47	0.39
SENIOR AMERICAN INS CO	PA	E-	1q 2019	7.2	1.5	1.5	-10.3	-1.44	-0.92
SENIOR HEALTH INS CO OF PENNSYLVANIA	PA	E-	1q 2019	2,137.4	85.9	85.9	-481.3	-1.47	-0.97
SENIOR LIFE INS CO	GA	D+	1q 2019	64.6	58.8	0.0	11.4	1.50	0.77
SENIOR WHOLE HEALTH OF NEW YORK INC	NY	• C-	1q 2019	178.6	688.2	688.2	42.8	0.63	0.53
SENTINEL SECURITY LIFE INS CO	UT	D	1q 2019	505.3	334.0	42.2	46.8	1.22	0.61
▼ SENTRY INS A MUTUAL CO	WI	B	1q 2019	8,944.7	513.8	1.4	5,596.1	2.99	2.43
SENTRY LIFE INS CO	WI	A	1q 2019	7,524.4	805.2	1.8	306.5	3.46	1.94
SENTRY LIFE INS CO OF NEW YORK	NY	B	1q 2019	122.2	16.8	0.0	10.4	1.17	1.05
SENTRY SELECT INS CO	WI	B	1q 2019	853.9	606.9	9.6	229.3	3.01	1.93
SEQUOIA HEALTH PLAN INC	CA	• E+	1q 2019	2.9	68.9	68.9	2.4	0.35	0.21
SERVICE LIFE & CAS INS CO	TX	U		--	--	--	--	--	--
SETON HEALTH PLAN INC	TX	• B	1q 2019	49.0	28.9	28.9	30.8	3.94	3.28
▲ SETON INSURANCE COMPANY	TX	• C+	1q 2019	8.2	0.2	0.2	7.8	3.18	2.65
SETTLERS LIFE INS CO	WI	B	1q 2019	430.4	54.7	0.2	49.1	2.95	1.60
▲ SHA LLC	TX	• D	1q 2019	142.8	568.5	568.5	56.5	1.08	0.90
▲ SHARP HEALTH PLAN	CA	• B+	1q 2019	177.2	744.8	744.8	92.9	1.52	0.99
SHELTER LIFE INS CO	MO	B	1q 2019	1,290.8	151.6	13.1	236.2	3.90	2.45
SHELTERPOINT INS CO	FL	B	1q 2019	9.1	1.9	1.9	8.0	3.95	3.55
SHELTERPOINT LIFE INS CO	NY	• A	1q 2019	183.5	186.1	184.6	65.3	1.85	1.56
SHENANDOAH LIFE INS CO	VA	B-	1q 2019	998.8	54.3	12.0	110.2	2.79	1.52
SHERIDAN LIFE INS CO	OK	U		--	--	--	--	--	--
SIDNEY HILLMAN HEALTH CENTRE	IL	U		--	--	--	--	--	--
SIERRA HEALTH AND LIFE INS CO INC	NV	• B	1q 2019	4,933.9	16,213.6	16,213.6	2,593.1	2.66	2.21
▼ SIGNATURE ADVANTAGE LLC	KY	• D	1q 2019	2.9	4.7	4.7	1.0	0.42	0.35
SILVERSCRIPT INS CO	TN	• D	1q 2019	2,971.8	2,720.5	2,720.5	865.4	5.68	4.74
SILVERSUMMIT HEALTHPLAN INC	NV	• C-	1q 2019	154.6	372.0	372.0	83.5	5.87	4.89
SIMPLY HEALTHCARE PLANS INC	FL	• B-	1q 2019	654.2	3,171.7	3,171.7	248.9	1.39	1.16
SIMPRA ADVANTAGE INC	AL	• D+	1q 2019	19.4	40.7	40.7	7.7	1.18	0.98
▼ SIRIUS AMERICA INS CO	NY	• C	1q 2019	1,257.7	202.8	190.8	519.8	0.91	0.57
SISTEMAS MEDICOS NACIONALES SA DE CV	CA	• B-	1q 2019	66.9	95.5	95.5	38.2	3.16	2.10
SOLIS HEALTH PLANS INC	FL	U		--	--	--	--	--	--
SOLSTICE HEALTH INS CO	NY	• C+	1q 2019	19.2	16.7	16.7	3.2	2.50	2.08

Arrows denote recent upgrades ▲ or downgrades▼

• Bullets denote a more detailed analysis is available in Section II.

INSURANCE COMPANY NAME	DOM. STATE	RATING	DATA DATE	TOTAL ASSETS ($MIL)	TOTAL PREMIUMS ($MIL)	HEALTH PREMIUMS ($MIL)	CAPITAL & SURPLUS ($MIL)	RISK ADJUSTED CAPITAL RATIO 1	RISK ADJUSTED CAPITAL RATIO 2
SOUNDPATH HEALTH	WA	• D	1q 2019	51.7	188.4	188.4	41.8	2.03	1.69
SOUTHEASTERN INDIANA HEALTH ORG INC	IN	• C+	1q 2019	15.2	33.8	33.8	9.4	1.80	1.50
SOUTHERN FARM BUREAU LIFE INS CO	MS	A	1q 2019	14,368.9	915.4	29.8	2,591.5	4.38	2.35
SOUTHERN FINANCIAL LIFE INS CO	KY	C	1q 2019	10.5	14.7	8.7	3.4	1.39	1.25
SOUTHERN GUARANTY INS CO	WI	• C+	1q 2019	30.2	1.3	1.3	29.0	4.86	3.09
SOUTHERN NATL LIFE INS CO INC	LA	B	1q 2019	17.7	7.0	1.7	14.0	2.70	2.09
SOUTHWEST L&H INS CO	TX	• D	1q 2019	9.8	9.5	9.5	7.6	3.88	3.23
SOUTHWEST SERVICE LIFE INS CO	TX	D-	1q 2019	11.7	13.3	11.7	4.7	0.80	0.69
SPARTAN PLAN IL INC	IL	• D+	1q 2019	2.9	0.6	0.6	2.1	1.50	1.25
SPARTAN PLAN NY INC	NY	• D	1q 2019	2.3	0.5	0.5	1.6	2.33	1.95
SPARTAN PLAN PA INC	PA	• D	1q 2019	2.4	0.7	0.7	1.2	1.74	1.45
SPARTAN PLAN VA INC	VA	• D+	1q 2019	3.2	0.4	0.4	2.6	1.24	1.03
SSM HEALTH PLAN	MO	U		--	--	--	--	--	--
STABLEVIEW HEALTH INC	KY	U		--	--	--	--	--	--
STANDARD GUARANTY INS CO	DE	B-	1q 2019	307.8	353.6	0.1	131.8	2.31	1.78
STANDARD INS CO	OR	• B+	1q 2019	25,172.5	5,828.3	1,605.3	1,342.9	2.32	1.21
STANDARD LIFE & ACCIDENT INS CO	TX	• A-	1q 2019	511.2	110.7	97.4	296.4	6.09	3.81
STANDARD LIFE & CAS INS CO	UT	D	1q 2019	35.3	15.4	4.8	6.5	1.32	1.19
STANDARD LIFE INS CO OF NY	NY	• A-	1q 2019	304.9	107.2	72.8	104.7	4.73	3.11
STANDARD SECURITY LIFE INS CO OF NY	NY	• B+	1q 2019	139.6	100.6	98.7	70.8	6.86	5.26
STANFORD HEALTH CARE ADVANTAGE	CA	• E	1q 2019	17.1	27.5	27.5	5.5	1.03	0.65
STARMOUNT LIFE INS CO	ME	• C	1q 2019	103.0	214.1	206.8	47.9	1.36	1.06
STARNET INS CO	IA	C+	1q 2019	260.4	382.9	3.4	120.5	12.88	11.59
STARR INDEMNITY & LIABILITY CO	TX	B-	1q 2019	5,434.2	2,090.6	29.0	2,073.5	1.25	0.90
STARR SURPLUS LINES INS CO	TX	C+	1q 2019	587.3	636.9	0.0	154.8	1.38	0.93
STARSTONE NATIONAL INS CO	DE	C-	1q 2019	537.8	344.4	0.3	111.8	1.14	0.56
STATE AUTOMOBILE MUTUAL INS CO	OH	C+	1q 2019	2,347.7	428.7	0.0	839.1	1.33	1.21
STATE FARM FIRE & CAS CO	IL	B	1q 2019	42,254.7	19,565.2	0.0	20,163.1	3.58	2.33
STATE FARM MUTUAL AUTOMOBILE INS CO	IL	B	1q 2019	167,779.7	40,650.9	1,019.2	107,505.6	2.24	1.93
STATE LIFE INS CO	IN	B	1q 2019	8,764.2	948.1	19.8	498.3	1.69	0.86
STATE MUTUAL INS CO	GA	• D	1q 2019	187.8	58.2	41.7	25.4	1.07	0.69
STERLING DENTAL OF MO INC	MO	U		--	--	--	--	--	--
STERLING INVESTORS LIFE INS CO	IN	B-	1q 2019	82.1	33.3	8.1	10.5	1.36	1.16
STERLING LIFE INS CO	IL	B-	1q 2019	35.3	61.0	59.6	15.8	0.93	0.72
STEWARD HEALTH CHOICE INC	AZ	U		--	--	--	--	--	--
STEWARD HEALTH CHOICE UTAH INC	UT	• E-	1q 2019	32.2	59.3	59.3	16.4	2.34	1.95
SUMMA INS CO	OH	• C-	1q 2019	51.4	170.8	170.8	24.6	1.40	1.17
SUMMACARE INC	OH	• C	1q 2019	86.1	258.8	258.8	42.1	1.26	1.05
SUN LIFE & HEALTH INS CO	MI	• D	1q 2019	932.6	200.7	136.2	99.0	2.22	1.32
SUN LIFE ASR CO OF CANADA	MI	• D+	1q 2019	18,892.8	3,102.8	2,047.9	1,374.7	0.79	0.46
SUNFLOWER STATE HEALTH PLAN INC	KS	• C	1q 2019	306.3	1,355.5	1,355.5	133.6	2.17	1.81
SUNSET LIFE INS CO OF AMERICA	MO	B-	1q 2019	303.0	17.4	0.0	25.6	2.68	1.40
SUNSHINE HEALTH	FL	• D+	1q 2019	794.0	3,945.8	3,945.8	351.5	1.53	1.27
SUNSHINE HEALTH COMMUNITY SOLUTIONS	FL	• C-	1q 2019	15.9	21.7	21.7	8.1	2.93	2.44
SUPERIOR HEALTHPLAN COMMUNITY SOLUTI	TX	• C-	1q 2019	12.9	10.3	10.3	3.8	2.77	2.31
SUPERIOR HEALTHPLAN INC	TX	• C+	1q 2019	862.6	4,327.9	4,327.9	442.5	1.84	1.53
SURENCY LIFE & HEALTH INS CO	KS	C-	1q 2019	12.6	12.0	12.0	10.1	3.52	2.64
SURETY LIFE & CASUALTY INS CO	ND	C-	1q 2019	12.9	1.4	0.6	5.3	2.06	1.69
SURETY LIFE INS CO	NE	D	1q 2019	19.4	32.3	0.0	18.1	3.17	1.54
SUTTER HEALTH PLAN	CA	• D	1q 2019	106.1	428.8	428.8	19.8	0.56	0.35
SWBC LIFE INS CO	TX	A-	1q 2019	33.5	15.1	8.8	23.6	3.83	2.68
SWISS RE LIFE & HEALTH AMER INC	MO	• C	1q 2019	14,338.0	0.3	0.3	2,720.9	2.70	1.72

INSURANCE COMPANY NAME	DOM. STATE	RATING	DATA DATE	TOTAL ASSETS ($MIL)	TOTAL PREMIUMS ($MIL)	HEALTH PREMIUMS ($MIL)	CAPITAL & SURPLUS ($MIL)	RISK ADJUSTED CAPITAL RATIO 1	RISK ADJUSTED CAPITAL RATIO 2
SYMETRA LIFE INS CO	IA	B	1q 2019	39,288.3	4,733.5	849.6	2,167.0	1.62	0.94
SYMPHONIX HEALTH INS INC	IL	• E+	1q 2019	203.8	541.5	541.5	115.9	5.48	4.56
TAKECARE INS CO	GU	• C	1q 2019	35.4	90.7	90.7	13.1	0.88	0.73
TALCOTT RESOLUTION LIFE	CT	B-	1q 2019	34,503.4	1,026.1	0.3	1,124.6	2.72	1.38
TALCOTT RESOLUTION LIFE INS CO	CT	C+	1q 2019	90,075.6	1,689.2	69.0	3,687.0	2.04	1.46
TEACHERS INS & ANNUITY ASN OF AM	NY	A+	1q 2019	307,655.9	15,047.2	13.0	38,367.4	3.79	2.23
TEXAS CHILDRENS HEALTH PLAN INC	TX	• D+	1q 2019	328.5	1,676.5	1,676.5	132.3	0.79	0.66
TEXAS FARM BUREAU MUTUAL INS CO	TX	B-	1q 2019	857.8	552.2	0.8	415.4	3.11	2.86
TEXAS HLTH + AETNA HLTH INS CO	TX	• C	1q 2019	157.3	278.7	278.7	88.1	4.67	3.89
TEXAS HLTH + AETNA HLTH PLAN	TX	• C	1q 2019	15.4	20.9	20.9	9.4	3.43	2.86
▼ TEXAS LIFE INS CO	TX	C+	1q 2019	1,274.3	267.3	0.0	107.2	1.75	0.91
THE UNION LABOR LIFE INS CO	MD	• B	1q 2019	3,999.1	209.5	140.7	112.0	2.12	1.38
THP INS CO	WV	• D+	1q 2019	59.7	112.1	112.1	21.7	1.44	1.20
THRIVENT LIFE INS CO	WI	B	1q 2019	3,876.7	135.7	0.0	166.7	1.84	0.91
TIAA-CREF LIFE INS CO	NY	B	1q 2019	13,848.4	797.7	7.0	502.6	1.98	1.04
TIMBER PRODUCTS MANUFACTURERS TRUST	WA	• C+	1q 2019	18.2	40.7	40.7	14.9	2.98	2.49
▼ TIME INS CO	PR	C	1q 2019	19.3	159.1	119.2	2.4	1.14	0.57
TOKIO MARINE GRV RE INC	OK	C+	1q 2019	37.2	22.2	0.3	35.5	55.11	49.60
TOKIO MARINE PACIFIC INS LTD	GU	• C	1q 2019	128.7	169.8	154.7	87.5	4.92	2.68
TOTAL HEALTH CARE INC	MI	• C+	1q 2019	98.7	183.4	183.4	53.0	1.81	1.51
TOTAL HEALTH CARE USA INC	MI	• B+	1q 2019	95.2	182.2	182.2	44.9	3.12	2.60
TOWN & COUNTRY LIFE INS CO	UT	C-	1q 2019	8.0	5.0	5.0	5.2	2.63	2.37
TPM LIFE INS CO	PA	B	1q 2019	22.2	1.3	1.1	4.6	1.44	1.21
TRANS CITY LIFE INS CO	AZ	C-	1q 2019	19.7	2.2	0.3	9.7	3.42	3.08
TRANS OCEANIC LIFE INS CO	PR	• A-	1q 2019	76.6	29.7	27.5	34.6	2.57	1.63
TRANSAMERICA CASUALTY INS CO	IA	C	1q 2019	156.2	26.0	0.3	123.3	8.03	6.42
TRANSAMERICA FINANCIAL LIFE INS CO	NY	B	1q 2019	30,736.6	5,759.0	114.1	1,136.0	3.13	1.51
TRANSAMERICA LIFE INS CO	IA	B	1q 2019	121,356.4	14,330.4	1,045.9	6,463.6	1.61	1.18
TRANSAMERICA PREMIER LIFE INS CO	IA	C+	1q 2019	49,886.2	3,540.9	654.5	2,120.7	2.36	1.25
▲ TRH HEALTH INS CO	TN	• C+	1q 2019	118.8	290.4	290.4	85.3	3.36	2.80
TRILLIUM COMMUNITY HEALTH PLAN INC	OR	• C+	1q 2019	150.1	536.1	536.1	55.0	1.97	1.64
TRILOGY HEALTH INS INC	WI	• C	1q 2019	7.5	28.3	28.3	3.9	0.86	0.71
TRINITY LIFE INS CO	OK	D-	1q 2019	278.1	49.4	0.0	11.4	0.59	0.40
TRIPLE S VIDA INC	PR	• B-	1q 2019	679.7	188.3	68.2	63.8	1.28	0.84
TRIPLE-S ADVANTAGE INC	PR	• C+	1q 2019	365.6	1,130.2	1,130.2	109.6	0.92	0.77
▲ TRIPLE-S BLUE II	PR	D+	1q 2019	15.3	10.2	9.8	2.9	1.00	0.84
TRIPLE-S SALUD INC	PR	• B+	1q 2019	827.7	1,565.7	1,565.7	366.7	2.06	1.72
TRITON INS CO	TX	• C+	1q 2019	463.0	129.2	35.4	123.4	4.81	2.82
▲ TRUE HEALTH NEW MEXICO INC	NM	• C	1q 2019	66.3	159.7	159.7	23.0	1.34	1.12
▲ TRUSTED HEALTH PLAN (MI) INC	MI	• C	1q 2019	16.7	26.9	26.9	6.3	1.74	1.45
▲ TRUSTED HEALTH PLAN INC	DC	• B	1q 2019	60.9	160.0	160.0	21.8	1.60	1.33
TRUSTMARK INS CO	IL	• B+	1q 2019	1,625.3	387.8	173.2	342.8	2.88	1.66
TRUSTMARK LIFE INS CO	IL	• B+	1q 2019	330.1	127.9	121.8	184.3	8.84	6.20
TSG GUARD INC	OH	U		--	--	--	--	--	--
TUFTS ASSOCIATED HEALTH MAINT ORG	MA	• C	1q 2019	1,112.4	2,582.0	2,582.0	668.7	3.90	3.25
TUFTS HEALTH FREEDOM INS CO	NH	• C-	1q 2019	47.2	95.5	95.5	19.0	2.90	2.42
TUFTS HEALTH PUBLIC PLANS INC	MA	• C	1q 2019	715.6	2,151.8	2,151.8	330.3	2.47	2.06
TUFTS INS CO	MA	• C	1q 2019	114.9	294.4	294.4	71.7	3.93	3.27
U S HEALTH & LIFE INS CO	MI	• B	1q 2019	28.6	32.4	32.4	14.4	4.68	3.90
UCARE HEALTH INC	WI	• C+	1q 2019	37.2	6.7	6.7	35.1	15.49	12.91
UCARE MINNESOTA	MN	• B	1q 2019	1,263.2	3,419.1	3,419.1	686.6	2.88	2.40
UHC OF CALIFORNIA INC	CA	• B-	1q 2019	988.2	6,693.4	6,693.4	361.8	1.20	0.75

Arrows denote recent upgrades ▲ or downgrades▼

• Bullets denote a more detailed analysis is available in Section II.

INSURANCE COMPANY NAME	DOM. STATE	RATING	DATA DATE	TOTAL ASSETS ($MIL)	TOTAL PREMIUMS ($MIL)	HEALTH PREMIUMS ($MIL)	CAPITAL & SURPLUS ($MIL)	RISK ADJUSTED CAPITAL RATIO 1	RISK ADJUSTED CAPITAL RATIO 2
ULTIMATE HEALTH PLANS INC	FL	• E-	1q 2019	16.6	62.2	62.2	2.6	0.22	0.19
UNDERWRITERS AT LLOYDS (KY)	KY	D-	1q 2019	161.6	44.2	0.3	33.4	0.33	0.22
UNDERWRITERS AT LLOYDS (VI)	VI	E+	1q 2019	337.7	87.1	0.5	75.0	0.35	0.23
UNICARE HEALTH PLAN OF WEST VIRGINIA	WV	• B+	1q 2019	150.9	449.0	449.0	93.7	3.73	3.11
UNICARE LIFE & HEALTH INS CO	IN	• B-	1q 2019	540.8	233.4	59.2	93.7	1.75	1.35
UNIFIED LIFE INS CO	TX	B	1q 2019	221.1	53.3	47.6	24.3	1.90	1.15
UNIMERICA INS CO	WI	• B	1q 2019	431.4	420.0	410.8	241.1	4.63	3.63
UNIMERICA LIFE INS CO OF NY	NY	B	1q 2019	40.8	4.3	1.4	23.2	4.72	4.25
UNION FIDELITY LIFE INS CO	KS	• E	1q 2019	20,654.0	24.2	14.1	658.3	1.36	0.69
UNION HEALTH SERVICE INC	IL	• C+	1q 2019	29.7	80.8	80.8	16.6	1.06	0.89
UNION MEDICAL CENTER	IL	U		--	--	--	--	--	--
UNION NATIONAL LIFE INS CO	LA	B	1q 2019	20.9	82.9	6.1	17.0	4.94	2.47
UNION SECURITY INS CO	KS	• B	1q 2019	2,637.1	748.7	564.1	131.1	2.91	1.50
UNION SECURITY LIFE INS CO OF NY	NY	• C+	1q 2019	60.6	26.9	24.6	48.5	6.77	6.09
UNITED AMERICAN INS CO	NE	• B-	1q 2019	760.7	481.1	450.0	145.5	1.44	1.08
UNITED FARM FAMILY LIFE INS CO	IN	A	1q 2019	2,373.1	142.6	0.6	342.8	3.40	2.01
UNITED FIDELITY LIFE INS CO	TX	C	1q 2019	826.1	6.1	0.2	556.4	0.85	0.81
UNITED HEALTHCARE INS CO	CT	• C	1q 2019	19,982.2	54,139.0	53,997.1	7,133.9	1.02	0.85
UNITED HEALTHCARE INS CO OF IL	IL	• B+	1q 2019	546.3	1,249.1	1,249.1	193.0	2.86	2.38
UNITED HEALTHCARE INS CO OF NY	NY	• B	1q 2019	1,381.2	2,257.0	2,257.0	642.1	7.70	6.42
UNITED HEALTHCARE OF ALABAMA INC	AL	• C	1q 2019	61.6	93.9	93.9	38.7	72.65	60.54
UNITED HEALTHCARE OF ARIZONA INC	AZ	• C	1q 2019	52.8	125.2	125.2	26.6	5.35	4.46
UNITED HEALTHCARE OF ARKANSAS INC	AR	• B-	1q 2019	37.7	65.2	65.2	20.3	4.89	4.08
UNITED HEALTHCARE OF COLORADO INC	CO	• C	1q 2019	48.3	92.3	92.3	16.3	3.32	2.77
UNITED HEALTHCARE OF FLORIDA INC	FL	• C+	1q 2019	521.9	2,493.0	2,493.0	251.3	1.85	1.54
UNITED HEALTHCARE OF GEORGIA INC	GA	• C+	1q 2019	96.0	363.7	363.7	39.0	1.86	1.55
UNITED HEALTHCARE OF ILLINOIS INC	IL	• B	1q 2019	67.6	178.6	178.6	34.1	4.41	3.67
UNITED HEALTHCARE OF KENTUCKY LTD	KY	• B-	1q 2019	47.4	158.6	158.6	21.4	2.30	1.91
UNITED HEALTHCARE OF LOUISIANA INC	LA	• B	1q 2019	560.0	2,252.3	2,252.3	158.2	1.58	1.32
UNITED HEALTHCARE OF MID-ATLANTIC	MD	• B-	1q 2019	421.3	980.8	980.8	121.0	2.43	2.02
UNITED HEALTHCARE OF MISSISSIPPI INC	MS	• B-	1q 2019	269.4	1,144.6	1,144.6	166.7	2.36	1.97
UNITED HEALTHCARE OF NC INC	NC	• C	1q 2019	192.5	496.9	496.9	95.5	3.46	2.88
UNITED HEALTHCARE OF NEW ENGLAND INC	RI	• B	1q 2019	358.8	1,160.8	1,160.8	142.4	2.40	2.00
UNITED HEALTHCARE OF NY INC	NY	• B+	1q 2019	1,443.0	5,344.2	5,344.2	597.1	1.91	1.60
UNITED HEALTHCARE OF OHIO INC	OH	• C	1q 2019	59.7	57.7	57.7	50.0	15.62	13.02
UNITED HEALTHCARE OF THE MIDLANDS	NE	• B	1q 2019	845.2	3,102.5	3,102.5	349.3	2.27	1.89
UNITED HEALTHCARE OF THE MIDWEST INC	MO	• C+	1q 2019	587.4	860.4	860.4	195.3	4.84	4.03
UNITED HEALTHCARE OF TX INC	TX	• B	1q 2019	65.4	122.1	122.1	26.5	12.37	10.31
UNITED HEALTHCARE OF UTAH	UT	• B	1q 2019	210.5	810.8	810.8	86.3	2.27	1.89
UNITED HEALTHCARE OF WISCONSIN INC	WI	• B+	1q 2019	2,025.5	6,426.8	6,426.8	1,006.8	3.06	2.55
UNITED HERITAGE LIFE INS CO	ID	B	1q 2019	605.8	90.6	5.5	67.6	2.41	1.18
UNITED HOME LIFE INS CO	IN	B	1q 2019	100.0	52.3	0.0	20.8	2.45	2.21
UNITED INS CO OF AMERICA	IL	B-	1q 2019	4,071.0	167.4	7.8	419.1	1.74	1.02
UNITED LIFE INS CO	IA	B	1q 2019	1,551.4	181.3	1.2	148.1	2.62	1.28
UNITED NATIONAL LIFE INS CO OF AM	IL	B	1q 2019	34.8	16.8	15.5	9.6	1.57	1.15
UNITED OF OMAHA LIFE INS CO	NE	• B	1q 2019	24,356.1	5,233.0	1,733.1	1,657.3	2.04	1.17
UNITED OHIO INS CO	OH	B-	1q 2019	370.6	170.0	0.0	192.9	7.12	5.18
UNITED SECURITY ASR CO OF PA	PA	E+	1q 2019	37.4	31.0	30.7	11.5	2.15	1.94
UNITED SECURITY HEALTH & CASUALTY	IL	C-	1q 2019	8.4	2.4	1.2	5.6	3.28	2.58
UNITED STATES LIFE INS CO IN NYC	NY	C+	1q 2019	28,422.8	1,687.4	39.4	1,382.7	1.95	0.90
UNITED SURETY & INDEMNITY CO	PR	C	1q 2019	117.6	48.5	0.6	64.9	2.05	1.35
UNITED WORLD LIFE INS CO	NE	• B+	1q 2019	132.1	437.5	436.3	45.0	3.82	1.60

INSURANCE COMPANY NAME	DOM. STATE	RATING	DATA DATE	TOTAL ASSETS ($MIL)	TOTAL PREMIUMS ($MIL)	HEALTH PREMIUMS ($MIL)	CAPITAL & SURPLUS ($MIL)	RISK ADJUSTED CAPITAL RATIO 1	RISK ADJUSTED CAPITAL RATIO 2
UNITEDHEALTHCARE BENEFITS OF TEXAS	TX	• B	1q 2019	622.5	3,566.8	3,566.8	304.4	2.27	1.90
UNITEDHEALTHCARE BENEFITS PLAN OF CA	CA	U		--	--	--	--	--	--
UNITEDHEALTHCARE COMMUNITY PLAN INC	MI	• B	1q 2019	272.1	872.2	872.2	146.2	3.05	2.54
UNITEDHEALTHCARE COMMUNITY PLAN TX	TX	• B-	1q 2019	586.7	2,567.2	2,567.2	200.7	1.24	1.04
UNITEDHEALTHCARE COMMUNITYPLAN OHIO	OH	• B	1q 2019	577.2	2,510.5	2,510.5	358.6	2.74	2.28
UNITEDHEALTHCARE INS CO RIVER VALLEY	IL	• B	1q 2019	426.7	1,395.6	1,395.6	185.4	2.38	1.98
UNITEDHEALTHCARE LIFE INS CO	WI	• C	1q 2019	253.1	471.7	471.6	170.1	2.89	2.28
▲ UNITEDHEALTHCARE OF NEW MEXICO INC	NM	• B-	1q 2019	225.5	543.6	543.6	174.3	10.51	8.75
UNITEDHEALTHCARE OF OKLAHOMA INC	OK	• B	1q 2019	138.5	490.1	490.1	77.0	2.82	2.35
UNITEDHEALTHCARE OF OREGON	OR	• B+	1q 2019	462.8	1,410.5	1,410.5	228.8	3.08	2.57
UNITEDHEALTHCARE OF PENNSYLVANIA INC	PA	• B	1q 2019	411.0	1,241.1	1,241.1	198.3	4.49	3.74
▲ UNITEDHEALTHCARE OF WASHINGTON INC	WA	• B	1q 2019	352.7	923.2	923.2	173.5	3.48	2.90
UNITEDHEALTHCARE PLAN RIVER VALLEY	IL	• B	1q 2019	1,413.7	6,121.5	6,121.5	410.7	1.23	1.03
UNITY HEALTH PLANS INS CORP	WI	• C	1q 2019	283.4	1,276.8	1,276.8	100.3	1.62	1.35
UNIV OF MD HEALTH ADVANTAGE INC	MD	• E-	1q 2019	23.9	154.3	154.3	5.8	0.25	0.21
UNIVERSAL CARE	CA	• E-	1q 2019	114.9	327.6	327.6	-15.1	0.00	0.00
▲ UNIVERSAL FIDELITY LIFE INS CO	OK	C	1q 2019	15.4	7.7	7.3	5.9	1.94	1.59
UNIVERSAL GUARANTY LIFE INS CO	OH	C+	1q 2019	359.6	8.1	0.0	71.7	1.99	1.16
UNIVERSAL LIFE INS CO	PR	B+	1q 2019	1,757.3	408.5	6.6	128.6	2.69	1.42
UNIVERSITY HEALTH ALLIANCE	HI	• C+	1q 2019	151.8	327.9	327.9	99.8	2.69	2.24
▼ UNIVERSITY HEALTH CARE INC	KY	• D	1q 2019	252.2	1,945.9	1,945.9	62.7	0.48	0.40
▲ UNIVERSITY OF UTAH HEALTH INS PLANS	UT	• C+	1q 2019	122.0	181.1	181.1	56.1	3.50	2.92
UNUM INS CO	ME	• C	1q 2019	65.3	7.1	4.8	46.7	6.89	4.10
UNUM LIFE INS CO OF AMERICA	ME	• C+	1q 2019	21,897.0	4,929.2	3,412.9	1,705.7	2.25	1.19
UPMC FOR YOU INC	PA	• B+	1q 2019	991.0	3,602.9	3,602.9	445.1	2.03	1.69
UPMC HEALTH BENEFITS INC	PA	• C	1q 2019	286.6	128.8	37.0	128.0	0.87	0.54
UPMC HEALTH COVERAGE INC	PA	• B-	1q 2019	20.2	27.5	27.5	16.4	7.00	5.84
UPMC HEALTH NETWORK INC	PA	• C+	1q 2019	48.7	97.8	97.8	37.6	3.78	3.15
UPMC HEALTH OPTIONS INC	PA	• C+	1q 2019	520.9	2,212.3	2,212.3	300.1	2.13	1.78
▼ UPMC HEALTH PLAN INC	PA	• C+	1q 2019	607.0	1,736.2	1,736.2	186.4	1.65	1.37
UPPER PENINSULA HEALTH PLAN INC	MI	• B+	1q 2019	110.1	254.4	254.4	56.8	3.82	3.19
US ALLIANCE LIFE & SECURITY CO	KS	D	3q 2018	28.0	4.8	0.1	4.3	0.91	0.56
US FIRE INS CO	DE	• C	1q 2019	4,122.9	1,109.1	340.5	1,366.6	1.23	0.99
▼ US SPECIALTY INS CO	TX	C	1q 2019	2,068.9	649.0	0.7	612.1	2.19	1.39
USA INS CO	MS	C-	1q 2019	4.1	0.3	0.2	3.2	2.55	2.30
USAA LIFE INS CO	TX	A	1q 2019	25,796.7	2,417.1	351.1	2,573.0	3.78	2.04
USABLE LIFE	AR	• A-	1q 2019	497.8	237.5	122.7	259.2	2.76	2.05
USABLE MUTUAL INS CO	AR	• B	1q 2019	1,801.4	2,480.2	2,480.2	872.7	5.02	4.19
▲ USIC LIFE INS CO	PR	B-	1q 2019	11.0	5.7	4.7	8.4	2.28	1.64
UTIC INS CO	AL	B+	1q 2019	106.7	15.3	15.3	23.4	2.53	1.57
UTMB HEALTH PLANS INC	TX	• B-	1q 2019	5.8	0.6	0.6	5.7	58.67	48.89
VALUEOPTIONS OF NEW JERSEY INC	NJ	• E	4q 2018	19.0	180.3	180.3	9.2	0.00	0.00
VALUEOPTIONS OF TEXAS INC	TX	• D	1q 2018	6.2	0.3	0.3	6.2	3.46	2.88
VANTAGE HEALTH PLAN INC	LA	• D+	1q 2019	90.4	402.9	402.9	34.8	0.67	0.56
VANTAGE HLTH PLAN AR INC		U		--	--	--	--	--	--
VANTIS LIFE INS CO	CT	C+	1q 2019	527.8	132.8	0.0	61.9	1.67	1.11
VENTURA COUNTY HEALTH CARE PLAN	CA	• E-	1q 2019	18.1	79.9	79.9	4.6	0.46	0.29
VERMONT HEALTH PLAN LLC	VT	• C+	1q 2019	40.3	31.9	31.9	31.4	8.21	6.84
VERSANT LIFE INS CO	MS	B-	1q 2019	6.4	0.6	0.1	5.2	2.94	2.64
▼ VIBRA HEALTH PLAN INC	PA	• E+	1q 2019	4.1	12.6	12.6	0.8	0.67	0.56
VIGILANT INS CO	NY	B	1q 2019	425.3	430.6	0.2	335.2	21.68	17.76
▼ VIRGINIA FARM BUREAU MUTUAL INS CO	VA	C	1q 2019	429.2	138.0	0.0	224.1	2.27	1.87

INSURANCE COMPANY NAME	DOM. STATE	RATING	DATA DATE	TOTAL ASSETS ($MIL)	TOTAL PREMIUMS ($MIL)	HEALTH PREMIUMS ($MIL)	CAPITAL & SURPLUS ($MIL)	RISK ADJUSTED CAPITAL RATIO 1	RISK ADJUSTED CAPITAL RATIO 2
VIRGINIA PREMIER HEALTH PLAN INC	VA	• C+	1q 2019	384.4	1,462.7	1,462.7	165.0	0.91	0.76
VISTA HEALTH PLAN INC	PA	• B+	1q 2019	1,254.9	5,009.8	5,009.8	329.2	2.01	1.68
VIVA HEALTH INC	AL	• B+	1q 2019	214.0	735.3	735.3	120.4	2.31	1.92
VOLUNTARY EMPLOYEES BENEFIT	HI	U		--	--	--	--	--	--
VOLUNTEER STATE HEALTH PLAN INC	TN	• A+	1q 2019	889.1	2,576.0	2,576.0	407.8	3.00	2.50
VOYA INS & ANNUITY CO	IA	B-	1q 2019	51,647.8	369.4	0.1	2,244.8	1.11	0.77
VOYA RETIREMENT INS & ANNUITY CO	CT	B+	1q 2019	106,305.7	12,148.1	0.1	2,081.5	2.18	1.06
WASHINGTON NATIONAL INS CO	IN	• D+	1q 2019	5,491.6	706.1	648.6	365.2	1.55	0.91
WEA INS CORP	WI	• C	1q 2019	698.8	608.0	608.0	192.1	1.69	1.22
WELLCALL INC	CA	• C-	1q 2019	3.6	1.0	1.0	2.7	2.06	1.35
WELLCARE HEALTH INS OF ARIZONA INC	AZ	• C	1q 2019	224.3	711.8	711.8	70.5	1.90	1.58
WELLCARE HEALTH INS OF KENTUCKY INC	KY	• B-	1q 2019	846.5	3,023.4	3,023.4	393.0	2.66	2.22
WELLCARE HEALTH INS OF NEW YORK INC	NY	• C	1q 2019	6.4	0.5	0.5	6.1	4.02	3.35
WELLCARE HEALTH INS OF TN INC	TN	U		--	--	--	--	--	--
WELLCARE HEALTH PLANS OF KENTUCKY	KY	U		--	--	--	--	--	--
WELLCARE HEALTH PLANS OF NEW JERSEY	NJ	• C+	1q 2019	198.7	717.0	717.0	89.0	2.48	2.07
WELLCARE HLTH INS CO AM	AR	U		--	--	--	--	--	--
WELLCARE HLTH INS CO OF NH INC	NH	U		--	--	--	--	--	--
WELLCARE HLTH INS OF CT INC	CT	U		--	--	--	--	--	--
WELLCARE HLTH PLANS OF AZ INC	AZ	U		--	--	--	--	--	--
WELLCARE HLTH PLANS OF VT INC	VT	U		--	--	--	--	--	--
WELLCARE HLTH PLANS TN INC	TN	U		--	--	--	--	--	--
WELLCARE NATL HLTH INS CO	TX	U		--	--	--	--	--	--
WELLCARE OF ALABAMA INC	AL	U		--	--	--	--	--	--
WELLCARE OF ARKANSAS INC	AR	U		--	--	--	--	--	--
WELLCARE OF CONNECTICUT INC	CT	• C	1q 2019	46.3	99.8	99.8	25.6	3.88	3.23
WELLCARE OF FLORIDA INC	FL	• B	1q 2019	1,091.0	3,757.4	3,757.4	300.4	1.71	1.43
WELLCARE OF GEORGIA INC	GA	• B	1q 2019	531.8	2,078.6	2,078.6	219.1	2.15	1.79
WELLCARE OF MAINE INC	ME	U		--	--	--	--	--	--
WELLCARE OF MISSISSIPPI INC	MS	U		--	--	--	--	--	--
WELLCARE OF MO HLTH INS CO	MO	U		--	--	--	--	--	--
WELLCARE OF NEBRASKA INC	NE	• C	1q 2019	170.9	341.3	341.3	51.1	3.56	2.97
WELLCARE OF NEVADA INC	NV	U		--	--	--	--	--	--
WELLCARE OF NEW HAMPSHIRE INC	NH	U		--	--	--	--	--	--
WELLCARE OF OHIO INC	OH	U		--	--	--	--	--	--
WELLCARE OF OKLAHOMA INC	OK	U		--	--	--	--	--	--
WELLCARE OF SOUTH CAROLINA INC	SC	• B-	1q 2019	107.3	304.2	304.2	61.2	3.78	3.15
WELLCARE OF TEXAS INC	TX	• B	1q 2019	149.2	423.2	423.2	67.5	3.09	2.57
WELLCARE PRESCRIPTION INS INC	FL	• C	1q 2019	1,378.7	762.4	762.4	161.6	7.12	5.93
WELLCENTRIC HEALTH GROUP DC	DC	U		--	--	--	--	--	--
WELLFLEET INS CO	IN	• C-	1q 2019	105.0	44.4	44.0	63.8	13.16	11.84
WELLFLEET NEW YORK INS CO	NY	• C	1q 2019	107.5	113.9	111.1	27.9	3.10	2.24
WELLMARK HEALTH PLAN OF IOWA	IA	• B	1q 2019	330.3	419.9	419.9	218.1	7.78	6.48
WELLMARK INC	IA	• B-	1q 2019	2,611.4	2,625.9	2,625.9	1,722.3	6.35	5.30
WELLMARK OF SOUTH DAKOTA INC	SD	• B+	1q 2019	508.1	779.1	779.1	313.1	7.31	6.10
WELLMARK SYNERGY HEALTH INC	IA	• C+	1q 2019	14.9	1.2	1.2	13.6	10.49	8.74
WELLMARK VALUE HEALTH PLAN INC	IA	• C+	1q 2019	15.1	1.2	1.2	8.6	6.68	5.57
WESCO INS CO	DE	C-	1q 2019	1,897.9	2,567.1	60.8	328.7	1.29	0.78
WEST COAST LIFE INS CO	NE	B-	1q 2019	5,361.8	513.9	0.0	396.5	2.44	1.17
WEST VIRGINIA FAMILY HEALTH PLAN INC	WV	• B-	1q 2019	82.8	337.7	337.7	36.6	2.55	2.12
WESTERN & SOUTHERN LIFE INS CO	OH	B	1q 2019	10,446.1	241.3	25.5	5,156.0	1.35	1.24
WESTERN AMERICAN LIFE INS CO	TX	D+	1q 2019	26.5	2.2	0.0	2.0	0.48	0.44

	INSURANCE COMPANY NAME	DOM. STATE	RATING	DATA DATE	TOTAL ASSETS ($MIL)	TOTAL PREMIUMS ($MIL)	HEALTH PREMIUMS ($MIL)	CAPITAL & SURPLUS ($MIL)	RISK ADJUSTED CAPITAL RATIO 1	RISK ADJUSTED CAPITAL RATIO 2
	WESTERN GROCERS EMPLOYEE BENEFITS	OR	• E+	1q 2019	8.0	21.2	21.2	3.1	N/A	N/A
	WESTERN HEALTH ADVANTAGE	CA	• E	1q 2019	74.5	760.7	760.7	11.0	0.24	0.15
	WESTERN SKY CMNTY CARE INC	NM	U		--	--	--	--	--	--
	WESTERN UNITED LIFE ASR CO	WA	B-	1q 2019	1,224.5	182.0	11.3	80.4	1.67	0.80
▼	WESTPORT INS CORP	MO	• C	1q 2019	5,367.9	876.0	357.5	1,809.0	1.52	0.91
	WICHITA NATIONAL LIFE INS CO	OK	C-	1q 2019	15.5	4.8	0.9	7.6	2.48	2.23
	WILCAC LIFE INS CO	IL	C	1q 2019	2,239.7	37.5	0.6	124.3	4.71	2.15
	WILCO LIFE INS CO	IN	C	1q 2019	2,783.9	166.7	20.8	166.9	1.62	0.83
	WILLIAM PENN LIFE INS CO OF NEW YORK	NY	C	1q 2019	1,183.1	217.2	0.0	97.0	2.10	1.02
▼	WILTON REASSURANCE LIFE CO OF NY	NY	C	1q 2019	879.4	46.1	0.1	102.2	2.47	1.20
	WINDSOR LIFE INS CO	TX	B-	1q 2019	3.2	0.5	0.5	3.0	2.82	2.54
	WISCONSIN COLLABORATIVE INSURANCE CO	WI	• B-	1q 2019	34.5	43.7	43.7	21.2	3.93	3.27
	WISCONSIN PHYSICIANS SERVICE INS	WI	• C	1q 2019	279.6	396.0	396.0	122.4	2.39	1.99
	WMI MUTUAL INS CO	UT	• B-	1q 2019	15.9	18.0	18.0	11.3	3.57	2.98
	WPS HEALTH PLAN INC	WI	• C-	1q 2019	26.3	89.1	89.1	12.7	1.75	1.46
	WV SENIOR ADVANTAGE INC	WV	• C-	1q 2019	6.0	10.3	10.3	2.8	1.66	1.38
▼	ZURICH AMERICAN INS CO	NY	C	1q 2019	31,186.9	5,969.1	222.5	7,085.7	1.44	1.07
	ZURICH AMERICAN LIFE INS CO	IL	C	1q 2019	14,823.7	444.1	18.7	126.5	2.83	1.58
	ZURICH AMERICAN LIFE INS CO OF NY	NY	B-	1q 2019	82.8	14.1	5.0	20.7	2.60	2.34

Section II

Analysis of Largest Companies

A summary analysis of all rated

U.S. Health Plans and Blue Cross Blue Shield Plans

plus other **U.S. Insurers**
with capital in excess of $25 million and health insurance premiums equaling at least 25% of total premiums.

Companies are listed in alphabetical order.

Section II Contents

This section contains rating factors, historical data, and general information on all rated health insurers and Blue Cross/Blue Shield plans plus other insurers with capital in excess of $25 million and health insurance premiums equaling at least 25% of total premiums.

A number of the contents listed below will only apply to health insurers filing the NAIC Health insurance financial statement.

1. **Safety Rating** The current Weiss rating appears to the right of the company name. Our ratings are designed to distinguish levels of insolvency risk and are measured on a scale from A (Excellent) to F (Failed). Highly rated companies are, in our opinion, less likely to experience financial difficulties than lower rated firms. See *About Weiss Safety Ratings* for more information.

2. **Major Rating Factors** A synopsis of the key indexes and sub-factors that have most influenced the rating of a particular insurer. Items are presented in the approximate order of their importance to the rating. There may be additional factors which have influenced the rating but do not appear due to space limitations or confidentiality agreements with insurers.

3. **Other Rating Factors** A summary of those Weiss Ratings indexes that were not included as Major Rating Factors, but nevertheless may have had some impact on the final grade.

4. **Principal Business** The major types of policies written by an insurer along with the percentages for each line in relation to the entire book of business, including direct premium, reinsurance assumed and deposit funds. Lines of business for health insurers include comprehensive medical, medical only, medicare supplemental, administrative service contracts, point of service, dental, vision, stop-loss, long-term care, disability, Federal Employee Health Benefits (FEHB), medicare, and medicaid.

5. **Member Physicians** The number of physicians who participated in the insurer's network of providers during the current and prior year.

6. **MLR (Medical Loss Ratio)** The percentage of total premium income paid out as benefits to members.

7. **Administrative Expense Ratio** The percentage of total premium income paid out for administrative expenses.

8. **Enrollment** The total number of members (policyholders) as of the current quarter, current year end and prior year end. The letter Q followed by a number represents the quarter (first, second, or third) from which the enrollment numbers were last available.

9. Medical Expenses Per Member Per Month — The average dollar amount the insurer spends on a per member per month basis. Calculated as total medical expenses divided by the reported member months.

10. Principal Investments — The major investments in an insurer's portfolio. These include investment grade bonds, noninvestment grade bonds, collateralized mortgage obligations (CMOs) and other structured securities, which consist primarily of mortgage-backed bonds, real estate, mortgages in good standing, nonperforming mortgages, common and preferred stocks, contract loans and other investments.

11. Provider Compensation — The total annual amount the health insurer pays its providers (e.g., physicians, hospitals, etc.) and manner in which they are paid, including:

- fee-for-service (FFS) – amount paid for the services provided where the payment base is not fixed by contract
- contractual fees – amount paid for services whereby the amount is fixed by contract, e.g., hospital per diems, DRGs, etc.
- salary – amount paid providers who are direct employees of the HMO
- capitation – amount paid to providers on a per member basis as defined by contract
- other – amount paid under various contracts including bonus arrangements, stop-loss arrangements, etc.

12. Total Member Encounters — The number of contacts members of the health insurer who are not confined to a health care facility have with the providers during the current year.

13. Investments in Affiliates — The percentage of bonds, common and preferred stocks, and other financial instruments an insurer has invested with affiliated companies. This is not a subcategory of "Principal Investments."

14. Group Affiliation — The name of the group of companies to which a particular insurer belongs.

15. Licensed in — List of the states in which an insurer is licensed to conduct business.

16. Address — The address of an insurer's corporate headquarters. This location may differ from the company's state of domicile.

17. Phone — The telephone number of an insurer's corporate headquarters.

18. Domicile State — The state that has primary regulatory responsibility for this company. You do not have to live in the domicile state to do business with this firm, provided it is registered to do business in your state.

19. Commenced Business The month and year the insurer started its operations

20. NAIC Code The identification number assigned to an insurer by the National Association of Insurance Commissioners (NAIC).

21. Historical Data Five years of background data for Weiss Safety Rating, risk-adjusted capital ratios (moderate and severe loss scenarios), total assets, capital (including capital stock and retained earnings), net premium, and net income. See the next page for more details on how to read the historical data table.

22. Customized Graph (or Table) A graph or table depicting one of the company's major strengths or weaknesses.

How to Read the Historical Data Table

Data Date:
The quarterly or annual date of the financial statements that provide the source of the data.

RACR#1:
Ratio of the capital resources an insurer currently has to the resources that would be needed to deal with a modest loss scenario.

Total Assets:
Total admitted assets in millions of dollars, including investments and other business assets.

Net Premiums:
The total volume of premium dollars, in millions, retained by an insurer. This figure is equal to direct premiums written plus deposit funds, and reinsurance assumed, less reinsurance ceded.

Data Date	Rating	RACR #1	RACR #2	Total Assets ($mil)	Capital ($mil)	Net Premium ($mil)	Net Income ($mil)
3-19	C+	2.54	2.12	143.7	72.6	153.0	2.3
3-18	C-	2.24	1.87	134.6	61.0	136.4	-8.6
2018	C+	2.48	2.07	129.0	70.8	544.8	0.3
2017	C-	1.49	1.24	116.7	63.9	529.3	6.2
2016	B+	4.01	2.67	56.0	46.8	10.8	1.3
2015	B+	3.91	2.59	54.0	45.3	10.6	2.2
2014	B+	3.64	2.40	53.5	44.0	9.9	2.9

Safety Rating:
Our opinion of the financial strength of an insurer based on data from that time period.

RACR #2:
Ratio of the capital resources an insurer currently has to the resources that would be needed to deal with a severe loss scenario.

Capital:
The equity or net worth of an insurer in millions of dollars.

Net Income:
Profit gained on operations and investments, after expenses, taxes, and capital gains

Row Descriptions:

Row 1 contains the most recent quarterly data as filed with state regulators and is presented on a year-to-date basis. For example, the figure for third quarter premiums includes premiums received through the third quarter. **Row 2** consists of data from the same quarter of the prior year. Compare current quarterly results to those of a year ago.

Row 3 contains data from the most recent annual statutory filing. **Rows 4-7** includes data from year-end statements going back four years from the most recent annual filing. Compare current year-end results to those of the previous four years. With the exception of Total Assets and Capital, quarterly data are not comparable with annual data.

Customized Graphs

In the lower right-hand corner of each company section, a customized graph or text block highlights a key factor affecting that company's financial strength. One of twenty five types of information is found, identified by one of the following headings:

# of Months of Claims and Expenses in Capital illustrates the number of months' worth of medical and administrative expenses the company could cover by drawing solely on its current capital position.

Adverse Trends in Operations lists changes in key balance sheet and income statement items which may be leading indicators of deteriorating business performance.

Allocation of Premium Income shows what portion of the company's premium income is being spent on medical benefits and administrative expenses. Any income left after the payment of these two types of expense, is used to pay taxes and extraordinary expenditures; the remainder is profit.

Capital History plots the company's reported capital and surplus in millions of dollars over the last five years. Volatile changes in capital levels may indicate unstable operations.

Detail of Risk-Adjusted Capital Ratio provides a percentage breakdown of target capital components based on lines of business and investments in a moderate or severe loss scenario. Target capital is our opinion of the level of capital the company should have, based on the risk it assumes. For example, if the percentage of target capital for individual life is 33%, this means that 33% of the company's target capital relates to individual life. C2 refers to the pricing risk element of the risk-adjusted capital formula. C3 refers to disintermediation (interest rate) risk.

Enrollment Trend charts an insurer's year-end membership levels over the last five years.

Exposure to Withdrawals Without Penalty answers the question: For each dollar of capital and surplus, how much does the company have in annuity and deposit funds that can be withdrawn by policyholders with minimal or no penalty? The figures do not include the effects of reinsurance or funds subject to withdrawals from cash value life insurance policies.

Group Ratings shows the group name, a composite Weiss Safety Rating for the group, and a list of the largest members with their ratings. The composite Weiss Safety Rating is made up of the weighted average, by assets, of the individual ratings of each company in the group (including life/health companies, property/casualty companies, or HMOs) plus a factor for the financial strength of the holding company, where applicable.

High Risk Assets as a % of Capital answers the question: For each dollar of capital and surplus, how much does the company have in junk bonds, nonperforming mortgages and repossessed real estate? Accumulations in the Asset Valuation Reserve or AVR, which provide some protection against investment losses, have not been included in the figure for capital. These figures are based on year-end data.

Income Trends shows underwriting and net income results over the last five years.

Investment Income Compared to Needs of Reserves answers the question: Is the company earning enough investment income to meet the expectations of actuaries when they priced their policies and set reserve levels? According to state insurance regulators, it would be "unusual" if an insurer were to have less than $1.25 in actual investment income for each dollar of investment income that it projected in its actuarial forecasts. This provides an excess margin of at least 25 cents on the dollar to cover any unexpected decline in income or increase in claims. This graph shows whether or not the company is maintaining the appropriate 25% margin and is based on year-end data.

Junk Bonds as a % of Capital answers the question: For each dollar of capital and surplus, how much does the company have in junk bonds? In addition, it shows a breakdown of the junk bond portfolio by bond rating – BB, B, CCC or in default. Accumulations in the Asset Valuation Reserve or AVR, which provide some protection against investment losses, have not been included in the figure for capital. These figures are based on year-end data.

Largest Net Exposure Per Risk shows the ratio of the largest net aggregate amount insured in any one risk (excluding workers' compensation) as a percent of capital.

Liquidity Index evaluates a company's ability to raise the cash necessary to pay claims. Various cash flow scenarios are modeled to determine how the company might fare in the event of an unexpected spike in claims costs.

Net Income History plots operating gains and losses over the most recent five-year period.

Nonperforming Mortgages (plus repossessed real estate) as a % of Capital answers the question: For each dollar of capital and surplus, how much does the company have in nonperforming mortgages and repossessed real estate? Nonperforming mortgages include those overdue more than 90 days and mortgages currently in process of foreclosure. Accumulations in the Asset Valuation Reserve or AVR, which provide some protection against investment losses, have not been included in the figure for capital. These figures are based on year-end data.

Policy Leverage answers the question: To what degree is this insurer capable of handling an unexpected spike in claims? Low leverage indicates low exposure; high leverage is high exposure.

Target leverage represents the maximum exposure we feel would be appropriate for a top-rated company.

Premium Growth History depicts the change in the insurer's net premiums written. Such changes may be the result of issuing more policies or changes in reinsurance arrangements. In either case, growth rates above 20% per year are considered excessive. "Standard" growth is under 20%; "shrinkage" refers to net declines.

Rating Indexes illustrate the score and range – strong, good, fair, or weak – on each of Weiss indexes.

Reserve Deficiency shows whether the company has set aside sufficient funds to pay claims. A positive number indicates insufficient reserving and a negative number adequate reserving.

Reserves to Capital analyzes the relationship between loss and loss expense reserves to capital. Operating results and capital levels for companies with a high ratio are more susceptible to fluctuations than those with lower ratios.

Risk-Adjusted Capital Ratio #1 answers the question: In each of the past five years, does the insurer have sufficient capital to cover potential losses in its investments and business operations in a *moderate* loss scenario?

Risk-Adjusted Capital Ratio #2 answers the question: In each of the past five years, does the insurer have sufficient capital to cover potential losses in its investments and business operations in a *severe* loss scenario?

Risk-Adjusted Capital Ratios answers these questions for both a moderate loss scenario (RACR #1 shown by the dark bar), and a severe loss scenario (RACR #2, light bar).

21ST CENTURY PREMIER INS CO B- Good

Major Rating Factors: Fair overall results on stability tests (3.8).
Other Rating Factors: Good overall profitability index (6.2). Weak expense controls. Return on equity has been low, averaging 2.0% over the past five years. Strong long-term capitalization index (10.0) based on excellent current risk adjusted capital (severe and moderate loss scenarios), despite some fluctuation in capital levels. Superior liquidity (10.0) with ample operational cash flow and liquid investments.
Principal Business: Auto liability (52%), group accident & health (27%), auto physical damage (21%), and other accident & health (8%).
Principal Investments: Investment grade bonds (75%) and misc. investments (25%).
Investments in Affiliates: 24%
Group Affiliation: Farmers Insurance Group of Companies
Licensed in: All states except PR
Commenced Business: April 1866
Address: 2595 INTERSTATE DRIVE STE 103, Harrisburg, PA 17110
Phone: (302) 252-2000 **Domicile State:** PA **NAIC Code:** 20796

Data Date	Rating	RACR #1	RACR #2	Loss Ratio %	Total Assets ($mil)	Capital ($mil)	Net Premium ($mil)	Net Income ($mil)
3-19	B-	4.59	4.54	N/A	296.4	296.4	0.0	1.0
3-18	B-	4.59	4.53	N/A	291.9	290.5	0.0	0.9
2018	B-	4.58	4.53	0.0	295.1	295.1	0.0	4.2
2017	B-	4.58	4.52	0.0	289.3	289.3	0.0	4.6
2016	B-	4.59	4.52	0.0	285.2	283.0	0.0	4.5
2015	B-	4.55	4.49	0.0	282.2	279.5	0.0	6.1
2014	B-	4.53	4.43	0.0	275.7	270.6	0.0	8.9

Rating Indexes

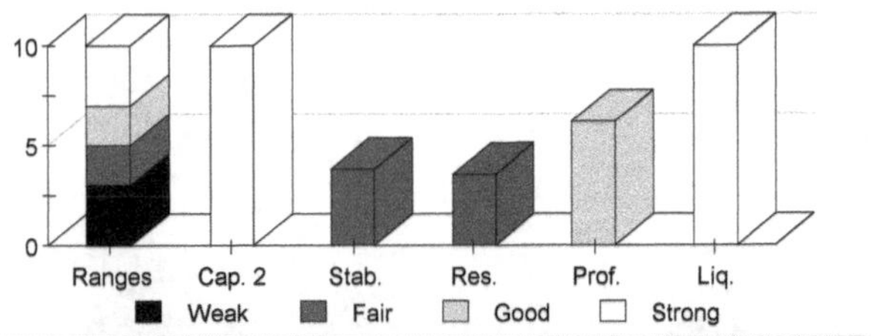

4 EVER LIFE INSURANCE COMPANY B Good

Major Rating Factors: Good quality investment portfolio (6.8 on a scale of 0 to 10) despite mixed results such as: no exposure to mortgages and substantial holdings of BBB bonds but minimal holdings in junk bonds. Good liquidity (6.9) with sufficient resources to handle a spike in claims. Fair overall results on stability tests (4.7) including negative cash flow from operations for 2018.
Other Rating Factors: Fair profitability (4.9). Strong capitalization (10.0) based on excellent risk adjusted capital (severe loss scenario).
Principal Business: Group health insurance (53%), reinsurance (45%), and group life insurance (2%).
Principal Investments: NonCMO investment grade bonds (43%), CMOs and structured securities (23%), cash (16%), common & preferred stock (5%), and noninv. grade bonds (4%).
Investments in Affiliates: None
Group Affiliation: BCS Financial Corp
Licensed in: All states, the District of Columbia and Puerto Rico
Commenced Business: November 1949
Address: 2 Mid America Plaza Suite 200, Oakbrook Terrace, IL 60181
Phone: (630) 472-7700 **Domicile State:** IL **NAIC Code:** 80985

Data Date	Rating	RACR #1	RACR #2	Total Assets ($mil)	Capital ($mil)	Net Premium ($mil)	Net Income ($mil)
3-19	B	7.17	4.74	171.1	82.8	17.2	0.8
3-18	B	6.51	4.28	193.3	86.2	17.5	1.4
2018	B	6.41	4.26	182.0	81.4	69.8	5.5
2017	B	5.81	3.83	212.5	85.0	76.8	5.1
2016	B	5.21	3.36	207.5	82.6	72.9	0.6
2015	A	5.63	3.67	200.0	93.1	86.9	5.5
2014	A	3.89	2.72	198.5	92.3	151.8	7.3

Rating Indexes

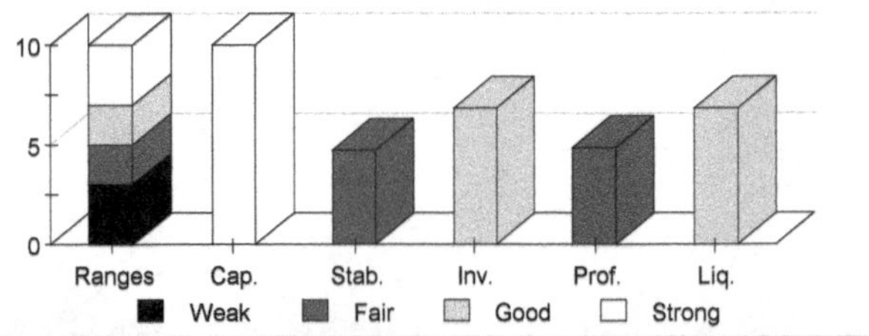

ABSOLUTE TOTAL CARE INC C+ Fair

Major Rating Factors: Fair profitability index (3.9 on a scale of 0 to 10). Good quality investment portfolio (6.5). Good liquidity (6.8) with sufficient resources (cash flows and marketable investments) to handle a spike in claims.
Other Rating Factors: Strong capitalization (8.5) based on excellent current risk-adjusted capital (severe loss scenario).
Principal Business: Medicaid (87%), Medicare (13%)
Mem Phys: 18: 16,458 **17:** 9,301 **18 MLR** 88.0% **/ 18 Admin Exp** N/A
Enroll(000): Q1 19: 131 **18:** 122 **17:** 121 **Med Exp PMPM:** $338
Principal Investments: Long-term bonds (74%), cash and equiv (25%), affiliate common stock (1%)
Provider Compensation ($000): Contr fee ($430,553), salary ($34,315), capitation ($6,496), bonus arrang ($1,882)
Total Member Encounters: Phys (254,163), non-phys (139,356)
Group Affiliation: None
Licensed in: SC
Address: 1441 Main St Ste 900, Columbia, SC 29201
Phone: (314) 725-4477 **Dom State:** SC **Commenced Bus:** N/A

Data Date	Rating	RACR #1	RACR #2	Total Assets ($mil)	Capital ($mil)	Net Premium ($mil)	Net Income ($mil)
3-19	C+	2.54	2.12	143.7	72.6	153.0	2.3
3-18	C-	2.24	1.87	134.6	61.0	136.4	-8.6
2018	C+	2.48	2.07	129.0	70.8	544.8	0.3
2017	C-	1.49	1.24	116.7	63.9	529.3	6.2
2016	C-	2.14	1.79	113.4	57.9	492.5	-1.7
2015	C-	2.09	1.74	107.9	50.1	435.7	-1.4
2014	C-	2.07	1.72	92.1	45.4	396.3	-8.4

Rating Indexes

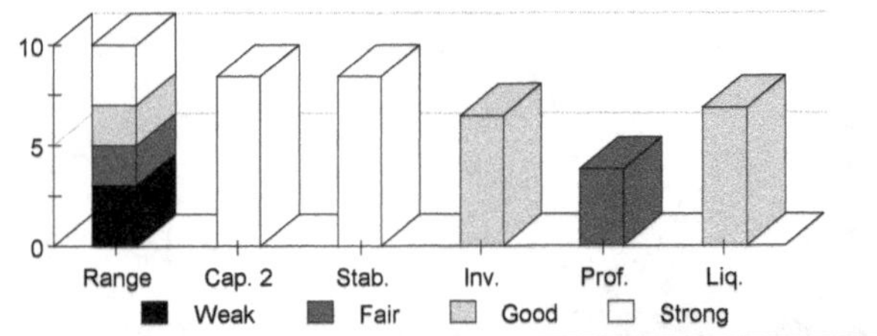

ACCESS SENIOR HEALTHCARE INC — E- Very Weak

Major Rating Factors: Weak profitability index (0.9 on a scale of 0 to 10). Poor capitalization index (0.0) based on weak current risk-adjusted capital (severe loss scenario). Weak overall results on stability tests (0.6).
Other Rating Factors: Weak liquidity (0.7) as a spike in claims may stretch capacity.
Principal Business: Managed care (100%)
Mem Phys: 18: N/A **17:** N/A **18 MLR** 98.2% **/ 18 Admin Exp** N/A
Enroll(000): Q1 19: 3 **18:** 3 **17:** 3 **Med Exp PMPM:** $3,063
Principal Investments ($000): Cash and equiv ($3,270)
Provider Compensation ($000): None
Total Member Encounters: N/A
Group Affiliation: None
Licensed in: CA
Address: 21031 Ventura Blvd Suite 210, Woodland Hills, CA 91364
Phone: (818) 710-0315 **Dom State:** CA **Commenced Bus:** July 2013

Data Date	Rating	RACR #1	RACR #2	Total Assets ($mil)	Capital ($mil)	Net Premium ($mil)	Net Income ($mil)
3-19	E-	0.30	0.19	5.3	1.5	7.2	-0.1
3-18	E-	0.35	0.22	5.2	1.8	7.0	-0.9
2018	E-	N/A	N/A	5.0	1.4	28.8	-1.8
2017	D	0.61	0.37	6.5	2.7	31.7	0.3
2016	N/A	N/A	N/A	N/A	N/A	N/A	N/A
2015	U	1.07	0.65	3.3	2.1	12.6	0.0
2014	N/A	N/A	N/A	2.1	2.1	N/A	N/A

ADVANCE INSURANCE COMPANY OF KANSAS * — B+ Good

Major Rating Factors: Good overall results on stability tests (6.8 on a scale of 0 to 10). Stability strengths include excellent operational trends and excellent risk diversification. Fair quality investment portfolio (4.5). Strong capitalization (9.4) based on excellent risk adjusted capital (severe loss scenario). Capital levels have been relatively consistent over the last five years.
Other Rating Factors: Excellent profitability (8.1) with operating gains in each of the last five years. Excellent liquidity (7.0).
Principal Business: Group life insurance (54%), group health insurance (34%), and individual life insurance (12%).
Principal Investments: CMOs and structured securities (35%), nonCMO investment grade bonds (31%), common & preferred stock (30%), noninv. grade bonds (1%), and cash (1%).
Investments in Affiliates: 2%
Group Affiliation: Blue Cross Blue Shield Kansas
Licensed in: KS
Commenced Business: July 2004
Address: 1133 SW Topeka Blvd, Topeka, KS 66629-0001
Phone: (785) 273-9804 **Domicile State:** KS **NAIC Code:** 12143

Data Date	Rating	RACR #1	RACR #2	Total Assets ($mil)	Capital ($mil)	Net Premium ($mil)	Net Income ($mil)
3-19	B+	3.93	2.57	61.2	51.7	2.7	0.2
3-18	B+	3.95	2.59	59.4	49.9	2.7	0.6
2018	B+	4.09	2.69	58.3	49.9	10.9	1.8
2017	B+	3.95	2.59	59.7	49.7	10.9	2.7
2016	B+	4.01	2.67	56.0	46.8	10.8	1.3
2015	B+	3.91	2.59	54.0	45.3	10.6	2.2
2014	B+	3.64	2.40	53.5	44.0	9.9	2.9

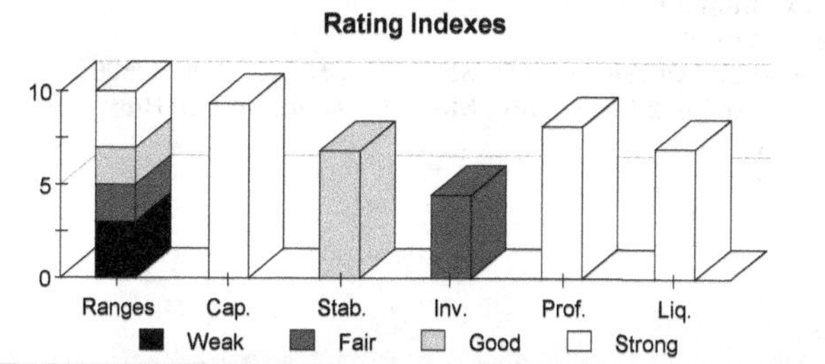

ADVENTIST HEALTH PLAN INC — D Weak

Major Rating Factors: Weak profitability index (0.7 on a scale of 0 to 10). Fair overall results on stability tests (4.0). Good capitalization index (6.2) based on fair current risk-adjusted capital (moderate loss scenario).
Other Rating Factors: Excellent liquidity (7.0) with sufficient resources (cash flows and marketable investments) to handle a spike in claims.
Principal Business: Managed care (100%)
Mem Phys: 18: N/A **17:** N/A **18 MLR** 94.3% **/ 18 Admin Exp** N/A
Enroll(000): Q1 19: 17 **18:** 17 **17:** 18 **Med Exp PMPM:** $137
Principal Investments ($000): Cash and equiv ($7,731)
Provider Compensation ($000): None
Total Member Encounters: N/A
Group Affiliation: None
Licensed in: CA
Address: 2100 Douglas Blvd, Roseville, CA 95661
Phone: (916) 789-4252 **Dom State:** CA **Commenced Bus:** N/A

Data Date	Rating	RACR #1	RACR #2	Total Assets ($mil)	Capital ($mil)	Net Premium ($mil)	Net Income ($mil)
3-19	D	0.93	0.59	7.1	3.1	7.4	0.4
3-18	D	0.98	0.62	7.4	3.0	7.7	0.4
2018	D	0.81	0.51	9.3	2.7	30.1	0.1
2017	D	0.83	0.53	5.0	2.6	28.1	0.8
2016	D	0.61	0.39	3.3	1.8	26.2	0.7
2015	E-	N/A	N/A	1.5	-1.9	N/A	-1.7
2014	N/A	N/A	N/A	1.1	-0.2	N/A	-1.8

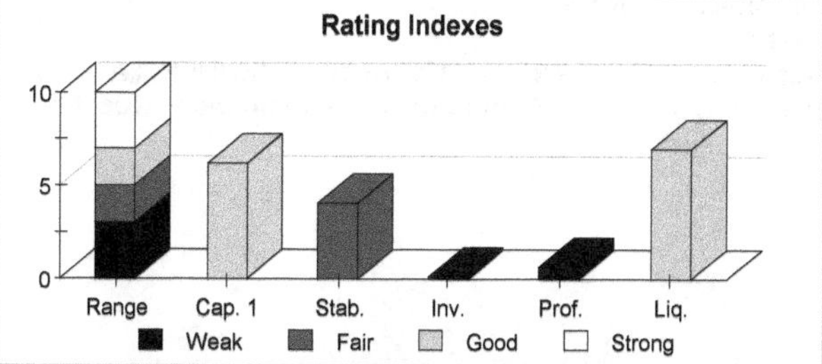

AETNA BETTER HEALTH (AN OHIO CORP) B Good

Major Rating Factors: Excellent profitability (7.1 on a scale of 0 to 10). Strong capitalization (10.0) based on excellent current risk-adjusted capital (severe loss scenario). High quality investment portfolio (9.1).
Other Rating Factors: Excellent liquidity (7.0) with sufficient resources (cash flows and marketable investments) to handle a spike in claims.
Principal Business: Medicaid (66%), Medicare (34%)
Mem Phys: 18: 23,790 **17:** 17,245 **18 MLR** 76.2% **/ 18 Admin Exp** N/A
Enroll(000): Q1 19: 26 **18:** 25 **17:** 24 **Med Exp PMPM:** $2,565
Principal Investments: Long-term bonds (81%), cash and equiv (16%), mortgs (3%)
Provider Compensation ($000): Contr fee ($636,271), FFS ($95,583), capitation ($13,063), bonus arrang ($604)
Total Member Encounters: Phys (913,046), non-phys (3,150,636)
Group Affiliation: None
Licensed in: OH
Address: 7400 W CAMPUS Rd, NEW ALBANY, OH 43054
Phone: (800) 872-3862 **Dom State:** OH **Commenced Bus:** N/A

Data Date	Rating	RACR #1	RACR #2	Total Assets ($mil)	Capital ($mil)	Net Premium ($mil)	Net Income ($mil)
3-19	B	4.34	3.62	371.6	206.6	239.4	17.6
3-18	B	N/A	N/A	328.2	144.4	231.7	12.4
2018	B	4.02	3.35	331.7	189.5	960.8	102.5
2017	B	N/A	N/A	286.6	134.3	936.8	65.7
2016	C+	4.01	3.34	319.8	166.2	858.2	40.4
2015	C+	2.86	2.38	310.5	107.4	783.0	-10.1
2014	U	1.69	1.41	159.1	44.7	335.3	-19.6

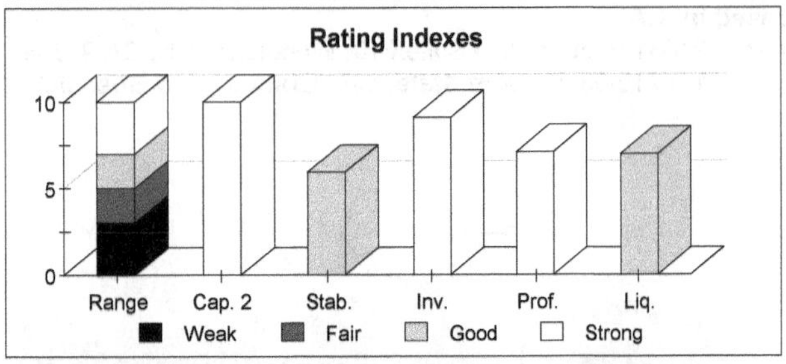

AETNA BETTER HEALTH INC C Fair

Major Rating Factors: Weak profitability index (2.3 on a scale of 0 to 10). Good quality investment portfolio (6.8). Good liquidity (5.8) with sufficient resources (cash flows and marketable investments) to handle a spike in claims.
Other Rating Factors: Strong capitalization (10.0) based on excellent current risk-adjusted capital (severe loss scenario).
Principal Business: Medicaid (51%), Medicare (49%)
Mem Phys: 18: 18,171 **17:** 26,717 **18 MLR** 81.3% **/ 18 Admin Exp** N/A
Enroll(000): Q1 19: 7 **18:** 7 **17:** 232 **Med Exp PMPM:** $1,874
Principal Investments: Long-term bonds (88%), cash and equiv (12%)
Provider Compensation ($000): Contr fee ($289,438), FFS ($74,223), capitation ($3,261), bonus arrang ($637)
Total Member Encounters: Phys (255,900), non-phys (230,333)
Group Affiliation: None
Licensed in: IL
Address: 333 W WACKER Dr Ste 2100, CHICAGO, IL 60606
Phone: (800) 872-3862 **Dom State:** IL **Commenced Bus:** N/A

Data Date	Rating	RACR #1	RACR #2	Total Assets ($mil)	Capital ($mil)	Net Premium ($mil)	Net Income ($mil)
3-19	C	4.99	4.16	116.3	61.5	47.4	12.7
3-18	B	1.75	1.46	402.2	195.9	48.5	-23.1
2018	C	3.82	3.19	134.1	46.9	197.3	-1.3
2017	B	1.45	1.20	586.8	222.6	1,815.9	23.1
2016	B-	1.97	1.64	591.8	189.5	1,539.8	-14.8
2015	B	2.00	1.67	483.0	165.0	1,361.9	-11.2
2014	B	2.42	2.02	252.6	87.3	645.5	10.3

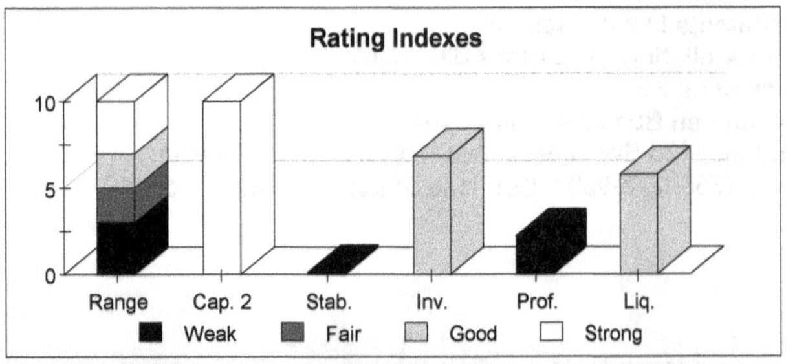

AETNA BETTER HEALTH INC (A LA CORP) C Fair

Major Rating Factors: Weak profitability index (0.9 on a scale of 0 to 10). Good liquidity (6.8) with sufficient resources (cash flows and marketable investments) to handle a spike in claims. Strong capitalization (8.6) based on excellent current risk-adjusted capital (severe loss scenario).
Other Rating Factors: High quality investment portfolio (9.9).
Principal Business: Medicaid (100%)
Mem Phys: 18: 18,255 **17:** 16,045 **18 MLR** 84.9% **/ 18 Admin Exp** N/A
Enroll(000): Q1 19: 126 **18:** 119 **17:** 117 **Med Exp PMPM:** $379
Principal Investments: Long-term bonds (87%), cash and equiv (13%)
Provider Compensation ($000): Contr fee ($512,345), FFS ($28,825), capitation ($7,594), bonus arrang ($2,424)
Total Member Encounters: Phys (905,000), non-phys (625,408)
Group Affiliation: None
Licensed in: AL, LA
Address: 2400 VETERANS MEMORIAL Blvd, KENNER, LA 70062
Phone: (504) 667-4461 **Dom State:** LA **Commenced Bus:** N/A

Data Date	Rating	RACR #1	RACR #2	Total Assets ($mil)	Capital ($mil)	Net Premium ($mil)	Net Income ($mil)
3-19	C	2.62	2.19	198.0	57.3	165.5	-4.1
3-18	C+	N/A	N/A	218.2	85.5	155.0	-2.9
2018	C	2.85	2.38	219.5	64.5	634.7	-14.4
2017	C+	N/A	N/A	224.6	87.9	592.0	22.8
2016	C+	2.94	2.45	213.9	65.1	421.9	-7.9
2015	C+	1.67	1.39	89.4	24.5	180.7	-11.9
2014	N/A	N/A	N/A	3.0	3.0	N/A	N/A

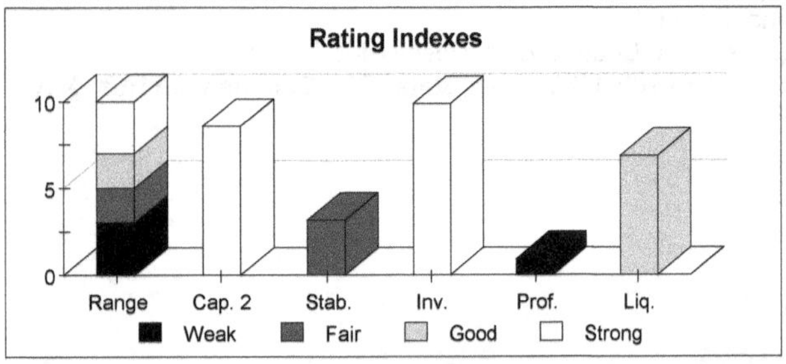

AETNA BETTER HEALTH INC (A NJ CORP) B Good

Major Rating Factors: Good liquidity (6.5 on a scale of 0 to 10) with sufficient resources (cash flows and marketable investments) to handle a spike in claims. Excellent profitability (7.5). Strong capitalization (8.3) based on excellent current risk-adjusted capital (severe loss scenario).
Other Rating Factors: High quality investment portfolio (9.7).
Principal Business: Medicaid (100%)
Mem Phys: 18: 10,804 **17:** 10,563 **18 MLR** 84.4% **/ 18 Admin Exp** N/A
Enroll(000): Q1 19: 63 **18:** 58 **17:** 46 **Med Exp PMPM:** $460
Principal Investments: Long-term bonds (84%), cash and equiv (16%)
Provider Compensation ($000): Contr fee ($220,103), FFS ($75,047), bonus arrang ($1,586), capitation ($1,155)
Total Member Encounters: Phys (227,378), non-phys (318,767)
Group Affiliation: None
Licensed in: NJ
Address: 3 INDEPENDENCE WAY Ste 400, PRINCETON, NJ 8540
Phone: (855) 232-3596 **Dom State:** NJ **Commenced Bus:** N/A

Data Date	Rating	RACR #1	RACR #2	Total Assets ($mil)	Capital ($mil)	Net Premium ($mil)	Net Income ($mil)
3-19	B	2.38	1.98	141.5	43.5	101.1	-1.9
3-18	B+	N/A	N/A	141.1	37.9	85.3	2.5
2018	B	2.50	2.08	133.3	46.3	364.1	10.7
2017	B+	N/A	N/A	134.6	36.3	233.8	16.2
2016	B	7.41	6.18	119.6	35.3	138.0	16.1
2015	C+	1.92	1.60	50.0	12.3	68.4	-2.6
2014	N/A	N/A	N/A	5.0	5.0	N/A	N/A

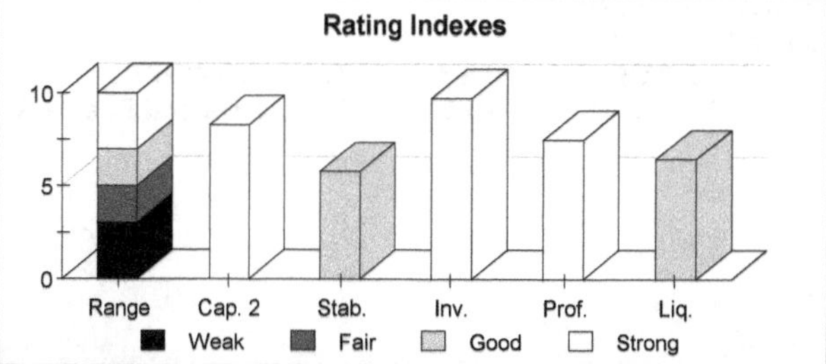

AETNA BETTER HEALTH INC (A PA CORP) C Fair

Major Rating Factors: Fair quality investment portfolio (3.8 on a scale of 0 to 10). Good liquidity (6.9) with sufficient resources (cash flows and marketable investments) to handle a spike in claims. Excellent profitability (8.7).
Other Rating Factors: Strong capitalization (9.1) based on excellent current risk-adjusted capital (severe loss scenario).
Principal Business: Medicaid (100%)
Mem Phys: 18: 39,650 **17:** 34,661 **18 MLR** 76.6% **/ 18 Admin Exp** N/A
Enroll(000): Q1 19: 202 **18:** 199 **17:** 205 **Med Exp PMPM:** $318
Principal Investments: Long-term bonds (93%), mortgs (5%), cash and equiv (1%)
Provider Compensation ($000): Contr fee ($686,014), FFS ($67,581), capitation ($35,571), bonus arrang ($1,899)
Total Member Encounters: Phys (961,833), non-phys (1,061,066)
Group Affiliation: None
Licensed in: PA
Address: 1425 UNION MEETING Rd, BLUE BELL, PA 19422
Phone: (800) 872-3862 **Dom State:** PA **Commenced Bus:** N/A

Data Date	Rating	RACR #1	RACR #2	Total Assets ($mil)	Capital ($mil)	Net Premium ($mil)	Net Income ($mil)
3-19	C	3.02	2.52	380.2	134.5	247.7	2.0
3-18	C	3.52	2.93	486.1	147.2	241.2	6.8
2018	C	2.97	2.47	353.8	131.6	1,013.9	56.1
2017	D-	2.41	2.01	480.5	141.2	936.5	63.0
2016	D-	3.76	3.13	574.8	141.3	867.8	58.2
2015	D-	2.57	2.14	419.0	111.4	818.5	32.7
2014	D-	4.38	3.65	304.8	108.6	467.1	11.1

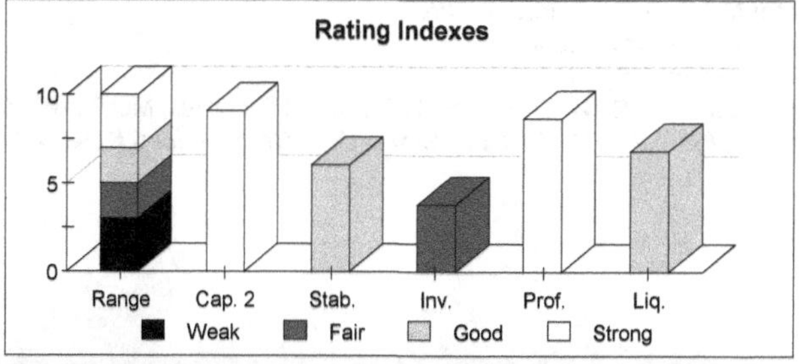

AETNA BETTER HEALTH OF CA INC D+ Weak

Major Rating Factors: Weak profitability index (0.9 on a scale of 0 to 10). Good overall results on stability tests (5.3) despite fair risk diversification due to the company's size. Strong capitalization index (10.0) based on excellent current risk-adjusted capital (severe loss scenario).
Other Rating Factors: Excellent liquidity (8.8) with ample operational cash flow and liquid investments.
Principal Business: Medicaid (100%)
Mem Phys: 18: N/A **17:** N/A **18 MLR** 43.5% **/ 18 Admin Exp** N/A
Enroll(000): Q1 19: 14 **18:** 11 **17:** N/A **Med Exp PMPM:** $122
Principal Investments ($000): Cash and equiv ($22,012)
Provider Compensation ($000): None
Total Member Encounters: N/A
Group Affiliation: Access Senior HealthCare Inc
Licensed in: (No states)
Address: , , CA 94598-2581
Phone: (Phone number **Dom State:** DE **Commenced Bus:** N/A

Data Date	Rating	RACR #1	RACR #2	Total Assets ($mil)	Capital ($mil)	Net Premium ($mil)	Net Income ($mil)
3-19	D+	6.28	3.87	30.9	17.1	11.3	0.7
3-18	U	19.75	13.81	20.1	10.4	1.3	2.2
2018	D+	5.41	3.40	27.0	16.3	21.2	8.1
2017	U	9.23	6.59	17.7	6.3	N/A	-8.7
2016	N/A	N/A	N/A	N/A	N/A	N/A	N/A
2015	N/A	N/A	N/A	N/A	N/A	N/A	N/A
2014	N/A	N/A	N/A	N/A	N/A	N/A	N/A

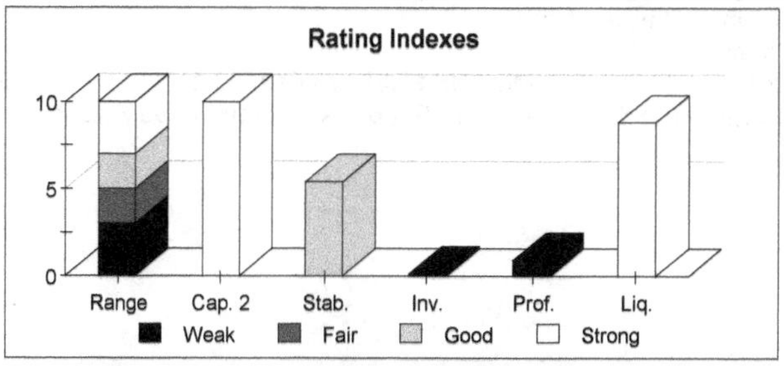

AETNA BETTER HEALTH OF MICHIGAN INC — B — Good

Major Rating Factors: Good overall profitability index (5.5 on a scale of 0 to 10). Strong capitalization (9.7) based on excellent current risk-adjusted capital (severe loss scenario). High quality investment portfolio (9.4).

Other Rating Factors: Excellent liquidity (7.2) with ample operational cash flow and liquid investments.

Principal Business: Medicare (53%), Medicaid (47%)

Mem Phys: 18: 16,880 **17:** 14,464 **18 MLR** 80.0% **/ 18 Admin Exp** N/A

Enroll(000): Q1 19: 44 **18:** 45 **17:** 50 **Med Exp PMPM:** $421

Principal Investments: Cash and equiv (84%), long-term bonds (16%)

Provider Compensation ($000): Contr fee ($204,195), FFS ($31,814), capitation ($6,076)

Total Member Encounters: Phys (273,229), non-phys (310,933)

Group Affiliation: None

Licensed in: ID, MI

Address: 1333 GRATIOT STE 400, DETROIT, MI 48207

Phone: (313) 465-1519 **Dom State:** MI **Commenced Bus:** N/A

Data Date	Rating	RACR #1	RACR #2	Total Assets ($mil)	Capital ($mil)	Net Premium ($mil)	Net Income ($mil)
3-19	B	3.48	2.90	130.7	50.8	79.8	-3.8
3-18	B	2.33	1.94	140.6	38.0	88.5	-2.7
2018	B	3.70	3.08	136.5	54.6	293.6	12.9
2017	B	1.51	1.26	121.5	41.5	349.5	3.2
2016	B	2.22	1.85	120.5	34.2	340.2	-3.5
2015	B+	3.04	2.53	110.4	36.9	282.1	5.6
2014	B	2.98	2.49	49.1	23.6	187.5	6.2

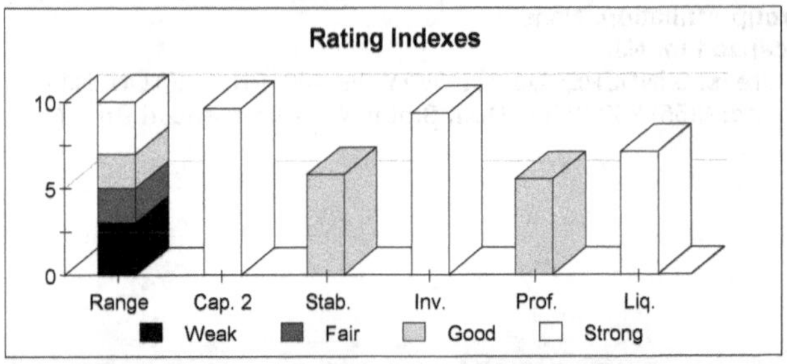

AETNA BETTER HEALTH OF MISSOURI LLC — C — Fair

Major Rating Factors: Weak overall results on stability tests (0.3 on a scale of 0 to 10) based on a steep decline in capital during 2018. Rating is significantly influenced by the good financial results of . Excellent profitability (7.4). Strong capitalization index (10.0) based on excellent current risk-adjusted capital (severe loss scenario).

Other Rating Factors: High quality investment portfolio (8.9). Excellent liquidity (10.0) with ample operational cash flow and liquid investments.

Principal Business: Medicaid (100%)

Mem Phys: 18: N/A **17:** N/A **18 MLR** -307.1% **/ 18 Admin Exp** N/A

Enroll(000): Q1 19: N/A **18:** N/A **17:** N/A **Med Exp PMPM:** N/A

Principal Investments: Long-term bonds (90%), cash and equiv (10%)

Provider Compensation ($000): Contr fee ($1,148)

Total Member Encounters: N/A

Group Affiliation: None

Licensed in: KS, MO

Address: 10 S BROADWAY SUITE 1200, ST. LOUIS, MO 63102-1713

Phone: (314) 241-5300 **Dom State:** MO **Commenced Bus:** N/A

Data Date	Rating	RACR #1	RACR #2	Total Assets ($mil)	Capital ($mil)	Net Premium ($mil)	Net Income ($mil)
3-19	C	38.20	31.83	41.4	41.1	0.1	-0.2
3-18	C	9.74	8.12	127.0	123.1	2.0	2.9
2018	C	37.78	31.48	40.9	40.5	1.0	1.0
2017	C	6.59	5.49	129.2	117.6	258.9	7.9
2016	B	4.66	3.88	280.3	164.4	780.7	32.7
2015	B	4.29	3.58	252.9	135.4	707.0	20.1
2014	A-	3.97	3.31	191.5	109.6	645.4	24.3

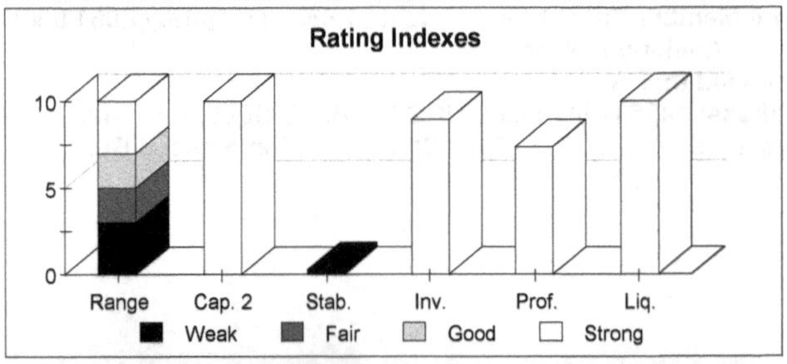

AETNA BETTER HEALTH OF TEXAS INC — B — Good

Major Rating Factors: Good liquidity (6.8 on a scale of 0 to 10) with sufficient resources (cash flows and marketable investments) to handle a spike in claims. Excellent profitability (9.2). Strong capitalization (9.3) based on excellent current risk-adjusted capital (severe loss scenario).

Other Rating Factors: High quality investment portfolio (9.9).

Principal Business: Medicaid (93%), comp med (7%)

Mem Phys: 18: 35,652 **17:** 31,056 **18 MLR** 80.7% **/ 18 Admin Exp** N/A

Enroll(000): Q1 19: 88 **18:** 88 **17:** 92 **Med Exp PMPM:** $234

Principal Investments: Long-term bonds (90%), cash and equiv (10%)

Provider Compensation ($000): Contr fee ($231,779), FFS ($18,215), capitation ($1,256), bonus arrang ($166)

Total Member Encounters: Phys (598,970), non-phys (480,559)

Group Affiliation: None

Licensed in: TX

Address: 2777 N STEMMONS FREEWAY #1450, DALLAS, TX 75207-2265

Phone: (800) 872-3862 **Dom State:** TX **Commenced Bus:** N/A

Data Date	Rating	RACR #1	RACR #2	Total Assets ($mil)	Capital ($mil)	Net Premium ($mil)	Net Income ($mil)
3-19	B	3.23	2.69	99.4	47.9	79.2	-2.2
3-18	B+	N/A	N/A	103.6	47.5	80.9	-5.8
2018	B	3.36	2.80	103.5	50.2	314.5	16.6
2017	B+	N/A	N/A	119.5	53.3	284.3	19.1
2016	C+	3.55	2.96	102.1	48.8	251.1	15.4
2015	U	5.62	4.68	92.7	30.7	70.3	4.6
2014	N/A	N/A	N/A	N/A	N/A	N/A	N/A

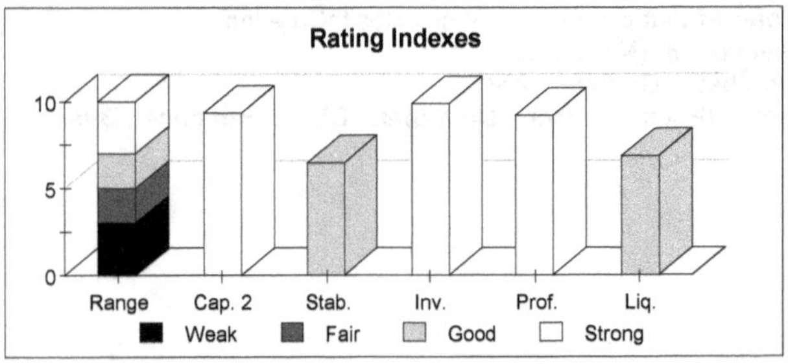

AETNA BETTER HLTH OF KY INS CO * B+ Good

Major Rating Factors: Good liquidity (6.7 on a scale of 0 to 10) with sufficient resources (cash flows and marketable investments) to handle a spike in claims. Excellent profitability (10.0). Strong capitalization (10.0) based on excellent current risk-adjusted capital (severe loss scenario).
Other Rating Factors: Fair quality investment portfolio (4.8).
Principal Business: Medicaid (97%), comp med (3%)
Mem Phys: 18: 30,303 **17:** 28,667 **18 MLR** 82.9% **/ 18 Admin Exp** N/A
Enroll(000): Q1 19: 214 **18:** 225 **17:** 243 **Med Exp PMPM:** $335
Principal Investments: Long-term bonds (93%), cash and equiv (4%), mortgs (3%)
Provider Compensation ($000): Contr fee ($909,602), FFS ($29,002), capitation ($11,496)
Total Member Encounters: Phys (1,659,127), non-phys (943,152)
Group Affiliation: None
Licensed in: KY
Address: 306 WEST MAIN St Ste 512, LOUISVILLE, KY 40202
Phone: (800) 627-4702 **Dom State:** KY **Commenced Bus:** N/A

Data Date	Rating	RACR #1	RACR #2	Total Assets ($mil)	Capital ($mil)	Net Premium ($mil)	Net Income ($mil)
3-19	B+	5.84	4.87	524.3	337.4	262.5	13.4
3-18	B+	N/A	N/A	532.8	258.6	282.8	4.1
2018	B+	5.67	4.72	496.0	326.5	1,121.8	59.1
2017	B+	N/A	N/A	526.8	261.9	1,124.5	55.7
2016	C+	3.29	2.74	563.5	213.4	1,111.9	122.2
2015	N/A	N/A	N/A	3.3	3.3	N/A	N/A
2014	N/A	N/A	N/A	N/A	N/A	N/A	N/A

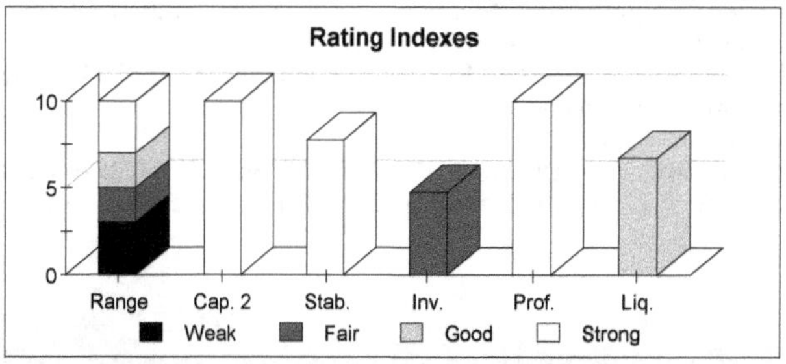

AETNA HEALTH & LIFE INSURANCE COMPANY C Fair

Major Rating Factors: Fair profitability (4.3 on a scale of 0 to 10) with operating losses during the first three months of 2019. Good quality investment portfolio (6.6) despite mixed results such as: no exposure to mortgages and substantial holdings of BBB bonds but minimal holdings in junk bonds. Good liquidity (6.9) with sufficient resources to handle a spike in claims.
Other Rating Factors: Weak overall results on stability tests (2.8) including weak results on operational trends, negative cash flow from operations for 2018. Strong capitalization (7.2) based on excellent risk adjusted capital (severe loss scenario).
Principal Business: Individual health insurance (95%) and group health insurance (5%).
Principal Investments: NonCMO investment grade bonds (88%), CMOs and structured securities (3%), and noninv. grade bonds (2%).
Investments in Affiliates: None
Group Affiliation: Aetna Inc
Licensed in: All states except PR
Commenced Business: October 1971
Address: 151 FARMINGTON AVENUE, HARTFORD, CT 6156
Phone: (800) 872-3862 **Domicile State:** CT **NAIC Code:** 78700

Data Date	Rating	RACR #1	RACR #2	Total Assets ($mil)	Capital ($mil)	Net Premium ($mil)	Net Income ($mil)
3-19	C	1.55	1.16	159.3	84.4	106.1	-20.2
3-18	C+	6.26	3.74	404.7	294.8	87.0	-6.0
2018	C	2.11	1.59	185.2	106.5	374.0	-13.0
2017	C+	5.60	3.55	388.4	307.3	-1,183.1	418.9
2016	B+	2.14	1.33	2,388.6	282.5	804.5	9.5
2015	B+	2.59	1.58	2,290.6	299.9	655.8	76.8
2014	B+	3.11	1.86	2,254.6	319.7	568.8	85.2

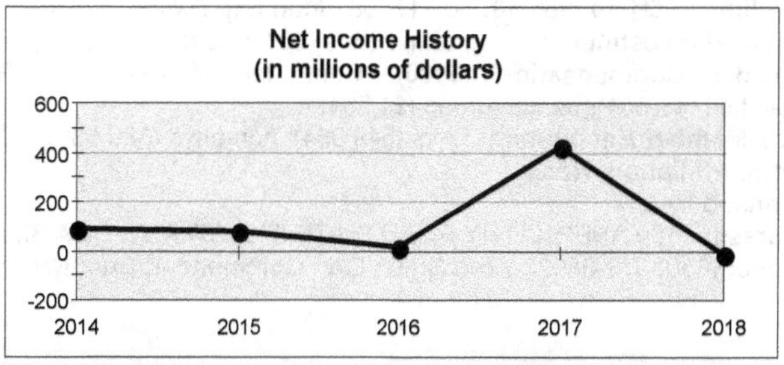

AETNA HEALTH INC (A CT CORP) C Fair

Major Rating Factors: Fair profitability index (2.9 on a scale of 0 to 10). Fair quality investment portfolio (3.8). Weak overall results on stability tests (1.9) based on a steep decline in premium revenue in 2018, a steep decline in capital during 2018 and a significant 41% decrease in enrollment during the period. Rating is significantly influenced by the good financial results of .
Other Rating Factors: Good liquidity (6.9) with sufficient resources (cash flows and marketable investments) to handle a spike in claims. Strong capitalization index (10.0) based on excellent current risk-adjusted capital (severe loss scenario).
Principal Business: Medicare (99%), comp med (1%)
Mem Phys: 18: 33,909 **17:** 26,364 **18 MLR** 87.5% **/ 18 Admin Exp** N/A
Enroll(000): Q1 19: 12 **18:** 15 **17:** 26 **Med Exp PMPM:** $712
Principal Investments: Long-term bonds (74%), cash and equiv (22%), mortgs (5%)
Provider Compensation ($000): Contr fee ($137,452), FFS ($5,106), bonus arrang ($2,918), capitation ($685)
Total Member Encounters: Phys (506,173), non-phys (305,587)
Group Affiliation: None
Licensed in: CT
Address: 151 FARMINGTON AVENUE, HARTFORD, CT 6156
Phone: (800) 872-3862 **Dom State:** CT **Commenced Bus:** N/A

Data Date	Rating	RACR #1	RACR #2	Total Assets ($mil)	Capital ($mil)	Net Premium ($mil)	Net Income ($mil)
3-19	C	4.75	3.96	71.8	47.2	34.8	1.4
3-18	C+	4.88	4.06	114.1	68.0	40.3	-6.4
2018	C	4.59	3.83	86.9	45.5	156.1	-3.5
2017	C	3.47	2.89	112.7	74.5	254.1	11.3
2016	C	6.11	5.09	122.2	82.2	245.6	13.0
2015	C	5.02	4.18	103.2	68.2	225.4	1.5
2014	C	3.68	3.07	102.8	67.2	298.1	-8.6

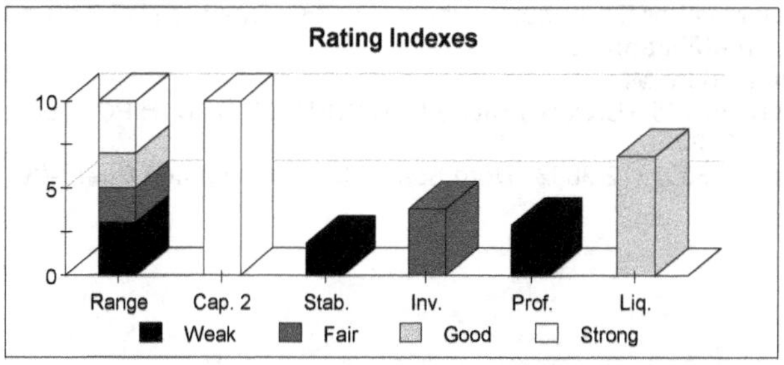

AETNA HEALTH INC (A FLORIDA CORP) B- Good

Major Rating Factors: Fair profitability index (4.6 on a scale of 0 to 10). Fair overall results on stability tests (4.5) based on a significant 18% decrease in enrollment during the period. Rating is significantly influenced by the good financial results of . Good liquidity (5.8) with sufficient resources (cash flows and marketable investments) to handle a spike in claims.
Other Rating Factors: Strong capitalization index (8.2) based on excellent current risk-adjusted capital (severe loss scenario). High quality investment portfolio (8.8).
Principal Business: Medicare (53%), comp med (47%)
Mem Phys: 18: 78,135 **17:** 55,308 **18 MLR** 87.7% **/ 18 Admin Exp** N/A
Enroll(000): Q1 19: 171 **18:** 191 **17:** 233 **Med Exp PMPM:** $597
Principal Investments: Long-term bonds (86%), cash and equiv (13%)
Provider Compensation ($000): Contr fee ($1,206,123), capitation ($155,743), FFS ($53,030), bonus arrang ($34,834)
Total Member Encounters: Phys (2,322,400), non-phys (2,111,301)
Group Affiliation: None
Licensed in: FL, IA
Address: 4630 WOODLANDS CORPORATE BOULE, TAMPA, FL 33614-2415
Phone: (813) 775-0000 **Dom State:** FL **Commenced Bus:** N/A

Data Date	Rating	RACR #1	RACR #2	Total Assets ($mil)	Capital ($mil)	Net Premium ($mil)	Net Income ($mil)
3-19	B-	2.31	1.92	434.2	199.7	387.2	45.1
3-18	B-	2.17	1.81	575.5	191.3	435.2	-24.3
2018	B-	2.05	1.71	499.9	174.5	1,673.8	-34.8
2017	B	1.64	1.37	431.4	200.9	1,843.4	52.5
2016	B+	2.58	2.15	541.2	249.8	1,982.9	69.6
2015	B	2.21	1.84	512.6	180.0	1,631.5	41.3
2014	A-	2.43	2.02	266.5	130.4	1,101.5	53.9

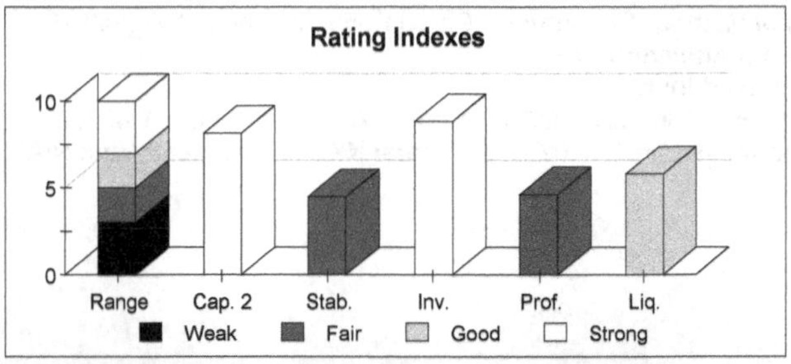

AETNA HEALTH INC (A GEORGIA CORP) C Fair

Major Rating Factors: Fair profitability index (4.1 on a scale of 0 to 10). Weak overall results on stability tests (2.0) based on a significant 25% decrease in enrollment during the period, a steep decline in capital during 2018. Rating is significantly influenced by the good financial results of . Good liquidity (6.6) with sufficient resources (cash flows and marketable investments) to handle a spike in claims.
Other Rating Factors: Strong capitalization index (10.0) based on excellent current risk-adjusted capital (severe loss scenario). High quality investment portfolio (9.3).
Principal Business: Comp med (71%), Medicare (21%), FEHB (6%), dental (1%)
Mem Phys: 18: 31,276 **17:** 29,710 **18 MLR** 83.7% **/ 18 Admin Exp** N/A
Enroll(000): Q1 19: 38 **18:** 50 **17:** 66 **Med Exp PMPM:** $320
Principal Investments: Long-term bonds (98%), cash and equiv (2%)
Provider Compensation ($000): Contr fee ($215,674), FFS ($6,305), capitation ($1,604), bonus arrang ($1,564)
Total Member Encounters: Phys (549,964), non-phys (396,539)
Group Affiliation: None
Licensed in: GA
Address: 1100 ABERNATHY ROAD SUITE 375, ATLANTA, GA 30328
Phone: (800) 872-3862 **Dom State:** GA **Commenced Bus:** N/A

Data Date	Rating	RACR #1	RACR #2	Total Assets ($mil)	Capital ($mil)	Net Premium ($mil)	Net Income ($mil)
3-19	C	4.99	4.16	188.6	68.7	47.4	3.8
3-18	C+	6.07	5.06	252.7	102.5	67.7	-3.5
2018	C	4.75	3.96	193.5	65.1	255.1	4.9
2017	C+	4.37	3.64	235.8	105.3	317.8	10.2
2016	B	3.66	3.05	284.8	131.4	605.1	18.9
2015	B	3.01	2.51	298.3	116.0	642.9	-4.6
2014	B	3.67	3.06	241.4	129.6	753.5	11.5

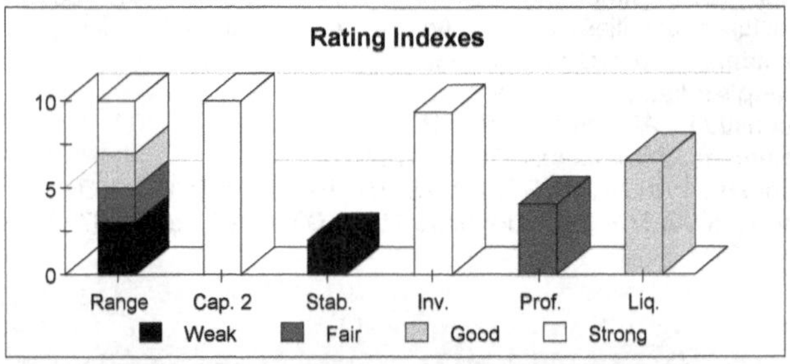

AETNA HEALTH INC (A MAINE CORP) B Good

Major Rating Factors: Good overall profitability index (6.6 on a scale of 0 to 10). Good overall results on stability tests (5.3). Rating is significantly influenced by the good financial results of . Strong capitalization index (10.0) based on excellent current risk-adjusted capital (severe loss scenario).
Other Rating Factors: High quality investment portfolio (7.9). Excellent liquidity (7.1) with ample operational cash flow and liquid investments.
Principal Business: Medicare (80%), comp med (20%)
Mem Phys: 18: 14,925 **17:** 11,740 **18 MLR** 75.0% **/ 18 Admin Exp** N/A
Enroll(000): Q1 19: 9 **18:** 8 **17:** 11 **Med Exp PMPM:** $481
Principal Investments: Long-term bonds (83%), cash and equiv (17%)
Provider Compensation ($000): Contr fee ($50,828), FFS ($1,664), capitation ($323)
Total Member Encounters: Phys (193,938), non-phys (127,353)
Group Affiliation: None
Licensed in: ME
Address: 175 RUNNING HILL ROAD SUITE 30, SOUTH PORTLAND, ME 04106-3220
Phone: (800) 872-3862 **Dom State:** ME **Commenced Bus:** N/A

Data Date	Rating	RACR #1	RACR #2	Total Assets ($mil)	Capital ($mil)	Net Premium ($mil)	Net Income ($mil)
3-19	B	5.86	4.88	34.8	23.6	19.6	0.9
3-18	B-	3.54	2.95	34.8	16.8	17.1	-0.7
2018	B	5.62	4.69	37.2	22.6	66.8	5.2
2017	B-	2.10	1.75	28.9	17.5	77.8	4.6
2016	B-	3.13	2.61	27.6	15.5	75.3	2.5
2015	B-	2.36	1.97	26.2	12.7	80.1	-1.2
2014	B	2.36	1.97	27.9	15.7	104.7	2.6

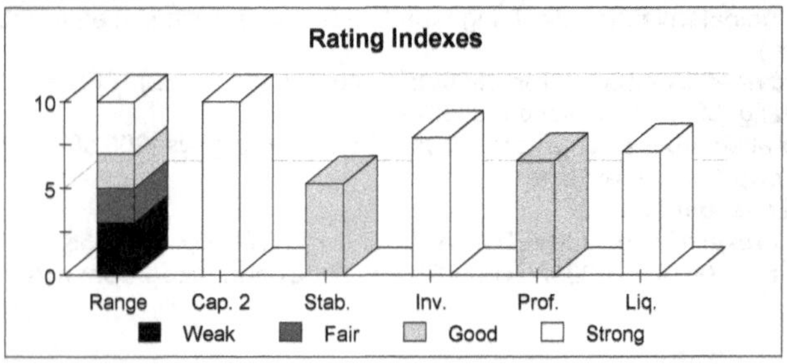

AETNA HEALTH INC (A NEW JERSEY CORP) B Good

Major Rating Factors: Good overall profitability index (5.2 on a scale of 0 to 10). Good liquidity (6.8) with sufficient resources (cash flows and marketable investments) to handle a spike in claims. Fair quality investment portfolio (4.2).
Other Rating Factors: Fair overall results on stability tests (4.9). Rating is significantly influenced by the good financial results of . Strong capitalization index (10.0) based on excellent current risk-adjusted capital (severe loss scenario).
Principal Business: Medicare (78%), comp med (17%), FEHB (5%)
Mem Phys: 18: 51,944 **17:** 41,987 **18 MLR** 86.3% **/ 18 Admin Exp** N/A
Enroll(000): Q1 19: 67 **18:** 62 **17:** 64 **Med Exp PMPM:** $781
Principal Investments: Long-term bonds (84%), cash and equiv (16%)
Provider Compensation ($000): Contr fee ($560,941), FFS ($34,452), capitation ($11,357), bonus arrang ($3,251)
Total Member Encounters: Phys (1,769,166), non-phys (1,131,899)
Group Affiliation: None
Licensed in: NJ
Address: 9 ENTIN ROAD SUITE 203, PARSIPPANY, NJ 7054
Phone: (800) 872-3862 **Dom State:** NJ **Commenced Bus:** N/A

Data Date	Rating	RACR #1	RACR #2	Total Assets ($mil)	Capital ($mil)	Net Premium ($mil)	Net Income ($mil)
3-19	B	4.35	3.63	283.8	167.0	187.4	-4.1
3-18	B	N/A	N/A	319.2	173.2	178.8	-10.7
2018	B	4.43	3.70	301.1	170.5	699.4	2.5
2017	B	N/A	N/A	271.1	184.5	653.8	17.5
2016	B	3.87	3.22	302.9	187.8	887.0	17.7
2015	B	2.94	2.45	340.4	171.6	1,123.5	13.4
2014	B	3.34	2.79	323.7	198.4	1,171.4	40.2

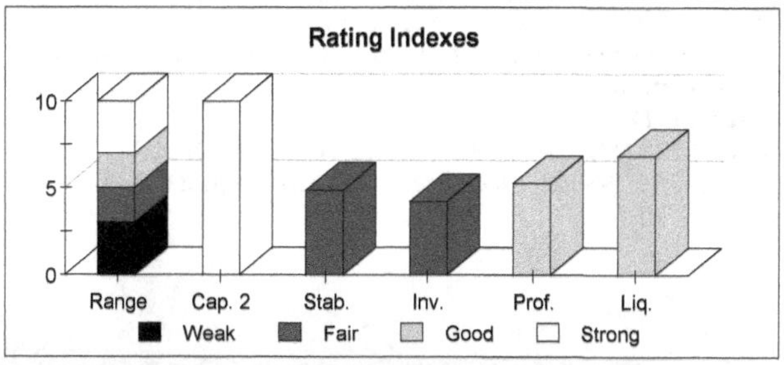

AETNA HEALTH INC (A NEW YORK CORP) B Good

Major Rating Factors: Good overall results on stability tests (5.2 on a scale of 0 to 10). Rating is significantly influenced by the good financial results of . Good liquidity (6.8) with sufficient resources (cash flows and marketable investments) to handle a spike in claims. Fair profitability index (4.5).
Other Rating Factors: Strong capitalization index (10.0) based on excellent current risk-adjusted capital (severe loss scenario). High quality investment portfolio (7.8).
Principal Business: Medicare (100%)
Mem Phys: 18: 109,884 **17:** 81,935 **18 MLR** 90.8% **/ 18 Admin Exp** N/A
Enroll(000): Q1 19: 22 **18:** 11 **17:** 10 **Med Exp PMPM:** $832
Principal Investments: Long-term bonds (80%), affiliate common stock (14%), cash and equiv (3%), mortgs (2%)
Provider Compensation ($000): Contr fee ($96,533), FFS ($4,940), capitation ($1,571), bonus arrang ($294)
Total Member Encounters: Phys (350,097), non-phys (235,265)
Group Affiliation: None
Licensed in: NY
Address: 100 PARK AVENUE 12TH FLOOR, NEW YORK, NY 10178
Phone: (800) 872-3862 **Dom State:** NY **Commenced Bus:** N/A

Data Date	Rating	RACR #1	RACR #2	Total Assets ($mil)	Capital ($mil)	Net Premium ($mil)	Net Income ($mil)
3-19	B	17.65	14.71	288.1	226.4	55.8	5.6
3-18	C+	19.02	15.85	288.0	221.2	28.6	-3.6
2018	B-	17.28	14.40	289.7	221.7	117.4	-5.8
2017	C+	14.16	11.80	270.1	225.5	120.3	6.1
2016	C+	18.31	15.26	264.7	214.4	172.3	13.2
2015	C+	13.32	11.10	276.0	198.4	300.9	15.2
2014	B	4.53	3.78	285.2	176.5	489.9	25.4

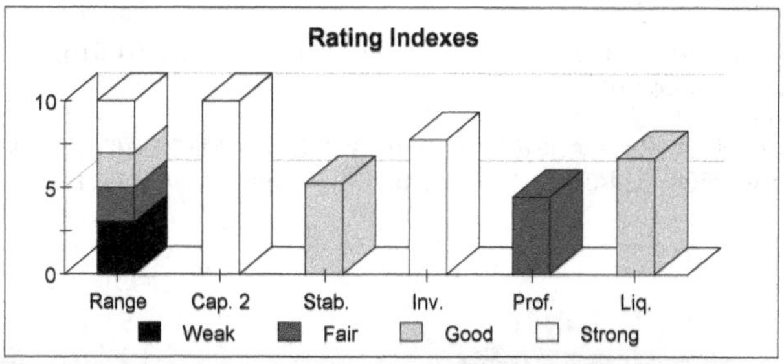

AETNA HEALTH INC (A PA CORP) B Good

Major Rating Factors: Good quality investment portfolio (6.6 on a scale of 0 to 10). Good overall results on stability tests (5.0) despite a decline in enrollment during 2018. Rating is significantly influenced by the good financial results of . Good liquidity (6.2) with sufficient resources (cash flows and marketable investments) to handle a spike in claims.
Other Rating Factors: Excellent profitability (7.2). Strong capitalization index (10.0) based on excellent current risk-adjusted capital (severe loss scenario).
Principal Business: Medicare (51%), comp med (25%), FEHB (23%), Medicaid (1%)
Mem Phys: 18: 554,080 **17:** 426,906 **18 MLR** 87.3% **/ 18 Admin Exp** N/A
Enroll(000): Q1 19: 470 **18:** 488 **17:** 598 **Med Exp PMPM:** $461
Principal Investments: Long-term bonds (86%), affiliate common stock (7%), cash and equiv (5%), mortgs (2%)
Provider Compensation ($000): Contr fee ($2,667,898), FFS ($109,752), capitation ($35,185), bonus arrang ($23,896)
Total Member Encounters: Phys (6,627,326), non-phys (4,472,013)
Group Affiliation: None
Licensed in: AZ, CO, DC, DE, IL, IN, KS, KY, MD, MA, MO, NE, NV, NC, OH, OK, PA, SC, TN, VA, WA, WV
Address: 1425 UNION MEETING ROAD, BLUE BELL, PA 19422
Phone: (800) 872-3862 **Dom State:** PA **Commenced Bus:** N/A

Data Date	Rating	RACR #1	RACR #2	Total Assets ($mil)	Capital ($mil)	Net Premium ($mil)	Net Income ($mil)
3-19	B	4.00	3.34	1,104.1	555.3	844.4	55.2
3-18	B-	3.21	2.68	1,261.4	473.7	784.2	-54.0
2018	B	3.56	2.97	1,064.3	489.5	3,153.5	96.3
2017	B-	2.88	2.40	1,152.6	525.3	3,521.2	129.5
2016	C+	2.69	2.24	1,380.0	458.2	3,951.7	83.4
2015	B	4.17	3.47	1,479.3	672.3	4,192.9	113.8
2014	B	3.64	3.04	1,322.6	662.2	4,568.7	117.0

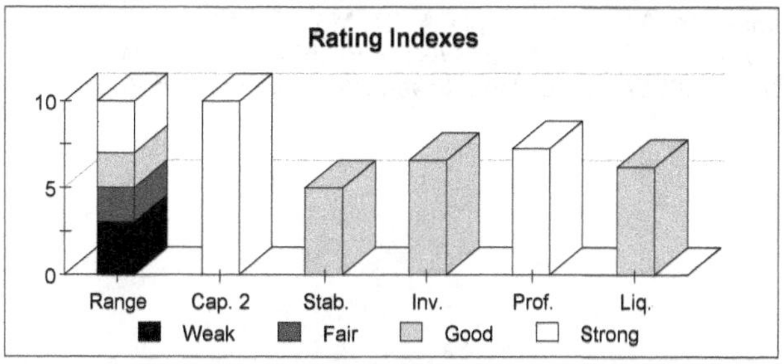

AETNA HEALTH INC (A TEXAS CORP) C Fair

Major Rating Factors: Fair overall results on stability tests (4.3 on a scale of 0 to 10). Rating is significantly influenced by the good financial results of . Weak profitability index (0.7). Good liquidity (6.5) with sufficient resources (cash flows and marketable investments) to handle a spike in claims.
Other Rating Factors: Strong capitalization index (7.8) based on excellent current risk-adjusted capital (severe loss scenario). High quality investment portfolio (9.9).
Principal Business: Medicare (79%), comp med (21%)
Mem Phys: 18: 66,203 **17:** 61,987 **18 MLR** 94.0% **/ 18 Admin Exp** N/A
Enroll(000): Q1 19: 54 **18:** 56 **17:** 53 **Med Exp PMPM:** $661
Principal Investments: Long-term bonds (63%), cash and equiv (37%)
Provider Compensation ($000): Contr fee ($381,229), FFS ($51,804), capitation ($3,914), bonus arrang ($1,035)
Total Member Encounters: Phys (507,283), non-phys (307,014)
Group Affiliation: None
Licensed in: TX
Address: 2777 N STEMMONS FREEWAY SUITE, DALLAS, TX 75207-2265
Phone: (800) 872-3862 **Dom State:** TX **Commenced Bus:** N/A

Data Date	Rating	RACR #1	RACR #2	Total Assets ($mil)	Capital ($mil)	Net Premium ($mil)	Net Income ($mil)
3-19	C	1.98	1.65	138.5	59.8	129.3	1.8
3-18	C	2.52	2.10	165.2	58.8	117.7	-9.6
2018	C	1.93	1.61	170.2	58.1	472.3	-23.6
2017	C	1.83	1.53	128.4	68.0	407.9	-18.1
2016	C+	3.83	3.19	161.0	96.7	430.1	-7.6
2015	B	4.13	3.44	166.9	116.0	514.8	13.9
2014	B	3.13	2.61	236.5	124.0	690.2	23.6

Rating Indexes

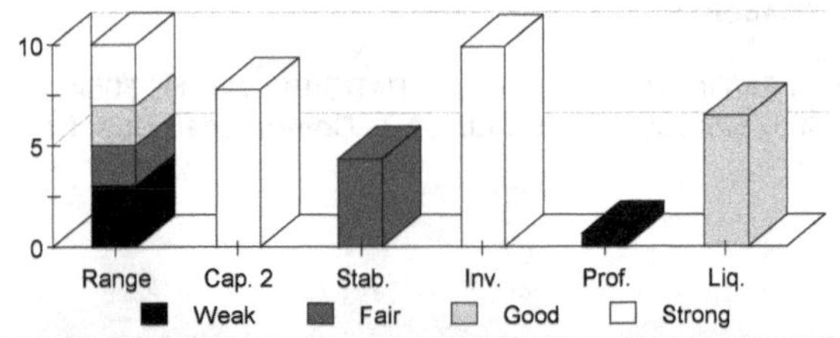

AETNA HEALTH INC (LA) B- Good

Major Rating Factors: Fair overall results on stability tests (4.6 on a scale of 0 to 10) based on a significant 15% decrease in enrollment during the period. Rating is significantly influenced by the good financial results of . Good overall profitability index (6.1). Strong capitalization index (10.0) based on excellent current risk-adjusted capital (severe loss scenario).
Other Rating Factors: High quality investment portfolio (9.7). Excellent liquidity (7.0) with ample operational cash flow and liquid investments.
Principal Business: Comp med (84%), Medicare (16%)
Mem Phys: 18: 11,233 **17:** 10,598 **18 MLR** 78.9% **/ 18 Admin Exp** N/A
Enroll(000): Q1 19: 10 **18:** 13 **17:** 16 **Med Exp PMPM:** $449
Principal Investments: Long-term bonds (59%), cash and equiv (41%)
Provider Compensation ($000): Contr fee ($68,063), FFS ($8,783), capitation ($739)
Total Member Encounters: Phys (211,711), non-phys (161,615)
Group Affiliation: None
Licensed in: LA
Address: 3838 N CAUSEWAY BLVD SUITE 335, METAIRIE, LA 70002
Phone: (504) 834-0840 **Dom State:** LA **Commenced Bus:** N/A

Data Date	Rating	RACR #1	RACR #2	Total Assets ($mil)	Capital ($mil)	Net Premium ($mil)	Net Income ($mil)
3-19	B-	4.68	3.90	36.7	26.8	18.9	1.6
3-18	C+	3.35	2.79	39.1	17.8	23.4	-2.4
2018	B-	4.43	3.69	35.2	25.3	95.5	5.1
2017	C+	2.15	1.79	33.7	20.3	102.0	8.8
2016	B-	4.51	3.76	43.7	24.4	111.1	6.1
2015	B-	2.29	1.91	45.9	17.6	139.7	-5.5
2014	B	2.06	1.72	55.0	21.0	190.4	2.0

Rating Indexes

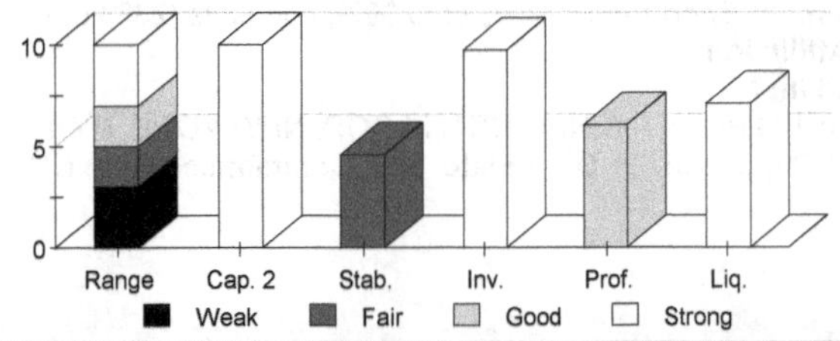

AETNA HEALTH INS CO C Fair

Major Rating Factors: Weak profitability index (1.1 on a scale of 0 to 10). Good quality investment portfolio (6.7). Strong capitalization (10.0) based on excellent current risk-adjusted capital (severe loss scenario).
Other Rating Factors: Excellent liquidity (7.0) with sufficient resources (cash flows and marketable investments) to handle a spike in claims.
Principal Business: Med supp (71%), comp med (29%)
Mem Phys: 18: N/A **17:** N/A **18 MLR** 76.5% **/ 18 Admin Exp** N/A
Enroll(000): Q1 19: 56 **18:** 70 **17:** 128 **Med Exp PMPM:** $22
Principal Investments: Long-term bonds (55%), cash and equiv (45%)
Provider Compensation ($000): Contr fee ($21,424), FFS ($19)
Total Member Encounters: N/A
Group Affiliation: None
Licensed in: All states except CA, CT, MS, NY, PR
Address: 1425 UNION MEETING Rd, BLUE BELL, PA 19422
Phone: (800) 872-3862 **Dom State:** PA **Commenced Bus:** N/A

Data Date	Rating	RACR #1	RACR #2	Total Assets ($mil)	Capital ($mil)	Net Premium ($mil)	Net Income ($mil)
3-19	C	5.86	4.88	20.5	13.3	10.1	-0.6
3-18	C	22.75	18.96	41.6	34.1	5.3	-0.6
2018	C	6.31	5.26	23.1	14.3	29.3	-2.4
2017	C	13.90	11.59	43.8	35.1	15.6	-0.2
2016	B-	9.96	8.30	43.1	34.8	34.8	0.6
2015	C+	6.42	5.35	59.0	32.3	33.8	-6.8
2014	B	7.50	6.25	59.1	38.9	52.4	-1.5

Rating Indexes

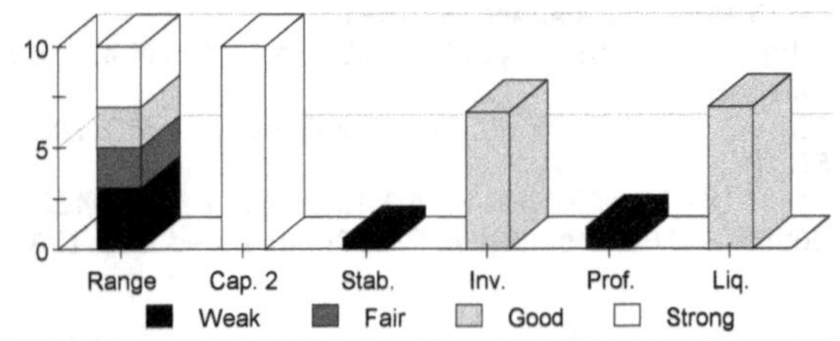

AETNA HEALTH OF CALIFORNIA INC — B — Good

Major Rating Factors: Good overall results on stability tests (5.4 on a scale of 0 to 10) despite a decline in enrollment during 2018. Rating is significantly influenced by the good financial results of Aetna Inc. Excellent profitability (7.7). Strong capitalization index (7.4) based on excellent current risk-adjusted capital (severe loss scenario).
Other Rating Factors: Excellent liquidity (7.0) with sufficient resources (cash flows and marketable investments) to handle a spike in claims.
Principal Business: Medicare (14%)
Mem Phys: 18: N/A **17:** N/A **18 MLR** 80.2% **/ 18 Admin Exp** N/A
Enroll(000): Q1 19: 220 **18:** 224 **17:** 269 **Med Exp PMPM:** $394
Principal Investments ($000): Cash and equiv ($75,797)
Provider Compensation ($000): None
Total Member Encounters: N/A
Group Affiliation: Aetna Inc
Licensed in: CA
Address: 2850 Shadelands Drive, Walnut Creek, CA 94598
Phone: (925) 948-4207 **Dom State:** CA **Commenced Bus:** October 1981

Data Date	Rating	RACR #1	RACR #2	Total Assets ($mil)	Capital ($mil)	Net Premium ($mil)	Net Income ($mil)
3-19	B	2.09	1.41	440.5	195.1	336.2	15.0
3-18	B	1.50	1.01	500.7	155.7	345.7	8.1
2018	B	1.90	1.29	406.7	176.6	1,389.2	70.8
2017	B	1.44	0.97	387.4	150.0	1,580.2	42.8
2016	C+	1.16	0.79	483.7	135.8	1,775.7	35.0
2015	C+	1.05	0.71	451.7	120.9	1,821.2	21.2
2014	B	1.12	0.74	448.5	128.6	1,958.3	36.1

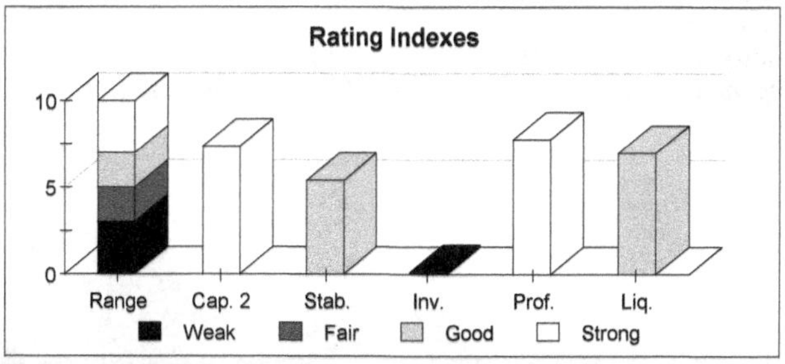

AETNA HEALTH OF IOWA INC — C+ — Fair

Major Rating Factors: Fair profitability index (3.5 on a scale of 0 to 10). Fair overall results on stability tests (3.4) based on a steep decline in premium revenue in 2018, a significant 89% decrease in enrollment during the period. Rating is significantly influenced by the good financial results of . Strong capitalization index (10.0) based on excellent current risk-adjusted capital (severe loss scenario).
Other Rating Factors: High quality investment portfolio (9.2). Excellent liquidity (7.3) with ample operational cash flow and liquid investments.
Principal Business: Comp med (102%)
Mem Phys: 18: 33,791 **17:** 31,138 **18 MLR** 58.6% **/ 18 Admin Exp** N/A
Enroll(000): Q1 19: 1 **18:** 4 **17:** 38 **Med Exp PMPM:** $275
Principal Investments: Long-term bonds (81%), cash and equiv (19%)
Provider Compensation ($000): Contr fee ($44,024), FFS ($693), capitation ($104)
Total Member Encounters: Phys (52,036), non-phys (40,755)
Group Affiliation: None
Licensed in: IA
Address: 15950 WEST DODGE ROAD, OMAHA, NE 68118
Phone: (800) 471-0240 **Dom State:** IA **Commenced Bus:** N/A

Data Date	Rating	RACR #1	RACR #2	Total Assets ($mil)	Capital ($mil)	Net Premium ($mil)	Net Income ($mil)
3-19	C+	21.53	17.94	53.6	41.6	1.9	1.6
3-18	C+	2.81	2.34	83.0	32.8	6.2	-6.2
2018	C+	20.69	17.24	54.0	39.9	31.8	2.0
2017	C+	1.90	1.59	97.0	37.5	209.6	8.3
2016	C+	1.92	1.60	87.5	29.4	240.4	-7.3
2015	B	2.13	1.78	96.9	39.1	311.4	-2.1
2014	B	2.16	1.80	70.9	25.6	198.5	-3.6

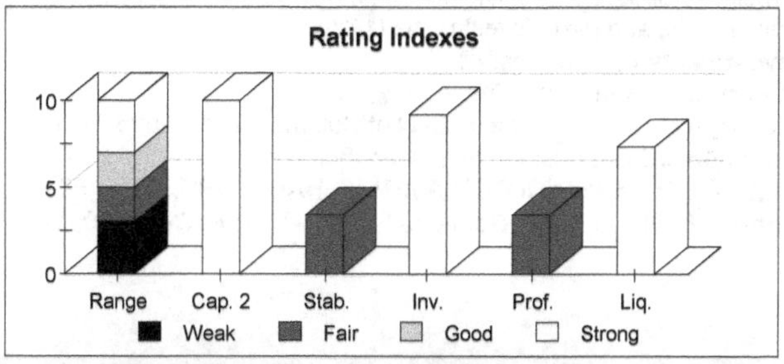

AETNA HEALTH OF UTAH INC — C — Fair

Major Rating Factors: Fair profitability index (4.4 on a scale of 0 to 10). Fair quality investment portfolio (3.7). Weak overall results on stability tests (2.9) based on a significant 23% decrease in enrollment during the period, an inordinate decline in premium revenue in 2018 and a steep decline in capital during 2018. Rating is significantly influenced by the good financial results of .
Other Rating Factors: Strong capitalization index (10.0) based on excellent current risk-adjusted capital (severe loss scenario). Excellent liquidity (6.9) with sufficient resources (cash flows and marketable investments) to handle a spike in claims.
Principal Business: FEHB (49%), comp med (28%), Medicare (23%)
Mem Phys: 18: 12,689 **17:** 12,941 **18 MLR** 81.1% **/ 18 Admin Exp** N/A
Enroll(000): Q1 19: 25 **18:** 35 **17:** 45 **Med Exp PMPM:** $387
Principal Investments: Long-term bonds (67%), cash and equiv (33%)
Provider Compensation ($000): Contr fee ($175,617), FFS ($8,986), capitation ($382)
Total Member Encounters: Phys (435,984), non-phys (284,697)
Group Affiliation: None
Licensed in: ID, NV, UT, WY
Address: 10150 S CENTENNIAL PARKWAY SUI, SANDY, UT 84070
Phone: (801) 933-3500 **Dom State:** UT **Commenced Bus:** N/A

Data Date	Rating	RACR #1	RACR #2	Total Assets ($mil)	Capital ($mil)	Net Premium ($mil)	Net Income ($mil)
3-19	C	5.22	4.35	83.3	41.7	46.1	3.1
3-18	C+	5.76	4.80	112.1	50.9	63.0	-2.7
2018	C	4.82	4.02	78.2	38.1	224.3	4.8
2017	C+	3.77	3.14	99.6	53.9	257.6	16.1
2016	B-	4.51	3.76	113.8	54.4	293.5	-2.7
2015	B	3.35	2.79	117.8	55.9	300.7	6.4
2014	B	1.93	1.61	124.2	50.6	477.8	5.0

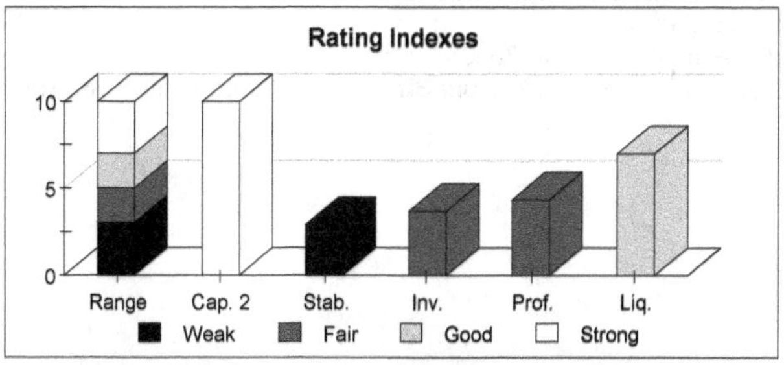

AETNA HEALTHASSURANCE PA INC — D — Weak

Major Rating Factors: Fair quality investment portfolio (3.7 on a scale of 0 to 10). Good overall profitability index (5.5). Good liquidity (6.2) with sufficient resources (cash flows and marketable investments) to handle a spike in claims.
Other Rating Factors: Strong capitalization (9.2) based on excellent current risk-adjusted capital (severe loss scenario).
Principal Business: Comp med (100%)
Mem Phys: 18: N/A **17:** 43,426 **18 MLR** 84.6% **/ 18 Admin Exp** N/A
Enroll(000): Q1 19: 40 **18:** 45 **17:** 53 **Med Exp PMPM:** $444
Principal Investments: Long-term bonds (99%), cash and equiv (1%)
Provider Compensation ($000): Contr fee ($244,003), FFS ($6,384)
Total Member Encounters: Phys (629,875), non-phys (492,325)
Group Affiliation: None
Licensed in: PA
Address: 980 JOLLY Rd, BLUE BELL, PA 19422
Phone: (800) 788-6445 **Dom State:** PA **Commenced Bus:** N/A

Data Date	Rating	RACR #1	RACR #2	Total Assets ($mil)	Capital ($mil)	Net Premium ($mil)	Net Income ($mil)
3-19	D	3.09	2.57	89.0	55.5	64.0	3.2
3-18	D	N/A	N/A	111.9	42.6	76.4	-7.2
2018	D	2.87	2.39	84.4	51.5	299.2	1.9
2017	D	N/A	N/A	102.3	49.8	280.7	-6.4
2016	C+	1.90	1.58	26.9	9.9	71.6	4.9
2015	N/A	N/A	N/A	5.0	5.0	N/A	N/A
2014	N/A	N/A	N/A	N/A	N/A	N/A	N/A

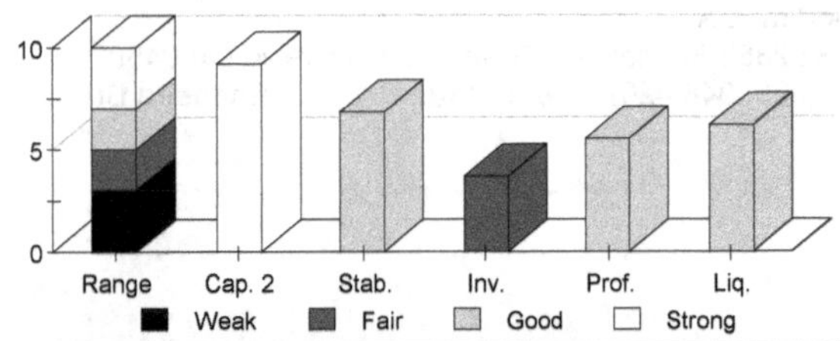

AETNA LIFE INSURANCE COMPANY — B — Good

Major Rating Factors: Good current capitalization (5.5 on a scale of 0 to 10) based on mixed results -- excessive policy leverage mitigated by excellent risk adjusted capital (severe loss scenario) reflecting improvement over results in 2017. Good quality investment portfolio (6.2) despite significant exposure to mortgages . Mortgage default rate has been low. large holdings of BBB rated bonds in addition to small junk bond holdings. Good liquidity (5.9).
Other Rating Factors: Good overall results on stability tests (5.4) excellent operational trends and excellent risk diversification. Excellent profitability (7.9).
Principal Business: Group health insurance (55%), individual health insurance (41%), group life insurance (3%), and reinsurance (1%).
Principal Investments: NonCMO investment grade bonds (56%), CMOs and structured securities (12%), mortgages in good standing (11%), noninv. grade bonds (7%), and misc. investments (14%).
Investments in Affiliates: 4%
Group Affiliation: Aetna Inc
Licensed in: All states, the District of Columbia and Puerto Rico
Commenced Business: December 1850
Address: 151 FARMINGTON AVENUE, HARTFORD, CT 6156
Phone: (800) 872-3862 **Domicile State:** CT **NAIC Code:** 60054

Data Date	Rating	RACR #1	RACR #2	Total Assets ($mil)	Capital ($mil)	Net Premium ($mil)	Net Income ($mil)
3-19	B	1.46	1.11	22,067.5	4,433.3	6,043.5	830.4
3-18	B	1.13	0.85	23,044.7	2,934.9	4,999.5	264.9
2018	B	1.28	0.97	20,230.7	3,697.1	19,837.6	1,933.0
2017	B	1.12	0.84	19,894.8	2,904.0	17,984.7	1,339.4
2016	B	1.34	1.00	22,376.2	3,479.2	18,556.4	1,251.7
2015	B	1.57	1.15	21,214.1	3,770.8	17,155.4	1,211.9
2014	B+	1.72	1.25	22,795.4	3,871.9	15,544.4	1,321.7

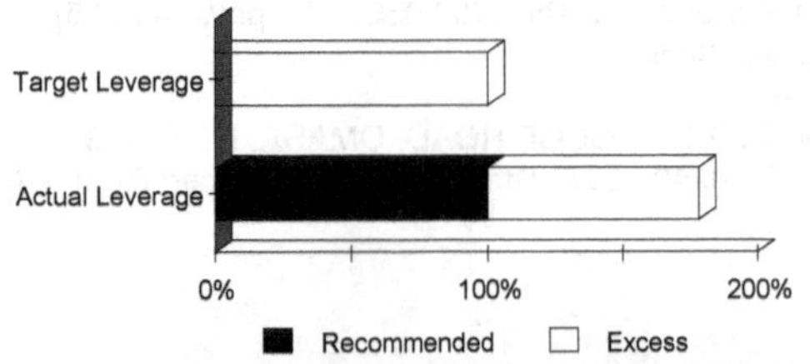

AHF MCO OF GEORGIA INC — D+ — Weak

Major Rating Factors: Weak profitability index (2.4 on a scale of 0 to 10). Strong capitalization (10.0) based on excellent current risk-adjusted capital (severe loss scenario). High quality investment portfolio (9.9).
Other Rating Factors: Excellent liquidity (10.0) with ample operational cash flow and liquid investments.
Principal Business: Medicare (100%)
Mem Phys: 18: N/A **17:** N/A **18 MLR** 91.1% **/ 18 Admin Exp** N/A
Enroll(000): Q1 19: 0 **18:** 0 **17:** N/A **Med Exp PMPM:** $3,271
Principal Investments: Cash and equiv (100%)
Provider Compensation ($000): FFS ($163)
Total Member Encounters: N/A
Group Affiliation: AIDS Healthcare Foundation
Licensed in: GA
Address: , Atlanta, GA 30308
Phone: (323) 860-5200 **Dom State:** GA **Commenced Bus:** N/A

Data Date	Rating	RACR #1	RACR #2	Total Assets ($mil)	Capital ($mil)	Net Premium ($mil)	Net Income ($mil)
3-19	D+	152.49	127.07	4.3	4.1	0.1	0.0
3-18	N/A	N/A	N/A	4.1	4.0	N/A	N/A
2018	D	150.80	125.70	4.2	4.0	0.2	0.0
2017	N/A	N/A	N/A	4.0	4.0	N/A	N/A
2016	N/A	N/A	N/A	N/A	N/A	N/A	N/A
2015	N/A	N/A	N/A	N/A	N/A	N/A	N/A
2014	N/A	N/A	N/A	N/A	N/A	N/A	N/A

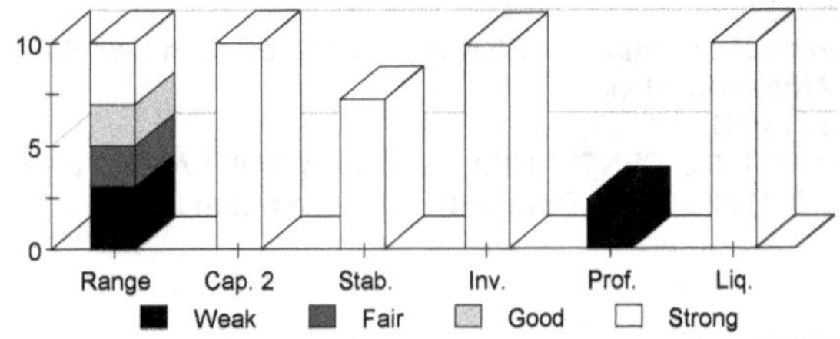

AIDS HEALTHCARE FOUNDATION MCO OF FL — E+ Very Weak

Major Rating Factors: Weak profitability index (0.9 on a scale of 0 to 10). Poor capitalization (2.9) based on weak current risk-adjusted capital (moderate loss scenario). Good liquidity (5.6) with sufficient resources (cash flows and marketable investments) to handle a spike in claims.
Other Rating Factors: High quality investment portfolio (9.3).
Principal Business: Medicare (64%), Medicaid (36%)
Mem Phys: 18: 3,803 **17:** N/A **18 MLR** 98.8% **/ 18 Admin Exp** N/A
Enroll(000): Q1 19: 2 **18:** 3 **17:** 4 **Med Exp PMPM:** $3,289
Principal Investments: Cash and equiv (54%), long-term bonds (35%), real estate (7%), nonaffiliate common stock (4%)
Provider Compensation ($000): Contr fee ($132,685)
Total Member Encounters: Phys (17,533), non-phys (13,757)
Group Affiliation: None
Licensed in: FL
Address: 110 SE 6th St Ste 1960, Ft. Lauderdale, FL 33316
Phone: (323) 860-5200 **Dom State:** FL **Commenced Bus:** N/A

Data Date	Rating	RACR #1	RACR #2	Total Assets ($mil)	Capital ($mil)	Net Premium ($mil)	Net Income ($mil)
3-19	E+	0.61	0.51	29.6	12.0	28.4	-3.0
3-18	E	0.77	0.64	58.3	12.0	33.0	-2.5
2018	E+	0.52	0.43	39.1	9.9	138.9	-14.5
2017	E-	0.91	0.76	51.4	14.5	134.5	1.0
2016	E+	0.41	0.34	37.9	7.1	121.8	-13.9
2015	E	0.17	0.14	18.9	2.8	111.2	-11.3
2014	D-	0.49	0.41	20.1	6.2	87.9	-5.6

Rating Indexes

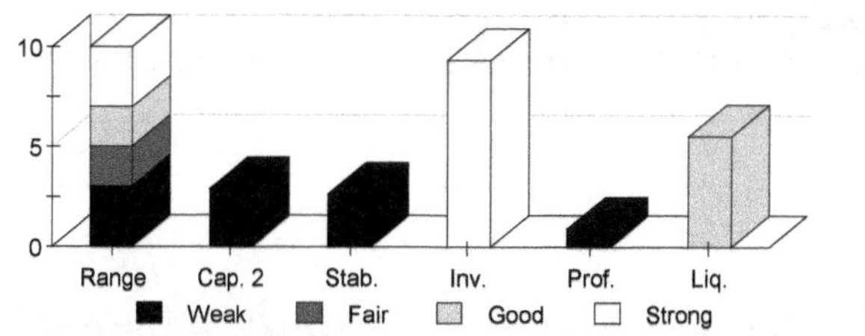

ALIGNMENT HEALTH PLAN — E Very Weak

Major Rating Factors: Weak profitability index (0.9 on a scale of 0 to 10). Poor capitalization index (0.0) based on weak current risk-adjusted capital (severe loss scenario). Weak liquidity (0.0) as a spike in claims may stretch capacity.
Other Rating Factors: Good overall results on stability tests (5.1) despite fair risk diversification due to the company's size.
Principal Business: Medicare (100%)
Mem Phys: 18: N/A **17:** N/A **18 MLR** 94.7% **/ 18 Admin Exp** N/A
Enroll(000): Q1 19: 47 **18:** 40 **17:** 35 **Med Exp PMPM:** $915
Principal Investments ($000): Cash and equiv ($20,245)
Provider Compensation ($000): None
Total Member Encounters: N/A
Group Affiliation: Alignment Healthcare USA LLC
Licensed in: CA
Address: 1100 W Town & Country Rd #1600, Orange, CA 92868
Phone: (657) 218-7731 **Dom State:** CA **Commenced Bus:** May 2004

Data Date	Rating	RACR #1	RACR #2	Total Assets ($mil)	Capital ($mil)	Net Premium ($mil)	Net Income ($mil)
3-19	E	0.02	0.01	96.9	14.7	162.4	-1.2
3-18	E	N/A	N/A	107.2	13.6	109.0	-14.7
2018	E	N/A	N/A	72.5	13.9	449.2	-61.3
2017	E	N/A	N/A	66.8	13.7	361.4	-58.2
2016	E	N/A	N/A	46.4	10.0	227.8	-24.6
2015	E	0.24	0.15	52.2	11.6	205.6	-32.2
2014	E	0.21	0.13	36.6	9.6	133.8	-18.0

Rating Indexes

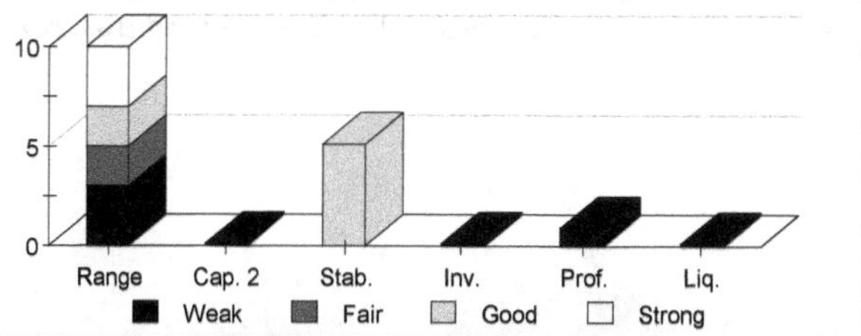

ALL SAVERS INSURANCE COMPANY — C Fair

Major Rating Factors: Weak profitability (2.8 on a scale of 0 to 10). Excellent expense controls. Weak overall results on stability tests (2.8) including excessive premium growth and weak results on operational trends. Strong overall capitalization (10.0) based on excellent risk adjusted capital (severe loss scenario). Nevertheless, capital levels have fluctuated during prior years.
Other Rating Factors: High quality investment portfolio (8.1). Excellent liquidity (7.5).
Principal Business: Group health insurance (99%) and individual health insurance (1%).
Principal Investments: NonCMO investment grade bonds (68%), CMOs and structured securities (26%), and cash (1%).
Investments in Affiliates: None
Group Affiliation: UnitedHealth Group Inc
Licensed in: All states except CA, MA, MN, NJ, NY, PR
Commenced Business: February 1986
Address: 7440 WOODLAND DRIVE, INDIANAPOLIS, IN 46278-1719
Phone: (317) 715-7056 **Domicile State:** IN **NAIC Code:** 82406

Data Date	Rating	RACR #1	RACR #2	Total Assets ($mil)	Capital ($mil)	Net Premium ($mil)	Net Income ($mil)
3-19	C	6.76	5.13	632.7	452.0	164.9	23.7
3-18	C	10.66	7.60	1,140.7	751.9	114.6	6.2
2018	C	9.17	6.84	733.4	579.7	493.8	57.6
2017	C	13.51	9.47	1,143.2	997.3	497.7	187.6
2016	C	5.31	3.99	1,551.5	1,054.2	1,603.1	-102.2
2015	C	5.60	4.41	1,067.5	600.8	891.4	-339.5
2014	B-	1.51	1.25	61.6	31.1	111.9	5.0

Net Income History
(in millions of dollars)

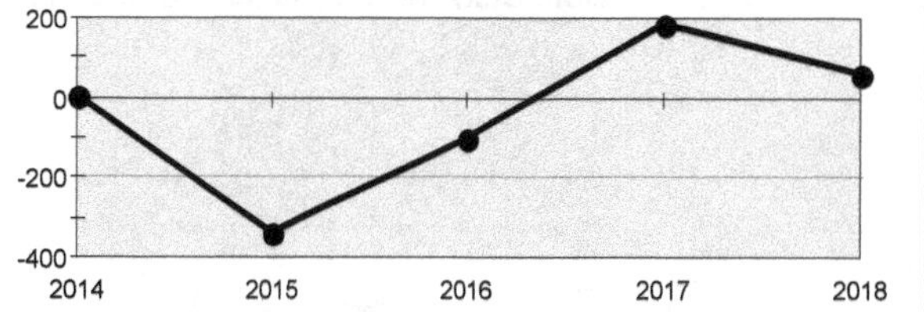

ALLCARE HEALTH PLAN INC — E — Very Weak

Major Rating Factors: Weak profitability index (1.1 on a scale of 0 to 10). Good capitalization (5.2) based on good current risk-adjusted capital (severe loss scenario). Good liquidity (6.5) with sufficient resources (cash flows and marketable investments) to handle a spike in claims.
Other Rating Factors: High quality investment portfolio (9.9).
Principal Business: Medicare (100%)
Mem Phys: 18: 1,679 **17:** 1,373 **18 MLR** 95.7% **/ 18 Admin Exp** N/A
Enroll(000): Q1 19: 3 **18:** 3 **17:** 4 **Med Exp PMPM:** $945
Principal Investments: Cash and equiv (53%), long-term bonds (47%)
Provider Compensation ($000): Contr fee ($27,883), FFS ($2,805), bonus arrang ($109)
Total Member Encounters: Phys (58,234), non-phys (22,453)
Group Affiliation: AllCare Health Inc
Licensed in: OR
Address: 740 SE 7th St, Grants Pass, OR 97526
Phone: (888) 460-0185 **Dom State:** OR **Commenced Bus:** N/A

Data Date	Rating	RACR #1	RACR #2	Total Assets ($mil)	Capital ($mil)	Net Premium ($mil)	Net Income ($mil)
3-19	E	0.96	0.80	12.2	7.2	11.1	0.5
3-18	E	0.84	0.70	14.2	6.1	7.2	-0.7
2018	E	0.77	0.64	11.2	5.6	33.1	-1.1
2017	E	0.99	0.82	12.7	6.9	35.8	0.4
2016	E	0.87	0.73	11.3	6.4	33.5	-0.8
2015	E	1.18	0.98	10.9	7.1	31.4	0.0
2014	E	0.67	0.56	11.8	6.5	41.2	-2.6

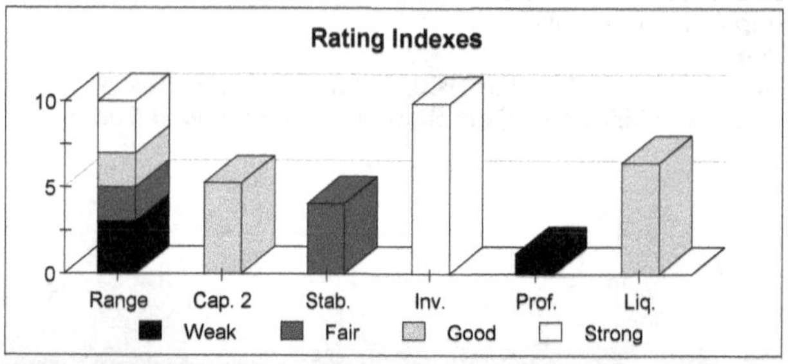

ALLEGIAN INS CO — C- — Fair

Major Rating Factors: Fair profitability index (4.2 on a scale of 0 to 10). Strong capitalization (8.5) based on excellent current risk-adjusted capital (severe loss scenario). High quality investment portfolio (9.9).
Other Rating Factors: Excellent liquidity (10.0) with ample operational cash flow and liquid investments.
Principal Business: Medicare (99%), comp med (1%)
Mem Phys: 18: N/A **17:** 5,397 **18 MLR** -989.4% **/ 18 Admin Exp** N/A
Enroll(000): Q1 19: N/A **18:** N/A **17:** N/A **Med Exp PMPM:** N/A
Principal Investments: Cash and equiv (98%), long-term bonds (2%)
Provider Compensation ($000): Contr fee ($338)
Total Member Encounters: N/A
Group Affiliation: Tenet Healthcare Corporation
Licensed in: TX
Address: 4801 NW Loop #410 Ste 380, Phoenix, AZ 85020
Phone: (602) 824-3700 **Dom State:** TX **Commenced Bus:** N/A

Data Date	Rating	RACR #1	RACR #2	Total Assets ($mil)	Capital ($mil)	Net Premium ($mil)	Net Income ($mil)
3-19	C-	2.58	2.15	5.8	5.5	N/A	0.5
3-18	D+	2.33	1.94	14.9	11.3	0.2	0.4
2018	C-	2.39	1.99	6.6	5.0	0.3	2.9
2017	D+	2.11	1.76	19.9	10.5	24.9	2.8
2016	D+	1.63	1.36	34.4	16.1	89.3	-3.9
2015	D+	3.40	2.83	29.7	20.4	55.5	2.0
2014	D+	2.72	2.27	26.1	18.3	57.0	1.4

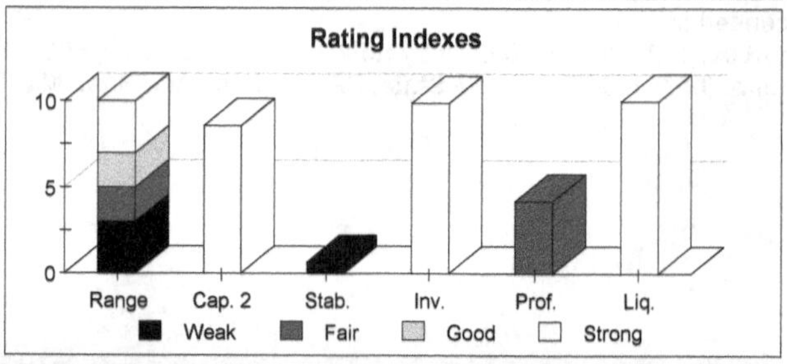

ALLEGIANCE L&H INS CO — C+ — Fair

Major Rating Factors: Excellent profitability (8.9 on a scale of 0 to 10). Strong capitalization (10.0) based on excellent current risk-adjusted capital (severe loss scenario). High quality investment portfolio (9.6).
Other Rating Factors: Excellent liquidity (7.5) with ample operational cash flow and liquid investments.
Principal Business: Comp med (96%), dental (3%)
Mem Phys: 18: N/A **17:** N/A **18 MLR** 79.3% **/ 18 Admin Exp** N/A
Enroll(000): Q1 19: 3 **18:** 3 **17:** 3 **Med Exp PMPM:** $324
Principal Investments: Long-term bonds (53%), cash and equiv (47%)
Provider Compensation ($000): FFS ($11,831)
Total Member Encounters: Phys (12,732), non-phys (39,930)
Group Affiliation: Cigna Corporation
Licensed in: MT
Address: 2806 S GARFIELD St, MISSOULA, MT 59801
Phone: (406) 721-2222 **Dom State:** MT **Commenced Bus:** N/A

Data Date	Rating	RACR #1	RACR #2	Total Assets ($mil)	Capital ($mil)	Net Premium ($mil)	Net Income ($mil)
3-19	C+	9.54	7.95	16.9	14.1	3.6	0.8
3-18	C+	9.51	7.93	15.3	12.6	3.7	0.4
2018	C+	9.02	7.52	16.7	13.3	14.4	1.1
2017	C	5.19	4.32	14.6	12.2	13.3	0.8
2016	C	10.64	8.87	13.7	11.4	13.6	1.9
2015	C	4.13	3.44	12.5	9.5	22.9	1.3
2014	C	2.64	2.20	15.2	8.7	36.8	0.2

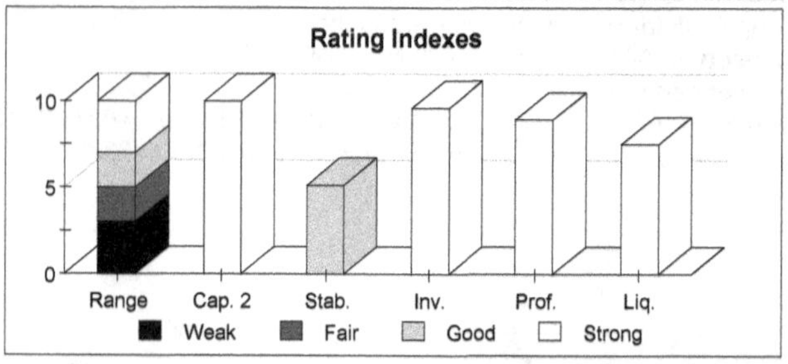

ALLIANCE HEALTH & LIFE INS CO — C — Fair

Major Rating Factors: Weak profitability index (1.9 on a scale of 0 to 10). Low quality investment portfolio (1.3). Strong capitalization (7.8) based on excellent current risk-adjusted capital (severe loss scenario).
Other Rating Factors: Excellent liquidity (7.2) with ample operational cash flow and liquid investments.
Principal Business: Comp med (69%), Medicare (14%), med supp (1%), other (15%)
Mem Phys: 18: 12,553 **17:** 12,296 **18 MLR** 65.8% **/ 18 Admin Exp** N/A
Enroll(000): Q1 19: 54 **18:** 53 **17:** 60 **Med Exp PMPM:** $355
Principal Investments: Cash and equiv (87%), long-term bonds (12%), nonaffiliate common stock (1%)
Provider Compensation ($000): Contr fee ($233,940), FFS ($3,935)
Total Member Encounters: Phys (298,235), non-phys (266,830)
Group Affiliation: Henry Ford Health System
Licensed in: MI
Address: 2850 West Grand Blvd, Detroit, MI 48202
Phone: (313) 872-8100 **Dom State:** MI **Commenced Bus:** N/A

Data Date	Rating	RACR #1	RACR #2	Total Assets ($mil)	Capital ($mil)	Net Premium ($mil)	Net Income ($mil)
3-19	C	1.98	1.65	143.1	54.7	81.1	0.9
3-18	C	1.31	1.09	143.7	40.3	85.4	-1.9
2018	C	1.94	1.62	134.0	53.8	347.5	12.1
2017	C	1.10	0.92	135.1	42.2	367.8	-10.0
2016	C	1.19	0.99	111.2	36.2	399.0	-17.0
2015	C+	1.26	1.05	86.0	24.4	293.2	-2.1
2014	B	1.60	1.33	70.1	26.0	235.6	-2.0

Rating Indexes

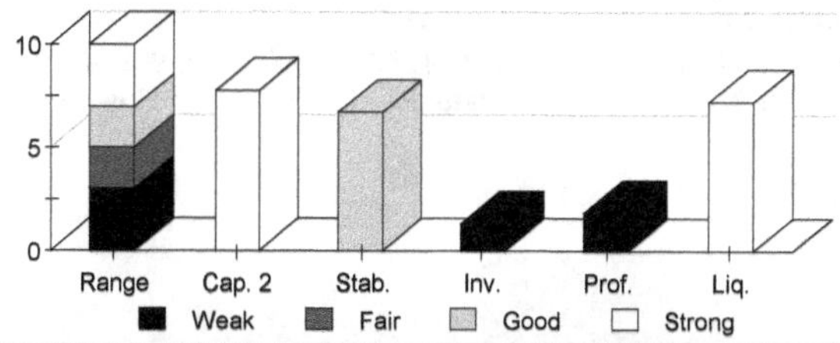

ALLIANT HEALTH PLANS INC — D- — Weak

Major Rating Factors: Good overall profitability index (6.8 on a scale of 0 to 10). Good overall results on stability tests (5.5). Strong capitalization index (7.8) based on excellent current risk-adjusted capital (severe loss scenario).
Other Rating Factors: High quality investment portfolio (9.9). Excellent liquidity (7.3) with ample operational cash flow and liquid investments.
Principal Business: Comp med (100%)
Mem Phys: 18: 16,307 **17:** 14,611 **18 MLR** 73.2% **/ 18 Admin Exp** N/A
Enroll(000): Q1 19: 38 **18:** 49 **17:** 34 **Med Exp PMPM:** $580
Principal Investments: Cash and equiv (100%)
Provider Compensation ($000): Contr fee ($311,861), capitation ($1,389)
Total Member Encounters: Phys (108,644), non-phys (22,585)
Group Affiliation: Health One Alliance LLC
Licensed in: GA
Address: 1503 N Tibbs Road, Dalton, GA 30720
Phone: (706) 629-8848 **Dom State:** GA **Commenced Bus:** N/A

Data Date	Rating	RACR #1	RACR #2	Total Assets ($mil)	Capital ($mil)	Net Premium ($mil)	Net Income ($mil)
3-19	D-	2.00	1.66	157.0	75.6	73.6	5.6
3-18	D-	1.00	0.83	108.2	25.3	115.2	10.2
2018	D-	1.86	1.55	156.1	71.1	481.8	55.7
2017	D-	0.61	0.51	54.2	15.2	253.2	3.6
2016	D-	1.08	0.90	33.4	12.8	114.3	-6.2
2015	C	1.19	0.99	36.0	15.2	129.8	-1.7
2014	C	1.25	1.04	35.1	16.9	118.8	-0.4

Rating Indexes

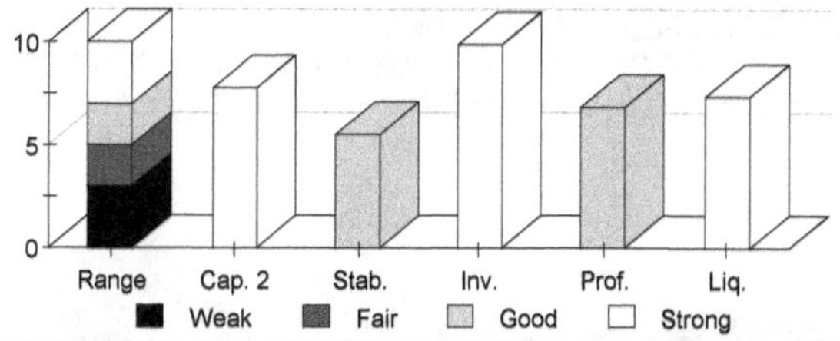

ALLINA HLTH & AETNA INS CO — C — Fair

Major Rating Factors: Weak profitability index (0.9 on a scale of 0 to 10). Good liquidity (6.2) with sufficient resources (cash flows and marketable investments) to handle a spike in claims. Strong capitalization (8.5) based on excellent current risk-adjusted capital (severe loss scenario).
Other Rating Factors: High quality investment portfolio (9.9).
Principal Business: Comp med (100%)
Mem Phys: 18: N/A **17:** N/A **18 MLR** 30.0% **/ 18 Admin Exp** N/A
Enroll(000): Q1 19: 12 **18:** 0 **17:** N/A **Med Exp PMPM:** $142
Principal Investments: Cash and equiv (90%), long-term bonds (10%)
Provider Compensation ($000): Contr fee ($58)
Total Member Encounters: Phys (443), non-phys (248)
Group Affiliation: Allina Health Aetna Insurance Holdin
Licensed in: MN
Address: , ST. LOUIS PARK, MN 55416-5380
Phone: (800) 872-3862 **Dom State:** MN **Commenced Bus:** N/A

Data Date	Rating	RACR #1	RACR #2	Total Assets ($mil)	Capital ($mil)	Net Premium ($mil)	Net Income ($mil)
3-19	C	2.57	2.14	15.1	4.6	16.8	-5.5
3-18	N/A	N/A	N/A	2.6	2.0	N/A	-0.7
2018	C	2.60	2.17	5.5	4.7	0.2	-9.8
2017	N/A	N/A	N/A	4.6	2.7	N/A	-1.8
2016	N/A	N/A	N/A	N/A	N/A	N/A	N/A
2015	N/A	N/A	N/A	N/A	N/A	N/A	N/A
2014	N/A	N/A	N/A	N/A	N/A	N/A	N/A

Rating Indexes

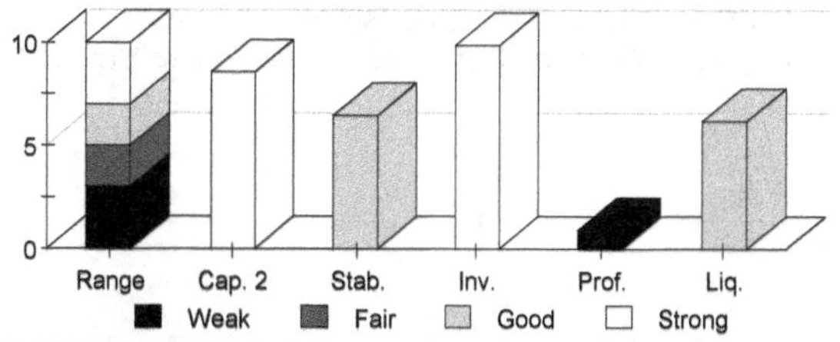

ALOHACARE B- Good

Major Rating Factors: Fair profitability index (4.2 on a scale of 0 to 10). Good overall results on stability tests (5.8). Strong capitalization index (8.8) based on excellent current risk-adjusted capital (severe loss scenario).
Other Rating Factors: High quality investment portfolio (9.9). Excellent liquidity (7.3) with ample operational cash flow and liquid investments.
Principal Business: Medicaid (93%), Medicare (7%)
Mem Phys: 18: 6,747 **17:** 6,780 **18 MLR** 88.8% **/ 18 Admin Exp** N/A
Enroll(000): Q1 19: 65 **18:** 66 **17:** 71 **Med Exp PMPM:** $404
Principal Investments: Cash and equiv (78%), long-term bonds (21%), nonaffiliate common stock (1%)
Provider Compensation ($000): Contr fee ($245,540), FFS ($83,627), capitation ($4,445)
Total Member Encounters: Phys (402,252), non-phys (262,258)
Group Affiliation: None
Licensed in: HI
Address: 1357 Kapiolani Blvd Suite 1250, Honolulu, HI 96814
Phone: (808) 973-1650 **Dom State:** HI **Commenced Bus:** N/A

Data Date	Rating	RACR #1	RACR #2	Total Assets ($mil)	Capital ($mil)	Net Premium ($mil)	Net Income ($mil)
3-19	B-	2.80	2.33	157.0	88.8	91.8	0.2
3-18	C+	2.69	2.25	174.0	88.6	92.6	2.4
2018	B-	2.78	2.32	163.1	88.3	372.3	2.4
2017	C+	2.38	1.98	174.5	86.3	377.0	12.4
2016	C+	2.27	1.89	141.4	67.2	317.3	15.6
2015	N/A	N/A	N/A	113.8	51.6	271.0	-19.2
2014	B	3.00	2.50	114.8	70.8	237.6	-5.3

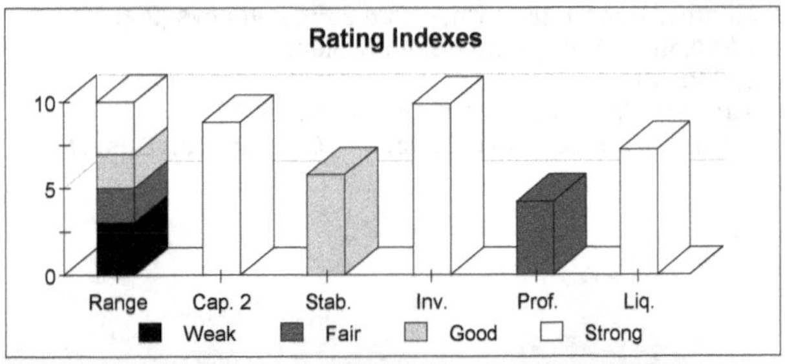

AMALGAMATED LIFE INSURANCE COMPANY * A Excellent

Major Rating Factors: Good liquidity (6.4 on a scale of 0 to 10) with sufficient resources to handle a spike in claims. Strong capitalization (10.0) based on excellent risk adjusted capital (severe loss scenario). Furthermore, this high level of risk adjusted capital has been consistently maintained over the last five years. High quality investment portfolio (8.2).
Other Rating Factors: Excellent profitability (8.4). Excellent overall results on stability tests (7.1) excellent operational trends and excellent risk diversification.
Principal Business: Group life insurance (35%), group health insurance (33%), reinsurance (29%), and individual health insurance (3%).
Principal Investments: NonCMO investment grade bonds (58%) and CMOs and structured securities (29%).
Investments in Affiliates: None
Group Affiliation: National Retirement Fund
Licensed in: All states except PR
Commenced Business: February 1944
Address: 333 WESTCHESTER AVENUE, WHITE PLAINS, NY 10604
Phone: (914) 367-5000 **Domicile State:** NY **NAIC Code:** 60216

Data Date	Rating	RACR #1	RACR #2	Total Assets ($mil)	Capital ($mil)	Net Premium ($mil)	Net Income ($mil)
3-19	A	4.07	3.10	148.4	66.9	24.7	1.2
3-18	A	4.34	3.31	132.3	63.3	23.7	2.0
2018	A	3.96	3.00	146.5	66.8	96.5	4.9
2017	A	4.24	3.24	127.5	61.7	82.7	5.5
2016	A-	4.85	3.74	122.9	57.8	80.7	3.5
2015	A-	4.12	3.27	119.9	55.6	75.6	3.0
2014	A-	3.82	3.03	111.8	51.0	72.4	3.5

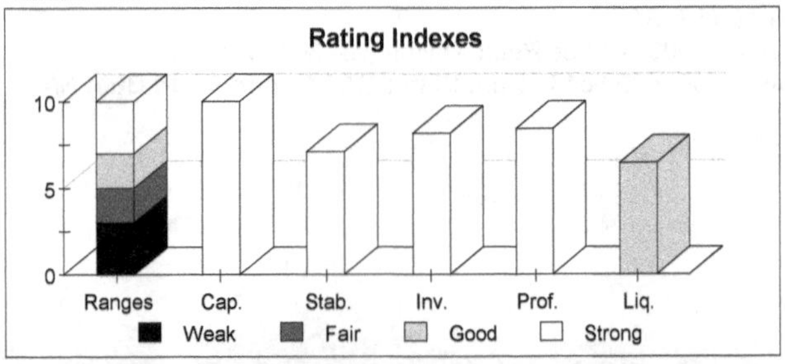

AMBETTER OF MAGNOLIA INC B- Good

Major Rating Factors: Good quality investment portfolio (6.2 on a scale of 0 to 10). Excellent profitability (9.5). Strong capitalization (10.0) based on excellent current risk-adjusted capital (severe loss scenario).
Other Rating Factors: Excellent liquidity (7.2) with ample operational cash flow and liquid investments.
Principal Business: Comp med (100%)
Mem Phys: 18: 14,510 **17:** 11,245 **18 MLR** 66.5% **/ 18 Admin Exp** N/A
Enroll(000): Q1 19: 80 **18:** 59 **17:** 48 **Med Exp PMPM:** $418
Principal Investments: Cash and equiv (67%), long-term bonds (33%)
Provider Compensation ($000): Contr fee ($299,997), bonus arrang ($17,490), capitation ($934), salary ($834)
Total Member Encounters: Phys (371,457), non-phys (464,635)
Group Affiliation: None
Licensed in: MS
Address: 111 East Capitol St Ste 500, Jackson, MS 39201
Phone: (314) 725-4477 **Dom State:** MS **Commenced Bus:** N/A

Data Date	Rating	RACR #1	RACR #2	Total Assets ($mil)	Capital ($mil)	Net Premium ($mil)	Net Income ($mil)
3-19	B-	5.89	4.91	177.3	71.3	142.5	13.4
3-18	C+	N/A	N/A	113.2	36.8	133.9	17.4
2018	B-	4.87	4.06	136.9	58.8	493.8	40.3
2017	C+	N/A	N/A	62.1	17.6	298.4	9.2
2016	C-	1.35	1.12	49.7	8.4	126.1	0.1
2015	U	8.82	7.35	40.3	4.3	35.7	0.9
2014	N/A	N/A	N/A	N/A	N/A	N/A	N/A

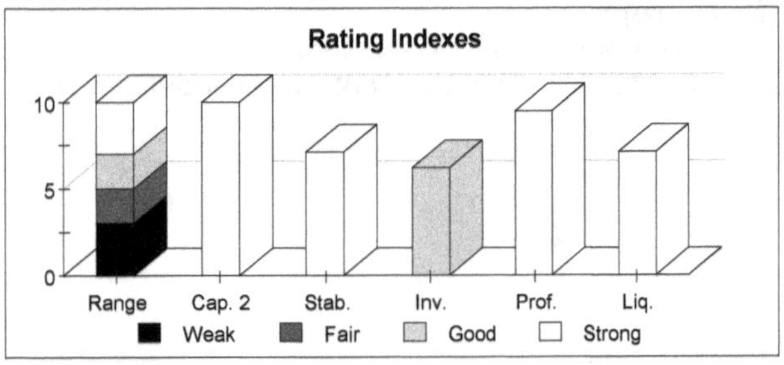

AMBETTER OF PEACH STATE INC B- Good

Major Rating Factors: Excellent profitability (9.4 on a scale of 0 to 10). Strong capitalization (10.0) based on excellent current risk-adjusted capital (severe loss scenario). High quality investment portfolio (7.7).
Other Rating Factors: Excellent liquidity (7.0) with sufficient resources (cash flows and marketable investments) to handle a spike in claims.
Principal Business: Comp med (100%)
Mem Phys: 18: 19,961 **17:** 16,291 **18 MLR** 70.9% **/ 18 Admin Exp** N/A
Enroll(000): Q1 19: 238 **18:** 170 **17:** 116 **Med Exp PMPM:** $353
Principal Investments: Long-term bonds (50%), cash and equiv (50%)
Provider Compensation ($000): Contr fee ($650,989), bonus arrang ($120,991), capitation ($3,483), salary ($1,622)
Total Member Encounters: Phys (1,015,187), non-phys (828,056)
Group Affiliation: None
Licensed in: GA
Address: 1100 Circle 75 Pkwy Ste 1100, Atlanta, GA 30339
Phone: (314) 725-4477 **Dom State:** GA **Commenced Bus:** N/A

Data Date	Rating	RACR #1	RACR #2	Total Assets ($mil)	Capital ($mil)	Net Premium ($mil)	Net Income ($mil)
3-19	B-	4.24	3.53	421.1	161.2	383.2	43.2
3-18	C+	N/A	N/A	329.2	65.4	287.1	28.6
2018	B-	3.07	2.56	328.7	116.7	1,136.9	84.6
2017	C+	N/A	N/A	198.8	33.4	489.4	17.7
2016	C-	2.91	2.42	165.8	17.9	197.2	13.6
2015	N/A	N/A	N/A	6.3	3.0	N/A	-0.2
2014	N/A	N/A	N/A	N/A	N/A	N/A	N/A

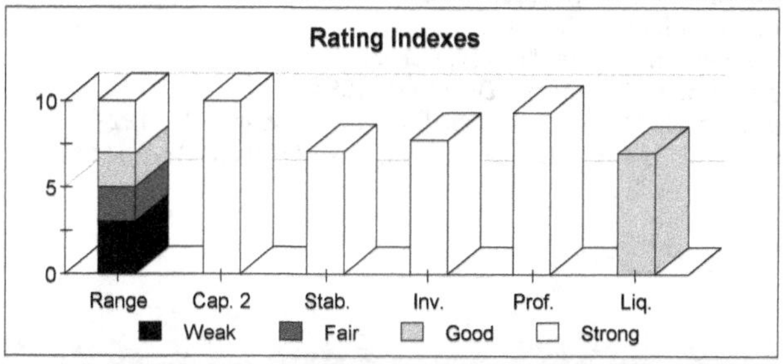

AMERICAN BANKERS LIFE ASSURANCE COMPANY OF FLORID. C+ Fair

Major Rating Factors: Fair overall results on stability tests (4.3 on a scale of 0 to 10) including excessive premium growth. Good quality investment portfolio (6.5) despite mixed results such as: minimal exposure to mortgages and substantial holdings of BBB bonds but minimal holdings in junk bonds. Strong capitalization (9.6) based on excellent risk adjusted capital (severe loss scenario).
Other Rating Factors: Excellent profitability (7.1). Excellent liquidity (8.0).
Principal Business: Credit life insurance (42%), credit health insurance (38%), reinsurance (14%), group health insurance (4%), and individual life insurance (2%).
Principal Investments: NonCMO investment grade bonds (54%), real estate (15%), cash (12%), CMOs and structured securities (8%), and misc. investments (6%).
Investments in Affiliates: None
Group Affiliation: Assurant Inc
Licensed in: All states except NY
Commenced Business: April 1952
Address: 11222 QUAIL ROOST DRIVE, MIAMI, FL 33157-6596
Phone: (305) 253-2244 **Domicile State:** FL **NAIC Code:** 60275

Data Date	Rating	RACR #1	RACR #2	Total Assets ($mil)	Capital ($mil)	Net Premium ($mil)	Net Income ($mil)
3-19	C+	4.78	2.74	328.9	51.9	26.3	5.4
3-18	C+	5.48	3.02	348.2	51.8	20.2	4.9
2018	C+	4.75	2.72	338.4	47.9	95.1	23.0
2017	C+	5.57	3.05	364.0	53.0	79.1	23.8
2016	C+	7.11	3.50	378.7	54.7	35.7	21.5
2015	C+	7.24	3.58	406.2	56.7	30.6	21.2
2014	B	5.37	2.87	489.6	55.9	67.9	18.6

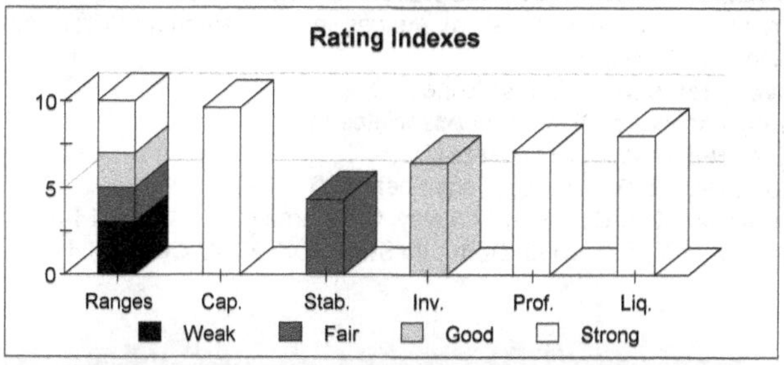

AMERICAN CONTINENTAL INSURANCE COMPANY C Fair

Major Rating Factors: Fair overall results on stability tests (4.2 on a scale of 0 to 10). Strong capitalization (6.0) based on excellent risk adjusted capital (severe loss scenario). Capital levels have been relatively consistent over the last five years. Good liquidity (5.6) with sufficient resources to handle a spike in claims.
Other Rating Factors: Weak profitability (1.9) with operating losses during the first three months of 2019. High quality investment portfolio (7.7).
Principal Business: Individual health insurance (91%) and individual life insurance (9%).
Principal Investments: NonCMO investment grade bonds (68%), CMOs and structured securities (35%), mortgages in good standing (2%), policy loans (1%), and noninv. grade bonds (1%).
Investments in Affiliates: None
Group Affiliation: Aetna Inc
Licensed in: AL, AZ, AR, CO, FL, GA, IL, IN, IA, KS, KY, LA, MI, MN, MS, MO, MT, NE, NV, NM, NC, ND, OH, OK, PA, SC, SD, TN, TX, UT, VA, WV, WI, WY
Commenced Business: September 2005
Address: 800 CRESENT CENTRE DR STE 200, FRANKLIN, TN 37067
Phone: (800) 264-4000 **Domicile State:** TN **NAIC Code:** 12321

Data Date	Rating	RACR #1	RACR #2	Total Assets ($mil)	Capital ($mil)	Net Premium ($mil)	Net Income ($mil)
3-19	C	1.74	1.30	306.9	110.5	124.1	-7.7
3-18	B-	1.68	1.26	270.7	106.4	127.2	-9.6
2018	C	1.86	1.39	285.8	118.3	499.4	-5.1
2017	B-	1.82	1.37	276.9	115.2	506.3	-15.0
2016	B-	1.60	1.21	229.0	94.0	472.9	-17.7
2015	B-	1.49	1.14	203.1	79.7	430.1	-15.3
2014	B	1.82	1.40	177.2	86.4	378.7	-12.7

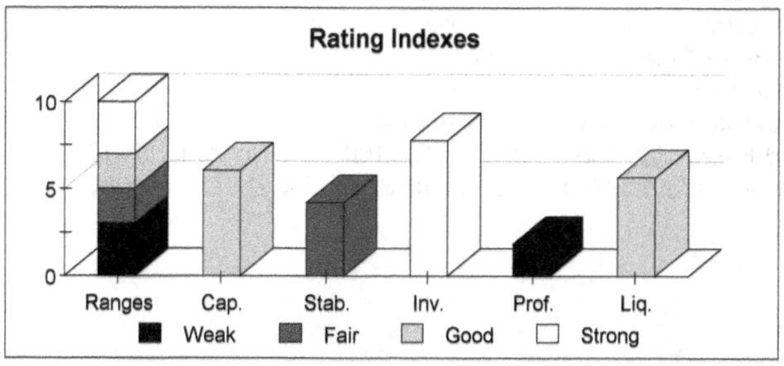

AMERICAN FAMILY LIFE ASSUR COMPANY OF NEW YORK * A- Excellent

Major Rating Factors: Excellent overall results on stability tests (7.3 on a scale of 0 to 10). Strengths that enhance stability include excellent operational trends and excellent risk diversification. Strong capitalization (10.0) based on excellent risk adjusted capital (severe loss scenario). Furthermore, this high level of risk adjusted capital has been consistently maintained over the last five years. High quality investment portfolio (7.9).
Other Rating Factors: Excellent profitability (8.7). Excellent liquidity (8.0).
Principal Business: Individual health insurance (94%), individual life insurance (4%), and group health insurance (2%).
Principal Investments: NonCMO investment grade bonds (89%), noninv. grade bonds (2%), and CMOs and structured securities (1%).
Investments in Affiliates: None
Group Affiliation: AFLAC Inc
Licensed in: CT, MA, NJ, NY, ND, VT
Commenced Business: December 1964
Address: 22 Corporate Woods Blvd Ste 2, Albany, NY 12211
Phone: (518) 438-0764 **Domicile State:** NY **NAIC Code:** 60526

Data Date	Rating	RACR #1	RACR #2	Total Assets ($mil)	Capital ($mil)	Net Premium ($mil)	Net Income ($mil)
3-19	A-	6.09	4.11	978.2	334.3	85.5	24.0
3-18	A-	5.93	3.95	956.9	319.1	83.5	18.4
2018	A-	5.55	3.65	965.2	310.1	335.4	66.6
2017	A-	5.60	3.74	915.6	300.6	326.8	58.9
2016	A-	5.91	3.97	870.1	304.3	315.9	51.6
2015	A-	6.11	4.20	817.9	298.5	304.2	47.4
2014	A-	5.39	3.76	735.9	250.1	293.5	26.8

Adverse Trends in Operations

Decrease in capital during 2017 (1%)
Increase in policy surrenders from 2014 to 2015 (30%)

AMERICAN FIDELITY ASSURANCE COMPANY * B+ Good

Major Rating Factors: Good quality investment portfolio (6.2 on a scale of 0 to 10) despite mixed results such as: minimal exposure to mortgages and large holdings of BBB rated bonds but small junk bond holdings. Good liquidity (6.4) with sufficient resources to cover a large increase in policy surrenders. Good overall results on stability tests (6.8) excellent operational trends and excellent risk diversification.
Other Rating Factors: Strong capitalization (7.3) based on excellent risk adjusted capital (severe loss scenario). Excellent profitability (8.5).
Principal Business: Group health insurance (40%), individual health insurance (25%), individual annuities (17%), individual life insurance (13%), and other lines (5%).
Principal Investments: NonCMO investment grade bonds (63%), CMOs and structured securities (17%), mortgages in good standing (10%), cash (7%), and misc. investments (4%).
Investments in Affiliates: None
Group Affiliation: Cameron Associates Inc
Licensed in: All states except NY
Commenced Business: December 1960
Address: 9000 Cameron Parkway, Oklahoma City, OK 73114-3701
Phone: (405) 523-2000 **Domicile State:** OK **NAIC Code:** 60410

Data Date	Rating	RACR #1	RACR #2	Total Assets ($mil)	Capital ($mil)	Net Premium ($mil)	Net Income ($mil)
3-19	B+	2.09	1.20	6,256.2	526.5	307.5	28.1
3-18	B+	1.86	1.08	5,974.7	459.4	272.1	27.8
2018	B+	2.05	1.17	6,101.2	505.2	1,091.7	98.9
2017	B+	1.78	1.04	5,896.7	430.6	957.4	66.2
2016	B+	1.88	1.07	5,446.8	414.6	906.6	76.4
2015	B+	1.97	1.13	5,181.1	408.5	957.9	75.4
2014	B+	1.93	1.11	4,959.0	380.4	822.5	69.3

Adverse Trends in Operations

Decrease in premium volume from 2015 to 2016 (5%)

AMERICAN HEALTH & LIFE INSURANCE COMPANY * A- Excellent

Major Rating Factors: Good overall results on stability tests (6.9 on a scale of 0 to 10). Strengths that enhance stability include excellent operational trends and excellent risk diversification. Good quality investment portfolio (6.3) despite mixed results such as: minimal exposure to mortgages and large holdings of BBB rated bonds but small junk bond holdings. Good overall profitability (6.9).
Other Rating Factors: Strong capitalization (7.8) based on excellent risk adjusted capital (severe loss scenario). Excellent liquidity (9.0).
Principal Business: Credit health insurance (40%), credit life insurance (38%), individual life insurance (9%), reinsurance (8%), and other lines (5%).
Principal Investments: NonCMO investment grade bonds (73%), CMOs and structured securities (21%), noninv. grade bonds (3%), and common & preferred stock (1%).
Investments in Affiliates: None
Group Affiliation: Citigroup Inc
Licensed in: All states except NY, PR
Commenced Business: June 1954
Address: 3001 Meacham Blvd Ste 100, Fort Worth, TX 76137
Phone: (800) 307-0048 **Domicile State:** TX **NAIC Code:** 60518

Data Date	Rating	RACR #1	RACR #2	Total Assets ($mil)	Capital ($mil)	Net Premium ($mil)	Net Income ($mil)
3-19	A-	2.38	1.51	1,083.3	148.4	84.1	17.3
3-18	A-	2.71	1.71	924.7	136.2	81.3	5.0
2018	A-	2.00	1.28	1,038.1	128.5	377.6	32.1
2017	A-	2.70	1.70	883.2	130.3	251.1	34.5
2016	A-	5.40	3.11	924.2	215.1	154.3	71.2
2015	A-	4.03	2.40	923.9	183.5	199.8	55.5
2014	B	2.88	1.96	912.8	188.6	209.9	70.0

Adverse Trends in Operations

Increase in policy surrenders from 2017 to 2018 (1066%)
Decrease in capital during 2017 (39%)
Increase in policy surrenders from 2016 to 2017 (36%)
Decrease in premium volume from 2015 to 2016 (23%)
Increase in policy surrenders from 2014 to 2015 (126%)

AMERICAN HERITAGE LIFE INSURANCE COMPANY B Good

Major Rating Factors: Good capitalization (6.6 on a scale of 0 to 10) based on good risk adjusted capital (severe loss scenario). Good quality investment portfolio (5.4) despite mixed results such as: large holdings of BBB rated bonds but moderate junk bond exposure. Good overall profitability (5.7) although investment income, in comparison to reserve requirements, is below regulatory standards.

Other Rating Factors: Good liquidity (6.4). Good overall results on stability tests (5.9) excellent operational trends and excellent risk diversification.

Principal Business: Group health insurance (65%), individual health insurance (19%), individual life insurance (8%), group life insurance (7%), and reinsurance (1%).

Principal Investments: NonCMO investment grade bonds (52%), policy loans (16%), common & preferred stock (10%), mortgages in good standing (10%), and misc. investments (12%).

Investments in Affiliates: 7%

Group Affiliation: Allstate Group

Licensed in: All states except NY

Commenced Business: December 1956

Address: 1776 AMERICAN HERITAGE LIFE DR, JACKSONVILLE, FL 32224-6688

Phone: (904) 992-1776 **Domicile State:** FL **NAIC Code:** 60534

Data Date	Rating	RACR #1	RACR #2	Total Assets ($mil)	Capital ($mil)	Net Premium ($mil)	Net Income ($mil)
3-19	B	1.24	0.95	2,056.9	339.0	233.5	6.5
3-18	B	1.09	0.83	1,977.8	313.5	238.6	5.8
2018	B	1.18	0.91	2,003.1	323.9	952.5	101.8
2017	B	1.08	0.82	1,922.0	306.0	905.3	55.3
2016	B	1.22	0.97	1,885.6	344.3	861.4	63.1
2015	B	1.19	0.96	1,830.9	329.7	785.9	56.3
2014	B	1.27	1.02	1,799.7	353.3	744.8	123.3

Risk-Adjusted Capital Ratio #2 (Severe Loss Scenario)

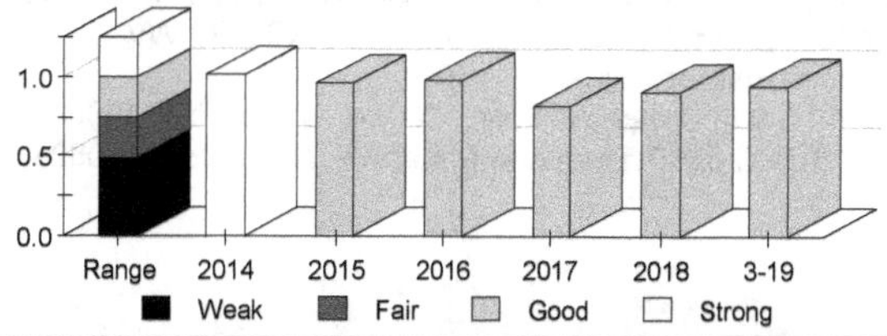

AMERICAN LIFE INSURANCE COMPANY C Fair

Major Rating Factors: Fair quality investment portfolio (3.0 on a scale of 0 to 10). Fair overall results on stability tests (3.4). Good overall profitability (6.1) despite operating losses during the first three months of 2019.

Other Rating Factors: Strong capitalization (7.0) based on excellent risk adjusted capital (severe loss scenario). Excellent liquidity (9.1).

Principal Business: Individual life insurance (49%), reinsurance (23%), group health insurance (18%), individual health insurance (6%), and other lines (5%).

Principal Investments: Common & preferred stock (56%), noninv. grade bonds (17%), nonCMO investment grade bonds (13%), cash (9%), and misc. investments (5%).

Investments in Affiliates: 58%

Group Affiliation: MetLife Inc

Licensed in: DE

Commenced Business: August 1921

Address: 1209 Orange Street, Wilmington, DE 19801

Phone: (302) 594-2000 **Domicile State:** DE **NAIC Code:** 60690

Data Date	Rating	RACR #1	RACR #2	Total Assets ($mil)	Capital ($mil)	Net Premium ($mil)	Net Income ($mil)
3-19	C	1.05	1.00	11,181.3	4,836.4	320.1	-98.8
3-18	C	1.31	1.23	13,053.3	6,609.8	397.9	-155.8
2018	C	1.03	0.99	10,807.1	4,920.6	1,441.1	2,085.5
2017	C	1.21	1.17	11,986.6	6,547.6	1,389.6	3,076.8
2016	C	1.03	0.99	10,377.8	5,235.3	1,373.6	341.5
2015	C	1.02	0.99	11,097.5	6,115.1	1,204.5	334.6
2014	C	0.93	0.89	8,215.9	3,358.5	1,409.1	-36.1

Rating Indexes

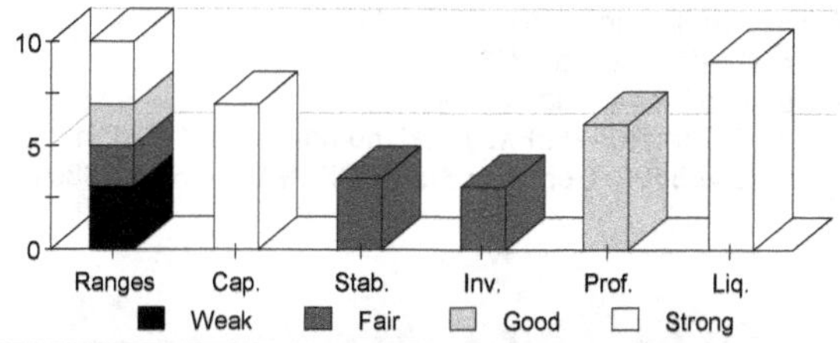

AMERICAN NATIONAL LIFE INSURANCE COMPANY OF TEXAS B- Good

Major Rating Factors: Good liquidity (6.2 on a scale of 0 to 10) with sufficient resources to handle a spike in claims. Good overall results on stability tests (5.0) despite excessive premium growth. Strengths include good financial support from affiliation with American National Group Inc, excellent operational trends and excellent risk diversification. Weak profitability (2.3).

Other Rating Factors: Strong capitalization (9.0) based on excellent risk adjusted capital (severe loss scenario). High quality investment portfolio (7.1).

Principal Business: Reinsurance (42%), group health insurance (40%), individual health insurance (15%), and individual life insurance (3%).

Principal Investments: NonCMO investment grade bonds (93%), noninv. grade bonds (3%), and policy loans (3%).

Investments in Affiliates: None

Group Affiliation: American National Group Inc

Licensed in: All states except ME, NJ, NY, VT, PR

Commenced Business: December 1954

Address: ONE MOODY PLAZA, GALVESTON, TX 77550

Phone: (409) 763-4661 **Domicile State:** TX **NAIC Code:** 71773

Data Date	Rating	RACR #1	RACR #2	Total Assets ($mil)	Capital ($mil)	Net Premium ($mil)	Net Income ($mil)
3-19	B-	3.48	2.32	127.1	32.9	11.6	0.1
3-18	B-	3.84	2.98	124.5	34.1	9.1	-0.2
2018	B-	3.59	2.39	127.7	33.0	39.2	-1.5
2017	B-	3.85	2.99	123.7	34.2	28.8	-0.5
2016	B-	3.95	3.48	122.5	35.2	26.8	-0.8
2015	B-	4.01	3.16	127.5	35.9	35.5	-5.3
2014	B-	4.06	3.10	136.3	36.8	38.4	0.6

American National Group Inc
Composite Group Rating: B

Largest Group Members	Assets ($mil)	Rating
AMERICAN NATIONAL INS CO	20468	B
FARM FAMILY LIFE INS CO	2367	B-
AMERICAN NATIONAL PROPERTY CAS CO	1464	B
FARM FAMILY CASUALTY INS CO	1304	B
STANDARD LIFE ACCIDENT INS CO	517	A-

AMERICAN PROGRESSIVE L&H INSURANCE COMPANY OF NY C Fair

Major Rating Factors: Good overall capitalization (5.6 on a scale of 0 to 10) based on mixed results -- excessive policy leverage mitigated by good risk adjusted capital (severe loss scenario). However, capital levels have fluctuated somewhat during past years. Good overall profitability (5.1). Excellent expense controls. Weak liquidity (0.8).

Other Rating Factors: Weak overall results on stability tests (2.8). High quality investment portfolio (7.4).

Principal Business: Individual health insurance (97%), credit health insurance (2%), and individual life insurance (1%).

Principal Investments: NonCMO investment grade bonds (81%), CMOs and structured securities (6%), common & preferred stock (2%), and noninv. grade bonds (1%).

Investments in Affiliates: None

Group Affiliation: WellCare Health Plans Inc

Licensed in: AL, AR, CO, CT, DC, DE, GA, HI, IL, IN, LA, ME, MD, MA, MN, MO, NH, NJ, NY, NC, OH, OK, OR, PA, RI, SC, TX, VT, VA, WV

Commenced Business: March 1946

Address: 44 South Broadway Suite 1200, New York, NY 10004

Phone: (813) 206-6200 **Domicile State:** NY **NAIC Code:** 80624

Data Date	Rating	RACR #1	RACR #2	Total Assets ($mil)	Capital ($mil)	Net Premium ($mil)	Net Income ($mil)
3-19	C	1.10	0.89	285.3	124.2	166.6	8.2
3-18	C	1.03	0.84	305.1	104.8	151.3	1.7
2018	C	1.05	0.86	250.8	116.5	602.8	12.0
2017	C	1.04	0.84	222.9	102.1	535.7	-6.6
2016	C	1.25	1.02	215.0	109.3	463.9	10.0
2015	C	1.29	1.03	211.5	101.3	420.8	-13.0
2014	B	1.49	1.18	227.7	116.4	412.9	2.7

Policy Leverage

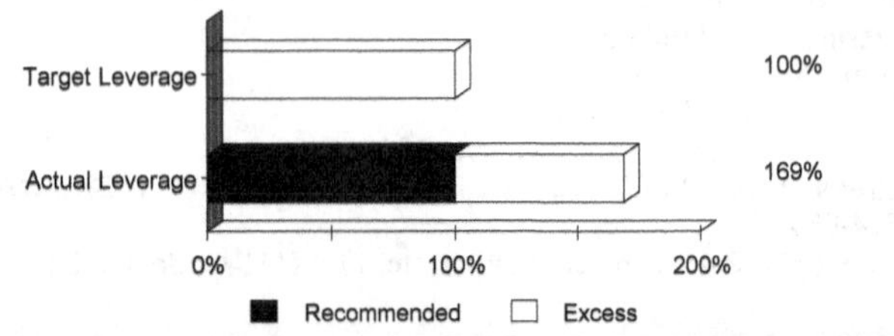

AMERICAN PUBLIC LIFE INSURANCE COMPANY B Good

Major Rating Factors: Good liquidity (6.7 on a scale of 0 to 10) with sufficient resources to handle a spike in claims. Good overall results on stability tests (6.1). Stability strengths include excellent operational trends and excellent risk diversification. Strong capitalization (8.3) based on excellent risk adjusted capital (severe loss scenario). Moreover, capital levels have been consistently high over the last five years.

Other Rating Factors: High quality investment portfolio (8.0). Excellent profitability (8.3).

Principal Business: Group health insurance (85%), individual health insurance (11%), reinsurance (2%), and individual life insurance (1%).

Principal Investments: NonCMO investment grade bonds (62%), CMOs and structured securities (24%), mortgages in good standing (8%), cash (3%), and misc. investments (3%).

Investments in Affiliates: None

Group Affiliation: Cameron Associates Inc

Licensed in: All states except NY, PR

Commenced Business: March 1946

Address: 9000 Cameron Parkway, Oklahoma City, OK 73114

Phone: (601) 936-6600 **Domicile State:** OK **NAIC Code:** 60801

Data Date	Rating	RACR #1	RACR #2	Total Assets ($mil)	Capital ($mil)	Net Premium ($mil)	Net Income ($mil)
3-19	B	2.43	1.84	103.0	36.7	24.7	1.5
3-18	B	2.04	1.54	102.2	30.7	25.5	-0.1
2018	B	2.34	1.77	100.8	35.2	96.6	5.2
2017	B	2.11	1.59	99.5	30.8	90.9	5.5
2016	B	1.96	1.47	90.3	26.4	74.4	5.9
2015	B	1.95	1.44	86.7	23.6	61.4	5.0
2014	B	1.92	1.41	83.2	21.6	52.8	4.4

Adverse Trends in Operations

Increase in policy surrenders from 2014 to 2015 (36%)

AMERICAN REPUBLIC INSURANCE COMPANY B- Good

Major Rating Factors: Good quality investment portfolio (5.8 on a scale of 0 to 10) despite mixed results such as: minimal exposure to mortgages and large holdings of BBB rated bonds but minimal holdings in junk bonds. Good liquidity (6.8) with sufficient resources to handle a spike in claims as well as a significant increase in policy surrenders. Fair overall results on stability tests (4.8) including fair financial strength of affiliated American Enterprise Mutual Holding.

Other Rating Factors: Strong capitalization (10.0) based on excellent risk adjusted capital (severe loss scenario). Excellent profitability (7.7).

Principal Business: Reinsurance (82%), individual health insurance (11%), group health insurance (5%), and individual life insurance (2%).

Principal Investments: NonCMO investment grade bonds (53%), CMOs and structured securities (21%), mortgages in good standing (9%), noninv. grade bonds (3%), and misc. investments (12%).

Investments in Affiliates: 6%

Group Affiliation: American Enterprise Mutual Holding

Licensed in: All states except NY, PR

Commenced Business: May 1929

Address: 601 Sixth Avenue, Des Moines, IA 50309

Phone: (800) 247-2190 **Domicile State:** IA **NAIC Code:** 60836

Data Date	Rating	RACR #1	RACR #2	Total Assets ($mil)	Capital ($mil)	Net Premium ($mil)	Net Income ($mil)
3-19	B-	5.95	3.69	1,095.7	487.3	161.5	3.5
3-18	A-	3.88	2.74	1,038.8	459.1	170.6	-1.2
2018	B-	5.87	3.64	1,057.0	481.8	675.9	26.3
2017	A-	4.18	2.99	937.4	445.0	442.0	23.3
2016	A-	5.06	3.60	937.6	511.1	392.1	33.1
2015	A-	5.21	3.70	820.0	477.9	328.1	21.6
2014	A-	5.26	3.89	802.5	468.1	297.9	34.1

American Enterprise Mutual Holding
Composite Group Rating: C

Largest Group Members	Assets ($mil)	Rating
GREAT WESTERN INS CO	1394	C-
AMERICAN REPUBLIC INS CO	1057	B-
MEDICO INS CO	84	B-
MEDICO CORP LIFE INS CO	74	B-
AMERICAN REPUBLIC CORP INS CO	22	C

AMERICAN RETIREMENT LIFE INSURANCE COMPANY C+ Fair

Major Rating Factors: Fair overall results on stability tests (3.3 on a scale of 0 to 10) including negative cash flow from operations for 2018, fair risk adjusted capital in prior years. Good current capitalization (5.1) based on mixed results -- excessive policy leverage mitigated by excellent risk adjusted capital (severe loss scenario) reflecting significant improvement over results in 2016. Weak profitability (1.4) with operating losses during the first three months of 2019.
Other Rating Factors: Weak liquidity (0.4). High quality investment portfolio (7.6).
Principal Business: Individual health insurance (100%).
Principal Investments: NonCMO investment grade bonds (112%) and noninv. grade bonds (1%).
Investments in Affiliates: None
Group Affiliation: CIGNA Corp
Licensed in: AL, AZ, AR, CA, CO, DE, FL, GA, IL, IN, IA, KS, KY, LA, MD, MN, MS, MO, MT, NE, NV, NH, NM, NC, ND, OH, OK, OR, PA, RI, SC, SD, TN, TX, UT, VA, WV, WI, WY
Commenced Business: November 1978
Address: 1300 East Ninth Street, Cleveland, OH 44114
Phone: (512) 451-2224 **Domicile State:** OH **NAIC Code:** 88366

Data Date	Rating	RACR #1	RACR #2	Total Assets ($mil)	Capital ($mil)	Net Premium ($mil)	Net Income ($mil)
3-19	C+	1.46	1.12	141.6	78.9	104.7	-9.6
3-18	C+	1.38	1.06	127.4	66.6	97.7	-13.4
2018	C+	1.17	0.91	123.9	63.1	401.2	-42.6
2017	C+	1.27	0.99	121.0	59.7	345.2	-38.1
2016	C+	0.91	0.71	76.9	40.7	255.5	-26.4
2015	C+	1.36	1.05	77.4	47.3	192.2	-22.1
2014	B-	1.11	0.86	55.7	31.0	120.4	-17.7

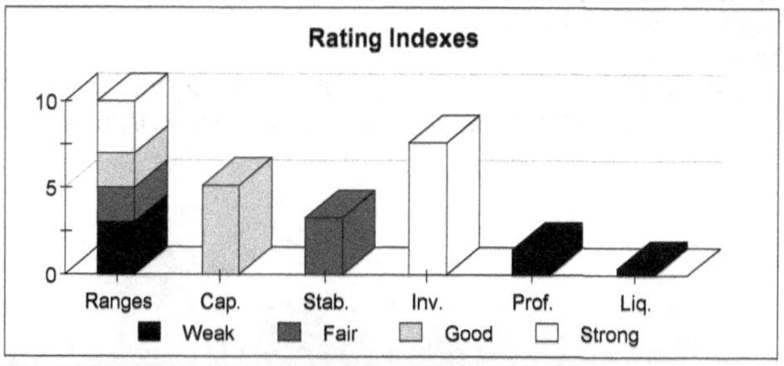

AMERICAN SPECIALTY HEALTH INS CO B Good

Major Rating Factors: Good overall profitability index (6.3 on a scale of 0 to 10). Strong capitalization (10.0) based on excellent current risk-adjusted capital (severe loss scenario). High quality investment portfolio (9.9).
Other Rating Factors: Excellent liquidity (10.0) with ample operational cash flow and liquid investments.
Principal Business: Other (100%)
Mem Phys: 18: 28,744 **17:** 27,647 **18 MLR** 58.7% **/ 18 Admin Exp** N/A
Enroll(000): Q1 19: 189 **18:** 189 **17:** 146 **Med Exp PMPM:** $0
Principal Investments: Cash and equiv (100%)
Provider Compensation ($000): FFS ($657)
Total Member Encounters: Non-phys (24,891)
Group Affiliation: American Specialty Health Incorporat
Licensed in: All states except AK, CT, ME, NJ, NY, NC, RI, PR
Address: 70 West Madison Ste 3800, Carmel, IN 46032
Phone: (800) 848-3555 **Dom State:** IN **Commenced Bus:** N/A

Data Date	Rating	RACR #1	RACR #2	Total Assets ($mil)	Capital ($mil)	Net Premium ($mil)	Net Income ($mil)
3-19	B	46.48	38.74	9.8	8.8	1.4	0.4
3-18	B-	41.66	34.72	8.9	8.4	0.3	0.0
2018	B	44.41	37.01	9.6	8.4	1.1	0.0
2017	B-	41.93	34.94	8.8	8.4	1.4	0.1
2016	B-	34.50	28.75	9.5	8.4	1.8	0.2
2015	B	27.13	22.61	8.5	8.1	3.0	0.7
2014	C-	19.15	15.96	8.1	7.5	3.0	0.4

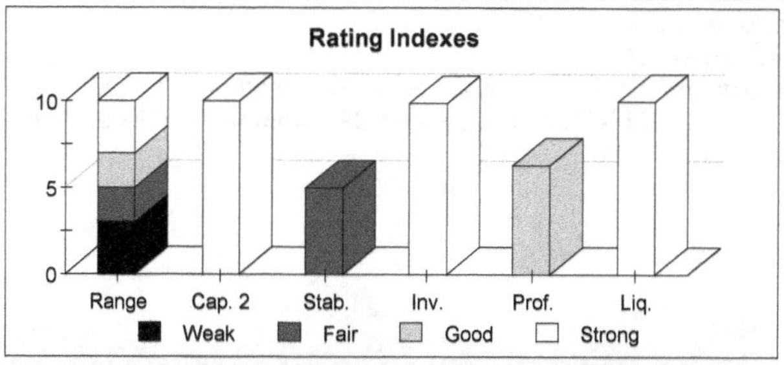

AMERICAN SPECIALTY HEALTH ODS OF NJ B Good

Major Rating Factors: Good capitalization (6.4 on a scale of 0 to 10) based on good current risk-adjusted capital (severe loss scenario). Excellent profitability (7.3). High quality investment portfolio (9.9).
Other Rating Factors: Excellent liquidity (6.9) with sufficient resources (cash flows and marketable investments) to handle a spike in claims.
Principal Business: Other (100%)
Mem Phys: 18: 1,018 **17:** 996 **18 MLR** 77.8% **/ 18 Admin Exp** N/A
Enroll(000): 18: 1,253 **17:** 1,182 **Med Exp PMPM:** $0
Principal Investments: Cash and equiv (100%)
Provider Compensation ($000): FFS ($8,615)
Total Member Encounters: Non-phys (216,847)
Group Affiliation: American Specialty Health Incorporat
Licensed in: NJ
Address: 830 Bear Tavern Rd, Dayton, NJ 8810
Phone: (800) 848-3555 **Dom State:** NJ **Commenced Bus:** N/A

Data Date	Rating	RACR #1	RACR #2	Total Assets ($mil)	Capital ($mil)	Net Premium ($mil)	Net Income ($mil)
2018	B	1.14	0.95	3.5	2.2	11.4	0.0
2017	C+	1.11	0.93	3.7	2.2	10.4	0.1
2016	C	1.26	1.05	2.7	2.1	10.1	0.1
2015	U	1.32	1.10	0.9	0.6	3.0	0.1
2014	U	1.19	0.99	0.7	0.5	2.9	0.1

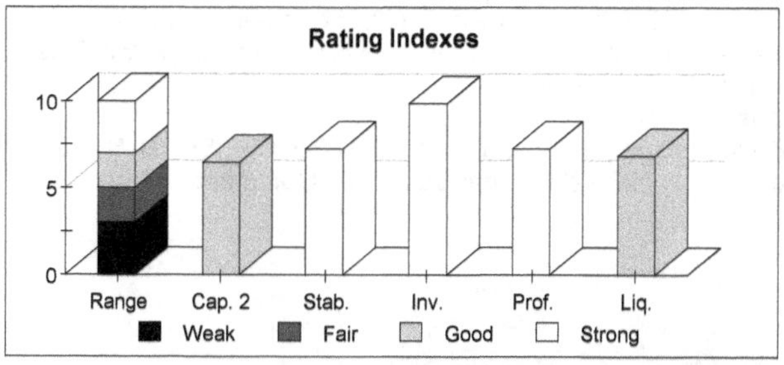

AMERICAS 1ST CHOICE SOUTH CAROLINA — C+ Fair

Major Rating Factors: Weak profitability index (0.9 on a scale of 0 to 10). Low quality investment portfolio (1.6). Strong capitalization (8.2) based on excellent current risk-adjusted capital (severe loss scenario).
Other Rating Factors: Excellent liquidity (7.0) with sufficient resources (cash flows and marketable investments) to handle a spike in claims.
Principal Business: Medicare (100%)
Mem Phys: 18: 310 **17:** 4,780 **18 MLR** 89.4% **/ 18 Admin Exp** N/A
Enroll(000): Q1 19: 1 **18:** 1 **17:** 1 **Med Exp PMPM:** $775
Principal Investments: Cash and equiv (100%)
Provider Compensation ($000): FFS ($7,035), capitation ($95), bonus arrang ($11)
Total Member Encounters: Phys (1,473), non-phys (1,339)
Group Affiliation: Anthem Inc
Licensed in: SC
Address: 250 Berryhill Rd Ste 311, COLUMBIA, SC 29210
Phone: (888) 563-3289 **Dom State:** SC **Commenced Bus:** N/A

Data Date	Rating	RACR #1	RACR #2	Total Assets ($mil)	Capital ($mil)	Net Premium ($mil)	Net Income ($mil)
3-19	C+	2.33	1.94	4.8	2.0	1.4	0.0
3-18	E-	N/A	N/A	5.2	2.8	1.8	-0.1
2018	C+	2.36	1.97	3.9	2.0	7.3	-0.9
2017	E-	N/A	N/A	3.1	1.2	7.6	-1.4
2016	D	4.32	3.60	2.3	1.8	1.9	0.1
2015	D-	3.77	3.14	2.2	1.7	1.2	0.1
2014	N/A	N/A	N/A	1.9	1.6	N/A	N/A

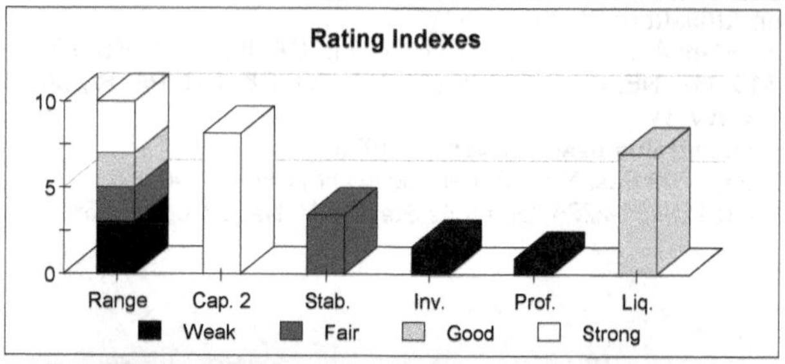

AMERICASHEALTH PLAN INC — D Weak

Major Rating Factors: Weak profitability index (0.9 on a scale of 0 to 10). Weak overall results on stability tests (2.6) based on an excessive 51% enrollment growth during the period. Strong capitalization index (9.3) based on excellent current risk-adjusted capital (severe loss scenario).
Other Rating Factors: Excellent liquidity (7.4) with ample operational cash flow and liquid investments.
Principal Business: Managed care (100%)
Mem Phys: 18: N/A **17:** N/A **18 MLR** 68.9% **/ 18 Admin Exp** N/A
Enroll(000): Q1 19: 2 **18:** 1 **17:** 1 **Med Exp PMPM:** $338
Principal Investments ($000): Cash and equiv ($4,221)
Provider Compensation ($000): None
Total Member Encounters: N/A
Group Affiliation: None
Licensed in: CA
Address: 200 South Wells Road Suite 200, Ventura, CA 93004
Phone: (615) 714-0232 **Dom State:** CA **Commenced Bus:** April 2013

Data Date	Rating	RACR #1	RACR #2	Total Assets ($mil)	Capital ($mil)	Net Premium ($mil)	Net Income ($mil)
3-19	D	3.77	2.66	5.2	2.0	2.8	0.4
3-18	E+	2.17	1.55	4.5	1.1	1.7	0.1
2018	D-	2.25	1.59	4.8	1.2	6.4	0.1
2017	E+	2.19	1.56	3.9	1.1	3.8	-0.6
2016	C-	14.90	9.82	2.3	1.7	0.9	-0.1
2015	N/A	N/A	N/A	1.4	1.4	N/A	N/A
2014	N/A	N/A	N/A	1.5	1.5	N/A	N/A

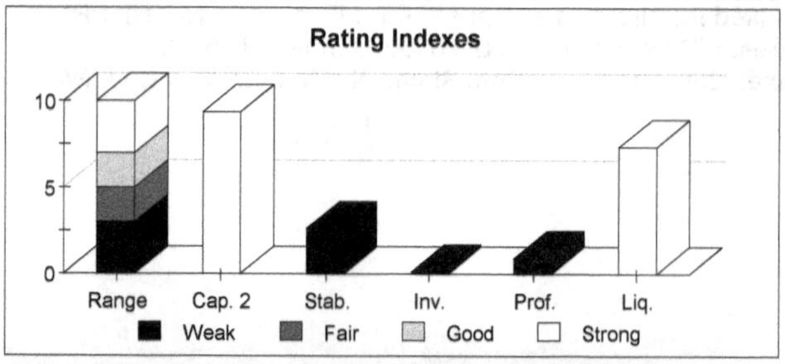

AMERICHOICE OF NEW JERSEY INC — B Good

Major Rating Factors: Good overall profitability index (5.0 on a scale of 0 to 10). Good liquidity (6.4) with sufficient resources (cash flows and marketable investments) to handle a spike in claims. Fair overall results on stability tests (4.7). Rating is significantly influenced by the good financial results of .
Other Rating Factors: Strong capitalization index (7.2) based on excellent current risk-adjusted capital (severe loss scenario). High quality investment portfolio (9.7).
Principal Business: Medicaid (99%), comp med (1%)
Mem Phys: 18: 17,377 **17:** 18,132 **18 MLR** 88.0% **/ 18 Admin Exp** N/A
Enroll(000): Q1 19: 460 **18:** 470 **17:** 483 **Med Exp PMPM:** $411
Principal Investments: Long-term bonds (77%), cash and equiv (23%)
Provider Compensation ($000): Contr fee ($1,830,716), FFS ($514,890), capitation ($28,540), bonus arrang ($3,012), other ($15,504)
Total Member Encounters: Phys (3,696,186), non-phys (2,597,823)
Group Affiliation: None
Licensed in: NJ
Address: 333 THORNALL STREET 9TH FLOOR, ISELIN, NJ 8830
Phone: (732) 623-1258 **Dom State:** NJ **Commenced Bus:** N/A

Data Date	Rating	RACR #1	RACR #2	Total Assets ($mil)	Capital ($mil)	Net Premium ($mil)	Net Income ($mil)
3-19	B	1.55	1.29	568.7	256.7	658.5	-33.8
3-18	B	1.87	1.56	580.4	283.1	664.4	-33.6
2018	B	1.70	1.42	587.7	283.3	2,714.5	-26.1
2017	B+	1.58	1.32	591.6	318.7	2,569.1	45.6
2016	B	2.05	1.71	547.6	272.9	2,549.2	87.7
2015	B	2.07	1.72	523.6	258.7	2,388.2	99.1
2014	B	2.45	2.04	532.7	247.6	1,989.5	97.1

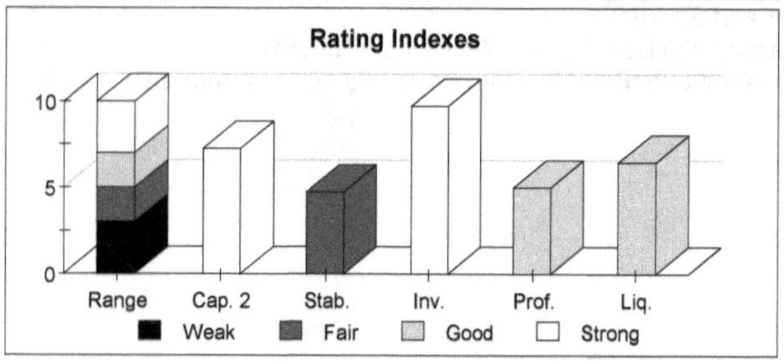

AMERIGROUP COMMUNITY CARE NM B Good

Major Rating Factors: Good overall profitability index (5.4 on a scale of 0 to 10). Good quality investment portfolio (6.5). Strong capitalization (10.0) based on excellent current risk-adjusted capital (severe loss scenario).
Other Rating Factors: Excellent liquidity (9.0) with ample operational cash flow and liquid investments.
Principal Business: Medicare (100%)
Mem Phys: 18: 6,471 **17:** 6,180 **18 MLR** 58.8% **/ 18 Admin Exp** N/A
Enroll(000): Q1 19: 1 **18:** 2 **17:** 2 **Med Exp PMPM:** $496
Principal Investments: Long-term bonds (73%), cash and equiv (24%), other (3%)
Provider Compensation ($000): Contr fee ($8,643), capitation ($1,126), FFS ($928)
Total Member Encounters: Phys (15,763), non-phys (22,300)
Group Affiliation: Anthem Inc
Licensed in: NM
Address: 6565 AMERICAS PARKWAY NE #200, ALBUQUERQUE, NM 87110
Phone: (757) 490-6900 **Dom State:** NM **Commenced Bus:** N/A

Data Date	Rating	RACR #1	RACR #2	Total Assets ($mil)	Capital ($mil)	Net Premium ($mil)	Net Income ($mil)
3-19	B	48.09	40.08	74.4	70.0	3.9	0.6
3-18	B-	33.66	28.05	71.4	64.6	4.0	0.5
2018	B	47.63	39.70	74.1	69.4	15.6	5.6
2017	B-	21.26	17.71	68.1	64.0	19.4	0.1
2016	B-	33.33	27.77	99.8	63.5	18.8	0.6
2015	B-	34.71	28.93	68.2	62.9	20.2	2.4
2014	B-	16.89	14.07	71.1	60.2	37.8	-2.5

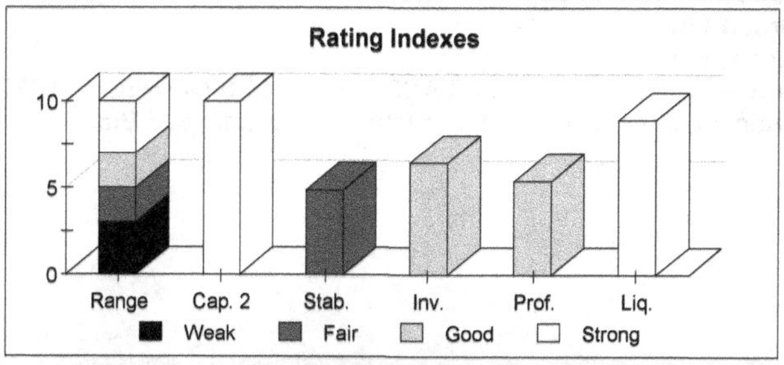

AMERIGROUP DISTRICT B- Good

Major Rating Factors: Excellent profitability (8.1 on a scale of 0 to 10). Strong capitalization (10.0) based on excellent current risk-adjusted capital (severe loss scenario). High quality investment portfolio (9.9).
Other Rating Factors: Excellent liquidity (8.3) with ample operational cash flow and liquid investments.
Principal Business: Medicaid (96%), comp med (4%)
Mem Phys: 18: 3,115 **17:** 3,008 **18 MLR** 56.3% **/ 18 Admin Exp** N/A
Enroll(000): Q1 19: 46 **18:** 47 **17:** 52 **Med Exp PMPM:** $212
Principal Investments: Cash and equiv (100%)
Provider Compensation ($000): Bonus arrang ($51,443), contr fee ($49,178), FFS ($31,942), capitation ($2,445)
Total Member Encounters: Phys (109,568), non-phys (142,947)
Group Affiliation: Anthem Inc
Licensed in: DC
Address: , WASHINGTON, DC 20002
Phone: (757) 490-6900 **Dom State:** DC **Commenced Bus:** N/A

Data Date	Rating	RACR #1	RACR #2	Total Assets ($mil)	Capital ($mil)	Net Premium ($mil)	Net Income ($mil)
3-19	B-	11.15	9.29	124.9	89.4	50.5	8.6
3-18	N/A	N/A	N/A	90.6	25.3	57.1	-5.4
2018	B-	10.23	8.53	124.8	80.6	220.1	50.7
2017	N/A	N/A	N/A	52.9	11.8	63.2	-4.5
2016	N/A	N/A	N/A	N/A	N/A	N/A	N/A
2015	N/A	N/A	N/A	N/A	N/A	N/A	N/A
2014	N/A	N/A	N/A	N/A	N/A	N/A	N/A

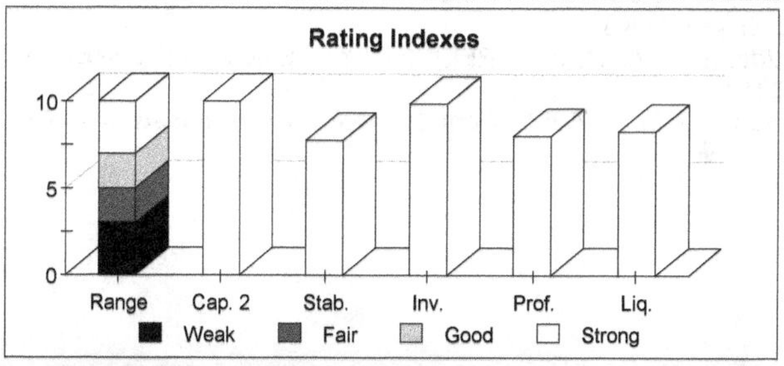

AMERIGROUP INS CO B Good

Major Rating Factors: Good quality investment portfolio (6.6 on a scale of 0 to 10). Good liquidity (6.4) with sufficient resources (cash flows and marketable investments) to handle a spike in claims. Excellent profitability (8.1).
Other Rating Factors: Strong capitalization (8.8) based on excellent current risk-adjusted capital (severe loss scenario).
Principal Business: Medicaid (100%)
Mem Phys: 18: 30,546 **17:** 28,103 **18 MLR** 82.1% **/ 18 Admin Exp** N/A
Enroll(000): Q1 19: 151 **18:** 152 **17:** 153 **Med Exp PMPM:** $456
Principal Investments: Long-term bonds (100%), other (1%)
Provider Compensation ($000): Bonus arrang ($512,121), contr fee ($255,532), FFS ($63,829), capitation ($1,962)
Total Member Encounters: Phys (650,836), non-phys (1,863,427)
Group Affiliation: Anthem Inc
Licensed in: AL, AZ, AR, DE, IA, LA, MD, MI, MS, NE, NM, ND, OR, PA, SD, TN, TX, UT, WA, WV, WY
Address: 3800 BUFFALO SPEEDWAY Ste 400, HOUSTON, TX 77098
Phone: (757) 490-6900 **Dom State:** TX **Commenced Bus:** N/A

Data Date	Rating	RACR #1	RACR #2	Total Assets ($mil)	Capital ($mil)	Net Premium ($mil)	Net Income ($mil)
3-19	B	2.82	2.35	289.2	153.2	256.3	7.2
3-18	B-	2.64	2.20	265.5	134.1	248.6	-10.0
2018	B	2.70	2.25	267.6	146.3	1,014.4	27.0
2017	B-	1.99	1.66	382.6	143.4	963.6	28.3
2016	B-	2.86	2.39	209.3	99.2	624.2	6.0
2015	B-	3.52	2.93	167.5	93.6	491.8	-0.1
2014	B-	4.51	3.76	141.7	96.9	383.1	1.5

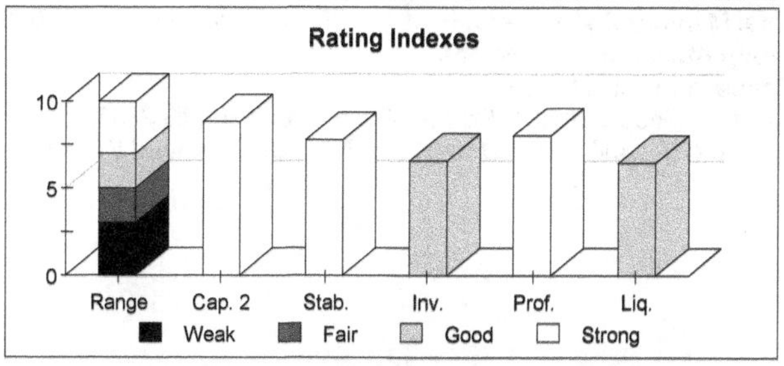

AMERIGROUP IOWA INC C Fair

Major Rating Factors: Weak profitability index (1.9 on a scale of 0 to 10). Low quality investment portfolio (0.0). Strong capitalization (7.8) based on excellent current risk-adjusted capital (severe loss scenario).
Other Rating Factors: Excellent liquidity (7.0) with ample operational cash flow and liquid investments.
Principal Business: Medicaid (99%), comp med (1%)
Mem Phys: 18: 35,218 **17:** 32,435 **18 MLR** 92.0% **/ 18 Admin Exp** N/A
Enroll(000): Q1 19: 209 **18:** 202 **17:** 190 **Med Exp PMPM:** $576
Principal Investments: Cash and equiv (100%)
Provider Compensation ($000): Bonus arrang ($637,108), contr fee ($631,260), FFS ($71,375), capitation ($8,350)
Total Member Encounters: Phys (1,111,306), non-phys (3,339,120)
Group Affiliation: Anthem Inc
Licensed in: IA
Address: 5550 WILD ROSE LANE Ste 400, DES MOINES, IA 50266
Phone: (757) 490-6900 **Dom State:** IA **Commenced Bus:** N/A

Data Date	Rating	RACR #1	RACR #2	Total Assets ($mil)	Capital ($mil)	Net Premium ($mil)	Net Income ($mil)
3-19	C	1.97	1.65	326.9	171.4	379.5	7.9
3-18	C	N/A	N/A	355.0	128.9	346.4	-31.7
2018	C	1.95	1.63	317.9	169.4	1,445.4	4.3
2017	C	N/A	N/A	309.7	149.1	1,231.2	-38.1
2016	B-	1.74	1.45	316.6	132.4	788.0	-133.3
2015	N/A	N/A	N/A	74.0	19.1	N/A	-50.5
2014	N/A	N/A	N/A	N/A	N/A	N/A	N/A

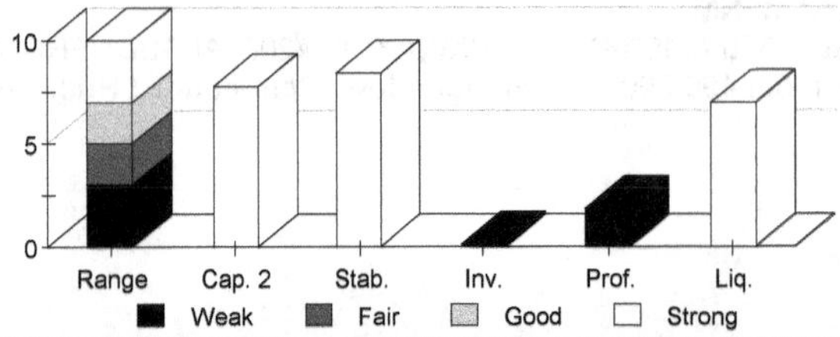

AMERIGROUP KANSAS INC B- Good

Major Rating Factors: Fair profitability index (3.8 on a scale of 0 to 10). Good liquidity (6.8) with sufficient resources (cash flows and marketable investments) to handle a spike in claims. Strong capitalization (8.8) based on excellent current risk-adjusted capital (severe loss scenario).
Other Rating Factors: High quality investment portfolio (7.2).
Principal Business: Medicaid (97%), comp med (3%)
Mem Phys: 18: 20,529 **17:** 19,367 **18 MLR** 87.0% **/ 18 Admin Exp** N/A
Enroll(000): Q1 19: N/A **18:** 118 **17:** 125 **Med Exp PMPM:** $631
Principal Investments: Long-term bonds (102%), other (2%)
Provider Compensation ($000): Contr fee ($879,227), FFS ($57,457)
Total Member Encounters: Phys (690,312), non-phys (2,439,290)
Group Affiliation: Anthem Inc
Licensed in: KS
Address: 9225 INDIAN CREEK PKWY STE 400, OVERLAND PARK, KS 66210
Phone: (913) 749-5955 **Dom State:** KS **Commenced Bus:** N/A

Data Date	Rating	RACR #1	RACR #2	Total Assets ($mil)	Capital ($mil)	Net Premium ($mil)	Net Income ($mil)
3-19	B-	2.83	2.36	206.8	177.8	-2.2	5.7
3-18	B-	N/A	N/A	300.5	164.0	267.4	-12.3
2018	B-	2.76	2.30	289.3	173.6	1,078.9	-4.3
2017	B-	N/A	N/A	313.4	176.2	986.5	-6.5
2016	B-	3.35	2.79	303.3	183.3	997.7	8.9
2015	B-	3.24	2.70	289.4	173.2	1,004.9	87.2
2014	B-	1.69	1.41	253.8	87.1	900.9	-68.5

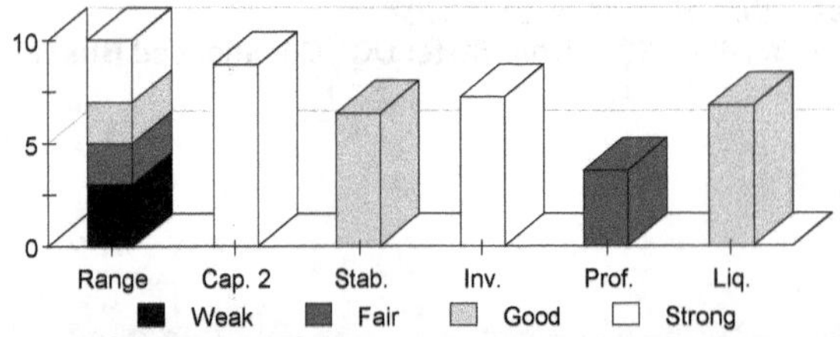

AMERIGROUP MARYLAND INC B- Good

Major Rating Factors: Fair quality investment portfolio (3.6 on a scale of 0 to 10). Excellent profitability (9.0). Strong capitalization (9.2) based on excellent current risk-adjusted capital (severe loss scenario).
Other Rating Factors: Excellent liquidity (7.1) with ample operational cash flow and liquid investments.
Principal Business: Medicaid (94%), comp med (6%)
Mem Phys: 18: 20,621 **17:** 18,496 **18 MLR** 78.7% **/ 18 Admin Exp** N/A
Enroll(000): Q1 19: 279 **18:** 275 **17:** 279 **Med Exp PMPM:** $265
Principal Investments: Long-term bonds (71%), cash and equiv (25%), other (4%)
Provider Compensation ($000): Bonus arrang ($547,315), contr fee ($238,518), FFS ($86,622), capitation ($5,984)
Total Member Encounters: Phys (1,419,340), non-phys (1,060,659)
Group Affiliation: Anthem Inc
Licensed in: AL, MD, RI
Address: 7550 TEAGUE Rd Ste 500, HANOVER, MD 21076
Phone: (757) 490-6900 **Dom State:** MD **Commenced Bus:** N/A

Data Date	Rating	RACR #1	RACR #2	Total Assets ($mil)	Capital ($mil)	Net Premium ($mil)	Net Income ($mil)
3-19	B-	3.08	2.57	486.2	188.4	284.2	28.2
3-18	B	2.58	2.15	439.0	157.3	288.1	1.6
2018	B-	2.66	2.22	448.6	162.1	1,113.1	82.7
2017	B	1.80	1.50	385.4	154.0	1,095.9	68.2
2016	B	2.14	1.78	346.3	128.7	1,088.1	54.3
2015	B	1.88	1.57	276.2	98.2	946.1	3.9
2014	B	2.09	1.74	307.2	114.2	1,069.6	51.3

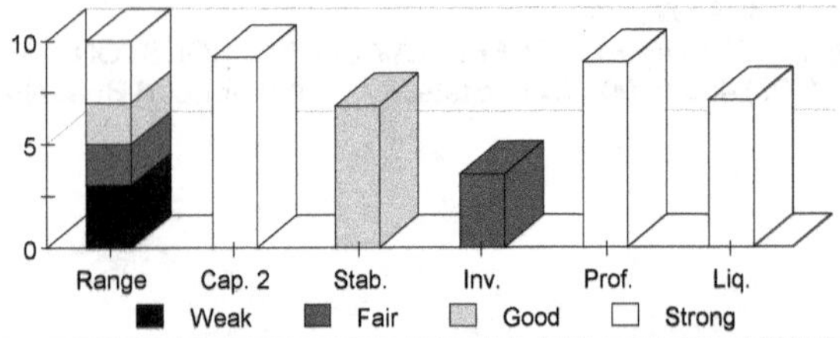

AMERIGROUP NEW JERSEY INC * A- Excellent

Major Rating Factors: Excellent profitability (8.3 on a scale of 0 to 10). Strong capitalization index (8.0) based on excellent current risk-adjusted capital (severe loss scenario). Good quality investment portfolio (6.8).
Other Rating Factors: Good overall results on stability tests (6.8) despite a decline in enrollment during 2018. Rating is significantly influenced by the good financial results of Anthem Inc. Good liquidity (6.9) with sufficient resources (cash flows and marketable investments) to handle a spike in claims.
Principal Business: Medicaid (79%), Medicare (19%), comp med (2%)
Mem Phys: 18: 17,706 **17:** 15,190 **18 MLR** 83.8% **/ 18 Admin Exp** N/A
Enroll(000): Q1 19: 180 **18:** 178 **17:** 194 **Med Exp PMPM:** $514
Principal Investments: Long-term bonds (79%), cash and equiv (20%)
Provider Compensation ($000): Bonus arrang ($607,952), contr fee ($283,158), FFS ($214,827), capitation ($58,143)
Total Member Encounters: Phys (1,390,294), non-phys (2,985,673)
Group Affiliation: Anthem Inc
Licensed in: NJ
Address: 101 WOOD AVENUE SOUTH 8TH FLOO, ISELIN, NJ 8830
Phone: (757) 490-6900 **Dom State:** NJ **Commenced Bus:** N/A

Data Date	Rating	RACR #1	RACR #2	Total Assets ($mil)	Capital ($mil)	Net Premium ($mil)	Net Income ($mil)
3-19	A-	2.15	1.79	324.9	167.0	339.3	4.2
3-18	A-	2.23	1.86	355.0	168.0	348.0	5.1
2018	A-	2.11	1.76	359.0	163.8	1,381.2	41.6
2017	B+	1.54	1.28	313.5	161.5	1,365.9	41.1
2016	A-	2.52	2.10	318.0	168.8	1,304.3	65.2
2015	B	2.54	2.12	386.5	154.3	1,208.2	59.1
2014	A-	3.82	3.18	290.8	174.5	965.4	77.7

Rating Indexes

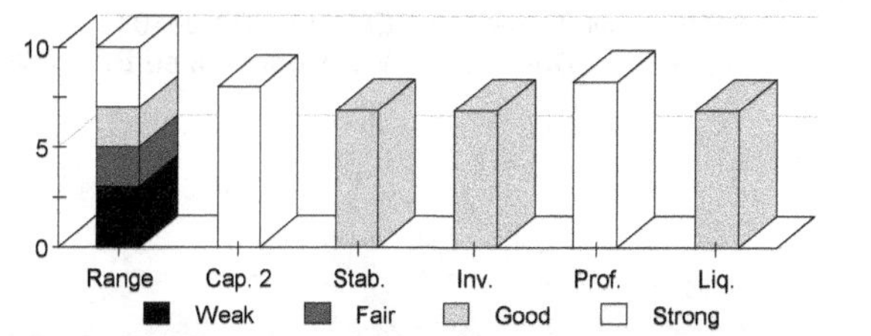

AMERIGROUP TENNESSEE INC B- Good

Major Rating Factors: Fair quality investment portfolio (3.7 on a scale of 0 to 10). Good liquidity (5.8) with sufficient resources (cash flows and marketable investments) to handle a spike in claims. Excellent profitability (7.5).
Other Rating Factors: Strong capitalization (7.9) based on excellent current risk-adjusted capital (severe loss scenario).
Principal Business: Medicaid (91%), Medicare (9%)
Mem Phys: 18: 27,529 **17:** 26,291 **18 MLR** 82.9% **/ 18 Admin Exp** N/A
Enroll(000): Q1 19: 387 **18:** 381 **17:** 414 **Med Exp PMPM:** $308
Principal Investments: Long-term bonds (93%), other (8%)
Provider Compensation ($000): Bonus arrang ($749,029), contr fee ($538,732), FFS ($115,765), capitation ($46,677)
Total Member Encounters: Phys (1,769,117), non-phys (3,816,284)
Group Affiliation: Anthem Inc
Licensed in: TN
Address: 22 CENTURY Blvd Ste 220, NASHVILLE, TN 37214
Phone: (757) 490-6900 **Dom State:** TN **Commenced Bus:** N/A

Data Date	Rating	RACR #1	RACR #2	Total Assets ($mil)	Capital ($mil)	Net Premium ($mil)	Net Income ($mil)
3-19	B-	2.09	1.74	508.1	191.9	409.7	1.1
3-18	B-	2.50	2.09	513.3	224.3	445.0	-7.2
2018	B-	2.05	1.71	515.5	187.2	1,739.0	14.8
2017	B-	1.90	1.58	488.9	233.2	1,777.3	56.2
2016	B-	1.76	1.47	531.9	178.2	1,905.9	13.4
2015	B	2.02	1.68	591.6	169.6	1,688.4	22.7
2014	B	3.21	2.68	429.0	156.6	1,006.3	26.1

Rating Indexes

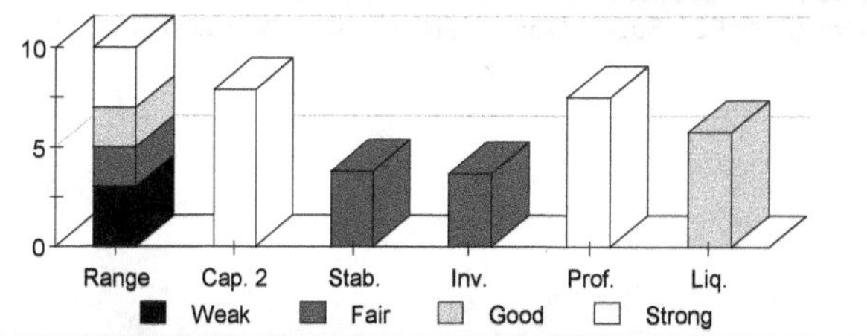

AMERIGROUP TEXAS INC * A- Excellent

Major Rating Factors: Excellent profitability (8.3 on a scale of 0 to 10). Strong capitalization index (7.8) based on excellent current risk-adjusted capital (severe loss scenario). Excellent overall results on stability tests (7.9). Rating is significantly influenced by the good financial results of Anthem Inc.
Other Rating Factors: Good quality investment portfolio (6.1). Good liquidity (6.1) with sufficient resources (cash flows and marketable investments) to handle a spike in claims.
Principal Business: Medicaid (74%), Medicare (23%), comp med (3%)
Mem Phys: 18: 84,085 **17:** 84,629 **18 MLR** 86.4% **/ 18 Admin Exp** N/A
Enroll(000): Q1 19: 697 **18:** 668 **17:** 685 **Med Exp PMPM:** $454
Principal Investments: Long-term bonds (87%), other (15%)
Provider Compensation ($000): Bonus arrang ($2,145,205), contr fee ($935,046), FFS ($418,911), capitation ($159,458)
Total Member Encounters: Phys (4,186,457), non-phys (6,736,484)
Group Affiliation: Anthem Inc
Licensed in: TX
Address: 3800 BUFFALO SPEEDWAY SUITE 40, HOUSTON, TX 77098
Phone: (757) 490-6900 **Dom State:** TX **Commenced Bus:** N/A

Data Date	Rating	RACR #1	RACR #2	Total Assets ($mil)	Capital ($mil)	Net Premium ($mil)	Net Income ($mil)
3-19	A-	2.02	1.68	1,025.7	456.8	1,221.2	17.8
3-18	A-	1.86	1.55	1,023.6	352.7	1,029.0	-67.5
2018	A-	1.97	1.64	946.1	443.8	4,245.1	47.5
2017	A-	1.65	1.38	923.3	409.2	3,838.7	87.5
2016	A-	2.06	1.72	912.7	400.5	3,861.6	87.0
2015	B	1.86	1.55	874.5	352.8	3,610.8	54.3
2014	B	2.15	1.79	629.8	312.0	2,747.5	37.7

Rating Indexes

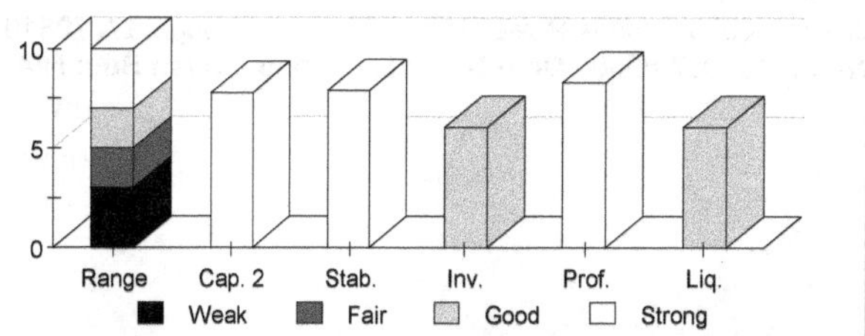

AMERIGROUP WASHINGTON INC * A- Excellent

Major Rating Factors: Strong capitalization (10.0 on a scale of 0 to 10) based on excellent current risk-adjusted capital (severe loss scenario). High quality investment portfolio (7.8). Good overall profitability index (6.8).
Other Rating Factors: Good liquidity (6.7) with sufficient resources (cash flows and marketable investments) to handle a spike in claims.
Principal Business: Medicaid (96%), Medicare (3%)
Mem Phys: 18: 29,993 **17:** 26,721 **18 MLR** 81.4% **/ 18 Admin Exp** N/A
Enroll(000): Q1 19: 168 **18:** 153 **17:** 147 **Med Exp PMPM:** $227
Principal Investments: Long-term bonds (97%), other (3%)
Provider Compensation ($000): Bonus arrang ($296,151), contr fee ($55,535), FFS ($38,158), capitation ($16,889)
Total Member Encounters: Phys (568,239), non-phys (626,611)
Group Affiliation: Anthem Inc
Licensed in: WA
Address: 705 FIFTH Ave S Ste 110, SEATTLE, WA 98104
Phone: (757) 490-6900 **Dom State:** WA **Commenced Bus:** N/A

Data Date	Rating	RACR #1	RACR #2	Total Assets ($mil)	Capital ($mil)	Net Premium ($mil)	Net Income ($mil)
3-19	A-	5.92	4.93	302.8	161.6	157.4	9.1
3-18	A-	4.19	3.49	267.4	139.2	135.6	-8.4
2018	A-	5.57	4.64	280.5	151.5	491.1	22.6
2017	A-	3.13	2.61	261.5	146.7	602.5	28.7
2016	A-	4.36	3.63	259.0	134.1	570.7	24.8
2015	B	4.33	3.60	240.5	120.9	509.6	18.7
2014	B-	5.11	4.26	413.2	103.4	389.9	-4.6

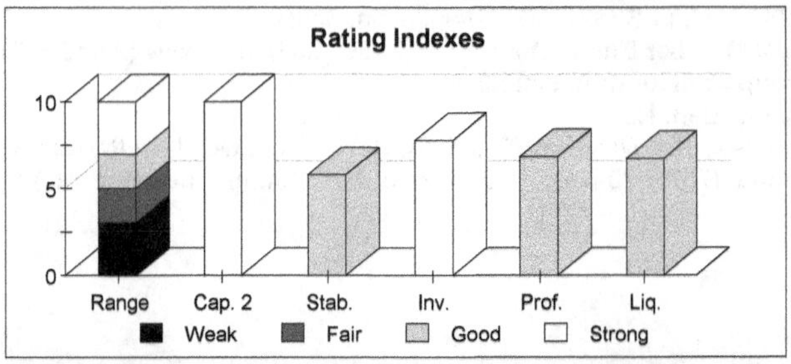

AMERIHEALTH CARITAS IOWA INC C Fair

Major Rating Factors: Weak profitability index (1.9 on a scale of 0 to 10). Strong capitalization (10.0) based on excellent current risk-adjusted capital (severe loss scenario). High quality investment portfolio (9.9).
Other Rating Factors: Excellent liquidity (10.0) with ample operational cash flow and liquid investments.
Principal Business: Medicaid (100%)
Mem Phys: 18: N/A **17:** 48,093 **18 MLR** -597.7% **/ 18 Admin Exp** N/A
Enroll(000): Q1 19: N/A **18:** N/A **17:** N/A **Med Exp PMPM:** N/A
Principal Investments: Cash and equiv (90%), long-term bonds (10%)
Provider Compensation ($000): Contr fee ($74,023), capitation ($1,104)
Total Member Encounters: N/A
Group Affiliation: Independence Health Group Inc
Licensed in: IA
Address: 601 Locust St Ste 900, Philadelphia, PA 19113
Phone: (215) 937-8000 **Dom State:** IA **Commenced Bus:** N/A

Data Date	Rating	RACR #1	RACR #2	Total Assets ($mil)	Capital ($mil)	Net Premium ($mil)	Net Income ($mil)
3-19	C	106.01	88.34	138.4	133.6	3.8	0.3
3-18	C	1.33	1.11	190.0	139.1	4.0	-4.5
2018	C	104.70	87.21	136.4	131.6	2.8	31.1
2017	C-	0.99	0.82	255.4	146.6	1,748.3	-169.3
2016	C-	1.18	0.99	453.6	140.1	1,398.0	-293.1
2015	N/A	N/A	N/A	41.2	8.2	N/A	-33.0
2014	N/A	N/A	N/A	N/A	N/A	N/A	N/A

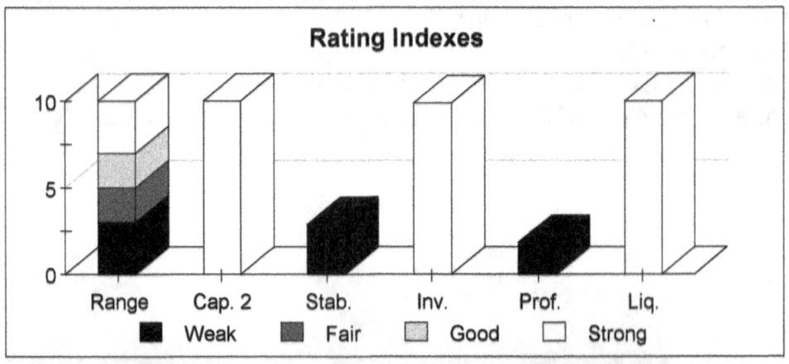

AMERIHEALTH CARITAS OF LOUISIANA INC B Good

Major Rating Factors: Excellent profitability (7.3 on a scale of 0 to 10). Strong capitalization (7.8) based on excellent current risk-adjusted capital (severe loss scenario). High quality investment portfolio (9.9).
Other Rating Factors: Excellent liquidity (7.0) with sufficient resources (cash flows and marketable investments) to handle a spike in claims.
Principal Business: Medicaid (100%)
Mem Phys: 18: 29,788 **17:** 33,543 **18 MLR** 84.6% **/ 18 Admin Exp** N/A
Enroll(000): Q1 19: 213 **18:** 209 **17:** 214 **Med Exp PMPM:** $367
Principal Investments: Cash and equiv (93%), long-term bonds (7%)
Provider Compensation ($000): Contr fee ($727,014), capitation ($198,213), bonus arrang ($4,959)
Total Member Encounters: Phys (1,069,461), non-phys (912,435)
Group Affiliation: Independence Health Group Inc
Licensed in: LA
Address: 10000 Perkins Rowe G Ste 400, Baton Rouge, LA 70810
Phone: (215) 937-8000 **Dom State:** LA **Commenced Bus:** N/A

Data Date	Rating	RACR #1	RACR #2	Total Assets ($mil)	Capital ($mil)	Net Premium ($mil)	Net Income ($mil)
3-19	B	2.00	1.67	249.0	83.9	270.0	-2.1
3-18	B	1.89	1.58	251.0	84.4	267.3	-9.8
2018	B	2.06	1.72	261.7	87.0	1,100.2	2.6
2017	C+	1.43	1.20	268.2	94.2	1,020.3	27.3
2016	C	1.56	1.30	276.8	67.9	908.3	6.2
2015	C	1.96	1.63	155.6	59.8	622.8	9.7
2014	C	1.67	1.40	183.0	48.7	537.3	-1.4

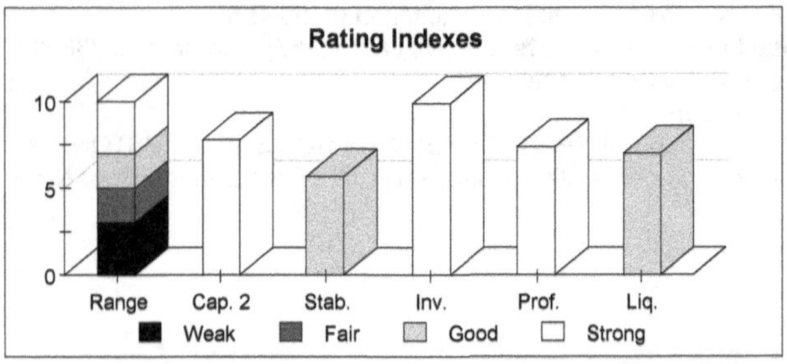

AMERIHEALTH DISTRICT OF COLUMBIA INC C+ Fair

Major Rating Factors: Fair profitability index (4.2 on a scale of 0 to 10). Strong capitalization (7.2) based on excellent current risk-adjusted capital (severe loss scenario). High quality investment portfolio (9.9).
Other Rating Factors: Excellent liquidity (6.9) with sufficient resources (cash flows and marketable investments) to handle a spike in claims.
Principal Business: Medicaid (93%), comp med (7%)
Mem Phys: 18: 6,505 **17:** 6,576 **18 MLR** 87.1% **/ 18 Admin Exp** N/A
Enroll(000): Q1 19: 124 **18:** 123 **17:** 117 **Med Exp PMPM:** $339
Principal Investments: Cash and equiv (93%), long-term bonds (7%)
Provider Compensation ($000): Contr fee ($487,178), capitation ($7,557)
Total Member Encounters: Phys (792,619), non-phys (83,424)
Group Affiliation: Independence Health Group Inc
Licensed in: DC
Address: 1120 Vermont Ave Ste 200, Washington, DC 20024
Phone: (215) 937-8000 **Dom State:** DC **Commenced Bus:** N/A

Data Date	Rating	RACR #1	RACR #2	Total Assets ($mil)	Capital ($mil)	Net Premium ($mil)	Net Income ($mil)
3-19	C+	1.47	1.23	118.2	40.0	136.0	-6.2
3-18	B-	N/A	N/A	130.0	53.8	135.1	-5.8
2018	C+	1.59	1.32	127.3	44.1	563.5	-15.2
2017	B-	N/A	N/A	145.2	59.9	507.2	21.1
2016	B-	2.95	2.46	155.1	72.2	493.9	19.2
2015	B	2.28	1.90	142.9	56.2	477.3	9.5
2014	B	2.25	1.87	115.5	45.1	447.0	16.4

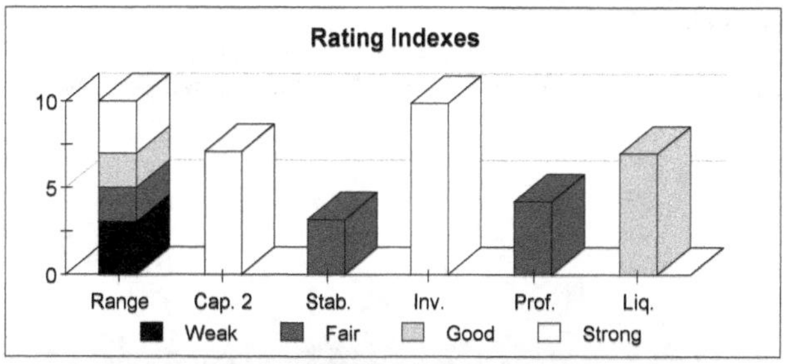

AMERIHEALTH HMO INC C+ Fair

Major Rating Factors: Fair overall results on stability tests (4.1 on a scale of 0 to 10) based on a steep decline in premium revenue in 2018. Rating is significantly influenced by the good financial results of Independence Health Group Inc. Good overall profitability index (5.2). Weak liquidity (2.9) as a spike in claims may stretch capacity.
Other Rating Factors: Strong capitalization index (10.0) based on excellent current risk-adjusted capital (severe loss scenario). High quality investment portfolio (9.9).
Principal Business: Comp med (100%)
Mem Phys: 18: 59,134 **17:** 45,785 **18 MLR** 1597.6% **/ 18 Admin Exp** N/A
Enroll(000): Q1 19: 29 **18:** 27 **17:** 31 **Med Exp PMPM:** $364
Principal Investments: Long-term bonds (82%), cash and equiv (18%)
Provider Compensation ($000): Contr fee ($114,148), FFS ($9,807), capitation ($2,249), bonus arrang ($439)
Total Member Encounters: Phys (351,768), non-phys (50,373)
Group Affiliation: Independence Health Group Inc
Licensed in: DE, NJ, PA
Address: 1901 Market Street, Philadelphia, PA 19103-1480
Phone: (215) 241-2400 **Dom State:** PA **Commenced Bus:** N/A

Data Date	Rating	RACR #1	RACR #2	Total Assets ($mil)	Capital ($mil)	Net Premium ($mil)	Net Income ($mil)
3-19	C+	13.93	11.61	114.4	23.7	1.8	0.5
3-18	C	14.42	12.02	121.6	20.8	2.1	0.1
2018	C+	13.73	11.44	107.8	23.3	7.7	1.0
2017	C	8.39	6.99	105.6	21.1	12.1	1.0
2016	C	9.04	7.53	162.0	18.6	14.9	1.9
2015	C	7.89	6.58	259.5	19.3	17.2	0.9
2014	C	3.25	2.71	293.8	51.4	335.9	-0.8

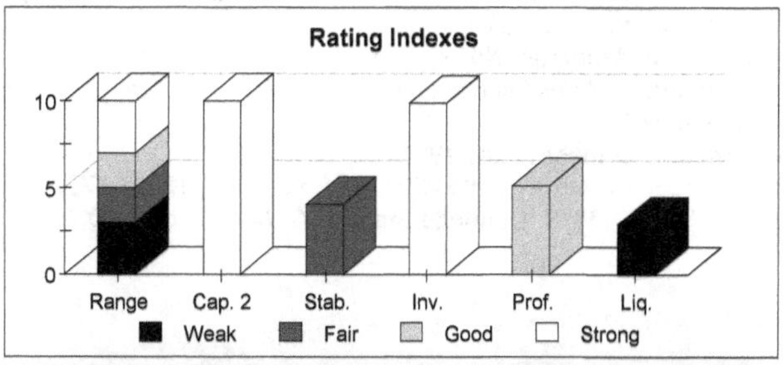

AMERIHEALTH INSURANCE CO OF NJ C Fair

Major Rating Factors: Fair profitability index (3.1 on a scale of 0 to 10). Good quality investment portfolio (6.5). Strong capitalization (10.0) based on excellent current risk-adjusted capital (severe loss scenario).
Other Rating Factors: Excellent liquidity (7.2) with ample operational cash flow and liquid investments.
Principal Business: Comp med (98%), med supp (2%)
Mem Phys: 18: 60,337 **17:** 44,494 **18 MLR** 65.6% **/ 18 Admin Exp** N/A
Enroll(000): 18: 160 **17:** 139 **Med Exp PMPM:** $362
Principal Investments: Long-term bonds (55%), cash and equiv (45%)
Provider Compensation ($000): Contr fee ($603,903), FFS ($105,199), capitation ($4,116), bonus arrang ($748)
Total Member Encounters: Phys (3,354,912), non-phys (348,993)
Group Affiliation: Independence Health Group Inc
Licensed in: NJ
Address: 8000 Midlantic Dr Ste 333, Cranbury, NJ 08512-3706
Phone: (609) 662-2400 **Dom State:** NJ **Commenced Bus:** N/A

Data Date	Rating	RACR #1	RACR #2	Total Assets ($mil)	Capital ($mil)	Net Premium ($mil)	Net Income ($mil)
2018	C	3.68	3.07	551.5	209.6	1,095.4	51.0
2017	C-	2.07	1.73	396.8	168.1	1,072.2	17.3
2016	C-	1.59	1.32	421.3	126.6	1,356.1	-63.5
2015	C-	2.41	2.01	492.6	173.8	1,241.3	-46.9
2014	C-	2.39	1.99	431.9	143.6	1,057.6	15.1

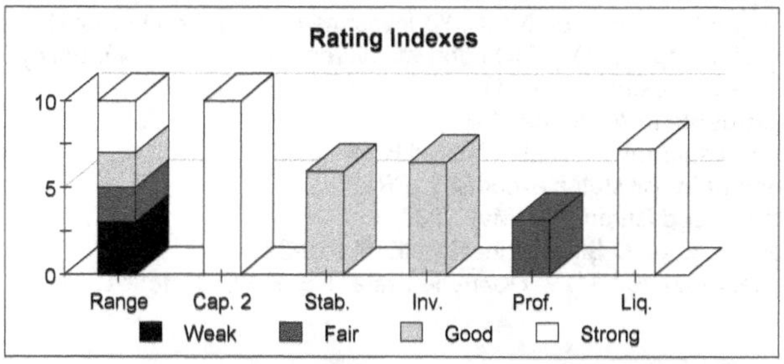

AMERIHEALTH MICHIGAN INC — C — Fair

Major Rating Factors: Weak profitability index (0.9 on a scale of 0 to 10). Good liquidity (6.9) with sufficient resources (cash flows and marketable investments) to handle a spike in claims. Strong capitalization (7.7) based on excellent current risk-adjusted capital (severe loss scenario).
Other Rating Factors: High quality investment portfolio (9.9).
Principal Business: Medicare (100%)
Mem Phys: 18: 8,567 **17:** 9,400 **18 MLR** 94.9% **/ 18 Admin Exp** N/A
Enroll(000): Q1 19: 3 **18:** 3 **17:** 3 **Med Exp PMPM:** $1,866
Principal Investments: Cash and equiv (89%), long-term bonds (11%)
Provider Compensation ($000): Contr fee ($70,567), capitation ($936)
Total Member Encounters: Phys (69,820), non-phys (10,887)
Group Affiliation: Independence Health Group Inc
Licensed in: MI
Address: 100 Galleria Officentre #210A, Southfield, MI 48034
Phone: (215) 937-8000 **Dom State:** MI **Commenced Bus:** N/A

Data Date	Rating	RACR #1	RACR #2	Total Assets ($mil)	Capital ($mil)	Net Premium ($mil)	Net Income ($mil)
3-19	C	1.94	1.62	22.8	8.9	15.9	-1.7
3-18	C-	N/A	N/A	27.6	9.9	17.2	-3.0
2018	C	2.23	1.86	26.0	10.7	75.4	-10.7
2017	C-	N/A	N/A	25.5	12.9	73.2	-2.9
2016	C-	2.03	1.69	28.4	11.9	78.1	-10.7
2015	U	1.96	1.63	27.5	8.7	40.1	-13.5
2014	N/A	N/A	N/A	2.1	2.0	N/A	-2.6

Rating Indexes

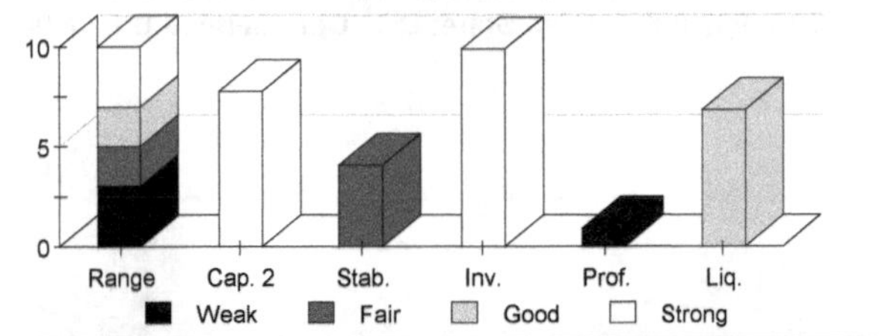

AMERITAS LIFE INSURANCE CORP OF NEW YORK — B- — Good

Major Rating Factors: Good current capitalization (6.6 on a scale of 0 to 10) based on good risk adjusted capital (severe loss scenario), although results have slipped from the excellent range over the last two years. Good quality investment portfolio (5.5) despite large holdings of BBB rated bonds in addition to moderate junk bond exposure. Exposure to mortgages is significant, but the mortgage default rate has been low. Good liquidity (5.5).
Other Rating Factors: Fair overall results on stability tests (4.9) including excessive premium growth. Weak profitability (2.5) with operating losses during the first three months of 2019.
Principal Business: N/A
Principal Investments: NonCMO investment grade bonds (62%), mortgages in good standing (17%), CMOs and structured securities (13%), policy loans (3%), and noninv. grade bonds (3%).
Investments in Affiliates: None
Group Affiliation: Ameritas Mutual Holding Co
Licensed in: NY
Commenced Business: May 1994
Address: 1350 Broadway Suite 2201, New York, NY 10018-7722
Phone: (845) 357-3816 **Domicile State:** NY **NAIC Code:** 60033

Data Date	Rating	RACR #1	RACR #2	Total Assets ($mil)	Capital ($mil)	Net Premium ($mil)	Net Income ($mil)
3-19	B-	1.79	0.95	1,680.9	92.5	54.6	-0.9
3-18	B-	2.31	1.22	1,295.7	107.6	31.3	1.5
2018	B-	1.82	0.97	1,648.4	92.5	129.2	-11.8
2017	B-	2.29	1.22	1,275.7	106.4	154.8	0.0
2016	B-	2.18	1.18	1,204.4	97.2	131.7	20.1
2015	B-	1.60	0.87	1,149.7	65.8	100.8	-17.1
2014	B-	2.15	1.18	1,128.8	86.9	95.3	-3.9

Risk-Adjusted Capital Ratio #2
(Severe Loss Scenario)

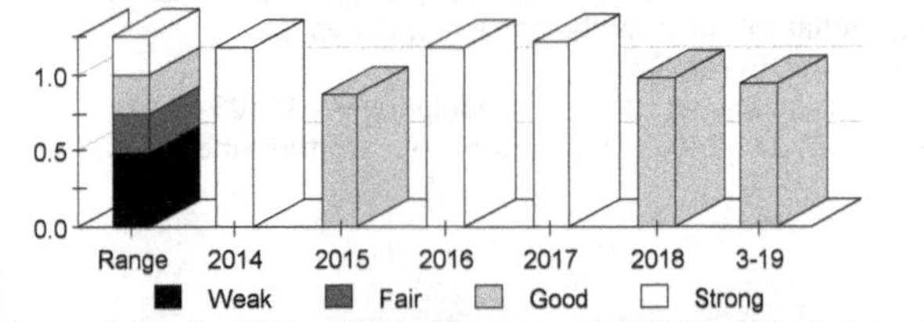

AMERITAS LIFE INSURANCE CORPORATION — B — Good

Major Rating Factors: Good liquidity (6.0 on a scale of 0 to 10) with sufficient resources to cover a large increase in policy surrenders. Good overall results on stability tests (5.6). Stability strengths include good operational trends and excellent risk diversification. Fair quality investment portfolio (4.9) with large holdings of BBB rated bonds in addition to moderate junk bond exposure. Exposure to mortgages is significant, but the mortgage default rate has been low.
Other Rating Factors: Fair profitability (4.7) with operating losses during the first three months of 2019. Strong capitalization (7.5) based on excellent risk adjusted capital (severe loss scenario).
Principal Business: Group retirement contracts (29%), group health insurance (23%), individual life insurance (20%), individual annuities (17%), and other lines (11%).
Principal Investments: NonCMO investment grade bonds (53%), mortgages in good standing (16%), CMOs and structured securities (15%), policy loans (4%), and misc. investments (11%).
Investments in Affiliates: 1%
Group Affiliation: Ameritas Mutual Holding Co
Licensed in: All states except NY, PR
Commenced Business: May 1887
Address: 5900 O Street, Lincoln, NE 68510-2234
Phone: (402) 467-1122 **Domicile State:** NE **NAIC Code:** 61301

Data Date	Rating	RACR #1	RACR #2	Total Assets ($mil)	Capital ($mil)	Net Premium ($mil)	Net Income ($mil)
3-19	B	2.28	1.33	22,844.0	1,544.4	815.5	-15.8
3-18	B	2.22	1.32	20,066.6	1,554.6	665.8	33.3
2018	B	2.27	1.33	21,734.8	1,510.6	2,781.7	71.3
2017	B	2.25	1.34	20,076.5	1,555.6	2,724.5	106.3
2016	B	2.22	1.34	18,696.6	1,484.1	4,421.9	-4.8
2015	B	2.40	1.45	18,148.8	1,511.5	3,359.6	-9.5
2014	B	2.67	1.67	16,822.0	1,623.5	2,119.7	129.8

Exposure to Withdrawals Without Penalty
(as a % of capital)

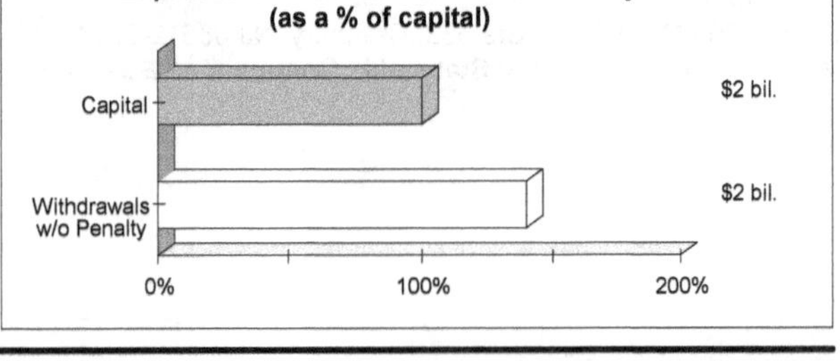

AMEX ASSURANCE CO B- Good

Major Rating Factors: Fair overall results on stability tests (3.5 on a scale of 0 to 10). History of adequate reserve strength (6.6) as reserves have been consistently at an acceptable level.
Other Rating Factors: Strong long-term capitalization index (10.0) based on excellent current risk adjusted capital (severe and moderate loss scenarios), despite some fluctuation in capital levels. Excellent profitability (8.5) with operating gains in each of the last five years. Return on equity has been excellent over the last five years averaging 34.0%. Excellent liquidity (7.6) with ample operational cash flow and liquid investments.
Principal Business: (Not applicable due to unusual reinsurance transactions.)
Principal Investments: Investment grade bonds (91%) and misc. investments (9%).
Investments in Affiliates: None
Group Affiliation: American Express Company
Licensed in: All states, the District of Columbia and Puerto Rico
Commenced Business: February 1973
Address: 2 Pierce Place Suite 900, Itasca, IL 60143
Phone: (602) 537-6511 **Domicile State:** IL **NAIC Code:** 27928

Data Date	Rating	RACR #1	RACR #2	Loss Ratio %	Total Assets ($mil)	Capital ($mil)	Net Premium ($mil)	Net Income ($mil)
3-19	B-	9.75	5.73	N/A	259.2	208.9	48.1	16.6
3-18	B-	10.40	6.05	N/A	243.8	196.0	46.4	20.1
2018	B	9.32	5.47	44.2	237.8	192.2	185.6	69.4
2017	B	9.14	5.34	46.0	218.2	175.8	176.5	53.4
2016	B	10.58	6.07	39.0	227.8	181.4	177.4	59.7
2015	B	9.75	5.62	36.6	256.3	184.3	188.2	62.5
2014	B	10.09	5.82	38.7	280.2	188.8	183.4	70.7

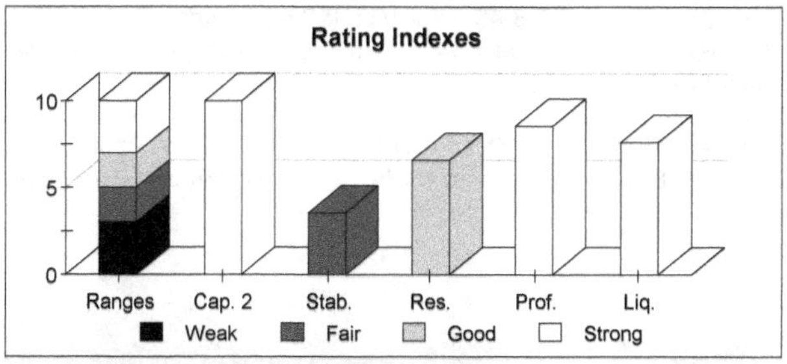

AMFIRST INS CO B Good

Major Rating Factors: Fair quality investment portfolio (3.1 on a scale of 0 to 10). Excellent profitability (7.9). Strong capitalization (9.3) based on excellent current risk-adjusted capital (severe loss scenario).
Other Rating Factors: Excellent liquidity (7.9) with ample operational cash flow and liquid investments.
Principal Business: Dental (41%), other (53%)
Mem Phys: 18: N/A **17:** N/A **18 MLR** 17.2% **/ 18 Admin Exp** N/A
Enroll(000): Q1 19: 54 **18:** 54 **17:** 41 **Med Exp PMPM:** $22
Principal Investments: Affiliate common stock (47%), long-term bonds (29%), cash and equiv (12%), real estate (3%), pref stock (3%), nonaffiliate common stock (2%), other (4%)
Provider Compensation ($000): FFS ($13,259)
Total Member Encounters: Phys (50,200), non-phys (139,198)
Group Affiliation: Wheaton Management LLC
Licensed in: AL, AZ, AR, CA, FL, GA, HI, KY, LA, MD, MI, MS, NC, OH, OK, PA, SC, TN, TX, VA, WV
Address: 201 Robert S Kerr Ave Ste 600, Oklahoma City, OK 73102
Phone: (601) 956-2028 **Dom State:** OK **Commenced Bus:** N/A

Data Date	Rating	RACR #1	RACR #2	Total Assets ($mil)	Capital ($mil)	Net Premium ($mil)	Net Income ($mil)
3-19	B	3.22	2.68	69.5	60.0	17.4	3.5
3-18	B+	N/A	N/A	66.1	50.3	17.3	1.8
2018	B	2.97	2.48	67.5	55.9	73.1	6.5
2017	B+	N/A	N/A	58.8	50.8	61.9	4.4
2016	B	3.24	2.70	52.5	45.3	53.3	2.8
2015	B	2.84	2.37	47.4	41.3	52.4	5.8
2014	B	2.54	2.11	41.5	35.0	35.6	4.3

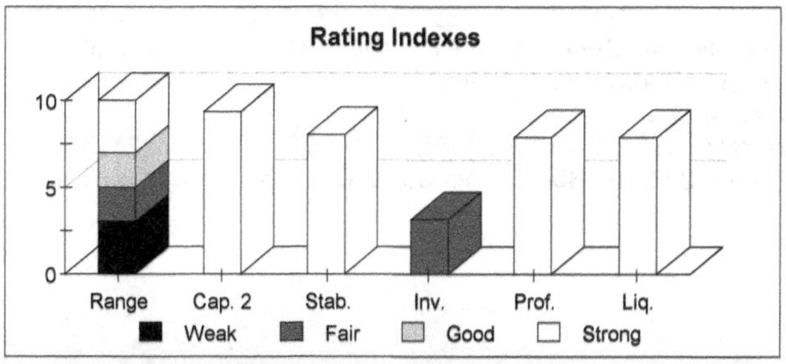

AMGP GEORGIA MANAGED CARE CO INC * A- Excellent

Major Rating Factors: Excellent profitability (7.6 on a scale of 0 to 10). Strong capitalization (8.2) based on excellent current risk-adjusted capital (severe loss scenario). High quality investment portfolio (7.3).
Other Rating Factors: Good liquidity (6.8) with sufficient resources (cash flows and marketable investments) to handle a spike in claims.
Principal Business: Medicaid (94%), comp med (6%)
Mem Phys: 18: 42,695 **17:** 33,102 **18 MLR** 78.9% **/ 18 Admin Exp** N/A
Enroll(000): Q1 19: 392 **18:** 385 **17:** 367 **Med Exp PMPM:** $211
Principal Investments: Long-term bonds (96%), other (4%)
Provider Compensation ($000): Bonus arrang ($515,297), contr fee ($344,936), FFS ($101,733), capitation ($11,774)
Total Member Encounters: Phys (1,698,082), non-phys (2,047,687)
Group Affiliation: Anthem Inc
Licensed in: GA
Address: 4170 ASHFORD DUNWOODY RD, ATLANTA, GA 30319
Phone: (678) 587-4840 **Dom State:** GA **Commenced Bus:** N/A

Data Date	Rating	RACR #1	RACR #2	Total Assets ($mil)	Capital ($mil)	Net Premium ($mil)	Net Income ($mil)
3-19	A-	2.31	1.92	310.5	148.9	300.8	-4.0
3-18	A-	2.08	1.73	294.1	127.2	301.8	-20.8
2018	A-	2.37	1.97	321.5	153.1	1,233.6	30.5
2017	A-	1.67	1.39	291.5	145.3	1,174.4	16.4
2016	A-	2.37	1.97	296.4	147.4	1,228.3	16.0
2015	A-	2.55	2.13	291.7	150.7	1,202.7	26.1
2014	A-	2.70	2.25	270.7	136.3	1,054.7	36.7

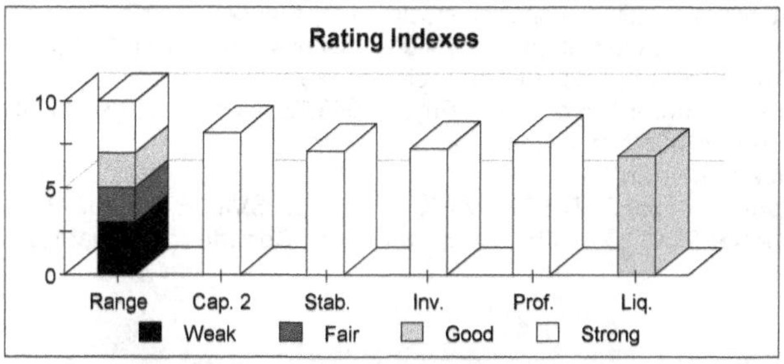

ANTHEM BLUE CROSS LIFE & HEALTH INS — B- — Good

Major Rating Factors: Fair quality investment portfolio (3.7 on a scale of 0 to 10). Good liquidity (6.8) with sufficient resources (cash flows and marketable investments) to handle a spike in claims. Excellent profitability (7.9).
Other Rating Factors: Strong capitalization (10.0) based on excellent current risk-adjusted capital (severe loss scenario).
Principal Business: Comp med (56%), dental (12%), Medicare (9%), vision (2%), other (21%)
Mem Phys: 18: 66,674 **17:** 63,100 **18 MLR** 82.5% **/ 18 Admin Exp** N/A
Enroll(000): Q1 19: 2,366 **18:** 2,320 **17:** 2,238 **Med Exp PMPM:** $54
Principal Investments: Long-term bonds (78%), cash and equiv (3%), nonaffiliate common stock (2%), other (17%)
Provider Compensation ($000): Contr fee ($488,842), bonus arrang ($444,225), FFS ($436,652), capitation ($3,432), other ($135,157)
Total Member Encounters: Phys (1,395,014), non-phys (1,571,945)
Group Affiliation: Anthem Inc
Licensed in: CA
Address: 21555 OXNARD St, WOODLAND HILLS, CA 91367
Phone: (818) 234-2345 **Dom State:** CA **Commenced Bus:** N/A

Data Date	Rating	RACR #1	RACR #2	Total Assets ($mil)	Capital ($mil)	Net Premium ($mil)	Net Income ($mil)
3-19	B-	8.12	6.77	2,445.3	1,320.7	453.7	74.4
3-18	B-	N/A	N/A	2,225.2	1,250.7	461.4	32.8
2018	B-	7.79	6.49	2,423.9	1,264.8	1,817.7	181.6
2017	B-	N/A	N/A	2,288.8	1,216.8	1,933.2	158.3
2016	B-	7.49	6.25	2,682.8	1,340.8	2,289.5	281.4
2015	B	5.69	4.75	2,521.6	1,274.7	3,631.5	243.6
2014	B	5.64	4.70	2,572.2	1,352.5	4,079.9	309.4

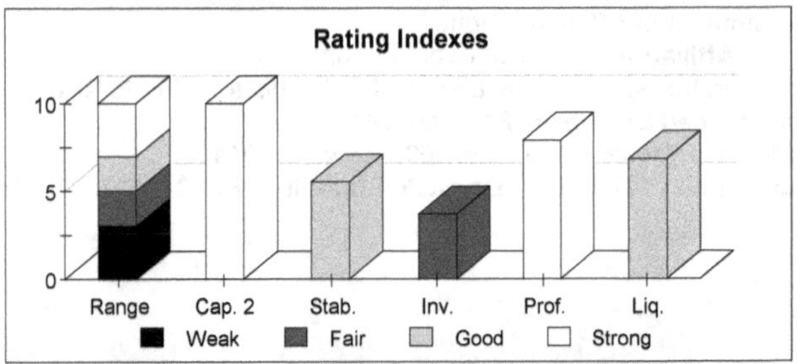

ANTHEM HEALTH PLANS INC — B — Good

Major Rating Factors: Good quality investment portfolio (6.6 on a scale of 0 to 10). Good liquidity (6.9) with sufficient resources (cash flows and marketable investments) to handle a spike in claims. Excellent profitability (8.1).
Other Rating Factors: Strong capitalization (8.9) based on excellent current risk-adjusted capital (severe loss scenario).
Principal Business: Comp med (51%), Medicare (21%), FEHB (15%), med supp (6%), dental (2%), other (4%)
Mem Phys: 18: 31,777 **17:** 28,745 **18 MLR** 83.4% **/ 18 Admin Exp** N/A
Enroll(000): Q1 19: 604 **18:** 609 **17:** 674 **Med Exp PMPM:** $218
Principal Investments: Long-term bonds (44%), nonaffiliate common stock (2%), other (55%)
Provider Compensation ($000): Bonus arrang ($1,148,675), contr fee ($239,957), FFS ($235,104), capitation ($19,945), other ($68,212)
Total Member Encounters: Phys (2,679,150), non-phys (2,077,410)
Group Affiliation: Anthem Inc
Licensed in: CT
Address: 108 LEIGUS Rd, WALLINGFORD, CT 06492-2518
Phone: (203) 677-4000 **Dom State:** CT **Commenced Bus:** N/A

Data Date	Rating	RACR #1	RACR #2	Total Assets ($mil)	Capital ($mil)	Net Premium ($mil)	Net Income ($mil)
3-19	B	2.86	2.39	749.1	370.8	441.8	29.8
3-18	B	2.41	2.01	800.2	288.3	508.3	-15.8
2018	B	2.79	2.32	770.2	360.3	1,996.1	79.8
2017	B	1.84	1.53	765.8	293.7	1,979.1	42.4
2016	B-	2.44	2.03	800.4	232.2	1,663.8	22.5
2015	B-	3.49	2.91	697.2	284.1	1,570.9	91.9
2014	B	3.39	2.82	719.5	311.7	1,801.1	108.4

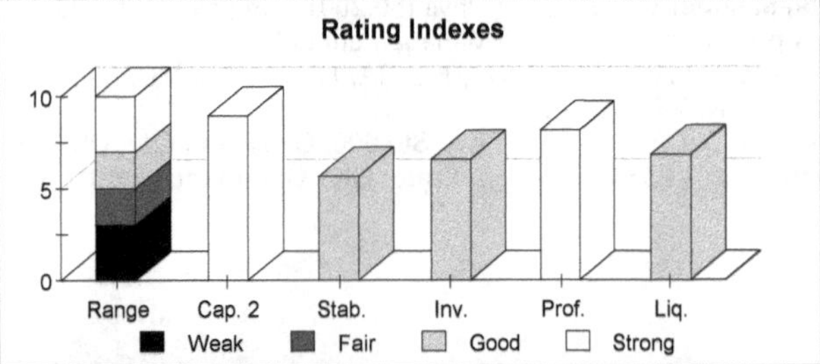

ANTHEM HEALTH PLANS OF KENTUCKY INC — B — Good

Major Rating Factors: Good overall results on stability tests (5.9 on a scale of 0 to 10). Rating is significantly influenced by the good financial results of Anthem Inc. Good liquidity (6.4) with sufficient resources (cash flows and marketable investments) to handle a spike in claims. Excellent profitability (9.1).
Other Rating Factors: Strong capitalization index (10.0) based on excellent current risk-adjusted capital (severe loss scenario). High quality investment portfolio (8.9).
Principal Business: Comp med (72%), FEHB (17%), med supp (9%), dental (1%)
Mem Phys: 18: 33,463 **17:** 31,585 **18 MLR** 83.8% **/ 18 Admin Exp** N/A
Enroll(000): Q1 19: 902 **18:** 772 **17:** 830 **Med Exp PMPM:** $184
Principal Investments: Long-term bonds (92%), real estate (4%), cash and equiv (2%), affiliate common stock (1%), other (2%)
Provider Compensation ($000): Bonus arrang ($933,633), contr fee ($485,991), FFS ($311,018), capitation ($37)
Total Member Encounters: Phys (3,056,736), non-phys (3,006,041)
Group Affiliation: Anthem Inc
Licensed in: KY
Address: 13550 TRITON PARK BLVD, LOUISVILLE, KY 40223
Phone: (800) 331-1476 **Dom State:** KY **Commenced Bus:** N/A

Data Date	Rating	RACR #1	RACR #2	Total Assets ($mil)	Capital ($mil)	Net Premium ($mil)	Net Income ($mil)
3-19	B	3.83	3.19	919.1	380.1	538.7	63.6
3-18	B+	3.03	2.52	900.5	352.6	507.1	22.8
2018	B	3.20	2.66	838.0	314.2	2,036.8	145.0
2017	B+	2.18	1.81	927.8	332.8	2,372.9	136.8
2016	B+	2.69	2.24	1,069.4	313.6	2,285.7	112.0
2015	B	2.85	2.38	866.8	299.3	2,161.2	101.8
2014	B	3.05	2.54	897.5	331.4	2,311.1	123.4

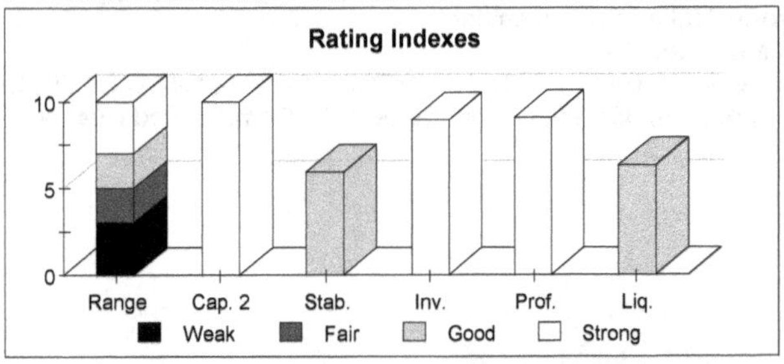

ANTHEM HEALTH PLANS OF MAINE INC B Good

Major Rating Factors: Excellent profitability (7.6 on a scale of 0 to 10). Strong capitalization (10.0) based on excellent current risk-adjusted capital (severe loss scenario). High quality investment portfolio (8.3).
Other Rating Factors: Excellent liquidity (6.9) with sufficient resources (cash flows and marketable investments) to handle a spike in claims.
Principal Business: Comp med (71%), FEHB (21%), med supp (5%)
Mem Phys: 18: 7,792 **17:** 7,455 **18 MLR** 85.9% **/ 18 Admin Exp** N/A
Enroll(000): Q1 19: 393 **18:** 362 **17:** 382 **Med Exp PMPM:** $197
Principal Investments: Long-term bonds (95%), cash and equiv (1%), other (5%)
Provider Compensation ($000): Bonus arrang ($743,701), FFS ($143,517), contr fee ($17,041), capitation ($35), other ($9,453)
Total Member Encounters: Phys (1,286,640), non-phys (890,494)
Group Affiliation: Anthem Inc
Licensed in: ME
Address: 2 GANNETT Dr, SOUTH PORTLAND, ME 04106-6911
Phone: (866) 583-6182 **Dom State:** ME **Commenced Bus:** N/A

Data Date	Rating	RACR #1	RACR #2	Total Assets ($mil)	Capital ($mil)	Net Premium ($mil)	Net Income ($mil)
3-19	B	4.03	3.36	489.8	143.7	298.9	25.7
3-18	A-	3.65	3.04	491.1	167.9	242.8	2.1
2018	B	3.41	2.84	493.9	120.1	991.7	58.6
2017	A-	2.57	2.14	498.0	165.4	1,139.5	37.7
2016	B	3.12	2.60	408.4	150.4	1,062.9	19.1
2015	B-	3.40	2.84	397.9	154.0	1,034.5	22.2
2014	B-	3.91	3.26	386.3	141.2	1,017.4	19.2

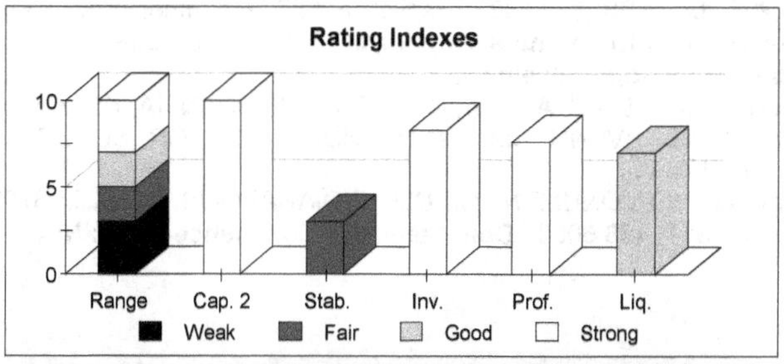

ANTHEM HEALTH PLANS OF NEW HAMPSHIRE B Good

Major Rating Factors: Fair quality investment portfolio (4.5 on a scale of 0 to 10). Excellent profitability (8.3). Strong capitalization (9.5) based on excellent current risk-adjusted capital (severe loss scenario).
Other Rating Factors: Excellent liquidity (6.9) with sufficient resources (cash flows and marketable investments) to handle a spike in claims.
Principal Business: FEHB (39%), Medicare (28%), comp med (19%), med supp (11%), other (1%)
Mem Phys: 18: 22,509 **17:** 19,911 **18 MLR** 85.3% **/ 18 Admin Exp** N/A
Enroll(000): Q1 19: 187 **18:** 170 **17:** 134 **Med Exp PMPM:** $319
Principal Investments: Long-term bonds (54%), affiliate common stock (47%)
Provider Compensation ($000): Bonus arrang ($319,580), contr fee ($205,786), FFS ($84,059), capitation ($4,394)
Total Member Encounters: N/A
Group Affiliation: Anthem Inc
Licensed in: GA, KY, NH
Address: 1155 ELM St, MANCHESTER, NH 3101
Phone: (603) 541-2000 **Dom State:** NH **Commenced Bus:** N/A

Data Date	Rating	RACR #1	RACR #2	Total Assets ($mil)	Capital ($mil)	Net Premium ($mil)	Net Income ($mil)
3-19	B	3.36	2.80	448.7	226.4	226.0	0.1
3-18	B	3.50	2.91	380.8	171.8	176.5	-7.0
2018	B	3.00	2.50	398.9	202.3	738.6	58.5
2017	B	2.26	1.88	322.7	155.3	515.8	43.9
2016	B	2.96	2.46	316.0	142.7	488.2	35.2
2015	B+	3.68	3.06	339.9	162.9	466.9	41.7
2014	B+	3.15	2.62	327.7	157.9	493.8	31.8

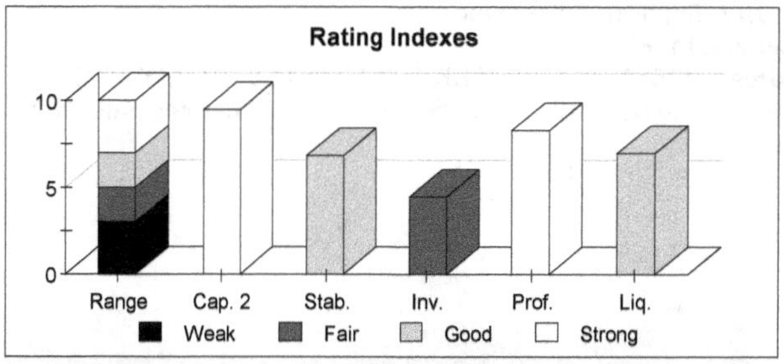

ANTHEM HEALTH PLANS OF VIRGINIA B Good

Major Rating Factors: Good quality investment portfolio (6.6 on a scale of 0 to 10). Good liquidity (6.6) with sufficient resources (cash flows and marketable investments) to handle a spike in claims. Excellent profitability (9.1).
Other Rating Factors: Strong capitalization (10.0) based on excellent current risk-adjusted capital (severe loss scenario).
Principal Business: FEHB (46%), comp med (37%), med supp (9%), dental (3%), other (5%)
Mem Phys: 18: 35,955 **17:** 34,415 **18 MLR** 94.2% **/ 18 Admin Exp** N/A
Enroll(000): Q1 19: 1,544 **18:** 1,484 **17:** 1,490 **Med Exp PMPM:** $170
Principal Investments: Long-term bonds (56%), cash and equiv (4%), real estate (3%), affiliate common stock (3%), nonaffiliate common stock (1%), other (33%)
Provider Compensation ($000): Bonus arrang ($2,155,842), FFS ($741,312), contr fee ($10,422), other ($107,324)
Total Member Encounters: Phys (5,782,046), non-phys (3,852,721)
Group Affiliation: Anthem Inc
Licensed in: VA
Address: 2015 STAPLES MILL Rd, RICHMOND, VA 23230
Phone: (804) 354-7000 **Dom State:** VA **Commenced Bus:** N/A

Data Date	Rating	RACR #1	RACR #2	Total Assets ($mil)	Capital ($mil)	Net Premium ($mil)	Net Income ($mil)
3-19	B	4.35	3.63	1,779.7	753.8	756.0	86.6
3-18	B	4.13	3.44	2,034.7	709.9	796.9	41.1
2018	B	3.84	3.20	1,799.8	661.7	3,210.7	293.6
2017	B-	3.55	2.96	2,271.8	698.2	3,658.1	241.0
2016	B-	3.52	2.93	1,941.2	655.3	3,825.9	230.2
2015	B-	3.09	2.58	1,991.9	594.2	3,740.6	216.1
2014	B	3.15	2.62	1,962.5	623.1	3,947.9	242.5

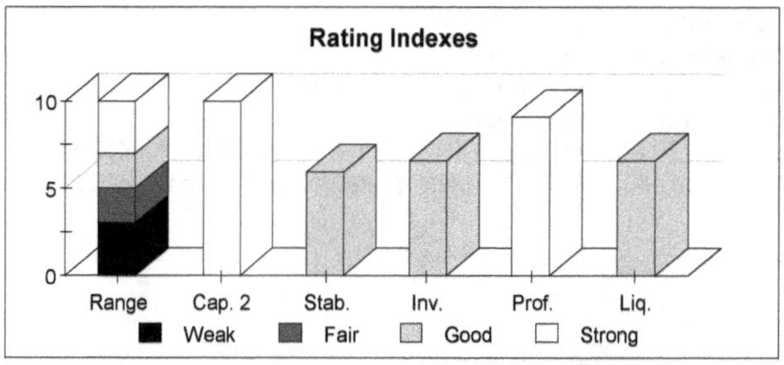

ANTHEM INS COMPANIES INC — B- — Good

Major Rating Factors: Fair quality investment portfolio (3.7 on a scale of 0 to 10). Good liquidity (6.9) with sufficient resources (cash flows and marketable investments) to handle a spike in claims. Excellent profitability (9.3).
Other Rating Factors: Strong capitalization (9.1) based on excellent current risk-adjusted capital (severe loss scenario).
Principal Business: Medicaid (39%), Medicare (22%), comp med (20%), FEHB (8%), med supp (2%), other (8%)
Mem Phys: 18: 43,911 **17:** 41,861 **18 MLR** 85.7% **/ 18 Admin Exp** N/A
Enroll(000): Q1 19: 2,626 **18:** 2,770 **17:** 2,631 **Med Exp PMPM:** $190
Principal Investments: Long-term bonds (75%), nonaffiliate common stock (5%), cash and equiv (2%), affiliate common stock (1%), other (18%)
Provider Compensation ($000): Bonus arrang ($3,666,493), contr fee ($1,266,266), FFS ($843,486), capitation ($87,362), other ($262,300)
Total Member Encounters: Phys (8,359,335), non-phys (8,181,265)
Group Affiliation: Anthem Inc
Licensed in: AL, AZ, AR, CA, CO, CT, GA, ID, IL, IN, IA, KS, KY, LA, ME, MS, MO, MT, NE, NV, NH, NM, NY, NC, ND, OH, OK, OR, SC, SD, TN, TX, UT, VA, WA, WI, WY
Address: 120 MONUMENT CIRCLE, INDIANAPOLIS, IN 46204-3709
Phone: (317) 488-6000 **Dom State:** IN **Commenced Bus:** N/A

Data Date	Rating	RACR #1	RACR #2	Total Assets ($mil)	Capital ($mil)	Net Premium ($mil)	Net Income ($mil)
3-19	B-	3.01	2.51	3,987.7	1,396.8	1,913.1	210.0
3-18	B-	2.77	2.31	3,892.2	1,232.4	1,712.6	71.8
2018	B-	2.56	2.14	3,480.9	1,180.3	7,116.0	498.9
2017	B-	2.67	2.22	3,337.6	1,186.4	6,933.8	420.0
2016	B-	2.42	2.02	2,947.5	968.6	6,126.1	431.0
2015	B-	2.36	1.97	2,853.0	816.5	5,320.0	405.5
2014	B-	2.90	2.42	3,231.7	832.9	4,869.8	389.1

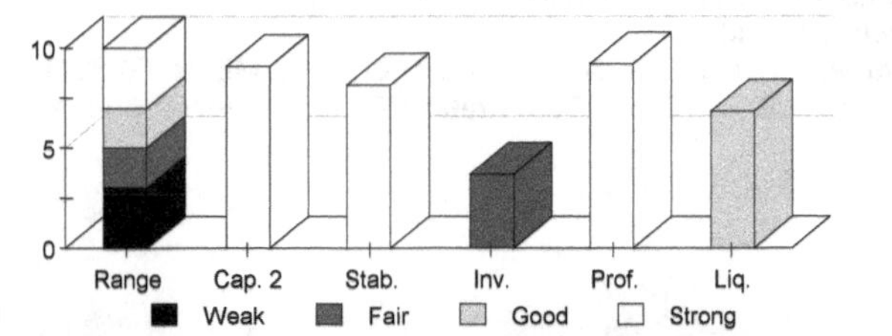

ANTHEM KENTUCKY MANAGED CARE PLAN * — A- — Excellent

Major Rating Factors: Excellent profitability (9.1 on a scale of 0 to 10). Strong capitalization (10.0) based on excellent current risk-adjusted capital (severe loss scenario). High quality investment portfolio (8.5).
Other Rating Factors: Good liquidity (6.6) with sufficient resources (cash flows and marketable investments) to handle a spike in claims.
Principal Business: Medicaid (99%)
Mem Phys: 18: 33,632 **17:** 24,526 **18 MLR** 86.1% **/ 18 Admin Exp** N/A
Enroll(000): Q1 19: 125 **18:** 131 **17:** 129 **Med Exp PMPM:** $410
Principal Investments: Long-term bonds (92%), cash and equiv (8%)
Provider Compensation ($000): Bonus arrang ($293,529), contr fee ($268,607), FFS ($81,862)
Total Member Encounters: Phys (884,514), non-phys (1,232,737)
Group Affiliation: Anthem Inc
Licensed in: KY
Address: 13550 TRITON PARK BLVD, LOUISVILLE, KY 40223
Phone: (800) 331-1476 **Dom State:** KY **Commenced Bus:** N/A

Data Date	Rating	RACR #1	RACR #2	Total Assets ($mil)	Capital ($mil)	Net Premium ($mil)	Net Income ($mil)
3-19	A-	3.67	3.06	243.4	158.6	187.7	-4.7
3-18	A-	N/A	N/A	252.1	150.5	178.9	-2.4
2018	A-	3.80	3.17	250.8	164.6	746.4	13.6
2017	A-	N/A	N/A	246.9	152.8	665.6	30.3
2016	A-	3.62	3.02	216.1	122.0	588.9	18.7
2015	B+	4.23	3.53	190.8	104.3	490.4	61.9
2014	U	4.39	3.66	70.7	26.9	87.5	8.9

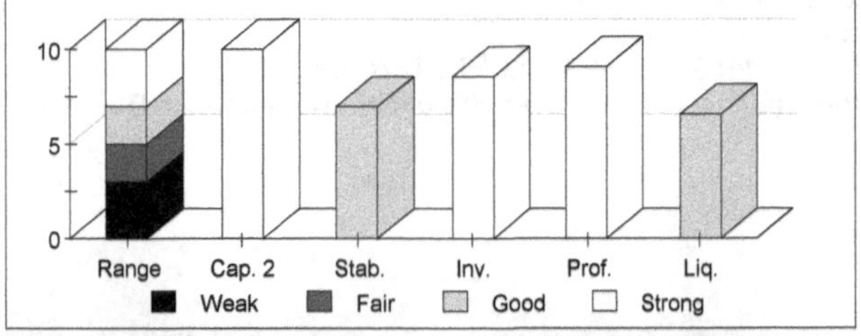

ANTHEM LIFE INSURANCE COMPANY * — B+ — Good

Major Rating Factors: Good overall results on stability tests (6.7 on a scale of 0 to 10) despite negative cash flow from operations for 2018. Other stability subfactors include excellent operational trends and excellent risk diversification. Good liquidity (5.8) with sufficient resources to handle a spike in claims. Strong capitalization (8.0) based on excellent risk adjusted capital (severe loss scenario).
Other Rating Factors: High quality investment portfolio (7.4). Excellent profitability (7.8).
Principal Business: Reinsurance (50%), group life insurance (28%), and group health insurance (22%).
Principal Investments: NonCMO investment grade bonds (52%), CMOs and structured securities (36%), cash (2%), and common & preferred stock (2%).
Investments in Affiliates: None
Group Affiliation: Anthem Inc
Licensed in: All states except NY, RI, VT, PR
Commenced Business: June 1956
Address: 120 MONUMENT CIRCLE, INDIANAPOLIS, IN 46204
Phone: (614) 433-8800 **Domicile State:** IN **NAIC Code:** 61069

Data Date	Rating	RACR #1	RACR #2	Total Assets ($mil)	Capital ($mil)	Net Premium ($mil)	Net Income ($mil)
3-19	B+	2.44	1.68	759.7	161.6	128.1	7.7
3-18	B	2.34	1.61	693.6	133.0	113.0	6.7
2018	B	2.11	1.46	732.3	148.9	430.8	21.9
2017	B-	1.98	1.37	674.7	125.1	412.0	12.3
2016	A-	1.85	1.28	623.3	108.9	362.3	28.3
2015	A-	1.64	1.16	633.7	95.9	368.9	18.2
2014	A-	1.92	1.34	582.4	109.1	357.8	34.4

Adverse Trends in Operations

Increase in policy surrenders from 2016 to 2017 (3256%)
Decrease in premium volume from 2015 to 2016 (2%)
Decrease in asset base during 2016 (2%)
Decrease in capital during 2015 (12%)

AR HEALTH & WELLNESS HLTH PLAN C- Fair

Major Rating Factors: Weak profitability index (0.9 on a scale of 0 to 10). Low quality investment portfolio (2.8). Strong capitalization (10.0) based on excellent current risk-adjusted capital (severe loss scenario).
Other Rating Factors: Excellent liquidity (7.0) with sufficient resources (cash flows and marketable investments) to handle a spike in claims.
Principal Business: Medicare (100%)
Mem Phys: 18: 19,565 **17:** N/A **18 MLR** 101.6% **/ 18 Admin Exp** N/A
Enroll(000): Q1 19: 14 **18:** 5 **17:** N/A **Med Exp PMPM:** $773
Principal Investments: Cash and equiv (62%), long-term bonds (3%), other (35%)
Provider Compensation ($000): Contr fee ($33,875), salary ($776), capitation ($588), bonus arrang ($168)
Total Member Encounters: Phys (100,744), non-phys (19,384)
Group Affiliation: None
Licensed in: AR
Address: , Little Rock, AR 72202
Phone: (314) 725-4477 **Dom State:** AR **Commenced Bus:** N/A

Data Date	Rating	RACR #1	RACR #2	Total Assets ($mil)	Capital ($mil)	Net Premium ($mil)	Net Income ($mil)
3-19	C-	3.69	3.08	38.5	15.5	31.5	-3.4
3-18	N/A	N/A	N/A	15.5	4.0	9.2	-1.1
2018	C-	1.77	1.48	21.8	7.4	42.6	-9.1
2017	N/A	N/A	N/A	5.5	5.2	N/A	N/A
2016	N/A	N/A	N/A	N/A	N/A	N/A	N/A
2015	N/A	N/A	N/A	N/A	N/A	N/A	N/A
2014	N/A	N/A	N/A	N/A	N/A	N/A	N/A

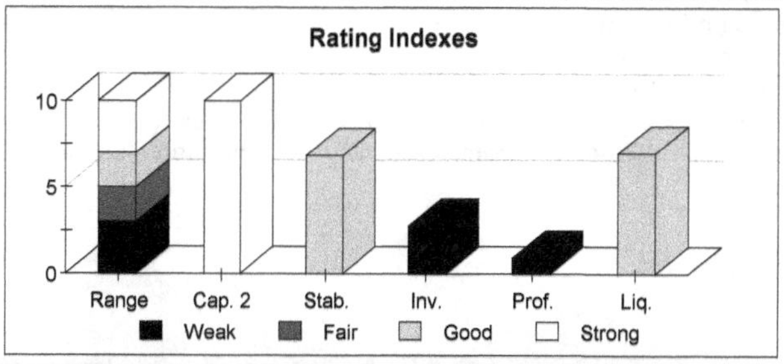

ARCADIAN HEALTH PLAN INC B- Good

Major Rating Factors: Good quality investment portfolio (6.7 on a scale of 0 to 10). Good liquidity (6.8) with sufficient resources (cash flows and marketable investments) to handle a spike in claims. Strong capitalization (10.0) based on excellent current risk-adjusted capital (severe loss scenario).
Other Rating Factors: Weak profitability index (2.0).
Principal Business: Medicare (100%)
Mem Phys: 18: 172,688 **17:** 42,788 **18 MLR** 84.0% **/ 18 Admin Exp** N/A
Enroll(000): Q1 19: 361 **18:** 323 **17:** 80 **Med Exp PMPM:** $757
Principal Investments: Long-term bonds (75%), cash and equiv (25%)
Provider Compensation ($000): Contr fee ($1,326,470), capitation ($1,324,952), FFS ($15,560), salary ($9,423)
Total Member Encounters: Phys (5,715,082), non-phys (2,873,565)
Group Affiliation: None
Licensed in: AL, AZ, AR, CA, ID, IN, KY, ME, MO, NE, NH, SC, TX, VA, WA, WV
Address: 300 DESCHUTES WAY SW Ste 304, TUMWATER, WA 98501
Phone: (502) 580-1000 **Dom State:** WA **Commenced Bus:** N/A

Data Date	Rating	RACR #1	RACR #2	Total Assets ($mil)	Capital ($mil)	Net Premium ($mil)	Net Income ($mil)
3-19	B-	4.10	3.42	1,073.7	613.3	1,063.1	47.2
3-18	B-	12.88	10.73	1,075.0	402.2	857.5	-46.6
2018	B-	3.42	2.85	834.3	511.5	3,417.7	59.7
2017	B-	5.62	4.68	305.9	237.5	803.6	29.0
2016	B-	4.86	4.05	275.8	171.0	812.9	-41.2
2015	C+	7.23	6.02	77.7	35.0	71.1	-32.7
2014	C	12.03	10.03	69.1	57.9	70.1	7.5

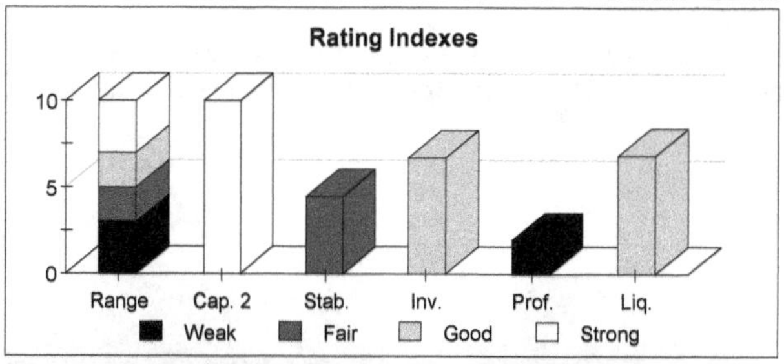

ARKANSAS SUPERIOR SELECT INC E Very Weak

Major Rating Factors: Weak profitability index (0.8 on a scale of 0 to 10). Weak liquidity (0.5) as a spike in claims may stretch capacity. Good capitalization (5.0) based on good current risk-adjusted capital (severe loss scenario).
Other Rating Factors: High quality investment portfolio (9.5).
Principal Business: Medicare (99%)
Mem Phys: 18: 2,611 **17:** 3,669 **18 MLR** 94.5% **/ 18 Admin Exp** N/A
Enroll(000): Q1 19: 3 **18:** 3 **17:** 1 **Med Exp PMPM:** $1,067
Principal Investments: Cash and equiv (91%), other (9%)
Provider Compensation ($000): Contr fee ($18,947), capitation ($1,760)
Total Member Encounters: Phys (18,766), non-phys (41,133)
Group Affiliation: Select Founders LLC
Licensed in: AR
Address: 1401 West Capital Ste 430, North Little Rock, AR 72114
Phone: (501) 372-1922 **Dom State:** AR **Commenced Bus:** N/A

Data Date	Rating	RACR #1	RACR #2	Total Assets ($mil)	Capital ($mil)	Net Premium ($mil)	Net Income ($mil)
3-19	E	0.93	0.77	13.6	5.1	6.9	-0.1
3-18	E	N/A	N/A	11.9	2.7	6.4	-0.3
2018	E	0.91	0.75	14.9	5.0	27.9	-4.2
2017	E	N/A	N/A	8.7	3.1	11.6	-4.5
2016	E	1.25	1.04	4.6	1.3	5.1	-3.5
2015	E	0.69	0.57	3.6	1.0	1.7	-4.1
2014	N/A	N/A	N/A	2.4	2.4	N/A	-1.2

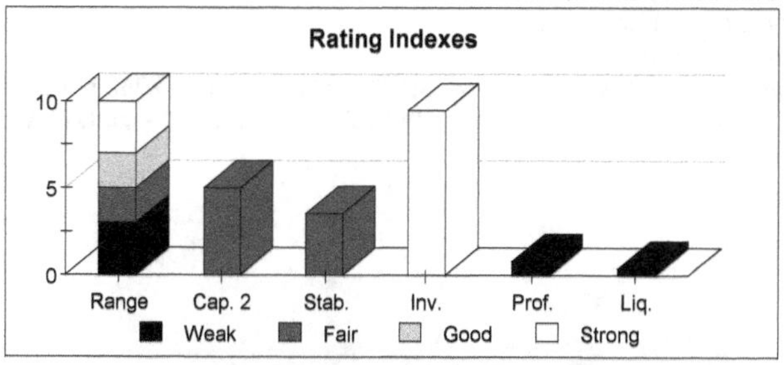

ASPIRE HEALTH PLAN E- Very Weak

Major Rating Factors: Weak profitability index (0.0 on a scale of 0 to 10). Poor capitalization index (0.0) based on weak current risk-adjusted capital (severe loss scenario). Weak overall results on stability tests (0.5) based on an excessive 39% enrollment growth during the period, a steep decline in capital during 2018.
Other Rating Factors: Weak liquidity (0.1) as a spike in claims may stretch capacity.
Principal Business: Medicare (100%)
Mem Phys: 18: N/A **17:** N/A **18 MLR** 98.7% **/ 18 Admin Exp** N/A
Enroll(000): Q1 19: 4 **18:** 3 **17:** 2 **Med Exp PMPM:** $847
Principal Investments ($000): Cash and equiv ($2,016)
Provider Compensation ($000): None
Total Member Encounters: N/A
Group Affiliation: None
Licensed in: CA
Address: 23625 Holman Highway, Monterey, CA 93940
Phone: (831) 625-4965 **Dom State:** CA **Commenced Bus:** April 2013

Data Date	Rating	RACR #1	RACR #2	Total Assets ($mil)	Capital ($mil)	Net Premium ($mil)	Net Income ($mil)
3-19	E-	N/A	N/A	6.0	-34.8	10.5	-2.0
3-18	E-	N/A	N/A	7.7	-24.6	8.8	-1.9
2018	E-	N/A	N/A	6.5	-32.8	34.1	-10.0
2017	E-	N/A	N/A	4.9	-22.7	23.4	-7.3
2016	E-	N/A	N/A	8.5	-15.2	13.7	1.6
2015	E-	N/A	N/A	3.8	-1.6	7.8	-6.0
2014	E-	N/A	N/A	2.6	-2.7	4.1	-4.3

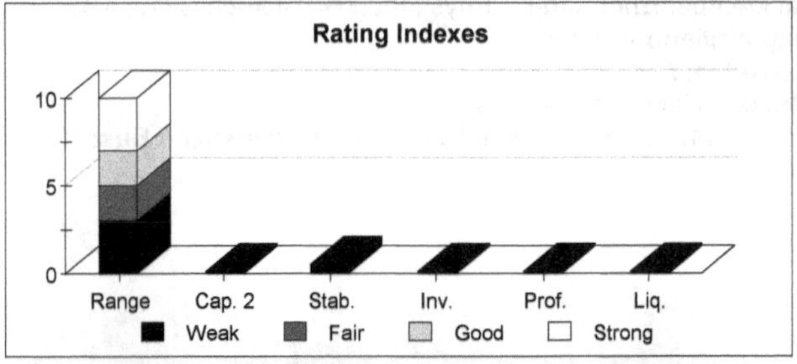

ASPIRUS ARISE HEALTH PLAN OF WISCONS C Fair

Major Rating Factors: Weak profitability index (0.9 on a scale of 0 to 10). Low quality investment portfolio (1.7). Strong capitalization (7.0) based on excellent current risk-adjusted capital (severe loss scenario).
Other Rating Factors: Excellent liquidity (7.1) with ample operational cash flow and liquid investments.
Principal Business: Comp med (100%)
Mem Phys: 18: 6,209 **17:** 6,209 **18 MLR** 90.1% **/ 18 Admin Exp** N/A
Enroll(000): Q1 19: 14 **18:** 14 **17:** 12 **Med Exp PMPM:** $489
Principal Investments: Cash and equiv (73%), long-term bonds (27%)
Provider Compensation ($000): Contr fee ($47,805), FFS ($32,290)
Total Member Encounters: Phys (73,871), non-phys (31,746)
Group Affiliation: Aspirus Inc
Licensed in: WI
Address: 3000 WESTHILL Dr Ste 303, WAUSAU, WI 54401
Phone: (715) 972-8135 **Dom State:** WI **Commenced Bus:** N/A

Data Date	Rating	RACR #1	RACR #2	Total Assets ($mil)	Capital ($mil)	Net Premium ($mil)	Net Income ($mil)
3-19	C	1.37	1.14	49.3	16.3	25.9	0.4
3-18	C-	1.23	1.02	39.9	11.3	20.9	-1.4
2018	C	1.34	1.11	43.2	15.9	92.5	-3.0
2017	U	1.10	0.92	30.8	12.9	65.1	-6.2
2016	N/A	N/A	N/A	2.4	1.1	N/A	-0.4
2015	N/A	N/A	N/A	N/A	N/A	N/A	N/A
2014	N/A	N/A	N/A	N/A	N/A	N/A	N/A

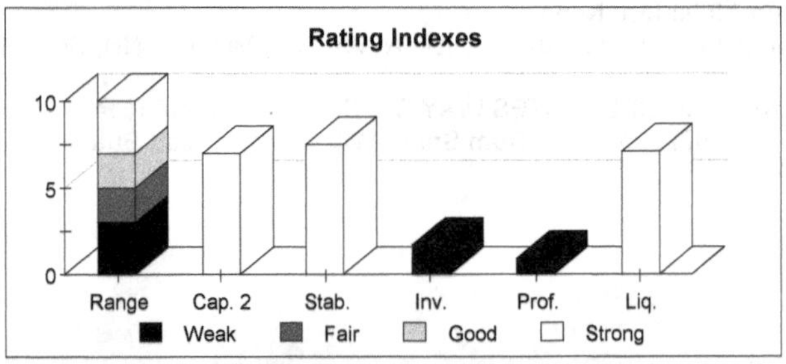

ASSN HEALTH CARE MGMT INC D Weak

Major Rating Factors: Weak profitability index (0.9 on a scale of 0 to 10). Poor capitalization index (2.6) based on weak current risk-adjusted capital (moderate loss scenario). Weak overall results on stability tests (2.1) based on an excessive 32% enrollment growth during the period.
Other Rating Factors: Excellent liquidity (7.0) with ample operational cash flow and liquid investments.
Principal Business: Indemnity (100%)
Mem Phys: 18: N/A **17:** N/A **18 MLR** N/A **/ 18 Admin Exp** N/A
Enroll(000): Q1 19: 7 **18:** 5 **17:** 4 **Med Exp PMPM:** N/A
Principal Investments ($000): Cash and equiv ($1,815)
Provider Compensation ($000): None
Total Member Encounters: N/A
Group Affiliation: None
Licensed in: (No states)
Address: 11111 Richmond Ave Ste 200, Houston, TX 77082-6602
Phone: (Phone number **Dom State:** CA **Commenced Bus:** N/A

Data Date	Rating	RACR #1	RACR #2	Total Assets ($mil)	Capital ($mil)	Net Premium ($mil)	Net Income ($mil)
3-19	D	0.47	0.47	1.8	0.5	9.3	1.3
3-18	D+	2.11	2.07	1.2	1.0	1.8	0.2
2018	D	0.43	0.43	1.9	0.5	10.8	-0.3
2017	U	1.75	1.71	1.0	0.8	6.1	-0.1
2016	N/A	N/A	N/A	N/A	N/A	N/A	N/A
2015	N/A	N/A	N/A	N/A	N/A	N/A	N/A
2014	N/A	N/A	N/A	N/A	N/A	N/A	N/A

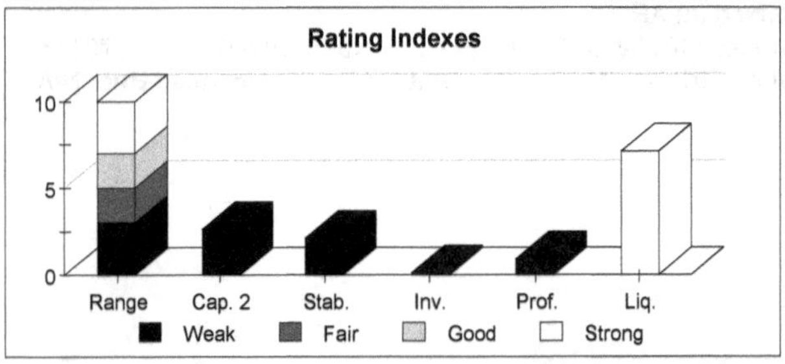

ASSURITY LIFE INSURANCE COMPANY * B+ Good

Major Rating Factors: Good quality investment portfolio (5.5 on a scale of 0 to 10) despite significant exposure to mortgages . Mortgage default rate has been low. large holdings of BBB rated bonds in addition to small junk bond holdings. Good overall profitability (6.1) despite operating losses during the first three months of 2019. Good liquidity (5.5).
Other Rating Factors: Good overall results on stability tests (6.6) excellent operational trends and excellent risk diversification. Strong capitalization (7.7) based on excellent risk adjusted capital (severe loss scenario).
Principal Business: Individual life insurance (47%), individual health insurance (27%), group health insurance (16%), individual annuities (5%), and other lines (6%).
Principal Investments: NonCMO investment grade bonds (56%), mortgages in good standing (18%), CMOs and structured securities (10%), policy loans (5%), and misc. investments (11%).
Investments in Affiliates: 1%
Group Affiliation: Assurity Security Group Inc
Licensed in: All states except NY, PR
Commenced Business: March 1964
Address: 2000 Q STREET, LINCOLN, NE 68503
Phone: (402) 476-6500 **Domicile State:** NE **NAIC Code:** 71439

Data Date	Rating	RACR #1	RACR #2	Total Assets ($mil)	Capital ($mil)	Net Premium ($mil)	Net Income ($mil)
3-19	B+	2.49	1.45	2,750.1	337.1	50.5	-1.2
3-18	B+	2.50	1.44	2,727.2	334.4	45.3	2.3
2018	B+	2.50	1.46	2,626.8	337.5	198.7	11.1
2017	B+	2.54	1.47	2,632.3	334.7	189.2	16.8
2016	B+	2.70	1.51	2,605.0	324.9	193.3	12.0
2015	B+	2.71	1.51	2,472.0	318.1	189.5	20.8
2014	B+	3.03	1.61	2,463.6	300.5	189.7	19.2

Rating Indexes

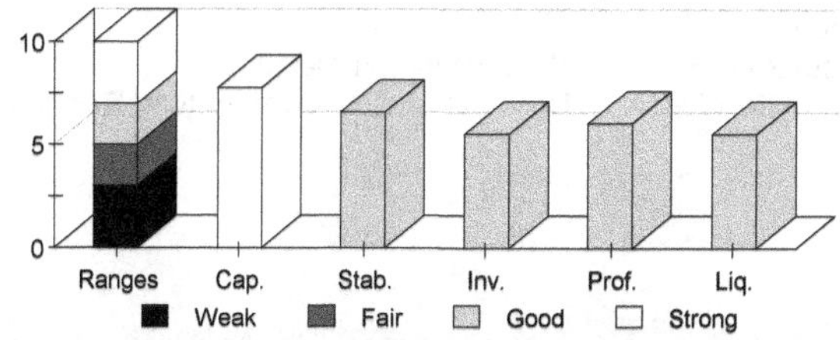

ASURIS NORTHWEST HEALTH B Good

Major Rating Factors: Good overall profitability index (6.1 on a scale of 0 to 10). Strong capitalization (10.0) based on excellent current risk-adjusted capital (severe loss scenario). High quality investment portfolio (9.8).
Other Rating Factors: Excellent liquidity (6.9) with sufficient resources (cash flows and marketable investments) to handle a spike in claims.
Principal Business: Comp med (80%), med supp (9%), Medicare (7%), other (4%)
Mem Phys: 18: 7,273 **17:** 6,723 **18 MLR** 75.2% **/ 18 Admin Exp** N/A
Enroll(000): Q1 19: 42 **18:** 44 **17:** 43 **Med Exp PMPM:** $231
Principal Investments: Long-term bonds (88%), cash and equiv (12%)
Provider Compensation ($000): Contr fee ($108,095), FFS ($17,642), bonus arrang ($76), capitation ($39)
Total Member Encounters: Phys (348,660), non-phys (457,696)
Group Affiliation: Cambia Health Solutions Inc
Licensed in: OR, WA
Address: 1800 NINTH Ave, SEATTLE, WA 98101
Phone: (206) 464-3600 **Dom State:** WA **Commenced Bus:** N/A

Data Date	Rating	RACR #1	RACR #2	Total Assets ($mil)	Capital ($mil)	Net Premium ($mil)	Net Income ($mil)
3-19	B	8.47	7.06	121.4	85.7	38.7	3.4
3-18	B-	5.16	4.30	105.4	65.8	43.1	-3.4
2018	B	8.14	6.78	112.3	82.2	168.7	11.0
2017	B-	3.46	2.89	98.7	68.5	185.4	2.2
2016	B-	6.94	5.79	92.1	65.8	141.6	0.8
2015	C+	6.94	5.78	91.7	64.5	145.4	5.1
2014	B-	5.47	4.56	90.5	60.2	167.0	-2.6

Rating Indexes

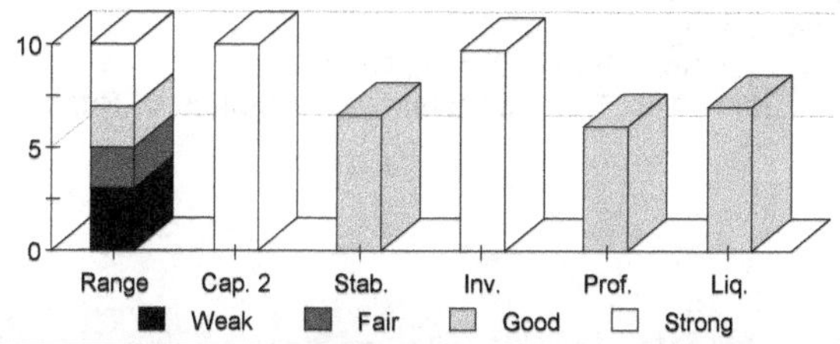

ATRIO HEALTH PLANS INC D Weak

Major Rating Factors: Weak profitability index (1.3 on a scale of 0 to 10). Good capitalization (6.2) based on good current risk-adjusted capital (severe loss scenario). High quality investment portfolio (7.2).
Other Rating Factors: Excellent liquidity (7.1) with ample operational cash flow and liquid investments.
Principal Business: Medicare (98%), comp med (2%)
Mem Phys: 18: 4,769 **17:** 5,292 **18 MLR** 80.5% **/ 18 Admin Exp** N/A
Enroll(000): Q1 19: 18 **18:** 20 **17:** 28 **Med Exp PMPM:** $689
Principal Investments: Long-term bonds (48%), cash and equiv (44%), other (8%)
Provider Compensation ($000): Capitation ($168,437), FFS ($6,718)
Total Member Encounters: Phys (635,682), non-phys (282,679)
Group Affiliation: ATRIO Health Plans Inc
Licensed in: OR
Address: 2270 NW Aviation Dr Ste 3, Roseburg, OR 97470
Phone: (541) 672-8620 **Dom State:** OR **Commenced Bus:** N/A

Data Date	Rating	RACR #1	RACR #2	Total Assets ($mil)	Capital ($mil)	Net Premium ($mil)	Net Income ($mil)
3-19	D	1.11	0.92	63.4	20.3	51.5	1.1
3-18	D	0.58	0.48	66.5	13.9	56.0	-1.3
2018	D	1.01	0.84	62.9	18.6	203.9	2.7
2017	D+	0.68	0.57	52.1	16.3	257.0	-9.4
2016	C-	1.68	1.40	50.4	25.5	203.3	-3.5
2015	C-	2.23	1.85	46.5	28.1	176.1	1.3
2014	C-	1.31	1.09	40.3	23.4	159.8	2.5

Rating Indexes

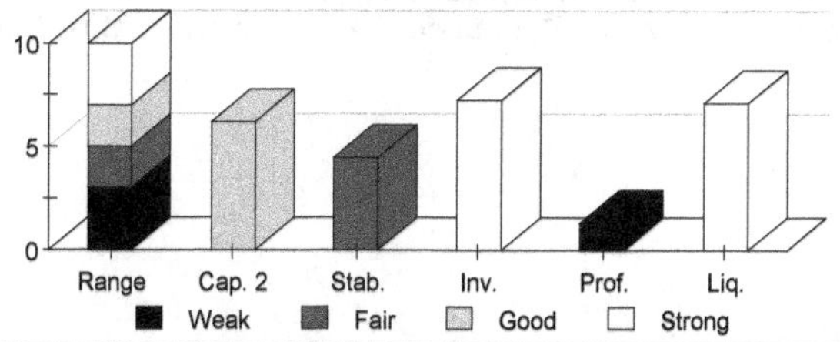

* Denotes a Weiss Ratings Recommended Company

AULTCARE HEALTH INSURING CORP B Good

Major Rating Factors: Good quality investment portfolio (4.9 on a scale of 0 to 10). Good liquidity (6.8) with sufficient resources (cash flows and marketable investments) to handle a spike in claims. Fair profitability index (4.7).
Other Rating Factors: Strong capitalization (7.8) based on excellent current risk-adjusted capital (severe loss scenario).
Principal Business: Medicare (100%)
Mem Phys: 18: 3,564 **17:** 3,619 **18 MLR** 84.4% **/ 18 Admin Exp** N/A
Enroll(000): Q1 19: 20 **18:** 20 **17:** 21 **Med Exp PMPM:** $850
Principal Investments: Affiliate common stock (49%), long-term bonds (28%), nonaffiliate common stock (9%), cash and equiv (2%), other (11%)
Provider Compensation ($000): Contr fee ($125,649), capitation ($61,305), FFS ($14,668)
Total Member Encounters: Phys (210,738), non-phys (447,197)
Group Affiliation: None
Licensed in: OH
Address: 2600 Sixth St SW, Canton, OH 44710
Phone: (330) 363-4057 **Dom State:** OH **Commenced Bus:** N/A

Data Date	Rating	RACR #1	RACR #2	Total Assets ($mil)	Capital ($mil)	Net Premium ($mil)	Net Income ($mil)
3-19	B	2.02	1.69	109.1	92.2	62.9	1.4
3-18	B	N/A	N/A	123.5	89.7	60.7	0.7
2018	B	1.91	1.59	105.8	87.1	242.6	7.1
2017	B	N/A	N/A	106.6	90.0	244.8	7.2
2016	B-	1.92	1.60	97.3	76.9	245.0	5.1
2015	C-	1.52	1.26	82.6	64.6	226.7	-3.9
2014	N/A	N/A	N/A	66.3	66.3	N/A	N/A

Rating Indexes

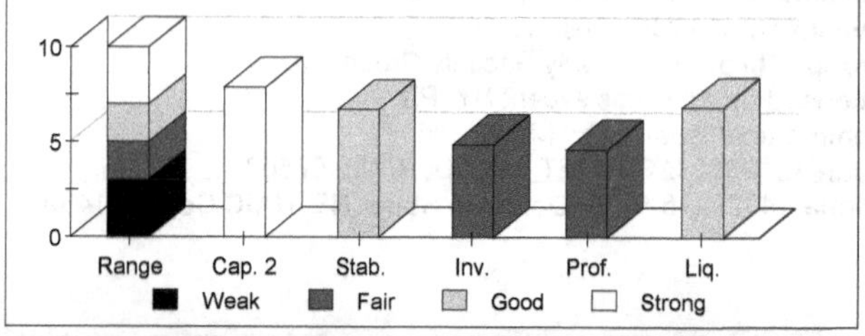

AULTCARE INS CO B Good

Major Rating Factors: Good liquidity (6.0 on a scale of 0 to 10) with sufficient resources (cash flows and marketable investments) to handle a spike in claims. Excellent profitability (7.6). Strong capitalization (7.8) based on excellent current risk-adjusted capital (severe loss scenario).
Other Rating Factors: High quality investment portfolio (8.6).
Principal Business: Comp med (85%), FEHB (5%), dental (1%), other (8%)
Mem Phys: 18: 3,564 **17:** 3,619 **18 MLR** 89.4% **/ 18 Admin Exp** N/A
Enroll(000): Q1 19: 74 **18:** 83 **17:** 85 **Med Exp PMPM:** $243
Principal Investments: Long-term bonds (38%), cash and equiv (25%), nonaffiliate common stock (12%), other (25%)
Provider Compensation ($000): Contr fee ($150,481), FFS ($39,356), capitation ($32,769)
Total Member Encounters: Phys (206,878), non-phys (409,657)
Group Affiliation: None
Licensed in: OH
Address: 2600 Sixth St SW, Canton, OH 44710
Phone: (330) 363-4057 **Dom State:** OH **Commenced Bus:** N/A

Data Date	Rating	RACR #1	RACR #2	Total Assets ($mil)	Capital ($mil)	Net Premium ($mil)	Net Income ($mil)
3-19	B	2.00	1.67	93.2	50.9	64.5	0.9
3-18	B	2.19	1.82	113.3	48.2	68.1	-1.1
2018	B	1.90	1.58	94.5	48.3	277.1	3.8
2017	C+	1.93	1.61	95.6	49.2	254.7	6.5
2016	C	2.01	1.68	86.1	42.7	259.3	5.5
2015	C-	1.79	1.49	84.0	36.0	250.2	7.7
2014	C-	1.59	1.33	116.1	62.4	465.7	5.4

Rating Indexes

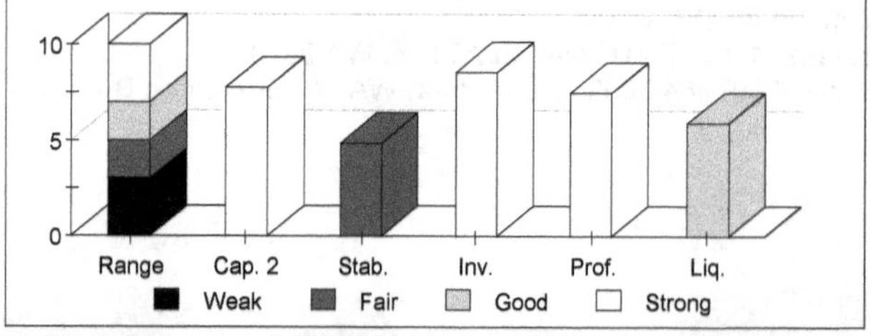

AVALON INS CO D+ Weak

Major Rating Factors: Weak profitability index (0.7 on a scale of 0 to 10). Weak liquidity (1.9) as a spike in claims may stretch capacity. Good quality investment portfolio (5.9).
Other Rating Factors: Strong capitalization (7.8) based on excellent current risk-adjusted capital (severe loss scenario).
Principal Business: Med supp (2%), vision (1%), other (97%)
Mem Phys: 18: 781 **17:** 786 **18 MLR** 103.8% **/ 18 Admin Exp** N/A
Enroll(000): Q1 19: 291 **18:** 347 **17:** 307 **Med Exp PMPM:** $16
Principal Investments: Long-term bonds (70%), cash and equiv (30%)
Provider Compensation ($000): Contr fee ($9,729), other ($52,891)
Total Member Encounters: Phys (13,909), non-phys (230,504)
Group Affiliation: None
Licensed in: DC, DE, MD, PA, VA, WV
Address: 2500 Elmerton Ave, Harrisburg, PA 17177-9799
Phone: (717) 541-7000 **Dom State:** PA **Commenced Bus:** N/A

Data Date	Rating	RACR #1	RACR #2	Total Assets ($mil)	Capital ($mil)	Net Premium ($mil)	Net Income ($mil)
3-19	D+	1.98	1.65	39.4	16.4	14.3	-2.1
3-18	C	3.44	2.87	35.0	17.8	15.0	-1.9
2018	D+	2.24	1.86	42.9	18.6	63.7	-18.7
2017	C	2.18	1.82	39.7	19.7	62.9	-4.0
2016	C	2.05	1.70	38.3	15.5	63.8	-9.3
2015	C	2.81	2.35	41.4	18.4	62.4	-4.7
2014	C	2.04	1.70	33.9	13.8	56.0	-6.1

Rating Indexes

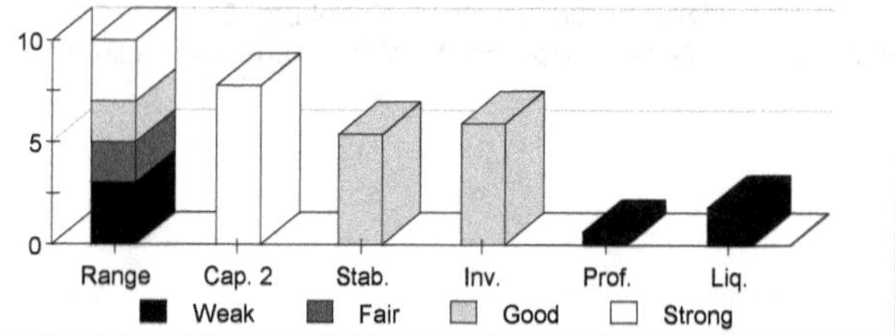

AVERA HEALTH PLANS INC — B — Good

Major Rating Factors: Good liquidity (6.7 on a scale of 0 to 10) with sufficient resources (cash flows and marketable investments) to handle a spike in claims. Fair profitability index (4.8). Strong capitalization index (7.5) based on excellent current risk-adjusted capital (severe loss scenario).
Other Rating Factors: High quality investment portfolio (7.2). Excellent overall results on stability tests (7.9) despite a decline in enrollment during 2018.
Principal Business: Comp med (92%), med supp (8%)
Mem Phys: 18: 6,810 **17:** 6,364 **18 MLR** 88.9% **/ 18 Admin Exp** N/A
Enroll(000): Q1 19: 54 **18:** 50 **17:** 53 **Med Exp PMPM:** $366
Principal Investments: Long-term bonds (57%), cash and equiv (24%), nonaffiliate common stock (19%)
Provider Compensation ($000): FFS ($120,686), contr fee ($98,393)
Total Member Encounters: Phys (76,230), non-phys (45,953)
Group Affiliation: None
Licensed in: IA, NE, SD
Address: 3816 S Elmwood Ave Suite 100, Sioux Falls, SD 57105-6538
Phone: (605) 322-4545 **Dom State:** SD **Commenced Bus:** N/A

Data Date	Rating	RACR #1	RACR #2	Total Assets ($mil)	Capital ($mil)	Net Premium ($mil)	Net Income ($mil)
3-19	B	1.78	1.49	89.5	49.2	62.3	7.6
3-18	C	1.18	0.99	80.5	34.4	59.4	2.2
2018	B	1.42	1.18	77.7	39.8	245.7	13.0
2017	C	1.09	0.90	77.1	31.8	249.8	8.2
2016	C-	0.91	0.76	56.6	22.2	191.6	0.6
2015	C-	1.19	0.99	47.7	22.1	123.5	-17.9
2014	N/A	N/A	N/A	32.5	11.5	118.0	0.6

Rating Indexes

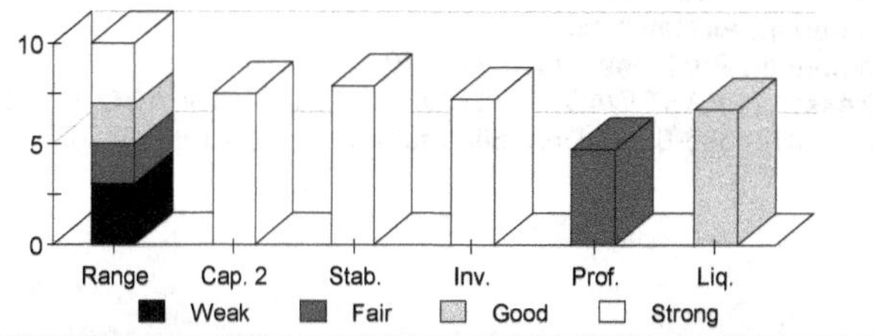

AVMED INC — C — Fair

Major Rating Factors: Weak profitability index (2.4 on a scale of 0 to 10). Good capitalization index (6.2) based on good current risk-adjusted capital (severe loss scenario). Good overall results on stability tests (5.3).
Other Rating Factors: Good liquidity (5.3) with sufficient resources (cash flows and marketable investments) to handle a spike in claims. High quality investment portfolio (7.3).
Principal Business: Comp med (59%), Medicare (39%), FEHB (2%)
Mem Phys: 18: 40,983 **17:** 39,993 **18 MLR** 86.4% **/ 18 Admin Exp** N/A
Enroll(000): Q1 19: 82 **18:** 105 **17:** 165 **Med Exp PMPM:** $547
Principal Investments: Long-term bonds (79%), nonaffiliate common stock (13%), cash and equiv (5%), real estate (4%)
Provider Compensation ($000): Contr fee ($466,521), FFS ($213,158), capitation ($124,455), bonus arrang ($1,922)
Total Member Encounters: N/A
Group Affiliation: SantaFe HealthCare Inc
Licensed in: FL
Address: 9400 South Dadeland Boulevard, Miami, FL 33156
Phone: (352) 372-8400 **Dom State:** FL **Commenced Bus:** N/A

Data Date	Rating	RACR #1	RACR #2	Total Assets ($mil)	Capital ($mil)	Net Premium ($mil)	Net Income ($mil)
3-19	C	1.11	0.92	264.8	98.9	186.6	4.1
3-18	C	0.72	0.60	338.0	76.9	242.3	-2.7
2018	C	1.03	0.86	251.8	94.0	923.8	14.9
2017	C	0.75	0.63	308.8	80.1	1,098.7	0.2
2016	C	0.99	0.83	281.1	81.7	967.8	-15.5
2015	B-	1.54	1.28	283.7	99.9	819.8	-6.0
2014	B	1.94	1.61	253.6	115.2	723.8	-48.5

Rating Indexes

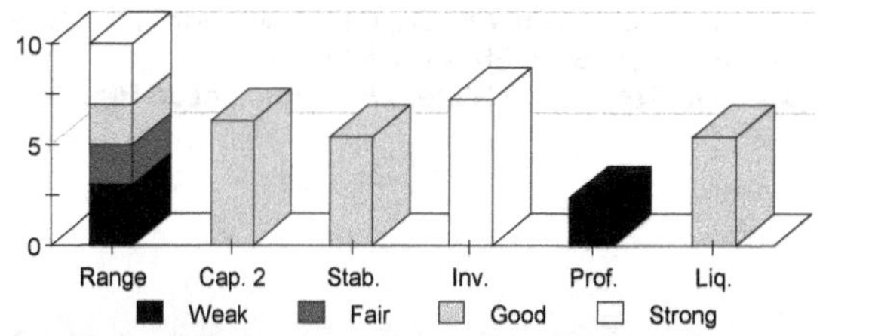

BANKERS FIDELITY LIFE INSURANCE COMPANY — C — Fair

Major Rating Factors: Fair quality investment portfolio (4.8 on a scale of 0 to 10). Fair liquidity (3.8) as cash from operations and sale of marketable assets may not be adequate to cover a spike in claims. Fair overall results on stability tests (3.8) including negative cash flow from operations for 2018.
Other Rating Factors: Good capitalization (5.6) based on good risk adjusted capital (severe loss scenario). Weak profitability (2.0) with operating losses during the first three months of 2019.
Principal Business: Individual health insurance (73%), reinsurance (21%), individual life insurance (5%), and group health insurance (1%).
Principal Investments: NonCMO investment grade bonds (72%), common & preferred stock (11%), noninv. grade bonds (6%), CMOs and structured securities (5%), and misc. investments (5%).
Investments in Affiliates: 9%
Group Affiliation: Atlantic American Corp
Licensed in: All states except CA, CT, NY, VT, PR
Commenced Business: November 1955
Address: 4370 Peachtree Road NE, Atlanta, GA 30319
Phone: (800) 241-1439 **Domicile State:** GA **NAIC Code:** 61239

Data Date	Rating	RACR #1	RACR #2	Total Assets ($mil)	Capital ($mil)	Net Premium ($mil)	Net Income ($mil)
3-19	C	1.04	0.82	151.8	33.2	31.8	-2.3
3-18	C+	1.11	0.85	146.8	31.7	29.9	-1.9
2018	C	1.09	0.87	152.5	34.2	119.0	-3.4
2017	B-	1.21	0.93	150.0	34.1	109.6	-2.9
2016	B	1.24	0.94	144.3	33.4	99.6	1.2
2015	B	1.28	0.96	143.9	35.3	96.1	4.0
2014	B	1.21	0.92	139.1	34.0	100.2	2.7

Rating Indexes

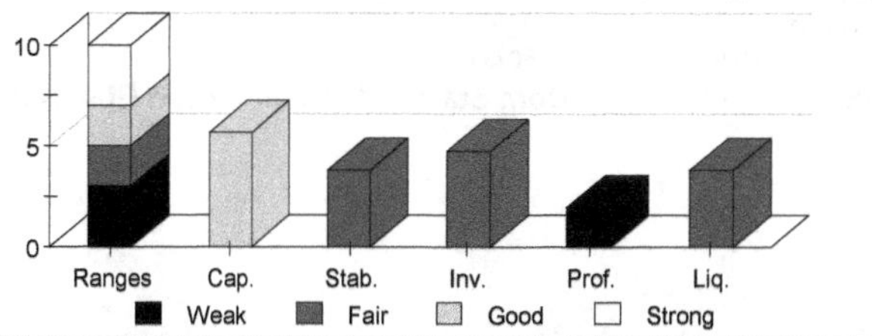

BANKERS LIFE & CASUALTY COMPANY D+ Weak

Major Rating Factors: Weak overall results on stability tests (2.7 on a scale of 0 to 10). Fair quality investment portfolio (4.4) with large holdings of BBB rated bonds in addition to junk bond exposure equal to 62% of capital. Fair profitability (3.4). Excellent expense controls.

Other Rating Factors: Good capitalization (6.7) based on good risk adjusted capital (severe loss scenario). Good liquidity (5.4).

Principal Business: Individual annuities (42%), individual health insurance (27%), individual life insurance (17%), reinsurance (14%), and group health insurance (1%).

Principal Investments: NonCMO investment grade bonds (51%), CMOs and structured securities (28%), mortgages in good standing (7%), noninv. grade bonds (5%), and misc. investments (8%).

Investments in Affiliates: 1%

Group Affiliation: CNO Financial Group Inc

Licensed in: All states except NY, PR

Commenced Business: January 1879

Address: 111 EAST WACKER DRIVE STE 2100, CHICAGO, IL 60601-4508

Phone: (312) 396-6000 **Domicile State:** IL **NAIC Code:** 61263

Data Date	Rating	RACR #1	RACR #2	Total Assets ($mil)	Capital ($mil)	Net Premium ($mil)	Net Income ($mil)
3-19	D+	1.71	0.96	15,753.0	1,168.3	654.3	76.9
3-18	D+	2.01	1.06	18,474.4	1,365.7	642.3	43.6
2018	D+	1.64	0.92	15,514.6	1,110.2	2,556.4	-299.9
2017	D+	2.10	1.11	18,273.9	1,336.8	2,581.5	249.3
2016	D+	2.32	1.20	17,602.0	1,300.3	2,535.9	171.2
2015	D+	2.23	1.16	16,905.4	1,238.6	2,385.0	188.7
2014	D+	2.12	1.10	16,590.7	1,193.1	2,387.1	211.6

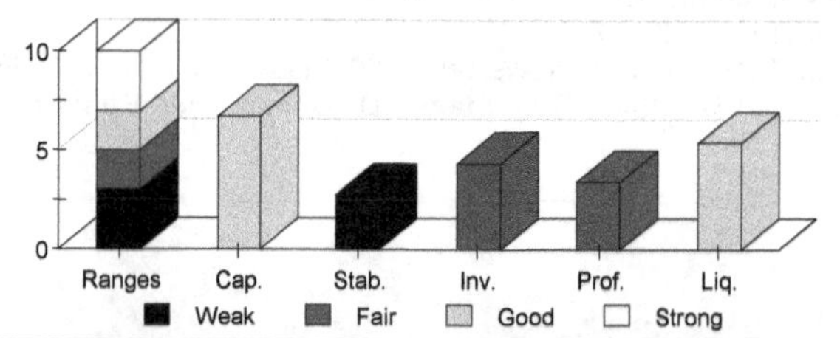

BANKERS RESERVE LIFE INS CO OF WI C- Fair

Major Rating Factors: Weak profitability index (1.1 on a scale of 0 to 10). Good liquidity (6.7) with sufficient resources (cash flows and marketable investments) to handle a spike in claims. Strong capitalization (7.9) based on excellent current risk-adjusted capital (severe loss scenario).

Other Rating Factors: High quality investment portfolio (7.8).

Principal Business: Medicaid (94%), comp med (6%)

Mem Phys: 18: 59,918 **17:** 55,538 **18 MLR** 89.9% **/ 18 Admin Exp** N/A

Enroll(000): Q1 19: 507 **18:** 512 **17:** 529 **Med Exp PMPM:** $302

Principal Investments: Long-term bonds (58%), cash and equiv (37%), affiliate common stock (3%), other (2%)

Provider Compensation ($000): Contr fee ($1,420,737), bonus arrang ($385,228), salary ($63,062), FFS ($16,804), capitation ($12,695)

Total Member Encounters: Phys (2,747,197), non-phys (9,603,546)

Group Affiliation: None

Licensed in: All states except AK, CA, CT, HI, MA, MN, NY, VT, PR

Address: 7700 Forsyth Blvd, St. Louis, MO 63105

Phone: (314) 505-6143 **Dom State:** WI **Commenced Bus:** N/A

Data Date	Rating	RACR #1	RACR #2	Total Assets ($mil)	Capital ($mil)	Net Premium ($mil)	Net Income ($mil)
3-19	C-	2.08	1.73	448.3	233.5	529.2	-1.4
3-18	C-	1.87	1.56	407.4	195.4	507.7	-21.7
2018	C-	2.06	1.71	436.3	230.8	2,110.2	14.1
2017	C-	1.32	1.10	409.9	191.0	1,904.0	-65.9
2016	C-	2.14	1.78	410.4	223.7	1,958.6	-20.7
2015	C-	2.17	1.81	425.9	244.4	2,102.0	-21.7
2014	C-	2.18	1.82	468.8	268.0	2,363.6	11.2

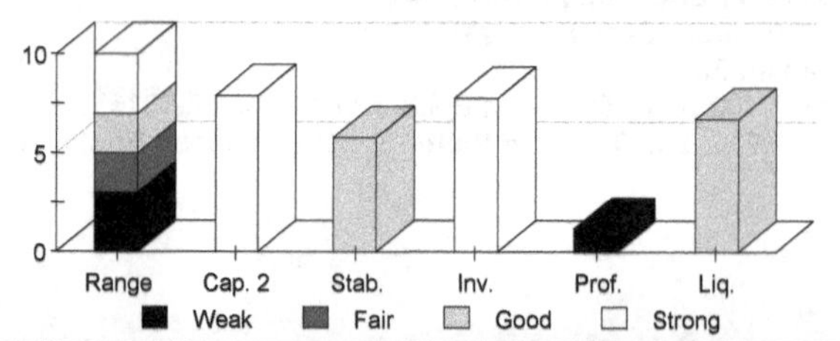

BANNER HEALTH & AETNA HLTH INS C Fair

Major Rating Factors: Weak profitability index (2.7 on a scale of 0 to 10). Good quality investment portfolio (6.8). Strong capitalization (10.0) based on excellent current risk-adjusted capital (severe loss scenario).

Other Rating Factors: Excellent liquidity (8.0) with ample operational cash flow and liquid investments.

Principal Business: Comp med (100%)

Mem Phys: 18: 14,484 **17:** N/A **18 MLR** 25.6% **/ 18 Admin Exp** N/A

Enroll(000): Q1 19: 36 **18:** 32 **17:** N/A **Med Exp PMPM:** $257

Principal Investments: Long-term bonds (52%), cash and equiv (34%), affiliate common stock (12%), nonaffiliate common stock (2%)

Provider Compensation ($000): Contr fee ($42,761), FFS ($5,820), bonus arrang ($4)

Total Member Encounters: Phys (203,025), non-phys (171,045)

Group Affiliation: None

Licensed in: AZ

Address: , PHOENIX, AZ 85040

Phone: (602) 659-1100 **Dom State:** AZ **Commenced Bus:** N/A

Data Date	Rating	RACR #1	RACR #2	Total Assets ($mil)	Capital ($mil)	Net Premium ($mil)	Net Income ($mil)
3-19	C	4.45	3.71	136.3	67.5	51.2	2.3
3-18	N/A	N/A	N/A	150.0	53.8	65.3	5.0
2018	C	3.97	3.31	133.1	59.5	233.3	-7.6
2017	N/A	N/A	N/A	113.3	41.3	179.3	6.7
2016	N/A	N/A	N/A	N/A	N/A	N/A	N/A
2015	N/A	N/A	N/A	N/A	N/A	N/A	N/A
2014	N/A	N/A	N/A	N/A	N/A	N/A	N/A

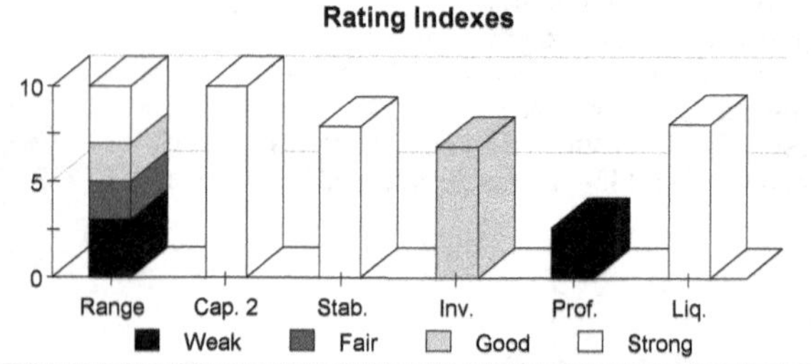

BANNER HLTH & AETNA HLTH PLAN B- Good

Major Rating Factors: Fair profitability index (4.3 on a scale of 0 to 10). Strong capitalization (10.0) based on excellent current risk-adjusted capital (severe loss scenario). High quality investment portfolio (9.0).
Other Rating Factors: Excellent liquidity (6.9) with sufficient resources (cash flows and marketable investments) to handle a spike in claims.
Principal Business: Comp med (100%)
Mem Phys: 18: 14,484 **17:** N/A **18 MLR** 52.3% **/ 18 Admin Exp** N/A
Enroll(000): Q1 19: 5 **18:** 5 **17:** N/A **Med Exp PMPM:** $272
Principal Investments: Long-term bonds (61%), cash and equiv (37%), nonaffiliate common stock (2%)
Provider Compensation ($000): Contr fee ($9,981), FFS ($1,895), capitation ($6)
Total Member Encounters: Phys (38,360), non-phys (32,832)
Group Affiliation: None
Licensed in: AZ
Address: , PHOENIX, AZ 85040
Phone: (602) 659-1100 **Dom State:** AZ **Commenced Bus:** N/A

Data Date	Rating	RACR #1	RACR #2	Total Assets ($mil)	Capital ($mil)	Net Premium ($mil)	Net Income ($mil)
3-19	B-	5.35	4.46	22.1	12.9	5.6	2.7
3-18	N/A	N/A	N/A	22.5	10.6	11.0	1.8
2018	C	4.22	3.51	25.9	9.8	27.5	-1.3
2017	N/A	N/A	N/A	14.8	6.5	16.6	1.6
2016	N/A	N/A	N/A	N/A	N/A	N/A	N/A
2015	N/A	N/A	N/A	N/A	N/A	N/A	N/A
2014	N/A	N/A	N/A	N/A	N/A	N/A	N/A

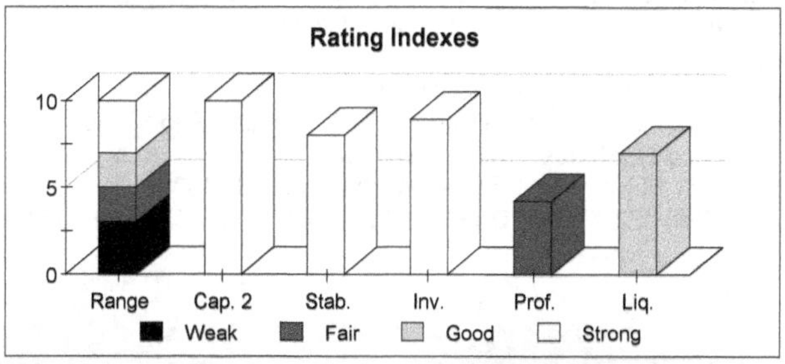

BAPTIST HEALTH PLAN INC D Weak

Major Rating Factors: Weak profitability index (0.2 on a scale of 0 to 10). Weak overall results on stability tests (2.1) based on a significant 100% decrease in enrollment during the period, a steep decline in capital during 2018. Fair capitalization index (2.9) based on good current risk-adjusted capital (moderate loss scenario
Other Rating Factors: Good quality investment portfolio (5.5). Good liquidity (5.5) with sufficient resources (cash flows and marketable investments) to handle a spike in claims.
Principal Business: Comp med (100%)
Mem Phys: 18: 44,773 **17:** 44,773 **18 MLR** 88.3% **/ 18 Admin Exp** N/A
Enroll(000): Q1 19: N/A **18:** N/A **17:** 22 **Med Exp PMPM:** N/A
Principal Investments: Long-term bonds (52%), nonaffiliate common stock (36%), cash and equiv (12%)
Provider Compensation ($000): Contr fee ($29,133), FFS ($704), capitation ($104)
Total Member Encounters: Phys (19,435), non-phys (4,852)
Group Affiliation: Baptist Healthcare System Inc
Licensed in: IL, IN, KY, OH, TN, WV
Address: 651 Perimeter Drive STE 300, Lexington, KY 40517
Phone: (859) 269-4475 **Dom State:** KY **Commenced Bus:** N/A

Data Date	Rating	RACR #1	RACR #2	Total Assets ($mil)	Capital ($mil)	Net Premium ($mil)	Net Income ($mil)
3-19	D	1.37	1.14	15.5	9.6	0.0	-0.2
3-18	E	0.32	0.26	33.0	10.2	9.0	-1.2
2018	D-	1.26	1.05	16.4	8.9	16.4	-4.2
2017	E	0.31	0.26	43.0	11.3	135.2	-11.8
2016	D+	0.63	0.53	76.2	19.1	153.1	-24.8
2015	C	2.71	2.26	68.0	34.9	129.8	-18.5
2014	B	4.08	3.40	100.6	71.7	145.8	-6.3

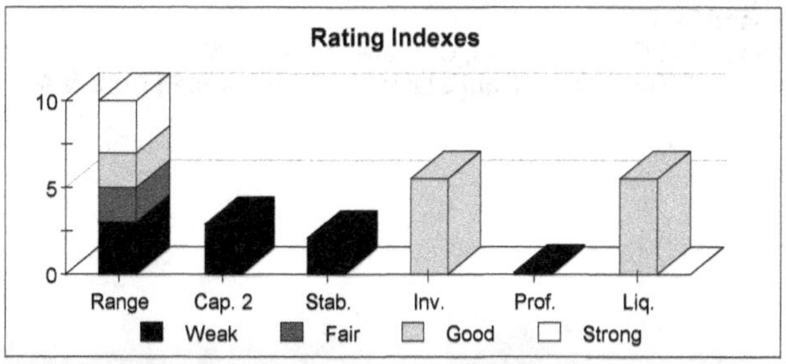

BAY AREA ACCOUNTABLE CARE D Weak

Major Rating Factors: Weak profitability index (0.9 on a scale of 0 to 10). Weak liquidity (0.0) as a spike in claims may stretch capacity. Fair capitalization index (4.2) based on weak current risk-adjusted capital (moderate loss scenario).
Other Rating Factors: Fair overall results on stability tests (4.2) in spite of healthy premium and capital growth during 2018 but an excessive 76% enrollment growth during the period.
Principal Business: Managed care (100%)
Mem Phys: 18: N/A **17:** N/A **18 MLR** 95.0% **/ 18 Admin Exp** N/A
Enroll(000): Q1 19: 44 **18:** 26 **17:** 15 **Med Exp PMPM:** $413
Principal Investments ($000): Cash and equiv ($26,611)
Provider Compensation ($000): None
Total Member Encounters: N/A
Group Affiliation: None
Licensed in: CA
Address: 6475 Christie Avenue Suite 360, Emeryville, CA 94608
Phone: (415) 299-7840 **Dom State:** CA **Commenced Bus:** N/A

Data Date	Rating	RACR #1	RACR #2	Total Assets ($mil)	Capital ($mil)	Net Premium ($mil)	Net Income ($mil)
3-19	D	0.68	0.42	46.4	12.7	57.7	-3.2
3-18	D-	0.22	0.14	25.2	6.9	31.8	-1.8
2018	D-	0.46	0.28	33.1	9.4	126.7	-12.4
2017	D-	0.11	0.07	20.5	5.7	87.6	-4.1
2016	D+	2.43	1.53	18.1	9.7	31.5	-1.9
2015	N/A	N/A	N/A	N/A	N/A	N/A	N/A
2014	N/A	N/A	N/A	N/A	N/A	N/A	N/A

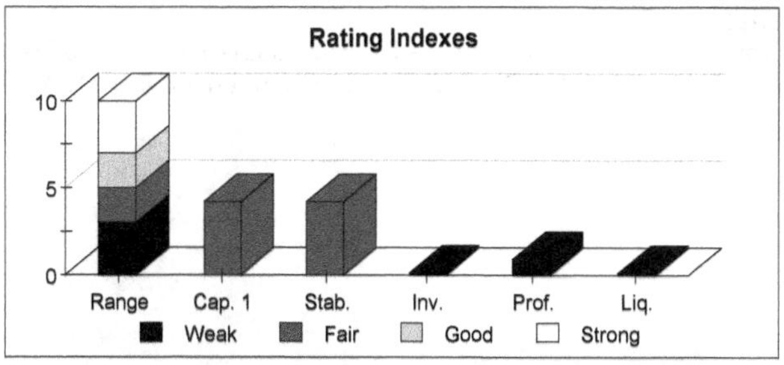

BCS INS CO B- Good

Major Rating Factors: Fair profitability index (3.8 on a scale of 0 to 10). Fair expense controls. Return on equity has been fair, averaging 7.9% over the past five years. Fair overall results on stability tests (3.5).
Other Rating Factors: Good liquidity (6.7) with sufficient resources (cash flows and marketable investments) to handle a spike in claims. Strong long-term capitalization index (10.0) based on excellent current risk adjusted capital (severe and moderate loss scenarios), despite some fluctuation in capital levels. Ample reserve history (7.0) that can protect against increases in claims costs.
Principal Business: Group accident & health (47%), inland marine (30%), other liability (13%), commercial multiple peril (9%), and aggregate write-ins for other lines of business (1%).
Principal Investments: Investment grade bonds (87%), misc. investments (13%), and non investment grade bonds (1%).
Investments in Affiliates: 0%
Group Affiliation: BCS Financial Corp
Licensed in: All states, the District of Columbia and Puerto Rico
Commenced Business: November 1952
Address: 6740 North High Street, Worthington, OH 43085
Phone: (630) 472-7700 **Domicile State:** OH **NAIC Code:** 38245

Data Date	Rating	RACR #1	RACR #2	Loss Ratio %	Total Assets ($mil)	Capital ($mil)	Net Premium ($mil)	Net Income ($mil)
3-19	B-	10.74	6.12	N/A	343.2	155.3	23.8	4.8
3-18	B-	10.82	5.97	N/A	284.0	150.6	23.5	3.9
2018	B	9.94	5.66	58.1	336.6	141.9	97.6	11.3
2017	B	10.47	5.80	57.9	276.6	147.0	98.6	13.9
2016	B	8.93	5.13	64.9	269.4	155.2	101.8	11.4
2015	B	8.58	4.87	60.5	272.2	161.3	95.3	13.3
2014	B	6.63	3.81	69.0	279.6	157.2	129.6	8.0

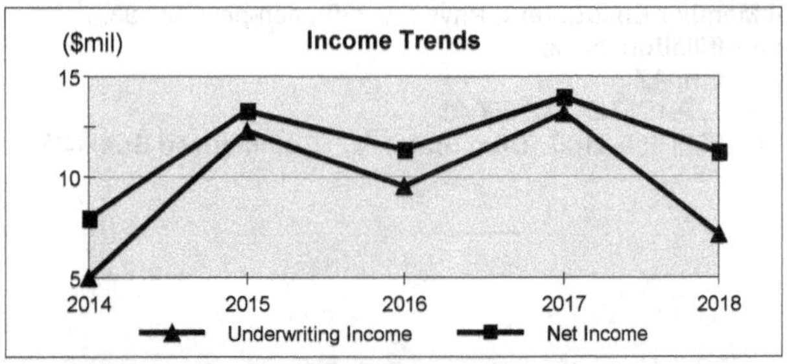

BEACON HEALTH OPTIONS OF PA E+ Very Weak

Major Rating Factors: Excellent profitability (8.2 on a scale of 0 to 10). Strong capitalization (10.0) based on excellent current risk-adjusted capital (severe loss scenario). High quality investment portfolio (9.9).
Other Rating Factors: Excellent liquidity (10.0) with ample operational cash flow and liquid investments.
Principal Business: Medicaid (100%)
Mem Phys: 18: 1,245 **17:** 1,164 **18 MLR** 71.5% **/ 18 Admin Exp** N/A
Enroll(000): Q1 19: 9 **18:** 9 **17:** 9 **Med Exp PMPM:** $81
Principal Investments: Cash and equiv (100%)
Provider Compensation ($000): Contr fee ($14,913)
Total Member Encounters: Phys (15,315), non-phys (544,481)
Group Affiliation: DCP 2014 GP-GP LLC
Licensed in: PA
Address: 240 Corporate Blvd, Chesapeake, VA 23320
Phone: (757) 459-5418 **Dom State:** PA **Commenced Bus:** N/A

Data Date	Rating	RACR #1	RACR #2	Total Assets ($mil)	Capital ($mil)	Net Premium ($mil)	Net Income ($mil)
3-19	E+	7.75	6.45	28.2	17.1	3.6	2.3
3-18	E	5.36	4.47	36.7	20.7	4.0	2.6
2018	E	6.74	5.62	24.3	14.8	12.5	10.2
2017	E	4.71	3.93	34.0	18.2	28.7	8.6
2016	E	2.26	1.89	43.8	19.7	83.8	7.5
2015	E	1.87	1.56	46.5	19.1	105.2	7.4
2014	E	1.57	1.31	34.8	16.2	101.4	3.7

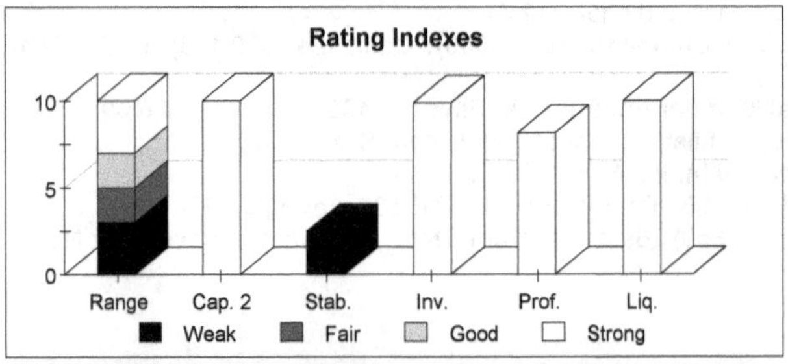

BEHEALTHY FLORIDA INC C- Fair

Major Rating Factors: Weak profitability index (1.9 on a scale of 0 to 10). Low quality investment portfolio (0.8). Strong capitalization (10.0) based on excellent current risk-adjusted capital (severe loss scenario).
Other Rating Factors: Excellent liquidity (7.7) with ample operational cash flow and liquid investments.
Principal Business: Medicare (100%)
Mem Phys: 18: N/A **17:** N/A **18 MLR** 87.4% **/ 18 Admin Exp** N/A
Enroll(000): Q1 19: 6 **18:** 10 **17:** 9 **Med Exp PMPM:** $812
Principal Investments: Cash and equiv (100%)
Provider Compensation ($000): Capitation ($94,607)
Total Member Encounters: Phys (120,877), non-phys (33,964)
Group Affiliation: None
Licensed in: FL
Address: 4800 Deerwood Campus Parkway, Jacksonville, FL 32246
Phone: (904) 791-6111 **Dom State:** FL **Commenced Bus:** N/A

Data Date	Rating	RACR #1	RACR #2	Total Assets ($mil)	Capital ($mil)	Net Premium ($mil)	Net Income ($mil)
3-19	C-	4.26	3.55	40.4	22.3	17.1	3.7
3-18	D+	N/A	N/A	47.5	15.7	27.0	-1.7
2018	C-	3.69	3.08	45.0	19.3	108.2	1.0
2017	D+	N/A	N/A	34.0	17.4	93.2	-0.8
2016	D	6.97	5.81	16.6	11.0	23.3	-1.5
2015	C-	5.23	4.36	8.8	5.3	7.0	-3.7
2014	D	0.88	0.74	3.6	2.2	5.1	-3.0

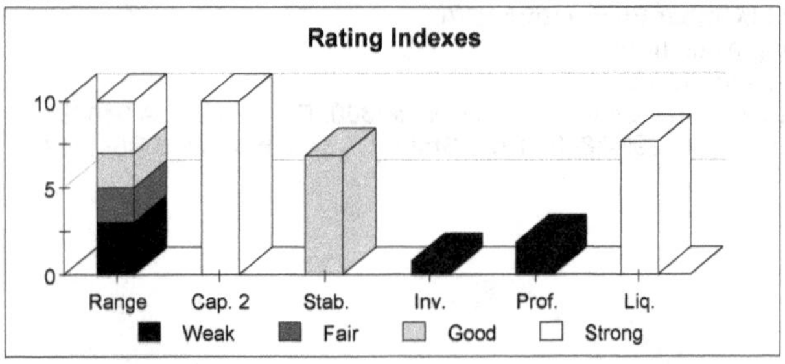

BERKLEY LIFE & HEALTH INSURANCE COMPANY * A Excellent

Major Rating Factors: Good liquidity (6.8 on a scale of 0 to 10) with sufficient resources to handle a spike in claims. Excellent overall results on stability tests (7.8). Strengths that enhance stability include excellent operational trends and excellent risk diversification. Strong capitalization (10.0) based on excellent risk adjusted capital (severe loss scenario). Furthermore, this high level of risk adjusted capital has been consistently maintained over the last five years.
Other Rating Factors: High quality investment portfolio (7.7). Excellent profitability (8.7).
Principal Business: Group health insurance (99%) and reinsurance (1%).
Principal Investments: CMOs and structured securities (54%) and nonCMO investment grade bonds (45%).
Investments in Affiliates: None
Group Affiliation: W R Berkley Corp
Licensed in: All states except PR
Commenced Business: July 1963
Address: 11201 DOUGLAS AVE, URBANDALE, IA 50322
Phone: (609) 584-6990 **Domicile State:** IA **NAIC Code:** 64890

Data Date	Rating	RACR #1	RACR #2	Total Assets ($mil)	Capital ($mil)	Net Premium ($mil)	Net Income ($mil)
3-19	A	4.83	3.53	336.2	174.8	66.4	8.4
3-18	A	4.80	3.57	280.3	154.2	63.0	4.5
2018	A	4.59	3.35	324.2	166.6	268.0	16.5
2017	A	4.73	3.50	277.3	150.7	238.1	8.2
2016	B	4.60	3.45	267.7	143.7	237.9	14.1
2015	B-	5.35	4.11	223.9	129.2	187.3	23.1
2014	B-	5.56	4.23	197.6	106.0	145.5	11.7

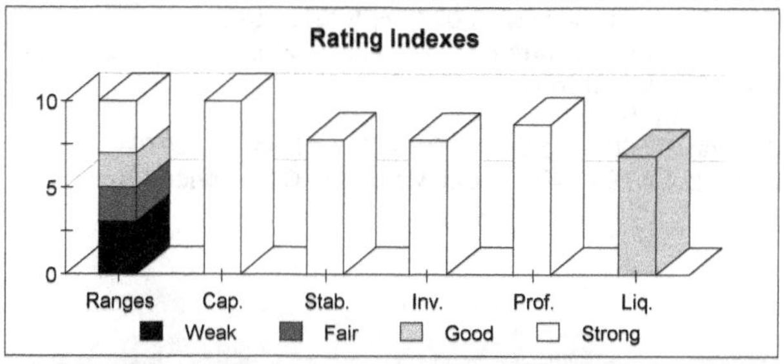

BERKSHIRE LIFE INSURANCE COMPANY OF AMERICA B Good

Major Rating Factors: Good overall profitability (5.7 on a scale of 0 to 10). Good overall results on stability tests (6.2). Strengths include potential support from affiliation with Guardian Group, excellent operational trends and excellent risk diversification. Fair quality investment portfolio (3.9) with large holdings of BBB rated bonds in addition to junk bond exposure equal to 56% of capital.
Other Rating Factors: Strong capitalization (7.1) based on excellent risk adjusted capital (severe loss scenario). Excellent liquidity (8.0).
Principal Business: Individual health insurance (77%), reinsurance (22%), and individual life insurance (1%).
Principal Investments: NonCMO investment grade bonds (93%), noninv. grade bonds (3%), and mortgages in good standing (1%).
Investments in Affiliates: None
Group Affiliation: Guardian Group
Licensed in: All states except PR
Commenced Business: July 2001
Address: 700 SOUTH STREET, PITTSFIELD, MA 1201
Phone: (413) 499-4321 **Domicile State:** MA **NAIC Code:** 71714

Data Date	Rating	RACR #1	RACR #2	Total Assets ($mil)	Capital ($mil)	Net Premium ($mil)	Net Income ($mil)
3-19	B	2.27	1.08	3,988.4	191.5	33.6	5.6
3-18	B	2.41	1.13	3,787.1	192.4	32.7	6.5
2018	B	2.44	1.16	3,927.6	192.7	131.4	-13.3
2017	B	2.57	1.20	3,717.7	189.1	126.9	10.2
2016	B	2.97	1.36	3,526.7	201.6	123.3	17.8
2015	B	3.34	1.58	3,381.4	207.9	118.2	14.2
2014	A-	4.53	2.24	3,377.3	269.5	114.0	16.9

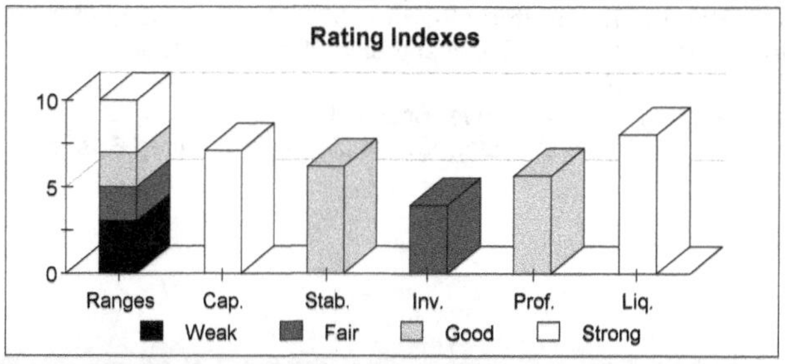

BLUE ADVANTAGE PLUS OF KANSAS CITY C Fair

Major Rating Factors: Fair capitalization (2.9 on a scale of 0 to 10) based on good current risk-adjusted capital (moderate loss scenario). Weak profitability index (0.5). Good liquidity (5.2) with sufficient resources (cash flows and marketable investments) to handle a spike in claims.
Other Rating Factors: High quality investment portfolio (8.7).
Principal Business: Medicare (100%)
Mem Phys: 18: 4,040 **17:** 3,059 **18 MLR** 93.1% **/ 18 Admin Exp** N/A
Enroll(000): Q1 19: 9 **18:** 10 **17:** 9 **Med Exp PMPM:** $779
Principal Investments: Long-term bonds (81%), cash and equiv (19%)
Provider Compensation ($000): Contr fee ($73,499), FFS ($18,374), capitation ($1,482)
Total Member Encounters: Phys (76,485), non-phys (17,550)
Group Affiliation: None
Licensed in: KS, MO
Address: 2301 Main St, Kansas City, MO 64108-2428
Phone: (816) 395-2222 **Dom State:** MO **Commenced Bus:** N/A

Data Date	Rating	RACR #1	RACR #2	Total Assets ($mil)	Capital ($mil)	Net Premium ($mil)	Net Income ($mil)
3-19	C	1.06	0.89	49.7	16.6	21.8	-15.7
3-18	C	N/A	N/A	46.4	14.3	24.6	-2.9
2018	C	0.65	0.54	34.0	10.0	100.6	-9.1
2017	C	N/A	N/A	41.3	17.4	79.8	-16.7
2016	C	1.00	0.83	16.8	9.3	29.3	-5.9
2015	N/A	N/A	N/A	21.2	15.3	N/A	-8.7
2014	N/A	N/A	N/A	26.2	24.0	N/A	-1.0

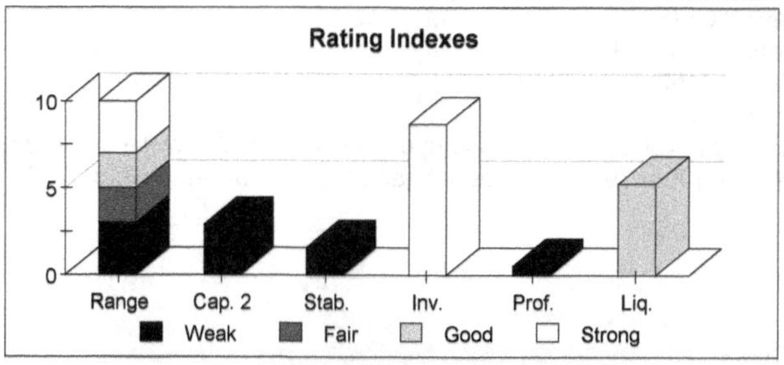

BLUE CARE NETWORK OF MICHIGAN B Good

Major Rating Factors: Good quality investment portfolio (6.7 on a scale of 0 to 10). Excellent profitability (7.5). Strong capitalization index (10.0) based on excellent current risk-adjusted capital (severe loss scenario).
Other Rating Factors: Excellent overall results on stability tests (8.4). Excellent liquidity (7.0) with sufficient resources (cash flows and marketable investments) to handle a spike in claims
Principal Business: Comp med (73%), Medicare (24%), FEHB (3%)
Mem Phys: 18: 58,949 **17:** 54,950 **18 MLR** 81.0% **/ 18 Admin Exp** N/A
Enroll(000): Q1 19: 747 **18:** 739 **17:** 689 **Med Exp PMPM:** $385
Principal Investments: Long-term bonds (65%), cash and equiv (23%), nonaffiliate common stock (9%), other (3%)
Provider Compensation ($000): Bonus arrang ($2,031,838), contr fee ($992,686), capitation ($236,007), FFS ($105,913)
Total Member Encounters: Phys (4,607,229), non-phys (2,213,247)
Group Affiliation: None
Licensed in: MI
Address: 20500 Civic Center Drive, Southfield, MI 48076
Phone: (248) 799-6400 **Dom State:** MI **Commenced Bus:** N/A

Data Date	Rating	RACR #1	RACR #2	Total Assets ($mil)	Capital ($mil)	Net Premium ($mil)	Net Income ($mil)
3-19	B	7.12	5.94	2,607.1	1,680.2	1,058.8	52.2
3-18	B	6.94	5.78	2,342.5	1,366.6	1,028.3	-1.1
2018	B	6.82	5.68	2,402.8	1,609.4	4,239.2	250.6
2017	A-	7.07	5.89	2,154.4	1,398.9	3,581.0	240.4
2016	B+	6.05	5.04	1,864.2	1,123.0	3,399.3	93.8
2015	B+	5.74	4.78	1,847.8	1,026.5	3,252.5	18.0
2014	B+	5.74	4.78	1,799.3	1,013.5	2,992.1	17.3

Rating Indexes

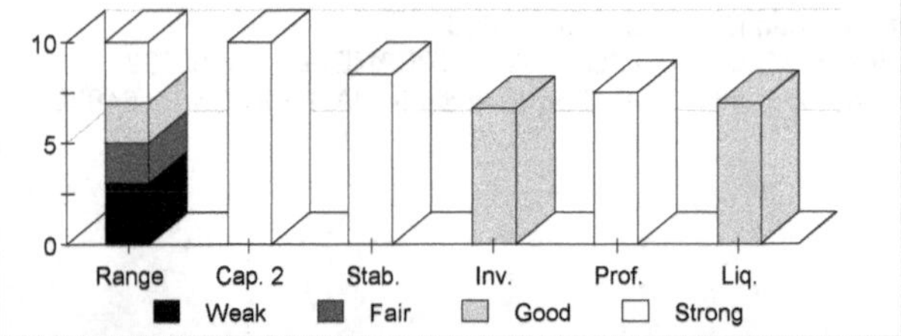

BLUE CROSS & BLUE SHIELD MA HMO BLUE * B+ Good

Major Rating Factors: Good overall profitability index (6.1 on a scale of 0 to 10). Good quality investment portfolio (5.9). Good liquidity (6.5) with sufficient resources (cash flows and marketable investments) to handle a spike in claims.
Other Rating Factors: Strong capitalization (10.0) based on excellent current risk-adjusted capital (severe loss scenario).
Principal Business: Comp med (90%), Medicare (10%)
Mem Phys: 18: 25,340 **17:** 24,968 **18 MLR** 87.6% **/ 18 Admin Exp** N/A
Enroll(000): Q1 19: 777 **18:** 803 **17:** 801 **Med Exp PMPM:** $465
Principal Investments: Long-term bonds (41%), nonaffiliate common stock (10%), real estate (4%), cash and equiv (1%), other (43%)
Provider Compensation ($000): Bonus arrang ($2,983,035), contr fee ($1,252,002), FFS ($235,399), capitation ($12,904)
Total Member Encounters: Phys (3,163,672), non-phys (3,050,539)
Group Affiliation: Blue Cross and Blue Shield of Massac
Licensed in: MA
Address: 101 Huntington Ave, Boston, MA 2199
Phone: (617) 246-5000 **Dom State:** MA **Commenced Bus:** N/A

Data Date	Rating	RACR #1	RACR #2	Total Assets ($mil)	Capital ($mil)	Net Premium ($mil)	Net Income ($mil)
3-19	B+	3.97	3.31	2,326.3	1,509.9	1,281.9	44.7
3-18	B+	3.85	3.21	2,372.3	1,379.7	1,267.6	-5.9
2018	B+	3.72	3.10	2,266.5	1,413.8	5,096.3	94.0
2017	A-	3.87	3.22	2,411.7	1,383.7	4,817.4	121.4
2016	B+	3.89	3.24	2,098.2	1,207.7	4,596.5	74.2
2015	B	3.91	3.26	1,908.1	1,089.6	4,358.1	2.4
2014	B	3.99	3.33	1,928.6	1,124.2	4,130.2	3.2

Rating Indexes

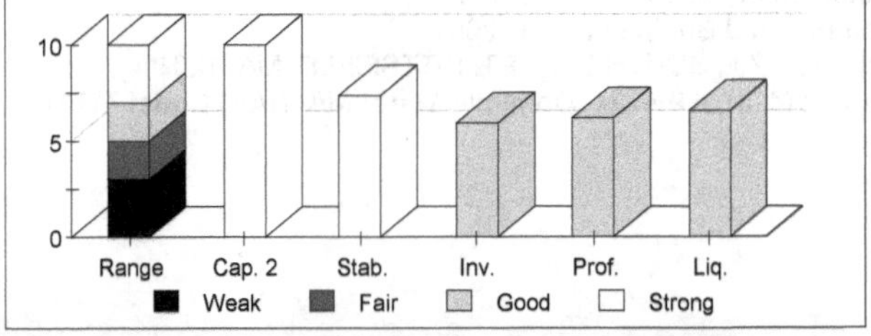

BLUE CROSS & BLUE SHIELD OF FLORIDA B Good

Major Rating Factors: Good quality investment portfolio (6.4 on a scale of 0 to 10). Excellent profitability (8.7). Strong capitalization (10.0) based on excellent current risk-adjusted capital (severe loss scenario).
Other Rating Factors: Excellent liquidity (7.0) with ample operational cash flow and liquid investments.
Principal Business: Comp med (66%), FEHB (22%), Medicare (6%), med supp (4%), other (1%)
Mem Phys: 18: 28,564 **17:** 28,564 **18 MLR** 79.0% **/ 18 Admin Exp** N/A
Enroll(000): Q1 19: 1,943 **18:** 1,861 **17:** 1,843 **Med Exp PMPM:** $384
Principal Investments: Long-term bonds (65%), cash and equiv (15%), nonaffiliate common stock (8%), real estate (6%), other (6%)
Provider Compensation ($000): Contr fee ($7,505,765), FFS ($987,955), capitation ($42,779), bonus arrang ($35,843)
Total Member Encounters: Phys (15,169,338), non-phys (11,697,160)
Group Affiliation: None
Licensed in: FL, PA
Address: 4800 Deerwood Campus Parkway, Jacksonville, FL 32246
Phone: (904) 791-6111 **Dom State:** FL **Commenced Bus:** N/A

Data Date	Rating	RACR #1	RACR #2	Total Assets ($mil)	Capital ($mil)	Net Premium ($mil)	Net Income ($mil)
3-19	B	3.85	3.20	6,126.3	1,952.0	2,851.4	126.2
3-18	B-	3.57	2.98	5,863.3	1,699.5	2,751.9	3.8
2018	B	3.80	3.17	5,645.2	1,927.5	10,872.4	694.6
2017	B-	3.77	3.14	5,730.6	1,792.8	10,018.8	474.0
2016	B-	5.46	4.55	5,974.6	2,271.7	9,387.5	552.8
2015	C	4.69	3.91	5,612.2	1,842.1	8,789.8	327.5
2014	C	3.89	3.24	4,969.1	1,439.0	8,102.4	64.9

Rating Indexes

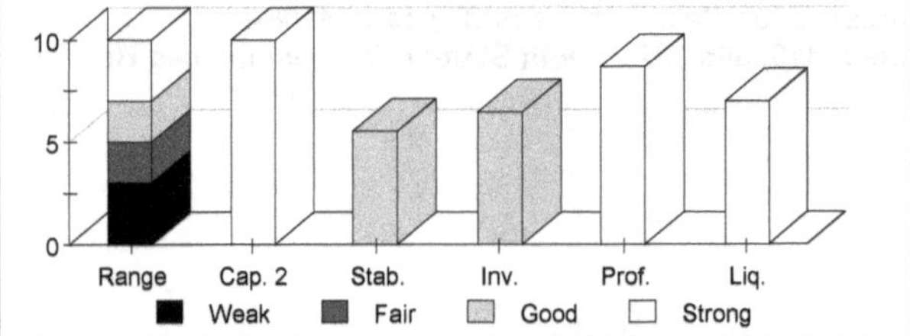

BLUE CROSS BLUE SHIELD HEALTHCARE GA * A- Excellent

Major Rating Factors: Excellent profitability (9.1 on a scale of 0 to 10). Strong capitalization index (10.0) based on excellent current risk-adjusted capital (severe loss scenario). High quality investment portfolio (7.3).
Other Rating Factors: Excellent overall results on stability tests (7.1). Rating is significantly influenced by the good financial results of Anthem Inc. Good liquidity (6.8) with sufficient resources (cash flows and marketable investments) to handle a spike in claims.
Principal Business: Comp med (61%), FEHB (36%), Medicare (1%), other (2%)
Mem Phys: 18: 21,858 **17:** 20,640 **18 MLR** 80.0% **/ 18 Admin Exp** N/A
Enroll(000): Q1 19: 1,907 **18:** 714 **17:** 690 **Med Exp PMPM:** $345
Principal Investments: Long-term bonds (81%), cash and equiv (2%), nonaffiliate common stock (1%), other (16%)
Provider Compensation ($000): Bonus arrang ($1,761,793), contr fee ($645,896), FFS ($508,362), capitation ($6,935), other ($48,020)
Total Member Encounters: Phys (3,910,256), non-phys (1,675,115)
Group Affiliation: Anthem Inc
Licensed in: GA
Address: 3350 PEACHTREE ROAD NE, ATLANTA, GA 30326
Phone: (404) 842-8000 **Dom State:** GA **Commenced Bus:** N/A

Data Date	Rating	RACR #1	RACR #2	Total Assets ($mil)	Capital ($mil)	Net Premium ($mil)	Net Income ($mil)
3-19	A-	6.71	5.59	2,584.7	1,132.8	1,148.9	130.1
3-18	A-	2.12	1.76	1,425.3	422.4	947.9	52.8
2018	A-	3.12	2.60	1,438.1	514.7	3,747.9	235.3
2017	A-	1.49	1.24	1,073.3	383.6	3,295.9	103.7
2016	A-	2.51	2.10	764.0	310.7	2,134.3	71.7
2015	A-	2.47	2.06	612.2	257.6	1,782.8	50.9
2014	A-	2.79	2.32	717.8	261.5	1,593.9	46.8

Rating Indexes

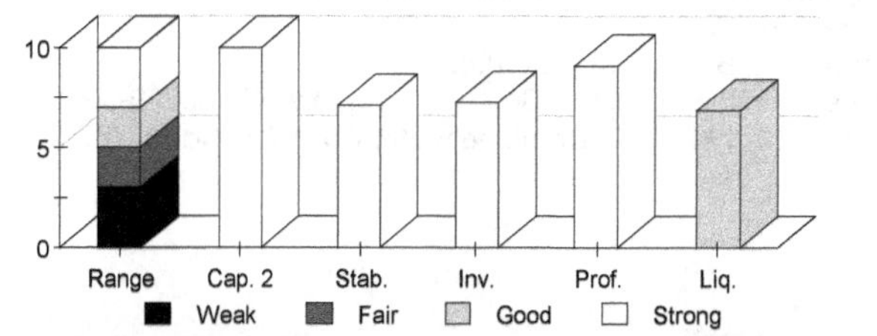

BLUE CROSS BLUE SHIELD OF ALABAMA * B+ Good

Major Rating Factors: Good overall profitability index (6.1 on a scale of 0 to 10). Good quality investment portfolio (6.8). Strong capitalization (10.0) based on excellent current risk-adjusted capital (severe loss scenario).
Other Rating Factors: Excellent liquidity (7.1) with ample operational cash flow and liquid investments.
Principal Business: Comp med (69%), FEHB (13%), Medicare (11%), med supp (4%), dental (2%)
Mem Phys: 18: 47,650 **17:** 46,529 **18 MLR** 84.7% **/ 18 Admin Exp** N/A
Enroll(000): Q1 19: 1,659 **18:** 1,635 **17:** 1,639 **Med Exp PMPM:** $259
Principal Investments: Long-term bonds (58%), nonaffiliate common stock (16%), cash and equiv (16%), real estate (3%), affiliate common stock (3%), other (4%)
Provider Compensation ($000): Contr fee ($5,054,161), capitation ($10,996), FFS ($1,956), bonus arrang ($1,463)
Total Member Encounters: Phys (22,841,105), non-phys (7,812,703)
Group Affiliation: None
Licensed in: AL
Address: 450 Riverchase Parkway East, Birmingham, AL 35244
Phone: (205) 220-2100 **Dom State:** AL **Commenced Bus:** N/A

Data Date	Rating	RACR #1	RACR #2	Total Assets ($mil)	Capital ($mil)	Net Premium ($mil)	Net Income ($mil)
3-19	B+	6.21	5.18	4,116.3	2,127.9	1,539.5	54.7
3-18	B	6.31	5.26	4,159.9	1,949.7	1,518.4	78.1
2018	B+	5.84	4.87	3,960.0	2,001.7	6,027.4	403.2
2017	B	6.10	5.08	3,936.4	1,881.7	5,770.9	343.4
2016	B-	4.68	3.90	3,031.4	1,257.9	5,155.8	83.9
2015	B	4.55	3.79	2,840.7	1,142.2	4,864.7	-138.3
2014	B	5.20	4.33	2,865.3	1,077.4	4,577.2	52.8

Rating Indexes

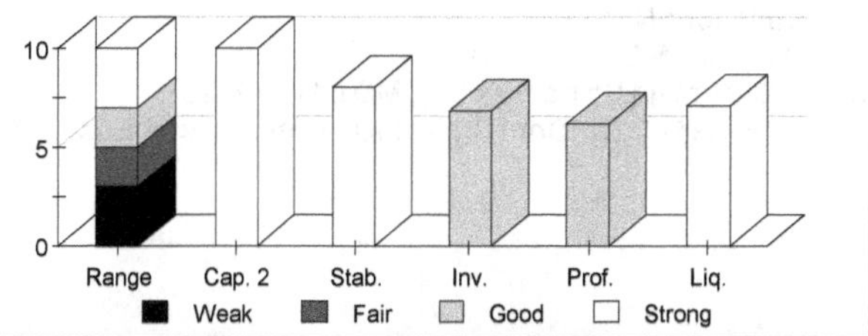

BLUE CROSS BLUE SHIELD OF ARIZONA * A+ Excellent

Major Rating Factors: Excellent profitability (7.4 on a scale of 0 to 10). Strong capitalization (10.0) based on excellent current risk-adjusted capital (severe loss scenario). Excellent liquidity (7.1) with ample operational cash flow and liquid investments.
Other Rating Factors: Good quality investment portfolio (6.5).
Principal Business: Comp med (62%), FEHB (29%), med supp (5%), other (4%)
Mem Phys: 18: 33,291 **17:** 26,871 **18 MLR** 79.2% **/ 18 Admin Exp** N/A
Enroll(000): Q1 19: 1,574 **18:** 1,529 **17:** 1,527 **Med Exp PMPM:** $95
Principal Investments: Long-term bonds (46%), nonaffiliate common stock (21%), cash and equiv (5%), affiliate common stock (4%), real estate (3%), other (21%)
Provider Compensation ($000): Contr fee ($1,338,511), FFS ($374,190), capitation ($4,232), bonus arrang ($3,073)
Total Member Encounters: Phys (2,759,132), non-phys (1,815,072)
Group Affiliation: Blue Cross Blue Shield of Arizona In
Licensed in: AZ
Address: 2444 W LAS PALMARITAS Dr, PHOENIX, AZ 85021
Phone: (602) 864-4100 **Dom State:** AZ **Commenced Bus:** N/A

Data Date	Rating	RACR #1	RACR #2	Total Assets ($mil)	Capital ($mil)	Net Premium ($mil)	Net Income ($mil)
3-19	A+	7.77	6.48	2,403.3	1,626.8	590.8	81.4
3-18	A+	7.31	6.09	2,216.8	1,384.6	555.7	62.1
2018	A+	7.19	5.99	2,268.1	1,504.8	2,207.4	158.7
2017	A+	7.05	5.87	2,104.4	1,335.3	2,106.9	196.7
2016	A+	6.02	5.02	1,782.4	1,084.4	2,048.1	61.0
2015	A+	5.92	4.94	1,627.1	1,004.2	1,975.8	2.6
2014	A+	6.42	5.35	1,657.1	1,030.1	1,716.5	4.4

Rating Indexes

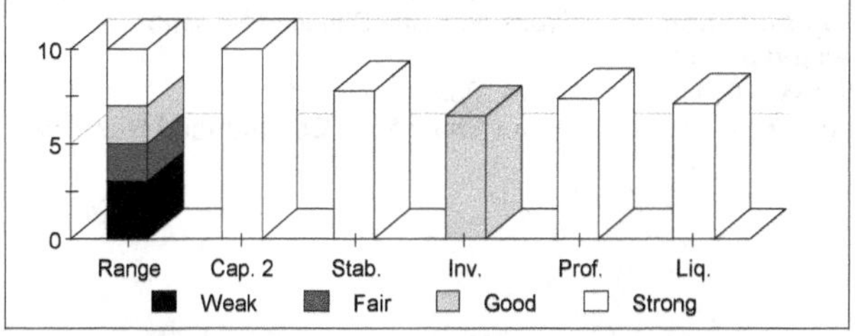

BLUE CROSS BLUE SHIELD OF KANSAS INCORPORATED B Good

Major Rating Factors: Good overall profitability (5.6 on a scale of 0 to 10). Excellent expense controls. Good liquidity (6.0) with sufficient resources to handle a spike in claims. Good overall results on stability tests (5.4). Stability strengths include excellent operational trends and excellent risk diversification.
Other Rating Factors: Fair quality investment portfolio (4.6). Strong capitalization (7.8) based on excellent risk adjusted capital (severe loss scenario).
Principal Business: Group health insurance (66%) and individual health insurance (34%).
Principal Investments: NonCMO investment grade bonds (33%), common & preferred stock (26%), CMOs and structured securities (21%), noninv. grade bonds (2%), and real estate (2%).
Investments in Affiliates: 7%
Group Affiliation: Blue Cross Blue Shield Kansas
Licensed in: KS
Commenced Business: July 1942
Address: 1133 SW Topeka Boulevard, Topeka, KS 66629-0001
Phone: (785) 291-7000 **Domicile State:** KS **NAIC Code:** 70729

Data Date	Rating	RACR #1	RACR #2	Total Assets ($mil)	Capital ($mil)	Net Premium ($mil)	Net Income ($mil)
3-19	B	2.02	1.53	1,917.1	925.7	591.2	18.0
3-18	B	2.01	1.51	1,752.0	808.9	567.6	10.1
2018	B	1.89	1.45	1,765.8	892.5	2,259.0	105.1
2017	B	2.06	1.54	1,730.4	791.6	1,775.0	3.4
2016	B	1.74	1.35	1,452.3	728.9	1,899.8	59.1
2015	B	1.84	1.39	1,404.1	686.7	1,854.4	-30.8
2014	B	2.05	1.50	1,555.1	753.6	1,797.7	-11.5

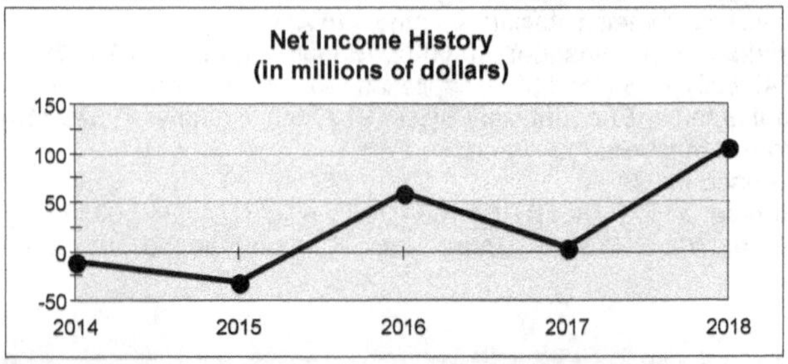

BLUE CROSS BLUE SHIELD OF KC C+ Fair

Major Rating Factors: Fair quality investment portfolio (3.9 on a scale of 0 to 10). Good overall profitability index (5.1). Good liquidity (6.8) with sufficient resources (cash flows and marketable investments) to handle a spike in claims.
Other Rating Factors: Strong capitalization (10.0) based on excellent current risk-adjusted capital (severe loss scenario).
Principal Business: Comp med (72%), FEHB (23%), med supp (4%), dental (1%)
Mem Phys: 18: 6,712 **17:** 6,621 **18 MLR** 81.0% **/ 18 Admin Exp** N/A
Enroll(000): Q1 19: 480 **18:** 474 **17:** 520 **Med Exp PMPM:** $228
Principal Investments: Long-term bonds (52%), nonaffiliate common stock (27%), affiliate common stock (8%), real estate (2%), other (11%)
Provider Compensation ($000): Contr fee ($1,107,223), FFS ($193,732), capitation ($10,389)
Total Member Encounters: Phys (1,719,178), non-phys (417,270)
Group Affiliation: None
Licensed in: KS, MO
Address: 2301 Main St, Kansas City, MO 64108-2428
Phone: (816) 395-2222 **Dom State:** MO **Commenced Bus:** N/A

Data Date	Rating	RACR #1	RACR #2	Total Assets ($mil)	Capital ($mil)	Net Premium ($mil)	Net Income ($mil)
3-19	C+	5.96	4.97	1,337.2	786.3	394.7	12.1
3-18	C+	4.61	3.84	1,333.2	650.7	385.6	7.6
2018	C+	5.67	4.72	1,246.0	758.1	1,590.0	66.6
2017	C+	4.94	4.12	1,265.9	706.6	1,834.0	106.1
2016	C	4.22	3.52	1,157.0	604.7	1,718.1	23.1
2015	C	4.05	3.38	1,108.9	562.2	1,484.8	-5.8
2014	C+	3.73	3.11	1,008.1	502.0	1,347.9	-82.5

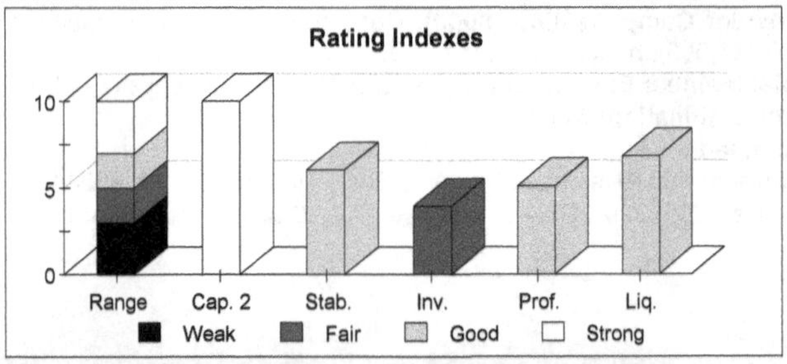

BLUE CROSS BLUE SHIELD OF MA C+ Fair

Major Rating Factors: Good liquidity (6.3 on a scale of 0 to 10) with sufficient resources (cash flows and marketable investments) to handle a spike in claims. Weak profitability index (2.7). Strong capitalization (9.0) based on excellent current risk-adjusted capital (severe loss scenario).
Other Rating Factors: High quality investment portfolio (7.3).
Principal Business: Comp med (37%), FEHB (26%), med supp (18%), dental (7%), other (12%)
Mem Phys: 18: 25,340 **17:** 24,968 **18 MLR** 94.4% **/ 18 Admin Exp** N/A
Enroll(000): Q1 19: 1,502 **18:** 1,480 **17:** 1,373 **Med Exp PMPM:** $156
Principal Investments: Long-term bonds (50%), nonaffiliate common stock (11%), real estate (6%), cash and equiv (3%), other (30%)
Provider Compensation ($000): Contr fee ($1,644,288), FFS ($846,673), bonus arrang ($220,490)
Total Member Encounters: Phys (3,588,252), non-phys (2,865,229)
Group Affiliation: Blue Cross and Blue Shield of Massac
Licensed in: MA
Address: 101 Huntington Ave, Boston, MA 2199
Phone: (617) 246-5000 **Dom State:** MA **Commenced Bus:** N/A

Data Date	Rating	RACR #1	RACR #2	Total Assets ($mil)	Capital ($mil)	Net Premium ($mil)	Net Income ($mil)
3-19	C+	2.96	2.47	2,471.4	823.0	783.9	47.0
3-18	C+	3.64	3.03	2,589.0	978.0	709.0	63.4
2018	C+	2.78	2.32	2,386.1	779.3	2,899.7	65.6
2017	C+	3.13	2.61	2,548.0	895.0	2,687.8	-128.4
2016	B	3.00	2.50	2,237.4	728.2	2,522.4	3.9
2015	B	3.14	2.61	2,005.4	618.7	2,439.3	12.6
2014	B	3.17	2.64	1,994.1	671.2	2,370.5	4.7

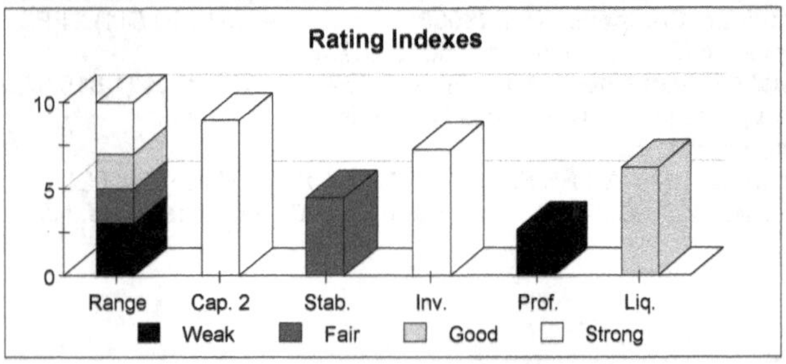

BLUE CROSS BLUE SHIELD OF MICHIGAN — B- Good

Major Rating Factors: Fair profitability index (3.8 on a scale of 0 to 10). Good quality investment portfolio (6.7). Strong capitalization (10.0) based on excellent current risk-adjusted capital (severe loss scenario).
Other Rating Factors: Excellent liquidity (6.9) with sufficient resources (cash flows and marketable investments) to handle a spike in claims.
Principal Business: Comp med (49%), Medicare (35%), FEHB (6%), med supp (5%), dental (1%), other (4%)
Mem Phys: 18: 66,090 **17:** 58,188 **18 MLR** 83.6% **/ 18 Admin Exp** N/A
Enroll(000): Q1 19: 1,416 **18:** 1,322 **17:** 1,279 **Med Exp PMPM:** $477
Principal Investments: Affiliate common stock (41%), long-term bonds (32%), cash and equiv (7%), nonaffiliate common stock (6%), real estate (1%), other (13%)
Provider Compensation ($000): Contr fee ($7,386,356), bonus arrang ($50,042), capitation ($1,455)
Total Member Encounters: N/A
Group Affiliation: None
Licensed in: MI
Address: 600 Lafayette East, Detroit, MI 48226
Phone: (313) 225-9000 **Dom State:** MI **Commenced Bus:** N/A

Data Date	Rating	RACR #1	RACR #2	Total Assets ($mil)	Capital ($mil)	Net Premium ($mil)	Net Income ($mil)
3-19	B-	4.24	3.54	9,399.2	5,322.4	2,251.6	335.8
3-18	C	3.85	3.21	8,788.6	4,345.5	2,226.2	180.3
2018	B-	3.93	3.28	8,990.4	4,933.2	9,086.6	559.5
2017	C	3.77	3.14	8,489.0	4,251.6	8,146.4	295.2
2016	C	3.17	2.64	7,543.7	3,432.5	7,899.3	-226.1
2015	C+	3.36	2.80	7,488.3	3,171.7	7,502.7	-344.3
2014	B	3.97	3.31	7,646.2	3,340.1	7,445.8	295.0

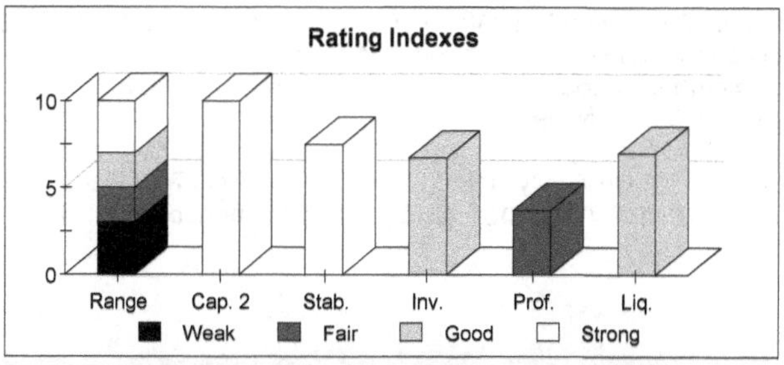

BLUE CROSS BLUE SHIELD OF MINNESOTA — C Fair

Major Rating Factors: Weak profitability index (2.5 on a scale of 0 to 10). Good quality investment portfolio (6.6). Good liquidity (6.8) with sufficient resources (cash flows and marketable investments) to handle a spike in claims.
Other Rating Factors: Strong capitalization (9.7) based on excellent current risk-adjusted capital (severe loss scenario).
Principal Business: Medicare (36%), comp med (35%), FEHB (15%), med supp (6%), other (8%)
Mem Phys: 18: 53,676 **17:** 50,238 **18 MLR** 83.9% **/ 18 Admin Exp** N/A
Enroll(000): Q1 19: 782 **18:** 812 **17:** 683 **Med Exp PMPM:** $341
Principal Investments: Long-term bonds (38%), nonaffiliate common stock (21%), affiliate common stock (3%), cash and equiv (2%), other (36%)
Provider Compensation ($000): Bonus arrang ($1,478,352), contr fee ($1,384,532), FFS ($309,545), other ($94,438)
Total Member Encounters: Phys (5,106,208), non-phys (1,843,061)
Group Affiliation: Aware Integrated Inc
Licensed in: MN
Address: 3535 Blue Cross Rd, Eagan, MN 55122
Phone: (651) 662-8000 **Dom State:** MN **Commenced Bus:** N/A

Data Date	Rating	RACR #1	RACR #2	Total Assets ($mil)	Capital ($mil)	Net Premium ($mil)	Net Income ($mil)
3-19	C	3.56	2.96	2,784.9	1,061.2	955.8	61.5
3-18	C	4.24	3.54	2,606.5	1,118.5	968.9	62.4
2018	C	3.47	2.89	2,582.2	1,034.5	3,956.2	36.6
2017	C	3.97	3.31	2,454.4	1,043.9	3,655.8	-12.0
2016	C	2.58	2.15	2,544.3	990.5	3,938.7	-103.5
2015	C+	3.69	3.07	2,751.4	1,100.7	3,762.9	-178.4
2014	B	3.37	2.81	1,942.1	726.5	3,277.2	-9.0

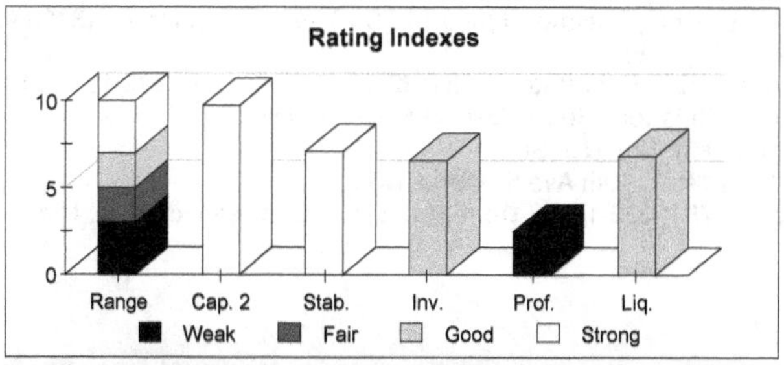

BLUE CROSS BLUE SHIELD OF MS, MUTUAL * — A Excellent

Major Rating Factors: Strong capitalization (10.0 on a scale of 0 to 10) based on excellent current risk-adjusted capital (severe loss scenario). High quality investment portfolio (6.9). Good overall profitability index (6.7).
Other Rating Factors: Good liquidity (6.9) with sufficient resources (cash flows and marketable investments) to handle a spike in claims.
Principal Business: Comp med (72%), FEHB (25%), med supp (2%)
Mem Phys: 18: 13,297 **17:** 12,575 **18 MLR** 87.1% **/ 18 Admin Exp** N/A
Enroll(000): Q1 19: 625 **18:** 627 **17:** 632 **Med Exp PMPM:** $158
Principal Investments: Long-term bonds (72%), cash and equiv (9%), affiliate common stock (8%), nonaffiliate common stock (7%), real estate (5%)
Provider Compensation ($000): Contr fee ($1,170,516), FFS ($22,548), bonus arrang ($312)
Total Member Encounters: Phys (2,057,325), non-phys (1,674,350)
Group Affiliation: Blue Cross & Blue Shield of Mississi
Licensed in: MS
Address: 3545 Lakeland Dr, Flowood, MS 39232
Phone: (601) 664-4590 **Dom State:** MS **Commenced Bus:** N/A

Data Date	Rating	RACR #1	RACR #2	Total Assets ($mil)	Capital ($mil)	Net Premium ($mil)	Net Income ($mil)
3-19	A	8.26	6.88	1,042.9	687.3	329.8	0.6
3-18	A-	7.64	6.36	999.5	613.5	322.8	-15.9
2018	A	8.09	6.74	1,000.6	676.7	1,374.7	43.2
2017	A-	7.67	6.40	962.1	627.6	1,359.3	49.7
2016	B	7.35	6.12	899.1	597.3	1,334.1	23.6
2015	B+	7.65	6.38	877.5	583.6	1,287.2	13.6
2014	B+	7.85	6.54	845.2	564.8	1,213.2	18.3

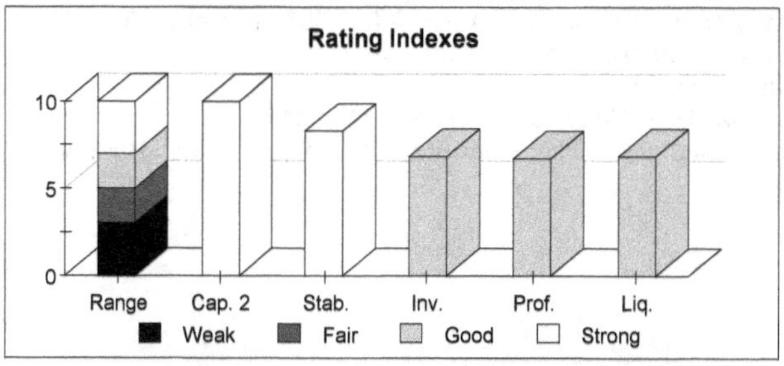

BLUE CROSS BLUE SHIELD OF NC * B+ Good

Major Rating Factors: Good overall profitability index (6.1 on a scale of 0 to 10). Good quality investment portfolio (6.2). Good liquidity (6.8) with sufficient resources (cash flows and marketable investments) to handle a spike in claims.
Other Rating Factors: Strong capitalization (10.0) based on excellent current risk-adjusted capital (severe loss scenario).
Principal Business: Comp med (71%), FEHB (13%), Medicare (9%), med supp (4%), other (2%)
Mem Phys: 18: 63,002 **17:** 60,163 **18 MLR** 74.9% **/ 18 Admin Exp** N/A
Enroll(000): Q1 19: 1,676 **18:** 1,580 **17:** 1,634 **Med Exp PMPM:** $354
Principal Investments: Long-term bonds (63%), nonaffiliate common stock (16%), affiliate common stock (4%), pref stock (4%), cash and equiv (2%), other (11%)
Provider Compensation ($000): Contr fee ($4,672,664), FFS ($2,102,125), bonus arrang ($35,852), capitation ($34,459)
Total Member Encounters: Phys (8,413,397)
Group Affiliation: None
Licensed in: NC
Address: 4705 University Dr Bldg 700, Durham, NC 27707-3460
Phone: (919) 489-7431 **Dom State:** NC **Commenced Bus:** N/A

Data Date	Rating	RACR #1	RACR #2	Total Assets ($mil)	Capital ($mil)	Net Premium ($mil)	Net Income ($mil)
3-19	B+	6.60	5.50	6,006.9	3,759.6	2,276.7	337.8
3-18	B	5.74	4.79	5,484.3	3,114.1	2,361.3	200.9
2018	B+	6.01	5.00	5,707.6	3,416.5	9,140.7	650.4
2017	B	5.45	4.54	5,210.5	2,954.5	8,732.1	699.6
2016	B-	4.85	4.04	4,110.2	2,210.5	7,189.0	272.0
2015	B-	4.16	3.47	4,102.7	2,067.1	7,457.1	-5.7
2014	B+	4.52	3.77	4,206.1	2,298.3	7,351.8	-137.6

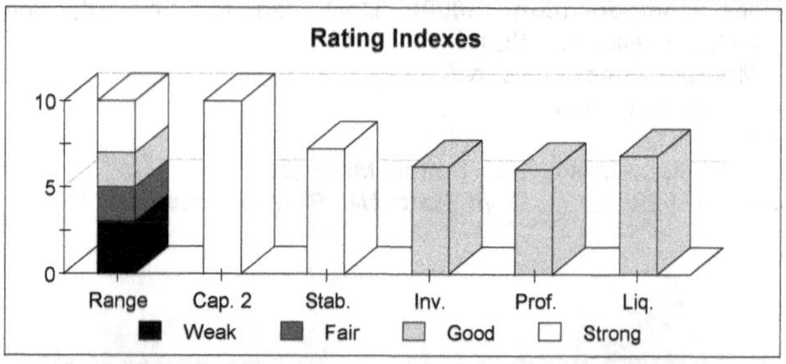

BLUE CROSS BLUE SHIELD OF ND B Good

Major Rating Factors: Good quality investment portfolio (5.3 on a scale of 0 to 10). Good liquidity (6.6) with sufficient resources (cash flows and marketable investments) to handle a spike in claims. Fair profitability index (4.8).
Other Rating Factors: Strong capitalization (10.0) based on excellent current risk-adjusted capital (severe loss scenario).
Principal Business: Comp med (68%), FEHB (11%), med supp (8%), dental (2%), other (11%)
Mem Phys: 18: 7,366 **17:** 6,807 **18 MLR** 88.6% **/ 18 Admin Exp** N/A
Enroll(000): Q1 19: 315 **18:** 323 **17:** 319 **Med Exp PMPM:** $272
Principal Investments: Long-term bonds (62%), nonaffiliate common stock (15%), affiliate common stock (10%), real estate (3%), pref stock (3%), cash and equiv (3%), other (4%)
Provider Compensation ($000): FFS ($509,292), contr fee ($496,932), bonus arrang ($13,019)
Total Member Encounters: Phys (2,542,585), non-phys (2,411,564)
Group Affiliation: HealthyDakota Mutual Holdings
Licensed in: MN, ND, SD
Address: 4510 13th Ave S, Fargo, ND 58121
Phone: (701) 282-1523 **Dom State:** ND **Commenced Bus:** N/A

Data Date	Rating	RACR #1	RACR #2	Total Assets ($mil)	Capital ($mil)	Net Premium ($mil)	Net Income ($mil)
3-19	B	3.64	3.03	777.4	476.9	305.4	19.3
3-18	B	4.55	3.79	811.0	535.9	293.6	-3.8
2018	B	3.80	3.17	793.6	495.7	1,185.0	-30.5
2017	B	4.61	3.84	798.8	541.2	1,099.3	51.0
2016	B	3.66	3.05	640.5	399.2	1,080.4	70.3
2015	B	2.49	2.07	521.5	302.9	1,243.3	63.8
2014	C+	1.68	1.40	513.5	231.1	1,328.2	26.8

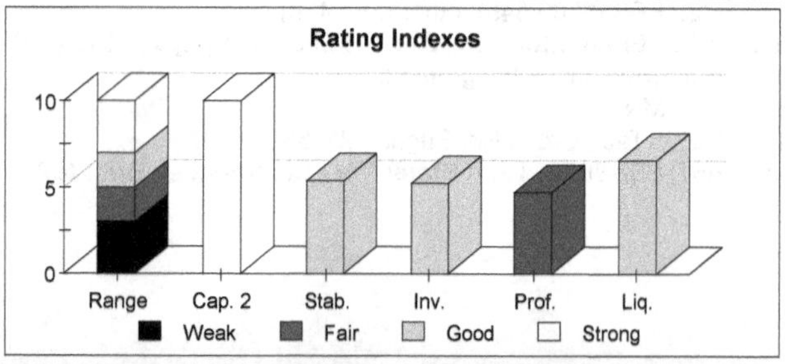

BLUE CROSS BLUE SHIELD OF NEBRASKA C Fair

Major Rating Factors: Fair profitability index (3.2 on a scale of 0 to 10). Good liquidity (6.8) with sufficient resources (cash flows and marketable investments) to handle a spike in claims. Strong capitalization (10.0) based on excellent current risk-adjusted capital (severe loss scenario).
Other Rating Factors: High quality investment portfolio (7.8).
Principal Business: Comp med (69%), FEHB (16%), med supp (11%), other (4%)
Mem Phys: 18: N/A **17:** 19,096 **18 MLR** 84.4% **/ 18 Admin Exp** N/A
Enroll(000): Q1 19: 313 **18:** 325 **17:** 359 **Med Exp PMPM:** $343
Principal Investments: Long-term bonds (68%), nonaffiliate common stock (15%), cash and equiv (4%), affiliate common stock (4%), other (9%)
Provider Compensation ($000): Contr fee ($1,389,482), other ($18,392)
Total Member Encounters: Phys (2,020,306), non-phys (86,185)
Group Affiliation: GoodLife Partners Inc
Licensed in: NE
Address: 1919 Aksarben Dr, Omaha, NE 68180
Phone: (402) 982-7000 **Dom State:** NE **Commenced Bus:** N/A

Data Date	Rating	RACR #1	RACR #2	Total Assets ($mil)	Capital ($mil)	Net Premium ($mil)	Net Income ($mil)
3-19	C	4.90	4.09	919.5	413.4	360.4	18.8
3-18	C	4.10	3.42	939.3	391.2	379.8	15.6
2018	C	4.56	3.80	912.3	387.7	1,601.0	6.3
2017	C	4.28	3.57	943.4	406.5	1,676.9	46.9
2016	C	3.57	2.98	875.3	355.7	1,744.1	-21.6
2015	B-	4.80	4.00	880.3	391.9	1,648.2	-31.5
2014	A-	5.91	4.92	896.8	429.9	1,636.0	5.4

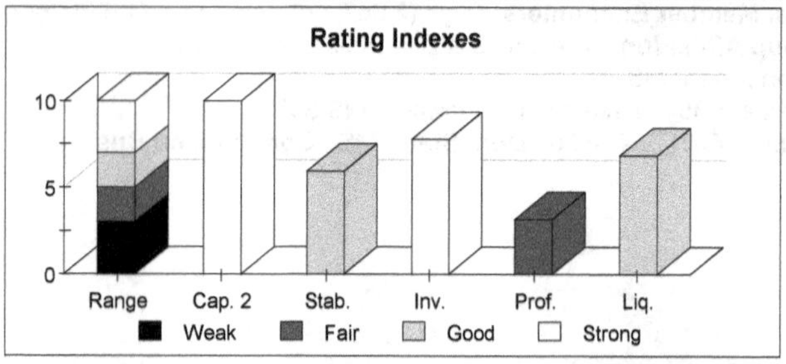

BLUE CROSS BLUE SHIELD OF RI — C — Fair

Major Rating Factors: Weak profitability index (1.9 on a scale of 0 to 10). Good liquidity (6.7) with sufficient resources (cash flows and marketable investments) to handle a spike in claims. Strong capitalization (8.6) based on excellent current risk-adjusted capital (severe loss scenario).
Other Rating Factors: High quality investment portfolio (8.0).
Principal Business: Comp med (51%), Medicare (35%), FEHB (7%), med supp (3%), dental (2%), other (1%)
Mem Phys: 18: 4,346 **17:** 4,374 **18 MLR** 83.0% **/ 18 Admin Exp** N/A
Enroll(000): Q1 19: 386 **18:** 391 **17:** 402 **Med Exp PMPM:** $301
Principal Investments: Long-term bonds (64%), nonaffiliate common stock (22%), real estate (8%), cash and equiv (3%), other (3%)
Provider Compensation ($000): Contr fee ($1,412,454)
Total Member Encounters: Phys (1,754,116), non-phys (1,296,498)
Group Affiliation: None
Licensed in: RI
Address: 500 EXCHANGE St, PROVIDENCE, RI 2903
Phone: (401) 459-5886 **Dom State:** RI **Commenced Bus:** N/A

Data Date	Rating	RACR #1	RACR #2	Total Assets ($mil)	Capital ($mil)	Net Premium ($mil)	Net Income ($mil)
3-19	C	2.62	2.19	654.0	328.5	428.3	30.0
3-18	C	2.02	1.68	695.0	266.5	434.2	-17.6
2018	C	2.37	1.98	638.2	298.7	1,708.9	9.4
2017	C	2.23	1.86	627.2	293.0	1,719.4	22.6
2016	C	2.01	1.68	618.4	266.5	1,714.1	-34.5
2015	C	2.40	2.00	623.7	293.7	1,661.3	-125.9
2014	C	2.02	1.68	614.6	264.0	1,640.5	0.1

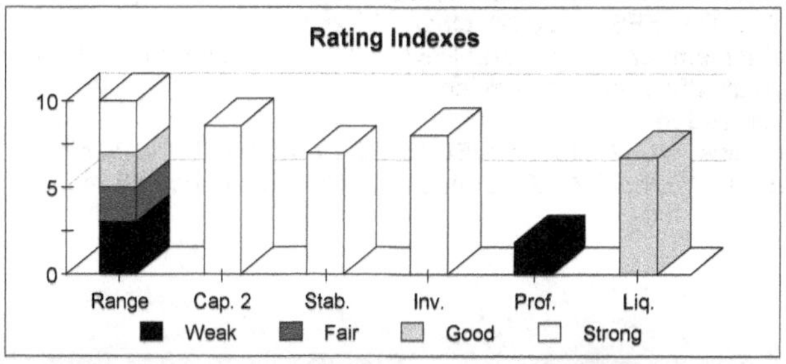

BLUE CROSS BLUE SHIELD OF SC INC * — B+ — Good

Major Rating Factors: Excellent profitability (8.3 on a scale of 0 to 10). Strong capitalization (10.0) based on excellent current risk-adjusted capital (severe loss scenario). Excellent liquidity (7.0) with ample operational cash flow and liquid investments.
Other Rating Factors: Fair quality investment portfolio (3.2).
Principal Business: Comp med (76%), FEHB (15%), med supp (4%), dental (3%), other (2%)
Mem Phys: 18: 23,112 **17:** 21,332 **18 MLR** 74.8% **/ 18 Admin Exp** N/A
Enroll(000): Q1 19: 1,521 **18:** 1,503 **17:** 1,426 **Med Exp PMPM:** $158
Principal Investments: Long-term bonds (26%), affiliate common stock (21%), nonaffiliate common stock (17%), cash and equiv (9%), real estate (4%), other (22%)
Provider Compensation ($000): Contr fee ($2,553,254), FFS ($229,719), bonus arrang ($9,122), capitation ($1,464), other ($2,805)
Total Member Encounters: Phys (5,151,333), non-phys (1,985,055)
Group Affiliation: None
Licensed in: SC
Address: 2501 Faraway Dr, Columbia, SC 29219
Phone: (803) 788-3860 **Dom State:** SC **Commenced Bus:** N/A

Data Date	Rating	RACR #1	RACR #2	Total Assets ($mil)	Capital ($mil)	Net Premium ($mil)	Net Income ($mil)
3-19	B+	6.16	5.14	4,742.7	3,075.1	1,026.1	87.9
3-18	B+	5.71	4.76	4,216.0	2,651.0	977.1	19.9
2018	B+	5.90	4.92	4,475.5	2,941.9	3,804.2	261.7
2017	B+	5.67	4.72	4,048.6	2,628.6	3,344.9	79.4
2016	A-	5.56	4.63	3,522.2	2,413.8	2,639.2	59.1
2015	A-	5.88	4.90	3,254.2	2,252.7	2,325.5	76.7
2014	A-	4.61	3.84	3,195.9	2,166.3	2,369.0	38.1

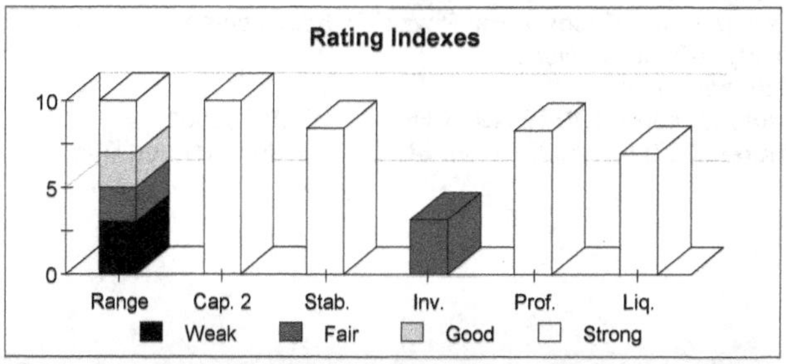

BLUE CROSS BLUE SHIELD OF VERMONT — C+ — Fair

Major Rating Factors: Fair quality investment portfolio (4.4 on a scale of 0 to 10). Good liquidity (6.8) with sufficient resources (cash flows and marketable investments) to handle a spike in claims. Weak profitability index (2.2).
Other Rating Factors: Strong capitalization (8.0) based on excellent current risk-adjusted capital (severe loss scenario).
Principal Business: Comp med (81%), FEHB (17%), med supp (2%)
Mem Phys: 18: 8,200 **17:** 8,096 **18 MLR** 93.3% **/ 18 Admin Exp** N/A
Enroll(000): Q1 19: 199 **18:** 198 **17:** 212 **Med Exp PMPM:** $202
Principal Investments: Long-term bonds (43%), affiliate common stock (37%), cash and equiv (10%), nonaffiliate common stock (6%), real estate (4%)
Provider Compensation ($000): FFS ($215,416), contr fee ($185,078), capitation ($1,954), other ($84,547)
Total Member Encounters: Phys (254,067), non-phys (335,351)
Group Affiliation: None
Licensed in: VT
Address: 445 Industrial Lane, Berlin, VT 5602
Phone: (802) 223-6131 **Dom State:** VT **Commenced Bus:** N/A

Data Date	Rating	RACR #1	RACR #2	Total Assets ($mil)	Capital ($mil)	Net Premium ($mil)	Net Income ($mil)
3-19	C+	2.13	1.77	252.3	110.7	130.5	6.9
3-18	B	2.22	1.85	278.5	124.8	132.3	0.0
2018	C+	2.12	1.77	257.6	110.2	517.4	-6.7
2017	B	2.36	1.96	288.3	134.1	578.3	7.6
2016	B	2.52	2.10	285.4	135.3	547.3	-9.7
2015	B+	2.81	2.34	266.6	148.4	539.9	12.2
2014	B+	2.81	2.34	256.1	138.4	470.6	9.9

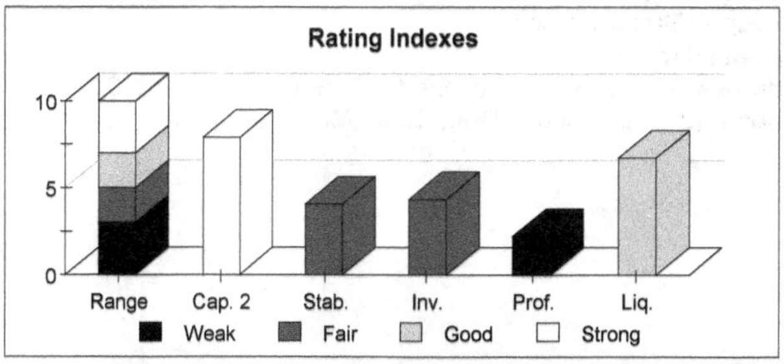

BLUE CROSS BLUE SHIELD OF WISCONSIN B- Good

Major Rating Factors: Excellent profitability (9.1 on a scale of 0 to 10). Strong capitalization (10.0) based on excellent current risk-adjusted capital (severe loss scenario). Excellent liquidity (6.9) with sufficient resources (cash flows and marketable investments) to handle a spike in claims.
Other Rating Factors: Low quality investment portfolio (0.7).
Principal Business: FEHB (57%), comp med (24%), med supp (9%), dental (3%), other (6%)
Mem Phys: 18: 44,905 **17:** 42,101 **18 MLR** 100.1% **/ 18 Admin Exp** N/A
Enroll(000): Q1 19: 403 **18:** 414 **17:** 354 **Med Exp PMPM:** $146
Principal Investments: Affiliate common stock (51%), long-term bonds (46%), cash and equiv (2%), real estate (2%)
Provider Compensation ($000): Bonus arrang ($405,076), contr fee ($191,995), FFS ($92,669), other ($30,283)
Total Member Encounters: Phys (729,992), non-phys (839,432)
Group Affiliation: Anthem Inc
Licensed in: WI
Address: N17 W24340 RIVERWOOD Dr, WAUKESHA, WI 53188
Phone: (262) 523-4020 **Dom State:** WI **Commenced Bus:** N/A

Data Date	Rating	RACR #1	RACR #2	Total Assets ($mil)	Capital ($mil)	Net Premium ($mil)	Net Income ($mil)
3-19	B-	3.97	3.31	608.3	347.5	172.3	30.2
3-18	B-	3.66	3.05	575.1	292.8	180.2	11.9
2018	B-	3.47	2.89	565.5	302.8	726.9	123.0
2017	B-	2.58	2.15	576.6	276.7	769.1	92.8
2016	B-	3.01	2.50	544.6	260.5	758.6	81.2
2015	B-	2.56	2.13	463.8	206.4	735.1	78.6
2014	B-	3.06	2.55	454.2	232.1	699.4	84.3

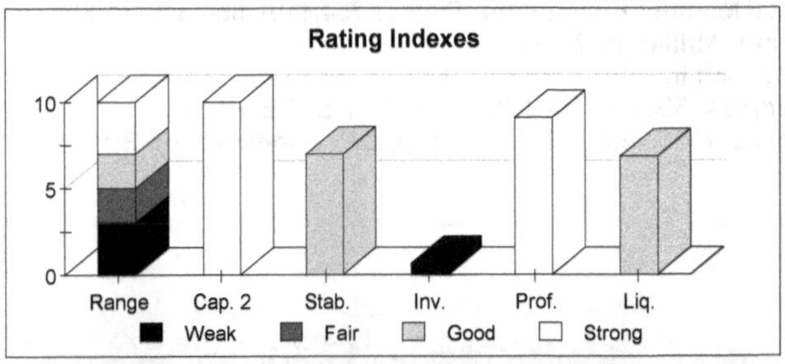

BLUE CROSS BLUE SHIELD OF WYOMING B- Good

Major Rating Factors: Fair quality investment portfolio (3.6 on a scale of 0 to 10). Good overall profitability index (5.2). Strong capitalization (10.0) based on excellent current risk-adjusted capital (severe loss scenario).
Other Rating Factors: Excellent liquidity (7.0) with ample operational cash flow and liquid investments.
Principal Business: Comp med (77%), FEHB (18%), med supp (4%)
Mem Phys: 18: 4,561 **17:** 4,432 **18 MLR** 75.5% **/ 18 Admin Exp** N/A
Enroll(000): Q1 19: 92 **18:** 89 **17:** 88 **Med Exp PMPM:** $432
Principal Investments: Nonaffiliate common stock (46%), long-term bonds (39%), cash and equiv (9%), real estate (1%), other (5%)
Provider Compensation ($000): FFS ($418,181), contr fee ($32,006), bonus arrang ($44)
Total Member Encounters: Phys (825,636), non-phys (965,576)
Group Affiliation: None
Licensed in: WY
Address: 4000 HOUSE Ave, CHEYENNE, WY 82001
Phone: (307) 634-1393 **Dom State:** WY **Commenced Bus:** N/A

Data Date	Rating	RACR #1	RACR #2	Total Assets ($mil)	Capital ($mil)	Net Premium ($mil)	Net Income ($mil)
3-19	B-	5.87	4.89	625.1	368.4	159.6	15.7
3-18	B-	5.19	4.33	544.4	323.0	153.1	10.6
2018	B-	5.28	4.40	547.8	335.4	612.2	40.5
2017	B-	5.07	4.22	525.8	315.9	484.0	23.4
2016	B	4.91	4.09	481.1	276.4	467.8	-15.1
2015	B	6.13	5.11	437.3	275.1	369.1	20.1
2014	B	5.97	4.97	405.0	251.3	286.3	12.7

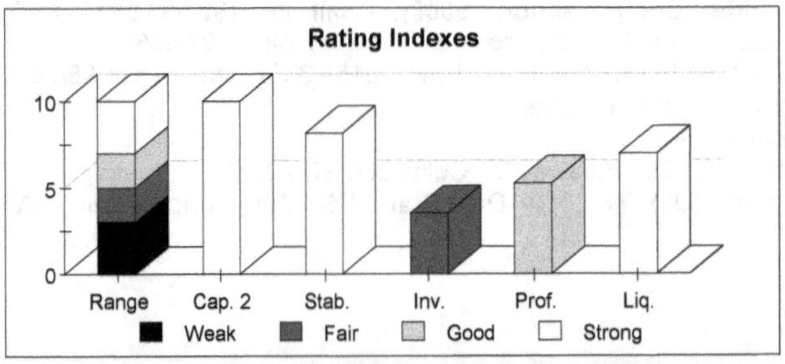

BLUE CROSS COMPLETE OF MICHIGAN B Good

Major Rating Factors: Good overall profitability index (6.9 on a scale of 0 to 10). Strong capitalization (9.0) based on excellent current risk-adjusted capital (severe loss scenario). High quality investment portfolio (9.9).
Other Rating Factors: Excellent liquidity (7.3) with ample operational cash flow and liquid investments.
Principal Business: Medicaid (100%)
Mem Phys: 18: 29,230 **17:** 27,346 **18 MLR** 78.8% **/ 18 Admin Exp** N/A
Enroll(000): Q1 19: 210 **18:** 210 **17:** 203 **Med Exp PMPM:** $238
Principal Investments: Cash and equiv (96%), long-term bonds (4%)
Provider Compensation ($000): Contr fee ($595,108), capitation ($2,760), bonus arrang ($1,383)
Total Member Encounters: Phys (1,505,287), non-phys (245,569)
Group Affiliation: None
Licensed in: MI
Address: 100 Galleria Officentre #210, Southfield, MI 48034
Phone: (215) 937-8000 **Dom State:** MI **Commenced Bus:** N/A

Data Date	Rating	RACR #1	RACR #2	Total Assets ($mil)	Capital ($mil)	Net Premium ($mil)	Net Income ($mil)
3-19	B	2.98	2.48	294.3	116.6	200.6	9.9
3-18	C	1.51	1.26	240.1	65.8	227.9	-9.1
2018	B	2.74	2.28	271.1	106.6	755.9	31.4
2017	E	1.12	0.93	229.9	74.9	884.8	17.1
2016	E	1.46	1.22	154.9	47.9	709.4	10.8
2015	E	1.95	1.63	115.5	37.9	418.5	-1.2
2014	E	1.33	1.11	89.2	30.7	259.3	-13.7

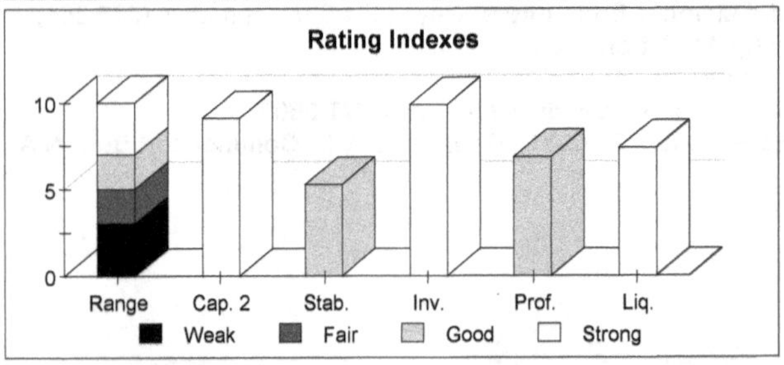

BLUE CROSS OF CALIFORNIA * A+ Excellent

Major Rating Factors: Excellent profitability (9.1 on a scale of 0 to 10). Strong capitalization index (9.0) based on excellent current risk-adjusted capital (severe loss scenario). Excellent overall results on stability tests (7.5).
Other Rating Factors: Excellent liquidity (7.3) with ample operational cash flow and liquid investments.
Principal Business: Medicaid (23%), Medicare (10%)
Mem Phys: 18: N/A **17:** N/A **18 MLR** 81.6% **/ 18 Admin Exp** N/A
Enroll(000): Q1 19: 3,555 **18:** 3,552 **17:** 3,884 **Med Exp PMPM:** $304
Principal Investments ($000): Cash and equiv ($2,973,111)
Provider Compensation ($000): None
Total Member Encounters: N/A
Group Affiliation: Anthem Inc
Licensed in: CA
Address: 1 Wellpoint Way, Thousand Oaks, CA 91362
Phone: (916) 403-0526 **Dom State:** CA **Commenced Bus:** July 1982

Data Date	Rating	RACR #1	RACR #2	Total Assets ($mil)	Capital ($mil)	Net Premium ($mil)	Net Income ($mil)
3-19	A+	3.91	2.49	7,997.8	3,429.6	4,041.6	348.8
3-18	A+	3.47	2.20	7,784.6	3,115.6	3,951.6	312.1
2018	A+	3.52	2.24	7,154.9	3,043.0	15,774.6	773.4
2017	A+	3.18	2.02	7,871.8	2,819.6	16,792.3	993.3
2016	A+	2.62	1.65	7,350.6	2,109.1	16,650.0	710.4
2015	A+	2.49	1.57	6,611.5	1,801.2	14,977.4	502.0
2014	A+	2.41	1.53	5,862.9	1,643.8	13,373.6	426.0

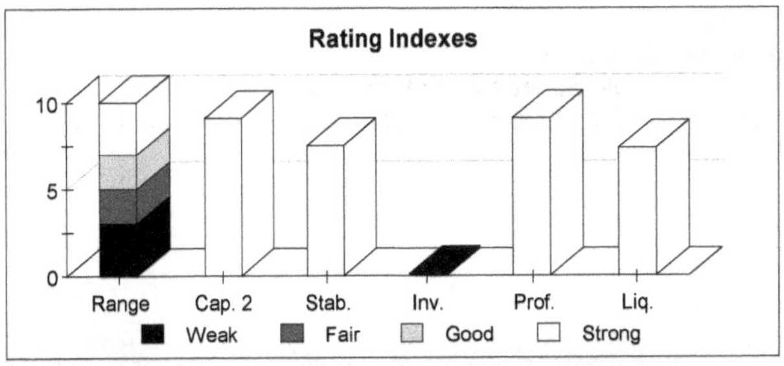

BLUE CROSS OF IDAHO CARE PLUS INC C+ Fair

Major Rating Factors: Good liquidity (6.5 on a scale of 0 to 10) with sufficient resources (cash flows and marketable investments) to handle a spike in claims. Weak profitability index (0.9). Strong capitalization (8.1) based on excellent current risk-adjusted capital (severe loss scenario).
Other Rating Factors: High quality investment portfolio (9.1).
Principal Business: Medicare (85%), Medicaid (14%), med supp (1%)
Mem Phys: 18: 9,068 **17:** 8,028 **18 MLR** 85.3% **/ 18 Admin Exp** N/A
Enroll(000): Q1 19: 35 **18:** 29 **17:** 25 **Med Exp PMPM:** $888
Principal Investments: Long-term bonds (67%), cash and equiv (18%), nonaffiliate common stock (12%), pref stock (1%), other (2%)
Provider Compensation ($000): Contr fee ($153,311), bonus arrang ($138,713), capitation ($474)
Total Member Encounters: Phys (302,973), non-phys (446,887)
Group Affiliation: Blue Cross of Idaho Health Service I
Licensed in: ID
Address: 3000 E Pine Ave, Meridian, ID 83642
Phone: (208) 345-4550 **Dom State:** ID **Commenced Bus:** N/A

Data Date	Rating	RACR #1	RACR #2	Total Assets ($mil)	Capital ($mil)	Net Premium ($mil)	Net Income ($mil)
3-19	C+	2.23	1.86	165.0	79.8	110.7	2.5
3-18	C	N/A	N/A	180.6	78.6	83.1	0.6
2018	C+	2.08	1.73	147.5	76.7	349.5	1.0
2017	C	N/A	N/A	144.9	78.0	305.7	17.5
2016	C	1.42	1.18	123.3	59.6	320.4	13.3
2015	C+	1.00	0.83	97.8	48.1	325.4	-5.7
2014	U	0.19	0.16	35.8	3.5	75.1	-14.2

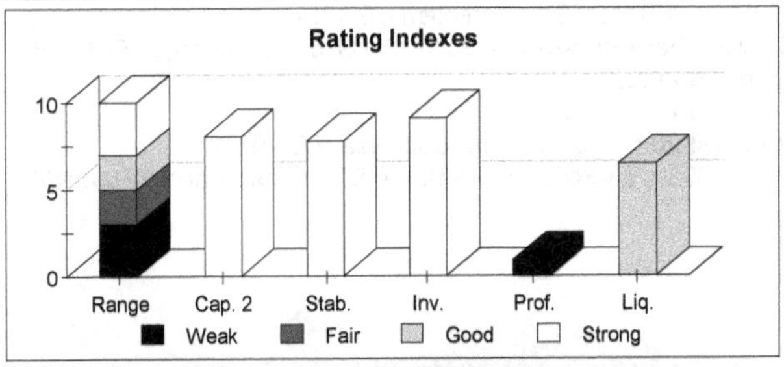

BLUE CROSS OF IDAHO HEALTH SERVICE B Good

Major Rating Factors: Good overall profitability index (5.8 on a scale of 0 to 10). Good quality investment portfolio (5.6). Good liquidity (6.8) with sufficient resources (cash flows and marketable investments) to handle a spike in claims.
Other Rating Factors: Strong capitalization (10.0) based on excellent current risk-adjusted capital (severe loss scenario).
Principal Business: Comp med (78%), FEHB (15%), dental (2%), med supp (1%), other (3%)
Mem Phys: 18: 15,349 **17:** 14,555 **18 MLR** 84.4% **/ 18 Admin Exp** N/A
Enroll(000): Q1 19: 263 **18:** 264 **17:** 244 **Med Exp PMPM:** $333
Principal Investments: Long-term bonds (57%), nonaffiliate common stock (25%), cash and equiv (8%), real estate (3%), other (8%)
Provider Compensation ($000): Contr fee ($778,649), bonus arrang ($265,903), capitation ($5,229)
Total Member Encounters: Phys (1,525,629), non-phys (1,397,212)
Group Affiliation: Blue Cross of Idaho Health Service I
Licensed in: ID
Address: 3000 E Pine Ave, Meridian, ID 83642
Phone: (208) 345-4550 **Dom State:** ID **Commenced Bus:** N/A

Data Date	Rating	RACR #1	RACR #2	Total Assets ($mil)	Capital ($mil)	Net Premium ($mil)	Net Income ($mil)
3-19	B	6.60	5.50	980.3	653.5	319.9	17.3
3-18	B	7.47	6.23	973.6	635.5	303.4	12.1
2018	B	6.34	5.28	937.4	632.9	1,244.2	48.5
2017	B	6.75	5.62	896.6	600.5	1,063.6	79.8
2016	B	5.47	4.56	770.1	486.6	1,173.6	11.0
2015	B	4.92	4.10	758.1	458.5	1,202.5	-3.1
2014	B+	4.89	4.08	821.5	524.8	1,367.2	5.9

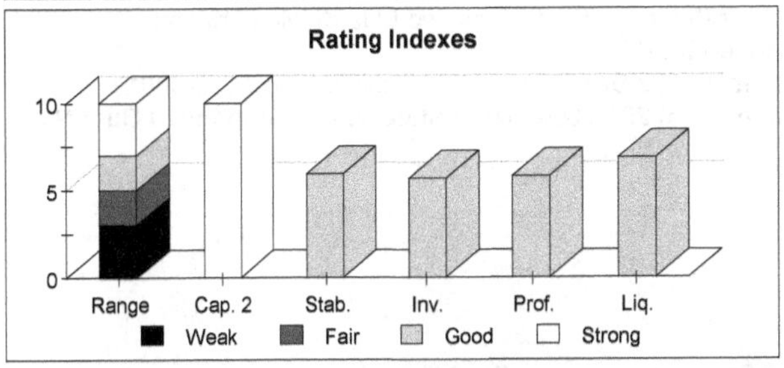

BLUE SHIELD OF CALIFORNIA LIFE & HEALTH INS COMPANY B Good

Major Rating Factors: Good overall profitability (6.2 on a scale of 0 to 10). Excellent expense controls. Good liquidity (6.7) with sufficient resources to handle a spike in claims. Fair overall results on stability tests (4.9) including negative cash flow from operations for 2018.
Other Rating Factors: Strong capitalization (10.0) based on excellent risk adjusted capital (severe loss scenario). High quality investment portfolio (8.1).
Principal Business: Individual health insurance (58%), group health insurance (38%), and group life insurance (4%).
Principal Investments: CMOs and structured securities (56%), nonCMO investment grade bonds (39%), and cash (2%).
Investments in Affiliates: None
Group Affiliation: Blue Shield of California
Licensed in: CA
Commenced Business: July 1954
Address: 50 Beale Street, San Francisco, CA 94105-0000
Phone: (800) 642-5599 **Domicile State:** CA **NAIC Code:** 61557

Data Date	Rating	RACR #1	RACR #2	Total Assets ($mil)	Capital ($mil)	Net Premium ($mil)	Net Income ($mil)
3-19	B	5.33	3.93	318.1	202.1	62.5	11.1
3-18	B	4.74	3.48	315.5	185.4	60.8	5.9
2018	B	5.09	3.75	303.2	191.1	242.3	12.4
2017	B	4.61	3.41	303.5	179.2	253.4	9.7
2016	B	5.28	4.03	463.6	323.0	310.2	22.9
2015	B	2.98	2.37	665.2	481.1	1,249.2	39.5
2014	A-	1.93	1.53	743.7	444.3	1,794.5	78.5

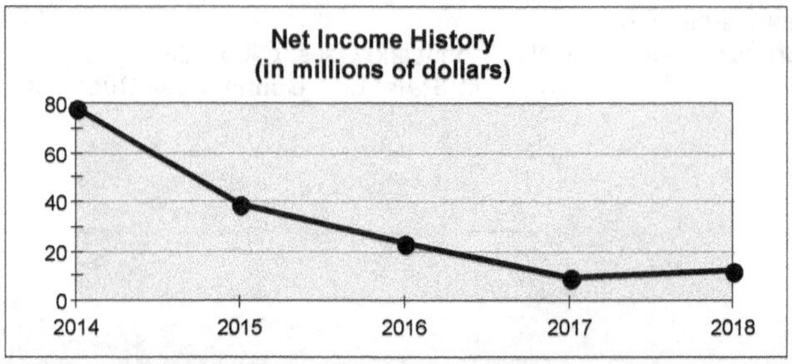

BLUECHOICE HEALTHPLAN OF SC INC B Good

Major Rating Factors: Good quality investment portfolio (5.9 on a scale of 0 to 10). Good overall results on stability tests (5.9). Good liquidity (6.2) with sufficient resources (cash flows and marketable investments) to handle a spike in claims.
Other Rating Factors: Fair profitability index (4.4). Strong capitalization index (10.0) based on excellent current risk-adjusted capital (severe loss scenario).
Principal Business: Comp med (72%), Medicaid (28%)
Mem Phys: 18: 24,823 **17:** 22,611 **18 MLR** 114.2% **/ 18 Admin Exp** N/A
Enroll(000): Q1 19: 195 **18:** 188 **17:** 183 **Med Exp PMPM:** $313
Principal Investments: Long-term bonds (56%), cash and equiv (27%), nonaffiliate common stock (12%), affiliate common stock (5%)
Provider Compensation ($000): Contr fee ($599,804), bonus arrang ($93,020), FFS ($2,732), capitation ($2,105)
Total Member Encounters: Phys (1,127,571), non-phys (523,328)
Group Affiliation: None
Licensed in: SC
Address: I-20 at Alpine Road, Columbia, SC 29219
Phone: (803) 786-8466 **Dom State:** SC **Commenced Bus:** N/A

Data Date	Rating	RACR #1	RACR #2	Total Assets ($mil)	Capital ($mil)	Net Premium ($mil)	Net Income ($mil)
3-19	B	7.51	6.26	386.7	258.6	160.9	4.6
3-18	B	7.68	6.40	376.2	231.2	147.2	-1.8
2018	B	7.21	6.01	368.7	247.6	609.8	19.8
2017	B	5.62	4.69	352.6	231.4	562.6	29.6
2016	B	3.36	2.80	346.9	197.9	969.9	-23.4
2015	A	5.95	4.96	347.4	225.4	664.4	14.4
2014	A-	7.25	6.04	306.2	215.1	490.4	11.3

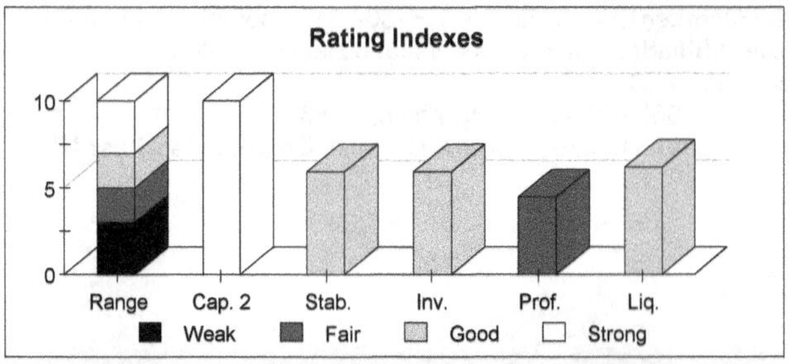

BLUECROSS BLUESHIELD KANSAS SOLUTION C+ Fair

Major Rating Factors: Good quality investment portfolio (5.8 on a scale of 0 to 10). Weak profitability index (0.5). Strong capitalization (10.0) based on excellent current risk-adjusted capital (severe loss scenario).
Other Rating Factors: Excellent liquidity (8.8) with ample operational cash flow and liquid investments.
Principal Business: Comp med (100%)
Mem Phys: 18: 13,439 **17:** 12,542 **18 MLR** -60.0% **/ 18 Admin Exp** N/A
Enroll(000): Q1 19: N/A **18:** N/A **17:** 64 **Med Exp PMPM:** N/A
Principal Investments: Long-term bonds (55%), cash and equiv (28%), nonaffiliate common stock (17%)
Provider Compensation ($000): Contr fee ($33,350)
Total Member Encounters: Phys (10,315), non-phys (10,684)
Group Affiliation: Blue Cross and Blue Shield of Kansas
Licensed in: KS
Address: 1133 SW Topeka Blvd, Topeka, KS 66629-0001
Phone: (785) 291-7000 **Dom State:** KS **Commenced Bus:** N/A

Data Date	Rating	RACR #1	RACR #2	Total Assets ($mil)	Capital ($mil)	Net Premium ($mil)	Net Income ($mil)
3-19	C+	24.52	20.43	60.1	56.7	0.0	0.4
3-18	C+	N/A	N/A	91.3	39.6	0.7	-6.7
2018	C+	23.17	19.31	56.6	53.5	3.9	3.9
2017	C+	N/A	N/A	143.6	40.7	338.9	-15.1
2016	C+	4.16	3.47	138.2	67.7	157.8	4.5
2015	C	2.53	2.11	98.4	17.0	43.1	-61.3
2014	N/A	N/A	N/A	10.9	10.2	N/A	-0.1

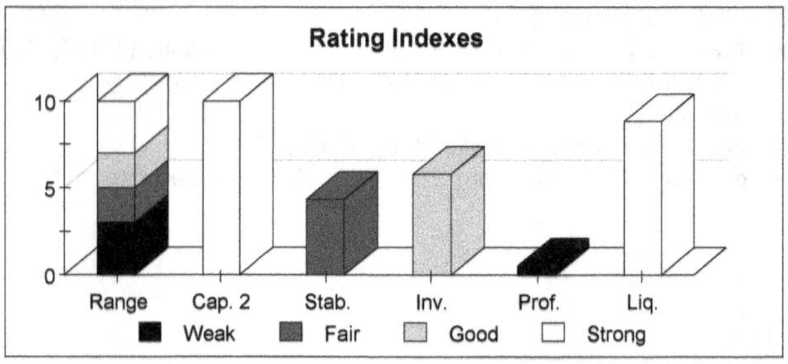

BLUECROSS BLUESHIELD OF TENNESSEE * B+ Good

Major Rating Factors: Good overall profitability index (6.3 on a scale of 0 to 10). Good quality investment portfolio (6.3). Strong capitalization (10.0) based on excellent current risk-adjusted capital (severe loss scenario).
Other Rating Factors: Excellent liquidity (7.1) with ample operational cash flow and liquid investments.
Principal Business: Comp med (58%), Medicare (24%), FEHB (13%), dental (3%), med supp (2%)
Mem Phys: 18: 33,337 **17:** 32,461 **18 MLR** 74.6% **/ 18 Admin Exp** N/A
Enroll(000): Q1 19: 1,763 **18:** 1,700 **17:** 1,599 **Med Exp PMPM:** $198
Principal Investments: Long-term bonds (54%), affiliate common stock (14%), nonaffiliate common stock (14%), cash and equiv (9%), pref stock (3%), real estate (2%), other (5%)
Provider Compensation ($000): Contr fee ($3,125,836), FFS ($859,577), capitation ($17,482), bonus arrang ($6,252)
Total Member Encounters: Phys (10,068,096), non-phys (1,641,710)
Group Affiliation: BlueCross BlueShield of Tennessee In
Licensed in: TN
Address: 1 Cameron Hill Circle, Chattanooga, TN 37402-0001
Phone: (423) 535-5600 **Dom State:** TN **Commenced Bus:** N/A

Data Date	Rating	RACR #1	RACR #2	Total Assets ($mil)	Capital ($mil)	Net Premium ($mil)	Net Income ($mil)
3-19	B+	7.15	5.96	4,339.8	3,436.7	1,313.5	226.5
3-18	B	8.61	7.17	3,360.5	2,309.3	1,382.5	196.8
2018	B+	6.54	5.45	3,995.9	3,139.3	5,411.3	679.2
2017	B	7.98	6.65	2,927.1	2,139.9	4,631.7	322.4
2016	B	6.32	5.27	2,556.7	1,733.5	4,739.9	2.4
2015	B+	6.19	5.16	2,465.5	1,678.6	4,525.2	-101.9
2014	A	6.86	5.72	2,442.4	1,733.5	4,222.3	63.4

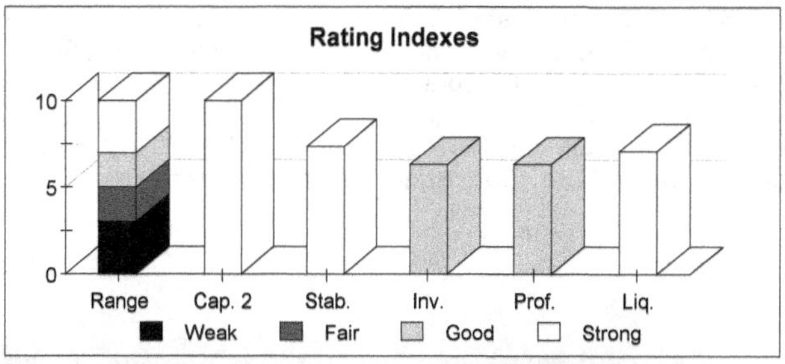

BOSTON MEDICAL CENTER HEALTH PLAN C Fair

Major Rating Factors: Fair quality investment portfolio (3.1 on a scale of 0 to 10). Weak profitability index (2.1). Good capitalization (6.6) based on good current risk-adjusted capital (severe loss scenario).
Other Rating Factors: Good liquidity (6.8) with sufficient resources (cash flows and marketable investments) to handle a spike in claims.
Principal Business: Medicaid (86%), comp med (13%), Medicare (1%)
Mem Phys: 18: 44,968 **17:** 30,597 **18 MLR** 93.5% **/ 18 Admin Exp** N/A
Enroll(000): Q1 19: 416 **18:** 395 **17:** 313 **Med Exp PMPM:** $458
Principal Investments: Nonaffiliate common stock (50%), cash and equiv (28%), long-term bonds (22%)
Provider Compensation ($000): Contr fee ($1,856,892), capitation ($238,026), bonus arrang ($1,402)
Total Member Encounters: Phys (2,567,717), non-phys (6,126,850)
Group Affiliation: BMC Health System Inc
Licensed in: MA, NH
Address: Two Copley Place Ste 600, Charlestown, MA 2129
Phone: (617) 748-6000 **Dom State:** MA **Commenced Bus:** N/A

Data Date	Rating	RACR #1	RACR #2	Total Assets ($mil)	Capital ($mil)	Net Premium ($mil)	Net Income ($mil)
3-19	C	1.16	0.97	524.9	227.6	634.9	6.5
3-18	B-	N/A	N/A	503.4	217.3	485.2	-3.7
2018	C	1.11	0.93	474.5	217.4	2,297.2	-17.5
2017	B-	N/A	N/A	463.5	233.2	1,618.5	-1.9
2016	B-	1.91	1.59	471.3	236.2	1,574.5	-4.5
2015	B-	2.12	1.77	459.4	253.6	1,564.1	47.8
2014	C+	1.40	1.17	392.0	204.2	1,791.5	-19.4

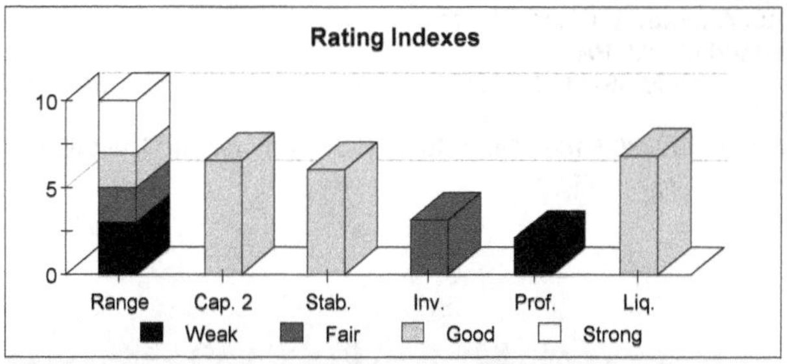

BOSTON MUTUAL LIFE INSURANCE COMPANY * B+ Good

Major Rating Factors: Good quality investment portfolio (5.9 on a scale of 0 to 10) despite significant exposure to mortgages . Mortgage default rate has been low. large holdings of BBB rated bonds in addition to minimal holdings in junk bonds. Good overall profitability (5.8) although investment income, in comparison to reserve requirements, is below regulatory standards. Good liquidity (5.6).
Other Rating Factors: Good overall results on stability tests (6.4) excellent operational trends and excellent risk diversification. Strong capitalization (7.5) based on excellent risk adjusted capital (severe loss scenario).
Principal Business: Individual life insurance (56%), group health insurance (23%), group life insurance (17%), and individual health insurance (3%).
Principal Investments: NonCMO investment grade bonds (57%), mortgages in good standing (14%), policy loans (12%), common & preferred stock (8%), and misc. investments (8%).
Investments in Affiliates: 3%
Group Affiliation: Boston Mutual Group
Licensed in: All states, the District of Columbia and Puerto Rico
Commenced Business: February 1892
Address: 120 Royall Street, Canton, MA 02021-1098
Phone: (781) 828-7000 **Domicile State:** MA **NAIC Code:** 61476

Data Date	Rating	RACR #1	RACR #2	Total Assets ($mil)	Capital ($mil)	Net Premium ($mil)	Net Income ($mil)
3-19	B+	2.06	1.36	1,484.3	225.4	55.4	3.9
3-18	B+	2.27	1.49	1,443.2	212.3	55.4	3.5
2018	B+	2.02	1.34	1,465.1	219.1	202.3	13.9
2017	B+	2.26	1.48	1,430.5	209.4	196.7	13.9
2016	B+	2.06	1.35	1,359.7	178.0	188.1	11.4
2015	B+	1.98	1.31	1,297.1	159.1	185.7	12.8
2014	B+	1.95	1.29	1,245.2	145.3	185.3	9.9

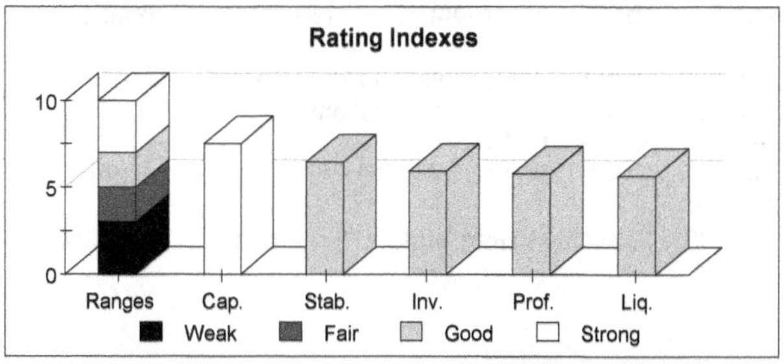

BRAVO HEALTH MID-ATLANTIC INC — C — Fair

Major Rating Factors: Fair quality investment portfolio (4.3 on a scale of 0 to 10). Fair overall results on stability tests (4.3) based on a decline in the number of member physicians during 2019. Rating is significantly influenced by the good financial results of Cigna Corporation. Weak profitability index (2.1).
Other Rating Factors: Weak liquidity (1.2) as a spike in claims may stretch capacity. Strong capitalization index (8.4) based on excellent current risk-adjusted capital (severe loss scenario).
Principal Business: Medicare (100%)
Mem Phys: 18: 9,209 **17:** 14,363 **18 MLR** 92.3% **/ 18 Admin Exp** N/A
Enroll(000): Q1 19: 18 **18:** 18 **17:** 16 **Med Exp PMPM:** $1,137
Principal Investments: Long-term bonds (101%)
Provider Compensation ($000): Contr fee ($172,433), capitation ($44,304), salary ($2,341), bonus arrang ($615), other ($17,742)
Total Member Encounters: Phys (291,648), non-phys (259,595)
Group Affiliation: Cigna Corporation
Licensed in: DC, DE, MD
Address: 3601 ODONNELL STREET, BALTIMORE, MD 21224-5238
Phone: (800) 235-9188 **Dom State:** MD **Commenced Bus:** N/A

Data Date	Rating	RACR #1	RACR #2	Total Assets ($mil)	Capital ($mil)	Net Premium ($mil)	Net Income ($mil)
3-19	C	2.44	2.04	84.4	37.2	74.0	2.6
3-18	C	2.37	1.97	99.3	31.3	65.7	9.4
2018	C	1.86	1.55	73.0	27.9	259.1	7.9
2017	C	1.07	0.89	77.4	24.2	222.3	-18.4
2016	C+	2.19	1.82	80.6	35.6	279.3	-1.4
2015	B-	2.50	2.08	94.2	38.1	288.2	3.4
2014	B-	2.23	1.86	84.0	35.4	306.6	10.2

Rating Indexes

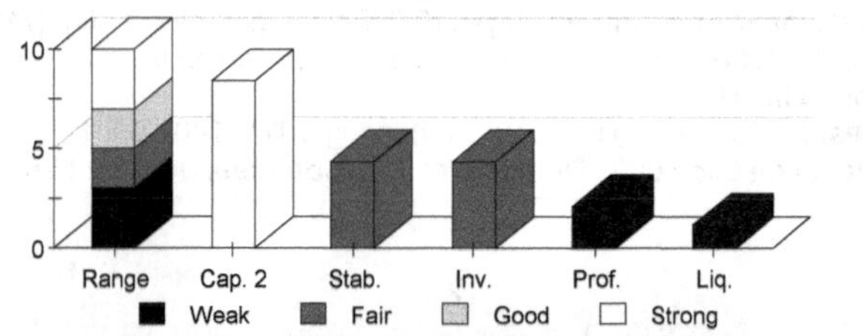

BRAVO HEALTH PENNSYLVANIA INC — C+ — Fair

Major Rating Factors: Fair profitability index (4.7 on a scale of 0 to 10). Fair quality investment portfolio (4.8). Good liquidity (6.2) with sufficient resources (cash flows and marketable investments) to handle a spike in claims.
Other Rating Factors: Strong capitalization (10.0) based on excellent current risk-adjusted capital (severe loss scenario).
Principal Business: Medicare (100%)
Mem Phys: 18: 19,494 **17:** 26,848 **18 MLR** 80.8% **/ 18 Admin Exp** N/A
Enroll(000): Q1 19: 45 **18:** 42 **17:** 41 **Med Exp PMPM:** $1,004
Principal Investments: Long-term bonds (102%)
Provider Compensation ($000): Contr fee ($373,734), capitation ($95,308), salary ($2,631), bonus arrang ($2,014), other ($40,309)
Total Member Encounters: Phys (767,319), non-phys (653,231)
Group Affiliation: Cigna Corporation
Licensed in: NJ, PA
Address: 1500 SPRING GARDEN St Ste 800, PHILADELPHIA, PA 19130-4071
Phone: (800) 235-9188 **Dom State:** PA **Commenced Bus:** N/A

Data Date	Rating	RACR #1	RACR #2	Total Assets ($mil)	Capital ($mil)	Net Premium ($mil)	Net Income ($mil)
3-19	C+	3.62	3.02	201.7	112.8	178.8	5.9
3-18	B	4.73	3.94	307.7	151.1	158.5	0.7
2018	C+	3.25	2.71	186.3	100.7	622.9	24.4
2017	B	3.33	2.78	236.9	149.8	596.7	9.8
2016	B	3.63	3.03	246.7	143.4	721.7	-4.8
2015	B	3.27	2.72	244.3	149.1	776.2	20.8
2014	B	2.82	2.35	236.3	131.2	904.4	14.8

Rating Indexes

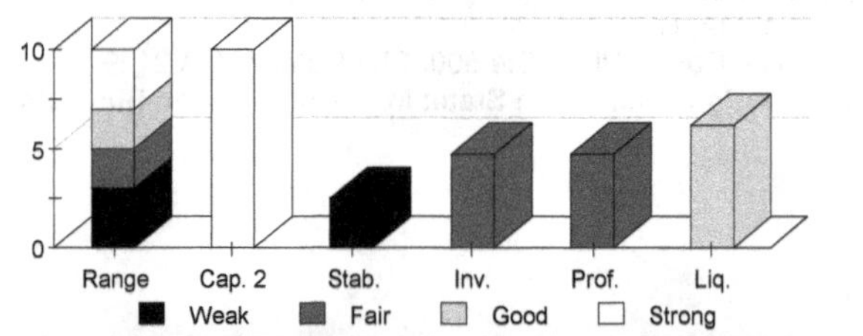

BRIDGESPAN HEALTH CO — B — Good

Major Rating Factors: Fair overall results on stability tests (4.4 on a scale of 0 to 10) based on a significant 95% decrease in enrollment during the period. Rating is significantly influenced by the good financial results of Cambia Health Solutions Inc. Strong capitalization index (10.0) based on excellent current risk-adjusted capital (severe loss scenario). High quality investment portfolio (9.2).
Other Rating Factors: Excellent liquidity (9.1) with ample operational cash flow and liquid investments. Weak profitability index (0.9).
Principal Business: Comp med (96%), med supp (4%)
Mem Phys: 18: N/A **17:** N/A **18 MLR** 17.8% **/ 18 Admin Exp** N/A
Enroll(000): Q1 19: 2 **18:** 2 **17:** 33 **Med Exp PMPM:** $126
Principal Investments: Long-term bonds (68%), cash and equiv (32%)
Provider Compensation ($000): Contr fee ($11,462), bonus arrang ($8,302), FFS ($1,298)
Total Member Encounters: Phys (16,215), non-phys (18,918)
Group Affiliation: Cambia Health Solutions Inc
Licensed in: ID, OR, UT, WA
Address: 2890 EAST COTTONWOOD PARKWAY, SALT LAKE CITY, UT 84121-7035
Phone: (801) 333-2000 **Dom State:** UT **Commenced Bus:** N/A

Data Date	Rating	RACR #1	RACR #2	Total Assets ($mil)	Capital ($mil)	Net Premium ($mil)	Net Income ($mil)
3-19	B	28.05	23.38	45.3	38.3	3.7	0.9
3-18	B-	2.29	1.91	49.9	27.3	4.0	-0.6
2018	B	27.38	22.82	42.9	37.3	16.2	9.1
2017	E	1.33	1.11	68.0	27.3	183.8	-0.4
2016	E	5.71	4.76	50.1	23.9	61.3	3.5
2015	E	3.06	2.55	45.1	19.6	67.9	-18.7
2014	E	0.91	0.76	17.0	3.0	22.1	-7.4

Rating Indexes

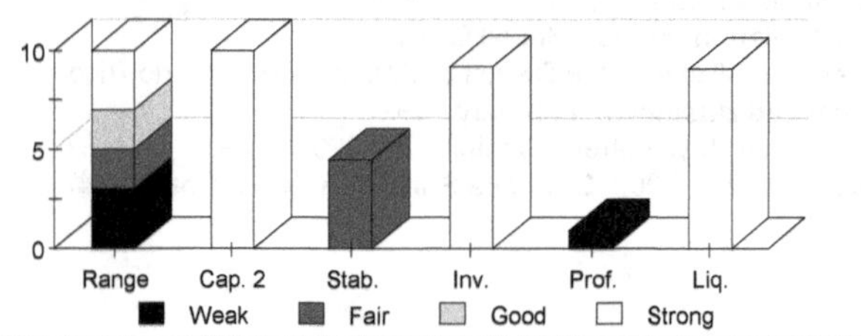

BRIDGEWAY HEALTH SOL OF AZ C Fair

Major Rating Factors: Good quality investment portfolio (6.5 on a scale of 0 to 10). Excellent profitability (8.5). Strong capitalization (10.0) based on excellent current risk-adjusted capital (severe loss scenario).
Other Rating Factors: Excellent liquidity (7.6) with ample operational cash flow and liquid investments.
Principal Business: Medicare (60%), Medicaid (40%)
Mem Phys: 18: 23,366 **17:** N/A **18 MLR** 8.3% **/ 18 Admin Exp** N/A
Enroll(000): Q1 19: 6 **18:** 1 **17:** N/A **Med Exp PMPM:** $178
Principal Investments: Long-term bonds (89%), cash and equiv (11%)
Provider Compensation ($000): Contr fee ($9,039), capitation ($940), salary ($293)
Total Member Encounters: Phys (14,080), non-phys (5,454)
Group Affiliation: Centene Corporation
Licensed in: AZ
Address: , Tempe, AZ 85281
Phone: (314) 725-4477 **Dom State:** AZ **Commenced Bus:** October 2006

Data Date	Rating	RACR #1	RACR #2	Total Assets ($mil)	Capital ($mil)	Net Premium ($mil)	Net Income ($mil)
3-19	C	12.49	10.41	32.1	10.9	21.5	0.0
3-18	N/A	N/A	N/A	N/A	N/A	N/A	N/A
2018	C-	11.57	9.64	17.1	9.7	13.8	4.1
2017	N/A	N/A	N/A	28.0	8.9	207.6	N/A
2016	N/A	N/A	N/A	N/A	N/A	N/A	N/A
2015	N/A	N/A	N/A	N/A	N/A	N/A	N/A
2014	N/A	N/A	N/A	N/A	N/A	N/A	N/A

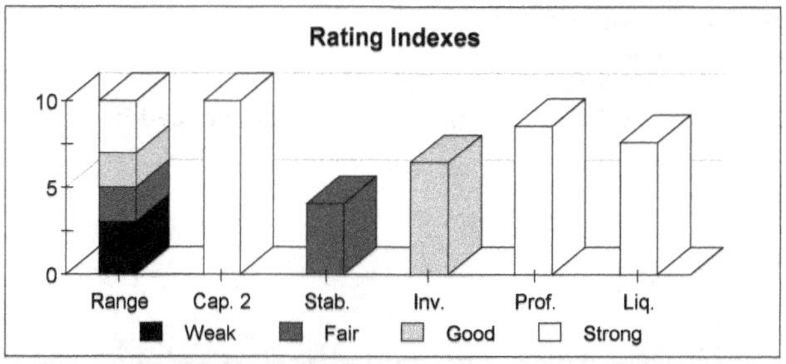

BRIGHT HEALTH CO OF ARIZONA D Weak

Major Rating Factors: Weak profitability index (0.9 on a scale of 0 to 10). Good liquidity (6.8) with sufficient resources (cash flows and marketable investments) to handle a spike in claims. Strong capitalization (10.0) based on excellent current risk-adjusted capital (severe loss scenario).
Other Rating Factors: High quality investment portfolio (9.8).
Principal Business: Medicare (100%)
Mem Phys: 18: 4,282 **17:** N/A **18 MLR** 84.6% **/ 18 Admin Exp** N/A
Enroll(000): Q1 19: 16 **18:** 1 **17:** N/A **Med Exp PMPM:** $614
Principal Investments: Cash and equiv (61%), long-term bonds (39%)
Provider Compensation ($000): Contr fee ($4,765), FFS ($1,782), capitation ($258)
Total Member Encounters: Phys (9,920), non-phys (1,618)
Group Affiliation: Bright Health Inc
Licensed in: AZ
Address: , PHOENIX, AZ 85018
Phone: (612) 238-1321 **Dom State:** AZ **Commenced Bus:** N/A

Data Date	Rating	RACR #1	RACR #2	Total Assets ($mil)	Capital ($mil)	Net Premium ($mil)	Net Income ($mil)
3-19	D	5.07	4.23	28.3	13.3	19.6	3.3
3-18	N/A	N/A	N/A	10.3	6.2	2.7	-1.1
2018	D	3.74	3.12	16.9	10.1	10.8	-7.9
2017	N/A	N/A	N/A	7.4	7.4	N/A	N/A
2016	N/A	N/A	N/A	N/A	N/A	N/A	N/A
2015	N/A	N/A	N/A	N/A	N/A	N/A	N/A
2014	N/A	N/A	N/A	N/A	N/A	N/A	N/A

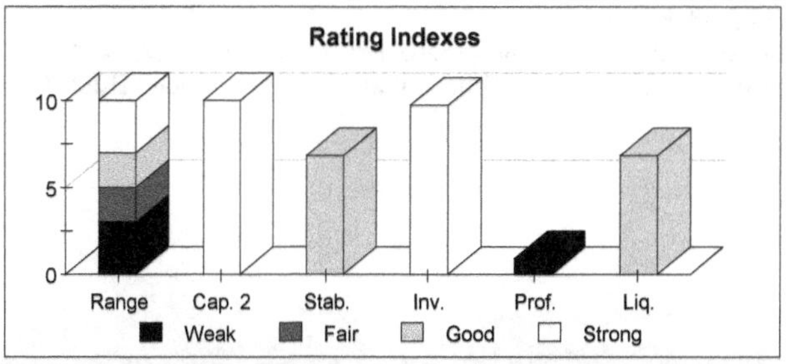

BRIGHT HEALTH INS CO E+ Very Weak

Major Rating Factors: Weak profitability index (0.9 on a scale of 0 to 10). Good liquidity (6.9) with sufficient resources (cash flows and marketable investments) to handle a spike in claims. Strong capitalization (8.0) based on excellent current risk-adjusted capital (severe loss scenario).
Other Rating Factors: High quality investment portfolio (9.9).
Principal Business: Comp med (95%), Medicare (5%)
Mem Phys: 18: 5,887 **17:** 5,804 **18 MLR** 75.4% **/ 18 Admin Exp** N/A
Enroll(000): Q1 19: 27 **18:** 22 **17:** 11 **Med Exp PMPM:** $300
Principal Investments: Long-term bonds (58%), cash and equiv (42%)
Provider Compensation ($000): Contr fee ($50,848), capitation ($13,808), FFS ($4,792)
Total Member Encounters: Phys (76,187), non-phys (14,195)
Group Affiliation: Bright Health Inc
Licensed in: AZ, CO
Address: 10333 E DRY CREEK Rd Ste 150, ENGLEWOOD, CO 80112
Phone: (612) 238-1321 **Dom State:** CO **Commenced Bus:** N/A

Data Date	Rating	RACR #1	RACR #2	Total Assets ($mil)	Capital ($mil)	Net Premium ($mil)	Net Income ($mil)
3-19	E+	2.17	1.81	85.0	23.3	17.2	7.8
3-18	N/A	N/A	N/A	44.6	14.9	26.5	1.4
2018	E	1.62	1.35	62.6	17.7	108.7	-7.4
2017	N/A	N/A	N/A	33.5	13.7	36.2	-17.5
2016	N/A	N/A	N/A	17.0	14.3	N/A	-0.4
2015	N/A	N/A	N/A	N/A	N/A	N/A	N/A
2014	N/A	N/A	N/A	N/A	N/A	N/A	N/A

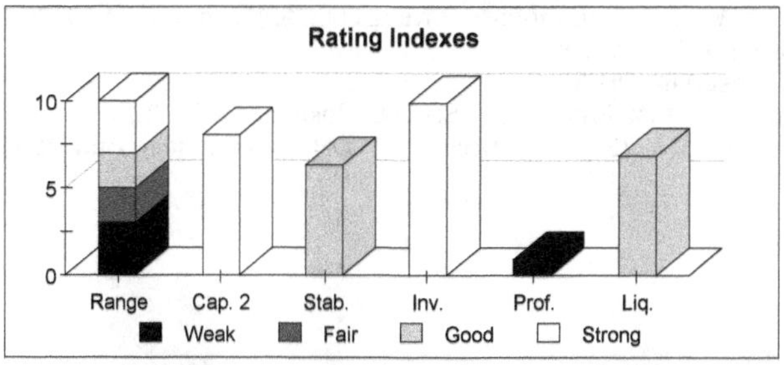

BRIGHT HLTH INS CO OF AL INC — D — Weak

Major Rating Factors: Weak profitability index (0.2 on a scale of 0 to 10). Strong capitalization (10.0) based on excellent current risk-adjusted capital (severe loss scenario). High quality investment portfolio (9.9).
Other Rating Factors: Excellent liquidity (6.9) with sufficient resources (cash flows and marketable investments) to handle a spike in claims.
Principal Business: Comp med (88%), Medicare (12%)
Mem Phys: 18: 435 **17:** N/A **18 MLR** 93.6% **/ 18 Admin Exp** N/A
Enroll(000): Q1 19: 3 **18:** 1 **17:** N/A **Med Exp PMPM:** $324
Principal Investments: Long-term bonds (54%), cash and equiv (46%)
Provider Compensation ($000): Contr fee ($2,413), capitation ($1,129), FFS ($289)
Total Member Encounters: Phys (3,043), non-phys (353)
Group Affiliation: Bright Health Inc
Licensed in: AL
Address: , HUNTSVILLE, AL 35801
Phone: (612) 238-1321 **Dom State:** AL **Commenced Bus:** N/A

Data Date	Rating	RACR #1	RACR #2	Total Assets ($mil)	Capital ($mil)	Net Premium ($mil)	Net Income ($mil)
3-19	D	5.63	4.69	13.1	6.5	4.6	0.3
3-18	N/A	N/A	N/A	7.4	6.2	1.9	0.1
2018	D	2.96	2.47	8.1	3.5	4.6	-2.6
2017	N/A	N/A	N/A	6.2	6.1	N/A	N/A
2016	N/A	N/A	N/A	N/A	N/A	N/A	N/A
2015	N/A	N/A	N/A	N/A	N/A	N/A	N/A
2014	N/A	N/A	N/A	N/A	N/A	N/A	N/A

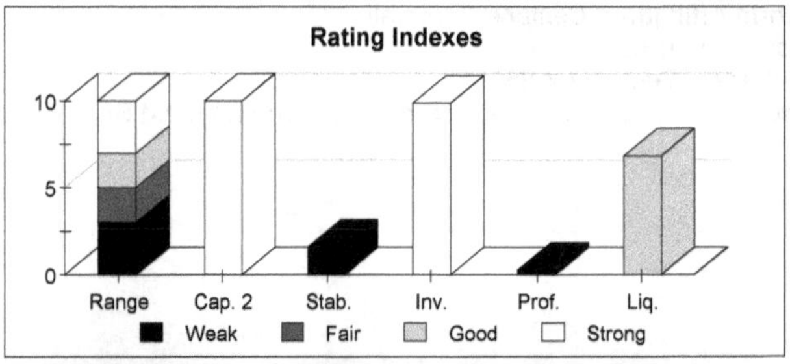

BROWN & TOLAND HEALTH SERVICES — E+ — Very Weak

Major Rating Factors: Weak profitability index (0.9 on a scale of 0 to 10). Fair capitalization index (4.6) based on weak current risk-adjusted capital (moderate loss scenario). Fair overall results on stability tests (4.3).
Other Rating Factors: Excellent liquidity (7.1) with ample operational cash flow and liquid investments.
Principal Business: Managed care (100%)
Mem Phys: 18: N/A **17:** N/A **18 MLR** 92.9% **/ 18 Admin Exp** N/A
Enroll(000): Q1 19: 13 **18:** 10 **17:** 10 **Med Exp PMPM:** $752
Principal Investments ($000): Cash and equiv ($19,897)
Provider Compensation ($000): None
Total Member Encounters: N/A
Group Affiliation: None
Licensed in: CA
Address: 1221 Broadway Street Suite 700, Oakland, CA 94612
Phone: (415) 322-9897 **Dom State:** CA **Commenced Bus:** April 2013

Data Date	Rating	RACR #1	RACR #2	Total Assets ($mil)	Capital ($mil)	Net Premium ($mil)	Net Income ($mil)
3-19	E+	0.72	0.44	35.3	6.5	34.0	1.0
3-18	E-	0.20	0.12	25.1	1.8	24.6	0.6
2018	E	0.60	0.37	27.5	5.5	99.2	4.3
2017	E-	0.13	0.08	22.2	1.1	93.9	4.2
2016	E-	N/A	N/A	24.1	-3.1	82.2	0.1
2015	E-	N/A	N/A	20.1	-3.3	85.3	-2.8
2014	E-	N/A	N/A	15.2	-0.5	19.4	-0.7

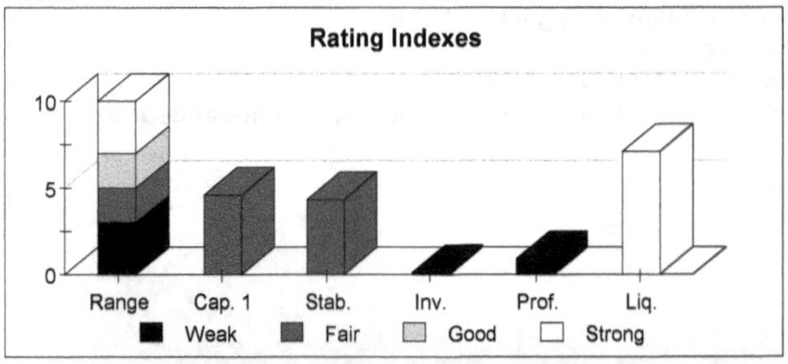

BUCKEYE COMMUNITY HEALTH PLAN INC — B — Good

Major Rating Factors: Good liquidity (6.9 on a scale of 0 to 10) with sufficient resources (cash flows and marketable investments) to handle a spike in claims. Excellent profitability (7.8). Strong capitalization (8.2) based on excellent current risk-adjusted capital (severe loss scenario).
Other Rating Factors: High quality investment portfolio (7.1).
Principal Business: Medicaid (86%), Medicare (10%), comp med (5%)
Mem Phys: 18: 43,775 **17:** 49,005 **18 MLR** 81.8% **/ 18 Admin Exp** N/A
Enroll(000): Q1 19: 370 **18:** 352 **17:** 346 **Med Exp PMPM:** $482
Principal Investments: Long-term bonds (66%), cash and equiv (30%), affiliate common stock (1%), other (3%)
Provider Compensation ($000): Contr fee ($1,292,580), bonus arrang ($538,724), capitation ($108,589), salary ($54,843), other ($33,634)
Total Member Encounters: Phys (2,606,792), non-phys (4,905,591)
Group Affiliation: None
Licensed in: OH
Address: 4349 Easton Way Ste 200, Columbus, OH 43219
Phone: (314) 725-4477 **Dom State:** OH **Commenced Bus:** N/A

Data Date	Rating	RACR #1	RACR #2	Total Assets ($mil)	Capital ($mil)	Net Premium ($mil)	Net Income ($mil)
3-19	B	2.34	1.95	611.8	290.5	655.4	16.3
3-18	B	2.44	2.03	593.1	256.7	623.8	1.9
2018	B	2.66	2.22	624.4	335.0	2,555.2	90.9
2017	B	1.78	1.48	473.3	253.5	2,207.3	44.2
2016	C+	2.26	1.88	429.4	211.0	2,048.4	22.8
2015	C+	1.96	1.63	454.5	178.3	1,981.9	25.9
2014	C+	2.01	1.68	368.2	123.1	1,325.9	-0.9

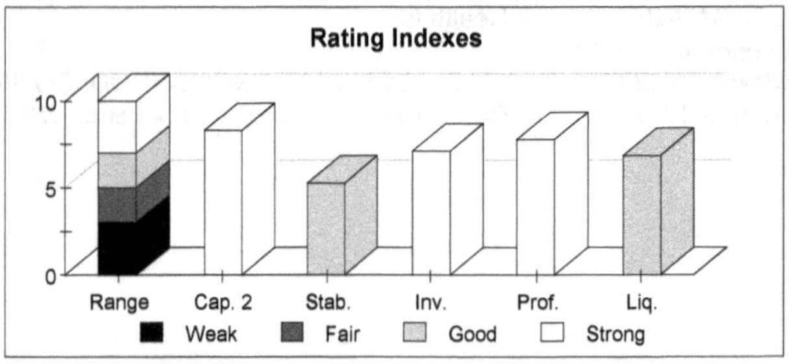

BUCKEYE HEALTH PLAN COMMUNITY — C- Fair

Major Rating Factors: Weak profitability index (0.9 on a scale of 0 to 10). Strong capitalization (8.4) based on excellent current risk-adjusted capital (severe loss scenario). High quality investment portfolio (9.9).
Other Rating Factors: Excellent liquidity (7.3) with ample operational cash flow and liquid investments.
Principal Business: Medicare (100%)
Mem Phys: 18: 43,775 **17:** N/A **18 MLR** 104.9% **/ 18 Admin Exp** N/A
Enroll(000): Q1 19: 2 **18:** 1 **17:** N/A **Med Exp PMPM:** $865
Principal Investments: Cash and equiv (89%), long-term bonds (11%)
Provider Compensation ($000): Contr fee ($7,132), salary ($364), capitation ($21)
Total Member Encounters: Phys (17,220), non-phys (5,755)
Group Affiliation: None
Licensed in: OH
Address: , Columbus, OH 43219
Phone: (314) 725-4477 **Dom State:** OH **Commenced Bus:** N/A

Data Date	Rating	RACR #1	RACR #2	Total Assets ($mil)	Capital ($mil)	Net Premium ($mil)	Net Income ($mil)
3-19	C-	2.45	2.05	8.2	3.3	4.3	0.4
3-18	N/A	N/A	N/A	4.5	2.3	1.8	-0.2
2018	C-	2.21	1.84	7.2	3.0	9.2	-2.7
2017	N/A	N/A	N/A	1.7	1.7	N/A	N/A
2016	N/A	N/A	N/A	N/A	N/A	N/A	N/A
2015	N/A	N/A	N/A	N/A	N/A	N/A	N/A
2014	N/A	N/A	N/A	N/A	N/A	N/A	N/A

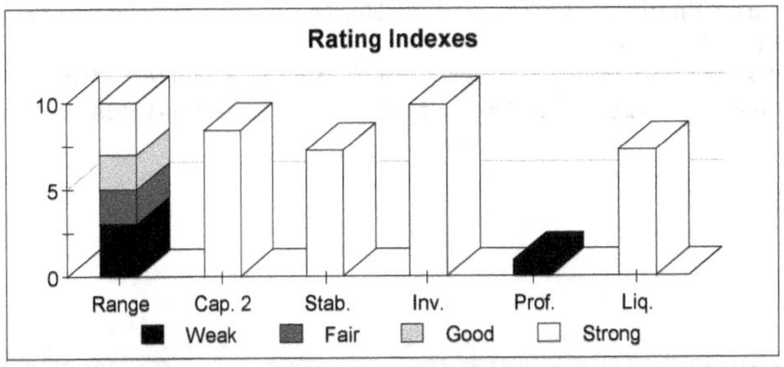

BUPA INS CO — B Good

Major Rating Factors: Fair profitability index (4.0 on a scale of 0 to 10). Strong capitalization (9.6) based on excellent current risk-adjusted capital (severe loss scenario). High quality investment portfolio (9.4).
Other Rating Factors: Excellent liquidity (7.7) with ample operational cash flow and liquid investments.
Principal Business: Comp med (100%)
Mem Phys: 18: 10,077 **17:** 13,895 **18 MLR** 27.5% **/ 18 Admin Exp** N/A
Enroll(000): Q1 19: 22 **18:** 22 **17:** 27 **Med Exp PMPM:** $248
Principal Investments: Long-term bonds (67%), cash and equiv (22%), affiliate common stock (5%), other (5%)
Provider Compensation ($000): FFS ($74,008)
Total Member Encounters: Phys (13,532), non-phys (6,027)
Group Affiliation: None
Licensed in: FL, PR
Address: 18001 Old Cutler Rd Ste 300, Palmetto Bay, FL 33157
Phone: (305) 275-1400 **Dom State:** FL **Commenced Bus:** N/A

Data Date	Rating	RACR #1	RACR #2	Total Assets ($mil)	Capital ($mil)	Net Premium ($mil)	Net Income ($mil)
3-19	B	3.40	2.84	313.8	140.3	75.3	-0.2
3-18	B	4.35	3.62	311.5	153.1	68.9	0.0
2018	B	3.42	2.85	312.2	140.9	260.9	-5.9
2017	B	4.33	3.61	322.2	152.5	295.6	0.9
2016	B	3.63	3.02	320.0	153.0	315.4	12.7
2015	C	3.60	3.00	379.4	170.4	367.7	45.9
2014	D+	2.70	2.25	401.2	124.7	413.2	17.9

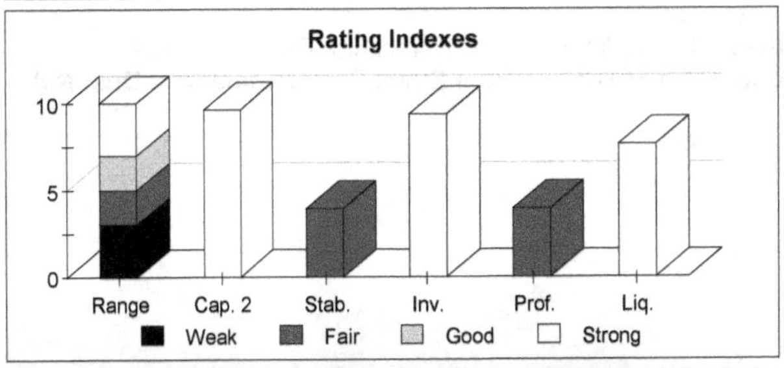

CALIFORNIA HEALTH & WELLNESS PLAN — D+ Weak

Major Rating Factors: Weak profitability index (1.0 on a scale of 0 to 10). Poor capitalization index (2.3) based on weak current risk-adjusted capital (moderate loss scenario). Fair overall results on stability tests (3.0) based on a steep decline in capital during 2018 but steady enrollment growth, averaging 5% over the past five years.
Other Rating Factors: Good liquidity (6.9) with sufficient resources (cash flows and marketable investments) to handle a spike in claims.
Principal Business: Medicaid (100%)
Mem Phys: 18: N/A **17:** N/A **18 MLR** 96.4% **/ 18 Admin Exp** N/A
Enroll(000): Q1 19: 196 **18:** 195 **17:** 192 **Med Exp PMPM:** $268
Principal Investments ($000): Cash and equiv ($29,939)
Provider Compensation ($000): None
Total Member Encounters: N/A
Group Affiliation: None
Licensed in: CA
Address: 1740 Creekside Oaks Drive, Sacramento, CA 95833
Phone: (818) 676-8486 **Dom State:** CA **Commenced Bus:** October 2013

Data Date	Rating	RACR #1	RACR #2	Total Assets ($mil)	Capital ($mil)	Net Premium ($mil)	Net Income ($mil)
3-19	D+	0.64	0.44	296.6	50.5	173.4	2.0
3-18	C	0.78	0.55	306.5	63.9	154.9	-0.9
2018	D+	0.59	0.41	324.3	47.6	656.8	-32.2
2017	C	0.81	0.57	297.2	65.7	627.7	0.7
2016	C+	1.11	0.78	320.4	84.4	610.6	27.2
2015	C	0.85	0.59	274.8	57.5	581.5	15.0
2014	C-	1.80	1.16	172.6	42.6	330.3	22.2

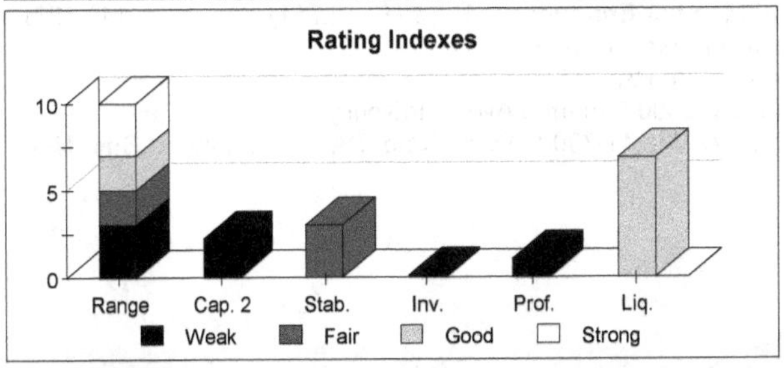

CALIFORNIA PHYSICIANS SERVICE * A+ Excellent

Major Rating Factors: Strong capitalization index (8.5 on a scale of 0 to 10) based on excellent current risk-adjusted capital (severe loss scenario). Excellent overall results on stability tests (8.0). Good overall profitability index (6.7).
Other Rating Factors: Good liquidity (6.6) with sufficient resources (cash flows and marketable investments) to handle a spike in claims.
Principal Business: Medicare (5%)
Mem Phys: 18: N/A **17:** N/A **18 MLR** 87.4% **/ 18 Admin Exp** N/A
Enroll(000): Q1 19: 3,516 **18:** 3,497 **17:** 3,274 **Med Exp PMPM:** $443
Principal Investments ($000): Cash and equiv ($1,423,371)
Provider Compensation ($000): None
Total Member Encounters: N/A
Group Affiliation: Blue Shield of California
Licensed in: CA
Address: 50 Beale Street 22nd Floor, San Francisco, CA 94105
Phone: (415) 229-5195 **Dom State:** CA **Commenced Bus:** February 1939

Data Date	Rating	RACR #1	RACR #2	Total Assets ($mil)	Capital ($mil)	Net Premium ($mil)	Net Income ($mil)
3-19	A+	3.15	2.13	9,021.3	5,445.4	4,374.5	473.2
3-18	A+	2.98	2.01	8,760.1	4,888.6	4,264.8	261.6
2018	A+	2.72	1.83	8,493.4	4,925.1	17,113.1	412.6
2017	A+	2.71	1.83	8,171.3	4,675.9	14,240.6	296.2
2016	A+	3.02	2.02	7,509.1	4,296.6	14,290.2	67.0
2015	A+	3.42	2.26	7,358.4	4,170.4	12,531.2	86.9
2014	A+	4.66	3.16	6,919.5	4,179.5	11,300.6	161.8

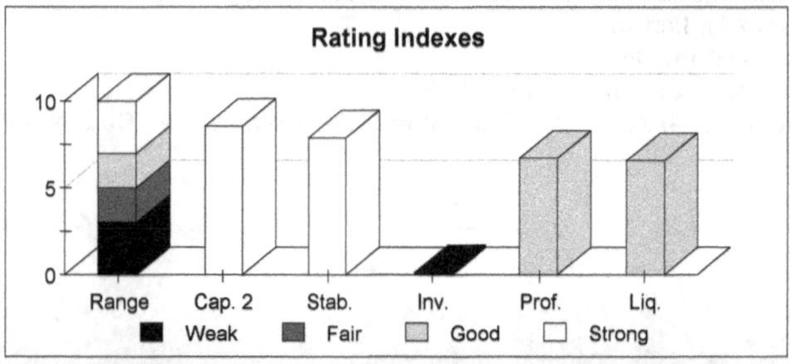

CAPITAL ADVANTAGE ASR CO C Fair

Major Rating Factors: Fair profitability index (4.1 on a scale of 0 to 10). Strong capitalization (10.0) based on excellent current risk-adjusted capital (severe loss scenario). High quality investment portfolio (8.6).
Other Rating Factors: Excellent liquidity (7.0) with ample operational cash flow and liquid investments.
Principal Business: Comp med (81%), dental (2%), other (17%)
Mem Phys: 18: 30,333 **17:** 28,708 **18 MLR** 76.4% **/ 18 Admin Exp** N/A
Enroll(000): Q1 19: 190 **18:** 175 **17:** 231 **Med Exp PMPM:** $476
Principal Investments: Long-term bonds (90%), cash and equiv (10%)
Provider Compensation ($000): Contr fee ($1,067,262), capitation ($73)
Total Member Encounters: Phys (1,879,297), non-phys (2,946,742)
Group Affiliation: None
Licensed in: PA
Address: 2500 Elmerton Ave, Harrisburg, PA 17177-9799
Phone: (717) 541-7000 **Dom State:** PA **Commenced Bus:** N/A

Data Date	Rating	RACR #1	RACR #2	Total Assets ($mil)	Capital ($mil)	Net Premium ($mil)	Net Income ($mil)
3-19	C	4.36	3.63	697.0	357.7	327.9	10.8
3-18	C-	N/A	N/A	621.6	263.0	344.7	5.1
2018	C	4.24	3.53	667.4	347.6	1,380.5	88.6
2017	C-	N/A	N/A	588.5	257.3	1,533.3	22.3
2016	C-	2.82	2.35	529.1	231.6	1,218.0	-44.7
2015	C-	1.94	1.62	423.6	185.8	965.1	-28.4
2014	C-	1.92	1.60	412.2	191.0	1,023.4	-38.3

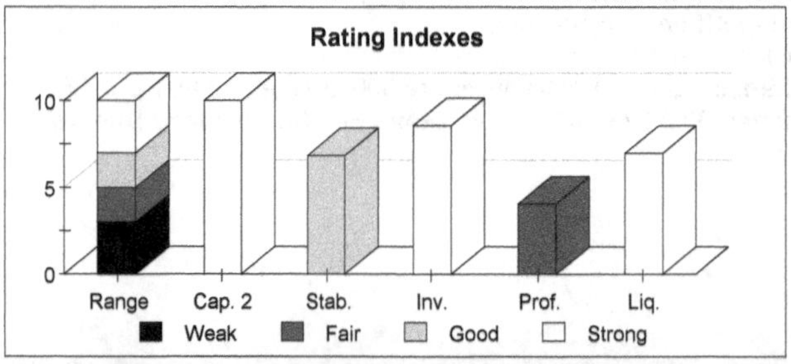

CAPITAL ADVANTAGE INS CO C Fair

Major Rating Factors: Low quality investment portfolio (2.3 on a scale of 0 to 10). Good profitability index (4.9). Strong capitalization (9.5) based on excellent current risk-adjusted capital (severe loss scenario).
Other Rating Factors: Excellent liquidity (7.5) with ample operational cash flow and liquid investments.
Principal Business: Medicare (65%), med supp (16%), comp med (3%), other (16%)
Mem Phys: 18: 30,333 **17:** 28,708 **18 MLR** 88.1% **/ 18 Admin Exp** N/A
Enroll(000): Q1 19: 79 **18:** 73 **17:** 58 **Med Exp PMPM:** $295
Principal Investments: Affiliate common stock (94%), long-term bonds (12%)
Provider Compensation ($000): Contr fee ($172,257), capitation ($5,920), bonus arrang ($667), other ($31,453)
Total Member Encounters: Phys (1,132,751), non-phys (149,183)
Group Affiliation: None
Licensed in: PA
Address: 2500 Elmerton Ave, Harrisburg, PA 17177-9799
Phone: (717) 541-7000 **Dom State:** PA **Commenced Bus:** N/A

Data Date	Rating	RACR #1	RACR #2	Total Assets ($mil)	Capital ($mil)	Net Premium ($mil)	Net Income ($mil)
3-19	C	3.34	2.78	674.3	429.6	71.0	-4.7
3-18	C	2.63	2.19	546.9	359.3	59.8	-4.0
2018	C	3.35	2.79	645.5	431.6	244.6	1.5
2017	C	2.06	1.72	579.5	367.6	233.4	-7.9
2016	C	2.73	2.27	464.2	349.0	219.2	4.2
2015	C	2.40	2.00	418.0	292.7	203.0	31.8
2014	C	2.73	2.28	442.9	319.2	258.4	22.7

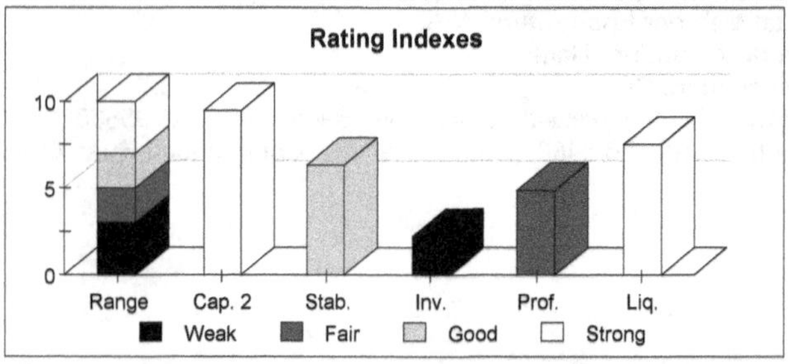

CAPITAL BLUE CROSS B- Good

Major Rating Factors: Fair profitability index (4.4 on a scale of 0 to 10). Strong capitalization (10.0) based on excellent current risk-adjusted capital (severe loss scenario). Excellent liquidity (7.4) with ample operational cash flow and liquid investments.
Other Rating Factors: Low quality investment portfolio (2.4).
Principal Business: FEHB (92%), med supp (6%), other (1%)
Mem Phys: 18: 784 **17:** 786 **18 MLR** 91.4% **/ 18 Admin Exp** N/A
Enroll(000): Q1 19: 89 **18:** 89 **17:** 91 **Med Exp PMPM:** $271
Principal Investments: Affiliate common stock (44%), long-term bonds (25%), nonaffiliate common stock (16%), real estate (3%), cash and equiv (3%), other (9%)
Provider Compensation ($000): Contr fee ($293,042)
Total Member Encounters: Non-phys (426,049)
Group Affiliation: None
Licensed in: PA
Address: 2500 Elmerton Ave, Harrisburg, PA 17177-9799
Phone: (717) 541-7000 **Dom State:** PA **Commenced Bus:** N/A

Data Date	Rating	RACR #1	RACR #2	Total Assets ($mil)	Capital ($mil)	Net Premium ($mil)	Net Income ($mil)
3-19	B-	4.17	3.48	1,168.7	722.2	88.1	4.1
3-18	B-	3.65	3.04	1,127.2	665.8	75.9	6.9
2018	B-	4.05	3.37	1,143.0	700.0	318.7	10.2
2017	B-	3.21	2.68	1,131.5	676.8	292.5	14.7
2016	B-	4.13	3.44	1,058.6	703.4	297.5	9.4
2015	B-	4.43	3.69	1,081.6	764.7	279.7	11.3
2014	B-	4.76	3.96	1,123.6	824.7	270.8	16.0

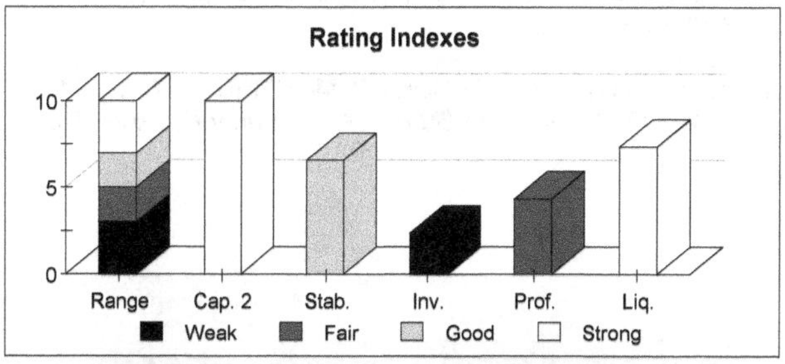

CAPITAL DISTRICT PHYSICIANS HEALTH P * A Excellent

Major Rating Factors: Excellent profitability (8.1 on a scale of 0 to 10). Strong capitalization index (9.1) based on excellent current risk-adjusted capital (severe loss scenario). High quality investment portfolio (7.3).
Other Rating Factors: Excellent overall results on stability tests (7.8). Good liquidity (6.9) with sufficient resources (cash flows and marketable investments) to handle a spike in claims.
Principal Business: Medicaid (33%), comp med (33%), Medicare (31%), other (3%)
Mem Phys: 18: 20,898 **17:** 20,195 **18 MLR** 86.3% **/ 18 Admin Exp** N/A
Enroll(000): Q1 19: 214 **18:** 210 **17:** 207 **Med Exp PMPM:** $522
Principal Investments: Long-term bonds (44%), cash and equiv (17%), affiliate common stock (7%), nonaffiliate common stock (5%), other (28%)
Provider Compensation ($000): Contr fee ($753,345), FFS ($414,276), bonus arrang ($69,757), capitation ($24,752), other ($29,555)
Total Member Encounters: Phys (1,860,051), non-phys (777,486)
Group Affiliation: Capital District Physicians Health P
Licensed in: CA, NY
Address: 500 Patroon Creek Boulevard, Albany, NY 12206-1057
Phone: (518) 641-3000 **Dom State:** NY **Commenced Bus:** N/A

Data Date	Rating	RACR #1	RACR #2	Total Assets ($mil)	Capital ($mil)	Net Premium ($mil)	Net Income ($mil)
3-19	A	3.02	2.52	621.6	395.2	394.2	10.6
3-18	B	2.53	2.11	580.1	321.5	367.6	-6.2
2018	A	2.88	2.40	586.0	378.8	1,511.9	43.0
2017	B	2.53	2.10	523.8	334.3	1,442.0	19.4
2016	B	2.47	2.05	506.9	308.4	1,444.6	33.8
2015	B-	2.33	1.94	478.7	292.9	1,512.3	85.7
2014	B-	2.06	1.72	440.7	248.9	1,426.9	23.7

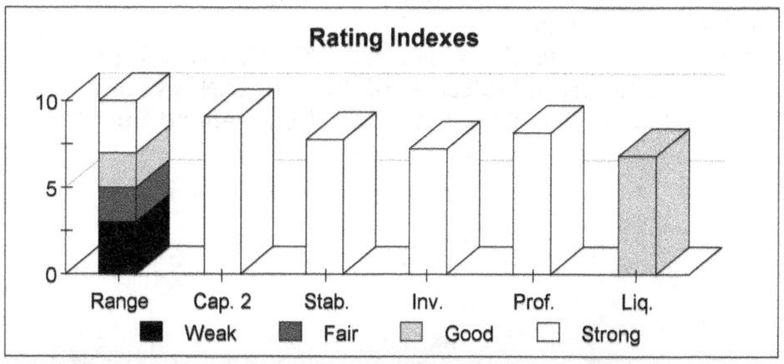

CAPITAL HEALTH PLAN INC * B+ Good

Major Rating Factors: Good overall profitability index (5.5 on a scale of 0 to 10). Good liquidity (6.7) with sufficient resources (cash flows and marketable investments) to handle a spike in claims. Strong capitalization index (10.0) based on excellent current risk-adjusted capital (severe loss scenario).
Other Rating Factors: High quality investment portfolio (8.5). Excellent overall results on stability tests (7.7).
Principal Business: Comp med (69%), Medicare (28%), FEHB (2%)
Mem Phys: 18: 585 **17:** 598 **18 MLR** 92.8% **/ 18 Admin Exp** N/A
Enroll(000): Q1 19: 134 **18:** 134 **17:** 134 **Med Exp PMPM:** $496
Principal Investments: Long-term bonds (76%), nonaffiliate common stock (18%), real estate (5%), cash and equiv (2%), other (1%)
Provider Compensation ($000): Contr fee ($441,115), FFS ($279,984), salary ($43,942), capitation ($32,190)
Total Member Encounters: Phys (1,124,463), non-phys (589,754)
Group Affiliation: None
Licensed in: FL
Address: 2140 Centerville Place, Tallahassee, FL 32308
Phone: (850) 383-3333 **Dom State:** FL **Commenced Bus:** N/A

Data Date	Rating	RACR #1	RACR #2	Total Assets ($mil)	Capital ($mil)	Net Premium ($mil)	Net Income ($mil)
3-19	B+	7.67	6.39	575.1	443.8	228.1	14.0
3-18	B	7.52	6.27	547.3	399.4	216.4	-5.0
2018	B+	7.24	6.04	546.7	419.0	865.0	25.0
2017	B	5.95	4.95	532.7	405.4	808.1	20.6
2016	B	7.32	6.10	489.9	371.0	766.3	4.6
2015	B	7.76	6.46	467.8	364.1	716.9	8.8
2014	N/A	N/A	N/A	461.3	368.8	679.2	3.6

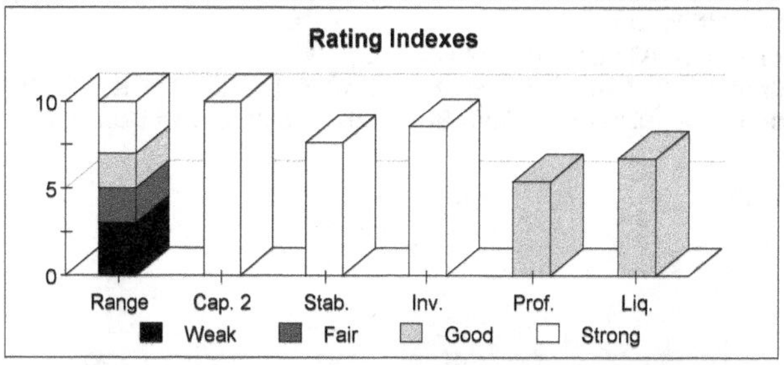

CARE 1ST HEALTH PLAN INC * A+ Excellent

Major Rating Factors: Excellent profitability (9.2 on a scale of 0 to 10). Strong capitalization (10.0) based on excellent current risk-adjusted capital (severe loss scenario). High quality investment portfolio (9.0).
Other Rating Factors: Good liquidity (6.8) with sufficient resources (cash flows and marketable investments) to handle a spike in claims.
Principal Business: Medicaid (62%), Medicare (38%)
Mem Phys: 18: N/A **17:** N/A **18 MLR** 88.6% **/ 18 Admin Exp** N/A
Enroll(000): Q1 19: 474 **18:** 493 **17:** 502 **Med Exp PMPM:** $347
Principal Investments: Long-term bonds (84%), cash and equiv (14%), real estate (2%)
Provider Compensation ($000): Contr fee ($1,390,391), capitation ($748,306)
Total Member Encounters: Phys (1,152,614), non-phys (9,344,505)
Group Affiliation: None
Licensed in: CA, TX
Address: 601 POTRERO GRANDE DR, MONTEREY PARK, CA 91755
Phone: (323) 889-6638 **Dom State:** CA **Commenced Bus:** N/A

Data Date	Rating	RACR #1	RACR #2	Total Assets ($mil)	Capital ($mil)	Net Premium ($mil)	Net Income ($mil)
3-19	A+	4.48	3.73	1,214.3	559.3	543.4	4.0
3-18	A+	N/A	N/A	1,258.3	523.5	568.5	28.8
2018	A+	4.33	3.60	1,007.1	543.2	2,348.5	50.8
2017	A+	N/A	N/A	1,085.5	486.6	2,153.3	65.8
2016	B+	2.63	2.19	1,212.5	404.8	2,405.0	234.5
2015	C	0.68	0.57	742.6	190.3	1,870.4	16.9
2014	U	0.97	0.81	435.2	90.6	1,345.8	48.5

Rating Indexes

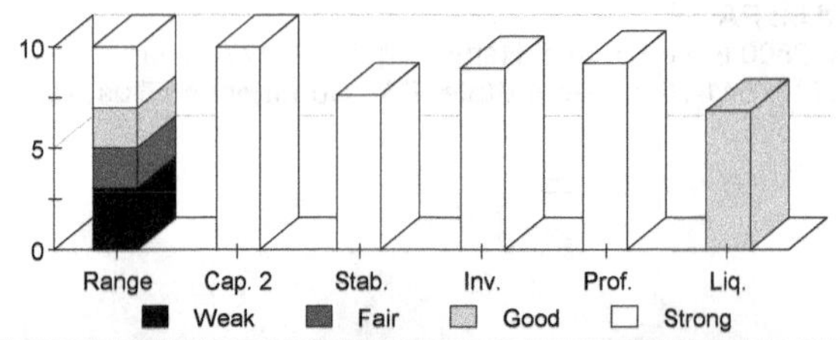

CARE IMPROVEMENT PLUS OF TEXAS INS B Good

Major Rating Factors: Good liquidity (5.1 on a scale of 0 to 10) with sufficient resources (cash flows and marketable investments) to handle a spike in claims. Excellent profitability (8.7). Strong capitalization (8.3) based on excellent current risk-adjusted capital (severe loss scenario).
Other Rating Factors: High quality investment portfolio (8.8).
Principal Business: Medicare (100%)
Mem Phys: 18: 257,761 **17:** 224,089 **18 MLR** 84.8% **/ 18 Admin Exp** N/A
Enroll(000): Q1 19: 124 **18:** 128 **17:** 109 **Med Exp PMPM:** $988
Principal Investments: Long-term bonds (99%), cash and equiv (1%)
Provider Compensation ($000): Contr fee ($1,006,856), FFS ($402,279), capitation ($18,846), bonus arrang ($3,221)
Total Member Encounters: Phys (3,017,167), non-phys (1,610,536)
Group Affiliation: None
Licensed in: AL, CO, IL, IN, IA, NE, NM, NC, PA, SC, TN, TX, VA
Address: 4350 LOCKHILL-SELMA Rd 3RD FL, SAN ANTONIO, TX 78249
Phone: (952) 936-1300 **Dom State:** TX **Commenced Bus:** N/A

Data Date	Rating	RACR #1	RACR #2	Total Assets ($mil)	Capital ($mil)	Net Premium ($mil)	Net Income ($mil)
3-19	B	2.38	1.98	607.9	248.0	478.4	20.9
3-18	B	2.67	2.22	689.0	188.2	415.4	-1.5
2018	B	2.15	1.79	557.5	223.6	1,701.8	48.9
2017	C+	1.94	1.62	497.8	189.9	1,376.9	59.2
2016	C	2.10	1.75	378.9	120.9	1,155.1	49.6
2015	B	2.17	1.81	377.0	140.5	1,297.7	34.6
2014	B	2.84	2.36	287.3	165.1	1,164.9	42.4

Rating Indexes

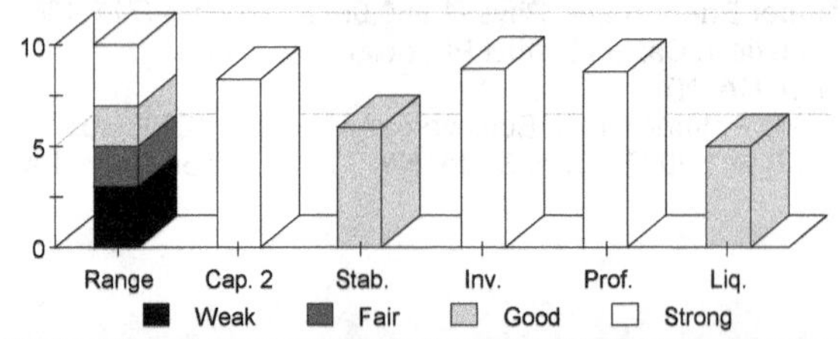

CARE IMPROVEMENT PLUS SOUTH CENTRAL B- Good

Major Rating Factors: Excellent profitability (9.0 on a scale of 0 to 10). Strong capitalization (10.0) based on excellent current risk-adjusted capital (severe loss scenario). High quality investment portfolio (9.1).
Other Rating Factors: Excellent liquidity (6.9) with sufficient resources (cash flows and marketable investments) to handle a spike in claims.
Principal Business: Medicare (100%)
Mem Phys: 18: 878,669 **17:** 732,877 **18 MLR** 78.4% **/ 18 Admin Exp** N/A
Enroll(000): Q1 19: 120 **18:** 121 **17:** 100 **Med Exp PMPM:** $961
Principal Investments: Long-term bonds (99%), cash and equiv (1%)
Provider Compensation ($000): Contr fee ($884,662), FFS ($320,297), capitation ($107,248), bonus arrang ($5,062)
Total Member Encounters: Phys (2,610,408), non-phys (1,425,251)
Group Affiliation: None
Licensed in: All states except CA, PR
Address: 1401 CAPITOL Ave 3RD Fll #375, LITTLE ROCK, AR 72201
Phone: (952) 936-1300 **Dom State:** AR **Commenced Bus:** N/A

Data Date	Rating	RACR #1	RACR #2	Total Assets ($mil)	Capital ($mil)	Net Premium ($mil)	Net Income ($mil)
3-19	B-	6.32	5.27	778.0	525.6	486.4	49.5
3-18	C	5.88	4.90	779.5	349.0	390.8	-0.4
2018	B-	5.70	4.75	727.7	473.0	1,673.8	125.9
2017	C	4.47	3.72	593.6	347.2	1,247.8	79.2
2016	C	2.17	1.81	1,029.5	423.1	3,705.3	241.4
2015	C	1.91	1.59	900.9	315.2	3,290.3	35.3
2014	C	2.30	1.92	646.9	348.6	2,985.4	78.0

Rating Indexes

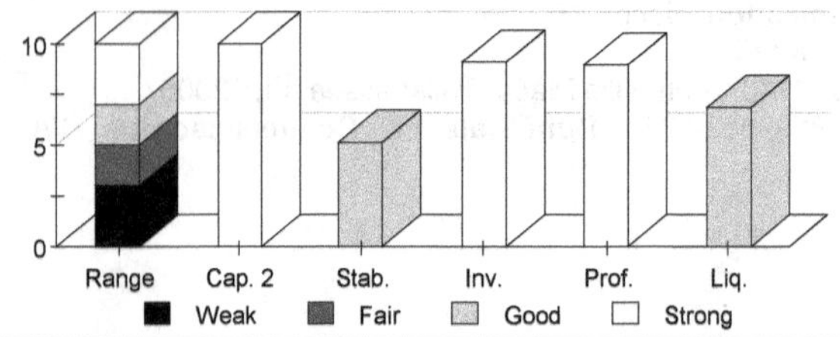

CARE IMPROVEMENT PLUS WI INS B Good

Major Rating Factors: Good overall profitability index (6.7 on a scale of 0 to 10). Strong capitalization (10.0) based on excellent current risk-adjusted capital (severe loss scenario). High quality investment portfolio (9.9).
Other Rating Factors: Excellent liquidity (7.2) with ample operational cash flow and liquid investments.
Principal Business: Medicare (100%)
Mem Phys: 18: 58,760 **17:** 25,196 **18 MLR** 77.5% **/ 18 Admin Exp** N/A
Enroll(000): Q1 19: 23 **18:** 20 **17:** 13 **Med Exp PMPM:** $857
Principal Investments: Cash and equiv (100%)
Provider Compensation ($000): Contr fee ($150,181), FFS ($27,405), capitation ($6,964), bonus arrang ($671)
Total Member Encounters: Phys (422,109), non-phys (215,516)
Group Affiliation: None
Licensed in: WI
Address: 10701 W RESEARCH DR, WAUWATOSA, WI 53266-0649
Phone: (952) 979-6137 **Dom State:** WI **Commenced Bus:** N/A

Data Date	Rating	RACR #1	RACR #2	Total Assets ($mil)	Capital ($mil)	Net Premium ($mil)	Net Income ($mil)
3-19	B	4.13	3.45	96.6	57.4	83.0	10.3
3-18	B	3.69	3.08	82.4	29.6	56.2	0.4
2018	B	3.39	2.83	78.2	47.1	242.8	18.2
2017	C+	1.82	1.52	50.5	25.2	131.0	5.3
2016	C	3.53	2.94	35.7	19.8	79.1	-0.9
2015	C	4.82	4.02	34.2	20.5	67.9	5.0
2014	C	3.36	2.80	22.2	11.6	45.1	-3.1

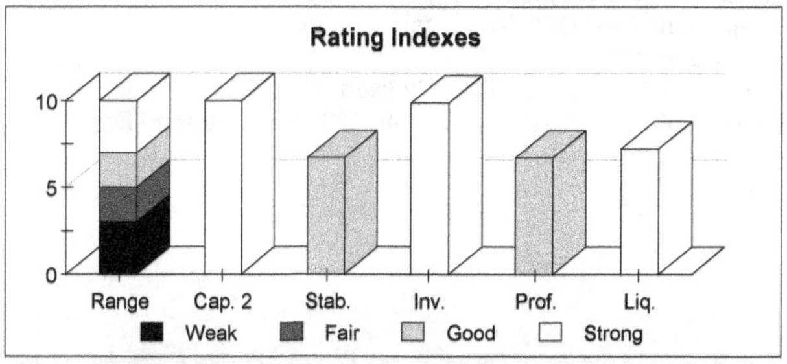

CARE N CARE INS CO C Fair

Major Rating Factors: Fair profitability index (3.1 on a scale of 0 to 10). Fair quality investment portfolio (3.1). Strong capitalization (7.3) based on excellent current risk-adjusted capital (severe loss scenario).
Other Rating Factors: Excellent liquidity (7.2) with ample operational cash flow and liquid investments.
Principal Business: Medicare (100%)
Mem Phys: 18: 4,766 **17:** 946 **18 MLR** 83.9% **/ 18 Admin Exp** N/A
Enroll(000): Q1 19: 13 **18:** 11 **17:** 11 **Med Exp PMPM:** $702
Principal Investments: Cash and equiv (100%)
Provider Compensation ($000): Contr fee ($80,853), capitation ($19,295)
Total Member Encounters: Phys (17,011)
Group Affiliation: The University of Texas Southwestern
Licensed in: TX
Address: 1701 River Run Rd Ste 402, Fort Worth, TX 76107
Phone: (817) 810-5213 **Dom State:** TX **Commenced Bus:** N/A

Data Date	Rating	RACR #1	RACR #2	Total Assets ($mil)	Capital ($mil)	Net Premium ($mil)	Net Income ($mil)
3-19	C	1.60	1.33	42.7	18.9	31.9	-1.9
3-18	C	1.78	1.48	55.3	21.2	25.5	0.8
2018	C	2.00	1.67	45.2	23.4	108.7	-0.8
2017	C	1.58	1.31	37.7	18.9	105.5	9.8
2016	C	1.16	0.97	30.0	14.4	113.8	-3.4
2015	C	1.31	1.09	30.3	16.6	101.6	-0.4
2014	D	1.64	1.36	25.0	17.9	90.4	0.9

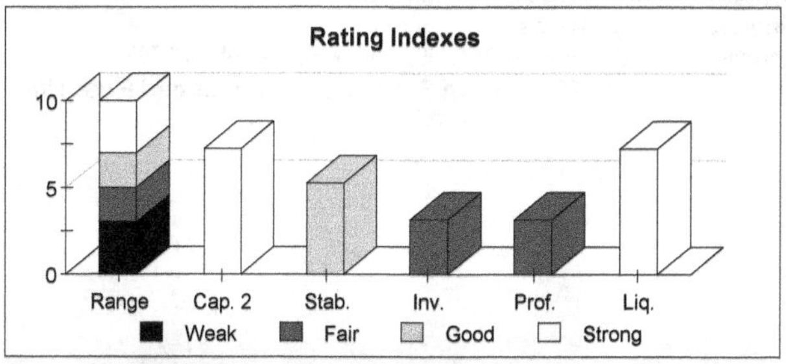

CARE N CARE INS CO OF NORTH CAROLINA E- Very Weak

Major Rating Factors: Weak profitability index (0.9 on a scale of 0 to 10). Poor capitalization (0.5) based on weak current risk-adjusted capital (moderate loss scenario). Weak liquidity (0.3) as a spike in claims may stretch capacity.
Other Rating Factors: High quality investment portfolio (9.9).
Principal Business: Medicare (100%)
Mem Phys: 18: 7,749 **17:** 3,412 **18 MLR** 91.0% **/ 18 Admin Exp** N/A
Enroll(000): Q1 19: 15 **18:** 15 **17:** 13 **Med Exp PMPM:** $679
Principal Investments: Cash and equiv (83%), long-term bonds (17%)
Provider Compensation ($000): Contr fee ($107,591)
Total Member Encounters: Phys (35,897)
Group Affiliation: The Moses H Cone Memorial Hospital
Licensed in: NC
Address: 7800 Airport Center Dr Ste 401, Greensboro, NC 27409
Phone: (336) 790-4386 **Dom State:** NC **Commenced Bus:** N/A

Data Date	Rating	RACR #1	RACR #2	Total Assets ($mil)	Capital ($mil)	Net Premium ($mil)	Net Income ($mil)
3-19	E-	0.35	0.29	34.9	10.5	37.3	-4.9
3-18	D+	N/A	N/A	56.8	10.7	30.6	-1.7
2018	D+	0.69	0.58	37.6	16.1	128.7	-11.4
2017	D+	N/A	N/A	57.3	13.4	103.3	-18.5
2016	D+	0.89	0.74	21.0	8.1	56.8	-3.6
2015	N/A	N/A	N/A	4.6	4.1	N/A	-1.4
2014	N/A	N/A	N/A	N/A	N/A	N/A	N/A

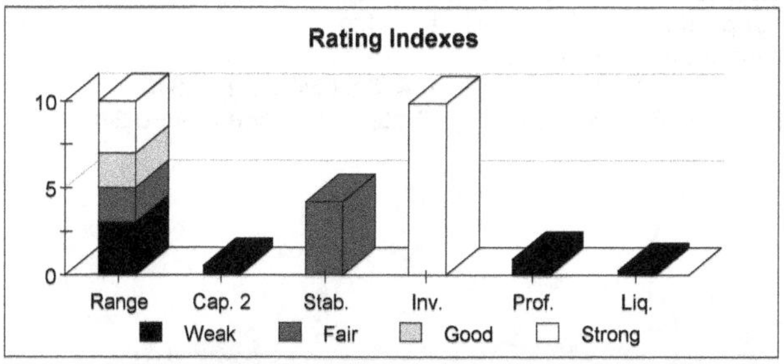

CARE WISCONSIN HEALTH PLAN INC * B+ Good

Major Rating Factors: Good overall profitability index (6.4 on a scale of 0 to 10). Strong capitalization (8.0) based on excellent current risk-adjusted capital (severe loss scenario). High quality investment portfolio (9.5).
Other Rating Factors: Excellent liquidity (7.0) with sufficient resources (cash flows and marketable investments) to handle a spike in claims.
Principal Business: Medicaid (63%), Medicare (37%)
Mem Phys: 18: 19,180 **17:** 16,440 **18 MLR** 85.8% **/ 18 Admin Exp** N/A
Enroll(000): Q1 19: 5 **18:** 5 **17:** 3 **Med Exp PMPM:** $2,383
Principal Investments: Cash and equiv (54%), long-term bonds (42%), nonaffiliate common stock (4%)
Provider Compensation ($000): Contr fee ($101,521), FFS ($25,200)
Total Member Encounters: Phys (178,563), non-phys (5,648,278)
Group Affiliation: Care Wisconsin First Inc
Licensed in: WI
Address: 1617 Sherman Ave, Madison, WI 53704
Phone: (608) 240-0020 **Dom State:** WI **Commenced Bus:** N/A

Data Date	Rating	RACR #1	RACR #2	Total Assets ($mil)	Capital ($mil)	Net Premium ($mil)	Net Income ($mil)
3-19	B+	2.17	1.81	61.5	36.6	40.0	-0.4
3-18	B	2.73	2.27	58.0	36.6	34.0	1.9
2018	B+	2.19	1.83	59.0	36.9	150.3	2.4
2017	B	2.60	2.17	51.8	35.0	129.3	7.1
2016	B	2.11	1.75	43.2	28.4	124.7	6.3
2015	C	1.63	1.36	34.5	21.8	118.8	11.0
2014	C	0.81	0.68	28.6	10.8	102.1	-9.4

Rating Indexes

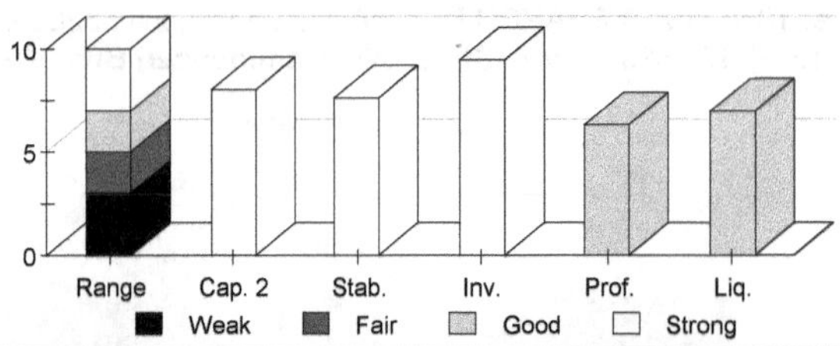

CARECENTRIX OF NEW JERSEY INC D Weak

Major Rating Factors: Fair profitability index (4.2 on a scale of 0 to 10). Fair capitalization (4.4) based on fair current risk-adjusted capital (moderate loss scenario). High quality investment portfolio (9.9).
Other Rating Factors: Excellent liquidity (7.8) with ample operational cash flow and liquid investments.
Principal Business: Other (100%)
Mem Phys: 18: 7,500 **17:** N/A **18 MLR** 85.0% **/ 18 Admin Exp** N/A
Enroll(000): 18: 821 **17:** 908 **Med Exp PMPM:** $2
Principal Investments: Cash and equiv (100%)
Provider Compensation ($000): FFS ($20,429)
Total Member Encounters: N/A
Group Affiliation: NDES Holdings LLC
Licensed in: (No states)
Address: 160 Greentree Dr Suite 101, Melville, NY 11747
Phone: (631) 501-7017 **Dom State:** NJ **Commenced Bus:** N/A

Data Date	Rating	RACR #1	RACR #2	Total Assets ($mil)	Capital ($mil)	Net Premium ($mil)	Net Income ($mil)
2018	D	0.84	0.70	10.8	4.6	24.0	0.8
2017	D-	N/A	N/A	9.0	3.8	22.5	0.4
2016	D-	0.66	0.55	30.9	3.4	18.0	-0.4
2015	U	0.43	0.36	9.9	0.8	7.1	-0.2
2014	N/A	N/A	N/A	2.8	0.9	0.6	0.1

Rating Indexes

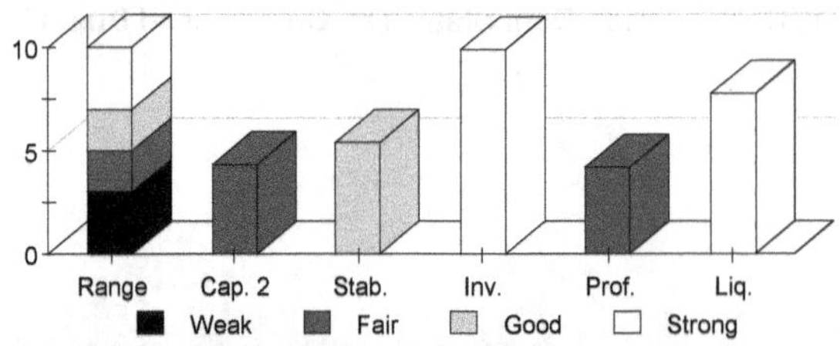

CARECONNECT INS CO E- Very Weak

Major Rating Factors: Weak profitability index (0.3 on a scale of 0 to 10). Weak liquidity (0.7) as a spike in claims may stretch capacity. Strong capitalization (10.0) based on excellent current risk-adjusted capital (severe loss scenario).
Other Rating Factors: High quality investment portfolio (9.8).
Principal Business: Comp med (86%)
Mem Phys: 18: 28,015 **17:** 27,364 **18 MLR** 133.0% **/ 18 Admin Exp** N/A
Enroll(000): Q1 19: N/A **18:** N/A **17:** 77 **Med Exp PMPM:** N/A
Principal Investments: Long-term bonds (96%), cash and equiv (4%)
Provider Compensation ($000): Contr fee ($62,702), capitation ($97), other ($1,148)
Total Member Encounters: Phys (59,968), non-phys (50,888)
Group Affiliation: Northwell Health Inc
Licensed in: (No states)
Address: 2200 Nern Blvd Ste 104, East Hills, NY 11548
Phone: (516) 405-7500 **Dom State:** NY **Commenced Bus:** N/A

Data Date	Rating	RACR #1	RACR #2	Total Assets ($mil)	Capital ($mil)	Net Premium ($mil)	Net Income ($mil)
3-19	E-	3.88	3.23	91.6	43.2	N/A	N/A
3-18	E-	N/A	N/A	267.3	70.8	40.1	-0.7
2018	E-	3.91	3.26	97.4	43.6	51.2	-29.3
2017	E-	N/A	N/A	326.7	73.5	555.6	-154.9
2016	E-	0.61	0.51	278.1	32.7	360.8	-156.2
2015	E	1.50	1.25	80.3	20.5	124.6	-29.8
2014	E-	N/A	N/A	28.5	-1.8	44.4	-26.8

Rating Indexes

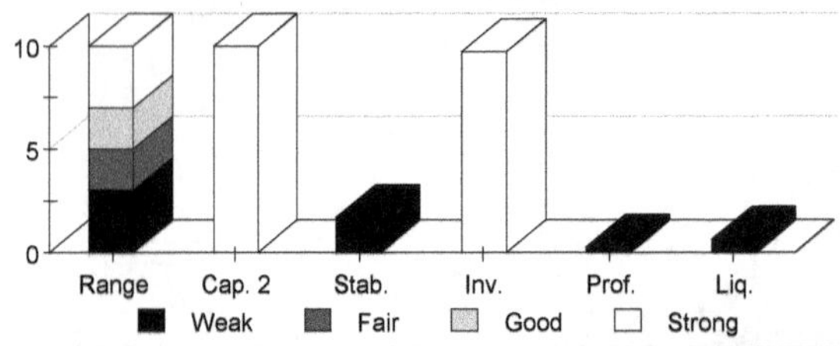

CARECORE NJ LLC D Weak

Major Rating Factors: Good liquidity (6.9 on a scale of 0 to 10) with sufficient resources (cash flows and marketable investments) to handle a spike in claims. Excellent profitability (7.9). Strong capitalization (10.0) based on excellent current risk-adjusted capital (severe loss scenario).
Other Rating Factors: High quality investment portfolio (8.1).
Principal Business: Other (100%)
Mem Phys: 18: 1,528 **17:** 1,012 **18 MLR** 89.8% **/ 18 Admin Exp** N/A
Enroll(000): 18: 1,337 **17:** 1,400 **Med Exp PMPM:** $8
Principal Investments: Cash and equiv (100%)
Provider Compensation ($000): Contr fee ($9,340), other ($122,967)
Total Member Encounters: N/A
Group Affiliation: Cigna Corporation
Licensed in: NJ
Address: 400 Buckwalter Place Blvd, Bluffton, SC 29910
Phone: (800) 918-8924 **Dom State:** NJ **Commenced Bus:** N/A

Data Date	Rating	RACR #1	RACR #2	Total Assets ($mil)	Capital ($mil)	Net Premium ($mil)	Net Income ($mil)
2018	D	3.76	3.13	30.4	7.9	147.2	0.3
2017	D-	N/A	N/A	23.1	7.6	158.0	1.4
2016	D-	1.77	1.48	26.4	6.3	148.4	3.7
2015	U	9.43	7.86	21.0	12.5	140.6	18.3
2014	N/A	N/A	N/A	16.7	11.7	155.8	31.3

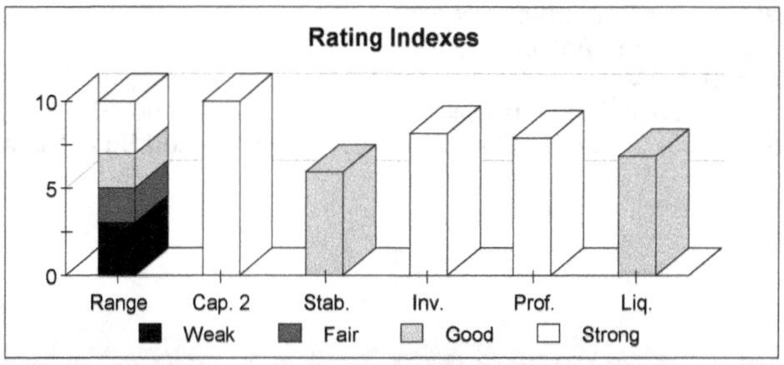

CAREFIRST BLUECHOICE INC C+ Fair

Major Rating Factors: Fair profitability index (3.0 on a scale of 0 to 10). Fair quality investment portfolio (4.8). Strong capitalization index (10.0) based on excellent current risk-adjusted capital (severe loss scenario).
Other Rating Factors: Excellent overall results on stability tests (6.9). Excellent liquidity (6.9) with sufficient resources (cash flows and marketable investments) to handle a spike in claims
Principal Business: Comp med (88%), FEHB (12%)
Mem Phys: 18: 48,386 **17:** 47,725 **18 MLR** 76.5% **/ 18 Admin Exp** N/A
Enroll(000): Q1 19: 626 **18:** 630 **17:** 657 **Med Exp PMPM:** $362
Principal Investments: Long-term bonds (48%), nonaffiliate common stock (13%), cash and equiv (3%), other (36%)
Provider Compensation ($000): Contr fee ($2,743,605), FFS ($18,226), capitation ($4,348)
Total Member Encounters: Phys (3,999,944), non-phys (3,096,872)
Group Affiliation: CareFirst Inc
Licensed in: DC, MD, VA
Address: 840 FIRST STREET NE, WASHINGTON, DC 20065
Phone: (410) 581-3000 **Dom State:** DC **Commenced Bus:** N/A

Data Date	Rating	RACR #1	RACR #2	Total Assets ($mil)	Capital ($mil)	Net Premium ($mil)	Net Income ($mil)
3-19	C+	3.82	3.18	1,272.7	741.3	880.7	47.0
3-18	C+	4.13	3.44	1,264.9	655.9	921.3	-6.3
2018	C+	3.72	3.10	1,213.8	721.1	3,620.5	63.9
2017	B	3.66	3.05	1,158.1	672.6	3,248.5	-27.8
2016	A-	4.72	3.93	1,145.5	697.5	3,102.9	-46.1
2015	A	5.30	4.42	1,177.0	741.1	2,986.5	-9.9
2014	A+	5.81	4.85	1,152.3	757.1	2,700.8	22.1

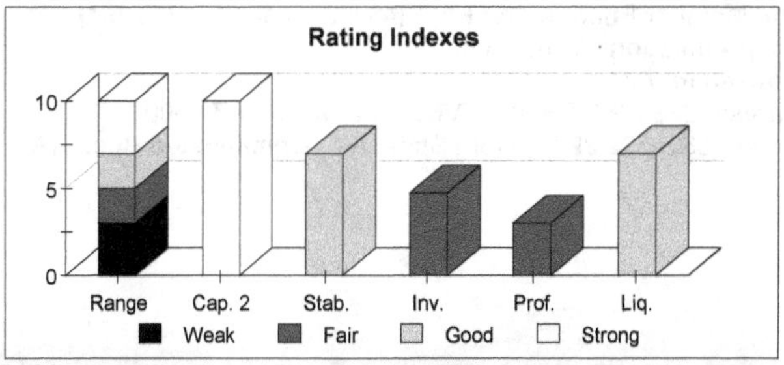

CAREFIRST OF MARYLAND INC C+ Fair

Major Rating Factors: Fair profitability index (4.2 on a scale of 0 to 10). Fair quality investment portfolio (3.9). Strong capitalization (10.0) based on excellent current risk-adjusted capital (severe loss scenario).
Other Rating Factors: Excellent liquidity (7.2) with ample operational cash flow and liquid investments.
Principal Business: FEHB (68%), comp med (19%), med supp (7%), dental (4%), other (2%)
Mem Phys: 18: 52,141 **17:** 51,525 **18 MLR** 84.3% **/ 18 Admin Exp** N/A
Enroll(000): Q1 19: 479 **18:** 504 **17:** 559 **Med Exp PMPM:** $272
Principal Investments: Long-term bonds (34%), nonaffiliate common stock (9%), cash and equiv (6%), other (51%)
Provider Compensation ($000): Contr fee ($1,607,967), FFS ($43,332), capitation ($4,529)
Total Member Encounters: Phys (5,713,426), non-phys (6,406,222)
Group Affiliation: CareFirst Inc
Licensed in: DC, MD
Address: 1501 S CLINTON St, BALTIMORE, MD 21224
Phone: (410) 581-3000 **Dom State:** MD **Commenced Bus:** N/A

Data Date	Rating	RACR #1	RACR #2	Total Assets ($mil)	Capital ($mil)	Net Premium ($mil)	Net Income ($mil)
3-19	C+	4.01	3.34	1,810.5	766.5	476.3	25.6
3-18	C+	3.82	3.19	1,559.8	626.9	480.2	-2.7
2018	C+	3.79	3.16	1,803.8	724.5	1,966.4	110.1
2017	C+	3.35	2.79	1,535.1	642.8	1,889.8	-28.9
2016	C+	3.65	3.04	1,412.3	556.2	1,946.6	-21.1
2015	C+	3.88	3.24	1,406.7	553.5	1,914.6	-9.8
2014	B-	3.78	3.15	1,369.0	537.6	1,950.4	-15.8

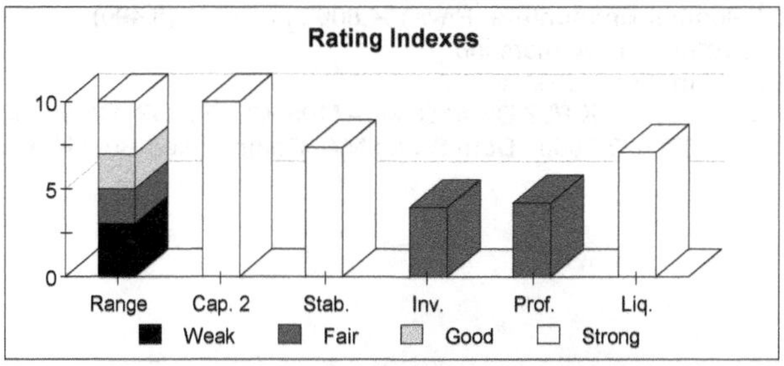

CAREMORE HEALTH PLAN — B- Good

Major Rating Factors: Fair overall results on stability tests (3.6 on a scale of 0 to 10) based on a steep decline in capital during 2018. Rating is significantly influenced by the good financial results of Anthem Inc. Good overall profitability index (6.1). Strong capitalization index (7.0) based on excellent current risk-adjusted capital (severe loss scenario).
Other Rating Factors: Excellent liquidity (7.1) with ample operational cash flow and liquid investments.
Principal Business: Managed care (100%)
Mem Phys: 18: N/A **17:** N/A **18 MLR** 93.1% **/ 18 Admin Exp** N/A
Enroll(000): Q1 19: 60 **18:** 59 **17:** 58 **Med Exp PMPM:** $1,203
Principal Investments ($000): Cash and equiv ($176,997)
Provider Compensation ($000): None
Total Member Encounters: N/A
Group Affiliation: Anthem Inc
Licensed in: CA
Address: 12900 Park Plaza Dr Suite 150, Cerritos, CA 90703
Phone: (562) 677-2455 **Dom State:** CA **Commenced Bus:** November 2002

Data Date	Rating	RACR #1	RACR #2	Total Assets ($mil)	Capital ($mil)	Net Premium ($mil)	Net Income ($mil)
3-19	B-	1.81	1.13	289.6	66.5	241.9	-0.5
3-18	B	2.30	1.43	273.9	70.6	226.2	1.1
2018	B-	1.74	1.09	285.4	63.8	910.4	14.8
2017	B	2.58	1.60	254.6	81.9	977.3	49.7
2016	B-	3.05	1.91	299.6	91.3	949.8	58.1
2015	B+	2.78	1.75	263.4	84.4	928.2	34.6
2014	B	2.82	1.78	292.6	80.5	835.7	27.1

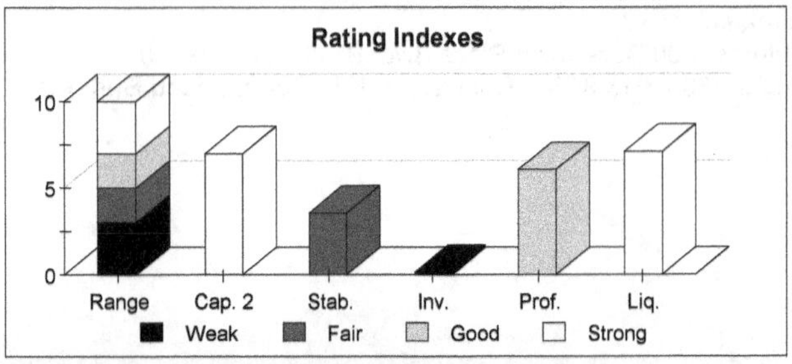

CAREMORE HEALTH PLAN OF ARIZONA INC — B Good

Major Rating Factors: Good liquidity (6.9 on a scale of 0 to 10) with sufficient resources (cash flows and marketable investments) to handle a spike in claims. Fair profitability index (4.4). Strong capitalization (10.0) based on excellent current risk-adjusted capital (severe loss scenario).
Other Rating Factors: High quality investment portfolio (8.6).
Principal Business: Medicare (100%)
Mem Phys: 18: 2,858 **17:** 3,279 **18 MLR** 77.0% **/ 18 Admin Exp** N/A
Enroll(000): Q1 19: N/A **18:** 14 **17:** 13 **Med Exp PMPM:** $799
Principal Investments: Long-term bonds (79%), cash and equiv (20%), other (1%)
Provider Compensation ($000): Contr fee ($88,004), salary ($26,878), capitation ($13,328), bonus arrang ($1,183)
Total Member Encounters: Phys (46,807), non-phys (13,894)
Group Affiliation: Anthem Inc
Licensed in: AZ
Address: 322 WEST ROOSEVELT, PHOENIX, AZ 85003
Phone: (562) 622-2900 **Dom State:** AZ **Commenced Bus:** N/A

Data Date	Rating	RACR #1	RACR #2	Total Assets ($mil)	Capital ($mil)	Net Premium ($mil)	Net Income ($mil)
3-19	B	5.36	4.46	61.5	38.6	39.5	1.9
3-18	B-	4.66	3.88	67.8	30.3	42.3	-1.9
2018	B	5.13	4.27	55.3	36.7	166.4	5.6
2017	C+	2.85	2.37	51.3	31.7	148.5	0.9
2016	B-	5.07	4.23	63.6	30.9	134.8	3.1
2015	B-	3.05	2.54	66.5	28.1	199.8	-7.6
2014	B-	3.96	3.30	67.2	34.6	187.6	2.0

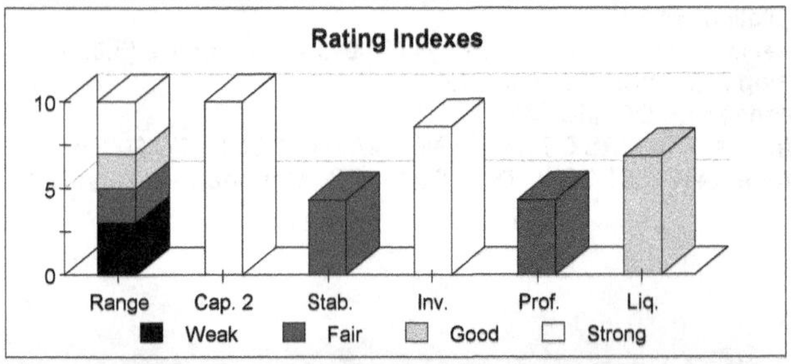

CAREMORE HEALTH PLAN OF NEVADA — B- Good

Major Rating Factors: Good liquidity (6.1 on a scale of 0 to 10) with sufficient resources (cash flows and marketable investments) to handle a spike in claims. Strong capitalization (9.7) based on excellent current risk-adjusted capital (severe loss scenario). High quality investment portfolio (8.5).
Other Rating Factors: Weak profitability index (1.7).
Principal Business: Medicare (100%)
Mem Phys: 18: 1,885 **17:** 2,183 **18 MLR** 91.2% **/ 18 Admin Exp** N/A
Enroll(000): Q1 19: N/A **18:** N/A **17:** 8 **Med Exp PMPM:** N/A
Principal Investments: Long-term bonds (97%), cash and equiv (2%), other (1%)
Provider Compensation ($000): Contr fee ($67,717), salary ($13,334), capitation ($6,727), bonus arrang ($846)
Total Member Encounters: Phys (34,809), non-phys (8,490)
Group Affiliation: Anthem Inc
Licensed in: (No states)
Address: 12900 PK PLZ DR #150 M/S-7105, CERRITOS, CA 90703
Phone: (562) 622-2900 **Dom State:** NV **Commenced Bus:** N/A

Data Date	Rating	RACR #1	RACR #2	Total Assets ($mil)	Capital ($mil)	Net Premium ($mil)	Net Income ($mil)
3-19	B-	3.50	2.92	31.4	19.6	26.0	-0.1
3-18	B-	3.42	2.85	38.8	18.0	24.0	0.9
2018	B-	3.47	2.89	30.5	19.4	96.6	2.5
2017	D	1.83	1.53	33.3	16.8	97.9	-4.3
2016	D	3.75	3.13	33.7	17.6	89.4	0.8
2015	D	3.64	3.04	36.3	16.8	83.7	-7.0
2014	D	3.94	3.29	32.7	17.9	72.0	1.0

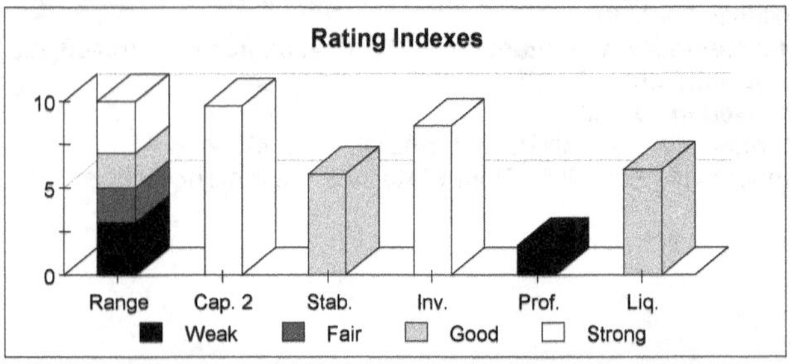

CAREPLUS HEALTH PLANS INC — B — Good

Major Rating Factors: Good overall results on stability tests (5.2 on a scale of 0 to 10) despite a decline in the number of member physicians during 2019. Rating is significantly influenced by the good financial results of . Good liquidity (6.8) with sufficient resources (cash flows and marketable investments) to handle a spike in claims. Excellent profitability (9.0).
Other Rating Factors: Strong capitalization index (10.0) based on excellent current risk-adjusted capital (severe loss scenario). High quality investment portfolio (8.3).
Principal Business: Medicare (100%)
Mem Phys: 18: 29,075 **17:** 34,108 **18 MLR** 81.2% **/ 18 Admin Exp** N/A
Enroll(000): Q1 19: 129 **18:** 118 **17:** 109 **Med Exp PMPM:** $1,034
Principal Investments: Long-term bonds (86%), cash and equiv (14%)
Provider Compensation ($000): Capitation ($807,188), salary ($337,560), contr fee ($300,040)
Total Member Encounters: Phys (2,593,766), non-phys (611,861)
Group Affiliation: None
Licensed in: FL
Address: 11430 NW 20TH STREET SUITE 300, MIAMI, FL 33172
Phone: (305) 441-9400 **Dom State:** FL **Commenced Bus:** N/A

Data Date	Rating	RACR #1	RACR #2	Total Assets ($mil)	Capital ($mil)	Net Premium ($mil)	Net Income ($mil)
3-19	B	3.63	3.02	538.2	173.1	518.6	20.1
3-18	B-	2.83	2.36	629.3	136.0	447.1	-12.5
2018	B	3.37	2.81	461.8	158.2	1,771.3	109.6
2017	B-	2.18	1.82	425.4	150.6	1,688.5	95.9
2016	B-	3.25	2.71	405.6	154.7	1,721.4	96.8
2015	B	3.86	3.21	450.5	199.7	1,754.0	142.9
2014	B-	3.25	2.71	336.1	111.4	1,379.2	56.9

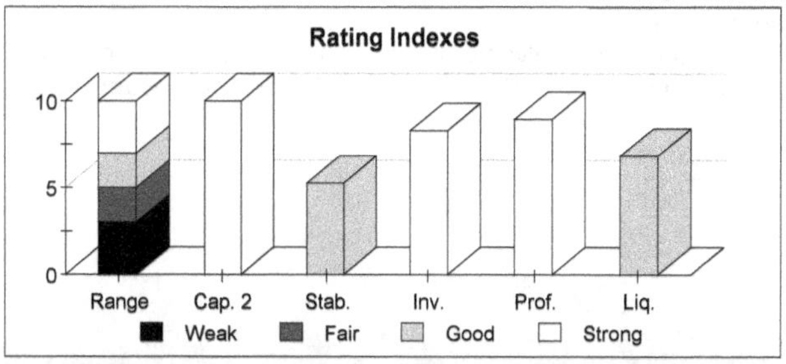

CARESOURCE — B- — Good

Major Rating Factors: Good quality investment portfolio (6.5 on a scale of 0 to 10). Good overall results on stability tests (5.5). Good liquidity (6.6) with sufficient resources (cash flows and marketable investments) to handle a spike in claims.
Other Rating Factors: Strong capitalization index (7.2) based on excellent current risk-adjusted capital (severe loss scenario). Weak profitability index (2.8).
Principal Business: Medicaid (91%), comp med (5%), Medicare (4%)
Mem Phys: 18: 43,825 **17:** 43,616 **18 MLR** 87.8% **/ 18 Admin Exp** N/A
Enroll(000): Q1 19: 1,309 **18:** 1,322 **17:** 1,366 **Med Exp PMPM:** $445
Principal Investments: Long-term bonds (65%), cash and equiv (20%), nonaffiliate common stock (15%)
Provider Compensation ($000): Contr fee ($6,786,277), capitation ($524,015)
Total Member Encounters: Phys (9,609,238), non-phys (12,183,520)
Group Affiliation: None
Licensed in: OH
Address: 230 North Main Street, Dayton, OH 45402
Phone: (937) 531-3300 **Dom State:** OH **Commenced Bus:** N/A

Data Date	Rating	RACR #1	RACR #2	Total Assets ($mil)	Capital ($mil)	Net Premium ($mil)	Net Income ($mil)
3-19	B-	1.50	1.25	1,651.2	736.8	2,124.9	-41.7
3-18	B-	2.12	1.77	1,837.0	912.3	2,052.8	107.8
2018	B-	1.53	1.28	1,655.8	753.0	8,334.8	76.1
2017	B-	1.74	1.45	1,721.0	804.0	7,784.4	28.1
2016	B	1.71	1.42	1,608.7	740.9	7,030.7	-186.2
2015	A-	2.32	1.93	1,762.0	929.2	6,723.9	191.0
2014	A-	2.19	1.82	1,720.9	743.5	5,607.9	160.7

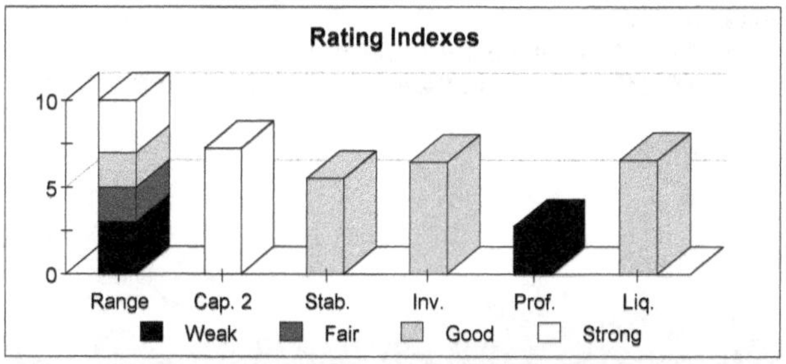

CARESOURCE GEORGIA CO — C — Fair

Major Rating Factors: Weak profitability index (2.4 on a scale of 0 to 10). Good capitalization (6.4) based on good current risk-adjusted capital (severe loss scenario). High quality investment portfolio (9.9).
Other Rating Factors: Excellent liquidity (6.9) with sufficient resources (cash flows and marketable investments) to handle a spike in claims.
Principal Business: Medicaid (100%)
Mem Phys: 18: 25,393 **17:** 24,049 **18 MLR** 93.4% **/ 18 Admin Exp** N/A
Enroll(000): Q1 19: 224 **18:** 216 **17:** 211 **Med Exp PMPM:** $237
Principal Investments: Cash and equiv (100%)
Provider Compensation ($000): Contr fee ($583,649), capitation ($1,387)
Total Member Encounters: Phys (1,464,158), non-phys (304,644)
Group Affiliation: None
Licensed in: GA
Address: 600 Galleria Parkway Ste 400, Atlanta, GA 30339
Phone: (678) 214-7500 **Dom State:** GA **Commenced Bus:** N/A

Data Date	Rating	RACR #1	RACR #2	Total Assets ($mil)	Capital ($mil)	Net Premium ($mil)	Net Income ($mil)
3-19	C	1.14	0.95	172.9	83.0	175.5	3.9
3-18	N/A	N/A	N/A	145.1	51.5	163.5	6.7
2018	C-	1.06	0.88	184.0	79.2	659.7	-20.7
2017	N/A	N/A	N/A	119.6	45.1	313.9	15.5
2016	N/A	N/A	N/A	3.5	2.7	N/A	-1.3
2015	N/A	N/A	N/A	4.0	4.0	N/A	N/A
2014	N/A	N/A	N/A	N/A	N/A	N/A	N/A

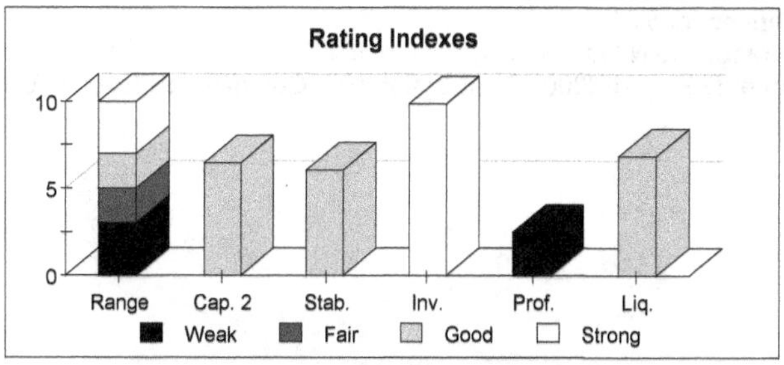

CARESOURCE INDIANA INC D+ Weak

Major Rating Factors: Weak profitability index (0.9 on a scale of 0 to 10). Strong capitalization (6.9) based on excellent current risk-adjusted capital (severe loss scenario). High quality investment portfolio (9.8).
Other Rating Factors: Excellent liquidity (7.1) with ample operational cash flow and liquid investments.
Principal Business: Medicaid (51%), comp med (49%)
Mem Phys: 18: 26,398 **17:** 20,667 **18 MLR** 88.7% **/ 18 Admin Exp** N/A
Enroll(000): Q1 19: 143 **18:** 161 **17:** 126 **Med Exp PMPM:** $330
Principal Investments: Cash and equiv (83%), long-term bonds (17%)
Provider Compensation ($000): Contr fee ($732,400), capitation ($1,583)
Total Member Encounters: Phys (976,944), non-phys (738,190)
Group Affiliation: None
Licensed in: IN
Address: 135 N Pennsylvania St Ste 1300, Indianapolis, IN 46204
Phone: (937) 531-3300 **Dom State:** IN **Commenced Bus:** N/A

Data Date	Rating	RACR #1	RACR #2	Total Assets ($mil)	Capital ($mil)	Net Premium ($mil)	Net Income ($mil)
3-19	D+	1.31	1.09	335.2	78.8	160.2	7.6
3-18	D+	N/A	N/A	337.8	66.9	213.8	29.7
2018	D+	1.20	1.00	302.1	73.4	782.1	9.7
2017	D+	N/A	N/A	201.3	39.1	350.5	5.7
2016	D+	2.15	1.79	64.6	15.9	92.4	-21.6
2015	B	2.05	1.71	49.8	8.6	55.6	-3.0
2014	N/A	N/A	N/A	3.0	2.2	N/A	-0.3

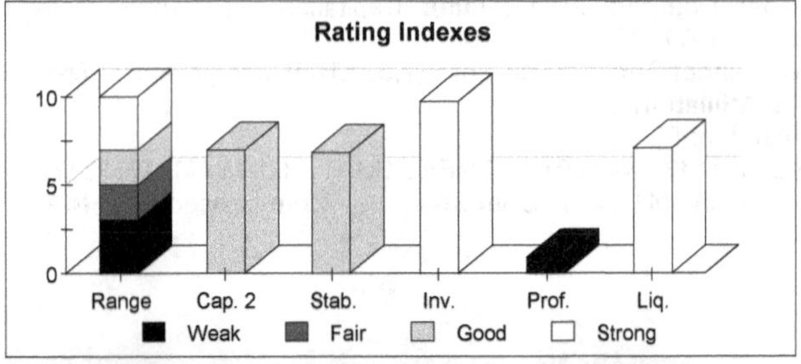

CARESOURCE KENTUCKY CO C Fair

Major Rating Factors: Weak profitability index (1.9 on a scale of 0 to 10). Strong capitalization (7.8) based on excellent current risk-adjusted capital (severe loss scenario). High quality investment portfolio (9.9).
Other Rating Factors: Excellent liquidity (7.0) with ample operational cash flow and liquid investments.
Principal Business: Comp med (100%)
Mem Phys: 18: 15,011 **17:** 12,207 **18 MLR** 85.2% **/ 18 Admin Exp** N/A
Enroll(000): Q1 19: 35 **18:** 45 **17:** 27 **Med Exp PMPM:** $414
Principal Investments: Cash and equiv (100%)
Provider Compensation ($000): Contr fee ($229,854), capitation ($454)
Total Member Encounters: Phys (289,673), non-phys (203,814)
Group Affiliation: None
Licensed in: KY
Address: 230 N Main St, Louisville, KY 40223
Phone: (937) 531-3300 **Dom State:** KY **Commenced Bus:** N/A

Data Date	Rating	RACR #1	RACR #2	Total Assets ($mil)	Capital ($mil)	Net Premium ($mil)	Net Income ($mil)
3-19	C	2.00	1.67	81.6	43.1	60.0	12.1
3-18	C	N/A	N/A	90.1	30.0	70.6	12.0
2018	C	1.38	1.15	85.5	32.2	281.3	0.1
2017	C	N/A	N/A	58.3	19.4	103.0	-6.0
2016	C	2.26	1.88	30.2	8.9	31.3	-8.8
2015	B	5.02	4.18	12.4	5.8	10.0	-3.6
2014	N/A	N/A	N/A	3.8	3.7	N/A	-0.3

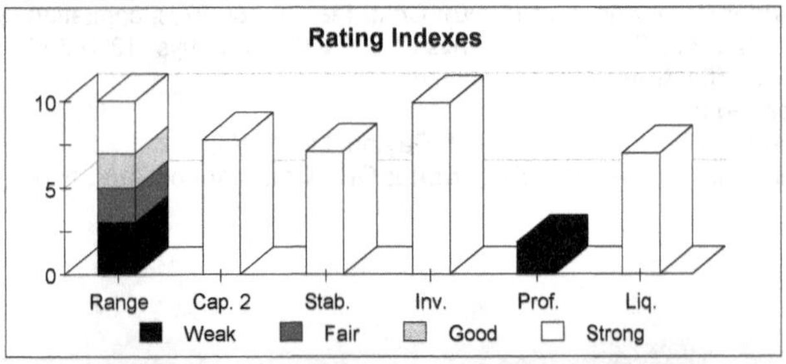

CARESOURCE WEST VIRGINIA CO C Fair

Major Rating Factors: Weak profitability index (0.9 on a scale of 0 to 10). Strong capitalization (7.3) based on excellent current risk-adjusted capital (severe loss scenario). High quality investment portfolio (9.9).
Other Rating Factors: Excellent liquidity (7.2) with ample operational cash flow and liquid investments.
Principal Business: Comp med (100%)
Mem Phys: 18: 6,663 **17:** 4,409 **18 MLR** 98.0% **/ 18 Admin Exp** N/A
Enroll(000): Q1 19: 7 **18:** 6 **17:** 5 **Med Exp PMPM:** $577
Principal Investments: Cash and equiv (100%)
Provider Compensation ($000): Contr fee ($48,699), capitation ($74)
Total Member Encounters: Phys (40,854), non-phys (24,472)
Group Affiliation: None
Licensed in: WV
Address: 230 N Main St, Dayton, OH 45402
Phone: (937) 531-3300 **Dom State:** WV **Commenced Bus:** N/A

Data Date	Rating	RACR #1	RACR #2	Total Assets ($mil)	Capital ($mil)	Net Premium ($mil)	Net Income ($mil)
3-19	C	1.59	1.33	35.6	12.1	13.8	1.2
3-18	C	N/A	N/A	30.1	10.1	14.5	1.4
2018	C	1.10	0.91	30.3	9.8	49.4	-6.0
2017	C	N/A	N/A	23.6	9.0	31.3	0.5
2016	C+	2.95	2.46	7.4	3.6	5.2	-0.5
2015	N/A	N/A	N/A	4.8	4.2	N/A	-0.3
2014	N/A	N/A	N/A	N/A	N/A	N/A	N/A

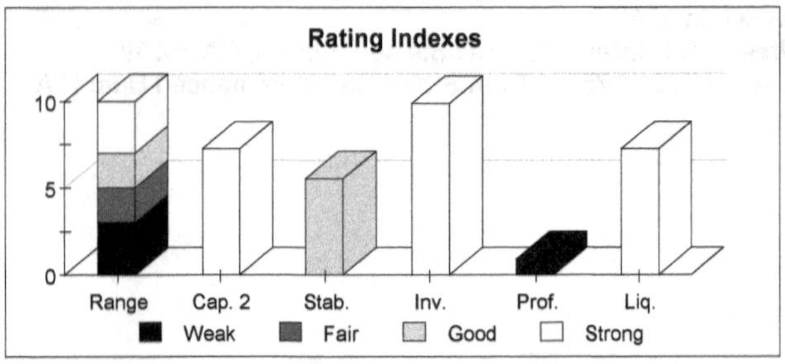

CARITEN HEALTH PLAN INC B Good

Major Rating Factors: Good overall results on stability tests (5.6 on a scale of 0 to 10). Rating is significantly influenced by the good financial results of . Excellent profitability (9.2). Strong capitalization index (10.0) based on excellent current risk-adjusted capital (severe loss scenario).
Other Rating Factors: High quality investment portfolio (8.6). Excellent liquidity (7.0) with sufficient resources (cash flows and marketable investments) to handle a spike in claims.
Principal Business: Medicare (100%)
Mem Phys: 18: 24,893 **17:** 19,449 **18 MLR** 79.0% **/ 18 Admin Exp** N/A
Enroll(000): Q1 19: 118 **18:** 118 **17:** 116 **Med Exp PMPM:** $784
Principal Investments: Long-term bonds (71%), cash and equiv (29%)
Provider Compensation ($000): Contr fee ($647,852), capitation ($425,907), FFS ($4,083)
Total Member Encounters: Phys (2,650,908), non-phys (1,243,058)
Group Affiliation: None
Licensed in: AL, TN
Address: 2160 LAKESIDE CENTRE WAY, KNOXVILLE, TN 37922
Phone: (865) 470-3993 **Dom State:** TN **Commenced Bus:** N/A

Data Date	Rating	RACR #1	RACR #2	Total Assets ($mil)	Capital ($mil)	Net Premium ($mil)	Net Income ($mil)
3-19	B	4.00	3.34	504.0	242.0	388.3	40.1
3-18	B+	3.92	3.27	594.7	223.4	356.8	1.6
2018	B	3.39	2.82	454.6	203.6	1,403.1	100.2
2017	B	2.83	2.36	457.2	221.0	1,356.1	90.3
2016	B	3.03	2.53	300.4	174.0	1,283.3	44.7
2015	B-	2.59	2.16	243.2	144.6	1,173.7	12.7
2014	B-	3.07	2.56	258.4	162.2	1,094.1	12.2

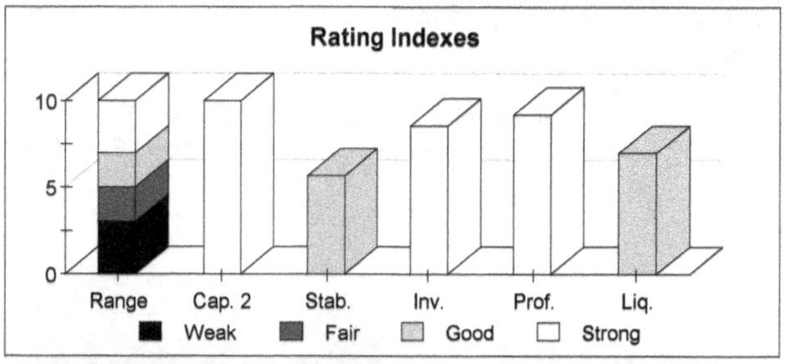

CATHOLIC SPECIAL NEEDS PLAN LLC C Fair

Major Rating Factors: Fair capitalization (3.4 on a scale of 0 to 10) based on weak current risk-adjusted capital (moderate loss scenario). Weak profitability index (1.3). High quality investment portfolio (9.9).
Other Rating Factors: Excellent liquidity (6.9) with sufficient resources (cash flows and marketable investments) to handle a spike in claims.
Principal Business: Medicare (100%)
Mem Phys: 18: N/A **17:** 1,127 **18 MLR** 90.9% **/ 18 Admin Exp** N/A
Enroll(000): Q1 19: 2 **18:** 2 **17:** 2 **Med Exp PMPM:** $2,051
Principal Investments: Cash and equiv (100%)
Provider Compensation ($000): Contr fee ($31,286), capitation ($10,067), bonus arrang ($476)
Total Member Encounters: N/A
Group Affiliation: Providence Health Foundation Inc
Licensed in: NY
Address: 205 Lexington Ave, New York, NY 10016
Phone: (855) 951-2273 **Dom State:** NY **Commenced Bus:** N/A

Data Date	Rating	RACR #1	RACR #2	Total Assets ($mil)	Capital ($mil)	Net Premium ($mil)	Net Income ($mil)
3-19	C	0.70	0.58	15.3	5.9	13.2	0.1
3-18	C+	0.80	0.66	18.1	6.0	11.9	-0.6
2018	C	0.69	0.58	14.3	5.9	47.3	-2.4
2017	C+	0.92	0.76	14.6	6.7	45.6	0.0
2016	C	0.83	0.69	15.1	6.3	48.3	0.4
2015	D+	0.71	0.59	14.9	5.8	46.1	0.8
2014	D	0.52	0.43	12.0	4.9	42.0	1.0

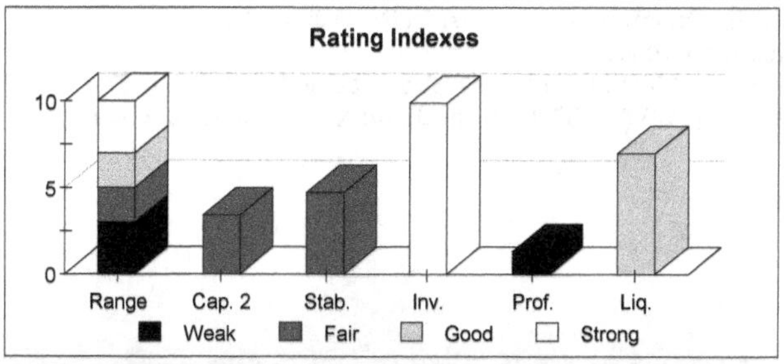

CATLIN INS CO C+ Fair

Major Rating Factors: Fair reserve development (3.1 on a scale of 0 to 10) as the level of reserves has at times been insufficient to cover claims. In 2015 and 2016 the two year reserve development was 18% and 19% deficient respectively. Fair overall results on stability tests (3.0). The largest net exposure for one risk is excessive at 5.2% of capital.
Other Rating Factors: Good overall long-term capitalization (6.5) based on good current risk adjusted capital (moderate loss scenario). However, capital levels have fluctuated during prior years. Weak profitability index (2.3) with operating losses during 2015, 2016, 2017 and 2018. Average return on equity over the last five years has been poor at -4.3%. Excellent liquidity (7.5) with ample operational cash flow and liquid investments.
Principal Business: Other liability (44%), group accident & health (43%), inland marine (8%), homeowners multiple peril (2%), fire (1%), and ocean marine (1%).
Principal Investments: Investment grade bonds (112%) and cash (18%).
Investments in Affiliates: None
Group Affiliation: XL Group Ltd
Licensed in: All states, the District of Columbia and Puerto Rico
Commenced Business: April 1913
Address: 1999 Bryan Street, Dallas, TX 75201
Phone: (203) 964-5200 **Domicile State:** TX **NAIC Code:** 19518

Data Date	Rating	RACR #1	RACR #2	Loss Ratio %	Total Assets ($mil)	Capital ($mil)	Net Premium ($mil)	Net Income ($mil)
3-19	C+	1.53	0.97	N/A	169.1	53.5	11.6	3.0
3-18	C+	1.42	0.83	N/A	165.9	59.8	16.1	5.8
2018	C+	1.45	0.92	85.3	209.7	50.8	46.9	-2.7
2017	C+	1.86	1.07	81.9	181.6	55.9	37.8	-7.6
2016	C	1.37	0.87	86.8	230.5	56.7	29.3	-0.9
2015	C	1.29	0.84	90.9	260.4	52.5	44.8	-5.3
2014	C	1.62	1.14	76.3	230.3	63.7	50.6	1.6

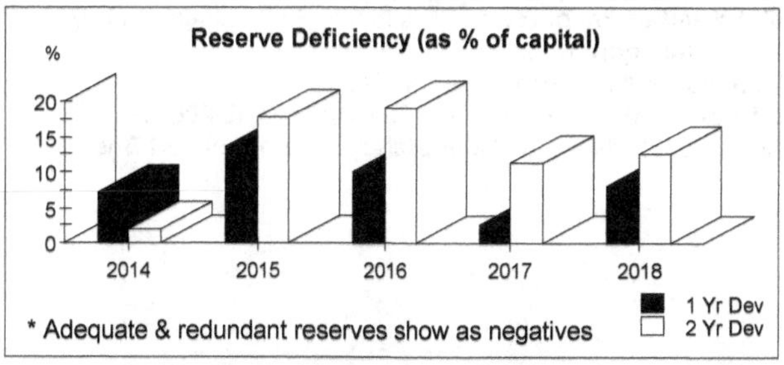

CDI GROUP INC E- Very Weak

Major Rating Factors: Weak profitability index (0.9 on a scale of 0 to 10). Fair overall results on stability tests (4.4) based on an excessive 30% enrollment growth during the period but healthy premium and capital growth during 2018. Good capitalization index (6.6) based on good current risk-adjusted capital (severe loss scenario)

Other Rating Factors: Excellent liquidity (7.3) with ample operational cash flow and liquid investments.

Principal Business: Managed care (100%)

Mem Phys: 18: N/A **17:** N/A **18 MLR** N/A **/ 18 Admin Exp** N/A

Enroll(000): Q1 19: 177 **18:** 170 **17:** 131 **Med Exp PMPM:** N/A

Principal Investments ($000): Cash and equiv ($704)

Provider Compensation ($000): None

Total Member Encounters: N/A

Group Affiliation: None

Licensed in: (No states)

Address: 601 Daily Dr Ste 215, Camarillo, CA 93010-5839

Phone: (800) 874-1986 **Dom State:** CA **Commenced Bus:** N/A

Data Date	Rating	RACR #1	RACR #2	Total Assets ($mil)	Capital ($mil)	Net Premium ($mil)	Net Income ($mil)
3-19	E-	1.00	0.97	2.9	1.7	4.4	1.1
3-18	E-	0.65	0.63	1.6	1.0	3.7	0.9
2018	E-	0.38	0.37	2.4	0.8	14.8	1.2
2017	E-	N/A	N/A	1.8	0.2	10.4	-0.6
2016	N/A	N/A	N/A	N/A	N/A	N/A	N/A
2015	N/A	N/A	N/A	N/A	N/A	N/A	N/A
2014	N/A	N/A	N/A	N/A	N/A	N/A	N/A

Rating Indexes

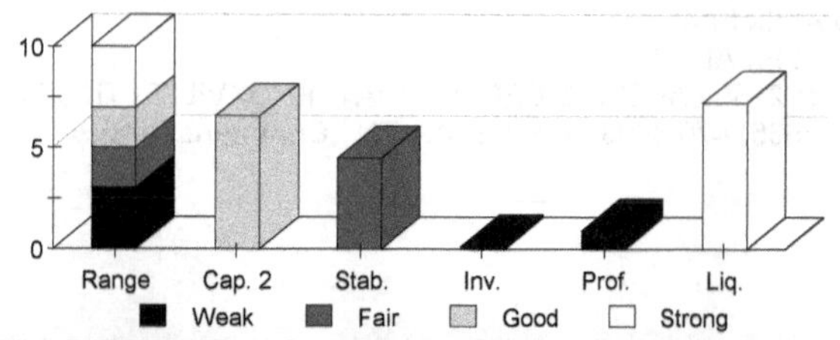

CDPHP UNIVERSAL BENEFITS INC B Good

Major Rating Factors: Good liquidity (6.9 on a scale of 0 to 10) with sufficient resources (cash flows and marketable investments) to handle a spike in claims. Strong capitalization (10.0) based on excellent current risk-adjusted capital (severe loss scenario). High quality investment portfolio (9.4).

Other Rating Factors: Weak profitability index (0.9).

Principal Business: Comp med (77%), FEHB (13%), Medicare (9%)

Mem Phys: 18: 20,930 **17:** 20,223 **18 MLR** 84.9% **/ 18 Admin Exp** N/A

Enroll(000): Q1 19: 92 **18:** 92 **17:** 93 **Med Exp PMPM:** $444

Principal Investments: Long-term bonds (70%), cash and equiv (29%)

Provider Compensation ($000): Contr fee ($447,110), bonus arrang ($13,147), capitation ($2,667), other ($14,582)

Total Member Encounters: Phys (720,261), non-phys (272,945)

Group Affiliation: Capital District Physicians Health P

Licensed in: NY

Address: 500 Patroon Creek Blvd, Albany, NY 12206-1057

Phone: (518) 641-3000 **Dom State:** NY **Commenced Bus:** N/A

Data Date	Rating	RACR #1	RACR #2	Total Assets ($mil)	Capital ($mil)	Net Premium ($mil)	Net Income ($mil)
3-19	B	3.84	3.20	206.5	140.1	142.3	5.7
3-18	C	3.00	2.50	193.9	120.5	138.7	-5.3
2018	B	3.67	3.05	198.0	134.9	567.2	9.1
2017	E+	2.77	2.31	179.5	124.8	588.1	11.1
2016	E+	2.23	1.86	175.3	113.7	703.4	-17.5
2015	E	1.37	1.15	176.2	82.0	795.0	-45.6
2014	E	1.35	1.12	154.0	77.5	759.3	-62.0

Rating Indexes

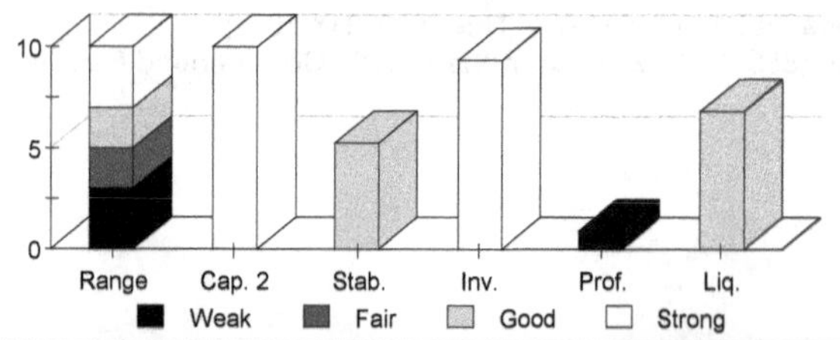

CELTIC INS CO B- Good

Major Rating Factors: Fair quality investment portfolio (4.8 on a scale of 0 to 10). Excellent profitability (8.5). Strong capitalization (8.9) based on excellent current risk-adjusted capital (severe loss scenario).

Other Rating Factors: Excellent liquidity (7.3) with ample operational cash flow and liquid investments.

Principal Business: Comp med (100%)

Mem Phys: 18: 114,998 **17:** 111,609 **18 MLR** 74.2% **/ 18 Admin Exp** N/A

Enroll(000): Q1 19: 1,137 **18:** 751 **17:** 532 **Med Exp PMPM:** $178

Principal Investments: Cash and equiv (46%), long-term bonds (44%), affiliate common stock (10%)

Provider Compensation ($000): Contr fee ($1,386,192), bonus arrang ($282,626), capitation ($27,861), salary ($15,946)

Total Member Encounters: Phys (4,634,952), non-phys (4,070,027)

Group Affiliation: None

Licensed in: All states except NY, PR

Address: 77 W Wacker Dr Ste 1200, Chicago, IL 60601

Phone: (800) 714-4658 **Dom State:** IL **Commenced Bus:** N/A

Data Date	Rating	RACR #1	RACR #2	Total Assets ($mil)	Capital ($mil)	Net Premium ($mil)	Net Income ($mil)
3-19	B-	2.91	2.42	2,461.8	441.3	806.8	85.8
3-18	C+	N/A	N/A	1,881.1	264.9	583.0	40.1
2018	B-	3.03	2.52	1,918.6	459.2	2,425.9	162.1
2017	C+	N/A	N/A	1,170.4	162.5	2,127.0	77.0
2016	C+	1.28	1.07	593.0	53.3	781.9	2.0
2015	C-	8.41	7.01	139.9	38.2	170.7	8.3
2014	N/A	N/A	N/A	136.6	29.4	129.8	N/A

Rating Indexes

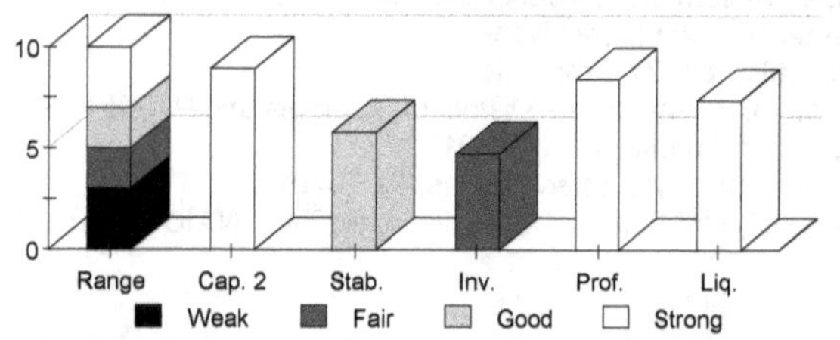

CELTICARE HEALTH PLAN OF MA INC C- Fair

Major Rating Factors: Excellent profitability (7.9 on a scale of 0 to 10). Strong capitalization (10.0) based on excellent current risk-adjusted capital (severe loss scenario). High quality investment portfolio (8.2).
Other Rating Factors: Excellent liquidity (8.0) with ample operational cash flow and liquid investments.
Principal Business: Medicaid (93%), comp med (7%)
Mem Phys: 18: N/A **17:** 11,391 **18 MLR** 59.2% **/ 18 Admin Exp** N/A
Enroll(000): Q1 19: N/A **18:** N/A **17:** 35 **Med Exp PMPM:** N/A
Principal Investments: Long-term bonds (46%), cash and equiv (26%), other (29%)
Provider Compensation ($000): Contr fee ($22,442), capitation ($3,660), salary ($579), bonus arrang ($354)
Total Member Encounters: Phys (21,859), non-phys (24,568)
Group Affiliation: None
Licensed in: MA
Address: 200 West St Ste 250, Bedford, NH 3110
Phone: (314) 725-4477 **Dom State:** MA **Commenced Bus:** N/A

Data Date	Rating	RACR #1	RACR #2	Total Assets ($mil)	Capital ($mil)	Net Premium ($mil)	Net Income ($mil)
3-19	C-	7.99	6.66	24.6	13.9	N/A	0.0
3-18	C	3.68	3.07	51.7	34.1	26.9	0.2
2018	C-	7.83	6.53	23.6	13.6	29.6	4.7
2017	C	2.17	1.81	69.3	33.9	173.9	2.4
2016	C+	4.70	3.92	80.7	46.4	174.2	5.6
2015	C+	6.11	5.09	99.6	55.7	220.1	26.6
2014	C+	3.67	3.05	62.9	29.4	179.5	14.6

Rating Indexes

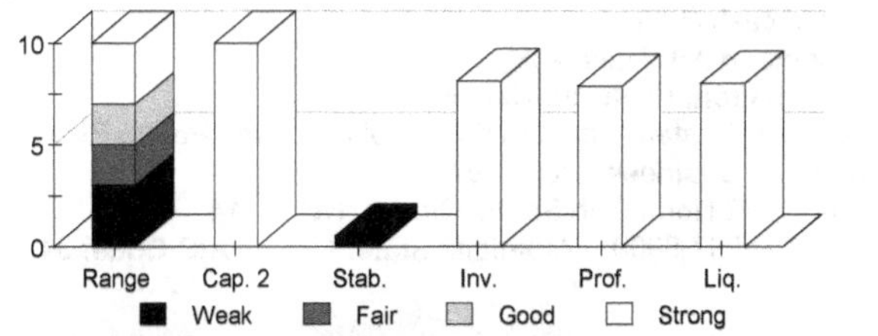

CENTRAL HEALTH PLAN OF CALIFORNIA E+ Very Weak

Major Rating Factors: Poor capitalization index (0.0 on a scale of 0 to 10) based on weak current risk-adjusted capital (severe loss scenario). Weak liquidity (0.0) as a spike in claims may stretch capacity. Fair profitability index (3.6).
Other Rating Factors: Fair overall results on stability tests (3.6) based on a steep decline in capital during 2018, fair risk diversification due to the company's size.
Principal Business: Medicare (100%)
Mem Phys: 18: N/A **17:** N/A **18 MLR** 88.5% **/ 18 Admin Exp** N/A
Enroll(000): Q1 19: 42 **18:** 41 **17:** 36 **Med Exp PMPM:** $760
Principal Investments ($000): Cash and equiv ($33,615)
Provider Compensation ($000): None
Total Member Encounters: N/A
Group Affiliation: AHMC Central Health LLC
Licensed in: CA
Address: 1540 Bridgegate Drive, Diamond Bar, CA 91765
Phone: (626) 388-2390 **Dom State:** CA **Commenced Bus:** October 2004

Data Date	Rating	RACR #1	RACR #2	Total Assets ($mil)	Capital ($mil)	Net Premium ($mil)	Net Income ($mil)
3-19	E+	0.37	0.23	60.2	12.6	113.6	-0.3
3-18	E+	0.49	0.30	102.7	14.9	97.6	0.9
2018	E+	0.38	0.23	51.1	13.0	408.2	-3.6
2017	E+	0.55	0.34	70.7	16.6	364.4	4.1
2016	E+	0.33	0.20	56.6	15.0	351.5	2.9
2015	E+	0.29	0.18	43.8	13.6	298.5	3.5
2014	E+	0.13	0.08	24.0	8.6	183.2	-0.2

Rating Indexes

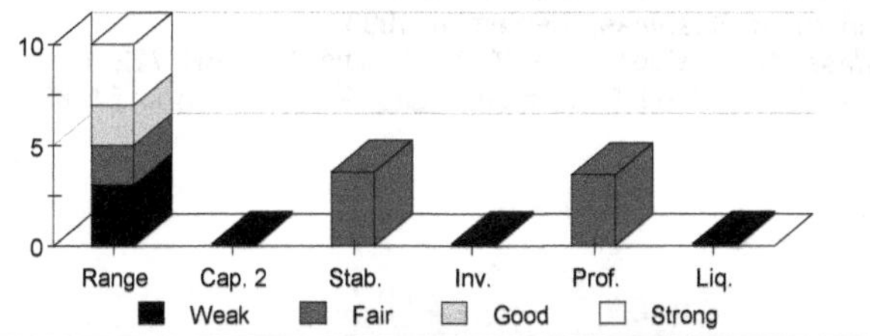

CENTRAL STATES HEALTH & LIFE COMPANY OF OMAHA B Good

Major Rating Factors: Good quality investment portfolio (5.8 on a scale of 0 to 10) despite mixed results such as: minimal exposure to mortgages and substantial holdings of BBB bonds but minimal holdings in junk bonds. Good liquidity (6.9) with sufficient resources to handle a spike in claims. Fair overall results on stability tests (4.0) including negative cash flow from operations for 2018.
Other Rating Factors: Strong capitalization (9.4) based on excellent risk adjusted capital (severe loss scenario). Excellent profitability (7.2) despite modest operating losses during 2018.
Principal Business: Reinsurance (57%), credit life insurance (22%), credit health insurance (12%), individual health insurance (6%), and other lines (3%).
Principal Investments: NonCMO investment grade bonds (41%), CMOs and structured securities (24%), common & preferred stock (12%), mortgages in good standing (5%), and misc. investments (17%).
Investments in Affiliates: 7%
Group Affiliation: Central States Group
Licensed in: All states except NY, PR
Commenced Business: June 1932
Address: 1212 North 96th Street, Omaha, NE 68114
Phone: (402) 397-1111 **Domicile State:** NE **NAIC Code:** 61751

Data Date	Rating	RACR #1	RACR #2	Total Assets ($mil)	Capital ($mil)	Net Premium ($mil)	Net Income ($mil)
3-19	B	3.53	2.63	382.3	142.3	27.1	2.7
3-18	B	4.03	2.92	402.0	128.2	27.8	-6.7
2018	B	3.45	2.58	383.8	137.1	111.3	-0.5
2017	A-	4.58	3.30	407.5	151.9	37.8	13.0
2016	A-	4.28	3.06	420.0	134.3	51.3	10.5
2015	A-	3.99	2.88	419.9	122.9	66.1	6.4
2014	A-	3.79	2.71	414.7	119.6	72.7	5.5

Rating Indexes

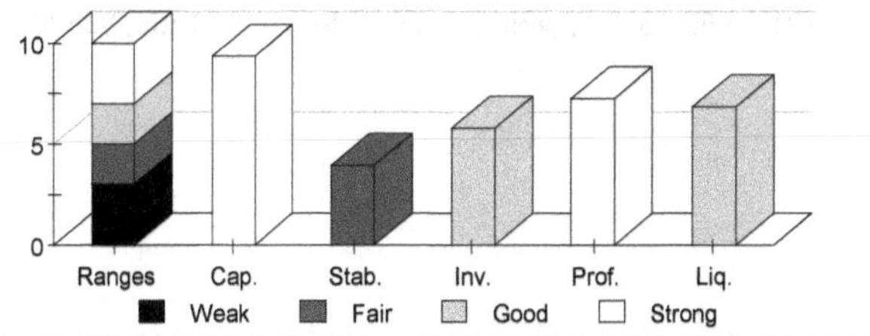

CENTRAL STATES INDEMNITY CO OF OMAHA C+ Fair

Major Rating Factors: Fair reserve development (4.6 on a scale of 0 to 10) as reserves have generally been sufficient to cover claims. Fair overall results on stability tests (3.6) including fair financial strength of affiliated Berkshire-Hathaway.

Other Rating Factors: Good overall profitability index (6.8). Excellent expense controls. Return on equity has been fair, averaging 5.2% over the past five years. Strong long-term capitalization index (9.7) based on excellent current risk adjusted capital (severe and moderate loss scenarios), despite some fluctuation in capital levels. Superior liquidity (10.0) with ample operational cash flow and liquid investments.

Principal Business: Other accident & health (61%), inland marine (29%), aggregate write-ins for other lines of business (5%), aircraft (2%), and credit accident & health (2%).

Principal Investments: Misc. investments (75%), investment grade bonds (24%), and cash (1%).

Investments in Affiliates: 4%

Group Affiliation: Berkshire-Hathaway

Licensed in: All states, the District of Columbia and Puerto Rico

Commenced Business: June 1977

Address: 1212 North 96th Street, Omaha, NE 68114

Phone: (402) 997-8000 **Domicile State:** NE **NAIC Code:** 34274

Data Date	Rating	RACR #1	RACR #2	Loss Ratio %	Total Assets ($mil)	Capital ($mil)	Net Premium ($mil)	Net Income ($mil)
3-19	C+	4.33	2.75	N/A	556.6	492.2	2.6	3.1
3-18	C	4.23	2.69	N/A	558.2	477.5	3.2	15.6
2018	C+	4.46	2.84	2.9	521.1	464.7	9.6	24.3
2017	C+	3.98	2.53	66.1	542.1	466.0	64.0	63.6
2016	C+	3.82	2.42	60.2	447.9	378.0	59.6	8.0
2015	C+	4.00	2.50	55.4	417.3	354.9	55.0	9.5
2014	C+	4.12	2.63	44.6	435.0	363.7	50.2	11.4

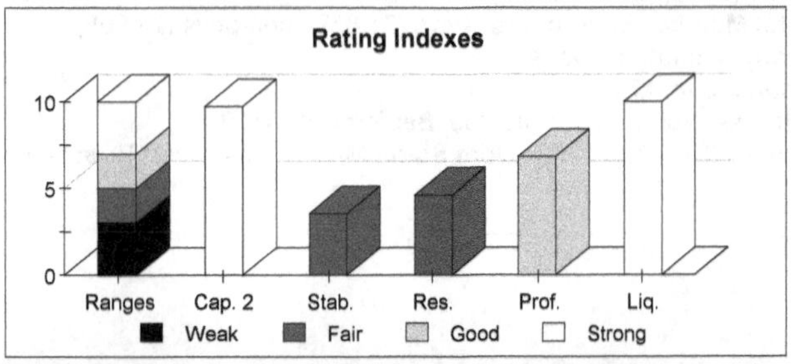

CENTRAL UNITED LIFE INSURANCE COMPANY C Fair

Major Rating Factors: Fair overall results on stability tests (3.8 on a scale of 0 to 10) including excessive premium growth and fair risk adjusted capital in prior years. Good current capitalization (5.2) based on good risk adjusted capital (severe loss scenario) reflecting some improvement over results in 2016. Good quality investment portfolio (5.2).

Other Rating Factors: Good overall profitability (6.4). Excellent liquidity (7.1).

Principal Business: Individual health insurance (49%), reinsurance (40%), group health insurance (7%), and individual life insurance (3%).

Principal Investments: NonCMO investment grade bonds (47%), common & preferred stock (22%), mortgages in good standing (7%), real estate (4%), and misc. investments (6%).

Investments in Affiliates: 22%

Group Affiliation: Manhattan Life Group Inc

Licensed in: All states except FL, NJ, NY, PR

Commenced Business: September 1963

Address: 425 W Capitol Ave Ste 1800, Little Rock, AR 72201

Phone: (713) 529-0045 **Domicile State:** AR **NAIC Code:** 61883

Data Date	Rating	RACR #1	RACR #2	Total Assets ($mil)	Capital ($mil)	Net Premium ($mil)	Net Income ($mil)
3-19	C	0.87	0.77	705.3	163.7	61.5	1.9
3-18	C	0.63	0.57	394.6	104.0	33.4	0.9
2018	C	0.82	0.73	700.5	153.7	251.4	19.3
2017	C	0.62	0.57	390.8	102.4	113.8	4.3
2016	C	0.61	0.55	385.0	95.6	99.9	-1.6
2015	C	0.64	0.59	327.0	92.9	100.0	2.6
2014	C	0.58	0.53	305.1	76.8	92.7	3.9

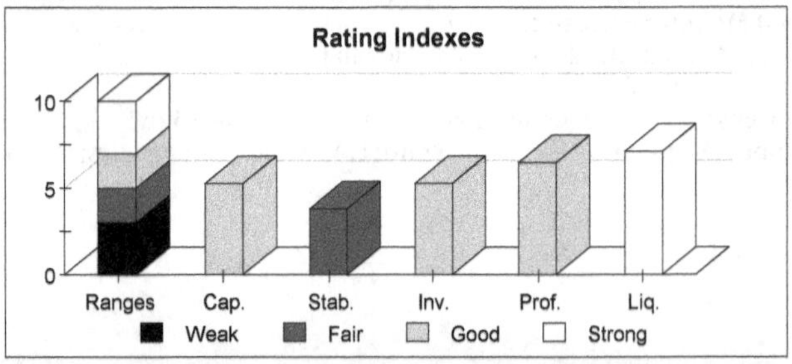

CENTRE LIFE INSURANCE COMPANY B- Good

Major Rating Factors: Good quality investment portfolio (6.7 on a scale of 0 to 10) with no exposure to mortgages and minimal holdings in junk bonds. Fair profitability (3.2). Fair overall results on stability tests (4.9) including excessive premium growth and negative cash flow from operations for 2018.

Other Rating Factors: Strong capitalization (9.3) based on excellent risk adjusted capital (severe loss scenario). Excellent liquidity (9.2).

Principal Business: Reinsurance (58%) and individual health insurance (42%).

Principal Investments: NonCMO investment grade bonds (80%), CMOs and structured securities (19%), and cash (1%).

Investments in Affiliates: None

Group Affiliation: Zurich Financial Services Group

Licensed in: All states except PR

Commenced Business: October 1927

Address: 1350 MAIN STREET SUITE 1600, SPRINGFIELD, MA 01103-1641

Phone: (212) 859-2640 **Domicile State:** MA **NAIC Code:** 80896

Data Date	Rating	RACR #1	RACR #2	Total Assets ($mil)	Capital ($mil)	Net Premium ($mil)	Net Income ($mil)
3-19	B-	4.24	2.55	1,655.3	94.6	0.6	0.6
3-18	B-	3.99	2.44	1,749.0	92.4	0.3	-0.4
2018	B-	4.22	2.46	1,680.2	93.9	1.3	0.5
2017	B-	4.04	2.40	1,790.7	93.6	1.4	-1.7
2016	B-	4.03	2.48	1,809.8	93.8	1.4	-0.5
2015	B-	3.94	2.57	1,884.1	94.5	1.9	-3.7
2014	B-	4.03	2.54	1,926.1	98.0	0.0	-2.7

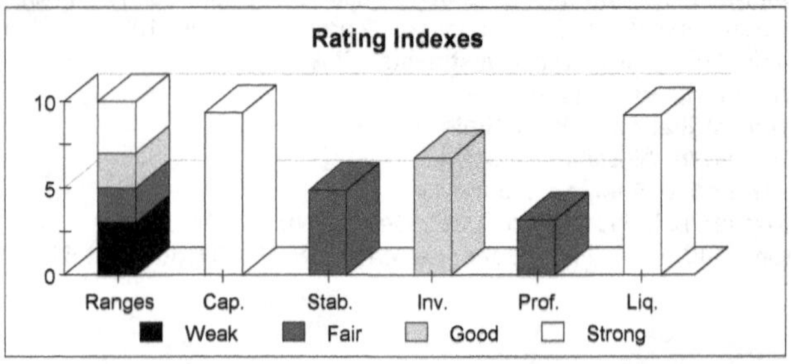

CENTURION LIFE INSURANCE COMPANY C Fair

Major Rating Factors: Fair profitability (4.5 on a scale of 0 to 10). Excellent expense controls. Good quality investment portfolio (6.8) despite mixed results such as: no exposure to mortgages and large holdings of BBB rated bonds but minimal holdings in junk bonds. Weak overall results on stability tests (2.4) including weak results on operational trends, negative cash flow from operations for 2018.
Other Rating Factors: Strong capitalization (10.0) based on excellent risk adjusted capital (severe loss scenario). Excellent liquidity (8.5).
Principal Business: Reinsurance (98%), credit health insurance (1%), and credit life insurance (1%).
Principal Investments: NonCMO investment grade bonds (81%), cash (11%), noninv. grade bonds (5%), and CMOs and structured securities (1%).
Investments in Affiliates: None
Group Affiliation: Wells Fargo Group
Licensed in: All states except ME, NY, VT, PR
Commenced Business: July 1956
Address: 800 WALNUT STREET, DES MOINES, IA 50309
Phone: (515) 557-7321 **Domicile State:** IA **NAIC Code:** 62383

Data Date	Rating	RACR #1	RACR #2	Total Assets ($mil)	Capital ($mil)	Net Premium ($mil)	Net Income ($mil)
3-19	C	24.64	11.06	501.7	315.9	0.0	4.3
3-18	C	33.92	14.66	1,048.4	802.5	0.7	7.9
2018	C	23.26	10.37	515.2	311.3	2.1	39.9
2017	C	30.33	13.00	1,249.2	793.7	37.2	489.3
2016	D	3.82	2.23	1,288.2	317.7	172.8	22.5
2015	D	3.59	2.17	1,262.6	293.9	179.0	52.0
2014	D	2.64	1.59	1,259.3	251.2	314.0	-165.5

Net Income History
(in millions of dollars)

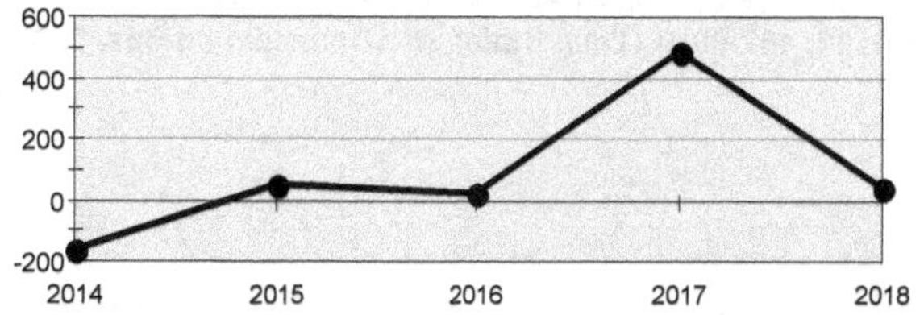

CHA HMO INC C+ Fair

Major Rating Factors: Fair overall results on stability tests (4.1 on a scale of 0 to 10). Rating is significantly influenced by the good financial results of . Good quality investment portfolio (6.8). Good liquidity (6.8) with sufficient resources (cash flows and marketable investments) to handle a spike in claims.
Other Rating Factors: Weak profitability index (2.4). Strong capitalization index (10.0) based on excellent current risk-adjusted capital (severe loss scenario).
Principal Business: Medicare (100%)
Mem Phys: 18: 26,568 **17:** 19,850 **18 MLR** 86.3% **/ 18 Admin Exp** N/A
Enroll(000): Q1 19: 314 **18:** 21 **17:** 19 **Med Exp PMPM:** $666
Principal Investments: Long-term bonds (88%), cash and equiv (12%)
Provider Compensation ($000): Contr fee ($91,725), capitation ($73,434), FFS ($2,547)
Total Member Encounters: Phys (358,279), non-phys (211,948)
Group Affiliation: None
Licensed in: HI, IN, IA, KY, NE, SD
Address: 500 WEST MAIN STREET, LOUISVILLE, KY 40202
Phone: (502) 580-1000 **Dom State:** KY **Commenced Bus:** N/A

Data Date	Rating	RACR #1	RACR #2	Total Assets ($mil)	Capital ($mil)	Net Premium ($mil)	Net Income ($mil)
3-19	C+	16.78	13.99	495.0	162.2	912.6	21.3
3-18	C+	N/A	N/A	62.8	16.6	48.2	-2.4
2018	C+	1.75	1.46	42.4	16.6	190.2	4.8
2017	C+	N/A	N/A	43.6	19.4	160.6	-4.5
2016	C+	3.79	3.16	33.0	23.3	128.3	0.0
2015	C+	6.07	5.06	32.6	24.0	77.6	-4.5
2014	C	10.04	8.37	32.7	27.2	33.3	-1.6

Rating Indexes

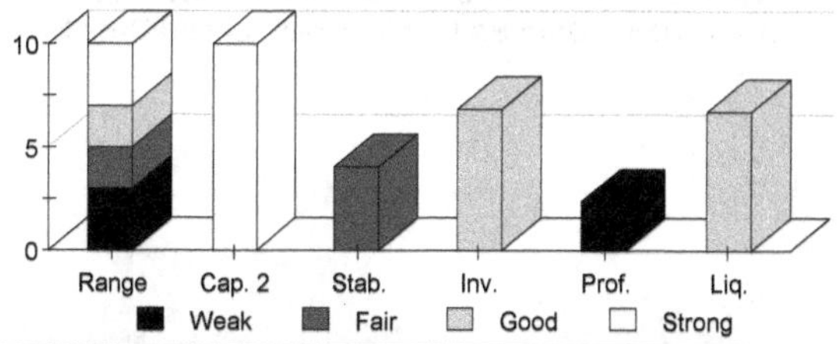

CHESAPEAKE LIFE INSURANCE COMPANY * A+ Excellent

Major Rating Factors: Excellent overall results on stability tests (7.9 on a scale of 0 to 10). Strengths that enhance stability include excellent operational trends and excellent risk diversification. Strong capitalization (9.4) based on excellent risk adjusted capital (severe loss scenario). Furthermore, this high level of risk adjusted capital has been consistently maintained over the last five years. High quality investment portfolio (8.8).
Other Rating Factors: Excellent profitability (8.1) despite modest operating losses during 2015. Excellent liquidity (8.0).
Principal Business: Individual health insurance (82%), individual life insurance (16%), and reinsurance (1%).
Principal Investments: NonCMO investment grade bonds (73%), CMOs and structured securities (5%), and cash (1%).
Investments in Affiliates: None
Group Affiliation: Blackstone Investor Group
Licensed in: All states except NJ, NY, VT, PR
Commenced Business: October 1956
Address: 1833 SOUTH MORGAN ROAD, OKLAHOMA CITY, OK 73128
Phone: (817) 255-3100 **Domicile State:** OK **NAIC Code:** 61832

Data Date	Rating	RACR #1	RACR #2	Total Assets ($mil)	Capital ($mil)	Net Premium ($mil)	Net Income ($mil)
3-19	A+	3.24	2.57	213.1	134.0	58.1	6.0
3-18	B	2.42	1.93	169.3	96.7	53.7	5.1
2018	A-	2.90	2.30	197.7	121.3	213.4	28.9
2017	B	2.21	1.76	158.7	86.7	200.8	16.6
2016	C+	1.85	1.47	133.3	69.7	184.3	11.6
2015	C+	1.38	1.11	99.8	46.8	159.6	-0.9
2014	C+	1.40	1.11	75.1	43.1	119.4	0.4

Adverse Trends in Operations

Change in asset mix during 2017 (5%)
Increase in policy surrenders from 2016 to 2017 (302%)
Increase in policy surrenders from 2015 to 2016 (122%)
Change in asset mix during 2016 (5.4%)
Increase in policy surrenders from 2014 to 2015 (922%)

* Denotes a Weiss Ratings Recommended Company

CHILDRENS COMMUNITY HEALTH PLAN INC * B+ Good

Major Rating Factors: Excellent profitability (7.6 on a scale of 0 to 10). Strong capitalization (8.1) based on excellent current risk-adjusted capital (severe loss scenario). High quality investment portfolio (9.9).
Other Rating Factors: Excellent liquidity (7.3) with ample operational cash flow and liquid investments.
Principal Business: Medicaid (55%), comp med (45%)
Mem Phys: 18: 16,676 **17:** 13,872 **18 MLR** 81.4% **/ 18 Admin Exp** N/A
Enroll(000): Q1 19: 134 **18:** 146 **17:** 130 **Med Exp PMPM:** $194
Principal Investments: Cash and equiv (86%), long-term bonds (14%)
Provider Compensation ($000): Contr fee ($310,783), FFS ($21,924), capitation ($1,103), bonus arrang ($627)
Total Member Encounters: Phys (404,454), non-phys (121,351)
Group Affiliation: Childrens Hospital and Health System
Licensed in: WI
Address: 9000 W Wisconsin Ave, Milwaukee, WI 53226
Phone: (800) 482-8010 **Dom State:** WI **Commenced Bus:** N/A

Data Date	Rating	RACR #1	RACR #2	Total Assets ($mil)	Capital ($mil)	Net Premium ($mil)	Net Income ($mil)
3-19	B+	2.22	1.85	161.7	81.5	86.2	11.1
3-18	B	1.62	1.35	118.2	42.2	115.9	2.7
2018	B+	1.90	1.58	159.0	71.4	434.4	32.9
2017	B	1.54	1.28	92.9	40.2	258.4	-4.0
2016	B	1.95	1.63	85.3	44.1	235.8	4.2
2015	B	1.72	1.43	81.3	39.7	237.6	10.7
2014	C-	1.31	1.09	70.3	29.8	314.2	9.7

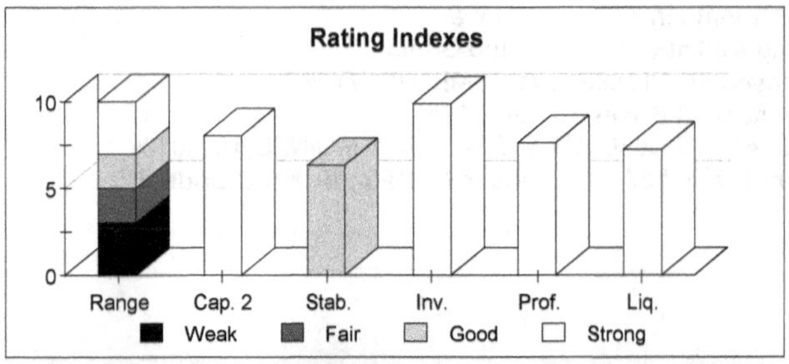

CHILDRENS MEDICAL CENTER HEALTH PLAN E- Very Weak

Major Rating Factors: Weak profitability index (0.9 on a scale of 0 to 10). Strong capitalization (7.1) based on excellent current risk-adjusted capital (severe loss scenario). High quality investment portfolio (9.9).
Other Rating Factors: Excellent liquidity (7.0) with sufficient resources (cash flows and marketable investments) to handle a spike in claims.
Principal Business: Medicaid (100%)
Mem Phys: 18: 7,614 **17:** 5,921 **18 MLR** 104.3% **/ 18 Admin Exp** N/A
Enroll(000): Q1 19: 9 **18:** 9 **17:** 10 **Med Exp PMPM:** $2,493
Principal Investments: Cash and equiv (100%)
Provider Compensation ($000): Contr fee ($263,896), capitation ($10,166)
Total Member Encounters: Phys (365,870), non-phys (55,665)
Group Affiliation: None
Licensed in: TX
Address: 1320 GREENWAY DR Ste 1000, IRVING, TX 75038
Phone: (214) 456-7000 **Dom State:** TX **Commenced Bus:** N/A

Data Date	Rating	RACR #1	RACR #2	Total Assets ($mil)	Capital ($mil)	Net Premium ($mil)	Net Income ($mil)
3-19	E-	1.42	1.18	89.4	47.0	67.9	7.6
3-18	E-	N/A	N/A	73.1	18.8	65.4	-11.3
2018	E-	1.21	1.01	101.0	40.7	264.6	-53.7
2017	E-	N/A	N/A	85.4	31.9	242.9	-69.7
2016	D+	1.16	0.97	31.7	3.9	38.2	-13.4
2015	N/A	N/A	N/A	4.5	3.7	N/A	-4.6
2014	N/A	N/A	N/A	4.8	3.3	N/A	-4.1

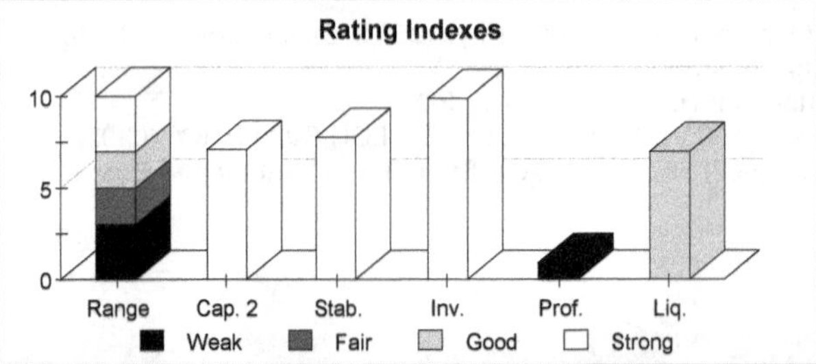

CHINESE COMMUNITY HEALTH PLAN E- Very Weak

Major Rating Factors: Weak profitability index (0.9 on a scale of 0 to 10). Poor capitalization index (0.0) based on weak current risk-adjusted capital (severe loss scenario). Weak overall results on stability tests (0.5).
Other Rating Factors: Excellent liquidity (7.1) with ample operational cash flow and liquid investments.
Principal Business: Medicare (38%)
Mem Phys: 18: N/A **17:** N/A **18 MLR** 89.5% **/ 18 Admin Exp** N/A
Enroll(000): Q1 19: 20 **18:** 20 **17:** 22 **Med Exp PMPM:** $1,941
Principal Investments ($000): Cash and equiv ($20,113)
Provider Compensation ($000): None
Total Member Encounters: N/A
Group Affiliation: Chinese Hospital Association
Licensed in: CA
Address: 445 Grant Avenue Suite 700, San Francisco, CA 94108
Phone: (415) 955-8800 **Dom State:** CA **Commenced Bus:** August 1987

Data Date	Rating	RACR #1	RACR #2	Total Assets ($mil)	Capital ($mil)	Net Premium ($mil)	Net Income ($mil)
3-19	E-	0.38	0.25	62.4	6.7	37.5	1.6
3-18	E	0.90	0.60	72.5	14.8	35.8	2.1
2018	E-	0.28	0.18	55.7	5.1	133.7	-5.5
2017	E	0.77	0.51	65.0	12.7	136.1	-20.1
2016	N/A	N/A	N/A	N/A	N/A	N/A	N/A
2015	B	2.69	1.78	92.1	41.9	155.4	4.7
2014	B	2.39	1.58	80.3	37.2	175.0	9.7

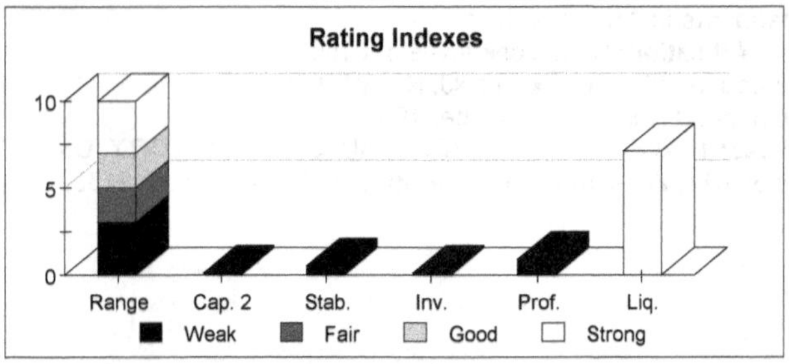

CHOICE PHYSICIANS NETWORK E Very Weak

Major Rating Factors: Poor capitalization index (0.0 on a scale of 0 to 10) based on weak current risk-adjusted capital (severe loss scenario). Fair profitability index (4.5). Fair overall results on stability tests (3.5).
Other Rating Factors: Good liquidity (6.9) with sufficient resources (cash flows and marketable investments) to handle a spike in claims.
Principal Business: Managed care (100%)
Mem Phys: 18: N/A **17:** N/A **18 MLR** 98.2% **/ 18 Admin Exp** N/A
Enroll(000): Q1 19: 15 **18:** 15 **17:** N/A **Med Exp PMPM:** $697
Principal Investments ($000): Cash and equiv ($19,458)
Provider Compensation ($000): None
Total Member Encounters: N/A
Group Affiliation: None
Licensed in: CA
Address: 18564 Hwy 18 Ste 105, Apple Valley, CA 92307
Phone: (626) 229-9828 **Dom State:** CA **Commenced Bus:** September 2009

Data Date	Rating	RACR #1	RACR #2	Total Assets ($mil)	Capital ($mil)	Net Premium ($mil)	Net Income ($mil)
3-19	E	0.41	0.25	28.8	5.7	33.2	2.5
3-18	U	34.68	21.70	18.7	1.3	30.2	-0.2
2018	E	0.22	0.13	25.4	3.2	130.6	1.7
2017	N/A	N/A	N/A	N/A	N/A	N/A	N/A
2016	E+	0.34	0.21	17.3	4.3	105.6	-0.5
2015	D-	0.38	0.23	12.0	3.4	78.5	0.0
2014	D	0.59	0.36	10.8	4.1	63.8	1.0

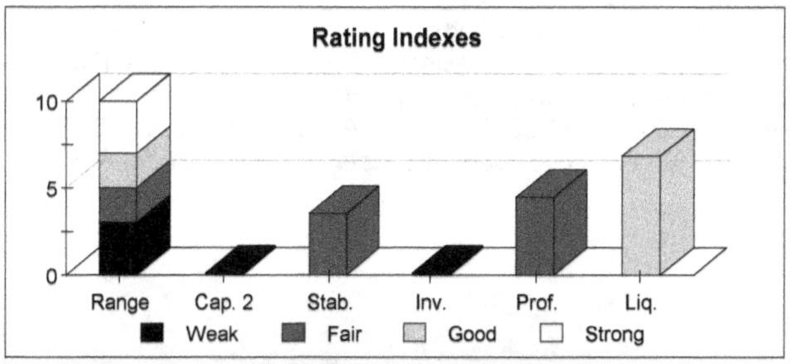

CHRISTIAN FIDELITY LIFE INSURANCE COMPANY * A- Excellent

Major Rating Factors: Good overall results on stability tests (6.5 on a scale of 0 to 10). Strengths that enhance stability include excellent operational trends and good risk diversification. Strong capitalization (9.3) based on excellent risk adjusted capital (severe loss scenario). Furthermore, this high level of risk adjusted capital has been consistently maintained over the last five years. High quality investment portfolio (7.9).
Other Rating Factors: Excellent profitability (7.8). Excellent liquidity (7.3).
Principal Business: Individual health insurance (87%), group health insurance (8%), and individual life insurance (5%).
Principal Investments: NonCMO investment grade bonds (88%), CMOs and structured securities (6%), mortgages in good standing (4%), cash (2%), and policy loans (1%).
Investments in Affiliates: None
Group Affiliation: Amerco Corp
Licensed in: AL, AZ, AR, CO, FL, GA, ID, IL, IN, KS, KY, LA, MS, MO, MT, NE, NV, NM, ND, OH, OK, OR, SC, SD, TN, TX, UT, VA, WA, WV, WY
Commenced Business: December 1935
Address: 1999 Bryan Street Suite 900, Dallas, TX 75201
Phone: (602) 263-6666 **Domicile State:** TX **NAIC Code:** 61859

Data Date	Rating	RACR #1	RACR #2	Total Assets ($mil)	Capital ($mil)	Net Premium ($mil)	Net Income ($mil)
3-19	A-	3.51	2.56	59.8	28.9	6.4	1.7
3-18	B+	3.05	2.23	61.6	28.2	7.3	1.6
2018	B+	3.28	2.39	58.2	27.2	26.9	8.7
2017	B	2.87	2.12	59.6	26.7	30.7	8.1
2016	B	2.75	2.03	63.9	28.0	34.5	8.1
2015	B	2.63	1.93	68.8	28.9	38.7	9.2
2014	B-	2.36	1.75	71.2	28.6	43.6	9.2

Adverse Trends in Operations

Decrease in asset base during 2018 (2%)
Decrease in premium volume from 2017 to 2018 (12%)
Decrease in premium volume from 2016 to 2017 (11%)
Decrease in premium volume from 2015 to 2016 (11%)
Decrease in premium volume from 2014 to 2015 (11%)

CHRISTUS HEALTH PLAN C- Fair

Major Rating Factors: Weak profitability index (1.7 on a scale of 0 to 10). Strong capitalization (8.3) based on excellent current risk-adjusted capital (severe loss scenario). High quality investment portfolio (8.4).
Other Rating Factors: Excellent liquidity (7.7) with ample operational cash flow and liquid investments.
Principal Business: Comp med (89%), Medicare (8%)
Mem Phys: 18: N/A **17:** N/A **18 MLR** 68.1% **/ 18 Admin Exp** N/A
Enroll(000): Q1 19: 32 **18:** 29 **17:** 34 **Med Exp PMPM:** $292
Principal Investments: Cash and equiv (100%)
Provider Compensation ($000): FFS ($117,713)
Total Member Encounters: Phys (309,816), non-phys (80,666)
Group Affiliation: None
Licensed in: NM, TX
Address: 919 Hidden Ridge Dr, Irving, TX 75038
Phone: (469) 282-2000 **Dom State:** TX **Commenced Bus:** N/A

Data Date	Rating	RACR #1	RACR #2	Total Assets ($mil)	Capital ($mil)	Net Premium ($mil)	Net Income ($mil)
3-19	C-	2.38	1.98	91.2	41.6	49.5	5.1
3-18	C-	1.31	1.09	66.5	21.6	41.3	1.9
2018	C-	2.06	1.72	84.3	36.5	168.5	16.8
2017	C-	1.19	0.99	51.6	19.7	135.9	-1.6
2016	C-	0.84	0.70	41.6	14.3	61.8	-11.4
2015	C-	1.44	1.20	10.7	7.6	21.2	-5.2
2014	C+	3.15	2.62	15.8	12.8	20.5	-2.8

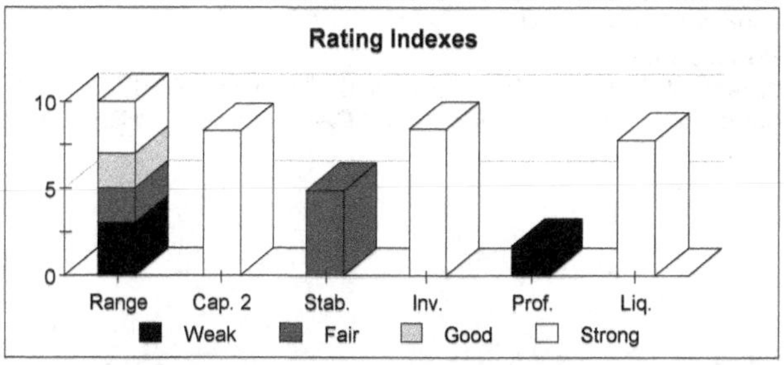

CIGNA HEALTH & LIFE INSURANCE COMPANY B Good

Major Rating Factors: Good overall results on stability tests (5.6 on a scale of 0 to 10). Stability strengths include excellent operational trends and excellent risk diversification. Good liquidity (6.0) with sufficient resources to handle a spike in claims. Fair quality investment portfolio (3.7).

Other Rating Factors: Strong capitalization (7.9) based on excellent risk adjusted capital (severe loss scenario). Excellent profitability (9.8).

Principal Business: Group health insurance (82%) and individual health insurance (18%).

Principal Investments: NonCMO investment grade bonds (55%), noninv. grade bonds (16%), mortgages in good standing (7%), common & preferred stock (5%), and CMOs and structured securities (2%).

Investments in Affiliates: 4%

Group Affiliation: CIGNA Corp

Licensed in: All states, the District of Columbia and Puerto Rico

Commenced Business: February 1964

Address: 900 COTTAGE GROVE ROAD, BLOOMFIELD, CT 6002

Phone: (860) 226-6000 **Domicile State:** CT **NAIC Code:** 67369

Data Date	Rating	RACR #1	RACR #2	Total Assets ($mil)	Capital ($mil)	Net Premium ($mil)	Net Income ($mil)
3-19	B	2.10	1.60	10,443.5	4,820.7	4,566.2	781.7
3-18	B	1.99	1.51	9,682.6	4,032.5	4,114.6	494.5
2018	B	2.09	1.59	10,489.2	4,801.1	16,629.8	2,197.3
2017	B	1.86	1.42	9,002.2	3,680.6	13,779.7	1,569.1
2016	B	1.86	1.43	7,410.9	3,390.1	11,625.2	1,396.6
2015	B	1.66	1.31	6,559.9	3,008.9	11,457.7	1,187.2
2014	B	1.89	1.48	6,204.5	2,799.7	9,789.3	1,047.0

Adverse Trends in Operations

Increase in policy surrenders from 2015 to 2016 (27%)

CIGNA HEALTHCARE OF ARIZONA INC C Fair

Major Rating Factors: Fair quality investment portfolio (3.8 on a scale of 0 to 10). Weak profitability index (1.9). Good overall results on stability tests (5.7). Rating is significantly influenced by the good financial results of Cigna Corporation.

Other Rating Factors: Good liquidity (6.1) with sufficient resources (cash flows and marketable investments) to handle a spike in claims. Strong capitalization index (8.1) based on excellent current risk-adjusted capital (severe loss scenario).

Principal Business: Medicare (97%), comp med (7%)

Mem Phys: 18: 28,338 **17:** 27,782 **18 MLR** 88.7% **/ 18 Admin Exp** N/A

Enroll(000): Q1 19: 55 **18:** 48 **17:** 48 **Med Exp PMPM:** $878

Principal Investments: Long-term bonds (95%), real estate (12%)

Provider Compensation ($000): Contr fee ($258,511), FFS ($109,258), salary ($58,760), capitation ($48,668), other ($24,874)

Total Member Encounters: Phys (254,652), non-phys (80,323)

Group Affiliation: Cigna Corporation

Licensed in: AZ

Address: 25500 NNORTERRA DR, PHOENIX, AZ 85085-8200

Phone: (860) 226-5076 **Dom State:** AZ **Commenced Bus:** N/A

Data Date	Rating	RACR #1	RACR #2	Total Assets ($mil)	Capital ($mil)	Net Premium ($mil)	Net Income ($mil)
3-19	C	2.27	1.89	145.9	73.8	162.2	3.7
3-18	C	1.80	1.50	178.5	48.1	144.9	-11.2
2018	C	2.28	1.90	131.1	74.3	571.2	11.3
2017	E-	1.41	1.18	121.9	60.4	444.4	-16.9
2016	E-	2.05	1.71	130.3	66.6	566.0	-36.2
2015	C	1.46	1.21	94.6	39.0	536.7	-19.7
2014	C	1.74	1.45	84.2	38.4	457.0	-16.9

Rating Indexes

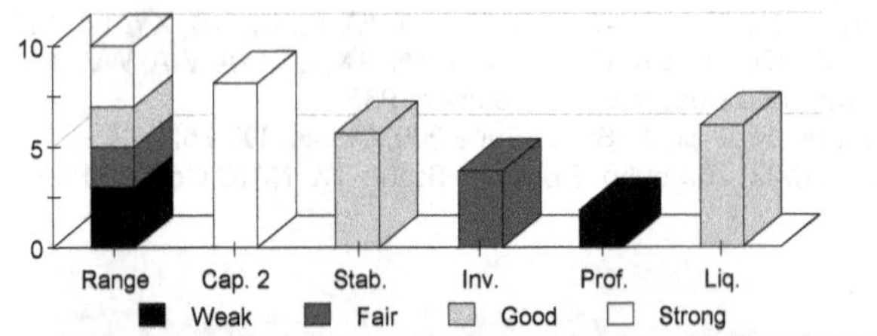

CIGNA HEALTHCARE OF CALIFORNIA INC C Fair

Major Rating Factors: Weak profitability index (0.9 on a scale of 0 to 10). Good overall results on stability tests (5.7). Rating is significantly influenced by the good financial results of CIGNA Corp. Good liquidity (6.9) with sufficient resources (cash flows and marketable investments) to handle a spike in claims.

Other Rating Factors: Strong capitalization index (7.2) based on good current risk-adjusted capital (moderate loss scenario).

Principal Business: Managed care (101%)

Mem Phys: 18: N/A **17:** N/A **18 MLR** 92.3% **/ 18 Admin Exp** N/A

Enroll(000): Q1 19: 154 **18:** 151 **17:** 176 **Med Exp PMPM:** $1,838

Principal Investments ($000): Cash and equiv ($81,326)

Provider Compensation ($000): None

Total Member Encounters: N/A

Group Affiliation: CIGNA Corp

Licensed in: CA

Address: 400 N Brand Blvd Suite #400, Glendale, CA 91203

Phone: (818) 500-6276 **Dom State:** CA **Commenced Bus:** November 1978

Data Date	Rating	RACR #1	RACR #2	Total Assets ($mil)	Capital ($mil)	Net Premium ($mil)	Net Income ($mil)
3-19	C	1.26	0.78	136.0	48.5	236.9	0.5
3-18	C	1.05	0.65	124.4	40.3	212.6	-4.9
2018	C	1.07	0.66	132.9	40.5	887.5	-14.6
2017	C	0.96	0.59	136.8	36.3	982.4	-20.4
2016	C	1.25	0.77	148.9	40.0	915.6	-16.5
2015	C	1.18	0.72	134.5	37.0	950.8	-18.6
2014	B	1.48	0.91	158.5	51.3	959.4	0.9

Rating Indexes

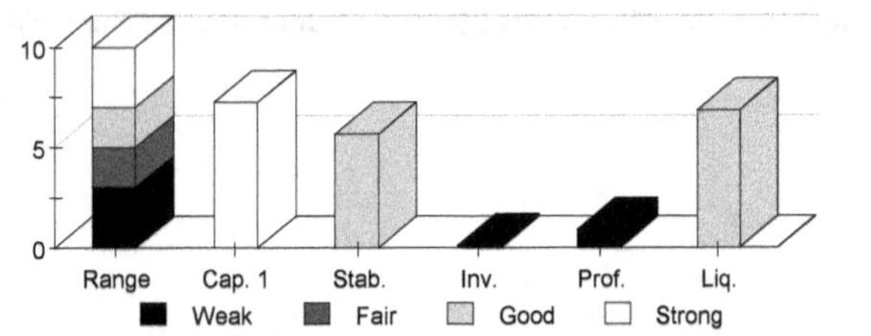

CIGNA HEALTHCARE OF COLORADO INC — C — Fair

Major Rating Factors: Fair overall results on stability tests (3.5 on a scale of 0 to 10) based on a significant 73% decrease in enrollment during the period, a steep decline in premium revenue in 2018. Rating is significantly influenced by the good financial results of Cigna Corporation. Weak profitability index (1.6). Strong capitalization index (10.0) based on excellent current risk-adjusted capital (severe loss scenario).
Other Rating Factors: High quality investment portfolio (9.9). Excellent liquidity (7.1) with ample operational cash flow and liquid investments.
Principal Business: Comp med (100%)
Mem Phys: 18: 17,257 **17:** 16,919 **18 MLR** 106.7% **/ 18 Admin Exp** N/A
Enroll(000): Q1 19: 0 **18:** 0 **17:** 1 **Med Exp PMPM:** $497
Principal Investments: Long-term bonds (63%), cash and equiv (37%)
Provider Compensation ($000): Contr fee ($2,449), FFS ($580), capitation ($98)
Total Member Encounters: Phys (2,060), non-phys (932)
Group Affiliation: Cigna Corporation
Licensed in: CO
Address: 3900 EAST MEXICO AVENUE SUITE, DENVER, CO 80210
Phone: (860) 226-6000 **Dom State:** CO **Commenced Bus:** N/A

Data Date	Rating	RACR #1	RACR #2	Total Assets ($mil)	Capital ($mil)	Net Premium ($mil)	Net Income ($mil)
3-19	C	6.30	5.25	3.3	3.1	0.3	-0.1
3-18	C	7.27	6.06	4.0	3.3	1.1	-0.3
2018	C	6.42	5.35	3.4	3.2	2.6	-0.5
2017	C	3.85	3.21	4.4	3.6	5.1	1.6
2016	C	3.99	3.32	4.3	2.0	4.8	-1.2
2015	C	3.88	3.24	4.1	2.3	7.1	-0.9
2014	C	6.00	5.00	4.8	3.2	7.6	0.2

Rating Indexes

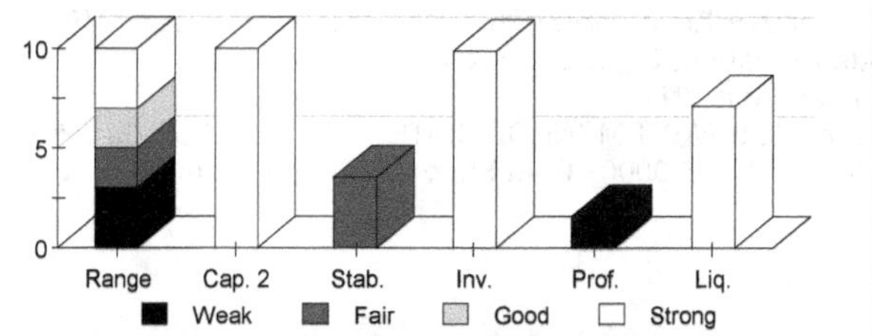

CIGNA HEALTHCARE OF FLORIDA INC — C — Fair

Major Rating Factors: Fair overall results on stability tests (4.8 on a scale of 0 to 10) based on a steep decline in premium revenue in 2018, a significant 16% decrease in enrollment during the period. Rating is significantly influenced by the good financial results of Cigna Corporation. Weak profitability index (1.9). Strong capitalization index (10.0) based on excellent current risk-adjusted capital (severe loss scenario).
Other Rating Factors: High quality investment portfolio (9.9). Excellent liquidity (7.1) with ample operational cash flow and liquid investments.
Principal Business: Comp med (100%)
Mem Phys: 18: 122,112 **17:** 119,718 **18 MLR** 97.4% **/ 18 Admin Exp** N/A
Enroll(000): Q1 19: 0 **18:** 0 **17:** 0 **Med Exp PMPM:** $414
Principal Investments: Long-term bonds (87%), cash and equiv (13%)
Provider Compensation ($000): Contr fee ($774), FFS ($193), capitation ($72)
Total Member Encounters: Phys (1,125), non-phys (280)
Group Affiliation: Cigna Corporation
Licensed in: FL
Address: 2701 NORTH ROCKY POINT DRIVE S, TAMPA, FL 33607
Phone: (860) 226-6000 **Dom State:** FL **Commenced Bus:** N/A

Data Date	Rating	RACR #1	RACR #2	Total Assets ($mil)	Capital ($mil)	Net Premium ($mil)	Net Income ($mil)
3-19	C	4.60	3.83	3.0	2.6	0.3	-0.1
3-18	C	5.17	4.31	3.2	2.8	0.2	0.0
2018	C	5.05	4.21	3.2	2.9	1.1	0.0
2017	C	2.54	2.12	3.3	2.9	1.5	0.1
2016	C	6.97	5.81	4.2	3.8	1.0	-0.1
2015	C	7.23	6.03	4.3	3.9	1.3	-0.1
2014	C	7.85	6.54	4.4	4.0	1.3	-0.2

Rating Indexes

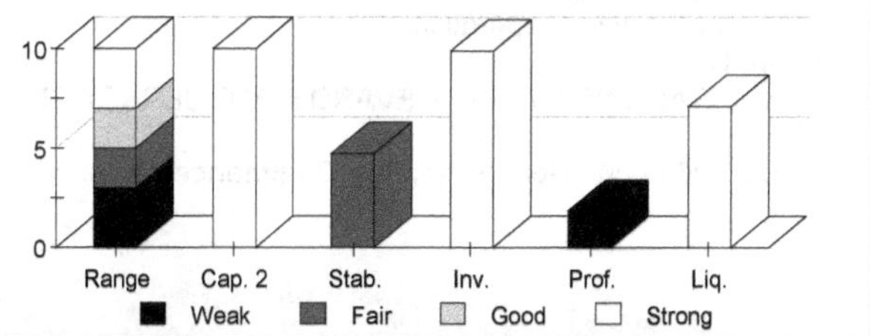

CIGNA HEALTHCARE OF GEORGIA INC — C — Fair

Major Rating Factors: Fair overall results on stability tests (3.5 on a scale of 0 to 10). Rating is significantly influenced by the good financial results of Cigna Corporation. Weak profitability index (1.7). Good quality investment portfolio (5.9).
Other Rating Factors: Good liquidity (6.2) with sufficient resources (cash flows and marketable investments) to handle a spike in claims. Strong capitalization index (8.5) based on excellent current risk-adjusted capital (severe loss scenario).
Principal Business: Medicare (99%), comp med (1%)
Mem Phys: 18: 49,702 **17:** 52,459 **18 MLR** 85.8% **/ 18 Admin Exp** N/A
Enroll(000): Q1 19: 21 **18:** 24 **17:** 26 **Med Exp PMPM:** $750
Principal Investments: Long-term bonds (95%), cash and equiv (5%)
Provider Compensation ($000): FFS ($213,524), capitation ($10,818)
Total Member Encounters: Phys (534,705), non-phys (157,407)
Group Affiliation: Cigna Corporation
Licensed in: GA
Address: TWO SECURITIES CENTRE 3500 PIE, ATLANTA, GA 30305
Phone: (404) 443-8800 **Dom State:** GA **Commenced Bus:** N/A

Data Date	Rating	RACR #1	RACR #2	Total Assets ($mil)	Capital ($mil)	Net Premium ($mil)	Net Income ($mil)
3-19	C	2.58	2.15	79.0	42.5	62.0	-1.1
3-18	C	2.57	2.14	118.6	45.8	66.9	2.2
2018	C	2.63	2.20	79.8	43.5	254.0	1.7
2017	E	1.49	1.24	93.9	43.7	269.6	-11.2
2016	E	1.85	1.54	111.7	54.5	383.6	-17.8
2015	E	1.50	1.25	78.8	20.8	173.7	-24.5
2014	E	2.70	2.25	13.2	3.8	12.5	-7.4

Rating Indexes

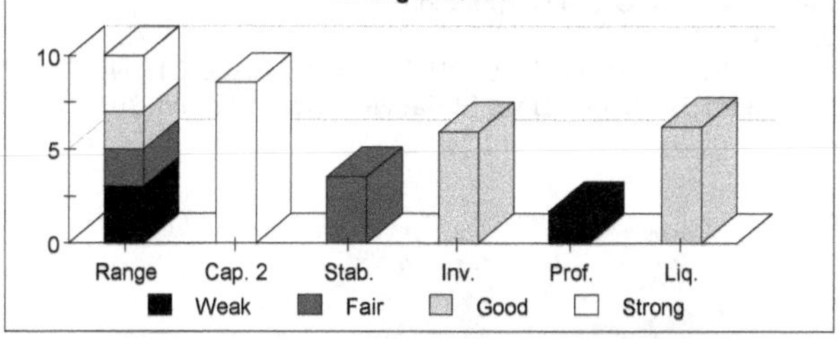

CIGNA HEALTHCARE OF ILLINOIS INC — C — Fair

Major Rating Factors: Fair overall results on stability tests (4.2 on a scale of 0 to 10) in spite of healthy premium and capital growth during 2018. Rating is significantly influenced by the good financial results of Cigna Corporation. Weak profitability index (0.9). Strong capitalization index (10.0) based on excellent current risk-adjusted capital (severe loss scenario).
Other Rating Factors: High quality investment portfolio (9.9). Excellent liquidity (6.9) with sufficient resources (cash flows and marketable investments) to handle a spike in claims.
Principal Business: Comp med (100%)
Mem Phys: 18: 61,398 **17:** 60,194 **18 MLR** 60.8% **/ 18 Admin Exp** N/A
Enroll(000): Q1 19: 18 **18:** 22 **17:** 21 **Med Exp PMPM:** $172
Principal Investments: Long-term bonds (88%), cash and equiv (12%)
Provider Compensation ($000): Contr fee ($39,098), FFS ($9,706), capitation ($87)
Total Member Encounters: Phys (101,704), non-phys (21,949)
Group Affiliation: Cigna Corporation
Licensed in: IL, IN
Address: 525 WEST MONROE SUITE 1650, CHICAGO, IL 60661
Phone: (860) 226-6000 **Dom State:** IL **Commenced Bus:** N/A

Data Date	Rating	RACR #1	RACR #2	Total Assets ($mil)	Capital ($mil)	Net Premium ($mil)	Net Income ($mil)
3-19	C	4.38	3.65	102.0	18.8	17.1	-0.4
3-18	C	3.43	2.86	102.0	12.8	21.1	1.3
2018	C	4.56	3.80	87.9	19.6	81.0	8.7
2017	C-	1.84	1.53	85.4	12.2	46.3	-10.9
2016	C	8.71	7.26	12.1	5.3	0.5	-4.1
2015	C	7.36	6.13	4.3	4.1	0.9	0.2
2014	C	7.07	5.89	4.1	3.9	1.1	-0.1

Rating Indexes

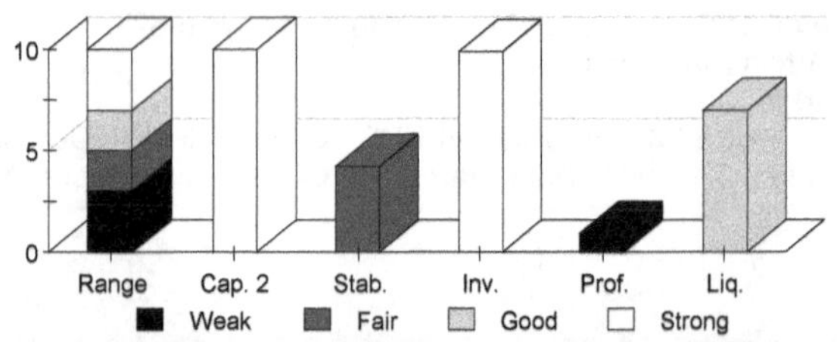

CIGNA HEALTHCARE OF NEW JERSEY INC — E — Very Weak

Major Rating Factors: Weak profitability index (0.0 on a scale of 0 to 10). Fair overall results on stability tests (4.8) based on a significant 36% decrease in enrollment during the period. Rating is significantly influenced by the good financial results of Cigna Corporation. Strong capitalization index (10.0) based on excellent current risk-adjusted capital (severe loss scenario).
Other Rating Factors: High quality investment portfolio (9.9). Excellent liquidity (7.6) with ample operational cash flow and liquid investments.
Principal Business: Comp med (100%)
Mem Phys: 18: 30,756 **17:** 30,153 **18 MLR** 220.3% **/ 18 Admin Exp** N/A
Enroll(000): Q1 19: 0 **18:** 0 **17:** 0 **Med Exp PMPM:** $6,847
Principal Investments: Cash and equiv (79%), long-term bonds (21%)
Provider Compensation ($000): Contr fee ($10,183), FFS ($324), capitation ($48)
Total Member Encounters: N/A
Group Affiliation: Cigna Corporation
Licensed in: NJ
Address: 499 WASHINGTON BOULEVARD 5TH F, JERSEY CITY, NJ 07310-1608
Phone: (860) 226-6000 **Dom State:** NJ **Commenced Bus:** N/A

Data Date	Rating	RACR #1	RACR #2	Total Assets ($mil)	Capital ($mil)	Net Premium ($mil)	Net Income ($mil)
3-19	E	13.32	11.10	13.5	11.5	0.1	1.4
3-18	E	N/A	N/A	5.6	4.0	0.5	2.1
2018	E	11.71	9.76	13.9	10.0	4.8	-0.8
2017	E	N/A	N/A	7.5	2.1	4.4	-3.4
2016	E	12.91	10.76	10.3	7.2	3.9	1.4
2015	C	5.19	4.33	5.2	2.9	1.6	-2.7
2014	C	8.10	6.75	5.3	4.6	1.3	-0.5

Rating Indexes

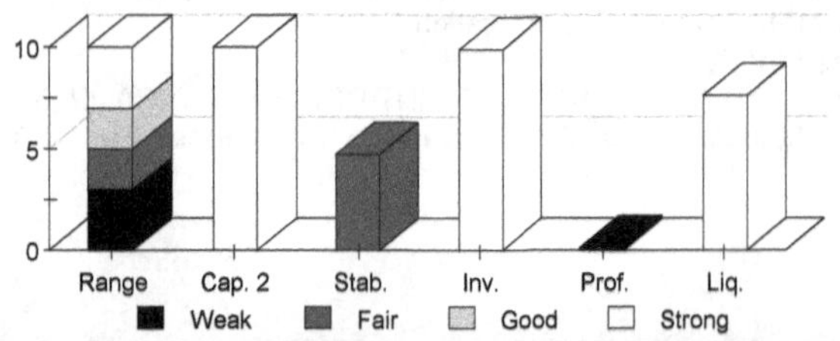

CIGNA HEALTHCARE OF NORTH CAROLINA — D — Weak

Major Rating Factors: Good overall profitability index (6.9 on a scale of 0 to 10). Strong capitalization index (10.0) based on excellent current risk-adjusted capital (severe loss scenario). High quality investment portfolio (7.5).
Other Rating Factors: Excellent overall results on stability tests (6.9) despite a decline in enrollment during 2018. Rating is significantly influenced by the good financial results of Cigna Corporation. Excellent liquidity (6.9) with sufficient resources (cash flows and marketable investments) to handle a spike in claims.
Principal Business: Comp med (63%), Medicare (37%)
Mem Phys: 18: 72,328 **17:** 71,012 **18 MLR** 68.1% **/ 18 Admin Exp** N/A
Enroll(000): Q1 19: 12 **18:** 21 **17:** 25 **Med Exp PMPM:** $428
Principal Investments: Long-term bonds (92%), cash and equiv (8%)
Provider Compensation ($000): FFS ($114,795), capitation ($2,144)
Total Member Encounters: Phys (224,150), non-phys (79,825)
Group Affiliation: Cigna Corporation
Licensed in: NC
Address: 701 CORPORATE CENTER DRIVE, RALEIGH, NC 27607
Phone: (860) 226-6000 **Dom State:** NC **Commenced Bus:** N/A

Data Date	Rating	RACR #1	RACR #2	Total Assets ($mil)	Capital ($mil)	Net Premium ($mil)	Net Income ($mil)
3-19	D	3.74	3.12	76.5	37.8	28.0	1.9
3-18	D	1.63	1.36	114.4	13.6	34.0	-7.4
2018	D	3.66	3.05	82.9	37.0	170.7	15.6
2017	C	1.46	1.22	95.2	21.5	149.9	7.8
2016	C	1.86	1.55	27.2	13.5	88.9	-4.2
2015	C	1.31	1.09	18.2	7.7	74.9	0.6
2014	C	2.99	2.49	14.0	5.7	23.0	-4.5

Rating Indexes

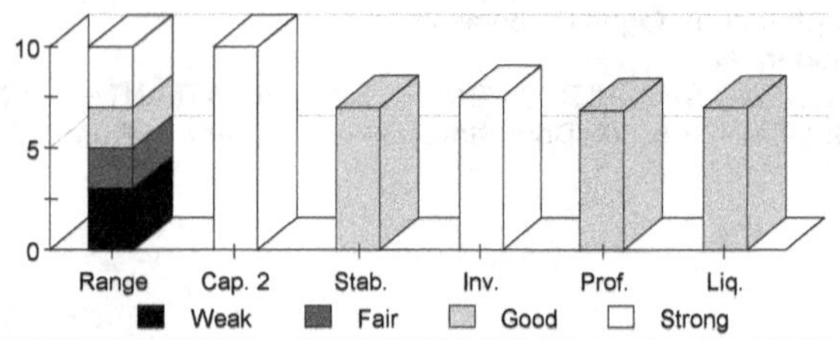

CIGNA HEALTHCARE OF SOUTH CAROLINA C Fair

Major Rating Factors: Weak profitability index (2.1 on a scale of 0 to 10). Good overall results on stability tests (5.5). Rating is significantly influenced by the good financial results of Cigna Corporation. Good liquidity (6.8) with sufficient resources (cash flows and marketable investments) to handle a spike in claims.
Other Rating Factors: Strong capitalization index (10.0) based on excellent current risk-adjusted capital (severe loss scenario). High quality investment portfolio (7.3).
Principal Business: Medicare (100%)
Mem Phys: 18: 20,477 **17:** 18,947 **18 MLR** 78.9% **/ 18 Admin Exp** N/A
Enroll(000): Q1 19: 5 **18:** 5 **17:** 6 **Med Exp PMPM:** $674
Principal Investments: Long-term bonds (95%), cash and equiv (5%)
Provider Compensation ($000): FFS ($44,822), capitation ($599), contr fee ($25)
Total Member Encounters: Phys (103,857), non-phys (34,371)
Group Affiliation: Cigna Corporation
Licensed in: SC
Address: 4000 FABER PLACE DRIVE SUITE #, GREENVILLE, SC 29601
Phone: (860) 226-6000 **Dom State:** SC **Commenced Bus:** N/A

Data Date	Rating	RACR #1	RACR #2	Total Assets ($mil)	Capital ($mil)	Net Premium ($mil)	Net Income ($mil)
3-19	C	4.94	4.11	28.8	21.6	12.4	1.7
3-18	C	3.87	3.23	34.5	18.1	14.9	0.3
2018	C	4.57	3.81	27.7	19.9	56.1	2.0
2017	D-	2.18	1.81	28.1	17.9	62.3	2.1
2016	D-	2.09	1.74	29.6	15.7	95.4	-2.4
2015	D+	1.07	0.89	16.2	6.6	80.2	-1.2
2014	D+	1.26	1.05	13.1	6.1	55.3	-2.2

Rating Indexes

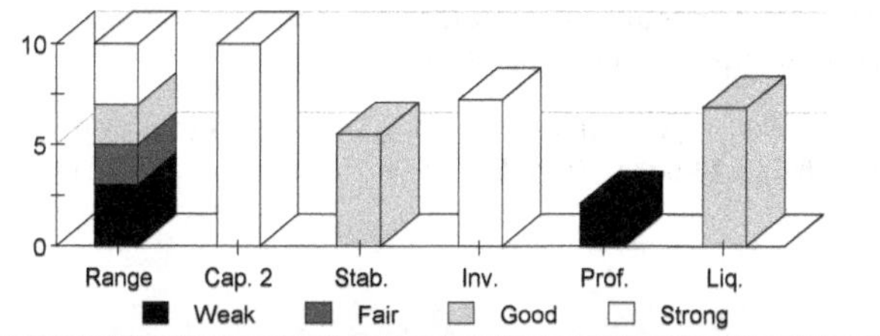

CIGNA HEALTHCARE OF ST LOUIS C Fair

Major Rating Factors: Fair profitability index (3.0 on a scale of 0 to 10). Fair overall results on stability tests (4.8). Rating is significantly influenced by the good financial results of Cigna Corporation. Strong capitalization index (10.0) based on excellent current risk-adjusted capital (severe loss scenario).
Other Rating Factors: High quality investment portfolio (9.3). Excellent liquidity (7.1) with ample operational cash flow and liquid investments.
Principal Business: Medicare (70%), comp med (30%)
Mem Phys: 18: 60,253 **17:** 59,076 **18 MLR** 75.6% **/ 18 Admin Exp** N/A
Enroll(000): Q1 19: 2 **18:** 2 **17:** 2 **Med Exp PMPM:** $544
Principal Investments: Long-term bonds (80%), cash and equiv (20%)
Provider Compensation ($000): FFS ($10,400), contr fee ($3,637), capitation ($684)
Total Member Encounters: Phys (28,438), non-phys (8,532)
Group Affiliation: Cigna Corporation
Licensed in: IL, KS, MO
Address: 231 S BEMISTON, CLAYTON, MO 63105
Phone: (860) 226-6000 **Dom State:** MO **Commenced Bus:** N/A

Data Date	Rating	RACR #1	RACR #2	Total Assets ($mil)	Capital ($mil)	Net Premium ($mil)	Net Income ($mil)
3-19	C	5.19	4.33	14.3	9.5	3.5	0.3
3-18	C	4.34	3.62	14.5	7.3	5.0	-0.3
2018	C	5.06	4.22	14.5	9.2	19.8	1.6
2017	D+	2.40	2.00	13.1	7.6	17.8	0.4
2016	D+	2.68	2.23	14.4	7.3	22.2	-1.4
2015	D+	15.69	13.07	13.3	8.9	6.3	0.0
2014	D+	2.58	2.15	6.4	2.1	5.2	-1.7

Rating Indexes

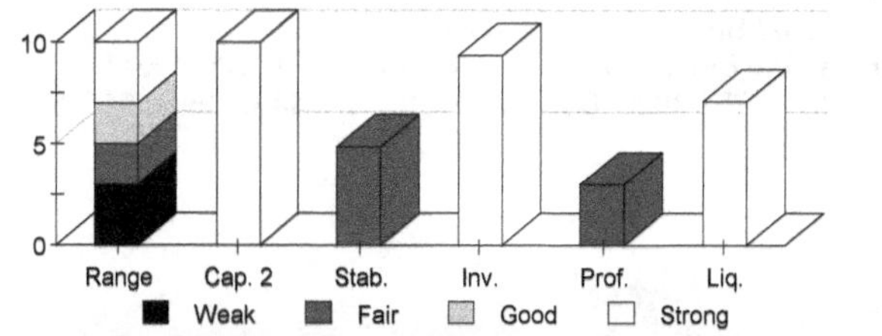

CIGNA HEALTHCARE OF TENNESSEE INC C- Fair

Major Rating Factors: Weak profitability index (1.4 on a scale of 0 to 10). Good overall results on stability tests (5.6). Rating is significantly influenced by the good financial results of Cigna Corporation. Good liquidity (6.9) with sufficient resources (cash flows and marketable investments) to handle a spike in claims.
Other Rating Factors: Strong capitalization index (9.5) based on excellent current risk-adjusted capital (severe loss scenario). High quality investment portfolio (9.9).
Principal Business: Comp med (100%)
Mem Phys: 18: 73,357 **17:** 71,919 **18 MLR** 79.4% **/ 18 Admin Exp** N/A
Enroll(000): Q1 19: 4 **18:** 4 **17:** 5 **Med Exp PMPM:** $334
Principal Investments: Long-term bonds (85%), cash and equiv (15%)
Provider Compensation ($000): Contr fee ($9,984), FFS ($4,926), capitation ($1,597)
Total Member Encounters: Phys (15,032), non-phys (5,067)
Group Affiliation: Cigna Corporation
Licensed in: MS, TN
Address: 1000 CORPORATE CENTRE DRIVE, FRANKLIN, TN 37067
Phone: (860) 226-5634 **Dom State:** TN **Commenced Bus:** N/A

Data Date	Rating	RACR #1	RACR #2	Total Assets ($mil)	Capital ($mil)	Net Premium ($mil)	Net Income ($mil)
3-19	C-	3.33	2.77	8.5	6.1	5.1	0.8
3-18	C-	2.19	1.83	8.2	3.5	5.1	-1.1
2018	C-	3.15	2.62	8.7	5.7	21.3	-1.2
2017	C-	1.44	1.20	8.9	4.8	22.0	-1.1
2016	C	3.22	2.69	7.0	4.0	16.5	-1.2
2015	C	3.52	2.94	7.8	4.6	19.0	0.2
2014	C	4.30	3.59	8.7	5.2	17.7	-1.4

Rating Indexes

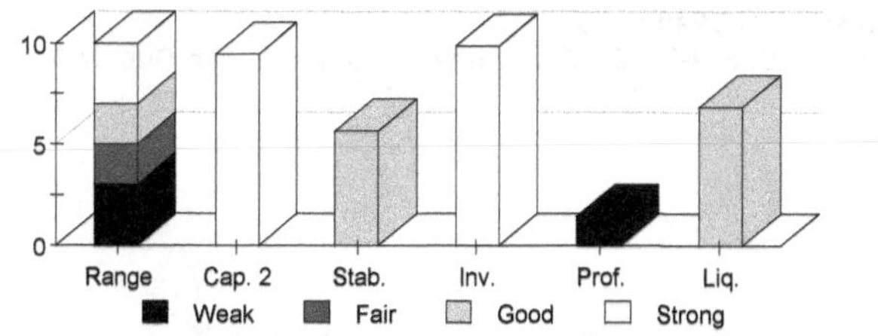

CIGNA HEALTHCARE OF TEXAS INC C- Fair

Major Rating Factors: Weak profitability index (2.6 on a scale of 0 to 10). Good overall results on stability tests (5.1) despite a decline in enrollment during 2018. Rating is significantly influenced by the good financial results of Cigna Corporation. Strong capitalization index (10.0) based on excellent current risk-adjusted capital (severe loss scenario).
Other Rating Factors: High quality investment portfolio (8.9). Excellent liquidity (7.0) with sufficient resources (cash flows and marketable investments) to handle a spike in claims.
Principal Business: Comp med (100%)
Mem Phys: 18: 159,775 **17:** 156,642 **18 MLR** 82.0% **/ 18 Admin Exp** N/A
Enroll(000): Q1 19: 8 **18:** 9 **17:** 10 **Med Exp PMPM:** $588
Principal Investments: Long-term bonds (75%), cash and equiv (25%)
Provider Compensation ($000): Contr fee ($41,723), FFS ($12,735), capitation ($10,446)
Total Member Encounters: Phys (24,681), non-phys (6,165)
Group Affiliation: Cigna Corporation
Licensed in: TX
Address: 6600 EAST CAMPUS CIRCLE DRIVE, PLANO, TX 75029
Phone: (860) 226-5634 **Dom State:** TX **Commenced Bus:** N/A

Data Date	Rating	RACR #1	RACR #2	Total Assets ($mil)	Capital ($mil)	Net Premium ($mil)	Net Income ($mil)
3-19	C-	5.83	4.86	34.1	25.1	16.8	2.0
3-18	C-	N/A	N/A	33.8	20.3	20.0	-0.7
2018	C-	5.44	4.53	32.7	23.2	76.4	1.9
2017	C-	N/A	N/A	32.7	20.6	79.9	0.2
2016	C-	2.39	1.99	37.6	15.6	110.8	-7.5
2015	B	3.26	2.72	27.0	15.4	83.1	-0.6
2014	B-	3.15	2.62	25.2	15.6	90.2	0.9

Rating Indexes

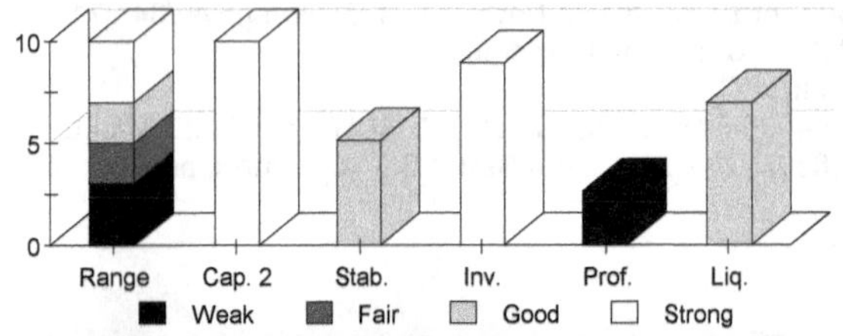

CIGNA LIFE INSURANCE COMPANY OF NEW YORK * A- Excellent

Major Rating Factors: Good quality investment portfolio (5.6 on a scale of 0 to 10) despite mixed results such as: large holdings of BBB rated bonds but moderate junk bond exposure. Good liquidity (6.8) with sufficient resources to handle a spike in claims. Excellent overall results on stability tests (7.0) excellent operational trends and excellent risk diversification.
Other Rating Factors: Strong capitalization (8.0) based on excellent risk adjusted capital (severe loss scenario). Excellent profitability (7.9).
Principal Business: Group health insurance (72%) and group life insurance (28%).
Principal Investments: NonCMO investment grade bonds (87%), noninv. grade bonds (10%), and CMOs and structured securities (3%).
Investments in Affiliates: None
Group Affiliation: CIGNA Corp
Licensed in: AL, DC, MO, NY, PA, TN
Commenced Business: December 1965
Address: 140 EAST 45TH STREET, NEW YORK, NY 10017
Phone: (215) 761-1000 **Domicile State:** NY **NAIC Code:** 64548

Data Date	Rating	RACR #1	RACR #2	Total Assets ($mil)	Capital ($mil)	Net Premium ($mil)	Net Income ($mil)
3-19	A-	2.56	1.69	419.6	111.7	55.3	0.3
3-18	A-	2.98	1.94	415.3	120.4	50.6	7.5
2018	A-	2.49	1.65	408.7	108.8	202.0	17.8
2017	A-	2.71	1.77	403.7	109.0	178.7	22.9
2016	A-	2.41	1.58	383.4	92.0	164.4	5.1
2015	A-	2.69	1.78	364.4	97.4	150.3	18.9
2014	A-	3.25	2.08	368.1	102.8	128.0	24.7

Adverse Trends in Operations

Decrease in capital during 2016 (5%)
Decrease in asset base during 2015 (1%)
Decrease in capital during 2015 (5%)

CLAREMONT BEHAVIORAL SVCS C- Fair

Major Rating Factors: Fair overall results on stability tests (4.4 on a scale of 0 to 10) based on poor risk diversification due to the company's size. Excellent profitability (8.6). Strong capitalization index (8.1) based on excellent current risk-adjusted capital (severe loss scenario).
Other Rating Factors: Excellent liquidity (7.4) with ample operational cash flow and liquid investments.
Principal Business: Managed care (93%), indemnity (7%)
Mem Phys: 18: N/A **17:** N/A **18 MLR** 32.9% **/ 18 Admin Exp** N/A
Enroll(000): Q1 19: 129 **18:** 129 **17:** N/A **Med Exp PMPM:** $12
Principal Investments ($000): Cash and equiv ($314)
Provider Compensation ($000): None
Total Member Encounters: N/A
Group Affiliation: Claremont Behavioral Services Inc
Licensed in: (No states)
Address: , , CA 94501-1075
Phone: (800) 834-3773 **Dom State:** **Commenced Bus:** N/A

Data Date	Rating	RACR #1	RACR #2	Total Assets ($mil)	Capital ($mil)	Net Premium ($mil)	Net Income ($mil)
3-19	C-	2.30	1.86	1.6	1.2	1.3	0.0
3-18	N/A	N/A	N/A	N/A	N/A	N/A	N/A
2018	C-	1.80	1.46	1.2	1.0	5.1	0.2
2017	N/A	N/A	N/A	N/A	N/A	N/A	N/A
2016	N/A	N/A	N/A	N/A	N/A	N/A	N/A
2015	N/A	N/A	N/A	N/A	N/A	N/A	N/A
2014	N/A	N/A	N/A	N/A	N/A	N/A	N/A

Rating Indexes

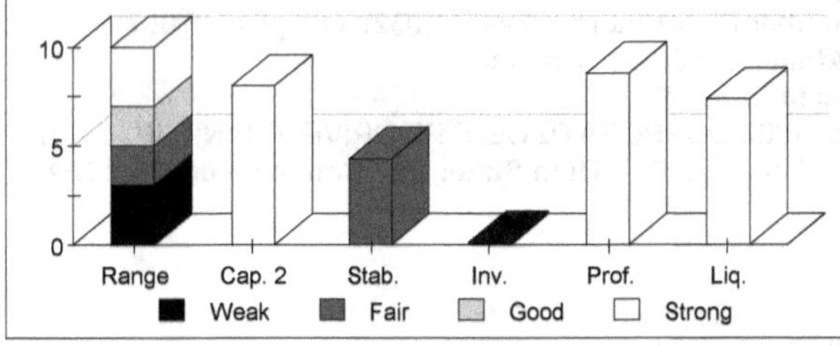

CLOVER INSURANCE COMPANY C Fair

Major Rating Factors: Weak profitability index (0.7 on a scale of 0 to 10). Poor capitalization (1.4) based on weak current risk-adjusted capital (moderate loss scenario). Weak liquidity (2.1) as a spike in claims may stretch capacity.
Other Rating Factors: High quality investment portfolio (9.9).
Principal Business: Medicare (100%)
Mem Phys: 18: 21,399 **17:** 8,979 **18 MLR** 116.6% **/ 18 Admin Exp** N/A
Enroll(000): Q1 19: 38 **18:** 32 **17:** 28 **Med Exp PMPM:** $895
Principal Investments: Cash and equiv (78%), long-term bonds (22%)
Provider Compensation ($000): Contr fee ($330,714)
Total Member Encounters: Phys (1,595,315), non-phys (92,003)
Group Affiliation: Clover Health Investments Corp
Licensed in: All states except MI, NH, NY, NC, VT, PR
Address: Harborside Plaza Ten 3 2nd St, Jersey City, NJ 7302
Phone: (201) 432-2133 **Dom State:** NJ **Commenced Bus:** N/A

Data Date	Rating	RACR #1	RACR #2	Total Assets ($mil)	Capital ($mil)	Net Premium ($mil)	Net Income ($mil)
3-19	C	0.44	0.37	115.3	34.0	110.2	-8.8
3-18	C+	N/A	N/A	116.0	30.1	89.2	-14.7
2018	C	0.46	0.38	107.7	35.1	290.1	-40.9
2017	C+	N/A	N/A	97.6	48.4	267.2	-21.5
2016	B-	6.41	5.34	189.0	67.9	46.0	-34.6
2015	N/A	N/A	N/A	35.5	10.2	52.5	N/A
2014	N/A	N/A	N/A	13.1	5.1	24.8	N/A

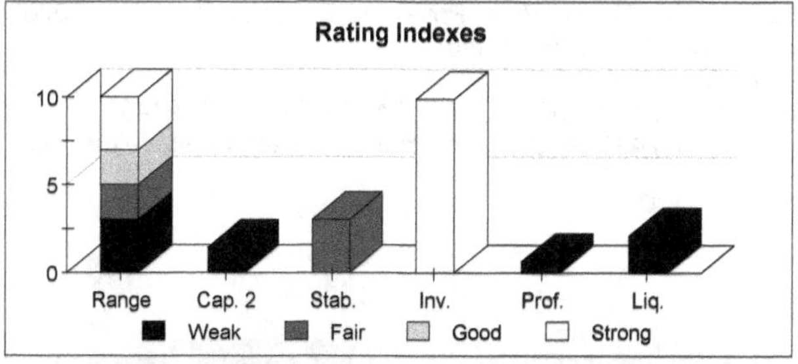

CMNTY CARE HLTH PLAN INC (WI) B- Good

Major Rating Factors: Fair profitability index (4.0 on a scale of 0 to 10). Strong capitalization (7.1) based on excellent current risk-adjusted capital (severe loss scenario). High quality investment portfolio (9.9).
Other Rating Factors: Excellent liquidity (7.0) with sufficient resources (cash flows and marketable investments) to handle a spike in claims.
Principal Business: Medicaid (62%), Medicare (38%)
Mem Phys: 18: N/A **17:** 14,992 **18 MLR** 90.6% **/ 18 Admin Exp** N/A
Enroll(000): Q1 19: 2 **18:** 2 **17:** 2 **Med Exp PMPM:** $3,221
Principal Investments: Cash and equiv (58%), long-term bonds (42%)
Provider Compensation ($000): Contr fee ($59,059), salary ($20,550)
Total Member Encounters: Phys (26,984), non-phys (49,457)
Group Affiliation: Community Care Inc
Licensed in: WI
Address: 205 Bishops Way, Brookfield, WI 53005
Phone: (414) 385-6600 **Dom State:** WI **Commenced Bus:** N/A

Data Date	Rating	RACR #1	RACR #2	Total Assets ($mil)	Capital ($mil)	Net Premium ($mil)	Net Income ($mil)
3-19	B-	1.44	1.20	22.8	14.6	22.0	0.0
3-18	C+	1.49	1.24	25.1	14.4	23.3	1.1
2018	B-	1.45	1.21	23.1	14.7	94.8	1.5
2017	C+	1.36	1.14	21.3	13.2	91.9	1.1
2016	C	1.31	1.09	20.3	12.5	94.6	3.2
2015	C-	0.87	0.73	16.8	8.8	96.2	-1.1
2014	C-	1.06	0.89	17.5	10.1	92.2	-5.6

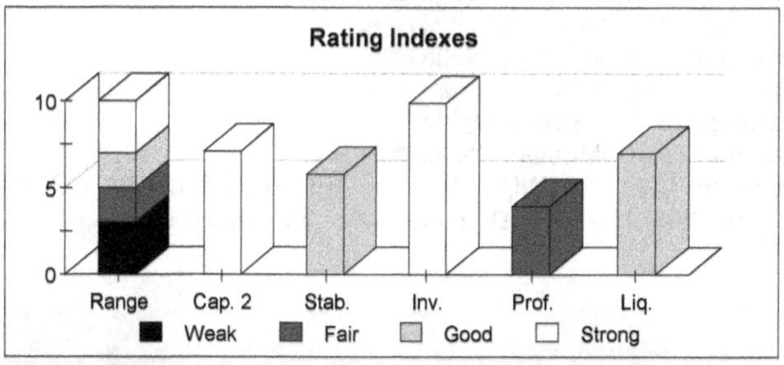

CMNTY CARE HLTH PLAN OF LA INC B- Good

Major Rating Factors: Fair quality investment portfolio (3.8 on a scale of 0 to 10). Strong capitalization (8.7) based on excellent current risk-adjusted capital (severe loss scenario). Excellent liquidity (7.0) with sufficient resources (cash flows and marketable investments) to handle a spike in claims.
Other Rating Factors: Weak profitability index (2.7).
Principal Business: Medicaid (96%), comp med (4%)
Mem Phys: 18: 18,617 **17:** 17,258 **18 MLR** 84.7% **/ 18 Admin Exp** N/A
Enroll(000): Q1 19: 277 **18:** 268 **17:** 246 **Med Exp PMPM:** $339
Principal Investments: Long-term bonds (67%), cash and equiv (32%), other (1%)
Provider Compensation ($000): Bonus arrang ($415,163), contr fee ($394,599), FFS ($134,053), capitation ($10,791)
Total Member Encounters: Phys (1,356,611), non-phys (2,006,269)
Group Affiliation: Anthem Inc
Licensed in: LA
Address: 3850 N CAUSEWAY BLVD Ste 600, METAIRIE, LA 70002
Phone: (757) 490-6900 **Dom State:** LA **Commenced Bus:** N/A

Data Date	Rating	RACR #1	RACR #2	Total Assets ($mil)	Capital ($mil)	Net Premium ($mil)	Net Income ($mil)
3-19	B-	2.72	2.27	385.7	170.9	311.7	-2.8
3-18	B	2.10	1.75	332.6	102.3	265.0	-20.3
2018	B-	2.77	2.31	394.5	174.5	1,138.8	-10.0
2017	B	1.76	1.47	333.7	124.0	947.5	12.5
2016	B-	1.61	1.34	282.8	68.9	785.3	-3.3
2015	B-	1.86	1.55	137.9	53.2	506.3	-3.9
2014	B-	2.15	1.79	102.7	47.5	396.0	-1.6

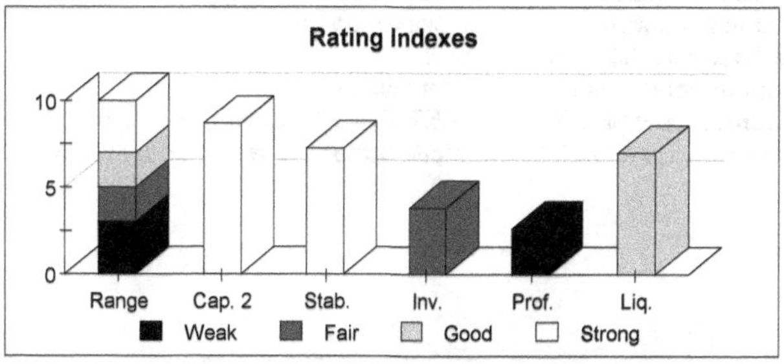

CMNTY CARE HLTH PLAN OF NV INC — B — Good

Major Rating Factors: Fair quality investment portfolio (4.6 on a scale of 0 to 10). Excellent profitability (9.0). Strong capitalization (8.3) based on excellent current risk-adjusted capital (severe loss scenario).
Other Rating Factors: Excellent liquidity (7.0) with sufficient resources (cash flows and marketable investments) to handle a spike in claims.
Principal Business: Medicaid (98%), comp med (2%)
Mem Phys: 18: 7,640 **17:** 7,040 **18 MLR** 81.1% **/ 18 Admin Exp** N/A
Enroll(000): Q1 19: 189 **18:** 187 **17:** 185 **Med Exp PMPM:** $244
Principal Investments: Long-term bonds (57%), cash and equiv (41%), other (2%)
Provider Compensation ($000): Bonus arrang ($338,248), contr fee ($110,296), FFS ($77,249), capitation ($3,694)
Total Member Encounters: Phys (988,507), non-phys (1,071,926)
Group Affiliation: Anthem Inc
Licensed in: NV
Address: 9133 W RUSSELL RD, LAS VEGAS, NV 89148
Phone: (757) 490-6900 **Dom State:** NV **Commenced Bus:** N/A

Data Date	Rating	RACR #1	RACR #2	Total Assets ($mil)	Capital ($mil)	Net Premium ($mil)	Net Income ($mil)
3-19	B	2.37	1.98	174.8	83.8	160.2	0.0
3-18	B	1.85	1.54	130.2	65.4	159.1	-8.4
2018	B	2.33	1.94	189.1	82.2	652.4	9.8
2017	B	1.31	1.09	138.6	71.8	645.3	8.2
2016	B	1.91	1.59	122.1	64.7	635.1	4.9
2015	B	2.19	1.82	114.8	61.3	560.0	9.5
2014	B	2.23	1.86	92.1	41.9	400.8	14.1

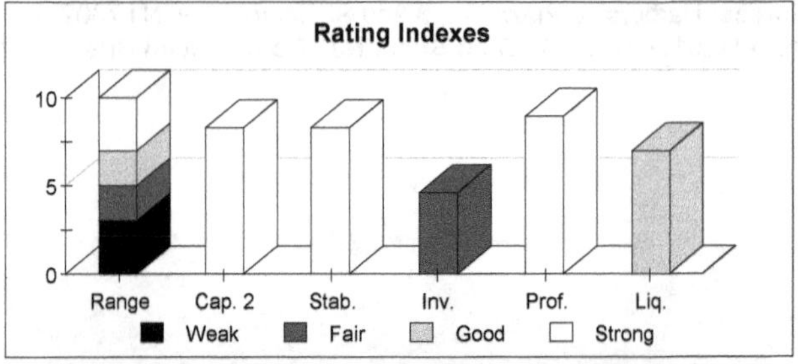

COLONIAL LIFE & ACCIDENT INSURANCE COMPANY — C+ — Fair

Major Rating Factors: Fair overall results on stability tests (4.6 on a scale of 0 to 10). Good quality investment portfolio (5.9) despite significant exposure to mortgages . Mortgage default rate has been low. large holdings of BBB rated bonds in addition to small junk bond holdings. Good liquidity (6.8) with sufficient resources to handle a spike in claims as well as a significant increase in policy surrenders.
Other Rating Factors: Strong capitalization (7.8) based on excellent risk adjusted capital (severe loss scenario). Excellent profitability (7.3).
Principal Business: Individual health insurance (65%), individual life insurance (21%), group health insurance (12%), and group life insurance (2%).
Principal Investments: NonCMO investment grade bonds (78%), mortgages in good standing (11%), noninv. grade bonds (3%), CMOs and structured securities (3%), and misc. investments (6%).
Investments in Affiliates: None
Group Affiliation: Unum Group
Licensed in: All states except NY
Commenced Business: September 1939
Address: 1200 COLONIAL LIFE BOULEVARD, COLUMBIA, SC 29210
Phone: (803) 798-7000 **Domicile State:** SC **NAIC Code:** 62049

Data Date	Rating	RACR #1	RACR #2	Total Assets ($mil)	Capital ($mil)	Net Premium ($mil)	Net Income ($mil)
3-19	C+	2.37	1.51	3,463.5	576.3	425.7	36.5
3-18	C+	2.10	1.33	3,285.8	490.3	418.9	30.1
2018	C+	2.20	1.40	3,421.9	528.0	1,589.6	200.4
2017	C+	2.14	1.35	3,220.0	490.4	1,503.0	157.9
2016	C+	2.53	1.57	3,143.9	562.1	1,414.5	151.5
2015	C+	2.65	1.64	3,018.8	566.0	1,333.8	157.8
2014	C+	2.44	1.53	2,922.0	567.1	1,277.5	160.9

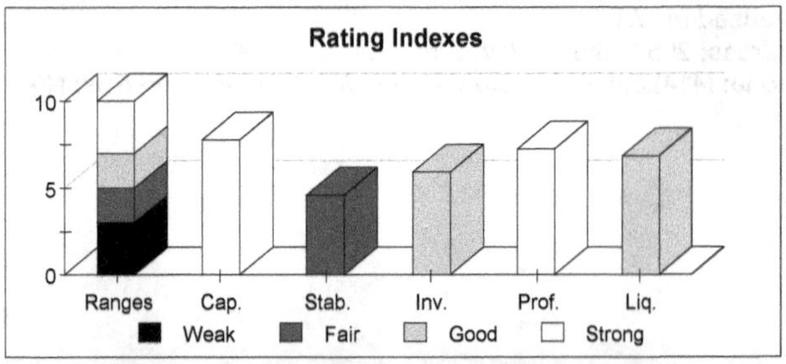

COLONIAL PENN LIFE INSURANCE COMPANY — D+ — Weak

Major Rating Factors: Weak overall results on stability tests (2.7 on a scale of 0 to 10) including weak financial strength of affiliated CNO Financial Group Inc and negative cash flow from operations for 2018. Weak profitability (1.9) with operating losses during the first three months of 2019. Weak liquidity (1.6).
Other Rating Factors: Fair quality investment portfolio (3.9). Good capitalization (5.3) based on good risk adjusted capital (moderate loss scenario).
Principal Business: Individual health insurance (63%), individual life insurance (23%), and group life insurance (13%).
Principal Investments: NonCMO investment grade bonds (73%), CMOs and structured securities (16%), policy loans (3%), noninv. grade bonds (3%), and misc. investments (4%).
Investments in Affiliates: None
Group Affiliation: CNO Financial Group Inc
Licensed in: All states except NY
Commenced Business: September 1959
Address: 399 MARKET STREET, PHILADELPHIA, PA 19181
Phone: (215) 928-8000 **Domicile State:** PA **NAIC Code:** 62065

Data Date	Rating	RACR #1	RACR #2	Total Assets ($mil)	Capital ($mil)	Net Premium ($mil)	Net Income ($mil)
3-19	D+	1.20	0.71	872.3	93.9	109.4	-7.3
3-18	D+	1.30	0.74	874.6	103.9	105.2	-4.8
2018	D+	1.19	0.69	869.9	92.4	379.0	-21.1
2017	D+	1.28	0.73	868.5	99.7	366.4	-11.7
2016	D+	1.27	0.72	854.7	95.8	352.5	-1.9
2015	D+	1.13	0.66	816.0	79.3	330.3	-18.8
2014	D+	1.16	0.67	742.8	73.3	303.7	-17.1

CNO Financial Group Inc Composite Group Rating: D+ Largest Group Members	Assets ($mil)	Rating
BANKERS LIFE CAS CO	15515	D+
WASHINGTON NATIONAL INS CO	5466	D+
COLONIAL PENN LIFE INS CO	870	D+
BANKERS CONSECO LIFE INS CO	496	D

COLORADO ACCESS D Weak

Major Rating Factors: Fair overall results on stability tests (4.7 on a scale of 0 to 10) based on an excessive 36% enrollment growth during the period, a decline in the number of member physicians during 2019. Good overall profitability index (5.0). Strong capitalization index (10.0) based on weak current risk-adjusted capital (severe loss scenario).
Other Rating Factors: High quality investment portfolio (9.9). Excellent liquidity (7.0) with ample operational cash flow and liquid investments.
Principal Business: Medicaid (69%), other (31%)
Mem Phys: 18: 13,957 **17:** 18,457 **18 MLR** 91.1% **/ 18 Admin Exp** N/A
Enroll(000): Q1 19: 528 **18:** 532 **17:** 393 **Med Exp PMPM:** $48
Principal Investments: Cash and equiv (117%)
Provider Compensation ($000): Contr fee ($195,935), capitation ($79,393)
Total Member Encounters: Phys (1,428,697), non-phys (23,425)
Group Affiliation: None
Licensed in: CO
Address: 11100 E BETHANY DR, AURORA, CO 80014-2630
Phone: (720) 744-5100 **Dom State:** CO **Commenced Bus:** N/A

Data Date	Rating	RACR #1	RACR #2	Total Assets ($mil)	Capital ($mil)	Net Premium ($mil)	Net Income ($mil)
3-19	D	N/A	N/A	57.8	22.0	91.5	-0.5
3-18	D	N/A	N/A	55.6	18.0	62.6	-1.7
2018	D	N/A	N/A	63.0	23.1	295.9	5.8
2017	D-	N/A	N/A	53.8	20.0	273.9	12.0
2016	E	0.23	0.19	62.9	10.9	244.1	7.9
2015	N/A	N/A	N/A	42.8	0.3	258.7	-13.4
2014	N/A	N/A	N/A	50.9	14.6	222.5	3.8

Rating Indexes

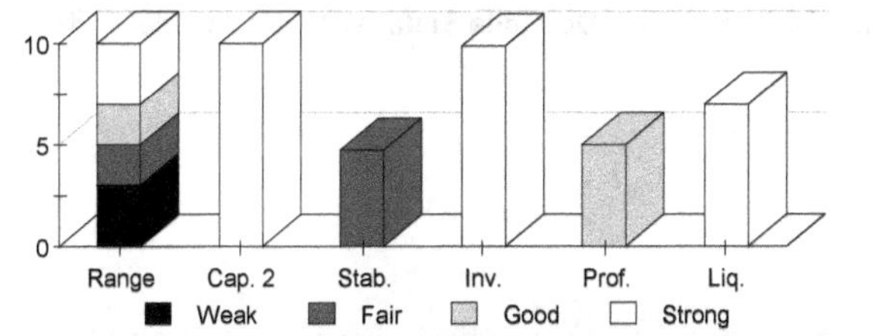

COMBINED INSURANCE COMPANY OF AMERICA C Fair

Major Rating Factors: Fair overall results on stability tests (4.1 on a scale of 0 to 10) including fair risk adjusted capital in prior years. Good capitalization (5.0) based on good risk adjusted capital (moderate loss scenario). Good quality investment portfolio (6.2) despite mixed results such as: substantial holdings of BBB bonds but junk bond exposure equal to 75% of capital.
Other Rating Factors: Weak profitability (1.9) with operating losses during the first three months of 2019. Excellent liquidity (8.3).
Principal Business: Individual health insurance (60%), group health insurance (29%), individual life insurance (6%), group life insurance (4%), and reinsurance (1%).
Principal Investments: NonCMO investment grade bonds (58%), CMOs and structured securities (26%), noninv. grade bonds (6%), common & preferred stock (2%), and misc. investments (5%).
Investments in Affiliates: 2%
Group Affiliation: Chubb Limited
Licensed in: All states except NY
Commenced Business: January 1922
Address: 111 E Wacker Drive, Chicago, IL 60601
Phone: (800) 225-4500 **Domicile State:** IL **NAIC Code:** 62146

Data Date	Rating	RACR #1	RACR #2	Total Assets ($mil)	Capital ($mil)	Net Premium ($mil)	Net Income ($mil)
3-19	C	1.02	0.73	2,328.5	182.0	272.0	-9.2
3-18	B-	1.53	1.09	1,526.5	205.8	127.6	19.1
2018	C	1.03	0.72	2,364.2	174.4	646.5	-158.7
2017	C+	1.37	0.97	1,495.7	178.7	480.2	33.4
2016	C+	1.15	0.80	1,432.1	131.5	447.5	30.7
2015	C	0.80	0.54	1,316.7	79.9	439.9	-14.1
2014	C+	1.10	0.78	1,378.3	134.4	434.5	60.1

Rating Indexes

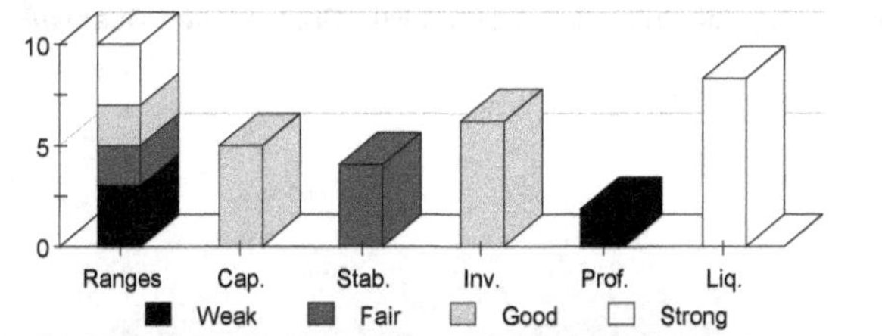

COMBINED LIFE INSURANCE COMPANY OF NEW YORK C+ Fair

Major Rating Factors: Fair overall results on stability tests (4.5 on a scale of 0 to 10) including weak risk adjusted capital in prior years. Weak profitability (2.9) with investment income below regulatory standards in relation to interest assumptions of reserves. Strong current capitalization (7.1) based on excellent risk adjusted capital (severe loss scenario) reflecting significant improvement over results in 2015.
Other Rating Factors: High quality investment portfolio (7.4). Excellent liquidity (7.4).
Principal Business: Individual health insurance (73%), individual life insurance (11%), group health insurance (7%), reinsurance (7%), and group life insurance (1%).
Principal Investments: NonCMO investment grade bonds (48%), CMOs and structured securities (47%), and policy loans (2%).
Investments in Affiliates: None
Group Affiliation: Chubb Limited
Licensed in: IL, NY
Commenced Business: June 1971
Address: 13 Cornell Road, Latham, NY 12110
Phone: (800) 951-6206 **Domicile State:** NY **NAIC Code:** 78697

Data Date	Rating	RACR #1	RACR #2	Total Assets ($mil)	Capital ($mil)	Net Premium ($mil)	Net Income ($mil)
3-19	C+	1.47	1.04	486.9	55.7	43.1	2.3
3-18	C+	1.29	0.91	450.1	47.3	41.7	2.6
2018	C+	1.42	1.01	472.3	52.7	167.2	7.8
2017	C+	1.21	0.86	441.6	44.3	163.4	10.0
2016	C+	0.95	0.67	420.3	33.4	155.2	7.6
2015	C	0.63	0.45	397.3	21.9	156.2	-9.7
2014	B	1.32	0.92	391.9	39.9	127.5	6.1

Rating Indexes

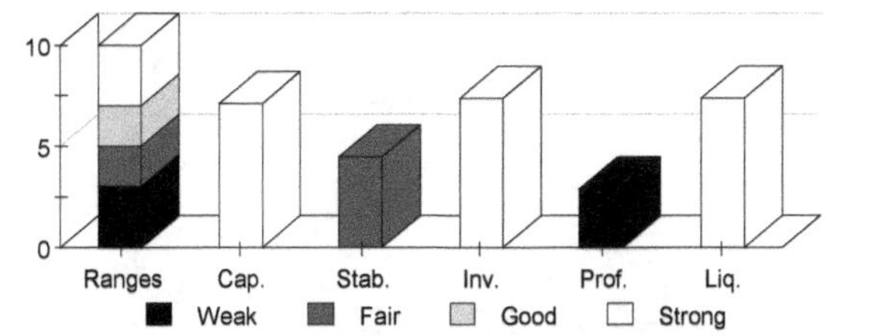

COMMENCEMENT BAY LIFE INSURANCE COMPANY B Good

Major Rating Factors: Good overall results on stability tests (5.9 on a scale of 0 to 10). Stability strengths include excellent operational trends and good risk diversification. Strong capitalization (10.0) based on excellent risk adjusted capital (severe loss scenario). Moreover, capital levels have been consistently high over the last five years. High quality investment portfolio (8.4).
Other Rating Factors: Excellent profitability (8.9). Excellent liquidity (10.0).
Principal Business: Group health insurance (100%).
Principal Investments: NonCMO investment grade bonds (57%) and CMOs and structured securities (38%).
Investments in Affiliates: None
Group Affiliation: Regence Group
Licensed in: OR, UT, WA
Commenced Business: September 1992
Address: 1800 NINTH AVENUE, SEATTLE, WA 98101
Phone: (206) 464-3600 **Domicile State:** WA **NAIC Code:** 78879

Data Date	Rating	RACR #1	RACR #2	Total Assets ($mil)	Capital ($mil)	Net Premium ($mil)	Net Income ($mil)
3-19	B	7.60	6.84	43.8	36.5	14.4	5.1
3-18	U	N/A	N/A	28.3	27.9	0.0	0.1
2018	B-	6.54	5.89	32.0	31.4	1.6	1.4
2017	U	6.36	5.72	28.0	27.8	0.0	0.3
2016	U	3.75	3.38	7.7	7.5	0.0	0.2
2015	U	3.71	3.34	7.7	7.4	0.0	0.1
2014	U	3.71	3.34	7.5	7.3	0.0	0.1

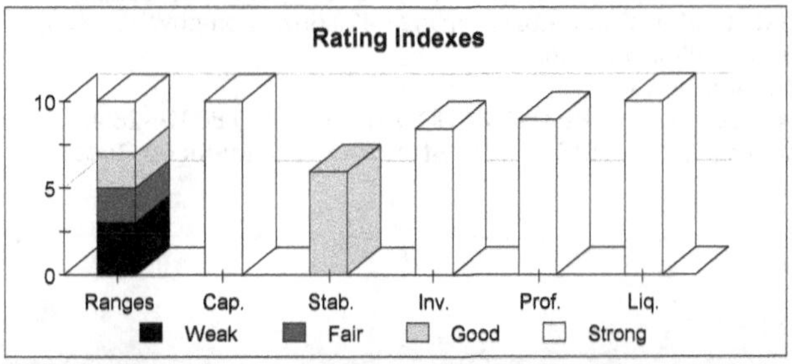

COMMON GROUND HEALTHCARE COOPERATIVE D Weak

Major Rating Factors: Weak profitability index (1.0 on a scale of 0 to 10). Fair quality investment portfolio (4.4). Strong capitalization (9.5) based on excellent current risk-adjusted capital (severe loss scenario).
Other Rating Factors: Excellent liquidity (8.0) with ample operational cash flow and liquid investments.
Principal Business: Comp med (100%)
Mem Phys: 18: 19,098 **17:** 16,574 **18 MLR** 68.4% **/ 18 Admin Exp** N/A
Enroll(000): Q1 19: 66 **18:** 52 **17:** 27 **Med Exp PMPM:** $579
Principal Investments: Cash and equiv (100%)
Provider Compensation ($000): FFS ($282,274), contr fee ($82,049)
Total Member Encounters: N/A
Group Affiliation: None
Licensed in: WI
Address: 120 BISHOPS WAY Ste 150, BROOKFIELD, WI 53005-6271
Phone: (262) 754-9690 **Dom State:** WI **Commenced Bus:** N/A

Data Date	Rating	RACR #1	RACR #2	Total Assets ($mil)	Capital ($mil)	Net Premium ($mil)	Net Income ($mil)
3-19	D	3.39	2.82	260.2	185.2	135.0	40.5
3-18	D	N/A	N/A	132.9	47.7	139.7	30.8
2018	D	2.40	2.00	217.9	144.8	557.5	135.5
2017	D	N/A	N/A	58.7	17.1	165.6	-11.1
2016	D	1.13	0.95	59.2	24.6	88.8	-36.0
2015	D	1.05	0.87	74.1	24.6	136.3	-28.2
2014	D	0.89	0.74	105.6	36.9	123.5	-36.5

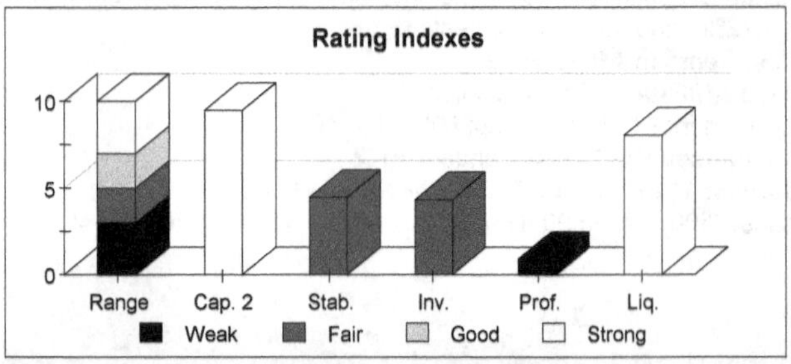

COMMUNITY CARE ALLIANCE OF ILLINOIS E- Very Weak

Major Rating Factors: Weak profitability index (0.0 on a scale of 0 to 10). Poor capitalization index (0.0) based on weak current risk-adjusted capital (severe loss scenario). Weak liquidity (0.1) as a spike in claims may stretch capacity.
Other Rating Factors: High quality investment portfolio (9.9).
Principal Business: Medicare (100%)
Mem Phys: 18: 9,889 **17:** 11,402 **18 MLR** 192.8% **/ 18 Admin Exp** N/A
Enroll(000): Q1 19: 5 **18:** 5 **17:** 6 **Med Exp PMPM:** $1,056
Principal Investments: Cash and equiv (76%), long-term bonds (24%)
Provider Compensation ($000): Contr fee ($56,056), capitation ($9,689)
Total Member Encounters: Phys (100,702), non-phys (301)
Group Affiliation: Delaware Life Partners LLC
Licensed in: IL
Address: 322 S Green St Ste 400, Chicago, IL 60607
Phone: (312) 605-9847 **Dom State:** IL **Commenced Bus:** N/A

Data Date	Rating	RACR #1	RACR #2	Total Assets ($mil)	Capital ($mil)	Net Premium ($mil)	Net Income ($mil)
3-19	E-	N/A	N/A	10.0	-11.3	15.6	21.3
3-18	C-	N/A	N/A	17.2	2.4	14.0	-0.2
2018	E-	N/A	N/A	6.8	-32.8	34.1	-39.3
2017	C-	N/A	N/A	13.5	4.2	62.5	-0.6
2016	D+	0.66	0.55	14.0	4.8	42.7	1.2
2015	D	0.29	0.24	8.6	2.7	19.6	0.1
2014	D+	1.38	1.15	5.2	2.6	7.2	-0.4

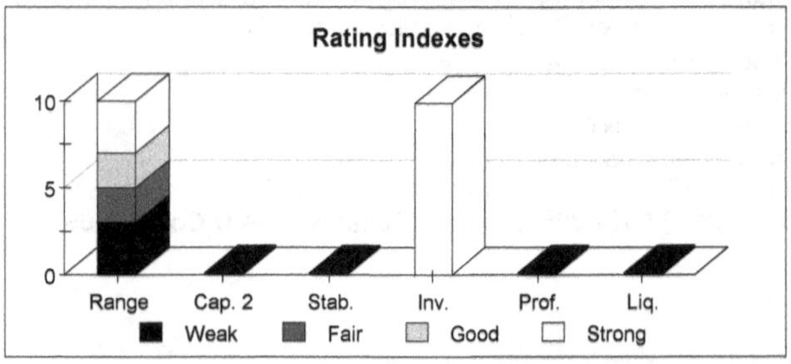

COMMUNITY CARE BEHAVIORAL HEALTH * B+ Good

Major Rating Factors: Excellent profitability (7.5 on a scale of 0 to 10). Strong capitalization (10.0) based on excellent current risk-adjusted capital (severe loss scenario). High quality investment portfolio (7.1).
Other Rating Factors: Excellent liquidity (7.0) with sufficient resources (cash flows and marketable investments) to handle a spike in claims.
Principal Business: Medicaid (100%)
Mem Phys: 18: 4,868 **17:** 4,272 **18 MLR** 86.1% **/ 18 Admin Exp** N/A
Enroll(000): Q1 19: 781 **18:** 740 **17:** 772 **Med Exp PMPM:** $93
Principal Investments: Long-term bonds (61%), cash and equiv (19%), nonaffiliate common stock (17%), other (3%)
Provider Compensation ($000): Contr fee ($816,280), capitation ($14,764)
Total Member Encounters: Phys (23,816,899)
Group Affiliation: None
Licensed in: PA
Address: 339 Sixth Ave Ste 1300, Pittsburgh, PA 15222
Phone: (412) 454-2120 **Dom State:** PA **Commenced Bus:** N/A

Data Date	Rating	RACR #1	RACR #2	Total Assets ($mil)	Capital ($mil)	Net Premium ($mil)	Net Income ($mil)
3-19	B+	4.39	3.66	386.8	249.2	279.0	17.3
3-18	B	4.08	3.40	347.2	213.2	239.7	0.6
2018	B+	4.03	3.36	347.1	227.7	970.5	18.6
2017	B	2.95	2.46	330.5	212.4	933.2	25.1
2016	C+	3.75	3.13	308.2	185.5	884.6	26.4
2015	C	3.10	2.59	244.5	156.9	811.3	4.5
2014	C	3.42	2.85	253.3	172.3	786.2	19.6

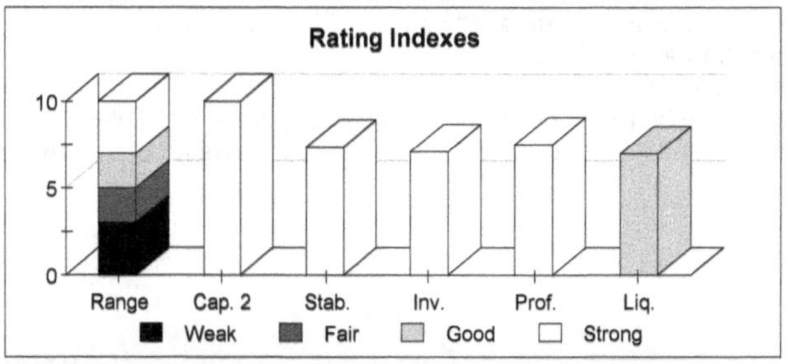

COMMUNITY CARE HEALTH PLAN C+ Fair

Major Rating Factors: Good overall results on stability tests (5.2 on a scale of 0 to 10) despite fair risk diversification due to the company's size but healthy premium and capital growth during 2018. Excellent profitability (8.7). Strong capitalization index (7.0) based on excellent current risk-adjusted capital (severe loss scenario).
Other Rating Factors: Excellent liquidity (7.4) with ample operational cash flow and liquid investments.
Principal Business: Managed care (100%)
Mem Phys: 18: N/A **17:** N/A **18 MLR** 80.6% **/ 18 Admin Exp** N/A
Enroll(000): Q1 19: 11 **18:** 10 **17:** 8 **Med Exp PMPM:** $346
Principal Investments ($000): Cash and equiv ($11,495)
Provider Compensation ($000): None
Total Member Encounters: N/A
Group Affiliation: Fresno Community Hosp & Med Center
Licensed in: CA
Address: 7370 N Palm Ave Ste 103, Fresno, CA 93711
Phone: (818) 458-2867 **Dom State:** CA **Commenced Bus:** March 2013

Data Date	Rating	RACR #1	RACR #2	Total Assets ($mil)	Capital ($mil)	Net Premium ($mil)	Net Income ($mil)
3-19	C+	1.84	1.15	13.6	9.4	13.4	1.5
3-18	C-	1.69	1.06	9.8	6.0	10.3	0.9
2018	C	1.50	0.93	12.2	7.9	46.4	2.8
2017	C-	1.42	0.89	8.7	5.1	30.3	1.2
2016	C-	1.79	1.14	6.9	4.7	20.8	0.1
2015	C-	1.91	1.21	7.5	4.6	19.2	0.3
2014	C-	2.70	1.72	6.5	3.9	12.1	0.2

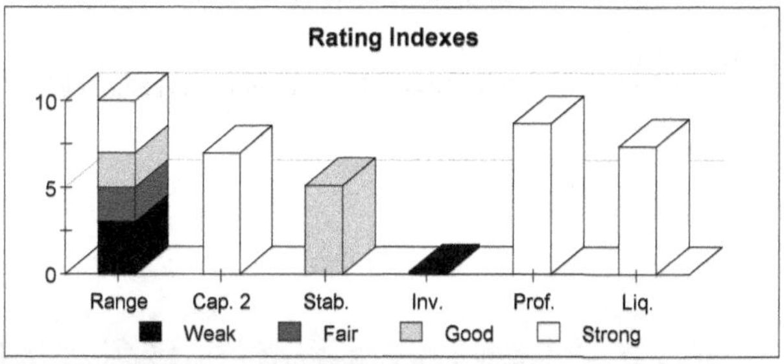

COMMUNITY FIRST HEALTH PLANS INC B- Good

Major Rating Factors: Fair overall results on stability tests (4.1 on a scale of 0 to 10). Good liquidity (6.8) with sufficient resources (cash flows and marketable investments) to handle a spike in claims. Strong capitalization index (7.0) based on excellent current risk-adjusted capital (severe loss scenario).
Other Rating Factors: High quality investment portfolio (8.7). Weak profitability index (2.7).
Principal Business: Medicaid (91%), comp med (9%)
Mem Phys: 18: 7,180 **17:** 7,248 **18 MLR** 92.8% **/ 18 Admin Exp** N/A
Enroll(000): Q1 19: 138 **18:** 139 **17:** 140 **Med Exp PMPM:** $300
Principal Investments: Cash and equiv (61%), long-term bonds (39%)
Provider Compensation ($000): Contr fee ($470,591), capitation ($22,256)
Total Member Encounters: Phys (617,056), non-phys (1,164,712)
Group Affiliation: None
Licensed in: TX
Address: 12238 Silicon Drive Ste 100, San Antonio, TX 78249
Phone: (210) 227-2347 **Dom State:** TX **Commenced Bus:** N/A

Data Date	Rating	RACR #1	RACR #2	Total Assets ($mil)	Capital ($mil)	Net Premium ($mil)	Net Income ($mil)
3-19	B-	1.32	1.10	126.0	66.8	140.6	-3.0
3-18	A-	1.76	1.46	136.2	77.8	131.3	-5.3
2018	B-	1.43	1.19	142.7	71.7	537.4	-14.6
2017	A-	1.97	1.64	155.7	86.2	509.8	-3.6
2016	A	2.78	2.32	155.1	92.3	424.2	19.0
2015	A-	2.53	2.11	117.8	74.5	356.3	14.6
2014	A-	2.22	1.85	104.9	58.9	310.6	13.7

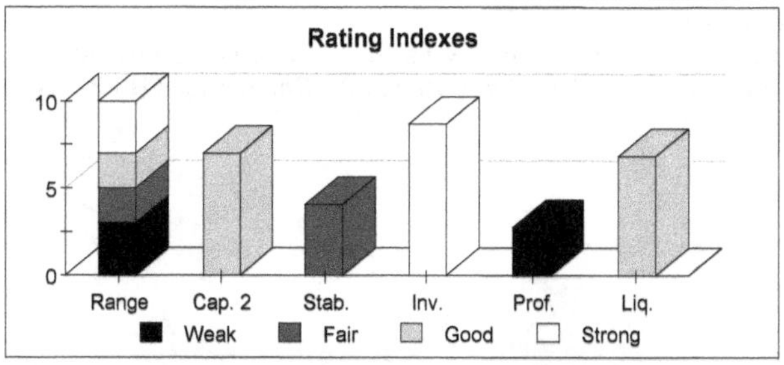

COMMUNITY HEALTH CHOICE INC — C — Fair

Major Rating Factors: Fair profitability index (3.0 on a scale of 0 to 10). Fair overall results on stability tests (4.1) based on a significant 20% decrease in enrollment during the period, an inordinate decline in premium revenue in 2018. Good capitalization index (5.1) based on good current risk-adjusted capital (severe loss scenario
Other Rating Factors: High quality investment portfolio (9.9). Excellent liquidity (7.2) with ample operational cash flow and liquid investments.
Principal Business: Comp med (100%)
Mem Phys: 18: 9,751 **17:** 9,751 **18 MLR** 81.3% **/ 18 Admin Exp** N/A
Enroll(000): Q1 19: 107 **18:** 111 **17:** 138 **Med Exp PMPM:** $400
Principal Investments: Cash and equiv (99%), long-term bonds (1%)
Provider Compensation ($000): Contr fee ($556,579), capitation ($19,790)
Total Member Encounters: Phys (966,692), non-phys (223,946)
Group Affiliation: None
Licensed in: TX
Address: 2636 South Loop West Ste 700, Houston, TX 77054
Phone: (713) 295-2200 **Dom State:** TX **Commenced Bus:** N/A

Data Date	Rating	RACR #1	RACR #2	Total Assets ($mil)	Capital ($mil)	Net Premium ($mil)	Net Income ($mil)
3-19	C	0.95	0.79	179.9	55.2	168.9	13.6
3-18	D	0.97	0.81	258.7	73.8	181.2	20.5
2018	C	0.98	0.82	175.1	57.3	706.2	35.4
2017	D	0.71	0.59	259.7	55.3	820.6	-24.9
2016	C+	0.84	0.70	305.1	81.5	1,126.9	-18.3
2015	B	1.47	1.23	239.9	101.6	850.6	5.4
2014	B-	1.67	1.39	192.1	100.4	720.2	16.3

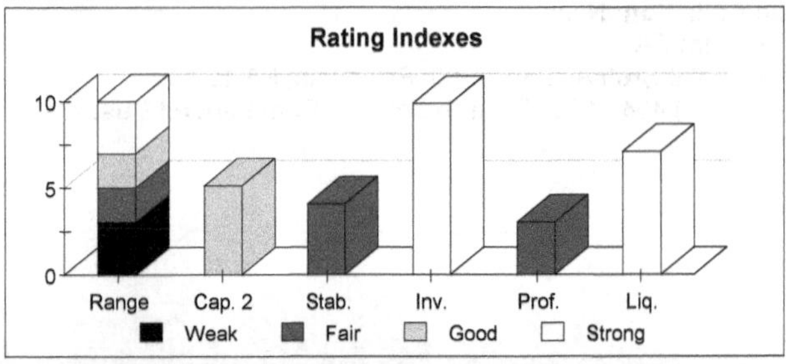

COMMUNITY HEALTH CHOICE TX INC — C — Fair

Major Rating Factors: Weak profitability index (2.1 on a scale of 0 to 10). Good capitalization (6.8) based on excellent current risk-adjusted capital (severe loss scenario). High quality investment portfolio (9.9).
Other Rating Factors: Excellent liquidity (6.9) with sufficient resources (cash flows and marketable investments) to handle a spike in claims.
Principal Business: Medicaid (92%), comp med (8%)
Mem Phys: 18: N/A **17:** 11,203 **18 MLR** 90.8% **/ 18 Admin Exp** N/A
Enroll(000): Q1 19: 268 **18:** 279 **17:** 290 **Med Exp PMPM:** $257
Principal Investments: Cash and equiv (91%), long-term bonds (9%)
Provider Compensation ($000): Contr fee ($863,960)
Total Member Encounters: Phys (2,751,307), non-phys (446,006)
Group Affiliation: Community Health Choice Texas Inc
Licensed in: TX
Address: , Houston, TX 77054
Phone: (713) 295-2200 **Dom State:** TX **Commenced Bus:** N/A

Data Date	Rating	RACR #1	RACR #2	Total Assets ($mil)	Capital ($mil)	Net Premium ($mil)	Net Income ($mil)
3-19	C	1.22	1.02	175.8	96.0	239.6	-2.4
3-18	N/A	N/A	N/A	133.8	35.9	234.1	-10.6
2018	C-	1.13	0.94	186.2	88.2	957.6	1.8
2017	N/A	N/A	N/A	143.6	51.0	688.3	-5.5
2016	N/A	N/A	N/A	N/A	N/A	N/A	N/A
2015	N/A	N/A	N/A	N/A	N/A	N/A	N/A
2014	N/A	N/A	N/A	N/A	N/A	N/A	N/A

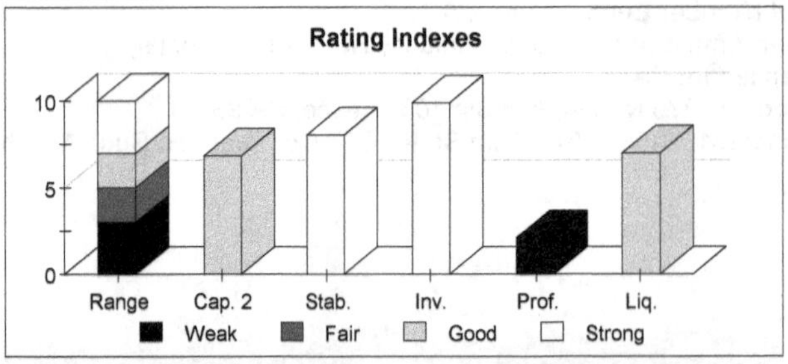

COMMUNITY HEALTH GROUP — B- — Good

Major Rating Factors: Fair overall results on stability tests (4.1 on a scale of 0 to 10). Excellent profitability (7.2). Strong capitalization index (10.0) based on excellent current risk-adjusted capital (severe loss scenario).
Other Rating Factors: Excellent liquidity (8.0) with ample operational cash flow and liquid investments.
Principal Business: Medicaid (100%)
Mem Phys: 18: N/A **17:** N/A **18 MLR** 102.6% **/ 18 Admin Exp** N/A
Enroll(000): Q1 19: 266 **18:** 272 **17:** 288 **Med Exp PMPM:** $290
Principal Investments ($000): Cash and equiv ($591,011)
Provider Compensation ($000): None
Total Member Encounters: N/A
Group Affiliation: None
Licensed in: CA
Address: 2420 Fenton Street Suite 100, Chula Vista, CA 91914
Phone: (619) 498-6516 **Dom State:** CA **Commenced Bus:** N/A

Data Date	Rating	RACR #1	RACR #2	Total Assets ($mil)	Capital ($mil)	Net Premium ($mil)	Net Income ($mil)
3-19	B-	6.99	4.25	895.6	482.1	258.3	-3.1
3-18	A-	8.89	5.39	838.5	587.5	280.3	41.9
2018	B-	7.04	4.28	754.2	485.2	950.4	-60.4
2017	A-	8.14	4.94	794.0	545.6	1,178.1	161.0
2016	B	5.72	3.46	776.0	384.5	1,184.5	197.3
2015	B-	3.02	1.83	529.4	187.3	1,038.5	113.7
2014	C+	1.28	0.80	231.4	73.6	683.6	35.2

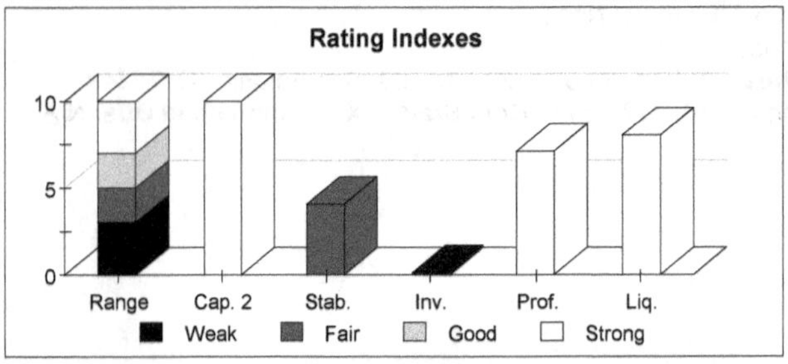

COMMUNITY HEALTH PLAN OF WASHINGTON — B — Good

Major Rating Factors: Good liquidity (6.8 on a scale of 0 to 10) with sufficient resources (cash flows and marketable investments) to handle a spike in claims. Fair profitability index (4.7). Fair quality investment portfolio (4.7).
Other Rating Factors: Strong capitalization (8.5) based on excellent current risk-adjusted capital (severe loss scenario).
Principal Business: Medicaid (88%), Medicare (11%), comp med (1%)
Mem Phys: 18: 26,446 **17:** 26,244 **18 MLR** 87.1% **/ 18 Admin Exp** N/A
Enroll(000): Q1 19: 276 **18:** 265 **17:** 292 **Med Exp PMPM:** $229
Principal Investments: Long-term bonds (56%), cash and equiv (27%), nonaffiliate common stock (16%)
Provider Compensation ($000): FFS ($616,012), capitation ($151,740)
Total Member Encounters: Phys (1,034,725), non-phys (774,905)
Group Affiliation: None
Licensed in: WA
Address: 1111 Third Ave Ste 400, Seattle, WA 98101
Phone: (206) 521-8833 **Dom State:** WA **Commenced Bus:** N/A

Data Date	Rating	RACR #1	RACR #2	Total Assets ($mil)	Capital ($mil)	Net Premium ($mil)	Net Income ($mil)
3-19	B	2.55	2.12	483.7	179.1	233.8	2.1
3-18	B	2.15	1.79	497.5	187.0	235.3	-0.1
2018	B	2.44	2.04	458.5	171.1	864.0	20.5
2017	B	2.17	1.81	458.1	188.8	1,087.3	24.2
2016	B	1.93	1.61	445.2	162.0	1,070.9	17.4
2015	B-	2.14	1.78	502.0	139.0	1,070.2	39.6
2014	B	1.62	1.35	562.1	98.6	999.1	-25.2

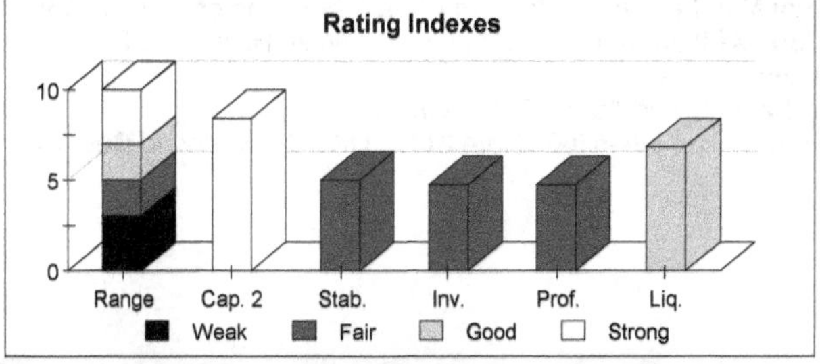

COMMUNITY INS CO — B- — Good

Major Rating Factors: Fair quality investment portfolio (3.5 on a scale of 0 to 10). Good liquidity (6.0) with sufficient resources (cash flows and marketable investments) to handle a spike in claims. Excellent profitability (9.0).
Other Rating Factors: Strong capitalization (9.2) based on excellent current risk-adjusted capital (severe loss scenario).
Principal Business: Comp med (41%), Medicare (34%), FEHB (17%), med supp (3%), dental (1%), other (4%)
Mem Phys: 18: 76,561 **17:** 72,646 **18 MLR** 87.1% **/ 18 Admin Exp** N/A
Enroll(000): Q1 19: 2,056 **18:** 1,959 **17:** 2,034 **Med Exp PMPM:** $199
Principal Investments: Long-term bonds (133%), nonaffiliate common stock (1%), other (9%)
Provider Compensation ($000): Bonus arrang ($3,112,723), contr fee ($814,223), FFS ($556,676), capitation ($106,534), other ($165,997)
Total Member Encounters: Phys (6,601,318), non-phys (6,032,409)
Group Affiliation: Anthem Inc
Licensed in: IN, OH
Address: 4361 IRWIN SIMPSON Rd, MASON, OH 45040-9498
Phone: (513) 872-8100 **Dom State:** OH **Commenced Bus:** N/A

Data Date	Rating	RACR #1	RACR #2	Total Assets ($mil)	Capital ($mil)	Net Premium ($mil)	Net Income ($mil)
3-19	B-	3.12	2.60	2,141.0	950.8	1,461.0	151.9
3-18	B	2.74	2.28	2,145.1	861.9	1,334.2	96.2
2018	B-	2.66	2.22	1,812.3	802.2	5,398.4	386.6
2017	B	2.45	2.04	1,990.4	830.0	5,714.2	348.6
2016	B+	2.64	2.20	2,138.7	807.8	5,297.0	319.1
2015	B+	2.56	2.13	2,091.4	754.1	5,255.4	266.3
2014	B+	2.74	2.28	2,014.3	812.2	5,309.2	276.9

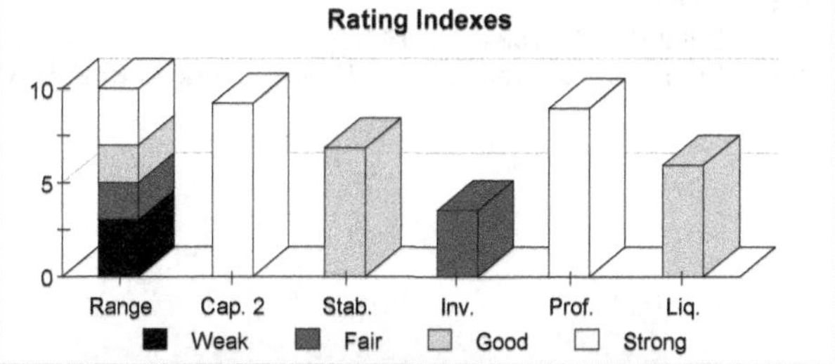

COMMUNITYCARE GOVERNMENT PROGRAMS — D — Weak

Major Rating Factors: Weak profitability index (0.9 on a scale of 0 to 10). Low quality investment portfolio (0.6). Good capitalization (6.9) based on excellent current risk-adjusted capital (severe loss scenario).
Other Rating Factors: Excellent liquidity (7.1) with ample operational cash flow and liquid investments.
Principal Business: Medicare (100%)
Mem Phys: 18: 3,148 **17:** 3,833 **18 MLR** 91.8% **/ 18 Admin Exp** N/A
Enroll(000): Q1 19: 5 **18:** 3 **17:** 2 **Med Exp PMPM:** $651
Principal Investments: Cash and equiv (94%), long-term bonds (6%)
Provider Compensation ($000): Capitation ($14,317), contr fee ($5,786), FFS ($170)
Total Member Encounters: Phys (30,242), non-phys (35,766)
Group Affiliation: CommunityCare Government Programs In
Licensed in: OK
Address: 218 W 6th St, Tulsa, OK 74103
Phone: (918) 594-5295 **Dom State:** OK **Commenced Bus:** N/A

Data Date	Rating	RACR #1	RACR #2	Total Assets ($mil)	Capital ($mil)	Net Premium ($mil)	Net Income ($mil)
3-19	D	1.24	1.03	10.2	4.3	8.5	-0.1
3-18	D+	N/A	N/A	10.0	3.9	6.1	-0.1
2018	D	1.28	1.06	9.0	4.4	26.3	0.2
2017	D+	N/A	N/A	6.5	4.4	13.8	0.6
2016	D+	1.16	0.96	3.6	2.9	5.6	-0.7
2015	N/A	N/A	N/A	1.8	1.7	N/A	-1.3
2014	N/A	N/A	N/A	N/A	N/A	N/A	N/A

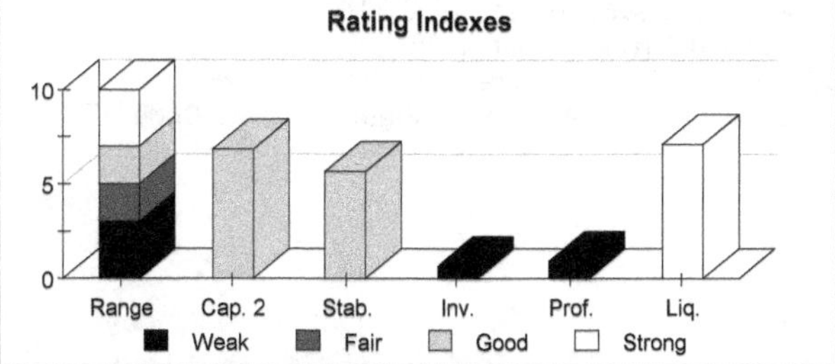

COMMUNITYCARE HMO INC B Good

Major Rating Factors: Good overall profitability index (5.8 on a scale of 0 to 10). Fair quality investment portfolio (3.7). Fair overall results on stability tests (4.8).
Other Rating Factors: Strong capitalization index (9.0) based on excellent current risk-adjusted capital (severe loss scenario). Excellent liquidity (7.0) with ample operational cash flow and liquid investments.
Principal Business: Comp med (52%), Medicare (48%)
Mem Phys: 18: 9,249 **17:** 9,764 **18 MLR** 87.7% **/ 18 Admin Exp** N/A
Enroll(000): Q1 19: 81 **18:** 85 **17:** 98 **Med Exp PMPM:** $484
Principal Investments: Cash and equiv (68%), long-term bonds (31%)
Provider Compensation ($000): Capitation ($270,225), contr fee ($264,363), FFS ($2,569)
Total Member Encounters: Phys (600,299), non-phys (614,405)
Group Affiliation: CommunityCare Managed Healthcare Pla
Licensed in: OK
Address: 218 W 6th St, Tulsa, OK 74103
Phone: (918) 594-5200 **Dom State:** OK **Commenced Bus:** N/A

Data Date	Rating	RACR #1	RACR #2	Total Assets ($mil)	Capital ($mil)	Net Premium ($mil)	Net Income ($mil)
3-19	B	2.98	2.48	199.9	107.1	142.9	0.5
3-18	B+	2.89	2.41	250.1	106.6	153.6	-7.7
2018	B	2.85	2.38	188.1	102.6	589.5	1.4
2017	B+	3.08	2.57	220.8	113.9	628.0	7.2
2016	B+	3.33	2.78	181.4	119.1	592.3	1.6
2015	A-	3.06	2.55	164.7	115.1	585.3	-0.1
2014	A	2.97	2.48	193.7	121.0	676.3	8.3

Rating Indexes

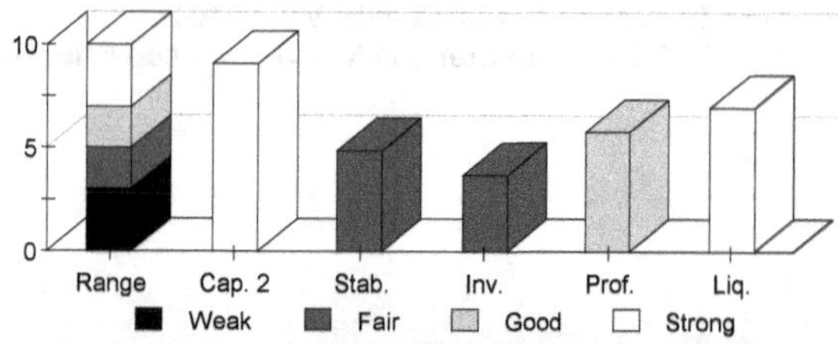

COMMUNITYCARE L&H INS CO C Fair

Major Rating Factors: Weak profitability index (0.9 on a scale of 0 to 10). Good capitalization (6.8) based on excellent current risk-adjusted capital (severe loss scenario). Good quality investment portfolio (6.6).
Other Rating Factors: Good liquidity (6.3) with sufficient resources (cash flows and marketable investments) to handle a spike in claims.
Principal Business: Comp med (97%), med supp (3%)
Mem Phys: 18: 12,280 **17:** 11,753 **18 MLR** 92.6% **/ 18 Admin Exp** N/A
Enroll(000): Q1 19: 9 **18:** 10 **17:** 12 **Med Exp PMPM:** $399
Principal Investments: Cash and equiv (84%), long-term bonds (16%)
Provider Compensation ($000): Contr fee ($48,077), FFS ($1,849)
Total Member Encounters: Phys (67,665), non-phys (49,593)
Group Affiliation: CommunityCare Managed Healthcare Pla
Licensed in: OK
Address: 218 W 6th St, Tulsa, OK 74103
Phone: (918) 594-5200 **Dom State:** OK **Commenced Bus:** N/A

Data Date	Rating	RACR #1	RACR #2	Total Assets ($mil)	Capital ($mil)	Net Premium ($mil)	Net Income ($mil)
3-19	C	1.22	1.02	17.5	6.7	11.5	0.1
3-18	B-	1.59	1.32	19.7	7.5	14.6	-1.1
2018	C	1.11	0.92	17.1	6.0	56.2	-2.3
2017	C	1.38	1.15	18.4	8.7	54.0	0.6
2016	B-	1.77	1.48	20.2	8.7	54.0	-1.3
2015	B-	1.68	1.40	20.0	10.1	66.0	-2.0
2014	B-	1.86	1.55	22.5	12.0	75.5	-1.0

Rating Indexes

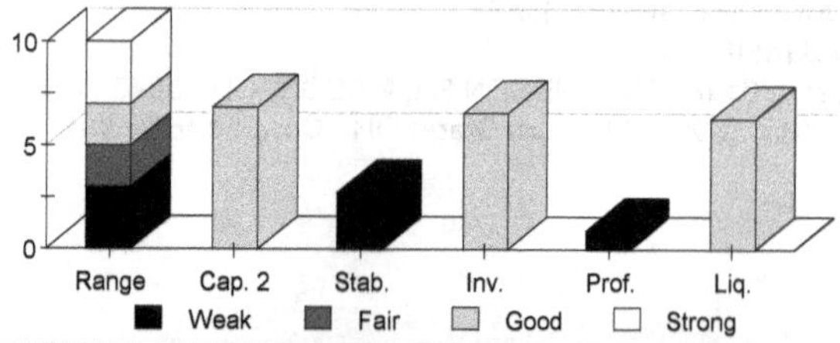

COMPANION LIFE INSURANCE COMPANY * B+ Good

Major Rating Factors: Good overall results on stability tests (6.6 on a scale of 0 to 10). Stability strengths include excellent operational trends and excellent risk diversification. Fair quality investment portfolio (4.9). Strong capitalization (8.8) based on excellent risk adjusted capital (severe loss scenario). Moreover, capital levels have been consistently high over the last five years.
Other Rating Factors: Excellent profitability (8.7). Excellent liquidity (7.0).
Principal Business: Group health insurance (77%), individual health insurance (11%), reinsurance (8%), and group life insurance (4%).
Principal Investments: NonCMO investment grade bonds (50%), common & preferred stock (32%), cash (8%), and CMOs and structured securities (8%).
Investments in Affiliates: 9%
Group Affiliation: Blue Cross Blue Shield of S Carolina
Licensed in: All states except CA, CT, HI, NJ, NY, PR
Commenced Business: July 1970
Address: 2501 Faraway Drive, Columbia, SC 29219
Phone: (800) 753-0404 **Domicile State:** SC **NAIC Code:** 77828

Data Date	Rating	RACR #1	RACR #2	Total Assets ($mil)	Capital ($mil)	Net Premium ($mil)	Net Income ($mil)
3-19	B+	2.86	2.20	420.6	235.4	74.4	4.7
3-18	B+	2.67	2.05	380.2	212.2	68.4	-0.2
2018	B+	2.80	2.17	395.7	228.1	279.8	18.8
2017	B+	2.71	2.08	373.6	212.4	253.2	19.4
2016	B+	2.55	1.99	338.7	186.2	237.4	16.4
2015	A-	3.15	2.44	300.4	160.4	221.6	13.7
2014	A-	2.95	2.30	284.9	149.0	220.5	15.6

Adverse Trends in Operations

Change in asset mix during 2015 (4.1%)

COMPCARE HEALTH SERVICES INS CORP * A- Excellent

Major Rating Factors: Excellent profitability (8.9 on a scale of 0 to 10). Strong capitalization index (10.0) based on excellent current risk-adjusted capital (severe loss scenario). High quality investment portfolio (7.9).
Other Rating Factors: Excellent overall results on stability tests (7.6). Rating is significantly influenced by the good financial results of Anthem Inc. Good liquidity (6.9) with sufficient resources (cash flows and marketable investments) to handle a spike in claims.
Principal Business: Comp med (48%), Medicaid (26%), Medicare (25%)
Mem Phys: 18: 15,733 **17:** 15,058 **18 MLR** 80.3% **/ 18 Admin Exp** N/A
Enroll(000): Q1 19: 232 **18:** 212 **17:** 217 **Med Exp PMPM:** $296
Principal Investments: Long-term bonds (88%), cash and equiv (11%)
Provider Compensation ($000): Contr fee ($330,155), bonus arrang ($305,989), FFS ($71,074), capitation ($15,281), other ($239)
Total Member Encounters: Phys (1,161,744), non-phys (1,479,364)
Group Affiliation: Anthem Inc
Licensed in: WI
Address: N17 W24340 RIVERWOOD DRIVE, WAUKESHA, WI 53188
Phone: (262) 523-4020 **Dom State:** WI **Commenced Bus:** N/A

Data Date	Rating	RACR #1	RACR #2	Total Assets ($mil)	Capital ($mil)	Net Premium ($mil)	Net Income ($mil)
3-19	A-	3.63	3.03	376.3	186.1	284.8	20.0
3-18	A-	3.52	2.93	361.4	157.0	216.0	2.7
2018	A-	3.29	2.74	329.3	167.9	914.3	59.1
2017	A-	2.44	2.04	308.5	152.9	798.4	41.5
2016	A-	3.11	2.60	265.3	135.4	769.1	45.8
2015	A-	2.50	2.09	233.6	100.7	681.2	6.8
2014	A-	2.85	2.38	228.6	107.6	660.8	29.1

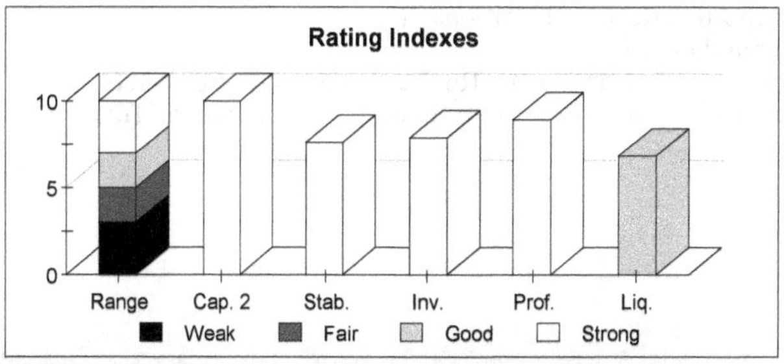

COMPREHENSIVE MOBILE INS CO B Good

Major Rating Factors: Excellent profitability (7.0 on a scale of 0 to 10). Strong capitalization (10.0) based on excellent current risk-adjusted capital (severe loss scenario). High quality investment portfolio (9.9).
Other Rating Factors: Excellent liquidity (7.7) with ample operational cash flow and liquid investments.
Principal Business: Other (100%)
Mem Phys: 18: 74 **17:** 45 **18 MLR** 47.2% **/ 18 Admin Exp** N/A
Enroll(000): Q1 19: 2 **18:** 2 **17:** 2 **Med Exp PMPM:** $87
Principal Investments: Cash and equiv (57%), long-term bonds (35%), nonaffiliate common stock (9%)
Provider Compensation ($000): FFS ($2,092)
Total Member Encounters: Non-phys (4,358)
Group Affiliation: None
Licensed in: AZ, NM, TX
Address: 19820 N 7TH St Ste 290, PHOENIX, AZ 85024
Phone: (877) 929-0030 **Dom State:** AZ **Commenced Bus:** N/A

Data Date	Rating	RACR #1	RACR #2	Total Assets ($mil)	Capital ($mil)	Net Premium ($mil)	Net Income ($mil)
3-19	B	4.38	3.65	2.6	2.5	1.2	0.2
3-18	B	N/A	N/A	2.2	2.1	1.0	N/A
2018	B	4.14	3.45	2.5	2.4	4.4	0.4
2017	B	N/A	N/A	2.6	2.1	4.0	0.2
2016	B	2.71	2.26	1.4	1.0	2.9	0.2
2015	C-	7.29	6.08	1.2	0.9	1.1	0.2
2014	U	5.59	4.66	0.7	0.7	0.1	-0.1

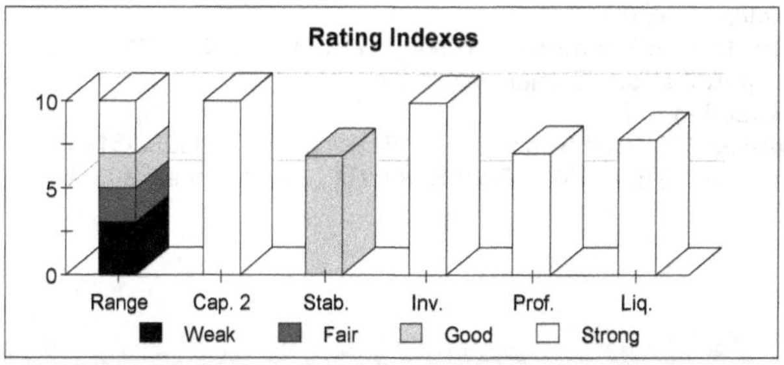

COMPREHENSIVE MOBILE PLAN UTAH INC C+ Fair

Major Rating Factors: Good overall profitability index (5.2 on a scale of 0 to 10). Strong capitalization (10.0) based on excellent current risk-adjusted capital (severe loss scenario). High quality investment portfolio (9.9).
Other Rating Factors: Excellent liquidity (8.8) with ample operational cash flow and liquid investments.
Principal Business: Other (100%)
Mem Phys: 18: 41 **17:** 19 **18 MLR** 49.0% **/ 18 Admin Exp** N/A
Enroll(000): Q1 19: 0 **18:** 1 **17:** 1 **Med Exp PMPM:** $90
Principal Investments: Cash and equiv (100%)
Provider Compensation ($000): FFS ($655)
Total Member Encounters: Non-phys (1,302)
Group Affiliation: None
Licensed in: UT
Address: 19820 N 7TH ST Ste 290, PHOENIX, AZ 85024
Phone: (877) 929-0030 **Dom State:** UT **Commenced Bus:** N/A

Data Date	Rating	RACR #1	RACR #2	Total Assets ($mil)	Capital ($mil)	Net Premium ($mil)	Net Income ($mil)
3-19	C+	6.13	5.10	1.1	1.0	0.3	0.0
3-18	U	N/A	N/A	0.9	0.8	0.3	N/A
2018	C+	5.88	4.90	1.0	1.0	1.3	0.2
2017	U	N/A	N/A	1.0	0.8	1.3	0.1
2016	U	5.11	4.26	0.8	0.7	1.0	0.1
2015	U	5.45	4.54	0.6	0.5	0.8	0.1
2014	U	3.51	2.93	0.4	0.4	0.0	-0.2

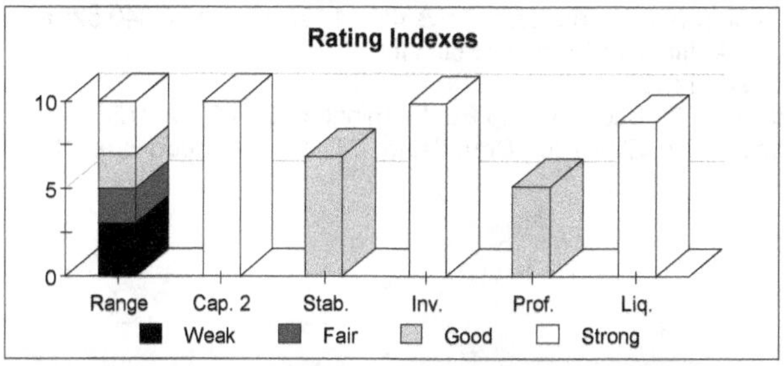

CONNECTICARE BENEFITS INC C Fair

Major Rating Factors: Good overall profitability index (6.2 on a scale of 0 to 10). Strong capitalization (8.1) based on excellent current risk-adjusted capital (severe loss scenario). High quality investment portfolio (8.8).
Other Rating Factors: Excellent liquidity (7.0) with sufficient resources (cash flows and marketable investments) to handle a spike in claims.
Principal Business: Comp med (100%)
Mem Phys: 18: 26,611 **17:** 25,734 **18 MLR** 72.1% **/ 18 Admin Exp** N/A
Enroll(000): Q1 19: 80 **18:** 68 **17:** 59 **Med Exp PMPM:** $465
Principal Investments: Long-term bonds (88%), cash and equiv (12%)
Provider Compensation ($000): Contr fee ($303,076), FFS ($74,186), capitation ($21,350)
Total Member Encounters: Phys (326,446), non-phys (280,390)
Group Affiliation: EmblemHealth Inc
Licensed in: CT
Address: 175 Scott Swamp Rd, Farmington, CT 06032-3124
Phone: (860) 674-5700 **Dom State:** CT **Commenced Bus:** N/A

Data Date	Rating	RACR #1	RACR #2	Total Assets ($mil)	Capital ($mil)	Net Premium ($mil)	Net Income ($mil)
3-19	C	2.21	1.84	207.7	63.0	139.4	16.5
3-18	D+	N/A	N/A	155.9	55.9	151.4	15.9
2018	C	1.64	1.37	173.7	46.7	566.4	56.6
2017	D+	N/A	N/A	121.7	40.5	390.7	1.3
2016	D+	1.78	1.49	84.1	27.2	272.1	-17.5
2015	C	4.80	4.00	81.5	42.4	198.8	13.6
2014	C-	3.34	2.79	59.5	29.7	140.1	12.3

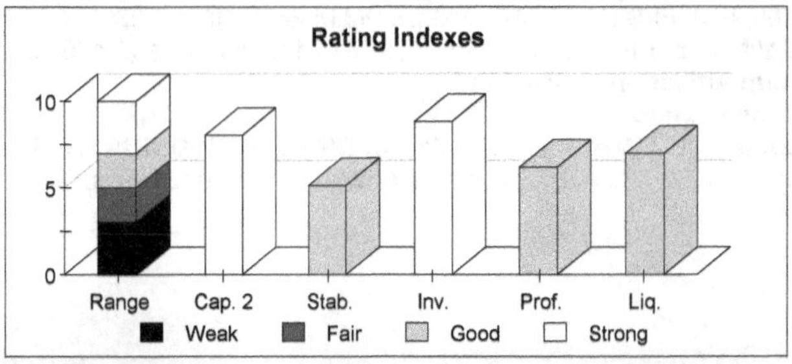

CONNECTICARE INC C- Fair

Major Rating Factors: Fair overall results on stability tests (3.4 on a scale of 0 to 10) based on a steep decline in capital during 2018. Weak profitability index (0.9). Good liquidity (6.8) with sufficient resources (cash flows and marketable investments) to handle a spike in claims.
Other Rating Factors: Strong capitalization index (7.6) based on excellent current risk-adjusted capital (severe loss scenario). High quality investment portfolio (9.2).
Principal Business: Medicare (70%), comp med (30%)
Mem Phys: 18: 26,611 **17:** 25,734 **18 MLR** 89.2% **/ 18 Admin Exp** N/A
Enroll(000): Q1 19: 75 **18:** 77 **17:** 79 **Med Exp PMPM:** $655
Principal Investments: Long-term bonds (84%), cash and equiv (16%)
Provider Compensation ($000): Contr fee ($482,603), FFS ($72,056), capitation ($56,096)
Total Member Encounters: Phys (662,501), non-phys (712,700)
Group Affiliation: EmblemHealth Inc
Licensed in: CT
Address: 175 Scott Swamp Road, Farmington, CT 06032-3124
Phone: (860) 674-5700 **Dom State:** CT **Commenced Bus:** N/A

Data Date	Rating	RACR #1	RACR #2	Total Assets ($mil)	Capital ($mil)	Net Premium ($mil)	Net Income ($mil)
3-19	C-	1.84	1.53	249.0	73.4	179.2	9.1
3-18	C	1.63	1.35	245.5	66.7	166.3	-18.2
2018	C-	1.67	1.39	216.5	66.8	679.9	-49.0
2017	C+	1.49	1.24	200.5	88.5	714.7	4.2
2016	C	2.19	1.82	209.2	94.5	793.8	7.1
2015	C+	2.51	2.09	214.0	108.9	835.4	5.1
2014	B	2.78	2.32	254.1	115.6	778.5	-0.9

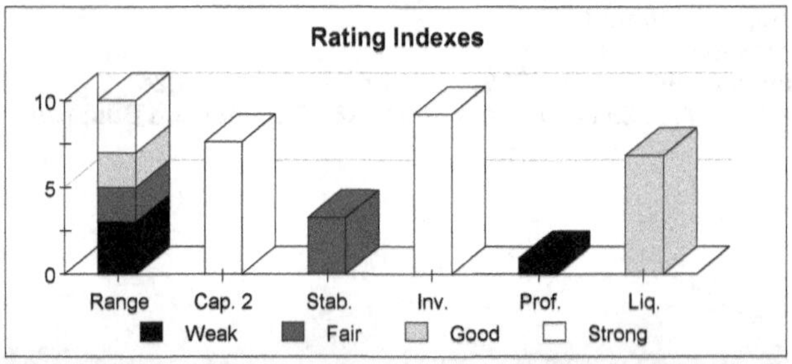

CONNECTICARE INS CO C Fair

Major Rating Factors: Weak profitability index (2.8 on a scale of 0 to 10). Strong capitalization (7.8) based on excellent current risk-adjusted capital (severe loss scenario). High quality investment portfolio (7.2).
Other Rating Factors: Excellent liquidity (7.0) with sufficient resources (cash flows and marketable investments) to handle a spike in claims.
Principal Business: Comp med (100%)
Mem Phys: 18: 26,611 **17:** 25,734 **18 MLR** 80.0% **/ 18 Admin Exp** N/A
Enroll(000): Q1 19: 77 **18:** 87 **17:** 92 **Med Exp PMPM:** $465
Principal Investments: Long-term bonds (63%), affiliate common stock (28%), cash and equiv (9%)
Provider Compensation ($000): Contr fee ($370,963), FFS ($75,456), capitation ($19,929)
Total Member Encounters: Phys (399,149), non-phys (340,525)
Group Affiliation: EmblemHealth Inc
Licensed in: CT
Address: 175 Scott Swamp Rd, Farmington, CT 06032-3124
Phone: (860) 674-5700 **Dom State:** CT **Commenced Bus:** N/A

Data Date	Rating	RACR #1	RACR #2	Total Assets ($mil)	Capital ($mil)	Net Premium ($mil)	Net Income ($mil)
3-19	C	2.01	1.67	247.9	126.6	137.6	1.3
3-18	C	1.50	1.25	217.1	99.0	138.3	-12.5
2018	C	1.71	1.42	245.1	108.4	591.2	54.8
2017	C	1.05	0.88	224.4	96.4	674.4	-3.1
2016	C	1.28	1.06	249.3	86.3	765.3	-49.8
2015	C	1.19	0.99	210.8	66.5	714.4	-19.7
2014	C	1.79	1.49	158.4	68.4	544.9	2.7

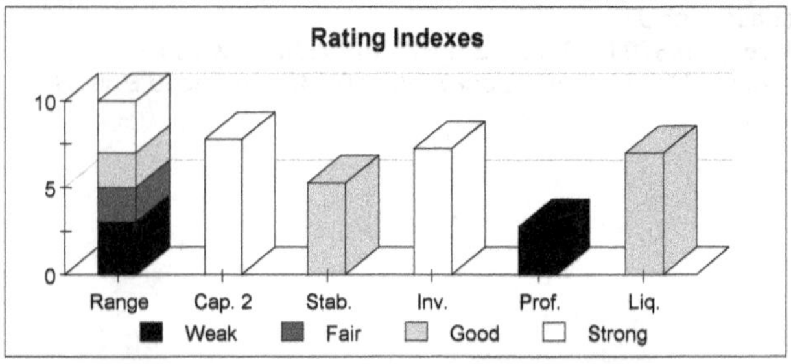

CONNECTICARE OF MASSACHUSETTS INC — C — Fair

Major Rating Factors: Fair profitability index (4.1 on a scale of 0 to 10). Fair overall results on stability tests (3.7) based on a significant 36% decrease in enrollment during the period, a steep decline in premium revenue in 2018. Rating is significantly influenced by the fair financial results of EmblemHealth Inc. Strong capitalization index (8.1) based on excellent current risk-adjusted capital (severe loss scenario).
Other Rating Factors: High quality investment portfolio (9.9). Excellent liquidity (8.5) with ample operational cash flow and liquid investments.
Principal Business: Comp med (100%)
Mem Phys: 18: 26,611 **17:** 25,734 **18 MLR** 53.4% **/ 18 Admin Exp** N/A
Enroll(000): Q1 19: 0 **18:** 0 **17:** 0 **Med Exp PMPM:** $390
Principal Investments: Long-term bonds (78%), cash and equiv (22%)
Provider Compensation ($000): Contr fee ($1,293), FFS ($493), capitation ($62)
Total Member Encounters: Phys (1,664), non-phys (1,308)
Group Affiliation: EmblemHealth Inc
Licensed in: MA
Address: c/o Leboeuf Lamb Greene & McRa, Boston, MA 02110-3173
Phone: (860) 674-5700 **Dom State:** MA **Commenced Bus:** N/A

Data Date	Rating	RACR #1	RACR #2	Total Assets ($mil)	Capital ($mil)	Net Premium ($mil)	Net Income ($mil)
3-19	C	2.26	1.88	3.6	3.0	0.6	0.3
3-18	D	1.59	1.33	2.8	2.1	0.7	0.2
2018	C	2.03	1.69	3.8	2.7	3.2	0.7
2017	E-	0.73	0.61	2.7	1.9	4.6	0.5
2016	E-	1.20	1.00	2.6	1.5	4.8	-0.7
2015	E-	1.74	1.45	3.7	2.1	8.3	-0.9
2014	C	2.55	2.13	6.7	3.1	10.1	-0.4

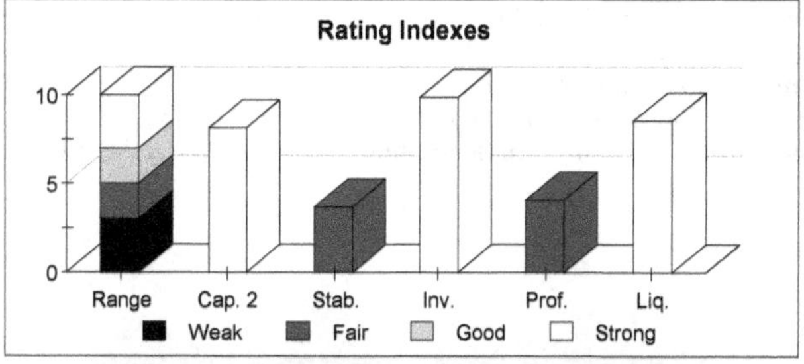

CONNECTICUT GENERAL LIFE INSURANCE COMPANY — B- — Good

Major Rating Factors: Good overall results on stability tests (5.2 on a scale of 0 to 10). Stability strengths include excellent operational trends and excellent risk diversification. Fair quality investment portfolio (4.4). Strong capitalization (7.2) based on excellent risk adjusted capital (severe loss scenario). Moreover, capital levels have been consistently high over the last five years.
Other Rating Factors: Excellent profitability (9.1). Excellent liquidity (7.8).
Principal Business: Individual life insurance (33%), group life insurance (32%), individual health insurance (24%), reinsurance (5%), and other lines (5%).
Principal Investments: Common & preferred stock (46%), nonCMO investment grade bonds (31%), policy loans (13%), mortgages in good standing (3%), and misc. investments (8%).
Investments in Affiliates: 47%
Group Affiliation: CIGNA Corp
Licensed in: All states, the District of Columbia and Puerto Rico
Commenced Business: October 1865
Address: 900 COTTAGE GROVE ROAD, BLOOMFIELD, CT 6002
Phone: (860) 226-6000 **Domicile State:** CT **NAIC Code:** 62308

Data Date	Rating	RACR #1	RACR #2	Total Assets ($mil)	Capital ($mil)	Net Premium ($mil)	Net Income ($mil)
3-19	B-	1.23	1.15	19,081.8	5,521.9	76.4	743.5
3-18	B-	1.35	1.23	18,502.4	4,766.4	85.8	217.0
2018	B-	1.25	1.17	19,056.7	5,494.5	333.7	1,239.4
2017	B-	1.32	1.22	18,137.2	4,412.2	346.3	1,013.8
2016	B-	1.32	1.20	17,646.3	4,074.4	402.2	1,180.4
2015	B-	1.33	1.19	17,374.4	3,631.0	490.7	916.2
2014	B-	1.34	1.19	17,768.9	3,473.3	1,107.4	212.6

Adverse Trends in Operations

Decrease in premium volume from 2016 to 2017 (14%)
Change in premium mix from 2015 to 2016 (4.3%)
Decrease in premium volume from 2015 to 2016 (17%)
Change in premium mix from 2014 to 2015 (4.7%)
Decrease in premium volume from 2014 to 2015 (56%)

CONSTITUTION LIFE INSURANCE COMPANY — D — Weak

Major Rating Factors: Weak overall results on stability tests (1.5 on a scale of 0 to 10) including potential financial drain due to affiliation with Nassau Reinsurance Group Holdings LP and negative cash flow from operations for 2018. Weak profitability (2.4) with investment income below regulatory standards in relation to interest assumptions of reserves. Fair quality investment portfolio (4.3).
Other Rating Factors: Good liquidity (6.6). Strong capitalization (7.6) based on excellent risk adjusted capital (severe loss scenario).
Principal Business: Individual health insurance (49%), reinsurance (30%), group health insurance (11%), and individual life insurance (9%).
Principal Investments: NonCMO investment grade bonds (59%), CMOs and structured securities (34%), noninv. grade bonds (3%), policy loans (1%), and cash (1%).
Investments in Affiliates: None
Group Affiliation: Nassau Reinsurance Group Holdings LP
Licensed in: All states except NJ, NY, PR
Commenced Business: June 1929
Address: 4888 Loop Central Dr Ste 700, Houston, TX 77081
Phone: (407) 547-3800 **Domicile State:** TX **NAIC Code:** 62359

Data Date	Rating	RACR #1	RACR #2	Total Assets ($mil)	Capital ($mil)	Net Premium ($mil)	Net Income ($mil)
3-19	D	2.64	1.40	388.3	40.6	11.4	1.2
3-18	D	2.29	1.26	403.1	34.5	11.0	-0.3
2018	D	2.62	1.40	390.7	39.6	42.5	5.2
2017	D	2.28	1.26	412.7	35.1	49.1	-4.0
2016	D	2.71	1.71	444.1	55.6	90.0	-11.8
2015	C+	2.75	1.84	394.8	66.6	123.3	34.9
2014	C+	1.88	1.23	316.5	37.0	94.4	11.1

Nassau Reinsurance Group Holdings LP
Composite Group Rating: D

Largest Group Members	Assets ($mil)	Rating
NASSAU LIFE INSURANCE CO	11960	D-
PHL VARIABLE INS CO	5914	D
CONSTITUTION LIFE INS CO	391	D
PYRAMID LIFE INS CO	74	D
NASSAU LIFE ANNUITY CO	35	D

CONTINENTAL AMERICAN INSURANCE COMPANY B Good

Major Rating Factors: Good liquidity (6.9 on a scale of 0 to 10) with sufficient resources to handle a spike in claims. Good overall results on stability tests (5.7) despite negative cash flow from operations for 2018. Strengths include good financial support from affiliation with AFLAC Inc, good operational trends and excellent risk diversification. Fair profitability (4.7).
Other Rating Factors: Strong capitalization (7.3) based on excellent risk adjusted capital (severe loss scenario). High quality investment portfolio (7.6).
Principal Business: Group health insurance (70%), reinsurance (27%), and group life insurance (3%).
Principal Investments: NonCMO investment grade bonds (85%), noninv. grade bonds (2%), and policy loans (1%).
Investments in Affiliates: None
Group Affiliation: AFLAC Inc
Licensed in: All states except NY, PR
Commenced Business: January 1969
Address: 1600 Williams Street, Omaha, NE 68114-3743
Phone: (888) 730-2244 **Domicile State:** SC **NAIC Code:** 71730

Data Date	Rating	RACR #1	RACR #2	Total Assets ($mil)	Capital ($mil)	Net Premium ($mil)	Net Income ($mil)
3-19	B	1.89	1.42	711.8	160.3	91.5	1.5
3-18	B	1.71	1.27	719.3	155.8	166.0	3.3
2018	B	1.70	1.28	665.1	157.3	587.6	5.9
2017	B	1.79	1.33	673.3	153.4	524.7	-21.7
2016	B	1.98	1.44	607.0	174.4	536.1	46.8
2015	B	1.84	1.37	512.3	138.0	436.8	26.2
2014	B	2.49	1.78	397.0	109.7	240.6	-17.3

AFLAC Inc
Composite Group Rating: B+

Largest Group Members	Assets ($mil)	Rating
AMERICAN FAMILY LIFE ASR CO OF NY	965	A-
CONTINENTAL AMERICAN INS CO	665	B

CONTINENTAL GENERAL INSURANCE COMPANY C+ Fair

Major Rating Factors: Fair quality investment portfolio (3.9 on a scale of 0 to 10) with large holdings of BBB rated bonds in addition to junk bond exposure equal to 71% of capital. Fair profitability (4.4) with investment income below regulatory standards in relation to interest assumptions of reserves. Fair overall results on stability tests (4.6) including excessive premium growth and fair risk adjusted capital in prior years.
Other Rating Factors: Strong capitalization (7.0) based on excellent risk adjusted capital (severe loss scenario). Excellent liquidity (8.1).
Principal Business: Individual health insurance (72%), group health insurance (16%), individual life insurance (7%), reinsurance (2%), and group life insurance (2%).
Principal Investments: NonCMO investment grade bonds (61%), CMOs and structured securities (17%), common & preferred stock (7%), noninv. grade bonds (5%), and misc. investments (4%).
Investments in Affiliates: 2%
Group Affiliation: HC2 Holdings Inc
Licensed in: All states except NY, PR
Commenced Business: July 1961
Address: 11001 Lakeline Blvd Ste 120, Austin, TX 78717
Phone: (866) 830-0607 **Domicile State:** OH **NAIC Code:** 71404

Data Date	Rating	RACR #1	RACR #2	Total Assets ($mil)	Capital ($mil)	Net Premium ($mil)	Net Income ($mil)
3-19	C+	1.86	1.01	4,240.2	274.2	30.2	26.8
3-18	C+	1.03	0.61	1,420.6	68.9	20.6	-5.6
2018	C+	1.78	0.96	4,206.9	255.5	126.2	-99.8
2017	C+	1.12	0.68	1,385.8	74.7	82.7	-0.1
2016	C+	1.10	0.72	1,344.1	76.9	82.2	-15.3
2015	C+	1.28	0.89	249.3	18.5	13.3	32.6
2014	C	2.35	1.38	242.4	21.5	14.3	1.9

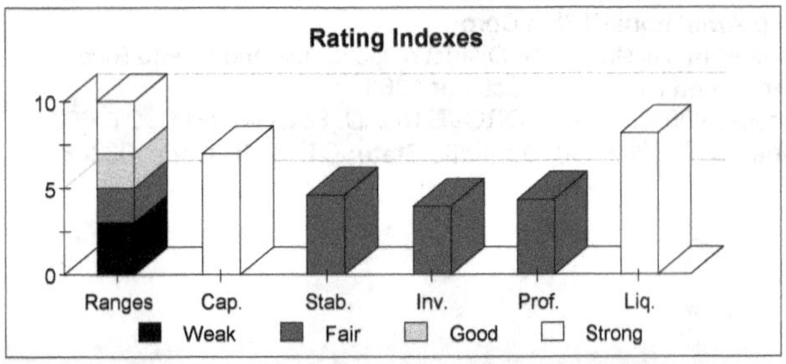

CONTINENTAL LIFE INSURANCE COMPANY OF BRENTWOOD C+ Fair

Major Rating Factors: Fair overall results on stability tests (4.5 on a scale of 0 to 10) including negative cash flow from operations for 2018. Good capitalization (5.2) based on good risk adjusted capital (severe loss scenario). Capital levels have been relatively consistent over the last five years. Good quality investment portfolio (5.4).
Other Rating Factors: Good liquidity (6.3). Weak profitability (2.0) with operating losses during the first three months of 2019.
Principal Business: Individual health insurance (99%), individual life insurance (1%), and group health insurance (1%).
Principal Investments: NonCMO investment grade bonds (41%), common & preferred stock (33%), CMOs and structured securities (27%), mortgages in good standing (2%), and noninv. grade bonds (1%).
Investments in Affiliates: 33%
Group Affiliation: Aetna Inc
Licensed in: All states except AK, DC, HI, ME, NY, PR
Commenced Business: December 1983
Address: 800 CRESCENT CENTRE DR STE 200, FRANKLIN, TN 37067
Phone: (800) 264-4000 **Domicile State:** TN **NAIC Code:** 68500

Data Date	Rating	RACR #1	RACR #2	Total Assets ($mil)	Capital ($mil)	Net Premium ($mil)	Net Income ($mil)
3-19	C+	0.86	0.77	364.4	160.0	139.6	-10.4
3-18	C+	0.98	0.88	336.5	175.0	125.2	-10.0
2018	C+	1.10	0.99	366.7	204.0	508.5	-13.5
2017	C+	1.10	0.99	345.6	194.4	468.0	-9.5
2016	B	1.16	1.03	307.1	173.8	427.2	-7.8
2015	B	1.11	0.99	274.0	144.3	380.6	-1.2
2014	B	1.19	1.08	277.8	156.4	330.6	3.0

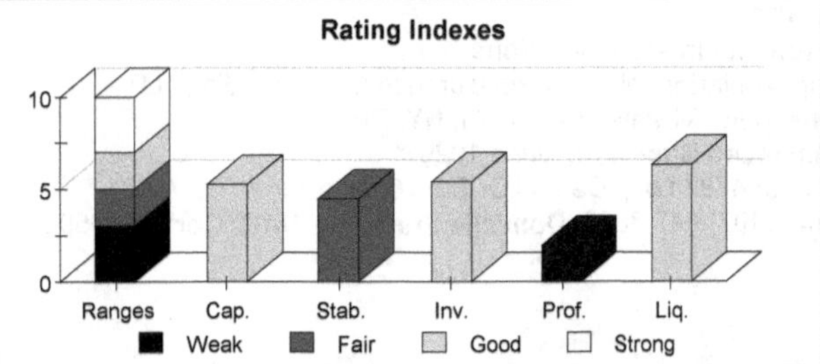

CONTRA COSTA HEALTH PLAN B Good

Major Rating Factors: Good overall results on stability tests (5.8 on a scale of 0 to 10). Excellent profitability (8.2). Strong capitalization index (7.0) based on excellent current risk-adjusted capital (severe loss scenario).
Other Rating Factors: Excellent liquidity (7.4) with ample operational cash flow and liquid investments.
Principal Business: Medicaid (92%)
Mem Phys: 18: N/A **17:** N/A **18 MLR** 103.4% **/ 18 Admin Exp** N/A
Enroll(000): Q1 19: 188 **18:** 188 **17:** 193 **Med Exp PMPM:** $350
Principal Investments ($000): Cash and equiv ($91,593)
Provider Compensation ($000): None
Total Member Encounters: N/A
Group Affiliation: None
Licensed in: CA
Address: 595 Center Avenue Suite 100, Martinez, CA 94553
Phone: (925) 313-6004 **Dom State:** CA **Commenced Bus:** November 1973

Data Date	Rating	RACR #1	RACR #2	Total Assets ($mil)	Capital ($mil)	Net Premium ($mil)	Net Income ($mil)
3-19	B	1.75	1.11	364.1	79.2	197.0	0.9
3-18	C	1.07	0.72	365.9	60.4	193.5	6.7
2018	B-	1.73	1.09	181.2	78.3	773.8	20.6
2017	C	0.94	0.63	392.9	53.7	743.6	6.9
2016	C	0.98	0.62	281.7	45.3	692.0	12.1
2015	C	1.16	0.74	206.2	45.5	622.6	24.6
2014	D	0.69	0.44	133.3	20.9	418.4	7.0

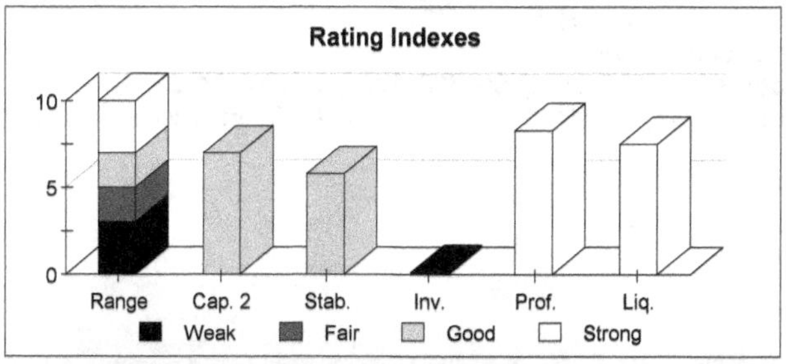

COOK CHILDRENS HEALTH PLAN E+ Very Weak

Major Rating Factors: Good overall profitability index (5.2 on a scale of 0 to 10). Strong capitalization index (7.5) based on excellent current risk-adjusted capital (severe loss scenario). High quality investment portfolio (9.9).
Other Rating Factors: Excellent overall results on stability tests (7.4). Excellent liquidity (7.0) with sufficient resources (cash flows and marketable investments) to handle a spike in claims
Principal Business: Medicaid (93%), comp med (7%)
Mem Phys: 18: 12,048 **17:** N/A **18 MLR** 87.5% **/ 18 Admin Exp** N/A
Enroll(000): Q1 19: 134 **18:** 138 **17:** 142 **Med Exp PMPM:** $287
Principal Investments: Cash and equiv (64%), long-term bonds (36%)
Provider Compensation ($000): Contr fee ($468,469), bonus arrang ($472)
Total Member Encounters: Phys (3,850,551), non-phys (394,218)
Group Affiliation: W I Cook Foundation
Licensed in: TX
Address: 801 Seventh Avenue, Fort Worth, TX 76104
Phone: (817) 334-2247 **Dom State:** TX **Commenced Bus:** N/A

Data Date	Rating	RACR #1	RACR #2	Total Assets ($mil)	Capital ($mil)	Net Premium ($mil)	Net Income ($mil)
3-19	E+	1.74	1.45	154.6	86.0	137.7	3.5
3-18	E+	1.35	1.13	123.2	64.3	133.7	-5.8
2018	E+	1.71	1.42	155.3	84.6	549.9	11.0
2017	E+	1.53	1.28	131.1	71.9	506.9	-4.0
2016	E+	2.71	2.25	129.7	75.9	345.7	18.5
2015	E+	2.35	1.96	118.7	63.9	297.1	11.3
2014	E+	1.97	1.65	96.3	54.4	295.7	18.3

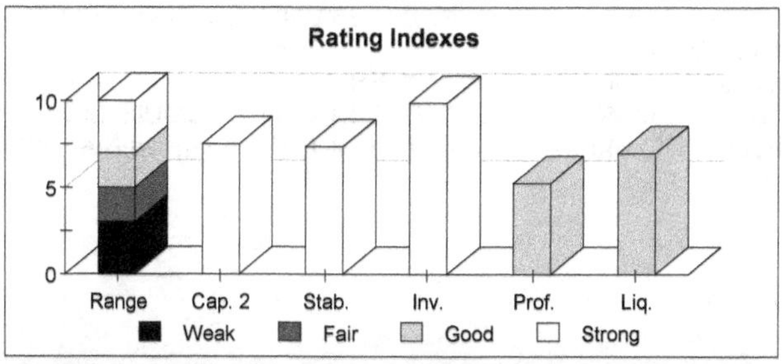

COORDINATED CARE CORP C+ Fair

Major Rating Factors: Fair quality investment portfolio (4.0 on a scale of 0 to 10). Good overall profitability index (6.5). Strong capitalization index (9.2) based on excellent current risk-adjusted capital (severe loss scenario).
Other Rating Factors: Excellent overall results on stability tests (7.3) based on healthy premium and capital growth during 2018. Rating is significantly influenced by the fair financial results of . Excellent liquidity (7.0) with ample operational cash flow and liquid investments.
Principal Business: Medicaid (85%), comp med (14%)
Mem Phys: 18: 27,626 **17:** 25,088 **18 MLR** 84.2% **/ 18 Admin Exp** N/A
Enroll(000): Q1 19: 300 **18:** 294 **17:** 294 **Med Exp PMPM:** $402
Principal Investments: Cash and equiv (61%), long-term bonds (32%), affiliate common stock (3%), other (4%)
Provider Compensation ($000): Contr fee ($1,342,945), capitation ($56,645), bonus arrang ($37,752), salary ($21,031)
Total Member Encounters: Phys (1,579,007), non-phys (1,598,444)
Group Affiliation: None
Licensed in: IN, WA
Address: 1099 N Meridian Street Suite 4, Indianapolis, IN 46204-1041
Phone: (314) 725-4477 **Dom State:** IN **Commenced Bus:** N/A

Data Date	Rating	RACR #1	RACR #2	Total Assets ($mil)	Capital ($mil)	Net Premium ($mil)	Net Income ($mil)
3-19	C+	3.15	2.62	574.7	237.0	457.8	25.8
3-18	C+	2.62	2.19	557.0	176.8	438.1	4.9
2018	C+	2.74	2.28	460.3	203.6	1,723.8	37.4
2017	C+	1.59	1.32	408.1	148.3	1,457.6	10.8
2016	C+	2.30	1.92	330.6	111.8	1,091.2	6.7
2015	C+	2.28	1.90	306.6	83.7	811.8	15.3
2014	C+	1.73	1.44	462.9	67.1	931.0	-3.1

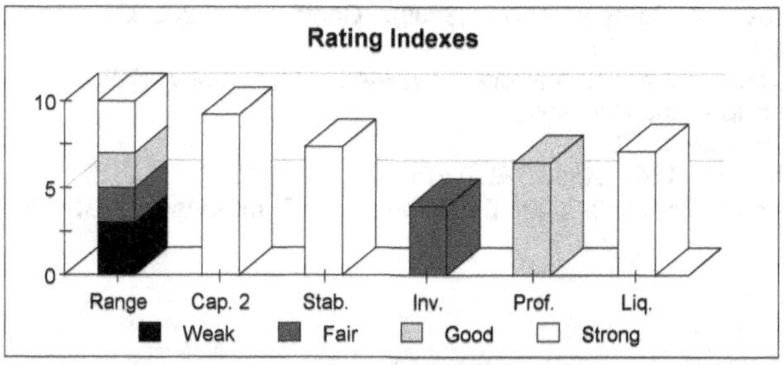

COORDINATED CARE OF WASHINGTON INC C- Fair

Major Rating Factors: Weak profitability index (0.9 on a scale of 0 to 10). Good liquidity (6.0) with sufficient resources (cash flows and marketable investments) to handle a spike in claims. Strong capitalization (8.3) based on excellent current risk-adjusted capital (severe loss scenario).
Other Rating Factors: High quality investment portfolio (7.4).
Principal Business: Medicaid (99%), comp med (1%)
Mem Phys: 18: 23,065 **17:** 25,488 **18 MLR** 94.5% **/ 18 Admin Exp** N/A
Enroll(000): Q1 19: 201 **18:** 191 **17:** 202 **Med Exp PMPM:** $234
Principal Investments: Long-term bonds (75%), cash and equiv (25%)
Provider Compensation ($000): Contr fee ($481,444), capitation ($31,542), bonus arrang ($21,282), salary ($14,008)
Total Member Encounters: Phys (801,129), non-phys (1,209,421)
Group Affiliation: None
Licensed in: WA
Address: 1145 BRdway Ste 300, Tacoma, WA 98402
Phone: (314) 725-4477 **Dom State:** WA **Commenced Bus:** N/A

Data Date	Rating	RACR #1	RACR #2	Total Assets ($mil)	Capital ($mil)	Net Premium ($mil)	Net Income ($mil)
3-19	C-	2.42	2.02	239.6	81.1	160.8	-11.0
3-18	D+	N/A	N/A	272.6	93.1	185.0	-15.6
2018	C-	2.51	2.09	229.9	84.5	596.6	-19.9
2017	D+	N/A	N/A	237.4	88.0	697.7	-11.2
2016	D+	1.90	1.59	247.2	60.6	680.3	-38.4
2015	D+	2.88	2.40	231.0	84.6	558.5	-8.6
2014	N/A	N/A	N/A	167.6	86.6	N/A	-30.3

Rating Indexes

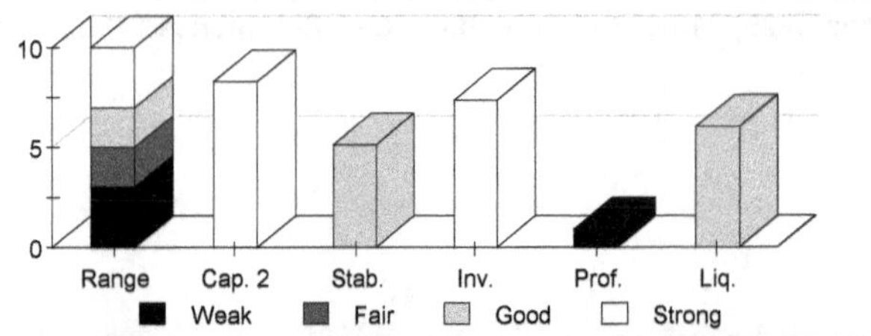

COVENTRY HEALTH & LIFE INS CO B- Good

Major Rating Factors: Fair quality investment portfolio (4.7 on a scale of 0 to 10). Good liquidity (6.8) with sufficient resources (cash flows and marketable investments) to handle a spike in claims. Excellent profitability (7.4).
Other Rating Factors: Strong capitalization (10.0) based on excellent current risk-adjusted capital (severe loss scenario).
Principal Business: Medicare (93%), comp med (7%)
Mem Phys: 18: N/A **17:** N/A **18 MLR** 82.6% **/ 18 Admin Exp** N/A
Enroll(000): Q1 19: 190 **18:** 180 **17:** 182 **Med Exp PMPM:** $656
Principal Investments: Long-term bonds (61%), affiliate common stock (29%), cash and equiv (7%), mortgs (3%)
Provider Compensation ($000): Contr fee ($1,254,647), FFS ($145,628), capitation ($23,782), bonus arrang ($6,269)
Total Member Encounters: Phys (1,888,243), non-phys (553,553)
Group Affiliation: None
Licensed in: All states except NY, PR
Address: 550 MARYVILLE CENTRE Dr #300, ST. LOUIS, MO 63141
Phone: (800) 843-7421 **Dom State:** MO **Commenced Bus:** N/A

Data Date	Rating	RACR #1	RACR #2	Total Assets ($mil)	Capital ($mil)	Net Premium ($mil)	Net Income ($mil)
3-19	B-	6.89	5.74	1,333.5	1,010.5	502.7	31.5
3-18	B	8.00	6.66	1,526.8	1,092.4	427.8	-12.3
2018	B-	6.61	5.51	1,251.2	963.9	1,728.0	47.6
2017	B	8.10	6.75	1,354.3	1,108.4	1,673.5	114.9
2016	B	7.51	6.26	1,512.5	1,145.3	2,484.5	77.6
2015	B	4.82	4.01	1,699.7	949.3	4,066.1	260.2
2014	B	2.89	2.41	1,616.3	704.2	4,565.5	159.1

Rating Indexes

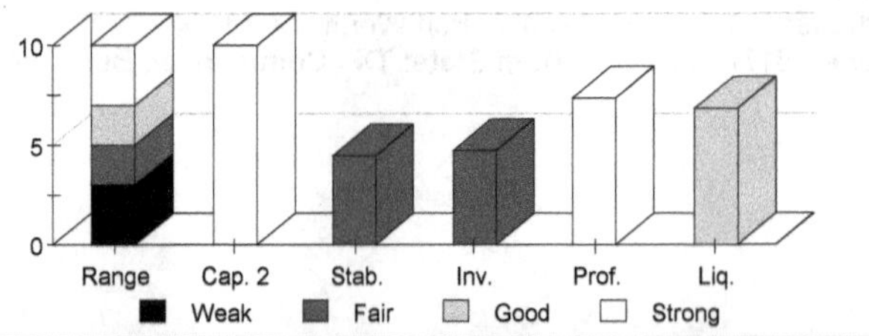

COVENTRY HEALTH CARE OF FLORIDA INC D Weak

Major Rating Factors: Weak profitability index (0.9 on a scale of 0 to 10). Weak overall results on stability tests (0.7). Rating is significantly influenced by the good financial results of . Weak liquidity (0.0) as a spike in claims may stretch capacity.
Other Rating Factors: Strong capitalization index (9.0) based on excellent current risk-adjusted capital (severe loss scenario). High quality investment portfolio (9.2).
Principal Business: Medicaid (83%), comp med (17%)
Mem Phys: 18: 41,044 **17:** 45,285 **18 MLR** 118.7% **/ 18 Admin Exp** N/A
Enroll(000): Q1 19: 138 **18:** 104 **17:** 108 **Med Exp PMPM:** $462
Principal Investments: Long-term bonds (65%), cash and equiv (34%), nonaffiliate common stock (1%)
Provider Compensation ($000): Contr fee ($282,824), FFS ($102,499), capitation ($47,500)
Total Member Encounters: Phys (448,110), non-phys (709,368)
Group Affiliation: None
Licensed in: FL
Address: 1340 CONCORD TERRACE, SUNRISE, FL 33323
Phone: (954) 858-3000 **Dom State:** FL **Commenced Bus:** N/A

Data Date	Rating	RACR #1	RACR #2	Total Assets ($mil)	Capital ($mil)	Net Premium ($mil)	Net Income ($mil)
3-19	D	2.99	2.49	384.4	127.2	137.2	53.5
3-18	C+	6.16	5.13	281.9	155.9	116.5	-6.2
2018	D	1.67	1.39	346.0	73.2	493.7	-113.1
2017	C+	4.52	3.77	298.6	160.7	511.7	32.0
2016	C+	3.05	2.54	547.7	195.6	1,368.1	42.9
2015	C+	2.10	1.75	515.7	128.7	1,280.5	6.9
2014	B	1.04	0.87	476.5	54.8	1,110.3	-44.6

Rating Indexes

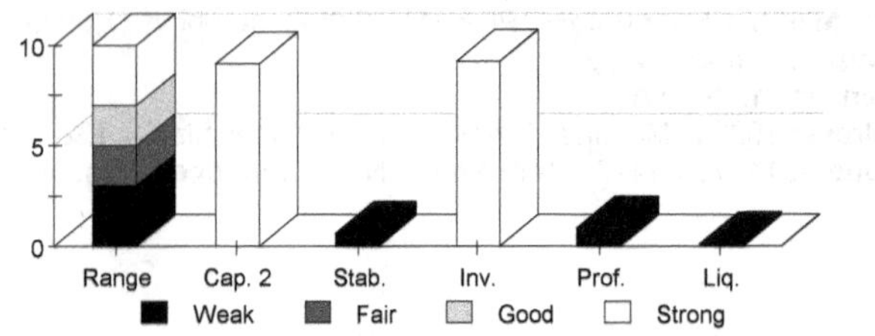

COVENTRY HEALTH CARE OF ILLINOIS INC C Fair

Major Rating Factors: Fair profitability index (4.4 on a scale of 0 to 10). Strong capitalization (10.0) based on excellent current risk-adjusted capital (severe loss scenario). High quality investment portfolio (9.5).
Other Rating Factors: Excellent liquidity (7.3) with ample operational cash flow and liquid investments.
Principal Business: Medicare (97%), comp med (3%)
Mem Phys: 18: 39,556 **17:** 34,250 **18 MLR** 59.6% **/ 18 Admin Exp** N/A
Enroll(000): Q1 19: 27 **18:** 25 **17:** 22 **Med Exp PMPM:** $647
Principal Investments: Long-term bonds (73%), cash and equiv (27%)
Provider Compensation ($000): Contr fee ($156,451), FFS ($19,336), bonus arrang ($7,453), capitation ($3,364)
Total Member Encounters: Phys (273,911), non-phys (94,735)
Group Affiliation: None
Licensed in: IL
Address: 2110 FOX Dr, CHAMPAIGN, IL 61820
Phone: (217) 366-1226 **Dom State:** IL **Commenced Bus:** N/A

Data Date	Rating	RACR #1	RACR #2	Total Assets ($mil)	Capital ($mil)	Net Premium ($mil)	Net Income ($mil)
3-19	C	4.23	3.53	159.6	81.6	95.3	15.5
3-18	C+	5.23	4.36	170.2	87.9	79.2	-5.2
2018	C	3.45	2.87	138.9	66.1	321.6	5.2
2017	C	3.75	3.12	135.5	92.3	308.3	14.0
2016	C	3.32	2.77	177.9	88.2	481.2	1.1
2015	B-	2.84	2.37	131.4	47.6	351.9	7.8
2014	B	2.20	1.83	117.6	34.3	320.1	-2.4

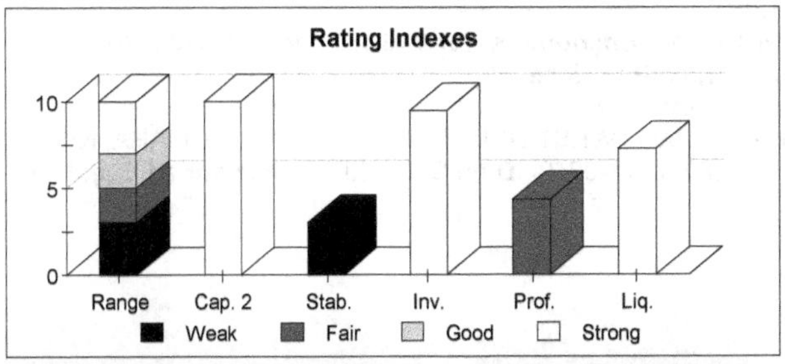

COVENTRY HEALTH CARE OF KANSAS INC C Fair

Major Rating Factors: Fair quality investment portfolio (3.7 on a scale of 0 to 10). Weak overall results on stability tests (0.0). Rating is significantly influenced by the good financial results of . Good overall profitability index (6.2).
Other Rating Factors: Strong capitalization index (10.0) based on excellent current risk-adjusted capital (severe loss scenario). Excellent liquidity (9.0) with ample operational cash flow and liquid investments.
Principal Business: Comp med (100%)
Mem Phys: 18: 32,064 **17:** 19,723 **18 MLR** 74.7% **/ 18 Admin Exp** N/A
Enroll(000): Q1 19: 0 **18:** 1 **17:** 2 **Med Exp PMPM:** $248
Principal Investments: Long-term bonds (59%), cash and equiv (39%), nonaffiliate common stock (3%)
Provider Compensation ($000): Contr fee ($4,484), capitation ($357), FFS ($195)
Total Member Encounters: Phys (6,392), non-phys (2,313)
Group Affiliation: None
Licensed in: AR, KS, MO, OK
Address: 8535 E 21ST STREET N, WICHITA, KS 67206
Phone: (913) 202-5400 **Dom State:** KS **Commenced Bus:** N/A

Data Date	Rating	RACR #1	RACR #2	Total Assets ($mil)	Capital ($mil)	Net Premium ($mil)	Net Income ($mil)
3-19	C	18.23	15.19	20.8	15.0	1.6	1.1
3-18	C	43.57	36.31	61.2	50.9	2.0	0.2
2018	C	17.31	14.43	21.7	13.7	6.0	3.0
2017	C-	27.26	22.72	61.9	51.8	13.1	5.0
2016	C+	4.28	3.57	116.0	73.8	367.9	25.7
2015	C+	3.43	2.86	211.3	93.1	573.7	28.2
2014	B	3.50	2.92	230.2	109.4	615.0	24.5

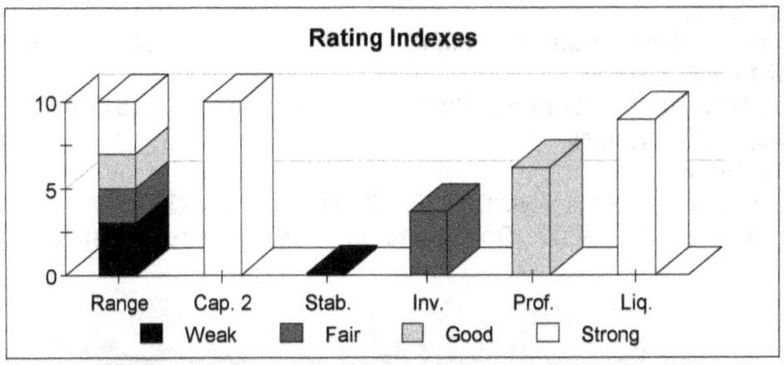

COVENTRY HEALTH CARE OF MISSOURI INC C+ Fair

Major Rating Factors: Fair quality investment portfolio (4.5 on a scale of 0 to 10). Fair overall results on stability tests (3.0). Rating is significantly influenced by the good financial results of . Good liquidity (6.1) with sufficient resources (cash flows and marketable investments) to handle a spike in claims.
Other Rating Factors: Excellent profitability (7.8). Strong capitalization index (9.6) based on excellent current risk-adjusted capital (severe loss scenario).
Principal Business: Medicare (100%)
Mem Phys: 18: 16,383 **17:** 15,361 **18 MLR** 93.5% **/ 18 Admin Exp** N/A
Enroll(000): Q1 19: 82 **18:** 83 **17:** 87 **Med Exp PMPM:** $750
Principal Investments: Long-term bonds (87%), cash and equiv (10%), mortgs (3%)
Provider Compensation ($000): Contr fee ($472,096), capitation ($189,094), bonus arrang ($62,460), FFS ($32,765)
Total Member Encounters: Phys (934,300), non-phys (236,772)
Group Affiliation: None
Licensed in: AR, IL, KS, MO, OK
Address: 550 MARYVILLE CENTRE DRIVE, ST. LOUIS, MO 63141
Phone: (314) 506-1700 **Dom State:** MO **Commenced Bus:** N/A

Data Date	Rating	RACR #1	RACR #2	Total Assets ($mil)	Capital ($mil)	Net Premium ($mil)	Net Income ($mil)
3-19	C+	3.45	2.88	281.1	139.0	222.8	19.9
3-18	B	3.79	3.16	400.5	152.2	210.8	-12.9
2018	C+	2.96	2.47	279.2	118.0	808.3	6.2
2017	B	2.91	2.43	309.5	163.8	883.6	61.9
2016	C+	5.72	4.76	323.0	154.4	588.3	37.1
2015	C+	4.55	3.79	236.3	116.9	563.5	32.4
2014	B	3.47	2.89	229.4	88.2	512.6	9.3

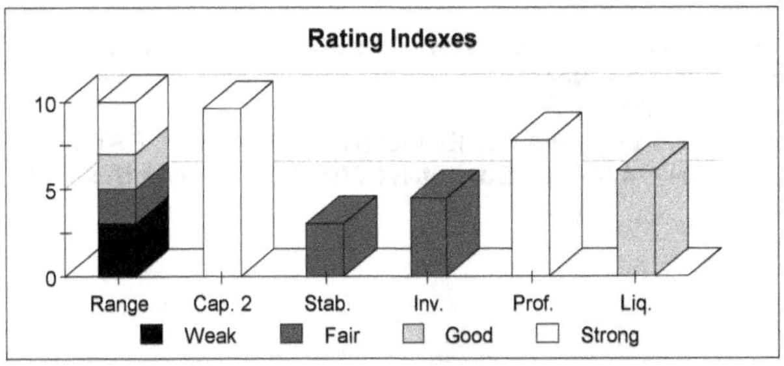

COVENTRY HEALTH CARE OF NEBRASKA INC C Fair

Major Rating Factors: Fair profitability index (3.7 on a scale of 0 to 10). Weak overall results on stability tests (0.0). Rating is significantly influenced by the good financial results of . Good quality investment portfolio (5.4).
Other Rating Factors: Strong capitalization index (10.0) based on excellent current risk-adjusted capital (severe loss scenario). Excellent liquidity (7.6) with ample operational cash flow and liquid investments.
Principal Business: Comp med (92%), Medicaid (8%)
Mem Phys: 18: N/A **17:** N/A **18 MLR** 65.4% **/ 18 Admin Exp** N/A
Enroll(000): Q1 19: N/A **18:** 2 **17:** 3 **Med Exp PMPM:** $291
Principal Investments: Long-term bonds (84%), mortgs (9%), cash and equiv (8%)
Provider Compensation ($000): Contr fee ($7,825), FFS ($3,431), capitation ($112)
Total Member Encounters: Phys (6,533), non-phys (3,056)
Group Affiliation: None
Licensed in: IA, NE
Address: 15950 WEST DODGE ROAD SUITE 40, OMAHA, NE 68118
Phone: (800) 471-0240 **Dom State:** NE **Commenced Bus:** N/A

Data Date	Rating	RACR #1	RACR #2	Total Assets ($mil)	Capital ($mil)	Net Premium ($mil)	Net Income ($mil)
3-19	C	22.06	18.38	23.7	23.0	0.0	0.4
3-18	B	64.83	54.02	99.6	94.4	1.9	-0.2
2018	C	21.40	17.83	36.1	22.1	9.8	2.8
2017	B	44.40	37.00	107.1	93.8	30.7	13.9
2016	B	2.80	2.34	200.5	81.7	567.0	-8.3
2015	B+	2.34	1.95	217.1	77.1	603.4	-4.2
2014	B+	2.78	2.32	148.6	60.4	422.1	11.1

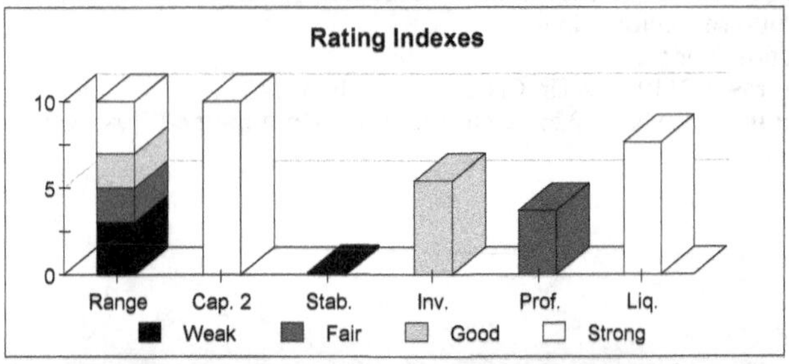

COVENTRY HEALTH CARE OF VIRGINIA INC B- Good

Major Rating Factors: Fair profitability index (3.6 on a scale of 0 to 10). Fair overall results on stability tests (4.9) based on an excessive 51% enrollment growth during the period. Rating is significantly influenced by the good financial results of . Good liquidity (6.8) with sufficient resources (cash flows and marketable investments) to handle a spike in claims.
Other Rating Factors: Strong capitalization index (7.2) based on excellent current risk-adjusted capital (severe loss scenario). High quality investment portfolio (9.5).
Principal Business: Medicaid (98%), Medicare (2%)
Mem Phys: 18: 6,735 **17:** 6,735 **18 MLR** 90.6% **/ 18 Admin Exp** N/A
Enroll(000): Q1 19: 135 **18:** 93 **17:** 61 **Med Exp PMPM:** $730
Principal Investments: Long-term bonds (63%), cash and equiv (36%), real estate (1%)
Provider Compensation ($000): Contr fee ($459,667), FFS ($165,299), capitation ($2,766)
Total Member Encounters: Phys (1,012,149), non-phys (817,422)
Group Affiliation: None
Licensed in: VA
Address: 9881 MAYLAND DRIVE, RICHMOND, VA 23233
Phone: (804) 747-3700 **Dom State:** VA **Commenced Bus:** N/A

Data Date	Rating	RACR #1	RACR #2	Total Assets ($mil)	Capital ($mil)	Net Premium ($mil)	Net Income ($mil)
3-19	B-	1.55	1.29	266.4	69.7	302.8	-8.7
3-18	C+	3.56	2.96	161.6	53.2	176.7	0.8
2018	B-	1.73	1.45	231.7	78.7	731.9	-10.3
2017	C+	2.21	1.84	127.2	53.3	277.5	15.4
2016	C+	1.88	1.57	109.5	40.1	348.4	-4.3
2015	B+	2.52	2.10	126.0	60.7	463.0	14.9
2014	B	2.38	1.98	125.7	59.4	414.2	2.6

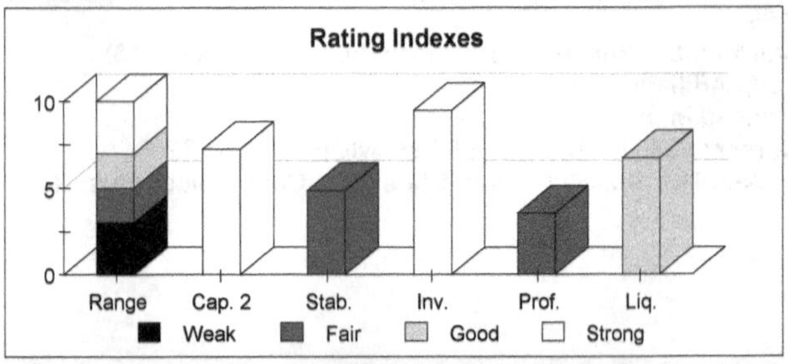

COVENTRY HEALTH CARE OF WEST VA INC B Good

Major Rating Factors: Good quality investment portfolio (6.4 on a scale of 0 to 10). Good overall results on stability tests (6.5) despite a decline in the number of member physicians during 2019. Rating is significantly influenced by the good financial results of . Good liquidity (6.5) with sufficient resources (cash flows and marketable investments) to handle a spike in claims.
Other Rating Factors: Excellent profitability (8.5). Strong capitalization index (9.3) based on excellent current risk-adjusted capital (severe loss scenario).
Principal Business: Medicaid (89%), Medicare (11%)
Mem Phys: 18: 5,207 **17:** 5,923 **18 MLR** 87.4% **/ 18 Admin Exp** N/A
Enroll(000): Q1 19: 121 **18:** 126 **17:** 132 **Med Exp PMPM:** $356
Principal Investments: Long-term bonds (80%), cash and equiv (20%)
Provider Compensation ($000): Contr fee ($478,538), FFS ($35,300), capitation ($11,545)
Total Member Encounters: Phys (956,748), non-phys (212,593)
Group Affiliation: None
Licensed in: WV
Address: 500 VIRGINIA STREET EAST SUITE, CHARLESTON, WV 25301
Phone: (804) 747-3700 **Dom State:** WV **Commenced Bus:** N/A

Data Date	Rating	RACR #1	RACR #2	Total Assets ($mil)	Capital ($mil)	Net Premium ($mil)	Net Income ($mil)
3-19	B	3.19	2.65	211.2	91.3	137.8	0.7
3-18	B	2.15	1.79	155.3	62.6	134.3	-5.8
2018	B	3.14	2.61	208.3	89.7	632.8	22.5
2017	B	1.49	1.24	148.7	68.2	555.9	12.6
2016	B+	2.41	2.01	171.0	72.5	546.4	22.6
2015	B+	3.56	2.97	120.5	64.5	342.8	18.6
2014	A	3.91	3.25	96.8	57.4	297.9	31.0

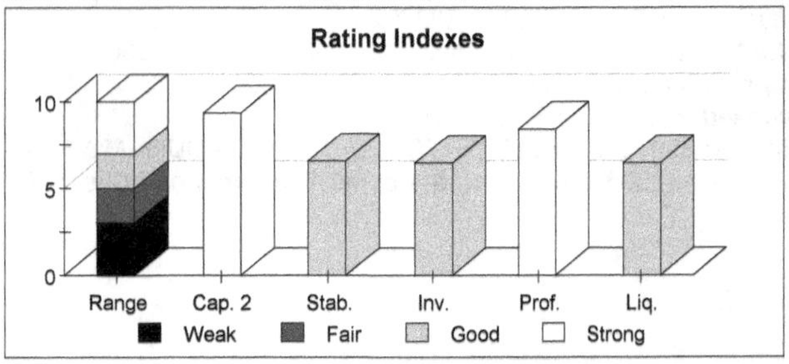

COX HEALTH SYSTEMS INS CO — D+ — Weak

Major Rating Factors: Weak profitability index (0.9 on a scale of 0 to 10). Fair capitalization (3.8) based on fair current risk-adjusted capital (moderate loss scenario). Good liquidity (6.6) with sufficient resources (cash flows and marketable investments) to handle a spike in claims.
Other Rating Factors: High quality investment portfolio (9.6).
Principal Business: Comp med (100%)
Mem Phys: 18: 3,495 **17:** 3,190 **18 MLR** 92.5% **/ 18 Admin Exp** N/A
Enroll(000): Q1 19: 28 **18:** 34 **17:** 35 **Med Exp PMPM:** $343
Principal Investments: Cash and equiv (64%), long-term bonds (35%)
Provider Compensation ($000): Contr fee ($136,535), FFS ($3,740)
Total Member Encounters: Phys (226,197), non-phys (29,783)
Group Affiliation: None
Licensed in: MO
Address: 3200 S National Bldg B, Springfield, MO 65801-5750
Phone: (417) 269-6762 **Dom State:** MO **Commenced Bus:** N/A

Data Date	Rating	RACR #1	RACR #2	Total Assets ($mil)	Capital ($mil)	Net Premium ($mil)	Net Income ($mil)
3-19	D+	0.75	0.63	51.9	18.8	32.3	0.3
3-18	D+	0.72	0.60	54.8	17.6	38.5	-0.6
2018	D+	0.74	0.62	53.8	18.7	153.5	-5.0
2017	D+	0.75	0.63	49.3	18.1	141.7	-14.6
2016	C	1.03	0.86	41.5	14.7	131.8	-3.7
2015	C+	1.15	0.96	38.3	17.5	120.5	-0.1
2014	B-	1.07	0.89	35.7	14.5	112.0	0.2

Rating Indexes

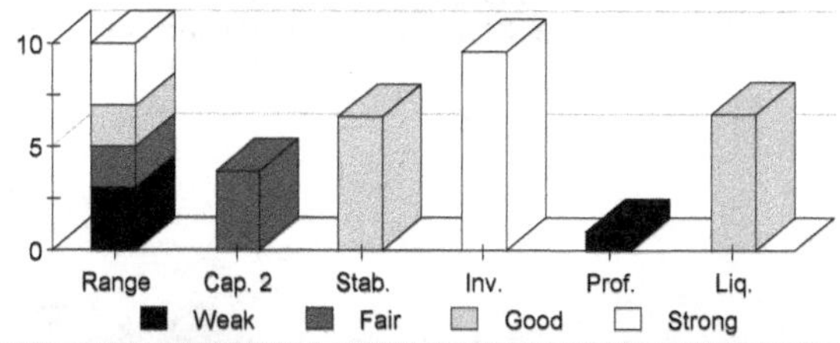

CRYSTAL RUN HEALTH INS CO INC — E — Very Weak

Major Rating Factors: Weak profitability index (0.0 on a scale of 0 to 10). Fair capitalization (3.1) based on weak current risk-adjusted capital (moderate loss scenario). Good liquidity (6.9) with sufficient resources (cash flows and marketable investments) to handle a spike in claims.
Other Rating Factors: High quality investment portfolio (9.9).
Principal Business: Comp med (100%)
Mem Phys: 18: 14,847 **17:** 11,287 **18 MLR** 112.4% **/ 18 Admin Exp** N/A
Enroll(000): Q1 19: 3 **18:** 3 **17:** 2 **Med Exp PMPM:** $468
Principal Investments: Cash and equiv (100%)
Provider Compensation ($000): Contr fee ($12,354)
Total Member Encounters: Phys (21,162), non-phys (8,276)
Group Affiliation: CRH Holdings II LLC
Licensed in: NY
Address: 109 Rykowski Lane, Middletown, NY 10941
Phone: (845) 703-6422 **Dom State:** NY **Commenced Bus:** N/A

Data Date	Rating	RACR #1	RACR #2	Total Assets ($mil)	Capital ($mil)	Net Premium ($mil)	Net Income ($mil)
3-19	E	0.64	0.54	13.0	2.5	3.9	-0.5
3-18	E-	N/A	N/A	12.0	4.1	3.5	-0.8
2018	E	0.82	0.68	12.0	3.0	12.7	-5.6
2017	E-	N/A	N/A	11.6	4.9	12.5	-4.0
2016	E-	0.13	0.11	6.7	0.3	9.4	-3.9
2015	E	2.17	1.81	6.9	2.4	2.1	-3.5
2014	N/A	N/A	N/A	N/A	N/A	N/A	N/A

Rating Indexes

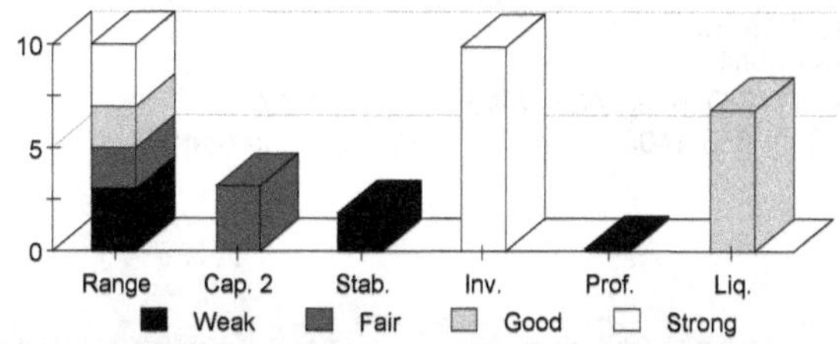

CRYSTAL RUN HEALTH PLAN LLC — E- — Very Weak

Major Rating Factors: Weak profitability index (0.0 on a scale of 0 to 10). Poor capitalization (0.4) based on weak current risk-adjusted capital (moderate loss scenario). Good liquidity (5.8) with sufficient resources (cash flows and marketable investments) to handle a spike in claims.
Other Rating Factors: High quality investment portfolio (9.9).
Principal Business: Comp med (54%), Medicaid (46%)
Mem Phys: 18: 14,847 **17:** 11,287 **18 MLR** 107.4% **/ 18 Admin Exp** N/A
Enroll(000): Q1 19: 4 **18:** 4 **17:** 4 **Med Exp PMPM:** $432
Principal Investments: Cash and equiv (100%)
Provider Compensation ($000): Contr fee ($17,023)
Total Member Encounters: N/A
Group Affiliation: CRH Holdings II LLC
Licensed in: NY
Address: 109 Rykowski Lane, Middletown, NY 10941
Phone: (845) 703-6422 **Dom State:** NY **Commenced Bus:** N/A

Data Date	Rating	RACR #1	RACR #2	Total Assets ($mil)	Capital ($mil)	Net Premium ($mil)	Net Income ($mil)
3-19	E-	0.34	0.28	12.4	0.5	4.0	-1.5
3-18	D-	N/A	N/A	12.1	4.8	5.1	-0.4
2018	D-	0.71	0.59	14.1	2.0	17.3	-6.8
2017	D-	N/A	N/A	11.0	5.1	17.6	1.4
2016	D-	1.21	1.01	12.0	3.5	13.2	-4.2
2015	N/A	N/A	N/A	9.0	7.9	0.1	N/A
2014	N/A	N/A	N/A	N/A	N/A	N/A	N/A

Rating Indexes

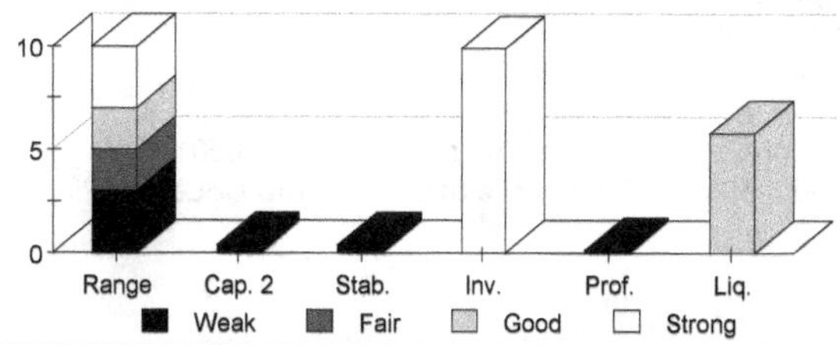

DAVITA HEALTHCARE PARTNERS PLAN INC E+ Very Weak

Major Rating Factors: Poor capitalization index (0.0 on a scale of 0 to 10) based on weak current risk-adjusted capital (severe loss scenario). Weak liquidity (0.0) as a spike in claims may stretch capacity. Fair overall results on stability tests (3.9).
Other Rating Factors: Good overall profitability index (5.9).
Principal Business: Managed care (95%)
Mem Phys: 18: N/A **17:** N/A **18 MLR** 99.0% **/ 18 Admin Exp** N/A
Enroll(000): Q1 19: 471 **18:** 477 **17:** 477 **Med Exp PMPM:** $363
Principal Investments ($000): Cash and equiv ($139,819)
Provider Compensation ($000): None
Total Member Encounters: N/A
Group Affiliation: HealthCare Partners Holdings LLC
Licensed in: CA
Address: 2220 E Gonzales Road Suite 210, Oxnard, CA 93036
Phone: (805) 981-5006 **Dom State:** CA **Commenced Bus:** January 2014

Data Date	Rating	RACR #1	RACR #2	Total Assets ($mil)	Capital ($mil)	Net Premium ($mil)	Net Income ($mil)
3-19	E+	0.34	0.21	236.3	53.7	593.0	15.3
3-18	E+	0.28	0.17	210.4	40.5	529.4	-6.9
2018	E+	0.24	0.14	183.8	38.4	2,125.6	-9.0
2017	D	0.33	0.20	187.4	47.4	1,947.3	-6.0
2016	D+	0.63	0.38	98.4	53.4	1,462.1	39.7
2015	D	0.51	0.31	79.0	43.6	1,458.0	40.8
2014	U	0.35	0.21	56.8	27.5	1,284.0	40.2

Rating Indexes

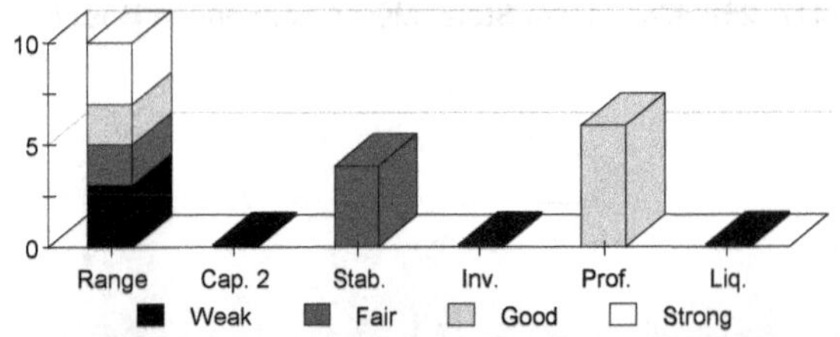

DEAN HEALTH PLAN INC * A Excellent

Major Rating Factors: Excellent profitability (8.6 on a scale of 0 to 10). Strong capitalization index (8.3) based on excellent current risk-adjusted capital (severe loss scenario). High quality investment portfolio (9.1).
Other Rating Factors: Excellent overall results on stability tests (8.3). Excellent liquidity (7.1) with ample operational cash flow and liquid investments
Principal Business: Comp med (80%), Medicare (10%), Medicaid (5%), med supp (3%), FEHB (2%)
Mem Phys: 18: 4,591 **17:** 4,111 **18 MLR** 86.0% **/ 18 Admin Exp** N/A
Enroll(000): Q1 19: 271 **18:** 264 **17:** 267 **Med Exp PMPM:** $368
Principal Investments: Cash and equiv (61%), long-term bonds (20%), nonaffiliate common stock (13%), real estate (6%)
Provider Compensation ($000): Capitation ($1,132,623), contr fee ($31,080), FFS ($23,498)
Total Member Encounters: Phys (890,314), non-phys (858,814)
Group Affiliation: None
Licensed in: WI
Address: 1277 Deming Way, Madison, WI 53717
Phone: (608) 836-1400 **Dom State:** WI **Commenced Bus:** N/A

Data Date	Rating	RACR #1	RACR #2	Total Assets ($mil)	Capital ($mil)	Net Premium ($mil)	Net Income ($mil)
3-19	A	2.39	1.99	305.3	160.8	348.6	3.5
3-18	B+	1.87	1.56	273.6	115.1	328.3	-16.4
2018	A	2.31	1.92	280.6	155.8	1,373.4	27.8
2017	B+	2.12	1.77	241.0	129.2	1,245.1	9.3
2016	B+	1.85	1.54	212.7	113.1	1,250.9	15.9
2015	B	1.60	1.33	209.0	95.9	1,220.6	5.3
2014	B	1.64	1.36	178.3	93.3	1,160.6	0.2

Rating Indexes

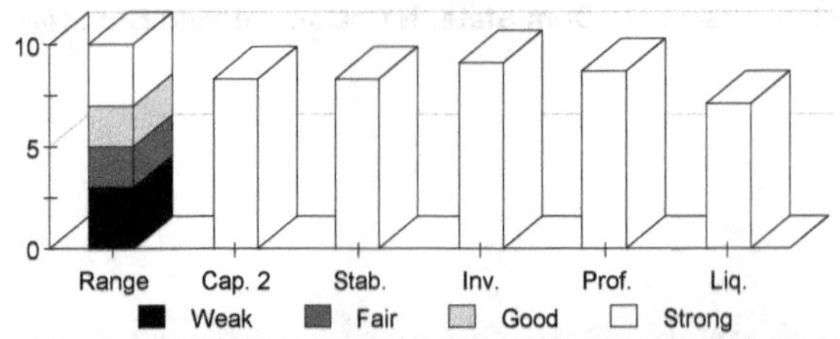

DEARBORN NATIONAL LIFE INSURANCE COMPANY * B+ Good

Major Rating Factors: Good overall results on stability tests (6.5 on a scale of 0 to 10) despite negative cash flow from operations for 2018. Other stability subfactors include good operational trends and excellent risk diversification. Good quality investment portfolio (6.1) despite mixed results such as: large holdings of BBB rated bonds but moderate junk bond exposure. Good overall profitability (5.6).
Other Rating Factors: Good liquidity (6.3). Strong capitalization (8.6) based on excellent risk adjusted capital (severe loss scenario).
Principal Business: Group life insurance (63%), group health insurance (35%), and individual life insurance (2%).
Principal Investments: NonCMO investment grade bonds (58%), CMOs and structured securities (19%), noninv. grade bonds (9%), mortgages in good standing (9%), and common & preferred stock (1%).
Investments in Affiliates: 1%
Group Affiliation: HCSC Group
Licensed in: All states except NY
Commenced Business: April 1969
Address: 300 East Randolph Street, Chicago, IL 60601-5099
Phone: (800) 633-3696 **Domicile State:** IL **NAIC Code:** 71129

Data Date	Rating	RACR #1	RACR #2	Total Assets ($mil)	Capital ($mil)	Net Premium ($mil)	Net Income ($mil)
3-19	B+	3.34	2.08	1,669.0	455.9	120.9	2.8
3-18	B+	3.41	2.10	1,763.3	476.4	111.6	3.5
2018	B+	3.33	2.06	1,676.5	453.0	462.0	25.7
2017	B+	3.40	2.09	1,785.1	474.3	437.9	34.0
2016	B+	3.36	2.11	1,872.5	497.0	408.0	19.7
2015	B+	3.63	2.25	1,990.5	522.1	382.5	59.1
2014	A-	2.86	1.91	2,145.5	514.7	379.9	54.8

Adverse Trends in Operations

Decrease in asset base during 2018 (6%)
Decrease in asset base during 2017 (5%)
Decrease in capital during 2017 (5%)
Decrease in asset base during 2016 (6%)
Decrease in asset base during 2015 (7%)

DELAWARE AMERICAN LIFE INSURANCE COMPANY * B+ Good

Major Rating Factors: Good overall results on stability tests (6.2 on a scale of 0 to 10). Stability strengths include good operational trends and excellent risk diversification. Good overall profitability (6.2). Strong capitalization (10.0) based on excellent risk adjusted capital (severe loss scenario).
Other Rating Factors: High quality investment portfolio (7.6). Excellent liquidity (7.1).
Principal Business: Group health insurance (67%), reinsurance (20%), group life insurance (12%), and individual life insurance (1%).
Principal Investments: NonCMO investment grade bonds (59%), CMOs and structured securities (27%), and cash (8%).
Investments in Affiliates: 5%
Group Affiliation: MetLife Inc
Licensed in: All states except PR
Commenced Business: August 1966
Address: 1209 Orange Street, Wilmington, DE 19801
Phone: (302) 594-2000 **Domicile State:** DE **NAIC Code:** 62634

Data Date	Rating	RACR #1	RACR #2	Total Assets ($mil)	Capital ($mil)	Net Premium ($mil)	Net Income ($mil)
3-19	B+	4.19	3.13	119.0	65.8	23.1	3.7
3-18	B+	3.53	2.66	124.5	65.2	25.1	3.5
2018	B+	4.07	3.02	117.0	65.1	93.0	12.5
2017	B+	3.36	2.53	120.2	61.8	96.4	7.2
2016	B+	4.56	3.33	132.8	72.5	89.9	15.2
2015	A-	3.53	2.60	136.6	63.5	108.7	1.8
2014	A-	3.88	2.81	136.7	69.3	102.1	10.0

Adverse Trends in Operations

Decrease in asset base during 2018 (3%)
Decrease in asset base during 2017 (9%)
Decrease in capital during 2017 (15%)
Change in premium mix from 2015 to 2016 (6.7%)
Decrease in premium volume from 2015 to 2016 (17%)

DENVER HEALTH MEDICAL PLAN INC B- Good

Major Rating Factors: Good capitalization index (6.3 on a scale of 0 to 10) based on good current risk-adjusted capital (severe loss scenario). Good overall results on stability tests (6.5). High quality investment portfolio (7.6).
Other Rating Factors: Excellent liquidity (7.1) with ample operational cash flow and liquid investments. Weak profitability index (2.6).
Principal Business: Comp med (49%), Medicaid (28%), Medicare (23%)
Mem Phys: 18: 20,921 **17:** 20,407 **18 MLR** 68.4% **/ 18 Admin Exp** N/A
Enroll(000): Q1 19: 24 **18:** 24 **17:** 29 **Med Exp PMPM:** $512
Principal Investments: Long-term bonds (93%), cash and equiv (7%)
Provider Compensation ($000): FFS ($78,837), contr fee ($56,622), capitation ($33,208)
Total Member Encounters: Phys (222,746), non-phys (86,172)
Group Affiliation: None
Licensed in: CO
Address: 777 Bannock Street MC 6000, Denver, CO 80204
Phone: (303) 602-2100 **Dom State:** CO **Commenced Bus:** N/A

Data Date	Rating	RACR #1	RACR #2	Total Assets ($mil)	Capital ($mil)	Net Premium ($mil)	Net Income ($mil)
3-19	B-	1.13	0.94	70.6	30.2	91.3	1.1
3-18	B-	1.76	1.47	62.7	30.8	42.4	0.7
2018	B-	1.08	0.90	66.5	28.9	244.4	-0.7
2017	B-	1.76	1.46	56.8	30.7	157.1	-1.1
2016	B	2.29	1.91	52.1	32.0	137.6	6.1
2015	B	2.50	2.08	48.5	31.0	119.3	1.2
2014	B	2.48	2.06	45.9	29.9	114.1	-5.0

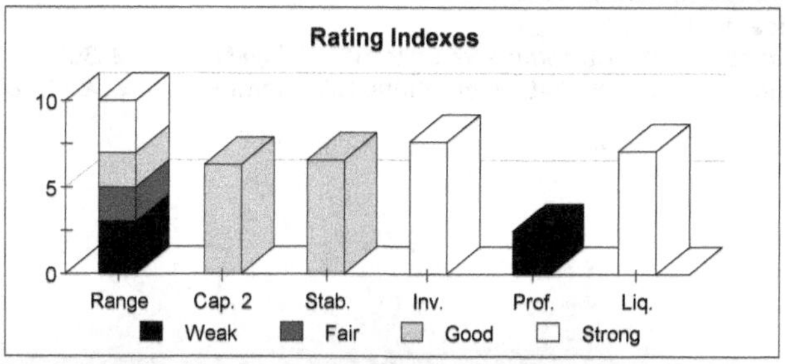

DIGNITY HEALTH PROVIDER RESOURCES E Very Weak

Major Rating Factors: Weak profitability index (0.9 on a scale of 0 to 10). Poor capitalization index (0.0) based on weak current risk-adjusted capital (severe loss scenario). Fair overall results on stability tests (3.8).
Other Rating Factors: Good liquidity (6.8) with sufficient resources (cash flows and marketable investments) to handle a spike in claims.
Principal Business: Managed care (100%)
Mem Phys: 18: N/A **17:** N/A **18 MLR** 99.6% **/ 18 Admin Exp** N/A
Enroll(000): Q1 19: 33 **18:** 32 **17:** 30 **Med Exp PMPM:** $389
Principal Investments ($000): Cash and equiv ($4,992)
Provider Compensation ($000): None
Total Member Encounters: N/A
Group Affiliation: None
Licensed in: CA
Address: 2175 Park Place, El Segundo, CA 90245
Phone: (310) 252-8834 **Dom State:** CA **Commenced Bus:** N/A

Data Date	Rating	RACR #1	RACR #2	Total Assets ($mil)	Capital ($mil)	Net Premium ($mil)	Net Income ($mil)
3-19	E	0.31	0.19	5.0	4.0	39.3	-0.1
3-18	E	0.41	0.25	5.5	4.8	37.1	0.1
2018	E	0.32	0.19	5.3	4.2	152.9	-0.5
2017	E	0.40	0.24	5.5	4.7	136.7	-0.7
2016	N/A	N/A	N/A	1.6	1.5	N/A	-0.3
2015	N/A	N/A	N/A	N/A	N/A	N/A	N/A
2014	N/A	N/A	N/A	N/A	N/A	N/A	N/A

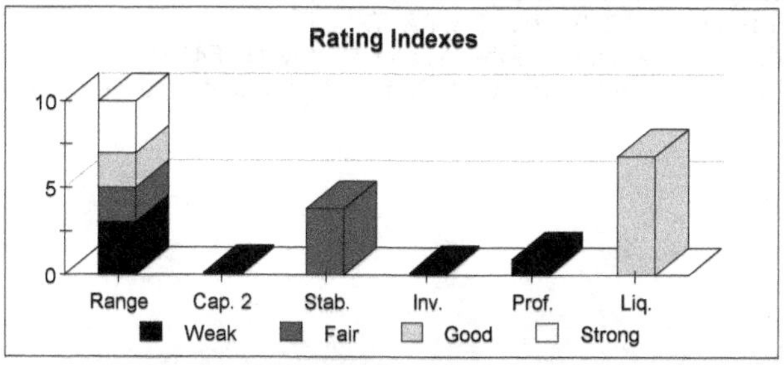

DRISCOLL CHILDRENS HEALTH PLAN — C- Fair

Major Rating Factors: Fair capitalization index (3.9 on a scale of 0 to 10) based on fair current risk-adjusted capital (moderate loss scenario). Fair overall results on stability tests (3.4) based on a steep decline in capital during 2018 but steady enrollment growth, averaging 6% over the past five years. Weak profitability index (1.5).

Other Rating Factors: Low quality investment portfolio (2.6). Good liquidity (6.8) with sufficient resources (cash flows and marketable investments) to handle a spike in claims.

Principal Business: Medicaid (97%), other (3%)

Mem Phys: 18: 3,378 **17:** 2,573 **18 MLR** 90.9% **/ 18 Admin Exp** N/A

Enroll(000): Q1 19: 178 **18:** 173 **17:** 171 **Med Exp PMPM:** $287

Principal Investments: Cash and equiv (65%), nonaffiliate common stock (35%)

Provider Compensation ($000): Contr fee ($402,664), FFS ($144,703), bonus arrang ($26,533), capitation ($15,788)

Total Member Encounters: Phys (1,753,574), non-phys (156,394)

Group Affiliation: Driscoll Childrens Hospital Inc

Licensed in: TX

Address: Corpus Christi, Corpus Christi, TX 78401

Phone: (361) 694-6432 **Dom State:** TX **Commenced Bus:** N/A

Data Date	Rating	RACR #1	RACR #2	Total Assets ($mil)	Capital ($mil)	Net Premium ($mil)	Net Income ($mil)
3-19	C-	0.76	0.64	127.9	52.1	170.8	-9.1
3-18	C	0.90	0.75	122.1	57.4	160.5	-13.7
2018	C-	0.86	0.71	142.7	58.2	664.1	-21.7
2017	C+	1.25	1.04	141.9	76.6	660.3	25.6
2016	C-	0.99	0.82	116.9	51.5	522.6	6.4
2015	C-	0.61	0.51	81.2	30.2	435.6	-15.6
2014	D	0.54	0.45	74.4	23.3	384.7	-9.3

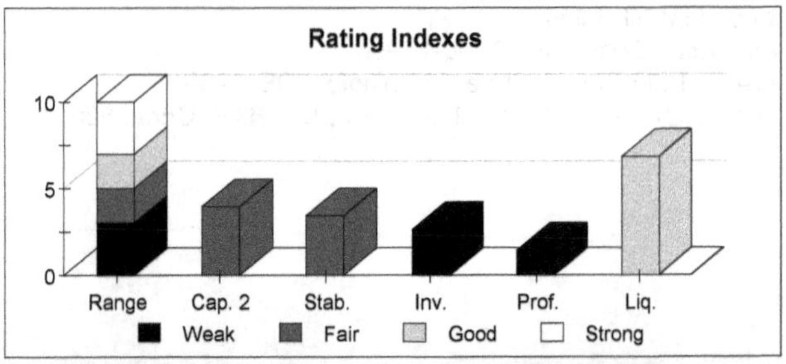

EASY CHOICE HEALTH PLAN — C Fair

Major Rating Factors: Fair profitability index (4.6 on a scale of 0 to 10). Fair overall results on stability tests (4.2). Strong capitalization index (7.0) based on good current risk-adjusted capital (moderate loss scenario).

Other Rating Factors: Excellent liquidity (7.0) with ample operational cash flow and liquid investments.

Principal Business: Medicare (100%)

Mem Phys: 18: N/A **17:** N/A **18 MLR** 83.9% **/ 18 Admin Exp** N/A

Enroll(000): Q1 19: 33 **18:** 31 **17:** 27 **Med Exp PMPM:** $917

Principal Investments ($000): Cash and equiv ($89,814)

Provider Compensation ($000): None

Total Member Encounters: N/A

Group Affiliation: None

Licensed in: CA

Address: 4550 California Ave Suite 100, Bakersfield, CA 93309

Phone: (310) 228-3745 **Dom State:** CA **Commenced Bus:** September 2006

Data Date	Rating	RACR #1	RACR #2	Total Assets ($mil)	Capital ($mil)	Net Premium ($mil)	Net Income ($mil)
3-19	C	1.11	0.71	118.0	31.6	116.1	1.4
3-18	C-	1.53	0.94	175.2	35.2	97.0	-0.3
2018	C	1.21	0.75	104.4	30.1	388.9	13.2
2017	C-	1.54	0.95	118.8	35.4	352.2	15.5
2016	D	0.68	0.42	100.4	20.1	382.1	0.8
2015	E	0.50	0.31	62.2	19.3	380.0	-13.0
2014	E	0.41	0.25	90.7	26.3	629.8	-32.9

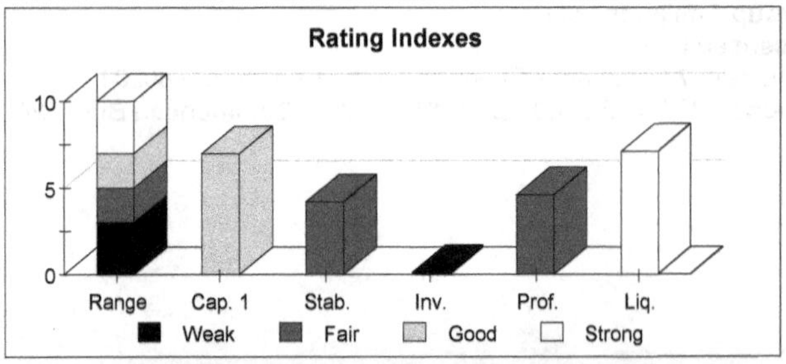

EDUCATORS HEALTH PLANS LIFE ACCIDENT * — B+ Good

Major Rating Factors: Good overall profitability index (5.6 on a scale of 0 to 10). Good liquidity (6.9) with sufficient resources (cash flows and marketable investments) to handle a spike in claims. Strong capitalization (8.6) based on excellent current risk-adjusted capital (severe loss scenario).

Other Rating Factors: High quality investment portfolio (9.2).

Principal Business: Dental (37%), comp med (15%), vision (3%), other (45%)

Mem Phys: 17: 18,168 **16:** 17,252 **17 MLR** 96.1% **/ 17 Admin Exp** N/A

Enroll(000): Q3 18: 189 **17:** 147 **16:** 117 **Med Exp PMPM:** $33

Principal Investments: Long-term bonds (71%), cash and equiv (29%)

Provider Compensation ($000): Contr fee ($41,345), FFS ($6,745)

Total Member Encounters: Phys (453,729), non-phys (377,618)

Group Affiliation: None

Licensed in: AZ, FL, NV, OH, PA, TX, UT

Address: 852 East Arrowhead Lane, Murray, UT 84107

Phone: (801) 262-7476 **Dom State:** UT **Commenced Bus:** N/A

Data Date	Rating	RACR #1	RACR #2	Total Assets ($mil)	Capital ($mil)	Net Premium ($mil)	Net Income ($mil)
9-18	B+	2.66	2.22	81.2	36.1	32.3	2.9
9-17	B	2.84	2.37	40.8	20.4	41.4	2.5
2017	B	2.08	1.74	60.5	33.6	57.4	1.5
2016	B	2.48	2.07	36.0	17.9	39.3	2.5
2015	B-	3.29	2.74	26.7	14.9	28.2	2.8
2014	C+	2.90	2.42	21.7	12.2	25.9	-2.0
2013	N/A	N/A	N/A	12.6	7.0	21.1	N/A

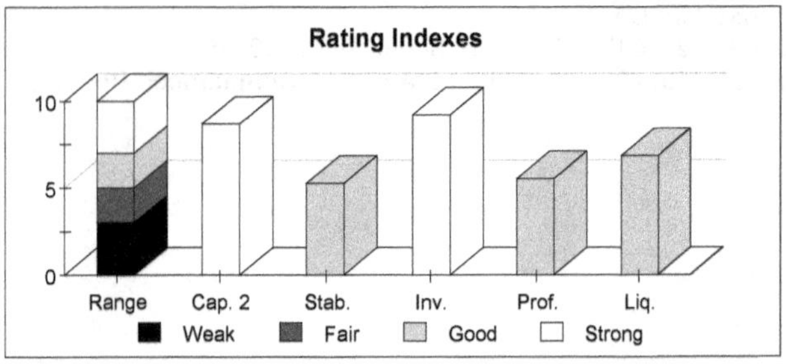

EL PASO FIRST HEALTH PLANS INC * B+ Good

Major Rating Factors: Good overall profitability index (6.4 on a scale of 0 to 10). Good overall results on stability tests (5.9). Strong capitalization index (8.1) based on excellent current risk-adjusted capital (severe loss scenario).
Other Rating Factors: High quality investment portfolio (9.5). Excellent liquidity (7.2) with ample operational cash flow and liquid investments.
Principal Business: Medicaid (92%), comp med (7%)
Mem Phys: 18: 1,993 **17:** 2,182 **18 MLR** 89.3% **/ 18 Admin Exp** N/A
Enroll(000): Q1 19: 73 **18:** 74 **17:** 76 **Med Exp PMPM:** $194
Principal Investments: Cash and equiv (85%), real estate (15%)
Provider Compensation ($000): Contr fee ($145,920), capitation ($19,611), FFS ($5,796), other ($2,107)
Total Member Encounters: Phys (570,910), non-phys (139,513)
Group Affiliation: None
Licensed in: TX
Address: 1145 Westmoreland, El Paso, TX 79925
Phone: (915) 298-7198 **Dom State:** TX **Commenced Bus:** N/A

Data Date	Rating	RACR #1	RACR #2	Total Assets ($mil)	Capital ($mil)	Net Premium ($mil)	Net Income ($mil)
3-19	B+	2.25	1.87	58.8	42.4	49.6	-2.7
3-18	A-	2.33	1.94	58.1	42.0	47.7	-2.7
2018	B+	2.42	2.02	61.7	45.4	196.2	0.1
2017	A-	2.55	2.12	60.5	45.6	190.3	8.5
2016	A-	2.20	1.83	60.3	42.5	201.0	8.6
2015	B	1.69	1.41	51.2	33.5	192.0	2.6
2014	B	2.08	1.74	47.8	30.8	150.6	5.2

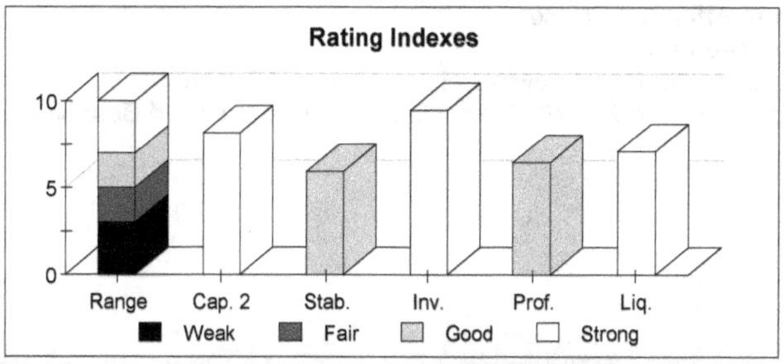

ELAN INSURANCE USVI INC E+ Very Weak

Major Rating Factors: Good overall profitability index (5.5 on a scale of 0 to 10). Strong capitalization (8.3) based on excellent current risk-adjusted capital (severe loss scenario). High quality investment portfolio (9.9).
Other Rating Factors: Excellent liquidity (7.5) with ample operational cash flow and liquid investments.
Principal Business: Comp med (99%), dental (1%)
Mem Phys: 18: 861 **17:** N/A **18 MLR** 70.8% **/ 18 Admin Exp** N/A
Enroll(000): Q1 19: 2 **18:** 2 **17:** 1 **Med Exp PMPM:** $293
Principal Investments: Cash and equiv (97%), nonaffiliate common stock (3%)
Provider Compensation ($000): FFS ($4,549)
Total Member Encounters: Phys (2,479), non-phys (421)
Group Affiliation: None
Licensed in: (No states)
Address: , St. Thomas, VI 802
Phone: (305) 890-1544 **Dom State:** VI **Commenced Bus:** N/A

Data Date	Rating	RACR #1	RACR #2	Total Assets ($mil)	Capital ($mil)	Net Premium ($mil)	Net Income ($mil)
3-19	E+	2.40	2.00	4.4	2.9	2.4	0.2
3-18	N/A	N/A	N/A	N/A	N/A	N/A	N/A
2018	B	2.26	1.88	4.1	2.7	6.7	0.0
2017	N/A	N/A	N/A	2.5	1.5	4.0	N/A
2016	N/A	N/A	N/A	2.3	0.7	1.9	N/A
2015	N/A	N/A	N/A	N/A	N/A	N/A	N/A
2014	N/A	N/A	N/A	N/A	N/A	N/A	N/A

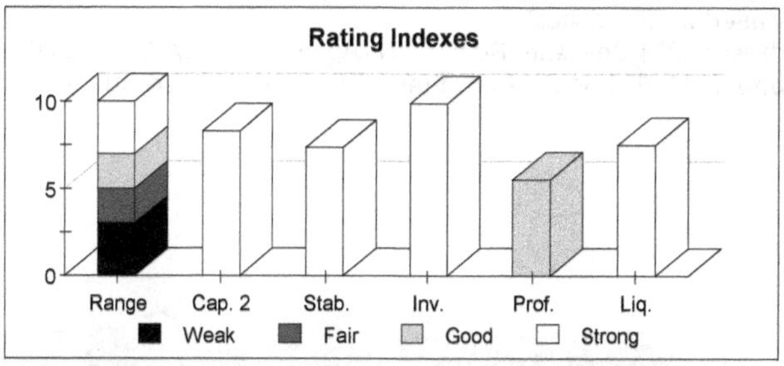

ELDERPLAN INC C Fair

Major Rating Factors: Fair profitability index (4.6 on a scale of 0 to 10). Good capitalization index (6.4) based on good current risk-adjusted capital (severe loss scenario). Good overall results on stability tests (5.7).
Other Rating Factors: Good liquidity (6.9) with sufficient resources (cash flows and marketable investments) to handle a spike in claims. High quality investment portfolio (9.9).
Principal Business: Medicaid (83%), Medicare (17%)
Mem Phys: 18: 29,743 **17:** 29,234 **18 MLR** 84.8% **/ 18 Admin Exp** N/A
Enroll(000): Q1 19: 26 **18:** 26 **17:** 24 **Med Exp PMPM:** $3,148
Principal Investments: Long-term bonds (54%), cash and equiv (39%), nonaffiliate common stock (7%)
Provider Compensation ($000): FFS ($845,376), contr fee ($53,961), capitation ($19,785)
Total Member Encounters: Phys (265,505), non-phys (82,657)
Group Affiliation: Elderplan Inc
Licensed in: NY
Address: 6323 Seventh Ave, Brooklyn, NY 11220
Phone: (718) 921-7990 **Dom State:** NY **Commenced Bus:** N/A

Data Date	Rating	RACR #1	RACR #2	Total Assets ($mil)	Capital ($mil)	Net Premium ($mil)	Net Income ($mil)
3-19	C	1.14	0.95	271.8	104.5	299.6	1.9
3-18	C	0.98	0.82	249.4	86.7	264.6	6.2
2018	C	1.10	0.92	256.3	101.2	1,081.6	21.2
2017	C	0.90	0.75	224.6	80.5	968.3	20.2
2016	C-	0.73	0.60	189.7	56.6	843.5	5.6
2015	D+	0.58	0.48	170.4	43.8	811.9	-30.7
2014	C	1.27	1.06	198.6	86.6	778.1	4.4

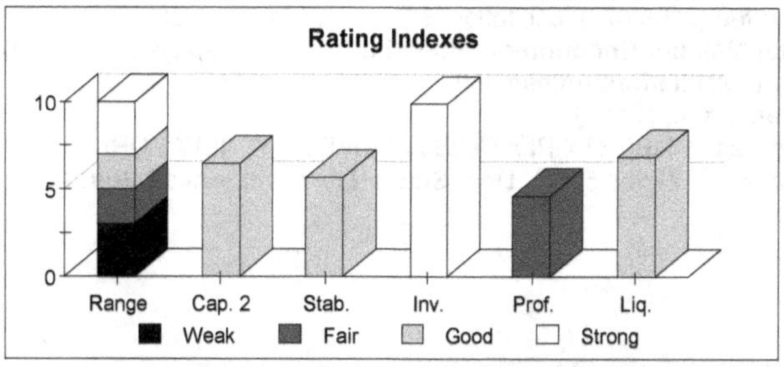

EMI HEALTH * A Excellent

Major Rating Factors: Excellent profitability (9.0 on a scale of 0 to 10). Strong capitalization (9.2) based on excellent current risk-adjusted capital (severe loss scenario). Excellent liquidity (8.6) with ample operational cash flow and liquid investments.
Other Rating Factors: Good quality investment portfolio (6.0).
Principal Business: Dental (6%), comp med (4%), med supp (4%), other (85%)
Mem Phys: 18: 19,257 **17:** 18,168 **18 MLR** 37.7% **/ 18 Admin Exp** N/A
Enroll(000): Q1 19: 56 **18:** 58 **17:** 55 **Med Exp PMPM:** $40
Principal Investments: Long-term bonds (29%), affiliate common stock (27%), cash and equiv (26%), real estate (16%), nonaffiliate common stock (1%)
Provider Compensation ($000): Contr fee ($22,057), FFS ($5,541)
Total Member Encounters: Phys (390,849), non-phys (243,403)
Group Affiliation: None
Licensed in: ID, UT
Address: 852 East Arrowhead Lane, Murray, UT 84107
Phone: (801) 262-7476 **Dom State:** UT **Commenced Bus:** N/A

Data Date	Rating	RACR #1	RACR #2	Total Assets ($mil)	Capital ($mil)	Net Premium ($mil)	Net Income ($mil)
3-19	A	3.08	2.57	158.9	102.2	18.3	1.7
3-18	A	N/A	N/A	133.0	88.6	19.6	1.2
2018	A	3.00	2.50	159.3	99.7	74.9	10.8
2017	A	N/A	N/A	118.7	84.9	30.6	7.9
2016	A	4.81	4.01	104.1	78.1	32.1	9.3
2015	A-	4.74	3.95	91.7	65.0	31.8	3.7
2014	B+	4.75	3.96	86.7	58.4	32.3	7.8

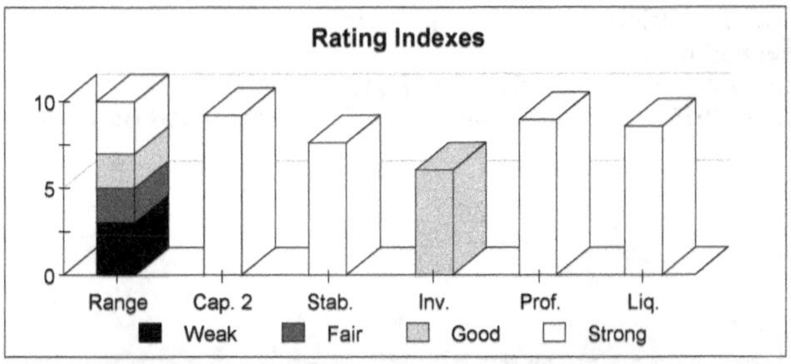

EMPATHIA PACIFIC INC C- Fair

Major Rating Factors: Fair overall results on stability tests (4.5 on a scale of 0 to 10). Excellent profitability (8.6). Strong capitalization index (10.0) based on excellent current risk-adjusted capital (severe loss scenario).
Other Rating Factors: Excellent liquidity (9.2) with ample operational cash flow and liquid investments.
Principal Business: Managed care (93%), indemnity (7%)
Mem Phys: 18: N/A **17:** N/A **18 MLR** 62.5% **/ 18 Admin Exp** N/A
Enroll(000): Q1 19: 134 **18:** 119 **17:** 132 **Med Exp PMPM:** $0
Principal Investments ($000): Cash and equiv ($2,253)
Provider Compensation ($000): None
Total Member Encounters: N/A
Group Affiliation: None
Licensed in: (No states)
Address: 5234 Chesebro Rd Ste 201, Agoura Hills, CA 91301-2268
Phone: (800) 634-6433 **Dom State:** CA **Commenced Bus:** N/A

Data Date	Rating	RACR #1	RACR #2	Total Assets ($mil)	Capital ($mil)	Net Premium ($mil)	Net Income ($mil)
3-19	C-	22.27	15.61	3.1	2.6	0.4	0.2
3-18	C-	18.46	13.19	2.5	2.2	0.4	0.1
2018	C-	20.97	14.76	2.8	2.4	1.5	0.3
2017	C-	18.05	13.01	2.4	2.1	1.5	0.3
2016	N/A	N/A	N/A	N/A	N/A	N/A	N/A
2015	N/A	N/A	N/A	N/A	N/A	N/A	N/A
2014	N/A	N/A	N/A	N/A	N/A	N/A	N/A

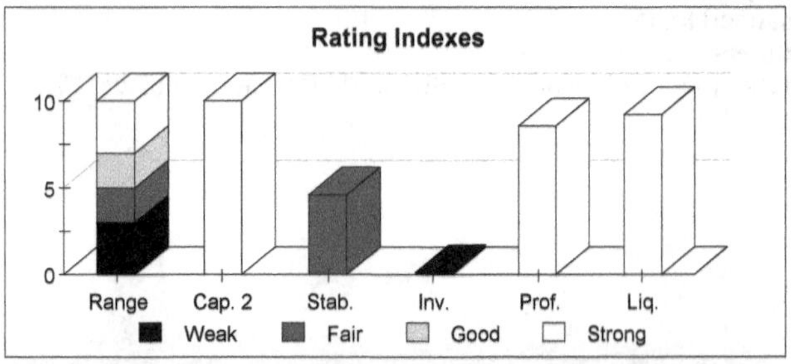

EMPIRE HEALTHCHOICE ASSURANCE INC B- Good

Major Rating Factors: Fair quality investment portfolio (3.7 on a scale of 0 to 10). Good overall profitability index (6.8). Good liquidity (6.8) with sufficient resources (cash flows and marketable investments) to handle a spike in claims.
Other Rating Factors: Strong capitalization (10.0) based on excellent current risk-adjusted capital (severe loss scenario).
Principal Business: Comp med (55%), FEHB (37%), med supp (2%), dental (2%), Medicare (1%), other (3%)
Mem Phys: 18: 90,836 **17:** 86,912 **18 MLR** 87.0% **/ 18 Admin Exp** N/A
Enroll(000): Q1 19: 980 **18:** 906 **17:** 766 **Med Exp PMPM:** $218
Principal Investments: Long-term bonds (70%), affiliate common stock (16%), other (16%)
Provider Compensation ($000): Bonus arrang ($1,583,191), FFS ($429,201), contr fee ($198,873), capitation ($2,355), other ($54,638)
Total Member Encounters: Phys (2,801,304), non-phys (1,802,269)
Group Affiliation: Anthem Inc
Licensed in: NY
Address: 1 LIBERTY PLAZA 165 BROADWAY, NEW YORK, NY 10005
Phone: (212) 563-5570 **Dom State:** NY **Commenced Bus:** N/A

Data Date	Rating	RACR #1	RACR #2	Total Assets ($mil)	Capital ($mil)	Net Premium ($mil)	Net Income ($mil)
3-19	B-	4.78	3.99	2,201.6	898.5	688.3	74.2
3-18	B-	4.89	4.08	2,279.6	955.2	630.5	6.9
2018	B-	4.39	3.66	1,982.6	821.0	2,634.3	164.7
2017	B-	4.85	4.04	2,177.0	963.8	2,104.0	106.1
2016	B-	4.54	3.78	2,501.0	877.4	2,228.7	193.0
2015	B-	4.23	3.52	2,378.9	928.5	2,598.2	145.1
2014	B-	5.55	4.62	2,709.0	1,130.7	2,493.0	326.0

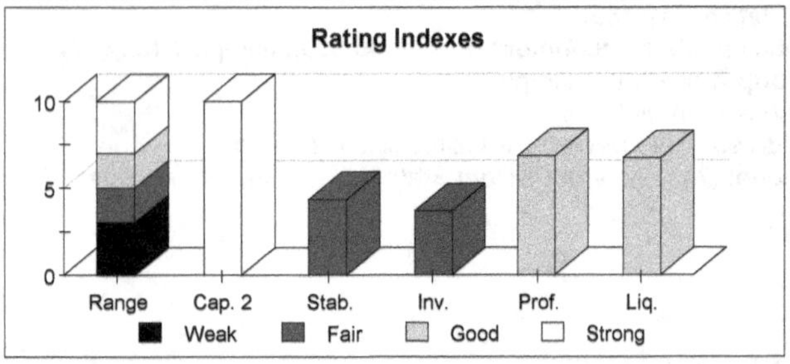

EMPIRE HEALTHCHOICE HMO INC B- Good

Major Rating Factors: Fair overall results on stability tests (4.7 on a scale of 0 to 10) based on a significant 37% decrease in enrollment during the period. Rating is significantly influenced by the good financial results of Anthem Inc. Good liquidity (6.2) with sufficient resources (cash flows and marketable investments) to handle a spike in claims. Strong capitalization index (10.0) based on excellent current risk-adjusted capital (severe loss scenario).
Other Rating Factors: High quality investment portfolio (7.9). Weak profitability index (0.9).
Principal Business: Medicare (87%), comp med (13%)
Mem Phys: 18: 89,941 **17:** 85,916 **18 MLR** 91.1% **/ 18 Admin Exp** N/A
Enroll(000): Q1 19: 83 **18:** 86 **17:** 135 **Med Exp PMPM:** $872
Principal Investments: Long-term bonds (97%), cash and equiv (1%), other (1%)
Provider Compensation ($000): Bonus arrang ($460,450), contr fee ($309,573), capitation ($109,952), FFS ($84,090)
Total Member Encounters: Phys (1,338,756), non-phys (927,452)
Group Affiliation: Anthem Inc
Licensed in: NY
Address: 1 LIBERTY PLAZA 165 BROADWAY, NEW YORK, NY 10005
Phone: (212) 563-5570 **Dom State:** NY **Commenced Bus:** N/A

Data Date	Rating	RACR #1	RACR #2	Total Assets ($mil)	Capital ($mil)	Net Premium ($mil)	Net Income ($mil)
3-19	B-	3.63	3.02	449.6	202.0	249.6	11.3
3-18	B-	2.70	2.25	551.7	200.8	247.7	-3.7
2018	B-	3.39	2.82	434.6	187.0	992.1	-15.8
2017	C	1.98	1.65	525.2	203.6	1,284.6	-38.4
2016	C+	2.96	2.47	616.1	223.9	1,381.4	-8.0
2015	B	3.53	2.94	615.5	241.8	1,248.0	-36.6
2014	B	3.83	3.19	692.9	295.0	1,390.9	-20.0

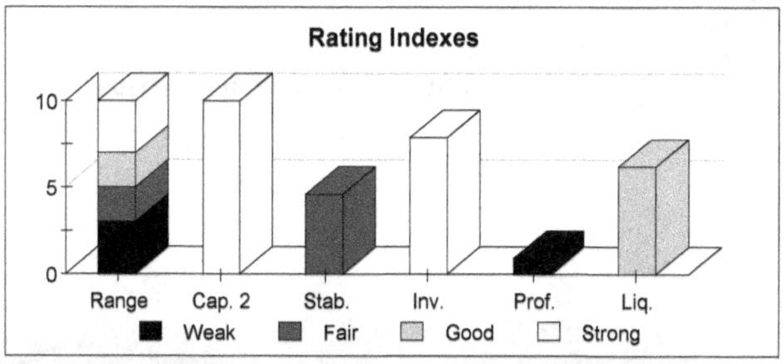

ENTERPRISE LIFE INSURANCE COMPANY B Good

Major Rating Factors: Good current capitalization (6.4 on a scale of 0 to 10) based on good risk adjusted capital (severe loss scenario) reflecting some improvement over results in 2017. Good quality investment portfolio (5.7) despite mixed results such as: no exposure to mortgages and substantial holdings of BBB bonds but no exposure to junk bonds. Good overall results on stability tests (5.5) despite excessive premium growth and fair risk adjusted capital in prior years excellent operational trends and good risk diversification.
Other Rating Factors: Excellent profitability (9.3). Excellent liquidity (7.5).
Principal Business: Reinsurance (99%).
Principal Investments: Common & preferred stock (47%), nonCMO investment grade bonds (25%), cash (14%), and CMOs and structured securities (13%).
Investments in Affiliates: 47%
Group Affiliation: Credit Suisse Group
Licensed in: AZ, AR, IL, KS, LA, MS, NE, NM, OK, OR, TX, WI
Commenced Business: September 1978
Address: 300 Burnett Street Suite 200, Fort Worth, TX 76102-2734
Phone: (817) 878-3300 **Domicile State:** TX **NAIC Code:** 89087

Data Date	Rating	RACR #1	RACR #2	Total Assets ($mil)	Capital ($mil)	Net Premium ($mil)	Net Income ($mil)
3-19	B	1.03	0.92	85.5	60.6	42.5	8.1
3-18	C+	0.94	0.84	57.5	35.9	33.1	3.6
2018	B	0.84	0.74	73.5	49.1	145.8	15.2
2017	C+	0.77	0.69	47.9	29.6	103.3	7.4
2016	B-	0.84	0.75	34.9	23.5	62.7	0.1
2015	C	0.88	0.79	28.2	19.9	38.9	0.0
2014	C	0.95	0.90	19.8	14.9	21.1	1.3

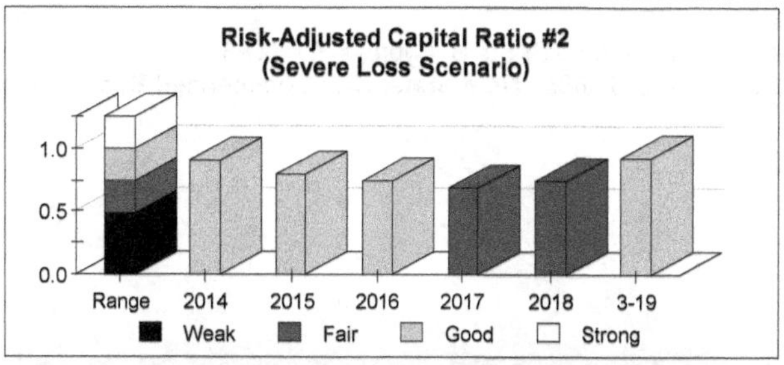

ENVISION INS CO C Fair

Major Rating Factors: Weak profitability index (2.5 on a scale of 0 to 10). Strong capitalization (7.5) based on excellent current risk-adjusted capital (severe loss scenario). High quality investment portfolio (9.9).
Other Rating Factors: Excellent liquidity (7.1) with ample operational cash flow and liquid investments.
Principal Business: Other (100%)
Mem Phys: 18: 60,938 **17:** 67,511 **18 MLR** 94.3% **/ 18 Admin Exp** N/A
Enroll(000): Q1 19: 643 **18:** 598 **17:** 402 **Med Exp PMPM:** $55
Principal Investments: Cash and equiv (94%), long-term bonds (6%)
Provider Compensation ($000): Other ($292,160)
Total Member Encounters: N/A
Group Affiliation: None
Licensed in: (No states)
Address: 2181 East Aurora Rd, Twinsburg, OH 44087
Phone: (330) 405-8089 **Dom State:** OH **Commenced Bus:** N/A

Data Date	Rating	RACR #1	RACR #2	Total Assets ($mil)	Capital ($mil)	Net Premium ($mil)	Net Income ($mil)
3-19	C	1.79	1.49	514.8	48.0	97.8	1.8
3-18	C	2.01	1.67	395.4	43.3	94.3	-5.3
2018	C	1.95	1.63	496.7	51.8	393.7	1.6
2017	C-	2.22	1.85	428.9	47.5	170.3	-2.6
2016	C-	1.77	1.48	309.9	49.6	235.9	-3.4
2015	C-	1.67	1.39	332.8	51.1	237.3	-6.8
2014	C	0.95	0.79	515.0	37.6	119.9	-3.1

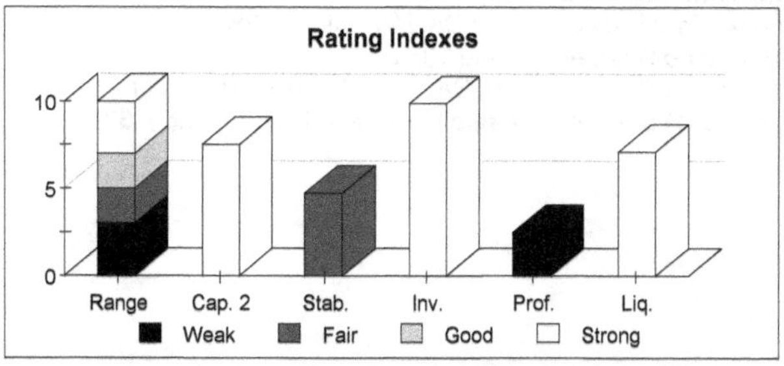

EON HEALTH INC (GA) C- Fair

Major Rating Factors: Weak profitability index (0.0 on a scale of 0 to 10). Good liquidity (6.9) with sufficient resources (cash flows and marketable investments) to handle a spike in claims. Strong capitalization (9.6) based on excellent current risk-adjusted capital (severe loss scenario).
Other Rating Factors: High quality investment portfolio (9.9).
Principal Business: Medicare (100%)
Mem Phys: 18: 3,194 **17:** 4,566 **18 MLR** 92.2% **/ 18 Admin Exp** N/A
Enroll(000): Q1 19: 0 **18:** 1 **17:** 0 **Med Exp PMPM:** $707
Principal Investments: Long-term bonds (98%), cash and equiv (2%)
Provider Compensation ($000): FFS ($4,444)
Total Member Encounters: Phys (1,090)
Group Affiliation: Delaware Life Partners LLC
Licensed in: GA
Address: , Atlanta, GA 30305
Phone: (847) 696-8521 **Dom State:** GA **Commenced Bus:** N/A

Data Date	Rating	RACR #1	RACR #2	Total Assets ($mil)	Capital ($mil)	Net Premium ($mil)	Net Income ($mil)
3-19	C-	3.43	2.86	9.2	3.4	1.1	0.0
3-18	N/A	N/A	N/A	5.8	1.2	1.3	N/A
2018	C-	3.41	2.84	9.6	3.3	4.8	-3.9
2017	N/A	N/A	N/A	5.7	1.0	4.7	-6.8
2016	N/A	N/A	N/A	8.1	8.1	N/A	N/A
2015	N/A	N/A	N/A	N/A	N/A	N/A	N/A
2014	N/A	N/A	N/A	N/A	N/A	N/A	N/A

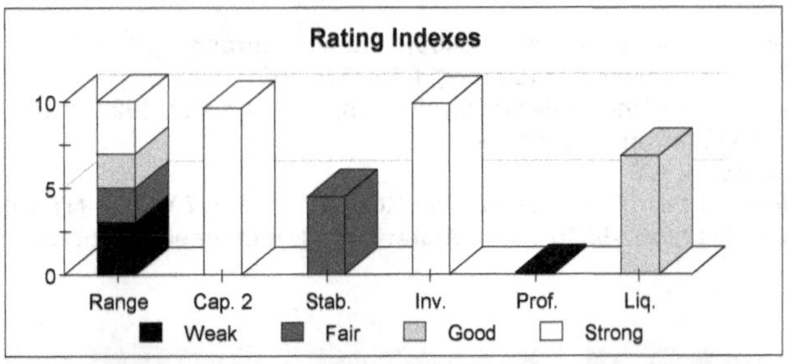

EPIC HEALTH PLAN D- Weak

Major Rating Factors: Poor capitalization index (0.0 on a scale of 0 to 10) based on weak current risk-adjusted capital (severe loss scenario). Weak liquidity (0.0) as a spike in claims may stretch capacity. Good overall results on stability tests (6.8) based on healthy premium and capital growth during 2018.
Other Rating Factors: Excellent profitability (8.8).
Principal Business: Managed care (100%)
Mem Phys: 18: N/A **17:** N/A **18 MLR** 94.0% **/ 18 Admin Exp** N/A
Enroll(000): Q1 19: 74 **18:** 72 **17:** 64 **Med Exp PMPM:** $524
Principal Investments ($000): Cash and equiv ($60,849)
Provider Compensation ($000): None
Total Member Encounters: N/A
Group Affiliation: None
Licensed in: CA
Address: 10803 Hope St Ste B, Cypress, CA 90630
Phone: (813) 206-7668 **Dom State:** CA **Commenced Bus:** October 2010

Data Date	Rating	RACR #1	RACR #2	Total Assets ($mil)	Capital ($mil)	Net Premium ($mil)	Net Income ($mil)
3-19	D-	0.35	0.21	73.3	31.0	131.2	3.2
3-18	D-	N/A	N/A	41.9	15.3	110.9	1.6
2018	D-	0.25	0.15	65.0	27.8	477.3	14.1
2017	D-	N/A	N/A	35.1	13.7	388.4	2.9
2016	D-	N/A	N/A	28.9	10.7	343.1	2.2
2015	D-	0.06	0.04	29.3	8.5	348.2	2.4
2014	D-	0.10	0.06	23.8	5.6	301.9	N/A

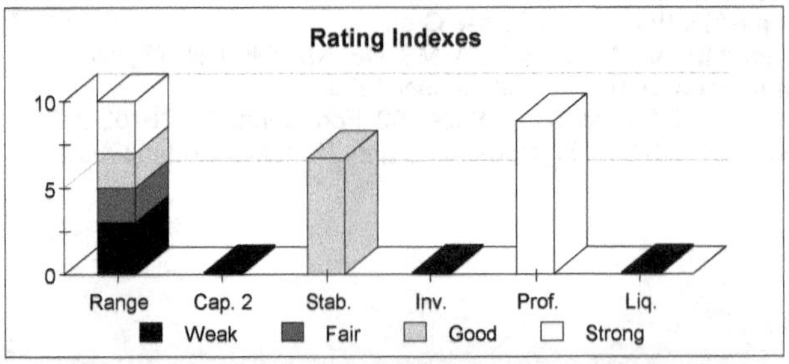

EQUITABLE LIFE & CASUALTY INSURANCE COMPANY C Fair

Major Rating Factors: Fair current capitalization (4.9 on a scale of 0 to 10) based on fair risk adjusted capital (moderate loss scenario), although results have slipped from the good range during the last year. Fair overall results on stability tests (3.8). Good quality investment portfolio (5.2).
Other Rating Factors: Good liquidity (6.9). Weak profitability (2.5).
Principal Business: Individual health insurance (58%), individual annuities (36%), individual life insurance (5%), and reinsurance (1%).
Principal Investments: NonCMO investment grade bonds (58%), mortgages in good standing (9%), CMOs and structured securities (9%), common & preferred stock (6%), and noninv. grade bonds (4%).
Investments in Affiliates: 6%
Group Affiliation: SILAC LLC
Licensed in: All states except CA, MN, NJ, NY, PR
Commenced Business: June 1935
Address: 3 TRIAD CENTER, SALT LAKE CITY, UT 84111
Phone: (801) 579-3400 **Domicile State:** UT **NAIC Code:** 62952

Data Date	Rating	RACR #1	RACR #2	Total Assets ($mil)	Capital ($mil)	Net Premium ($mil)	Net Income ($mil)
3-19	C	0.99	0.70	647.2	59.1	46.6	0.8
3-18	C+	1.01	0.82	330.3	44.8	12.7	0.2
2018	C	1.11	0.83	485.3	57.7	100.3	-4.2
2017	C+	0.98	0.80	351.6	43.3	59.7	-6.7
2016	B	2.86	1.90	313.6	44.8	64.7	-2.1
2015	B	2.94	1.96	306.4	46.2	69.7	9.5
2014	B	2.72	1.84	295.9	41.8	70.4	10.3

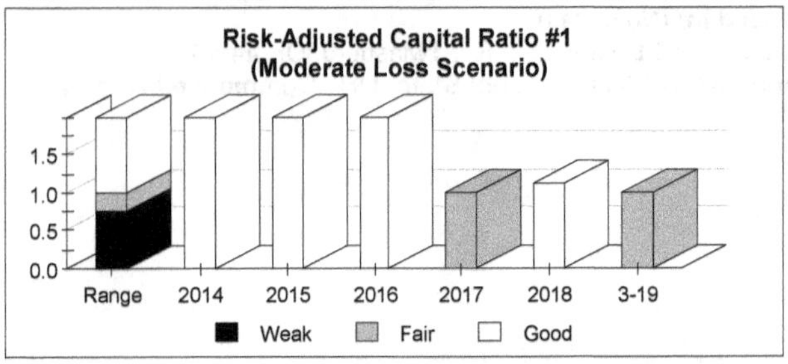

ESSENCE HEALTHCARE INC * A- Excellent

Major Rating Factors: Excellent profitability (8.7 on a scale of 0 to 10). Strong capitalization (7.3) based on excellent current risk-adjusted capital (severe loss scenario). High quality investment portfolio (9.3).
Other Rating Factors: Good liquidity (6.8) with sufficient resources (cash flows and marketable investments) to handle a spike in claims.
Principal Business: Medicare (100%)
Mem Phys: 18: 1,514 **17:** 2,952 **18 MLR** 84.0% **/ 18 Admin Exp** N/A
Enroll(000): Q1 19: 64 **18:** 65 **17:** 64 **Med Exp PMPM:** $797
Principal Investments: Long-term bonds (72%), cash and equiv (28%), nonaffiliate common stock (1%)
Provider Compensation ($000): Contr fee ($501,025), capitation ($117,997)
Total Member Encounters: Phys (492,940), non-phys (127,162)
Group Affiliation: None
Licensed in: IL, MO, TX, WA
Address: 13900 Riverport Dr, St. Louis, MO 63043
Phone: (314) 209-2780 **Dom State:** MO **Commenced Bus:** N/A

Data Date	Rating	RACR #1	RACR #2	Total Assets ($mil)	Capital ($mil)	Net Premium ($mil)	Net Income ($mil)
3-19	A-	1.57	1.31	223.8	93.5	199.1	6.5
3-18	B+	1.51	1.26	238.2	85.8	188.3	0.3
2018	A-	1.42	1.18	212.7	86.8	738.8	10.8
2017	B+	1.54	1.28	225.4	86.3	694.6	21.1
2016	B+	1.53	1.27	193.0	81.4	657.2	22.9
2015	B+	1.36	1.13	132.6	65.3	552.5	11.4
2014	B	1.33	1.11	106.6	51.3	435.8	10.7

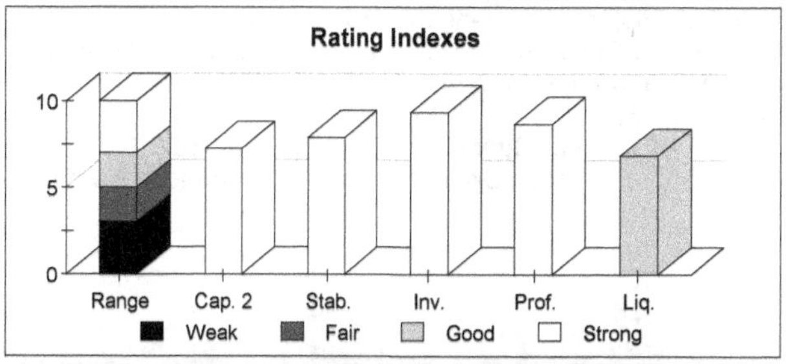

EXCELLUS HEALTH PLAN INC B Good

Major Rating Factors: Good overall profitability index (6.1 on a scale of 0 to 10). Good liquidity (6.9) with sufficient resources (cash flows and marketable investments) to handle a spike in claims. Strong capitalization (9.7) based on excellent current risk-adjusted capital (severe loss scenario).
Other Rating Factors: High quality investment portfolio (7.0).
Principal Business: Comp med (51%), Medicare (25%), Medicaid (18%), FEHB (3%), dental (1%), other (1%)
Mem Phys: 18: 28,403 **17:** 28,619 **18 MLR** 86.5% **/ 18 Admin Exp** N/A
Enroll(000): Q1 19: 1,099 **18:** 1,083 **17:** 1,104 **Med Exp PMPM:** $383
Principal Investments: Long-term bonds (69%), nonaffiliate common stock (18%), affiliate common stock (6%), cash and equiv (3%), real estate (1%), pref stock (1%), other (2%)
Provider Compensation ($000): Contr fee ($4,824,516), FFS ($98,837), capitation ($54,142), bonus arrang ($9,149), other ($56,015)
Total Member Encounters: Phys (9,300,288), non-phys (2,309,800)
Group Affiliation: Lifetime Healthcare Inc
Licensed in: NY
Address: 165 Court St, Rochester, NY 14647
Phone: (585) 453-6325 **Dom State:** NY **Commenced Bus:** N/A

Data Date	Rating	RACR #1	RACR #2	Total Assets ($mil)	Capital ($mil)	Net Premium ($mil)	Net Income ($mil)
3-19	B	3.48	2.90	3,365.7	1,312.3	1,497.5	102.5
3-18	B+	4.00	3.33	3,687.4	1,411.2	1,424.3	5.1
2018	B	3.04	2.54	3,385.4	1,137.5	5,746.6	150.1
2017	B+	4.07	3.39	3,348.9	1,438.1	5,617.8	182.3
2016	B+	3.29	2.74	3,086.3	1,210.7	5,983.7	99.5
2015	A-	2.99	2.50	3,026.5	1,059.4	5,923.2	57.9
2014	A-	3.23	2.69	3,046.4	1,157.6	5,944.0	24.2

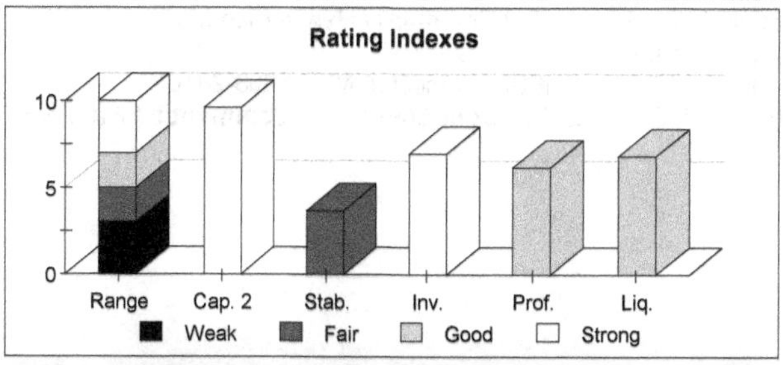

FAIR AMERICAN INS & REINS CO B Good

Major Rating Factors: History of adequate reserve strength (5.1 on a scale of 0 to 10) as reserves have been consistently at an acceptable level. Fair profitability index (4.7). Weak expense controls. Return on equity has been low, averaging 2.5% over the past five years.
Other Rating Factors: Fair overall results on stability tests (4.1) including excessive premium growth. Strong long-term capitalization index (10.0) based on excellent current risk adjusted capital (severe and moderate loss scenarios), despite some fluctuation in capital levels. Excellent liquidity (7.4) with ample operational cash flow and liquid investments.
Principal Business: Medical malpractice (52%), group accident & health (45%), and surety (3%).
Principal Investments: Investment grade bonds (96%) and misc. investments (4%).
Investments in Affiliates: None
Group Affiliation: Alleghany Corp Group
Licensed in: All states except PR
Commenced Business: September 1985
Address: ONE LIBERTY PLAZA 165 BROADWAY, New York, NY 10006
Phone: (212) 365-2200 **Domicile State:** NY **NAIC Code:** 35157

Data Date	Rating	RACR #1	RACR #2	Loss Ratio %	Total Assets ($mil)	Capital ($mil)	Net Premium ($mil)	Net Income ($mil)
3-19	B	46.10	34.44	N/A	229.2	201.2	2.1	1.9
3-18	B-	50.58	34.76	N/A	217.3	194.9	1.6	1.0
2018	B	43.21	35.19	72.3	229.7	199.4	7.8	5.5
2017	B-	55.78	37.50	50.7	211.3	193.9	4.0	3.8
2016	B-	56.35	38.56	52.3	205.6	187.7	3.9	5.7
2015	B	81.08	49.01	52.8	256.9	241.8	3.5	6.0
2014	B	5.55	5.32	64.2	256.9	243.1	3.7	4.6

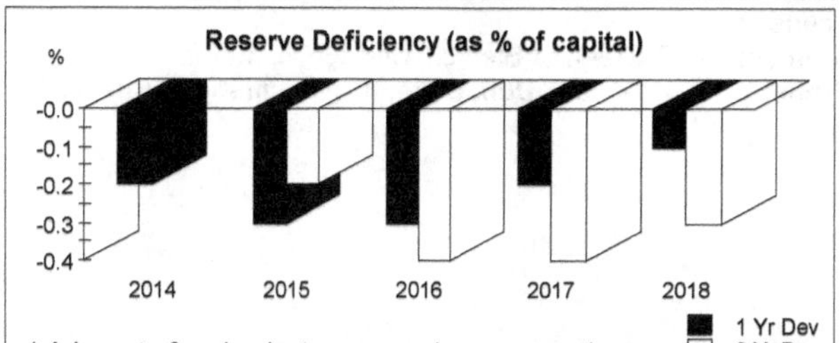

* Adequate & redundant reserves show as negatives

FALLON COMMUNITY HEALTH PLAN — B- Good

Major Rating Factors: Fair profitability index (3.3 on a scale of 0 to 10). Good liquidity (6.1) with sufficient resources (cash flows and marketable investments) to handle a spike in claims. Strong capitalization index (7.2) based on excellent current risk-adjusted capital (severe loss scenario).
Other Rating Factors: High quality investment portfolio (7.3). Excellent overall results on stability tests (7.3).
Principal Business: Comp med (56%), Medicaid (33%), Medicare (11%)
Mem Phys: 18: 64,400 **17:** 58,760 **18 MLR** 91.2% **/ 18 Admin Exp** N/A
Enroll(000): Q1 19: 167 **18:** 170 **17:** 135 **Med Exp PMPM:** $676
Principal Investments: Long-term bonds (48%), nonaffiliate common stock (30%), cash and equiv (19%), affiliate common stock (2%), other (1%)
Provider Compensation ($000): Contr fee ($1,024,436), capitation ($312,626), salary ($23,368), bonus arrang ($2,733)
Total Member Encounters: Phys (557,535), non-phys (931,656)
Group Affiliation: Fallon Community Health Plan Inc
Licensed in: MA
Address: 10 Chestnut Street, Worcester, MA 01608-2810
Phone: (508) 799-2100 **Dom State:** MA **Commenced Bus:** N/A

Data Date	Rating	RACR #1	RACR #2	Total Assets ($mil)	Capital ($mil)	Net Premium ($mil)	Net Income ($mil)
3-19	B-	1.49	1.24	407.3	172.8	379.8	3.0
3-18	B-	1.50	1.25	419.3	149.7	333.7	-8.9
2018	B-	1.38	1.15	401.2	160.3	1,514.4	8.8
2017	B-	1.63	1.36	383.6	163.1	1,242.2	17.9
2016	B-	1.59	1.33	347.2	145.8	1,149.0	-21.3
2015	B	1.82	1.52	368.4	151.3	1,095.9	8.8
2014	B	1.96	1.64	390.9	168.4	1,103.7	26.7

Rating Indexes

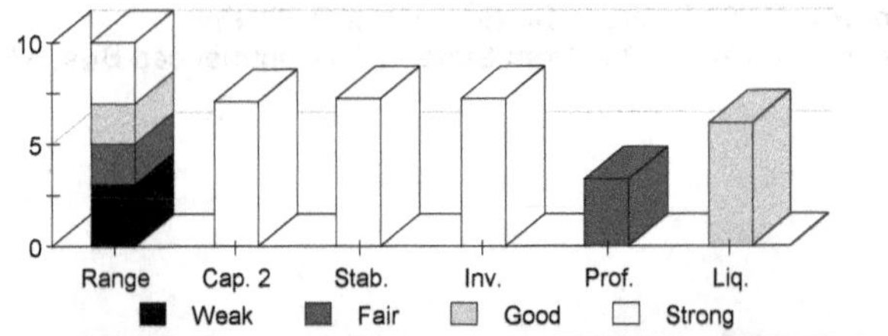

FALLON HEALTH & LIFE ASR CO — C Fair

Major Rating Factors: Weak profitability index (0.6 on a scale of 0 to 10). Strong capitalization (7.1) based on excellent current risk-adjusted capital (severe loss scenario). High quality investment portfolio (9.9).
Other Rating Factors: Excellent liquidity (7.1) with ample operational cash flow and liquid investments.
Principal Business: Comp med (64%), med supp (36%)
Mem Phys: 18: 64,400 **17:** 58,760 **18 MLR** 115.5% **/ 18 Admin Exp** N/A
Enroll(000): Q1 19: 5 **18:** 5 **17:** 6 **Med Exp PMPM:** $446
Principal Investments: Cash and equiv (100%), affiliate common stock (37%)
Provider Compensation ($000): Contr fee ($28,005), bonus arrang ($42), capitation ($42)
Total Member Encounters: Phys (22,875), non-phys (7,956)
Group Affiliation: Fallon Community Health Plan Inc
Licensed in: MA
Address: 10 Chestnut St, Worcester, MA 01608-2810
Phone: (508) 799-2100 **Dom State:** MA **Commenced Bus:** N/A

Data Date	Rating	RACR #1	RACR #2	Total Assets ($mil)	Capital ($mil)	Net Premium ($mil)	Net Income ($mil)
3-19	C	1.41	1.18	16.3	6.1	5.6	-0.7
3-18	C	1.19	0.99	20.4	5.3	6.3	-2.3
2018	C	1.57	1.31	18.8	6.8	23.6	-5.5
2017	E	1.05	0.88	24.0	6.5	28.7	-6.1
2016	E	2.02	1.68	25.9	8.4	30.1	1.8
2015	E	0.97	0.81	31.6	5.7	37.3	-11.0
2014	E	1.10	0.92	31.4	6.4	40.2	-12.1

Rating Indexes

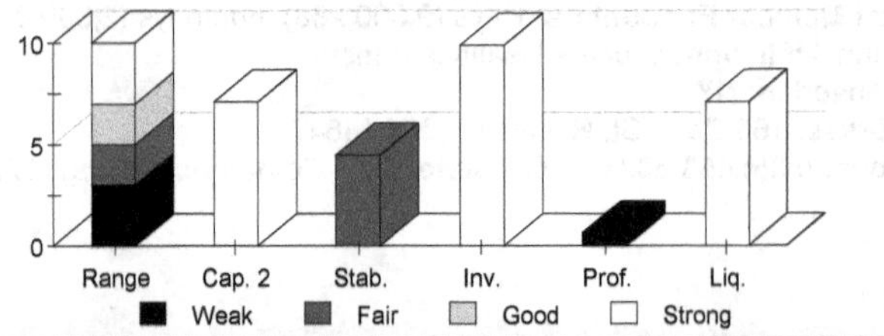

FAMILY HEALTH NETWORK INC — D- Weak

Major Rating Factors: Weak profitability index (1.0 on a scale of 0 to 10). Poor capitalization (0.0) based on weak current risk-adjusted capital (severe loss scenario). Weak liquidity (0.0) as a spike in claims may stretch capacity.
Other Rating Factors: High quality investment portfolio (9.8).
Principal Business: Medicaid (100%)
Mem Phys: 17: 13,356 **16:** 13,123 **17 MLR** 102.6% **/ 17 Admin Exp** N/A
Enroll(000): Q1 18: N/A **17:** 100 **16:** 239 **Med Exp PMPM:** $188
Principal Investments: Cash and equiv (95%), affiliate common stock (4%), long-term bonds (1%)
Provider Compensation ($000): Contr fee ($410,908), capitation ($38,885)
Total Member Encounters: N/A
Group Affiliation: None
Licensed in: IL
Address: 322 S Green St Ste 400, Chicago, IL 60607
Phone: (312) 491-1956 **Dom State:** IL **Commenced Bus:** N/A

Data Date	Rating	RACR #1	RACR #2	Total Assets ($mil)	Capital ($mil)	Net Premium ($mil)	Net Income ($mil)
3-18	D-	0.14	0.11	69.4	27.3	12.0	3.7
3-17	C	0.81	0.67	212.0	59.4	121.7	0.7
2017	D	0.15	0.12	102.9	28.8	419.3	-12.3
2016	C-	0.84	0.70	197.8	60.9	504.1	2.3
2015	U	0.43	0.36	171.7	27.6	466.1	1.8
2014	N/A	N/A	N/A	N/A	N/A	N/A	N/A
2013	N/A	N/A	N/A	N/A	N/A	N/A	N/A

Rating Indexes

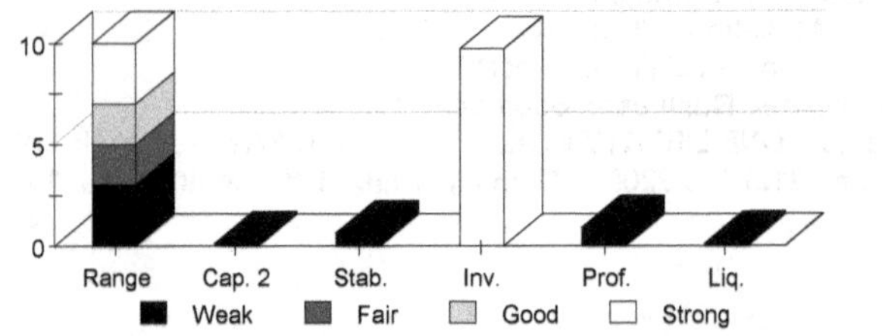

FAMILY HERITAGE LIFE INSURANCE COMPANY OF AMERICA B- Good

Major Rating Factors: Good quality investment portfolio (5.9 on a scale of 0 to 10) despite mixed results such as: minimal exposure to mortgages and large holdings of BBB rated bonds but small junk bond holdings. Good profitability (5.0) although investment income, in comparison to reserve requirements, is below regulatory standards. Fair overall results on stability tests (3.7).
Other Rating Factors: Strong capitalization (7.1) based on excellent risk adjusted capital (severe loss scenario). Excellent liquidity (7.7).
Principal Business: Individual health insurance (76%), reinsurance (19%), group health insurance (4%), and individual life insurance (1%).
Principal Investments: NonCMO investment grade bonds (93%), CMOs and structured securities (2%), noninv. grade bonds (1%), and mortgages in good standing (1%).
Investments in Affiliates: None
Group Affiliation: Torchmark Corp
Licensed in: All states except NY
Commenced Business: November 1989
Address: 6001 East Royalton Rd Ste 200, Cleveland, OH 44147-3529
Phone: (440) 922-5200 **Domicile State:** OH **NAIC Code:** 77968

Data Date	Rating	RACR #1	RACR #2	Total Assets ($mil)	Capital ($mil)	Net Premium ($mil)	Net Income ($mil)
3-19	B-	1.69	1.04	1,231.3	119.5	72.5	8.8
3-18	B+	1.70	1.05	1,347.8	104.0	74.6	7.6
2018	B-	2.04	1.25	1,196.8	125.4	170.0	31.5
2017	B+	1.65	1.01	1,290.4	100.3	284.3	23.0
2016	B+	1.96	1.25	1,108.8	104.2	264.6	23.8
2015	A-	1.92	1.27	921.0	78.3	254.1	19.1
2014	A-	1.87	1.27	775.2	67.4	237.0	18.1

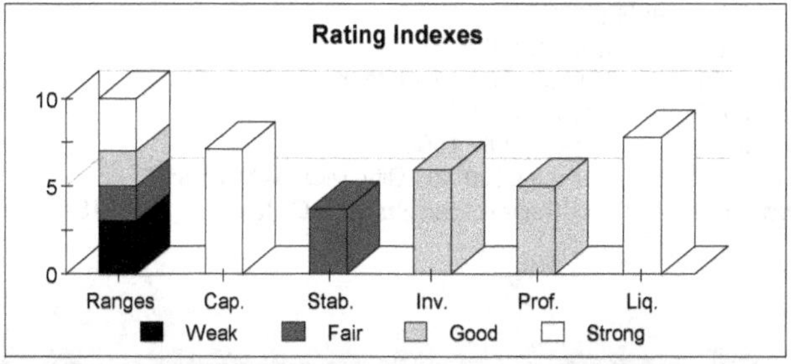

FAMILY LIFE INSURANCE COMPANY C Fair

Major Rating Factors: Fair profitability (3.0 on a scale of 0 to 10) with investment income below regulatory standards in relation to interest assumptions of reserves. Fair overall results on stability tests (4.2) including negative cash flow from operations for 2018. Good liquidity (5.6) with sufficient resources to handle a spike in claims.
Other Rating Factors: Strong capitalization (9.1) based on excellent risk adjusted capital (severe loss scenario). High quality investment portfolio (8.2).
Principal Business: Individual health insurance (67%) and individual life insurance (33%).
Principal Investments: NonCMO investment grade bonds (75%), policy loans (10%), mortgages in good standing (3%), CMOs and structured securities (2%), and common & preferred stock (1%).
Investments in Affiliates: None
Group Affiliation: Manhattan Life Group Inc
Licensed in: All states except NY, PR
Commenced Business: June 1949
Address: 10777 Northwest Freeway, Houston, TX 77092
Phone: (713) 529-0045 **Domicile State:** TX **NAIC Code:** 63053

Data Date	Rating	RACR #1	RACR #2	Total Assets ($mil)	Capital ($mil)	Net Premium ($mil)	Net Income ($mil)
3-19	C	3.07	2.42	143.7	28.4	6.5	0.4
3-18	C	3.28	2.66	149.6	30.6	6.7	0.4
2018	C	3.06	2.40	146.8	28.4	25.6	1.6
2017	C	3.33	2.72	150.8	31.1	25.6	2.7
2016	C	3.61	3.03	155.8	34.0	26.0	1.0
2015	C	3.79	3.13	158.7	35.8	26.5	2.7
2014	C	3.87	3.33	146.5	36.2	25.2	1.7

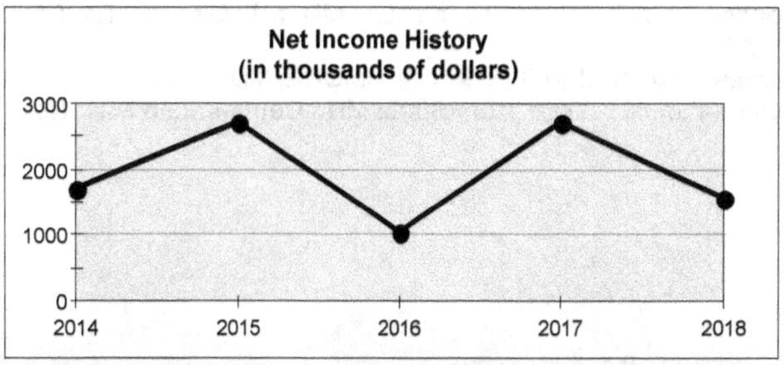

FAMILYCARE HEALTH PLANS INC E- Very Weak

Major Rating Factors: Weak profitability index (1.4 on a scale of 0 to 10). Strong capitalization (10.0) based on excellent current risk-adjusted capital (severe loss scenario). High quality investment portfolio (9.9).
Other Rating Factors: Excellent liquidity (7.2) with ample operational cash flow and liquid investments.
Principal Business: Medicare (100%)
Mem Phys: 18: N/A **17:** 2,514 **18 MLR** 96.9% **/ 18 Admin Exp** N/A
Enroll(000): Q1 19: N/A **18:** N/A **17:** 4 **Med Exp PMPM:** N/A
Principal Investments: Long-term bonds (57%), cash and equiv (43%)
Provider Compensation ($000): Contr fee ($23,027), FFS ($2,740), capitation ($94), bonus arrang ($14)
Total Member Encounters: N/A
Group Affiliation: FamilyCare Inc
Licensed in: OR
Address: 825 NE Multnomah Ste 1400, Portland, OR 97201
Phone: (503) 471-2103 **Dom State:** OR **Commenced Bus:** N/A

Data Date	Rating	RACR #1	RACR #2	Total Assets ($mil)	Capital ($mil)	Net Premium ($mil)	Net Income ($mil)
3-19	E-	4.62	3.85	19.0	18.7	N/A	0.1
3-18	E-	2.44	2.03	29.9	16.3	11.0	1.0
2018	E-	4.41	3.68	18.6	17.9	20.3	2.7
2017	E-	2.29	1.91	27.2	15.4	41.6	-10.0
2016	E-	1.14	0.95	19.4	9.8	47.3	-13.4
2015	D	1.26	1.05	17.9	8.6	39.3	-9.9
2014	C-	3.50	2.92	26.2	19.5	32.1	-5.0

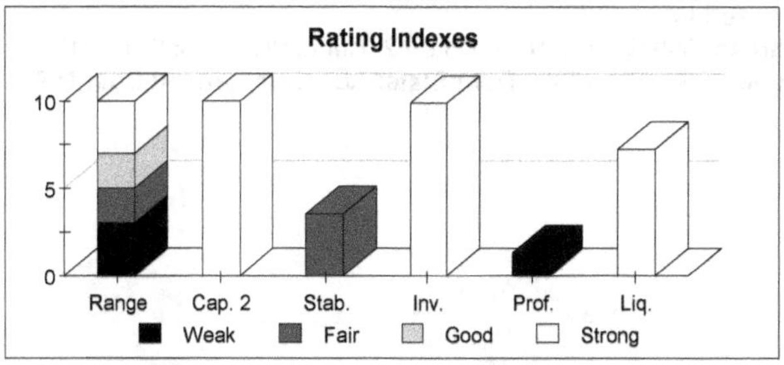

FIDELITY SECURITY LIFE INSURANCE COMPANY * A- Excellent

Major Rating Factors: Good quality investment portfolio (6.7 on a scale of 0 to 10) despite mixed results such as: minimal exposure to mortgages and large holdings of BBB rated bonds but minimal holdings in junk bonds. Good liquidity (6.7) with sufficient resources to cover a large increase in policy surrenders. Good overall results on stability tests (5.7) good operational trends and excellent risk diversification.
Other Rating Factors: Strong capitalization (9.8) based on excellent risk adjusted capital (severe loss scenario). Excellent profitability (7.7).
Principal Business: Group health insurance (89%), reinsurance (5%), individual health insurance (2%), individual life insurance (1%), and other lines (3%).
Principal Investments: NonCMO investment grade bonds (53%), CMOs and structured securities (30%), cash (4%), common & preferred stock (2%), and misc. investments (4%).
Investments in Affiliates: 2%
Group Affiliation: Fidelity Security Group
Licensed in: All states except PR
Commenced Business: July 1969
Address: 3130 Broadway, Kansas City, MO 64111-2452
Phone: (816) 750-1060 **Domicile State:** MO **NAIC Code:** 71870

Data Date	Rating	RACR #1	RACR #2	Total Assets ($mil)	Capital ($mil)	Net Premium ($mil)	Net Income ($mil)
3-19	A-	4.71	2.88	970.0	249.8	31.6	7.9
3-18	B	3.98	2.43	936.3	209.5	29.6	7.0
2018	A-	4.60	2.81	999.4	242.3	119.4	39.2
2017	B	3.87	2.36	949.5	204.4	115.0	22.8
2016	B	3.46	2.07	875.1	186.8	121.6	17.5
2015	B	2.02	1.44	864.2	169.0	420.4	18.1
2014	B-	2.65	1.73	831.7	151.9	204.6	18.4

Adverse Trends in Operations

Decrease in premium volume from 2016 to 2017 (5%)
Decrease in premium volume from 2015 to 2016 (71%)
Change in premium mix from 2015 to 2016 (5.8%)

FIRST CARE INC D Weak

Major Rating Factors: Weak profitability index (0.1 on a scale of 0 to 10). Good liquidity (5.1) with sufficient resources (cash flows and marketable investments) to handle a spike in claims. Strong capitalization (10.0) based on excellent current risk-adjusted capital (severe loss scenario).
Other Rating Factors: High quality investment portfolio (9.9).
Principal Business: Med supp (100%)
Mem Phys: 18: 46,809 **17:** 46,349 **18 MLR** 88.0% **/ 18 Admin Exp** N/A
Enroll(000): Q1 19: 12 **18:** 10 **17:** 6 **Med Exp PMPM:** $130
Principal Investments: Long-term bonds (81%), cash and equiv (19%)
Provider Compensation ($000): Contr fee ($11,906), FFS ($737)
Total Member Encounters: Phys (108,214), non-phys (49,914)
Group Affiliation: CareFirst Inc
Licensed in: AZ, DC, FL, ID, KY, LA, MD, MT, OK, OR, RI, TX, UT, VT, VA, WV, WY
Address: 1501 S CLINTON St, BALTIMORE, MD 21224
Phone: (410) 581-3000 **Dom State:** MD **Commenced Bus:** N/A

Data Date	Rating	RACR #1	RACR #2	Total Assets ($mil)	Capital ($mil)	Net Premium ($mil)	Net Income ($mil)
3-19	D	8.57	7.14	13.9	10.3	5.3	-4.2
3-18	C+	N/A	N/A	4.1	1.7	3.2	-2.8
2018	C	12.07	10.06	17.6	14.5	15.2	-12.5
2017	C+	N/A	N/A	6.3	4.5	7.5	-3.1
2016	C	106.20	88.46	14.0	6.2	0.6	0.0
2015	N/A	N/A	N/A	13.2	5.9	N/A	0.1
2014	N/A	N/A	N/A	11.1	5.2	N/A	0.8

Rating Indexes

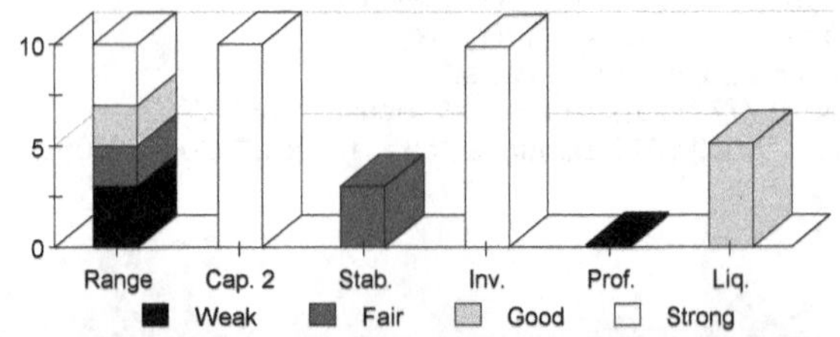

FIRST COMMUNITY HEALTH PLAN INC B Good

Major Rating Factors: Excellent profitability (8.4 on a scale of 0 to 10). Strong capitalization (10.0) based on excellent current risk-adjusted capital (severe loss scenario). High quality investment portfolio (9.5).
Other Rating Factors: Excellent liquidity (7.7) with ample operational cash flow and liquid investments.
Principal Business: Med supp (100%)
Mem Phys: 17: N/A **16:** N/A **17 MLR** 74.3% **/ 17 Admin Exp** N/A
Enroll(000): Q3 18: 4 **17:** 4 **16:** 4 **Med Exp PMPM:** $126
Principal Investments: Cash and equiv (57%), long-term bonds (43%)
Provider Compensation ($000): Contr fee ($5,883)
Total Member Encounters: Phys (102,246), non-phys (24,829)
Group Affiliation: None
Licensed in: AL
Address: 699 Gallatin St SW Ste A2, Huntsville, AL 35801-4912
Phone: (256) 532-2780 **Dom State:** AL **Commenced Bus:** N/A

Data Date	Rating	RACR #1	RACR #2	Total Assets ($mil)	Capital ($mil)	Net Premium ($mil)	Net Income ($mil)
9-18	B	10.66	8.89	8.7	7.4	6.0	0.9
9-17	B	9.09	7.57	7.8	6.3	6.0	0.1
2017	B	9.23	7.69	8.0	6.5	7.9	0.3
2016	B	8.93	7.44	7.6	6.2	7.7	0.2
2015	B	9.58	7.99	7.4	6.0	7.5	0.5
2014	B	8.91	7.42	6.9	5.6	7.1	0.3
2013	B	8.35	6.96	6.5	5.3	6.8	0.8

Rating Indexes

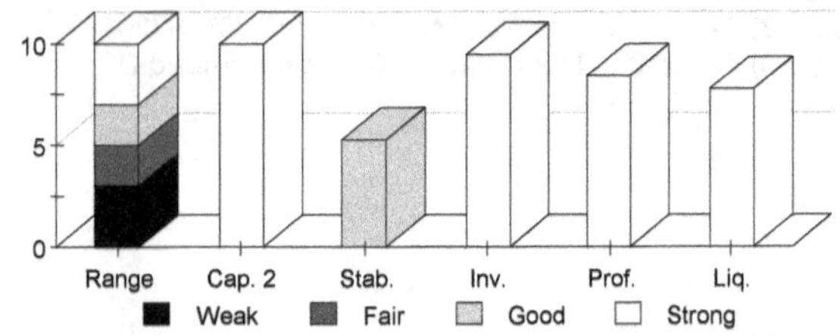

FIRST HEALTH LIFE & HEALTH INSURANCE COMPANY C+ Fair

Major Rating Factors: Fair profitability (3.9 on a scale of 0 to 10) with operating losses during the first three months of 2019. Fair overall results on stability tests (3.2) including weak results on operational trends. Good quality investment portfolio (6.4) with no exposure to mortgages and minimal holdings in junk bonds.
Other Rating Factors: Strong capitalization (7.8) based on excellent risk adjusted capital (severe loss scenario). Excellent liquidity (7.0).
Principal Business: Individual health insurance (97%) and group health insurance (3%).
Principal Investments: NonCMO investment grade bonds (62%), cash (29%), CMOs and structured securities (5%), and noninv. grade bonds (2%).
Investments in Affiliates: None
Group Affiliation: Aetna Inc
Licensed in: All states except PR
Commenced Business: June 1979
Address: DOWNERS GROVE, IL 60515
Phone: (630) 737-7900 **Domicile State:** TX **NAIC Code:** 90328

Data Date	Rating	RACR #1	RACR #2	Total Assets ($mil)	Capital ($mil)	Net Premium ($mil)	Net Income ($mil)
3-19	C+	1.89	1.55	422.3	171.2	144.4	-19.8
3-18	B-	1.60	1.31	526.7	198.1	138.9	-29.5
2018	C+	1.86	1.53	363.2	181.3	552.6	41.8
2017	B-	1.70	1.39	400.7	227.8	761.1	16.5
2016	B-	1.50	1.24	454.9	211.1	798.3	-1.7
2015	B-	2.24	1.85	581.8	289.2	700.0	16.1
2014	B	1.15	0.96	475.0	226.0	925.3	-6.6

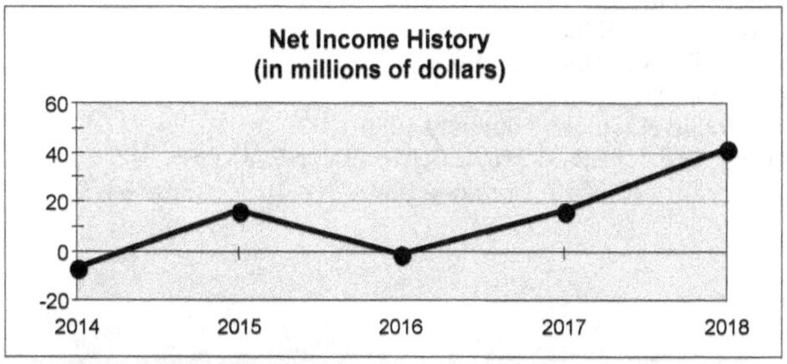

FIRST MEDICAL HEALTH PLAN INC D Weak

Major Rating Factors: Fair profitability index (4.7 on a scale of 0 to 10). Fair capitalization index (3.1) based on weak current risk-adjusted capital (moderate loss scenario). Good overall results on stability tests (5.4) despite a decline in enrollment during 2018.
Other Rating Factors: Good liquidity (6.9) with sufficient resources (cash flows and marketable investments) to handle a spike in claims. High quality investment portfolio (7.9).
Principal Business: Medicaid (56%), comp med (44%)
Mem Phys: 18: N/A **17:** N/A **18 MLR** 89.7% **/ 18 Admin Exp** N/A
Enroll(000): Q1 19: 528 **18:** 508 **17:** 556 **Med Exp PMPM:** $146
Principal Investments: Cash and equiv (87%), nonaffiliate common stock (13%)
Provider Compensation ($000): Capitation ($551,430), contr fee ($415,177)
Total Member Encounters: Phys (3,110,724), non-phys (6,259)
Group Affiliation: First Medical Health Plan Inc
Licensed in: PR
Address: 530 Marginal Buchanan, Guaynabo,
Phone: (787) 474-3999 **Dom State:** PR **Commenced Bus:** N/A

Data Date	Rating	RACR #1	RACR #2	Total Assets ($mil)	Capital ($mil)	Net Premium ($mil)	Net Income ($mil)
3-19	D	0.65	0.54	232.6	61.2	252.9	4.6
3-18	E	0.58	0.48	210.7	54.3	269.5	5.3
2018	D-	0.59	0.49	217.8	57.3	1,080.5	6.9
2017	E	0.51	0.42	205.9	49.4	1,074.2	16.2
2016	E-	0.28	0.23	183.5	32.8	1,048.9	10.6
2015	E-	0.12	0.10	191.9	21.5	882.7	-12.5
2014	E+	0.41	0.34	123.6	35.3	586.2	2.7

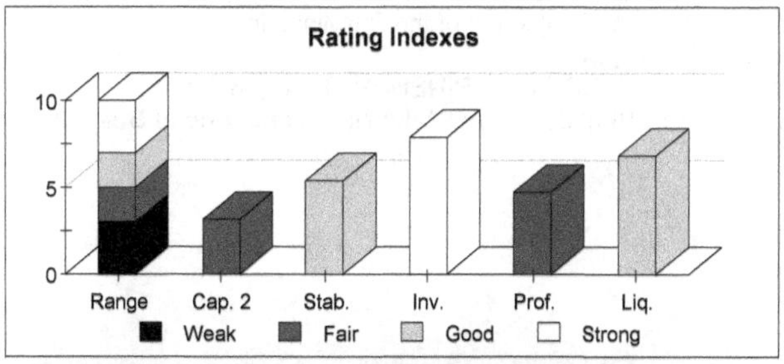

FIRST RELIANCE STANDARD LIFE INSURANCE COMPANY * A- Excellent

Major Rating Factors: Good overall results on stability tests (5.8 on a scale of 0 to 10) despite fair financial strength of affiliated Tokio Marine Holdings Inc. Strengths that enhance stability include excellent operational trends and excellent risk diversification. Good liquidity (6.8) with sufficient resources to handle a spike in claims. Fair profitability (3.6).
Other Rating Factors: Strong capitalization (10.0) based on excellent risk adjusted capital (severe loss scenario). High quality investment portfolio (7.8).
Principal Business: Group health insurance (66%) and group life insurance (34%).
Principal Investments: NonCMO investment grade bonds (81%), CMOs and structured securities (13%), and noninv. grade bonds (3%).
Investments in Affiliates: None
Group Affiliation: Tokio Marine Holdings Inc
Licensed in: DC, DE, NY
Commenced Business: October 1984
Address: 590 Madison Avenue 29th Floor, New York, NY 10022
Phone: (215) 787-4000 **Domicile State:** NY **NAIC Code:** 71005

Data Date	Rating	RACR #1	RACR #2	Total Assets ($mil)	Capital ($mil)	Net Premium ($mil)	Net Income ($mil)
3-19	A-	4.82	3.21	218.0	62.3	20.9	1.5
3-18	A	5.22	3.39	204.3	61.8	16.9	0.7
2018	A-	4.81	3.19	212.1	61.0	74.7	-0.5
2017	A	5.19	3.33	199.1	61.2	61.8	-5.8
2016	A	6.14	4.05	188.9	68.3	63.0	9.5
2015	A	5.72	3.61	184.0	65.5	57.9	6.5
2014	A	5.62	3.53	184.1	66.4	57.0	7.8

Tokio Marine Holdings Inc
Composite Group Rating: C+

Largest Group Members	Assets ($mil)	Rating
RELIANCE STANDARD LIFE INS CO	13875	C+
PHILADELPHIA INDEMNITY INS CO	9058	B-
SAFETY NATIONAL CASUALTY CORP	8028	C+
HOUSTON CASUALTY CO	3437	B-
US SPECIALTY INS CO	2042	B

FIRST UNUM LIFE INSURANCE COMPANY C+ Fair

Major Rating Factors: Fair overall results on stability tests (4.8 on a scale of 0 to 10) including fair financial strength of affiliated Unum Group. Fair quality investment portfolio (3.9) with large holdings of BBB rated bonds in addition to junk bond exposure equal to 95% of capital. Fair profitability (4.8) with operating losses during the first three months of 2019.
Other Rating Factors: Strong capitalization (7.3) based on excellent risk adjusted capital (severe loss scenario). Excellent liquidity (7.0).
Principal Business: Group health insurance (55%), group life insurance (22%), individual health insurance (20%), and individual life insurance (2%).
Principal Investments: NonCMO investment grade bonds (80%), mortgages in good standing (7%), noninv. grade bonds (7%), and CMOs and structured securities (5%).
Investments in Affiliates: None
Group Affiliation: Unum Group
Licensed in: NY
Commenced Business: January 1960
Address: 666 THIRD AVENUE SUITE 301, NEW YORK, NY 10017
Phone: (212) 328-8830 **Domicile State:** NY **NAIC Code:** 64297

Data Date	Rating	RACR #1	RACR #2	Total Assets ($mil)	Capital ($mil)	Net Premium ($mil)	Net Income ($mil)
3-19	C+	2.27	1.17	3,843.8	273.0	119.4	-1.7
3-18	C+	2.53	1.29	3,524.5	291.6	117.8	5.0
2018	C+	2.33	1.21	3,760.8	274.4	453.9	-13.6
2017	C+	2.66	1.36	3,457.4	299.1	392.7	27.4
2016	C+	2.63	1.32	3,260.8	282.4	375.7	82.4
2015	C+	2.54	1.27	3,130.4	263.5	363.2	26.5
2014	C+	2.63	1.33	2,976.2	272.1	360.0	-5.4

Unum Group
Composite Group Rating: C+

Largest Group Members	Assets ($mil)	Rating
UNUM LIFE INS CO OF AMERICA	22022	C+
PROVIDENT LIFE ACCIDENT INS CO	7994	C+
FIRST UNUM LIFE INS CO	3761	C+
COLONIAL LIFE ACCIDENT INS CO	3422	C+
PAUL REVERE LIFE INS CO	3410	C+

FIRSTCAROLINACARE INS CO D Weak

Major Rating Factors: Weak profitability index (1.0 on a scale of 0 to 10). Fair capitalization (4.2) based on fair current risk-adjusted capital (moderate loss scenario). Fair liquidity (2.9) as a spike in claims may stretch capacity.
Other Rating Factors: Good quality investment portfolio (6.5).
Principal Business: Medicare (59%), comp med (41%)
Mem Phys: 18: 3,250 **17:** 3,100 **18 MLR** 89.4% **/ 18 Admin Exp** N/A
Enroll(000): Q1 19: 15 **18:** 16 **17:** 18 **Med Exp PMPM:** $582
Principal Investments: Long-term bonds (57%), cash and equiv (27%), nonaffiliate common stock (16%)
Provider Compensation ($000): Contr fee ($107,435), capitation ($6,781), FFS ($5,250)
Total Member Encounters: Phys (305,532), non-phys (45,372)
Group Affiliation: FirstHealth of the Carolinas Inc
Licensed in: NC, SC
Address: 42 MEMORIAL Dr, PINEHURST, NC 28374
Phone: (910) 715-8100 **Dom State:** NC **Commenced Bus:** N/A

Data Date	Rating	RACR #1	RACR #2	Total Assets ($mil)	Capital ($mil)	Net Premium ($mil)	Net Income ($mil)
3-19	D	0.80	0.67	25.1	12.6	30.5	-0.5
3-18	D	1.00	0.83	37.6	17.1	33.9	0.1
2018	D	0.77	0.64	26.9	12.1	132.2	-5.0
2017	D	1.00	0.83	34.1	17.0	134.4	-9.7
2016	D	0.47	0.39	25.9	7.9	117.7	-17.6
2015	B-	1.11	0.92	30.1	13.7	98.0	-12.7
2014	B	1.01	0.85	23.2	9.7	74.2	-10.1

Rating Indexes

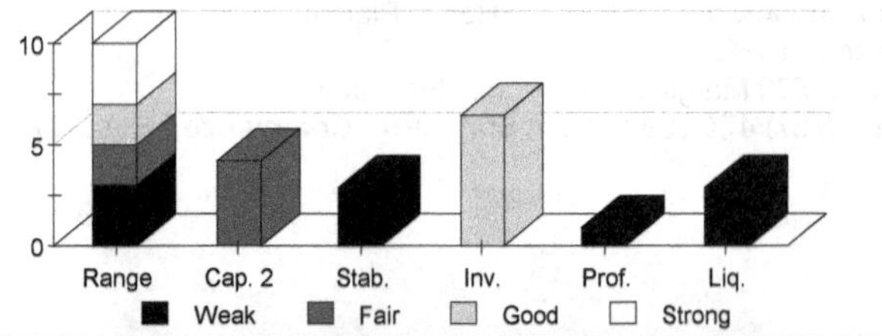

FLORIDA HEALTH CARE PLAN INC * A- Excellent

Major Rating Factors: Excellent profitability (9.0 on a scale of 0 to 10). Strong capitalization (10.0) based on excellent current risk-adjusted capital (severe loss scenario). High quality investment portfolio (9.5).
Other Rating Factors: Excellent liquidity (6.9) with sufficient resources (cash flows and marketable investments) to handle a spike in claims.
Principal Business: Comp med (71%), Medicare (29%)
Mem Phys: 18: 1,072 **17:** 1,020 **18 MLR** 82.1% **/ 18 Admin Exp** N/A
Enroll(000): Q1 19: 76 **18:** 84 **17:** 77 **Med Exp PMPM:** $488
Principal Investments: Long-term bonds (48%), cash and equiv (44%), real estate (9%)
Provider Compensation ($000): Contr fee ($303,813), salary ($58,906), FFS ($48,516), capitation ($15,656), other ($72,328)
Total Member Encounters: Phys (328,821), non-phys (122,159)
Group Affiliation: None
Licensed in: FL
Address: 1340 Ridgewood Ave, Holly Hill, FL 32117
Phone: (386) 676-7100 **Dom State:** FL **Commenced Bus:** N/A

Data Date	Rating	RACR #1	RACR #2	Total Assets ($mil)	Capital ($mil)	Net Premium ($mil)	Net Income ($mil)
3-19	A-	3.66	3.05	213.3	115.7	165.3	12.6
3-18	B+	4.06	3.38	226.5	93.8	154.2	2.5
2018	A-	3.30	2.75	202.4	103.8	611.9	25.6
2017	B+	2.57	2.15	192.6	87.8	501.7	16.4
2016	B-	5.50	4.58	166.4	87.4	428.0	12.0
2015	N/A	N/A	N/A	115.8	75.5	358.1	7.5
2014	B-	4.20	3.50	117.3	74.6	342.7	5.0

Rating Indexes

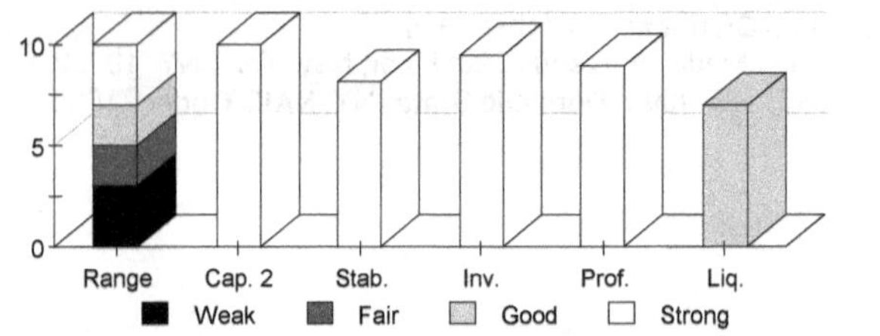

FLORIDA MHS INC — D — Weak

Major Rating Factors: Fair capitalization (3.9 on a scale of 0 to 10) based on fair current risk-adjusted capital (moderate loss scenario). Good overall profitability index (5.5). High quality investment portfolio (9.9).
Other Rating Factors: Excellent liquidity (7.0) with ample operational cash flow and liquid investments.
Principal Business: Medicaid (100%)
Mem Phys: 18: 35,675 **17:** 34,243 **18 MLR** 81.8% **/ 18 Admin Exp** N/A
Enroll(000): Q1 19: 26 **18:** 52 **17:** 79 **Med Exp PMPM:** $534
Principal Investments: Cash and equiv (92%), long-term bonds (8%)
Provider Compensation ($000): Contr fee ($500,457), capitation ($22,878)
Total Member Encounters: Phys (651,570), non-phys (1,800,339)
Group Affiliation: Magellan Health Inc
Licensed in: FL
Address: 6950 Columbia Gateway Dr, Columbia, MD 21046
Phone: (314) 387-5044 **Dom State:** FL **Commenced Bus:** N/A

Data Date	Rating	RACR #1	RACR #2	Total Assets ($mil)	Capital ($mil)	Net Premium ($mil)	Net Income ($mil)
3-19	D	0.77	0.64	86.1	28.0	63.1	-3.3
3-18	D	N/A	N/A	184.4	64.1	152.4	-8.9
2018	D	0.83	0.69	104.3	31.1	618.1	23.6
2017	D	N/A	N/A	241.2	111.4	605.6	34.9
2016	D	1.81	1.51	177.5	76.1	549.1	38.5
2015	D	0.90	0.75	122.9	39.2	440.9	-21.5
2014	U	1.33	1.11	124.5	29.3	190.1	-14.8

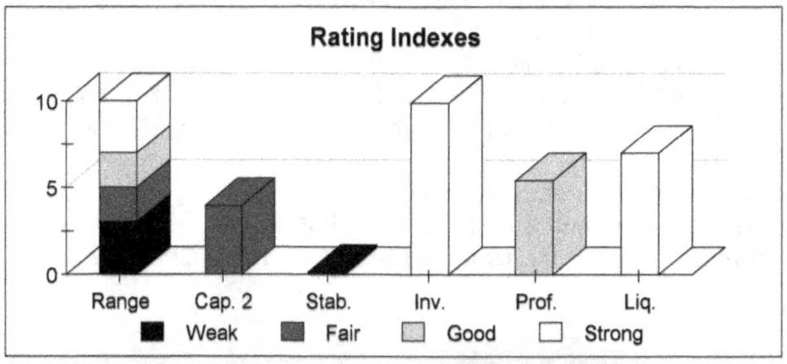

FLORIDA TRUE HEALTH INC — D — Weak

Major Rating Factors: Weak profitability index (0.8 on a scale of 0 to 10). Poor capitalization (2.9) based on weak current risk-adjusted capital (moderate loss scenario). Weak liquidity (0.0) as a spike in claims may stretch capacity.
Other Rating Factors: High quality investment portfolio (9.9).
Principal Business: Medicaid (100%)
Mem Phys: 18: 38,510 **17:** 36,020 **18 MLR** 92.9% **/ 18 Admin Exp** N/A
Enroll(000): Q1 19: 79 **18:** 321 **17:** 332 **Med Exp PMPM:** $290
Principal Investments: Cash and equiv (92%), long-term bonds (7%)
Provider Compensation ($000): Contr fee ($933,770), capitation ($192,210)
Total Member Encounters: Phys (2,756,560), non-phys (1,064,047)
Group Affiliation: Independence Health Group Inc
Licensed in: FL
Address: 11631 Kew Gardens Ave Ste 200, Palm Beach Gardens, FL 33410
Phone: (215) 937-8000 **Dom State:** FL **Commenced Bus:** N/A

Data Date	Rating	RACR #1	RACR #2	Total Assets ($mil)	Capital ($mil)	Net Premium ($mil)	Net Income ($mil)
3-19	D	0.61	0.51	86.9	31.4	109.2	-11.7
3-18	C	1.30	1.08	231.4	81.5	301.4	-17.9
2018	C	0.77	0.64	166.1	42.6	1,211.4	-241.0
2017	E	1.09	0.91	229.9	99.8	1,227.9	6.5
2016	E	1.68	1.40	219.2	95.2	1,104.9	18.3
2015	E	1.31	1.09	247.0	78.4	942.3	-152.5
2014	N/A	N/A	N/A	139.5	-1.7	648.0	-14.7

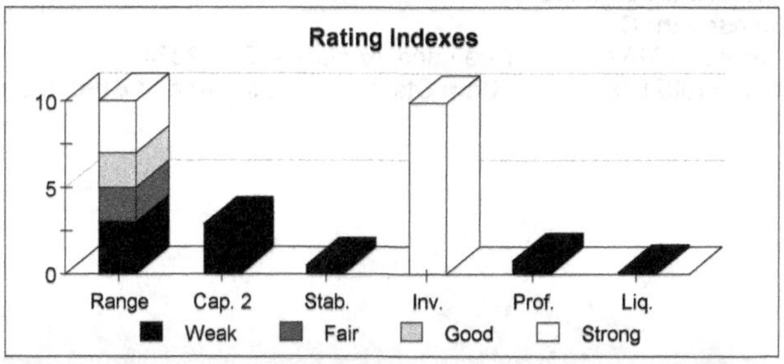

FREEDOM HEALTH INC — B — Good

Major Rating Factors: Good liquidity (6.2 on a scale of 0 to 10) with sufficient resources (cash flows and marketable investments) to handle a spike in claims. Excellent profitability (8.2). Strong capitalization (7.2) based on excellent current risk-adjusted capital (severe loss scenario).
Other Rating Factors: High quality investment portfolio (8.7).
Principal Business: Medicare (100%)
Mem Phys: 18: 19,350 **17:** 30,024 **18 MLR** 84.1% **/ 18 Admin Exp** N/A
Enroll(000): Q1 19: 78 **18:** 79 **17:** 75 **Med Exp PMPM:** $983
Principal Investments: Long-term bonds (69%), cash and equiv (30%), other (1%)
Provider Compensation ($000): Capitation ($619,070), contr fee ($273,216), FFS ($11,399)
Total Member Encounters: Phys (62,634), non-phys (65,025)
Group Affiliation: Anthem Inc
Licensed in: FL
Address: 5600 Mariner St Ste 227, Tampa, FL 33609
Phone: (813) 506-6000 **Dom State:** FL **Commenced Bus:** N/A

Data Date	Rating	RACR #1	RACR #2	Total Assets ($mil)	Capital ($mil)	Net Premium ($mil)	Net Income ($mil)
3-19	B	1.51	1.26	260.8	76.0	289.2	27.5
3-18	D	0.86	0.72	297.5	52.6	266.4	0.1
2018	B	0.95	0.80	196.8	49.5	1,093.3	6.7
2017	D-	0.47	0.39	182.7	38.3	938.8	15.3
2016	E	0.32	0.27	165.5	32.2	871.2	3.4
2015	E	0.40	0.33	135.0	33.7	770.8	10.4
2014	E+	0.32	0.26	103.7	25.0	663.7	0.5

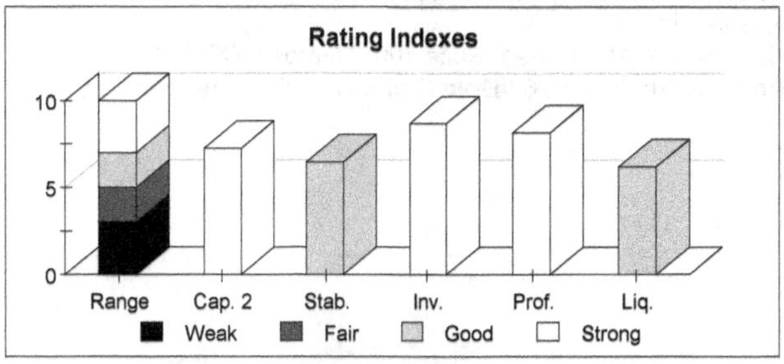

FREEDOM LIFE INSURANCE COMPANY OF AMERICA * B+ Good

Major Rating Factors: Good quality investment portfolio (6.7 on a scale of 0 to 10) despite mixed results such as: no exposure to mortgages and substantial holdings of BBB bonds but no exposure to junk bonds. Good overall results on stability tests (6.5) despite excessive premium growth and fair risk adjusted capital in prior years. Other stability subfactors include excellent operational trends and excellent risk diversification. Strong capitalization (7.3) based on excellent risk adjusted capital (severe loss scenario).
Other Rating Factors: Excellent profitability (8.5). Excellent liquidity (7.1).
Principal Business: Group health insurance (66%), individual health insurance (24%), and individual life insurance (11%).
Principal Investments: NonCMO investment grade bonds (44%), common & preferred stock (25%), CMOs and structured securities (25%), and cash (4%).
Investments in Affiliates: 25%
Group Affiliation: Credit Suisse Group
Licensed in: AL, AZ, AR, CO, DE, FL, GA, IL, IN, IA, KS, KY, LA, MD, MI, MN, MS, MO, NE, NV, NM, NC, OH, OK, OR, PA, SC, SD, TN, TX, UT, VA, WA, WV, WY
Commenced Business: June 1956
Address: 300 Burnett Street Suite 200, Fort Worth, TX 76102-2734
Phone: (817) 878-3300 **Domicile State:** TX **NAIC Code:** 62324

Data Date	Rating	RACR #1	RACR #2	Total Assets ($mil)	Capital ($mil)	Net Premium ($mil)	Net Income ($mil)
3-19	B+	1.40	1.20	247.5	153.2	123.4	18.9
3-18	B	1.21	1.03	168.5	89.3	94.4	5.0
2018	B+	1.18	1.03	211.5	122.8	422.3	37.6
2017	C+	1.11	0.96	148.3	76.4	282.2	19.4
2016	C+	0.83	0.71	100.2	51.1	196.9	12.0
2015	C+	0.75	0.65	77.3	37.0	140.1	14.9
2014	C	0.69	0.60	59.9	25.7	109.7	10.1

Adverse Trends in Operations

Change in asset mix during 2017 (6%)

FRESNO-KINGS-MADERA REGIONAL HEALTH C+ Fair

Major Rating Factors: Excellent profitability (9.6 on a scale of 0 to 10). Strong capitalization index (6.9) based on good current risk-adjusted capital (moderate loss scenario). Excellent overall results on stability tests (7.3).
Other Rating Factors: Excellent liquidity (6.9) with sufficient resources (cash flows and marketable investments) to handle a spike in claims.
Principal Business: Medicaid (100%)
Mem Phys: 18: N/A **17:** N/A **18 MLR** 84.4% **/ 18 Admin Exp** N/A
Enroll(000): Q1 19: 357 **18:** 356 **17:** 361 **Med Exp PMPM:** $232
Principal Investments ($000): Cash and equiv ($163,584)
Provider Compensation ($000): None
Total Member Encounters: N/A
Group Affiliation: None
Licensed in: CA
Address: 1615 Orange Tree Lane, Redlands, CA 92374
Phone: (909) 786-0702 **Dom State:** CA **Commenced Bus:** March 2011

Data Date	Rating	RACR #1	RACR #2	Total Assets ($mil)	Capital ($mil)	Net Premium ($mil)	Net Income ($mil)
3-19	C+	1.07	0.65	462.6	66.8	289.9	2.4
3-18	C	0.96	0.59	251.8	56.8	302.1	1.5
2018	C+	1.03	0.63	283.8	64.4	1,178.2	9.1
2017	C	0.93	0.57	167.7	55.4	1,089.3	10.4
2016	E+	0.58	0.35	151.4	38.4	1,092.6	11.5
2015	E+	0.43	0.26	124.8	26.8	1,010.4	13.3
2014	E	0.36	0.22	86.1	13.5	573.2	3.6

Rating Indexes

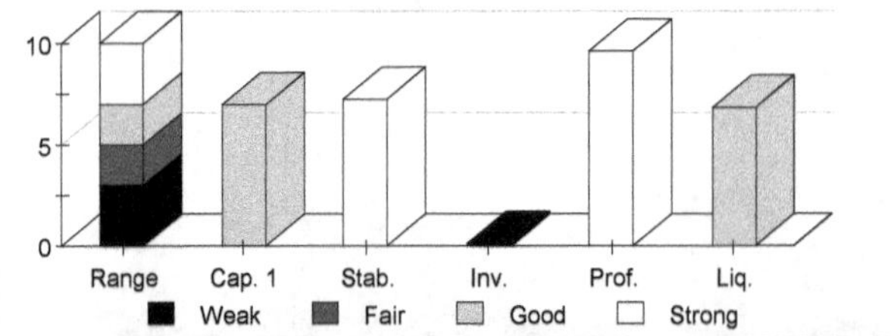

FRIDAY HEALTH PLANS OF CO INC E Very Weak

Major Rating Factors: Weak profitability index (1.1 on a scale of 0 to 10). Fair capitalization index (4.2) based on fair current risk-adjusted capital (moderate loss scenario). Good overall results on stability tests (5.2).
Other Rating Factors: High quality investment portfolio (7.7). Excellent liquidity (7.1) with ample operational cash flow and liquid investments.
Principal Business: Comp med (91%), Medicaid (5%), Medicare (4%)
Mem Phys: 18: 13,450 **17:** 11,055 **18 MLR** 70.4% **/ 18 Admin Exp** N/A
Enroll(000): Q1 19: 11 **18:** 12 **17:** 18 **Med Exp PMPM:** $361
Principal Investments: Cash and equiv (100%)
Provider Compensation ($000): Contr fee ($64,779), FFS ($194)
Total Member Encounters: N/A
Group Affiliation: Friday Health Plans Inc
Licensed in: CO
Address: 700 Main Street Suite 100, Alamosa, CO 81101
Phone: (719) 589-3696 **Dom State:** CO **Commenced Bus:** N/A

Data Date	Rating	RACR #1	RACR #2	Total Assets ($mil)	Capital ($mil)	Net Premium ($mil)	Net Income ($mil)
3-19	E	0.80	0.67	20.6	7.3	15.8	-0.3
3-18	E-	0.32	0.27	18.4	5.7	20.3	2.2
2018	E	0.93	0.77	20.9	8.3	82.2	2.3
2017	E-	0.18	0.15	22.6	4.0	96.3	-2.1
2016	E-	0.07	0.06	24.3	1.6	92.5	-4.8
2015	C	0.68	0.57	22.2	5.1	49.5	-1.9
2014	C+	1.13	0.94	19.7	7.7	49.1	2.4

Rating Indexes

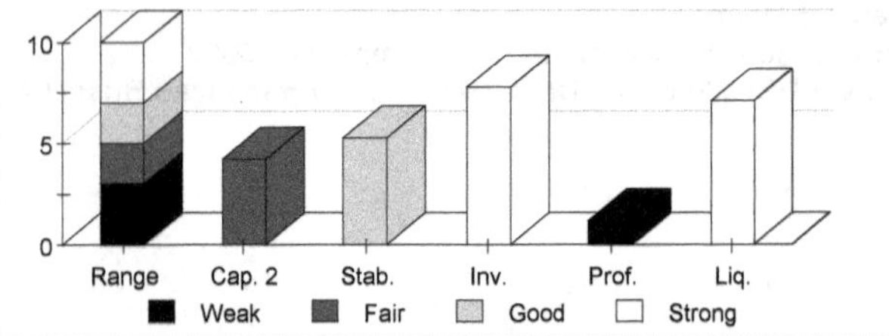

GATEWAY HEALTH PLAN INC — B- Good

Major Rating Factors: Fair quality investment portfolio (4.5 on a scale of 0 to 10). Good overall profitability index (6.8). Strong capitalization index (10.0) based on excellent current risk-adjusted capital (severe loss scenario).
Other Rating Factors: Excellent overall results on stability tests (8.1). Fair financial strength from affiliates. Excellent liquidity (6.9) with sufficient resources (cash flows and marketable investments) to handle a spike in claims.
Principal Business: Medicaid (68%), Medicare (32%)
Mem Phys: 18: 27,374 **17:** 23,846 **18 MLR** 85.0% **/ 18 Admin Exp** N/A
Enroll(000): Q1 19: 332 **18:** 336 **17:** 346 **Med Exp PMPM:** $485
Principal Investments: Long-term bonds (50%), nonaffiliate common stock (37%), cash and equiv (13%)
Provider Compensation ($000): Contr fee ($1,922,623), capitation ($98,087)
Total Member Encounters: Phys (1,591,756), non-phys (561,922)
Group Affiliation: Gateway Health Plan LP
Licensed in: PA
Address: 4 Gateway Center 444 Liberty, Pittsburgh, PA 15222-1222
Phone: (412) 255-4640 **Dom State:** PA **Commenced Bus:** N/A

Data Date	Rating	RACR #1	RACR #2	Total Assets ($mil)	Capital ($mil)	Net Premium ($mil)	Net Income ($mil)
3-19	B-	3.61	3.01	754.8	444.4	603.9	31.2
3-18	B-	3.05	2.54	800.0	371.0	602.9	31.2
2018	B-	3.30	2.75	702.4	403.0	2,357.3	85.1
2017	B-	2.09	1.74	652.6	331.5	2,329.6	75.9
2016	B-	2.34	1.95	754.7	299.6	2,380.6	57.9
2015	B-	1.91	1.59	581.7	236.2	2,168.8	10.9
2014	B	1.94	1.62	448.4	207.4	1,910.6	-22.5

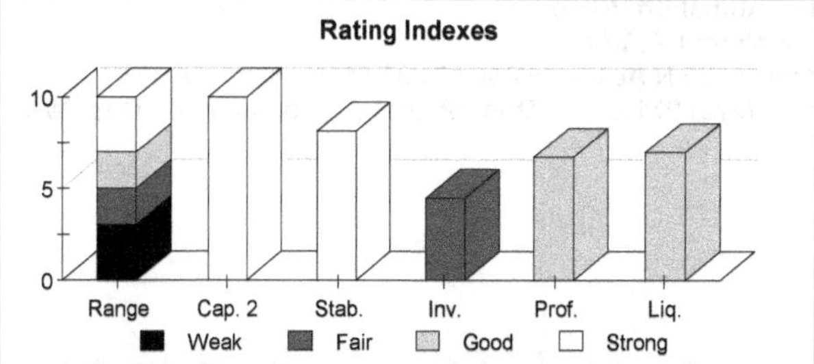

GATEWAY HEALTH PLAN OF OHIO INC — C Fair

Major Rating Factors: Weak profitability index (0.9 on a scale of 0 to 10). Low quality investment portfolio (1.2). Strong capitalization (7.6) based on excellent current risk-adjusted capital (severe loss scenario).
Other Rating Factors: Excellent liquidity (6.9) with sufficient resources (cash flows and marketable investments) to handle a spike in claims.
Principal Business: Medicare (100%)
Mem Phys: 18: 50,967 **17:** 27,375 **18 MLR** 88.9% **/ 18 Admin Exp** N/A
Enroll(000): Q1 19: 2 **18:** 10 **17:** 10 **Med Exp PMPM:** $772
Principal Investments: Cash and equiv (95%), long-term bonds (5%)
Provider Compensation ($000): Contr fee ($95,215), capitation ($2,751)
Total Member Encounters: Phys (81,500), non-phys (45,295)
Group Affiliation: Gateway Health Plan LP
Licensed in: KY, NC, OH
Address: 444 Liberty Ave Ste 2100, Pittsburgh, PA 15222-1222
Phone: (412) 255-4640 **Dom State:** OH **Commenced Bus:** N/A

Data Date	Rating	RACR #1	RACR #2	Total Assets ($mil)	Capital ($mil)	Net Premium ($mil)	Net Income ($mil)
3-19	C	1.83	1.53	19.0	11.7	9.1	-2.2
3-18	C	N/A	N/A	50.5	18.3	28.9	2.3
2018	C	2.14	1.78	29.0	14.0	109.2	-1.5
2017	C	N/A	N/A	37.5	16.2	106.5	-4.0
2016	C	2.69	2.24	29.6	12.7	78.5	0.8
2015	C	1.78	1.48	26.0	8.2	59.9	-1.0
2014	U	3.73	3.11	9.0	4.2	7.5	-6.6

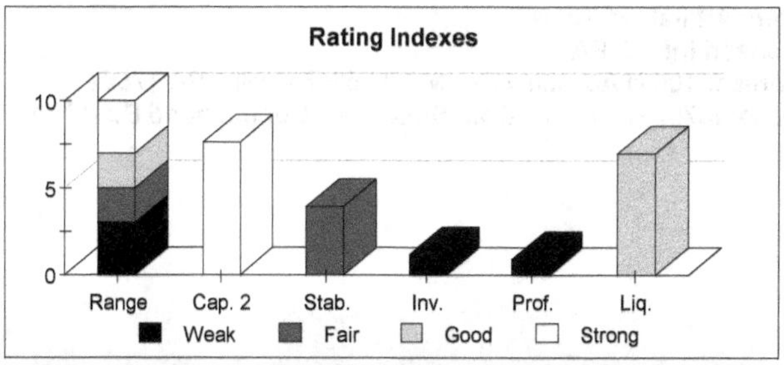

GEISINGER HEALTH PLAN * — B+ Good

Major Rating Factors: Excellent profitability (8.0 on a scale of 0 to 10). Strong capitalization index (7.3) based on excellent current risk-adjusted capital (severe loss scenario). High quality investment portfolio (7.3).
Other Rating Factors: Excellent overall results on stability tests (8.4) based on steady enrollment growth, averaging 7% over the past five years. Excellent liquidity (6.9) with sufficient resources (cash flows and marketable investments) to handle a spike in claims.
Principal Business: Medicaid (36%), Medicare (33%), comp med (30%)
Mem Phys: 18: 47,329 **17:** 44,024 **18 MLR** 84.9% **/ 18 Admin Exp** N/A
Enroll(000): Q1 19: 344 **18:** 364 **17:** 354 **Med Exp PMPM:** $510
Principal Investments: Long-term bonds (51%), nonaffiliate common stock (31%), cash and equiv (15%), real estate (3%)
Provider Compensation ($000): Contr fee ($1,833,381), FFS ($302,484), capitation ($95,039), bonus arrang ($40,168)
Total Member Encounters: Phys (3,189,117), non-phys (519,762)
Group Affiliation: None
Licensed in: NJ, PA
Address: 100 North Academy Avenue, Danville, PA 17822
Phone: (570) 271-8777 **Dom State:** PA **Commenced Bus:** N/A

Data Date	Rating	RACR #1	RACR #2	Total Assets ($mil)	Capital ($mil)	Net Premium ($mil)	Net Income ($mil)
3-19	B+	1.62	1.35	663.7	324.8	638.8	25.0
3-18	B+	1.47	1.22	674.3	266.8	678.1	20.8
2018	B+	1.40	1.17	635.2	286.4	2,671.9	100.3
2017	B+	1.35	1.12	535.2	251.3	2,375.4	86.5
2016	B	1.33	1.11	545.3	216.5	2,132.4	50.3
2015	B	1.32	1.10	465.4	195.5	1,884.8	16.3
2014	B	1.32	1.10	388.9	170.4	1,612.8	8.1

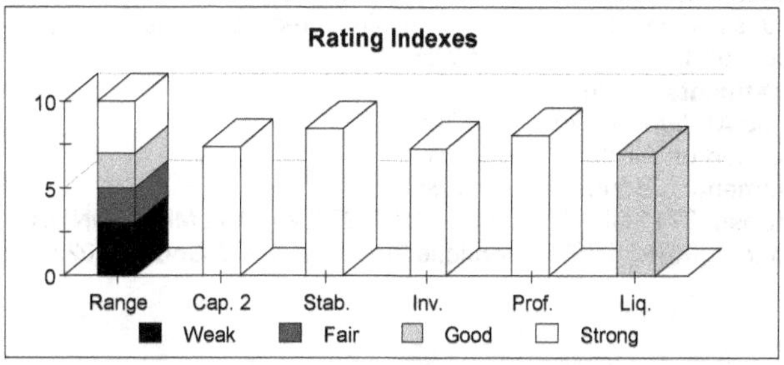

GEISINGER INDEMNITY INS CO — B- Good

Major Rating Factors: Good capitalization (6.2 on a scale of 0 to 10) based on good current risk-adjusted capital (severe loss scenario). High quality investment portfolio (9.9). Weak profitability index (0.9).
Other Rating Factors: Weak liquidity (0.0) as a spike in claims may stretch capacity.
Principal Business: Medicare (98%), med supp (1%)
Mem Phys: 18: 48,255 **17:** 50,346 **18 MLR** 89.8% **/ 18 Admin Exp** N/A
Enroll(000): Q1 19: 29 **18:** 31 **17:** 28 **Med Exp PMPM:** $591
Principal Investments: Long-term bonds (58%), cash and equiv (42%)
Provider Compensation ($000): Contr fee ($212,155), FFS ($11,157), bonus arrang ($2,305), capitation ($1,819)
Total Member Encounters: Phys (300,718), non-phys (70,853)
Group Affiliation: None
Licensed in: PA, WV
Address: 100 N Academy Ave MC 32-51, Danville, PA 17822
Phone: (570) 271-8777 **Dom State:** PA **Commenced Bus:** N/A

Data Date	Rating	RACR #1	RACR #2	Total Assets ($mil)	Capital ($mil)	Net Premium ($mil)	Net Income ($mil)
3-19	B-	1.11	0.93	86.0	30.6	60.9	-1.0
3-18	B-	1.56	1.30	101.0	34.6	58.9	-3.6
2018	B-	1.23	1.03	78.7	33.6	241.3	-13.2
2017	C-	1.38	1.15	77.1	38.1	205.5	-2.1
2016	C	1.13	0.94	58.3	19.6	138.8	-8.1
2015	C	1.07	0.89	44.8	14.6	128.3	7.7
2014	C	1.13	0.94	63.0	20.4	199.6	0.6

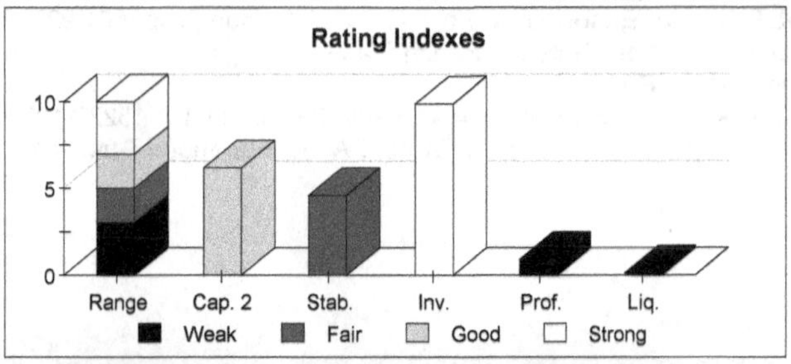

GEISINGER QUALITY OPTIONS INC — B- Good

Major Rating Factors: Good liquidity (6.5 on a scale of 0 to 10) with sufficient resources (cash flows and marketable investments) to handle a spike in claims. Strong capitalization (7.5) based on excellent current risk-adjusted capital (severe loss scenario). High quality investment portfolio (9.8).
Other Rating Factors: Weak profitability index (2.4).
Principal Business: Comp med (100%)
Mem Phys: 18: 45,328 **17:** 43,984 **18 MLR** 88.9% **/ 18 Admin Exp** N/A
Enroll(000): Q1 19: 50 **18:** 43 **17:** 53 **Med Exp PMPM:** $424
Principal Investments: Long-term bonds (82%), cash and equiv (18%)
Provider Compensation ($000): Contr fee ($153,933), FFS ($78,997), capitation ($4,419), bonus arrang ($3,589)
Total Member Encounters: Phys (236,666), non-phys (29,208)
Group Affiliation: None
Licensed in: NJ, PA
Address: 100 N Academy Ave MC 32-51, Danville, PA 17822
Phone: (570) 271-8777 **Dom State:** PA **Commenced Bus:** N/A

Data Date	Rating	RACR #1	RACR #2	Total Assets ($mil)	Capital ($mil)	Net Premium ($mil)	Net Income ($mil)
3-19	B-	1.72	1.43	75.6	39.5	75.5	5.4
3-18	B-	1.38	1.15	76.8	32.3	68.1	-5.6
2018	B-	1.41	1.18	66.2	32.8	264.1	-2.4
2017	C+	1.25	1.04	72.1	37.5	284.4	6.1
2016	C	1.30	1.08	83.7	31.9	265.0	-6.2
2015	C	1.53	1.28	68.6	30.5	231.1	0.4
2014	C	1.53	1.27	87.8	38.6	287.8	-6.2

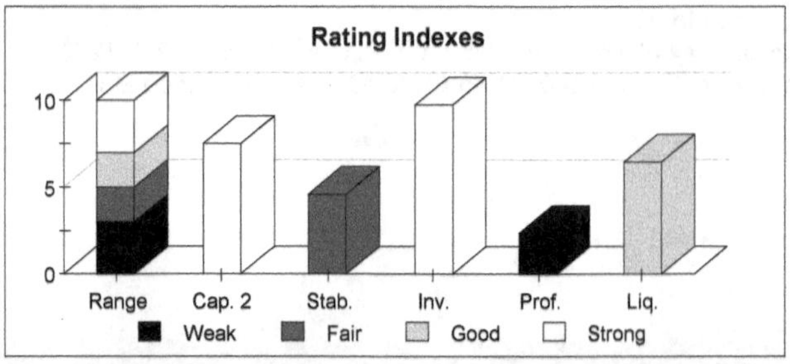

GENWORTH LIFE INSURANCE COMPANY — C Fair

Major Rating Factors: Fair current capitalization (4.4 on a scale of 0 to 10) based on fair risk adjusted capital (moderate loss scenario), although results have slipped from the good range over the last two years. Fair quality investment portfolio (3.8) with large holdings of BBB rated bonds in addition to junk bond exposure equal to 95% of capital. Exposure to mortgages is significant, but the mortgage default rate has been low. Fair overall results on stability tests (4.0) including fair risk adjusted capital in prior years.
Other Rating Factors: Weak profitability (1.8) with operating losses during the first three months of 2019. Excellent liquidity (7.2).
Principal Business: Individual health insurance (71%), reinsurance (11%), group health insurance (9%), and individual life insurance (9%).
Principal Investments: NonCMO investment grade bonds (63%), mortgages in good standing (11%), CMOs and structured securities (11%), noninv. grade bonds (5%), and misc. investments (9%).
Investments in Affiliates: 4%
Group Affiliation: Genworth Financial
Licensed in: All states except NY
Commenced Business: October 1956
Address: 2711 CENTERVILLE ROAD STE 400, WILMINGTON, DE 19808
Phone: (800) 255-7836 **Domicile State:** DE **NAIC Code:** 70025

Data Date	Rating	RACR #1	RACR #2	Total Assets ($mil)	Capital ($mil)	Net Premium ($mil)	Net Income ($mil)
3-19	C	0.93	0.64	40,255.7	1,876.9	558.4	-86.7
3-18	C+	1.18	0.84	39,992.3	2,663.9	552.3	-110.7
2018	C	0.94	0.65	39,995.4	1,871.0	2,287.8	-625.0
2017	C+	1.20	0.86	40,012.0	2,727.7	2,308.7	-39.1
2016	C+	1.17	0.87	40,225.8	3,152.9	2,084.8	-39.1
2015	B-	1.02	0.78	38,504.3	2,740.7	1,587.2	35.2
2014	B-	1.02	0.81	38,163.2	3,224.4	1,713.3	-179.7

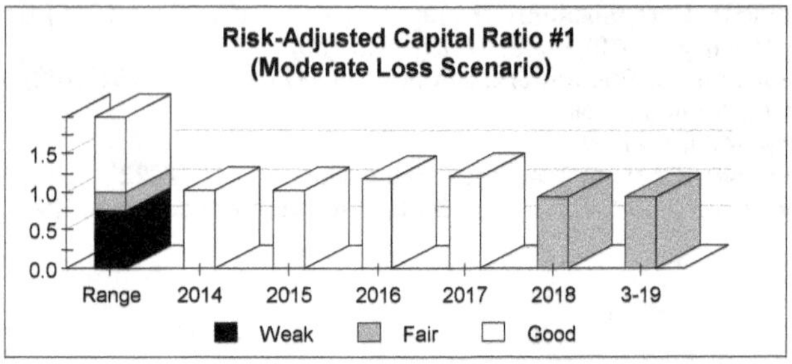

GENWORTH LIFE INSURANCE COMPANY OF NEW YORK C Fair

Major Rating Factors: Fair overall results on stability tests (3.7 on a scale of 0 to 10) including fair financial strength of affiliated Genworth Financial and negative cash flow from operations for 2018, fair risk adjusted capital in prior years. Fair quality investment portfolio (3.7) with large holdings of BBB rated bonds in addition to junk bond exposure equal to 76% of capital. Good capitalization (5.5) based on good risk adjusted capital (moderate loss scenario).
Other Rating Factors: Good liquidity (6.0). Weak profitability (1.4).
Principal Business: Individual health insurance (62%), reinsurance (17%), individual life insurance (17%), and group health insurance (3%).
Principal Investments: NonCMO investment grade bonds (61%), CMOs and structured securities (22%), mortgages in good standing (9%), noninv. grade bonds (3%), and common & preferred stock (1%).
Investments in Affiliates: None
Group Affiliation: Genworth Financial
Licensed in: CT, DC, DE, FL, IL, NJ, NY, RI, VA
Commenced Business: October 1988
Address: 600 THIRD AVENUE SUITE 2400, NEW YORK, NY 10016
Phone: (800) 357-1066 **Domicile State:** NY **NAIC Code:** 72990

Data Date	Rating	RACR #1	RACR #2	Total Assets ($mil)	Capital ($mil)	Net Premium ($mil)	Net Income ($mil)
3-19	C	1.32	0.68	7,727.9	247.6	62.0	16.6
3-18	C	1.43	0.73	7,906.5	293.1	63.1	5.8
2018	C	1.26	0.64	7,664.4	233.8	251.8	-56.0
2017	C	1.41	0.72	7,985.9	288.4	260.0	-168.1
2016	C	2.20	1.12	8,495.5	481.2	276.9	-20.0
2015	C+	2.22	1.12	8,372.2	494.8	356.1	-39.8
2014	B-	2.14	1.08	8,474.6	481.1	521.7	-93.3

Genworth Financial
Composite Group Rating: C

Largest Group Members	Assets ($mil)	Rating
GENWORTH LIFE INS CO	39995	C
GENWORTH LIFE ANNUITY INS CO	21184	C-
GENWORTH LIFE INS CO OF NEW YORK	7664	C
GENWORTH MORTGAGE INS CORP	3574	C
RIVERMONT LIFE INS CO I	607	C

GERBER LIFE INSURANCE COMPANY * B+ Good

Major Rating Factors: Good overall results on stability tests (6.4 on a scale of 0 to 10). Stability strengths include excellent operational trends and excellent risk diversification. Good quality investment portfolio (6.6) despite mixed results such as: large holdings of BBB rated bonds but moderate junk bond exposure. Fair profitability (4.2) with operating losses during the first three months of 2019.
Other Rating Factors: Fair liquidity (4.7). Strong capitalization (7.6) based on excellent risk adjusted capital (severe loss scenario).
Principal Business: Individual life insurance (46%), group health insurance (40%), individual health insurance (9%), and reinsurance (4%).
Principal Investments: NonCMO investment grade bonds (66%), CMOs and structured securities (24%), policy loans (5%), and noninv. grade bonds (4%).
Investments in Affiliates: None
Group Affiliation: Nestle SA
Licensed in: All states, the District of Columbia and Puerto Rico
Commenced Business: September 1968
Address: 1311 Mamaroneck Avenue, White Plains, NY 10605
Phone: (914) 272-4000 **Domicile State:** NY **NAIC Code:** 70939

Data Date	Rating	RACR #1	RACR #2	Total Assets ($mil)	Capital ($mil)	Net Premium ($mil)	Net Income ($mil)
3-19	B+	2.40	1.39	4,180.6	398.9	211.6	-2.5
3-18	B+	1.75	1.02	3,772.3	288.8	190.3	-7.8
2018	B+	1.81	1.05	3,992.2	311.7	745.1	-1.1
2017	B+	1.83	1.07	3,703.2	300.7	727.1	-2.7
2016	B+	1.78	1.06	3,397.6	307.0	690.0	15.3
2015	B+	1.90	1.14	3,088.3	295.8	604.2	18.5
2014	A-	1.97	1.20	2,812.2	285.3	565.3	24.2

Adverse Trends in Operations

Decrease in capital during 2017 (2%)

GHS HEALTH MAINTENANCE ORGANIZATION B- Good

Major Rating Factors: Fair overall results on stability tests (4.1 on a scale of 0 to 10) based on a significant 57% decrease in enrollment during the period. Rating is significantly influenced by the good financial results of Health Care Service Corporation a Mu. Good liquidity (5.5) with sufficient resources (cash flows and marketable investments) to handle a spike in claims. Strong capitalization index (10.0) based on excellent current risk-adjusted capital (severe loss scenario).
Other Rating Factors: High quality investment portfolio (9.9). Weak profitability index (0.9).
Principal Business: Medicare (100%)
Mem Phys: 18: 13,575 **17:** 12,424 **18 MLR** 92.4% **/ 18 Admin Exp** N/A
Enroll(000): Q1 19: 19 **18:** 4 **17:** 10 **Med Exp PMPM:** $630
Principal Investments: Long-term bonds (77%), cash and equiv (17%), affiliate common stock (6%)
Provider Compensation ($000): Contr fee ($41,415), FFS ($2,930), bonus arrang ($951), capitation ($26), other ($46)
Total Member Encounters: Phys (60,709), non-phys (23,521)
Group Affiliation: Health Care Service Corporation a Mu
Licensed in: OK
Address: 1400 South Boston, Tulsa, OK 74119
Phone: (312) 653-6000 **Dom State:** OK **Commenced Bus:** N/A

Data Date	Rating	RACR #1	RACR #2	Total Assets ($mil)	Capital ($mil)	Net Premium ($mil)	Net Income ($mil)
3-19	B-	8.38	6.98	56.9	26.4	6.9	-0.2
3-18	B-	N/A	N/A	66.3	26.3	9.2	9.4
2018	B-	8.56	7.13	50.1	27.0	36.7	-23.3
2017	B-	N/A	N/A	70.8	26.2	65.1	-10.5
2016	C+	3.57	2.97	43.5	28.5	38.7	-3.8
2015	B-	4.10	3.42	42.2	29.8	27.6	-15.5
2014	B	11.36	9.47	42.1	38.2	4.2	-1.1

Rating Indexes

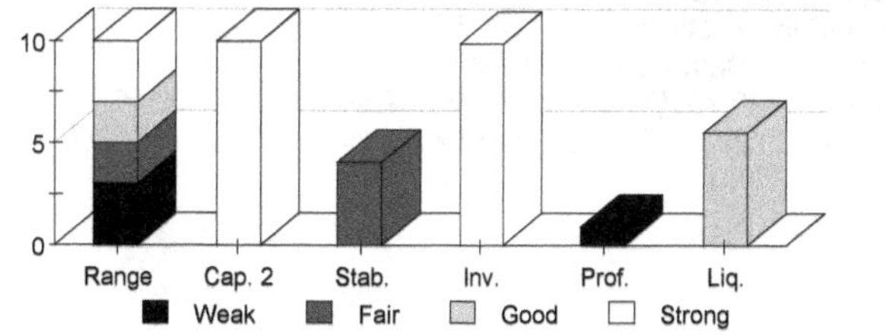

GHS INS CO E- Very Weak

Major Rating Factors: Weak profitability index (0.8 on a scale of 0 to 10). Good liquidity (6.3) with sufficient resources (cash flows and marketable investments) to handle a spike in claims. Strong capitalization (9.0) based on excellent current risk-adjusted capital (severe loss scenario).
Other Rating Factors: High quality investment portfolio (9.9).
Principal Business: Medicare (99%)
Mem Phys: 18: 27,955 **17:** 17,939 **18 MLR** 96.8% **/ 18 Admin Exp** N/A
Enroll(000): Q1 19: 4 **18:** 6 **17:** 6 **Med Exp PMPM:** $740
Principal Investments: Long-term bonds (63%), cash and equiv (37%)
Provider Compensation ($000): Contr fee ($37,596), capitation ($8,070), FFS ($5,211), bonus arrang ($359), other ($869)
Total Member Encounters: Phys (34,837), non-phys (14,032)
Group Affiliation: Health Care Service Corporation a Mu
Licensed in: AR, CO, IL, IN, KS, NM, OK, TX
Address: 3817 Nwest Expressway Ste 300, Oklahoma City, OK 73112
Phone: (312) 653-6000 **Dom State:** OK **Commenced Bus:** N/A

Data Date	Rating	RACR #1	RACR #2	Total Assets ($mil)	Capital ($mil)	Net Premium ($mil)	Net Income ($mil)
3-19	E-	2.98	2.48	34.8	12.1	10.7	-1.7
3-18	E-	N/A	N/A	43.2	7.6	12.7	-5.1
2018	E-	3.47	2.89	39.5	14.3	53.5	-14.2
2017	E-	N/A	N/A	34.6	13.6	45.4	5.7
2016	E	4.46	3.71	30.9	8.5	27.4	1.7
2015	E	4.59	3.83	24.6	4.4	6.8	-13.6
2014	N/A	N/A	N/A	18.5	8.1	0.6	N/A

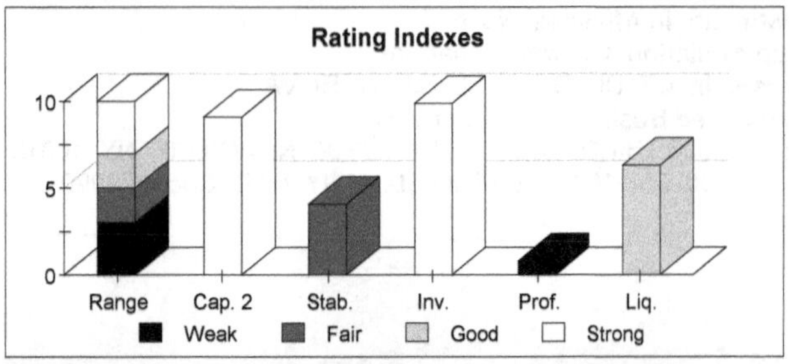

GLOBALHEALTH INC D Weak

Major Rating Factors: Weak profitability index (0.8 on a scale of 0 to 10). Poor capitalization (1.1) based on weak current risk-adjusted capital (moderate loss scenario). Low quality investment portfolio (2.1).
Other Rating Factors: Excellent liquidity (6.9) with sufficient resources (cash flows and marketable investments) to handle a spike in claims.
Principal Business: Comp med (52%), Medicare (44%), FEHB (3%)
Mem Phys: 18: 3,998 **17:** 3,533 **18 MLR** 84.5% **/ 18 Admin Exp** N/A
Enroll(000): Q1 19: 30 **18:** 44 **17:** 43 **Med Exp PMPM:** $533
Principal Investments: Cash and equiv (63%), long-term bonds (3%), other (34%)
Provider Compensation ($000): Capitation ($161,089), contr fee ($109,654), FFS ($365)
Total Member Encounters: Phys (140,926), non-phys (9,043)
Group Affiliation: Kinderhook Capital Fund III LP
Licensed in: OK
Address: 701 NE 10TH St Ste 300, OKLAHOMA CITY, OK 73102
Phone: (405) 280-5656 **Dom State:** OK **Commenced Bus:** N/A

Data Date	Rating	RACR #1	RACR #2	Total Assets ($mil)	Capital ($mil)	Net Premium ($mil)	Net Income ($mil)
3-19	D	0.41	0.34	57.1	9.1	67.8	-2.9
3-18	D	0.71	0.59	64.1	15.4	81.0	-3.2
2018	D	0.49	0.41	62.7	11.0	329.4	0.3
2017	D	0.88	0.73	45.8	19.1	283.9	-6.4
2016	D	1.04	0.87	35.3	18.5	256.4	-1.4
2015	D	1.02	0.85	36.7	20.4	245.4	-5.9
2014	C+	1.00	0.83	36.1	17.8	246.4	-1.4

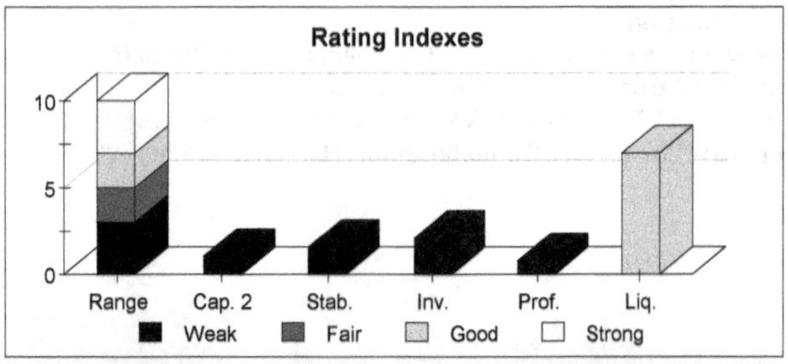

GOLDEN RULE INSURANCE COMPANY B Good

Major Rating Factors: Good overall results on stability tests (5.4 on a scale of 0 to 10) despite fair financial strength of affiliated UnitedHealth Group Inc. Other stability subfactors include excellent operational trends and excellent risk diversification. Good current capitalization (5.6) based on mixed results -- excessive policy leverage mitigated by excellent risk adjusted capital (severe loss scenario) reflecting improvement over results in 2016. Good liquidity (6.8).
Other Rating Factors: High quality investment portfolio (8.0). Excellent profitability (8.2).
Principal Business: Group health insurance (74%), individual health insurance (24%), and individual life insurance (2%).
Principal Investments: NonCMO investment grade bonds (74%) and CMOs and structured securities (22%).
Investments in Affiliates: None
Group Affiliation: UnitedHealth Group Inc
Licensed in: All states except NY, PR
Commenced Business: June 1961
Address: 7440 WOODLAND DRIVE, INDIANAPOLIS, IN 46278
Phone: (317) 290-8100 **Domicile State:** IN **NAIC Code:** 62286

Data Date	Rating	RACR #1	RACR #2	Total Assets ($mil)	Capital ($mil)	Net Premium ($mil)	Net Income ($mil)
3-19	B	1.76	1.37	593.8	307.6	350.3	69.8
3-18	B	1.35	1.06	535.3	232.8	305.5	36.1
2018	B	1.44	1.12	522.6	242.0	1,264.0	130.6
2017	B	1.14	0.89	499.2	198.6	1,338.1	82.6
2016	B	0.99	0.78	529.5	170.1	1,354.2	65.2
2015	B	1.37	1.07	635.6	268.0	1,501.3	106.8
2014	B	1.30	1.03	718.2	313.2	1,850.6	76.7

UnitedHealth Group Inc
Composite Group Rating: C+

Largest Group Members	Assets ($mil)	Rating
UNITED HEALTHCARE INS CO	20752	C
SIERRA HEALTH AND LIFE INS CO INC	3270	B
OXFORD HEALTH INS INC	2570	B
UNITED HEALTHCARE OF WISCONSIN INC	1760	B+
UNITED HEALTHCARE INS CO OF NY	1262	B-

GOLDEN SECURITY INS CO — B — Good

Major Rating Factors: Good liquidity (6.8 on a scale of 0 to 10) with sufficient resources (cash flows and marketable investments) to handle a spike in claims. Excellent profitability (9.5). Strong capitalization (8.1) based on excellent current risk-adjusted capital (severe loss scenario).
Other Rating Factors: High quality investment portfolio (8.5).
Principal Business: Other (100%)
Mem Phys: 18: N/A **17:** N/A **18 MLR** 80.6% **/ 18 Admin Exp** N/A
Enroll(000): Q1 19: 282 **18:** 272 **17:** 266 **Med Exp PMPM:** $16
Principal Investments: Long-term bonds (81%), cash and equiv (11%), nonaffiliate common stock (8%)
Provider Compensation ($000): Other ($52,342)
Total Member Encounters: N/A
Group Affiliation: BlueCross BlueShield of Tennessee In
Licensed in: AR, MS, TN
Address: 1 Cameron Hill Circle, Chattanooga, TN 37402-0001
Phone: (423) 535-5600 **Dom State:** TN **Commenced Bus:** N/A

Data Date	Rating	RACR #1	RACR #2	Total Assets ($mil)	Capital ($mil)	Net Premium ($mil)	Net Income ($mil)
3-19	B	2.24	1.86	58.0	38.8	18.5	0.9
3-18	B	2.14	1.78	47.6	32.2	16.5	0.6
2018	B	1.92	1.60	49.2	33.3	67.9	2.0
2017	B	1.25	1.04	43.1	31.9	60.0	3.4
2016	B	2.38	1.98	43.0	28.3	56.6	5.2
2015	B	2.18	1.82	34.2	22.9	51.3	5.6
2014	B	1.57	1.31	20.8	10.5	35.7	4.2

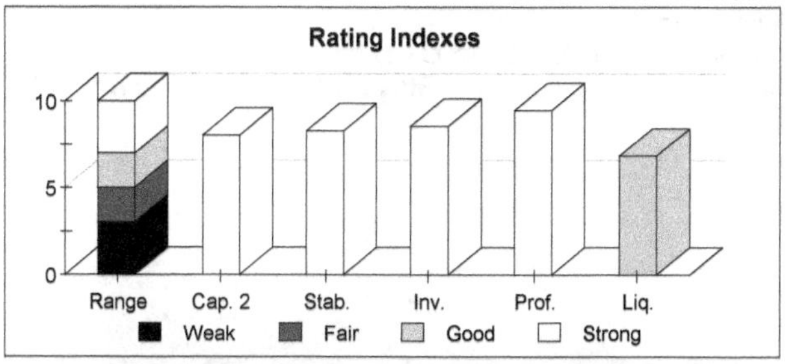

GOLDEN STATE MEDICARE HEALTH PLAN — D- — Weak

Major Rating Factors: Weak profitability index (0.9 on a scale of 0 to 10). Weak overall results on stability tests (2.6) in spite of healthy premium and capital growth during 2018. Weak liquidity (0.0) as a spike in claims may stretch capacity.
Other Rating Factors: Fair capitalization index (3.3) based on weak current risk-adjusted capital (moderate loss scenario).
Principal Business: Medicare (100%)
Mem Phys: 18: N/A **17:** N/A **18 MLR** 107.7% **/ 18 Admin Exp** N/A
Enroll(000): Q1 19: 6 **18:** 10 **17:** 8 **Med Exp PMPM:** $751
Principal Investments ($000): Cash and equiv ($20,532)
Provider Compensation ($000): None
Total Member Encounters: N/A
Group Affiliation: None
Licensed in: CA
Address: 3030 Old Ranch Pkwy Suite 155, Seal Beach, CA 90740
Phone: (608) 347-4897 **Dom State:** CA **Commenced Bus:** May 2009

Data Date	Rating	RACR #1	RACR #2	Total Assets ($mil)	Capital ($mil)	Net Premium ($mil)	Net Income ($mil)
3-19	D-	0.56	0.34	22.8	6.3	13.5	-1.1
3-18	D-	0.92	0.56	18.1	6.6	19.2	-1.0
2018	D-	0.60	0.37	24.2	6.8	81.7	-14.5
2017	E+	0.20	0.12	9.8	1.6	68.2	-4.3
2016	D-	0.50	0.31	8.3	3.4	66.0	-0.4
2015	D+	1.55	0.96	7.6	6.4	33.4	-1.0
2014	C-	2.41	1.51	5.8	5.5	18.1	-2.1

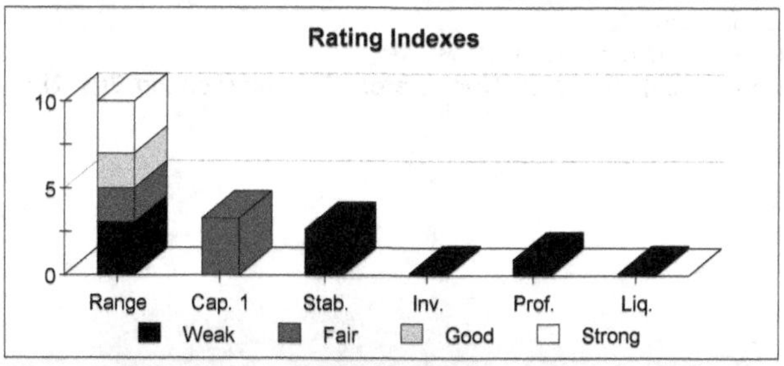

GOOD HEALTH HMO INC — C — Fair

Major Rating Factors: Fair quality investment portfolio (4.5 on a scale of 0 to 10). Weak profitability index (2.6). Good overall results on stability tests (5.3) despite inconsistent enrollment growth in the past five years due to declines in 2017 and 2018.
Other Rating Factors: Good liquidity (6.7) with sufficient resources (cash flows and marketable investments) to handle a spike in claims. Strong capitalization index (10.0) based on excellent current risk-adjusted capital (severe loss scenario).
Principal Business: Comp med (100%)
Mem Phys: 18: 5,645 **17:** 5,596 **18 MLR** 84.0% **/ 18 Admin Exp** N/A
Enroll(000): Q1 19: 36 **18:** 39 **17:** 50 **Med Exp PMPM:** $271
Principal Investments: Long-term bonds (95%), cash and equiv (5%)
Provider Compensation ($000): Contr fee ($122,982), FFS ($12,163), capitation ($3,510)
Total Member Encounters: Phys (207,881), non-phys (113,393)
Group Affiliation: None
Licensed in: KS, MO
Address: 2301 Main Street, Kansas City, MO 64108-2428
Phone: (816) 395-2222 **Dom State:** MO **Commenced Bus:** N/A

Data Date	Rating	RACR #1	RACR #2	Total Assets ($mil)	Capital ($mil)	Net Premium ($mil)	Net Income ($mil)
3-19	C	5.33	4.44	79.4	58.3	38.2	1.5
3-18	C	3.94	3.28	77.7	53.8	43.1	-2.9
2018	C	5.29	4.41	75.1	58.7	163.5	1.7
2017	C	2.90	2.42	80.8	56.4	187.7	-0.8
2016	C	4.13	3.44	86.7	57.7	189.5	-3.8
2015	C	5.86	4.88	73.9	56.0	138.0	0.5
2014	C	4.39	3.66	67.5	51.8	155.5	-6.8

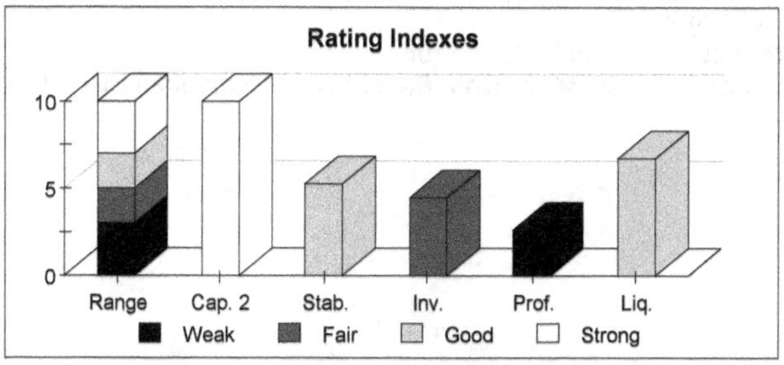

GOOD SAMARITAN INS PLAN OF ND — D — Weak

Major Rating Factors: Weak profitability index (0.4 on a scale of 0 to 10). Weak liquidity (2.2) as a spike in claims may stretch capacity. Strong capitalization (7.0) based on excellent current risk-adjusted capital (severe loss scenario).
Other Rating Factors: High quality investment portfolio (9.9).
Principal Business: Medicare (100%)
Mem Phys: 18: 8,906 **17:** N/A **18 MLR** 241.9% **/ 18 Admin Exp** N/A
Enroll(000): Q1 19: 0 **18:** 0 **17:** N/A **Med Exp PMPM:** $1,586
Principal Investments: Cash and equiv (80%), long-term bonds (20%)
Provider Compensation ($000): Capitation ($1,252), contr fee ($515)
Total Member Encounters: Phys (2,323), non-phys (3,900)
Group Affiliation: None
Licensed in: ND
Address: , Bismarck, ND 58503-0311
Phone: (804) 396-6412 **Dom State:** ND **Commenced Bus:** N/A

Data Date	Rating	RACR #1	RACR #2	Total Assets ($mil)	Capital ($mil)	Net Premium ($mil)	Net Income ($mil)
3-19	D	1.33	1.11	1.8	1.0	1.1	-0.2
3-18	N/A	N/A	N/A	1.7	0.9	0.5	-0.2
2018	D	1.41	1.18	1.7	1.1	1.2	-0.2
2017	N/A	N/A	N/A	1.1	1.1	N/A	-0.8
2016	N/A	N/A	N/A	N/A	N/A	N/A	N/A
2015	N/A	N/A	N/A	N/A	N/A	N/A	N/A
2014	N/A	N/A	N/A	N/A	N/A	N/A	N/A

Rating Indexes

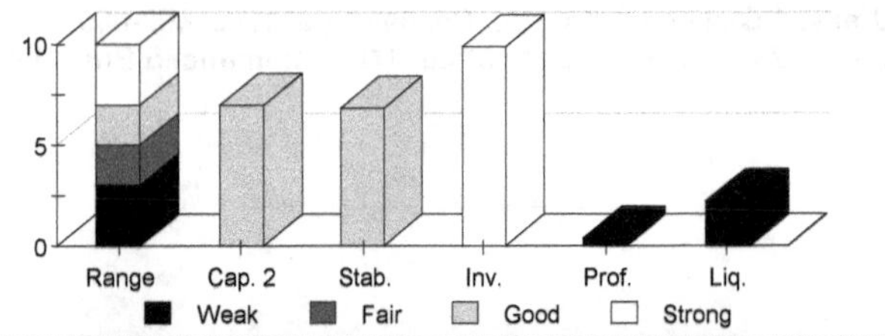

GOOD SAMARITAN INS PLAN OF NE — D — Weak

Major Rating Factors: Weak profitability index (0.0 on a scale of 0 to 10). Weak liquidity (1.4) as a spike in claims may stretch capacity. Strong capitalization (6.9) based on excellent current risk-adjusted capital (severe loss scenario).
Other Rating Factors: High quality investment portfolio (9.9).
Principal Business: Medicare (100%)
Mem Phys: 18: 8,959 **17:** N/A **18 MLR** 262.2% **/ 18 Admin Exp** N/A
Enroll(000): Q1 19: 1 **18:** 0 **17:** N/A **Med Exp PMPM:** $1,609
Principal Investments: Cash and equiv (81%), long-term bonds (19%)
Provider Compensation ($000): Capitation ($3,553), contr fee ($2,433)
Total Member Encounters: Phys (2,929), non-phys (12,069)
Group Affiliation: None
Licensed in: NE
Address: , Omaha, NE 68137-3204
Phone: (804) 396-6412 **Dom State:** NE **Commenced Bus:** N/A

Data Date	Rating	RACR #1	RACR #2	Total Assets ($mil)	Capital ($mil)	Net Premium ($mil)	Net Income ($mil)
3-19	D	1.28	1.07	3.1	1.0	2.8	-0.3
3-18	N/A	N/A	N/A	3.7	1.3	1.7	-0.8
2018	D	1.43	1.19	2.3	1.1	3.1	-1.2
2017	N/A	N/A	N/A	2.1	2.1	N/A	-0.9
2016	N/A	N/A	N/A	N/A	N/A	N/A	N/A
2015	N/A	N/A	N/A	N/A	N/A	N/A	N/A
2014	N/A	N/A	N/A	N/A	N/A	N/A	N/A

Rating Indexes

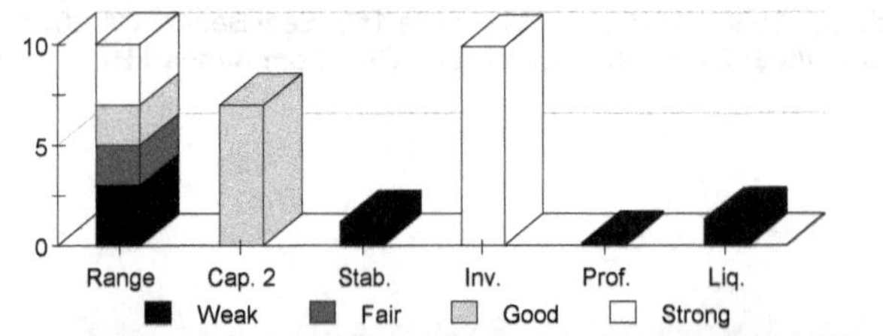

GOOD SAMARITAN INS PLAN OF SD — D — Weak

Major Rating Factors: Weak profitability index (0.8 on a scale of 0 to 10). Weak liquidity (2.2) as a spike in claims may stretch capacity. Good capitalization (6.2) based on good current risk-adjusted capital (severe loss scenario).
Other Rating Factors: High quality investment portfolio (9.9).
Principal Business: Medicare (100%)
Mem Phys: 18: 8,918 **17:** N/A **18 MLR** 238.9% **/ 18 Admin Exp** N/A
Enroll(000): Q1 19: 0 **18:** 0 **17:** N/A **Med Exp PMPM:** $1,373
Principal Investments: Cash and equiv (89%), long-term bonds (11%)
Provider Compensation ($000): Capitation ($1,748), contr fee ($710)
Total Member Encounters: Phys (1,742), non-phys (4,479)
Group Affiliation: None
Licensed in: SD
Address: , Sioux Falls, SD 57108
Phone: (804) 396-6412 **Dom State:** SD **Commenced Bus:** N/A

Data Date	Rating	RACR #1	RACR #2	Total Assets ($mil)	Capital ($mil)	Net Premium ($mil)	Net Income ($mil)
3-19	D	1.12	0.93	2.4	0.8	1.4	-0.3
3-18	N/A	N/A	N/A	1.6	0.4	0.8	-0.2
2018	D+	1.54	1.28	2.2	1.2	1.6	-0.4
2017	N/A	N/A	N/A	0.6	0.6	N/A	-0.8
2016	N/A	N/A	N/A	N/A	N/A	N/A	N/A
2015	N/A	N/A	N/A	N/A	N/A	N/A	N/A
2014	N/A	N/A	N/A	N/A	N/A	N/A	N/A

Rating Indexes

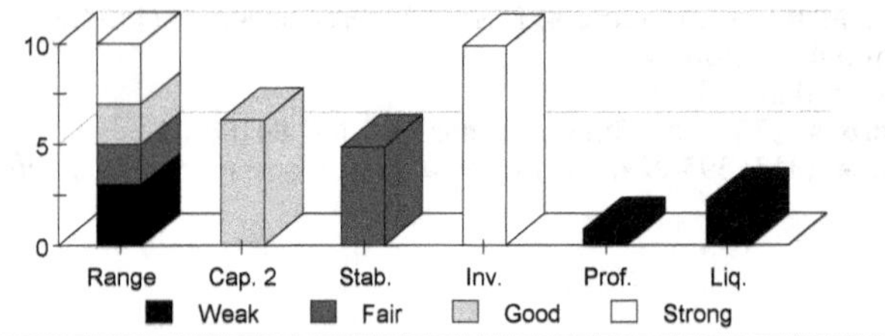

GOVERNMENT PERSONNEL MUTUAL LIFE INSURANCE CO B Good

Major Rating Factors: Good quality investment portfolio (6.6 on a scale of 0 to 10) despite significant exposure to mortgages . Mortgage default rate has been low. large holdings of BBB rated bonds in addition to small junk bond holdings. Good liquidity (6.2) with sufficient resources to handle a spike in claims as well as a significant increase in policy surrenders. Good overall results on stability tests (5.8) despite negative cash flow from operations for 2018 excellent operational trends and excellent risk diversification.
Other Rating Factors: Fair profitability (4.7) with operating losses during the first three months of 2019. Strong capitalization (8.0) based on excellent risk adjusted capital (severe loss scenario).
Principal Business: Individual life insurance (65%), individual health insurance (34%), individual annuities (1%), and reinsurance (1%).
Principal Investments: NonCMO investment grade bonds (62%), mortgages in good standing (16%), policy loans (8%), common & preferred stock (3%), and misc. investments (8%).
Investments in Affiliates: 2%
Group Affiliation: GPM Life Group
Licensed in: All states except NJ, NY, PR
Commenced Business: October 1934
Address: 2211 NE Loop 410, San Antonio, TX 78217
Phone: (800) 938-9765 **Domicile State:** TX **NAIC Code:** 63967

Data Date	Rating	RACR #1	RACR #2	Total Assets ($mil)	Capital ($mil)	Net Premium ($mil)	Net Income ($mil)
3-19	B	2.59	1.65	819.5	111.2	12.3	-2.1
3-18	B	2.14	1.17	823.5	115.6	11.6	-2.3
2018	B	2.68	1.70	820.2	114.8	46.1	-0.9
2017	B+	2.64	1.69	825.7	116.8	44.2	5.3
2016	B+	2.51	1.62	835.1	120.9	44.9	4.0
2015	B+	2.81	1.76	836.1	116.2	46.3	2.6
2014	B+	2.72	1.73	837.5	112.4	46.2	3.3

Adverse Trends in Operations

Decrease in capital during 2018 (2%)
Decrease in premium volume from 2016 to 2017 (2%)
Decrease in asset base during 2017 (1%)
Decrease in capital during 2017 (3%)
Decrease in premium volume from 2015 to 2016 (3%)

GRANITE STATE HEALTH PLAN INC C- Fair

Major Rating Factors: Weak profitability index (0.9 on a scale of 0 to 10). Strong capitalization (7.7) based on excellent current risk-adjusted capital (severe loss scenario). High quality investment portfolio (9.9).
Other Rating Factors: Excellent liquidity (6.9) with sufficient resources (cash flows and marketable investments) to handle a spike in claims.
Principal Business: Medicaid (100%)
Mem Phys: 18: 4,810 **17:** 7,391 **18 MLR** 92.3% **/ 18 Admin Exp** N/A
Enroll(000): Q1 19: 82 **18:** 60 **17:** 60 **Med Exp PMPM:** $373
Principal Investments: Cash and equiv (100%)
Provider Compensation ($000): Contr fee ($148,174), capitation ($51,957), bonus arrang ($49,225), salary ($8,600)
Total Member Encounters: Phys (306,141), non-phys (515,764)
Group Affiliation: None
Licensed in: NH
Address: 2 Executive Park Dr, Bedford, NH 3110
Phone: (314) 725-4477 **Dom State:** NH **Commenced Bus:** N/A

Data Date	Rating	RACR #1	RACR #2	Total Assets ($mil)	Capital ($mil)	Net Premium ($mil)	Net Income ($mil)
3-19	C-	1.94	1.62	67.5	24.9	98.2	-2.4
3-18	D+	N/A	N/A	66.4	22.3	69.5	-3.9
2018	C-	2.28	1.90	70.6	29.9	289.5	-6.5
2017	D+	N/A	N/A	94.9	24.2	276.1	-16.8
2016	D+	6.52	5.43	82.4	22.7	280.8	-15.7
2015	D+	4.31	3.59	91.1	25.1	325.8	-16.7
2014	D+	2.03	1.69	59.5	21.3	204.2	-7.0

Rating Indexes

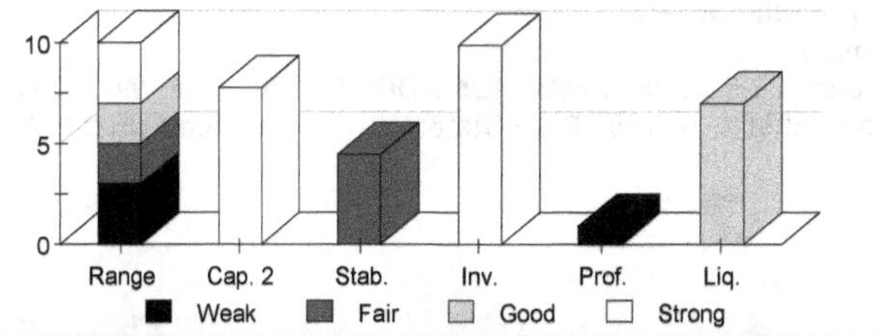

GREAT MIDWEST INS CO B- Good

Major Rating Factors: Fair reserve development (3.7 on a scale of 0 to 10) as reserves have generally been sufficient to cover claims. In 2017, the two year reserve development was 16% deficient. Fair profitability index (4.7) with operating losses during 2016 and 2017. Average return on equity over the last five years has been poor at -1.1%.
Other Rating Factors: Fair overall results on stability tests (3.9) including negative cash flow from operations for 2018. The largest net exposure for one risk is conservative at 1.1% of capital. Good liquidity (6.9) with sufficient resources (cash flows and marketable investments) to handle a spike in claims. Strong long-term capitalization index (7.8) based on excellent current risk adjusted capital (severe and moderate loss scenarios), despite some fluctuation in capital levels.
Principal Business: Group accident & health (54%), other liability (25%), auto liability (6%), workers compensation (6%), surety (3%), inland marine (3%), and other lines (3%).
Principal Investments: Investment grade bonds (70%), misc. investments (27%), and cash (3%).
Investments in Affiliates: 15%
Group Affiliation: Houston International Ins Group Ltd
Licensed in: All states except PR
Commenced Business: November 1985
Address: 800 Gessner Suite 600, Houston, TX 77024
Phone: (713) 935-0226 **Domicile State:** TX **NAIC Code:** 18694

Data Date	Rating	RACR #1	RACR #2	Loss Ratio %	Total Assets ($mil)	Capital ($mil)	Net Premium ($mil)	Net Income ($mil)
3-19	B-	2.70	1.88	N/A	216.4	129.8	18.6	0.3
3-18	B-	2.78	1.80	N/A	197.9	107.8	16.8	1.2
2018	B-	2.72	1.89	74.6	220.5	129.2	67.4	3.5
2017	B	2.62	1.69	75.8	215.3	107.0	73.0	-1.0
2016	B	2.29	1.51	94.5	215.8	104.8	86.2	-20.2
2015	B	2.42	1.50	63.8	211.1	107.6	93.5	6.1
2014	B-	3.37	2.10	59.1	191.8	103.0	71.2	5.8

Reserve Deficiency (as % of capital)

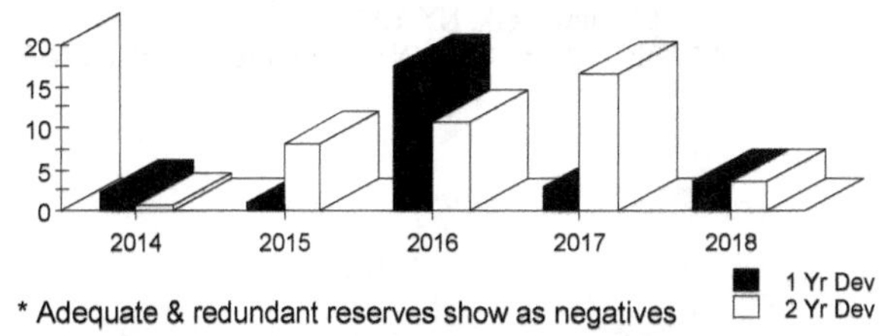

* Adequate & redundant reserves show as negatives

GROUP HEALTH COOP OF EAU CLAIRE E+ Very Weak

Major Rating Factors: Weak profitability index (2.3 on a scale of 0 to 10). Good overall results on stability tests (5.2) based on steady enrollment growth, averaging 10% over the past five years. Good liquidity (6.1) with sufficient resources (cash flows and marketable investments) to handle a spike in claims.
Other Rating Factors: Strong capitalization index (7.1) based on excellent current risk-adjusted capital (severe loss scenario). High quality investment portfolio (8.5).
Principal Business: Medicaid (73%), comp med (27%)
Mem Phys: 18: 10,268 **17:** 10,713 **18 MLR** 88.2% **/ 18 Admin Exp** N/A
Enroll(000): Q1 19: 54 **18:** 56 **17:** 48 **Med Exp PMPM:** $206
Principal Investments: Long-term bonds (85%), cash and equiv (15%)
Provider Compensation ($000): Contr fee ($98,977), FFS ($44,561), capitation ($627)
Total Member Encounters: Phys (330,158), non-phys (293,022)
Group Affiliation: None
Licensed in: WI
Address: 2503 N Hillcrest Parkway, Altoona, WI 54720
Phone: (715) 552-4300 **Dom State:** WI **Commenced Bus:** N/A

Data Date	Rating	RACR #1	RACR #2	Total Assets ($mil)	Capital ($mil)	Net Premium ($mil)	Net Income ($mil)
3-19	E+	1.40	1.17	50.7	24.7	38.0	1.9
3-18	E+	1.12	0.93	48.2	20.8	41.8	-0.9
2018	E+	1.30	1.08	52.0	22.7	163.8	0.4
2017	E+	1.20	1.00	51.2	22.4	176.9	-5.6
2016	E+	1.46	1.22	56.5	28.0	174.1	-2.9
2015	E+	1.81	1.51	58.2	31.0	163.7	6.5
2014	E+	1.73	1.44	49.0	24.3	138.7	12.5

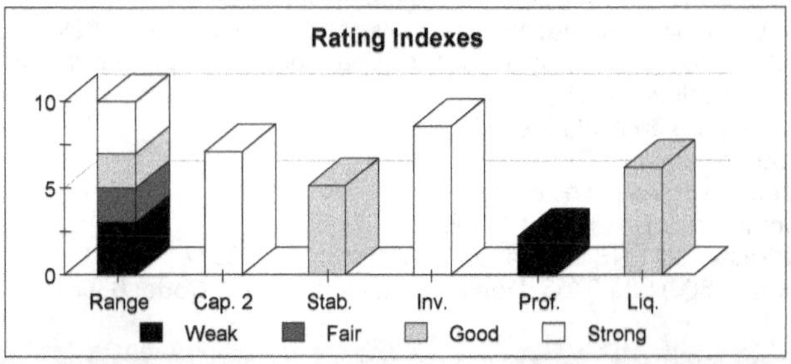

GROUP HEALTH COOP OF S CENTRAL WI C Fair

Major Rating Factors: Fair profitability index (3.0 on a scale of 0 to 10). Fair quality investment portfolio (3.9). Good liquidity (6.5) with sufficient resources (cash flows and marketable investments) to handle a spike in claims.
Other Rating Factors: Strong capitalization index (7.0) based on excellent current risk-adjusted capital (severe loss scenario). Excellent overall results on stability tests (7.0).
Principal Business: Comp med (89%), FEHB (8%), Medicaid (3%)
Mem Phys: 18: 3,502 **17:** 3,585 **18 MLR** 90.1% **/ 18 Admin Exp** N/A
Enroll(000): Q1 19: 77 **18:** 77 **17:** 75 **Med Exp PMPM:** $387
Principal Investments: Long-term bonds (42%), cash and equiv (22%), real estate (18%), nonaffiliate common stock (18%)
Provider Compensation ($000): FFS ($138,437), contr fee ($85,592), salary ($74,009), capitation ($58,500)
Total Member Encounters: Phys (349,976), non-phys (196,554)
Group Affiliation: None
Licensed in: WI
Address: 1265 JOHN Q HAMMONS DRIVE, MADISON, WI 53717
Phone: (608) 251-4156 **Dom State:** WI **Commenced Bus:** N/A

Data Date	Rating	RACR #1	RACR #2	Total Assets ($mil)	Capital ($mil)	Net Premium ($mil)	Net Income ($mil)
3-19	C	1.36	1.13	96.3	44.9	101.9	-0.8
3-18	D+	1.61	1.34	95.8	45.3	98.2	0.1
2018	C	1.37	1.14	95.0	45.1	395.7	2.6
2017	D+	1.64	1.36	88.1	46.0	363.1	5.5
2016	D	1.25	1.04	86.0	39.6	364.9	0.9
2015	D	1.17	0.97	84.3	39.2	383.6	0.2
2014	D	1.02	0.85	87.6	38.1	372.8	-18.7

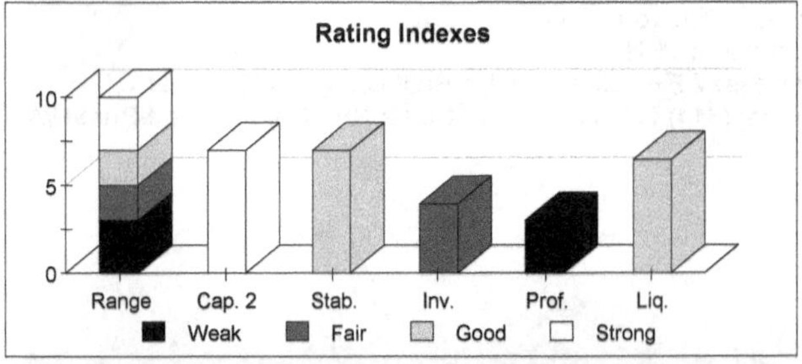

GROUP HEALTH INCORPORATED D+ Weak

Major Rating Factors: Good profitability index (5.0 on a scale of 0 to 10). Good liquidity (6.9) with sufficient resources (cash flows and marketable investments) to handle a spike in claims. Strong capitalization (10.0) based on excellent current risk-adjusted capital (severe loss scenario).
Other Rating Factors: High quality investment portfolio (9.1).
Principal Business: Comp med (35%), FEHB (23%), dental (21%), other (20%)
Mem Phys: 18: 104,191 **17:** 90,068 **18 MLR** 81.7% **/ 18 Admin Exp** N/A
Enroll(000): Q1 19: 1,679 **18:** 1,724 **17:** 1,716 **Med Exp PMPM:** $31
Principal Investments: Long-term bonds (84%), cash and equiv (16%)
Provider Compensation ($000): FFS ($352,698), contr fee ($209,060), other ($90,372)
Total Member Encounters: N/A
Group Affiliation: EmblemHealth Inc
Licensed in: NY
Address: 55 Water St, New York, NY 10041-8190
Phone: (646) 447-5000 **Dom State:** NY **Commenced Bus:** N/A

Data Date	Rating	RACR #1	RACR #2	Total Assets ($mil)	Capital ($mil)	Net Premium ($mil)	Net Income ($mil)
3-19	D+	4.62	3.85	694.1	348.0	189.9	-12.2
3-18	D	5.27	4.39	715.4	336.7	198.8	-0.4
2018	D+	4.15	3.45	661.6	320.2	808.1	-17.8
2017	E	4.15	3.46	723.1	336.1	774.1	34.1
2016	E	3.65	3.04	672.2	260.8	908.8	260.3
2015	E	2.86	2.39	602.4	213.8	912.7	30.2
2014	E	0.89	0.74	722.8	127.5	1,894.7	-128.6

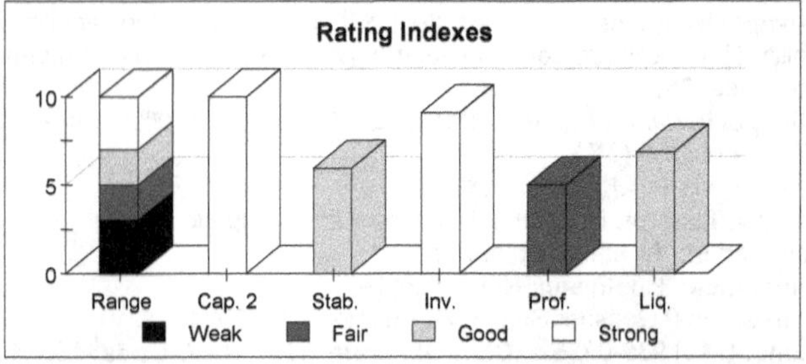

GROUP HEALTH PLAN INC — B — Good

Major Rating Factors: Good capitalization index (6.9 on a scale of 0 to 10) based on excellent current risk-adjusted capital (severe loss scenario). Excellent liquidity (7.0) with sufficient resources (cash flows and marketable investments) to handle a spike in claims. Weak profitability index (2.0).
Other Rating Factors: Low quality investment portfolio (1.6). Weak overall results on stability tests (2.3) based on a steep decline in capital during 2018, an excessive 38% enrollment growth during the period. Potentially strong support from affiliation with HealthPartners Inc.
Principal Business: Comp med (63%), Medicare (30%), FEHB (3%), dental (3%)
Mem Phys: 18: 74,128 **17:** 64,829 **18 MLR** 97.2% **/ 18 Admin Exp** N/A
Enroll(000): Q1 19: 69 **18:** 122 **17:** 89 **Med Exp PMPM:** $1,002
Principal Investments: Real estate (31%), long-term bonds (31%), nonaffiliate common stock (26%), cash and equiv (9%), affiliate common stock (2%)
Provider Compensation ($000): Bonus arrang ($509,787), contr fee ($116,876)
Total Member Encounters: Phys (1,745,191), non-phys (192,180)
Group Affiliation: HealthPartners Inc
Licensed in: MN
Address: 8170 33RD AVENUE SOUTH POBOX 1, MINNEAPOLIS, MN 55440-1309
Phone: (952) 883-6000 **Dom State:** MN **Commenced Bus:** N/A

Data Date	Rating	RACR #1	RACR #2	Total Assets ($mil)	Capital ($mil)	Net Premium ($mil)	Net Income ($mil)
3-19	B	1.25	1.04	851.7	91.3	280.7	-20.7
3-18	A-	2.44	2.03	911.4	163.9	383.8	-1.4
2018	B	1.44	1.20	837.8	105.9	1,554.9	-21.5
2017	A-	1.74	1.45	831.3	163.7	1,424.9	27.2
2016	A-	2.84	2.37	822.2	168.2	1,262.9	-13.9
2015	A+	4.68	3.90	882.2	206.8	1,130.3	12.1
2014	A+	4.75	3.96	844.0	188.4	1,088.6	41.7

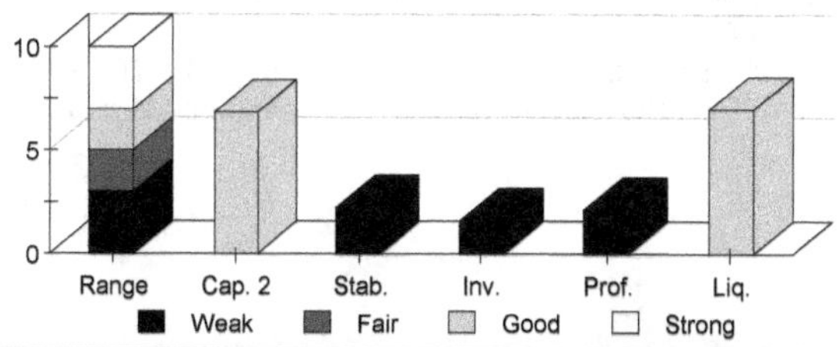

GROUP HOSP & MEDICAL SERVICES INC — B — Good

Major Rating Factors: Good overall profitability index (5.2 on a scale of 0 to 10). Fair quality investment portfolio (4.4). Strong capitalization (10.0) based on excellent current risk-adjusted capital (severe loss scenario).
Other Rating Factors: Excellent liquidity (7.0) with sufficient resources (cash flows and marketable investments) to handle a spike in claims.
Principal Business: FEHB (65%), comp med (31%), dental (2%)
Mem Phys: 18: 52,141 **17:** 51,525 **18 MLR** 87.8% **/ 18 Admin Exp** N/A
Enroll(000): Q1 19: 591 **18:** 565 **17:** 677 **Med Exp PMPM:** $442
Principal Investments: Long-term bonds (40%), nonaffiliate common stock (11%), cash and equiv (11%), other (38%)
Provider Compensation ($000): Contr fee ($2,925,300), FFS ($93,214), capitation ($6,678)
Total Member Encounters: Phys (8,577,241), non-phys (7,014,927)
Group Affiliation: CareFirst Inc
Licensed in: DC, MD, VA
Address: 840 FIRST St NE, WASHINGTON, DC 20065
Phone: (410) 581-3000 **Dom State:** DC **Commenced Bus:** N/A

Data Date	Rating	RACR #1	RACR #2	Total Assets ($mil)	Capital ($mil)	Net Premium ($mil)	Net Income ($mil)
3-19	B	5.53	4.61	2,755.1	1,252.3	838.5	33.7
3-18	B	5.59	4.66	2,669.1	1,112.5	859.7	-8.0
2018	B	5.30	4.42	2,761.6	1,200.1	3,463.1	100.2
2017	B	5.84	4.86	2,550.3	1,161.2	3,352.0	34.5
2016	B-	4.89	4.07	2,284.1	963.2	3,502.0	-9.5
2015	B-	5.06	4.22	2,292.7	960.2	3,465.3	35.0
2014	B-	5.02	4.18	2,209.6	934.4	3,347.3	-15.7

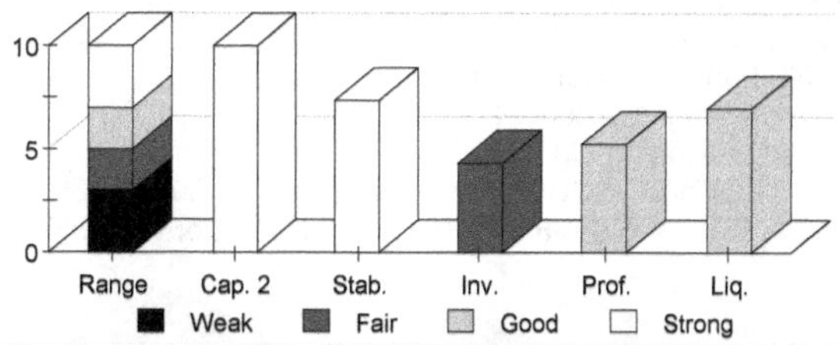

GUARANTEE TRUST LIFE INSURANCE COMPANY — B — Good

Major Rating Factors: Good quality investment portfolio (6.5 on a scale of 0 to 10) despite mixed results such as: minimal exposure to mortgages and large holdings of BBB rated bonds but small junk bond holdings. Good overall results on stability tests (5.5). Stability strengths include excellent operational trends and excellent risk diversification. Strong capitalization (7.6) based on excellent risk adjusted capital (severe loss scenario).
Other Rating Factors: Excellent profitability (7.7). Excellent liquidity (7.2).
Principal Business: Individual health insurance (75%), group health insurance (18%), individual life insurance (6%), and reinsurance (1%).
Principal Investments: NonCMO investment grade bonds (51%), CMOs and structured securities (32%), mortgages in good standing (9%), noninv. grade bonds (2%), and misc. investments (3%).
Investments in Affiliates: 1%
Group Affiliation: Guarantee Trust
Licensed in: All states except NY
Commenced Business: June 1936
Address: 1275 Milwaukee Avenue, Glenview, IL 60025
Phone: (847) 699-0600 **Domicile State:** IL **NAIC Code:** 64211

Data Date	Rating	RACR #1	RACR #2	Total Assets ($mil)	Capital ($mil)	Net Premium ($mil)	Net Income ($mil)
3-19	B	2.11	1.37	648.1	98.6	55.2	6.0
3-18	B	1.96	1.28	605.3	85.3	54.2	6.1
2018	B	2.01	1.32	638.9	92.3	229.6	20.3
2017	B	1.84	1.21	594.8	79.2	218.7	12.4
2016	B	1.85	1.23	550.7	77.0	219.2	9.1
2015	B	1.75	1.18	495.8	70.0	221.4	8.7
2014	B	1.67	1.15	433.3	62.3	210.7	9.7

Adverse Trends in Operations

Increase in policy surrenders from 2016 to 2017 (32%)
Increase in policy surrenders from 2015 to 2016 (46%)

GUARANTY ASSURANCE CO — E+ Very Weak

Major Rating Factors: Weak profitability index (0.4 on a scale of 0 to 10). Weak liquidity (0.1) as a spike in claims may stretch capacity. Good capitalization (5.7) based on good current risk-adjusted capital (severe loss scenario).
Other Rating Factors: High quality investment portfolio (8.0).
Principal Business: Dental (100%)
Mem Phys: 18: N/A **17:** N/A **18 MLR** 198.7% **/ 18 Admin Exp** N/A
Enroll(000): Q1 19: 34 **18:** 38 **17:** 39 **Med Exp PMPM:** $32
Principal Investments: Cash and equiv (37%), real estate (35%), long-term bonds (28%)
Provider Compensation ($000): FFS ($9,172), contr fee ($5,607), capitation ($214)
Total Member Encounters: N/A
Group Affiliation: Dental Economics Holdings Inc
Licensed in: LA
Address: 11969 Bricksome Ave Ste A, Baton Rouge, LA 70816
Phone: (281) 276-7150 **Dom State:** LA **Commenced Bus:** N/A

Data Date	Rating	RACR #1	RACR #2	Total Assets ($mil)	Capital ($mil)	Net Premium ($mil)	Net Income ($mil)
3-19	E+	1.03	0.86	2.3	1.1	3.8	0.7
3-18	U	N/A	N/A	0.9	0.7	1.9	N/A
2018	U	0.12	0.10	0.8	0.1	7.8	-0.6
2017	U	N/A	N/A	1.2	0.6	4.1	-0.8
2016	D+	2.87	2.39	1.8	1.2	3.1	0.1
2015	D+	17.09	14.24	1.4	1.1	0.6	-0.3
2014	E	3.31	2.76	1.7	1.4	3.0	0.3

Rating Indexes

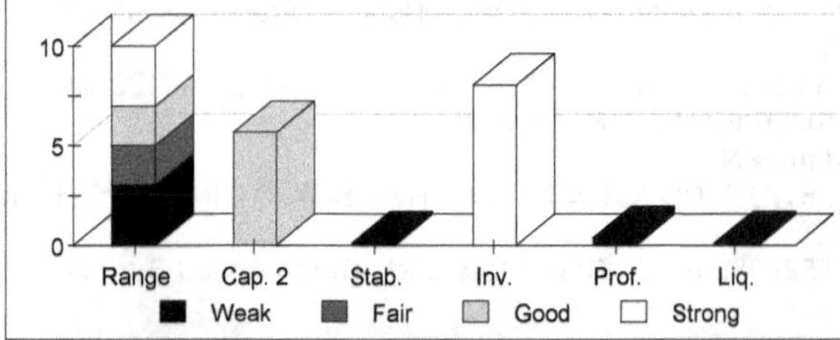

GUARDIAN LIFE INSURANCE COMPANY OF AMERICA * — A Excellent

Major Rating Factors: Good quality investment portfolio (6.5 on a scale of 0 to 10) despite mixed results such as: large holdings of BBB rated bonds but moderate junk bond exposure. Good overall profitability (6.7). Good liquidity (6.1) with sufficient resources to handle a spike in claims as well as a significant increase in policy surrenders.
Other Rating Factors: Strong capitalization (8.1) based on excellent risk adjusted capital (severe loss scenario). Excellent overall results on stability tests (7.5) excellent operational trends and excellent risk diversification.
Principal Business: Individual life insurance (49%), group health insurance (36%), group life insurance (7%), reinsurance (6%), and individual health insurance (2%).
Principal Investments: NonCMO investment grade bonds (63%), mortgages in good standing (9%), CMOs and structured securities (9%), policy loans (7%), and misc. investments (12%).
Investments in Affiliates: 2%
Group Affiliation: Guardian Group
Licensed in: All states except PR
Commenced Business: July 1860
Address: 7 HANOVER SQUARE, NEW YORK, NY 10004-4025
Phone: (212) 598-8000 **Domicile State:** NY **NAIC Code:** 64246

Data Date	Rating	RACR #1	RACR #2	Total Assets ($mil)	Capital ($mil)	Net Premium ($mil)	Net Income ($mil)
3-19	A	2.72	1.75	59,690.7	7,209.7	2,348.7	57.0
3-18	A	2.80	1.79	56,750.9	6,731.9	2,246.3	0.2
2018	A	2.77	1.80	58,488.7	7,171.8	8,387.5	310.4
2017	A	2.84	1.83	55,568.8	6,683.7	8,116.1	423.1
2016	A	2.77	1.79	51,883.7	6,172.5	7,772.7	367.7
2015	A	2.55	1.66	48,120.9	6,089.7	7,337.7	433.1
2014	A	2.76	1.80	45,297.4	5,691.6	7,000.0	711.8

Rating Indexes

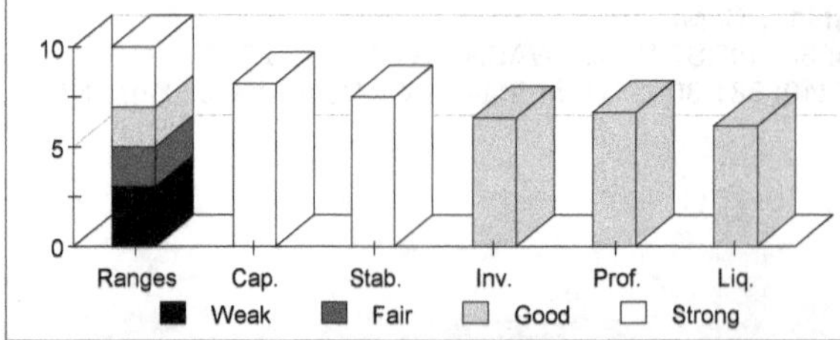

GUNDERSEN HEALTH PLAN INC — C- Fair

Major Rating Factors: Fair quality investment portfolio (3.6 on a scale of 0 to 10). Fair overall results on stability tests (3.6) based on a steep decline in capital during 2018, a steep decline in premium revenue in 2018. Weak profitability index (0.9).
Other Rating Factors: Good liquidity (6.8) with sufficient resources (cash flows and marketable investments) to handle a spike in claims. Strong capitalization index (7.7) based on excellent current risk-adjusted capital (severe loss scenario).
Principal Business: Medicare (70%), Medicaid (26%), comp med (2%), med supp (2%)
Mem Phys: 18: 9,567 **17:** 7,064 **18 MLR** 94.4% **/ 18 Admin Exp** N/A
Enroll(000): Q1 19: 57 **18:** 47 **17:** 46 **Med Exp PMPM:** $352
Principal Investments: Cash and equiv (77%), long-term bonds (16%), affiliate common stock (7%)
Provider Compensation ($000): Capitation ($183,176)
Total Member Encounters: Phys (272,070), non-phys (334,107)
Group Affiliation: University Health Care Inc
Licensed in: IA, WI
Address: 1836 South Avenue, La Crosse, WI 54601
Phone: (608) 643-2491 **Dom State:** WI **Commenced Bus:** N/A

Data Date	Rating	RACR #1	RACR #2	Total Assets ($mil)	Capital ($mil)	Net Premium ($mil)	Net Income ($mil)
3-19	C-	1.92	1.60	54.6	20.9	63.7	1.1
3-18	C-	N/A	N/A	69.0	19.7	53.6	-1.8
2018	C-	1.54	1.28	45.4	17.0	215.2	-2.1
2017	C-	N/A	N/A	36.2	21.8	269.7	-0.8
2016	C-	1.20	1.00	47.3	20.8	301.4	-5.7
2015	C+	0.65	0.54	38.9	16.1	297.4	-5.0
2014	B	1.12	0.93	39.7	22.1	295.5	2.3

Rating Indexes

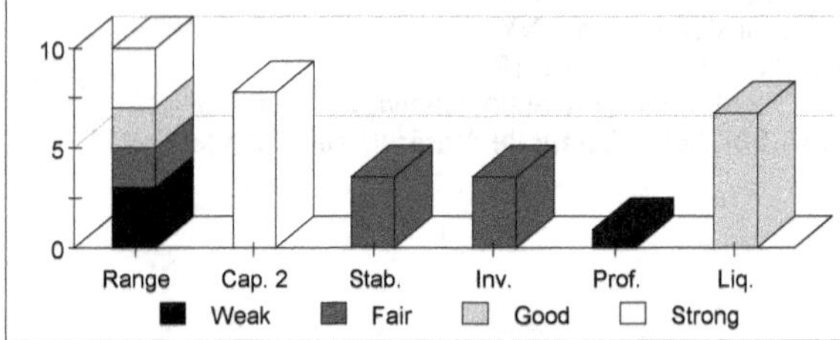

GUNDERSEN HLTH PLAN MN INC — C — Fair

Major Rating Factors: Weak profitability index (1.4 on a scale of 0 to 10). Strong capitalization (7.2) based on excellent current risk-adjusted capital (severe loss scenario). High quality investment portfolio (9.4).
Other Rating Factors: Excellent liquidity (7.3) with ample operational cash flow and liquid investments.
Principal Business: Medicare (73%), comp med (27%)
Mem Phys: 18: 847 **17:** 758 **18 MLR** 93.6% **/ 18 Admin Exp** N/A
Enroll(000): Q1 19: 2 **18:** 1 **17:** 1 **Med Exp PMPM:** $544
Principal Investments: Cash and equiv (100%)
Provider Compensation ($000): Capitation ($7,679)
Total Member Encounters: Phys (7,018), non-phys (10,603)
Group Affiliation: University Health Care Inc
Licensed in: MN
Address: 1900 S Ave, La Crescent, MN 55947
Phone: (608) 643-2491 **Dom State:** MN **Commenced Bus:** N/A

Data Date	Rating	RACR #1	RACR #2	Total Assets ($mil)	Capital ($mil)	Net Premium ($mil)	Net Income ($mil)
3-19	C	1.47	1.23	6.2	2.8	4.1	0.0
3-18	C	N/A	N/A	3.8	1.9	2.3	N/A
2018	C	1.45	1.20	4.9	2.7	8.8	-0.2
2017	C	N/A	N/A	2.4	1.9	8.1	-0.1
2016	C	1.20	1.00	2.4	2.1	6.4	0.2
2015	C	1.00	0.83	2.5	1.9	5.3	-0.7
2014	B-	0.78	0.65	1.7	1.5	4.1	0.1

Rating Indexes

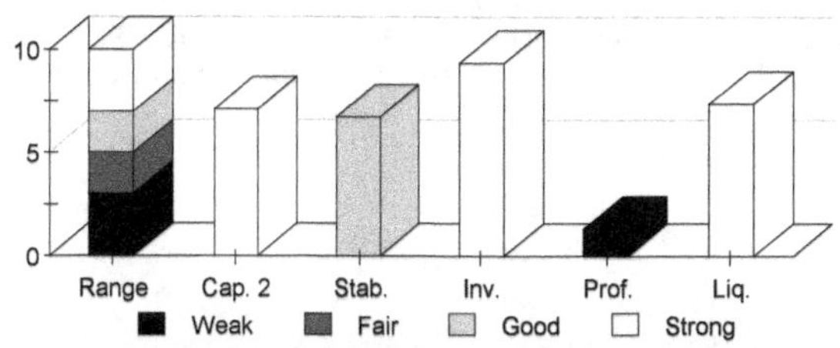

HALLMARK LIFE INSURANCE CO — D — Weak

Major Rating Factors: Weak profitability index (0.9 on a scale of 0 to 10). Low quality investment portfolio (2.7). Strong capitalization (7.5) based on excellent current risk-adjusted capital (severe loss scenario).
Other Rating Factors: Excellent liquidity (7.4) with ample operational cash flow and liquid investments.
Principal Business: Medicare (65%), comp med (35%)
Mem Phys: 18: N/A **17:** N/A **18 MLR** 91.6% **/ 18 Admin Exp** N/A
Enroll(000): Q1 19: 48 **18:** 172 **17:** N/A **Med Exp PMPM:** $576
Principal Investments: Cash and equiv (100%)
Provider Compensation ($000): Contr fee ($405,716), salary ($4,127), capitation ($143)
Total Member Encounters: Phys (1,182,830), non-phys (703,869)
Group Affiliation: None
Licensed in: AZ, NY
Address: , Phoenix, AZ 85016
Phone: (Phone number **Dom State:** AZ **Commenced Bus:** N/A

Data Date	Rating	RACR #1	RACR #2	Total Assets ($mil)	Capital ($mil)	Net Premium ($mil)	Net Income ($mil)
3-19	D	1.76	1.46	403.5	105.9	155.2	10.1
3-18	N/A	N/A	N/A	N/A	N/A	N/A	N/A
2018	D	1.71	1.43	494.5	103.2	658.4	-51.9
2017	N/A	N/A	N/A	4.3	4.2	N/A	N/A
2016	N/A	N/A	N/A	17.9	11.9	14.1	N/A
2015	N/A	N/A	N/A	19.7	11.3	14.5	N/A
2014	N/A	N/A	N/A	23.7	16.2	9.4	N/A

Rating Indexes

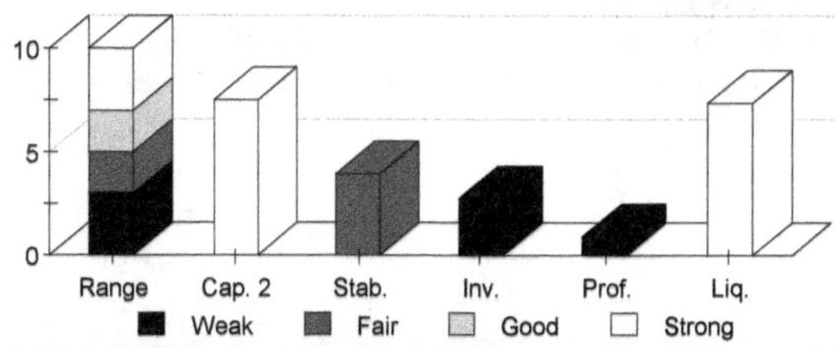

HAP MIDWEST HEALTH PLAN INC — C- — Fair

Major Rating Factors: Fair profitability index (3.9 on a scale of 0 to 10). Fair overall results on stability tests (3.0) based on a steep decline in capital during 2018. Low quality investment portfolio (1.2).
Other Rating Factors: Strong capitalization index (8.5) based on excellent current risk-adjusted capital (severe loss scenario). Excellent liquidity (7.1) with ample operational cash flow and liquid investments.
Principal Business: Medicare (92%), Medicaid (8%)
Mem Phys: 18: N/A **17:** 2,341 **18 MLR** 86.4% **/ 18 Admin Exp** N/A
Enroll(000): Q1 19: 8 **18:** 8 **17:** 8 **Med Exp PMPM:** $1,082
Principal Investments: Cash and equiv (100%)
Provider Compensation ($000): Contr fee ($95,992), capitation ($5,125)
Total Member Encounters: Phys (125,319), non-phys (149,411)
Group Affiliation: Henry Ford Health System
Licensed in: MI
Address: 2850 West Grand Blvd, Detroit, MI 48202
Phone: (888) 654-2200 **Dom State:** MI **Commenced Bus:** N/A

Data Date	Rating	RACR #1	RACR #2	Total Assets ($mil)	Capital ($mil)	Net Premium ($mil)	Net Income ($mil)
3-19	C-	2.54	2.12	49.0	20.3	26.6	-0.6
3-18	C-	3.26	2.72	59.7	26.6	26.5	0.3
2018	C-	2.59	2.16	55.7	21.0	115.6	-5.4
2017	C-	2.53	2.11	54.8	26.5	115.4	1.8
2016	C	2.73	2.28	85.4	24.3	122.4	23.0
2015	B	1.91	1.59	180.6	57.4	501.9	27.5
2014	B-	1.70	1.42	101.4	39.8	381.7	19.1

Rating Indexes

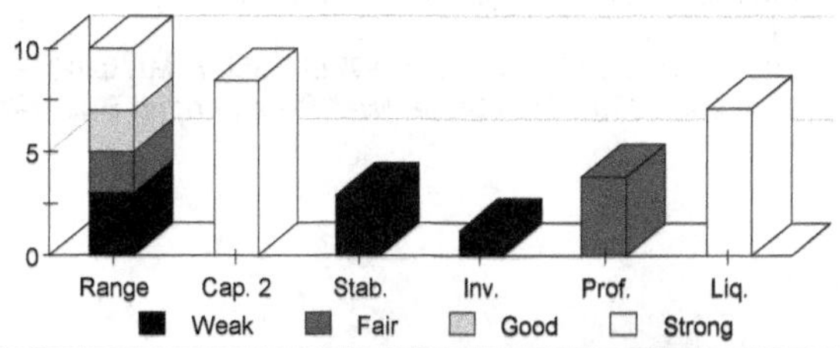

HARMONY HEALTH PLAN INC — C — Fair

Major Rating Factors: Fair profitability index (4.5 on a scale of 0 to 10). Low quality investment portfolio (2.3). Good overall results on stability tests (5.2).
Other Rating Factors: Strong capitalization index (8.3) based on excellent current risk-adjusted capital (severe loss scenario). Excellent liquidity (7.1) with ample operational cash flow and liquid investments.
Principal Business: Medicare (58%), Medicaid (42%)
Mem Phys: 18: 70,800 **17:** 67,000 **18 MLR** 81.5% **/ 18 Admin Exp** N/A
Enroll(000): Q1 19: 82 **18:** 309 **17:** 218 **Med Exp PMPM:** $369
Principal Investments: Cash and equiv (99%), long-term bonds (1%)
Provider Compensation ($000): Contr fee ($1,145,110), capitation ($90,382), bonus arrang ($9,516)
Total Member Encounters: Phys (1,764,254), non-phys (912,942)
Group Affiliation: WellCare Health Plans Inc
Licensed in: AL, AR, IL, IN, MS, MO, MT, OK, SC, TN, VA
Address: 29 North Wacker Drive Suite 30, Chicago, IL 60606
Phone: (813) 206-6200 **Dom State:** IL **Commenced Bus:** N/A

Data Date	Rating	RACR #1	RACR #2	Total Assets ($mil)	Capital ($mil)	Net Premium ($mil)	Net Income ($mil)
3-19	C	2.37	1.97	536.4	189.9	254.0	40.6
3-18	C	1.91	1.59	577.2	113.7	328.4	-17.1
2018	C	2.52	2.10	595.2	203.2	1,654.1	88.8
2017	C	1.56	1.30	468.6	133.8	1,209.6	-57.2
2016	C	3.07	2.56	384.3	151.7	1,069.7	16.6
2015	C	3.78	3.15	334.1	180.9	968.2	30.4
2014	B-	3.54	2.95	340.9	192.2	877.3	9.3

Rating Indexes

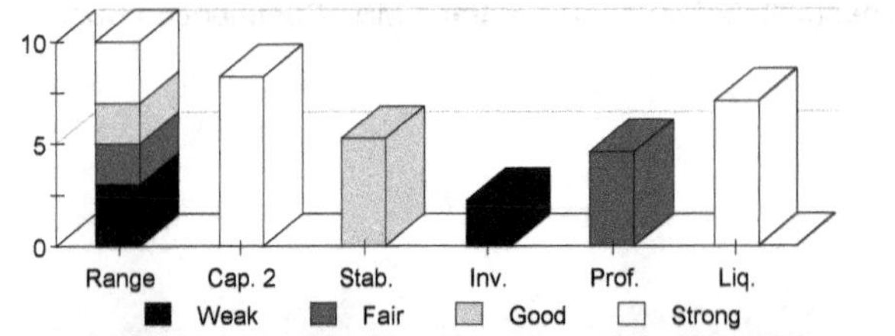

HARTFORD LIFE & ACCIDENT INSURANCE COMPANY — C — Fair

Major Rating Factors: Fair overall results on stability tests (3.6 on a scale of 0 to 10). Good liquidity (6.6) with sufficient resources to handle a spike in claims as well as a significant increase in policy surrenders. Weak profitability (2.8).
Other Rating Factors: Strong capitalization (9.2) based on excellent risk adjusted capital (severe loss scenario). High quality investment portfolio (7.0).
Principal Business: Reinsurance (39%), group health insurance (36%), and group life insurance (24%).
Principal Investments: NonCMO investment grade bonds (65%), CMOs and structured securities (17%), mortgages in good standing (9%), noninv. grade bonds (2%), and common & preferred stock (1%).
Investments in Affiliates: None
Group Affiliation: Hartford Financial Services Inc
Licensed in: All states, the District of Columbia and Puerto Rico
Commenced Business: February 1967
Address: One Hartford Plaza, Hartford, CT 06155-0001
Phone: (860) 547-5000 **Domicile State:** CT **NAIC Code:** 70815

Data Date	Rating	RACR #1	RACR #2	Total Assets ($mil)	Capital ($mil)	Net Premium ($mil)	Net Income ($mil)
3-19	C	3.85	2.48	12,747.8	2,494.4	1,030.5	144.5
3-18	C	3.61	2.29	13,038.8	2,112.1	1,132.1	96.3
2018	C	3.70	2.40	12,909.5	2,407.4	4,495.6	398.1
2017	C	3.42	2.19	12,935.8	2,028.5	5,777.5	-1,065.7
2016	B-	4.15	2.61	8,785.9	1,623.8	2,241.9	208.3
2015	C	3.96	2.47	8,992.2	1,651.4	2,296.5	168.1
2014	C	3.43	2.15	9,086.9	1,592.3	2,486.3	-331.3

Rating Indexes

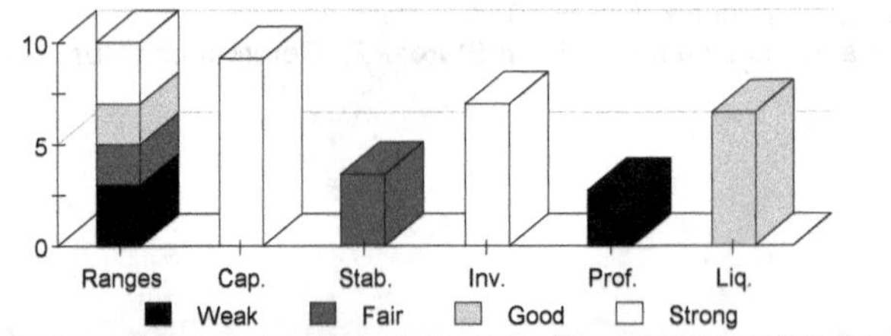

HARVARD PILGRIM HC OF NEW ENGLAND — C — Fair

Major Rating Factors: Weak profitability index (2.7 on a scale of 0 to 10). Good overall results on stability tests (6.6). Good liquidity (6.6) with sufficient resources (cash flows and marketable investments) to handle a spike in claims.
Other Rating Factors: Strong capitalization index (8.4) based on excellent current risk-adjusted capital (severe loss scenario). High quality investment portfolio (7.9).
Principal Business: Comp med (91%), Medicare (9%)
Mem Phys: 18: 83,960 **17:** 81,621 **18 MLR** 84.3% **/ 18 Admin Exp** N/A
Enroll(000): Q1 19: 70 **18:** 77 **17:** 93 **Med Exp PMPM:** $477
Principal Investments: Long-term bonds (91%), cash and equiv (9%)
Provider Compensation ($000): Capitation ($264,783), contr fee ($109,830), bonus arrang ($60,170), FFS ($23,867)
Total Member Encounters: Phys (326,738), non-phys (290,947)
Group Affiliation: Harvard Pilgrim Health Care Inc
Licensed in: MA, NH
Address: 93 WORCESTER STREET, WELLESLEY, MA 02481-9181
Phone: (781) 263-6000 **Dom State:** MA **Commenced Bus:** N/A

Data Date	Rating	RACR #1	RACR #2	Total Assets ($mil)	Capital ($mil)	Net Premium ($mil)	Net Income ($mil)
3-19	C	2.51	2.09	148.0	61.1	123.4	9.6
3-18	C	1.90	1.59	135.9	50.0	140.0	3.1
2018	C	2.38	1.98	154.5	58.9	552.2	2.5
2017	C	1.57	1.31	142.0	56.0	563.0	-2.9
2016	C	2.59	2.15	151.3	60.1	482.2	-7.7
2015	B	2.94	2.45	127.9	68.0	374.6	18.4
2014	B+	3.43	2.86	103.1	59.1	284.1	6.9

Rating Indexes

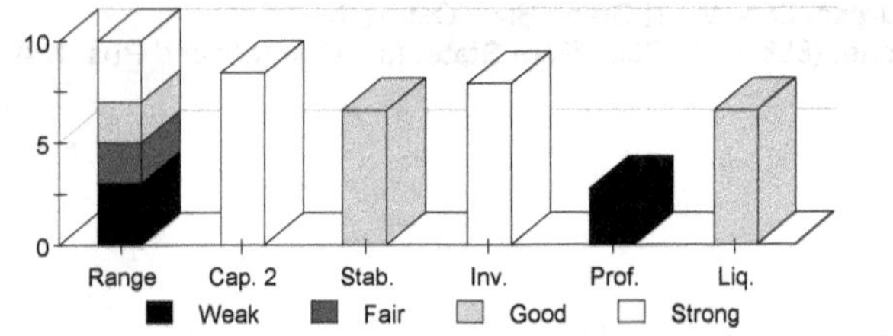

HARVARD PILGRIM HEALTH CARE INC — C+ Fair

Major Rating Factors: Fair profitability index (3.8 on a scale of 0 to 10). Fair quality investment portfolio (3.4). Good overall results on stability tests (6.1).
Other Rating Factors: Good liquidity (6.8) with sufficient resources (cash flows and marketable investments) to handle a spike in claims. Strong capitalization index (9.0) based on excellent current risk-adjusted capital (severe loss scenario).
Principal Business: Comp med (96%), Medicare (4%)
Mem Phys: 18: 83,960 **17:** 81,621 **18 MLR** 83.4% **/ 18 Admin Exp** N/A
Enroll(000): Q1 19: 234 **18:** 256 **17:** 250 **Med Exp PMPM:** $489
Principal Investments: Long-term bonds (36%), affiliate common stock (25%), nonaffiliate common stock (14%), cash and equiv (8%), real estate (3%), other (14%)
Provider Compensation ($000): Bonus arrang ($630,958), contr fee ($512,618), capitation ($267,520), FFS ($77,579), other ($13,212)
Total Member Encounters: Phys (1,117,302), non-phys (959,209)
Group Affiliation: Harvard Pilgrim Health Care Inc
Licensed in: ME, MA
Address: 93 WORCESTER STREET, WELLESLEY, MA 02481-9181
Phone: (781) 263-6000 **Dom State:** MA **Commenced Bus:** N/A

Data Date	Rating	RACR #1	RACR #2	Total Assets ($mil)	Capital ($mil)	Net Premium ($mil)	Net Income ($mil)
3-19	C+	2.97	2.47	971.2	588.7	413.1	9.0
3-18	C+	2.22	1.85	890.7	465.4	450.3	-5.0
2018	C+	2.74	2.28	970.7	552.7	1,822.8	42.2
2017	C+	2.17	1.81	917.8	477.8	1,647.1	-8.2
2016	C+	2.30	1.92	916.8	456.8	1,782.3	18.5
2015	B-	2.41	2.01	930.6	458.1	1,684.1	-35.2
2014	B+	3.36	2.80	921.6	548.7	1,645.1	14.3

Rating Indexes

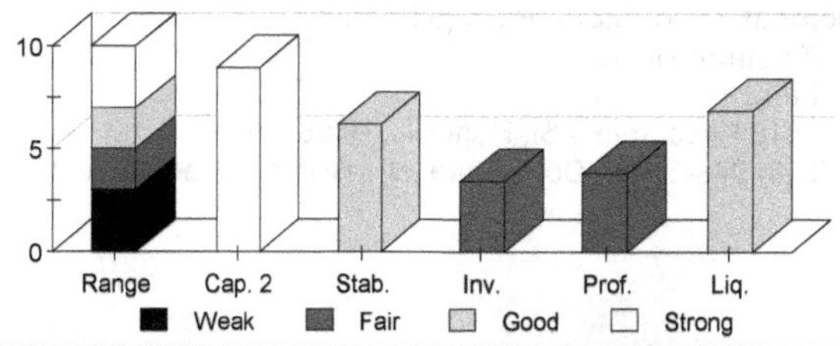

HARVARD PILGRIM HEALTH CARE OF CT — D+ Weak

Major Rating Factors: Weak profitability index (0.5 on a scale of 0 to 10). Good quality investment portfolio (6.8). Strong capitalization (10.0) based on excellent current risk-adjusted capital (severe loss scenario).
Other Rating Factors: Excellent liquidity (7.1) with ample operational cash flow and liquid investments.
Principal Business: Comp med (100%)
Mem Phys: 18: 83,960 **17:** 81,621 **18 MLR** 88.7% **/ 18 Admin Exp** N/A
Enroll(000): Q1 19: 6 **18:** 5 **17:** 0 **Med Exp PMPM:** $395
Principal Investments: Long-term bonds (77%), cash and equiv (23%)
Provider Compensation ($000): Contr fee ($8,588), FFS ($450), capitation ($265), bonus arrang ($66), other ($14)
Total Member Encounters: Phys (7,470), non-phys (5,571)
Group Affiliation: Harvard Pilgrim Health Care Inc
Licensed in: CT
Address: CITYPLACE II 185 ASYLUM St, HARTFORD, CT 6103
Phone: (781) 263-6000 **Dom State:** CT **Commenced Bus:** N/A

Data Date	Rating	RACR #1	RACR #2	Total Assets ($mil)	Capital ($mil)	Net Premium ($mil)	Net Income ($mil)
3-19	D+	9.56	7.97	19.4	14.4	9.3	1.1
3-18	D+	N/A	N/A	15.6	14.8	1.8	0.2
2018	D+	8.66	7.22	18.2	13.3	12.1	-1.2
2017	D+	N/A	N/A	14.9	14.6	2.7	-0.2
2016	C-	9.45	7.87	15.4	14.8	4.0	-0.5
2015	C	9.72	8.10	16.6	15.4	1.4	-1.6
2014	U	7.89	6.58	14.1	14.0	0.0	-2.0

Rating Indexes

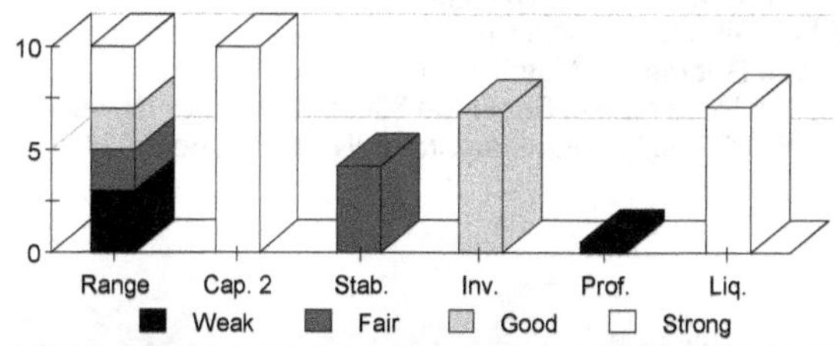

HAWAII MANAGEMENT ALLIANCE ASSOC — C Fair

Major Rating Factors: Weak liquidity (2.1 on a scale of 0 to 10) as a spike in claims may stretch capacity. Good overall profitability index (5.1). Good capitalization (5.0) based on good current risk-adjusted capital (severe loss scenario).
Other Rating Factors: High quality investment portfolio (9.4).
Principal Business: Comp med (80%), dental (4%), other (16%)
Mem Phys: 18: N/A **17:** 8,670 **18 MLR** 109.2% **/ 18 Admin Exp** N/A
Enroll(000): Q1 19: 42 **18:** 43 **17:** 42 **Med Exp PMPM:** $345
Principal Investments: Cash and equiv (64%), long-term bonds (32%), nonaffiliate common stock (4%)
Provider Compensation ($000): Contr fee ($170,975), FFS ($3,485)
Total Member Encounters: Phys (4,142), non-phys (5,142)
Group Affiliation: None
Licensed in: HI
Address: 733 Bishop St Ste 1560, Honolulu, HI 96813-4018
Phone: (808) 791-7550 **Dom State:** HI **Commenced Bus:** N/A

Data Date	Rating	RACR #1	RACR #2	Total Assets ($mil)	Capital ($mil)	Net Premium ($mil)	Net Income ($mil)
3-19	C	0.92	0.77	48.5	20.7	42.2	1.0
3-18	C	0.87	0.73	45.9	17.5	39.4	-1.3
2018	C	0.86	0.72	45.8	19.5	161.1	0.7
2017	C	0.87	0.73	42.7	18.7	150.3	3.8
2016	C-	0.84	0.70	36.2	15.1	131.3	1.0
2015	C-	0.79	0.66	38.2	13.7	127.0	0.2
2014	C-	0.79	0.66	33.0	11.6	90.8	-4.4

Rating Indexes

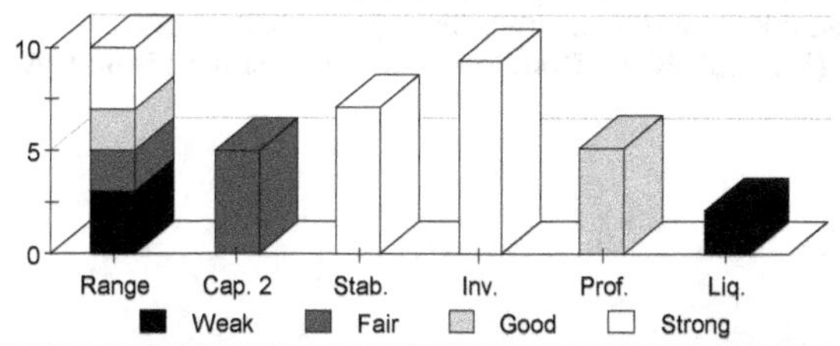

HAWAII MEDICAL SERVICE ASSOCIATION — B — Good

Major Rating Factors: Good overall profitability index (6.4 on a scale of 0 to 10). Fair quality investment portfolio (4.3). Strong capitalization (8.5) based on excellent current risk-adjusted capital (severe loss scenario).
Other Rating Factors: Excellent liquidity (7.0) with sufficient resources (cash flows and marketable investments) to handle a spike in claims.
Principal Business: Comp med (55%), Medicaid (21%), Medicare (13%), FEHB (11%)
Mem Phys: **18:** 7,942 **17:** 7,965 **18 MLR** 88.1% **/ 18 Admin Exp** N/A
Enroll(000): **Q1 19:** 707 **18:** 715 **17:** 723 **Med Exp PMPM:** $360
Principal Investments: Cash and equiv (45%), nonaffiliate common stock (19%), long-term bonds (18%), real estate (11%), affiliate common stock (5%), other (2%)
Provider Compensation ($000): Contr fee ($2,255,741), bonus arrang ($494,910), capitation ($175,951), salary ($140,117)
Total Member Encounters: Phys (5,367,639)
Group Affiliation: None
Licensed in: HI
Address: 818 Keeaumoku St, Honolulu, HI 96814
Phone: (808) 948-5145 **Dom State:** HI **Commenced Bus:** N/A

Data Date	Rating	RACR #1	RACR #2	Total Assets ($mil)	Capital ($mil)	Net Premium ($mil)	Net Income ($mil)
3-19	B	2.59	2.16	1,353.3	598.0	889.6	42.7
3-18	B-	2.00	1.67	1,281.9	462.1	876.3	-17.6
2018	B-	2.40	2.00	1,295.2	562.4	3,539.8	68.9
2017	B-	2.08	1.73	1,173.6	478.0	3,332.7	58.0
2016	C+	1.92	1.60	1,004.0	417.6	3,158.0	28.5
2015	C	1.70	1.42	972.6	371.9	2,978.7	7.6
2014	C	1.81	1.50	932.8	393.4	2,873.0	4.2

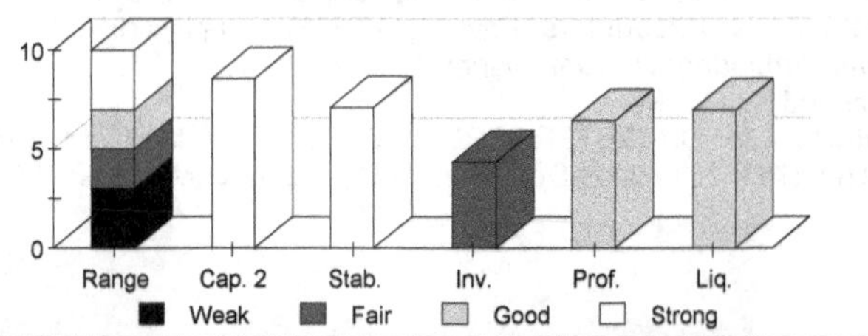

HCC LIFE INSURANCE COMPANY — B — Good

Major Rating Factors: Good overall results on stability tests (5.8 on a scale of 0 to 10) despite fair financial strength of affiliated HCC Ins Holdings Inc. Other stability subfactors include good operational trends and excellent risk diversification. Good liquidity (6.5) with sufficient resources to handle a spike in claims. Strong capitalization (9.7) based on excellent risk adjusted capital (severe loss scenario).
Other Rating Factors: High quality investment portfolio (7.8). Excellent profitability (7.7).
Principal Business: Group health insurance (82%), reinsurance (16%), and individual health insurance (1%).
Principal Investments: CMOs and structured securities (49%) and nonCMO investment grade bonds (49%).
Investments in Affiliates: None
Group Affiliation: HCC Ins Holdings Inc
Licensed in: All states except PR
Commenced Business: March 1981
Address: 150 West Market Street Ste 800, Indianapolis, IN 46204
Phone: (770) 973-9851 **Domicile State:** IN **NAIC Code:** 92711

Data Date	Rating	RACR #1	RACR #2	Total Assets ($mil)	Capital ($mil)	Net Premium ($mil)	Net Income ($mil)
3-19	B	3.63	2.78	1,059.6	587.2	309.2	28.1
3-18	B	3.26	2.57	1,003.8	447.6	340.9	36.8
2018	B	3.35	2.56	1,097.0	561.5	1,365.8	121.4
2017	B	3.06	2.40	994.8	406.2	1,095.5	90.9
2016	B	4.81	3.71	981.6	601.8	987.7	104.8
2015	B	4.44	3.40	921.5	552.7	973.3	112.1
2014	B	4.61	3.60	923.5	554.3	956.4	116.1

HCC Ins Holdings Inc
Composite Group Rating: C+

Largest Group Members	Assets ($mil)	Rating
RELIANCE STANDARD LIFE INS CO	13875	C+
PHILADELPHIA INDEMNITY INS CO	9058	B-
SAFETY NATIONAL CASUALTY CORP	8028	C+
HOUSTON CASUALTY CO	3437	B-
US SPECIALTY INS CO	2042	B

HCSC INS SERVICES CO — D- — Weak

Major Rating Factors: Weak profitability index (0.9 on a scale of 0 to 10). Strong capitalization (7.6) based on excellent current risk-adjusted capital (severe loss scenario). High quality investment portfolio (7.7).
Other Rating Factors: Excellent liquidity (7.0) with sufficient resources (cash flows and marketable investments) to handle a spike in claims.
Principal Business: Medicaid (66%), Medicare (10%), other (24%)
Mem Phys: **18:** 61,714 **17:** 53,413 **18 MLR** 86.9% **/ 18 Admin Exp** N/A
Enroll(000): **Q1 19:** 549 **18:** 540 **17:** 528 **Med Exp PMPM:** $208
Principal Investments: Long-term bonds (59%), cash and equiv (41%)
Provider Compensation ($000): Contr fee ($838,897), FFS ($159,251), capitation ($17,467), bonus arrang ($45), other ($315,937)
Total Member Encounters: Phys (936,881), non-phys (1,488,907)
Group Affiliation: Health Care Service Corporation a Mu
Licensed in: All states except CT, HI, ME, NH, NJ, NY, VT, PR
Address: 300 East Randolph St, Chicago, IL 60601-5099
Phone: (312) 653-6000 **Dom State:** IL **Commenced Bus:** N/A

Data Date	Rating	RACR #1	RACR #2	Total Assets ($mil)	Capital ($mil)	Net Premium ($mil)	Net Income ($mil)
3-19	D-	1.86	1.55	1,022.8	216.8	140.5	-32.5
3-18	D-	1.39	1.16	887.7	151.3	351.0	-93.9
2018	D-	2.12	1.77	1,043.9	247.8	1,523.2	-156.3
2017	D-	1.74	1.45	900.7	259.5	1,393.5	-114.3
2016	D	2.19	1.83	581.5	189.8	1,391.7	-37.3
2015	D	2.79	2.33	560.2	225.0	1,306.9	-122.1
2014	B	3.81	3.18	464.9	249.7	1,020.7	-45.0

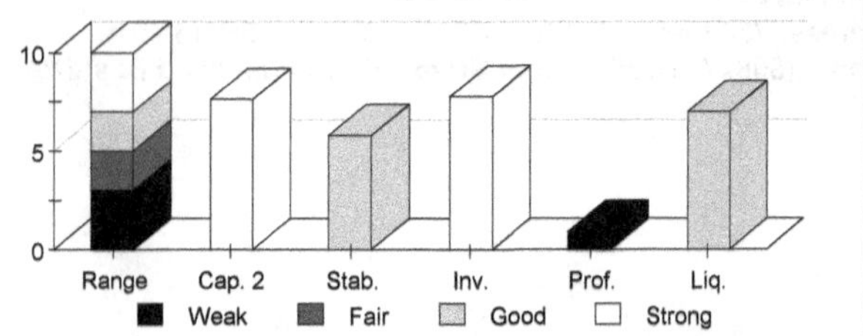

HEALTH ALLIANCE CONNECT INC — C — Fair

Major Rating Factors: Weak profitability index (2.5 on a scale of 0 to 10). Good liquidity (6.9) with sufficient resources (cash flows and marketable investments) to handle a spike in claims. Strong capitalization (7.5) based on excellent current risk-adjusted capital (severe loss scenario).
Other Rating Factors: High quality investment portfolio (9.2).
Principal Business: Medicare (98%), Medicaid (2%)
Mem Phys: 18: 41,526 **17:** 37,183 **18 MLR** 85.4% **/ 18 Admin Exp** N/A
Enroll(000): Q1 19: 23 **18:** 21 **17:** 20 **Med Exp PMPM:** $777
Principal Investments: Long-term bonds (58%), cash and equiv (42%)
Provider Compensation ($000): Contr fee ($138,566), capitation ($53,790), FFS ($4,472)
Total Member Encounters: Phys (126,019), non-phys (505,369)
Group Affiliation: None
Licensed in: IL, IN, OH
Address: 301 S Vine St, Champaign, IL 61822
Phone: (800) 851-3379 **Dom State:** IL **Commenced Bus:** N/A

Data Date	Rating	RACR #1	RACR #2	Total Assets ($mil)	Capital ($mil)	Net Premium ($mil)	Net Income ($mil)
3-19	C	1.76	1.46	55.7	24.0	60.0	0.4
3-18	C	N/A	N/A	84.1	30.5	53.2	-1.0
2018	C	1.81	1.51	54.4	25.1	227.5	6.6
2017	C	N/A	N/A	70.8	32.7	206.4	1.7
2016	C	0.96	0.80	166.1	72.3	647.4	4.9
2015	N/A	N/A	N/A	183.0	58.9	547.3	N/A
2014	U	1.97	1.64	39.8	11.4	31.5	-6.5

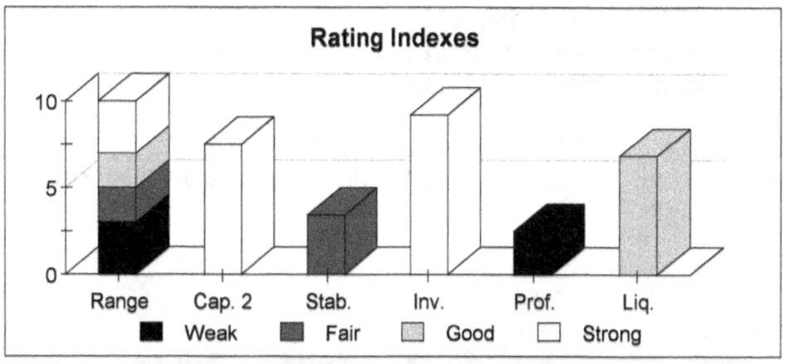

HEALTH ALLIANCE MEDICAL PLANS — B- — Good

Major Rating Factors: Fair profitability index (4.3 on a scale of 0 to 10). Good quality investment portfolio (5.1). Strong capitalization (8.9) based on excellent current risk-adjusted capital (severe loss scenario).
Other Rating Factors: Excellent liquidity (7.1) with ample operational cash flow and liquid investments.
Principal Business: Comp med (95%), Medicare (3%), FEHB (1%)
Mem Phys: 18: 50,222 **17:** 47,358 **18 MLR** 83.9% **/ 18 Admin Exp** N/A
Enroll(000): Q1 19: 146 **18:** 156 **17:** 169 **Med Exp PMPM:** $542
Principal Investments: Long-term bonds (48%), nonaffiliate common stock (43%), cash and equiv (7%), affiliate common stock (2%)
Provider Compensation ($000): Contr fee ($723,911), capitation ($350,192), FFS ($9,685)
Total Member Encounters: Phys (453,611), non-phys (1,550,545)
Group Affiliation: None
Licensed in: IL, MO
Address: 301 S Vine, Champaign, IL 61822
Phone: (800) 851-3379 **Dom State:** IL **Commenced Bus:** N/A

Data Date	Rating	RACR #1	RACR #2	Total Assets ($mil)	Capital ($mil)	Net Premium ($mil)	Net Income ($mil)
3-19	B-	2.84	2.37	511.1	239.3	300.8	8.2
3-18	B-	2.50	2.09	593.9	207.9	315.6	-14.0
2018	B-	2.61	2.18	507.9	220.6	1,226.3	17.1
2017	B-	2.61	2.18	641.0	223.0	1,229.8	16.6
2016	B-	2.52	2.10	505.1	195.7	1,133.1	2.2
2015	N/A	N/A	N/A	526.3	184.5	1,156.4	N/A
2014	B+	2.13	1.78	517.1	179.1	1,234.7	-14.0

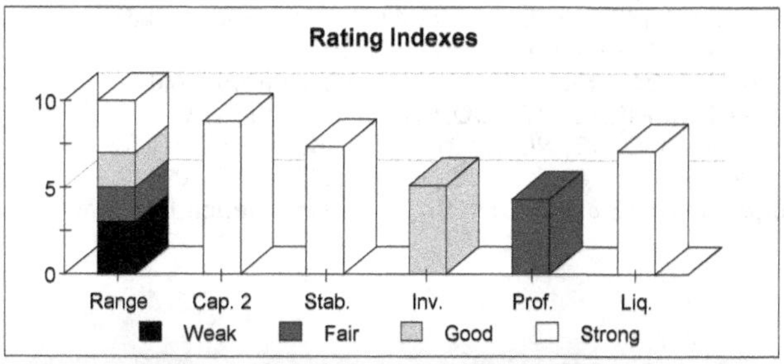

HEALTH ALLIANCE NORTHWEST HEALTH PL — B — Good

Major Rating Factors: Fair profitability index (4.4 on a scale of 0 to 10). Strong capitalization (8.1) based on excellent current risk-adjusted capital (severe loss scenario). High quality investment portfolio (9.3).
Other Rating Factors: Excellent liquidity (7.0) with sufficient resources (cash flows and marketable investments) to handle a spike in claims.
Principal Business: Medicare (100%)
Mem Phys: 18: 11,200 **17:** 9,369 **18 MLR** 88.0% **/ 18 Admin Exp** N/A
Enroll(000): Q1 19: 11 **18:** 8 **17:** 7 **Med Exp PMPM:** $633
Principal Investments: Long-term bonds (56%), cash and equiv (44%)
Provider Compensation ($000): Capitation ($39,488), contr fee ($16,446), FFS ($698)
Total Member Encounters: Phys (19,949), non-phys (160,203)
Group Affiliation: None
Licensed in: WA
Address: 316 Fifth St, Wenatchee, WA 98801
Phone: (800) 851-3379 **Dom State:** WA **Commenced Bus:** N/A

Data Date	Rating	RACR #1	RACR #2	Total Assets ($mil)	Capital ($mil)	Net Premium ($mil)	Net Income ($mil)
3-19	B	2.27	1.89	14.9	10.0	23.1	0.7
3-18	B-	N/A	N/A	20.4	9.7	15.5	N/A
2018	B	2.60	2.16	15.6	11.5	64.7	0.8
2017	B-	N/A	N/A	16.8	10.8	57.2	1.3
2016	C+	3.39	2.82	16.0	9.5	44.5	0.5
2015	C	3.79	3.16	16.5	9.1	30.1	-0.2
2014	B-	2.49	2.07	9.3	4.5	23.8	-0.3

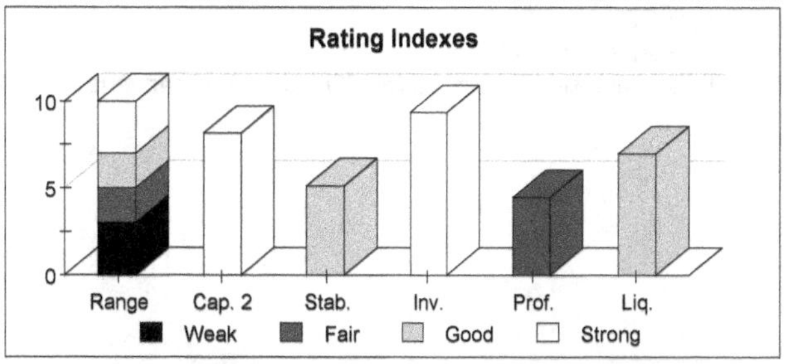

HEALTH ALLIANCE PLAN OF MICHIGAN C- Fair

Major Rating Factors: Fair profitability index (3.5 on a scale of 0 to 10). Low quality investment portfolio (2.5). Good overall results on stability tests (5.1).
Other Rating Factors: Strong capitalization index (7.6) based on excellent current risk-adjusted capital (severe loss scenario). Excellent liquidity (7.0) with sufficient resources (cash flows and marketable investments) to handle a spike in claims.
Principal Business: Comp med (46%), Medicare (46%), FEHB (8%)
Mem Phys: 18: 12,080 **17:** 11,900 **18 MLR** 88.4% **/ 18 Admin Exp** N/A
Enroll(000): Q1 19: 182 **18:** 181 **17:** 258 **Med Exp PMPM:** $580
Principal Investments: Cash and equiv (50%), long-term bonds (24%), affiliate common stock (23%), nonaffiliate common stock (2%), real estate (1%)
Provider Compensation ($000): Contr fee ($1,065,595), capitation ($253,454), FFS ($13,377), bonus arrang ($10,457)
Total Member Encounters: Phys (1,264,702), non-phys (1,495,759)
Group Affiliation: Henry Ford Health System
Licensed in: MI
Address: 2850 West Grand Boulevard, Detroit, MI 48202
Phone: (313) 872-8100 **Dom State:** MI **Commenced Bus:** N/A

Data Date	Rating	RACR #1	RACR #2	Total Assets ($mil)	Capital ($mil)	Net Premium ($mil)	Net Income ($mil)
3-19	C-	1.87	1.56	518.4	266.0	376.1	5.6
3-18	C	1.28	1.07	579.3	217.9	370.9	-16.6
2018	C-	1.78	1.49	515.8	254.7	1,468.0	3.5
2017	C	1.32	1.10	562.2	229.3	1,827.5	8.7
2016	C+	1.20	1.00	515.5	204.4	1,924.3	38.4
2015	C+	1.31	1.09	530.9	206.5	2,069.8	-33.1
2014	B	1.33	1.11	469.0	208.3	1,749.5	-5.0

Rating Indexes

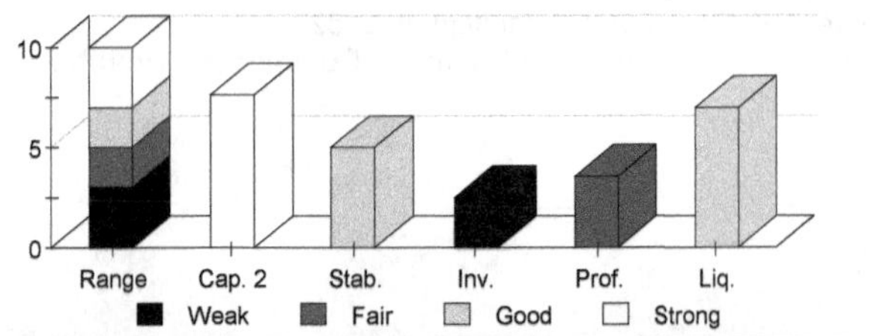

HEALTH CARE SVC CORP A MUT LEG RES B Good

Major Rating Factors: Good overall profitability index (5.8 on a scale of 0 to 10). Good quality investment portfolio (6.6). Strong capitalization (10.0) based on excellent current risk-adjusted capital (severe loss scenario).
Other Rating Factors: Excellent liquidity (7.0) with ample operational cash flow and liquid investments.
Principal Business: Comp med (66%), FEHB (15%), Medicaid (8%), med supp (4%), Medicare (4%), other (2%)
Mem Phys: 18: 251,046 **17:** 212,092 **18 MLR** 81.4% **/ 18 Admin Exp** N/A
Enroll(000): Q1 19: 9,431 **18:** 8,817 **17:** 8,437 **Med Exp PMPM:** $277
Principal Investments: Long-term bonds (80%), nonaffiliate common stock (7%), affiliate common stock (7%), real estate (6%), other (2%)
Provider Compensation ($000): Contr fee ($20,897,063), FFS ($6,238,234), capitation ($1,182,069), bonus arrang ($263,907), other ($655,488)
Total Member Encounters: Phys (51,525,353), non-phys (21,419,042)
Group Affiliation: Health Care Service Corporation a Mu
Licensed in: AK, AZ, AR, CO, CT, DC, DE, FL, GA, ID, IL, IN, KY, ME, MD, MA, MI, MN, MO, MT, NE, NJ, NM, OH, OK, OR, PA, SC, TX, UT, VA, WV, WI
Address: 300 East Randolph St, Chicago, IL 60601-5099
Phone: (312) 653-6000 **Dom State:** IL **Commenced Bus:** N/A

Data Date	Rating	RACR #1	RACR #2	Total Assets ($mil)	Capital ($mil)	Net Premium ($mil)	Net Income ($mil)
3-19	B	8.25	6.88	28,520.6	18,649.0	9,507.0	1,524.0
3-18	B	6.50	5.42	23,483.1	13,432.4	8,879.3	1,362.0
2018	B	7.47	6.23	26,725.6	16,859.3	35,927.2	4,114.7
2017	B	5.85	4.87	22,028.2	12,049.0	32,603.5	1,262.6
2016	B	4.74	3.95	18,036.1	9,535.9	30,335.8	106.3
2015	B	4.47	3.72	17,661.1	9,445.0	31,185.3	-65.9
2014	A+	5.55	4.63	17,829.4	9,942.2	27,705.5	-281.9

Rating Indexes

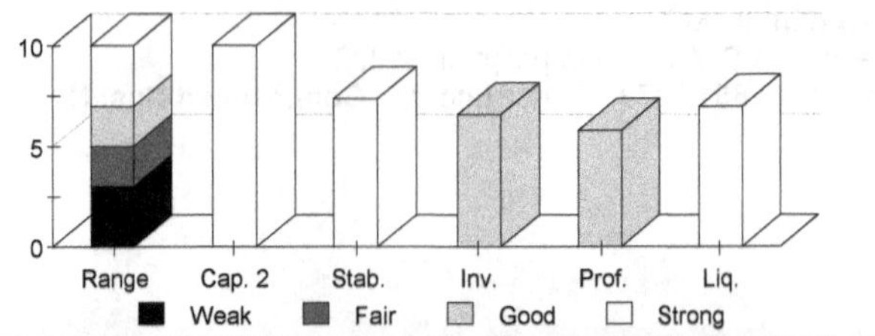

HEALTH COLORADO INC C Fair

Major Rating Factors: Fair capitalization (3.4 on a scale of 0 to 10) based on weak current risk-adjusted capital (moderate loss scenario). Good overall profitability index (6.9). High quality investment portfolio (9.9).
Other Rating Factors: Excellent liquidity (7.2) with ample operational cash flow and liquid investments.
Principal Business: Medicaid (100%)
Mem Phys: 18: 90 **17:** N/A **18 MLR** 81.5% **/ 18 Admin Exp** N/A
Enroll(000): Q1 19: 131 **18:** 133 **17:** N/A **Med Exp PMPM:** $45
Principal Investments: Cash and equiv (100%)
Provider Compensation ($000): Contr fee ($27,564), other ($6,421)
Total Member Encounters: Non-phys (296,626)
Group Affiliation: None
Licensed in: CO
Address: , Pueblo, CO 81008
Phone: (Phone number **Dom State:** CO **Commenced Bus:** N/A

Data Date	Rating	RACR #1	RACR #2	Total Assets ($mil)	Capital ($mil)	Net Premium ($mil)	Net Income ($mil)
3-19	C	0.69	0.58	9.2	4.8	24.8	-0.6
3-18	N/A	N/A	N/A	N/A	N/A	N/A	N/A
2018	C	0.79	0.66	10.3	5.4	44.1	1.1
2017	N/A	N/A	N/A	N/A	N/A	N/A	N/A
2016	N/A	N/A	N/A	N/A	N/A	N/A	N/A
2015	N/A	N/A	N/A	N/A	N/A	N/A	N/A
2014	N/A	N/A	N/A	N/A	N/A	N/A	N/A

Rating Indexes

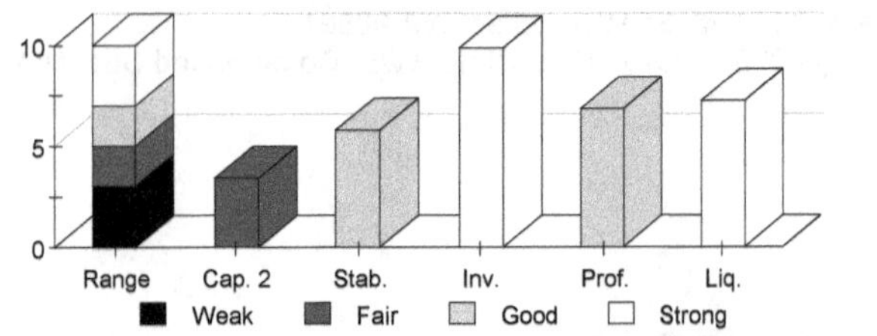

HEALTH FIRST COMM PLANS INC — C+ Fair

Major Rating Factors: Excellent profitability (9.2 on a scale of 0 to 10). Strong capitalization (8.3) based on excellent current risk-adjusted capital (severe loss scenario). High quality investment portfolio (9.1).
Other Rating Factors: Excellent liquidity (7.0) with sufficient resources (cash flows and marketable investments) to handle a spike in claims.
Principal Business: Comp med (100%)
Mem Phys: 18: 1,947 **17:** N/A **18 MLR** 77.4% **/ 18 Admin Exp** N/A
Enroll(000): Q1 19: 37 **18:** 40 **17:** N/A **Med Exp PMPM:** $408
Principal Investments: Long-term bonds (55%), cash and equiv (40%), nonaffiliate common stock (6%)
Provider Compensation ($000): Contr fee ($135,692), FFS ($63,159), capitation ($998)
Total Member Encounters: Phys (277,229), non-phys (106,087)
Group Affiliation: Health First Inc
Licensed in: FL
Address: , , FL 32955
Phone: (321) 434-5600 **Dom State:** FL **Commenced Bus:** January 2018

Data Date	Rating	RACR #1	RACR #2	Total Assets ($mil)	Capital ($mil)	Net Premium ($mil)	Net Income ($mil)
3-19	C+	2.36	1.97	95.9	49.9	60.7	1.2
3-18	N/A	N/A	N/A	91.6	41.8	61.4	3.6
2018	C	2.23	1.86	87.1	47.0	259.8	12.6
2017	N/A	N/A	N/A	2.0	2.0	N/A	N/A
2016	N/A	N/A	N/A	N/A	N/A	N/A	N/A
2015	N/A	N/A	N/A	N/A	N/A	N/A	N/A
2014	N/A	N/A	N/A	N/A	N/A	N/A	N/A

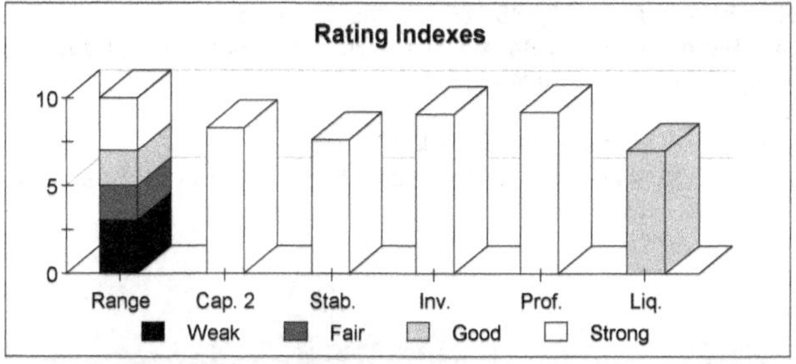

HEALTH FIRST HEALTH PLANS INC — B Good

Major Rating Factors: Excellent profitability (7.5 on a scale of 0 to 10). Strong capitalization (8.8) based on excellent current risk-adjusted capital (severe loss scenario). High quality investment portfolio (8.8).
Other Rating Factors: Excellent liquidity (7.0) with ample operational cash flow and liquid investments.
Principal Business: Medicare (100%)
Mem Phys: 18: 5,217 **17:** 5,301 **18 MLR** 82.7% **/ 18 Admin Exp** N/A
Enroll(000): Q1 19: 39 **18:** 38 **17:** 37 **Med Exp PMPM:** $739
Principal Investments: Long-term bonds (46%), cash and equiv (44%), nonaffiliate common stock (10%)
Provider Compensation ($000): Contr fee ($261,505), FFS ($77,656), capitation ($4,564)
Total Member Encounters: Phys (689,665), non-phys (346,270)
Group Affiliation: Health First Inc
Licensed in: FL
Address: 6450 US HIGHWAY 1, ROCKLEDGE, FL 32955
Phone: (321) 434-5600 **Dom State:** FL **Commenced Bus:** N/A

Data Date	Rating	RACR #1	RACR #2	Total Assets ($mil)	Capital ($mil)	Net Premium ($mil)	Net Income ($mil)
3-19	B	2.82	2.35	156.7	98.4	110.1	5.2
3-18	B	2.43	2.03	175.7	79.1	102.0	4.3
2018	B	2.66	2.21	143.9	93.0	408.1	17.9
2017	B	1.94	1.61	120.6	65.8	373.5	17.2
2016	C-	2.01	1.68	130.8	70.6	443.3	22.5
2015	N/A	N/A	N/A	1.8	1.8	N/A	N/A
2014	N/A	N/A	N/A	N/A	N/A	N/A	N/A

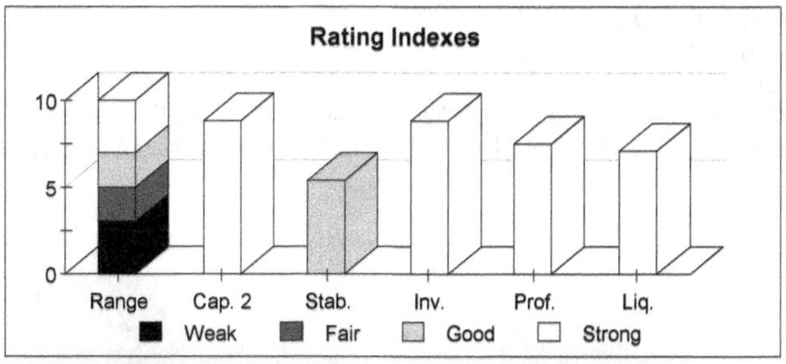

HEALTH FIRST INS INC — C Fair

Major Rating Factors: Weak profitability index (1.3 on a scale of 0 to 10). Strong capitalization (10.0) based on excellent current risk-adjusted capital (severe loss scenario). High quality investment portfolio (9.9).
Other Rating Factors: Excellent liquidity (10.0) with ample operational cash flow and liquid investments.
Principal Business: Comp med (94%), med supp (6%)
Mem Phys: 18: 1,734 **17:** 2,371 **18 MLR** 58.8% **/ 18 Admin Exp** N/A
Enroll(000): Q1 19: 0 **18:** 0 **17:** 1 **Med Exp PMPM:** $222
Principal Investments: Cash and equiv (100%)
Provider Compensation ($000): FFS ($734), contr fee ($702), capitation ($2)
Total Member Encounters: Phys (2,216), non-phys (1,197)
Group Affiliation: Health First Inc
Licensed in: FL
Address: 6450 US HIGHWAY 1, ROCKLEDGE, FL 32955
Phone: (321) 434-5600 **Dom State:** FL **Commenced Bus:** N/A

Data Date	Rating	RACR #1	RACR #2	Total Assets ($mil)	Capital ($mil)	Net Premium ($mil)	Net Income ($mil)
3-19	C	3.84	3.20	5.2	4.9	0.0	0.0
3-18	C+	3.48	2.90	5.4	4.6	0.5	-0.1
2018	C	3.82	3.19	5.3	4.9	1.4	0.2
2017	D	1.96	1.64	4.4	3.5	3.5	0.2
2016	E	4.06	3.38	6.0	4.7	5.3	0.3
2015	E-	1.58	1.32	6.4	3.6	10.4	-2.0
2014	D+	0.86	0.71	10.2	2.8	22.1	-1.9

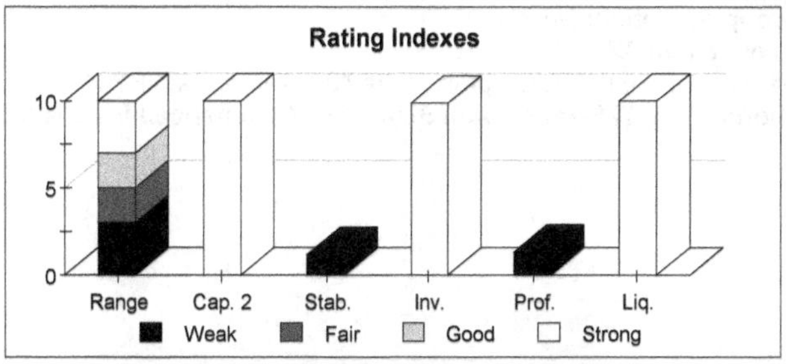

HEALTH INSURANCE PLAN OF GREATER NY — C- Fair

Major Rating Factors: Fair capitalization (4.6 on a scale of 0 to 10) based on fair current risk-adjusted capital (moderate loss scenario). Fair quality investment portfolio (4.2). Weak profitability index (0.8).
Other Rating Factors: Good liquidity (4.9) as cash resources may not be adequate to cover a spike in claims.
Principal Business: Comp med (45%), Medicare (32%), Medicaid (21%), FEHB (2%)
Mem Phys: 18: 110,096 **17:** 104,206 **18 MLR** 89.6% **/ 18 Admin Exp** N/A
Enroll(000): Q1 19: 582 **18:** 604 **17:** 600 **Med Exp PMPM:** $615
Principal Investments: Affiliate common stock (51%), cash and equiv (25%), real estate (18%), long-term bonds (1%), other (6%)
Provider Compensation ($000): Capitation ($1,801,568), contr fee ($1,488,126), FFS ($1,138,189), bonus arrang ($14,532)
Total Member Encounters: Phys (7,767,248), non-phys (4,092,555)
Group Affiliation: EmblemHealth Inc
Licensed in: NY
Address: 55 Water St, New York, NY 10041-8190
Phone: (646) 447-5000 **Dom State:** NY **Commenced Bus:** N/A

Data Date	Rating	RACR #1	RACR #2	Total Assets ($mil)	Capital ($mil)	Net Premium ($mil)	Net Income ($mil)
3-19	C-	0.87	0.73	1,215.2	361.3	1,234.7	-9.9
3-18	C-	0.81	0.68	1,451.0	318.6	1,224.4	-59.1
2018	C-	0.87	0.72	1,220.8	360.7	5,008.6	-48.8
2017	C-	0.81	0.68	1,252.9	391.8	4,754.2	-199.5
2016	C-	1.15	0.96	1,424.4	469.9	4,855.3	-239.2
2015	C-	1.70	1.42	1,644.4	684.1	5,065.0	-143.2
2014	B-	2.45	2.04	1,894.6	897.6	5,088.7	-365.3

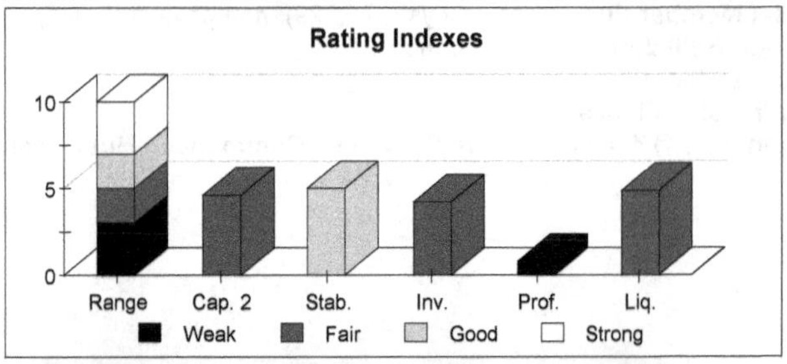

HEALTH NET COMMUNITY SOLUTIONS INC — B Good

Major Rating Factors: Fair overall results on stability tests (4.3 on a scale of 0 to 10) based on inconsistent enrollment growth in the past five years due to declines in 2015 and 2018. Excellent profitability (8.7). Strong capitalization index (8.2) based on excellent current risk-adjusted capital (severe loss scenario).
Other Rating Factors: Excellent liquidity (7.0) with ample operational cash flow and liquid investments.
Principal Business: Medicaid (79%), Medicare (5%)
Mem Phys: 18: N/A **17:** N/A **18 MLR** 84.0% **/ 18 Admin Exp** N/A
Enroll(000): Q1 19: 1,775 **18:** 1,792 **17:** 1,879 **Med Exp PMPM:** $235
Principal Investments ($000): Cash and equiv ($94,728)
Provider Compensation ($000): None
Total Member Encounters: N/A
Group Affiliation: Health Net Inc
Licensed in: CA
Address: 11971 Foundation Place, Rancho Cordova, CA 95670
Phone: (818) 676-8394 **Dom State:** CA **Commenced Bus:** June 2005

Data Date	Rating	RACR #1	RACR #2	Total Assets ($mil)	Capital ($mil)	Net Premium ($mil)	Net Income ($mil)
3-19	B	2.91	1.96	2,833.4	1,233.5	1,622.6	110.6
3-18	B	2.06	1.38	3,247.4	963.4	1,588.5	147.0
2018	B	2.59	1.74	2,394.5	1,107.7	6,244.4	493.9
2017	B+	2.19	1.47	3,107.0	1,029.0	7,518.8	433.2
2016	B	1.62	1.09	3,043.0	737.2	7,482.8	541.9
2015	B	2.03	1.26	2,321.8	549.1	6,467.1	533.2
2014	B-	1.75	1.08	1,593.8	369.1	4,427.6	195.7

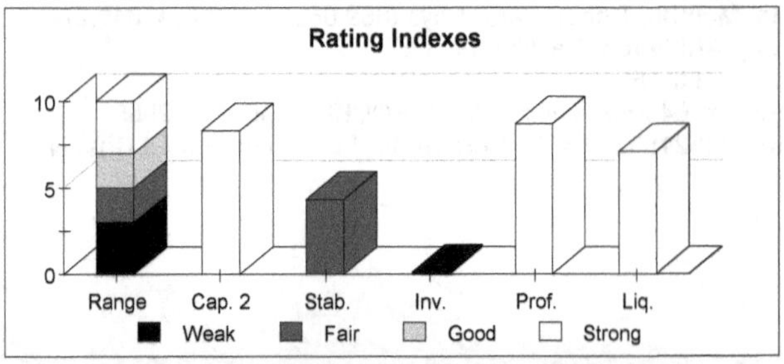

HEALTH NET COMMUNITY SOLUTIONS OF AR — C- Fair

Major Rating Factors: Weak profitability index (0.9 on a scale of 0 to 10). Strong capitalization (9.1) based on excellent current risk-adjusted capital (severe loss scenario). High quality investment portfolio (9.9).
Other Rating Factors: Excellent liquidity (7.2) with ample operational cash flow and liquid investments.
Principal Business: Medicare (100%)
Mem Phys: 18: 23,660 **17:** 19,324 **18 MLR** 77.5% **/ 18 Admin Exp** N/A
Enroll(000): Q1 19: 3 **18:** 36 **17:** 2 **Med Exp PMPM:** $683
Principal Investments: Cash and equiv (58%), long-term bonds (42%)
Provider Compensation ($000): Contr fee ($22,627), capitation ($431), salary ($256)
Total Member Encounters: Phys (57,867), non-phys (3,907)
Group Affiliation: None
Licensed in: AZ
Address: 1230 W Washington St Ste 400, Tempe, AZ 85281
Phone: (314) 725-4477 **Dom State:** AZ **Commenced Bus:** N/A

Data Date	Rating	RACR #1	RACR #2	Total Assets ($mil)	Capital ($mil)	Net Premium ($mil)	Net Income ($mil)
3-19	C-	3.06	2.55	15.3	6.5	6.8	-1.3
3-18	N/A	N/A	N/A	15.0	3.8	7.4	0.6
2018	C-	3.69	3.07	15.0	8.1	32.0	4.6
2017	N/A	N/A	N/A	9.7	3.8	17.8	-3.5
2016	N/A	N/A	N/A	1.6	1.6	N/A	N/A
2015	N/A	N/A	N/A	N/A	N/A	N/A	N/A
2014	N/A	N/A	N/A	N/A	N/A	N/A	N/A

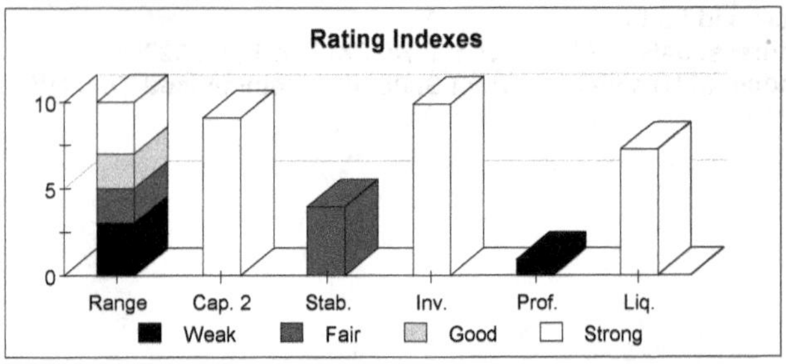

HEALTH NET HEALTH PLAN OF OREGON INC D Weak

Major Rating Factors: Weak profitability index (0.7 on a scale of 0 to 10). Good overall results on stability tests (5.1). Rating is significantly influenced by the fair financial results of . Good liquidity (5.3) with sufficient resources (cash flows and marketable investments) to handle a spike in claims.
Other Rating Factors: Strong capitalization index (7.8) based on excellent current risk-adjusted capital (severe loss scenario). High quality investment portfolio (9.1).
Principal Business: Medicare (68%), comp med (31%)
Mem Phys: 18: 66,617 **17:** 60,722 **18 MLR** 90.6% **/ 18 Admin Exp** N/A
Enroll(000): Q1 19: 63 **18:** 66 **17:** 77 **Med Exp PMPM:** $543
Principal Investments: Long-term bonds (93%), cash and equiv (7%)
Provider Compensation ($000): Contr fee ($420,776), capitation ($17,868), bonus arrang ($6,199), salary ($5,381)
Total Member Encounters: Phys (832,763), non-phys (322,855)
Group Affiliation: None
Licensed in: OR, WA
Address: 13221 SW 68th Parkway Suite 20, Tigard, OR 97223
Phone: (314) 724-4477 **Dom State:** OR **Commenced Bus:** N/A

Data Date	Rating	RACR #1	RACR #2	Total Assets ($mil)	Capital ($mil)	Net Premium ($mil)	Net Income ($mil)
3-19	D	1.97	1.64	157.2	62.4	119.2	-2.6
3-18	D	2.00	1.67	188.1	67.2	122.2	2.5
2018	D	2.33	1.94	155.6	73.7	499.0	-0.1
2017	F	1.42	1.18	182.9	73.1	526.5	-23.5
2016	E-	2.53	2.11	181.6	99.7	506.2	-31.8
2015	E+	1.68	1.40	152.1	68.1	418.8	-25.4
2014	E	1.92	1.60	131.6	55.7	327.9	-43.8

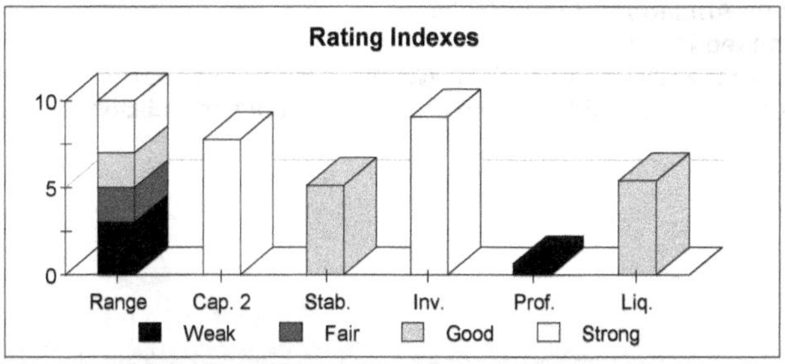

HEALTH NET LIFE INSURANCE COMPANY C Fair

Major Rating Factors: Fair overall results on stability tests (3.0 on a scale of 0 to 10) including negative cash flow from operations for 2018. Good liquidity (5.3) with sufficient resources to handle a spike in claims. Weak profitability (1.9) with operating losses during the first three months of 2019.
Other Rating Factors: Strong capitalization (9.0) based on excellent risk adjusted capital (severe loss scenario). High quality investment portfolio (8.2).
Principal Business: Individual health insurance (59%) and group health insurance (41%).
Principal Investments: NonCMO investment grade bonds (66%), CMOs and structured securities (24%), and cash (7%).
Investments in Affiliates: None
Group Affiliation: Centene Corporation
Licensed in: All states except MI, NY, PR
Commenced Business: January 1987
Address: 21281 Burbank Boulevard B3, Woodland Hills, CA 91367
Phone: (314) 725-4477 **Domicile State:** CA **NAIC Code:** 66141

Data Date	Rating	RACR #1	RACR #2	Total Assets ($mil)	Capital ($mil)	Net Premium ($mil)	Net Income ($mil)
3-19	C	2.94	2.33	685.2	353.0	175.3	-4.3
3-18	C	3.20	2.59	777.5	376.1	195.2	-27.6
2018	C	2.98	2.36	704.7	363.0	752.6	-53.1
2017	C	3.44	2.79	691.4	399.9	763.3	-16.4
2016	C	3.59	2.94	727.2	410.0	809.8	-171.8
2015	C	1.84	1.52	618.5	331.3	1,181.3	-93.2
2014	C	2.26	1.84	624.0	363.9	1,040.9	-9.3

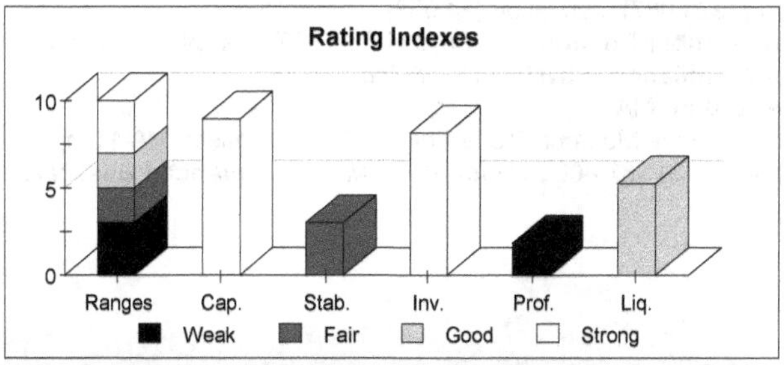

HEALTH NET OF ARIZONA INC C Fair

Major Rating Factors: Fair overall results on stability tests (4.8 on a scale of 0 to 10) based on a decline in the number of member physicians during 2019. Rating is significantly influenced by the fair financial results of . Weak profitability index (1.5). Good liquidity (6.6) with sufficient resources (cash flows and marketable investments) to handle a spike in claims.
Other Rating Factors: Strong capitalization index (10.0) based on excellent current risk-adjusted capital (severe loss scenario). High quality investment portfolio (8.4).
Principal Business: Comp med (76%), Medicare (21%), FEHB (2%)
Mem Phys: 18: 12,471 **17:** 18,450 **18 MLR** 78.1% **/ 18 Admin Exp** N/A
Enroll(000): Q1 19: 95 **18:** 122 **17:** 122 **Med Exp PMPM:** $470
Principal Investments: Long-term bonds (70%), cash and equiv (30%)
Provider Compensation ($000): Contr fee ($531,356), capitation ($102,726), salary ($11,667)
Total Member Encounters: Phys (747,760), non-phys (527,184)
Group Affiliation: None
Licensed in: AZ
Address: 1230 West Washington St Suite, Tempe, AZ 85281
Phone: (314) 725-4477 **Dom State:** AZ **Commenced Bus:** N/A

Data Date	Rating	RACR #1	RACR #2	Total Assets ($mil)	Capital ($mil)	Net Premium ($mil)	Net Income ($mil)
3-19	C	9.16	7.64	442.0	203.0	144.8	42.4
3-18	C	3.89	3.24	417.2	152.4	253.7	15.5
2018	C	7.37	6.14	419.8	163.9	932.6	43.0
2017	C	2.66	2.22	344.1	146.9	1,005.6	40.3
2016	C	2.63	2.19	455.4	130.5	360.9	-54.8
2015	C	1.39	1.16	451.0	65.8	684.2	-55.2
2014	D+	2.25	1.87	538.4	120.5	838.1	-79.0

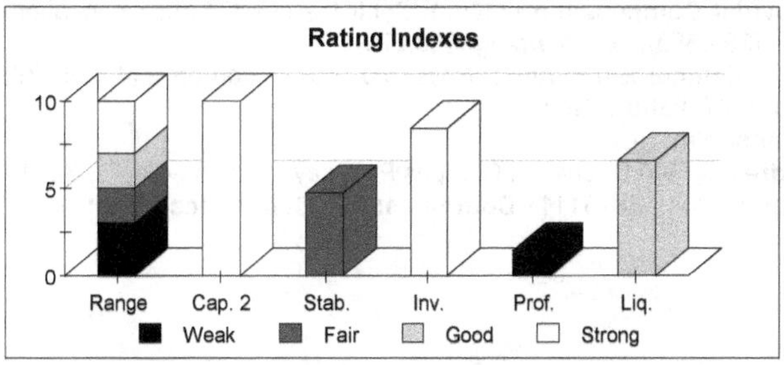

HEALTH NET OF CALIFORNIA INC C Fair

Major Rating Factors: Weak profitability index (1.9 on a scale of 0 to 10). Good overall results on stability tests (6.5) based on healthy premium and capital growth during 2018. Strong capitalization index (7.6) based on excellent current risk-adjusted capital (severe loss scenario).
Other Rating Factors: Excellent liquidity (6.9) with sufficient resources (cash flows and marketable investments) to handle a spike in claims.
Principal Business: Medicare (24%)
Mem Phys: 18: N/A **17:** N/A **18 MLR** 81.1% **/ 18 Admin Exp** N/A
Enroll(000): Q1 19: 953 **18:** 960 **17:** 1,010 **Med Exp PMPM:** $592
Principal Investments ($000): Cash and equiv ($400,461)
Provider Compensation ($000): None
Total Member Encounters: N/A
Group Affiliation: Health Net Inc
Licensed in: CA
Address: 21281 Burbank Blvd, Woodland Hills, CA 91367
Phone: (818) 676-8394 **Dom State:** CA **Commenced Bus:** March 1979

Data Date	Rating	RACR #1	RACR #2	Total Assets ($mil)	Capital ($mil)	Net Premium ($mil)	Net Income ($mil)
3-19	C	2.27	1.55	2,891.9	1,338.9	2,421.4	101.7
3-18	C	2.08	1.41	2,843.5	960.7	2,216.8	23.5
2018	C	2.08	1.41	2,620.3	1,218.6	8,784.6	94.3
2017	C	2.05	1.39	2,048.7	949.7	6,300.2	-59.8
2016	C	1.88	1.25	2,280.5	1,001.6	6,751.6	-459.2
2015	C+	2.42	1.51	2,592.5	1,045.0	7,591.8	-189.6
2014	B-	2.35	1.46	2,312.8	977.9	7,418.6	6.6

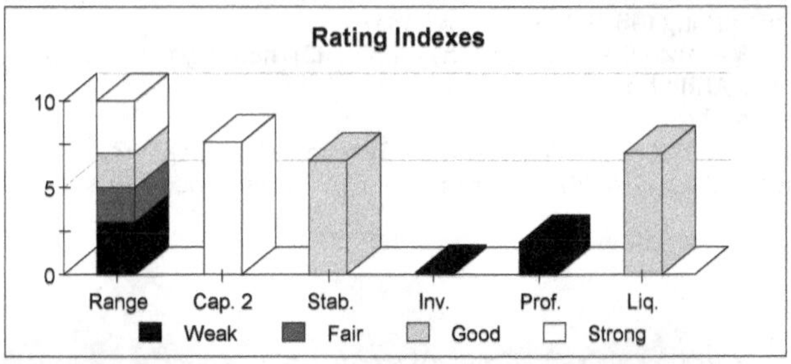

HEALTH NEW ENGLAND INC B Good

Major Rating Factors: Good capitalization index (6.8 on a scale of 0 to 10) based on excellent current risk-adjusted capital (severe loss scenario). Good overall results on stability tests (5.1). Good liquidity (6.7) with sufficient resources (cash flows and marketable investments) to handle a spike in claims.
Other Rating Factors: Fair profitability index (4.5). High quality investment portfolio (9.0).
Principal Business: Comp med (54%), Medicaid (35%), Medicare (12%)
Mem Phys: 18: 11,353 **17:** N/A **18 MLR** 89.8% **/ 18 Admin Exp** N/A
Enroll(000): Q1 19: 107 **18:** 106 **17:** 155 **Med Exp PMPM:** $473
Principal Investments: Long-term bonds (73%), cash and equiv (10%), nonaffiliate common stock (9%), affiliate common stock (4%), other (3%)
Provider Compensation ($000): Contr fee ($541,243), FFS ($195,879), bonus arrang ($29,967), capitation ($4,038)
Total Member Encounters: Phys (1,239,265), non-phys (148,890)
Group Affiliation: Baystate Health Inc
Licensed in: MA
Address: One Monarch Place Suite 1500, Springfield, MA 1144
Phone: (413) 787-4000 **Dom State:** MA **Commenced Bus:** N/A

Data Date	Rating	RACR #1	RACR #2	Total Assets ($mil)	Capital ($mil)	Net Premium ($mil)	Net Income ($mil)
3-19	B	1.21	1.01	202.7	91.7	173.8	-2.4
3-18	C	0.84	0.70	224.1	74.6	214.3	-9.9
2018	B-	1.04	0.87	185.7	80.9	771.1	6.5
2017	C	0.88	0.74	224.9	83.9	898.0	20.9
2016	D	0.53	0.44	185.2	57.5	936.9	18.1
2015	D	0.36	0.30	165.5	40.1	898.5	-20.5
2014	B-	0.84	0.70	151.0	48.0	585.0	-6.7

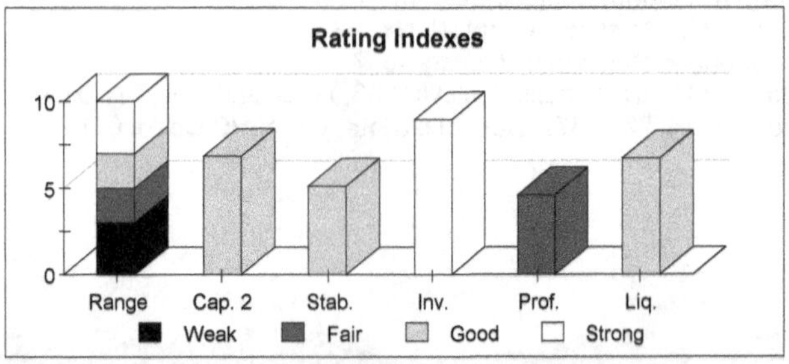

HEALTH OPTIONS INC * A- Excellent

Major Rating Factors: Excellent profitability (10.0 on a scale of 0 to 10). Strong capitalization index (10.0) based on excellent current risk-adjusted capital (severe loss scenario). Excellent overall results on stability tests (7.6) based on healthy premium and capital growth during 2018.
Other Rating Factors: Excellent liquidity (6.9) with sufficient resources (cash flows and marketable investments) to handle a spike in claims. Good quality investment portfolio (6.5).
Principal Business: Comp med (92%), Medicare (8%)
Mem Phys: 18: N/A **17:** N/A **18 MLR** 74.4% **/ 18 Admin Exp** N/A
Enroll(000): Q1 19: 883 **18:** 899 **17:** 712 **Med Exp PMPM:** $363
Principal Investments: Long-term bonds (63%), nonaffiliate common stock (19%), cash and equiv (14%), other (4%)
Provider Compensation ($000): Contr fee ($3,604,605), capitation ($266,106), FFS ($99,583), bonus arrang ($43,674)
Total Member Encounters: Phys (6,032,672), non-phys (4,656,579)
Group Affiliation: None
Licensed in: FL
Address: 4800 Deerwood Campus Parkway, Jacksonville, FL 32246
Phone: (904) 791-6111 **Dom State:** FL **Commenced Bus:** N/A

Data Date	Rating	RACR #1	RACR #2	Total Assets ($mil)	Capital ($mil)	Net Premium ($mil)	Net Income ($mil)
3-19	A-	4.01	3.34	2,415.5	1,115.3	1,473.9	99.5
3-18	B+	2.87	2.39	1,759.7	566.4	1,516.5	18.8
2018	A-	3.58	2.98	2,077.4	992.9	5,477.0	415.3
2017	B+	2.51	2.09	1,337.0	591.5	3,768.2	171.6
2016	C	3.15	2.63	879.8	412.0	2,585.6	101.0
2015	U	3.01	2.50	689.5	326.9	2,014.2	24.6
2014	N/A	N/A	N/A	560.2	241.0	1,592.5	19.6

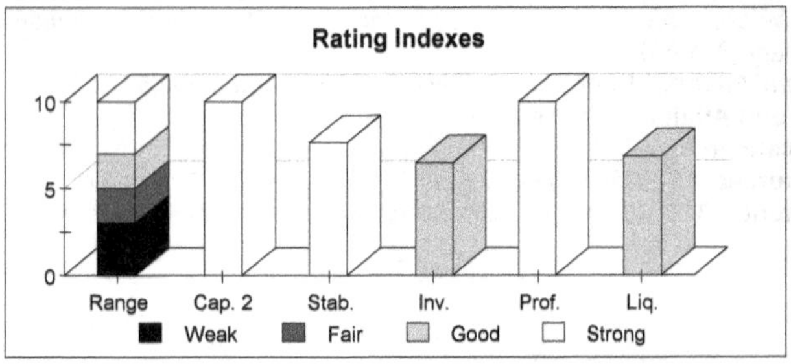

HEALTH PARTNERS PLANS INC — B — Good

Major Rating Factors: Good capitalization index (5.4 on a scale of 0 to 10) based on good current risk-adjusted capital (severe loss scenario). Fair profitability index (4.8). High quality investment portfolio (9.9).
Other Rating Factors: Excellent overall results on stability tests (7.1). Excellent liquidity (7.1) with ample operational cash flow and liquid investments
Principal Business: Medicaid (84%), Medicare (15%), comp med (1%)
Mem Phys: 18: 8,482 **17:** 8,644 **18 MLR** 81.6% **/ 18 Admin Exp** N/A
Enroll(000): Q1 19: 264 **18:** 275 **17:** 283 **Med Exp PMPM:** $475
Principal Investments: Cash and equiv (73%), long-term bonds (27%)
Provider Compensation ($000): Contr fee ($1,501,207), capitation ($66,580)
Total Member Encounters: Phys (2,214,700), non-phys (508,837)
Group Affiliation: Health Partners Plans Inc
Licensed in: PA
Address: 901 MARKET STREET SUITE 500, PHILADELPHIA, PA 19107
Phone: (215) 849-9606 **Dom State:** PA **Commenced Bus:** N/A

Data Date	Rating	RACR #1	RACR #2	Total Assets ($mil)	Capital ($mil)	Net Premium ($mil)	Net Income ($mil)
3-19	B	0.99	0.83	614.7	153.9	461.8	-5.0
3-18	B-	0.93	0.77	630.2	138.8	514.3	2.0
2018	B	1.03	0.86	556.7	159.3	1,956.2	20.2
2017	B-	0.93	0.77	579.2	138.8	1,943.5	11.0
2016	B-	0.90	0.75	620.7	126.8	1,917.0	27.3
2015	B-	0.83	0.69	469.9	96.9	1,502.9	N/A
2014	N/A	N/A	N/A	294.8	79.2	909.7	-8.5

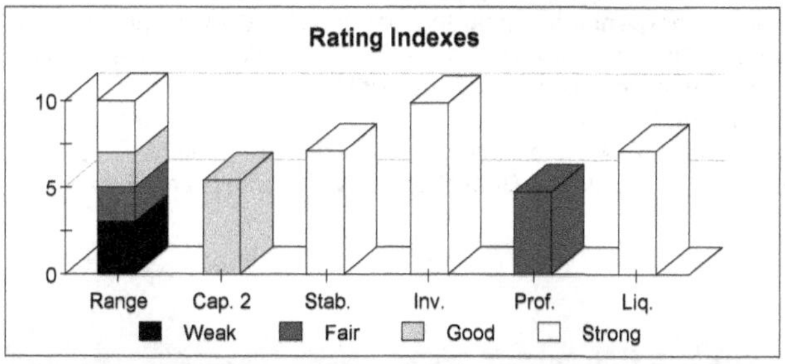

HEALTH PLAN OF CAREOREGON INC — C — Fair

Major Rating Factors: Weak profitability index (0.9 on a scale of 0 to 10). Good liquidity (6.0) with sufficient resources (cash flows and marketable investments) to handle a spike in claims. Strong capitalization (7.5) based on excellent current risk-adjusted capital (severe loss scenario).
Other Rating Factors: High quality investment portfolio (8.5).
Principal Business: Medicare (100%)
Mem Phys: 18: 1,472 **17:** 1,645 **18 MLR** 89.2% **/ 18 Admin Exp** N/A
Enroll(000): Q1 19: 11 **18:** 13 **17:** 13 **Med Exp PMPM:** $1,079
Principal Investments: Long-term bonds (85%), cash and equiv (15%)
Provider Compensation ($000): Contr fee ($125,291), FFS ($42,303)
Total Member Encounters: Phys (88,374), non-phys (66,850)
Group Affiliation: CareOregon Inc
Licensed in: OR
Address: 315 SW FIFTH AVE Ste 900, PORTLAND, OR 97204-1753
Phone: (503) 416-4100 **Dom State:** OR **Commenced Bus:** N/A

Data Date	Rating	RACR #1	RACR #2	Total Assets ($mil)	Capital ($mil)	Net Premium ($mil)	Net Income ($mil)
3-19	C	1.74	1.45	72.1	36.1	46.2	3.5
3-18	C	1.42	1.18	81.0	28.6	44.1	-1.2
2018	C	1.56	1.30	67.2	32.4	187.4	-1.5
2017	C	1.50	1.25	65.8	30.3	178.1	-15.6
2016	C	1.59	1.32	60.5	30.4	163.3	-8.6
2015	C	2.27	1.89	69.9	40.5	145.3	-16.2
2014	B	2.24	1.86	57.8	34.5	130.9	-5.0

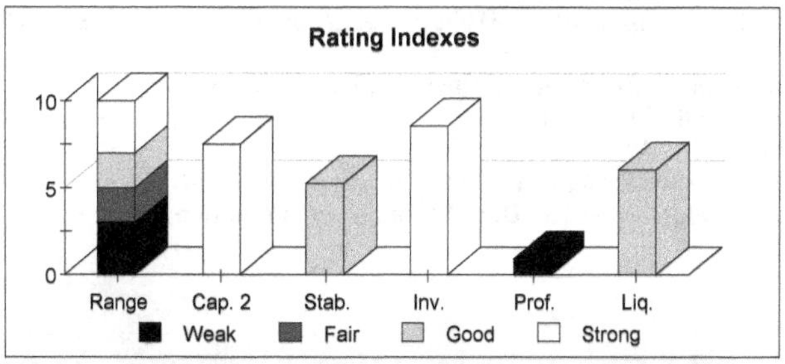

HEALTH PLAN OF NEVADA INC * — B+ — Good

Major Rating Factors: Good overall results on stability tests (6.6 on a scale of 0 to 10) despite a decline in the number of member physicians during 2019. Rating is significantly influenced by the good financial results of . Good liquidity (6.9) with sufficient resources (cash flows and marketable investments) to handle a spike in claims. Excellent profitability (9.0).
Other Rating Factors: Strong capitalization index (9.0) based on excellent current risk-adjusted capital (severe loss scenario). High quality investment portfolio (8.1).
Principal Business: Comp med (40%), Medicaid (33%), Medicare (26%)
Mem Phys: 18: 9,364 **17:** 12,639 **18 MLR** 80.3% **/ 18 Admin Exp** N/A
Enroll(000): Q1 19: 516 **18:** 581 **17:** 595 **Med Exp PMPM:** $331
Principal Investments: Long-term bonds (85%), cash and equiv (11%), real estate (3%), pref stock (1%)
Provider Compensation ($000): Contr fee ($1,006,500), capitation ($973,145), FFS ($354,549), bonus arrang ($2,210)
Total Member Encounters: Phys (3,974,299), non-phys (1,440,049)
Group Affiliation: None
Licensed in: NV
Address: 2720 NORTH TENAYA WAY, LAS VEGAS, NV 89128
Phone: (702) 242-7732 **Dom State:** NV **Commenced Bus:** N/A

Data Date	Rating	RACR #1	RACR #2	Total Assets ($mil)	Capital ($mil)	Net Premium ($mil)	Net Income ($mil)
3-19	B+	2.99	2.49	708.2	392.2	520.8	47.1
3-18	B+	2.42	2.02	808.5	293.1	751.6	1.3
2018	B+	2.67	2.22	672.4	348.1	2,943.4	201.1
2017	B+	1.80	1.50	621.9	291.3	2,763.9	155.2
2016	B	1.94	1.62	524.4	216.4	2,569.9	78.0
2015	B	2.43	2.02	505.6	226.5	2,345.0	99.5
2014	B	2.82	2.35	454.5	213.4	1,931.3	89.2

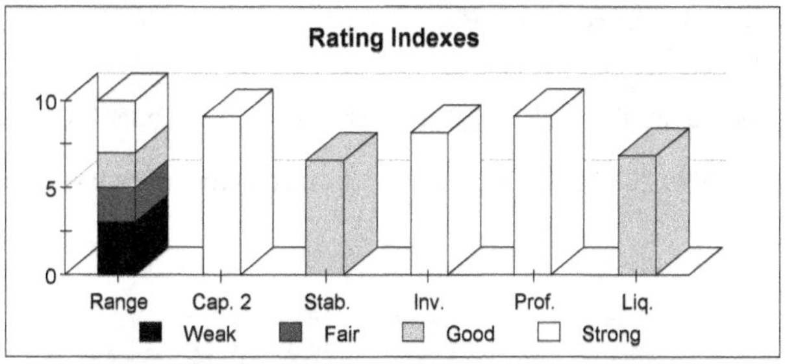

HEALTH PLAN OF WV INC — C Fair

Major Rating Factors: Fair quality investment portfolio (3.8 on a scale of 0 to 10). Fair overall results on stability tests (3.6) based on a steep decline in capital during 2018. Weak profitability index (1.1).
Other Rating Factors: Good liquidity (6.3) with sufficient resources (cash flows and marketable investments) to handle a spike in claims. Strong capitalization index (7.6) based on excellent current risk-adjusted capital (severe loss scenario).
Principal Business: Medicaid (50%), Medicare (31%), comp med (19%)
Mem Phys: 18: 22,982 **17:** 19,746 **18 MLR** 93.6% **/ 18 Admin Exp** N/A
Enroll(000): Q1 19: 113 **18:** 116 **17:** 122 **Med Exp PMPM:** $377
Principal Investments: Long-term bonds (46%), nonaffiliate common stock (22%), cash and equiv (17%), affiliate common stock (12%), real estate (2%)
Provider Compensation ($000): Contr fee ($530,112), capitation ($1,053)
Total Member Encounters: Phys (1,697,574), non-phys (496,714)
Group Affiliation: Health Plan of West Virginia Inc
Licensed in: OH, WV
Address: 52160 National Road E, Wheeling, WV 26003
Phone: (740) 695-3585 **Dom State:** WV **Commenced Bus:** N/A

Data Date	Rating	RACR #1	RACR #2	Total Assets ($mil)	Capital ($mil)	Net Premium ($mil)	Net Income ($mil)
3-19	C	1.85	1.54	240.3	131.3	148.9	-2.2
3-18	C	2.35	1.95	256.9	157.8	145.8	-3.2
2018	C	1.77	1.48	232.4	126.0	575.1	-14.9
2017	C	2.38	1.98	257.3	161.4	608.9	-4.2
2016	C	2.37	1.98	265.2	149.7	567.1	-18.0
2015	B	3.81	3.17	274.0	171.0	407.7	-8.4
2014	B+	3.60	3.00	259.9	194.8	381.5	10.9

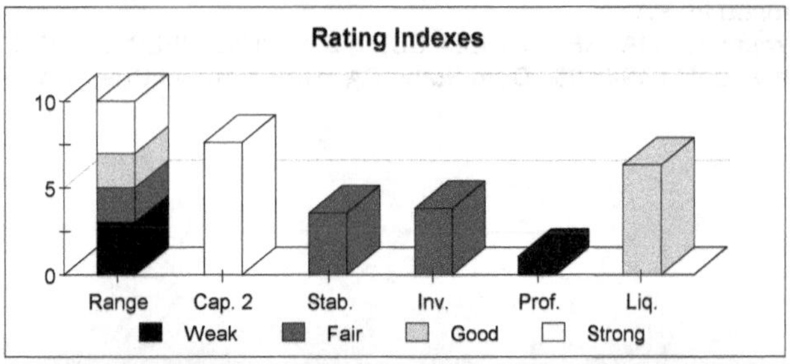

HEALTH TRADITION HEALTH PLAN — C- Fair

Major Rating Factors: Fair overall results on stability tests (4.2 on a scale of 0 to 10) based on a significant 84% decrease in enrollment during the period, a steep decline in premium revenue in 2018. Rating is significantly influenced by the fair financial results of . Weak profitability index (0.8). Strong capitalization index (7.4) based on excellent current risk-adjusted capital (severe loss scenario).
Other Rating Factors: High quality investment portfolio (9.9). Excellent liquidity (7.2) with ample operational cash flow and liquid investments.
Principal Business: Comp med (87%), med supp (13%)
Mem Phys: 18: 2,036 **17:** 1,834 **18 MLR** 90.2% **/ 18 Admin Exp** N/A
Enroll(000): Q1 19: 4 **18:** 5 **17:** 34 **Med Exp PMPM:** $389
Principal Investments: Cash and equiv (100%)
Provider Compensation ($000): Capitation ($18,397), FFS ($9,241), other ($4,066)
Total Member Encounters: Phys (38,915), non-phys (33,290)
Group Affiliation: None
Licensed in: WI
Address: 1808 East Main Street, Onalaska, WI 54650
Phone: (608) 276-4000 **Dom State:** WI **Commenced Bus:** N/A

Data Date	Rating	RACR #1	RACR #2	Total Assets ($mil)	Capital ($mil)	Net Premium ($mil)	Net Income ($mil)
3-19	C-	1.70	1.42	16.3	9.1	5.1	-0.7
3-18	C	0.80	0.66	49.7	8.5	9.8	-1.6
2018	C-	1.43	1.19	17.2	9.8	33.2	-3.9
2017	C+	0.98	0.81	54.3	10.1	150.1	-1.3
2016	B	1.20	1.00	40.6	12.1	142.2	0.0
2015	B	1.27	1.06	30.1	12.1	142.3	-0.3
2014	B	1.09	0.90	35.8	12.8	168.3	0.4

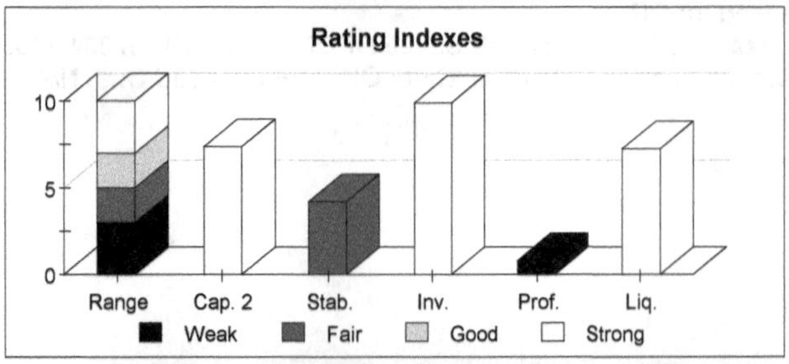

HEALTHASSURANCE PENNSYLVANIA INC — C Fair

Major Rating Factors: Fair quality investment portfolio (3.8 on a scale of 0 to 10). Weak overall results on stability tests (1.4). Rating is significantly influenced by the good financial results of . Good liquidity (6.8) with sufficient resources (cash flows and marketable investments) to handle a spike in claims.
Other Rating Factors: Excellent profitability (7.1). Strong capitalization index (8.9) based on excellent current risk-adjusted capital (severe loss scenario).
Principal Business: Medicare (97%), comp med (3%)
Mem Phys: 18: 61,931 **17:** 58,946 **18 MLR** 79.7% **/ 18 Admin Exp** N/A
Enroll(000): Q1 19: 70 **18:** 71 **17:** 74 **Med Exp PMPM:** $712
Principal Investments: Long-term bonds (97%), mortgs (4%)
Provider Compensation ($000): Contr fee ($579,998), FFS ($33,691), capitation ($11,907)
Total Member Encounters: Phys (844,344), non-phys (203,606)
Group Affiliation: None
Licensed in: PA
Address: 3721 TECPORT DRIVE PO BOX 6710, HARRISBURG, PA 17106-7103
Phone: (800) 788-6445 **Dom State:** PA **Commenced Bus:** N/A

Data Date	Rating	RACR #1	RACR #2	Total Assets ($mil)	Capital ($mil)	Net Premium ($mil)	Net Income ($mil)
3-19	C	2.86	2.38	237.0	109.2	191.7	8.0
3-18	B-	4.41	3.67	387.2	174.0	203.2	-3.8
2018	C	2.65	2.21	239.2	100.0	792.4	31.1
2017	B-	3.25	2.71	315.2	179.1	791.0	43.6
2016	B-	3.56	2.97	323.3	180.7	1,015.7	43.3
2015	B-	2.56	2.13	335.6	162.4	1,243.3	25.6
2014	B	2.77	2.31	318.7	159.8	1,124.5	19.6

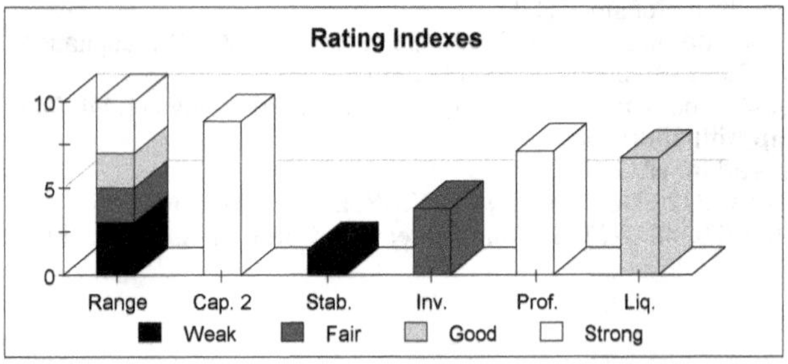

HEALTHFIRST HEALTH PLAN INC — B — Good

Major Rating Factors: Good liquidity (5.9 on a scale of 0 to 10) with sufficient resources (cash flows and marketable investments) to handle a spike in claims. Fair profitability index (4.4). Strong capitalization index (7.5) based on excellent current risk-adjusted capital (severe loss scenario).
Other Rating Factors: High quality investment portfolio (7.6). Excellent overall results on stability tests (8.3) based on steady enrollment growth, averaging 6% over the past five years.
Principal Business: Medicare (100%)
Mem Phys: 18: 39,287 **17:** 34,594 **18 MLR** 84.9% **/ 18 Admin Exp** N/A
Enroll(000): Q1 19: 163 **18:** 158 **17:** 149 **Med Exp PMPM:** $1,203
Principal Investments: Long-term bonds (90%), nonaffiliate common stock (7%), cash and equiv (2%), affiliate common stock (1%)
Provider Compensation ($000): Contr fee ($2,087,646), FFS ($72,481), capitation ($47,479)
Total Member Encounters: Phys (4,928,771), non-phys (5,738,967)
Group Affiliation: HealthFirst Inc
Licensed in: NY
Address: 100 Church St, New York, NY 10007
Phone: (212) 801-6000 **Dom State:** NY **Commenced Bus:** N/A

Data Date	Rating	RACR #1	RACR #2	Total Assets ($mil)	Capital ($mil)	Net Premium ($mil)	Net Income ($mil)
3-19	B	1.75	1.46	888.6	358.8	732.8	17.8
3-18	C+	1.64	1.37	1,028.8	311.6	648.5	8.4
2018	B	1.64	1.36	775.9	339.0	2,620.6	28.7
2017	C+	1.56	1.30	751.4	299.0	2,283.8	-3.6
2016	B-	1.38	1.15	782.8	262.5	2,238.2	6.5
2015	B-	1.45	1.21	614.3	241.5	2,022.5	5.8
2014	B-	1.43	1.19	548.7	206.9	1,775.9	-32.3

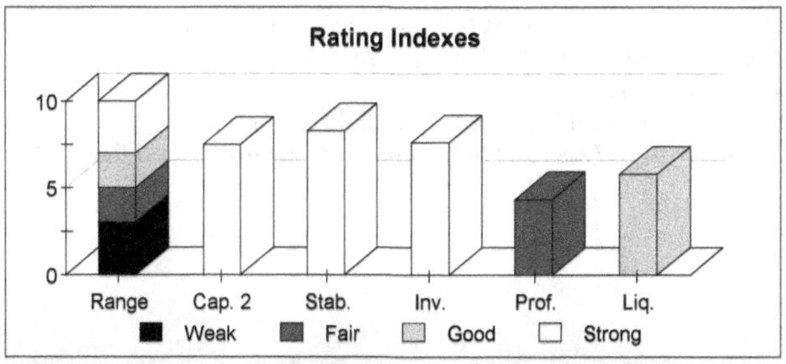

HEALTHFIRST INSURANCE CO — C+ — Fair

Major Rating Factors: Fair quality investment portfolio (4.4 on a scale of 0 to 10). Weak profitability index (0.0). Strong capitalization (9.7) based on excellent current risk-adjusted capital (severe loss scenario).
Other Rating Factors: Excellent liquidity (8.1) with ample operational cash flow and liquid investments.
Principal Business: Comp med (100%)
Mem Phys: 18: N/A **17:** N/A **18 MLR** 87.2% **/ 18 Admin Exp** N/A
Enroll(000): Q1 19: 8 **18:** 9 **17:** 4 **Med Exp PMPM:** $353
Principal Investments: Cash and equiv (99%), long-term bonds (1%)
Provider Compensation ($000): Contr fee ($22,875), FFS ($2,350), capitation ($435)
Total Member Encounters: Phys (20,086), non-phys (26,108)
Group Affiliation: HealthFirst Inc
Licensed in: NY
Address: , New York, NY 10007
Phone: (212) 801-6000 **Dom State:** NY **Commenced Bus:** N/A

Data Date	Rating	RACR #1	RACR #2	Total Assets ($mil)	Capital ($mil)	Net Premium ($mil)	Net Income ($mil)
3-19	C+	3.52	2.93	46.1	14.3	13.7	-0.7
3-18	N/A	N/A	N/A	33.2	18.7	7.4	-1.1
2018	C+	3.62	3.01	40.1	14.8	34.2	-5.3
2017	N/A	N/A	N/A	24.5	19.6	1.4	-5.4
2016	N/A	N/A	N/A	25.1	25.0	N/A	N/A
2015	N/A	N/A	N/A	N/A	N/A	N/A	N/A
2014	N/A	N/A	N/A	N/A	N/A	N/A	N/A

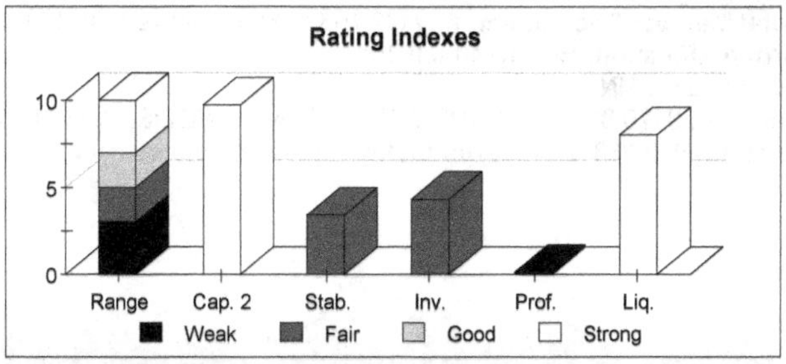

HEALTHKEEPERS INC — B — Good

Major Rating Factors: Good liquidity (6.9 on a scale of 0 to 10) with sufficient resources (cash flows and marketable investments) to handle a spike in claims. Fair quality investment portfolio (3.0). Excellent profitability (8.9).
Other Rating Factors: Strong capitalization index (9.0) based on excellent current risk-adjusted capital (severe loss scenario). Excellent overall results on stability tests (7.0). Rating is significantly influenced by the good financial results of Anthem Inc.
Principal Business: Medicaid (57%), comp med (39%), Medicare (4%)
Mem Phys: 18: 29,248 **17:** 28,352 **18 MLR** 83.4% **/ 18 Admin Exp** N/A
Enroll(000): Q1 19: 682 **18:** 533 **17:** 670 **Med Exp PMPM:** $442
Principal Investments: Long-term bonds (31%), nonaffiliate common stock (22%), cash and equiv (1%), other (46%)
Provider Compensation ($000): Bonus arrang ($1,698,912), contr fee ($742,643), FFS ($383,119), capitation ($83,205)
Total Member Encounters: Phys (3,834,216), non-phys (3,804,736)
Group Affiliation: Anthem Inc
Licensed in: VA
Address: 2015 STAPLES MILL ROAD, RICHMOND, VA 23230
Phone: (804) 354-7000 **Dom State:** VA **Commenced Bus:** N/A

Data Date	Rating	RACR #1	RACR #2	Total Assets ($mil)	Capital ($mil)	Net Premium ($mil)	Net Income ($mil)
3-19	B	2.98	2.48	1,568.7	665.7	1,232.8	106.9
3-18	B	3.08	2.57	1,193.9	635.6	857.3	38.7
2018	B	2.57	2.15	1,234.6	566.9	3,484.9	146.8
2017	B	2.43	2.02	1,188.2	595.1	3,460.7	183.9
2016	B+	2.46	2.05	1,132.9	442.7	3,120.5	123.8
2015	A-	2.17	1.81	896.5	340.7	2,806.1	46.2
2014	A-	2.50	2.09	716.9	281.5	2,081.4	65.3

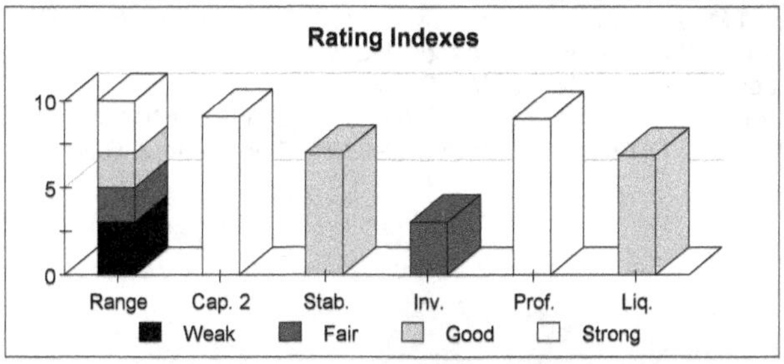

HEALTHNOW NY INC B Good

Major Rating Factors: Good liquidity (6.8 on a scale of 0 to 10) with sufficient resources (cash flows and marketable investments) to handle a spike in claims. Fair profitability index (4.3). Strong capitalization (10.0) based on excellent current risk-adjusted capital (severe loss scenario).
Other Rating Factors: High quality investment portfolio (8.2).
Principal Business: Comp med (59%), Medicare (28%), Medicaid (8%), FEHB (3%)
Mem Phys: 18: 25,306 **17:** 24,095 **18 MLR** 85.4% **/ 18 Admin Exp** N/A
Enroll(000): Q1 19: 414 **18:** 402 **17:** 398 **Med Exp PMPM:** $471
Principal Investments: Long-term bonds (79%), nonaffiliate common stock (17%), cash and equiv (1%), pref stock (1%), other (2%)
Provider Compensation ($000): Contr fee ($2,011,979), capitation ($236,962)
Total Member Encounters: Phys (2,955,321), non-phys (1,269,129)
Group Affiliation: HealthNow Systems Inc
Licensed in: NY
Address: 257 West Genesee St, Buffalo, NY 14202
Phone: (716) 887-6900 **Dom State:** NY **Commenced Bus:** N/A

Data Date	Rating	RACR #1	RACR #2	Total Assets ($mil)	Capital ($mil)	Net Premium ($mil)	Net Income ($mil)
3-19	B	4.23	3.53	1,194.8	696.1	706.4	64.7
3-18	B-	3.60	3.00	1,219.3	587.5	657.7	-8.7
2018	B-	3.71	3.09	1,113.3	624.6	2,647.1	47.0
2017	B-	3.78	3.15	1,072.5	611.7	2,484.3	54.9
2016	C+	3.37	2.81	1,062.3	541.5	2,311.2	4.2
2015	C+	3.53	2.94	1,037.8	544.4	2,242.3	63.8
2014	B-	2.64	2.20	1,041.3	486.5	2,443.8	-53.2

Rating Indexes

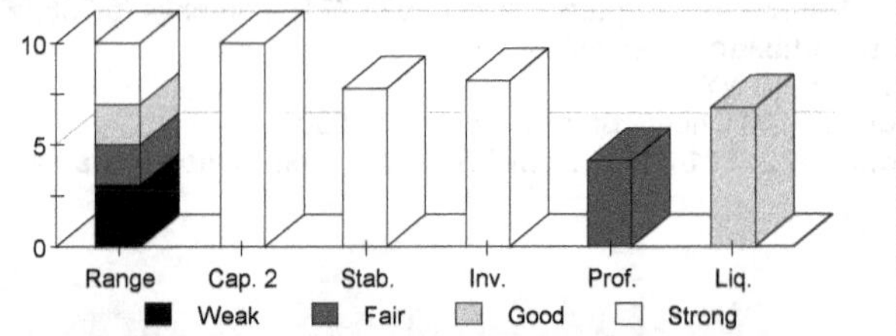

HEALTHPARTNERS * B+ Good

Major Rating Factors: Good quality investment portfolio (4.9 on a scale of 0 to 10). Strong capitalization index (9.7) based on excellent current risk-adjusted capital (severe loss scenario). Excellent overall results on stability tests (7.6).
Other Rating Factors: Excellent liquidity (7.2) with ample operational cash flow and liquid investments. Fair profitability index (4.2).
Principal Business: Medicaid (56%), comp med (40%), dental (3%)
Mem Phys: 18: 74,128 **17:** 64,829 **18 MLR** 90.1% **/ 18 Admin Exp** N/A
Enroll(000): Q1 19: 324 **18:** 305 **17:** 330 **Med Exp PMPM:** $466
Principal Investments: Affiliate common stock (38%), cash and equiv (25%), long-term bonds (23%), nonaffiliate common stock (7%), other (6%)
Provider Compensation ($000): Bonus arrang ($1,235,233), contr fee ($466,962)
Total Member Encounters: Phys (2,708,158), non-phys (391,141)
Group Affiliation: HealthPartners Inc
Licensed in: MN
Address: 8170 33RD AVENUE SOUTH, MINNEAPOLIS, MN 55440-1309
Phone: (952) 883-6000 **Dom State:** MN **Commenced Bus:** N/A

Data Date	Rating	RACR #1	RACR #2	Total Assets ($mil)	Capital ($mil)	Net Premium ($mil)	Net Income ($mil)
3-19	B+	3.55	2.96	1,327.1	982.4	513.5	12.9
3-18	B+	3.24	2.70	1,292.3	965.6	475.5	-1.4
2018	B+	3.42	2.85	1,358.7	944.8	1,950.3	57.6
2017	B+	3.07	2.56	1,300.1	940.1	1,696.6	-36.4
2016	A+	3.40	2.83	1,179.5	911.4	1,371.7	22.2
2015	A+	3.89	3.24	1,247.4	938.1	1,425.0	76.8
2014	A	3.60	3.00	1,236.0	908.6	1,350.2	16.8

Rating Indexes

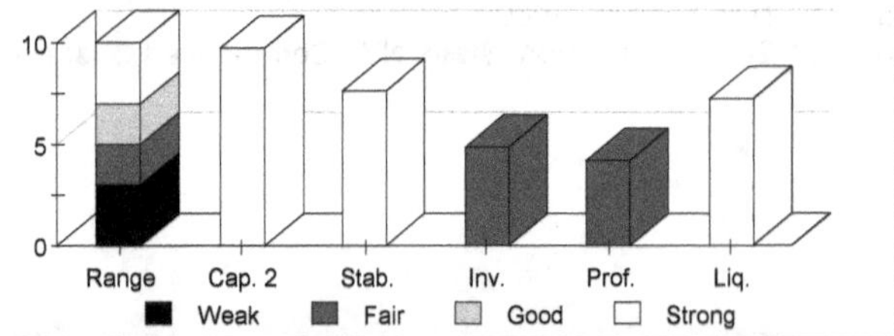

HEALTHPARTNERS INS CO * B+ Good

Major Rating Factors: Good liquidity (6.9 on a scale of 0 to 10) with sufficient resources (cash flows and marketable investments) to handle a spike in claims. Strong capitalization (10.0) based on excellent current risk-adjusted capital (severe loss scenario). High quality investment portfolio (9.9).
Other Rating Factors: Fair profitability index (4.8).
Principal Business: Comp med (89%), other (10%)
Mem Phys: 18: 74,128 **17:** 64,829 **18 MLR** 84.2% **/ 18 Admin Exp** N/A
Enroll(000): Q1 19: 687 **18:** 682 **17:** 702 **Med Exp PMPM:** $99
Principal Investments: Long-term bonds (57%), cash and equiv (32%), nonaffiliate common stock (11%)
Provider Compensation ($000): Bonus arrang ($473,240), contr fee ($369,724)
Total Member Encounters: Phys (1,007,770), non-phys (126,884)
Group Affiliation: HealthPartners Inc
Licensed in: IA, MN, NE, ND, SD, WI
Address: 8170 33RD Ave S, MINNEAPOLIS, MN 55440-1309
Phone: (952) 883-6000 **Dom State:** MN **Commenced Bus:** N/A

Data Date	Rating	RACR #1	RACR #2	Total Assets ($mil)	Capital ($mil)	Net Premium ($mil)	Net Income ($mil)
3-19	B+	3.74	3.11	416.8	258.2	270.3	18.8
3-18	B	3.11	2.59	429.9	225.5	247.3	22.9
2018	B+	3.39	2.83	375.8	233.2	992.7	31.8
2017	B	2.03	1.69	381.7	202.0	1,075.2	38.6
2016	B	2.33	1.94	372.7	159.1	1,053.8	-11.8
2015	B+	2.35	1.96	331.1	148.8	1,014.0	-10.5
2014	A-	2.89	2.41	319.0	160.5	943.2	10.1

Rating Indexes

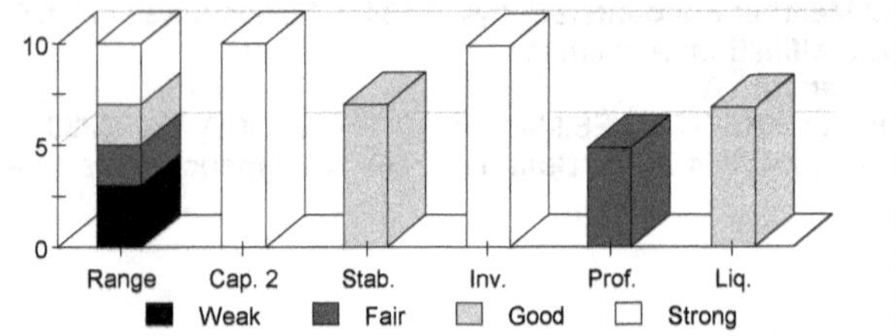

HEALTHPARTNERS UNITYPOINT HLTH — D- — Weak

Major Rating Factors: Weak profitability index (0.9 on a scale of 0 to 10). Low quality investment portfolio (0.0). Good liquidity (6.2) with sufficient resources (cash flows and marketable investments) to handle a spike in claims.
Other Rating Factors: Strong capitalization (7.7) based on excellent current risk-adjusted capital (severe loss scenario).
Principal Business: Comp med (57%), Medicare (17%)
Mem Phys: 18: 74,128 **17:** 64,829 **18 MLR** 77.5% **/ 18 Admin Exp** N/A
Enroll(000): Q1 19: 57 **18:** 8 **17:** 1 **Med Exp PMPM:** $461
Principal Investments: Cash and equiv (100%)
Provider Compensation ($000): Contr fee ($29,489), bonus arrang ($1,038)
Total Member Encounters: Phys (50,084), non-phys (8,528)
Group Affiliation: HealthPartners UnityPoint Health Inc
Licensed in: IL, IA
Address: 1776 WEST LAKES PARKWAY #100, WEST DES MOINES, IA 50266
Phone: (515) 695-3801 **Dom State:** IA **Commenced Bus:** N/A

Data Date	Rating	RACR #1	RACR #2	Total Assets ($mil)	Capital ($mil)	Net Premium ($mil)	Net Income ($mil)
3-19	D-	1.91	1.59	30.2	12.1	15.3	-1.3
3-18	N/A	N/A	N/A	25.3	14.1	6.8	-0.8
2018	U	2.12	1.77	22.7	13.4	45.1	-5.6
2017	N/A	N/A	N/A	21.7	15.0	15.1	-3.4
2016	N/A	N/A	N/A	19.2	18.4	N/A	-2.5
2015	N/A	N/A	N/A	7.0	7.0	N/A	N/A
2014	N/A	N/A	N/A	N/A	N/A	N/A	N/A

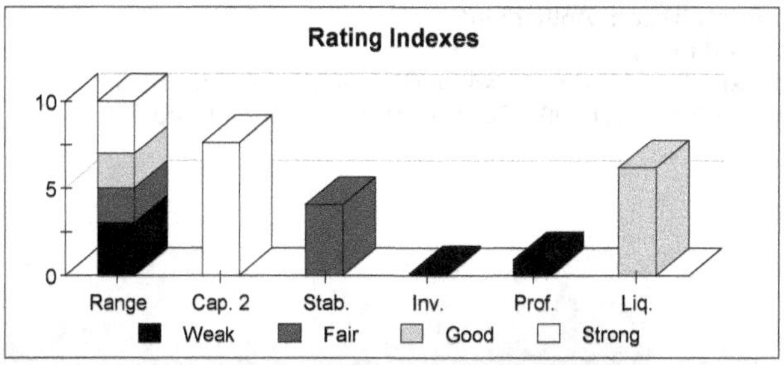

HEALTHSPRING L&H INS CO — B- — Good

Major Rating Factors: Fair profitability index (4.3 on a scale of 0 to 10). Fair quality investment portfolio (4.7). Good liquidity (6.5) with sufficient resources (cash flows and marketable investments) to handle a spike in claims.
Other Rating Factors: Strong capitalization (8.8) based on excellent current risk-adjusted capital (severe loss scenario).
Principal Business: Medicare (77%), Medicaid (23%)
Mem Phys: 18: 57,688 **17:** 22,539 **18 MLR** 81.6% **/ 18 Admin Exp** N/A
Enroll(000): Q1 19: 301 **18:** 299 **17:** 300 **Med Exp PMPM:** $948
Principal Investments: Long-term bonds (101%)
Provider Compensation ($000): FFS ($2,214,733), capitation ($921,881), contr fee ($249,320)
Total Member Encounters: Phys (10,450,405), non-phys (2,763,960)
Group Affiliation: None
Licensed in: All states except CA, PR
Address: 2900 N LOOP WEST Ste 1300, HOUSTON, TX 77092
Phone: (615) 291-7000 **Dom State:** TX **Commenced Bus:** N/A

Data Date	Rating	RACR #1	RACR #2	Total Assets ($mil)	Capital ($mil)	Net Premium ($mil)	Net Income ($mil)
3-19	B-	2.77	2.31	1,154.9	610.3	1,140.0	49.3
3-18	C+	4.59	3.83	1,408.6	549.8	1,050.6	-13.6
2018	B-	2.56	2.14	1,060.3	562.7	4,142.2	90.3
2017	C+	1.66	1.39	1,047.7	550.7	4,087.0	-21.7
2016	B	2.16	1.80	602.8	280.2	2,367.0	-50.8
2015	B	2.78	2.32	614.0	327.4	2,213.5	46.1
2014	B-	3.04	2.54	586.1	328.7	2,205.4	-7.9

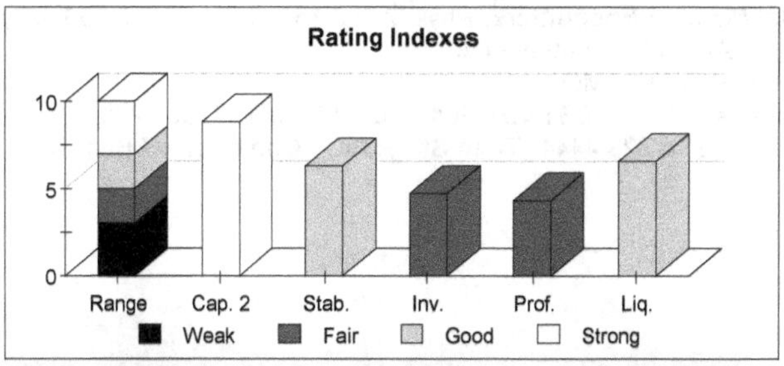

HEALTHSPRING OF FLORIDA INC — B — Good

Major Rating Factors: Good quality investment portfolio (5.6 on a scale of 0 to 10). Good liquidity (6.3) with sufficient resources (cash flows and marketable investments) to handle a spike in claims. Excellent profitability (8.0).
Other Rating Factors: Strong capitalization (8.1) based on excellent current risk-adjusted capital (severe loss scenario).
Principal Business: Medicare (100%)
Mem Phys: 18: 1,822 **17:** 2,192 **18 MLR** 83.4% **/ 18 Admin Exp** N/A
Enroll(000): Q1 19: 48 **18:** 47 **17:** 47 **Med Exp PMPM:** $1,219
Principal Investments: Long-term bonds (102%)
Provider Compensation ($000): Capitation ($390,577), contr fee ($197,214), FFS ($113,441)
Total Member Encounters: Phys (1,048,248), non-phys (610,285)
Group Affiliation: Cigna Corporation
Licensed in: FL
Address: 8600 NW 41ST St Ste 201, DORAL, FL 33166
Phone: (305) 229-7461 **Dom State:** FL **Commenced Bus:** N/A

Data Date	Rating	RACR #1	RACR #2	Total Assets ($mil)	Capital ($mil)	Net Premium ($mil)	Net Income ($mil)
3-19	B	2.23	1.86	150.0	82.7	213.2	7.8
3-18	B	1.76	1.47	231.5	62.8	211.7	-1.6
2018	B	2.31	1.92	153.3	85.5	826.4	26.2
2017	B+	1.86	1.55	169.2	95.9	776.1	6.6
2016	B+	2.42	2.02	157.0	89.5	866.7	26.9
2015	B	1.62	1.35	144.1	62.3	886.0	9.2
2014	B	1.56	1.30	123.7	54.7	784.0	6.4

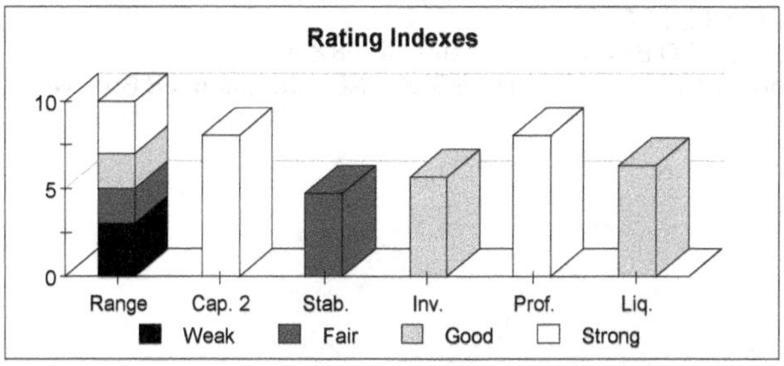

HEALTHSUN HEALTH PLANS INC — B- — Good

Major Rating Factors: Fair quality investment portfolio (3.5 on a scale of 0 to 10). Excellent profitability (7.5). Strong capitalization (9.0) based on excellent current risk-adjusted capital (severe loss scenario).
Other Rating Factors: Excellent liquidity (7.0) with sufficient resources (cash flows and marketable investments) to handle a spike in claims.
Principal Business: Medicare (100%)
Mem Phys: 18: 1,716 **17:** N/A **18 MLR** 84.0% **/ 18 Admin Exp** N/A
Enroll(000): Q1 19: 47 **18:** 47 **17:** 40 **Med Exp PMPM:** $1,440
Principal Investments: Cash and equiv (39%), long-term bonds (38%), other (23%)
Provider Compensation ($000): Capitation ($752,601)
Total Member Encounters: Phys (980,014), non-phys (629,516)
Group Affiliation: Anthem Inc
Licensed in: FL
Address: 3250 MARY ST #400, COCONUT GROVE, FL 33133
Phone: (305) 448-8100 **Dom State:** FL **Commenced Bus:** N/A

Data Date	Rating	RACR #1	RACR #2	Total Assets ($mil)	Capital ($mil)	Net Premium ($mil)	Net Income ($mil)
3-19	B-	2.96	2.46	214.7	94.8	267.5	-0.3
3-18	C-	N/A	N/A	275.8	66.8	216.8	-4.6
2018	B-	2.97	2.48	249.6	95.3	897.0	44.0
2017	C-	N/A	N/A	186.0	71.5	796.7	18.7
2016	N/A	N/A	N/A	134.8	29.9	709.0	N/A
2015	C-	0.62	0.51	130.1	30.8	695.7	23.5
2014	C	0.64	0.53	74.0	23.3	503.8	20.7

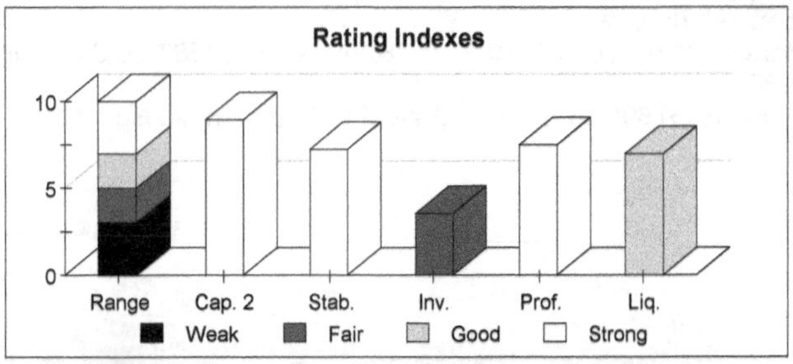

HEALTHY ALLIANCE LIFE INS CO — B — Good

Major Rating Factors: Good quality investment portfolio (6.8 on a scale of 0 to 10). Excellent profitability (8.7). Strong capitalization (10.0) based on excellent current risk-adjusted capital (severe loss scenario).
Other Rating Factors: Excellent liquidity (6.9) with sufficient resources (cash flows and marketable investments) to handle a spike in claims.
Principal Business: Comp med (75%), FEHB (18%), med supp (4%), dental (1%), other (2%)
Mem Phys: 18: 23,445 **17:** 22,014 **18 MLR** 77.7% **/ 18 Admin Exp** N/A
Enroll(000): Q1 19: 693 **18:** 706 **17:** 815 **Med Exp PMPM:** $208
Principal Investments: Long-term bonds (82%), other (17%)
Provider Compensation ($000): Bonus arrang ($1,218,852), contr fee ($337,809), FFS ($258,305), other ($404)
Total Member Encounters: Phys (2,286,155), non-phys (2,256,422)
Group Affiliation: Anthem Inc
Licensed in: KS, MO
Address: 1831 CHESTNUT St, ST. LOUIS, MO 63103-2275
Phone: (314) 923-4444 **Dom State:** MO **Commenced Bus:** N/A

Data Date	Rating	RACR #1	RACR #2	Total Assets ($mil)	Capital ($mil)	Net Premium ($mil)	Net Income ($mil)
3-19	B	4.00	3.33	1,044.1	439.4	570.4	77.3
3-18	A	4.38	3.65	1,173.4	535.6	581.1	46.7
2018	B	3.35	2.79	985.6	365.8	2,303.2	198.6
2017	A	3.23	2.69	1,087.1	489.4	2,566.9	194.3
2016	A-	4.13	3.44	890.1	420.4	1,942.0	142.8
2015	A-	4.25	3.54	829.4	379.6	1,811.5	106.3
2014	A-	4.50	3.75	870.8	397.8	1,872.9	109.8

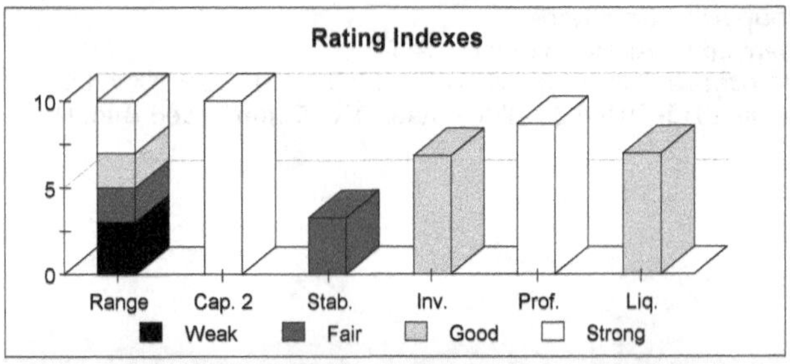

HEARTLANDPLAINS HEALTH — E — Very Weak

Major Rating Factors: Weak profitability index (1.1 on a scale of 0 to 10). Good liquidity (6.9) with sufficient resources (cash flows and marketable investments) to handle a spike in claims. Strong capitalization (10.0) based on excellent current risk-adjusted capital (severe loss scenario).
Other Rating Factors: High quality investment portfolio (9.9).
Principal Business: Medicare (100%)
Mem Phys: 18: 4,906 **17:** 4,806 **18 MLR** 93.2% **/ 18 Admin Exp** N/A
Enroll(000): Q1 19: N/A **18:** 1 **17:** 1 **Med Exp PMPM:** $701
Principal Investments: Long-term bonds (84%), cash and equiv (16%)
Provider Compensation ($000): Contr fee ($4,724), capitation ($77)
Total Member Encounters: Phys (5,292), non-phys (4,787)
Group Affiliation: None
Licensed in: NE
Address: PO Box 31457, Omaha, NE 68124
Phone: (866) 789-7747 **Dom State:** NE **Commenced Bus:** N/A

Data Date	Rating	RACR #1	RACR #2	Total Assets ($mil)	Capital ($mil)	Net Premium ($mil)	Net Income ($mil)
3-19	E	4.81	4.00	4.1	3.5	0.0	-0.1
3-18	E-	N/A	N/A	5.3	3.8	1.2	0.1
2018	E	4.92	4.10	4.3	3.6	5.0	0.0
2017	E-	N/A	N/A	5.5	3.6	5.7	N/A
2016	E-	1.59	1.33	4.6	1.7	6.3	-2.0
2015	N/A	N/A	N/A	4.4	2.2	3.5	-1.9
2014	N/A	N/A	N/A	3.3	3.3	N/A	N/A

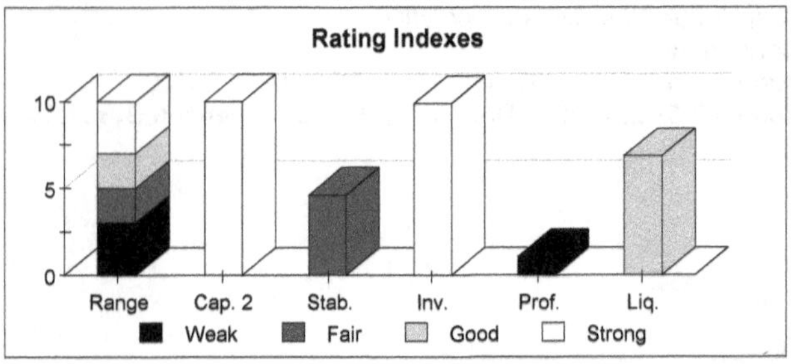

HENNEPIN HEALTH B Good

Major Rating Factors: Good overall profitability index (5.3 on a scale of 0 to 10). Good overall results on stability tests (6.1) despite a decline in enrollment during 2018. Strong capitalization index (7.9) based on excellent current risk-adjusted capital (severe loss scenario).
Other Rating Factors: High quality investment portfolio (8.5). Excellent liquidity (7.3) with ample operational cash flow and liquid investments.
Principal Business: Medicaid (96%), other (4%)
Mem Phys: 18: 1,628 **17:** 1,725 **18 MLR** 85.7% **/ 18 Admin Exp** N/A
Enroll(000): Q1 19: 24 **18:** 26 **17:** 31 **Med Exp PMPM:** $610
Principal Investments: Cash and equiv (99%), real estate (1%)
Provider Compensation ($000): Bonus arrang ($108,486), contr fee ($100,488)
Total Member Encounters: Phys (132,780), non-phys (115,118)
Group Affiliation: None
Licensed in: MN
Address: 400 South 4th Street Suite 201, Minneapolis, MN 55415
Phone: (612) 596-1036 **Dom State:** MN **Commenced Bus:** N/A

Data Date	Rating	RACR #1	RACR #2	Total Assets ($mil)	Capital ($mil)	Net Premium ($mil)	Net Income ($mil)
3-19	B	2.04	1.70	81.1	47.7	51.7	0.8
3-18	C	1.79	1.49	83.4	41.6	58.7	2.0
2018	B-	2.00	1.66	100.0	46.8	235.0	6.5
2017	C	1.71	1.42	105.6	39.8	231.5	4.8
2016	C-	2.60	2.17	72.1	34.6	127.0	0.6
2015	C-	2.57	2.14	93.0	34.1	143.6	-3.4
2014	N/A	N/A	N/A	86.7	28.5	158.2	-0.3

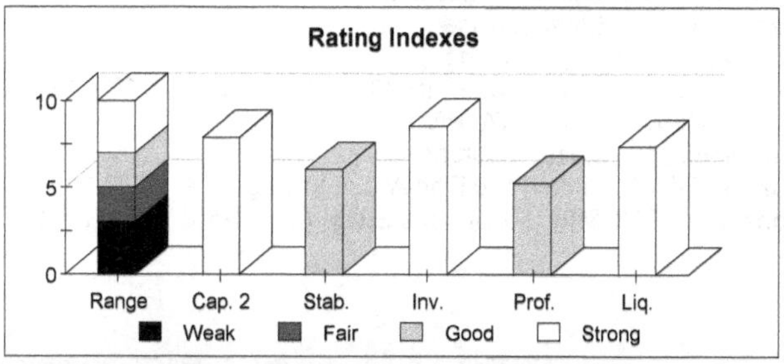

HERITAGE PROVIDER NETWORK INC D Weak

Major Rating Factors: Fair capitalization index (4.6 on a scale of 0 to 10) based on weak current risk-adjusted capital (moderate loss scenario). Good overall profitability index (6.8). Good overall results on stability tests (6.4) based on steady enrollment growth, averaging 9% over the past five years.
Other Rating Factors: Good liquidity (6.9) with sufficient resources (cash flows and marketable investments) to handle a spike in claims.
Principal Business: Managed care (100%)
Mem Phys: 18: N/A **17:** N/A **18 MLR** 93.9% **/ 18 Admin Exp** N/A
Enroll(000): Q1 19: 691 **18:** 697 **17:** 659 **Med Exp PMPM:** $326
Principal Investments ($000): Cash and equiv ($428,954)
Provider Compensation ($000): None
Total Member Encounters: N/A
Group Affiliation: Heritage California Medical Groups
Licensed in: CA
Address: 1 Park Plaza Suite 450, Irvine, CA 92614
Phone: (502) 580-1575 **Dom State:** CA **Commenced Bus:** May 1996

Data Date	Rating	RACR #1	RACR #2	Total Assets ($mil)	Capital ($mil)	Net Premium ($mil)	Net Income ($mil)
3-19	D	0.72	0.45	618.9	160.3	737.7	1.5
3-18	D	0.55	0.34	529.9	121.5	707.1	0.2
2018	D	0.70	0.43	623.5	155.7	2,866.4	4.1
2017	D	0.54	0.33	528.0	120.3	2,734.4	2.5
2016	D	0.66	0.41	575.3	127.8	2,432.2	2.3
2015	D	0.69	0.42	661.8	131.5	2,380.8	14.5
2014	D	0.72	0.44	496.1	123.4	2,098.1	17.7

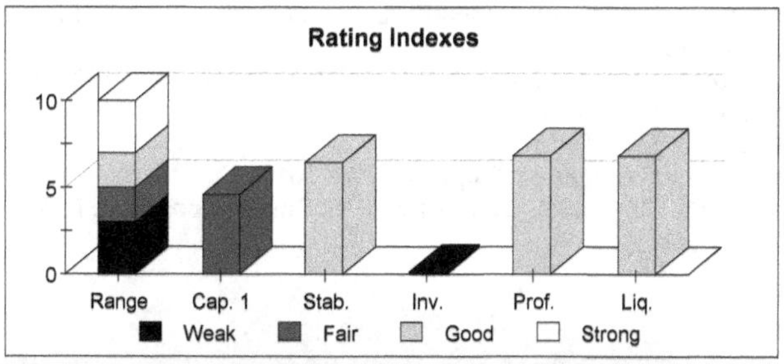

HIGHMARK BCBSD INC B Good

Major Rating Factors: Good overall profitability index (5.4 on a scale of 0 to 10). Good quality investment portfolio (6.5). Strong capitalization (10.0) based on excellent current risk-adjusted capital (severe loss scenario).
Other Rating Factors: Excellent liquidity (7.0) with ample operational cash flow and liquid investments.
Principal Business: Comp med (77%), FEHB (20%), med supp (2%)
Mem Phys: 18: 15,418 **17:** 10,885 **18 MLR** 79.3% **/ 18 Admin Exp** N/A
Enroll(000): Q1 19: 108 **18:** 106 **17:** 104 **Med Exp PMPM:** $442
Principal Investments: Long-term bonds (65%), nonaffiliate common stock (25%), cash and equiv (8%), other (2%)
Provider Compensation ($000): Contr fee ($552,456), FFS ($17,259), capitation ($1,454), bonus arrang ($823)
Total Member Encounters: Phys (773,063), non-phys (594,764)
Group Affiliation: None
Licensed in: DE
Address: 800 Delaware Ave, Wilmington, DE 19801
Phone: (302) 421-3000 **Dom State:** DE **Commenced Bus:** N/A

Data Date	Rating	RACR #1	RACR #2	Total Assets ($mil)	Capital ($mil)	Net Premium ($mil)	Net Income ($mil)
3-19	B	8.31	6.93	619.6	345.3	192.6	37.4
3-18	B	8.16	6.80	557.4	293.0	190.3	41.3
2018	B	7.34	6.12	543.8	304.2	724.5	85.2
2017	B	5.23	4.36	442.7	253.9	634.6	58.4
2016	B-	3.61	3.01	363.0	149.6	705.8	19.1
2015	B-	3.13	2.61	336.9	120.8	638.8	-26.5
2014	B	4.14	3.45	335.7	138.4	583.2	-4.2

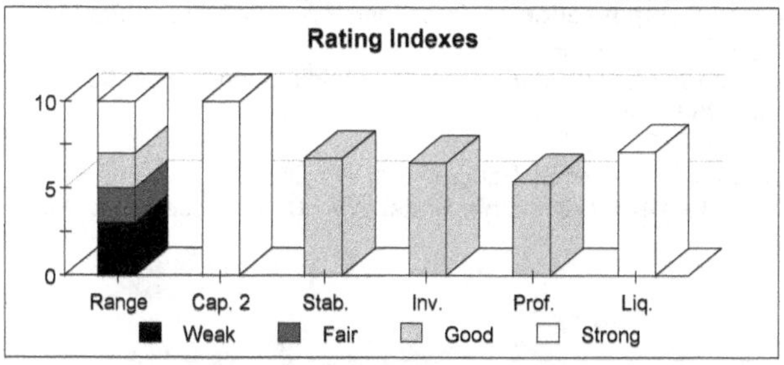

HIGHMARK CASUALTY INS CO — C — Fair

Major Rating Factors: Fair overall results on stability tests (3.1 on a scale of 0 to 10) including fair financial strength of affiliated Highmark Inc. History of adequate reserve strength (6.7) as reserves have been consistently at an acceptable level.

Other Rating Factors: Good liquidity (6.1) with sufficient resources (cash flows and marketable investments) to handle a spike in claims. Strong long-term capitalization index (10.0) based on excellent current risk adjusted capital (severe and moderate loss scenarios), despite some fluctuation in capital levels. Excellent profitability (7.8) with operating gains in each of the last five years.

Principal Business: Group accident & health (100%).

Principal Investments: Investment grade bonds (76%), misc. investments (12%), and non investment grade bonds (12%).

Investments in Affiliates: None

Group Affiliation: Highmark Inc

Licensed in: AL, FL, GA, ID, IL, IN, KS, KY, MD, MI, MS, MO, NV, NJ, NM, NC, OR, PA, SC, TX, UT, VA, WA, WV

Commenced Business: February 1978

Address: Fifth Ave Place 120 Fifth Ave, Pittsburgh, PA 15222-3099

Phone: (800) 328-5433 **Domicile State:** PA **NAIC Code:** 35599

Data Date	Rating	RACR #1	RACR #2	Loss Ratio %	Total Assets ($mil)	Capital ($mil)	Net Premium ($mil)	Net Income ($mil)
3-19	C	5.22	3.03	N/A	317.9	194.9	69.6	4.0
3-18	C	6.36	3.62	N/A	277.5	185.4	56.7	0.6
2018	C	5.92	3.40	69.1	293.1	189.3	244.9	15.5
2017	C	7.00	3.98	78.9	268.1	185.3	185.7	6.1
2016	C	4.28	2.84	74.5	274.7	179.2	218.0	1.9
2015	C	2.56	1.77	76.6	457.2	173.1	282.9	7.2
2014	C	2.11	1.47	80.1	439.0	166.3	298.4	5.0

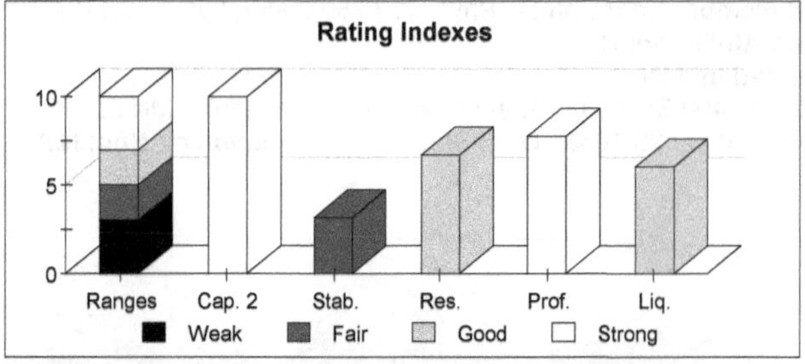

HIGHMARK INC — C — Fair

Major Rating Factors: Fair profitability index (3.4 on a scale of 0 to 10). Fair quality investment portfolio (3.6). Strong capitalization (10.0) based on excellent current risk-adjusted capital (severe loss scenario).

Other Rating Factors: Excellent liquidity (8.3) with ample operational cash flow and liquid investments.

Principal Business: Comp med (42%), Medicare (41%), FEHB (12%), med supp (3%), other (1%)

Mem Phys: 18: 99,130 **17:** 90,976 **18 MLR** 39.2% **/ 18 Admin Exp** N/A

Enroll(000): Q1 19: 817 **18:** 820 **17:** 844 **Med Exp PMPM:** $313

Principal Investments: Long-term bonds (32%), nonaffiliate common stock (21%), affiliate common stock (7%), cash and equiv (6%), real estate (1%), other (32%)

Provider Compensation ($000): Contr fee ($2,809,640), FFS ($288,946), bonus arrang ($24,966), capitation ($191)

Total Member Encounters: Phys (6,747,761), non-phys (4,450,424)

Group Affiliation: None

Licensed in: PA

Address: 1800 Center St, Camp Hill, PA 17011

Phone: (412) 544-7000 **Dom State:** PA **Commenced Bus:** N/A

Data Date	Rating	RACR #1	RACR #2	Total Assets ($mil)	Capital ($mil)	Net Premium ($mil)	Net Income ($mil)
3-19	C	4.08	3.40	7,290.6	3,872.0	1,902.1	36.9
3-18	C	4.00	3.34	7,326.0	3,816.1	2,018.3	76.0
2018	C	3.91	3.26	6,935.4	3,704.2	7,988.7	163.3
2017	C	3.99	3.32	6,923.1	3,799.4	7,962.6	660.1
2016	C	3.24	2.70	7,526.6	3,886.3	8,742.8	-73.9
2015	C	3.18	2.65	7,565.3	3,860.6	8,745.5	-405.2
2014	B-	3.44	2.86	7,729.6	4,252.0	9,259.3	-81.1

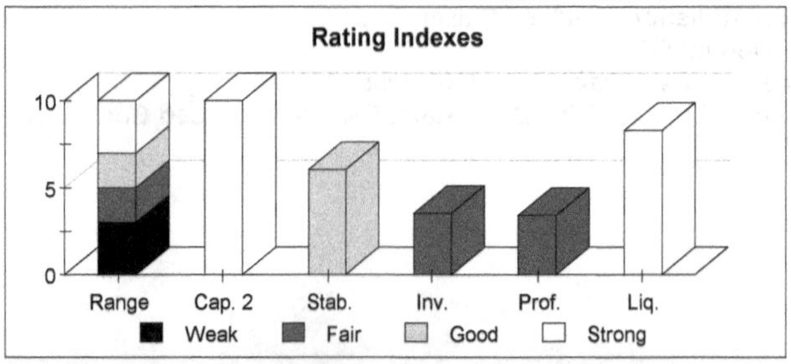

HIGHMARK WEST VIRGINIA INC — B — Good

Major Rating Factors: Good overall profitability index (5.5 on a scale of 0 to 10). Good quality investment portfolio (6.6). Strong capitalization (10.0) based on excellent current risk-adjusted capital (severe loss scenario).

Other Rating Factors: Excellent liquidity (7.0) with ample operational cash flow and liquid investments.

Principal Business: Comp med (61%), FEHB (32%), Medicare (2%), med supp (2%), other (3%)

Mem Phys: 18: 23,227 **17:** 18,294 **18 MLR** 80.9% **/ 18 Admin Exp** N/A

Enroll(000): Q1 19: 164 **18:** 164 **17:** 176 **Med Exp PMPM:** $479

Principal Investments: Long-term bonds (76%), nonaffiliate common stock (6%), cash and equiv (5%), affiliate common stock (3%), real estate (3%), other (7%)

Provider Compensation ($000): Contr fee ($943,130), FFS ($16,338), bonus arrang ($6,192), capitation ($207)

Total Member Encounters: Phys (1,190,292), non-phys (1,000,643)

Group Affiliation: None

Licensed in: PA, WV

Address: 614 Market St, Parkersburg, WV 26101

Phone: (304) 424-7700 **Dom State:** WV **Commenced Bus:** N/A

Data Date	Rating	RACR #1	RACR #2	Total Assets ($mil)	Capital ($mil)	Net Premium ($mil)	Net Income ($mil)
3-19	B	6.74	5.62	912.7	517.6	291.7	36.0
3-18	B	7.33	6.11	812.2	442.3	297.3	27.7
2018	B	6.17	5.15	837.0	473.3	1,197.8	95.0
2017	B	5.49	4.57	762.5	421.9	1,171.1	72.3
2016	B	4.62	3.85	677.2	314.2	1,192.5	-4.2
2015	B	4.59	3.82	617.5	290.2	1,121.8	-12.6
2014	B+	5.82	4.85	598.1	308.1	991.6	9.5

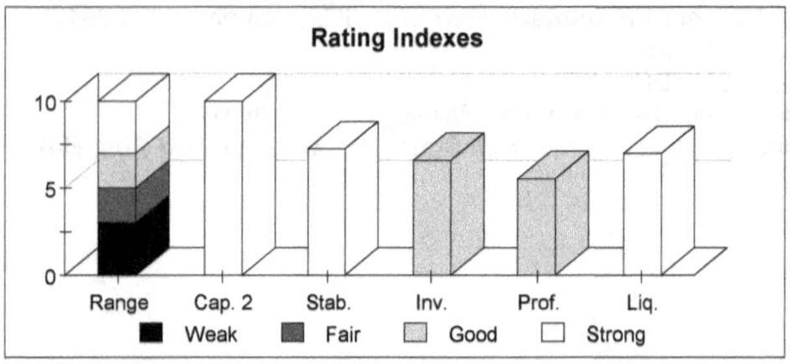

HIP INS CO OF NEW YORK D Weak

Major Rating Factors: Weak profitability index (2.5 on a scale of 0 to 10). Strong capitalization (10.0) based on excellent current risk-adjusted capital (severe loss scenario). High quality investment portfolio (8.9).
Other Rating Factors: Excellent liquidity (8.6) with ample operational cash flow and liquid investments.
Principal Business: Comp med (100%)
Mem Phys: 18: 63,923 **17:** 66,713 **18 MLR** 91.4% **/ 18 Admin Exp** N/A
Enroll(000): Q1 19: 8 **18:** 6 **17:** 7 **Med Exp PMPM:** $101
Principal Investments: Long-term bonds (76%), cash and equiv (24%)
Provider Compensation ($000): Contr fee ($3,122), FFS ($2,882), capitation ($608)
Total Member Encounters: Phys (37,207), non-phys (20,713)
Group Affiliation: EmblemHealth Inc
Licensed in: NY
Address: 55 Water St, New York, NY 10041-8190
Phone: (646) 447-5000 **Dom State:** NY **Commenced Bus:** N/A

Data Date	Rating	RACR #1	RACR #2	Total Assets ($mil)	Capital ($mil)	Net Premium ($mil)	Net Income ($mil)
3-19	D	32.32	26.93	45.6	41.6	5.4	1.2
3-18	D	32.76	27.30	54.1	39.5	2.4	-0.5
2018	D	31.61	26.35	49.1	41.0	8.4	0.2
2017	D-	20.47	17.05	53.4	39.7	9.2	-0.9
2016	D-	38.10	31.75	53.7	41.6	8.3	1.2
2015	D-	28.95	24.12	51.6	42.5	20.1	4.4
2014	D-	9.63	8.02	68.5	39.5	60.1	-5.1

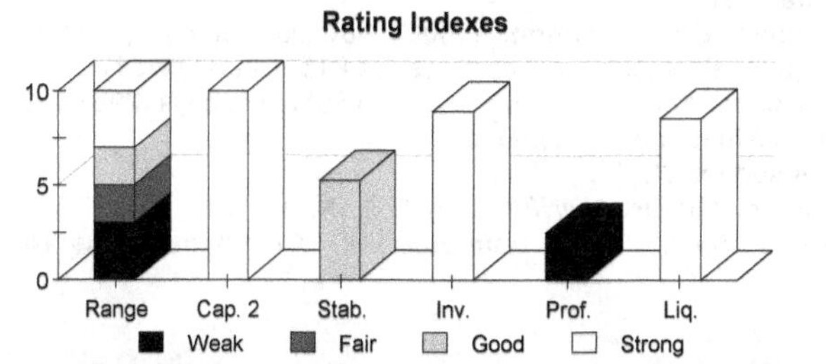

HM LIFE INSURANCE COMPANY B Good

Major Rating Factors: Good overall results on stability tests (5.4 on a scale of 0 to 10) despite fair financial strength of affiliated Highmark Inc. Other stability subfactors include good operational trends and excellent risk diversification. Good overall profitability (6.5). Good liquidity (6.9).
Other Rating Factors: Fair quality investment portfolio (4.8). Strong capitalization (9.9) based on excellent risk adjusted capital (severe loss scenario).
Principal Business: Group health insurance (95%) and reinsurance (5%).
Principal Investments: NonCMO investment grade bonds (44%), common & preferred stock (18%), CMOs and structured securities (14%), and noninv. grade bonds (10%).
Investments in Affiliates: None
Group Affiliation: Highmark Inc
Licensed in: All states except NY, PR
Commenced Business: May 1981
Address: Fifth AvePlace 120 Fifth Ave, Pittsburgh, PA 15222-3099
Phone: (800) 328-5433 **Domicile State:** PA **NAIC Code:** 93440

Data Date	Rating	RACR #1	RACR #2	Total Assets ($mil)	Capital ($mil)	Net Premium ($mil)	Net Income ($mil)
3-19	B	4.44	2.92	741.1	405.9	100.8	12.0
3-18	B	3.12	2.16	687.9	369.3	112.3	9.7
2018	B	4.28	2.84	677.8	391.3	421.9	56.1
2017	B-	3.20	2.29	674.0	360.1	720.9	-23.8
2016	B-	3.39	2.43	643.3	360.7	673.4	17.8
2015	B	3.73	2.73	620.8	348.6	640.3	37.3
2014	B	3.28	2.49	574.5	309.2	647.9	24.1

Highmark Inc
Composite Group Rating: C+

Largest Group Members	Assets ($mil)	Rating
HIGHMARK INC	6922	C
HIGHMARK WEST VIRGINIA INC	762	B
HM LIFE INS CO	678	B
GATEWAY HEALTH PLAN INC	653	B-
HIGHMARK BCBSD INC	443	B

HM LIFE INSURANCE COMPANY OF NEW YORK B Good

Major Rating Factors: Good liquidity (6.8 on a scale of 0 to 10) with sufficient resources to handle a spike in claims. Fair overall results on stability tests (4.6) including fair financial strength of affiliated Highmark Inc and negative cash flow from operations for 2018. Fair profitability (4.3) with operating losses during the first three months of 2019.
Other Rating Factors: Strong capitalization (10.0) based on excellent risk adjusted capital (severe loss scenario). High quality investment portfolio (8.4).
Principal Business: Group health insurance (95%) and reinsurance (5%).
Principal Investments: NonCMO investment grade bonds (46%), CMOs and structured securities (36%), and cash (3%).
Investments in Affiliates: None
Group Affiliation: Highmark Inc
Licensed in: DC, NY, RI
Commenced Business: March 1997
Address: 420 Fifth Avenue 3rd Floor, New York, NY 10119
Phone: (800) 328-5433 **Domicile State:** NY **NAIC Code:** 60213

Data Date	Rating	RACR #1	RACR #2	Total Assets ($mil)	Capital ($mil)	Net Premium ($mil)	Net Income ($mil)
3-19	B	5.37	3.70	62.5	41.2	10.0	-2.8
3-18	B	4.35	3.44	68.1	47.4	8.8	2.2
2018	B	5.77	3.94	66.2	43.8	36.2	-1.1
2017	B	3.64	2.90	67.3	45.1	72.8	5.1
2016	B	3.23	2.57	67.0	40.2	72.4	1.7
2015	B	3.33	2.64	65.7	38.9	66.2	-1.1
2014	B+	3.12	2.47	71.4	39.2	75.4	8.0

Highmark Inc
Composite Group Rating: C+

Largest Group Members	Assets ($mil)	Rating
HIGHMARK INC	6922	C
HIGHMARK WEST VIRGINIA INC	762	B
HM LIFE INS CO	678	B
GATEWAY HEALTH PLAN INC	653	B-
HIGHMARK BCBSD INC	443	B

HMO COLORADO — B — Good

Major Rating Factors: Good quality investment portfolio (5.2 on a scale of 0 to 10). Good overall results on stability tests (6.7) based on healthy premium and capital growth during 2018 but a decline in enrollment during 2018. Rating is significantly influenced by the good financial results of Anthem Inc. Excellent profitability (7.1).
Other Rating Factors: Strong capitalization index (10.0) based on excellent current risk-adjusted capital (severe loss scenario). Excellent liquidity (7.2) with ample operational cash flow and liquid investments.
Principal Business: Comp med (83%), Medicare (17%)
Mem Phys: 18: 21,963 **17:** 21,044 **18 MLR** 72.8% **/ 18 Admin Exp** N/A
Enroll(000): Q1 19: 101 **18:** 89 **17:** 111 **Med Exp PMPM:** $536
Principal Investments: Long-term bonds (64%), cash and equiv (34%), real estate (2%)
Provider Compensation ($000): Bonus arrang ($374,700), capitation ($98,005), FFS ($84,231), contr fee ($44,188), other ($151)
Total Member Encounters: Phys (453,501), non-phys (295,696)
Group Affiliation: Anthem Inc
Licensed in: CO, NV
Address: 700 BROADWAY, DENVER, CO 80273
Phone: (303) 831-2131 **Dom State:** CO **Commenced Bus:** N/A

Data Date	Rating	RACR #1	RACR #2	Total Assets ($mil)	Capital ($mil)	Net Premium ($mil)	Net Income ($mil)
3-19	B	4.98	4.15	357.3	196.8	219.9	36.8
3-18	B	2.45	2.04	220.7	95.3	202.8	25.1
2018	B	4.08	3.40	285.3	160.6	820.6	96.8
2017	B-	1.19	0.99	185.4	71.0	651.2	18.2
2016	B-	2.85	2.38	153.5	51.4	285.2	2.3
2015	C+	2.53	2.11	102.1	37.0	240.4	-4.1
2014	B-	3.25	2.71	92.9	42.2	209.2	3.9

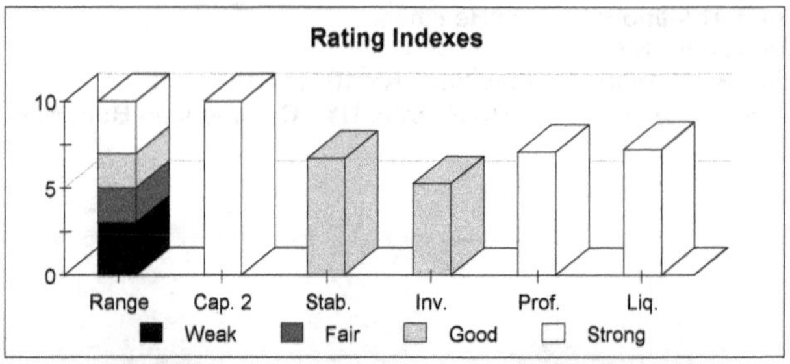

HMO LOUISIANA INC * — A+ — Excellent

Major Rating Factors: Strong capitalization index (10.0 on a scale of 0 to 10) based on excellent current risk-adjusted capital (severe loss scenario). High quality investment portfolio (7.5). Excellent overall results on stability tests (7.2).
Other Rating Factors: Excellent liquidity (7.1) with ample operational cash flow and liquid investments. Fair profitability index (4.5).
Principal Business: Comp med (92%), Medicare (8%)
Mem Phys: 18: 33,837 **17:** 29,260 **18 MLR** 78.6% **/ 18 Admin Exp** N/A
Enroll(000): Q1 19: 185 **18:** 175 **17:** 159 **Med Exp PMPM:** $409
Principal Investments: Long-term bonds (70%), nonaffiliate common stock (22%), cash and equiv (7%), other (1%)
Provider Compensation ($000): Contr fee ($895,009)
Total Member Encounters: Phys (1,891,689), non-phys (895,175)
Group Affiliation: None
Licensed in: LA
Address: 5525 Reitz Avenue, Baton Rouge, LA 70809
Phone: (225) 295-3307 **Dom State:** LA **Commenced Bus:** N/A

Data Date	Rating	RACR #1	RACR #2	Total Assets ($mil)	Capital ($mil)	Net Premium ($mil)	Net Income ($mil)
3-19	A+	6.82	5.69	801.6	454.1	278.3	30.7
3-18	A+	6.80	5.67	756.1	405.8	306.2	27.7
2018	A+	6.28	5.23	762.3	417.7	1,141.4	53.9
2017	A+	4.98	4.15	699.4	383.9	940.5	18.1
2016	A+	7.53	6.27	570.5	347.5	719.2	10.3
2015	A+	8.70	7.25	513.2	334.4	584.5	-28.8
2014	A+	10.84	9.04	502.3	362.4	508.9	15.3

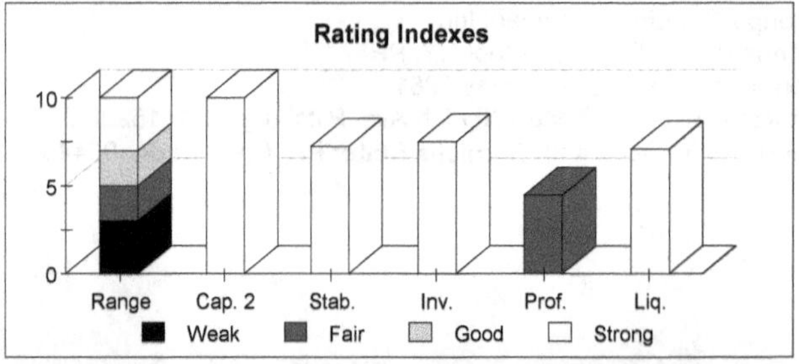

HMO MINNESOTA — C+ — Fair

Major Rating Factors: Fair profitability index (4.2 on a scale of 0 to 10). Fair quality investment portfolio (4.3). Good overall results on stability tests (4.9).
Other Rating Factors: Good liquidity (6.9) with sufficient resources (cash flows and marketable investments) to handle a spike in claims. Strong capitalization index (10.0) based on excellent current risk-adjusted capital (severe loss scenario).
Principal Business: Medicaid (92%), comp med (8%)
Mem Phys: 18: 32,563 **17:** 11,668 **18 MLR** 87.7% **/ 18 Admin Exp** N/A
Enroll(000): Q1 19: 373 **18:** 385 **17:** 409 **Med Exp PMPM:** $455
Principal Investments: Long-term bonds (62%), cash and equiv (20%), nonaffiliate common stock (18%)
Provider Compensation ($000): Contr fee ($1,251,933), bonus arrang ($740,149), FFS ($158,412)
Total Member Encounters: Phys (2,209,749), non-phys (2,608,577)
Group Affiliation: Aware Integrated Inc
Licensed in: MN
Address: 3535 Blue Cross Road, Eagan, MN 55122
Phone: (651) 662-8000 **Dom State:** MN **Commenced Bus:** N/A

Data Date	Rating	RACR #1	RACR #2	Total Assets ($mil)	Capital ($mil)	Net Premium ($mil)	Net Income ($mil)
3-19	C+	4.14	3.45	1,105.9	614.6	574.4	10.4
3-18	C	3.37	2.81	964.1	496.8	608.3	24.5
2018	C+	3.96	3.30	1,103.2	587.4	2,445.3	141.0
2017	C	2.57	2.14	1,011.3	473.0	2,406.5	32.2
2016	C	3.46	2.88	858.3	426.8	1,816.2	-156.7
2015	B-	9.49	7.91	825.1	570.2	895.0	52.0
2014	B	10.04	8.37	725.4	530.6	820.4	85.7

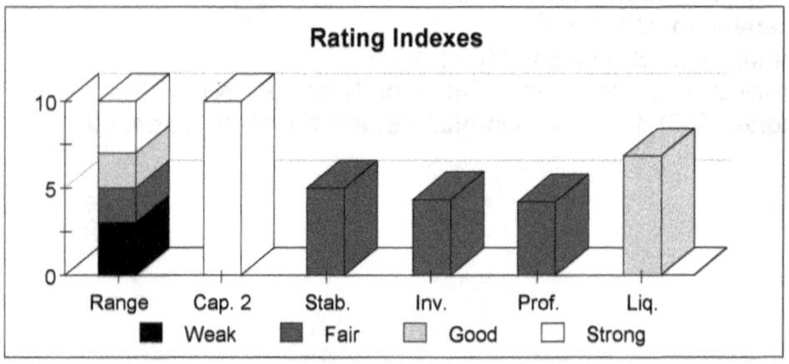

HMO MISSOURI INC B Good

Major Rating Factors: Good overall results on stability tests (5.2 on a scale of 0 to 10). Rating is significantly influenced by the good financial results of Anthem Inc. Good liquidity (6.8) with sufficient resources (cash flows and marketable investments) to handle a spike in claims. Excellent profitability (8.5).
Other Rating Factors: Strong capitalization index (10.0) based on excellent current risk-adjusted capital (severe loss scenario). High quality investment portfolio (8.1).
Principal Business: Medicare (46%), FEHB (30%), comp med (24%)
Mem Phys: 18: 19,000 **17:** 18,592 **18 MLR** 82.0% **/ 18 Admin Exp** N/A
Enroll(000): Q1 19: 17 **18:** 29 **17:** 28 **Med Exp PMPM:** $502
Principal Investments: Long-term bonds (99%), cash and equiv (1%)
Provider Compensation ($000): Bonus arrang ($99,041), FFS ($35,190), contr fee ($30,111), capitation ($2,673)
Total Member Encounters: Phys (215,923), non-phys (211,271)
Group Affiliation: Anthem Inc
Licensed in: IL, MO
Address: 1831 CHESTNUT STREET, ST. LOUIS, MO 63103-2275
Phone: (314) 923-4444 **Dom State:** MO **Commenced Bus:** N/A

Data Date	Rating	RACR #1	RACR #2	Total Assets ($mil)	Capital ($mil)	Net Premium ($mil)	Net Income ($mil)
3-19	B	3.73	3.11	86.1	36.8	27.7	0.7
3-18	B-	2.81	2.34	81.1	26.0	49.4	-3.5
2018	B	3.60	3.00	88.2	35.6	207.1	5.8
2017	C+	1.88	1.57	79.0	29.7	182.1	8.8
2016	B	6.74	5.61	75.1	45.2	149.5	8.8
2015	B-	7.08	5.90	68.9	38.3	134.8	9.9
2014	B-	5.72	4.77	61.2	29.7	135.6	10.4

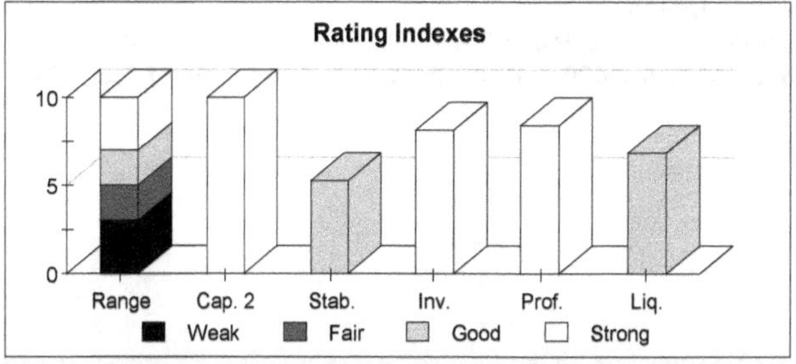

HMO PARTNERS INC * A+ Excellent

Major Rating Factors: Strong capitalization index (10.0 on a scale of 0 to 10) based on excellent current risk-adjusted capital (severe loss scenario). High quality investment portfolio (9.4). Good overall profitability index (5.7).
Other Rating Factors: Good overall results on stability tests (5.7). Weak liquidity (2.8) as a spike in claims may stretch capacity.
Principal Business: Comp med (92%), Medicare (8%)
Mem Phys: 18: 17,795 **17:** 16,862 **18 MLR** 123.0% **/ 18 Admin Exp** N/A
Enroll(000): Q1 19: 64 **18:** 69 **17:** 71 **Med Exp PMPM:** $329
Principal Investments: Long-term bonds (51%), cash and equiv (33%), nonaffiliate common stock (6%), other (9%)
Provider Compensation ($000): Bonus arrang ($196,869), contr fee ($88,173), FFS ($1,985)
Total Member Encounters: Phys (65,176), non-phys (81,739)
Group Affiliation: HMO Partners Inc
Licensed in: AR
Address: 320 West Capitol, Little Rock, AR 72203-8069
Phone: (501) 221-1800 **Dom State:** AR **Commenced Bus:** N/A

Data Date	Rating	RACR #1	RACR #2	Total Assets ($mil)	Capital ($mil)	Net Premium ($mil)	Net Income ($mil)
3-19	A+	4.83	4.03	127.5	71.0	53.9	3.0
3-18	A+	N/A	N/A	143.2	69.6	57.5	5.9
2018	A+	4.64	3.87	128.3	68.1	226.8	6.4
2017	A+	N/A	N/A	129.6	67.5	206.7	6.7
2016	A+	4.93	4.11	114.1	58.3	191.1	0.7
2015	A+	5.38	4.48	113.7	56.7	177.3	4.8
2014	A+	10.48	8.73	186.7	119.4	171.5	3.1

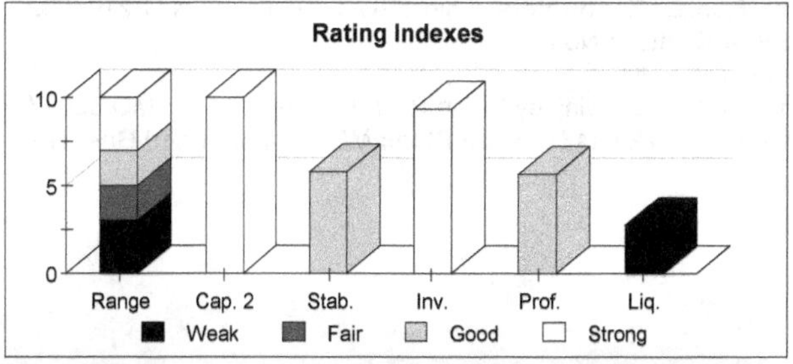

HN1 THERAPY NETWORK NEW JERSEY LLC C Fair

Major Rating Factors: Fair capitalization (4.3 on a scale of 0 to 10) based on fair current risk-adjusted capital (moderate loss scenario). Excellent profitability (8.2). High quality investment portfolio (9.9).
Other Rating Factors: Excellent liquidity (8.9) with ample operational cash flow and liquid investments.
Principal Business: Medicaid (93%), Medicare (7%)
Mem Phys: 18: 362 **17:** 287 **18 MLR** 45.2% **/ 18 Admin Exp** N/A
Enroll(000): 18: 182 **17:** 197 **Med Exp PMPM:** $0
Principal Investments: Cash and equiv (100%)
Provider Compensation ($000): FFS ($1,163), bonus arrang ($99)
Total Member Encounters: N/A
Group Affiliation: HN1 Therapy Network LLC
Licensed in: NJ
Address: 801 E Hallandale Beach Blv 200, Fort Lauderdale, FL 33316
Phone: (305) 614-0109 **Dom State:** NJ **Commenced Bus:** N/A

Data Date	Rating	RACR #1	RACR #2	Total Assets ($mil)	Capital ($mil)	Net Premium ($mil)	Net Income ($mil)
2018	C	0.83	0.69	2.6	2.3	2.7	0.5
2017	C-	N/A	N/A	2.8	2.5	2.9	0.9
2016	C-	0.86	0.71	2.8	2.3	3.0	0.9
2015	N/A	N/A	N/A	3.7	3.0	3.7	1.6
2014	N/A	N/A	N/A	4.8	2.0	5.8	1.8

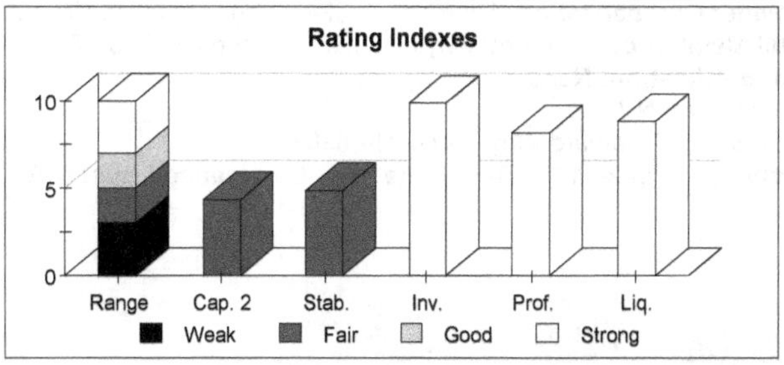

HNE INS CO — B — Good

Major Rating Factors: Fair profitability index (4.5 on a scale of 0 to 10). Strong capitalization (10.0) based on excellent current risk-adjusted capital (severe loss scenario). High quality investment portfolio (9.9).
Other Rating Factors: Excellent liquidity (9.0) with ample operational cash flow and liquid investments.
Principal Business: Med supp (100%)
Mem Phys: 18: 5,660 **17:** 5,845 **18 MLR** 89.8% **/ 18 Admin Exp** N/A
Enroll(000): Q1 19: 1 **18:** 1 **17:** 0 **Med Exp PMPM:** $156
Principal Investments: Cash and equiv (100%)
Provider Compensation ($000): Bonus arrang ($1,018)
Total Member Encounters: Phys (6,341), non-phys (669)
Group Affiliation: Baystate Health Inc
Licensed in: MA
Address: 1 Monarch Place Ste 1500, Springfield, MA 1144
Phone: (413) 787-4000 **Dom State:** MA **Commenced Bus:** N/A

Data Date	Rating	RACR #1	RACR #2	Total Assets ($mil)	Capital ($mil)	Net Premium ($mil)	Net Income ($mil)
3-19	B	29.20	24.33	5.5	5.1	0.4	0.0
3-18	C	N/A	N/A	5.1	4.9	0.3	-0.1
2018	B-	28.44	23.70	5.4	5.1	1.4	0.1
2017	C	N/A	N/A	5.1	5.0	0.7	0.1
2016	D+	68.24	56.87	5.0	4.9	0.5	0.1
2015	D+	65.74	54.79	5.0	4.9	0.4	0.0
2014	C	65.52	54.60	5.0	4.9	0.2	-0.1

Rating Indexes

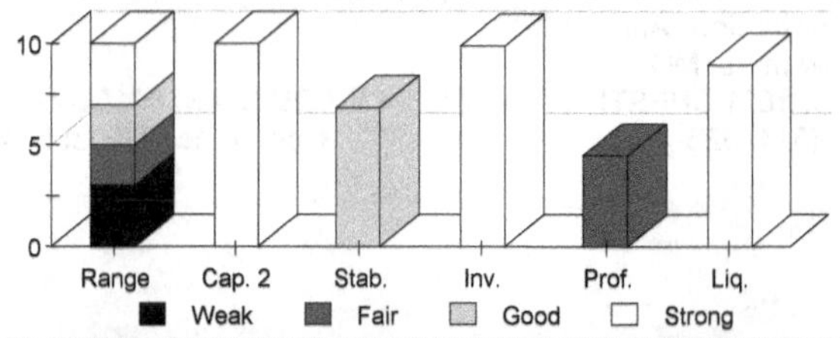

HOME STATE HEALTH PLAN INC — C- — Fair

Major Rating Factors: Weak profitability index (0.9 on a scale of 0 to 10). Good quality investment portfolio (5.8). Good liquidity (6.8) with sufficient resources (cash flows and marketable investments) to handle a spike in claims.
Other Rating Factors: Strong capitalization (8.5) based on excellent current risk-adjusted capital (severe loss scenario).
Principal Business: Medicaid (100%)
Mem Phys: 18: 16,281 **17:** 25,785 **18 MLR** 91.3% **/ 18 Admin Exp** N/A
Enroll(000): Q1 19: 227 **18:** 235 **17:** 270 **Med Exp PMPM:** $268
Principal Investments: Long-term bonds (57%), cash and equiv (40%), affiliate common stock (3%)
Provider Compensation ($000): Contr fee ($586,611), salary ($172,346), bonus arrang ($43,554), capitation ($17,568)
Total Member Encounters: Phys (885,637), non-phys (1,210,849)
Group Affiliation: None
Licensed in: MO
Address: 16090 Swingley Ridge Rd #450, Chesterfield, MO 63017
Phone: (314) 725-4477 **Dom State:** MO **Commenced Bus:** N/A

Data Date	Rating	RACR #1	RACR #2	Total Assets ($mil)	Capital ($mil)	Net Premium ($mil)	Net Income ($mil)
3-19	C-	2.59	2.16	216.5	104.7	200.7	-4.8
3-18	C-	2.23	1.86	217.5	85.9	227.3	-21.3
2018	C-	2.68	2.23	227.3	108.4	914.1	1.0
2017	C-	1.31	1.10	195.5	76.4	729.3	-34.9
2016	C-	2.21	1.84	102.3	43.4	344.4	-12.9
2015	C-	2.35	1.96	86.4	34.3	266.6	-15.6
2014	C-	2.58	2.15	60.2	22.6	179.2	-19.8

Rating Indexes

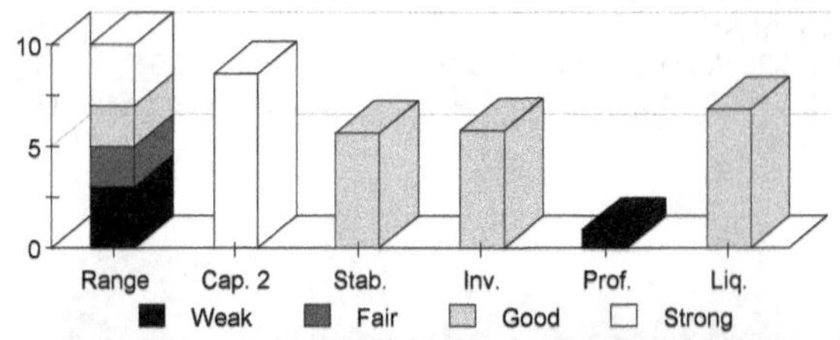

HOMETOWN HEALTH PLAN INC — D — Weak

Major Rating Factors: Weak profitability index (0.9 on a scale of 0 to 10). Fair overall results on stability tests (4.5) based on a significant 21% decrease in enrollment during the period. Good capitalization index (6.5) based on good current risk-adjusted capital (severe loss scenario).
Other Rating Factors: Good liquidity (6.8) with sufficient resources (cash flows and marketable investments) to handle a spike in claims. High quality investment portfolio (9.7).
Principal Business: Medicare (69%), comp med (30%)
Mem Phys: 18: 3,894 **17:** 2,254 **18 MLR** 94.0% **/ 18 Admin Exp** N/A
Enroll(000): Q1 19: 27 **18:** 27 **17:** 35 **Med Exp PMPM:** $639
Principal Investments: Cash and equiv (48%), long-term bonds (39%), real estate (14%)
Provider Compensation ($000): FFS ($244,365), capitation ($3,198)
Total Member Encounters: Phys (388,865), non-phys (275,778)
Group Affiliation: None
Licensed in: NV
Address: 830 Harvard Way, Reno, NV 89521
Phone: (775) 982-3100 **Dom State:** NV **Commenced Bus:** N/A

Data Date	Rating	RACR #1	RACR #2	Total Assets ($mil)	Capital ($mil)	Net Premium ($mil)	Net Income ($mil)
3-19	D	1.15	0.96	97.4	36.2	59.1	-0.6
3-18	C	1.17	0.98	112.2	35.2	72.3	-4.0
2018	D	1.13	0.94	91.8	35.9	259.5	-16.0
2017	C	1.29	1.07	94.6	41.3	275.3	12.7
2016	C-	1.01	0.84	86.1	30.6	266.5	-7.5
2015	C-	1.29	1.07	79.0	38.9	271.5	2.7
2014	C	0.75	0.62	69.0	22.2	254.2	-15.2

Rating Indexes

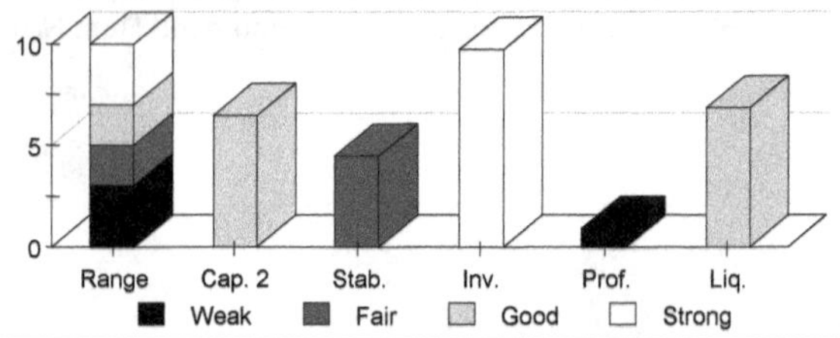

HOMETOWN HEALTH PROVIDERS INS CO — C+ — Fair

Major Rating Factors: Good overall profitability index (5.6 on a scale of 0 to 10). Strong capitalization (7.6) based on excellent current risk-adjusted capital (severe loss scenario). High quality investment portfolio (9.2).
Other Rating Factors: Excellent liquidity (6.9) with sufficient resources (cash flows and marketable investments) to handle a spike in claims.
Principal Business: Comp med (99%)
Mem Phys: 18: 3,899 **17:** 2,270 **18 MLR** 79.5% **/ 18 Admin Exp** N/A
Enroll(000): Q1 19: 31 **18:** 39 **17:** 39 **Med Exp PMPM:** $296
Principal Investments: Cash and equiv (43%), long-term bonds (42%), real estate (14%)
Provider Compensation ($000): FFS ($139,936)
Total Member Encounters: Phys (212,695), non-phys (108,759)
Group Affiliation: None
Licensed in: NV
Address: 830 Harvard Way, Reno, NV 89521
Phone: (775) 982-3100 **Dom State:** NV **Commenced Bus:** N/A

Data Date	Rating	RACR #1	RACR #2	Total Assets ($mil)	Capital ($mil)	Net Premium ($mil)	Net Income ($mil)
3-19	C+	1.80	1.50	75.6	34.6	43.6	1.6
3-18	B	2.07	1.73	73.7	30.5	46.5	2.1
2018	C+	1.73	1.44	68.5	33.3	180.5	4.9
2017	B-	1.79	1.49	60.0	28.8	133.3	-0.5
2016	B-	2.75	2.29	50.3	30.9	97.4	0.2
2015	B-	3.48	2.90	45.6	30.9	72.4	0.8
2014	B	4.14	3.45	44.5	30.7	58.1	2.2

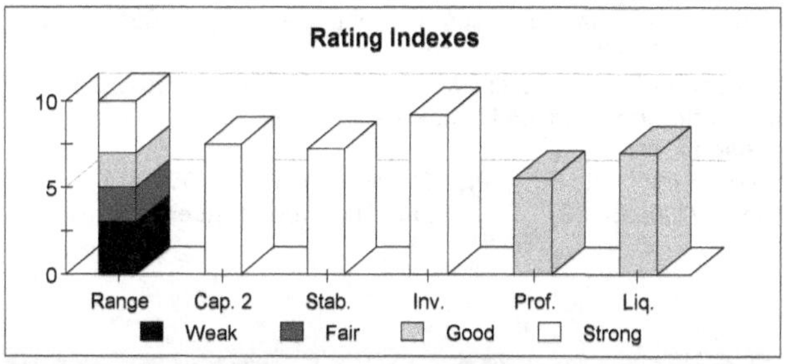

HOOSIER MOTOR MUTUAL INS CO — C+ — Fair

Major Rating Factors: Good quality investment portfolio (5.2 on a scale of 0 to 10). Weak profitability index (2.5). Strong capitalization (10.0) based on excellent current risk-adjusted capital (severe loss scenario).
Other Rating Factors: Excellent liquidity (10.0) with ample operational cash flow and liquid investments.
Principal Business: Other (100%)
Mem Phys: 18: N/A **17:** N/A **18 MLR** 0.2% **/ 18 Admin Exp** N/A
Enroll(000): Q1 19: 445 **18:** 446 **17:** 439 **Med Exp PMPM:** N/A
Principal Investments: Long-term bonds (43%), nonaffiliate common stock (40%), real estate (13%), cash and equiv (4%)
Provider Compensation ($000): Other ($3)
Total Member Encounters: N/A
Group Affiliation: None
Licensed in: IN
Address: 3750 Guion Rd, Indianapolis, IN 46222
Phone: (317) 923-1500 **Dom State:** IN **Commenced Bus:** N/A

Data Date	Rating	RACR #1	RACR #2	Total Assets ($mil)	Capital ($mil)	Net Premium ($mil)	Net Income ($mil)
3-19	C+	8.34	6.95	11.0	10.5	0.2	0.1
3-18	B-	8.10	6.75	11.4	10.9	0.2	0.2
2018	C+	7.98	6.65	10.5	10.0	0.6	-0.4
2017	B-	7.96	6.64	11.4	10.8	0.6	0.0
2016	C+	10.33	8.61	11.4	10.7	0.6	-0.3
2015	C-	10.58	8.81	11.2	10.8	0.6	-0.2
2014	C+	5.98	3.15	11.7	11.2	0.6	0.1

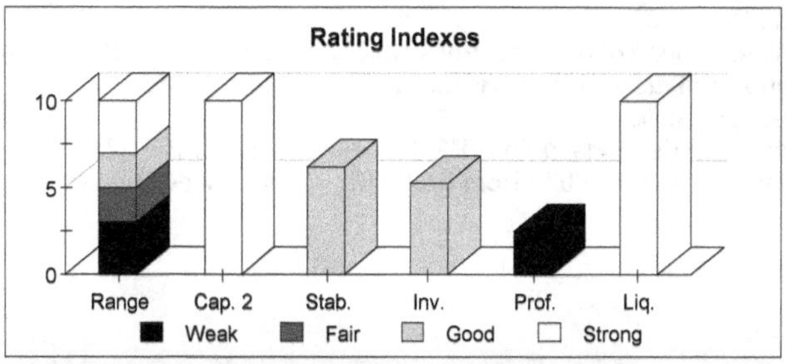

HOPKINS HEALTH ADV INC — E+ — Very Weak

Major Rating Factors: Weak profitability index (1.1 on a scale of 0 to 10). Fair capitalization (3.4) based on weak current risk-adjusted capital (moderate loss scenario). High quality investment portfolio (9.9).
Other Rating Factors: Excellent liquidity (6.9) with sufficient resources (cash flows and marketable investments) to handle a spike in claims.
Principal Business: Medicare (100%)
Mem Phys: 18: N/A **17:** N/A **18 MLR** 106.5% **/ 18 Admin Exp** N/A
Enroll(000): Q1 19: 19 **18:** 13 **17:** 8 **Med Exp PMPM:** $983
Principal Investments: Cash and equiv (99%), other (1%)
Provider Compensation ($000): Contr fee ($137,737), capitation ($1,587)
Total Member Encounters: Phys (1,124,589), non-phys (1,469,026)
Group Affiliation: None
Licensed in: MD
Address: 6704 Curtis Court, Glen Burnie, MD 21060
Phone: (410) 424-4948 **Dom State:** MD **Commenced Bus:** N/A

Data Date	Rating	RACR #1	RACR #2	Total Assets ($mil)	Capital ($mil)	Net Premium ($mil)	Net Income ($mil)
3-19	E+	0.68	0.57	66.6	13.4	55.9	-2.5
3-18	E	N/A	N/A	46.0	7.5	33.4	-1.1
2018	E+	0.84	0.70	61.5	16.5	137.8	-32.1
2017	E	N/A	N/A	38.5	8.7	85.2	-23.8
2016	D+	0.69	0.57	22.4	6.1	42.4	-19.7
2015	N/A	N/A	N/A	1.9	1.9	N/A	N/A
2014	N/A	N/A	N/A	N/A	N/A	N/A	N/A

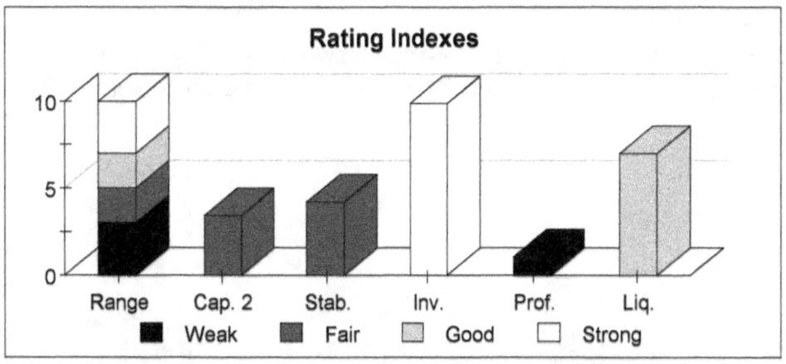

HORIZON HEALTHCARE OF NEW JERSEY INC C+ Fair

Major Rating Factors: Good overall profitability index (6.4 on a scale of 0 to 10). Good overall results on stability tests (5.6). Potentially strong support from affiliation with Horizon Healthcare Services Inc. Weak liquidity (2.1) as a spike in claims may stretch capacity.
Other Rating Factors: Strong capitalization index (10.0) based on excellent current risk-adjusted capital (severe loss scenario). High quality investment portfolio (9.2).
Principal Business: Medicaid (96%), Medicare (3%)
Mem Phys: 18: 22,908 **17:** 22,457 **18 MLR** 870.1% **/ 18 Admin Exp** N/A
Enroll(000): Q1 19: 854 **18:** 866 **17:** 878 **Med Exp PMPM:** $441
Principal Investments: Long-term bonds (82%), nonaffiliate common stock (13%), cash and equiv (5%)
Provider Compensation ($000): Contr fee ($4,242,055), FFS ($334,200), capitation ($177,822)
Total Member Encounters: Phys (10,218,779), non-phys (5,247,098)
Group Affiliation: Horizon Healthcare Services Inc
Licensed in: NJ
Address: 3 Penn Plz E Ste PP-15D, Newark, NJ 07105-2248
Phone: (973) 466-5607 **Dom State:** NJ **Commenced Bus:** N/A

Data Date	Rating	RACR #1	RACR #2	Total Assets ($mil)	Capital ($mil)	Net Premium ($mil)	Net Income ($mil)
3-19	C+	26.36	21.96	1,226.7	1,059.5	132.2	28.8
3-18	C+	19.88	16.57	1,252.2	1,054.6	131.3	3.2
2018	C+	26.28	21.90	1,228.0	1,055.9	539.7	26.3
2017	B	19.71	16.42	1,354.7	1,044.6	506.2	44.2
2016	A-	3.58	2.99	1,601.5	998.0	4,868.0	151.2
2015	A-	3.24	2.70	1,439.4	850.1	4,561.5	72.0
2014	A-	2.63	2.19	1,339.5	585.9	3,916.6	21.4

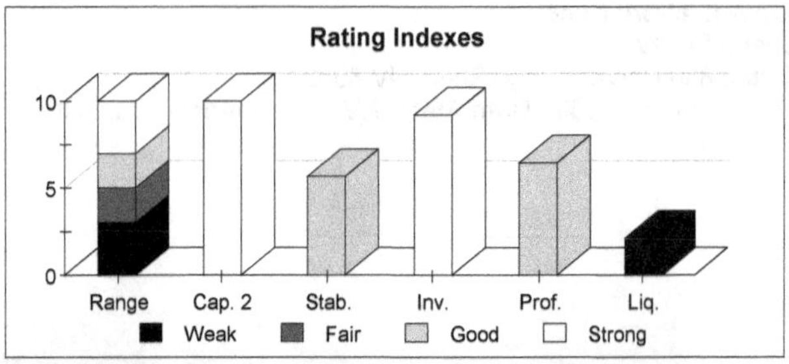

HORIZON HEALTHCARE SERVICES INC B Good

Major Rating Factors: Good overall profitability index (5.2 on a scale of 0 to 10). Good quality investment portfolio (6.1). Strong capitalization (10.0) based on excellent current risk-adjusted capital (severe loss scenario).
Other Rating Factors: Excellent liquidity (7.4) with ample operational cash flow and liquid investments.
Principal Business: Comp med (43%), Medicaid (38%), Medicare (9%), FEHB (7%), med supp (2%), dental (1%)
Mem Phys: 18: 95,620 **17:** 88,389 **18 MLR** 43.4% **/ 18 Admin Exp** N/A
Enroll(000): 18: 1,256 **17:** 1,371 **Med Exp PMPM:** $347
Principal Investments: Long-term bonds (61%), affiliate common stock (37%), nonaffiliate common stock (7%), other (2%)
Provider Compensation ($000): Contr fee ($5,007,450), capitation ($269,668), FFS ($190,203)
Total Member Encounters: Phys (12,657,634), non-phys (10,590,320)
Group Affiliation: Horizon Healthcare Services Inc
Licensed in: NJ
Address: 3 Penn Plaza East, PP-15D, Newark, NJ 07105-2248
Phone: (973) 466-5607 **Dom State:** NJ **Commenced Bus:** N/A

Data Date	Rating	RACR #1	RACR #2	Total Assets ($mil)	Capital ($mil)	Net Premium ($mil)	Net Income ($mil)
2018	B	3.79	3.16	5,527.8	2,985.3	12,456.5	336.1
2017	B	3.58	2.98	5,437.9	2,772.2	12,222.8	56.7
2016	B	3.59	3.00	4,257.6	2,385.9	6,692.7	-83.0
2015	B+	3.79	3.16	4,089.2	2,305.9	6,123.6	20.6
2014	B+	4.03	3.36	3,795.8	2,230.2	5,812.8	59.7

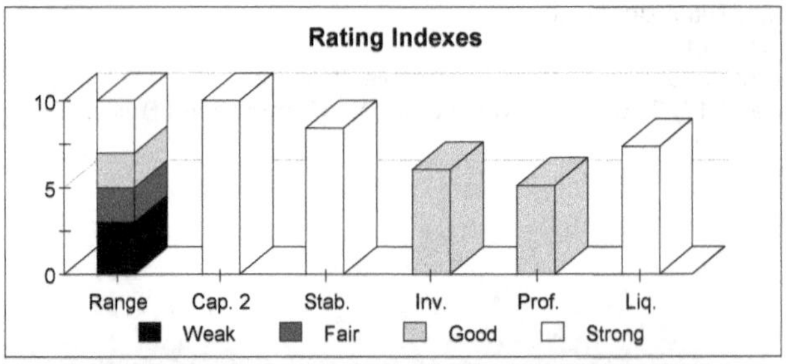

HORIZON INS CO C+ Fair

Major Rating Factors: Fair profitability index (4.9 on a scale of 0 to 10). Weak liquidity (1.7) as a spike in claims may stretch capacity. Strong capitalization (9.1) based on excellent current risk-adjusted capital (severe loss scenario).
Other Rating Factors: High quality investment portfolio (8.2).
Principal Business: Medicare (69%), med supp (18%), vision (6%), other (7%)
Mem Phys: 18: 46,637 **17:** 42,907 **18 MLR** 841.9% **/ 18 Admin Exp** N/A
Enroll(000): 18: 365 **17:** 300 **Med Exp PMPM:** $293
Principal Investments: Long-term bonds (96%), cash and equiv (4%)
Provider Compensation ($000): Contr fee ($1,129,450), capitation ($63,767), FFS ($48,165)
Total Member Encounters: Phys (2,565,147), non-phys (1,321,118)
Group Affiliation: Horizon Healthcare Services Inc
Licensed in: NJ
Address: 3 Penn Plaza East PP-15D, Newark, NJ 07105-2248
Phone: (973) 466-5607 **Dom State:** NJ **Commenced Bus:** N/A

Data Date	Rating	RACR #1	RACR #2	Total Assets ($mil)	Capital ($mil)	Net Premium ($mil)	Net Income ($mil)
2018	C+	3.03	2.52	155.7	29.9	149.5	-1.6
2017	B-	N/A	N/A	201.4	31.2	139.9	4.0
2016	B-	8.75	7.29	123.8	27.3	64.1	3.2
2015	B	3.79	3.16	141.4	25.5	220.3	9.1
2014	B+	1.68	1.40	71.5	16.3	258.7	7.4

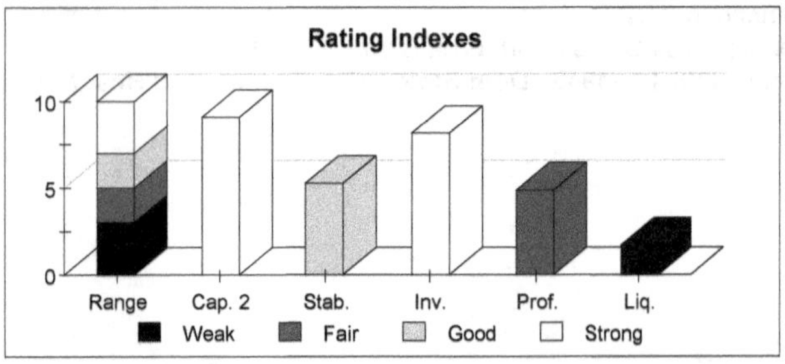

HPHC INS CO D+ Weak

Major Rating Factors: Weak profitability index (1.9 on a scale of 0 to 10). Good liquidity (6.7) with sufficient resources (cash flows and marketable investments) to handle a spike in claims. Strong capitalization (8.3) based on excellent current risk-adjusted capital (severe loss scenario).
Other Rating Factors: High quality investment portfolio (8.2).
Principal Business: Comp med (75%), med supp (23%), other (2%)
Mem Phys: 18: 83,960 **17:** 81,621 **18 MLR** 81.9% **/ 18 Admin Exp** N/A
Enroll(000): Q1 19: 147 **18:** 154 **17:** 189 **Med Exp PMPM:** $302
Principal Investments: Long-term bonds (93%), cash and equiv (6%), other (1%)
Provider Compensation ($000): Contr fee ($523,469), capitation ($57,143), FFS ($18,401), other ($25,473)
Total Member Encounters: Phys (1,121,006), non-phys (822,238)
Group Affiliation: Harvard Pilgrim Health Care Inc
Licensed in: CT, ME, MA, NH
Address: 93 WORCESTER St, WELLESLEY, MA 02481-9181
Phone: (781) 263-6000 **Dom State:** MA **Commenced Bus:** N/A

Data Date	Rating	RACR #1	RACR #2	Total Assets ($mil)	Capital ($mil)	Net Premium ($mil)	Net Income ($mil)
3-19	D+	2.38	1.98	250.0	106.2	173.1	7.8
3-18	D+	1.30	1.09	251.0	69.0	192.2	0.6
2018	D+	2.23	1.85	255.6	100.8	752.7	29.5
2017	D-	1.02	0.85	249.2	70.4	810.2	-0.1
2016	D-	1.43	1.19	268.9	70.6	774.5	-57.8
2015	C	1.23	1.02	226.3	51.8	665.4	-37.3
2014	B-	1.48	1.24	194.7	51.1	610.1	-12.1

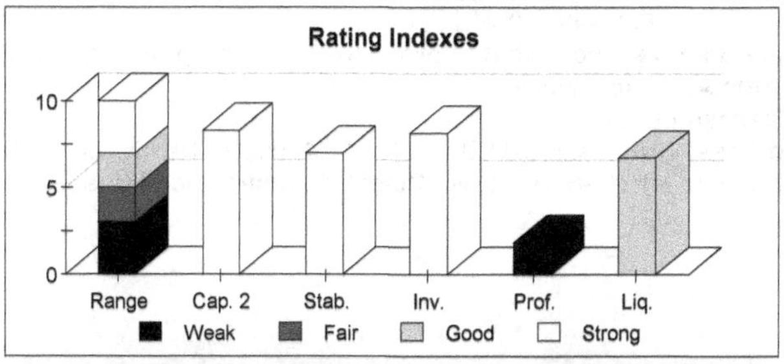

HUMANA BENEFIT PLAN OF ILLINOIS * B+ Good

Major Rating Factors: Good quality investment portfolio (6.7 on a scale of 0 to 10). Good liquidity (6.8) with sufficient resources (cash flows and marketable investments) to handle a spike in claims. Excellent profitability (8.8).
Other Rating Factors: Strong capitalization (10.0) based on excellent current risk-adjusted capital (severe loss scenario).
Principal Business: Medicare (100%)
Mem Phys: 18: 397,770 **17:** 218,504 **18 MLR** 85.2% **/ 18 Admin Exp** N/A
Enroll(000): Q1 19: 226 **18:** 178 **17:** 88 **Med Exp PMPM:** $792
Principal Investments: Long-term bonds (80%), cash and equiv (20%)
Provider Compensation ($000): Contr fee ($937,463), capitation ($502,593), salary ($78,576), FFS ($23,616)
Total Member Encounters: Phys (3,378,127), non-phys (1,743,124)
Group Affiliation: None
Licensed in: All states except FL, NY, UT, PR
Address: 7915 N HALE AVE STE D, PEORIA, IL 61615
Phone: (502) 580-1000 **Dom State:** IL **Commenced Bus:** N/A

Data Date	Rating	RACR #1	RACR #2	Total Assets ($mil)	Capital ($mil)	Net Premium ($mil)	Net Income ($mil)
3-19	B+	3.79	3.16	693.4	339.9	625.3	17.4
3-18	B	3.41	2.85	558.8	181.2	474.2	-22.0
2018	B+	3.66	3.05	551.0	328.5	1,906.1	40.2
2017	A-	2.85	2.38	367.0	208.9	1,016.5	51.8
2016	A-	3.13	2.61	248.6	161.8	969.5	32.1
2015	B	3.29	2.74	197.6	130.4	700.1	-0.9
2014	B-	4.36	3.63	88.5	61.9	280.2	19.5

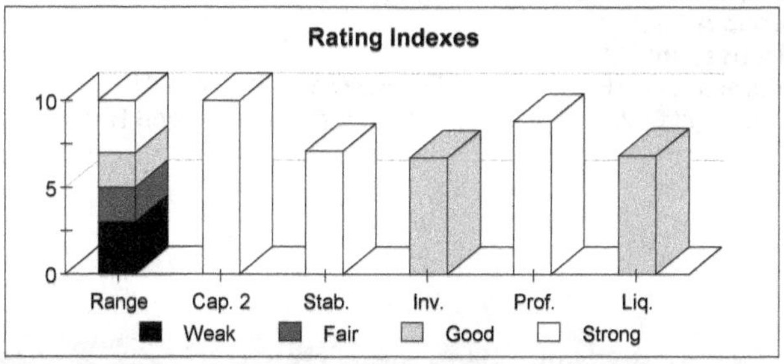

HUMANA EMPLOYERS HEALTH PLAN OF GA C+ Fair

Major Rating Factors: Fair overall results on stability tests (3.0 on a scale of 0 to 10) based on a steep decline in capital during 2018. Rating is significantly influenced by the good financial results of . Good liquidity (6.5) with sufficient resources (cash flows and marketable investments) to handle a spike in claims. Weak profitability index (1.2).
Other Rating Factors: Strong capitalization index (10.0) based on excellent current risk-adjusted capital (severe loss scenario). High quality investment portfolio (8.5).
Principal Business: Comp med (58%), Medicare (40%), FEHB (1%)
Mem Phys: 18: 53,096 **17:** 44,622 **18 MLR** 83.8% **/ 18 Admin Exp** N/A
Enroll(000): Q1 19: 242 **18:** 249 **17:** 255 **Med Exp PMPM:** $362
Principal Investments: Long-term bonds (98%), cash and equiv (2%)
Provider Compensation ($000): Contr fee ($726,946), FFS ($193,767), capitation ($169,929), salary ($22,169)
Total Member Encounters: Phys (2,074,223), non-phys (850,463)
Group Affiliation: None
Licensed in: GA
Address: 1200 ASHWOOD PKWY STE 250, ATLANTA, GA 30338
Phone: (770) 393-9226 **Dom State:** GA **Commenced Bus:** N/A

Data Date	Rating	RACR #1	RACR #2	Total Assets ($mil)	Capital ($mil)	Net Premium ($mil)	Net Income ($mil)
3-19	C+	5.30	4.42	577.8	377.8	367.8	12.4
3-18	B-	8.33	6.94	774.7	511.7	332.5	2.7
2018	C+	5.15	4.29	533.3	367.0	1,323.8	16.2
2017	C	6.74	5.62	694.3	510.7	1,198.2	17.1
2016	C	4.23	3.52	862.2	557.2	1,903.8	-118.4
2015	C-	2.17	1.81	985.9	300.8	2,273.5	-205.7
2014	D	2.20	1.83	408.3	196.9	1,623.8	-6.5

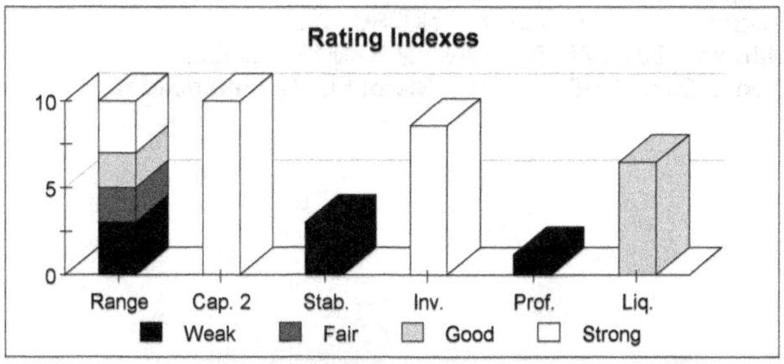

HUMANA HEALTH BENEFIT PLAN LA C+ Fair

Major Rating Factors: Fair overall results on stability tests (4.4 on a scale of 0 to 10). Rating is significantly influenced by the good financial results of . Good liquidity (6.3) with sufficient resources (cash flows and marketable investments) to handle a spike in claims. Excellent profitability (8.0).
Other Rating Factors: Strong capitalization index (8.8) based on excellent current risk-adjusted capital (severe loss scenario). High quality investment portfolio (9.2).
Principal Business: Medicare (82%), comp med (16%)
Mem Phys: 18: 36,720 **17:** 29,787 **18 MLR** 83.6% **/ 18 Admin Exp** N/A
Enroll(000): Q1 19: 376 **18:** 371 **17:** 330 **Med Exp PMPM:** $394
Principal Investments: Long-term bonds (101%)
Provider Compensation ($000): Contr fee ($1,072,025), capitation ($499,166), FFS ($103,466), salary ($21,250)
Total Member Encounters: Phys (3,875,923), non-phys (2,056,499)
Group Affiliation: None
Licensed in: LA
Address: ONE GALLERIA BLVD SUITE 1200, METAIRIE, LA 70001-7542
Phone: (504) 219-6600 **Dom State:** LA **Commenced Bus:** N/A

Data Date	Rating	RACR #1	RACR #2	Total Assets ($mil)	Capital ($mil)	Net Premium ($mil)	Net Income ($mil)
3-19	C+	2.81	2.34	538.6	268.8	554.3	19.3
3-18	B	3.11	2.59	763.6	290.5	501.8	-1.6
2018	C+	2.66	2.21	504.3	252.9	2,000.0	45.2
2017	B	2.36	1.96	595.6	294.3	2,080.3	81.9
2016	B	2.65	2.21	495.5	244.2	2,031.7	60.2
2015	B-	2.09	1.75	396.4	179.7	1,837.4	36.6
2014	B-	2.95	2.46	406.4	223.3	1,646.3	56.2

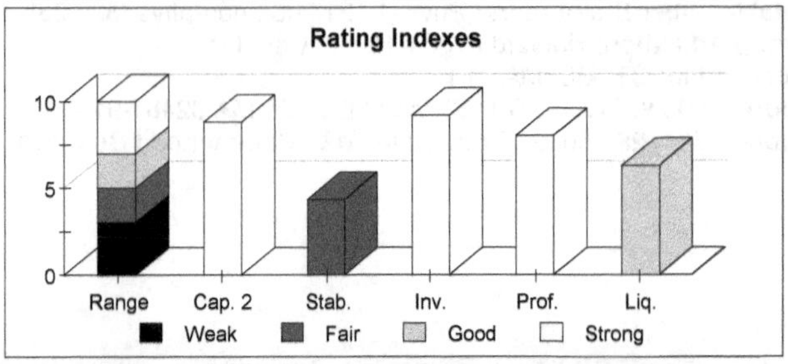

HUMANA HEALTH CO OF NEW YORK INC C+ Fair

Major Rating Factors: Weak profitability index (0.9 on a scale of 0 to 10). Low quality investment portfolio (0.6). Strong capitalization (8.3) based on excellent current risk-adjusted capital (severe loss scenario).
Other Rating Factors: Excellent liquidity (7.1) with ample operational cash flow and liquid investments.
Principal Business: Medicare (100%)
Mem Phys: 18: 30,078 **17:** 27,668 **18 MLR** 97.9% **/ 18 Admin Exp** N/A
Enroll(000): Q1 19: 28 **18:** 21 **17:** 14 **Med Exp PMPM:** $822
Principal Investments: Cash and equiv (100%)
Provider Compensation ($000): Contr fee ($146,202), capitation ($35,748), FFS ($3,633)
Total Member Encounters: Phys (406,498), non-phys (185,650)
Group Affiliation: None
Licensed in: NY
Address: 845 THIRD Ave 7TH Fl, NEW YORK, NY 10019
Phone: (800) 201-3687 **Dom State:** NY **Commenced Bus:** N/A

Data Date	Rating	RACR #1	RACR #2	Total Assets ($mil)	Capital ($mil)	Net Premium ($mil)	Net Income ($mil)
3-19	C+	2.39	1.99	99.3	30.8	76.3	-4.3
3-18	B-	2.40	2.00	77.6	19.3	46.8	-0.4
2018	C+	2.85	2.37	95.4	36.9	197.4	-32.8
2017	D-	1.45	1.21	56.9	20.4	128.1	-20.3
2016	D-	3.10	2.58	40.1	21.3	108.1	-12.1
2015	D-	6.33	5.27	27.9	22.5	42.6	-1.0
2014	E	17.18	14.32	28.3	24.1	13.2	-2.5

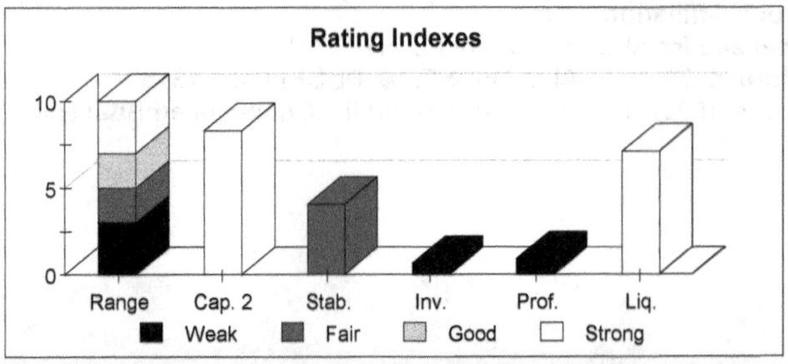

HUMANA HEALTH INS CO OF FL INC B- Good

Major Rating Factors: Fair profitability index (4.0 on a scale of 0 to 10). Good quality investment portfolio (6.7). Strong capitalization (10.0) based on excellent current risk-adjusted capital (severe loss scenario).
Other Rating Factors: Excellent liquidity (9.1) with ample operational cash flow and liquid investments.
Principal Business: Comp med (42%), med supp (35%), other (24%)
Mem Phys: 18: 77,529 **17:** 112,374 **18 MLR** 79.3% **/ 18 Admin Exp** N/A
Enroll(000): Q1 19: 39 **18:** 41 **17:** 178 **Med Exp PMPM:** $73
Principal Investments: Long-term bonds (77%), cash and equiv (23%)
Provider Compensation ($000): Contr fee ($91,832), FFS ($8,866)
Total Member Encounters: Phys (335,276), non-phys (142,250)
Group Affiliation: None
Licensed in: AL, FL, GA, KY, NC, SC, VA
Address: 3501 SW 160TH Ave, MIRAMAR, FL 33027
Phone: (305) 626-5616 **Dom State:** FL **Commenced Bus:** N/A

Data Date	Rating	RACR #1	RACR #2	Total Assets ($mil)	Capital ($mil)	Net Premium ($mil)	Net Income ($mil)
3-19	B-	24.12	20.10	199.0	122.2	17.4	-4.7
3-18	B-	N/A	N/A	210.5	122.3	9.1	5.9
2018	B-	25.12	20.93	212.5	127.4	41.0	13.8
2017	B-	N/A	N/A	277.9	116.2	976.3	-10.5
2016	B-	4.03	3.36	107.3	52.6	206.8	8.0
2015	C+	4.43	3.69	133.5	72.5	265.6	12.8
2014	C+	3.56	2.97	134.6	59.1	287.2	6.0

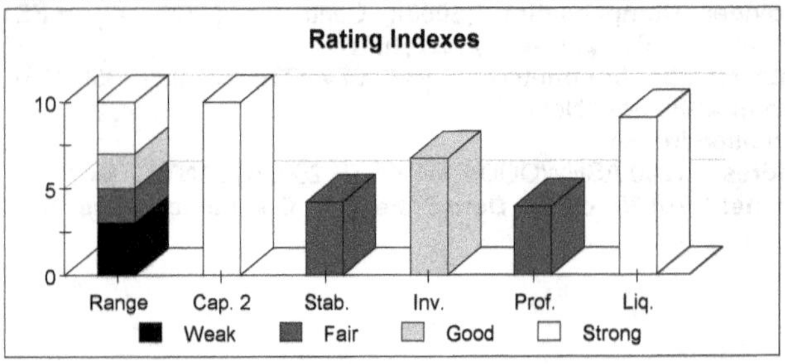

HUMANA HEALTH PLAN INC C+ Fair

Major Rating Factors: Fair profitability index (4.1 on a scale of 0 to 10). Fair overall results on stability tests (3.4) based on a significant 34% decrease in enrollment during the period, a steep decline in premium revenue in 2018 and a steep decline in capital during 2018. Fair liquidity (3.6) as cash resources may not be adequate to cover a spike in claims.
Other Rating Factors: Strong capitalization index (10.0) based on excellent current risk-adjusted capital (severe loss scenario). High quality investment portfolio (8.2).
Principal Business: Medicare (75%), comp med (21%), FEHB (2%), Medicaid (2%)
Mem Phys: 18: 472,557 **17:** 459,416 **18 MLR** 106.7% **/ 18 Admin Exp** N/A
Enroll(000): Q1 19: 340 **18:** 622 **17:** 948 **Med Exp PMPM:** $565
Principal Investments: Long-term bonds (89%), cash and equiv (7%), mortgs (2%), affiliate common stock (1%)
Provider Compensation ($000): Contr fee ($3,065,610), capitation ($690,973), salary ($460,815), FFS ($244,583)
Total Member Encounters: Phys (10,763,567), non-phys (5,909,250)
Group Affiliation: None
Licensed in: AL, AZ, AR, CO, ID, IL, IN, KS, KY, MO, NE, NV, NM, OH, SC, TN, TX, VA, WA, WV
Address: 321 WEST MAIN STREET - 12TH FL, LOUISVILLE, KY 40202
Phone: (502) 580-1000 **Dom State:** KY **Commenced Bus:** N/A

Data Date	Rating	RACR #1	RACR #2	Total Assets ($mil)	Capital ($mil)	Net Premium ($mil)	Net Income ($mil)
3-19	C+	4.15	3.46	1,381.4	804.6	269.5	31.2
3-18	B	3.03	2.52	2,099.0	982.1	972.5	-16.8
2018	C+	3.92	3.27	1,430.7	757.9	3,931.9	125.7
2017	B	3.08	2.56	2,029.1	998.9	7,259.6	117.2
2016	B-	2.65	2.21	1,678.6	866.7	7,278.9	37.0
2015	C+	2.15	1.79	1,385.6	601.3	5,790.9	-102.9
2014	C	2.55	2.13	1,275.1	585.6	4,947.1	-49.1

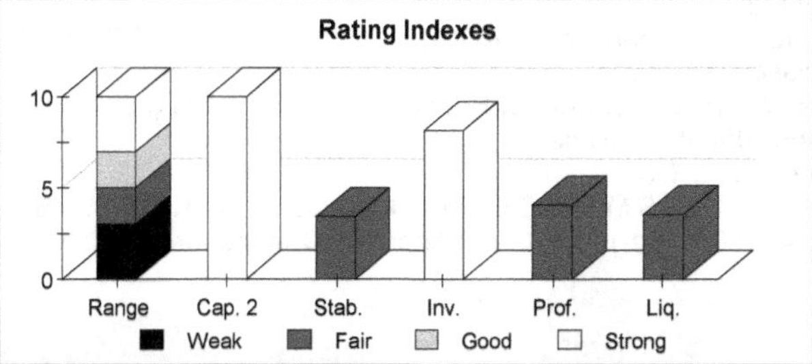

HUMANA HEALTH PLAN OF CALIFORNIA INC C+ Fair

Major Rating Factors: Weak profitability index (0.0 on a scale of 0 to 10). Weak overall results on stability tests (0.6) based on a steep decline in capital during 2017. Rating is significantly influenced by the good financial results of Humana Inc. Strong capitalization index (10.0) based on excellent current risk-adjusted capital (severe loss scenario).
Other Rating Factors: Excellent liquidity (7.4) with ample operational cash flow and liquid investments.
Principal Business: Medicare (100%)
Mem Phys: 17: N/A **16:** N/A **17 MLR** 7.4% **/ 17 Admin Exp** N/A
Enroll(000): Q1 18: N/A **17:** N/A **16:** N/A **Med Exp PMPM:** N/A
Principal Investments ($000): Cash and equiv ($11,071)
Provider Compensation ($000): None
Total Member Encounters: N/A
Group Affiliation: Humana Inc
Licensed in: CA
Address: 600 South Lake Ave Suite 308, Pasadena, CA 91106
Phone: (916) 441-2430 **Dom State:** CA **Commenced Bus:** May 2009

Data Date	Rating	RACR #1	RACR #2	Total Assets ($mil)	Capital ($mil)	Net Premium ($mil)	Net Income ($mil)
3-18	C+	9.07	7.42	24.4	14.5	0.1	0.1
3-17	C	N/A	N/A	53.1	35.9	-0.2	2.9
2017	C+	8.45	6.91	24.8	14.5	5.4	3.3
2016	C	0.74	0.48	54.3	32.9	-0.6	1.9
2015	C	0.74	0.48	104.3	30.9	616.9	-52.5
2014	C-	1.59	1.05	100.5	49.2	342.5	-23.3
2013	C-	2.22	1.51	64.0	38.0	205.0	-7.3

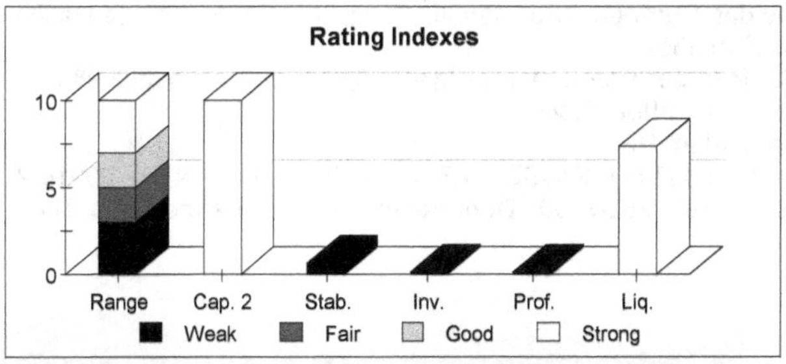

HUMANA HEALTH PLAN OF OHIO INC C+ Fair

Major Rating Factors: Weak profitability index (1.7 on a scale of 0 to 10). Weak overall results on stability tests (1.3) based on a decline in the number of member physicians during 2019. Rating is significantly influenced by the good financial results of . Strong capitalization index (10.0) based on excellent current risk-adjusted capital (severe loss scenario).
Other Rating Factors: High quality investment portfolio (8.7). Excellent liquidity (6.9) with sufficient resources (cash flows and marketable investments) to handle a spike in claims.
Principal Business: Comp med (99%), FEHB (1%)
Mem Phys: 18: 47,103 **17:** 78,165 **18 MLR** 81.7% **/ 18 Admin Exp** N/A
Enroll(000): Q1 19: 39 **18:** 44 **17:** 51 **Med Exp PMPM:** $320
Principal Investments: Long-term bonds (89%), cash and equiv (11%)
Provider Compensation ($000): Contr fee ($124,578), FFS ($53,617), capitation ($7,618)
Total Member Encounters: Phys (306,654), non-phys (124,576)
Group Affiliation: None
Licensed in: IN, KY, OH
Address: 640 EDEN PARK DRIVE, CINCINNATI, OH 45202-6056
Phone: (513) 784-5320 **Dom State:** OH **Commenced Bus:** N/A

Data Date	Rating	RACR #1	RACR #2	Total Assets ($mil)	Capital ($mil)	Net Premium ($mil)	Net Income ($mil)
3-19	C+	4.63	3.86	97.7	62.3	59.0	1.5
3-18	B-	8.92	7.44	164.8	115.5	60.5	2.6
2018	C+	4.60	3.83	91.6	61.8	225.3	5.4
2017	C	6.15	5.12	160.9	113.2	230.8	8.8
2016	B-	2.68	2.23	180.5	102.5	728.8	8.4
2015	C+	2.32	1.93	176.8	77.3	591.0	-27.3
2014	C	2.22	1.85	140.9	63.5	497.0	-25.5

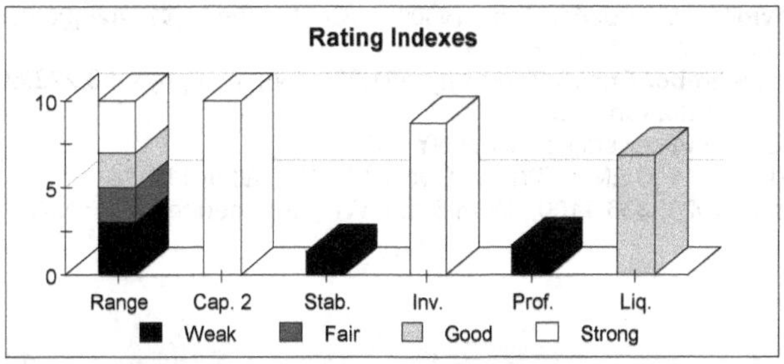

HUMANA HEALTH PLAN OF TEXAS INC C+ Fair

Major Rating Factors: Fair overall results on stability tests (3.8 on a scale of 0 to 10) based on a significant 17% decrease in enrollment during the period. Rating is significantly influenced by the good financial results of . Good liquidity (6.8) with sufficient resources (cash flows and marketable investments) to handle a spike in claims. Weak profitability index (0.8).
Other Rating Factors: Strong capitalization index (8.7) based on excellent current risk-adjusted capital (severe loss scenario). High quality investment portfolio (9.9).
Principal Business: Comp med (93%), FEHB (8%)
Mem Phys: 18: 75,176 **17:** 69,132 **18 MLR** 81.9% **/ 18 Admin Exp** N/A
Enroll(000): Q1 19: 139 **18:** 150 **17:** 181 **Med Exp PMPM:** $307
Principal Investments: Long-term bonds (93%), cash and equiv (5%), real estate (2%)
Provider Compensation ($000): Contr fee ($370,787), FFS ($205,235), capitation ($44,022)
Total Member Encounters: Phys (996,430), non-phys (326,250)
Group Affiliation: None
Licensed in: TX
Address: 1221 S MO PAC EXPY SUITE 200, AUSTIN, TX 78746-7625
Phone: (502) 580-1000 **Dom State:** TX **Commenced Bus:** N/A

Data Date	Rating	RACR #1	RACR #2	Total Assets ($mil)	Capital ($mil)	Net Premium ($mil)	Net Income ($mil)
3-19	C+	2.73	2.27	211.2	105.0	176.4	13.7
3-18	B-	3.28	2.73	263.3	127.4	194.9	8.8
2018	C+	2.48	2.07	206.2	94.6	749.9	-6.6
2017	C-	2.13	1.77	244.5	116.8	775.4	15.1
2016	C	4.65	3.87	404.6	233.9	805.9	-69.0
2015	C	2.28	1.90	584.5	199.6	2,044.9	-86.4
2014	B-	2.91	2.43	473.8	237.4	1,838.5	6.7

Rating Indexes

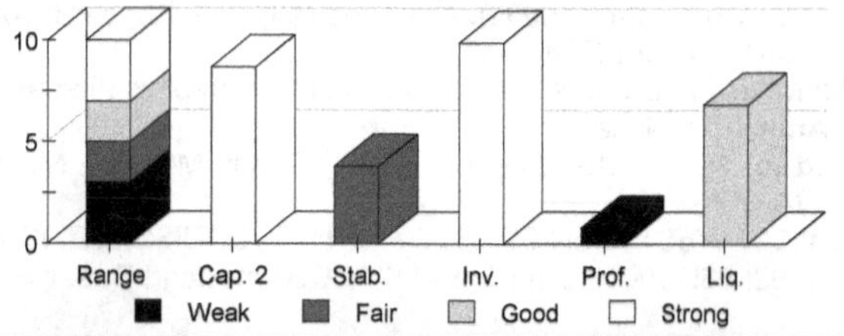

HUMANA HEALTH PLANS OF PUERTO RICO D Weak

Major Rating Factors: Weak profitability index (0.6 on a scale of 0 to 10). Weak overall results on stability tests (2.8) based on a steep decline in capital during 2018. Rating is significantly influenced by the good financial results of . Fair capitalization index (4.6) based on fair current risk-adjusted capital (moderate loss scenario).
Other Rating Factors: Good liquidity (6.0) with sufficient resources (cash flows and marketable investments) to handle a spike in claims. High quality investment portfolio (7.2).
Principal Business: Medicare (90%), FEHB (7%), comp med (3%)
Mem Phys: 18: 22,871 **17:** 22,560 **18 MLR** 90.3% **/ 18 Admin Exp** N/A
Enroll(000): Q1 19: 46 **18:** 43 **17:** 47 **Med Exp PMPM:** $565
Principal Investments: Long-term bonds (66%), cash and equiv (34%)
Provider Compensation ($000): Contr fee ($148,188), capitation ($130,802), FFS ($16,465)
Total Member Encounters: Phys (818,611), non-phys (383,983)
Group Affiliation: None
Licensed in: PR
Address: 383 FD ROOSEVELT AVENUE, SAN JUAN, PR 00918-2131
Phone: (787) 282-7900 **Dom State:** PR **Commenced Bus:** N/A

Data Date	Rating	RACR #1	RACR #2	Total Assets ($mil)	Capital ($mil)	Net Premium ($mil)	Net Income ($mil)
3-19	D	0.86	0.72	137.8	18.9	95.2	-4.2
3-18	D	1.63	1.36	144.7	18.3	83.4	-14.0
2018	D	1.12	0.93	128.5	23.1	324.6	-23.6
2017	C	1.55	1.29	124.1	33.0	304.2	-12.9
2016	C+	3.21	2.67	114.7	42.8	312.2	-32.2
2015	C+	4.97	4.14	140.8	75.6	417.7	7.7
2014	C	4.49	3.74	150.1	69.5	391.5	-18.2

Rating Indexes

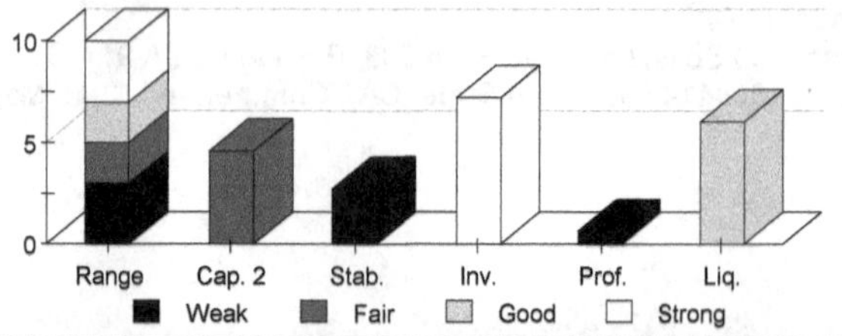

HUMANA INS CO (WI) B Good

Major Rating Factors: Excellent profitability (7.6 on a scale of 0 to 10). Strong capitalization (8.5) based on excellent current risk-adjusted capital (severe loss scenario). High quality investment portfolio (7.3).
Other Rating Factors: Excellent liquidity (6.9) with sufficient resources (cash flows and marketable investments) to handle a spike in claims.
Principal Business: Medicare (76%), comp med (6%), med supp (2%), dental (2%), other (15%)
Mem Phys: 18: 1,455,033 **17:** 1,016,412 **18 MLR** 81.7% **/ 18 Admin Exp** N/A
Enroll(000): Q1 19: 10,415 **18:** 10,813 **17:** 10,554 **Med Exp PMPM:** $157
Principal Investments: Long-term bonds (67%), cash and equiv (17%), affiliate common stock (15%)
Provider Compensation ($000): Contr fee ($17,426,955), capitation ($1,877,697), FFS ($896,995)
Total Member Encounters: Phys (41,276,466), non-phys (23,222,691)
Group Affiliation: None
Licensed in: All states except NY, PR
Address: 1100 EMPLOYERS Blvd, DEPERE, WI 54115
Phone: (920) 336-1100 **Dom State:** WI **Commenced Bus:** N/A

Data Date	Rating	RACR #1	RACR #2	Total Assets ($mil)	Capital ($mil)	Net Premium ($mil)	Net Income ($mil)
3-19	B	2.54	2.11	8,213.3	3,903.8	6,699.8	243.6
3-18	A-	2.90	2.42	11,021.5	3,927.5	6,235.9	-169.5
2018	B	2.42	2.02	7,233.4	3,720.7	24,820.0	1,140.0
2017	A	3.09	2.57	8,716.6	4,184.5	22,921.2	891.7
2016	A-	2.88	2.40	6,870.6	4,224.7	22,960.9	506.1
2015	B+	2.47	2.06	6,583.3	3,642.1	23,141.9	421.8
2014	C-	2.47	2.06	6,237.0	3,307.5	22,315.2	505.3

Rating Indexes

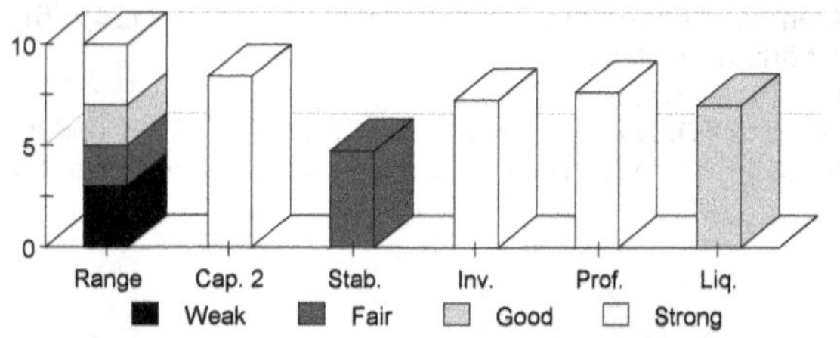

HUMANA INS CO OF NY B- Good

Major Rating Factors: Fair profitability index (3.9 on a scale of 0 to 10). Good liquidity (6.9) with sufficient resources (cash flows and marketable investments) to handle a spike in claims. Strong capitalization (10.0) based on excellent current risk-adjusted capital (severe loss scenario).
Other Rating Factors: High quality investment portfolio (9.6).
Principal Business: Medicare (38%), med supp (6%), dental (1%), other (55%)
Mem Phys: 18: 36,744 **17:** 20,369 **18 MLR** 79.2% **/ 18 Admin Exp** N/A
Enroll(000): Q1 19: 172 **18:** 173 **17:** 178 **Med Exp PMPM:** $102
Principal Investments: Long-term bonds (101%)
Provider Compensation ($000): Contr fee ($212,923), capitation ($3,845), FFS ($2,066)
Total Member Encounters: Phys (392,198), non-phys (177,396)
Group Affiliation: None
Licensed in: NY
Address: 845 THIRD Ave 7TH Fl, NEW YORK, NY 10019
Phone: (800) 201-3687 **Dom State:** NY **Commenced Bus:** N/A

Data Date	Rating	RACR #1	RACR #2	Total Assets ($mil)	Capital ($mil)	Net Premium ($mil)	Net Income ($mil)
3-19	B-	5.72	4.77	153.1	77.9	92.1	-0.3
3-18	B-	4.48	3.73	205.6	64.0	65.1	-6.6
2018	B-	5.91	4.92	134.0	80.4	270.9	8.9
2017	B-	3.26	2.72	154.4	71.9	277.2	4.0
2016	B-	4.49	3.74	105.5	68.1	291.8	-3.4
2015	C+	4.40	3.66	106.4	56.6	253.4	-4.9
2014	B-	5.20	4.34	98.5	59.4	230.7	-2.0

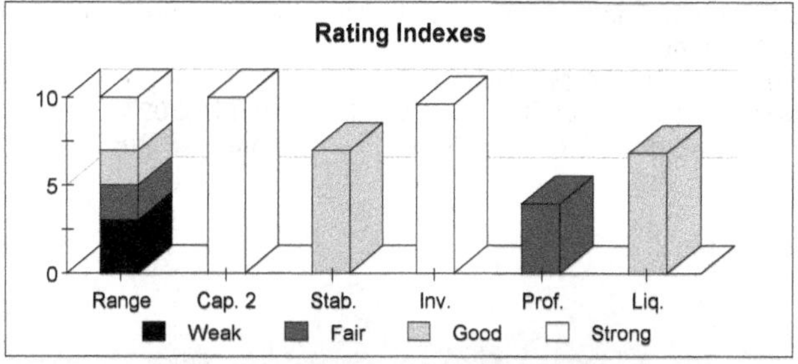

HUMANA INSURANCE COMPANY OF KENTUCKY * B+ Good

Major Rating Factors: Good overall results on stability tests (6.4 on a scale of 0 to 10) despite excessive premium growth. Other stability subfactors include good operational trends and excellent risk diversification. Good liquidity (6.9) with sufficient resources to handle a spike in claims. Strong capitalization (10.0) based on excellent risk adjusted capital (severe loss scenario).
Other Rating Factors: High quality investment portfolio (7.3). Excellent profitability (7.0) despite modest operating losses during 2015.
Principal Business: Reinsurance (57%), individual health insurance (34%), and group life insurance (9%).
Principal Investments: NonCMO investment grade bonds (62%), CMOs and structured securities (32%), and noninv. grade bonds (3%).
Investments in Affiliates: None
Group Affiliation: Humana Inc
Licensed in: CA, CO, KY, TX
Commenced Business: January 2001
Address: 500 WEST MAIN STREET, LOUISVILLE, KY 40202
Phone: (502) 580-1000 **Domicile State:** KY **NAIC Code:** 60219

Data Date	Rating	RACR #1	RACR #2	Total Assets ($mil)	Capital ($mil)	Net Premium ($mil)	Net Income ($mil)
3-19	B+	6.61	4.87	222.0	189.6	49.6	5.9
3-18	B-	6.45	4.76	214.8	168.3	34.5	3.5
2018	B+	6.78	4.98	216.7	185.0	135.4	20.9
2017	B-	6.34	4.65	215.3	164.9	126.5	17.3
2016	C	6.43	4.69	204.5	149.9	90.9	37.4
2015	C	2.61	1.95	432.9	122.2	269.9	-2.8
2014	B-	2.71	2.11	418.0	107.6	157.8	-5.8

Adverse Trends in Operations

Decrease in premium volume from 2015 to 2016 (66%)
Decrease in asset base during 2016 (53%)
Change in premium mix from 2014 to 2015 (4.4%)
Increase in policy surrenders from 2014 to 2015 (501%)
Change in asset mix during 2015 (6.3%)

HUMANA INSURANCE COMPANY OF PUERTO RICO INCORPOR/ C+ Fair

Major Rating Factors: Fair overall results on stability tests (4.7 on a scale of 0 to 10) including negative cash flow from operations for 2018. Good quality investment portfolio (6.9) despite mixed results such as: no exposure to mortgages and substantial holdings of BBB bonds but minimal holdings in junk bonds. Good liquidity (5.5) with sufficient resources to handle a spike in claims.
Other Rating Factors: Weak profitability (2.4) with operating losses during the first three months of 2019. Strong capitalization (7.8) based on excellent risk adjusted capital (severe loss scenario).
Principal Business: Group health insurance (90%) and individual health insurance (10%).
Principal Investments: NonCMO investment grade bonds (38%), CMOs and structured securities (27%), and noninv. grade bonds (1%).
Investments in Affiliates: None
Group Affiliation: Humana Inc
Licensed in: PR
Commenced Business: September 1971
Address: 383 FD ROOSEVELT AVENUE, SAN JUAN, PR 00918-2131
Phone: (787) 282-7900 **Domicile State:** PR **NAIC Code:** 84603

Data Date	Rating	RACR #1	RACR #2	Total Assets ($mil)	Capital ($mil)	Net Premium ($mil)	Net Income ($mil)
3-19	C+	1.98	1.52	78.6	45.6	35.5	-2.8
3-18	C	2.15	1.72	79.3	46.6	33.1	-3.4
2018	C+	2.06	1.58	83.4	48.7	133.2	-2.3
2017	B-	2.18	1.74	77.0	49.4	130.9	4.4
2016	C+	2.29	1.84	67.3	46.2	110.8	-4.4
2015	B-	2.85	2.28	69.3	51.2	96.9	1.5
2014	B-	2.80	2.22	70.2	49.8	93.3	-6.6

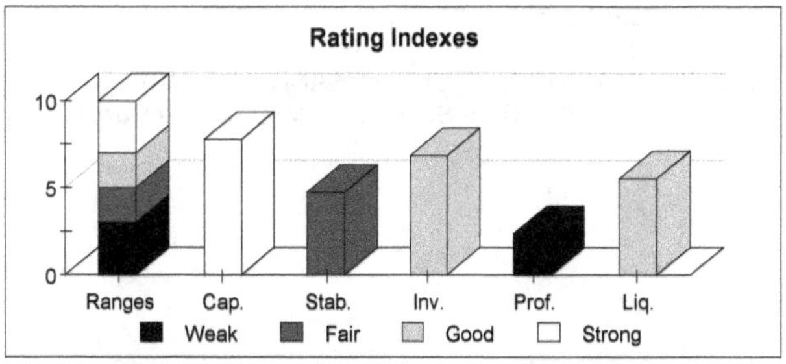

HUMANA MEDICAL PLAN INC * A- Excellent

Major Rating Factors: Excellent profitability (8.5 on a scale of 0 to 10). Strong capitalization index (8.8) based on excellent current risk-adjusted capital (severe loss scenario). High quality investment portfolio (9.0).
Other Rating Factors: Excellent overall results on stability tests (7.3). Good liquidity (6.6) with sufficient resources (cash flows and marketable investments) to handle a spike in claims.
Principal Business: Medicare (69%), Medicaid (23%), comp med (8%)
Mem Phys: 18: 141,455 **17:** 88,391 **18 MLR** 83.8% **/ 18 Admin Exp** N/A
Enroll(000): Q1 19: 1,082 **18:** 935 **17:** 941 **Med Exp PMPM:** $677
Principal Investments: Long-term bonds (88%), cash and equiv (12%)
Provider Compensation ($000): Capitation ($3,236,907), contr fee ($2,803,429), salary ($1,174,623), FFS ($311,869)
Total Member Encounters: Phys (14,834,546), non-phys (11,651,138)
Group Affiliation: None
Licensed in: FL, KY, MS, NC, OR, VA
Address: 3501 SW 160TH AVENUE, MIRAMAR, FL 33027
Phone: (305) 626-5616 **Dom State:** FL **Commenced Bus:** N/A

Data Date	Rating	RACR #1	RACR #2	Total Assets ($mil)	Capital ($mil)	Net Premium ($mil)	Net Income ($mil)
3-19	A-	2.76	2.30	2,319.2	921.7	2,579.9	68.1
3-18	B+	2.66	2.22	2,790.4	852.4	2,247.4	-42.7
2018	B+	2.61	2.17	2,108.1	867.4	8,928.2	281.6
2017	B+	2.68	2.23	2,037.6	900.2	8,736.0	252.0
2016	B	2.32	1.93	1,939.0	768.5	9,065.9	153.3
2015	B	2.21	1.84	2,013.8	683.1	8,867.8	328.3
2014	B-	2.60	2.17	1,742.2	591.5	6,965.8	332.9

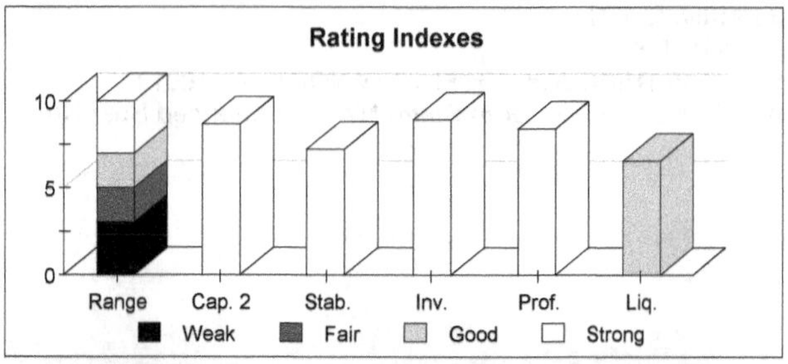

HUMANA MEDICAL PLAN OF MICHIGAN INC C+ Fair

Major Rating Factors: Good liquidity (6.9 on a scale of 0 to 10) with sufficient resources (cash flows and marketable investments) to handle a spike in claims. Weak profitability index (1.9). Strong capitalization (10.0) based on excellent current risk-adjusted capital (severe loss scenario).
Other Rating Factors: High quality investment portfolio (9.9).
Principal Business: Medicare (98%), comp med (2%)
Mem Phys: 18: 33,333 **17:** 66,271 **18 MLR** 85.7% **/ 18 Admin Exp** N/A
Enroll(000): Q1 19: 12 **18:** 10 **17:** 11 **Med Exp PMPM:** $645
Principal Investments: Long-term bonds (57%), cash and equiv (43%)
Provider Compensation ($000): Contr fee ($56,735), capitation ($18,167), FFS ($643)
Total Member Encounters: Phys (174,248), non-phys (87,643)
Group Affiliation: None
Licensed in: MI
Address: 250 MONROE NW STE 400, GRAND RAPIDS, MI 49503
Phone: (502) 580-1000 **Dom State:** MI **Commenced Bus:** N/A

Data Date	Rating	RACR #1	RACR #2	Total Assets ($mil)	Capital ($mil)	Net Premium ($mil)	Net Income ($mil)
3-19	C+	6.06	5.05	51.6	32.4	33.3	3.1
3-18	C+	N/A	N/A	48.9	25.2	20.7	1.1
2018	C+	5.50	4.58	41.3	29.3	88.7	3.7
2017	C+	N/A	N/A	39.8	24.3	77.3	-2.0
2016	C+	4.26	3.55	70.0	31.1	115.1	-8.0
2015	C+	4.10	3.41	56.6	21.0	80.1	1.3
2014	C	8.15	6.80	69.4	31.0	50.5	-4.3

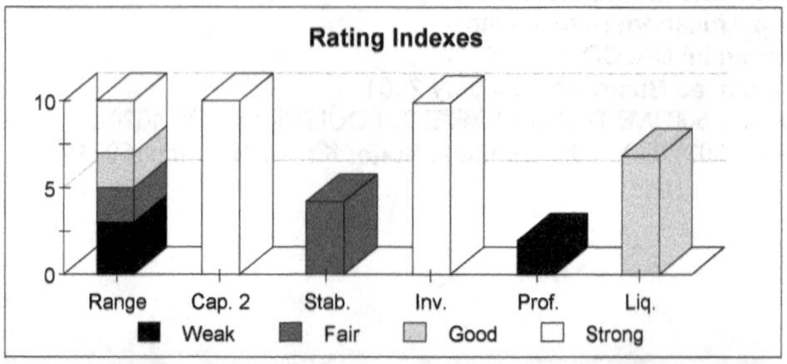

HUMANA MEDICAL PLAN OF UTAH INC C+ Fair

Major Rating Factors: Good liquidity (6.8 on a scale of 0 to 10) with sufficient resources (cash flows and marketable investments) to handle a spike in claims. Weak profitability index (0.8). Strong capitalization (10.0) based on excellent current risk-adjusted capital (severe loss scenario).
Other Rating Factors: High quality investment portfolio (9.1).
Principal Business: Medicare (99%)
Mem Phys: 18: 10,969 **17:** 8,591 **18 MLR** 75.1% **/ 18 Admin Exp** N/A
Enroll(000): Q1 19: 3 **18:** 4 **17:** 6 **Med Exp PMPM:** $472
Principal Investments: Long-term bonds (98%), cash and equiv (2%)
Provider Compensation ($000): Contr fee ($13,113), capitation ($10,209), FFS ($71)
Total Member Encounters: Phys (53,669), non-phys (28,618)
Group Affiliation: None
Licensed in: UT
Address: 9815 S MONROE St Ste 300, SANDY, UT 84070
Phone: (801) 256-6200 **Dom State:** UT **Commenced Bus:** N/A

Data Date	Rating	RACR #1	RACR #2	Total Assets ($mil)	Capital ($mil)	Net Premium ($mil)	Net Income ($mil)
3-19	C+	7.13	5.94	18.5	12.7	7.1	0.8
3-18	B-	8.40	7.00	29.5	20.4	7.6	0.4
2018	C+	6.74	5.62	17.4	12.0	29.8	2.0
2017	C	4.74	3.95	27.1	20.1	39.9	2.6
2016	C+	4.44	3.70	31.8	17.2	46.0	-10.9
2015	C-	4.47	3.73	43.4	19.2	68.6	-8.3
2014	D	7.59	6.32	40.2	27.5	75.5	0.5

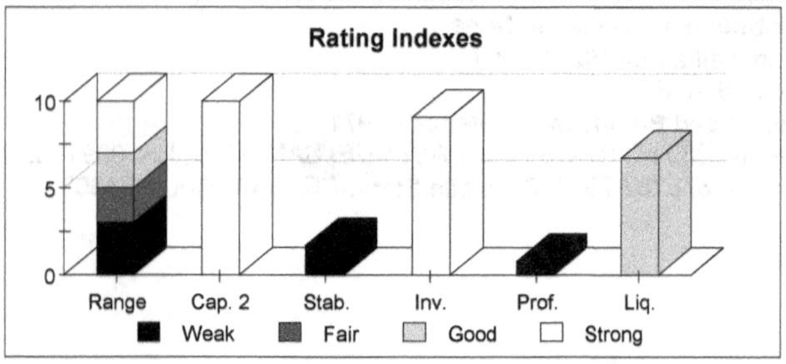

HUMANA WISCONSIN HEALTH ORGANIZATION — B — Good

Major Rating Factors: Good liquidity (6.7 on a scale of 0 to 10) with sufficient resources (cash flows and marketable investments) to handle a spike in claims. Fair profitability index (4.6). Strong capitalization index (8.8) based on excellent current risk-adjusted capital (severe loss scenario).

Other Rating Factors: High quality investment portfolio (9.1). Excellent overall results on stability tests (7.2) based on healthy premium and capital growth during 2018. Rating is significantly influenced by the good financial results of .

Principal Business: Medicare (96%), comp med (4%)

Mem Phys: 18: 218,700 **17:** 104,307 **18 MLR** 86.0% **/ 18 Admin Exp** N/A

Enroll(000): Q1 19: 284 **18:** 246 **17:** 135 **Med Exp PMPM:** $772

Principal Investments: Long-term bonds (68%), cash and equiv (32%)

Provider Compensation ($000): Capitation ($1,130,950), contr fee ($886,721), salary ($51,914), FFS ($37,325)

Total Member Encounters: Phys (4,284,414), non-phys (2,244,799)

Group Affiliation: None

Licensed in: DE, KY, MT, NJ, OH, RI, VA, WI

Address: N19W24133 RIVERWOOD DR SUITE 3, WAUKESHA, WI 53188-1145

Phone: (262) 408-4300 **Dom State:** WI **Commenced Bus:** N/A

Data Date	Rating	RACR #1	RACR #2	Total Assets ($mil)	Capital ($mil)	Net Premium ($mil)	Net Income ($mil)
3-19	B	2.82	2.35	818.9	313.2	828.3	28.1
3-18	B-	1.84	1.53	671.1	113.1	636.7	-26.9
2018	B	2.67	2.23	679.6	296.4	2,572.1	11.5
2017	B-	1.74	1.45	334.7	150.6	1,302.3	25.4
2016	B-	3.27	2.73	200.3	113.2	614.4	2.7
2015	C+	2.43	2.02	179.4	87.4	592.9	-17.6
2014	B-	2.14	1.78	69.9	35.7	287.6	-0.9

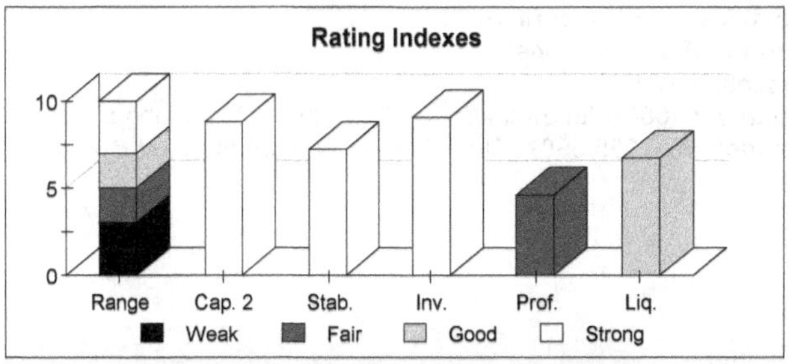

ILLINICARE HEALTH PLAN INC — C- — Fair

Major Rating Factors: Weak profitability index (2.0 on a scale of 0 to 10). Strong capitalization (7.8) based on excellent current risk-adjusted capital (severe loss scenario). High quality investment portfolio (8.7).

Other Rating Factors: Excellent liquidity (7.0) with sufficient resources (cash flows and marketable investments) to handle a spike in claims.

Principal Business: Medicaid (94%), Medicare (6%)

Mem Phys: 18: 24,949 **17:** 23,243 **18 MLR** 90.0% **/ 18 Admin Exp** N/A

Enroll(000): Q1 19: 355 **18:** 360 **17:** 216 **Med Exp PMPM:** $429

Principal Investments: Cash and equiv (69%), long-term bonds (22%), affiliate common stock (4%), other (6%)

Provider Compensation ($000): Contr fee ($1,233,534), bonus arrang ($252,989), salary ($58,294), capitation ($39,443), other ($21,162)

Total Member Encounters: Phys (1,549,701), non-phys (2,102,319)

Group Affiliation: None

Licensed in: IL

Address: 999 Oakmont Plaza Dr, Westmont, IL 60559

Phone: (314) 725-4477 **Dom State:** IL **Commenced Bus:** N/A

Data Date	Rating	RACR #1	RACR #2	Total Assets ($mil)	Capital ($mil)	Net Premium ($mil)	Net Income ($mil)
3-19	C-	2.02	1.68	473.1	184.7	521.2	18.9
3-18	C-	2.05	1.71	376.6	145.3	370.2	13.5
2018	C-	1.83	1.52	450.0	165.3	1,830.8	30.2
2017	C-	1.30	1.08	352.6	128.8	1,367.1	4.4
2016	C-	1.85	1.54	360.9	123.9	1,201.2	-73.7
2015	C-	1.69	1.41	295.8	95.0	1,078.8	-33.4
2014	C+	2.83	2.36	199.9	67.8	528.0	10.9

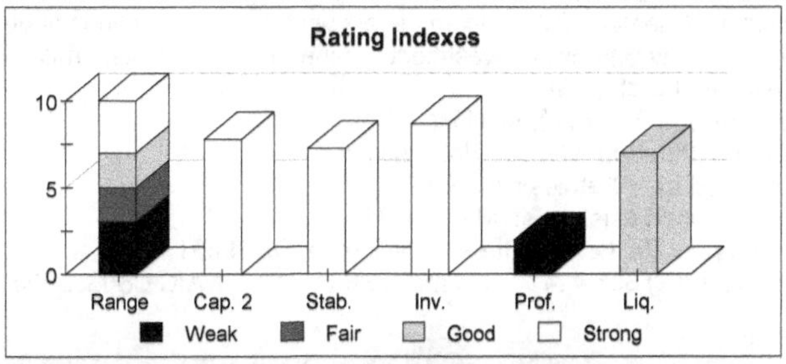

ILLINOIS MUTUAL LIFE INSURANCE COMPANY * — B+ — Good

Major Rating Factors: Good quality investment portfolio (6.4 on a scale of 0 to 10) despite mixed results such as: minimal exposure to mortgages and large holdings of BBB rated bonds but small junk bond holdings. Good overall profitability (6.3) despite operating losses during the first three months of 2019. Good liquidity (6.5).

Other Rating Factors: Good overall results on stability tests (6.7) excellent operational trends and excellent risk diversification. Strong capitalization (8.6) based on excellent risk adjusted capital (severe loss scenario).

Principal Business: Individual life insurance (50%), individual health insurance (47%), group health insurance (3%), and individual annuities (1%).

Principal Investments: NonCMO investment grade bonds (61%), CMOs and structured securities (23%), noninv. grade bonds (4%), common & preferred stock (4%), and misc. investments (7%).

Investments in Affiliates: None

Group Affiliation: None

Licensed in: All states except AK, DC, HI, NY, PR

Commenced Business: July 1912

Address: 300 SW Adams Street, Peoria, IL 61634

Phone: (309) 674-8255 **Domicile State:** IL **NAIC Code:** 64580

Data Date	Rating	RACR #1	RACR #2	Total Assets ($mil)	Capital ($mil)	Net Premium ($mil)	Net Income ($mil)
3-19	B+	3.69	2.06	1,507.2	241.5	24.7	-1.8
3-18	B	3.70	2.09	1,439.2	229.8	25.6	2.8
2018	B+	3.75	2.09	1,460.5	240.1	101.5	27.4
2017	B	3.74	2.12	1,442.3	229.8	105.4	12.7
2016	B	3.70	2.08	1,434.3	226.0	102.8	9.4
2015	A-	3.53	1.99	1,388.9	211.7	100.3	14.8
2014	A-	3.27	1.84	1,367.7	196.3	100.5	28.2

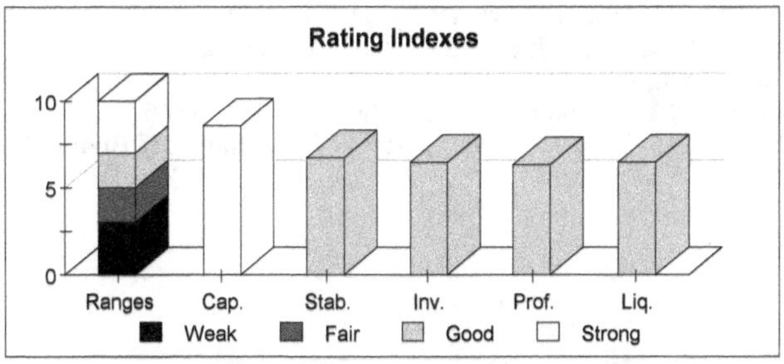

IMPERIAL HEALTH PLAN OF CALIFORNIA C- Fair

Major Rating Factors: Fair overall results on stability tests (3.2 on a scale of 0 to 10) based on an excessive 39% enrollment growth during the period but healthy premium and capital growth during 2018. Excellent profitability (8.4). Strong capitalization index (6.9) based on good current risk-adjusted capital (moderate loss scenario).
Other Rating Factors: Excellent liquidity (7.0) with ample operational cash flow and liquid investments.
Principal Business: Medicare (13%)
Mem Phys: 18: N/A **17:** N/A **18 MLR** 90.3% **/ 18 Admin Exp** N/A
Enroll(000): Q1 19: 6 **18:** 2 **17:** 2 **Med Exp PMPM:** $605
Principal Investments ($000): Cash and equiv ($7,989)
Provider Compensation ($000): None
Total Member Encounters: N/A
Group Affiliation: None
Licensed in: CA
Address: 10801 6th Street Suite 120, Rancho Cucamonga, CA 91730
Phone: (951) 335-3987 **Dom State:** CA **Commenced Bus:** N/A

Data Date	Rating	RACR #1	RACR #2	Total Assets ($mil)	Capital ($mil)	Net Premium ($mil)	Net Income ($mil)
3-19	C-	1.07	0.71	12.8	4.1	11.7	1.7
3-18	C-	1.30	0.86	5.0	2.3	4.0	1.0
2018	D+	0.60	0.40	9.5	2.4	24.9	1.1
2017	C-	0.71	0.47	3.3	1.3	15.6	0.0
2016	C-	2.38	1.57	3.0	1.3	5.1	0.1
2015	N/A	N/A	N/A	N/A	N/A	N/A	N/A
2014	N/A	N/A	N/A	N/A	N/A	N/A	N/A

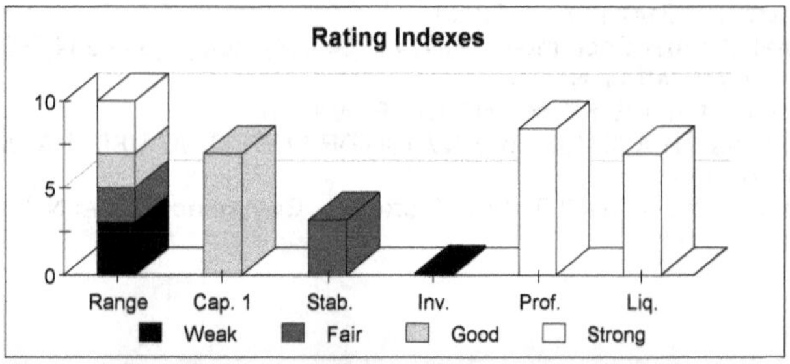

INDEPENDENCE AMERICAN INS CO B- Good

Major Rating Factors: Fair overall results on stability tests (3.7 on a scale of 0 to 10) including excessive premium growth. The largest net exposure for one risk is conservative at 1.7% of capital. History of adequate reserve strength (5.8) as reserves have been consistently at an acceptable level.
Other Rating Factors: Good liquidity (5.7) with sufficient resources (cash flows and marketable investments) to handle a spike in claims. Strong long-term capitalization index (8.0) based on excellent current risk adjusted capital (severe and moderate loss scenarios). Moreover, capital levels have been consistent in recent years. Excellent profitability (8.7) with operating gains in each of the last five years. Return on equity has been good over the last five years, averaging 10.5%.
Principal Business: Group accident & health (57%), inland marine (27%), other accident & health (10%), and aggregate write-ins for other lines of business (6%).
Principal Investments: Investment grade bonds (83%), misc. investments (14%), and cash (3%).
Investments in Affiliates: None
Group Affiliation: Geneve Holdings Inc
Licensed in: All states except PR
Commenced Business: March 1973
Address: 1209 Orange Street, Wilmington, DE 19801
Phone: (212) 355-4141 **Domicile State:** DE **NAIC Code:** 26581

Data Date	Rating	RACR #1	RACR #2	Loss Ratio %	Total Assets ($mil)	Capital ($mil)	Net Premium ($mil)	Net Income ($mil)
3-19	B-	2.15	1.65	N/A	135.2	88.1	38.9	4.6
3-18	B-	2.50	1.78	N/A	114.5	74.1	31.0	2.8
2018	B-	2.16	1.66	35.3	126.5	83.0	137.4	18.0
2017	B-	2.53	1.79	47.0	112.9	72.1	110.8	8.7
2016	B-	4.41	2.55	62.5	114.4	66.8	91.2	4.0
2015	C+	2.35	1.39	66.8	115.9	63.4	149.8	3.0
2014	C	2.34	1.39	66.7	102.9	60.2	133.6	3.1

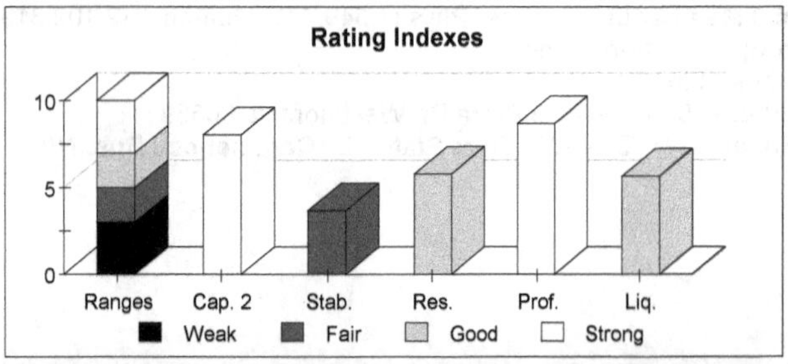

INDEPENDENCE BLUE CROSS C+ Fair

Major Rating Factors: Weak profitability index (0.6 on a scale of 0 to 10). Strong capitalization (9.5) based on excellent current risk-adjusted capital (severe loss scenario). High quality investment portfolio (7.3).
Other Rating Factors: Excellent liquidity (7.0) with sufficient resources (cash flows and marketable investments) to handle a spike in claims.
Principal Business: FEHB (82%), med supp (14%), comp med (3%)
Mem Phys: 18: 814 **17:** 794 **18 MLR** 97.6% **/ 18 Admin Exp** N/A
Enroll(000): Q1 19: 116 **18:** 117 **17:** 120 **Med Exp PMPM:** $242
Principal Investments: Long-term bonds (60%), cash and equiv (13%), nonaffiliate common stock (11%), other (16%)
Provider Compensation ($000): Contr fee ($302,622), FFS ($33,340), bonus arrang ($2,215), other ($5,052)
Total Member Encounters: Non-phys (747,246)
Group Affiliation: Independence Health Group Inc
Licensed in: PA
Address: 1901 Market St, Philadelphia, PA 19103-1480
Phone: (215) 241-2400 **Dom State:** PA **Commenced Bus:** N/A

Data Date	Rating	RACR #1	RACR #2	Total Assets ($mil)	Capital ($mil)	Net Premium ($mil)	Net Income ($mil)
3-19	C+	3.34	2.78	269.1	33.1	87.6	-2.6
3-18	C	5.91	4.93	303.9	56.6	86.8	-5.7
2018	C	3.32	2.77	272.3	32.9	351.4	-27.8
2017	C-	4.15	3.46	299.6	64.3	365.6	-9.1
2016	C-	6.74	5.62	285.0	68.7	391.8	7.0
2015	C-	5.44	4.53	303.9	56.0	358.8	-24.4
2014	C	6.57	5.48	423.1	81.4	373.2	18.8

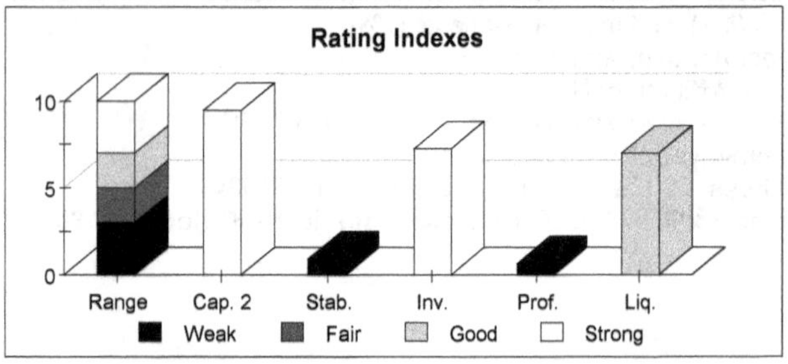

INDEPENDENT CARE HEALTH PLAN * B+ Good

Major Rating Factors: Good liquidity (6.7 on a scale of 0 to 10) with sufficient resources (cash flows and marketable investments) to handle a spike in claims. Excellent profitability (7.7). Strong capitalization (8.5) based on excellent current risk-adjusted capital (severe loss scenario).
Other Rating Factors: High quality investment portfolio (9.9).
Principal Business: Medicaid (51%), Medicare (49%)
Mem Phys: 18: 5,603 **17:** 5,187 **18 MLR** 80.4% **/ 18 Admin Exp** N/A
Enroll(000): Q1 19: 36 **18:** 35 **17:** 30 **Med Exp PMPM:** $566
Principal Investments: Long-term bonds (71%), cash and equiv (29%)
Provider Compensation ($000): Contr fee ($230,186), capitation ($2,454)
Total Member Encounters: Phys (357,713), non-phys (313,976)
Group Affiliation: None
Licensed in: IL, WI
Address: 1555 N RiverCenter Dr Ste 206, Milwaukee, WI 53212
Phone: (414) 223-4847 **Dom State:** WI **Commenced Bus:** N/A

Data Date	Rating	RACR #1	RACR #2	Total Assets ($mil)	Capital ($mil)	Net Premium ($mil)	Net Income ($mil)
3-19	B+	2.59	2.16	86.5	32.1	75.4	-0.2
3-18	A-	2.65	2.21	92.9	27.1	64.4	-1.6
2018	B+	2.61	2.18	87.3	32.5	285.1	4.6
2017	A-	1.64	1.37	78.5	29.3	228.0	2.8
2016	A-	2.68	2.23	71.2	27.4	215.1	-0.5
2015	B+	2.92	2.43	68.2	27.5	210.9	5.3
2014	B	2.87	2.39	55.4	22.2	175.5	1.8

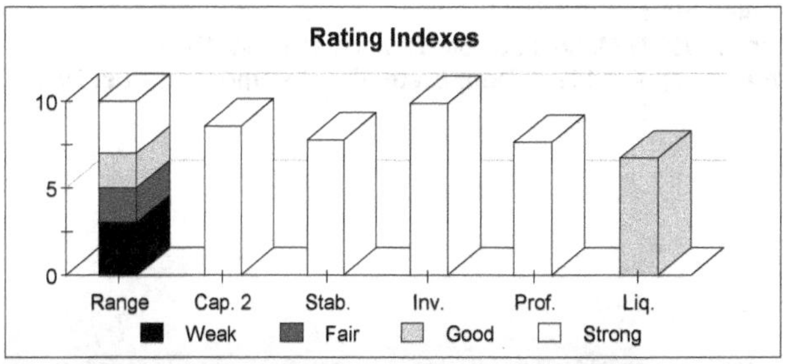

INDEPENDENT HEALTH ASSOC INC B- Good

Major Rating Factors: Fair profitability index (3.4 on a scale of 0 to 10). Good overall results on stability tests (6.5). Good liquidity (6.9) with sufficient resources (cash flows and marketable investments) to handle a spike in claims.
Other Rating Factors: Strong capitalization index (10.0) based on excellent current risk-adjusted capital (severe loss scenario). High quality investment portfolio (8.5).
Principal Business: Medicare (56%), Medicaid (27%), comp med (16%)
Mem Phys: 18: 4,278 **17:** 4,260 **18 MLR** 89.0% **/ 18 Admin Exp** N/A
Enroll(000): Q1 19: 161 **18:** 163 **17:** 170 **Med Exp PMPM:** $628
Principal Investments: Long-term bonds (59%), nonaffiliate common stock (9%), cash and equiv (6%), real estate (4%), affiliate common stock (3%), other (19%)
Provider Compensation ($000): Capitation ($889,499), FFS ($342,105), other ($16,128)
Total Member Encounters: Phys (332,353), non-phys (614,849)
Group Affiliation: Independent Health Association Inc
Licensed in: NY
Address: 511 Farber Lakes Drive, Buffalo, NY 14221
Phone: (716) 631-3001 **Dom State:** NY **Commenced Bus:** N/A

Data Date	Rating	RACR #1	RACR #2	Total Assets ($mil)	Capital ($mil)	Net Premium ($mil)	Net Income ($mil)
3-19	B-	3.82	3.19	711.8	404.9	357.5	7.9
3-18	B-	3.11	2.59	682.7	333.7	343.0	-3.1
2018	B-	3.63	3.02	688.8	387.1	1,403.3	26.5
2017	B-	3.37	2.81	722.0	367.5	1,386.1	23.7
2016	B-	3.23	2.69	710.1	367.1	1,511.3	26.1
2015	B-	2.99	2.49	764.7	337.3	1,507.7	-43.9
2014	B-	4.05	3.38	668.6	384.2	1,339.4	-72.8

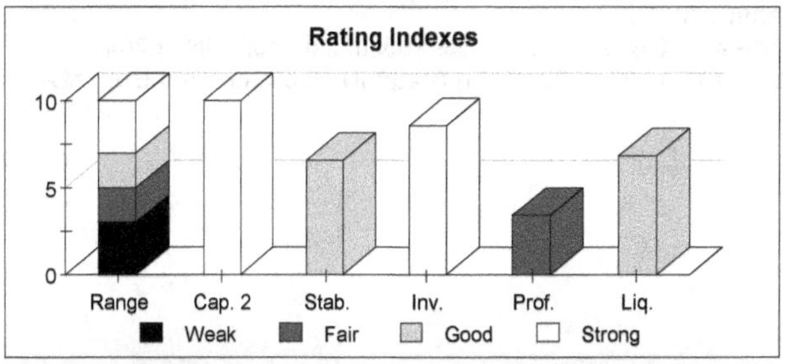

INDEPENDENT HEALTH BENEFITS CORP C Fair

Major Rating Factors: Weak profitability index (2.3 on a scale of 0 to 10). Strong capitalization (7.9) based on excellent current risk-adjusted capital (severe loss scenario). High quality investment portfolio (9.1).
Other Rating Factors: Excellent liquidity (7.2) with ample operational cash flow and liquid investments.
Principal Business: Comp med (77%), FEHB (12%), Medicare (11%)
Mem Phys: 18: 4,270 **17:** 4,248 **18 MLR** 87.0% **/ 18 Admin Exp** N/A
Enroll(000): Q1 19: 86 **18:** 100 **17:** 116 **Med Exp PMPM:** $429
Principal Investments: Long-term bonds (89%), cash and equiv (11%)
Provider Compensation ($000): FFS ($539,599), capitation ($1,770), other ($17,796)
Total Member Encounters: Phys (1,709,027), non-phys (3,798,075)
Group Affiliation: Independent Health Association Inc
Licensed in: NY
Address: 511 Farber Lakes Dr, Buffalo, NY 14221
Phone: (716) 631-3001 **Dom State:** NY **Commenced Bus:** N/A

Data Date	Rating	RACR #1	RACR #2	Total Assets ($mil)	Capital ($mil)	Net Premium ($mil)	Net Income ($mil)
3-19	C	2.04	1.70	256.6	101.0	138.5	4.6
3-18	C	1.54	1.28	235.2	78.5	159.8	-14.3
2018	C	1.93	1.61	247.3	96.4	632.6	2.2
2017	C	1.58	1.32	290.8	92.5	637.9	-1.3
2016	C	1.75	1.46	238.3	96.0	606.8	-13.1
2015	B-	2.48	2.07	270.2	107.0	584.3	-0.1
2014	B-	2.63	2.19	167.8	107.1	504.8	12.6

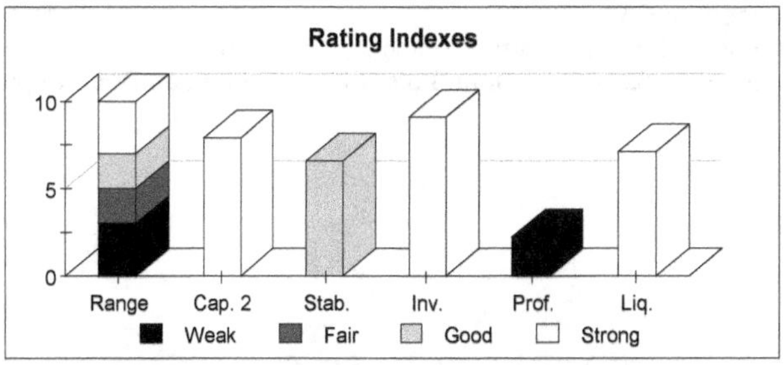

INDIANA UNIVERSITY HEALTH PLANS INC E- Very Weak

Major Rating Factors: Weak profitability index (0.6 on a scale of 0 to 10). Low quality investment portfolio (0.2). Good capitalization (6.6) based on good current risk-adjusted capital (severe loss scenario).
Other Rating Factors: Excellent liquidity (7.3) with ample operational cash flow and liquid investments.
Principal Business: Comp med (100%)
Mem Phys: 18: 14,275 **17:** 13,843 **18 MLR** 84.9% **/ 18 Admin Exp** N/A
Enroll(000): Q1 19: 9 **18:** 8 **17:** 13 **Med Exp PMPM:** $374
Principal Investments: Cash and equiv (100%)
Provider Compensation ($000): Capitation ($33,399)
Total Member Encounters: N/A
Group Affiliation: Indiana University Health Inc
Licensed in: IN
Address: 950 N Meridian St Ste 200, Indianapolis, IN 46204
Phone: (317) 963-4822 **Dom State:** IN **Commenced Bus:** N/A

Data Date	Rating	RACR #1	RACR #2	Total Assets ($mil)	Capital ($mil)	Net Premium ($mil)	Net Income ($mil)
3-19	E-	1.18	0.98	14.8	3.5	13.5	-0.3
3-18	E-	N/A	N/A	35.9	6.6	10.5	-0.4
2018	E-	1.19	0.99	14.3	3.6	39.3	-3.4
2017	E-	N/A	N/A	36.3	7.2	60.9	-7.8
2016	E-	1.88	1.57	41.7	7.8	73.9	-19.7
2015	D	1.92	1.60	22.2	14.2	141.9	-3.7
2014	D-	1.22	1.02	13.2	10.0	134.8	-2.0

Rating Indexes

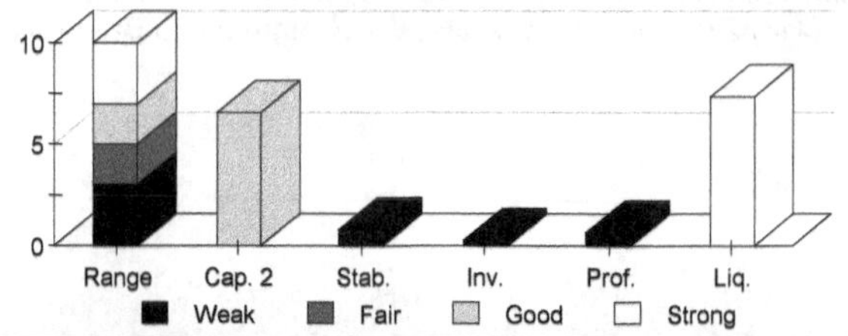

INDIANA UNIVERSITY HEALTH PLANS NFP D Weak

Major Rating Factors: Weak profitability index (0.9 on a scale of 0 to 10). Low quality investment portfolio (0.1). Fair capitalization (3.6) based on weak current risk-adjusted capital (moderate loss scenario).
Other Rating Factors: Excellent liquidity (7.2) with ample operational cash flow and liquid investments.
Principal Business: Medicare (100%)
Mem Phys: 18: 15,533 **17:** 14,231 **18 MLR** 88.7% **/ 18 Admin Exp** N/A
Enroll(000): Q1 19: 14 **18:** 14 **17:** 15 **Med Exp PMPM:** $812
Principal Investments: Cash and equiv (100%)
Provider Compensation ($000): Capitation ($128,498), FFS ($13,936)
Total Member Encounters: N/A
Group Affiliation: Indiana University Health Inc
Licensed in: IN
Address: 950 N Meridian St Ste 200, Indianapolis, IN 46204
Phone: (317) 963-4822 **Dom State:** IN **Commenced Bus:** N/A

Data Date	Rating	RACR #1	RACR #2	Total Assets ($mil)	Capital ($mil)	Net Premium ($mil)	Net Income ($mil)
3-19	D	0.72	0.60	38.2	10.9	35.6	-1.6
3-18	C+	N/A	N/A	33.3	11.6	39.3	-1.1
2018	C-	0.96	0.80	38.1	13.5	157.1	-4.3
2017	C+	N/A	N/A	33.1	13.0	162.3	-4.4
2016	C	1.46	1.21	19.1	15.2	180.0	0.6
2015	N/A	N/A	N/A	1.5	1.5	N/A	N/A
2014	N/A	N/A	N/A	1.5	1.5	N/A	N/A

Rating Indexes

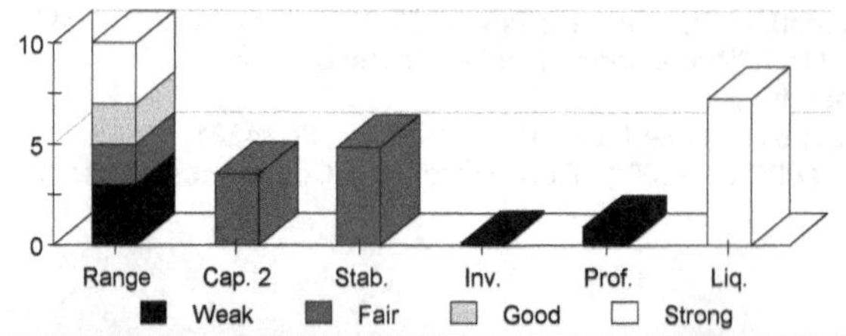

INLAND EMPIRE HEALTH PLAN * A Excellent

Major Rating Factors: Excellent profitability (8.9 on a scale of 0 to 10). Strong capitalization index (8.7) based on excellent current risk-adjusted capital (severe loss scenario). Excellent liquidity (7.0) with ample operational cash flow and liquid investments.
Other Rating Factors: Good overall results on stability tests (6.2).
Principal Business: Medicaid (91%), Medicare (9%)
Mem Phys: 18: N/A **17:** N/A **18 MLR** 91.5% **/ 18 Admin Exp** N/A
Enroll(000): Q1 19: 1,247 **18:** 1,245 **17:** 1,419 **Med Exp PMPM:** $296
Principal Investments ($000): Cash and equiv ($373,062)
Provider Compensation ($000): None
Total Member Encounters: N/A
Group Affiliation: None
Licensed in: CA
Address: 300 S Park Avenue, Pomona, CA 91769
Phone: (909) 623-6333 **Dom State:** CA **Commenced Bus:** September 1996

Data Date	Rating	RACR #1	RACR #2	Total Assets ($mil)	Capital ($mil)	Net Premium ($mil)	Net Income ($mil)
3-19	A	3.49	2.23	1,855.4	894.2	1,294.8	-0.8
3-18	A	3.31	2.09	1,432.7	848.2	1,166.0	0.9
2018	A	3.50	2.24	1,402.6	895.0	4,845.7	47.8
2017	A	3.32	2.10	1,381.7	847.3	5,099.5	68.0
2016	A	3.02	1.95	1,782.2	688.7	4,298.5	216.7
2015	B+	2.31	1.46	1,402.3	472.0	3,887.3	317.3
2014	B	1.31	0.83	476.0	160.3	1,847.9	41.9

Rating Indexes

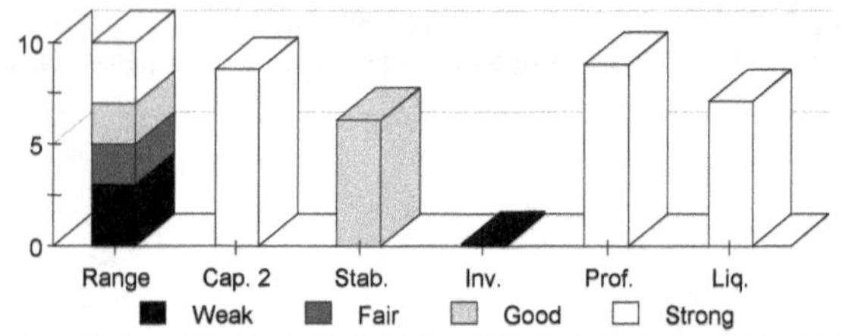

INNOVATION HEALTH INS CO — C- — Fair

Major Rating Factors: Weak profitability index (0.9 on a scale of 0 to 10). Good quality investment portfolio (6.8). Strong capitalization (10.0) based on excellent current risk-adjusted capital (severe loss scenario).
Other Rating Factors: Excellent liquidity (8.1) with ample operational cash flow and liquid investments.
Principal Business: Medicare (57%), comp med (43%)
Mem Phys: 18: 76,024 **17:** 74,673 **18 MLR** 28.4% **/ 18 Admin Exp** N/A
Enroll(000): Q1 19: 12 **18:** 11 **17:** 75 **Med Exp PMPM:** $322
Principal Investments: Long-term bonds (59%), affiliate common stock (33%), cash and equiv (8%)
Provider Compensation ($000): Contr fee ($70,601), FFS ($12,125), capitation ($7)
Total Member Encounters: Phys (174,414), non-phys (122,738)
Group Affiliation: Innovation Health Holdings LLC
Licensed in: DC, MD, VA
Address: 3190 FAIRVIEW PARK Dr Ste 570, FALLS CHURCH, VA 22042
Phone: (703) 914-2925 **Dom State:** VA **Commenced Bus:** N/A

Data Date	Rating	RACR #1	RACR #2	Total Assets ($mil)	Capital ($mil)	Net Premium ($mil)	Net Income ($mil)
3-19	C-	5.73	4.78	131.9	91.2	42.4	7.3
3-18	C-	N/A	N/A	173.6	65.6	36.6	1.5
2018	C-	5.25	4.37	119.3	82.7	163.2	12.4
2017	C-	N/A	N/A	198.7	62.5	315.8	-30.0
2016	C+	1.97	1.64	157.4	44.2	244.0	-26.0
2015	C+	3.52	2.93	120.4	63.2	204.6	3.1
2014	B	3.42	2.85	76.2	41.1	129.5	-1.0

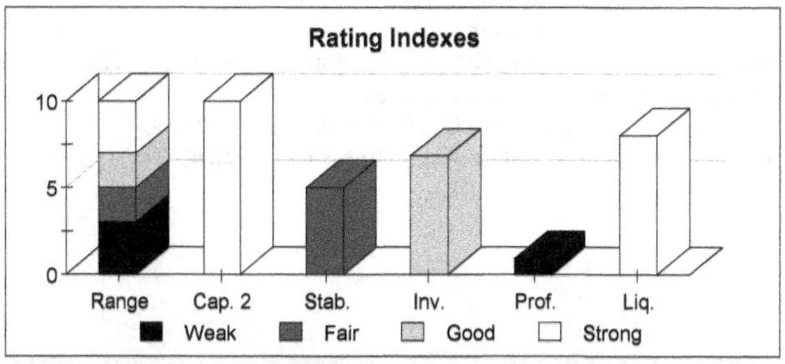

INNOVATION HEALTH PLAN INC — C- — Fair

Major Rating Factors: Good overall profitability index (5.0 on a scale of 0 to 10). Strong capitalization (10.0) based on excellent current risk-adjusted capital (severe loss scenario). High quality investment portfolio (9.9).
Other Rating Factors: Excellent liquidity (7.3) with ample operational cash flow and liquid investments.
Principal Business: Comp med (75%), Medicare (25%)
Mem Phys: 18: 84,706 **17:** 79,982 **18 MLR** 66.9% **/ 18 Admin Exp** N/A
Enroll(000): Q1 19: 15 **18:** 15 **17:** 21 **Med Exp PMPM:** $330
Principal Investments: Cash and equiv (50%), long-term bonds (50%)
Provider Compensation ($000): Contr fee ($48,426), FFS ($28,331), capitation ($107)
Total Member Encounters: Phys (204,613), non-phys (167,922)
Group Affiliation: Innovation Health Holdings LLC
Licensed in: DC, MD, VA
Address: 3190 FAIRVIEW PARK Dr Ste 570, FALLS CHURCH, VA 22042
Phone: (703) 914-2925 **Dom State:** VA **Commenced Bus:** N/A

Data Date	Rating	RACR #1	RACR #2	Total Assets ($mil)	Capital ($mil)	Net Premium ($mil)	Net Income ($mil)
3-19	C-	3.92	3.27	56.7	27.7	24.6	0.6
3-18	C-	N/A	N/A	57.8	23.0	29.6	0.5
2018	C-	3.82	3.18	53.1	26.9	112.2	3.3
2017	C-	N/A	N/A	46.0	22.5	104.7	0.3
2016	C-	2.74	2.28	44.1	18.4	95.7	-4.9
2015	C+	3.85	3.21	30.7	17.6	79.6	3.4
2014	B	3.60	3.00	20.8	12.1	51.3	1.1

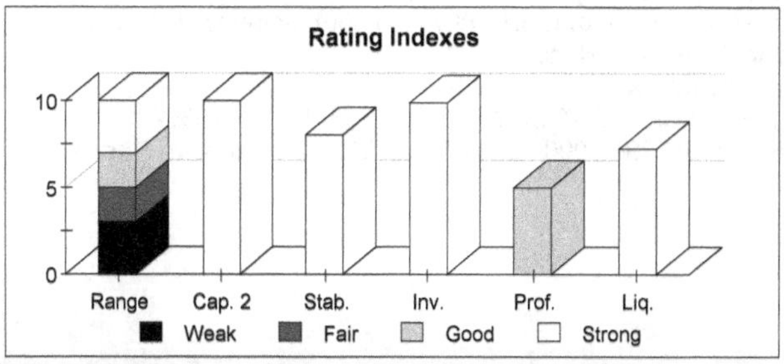

INOVA HEALTH PLAN LLC — D — Weak

Major Rating Factors: Fair profitability index (3.6 on a scale of 0 to 10). Strong capitalization (7.7) based on excellent current risk-adjusted capital (severe loss scenario). High quality investment portfolio (9.9).
Other Rating Factors: Excellent liquidity (6.9) with sufficient resources (cash flows and marketable investments) to handle a spike in claims.
Principal Business: Medicaid (100%)
Mem Phys: 17: N/A **16:** 15,151 **17 MLR** 90.5% **/ 17 Admin Exp** N/A
Enroll(000): Q3 18: N/A **17:** N/A **16:** 61 **Med Exp PMPM:** N/A
Principal Investments: Cash and equiv (65%), long-term bonds (35%)
Provider Compensation ($000): Capitation ($4,188), other ($167,478)
Total Member Encounters: Phys (394,110), non-phys (152,990)
Group Affiliation: Inova Health System Foundation
Licensed in: VA
Address: 8110 Gatehouse Rd Ste 400W, Falls Church, VA 22042
Phone: (703) 289-2455 **Dom State:** VA **Commenced Bus:** N/A

Data Date	Rating	RACR #1	RACR #2	Total Assets ($mil)	Capital ($mil)	Net Premium ($mil)	Net Income ($mil)
9-18	D	1.90	1.58	18.1	16.2	-0.3	5.5
9-17	C	2.50	2.09	61.3	23.9	157.4	-1.2
2017	C	2.66	2.22	38.8	23.1	175.7	2.9
2016	C+	2.56	2.13	56.3	24.5	196.3	-2.2
2015	B	2.95	2.46	51.5	26.5	188.6	1.9
2014	B	2.85	2.38	50.7	25.5	176.7	-4.1
2013	B+	3.75	3.12	54.4	32.1	178.2	0.4

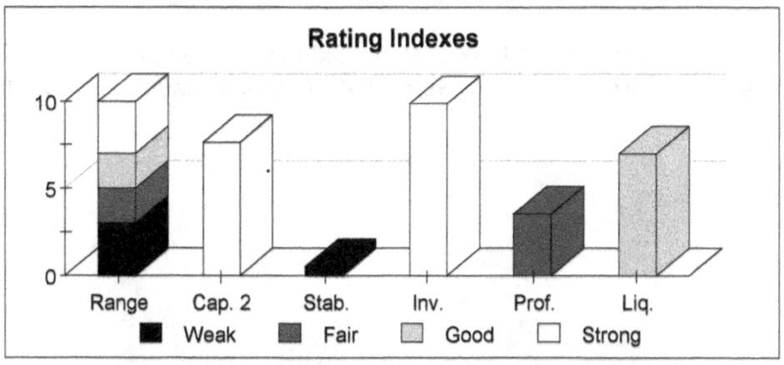

INS CO OF NORTH AMERICA C Fair

Major Rating Factors: Fair overall results on stability tests (3.5) including fair financial strength of affiliated Chubb Limited and negative cash flow from operations for 2018.

Other Rating Factors: Vulnerable liquidity (2.0) as a spike in claims may stretch capacity. Strong long-term capitalization index (10.0) based on excellent current risk adjusted capital (severe and moderate loss scenarios). Moreover, capital levels have been consistent in recent years. Excellent profitability (7.8) with operating gains in each of the last five years.

Principal Business: (Not applicable due to unusual reinsurance transactions.)

Principal Investments: Investment grade bonds (75%), cash (19%), and real estate (7%).

Investments in Affiliates: None

Group Affiliation: Chubb Limited

Licensed in: All states, the District of Columbia and Puerto Rico

Commenced Business: January 1792

Address: 436 WALNUT STREET, Philadelphia, PA 19106

Phone: (215) 640-1000 **Domicile State:** PA **NAIC Code:** 22713

Data Date	Rating	RACR #1	RACR #2	Loss Ratio %	Total Assets ($mil)	Capital ($mil)	Net Premium ($mil)	Net Income ($mil)
3-19	C	82.17	30.07	N/A	362.9	343.0	0.0	1.4
3-18	C	9.52	6.25	N/A	396.4	348.2	0.0	11.2
2018	C	119.30	37.10	0.0	357.3	343.1	-86.9	4.7
2017	C	2.20	1.45	83.9	999.4	251.2	270.6	6.0
2016	C	2.29	1.53	76.5	944.2	250.2	249.8	16.5
2015	C	2.08	1.40	72.8	883.8	233.6	237.9	8.6
2014	C	2.29	1.53	77.6	869.9	225.2	223.9	12.7

Rating Indexes

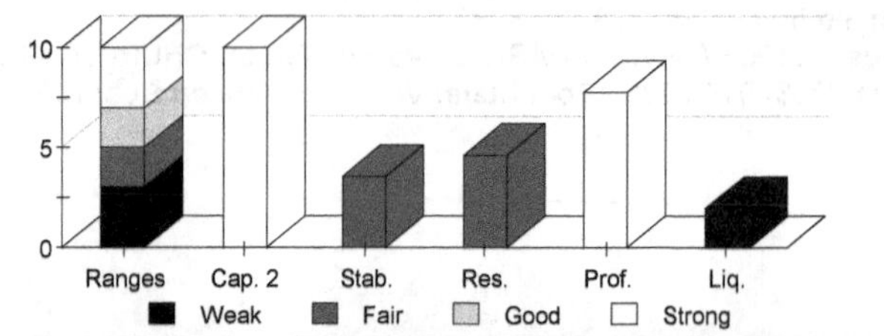

INS CO OF SCOTT & WHITE D Weak

Major Rating Factors: Weak profitability index (0.6 on a scale of 0 to 10). Fair liquidity (3.3) as cash resources may not be adequate to cover a spike in claims. Strong capitalization (7.2) based on excellent current risk-adjusted capital (severe loss scenario).

Other Rating Factors: High quality investment portfolio (9.6).

Principal Business: Medicare (57%), comp med (43%)

Mem Phys: 18: 15,215 **17:** 9,028 **18 MLR** 100.3% **/ 18 Admin Exp** N/A

Enroll(000): Q1 19: 9 **18:** 13 **17:** 15 **Med Exp PMPM:** $594

Principal Investments: Cash and equiv (66%), long-term bonds (26%), nonaffiliate common stock (7%)

Provider Compensation ($000): Contr fee ($82,276), FFS ($6,466), capitation ($418), bonus arrang ($141)

Total Member Encounters: Phys (48,350), non-phys (17,625)

Group Affiliation: None

Licensed in: TX

Address: 1206 WEST CAMPUS Dr, TEMPLE, TX 76502

Phone: (254) 298-3000 **Dom State:** TX **Commenced Bus:** N/A

Data Date	Rating	RACR #1	RACR #2	Total Assets ($mil)	Capital ($mil)	Net Premium ($mil)	Net Income ($mil)
3-19	D	1.55	1.29	30.4	16.7	15.6	0.5
3-18	E-	1.17	0.97	46.9	16.1	20.1	-3.7
2018	D	1.39	1.16	31.9	15.5	87.1	-4.4
2017	E-	1.14	0.95	49.8	19.2	125.3	-7.2
2016	E-	0.82	0.68	155.1	70.1	293.8	-128.8
2015	E	1.36	1.13	17.5	6.8	40.5	-5.3
2014	C-	1.37	1.15	9.8	3.6	24.7	-3.5

Rating Indexes

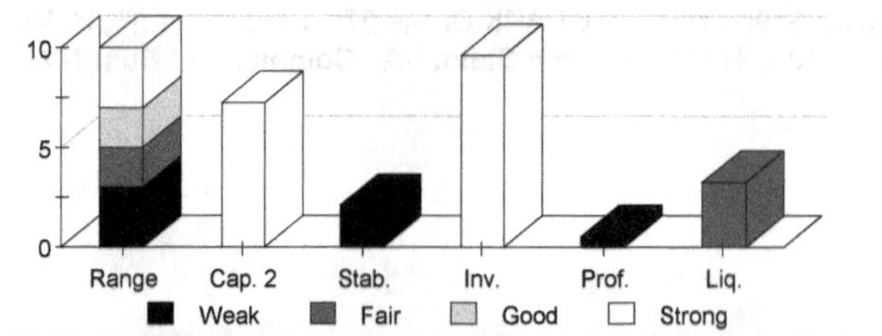

INTERVALLEY HEALTH PLAN D Weak

Major Rating Factors: Weak profitability index (1.5 on a scale of 0 to 10). Fair capitalization index (4.2) based on weak current risk-adjusted capital (moderate loss scenario). Fair overall results on stability tests (3.8).

Other Rating Factors: Excellent liquidity (6.9) with sufficient resources (cash flows and marketable investments) to handle a spike in claims.

Principal Business: Medicare (100%)

Mem Phys: 18: N/A **17:** N/A **18 MLR** 92.2% **/ 18 Admin Exp** N/A

Enroll(000): Q1 19: 20 **18:** 22 **17:** 25 **Med Exp PMPM:** $1,012

Principal Investments ($000): Cash and equiv ($19,283)

Provider Compensation ($000): None

Total Member Encounters: N/A

Group Affiliation: None

Licensed in: CA

Address: 1800 Harrison Street 20th Fl, Oakland, CA 94612

Phone: (510) 393-6574 **Dom State:** CA **Commenced Bus:** July 1979

Data Date	Rating	RACR #1	RACR #2	Total Assets ($mil)	Capital ($mil)	Net Premium ($mil)	Net Income ($mil)
3-19	D	0.68	0.43	35.0	18.6	71.7	-0.5
3-18	D	0.66	0.41	64.5	17.4	77.2	-1.6
2018	D	0.70	0.44	33.7	18.9	293.7	-0.1
2017	D	0.72	0.45	36.8	19.1	287.3	-6.1
2016	D	1.00	0.63	41.6	26.0	289.7	2.8
2015	D	1.01	0.64	38.6	23.2	262.5	2.4
2014	D	0.95	0.60	26.1	20.8	238.4	-2.1

Rating Indexes

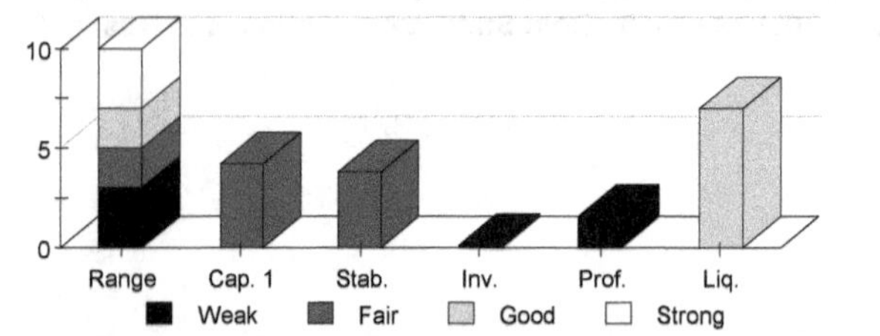

JOHN HANCOCK LIFE & HEALTH INSURANCE COMPANY B Good

Major Rating Factors: Good overall results on stability tests (5.0 on a scale of 0 to 10). Stability strengths include good operational trends and excellent risk diversification. Good quality investment portfolio (5.5) with minimal exposure to mortgages and minimal holdings in junk bonds. Strong capitalization (8.7) based on excellent risk adjusted capital (severe loss scenario).
Other Rating Factors: Excellent profitability (9.0). Excellent liquidity (9.1).
Principal Business: Group health insurance (75%), individual health insurance (21%), and reinsurance (4%).
Principal Investments: NonCMO investment grade bonds (59%), mortgages in good standing (7%), CMOs and structured securities (4%), real estate (3%), and misc. investments (20%).
Investments in Affiliates: 1%
Group Affiliation: Manulife Financial Group
Licensed in: All states, the District of Columbia and Puerto Rico
Commenced Business: October 1981
Address: 197 Clarendon Street, Boston, MA 02116-5010
Phone: (617) 572-6000 **Domicile State:** MA **NAIC Code:** 93610

Data Date	Rating	RACR #1	RACR #2	Total Assets ($mil)	Capital ($mil)	Net Premium ($mil)	Net Income ($mil)
3-19	B	3.88	2.10	14,564.1	1,009.2	169.5	11.7
3-18	B	3.52	1.92	13,731.3	901.9	170.4	36.9
2018	B	3.87	2.11	13,819.8	992.8	690.3	144.7
2017	B	3.56	1.95	14,006.8	891.9	686.5	104.6
2016	B	3.12	1.71	11,875.2	723.6	351.9	101.6
2015	B	3.22	1.76	11,150.5	704.6	575.4	40.3
2014	B	3.85	2.14	10,700.1	745.8	576.0	2.8

Adverse Trends in Operations

Decrease in asset base during 2018 (1%)
Change in premium mix from 2015 to 2016 (15.2%)
Increase in policy surrenders from 2015 to 2016 (579%)
Decrease in premium volume from 2015 to 2016 (39%)
Decrease in capital during 2015 (6%)

K S PLAN ADMINISTRATORS LLC * B+ Good

Major Rating Factors: Good quality investment portfolio (5.9 on a scale of 0 to 10). Excellent profitability (8.0). Strong capitalization (7.8) based on excellent current risk-adjusted capital (severe loss scenario).
Other Rating Factors: Excellent liquidity (7.0) with sufficient resources (cash flows and marketable investments) to handle a spike in claims.
Principal Business: Medicare (100%)
Mem Phys: 18: 776 **17:** 742 **18 MLR** 92.1% **/ 18 Admin Exp** N/A
Enroll(000): Q1 19: 34 **18:** 34 **17:** 32 **Med Exp PMPM:** $879
Principal Investments: Cash and equiv (52%), nonaffiliate common stock (48%)
Provider Compensation ($000): FFS ($173,652), capitation ($163,774), bonus arrang ($447)
Total Member Encounters: Phys (576,082), non-phys (13,794)
Group Affiliation: Kelsey-Seybold Medical Group PLLC
Licensed in: TX
Address: 2727 West Holcombe Blvd, Houston, TX 77025
Phone: (713) 442-0757 **Dom State:** TX **Commenced Bus:** N/A

Data Date	Rating	RACR #1	RACR #2	Total Assets ($mil)	Capital ($mil)	Net Premium ($mil)	Net Income ($mil)
3-19	B+	1.95	1.63	113.3	68.8	106.6	0.5
3-18	B+	1.94	1.61	129.9	61.3	93.6	-3.3
2018	B+	1.86	1.55	104.3	66.0	375.6	2.2
2017	B+	2.07	1.72	99.9	65.0	345.5	6.5
2016	B+	1.87	1.56	83.5	57.2	334.8	5.9
2015	B+	1.77	1.47	77.2	50.3	320.2	11.5
2014	B+	1.42	1.18	65.8	39.5	295.0	2.8

Rating Indexes

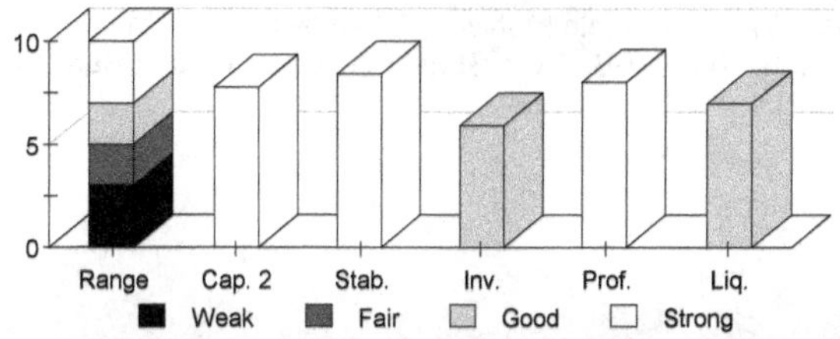

KAISER FNDTN HLTH PLAN OF WA B Good

Major Rating Factors: Good overall results on stability tests (5.7 on a scale of 0 to 10). Rating is significantly influenced by the strong financial results of Kaiser Foundation Health Plan Inc. Good liquidity (6.5) with sufficient resources (cash flows and marketable investments) to handle a spike in claims. Fair quality investment portfolio (4.8).
Other Rating Factors: Strong capitalization index (10.0) based on excellent current risk-adjusted capital (severe loss scenario). Weak profitability index (2.8).
Principal Business: Comp med (57%), Medicare (37%), FEHB (8%)
Mem Phys: 18: 16,395 **17:** 16,717 **18 MLR** 91.3% **/ 18 Admin Exp** N/A
Enroll(000): Q1 19: 433 **18:** 430 **17:** 386 **Med Exp PMPM:** $513
Principal Investments: Long-term bonds (44%), real estate (31%), nonaffiliate common stock (8%), affiliate common stock (8%), cash and equiv (1%), other (7%)
Provider Compensation ($000): Contr fee ($945,610), FFS ($644,281), capitation ($427,042), bonus arrang ($5,142), other ($619,500)
Total Member Encounters: Phys (2,096,489), non-phys (33,457)
Group Affiliation: Kaiser Foundation Health Plan Inc
Licensed in: WA
Address: 320 Westlake Ave N Suite 100, Seattle, WA 98101-1374
Phone: (206) 448-5600 **Dom State:** WA **Commenced Bus:** N/A

Data Date	Rating	RACR #1	RACR #2	Total Assets ($mil)	Capital ($mil)	Net Premium ($mil)	Net Income ($mil)
3-19	B	3.63	3.03	1,690.2	861.1	752.4	52.6
3-18	B+	N/A	N/A	1,630.2	801.5	755.0	30.0
2018	B	3.47	2.89	1,631.0	822.6	2,924.2	-24.5
2017	B+	N/A	N/A	1,537.6	803.6	2,636.5	-45.8
2016	A-	4.69	3.91	1,718.3	970.5	2,447.0	81.1
2015	A-	5.10	4.25	1,692.2	879.3	2,334.4	118.4
2014	A-	4.46	3.72	1,645.5	792.1	2,338.0	112.5

Rating Indexes

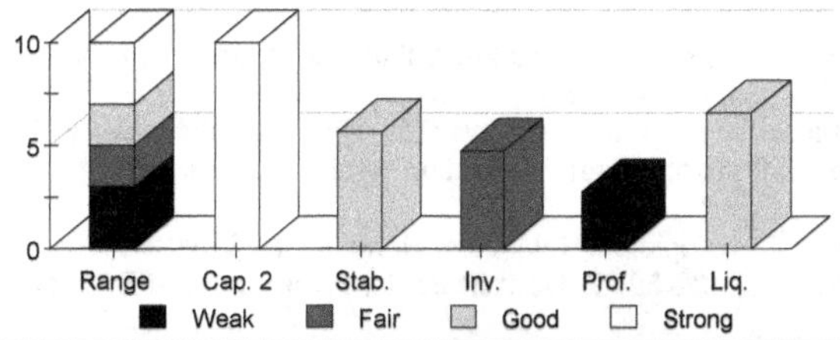

KAISER FNDTN HLTH PLAN WA OPTN B Good

Major Rating Factors: Good liquidity (6.3 on a scale of 0 to 10) with sufficient resources (cash flows and marketable investments) to handle a spike in claims. Strong capitalization (8.8) based on excellent current risk-adjusted capital (severe loss scenario). High quality investment portfolio (9.2).
Other Rating Factors: Weak profitability index (1.9).
Principal Business: Comp med (94%), FEHB (6%)
Mem Phys: 18: 46,058 **17:** 45,354 **18 MLR** 85.3% **/ 18 Admin Exp** N/A
Enroll(000): Q1 19: 164 **18:** 164 **17:** 187 **Med Exp PMPM:** $402
Principal Investments: Long-term bonds (76%), cash and equiv (23%), real estate (1%)
Provider Compensation ($000): FFS ($797,350), capitation ($947)
Total Member Encounters: Phys (783,779), non-phys (3,319)
Group Affiliation: Kaiser Foundation Health Plan Inc
Licensed in: ID, WA
Address: 320 Westlake Ave N Ste 100, Seattle, WA 98101-1374
Phone: (206) 448-5600 **Dom State:** WA **Commenced Bus:** N/A

Data Date	Rating	RACR #1	RACR #2	Total Assets ($mil)	Capital ($mil)	Net Premium ($mil)	Net Income ($mil)
3-19	B	2.76	2.30	317.5	131.2	235.7	12.8
3-18	B	2.22	1.85	299.1	117.7	233.5	-7.3
2018	B	2.53	2.11	289.9	119.7	935.6	-7.3
2017	B-	1.67	1.39	282.9	125.4	966.2	-5.9
2016	B	2.59	2.16	289.3	131.0	903.9	-7.7
2015	B	3.73	3.11	292.3	142.3	842.1	1.4
2014	B-	3.66	3.05	299.0	143.0	859.6	10.4

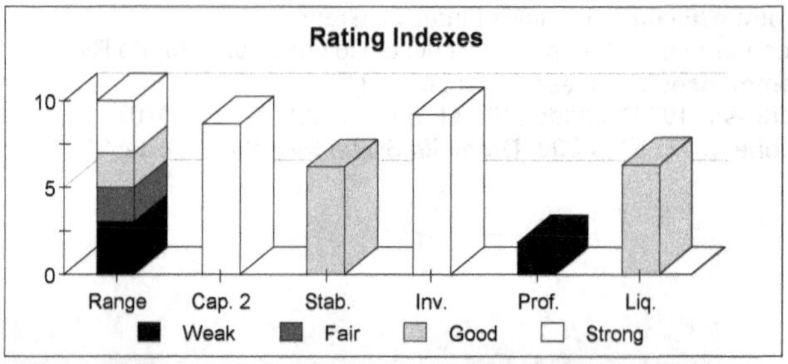

KAISER FOUNDATION HEALTH PLAN INC * A Excellent

Major Rating Factors: Excellent profitability (8.0 on a scale of 0 to 10). Strong capitalization index (9.6) based on excellent current risk-adjusted capital (severe loss scenario). Excellent overall results on stability tests (8.3) based on steady enrollment growth, averaging 4% over the past five years.
Other Rating Factors: Excellent liquidity (7.1) with ample operational cash flow and liquid investments.
Principal Business: Medicare (24%), Medicaid (4%)
Mem Phys: 18: N/A **17:** N/A **18 MLR** 97.4% **/ 18 Admin Exp** N/A
Enroll(000): Q1 19: 9,116 **18:** 8,944 **17:** 8,679 **Med Exp PMPM:** $683
Principal Investments ($000): Cash and equiv ($8,671,614)
Provider Compensation ($000): None
Total Member Encounters: N/A
Group Affiliation: Kaiser Foundation
Licensed in: CA
Address: 9700 Stockdale Highway, Bakersfield, CA 93311
Phone: (661) 664-5016 **Dom State:** CA **Commenced Bus:** N/A

Data Date	Rating	RACR #1	RACR #2	Total Assets ($mil)	Capital ($mil)	Net Premium ($mil)	Net Income ($mil)
3-19	A	4.00	2.88	80,034.0	35,872.8	20,141.1	3,155.2
3-18	A	3.51	2.53	75,442.7	29,737.1	19,086.4	1,386.9
2018	A	3.73	2.67	74,754.5	32,235.5	75,176.3	2,503.0
2017	A	3.39	2.44	73,382.8	28,953.4	68,459.4	3,798.0
2016	A	3.86	2.76	64,612.7	27,089.8	60,874.0	3,119.6
2015	A-	3.58	2.57	62,625.8	24,897.0	57,241.2	1,867.9
2014	B+	3.08	2.21	61,914.6	20,827.2	53,137.7	3,073.3

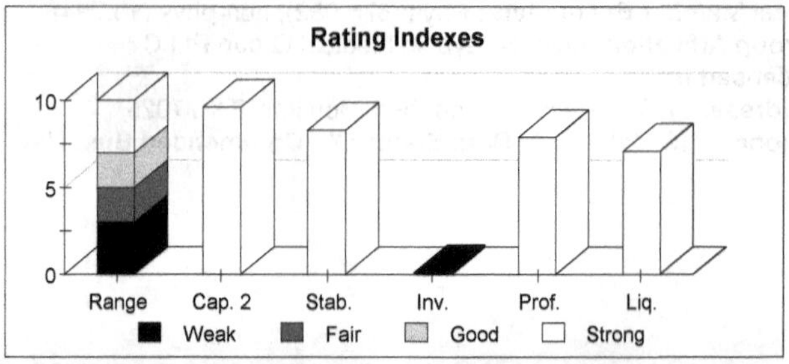

KAISER FOUNDATION HP INC HI B Good

Major Rating Factors: Good overall results on stability tests (6.8 on a scale of 0 to 10) based on steady enrollment growth, averaging 2% over the past five years. Rating is significantly influenced by the strong financial results of Kaiser Foundation Health Plan Inc. Good liquidity (6.8) with sufficient resources (cash flows and marketable investments) to handle a spike in claims. Strong capitalization index (8.9) based on excellent current risk-adjusted capital (severe loss scenario).
Other Rating Factors: High quality investment portfolio (9.5). Weak profitability index (0.9).
Principal Business: Comp med (62%), Medicare (26%), Medicaid (7%), FEHB (5%)
Mem Phys: 18: 471 **17:** 462 **18 MLR** 96.0% **/ 18 Admin Exp** N/A
Enroll(000): Q1 19: 254 **18:** 252 **17:** 251 **Med Exp PMPM:** $499
Principal Investments: Long-term bonds (54%), real estate (33%), cash and equiv (13%)
Provider Compensation ($000): Salary ($871,946), contr fee ($189,081), FFS ($14,231), other ($448,324)
Total Member Encounters: Phys (711,785), non-phys (521,079)
Group Affiliation: Kaiser Foundation Health Plan Inc
Licensed in: HI
Address: 711 Kapiolani Boulevard, Honolulu, HI 96813
Phone: (808) 432-5955 **Dom State:** HI **Commenced Bus:** N/A

Data Date	Rating	RACR #1	RACR #2	Total Assets ($mil)	Capital ($mil)	Net Premium ($mil)	Net Income ($mil)
3-19	B	2.86	2.38	571.1	138.6	407.2	-9.7
3-18	B	2.59	2.16	528.4	117.9	406.9	9.1
2018	B	2.99	2.49	584.3	144.7	1,582.2	-26.7
2017	C-	2.15	1.79	471.3	137.9	1,470.4	-85.5
2016	C	2.19	1.83	421.6	86.2	1,369.0	-22.8
2015	B-	2.02	1.69	424.5	75.2	1,270.6	-17.4
2014	B	2.26	1.88	380.8	81.7	1,203.5	-2.1

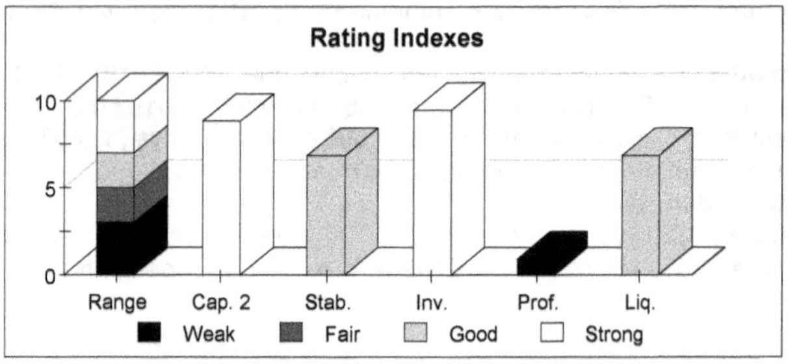

KAISER FOUNDATION HP MID-ATL STATES B Good

Major Rating Factors: Good overall results on stability tests (5.3 on a scale of 0 to 10) based on steady enrollment growth, averaging 9% over the past five years. Rating is significantly influenced by the strong financial results of Kaiser Foundation Health Plan Inc. Good liquidity (6.8) with sufficient resources (cash flows and marketable investments) to handle a spike in claims. Fair capitalization index (2.9) based on good current risk-adjusted capital (moderate loss scenario).
Other Rating Factors: High quality investment portfolio (7.8). Weak profitability index (1.1).
Principal Business: Comp med (60%), FEHB (18%), Medicare (15%), Medicaid (7%)
Mem Phys: 18: 21,018 **17:** 21,796 **18 MLR** 91.7% **/ 18 Admin Exp** N/A
Enroll(000): Q1 19: 736 **18:** 749 **17:** 701 **Med Exp PMPM:** $419
Principal Investments: Real estate (52%), long-term bonds (43%), cash and equiv (2%), other (3%)
Provider Compensation ($000): Contr fee ($813,095), salary ($773,191), FFS ($115,361), capitation ($11,609), other ($2,148,091)
Total Member Encounters: Phys (2,161,382), non-phys (1,018,709)
Group Affiliation: Kaiser Foundation Health Plan Inc
Licensed in: DC, MD, VA
Address: 2101 East Jefferson Street, Rockville, MD 20852
Phone: (301) 816-2424 **Dom State:** MD **Commenced Bus:** N/A

Data Date	Rating	RACR #1	RACR #2	Total Assets ($mil)	Capital ($mil)	Net Premium ($mil)	Net Income ($mil)
3-19	B	1.76	1.47	1,677.7	500.8	1,158.3	66.7
3-18	B	1.19	0.99	1,327.4	285.6	1,135.7	82.7
2018	B	1.54	1.28	1,654.8	437.0	4,196.9	23.8
2017	C	0.48	0.40	1,352.8	160.2	3,556.5	-85.0
2016	B	0.97	0.80	1,172.5	198.7	3,264.8	16.8
2015	B	1.10	0.91	1,148.5	209.2	2,981.7	-5.1
2014	B	0.80	0.66	1,196.4	147.2	2,621.1	-12.3

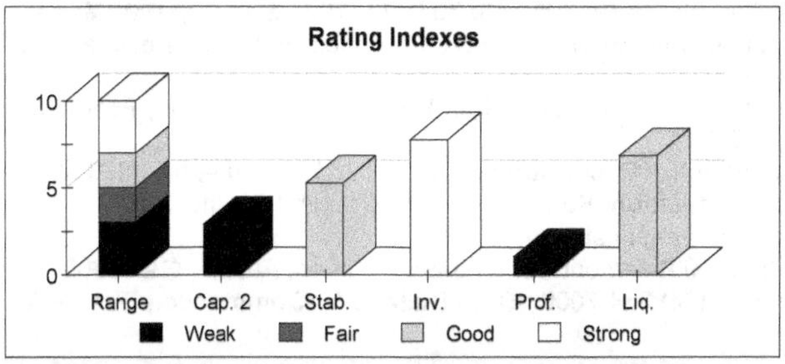

KAISER FOUNDATION HP NORTHWEST B Good

Major Rating Factors: Good overall results on stability tests (6.0 on a scale of 0 to 10) based on steady enrollment growth, averaging 4% over the past five years. Rating is significantly influenced by the strong financial results of Kaiser Foundation Health Plan Inc. Good liquidity (6.7) with sufficient resources (cash flows and marketable investments) to handle a spike in claims. Fair profitability index (3.1).
Other Rating Factors: Strong capitalization index (10.0) based on excellent current risk-adjusted capital (severe loss scenario). High quality investment portfolio (8.1).
Principal Business: Comp med (60%), Medicare (28%), dental (4%), FEHB (4%), other (5%)
Mem Phys: 18: 1,483 **17:** 1,404 **18 MLR** 92.4% **/ 18 Admin Exp** N/A
Enroll(000): Q1 19: 555 **18:** 541 **17:** 523 **Med Exp PMPM:** $575
Principal Investments: Long-term bonds (69%), real estate (30%), cash and equiv (1%)
Provider Compensation ($000): Salary ($1,710,019), contr fee ($497,829), FFS ($140,748), capitation ($6,445), other ($1,352,891)
Total Member Encounters: Phys (2,156,216), non-phys (730,439)
Group Affiliation: Kaiser Foundation Health Plan Inc
Licensed in: OR, WA
Address: 500 NE Multnomah Street Suite, Portland, OR 97232-2099
Phone: (503) 813-2800 **Dom State:** OR **Commenced Bus:** N/A

Data Date	Rating	RACR #1	RACR #2	Total Assets ($mil)	Capital ($mil)	Net Premium ($mil)	Net Income ($mil)
3-19	B	3.95	3.29	1,301.7	516.2	1,067.6	46.9
3-18	B	2.82	2.35	1,306.5	329.5	1,018.2	-9.2
2018	B	3.54	2.95	1,254.5	463.1	4,027.1	-7.0
2017	B-	2.31	1.93	1,192.0	353.2	3,765.2	-1.6
2016	B	4.39	3.66	1,399.4	479.9	3,558.6	40.4
2015	B-	3.99	3.32	1,477.6	419.3	3,357.5	-13.5
2014	B	2.03	1.69	1,300.8	203.2	3,137.6	-15.6

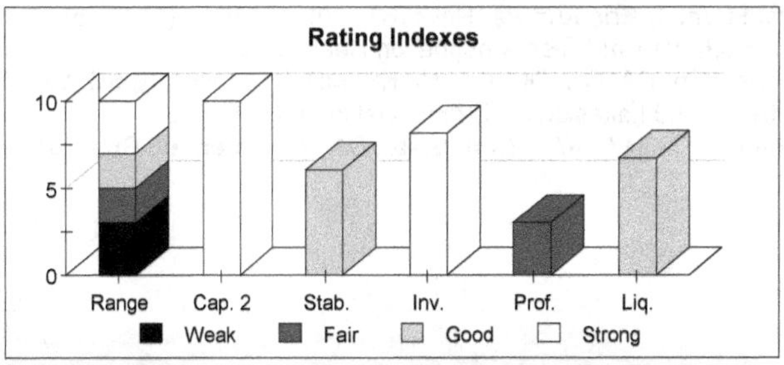

KAISER FOUNDATION HP OF CO B Good

Major Rating Factors: Good overall results on stability tests (5.5 on a scale of 0 to 10). Rating is significantly influenced by the strong financial results of Kaiser Foundation Health Plan Inc. Good liquidity (6.4) with sufficient resources (cash flows and marketable investments) to handle a spike in claims. Strong capitalization index (8.9) based on excellent current risk-adjusted capital (severe loss scenario).
Other Rating Factors: High quality investment portfolio (9.4). Weak profitability index (0.9).
Principal Business: Comp med (62%), Medicare (32%), FEHB (5%), other (1%)
Mem Phys: 18: 1,225 **17:** 1,199 **18 MLR** 97.3% **/ 18 Admin Exp** N/A
Enroll(000): Q1 19: 593 **18:** 589 **17:** 589 **Med Exp PMPM:** $524
Principal Investments: Long-term bonds (78%), real estate (20%), cash and equiv (2%)
Provider Compensation ($000): Contr fee ($1,452,999), salary ($643,479), FFS ($111,501), capitation ($24,051), other ($1,525,360)
Total Member Encounters: Phys (3,953,494), non-phys (1,802,497)
Group Affiliation: Kaiser Foundation Health Plan Inc
Licensed in: CO
Address: 10350 E DAKOTA AVENUE, DENVER, CO 80231-1314
Phone: (800) 632-9700 **Dom State:** CO **Commenced Bus:** N/A

Data Date	Rating	RACR #1	RACR #2	Total Assets ($mil)	Capital ($mil)	Net Premium ($mil)	Net Income ($mil)
3-19	B	2.89	2.41	1,609.3	473.6	1,012.4	25.8
3-18	B	2.46	2.05	1,549.1	399.2	987.2	26.7
2018	B	2.66	2.21	1,698.7	437.5	3,858.4	-147.9
2017	C	0.82	0.69	1,300.4	184.6	3,689.2	-49.6
2016	B	2.53	2.10	1,383.0	375.5	3,507.4	1.1
2015	B-	2.82	2.35	1,392.5	393.6	3,285.8	-17.0
2014	B	1.83	1.52	1,305.1	222.0	3,190.3	78.7

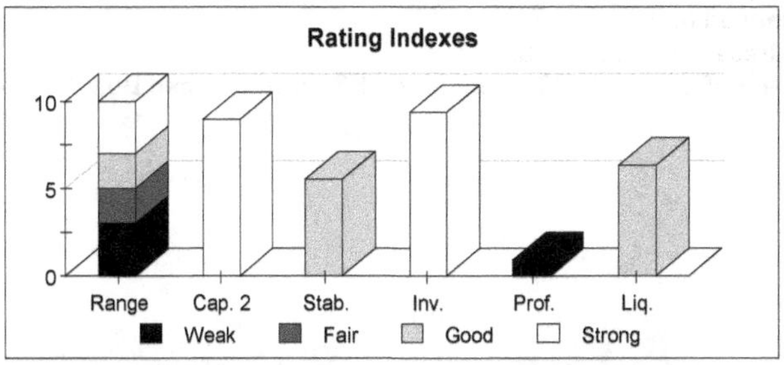

KAISER FOUNDATION HP OF GA B Good

Major Rating Factors: Good overall results on stability tests (5.6 on a scale of 0 to 10) based on steady enrollment growth, averaging 8% over the past five years. Rating is significantly influenced by the strong financial results of Kaiser Foundation Health Plan Inc. Good liquidity (6.3) with sufficient resources (cash flows and marketable investments) to handle a spike in claims. Fair capitalization index (2.9) based on fair current risk-adjusted capital (moderate loss scenario).
Other Rating Factors: High quality investment portfolio (9.0). Weak profitability index (0.9).
Principal Business: Comp med (75%), Medicare (16%), FEHB (8%), other (1%)
Mem Phys: 18: 837 **17:** 727 **18 MLR** 94.9% **/ 18 Admin Exp** N/A
Enroll(000): Q1 19: 306 **18:** 337 **17:** 292 **Med Exp PMPM:** $471
Principal Investments: Long-term bonds (66%), real estate (30%), cash and equiv (4%)
Provider Compensation ($000): Contr fee ($533,687), FFS ($166,121), other ($1,243,233)
Total Member Encounters: Phys (1,502,957), non-phys (373,394)
Group Affiliation: Kaiser Foundation Health Plan Inc
Licensed in: (No states)
Address: 9 Piedmont Center 3495 Piedmon, Atlanta, GA 30305-1736
Phone: (404) 364-7000 **Dom State:** GA **Commenced Bus:** N/A

Data Date	Rating	RACR #1	RACR #2	Total Assets ($mil)	Capital ($mil)	Net Premium ($mil)	Net Income ($mil)
3-19	B	0.93	0.78	665.2	149.7	485.5	-29.5
3-18	B	1.29	1.07	530.6	142.9	549.1	18.3
2018	B	1.14	0.95	720.5	182.9	2,065.2	-201.3
2017	C-	0.79	0.65	499.3	123.3	1,659.3	2.2
2016	C-	1.08	0.90	494.4	125.7	1,458.6	-9.1
2015	D	1.12	0.93	487.8	118.5	1,319.7	-30.1
2014	D	1.04	0.86	511.1	106.2	1,200.1	-170.2

Rating Indexes

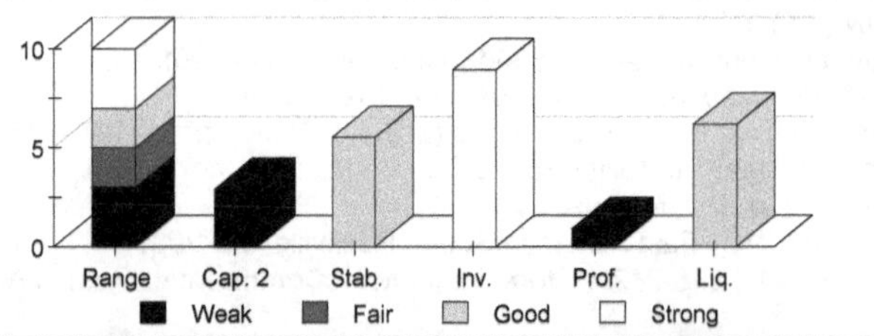

KAISER PERMANENTE INS CO * A- Excellent

Major Rating Factors: Excellent profitability (7.7 on a scale of 0 to 10). Strong capitalization (10.0) based on excellent current risk-adjusted capital (severe loss scenario). High quality investment portfolio (9.6).
Other Rating Factors: Excellent liquidity (7.0) with sufficient resources (cash flows and marketable investments) to handle a spike in claims.
Principal Business: Comp med (68%), dental (31%)
Mem Phys: 18: 924,558 **17:** 862,760 **18 MLR** 83.1% **/ 18 Admin Exp** N/A
Enroll(000): Q1 19: 240 **18:** 237 **17:** 228 **Med Exp PMPM:** $34
Principal Investments: Long-term bonds (86%), cash and equiv (11%), other (2%)
Provider Compensation ($000): Contr fee ($70,953), bonus arrang ($14,132), FFS ($10,559), other ($649)
Total Member Encounters: Phys (69,010), non-phys (163,775)
Group Affiliation: Kaiser Foundation Health Plan Inc
Licensed in: CA, CO, DC, GA, HI, KS, MD, MO, OH, OR, SC, VA, WA
Address: 300 Lakeside Dr 13th Fl, Oakland, CA 94612
Phone: (877) 847-7572 **Dom State:** CA **Commenced Bus:** N/A

Data Date	Rating	RACR #1	RACR #2	Total Assets ($mil)	Capital ($mil)	Net Premium ($mil)	Net Income ($mil)
3-19	A-	12.21	10.17	197.7	120.2	33.7	-0.5
3-18	B	13.66	11.38	182.2	112.4	27.9	-5.9
2018	A-	12.17	10.14	181.5	119.8	118.2	2.1
2017	B	10.10	8.41	188.1	118.1	115.5	6.5
2016	B	13.54	11.28	179.2	111.7	123.1	8.4
2015	B	12.65	10.54	174.3	103.7	126.2	7.2
2014	B+	10.19	8.50	169.6	94.8	141.2	8.2

Rating Indexes

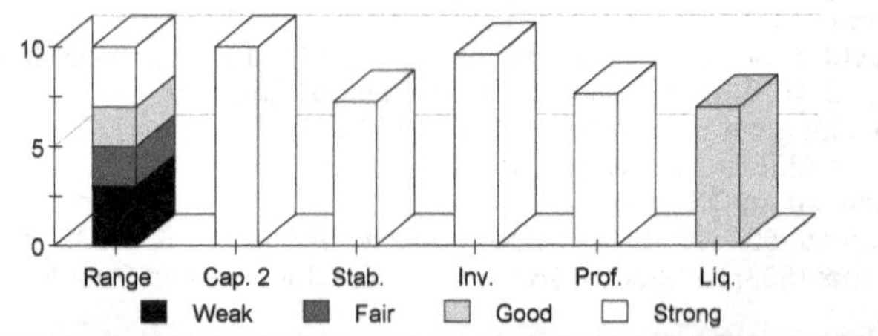

KANSAS SUPERIOR SELECT INC D+ Weak

Major Rating Factors: Weak profitability index (0.3 on a scale of 0 to 10). Fair capitalization (4.6) based on fair current risk-adjusted capital (moderate loss scenario). Good liquidity (6.2) with sufficient resources (cash flows and marketable investments) to handle a spike in claims.
Other Rating Factors: High quality investment portfolio (9.9).
Principal Business: Medicare (100%)
Mem Phys: 18: 3,262 **17:** N/A **18 MLR** 83.0% **/ 18 Admin Exp** N/A
Enroll(000): Q1 19: 0 **18:** 0 **17:** N/A **Med Exp PMPM:** $1,586
Principal Investments: Cash and equiv (86%), long-term bonds (14%)
Provider Compensation ($000): Contr fee ($1,460)
Total Member Encounters: Phys (3,277), non-phys (694)
Group Affiliation: Kansas Superior Select Inc
Licensed in: KS
Address: , Topeka, KS 66603
Phone: (620) 251-6700 **Dom State:** KS **Commenced Bus:** N/A

Data Date	Rating	RACR #1	RACR #2	Total Assets ($mil)	Capital ($mil)	Net Premium ($mil)	Net Income ($mil)
3-19	D+	0.87	0.73	3.0	1.2	1.6	-0.2
3-18	N/A	N/A	N/A	1.6	1.2	0.2	-0.3
2018	D+	1.04	0.87	2.9	1.4	3.3	-0.7
2017	N/A	N/A	N/A	1.6	1.4	N/A	-1.0
2016	N/A	N/A	N/A	N/A	N/A	N/A	N/A
2015	N/A	N/A	N/A	N/A	N/A	N/A	N/A
2014	N/A	N/A	N/A	N/A	N/A	N/A	N/A

Rating Indexes

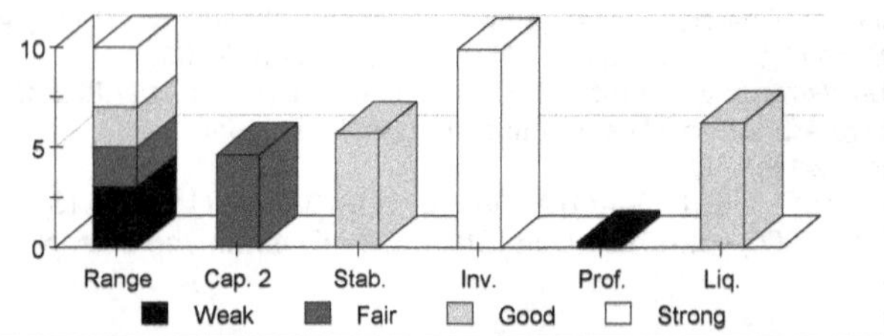

KERN HEALTH SYSTEMS * B+ Good

Major Rating Factors: Good overall results on stability tests (6.5 on a scale of 0 to 10) based on steady enrollment growth, averaging 8% over the past five years. Excellent profitability (9.0). Strong capitalization index (9.3) based on excellent current risk-adjusted capital (severe loss scenario).
Other Rating Factors: Excellent liquidity (7.5) with ample operational cash flow and liquid investments.
Principal Business: Medicaid (100%)
Mem Phys: 18: N/A **17:** N/A **18 MLR** 85.2% **/ 18 Admin Exp** N/A
Enroll(000): Q1 19: 248 **18:** 245 **17:** 242 **Med Exp PMPM:** $222
Principal Investments ($000): Cash and equiv ($232,362)
Provider Compensation ($000): None
Total Member Encounters: N/A
Group Affiliation: None
Licensed in: CA
Address: 1055 West 7th Street, Los Angeles, CA 90017
Phone: (213) 694-1250 **Dom State:** CA **Commenced Bus:** June 1996

Data Date	Rating	RACR #1	RACR #2	Total Assets ($mil)	Capital ($mil)	Net Premium ($mil)	Net Income ($mil)
3-19	B+	4.34	2.65	467.7	204.1	200.7	1.4
3-18	B-	4.80	2.93	355.6	193.2	177.7	1.6
2018	B	4.39	2.69	388.4	202.7	767.9	11.1
2017	B-	4.80	2.93	341.3	191.6	719.9	19.3
2016	B-	4.85	2.96	349.3	172.3	671.5	61.3
2015	C+	3.41	2.08	267.4	111.0	559.6	33.8
2014	C	3.02	1.85	205.9	81.7	407.1	3.8

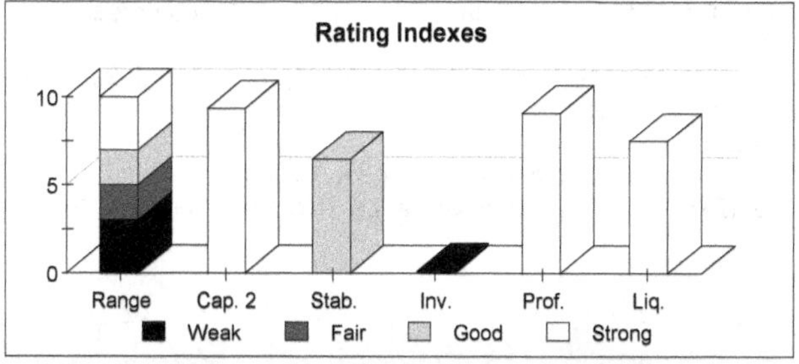

KEYSTONE HEALTH PLAN CENTRAL INC C- Fair

Major Rating Factors: Fair overall results on stability tests (4.4 on a scale of 0 to 10). Rating is significantly influenced by the fair financial results of . Weak profitability index (0.9). Good quality investment portfolio (6.0).
Other Rating Factors: Good liquidity (6.8) with sufficient resources (cash flows and marketable investments) to handle a spike in claims. Strong capitalization index (8.8) based on excellent current risk-adjusted capital (severe loss scenario).
Principal Business: Medicare (78%), comp med (21%), other (1%)
Mem Phys: 18: 4,705 **17:** 4,205 **18 MLR** 84.6% **/ 18 Admin Exp** N/A
Enroll(000): Q1 19: 35 **18:** 35 **17:** 35 **Med Exp PMPM:** $490
Principal Investments: Long-term bonds (74%), cash and equiv (26%)
Provider Compensation ($000): Contr fee ($195,690), capitation ($16,566), bonus arrang ($1,032)
Total Member Encounters: Phys (556,478), non-phys (139,293)
Group Affiliation: None
Licensed in: PA
Address: 2500 Elmerton Avenue, Harrisburg, PA 17177-9799
Phone: (717) 541-7000 **Dom State:** PA **Commenced Bus:** N/A

Data Date	Rating	RACR #1	RACR #2	Total Assets ($mil)	Capital ($mil)	Net Premium ($mil)	Net Income ($mil)
3-19	C-	2.78	2.32	82.5	39.4	67.2	-1.2
3-18	C	3.26	2.72	86.7	42.1	63.8	-6.5
2018	C-	3.00	2.50	81.1	42.8	250.6	-5.4
2017	C	2.34	1.95	88.4	49.6	229.1	1.6
2016	C+	2.32	1.93	146.1	45.1	307.9	-14.0
2015	C+	4.03	3.35	119.0	55.8	239.0	-11.3
2014	B	6.50	5.42	125.7	84.9	228.2	5.9

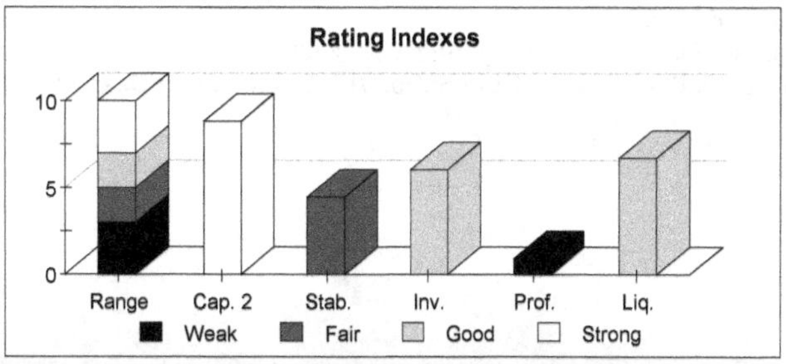

KEYSTONE HEALTH PLAN EAST INC B Good

Major Rating Factors: Good quality investment portfolio (6.2 on a scale of 0 to 10). Good overall results on stability tests (5.5). Good liquidity (6.9) with sufficient resources (cash flows and marketable investments) to handle a spike in claims.
Other Rating Factors: Excellent profitability (8.0). Strong capitalization index (9.6) based on excellent current risk-adjusted capital (severe loss scenario).
Principal Business: Comp med (65%), Medicare (35%)
Mem Phys: 18: 36,352 **17:** 35,173 **18 MLR** 76.7% **/ 18 Admin Exp** N/A
Enroll(000): Q1 19: 425 **18:** 429 **17:** 444 **Med Exp PMPM:** $476
Principal Investments: Long-term bonds (68%), nonaffiliate common stock (10%), cash and equiv (7%), pref stock (6%), affiliate common stock (5%), other (4%)
Provider Compensation ($000): Contr fee ($1,477,420), capitation ($972,702), FFS ($45,053), bonus arrang ($27,854)
Total Member Encounters: Phys (5,237,908), non-phys (1,724,677)
Group Affiliation: Independence Health Group Inc
Licensed in: PA
Address: 1901 Market Street, Philadelphia, PA 19103-1480
Phone: (215) 241-2400 **Dom State:** PA **Commenced Bus:** N/A

Data Date	Rating	RACR #1	RACR #2	Total Assets ($mil)	Capital ($mil)	Net Premium ($mil)	Net Income ($mil)
3-19	B	3.44	2.86	1,299.0	537.7	798.2	50.8
3-18	B-	3.10	2.59	1,474.9	460.7	822.7	-5.0
2018	B	3.07	2.56	1,203.0	476.7	3,274.5	154.5
2017	B-	2.57	2.14	1,246.5	477.9	3,089.8	131.3
2016	C+	2.64	2.20	1,221.4	397.5	3,072.9	44.3
2015	C	3.26	2.71	1,179.9	465.8	2,959.7	32.9
2014	B-	4.13	3.44	1,267.7	636.3	2,938.4	87.3

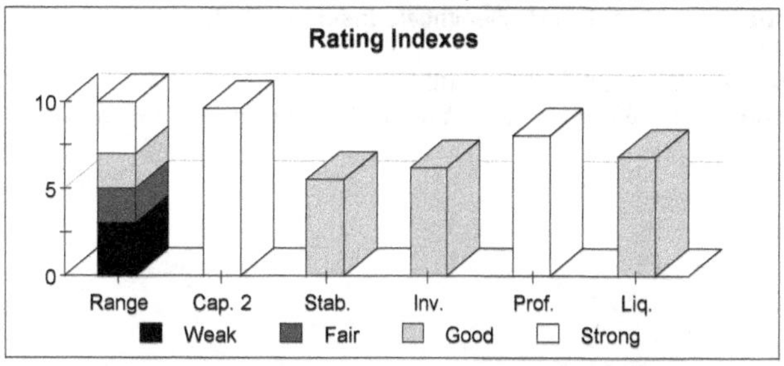

LA HEALTH SERVICE & INDEMNITY CO B Good

Major Rating Factors: Fair profitability index (4.9 on a scale of 0 to 10). Fair quality investment portfolio (4.1). Strong capitalization (10.0) based on excellent current risk-adjusted capital (severe loss scenario).
Other Rating Factors: Excellent liquidity (7.1) with ample operational cash flow and liquid investments.
Principal Business: Comp med (75%), FEHB (18%), med supp (5%), other (1%)
Mem Phys: 18: 38,537 **17:** 33,787 **18 MLR** 81.6% **/ 18 Admin Exp** N/A
Enroll(000): Q1 19: 718 **18:** 728 **17:** 675 **Med Exp PMPM:** $223
Principal Investments: Long-term bonds (45%), affiliate common stock (29%), nonaffiliate common stock (13%), cash and equiv (8%), real estate (3%), other (2%)
Provider Compensation ($000): FFS ($1,171,251), contr fee ($799,922), other ($16,002)
Total Member Encounters: Phys (5,199,081), non-phys (2,226,923)
Group Affiliation: None
Licensed in: LA
Address: 5525 Reitz Ave, Baton Rouge, LA 70809
Phone: (225) 295-3307 **Dom State:** LA **Commenced Bus:** N/A

Data Date	Rating	RACR #1	RACR #2	Total Assets ($mil)	Capital ($mil)	Net Premium ($mil)	Net Income ($mil)
3-19	B	6.61	5.51	2,178.7	1,488.7	589.6	63.2
3-18	B	5.92	4.93	2,045.0	1,275.7	589.9	24.5
2018	B	6.09	5.08	2,094.5	1,371.7	2,402.6	127.5
2017	B	5.81	4.84	1,993.4	1,252.2	2,392.0	95.0
2016	B	5.54	4.62	1,789.8	1,113.1	2,526.0	-4.8
2015	B	5.46	4.55	1,671.2	1,080.1	2,555.3	-50.6
2014	A-	6.44	5.37	1,736.9	1,145.3	2,408.8	36.3

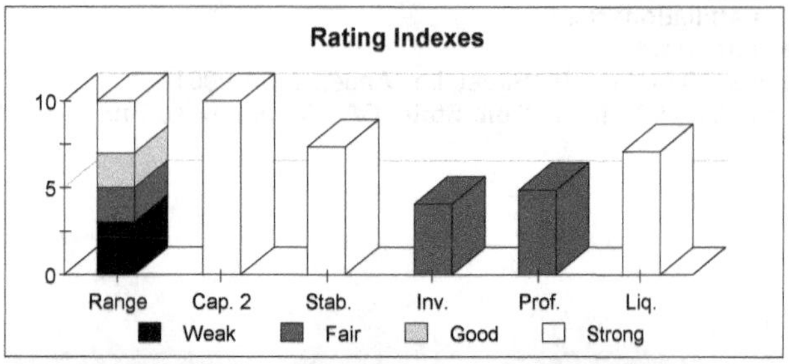

LEGAL SERVICE PLANS OF VIRGINIA INC B Good

Major Rating Factors: Excellent profitability (8.0 on a scale of 0 to 10). Strong capitalization (7.2) based on excellent current risk-adjusted capital (severe loss scenario). High quality investment portfolio (9.3).
Other Rating Factors: Excellent liquidity (7.8) with ample operational cash flow and liquid investments.
Principal Business: Other (100%)
Mem Phys: 18: N/A **17:** N/A **18 MLR** 31.9% **/ 18 Admin Exp** N/A
Enroll(000): Q1 19: 38 **18:** 38 **17:** 38 **Med Exp PMPM:** $80
Principal Investments: Long-term bonds (90%), cash and equiv (10%)
Provider Compensation ($000): Capitation ($3,034)
Total Member Encounters: N/A
Group Affiliation: Trident
Licensed in: VA
Address: One Pre-Paid Way, Ada, OK 74820
Phone: (580) 436-1234 **Dom State:** VA **Commenced Bus:** N/A

Data Date	Rating	RACR #1	RACR #2	Total Assets ($mil)	Capital ($mil)	Net Premium ($mil)	Net Income ($mil)
3-19	B	1.55	1.29	1.4	0.9	2.4	0.6
3-18	B	N/A	N/A	2.3	1.3	2.3	0.4
2018	B	2.16	1.80	1.7	1.2	9.5	2.5
2017	B	N/A	N/A	2.0	1.1	9.3	1.3
2016	B	2.05	1.71	2.4	1.3	9.1	1.1
2015	B	1.72	1.43	2.4	1.1	8.7	0.8
2014	N/A	N/A	N/A	2.4	1.0	8.4	1.0

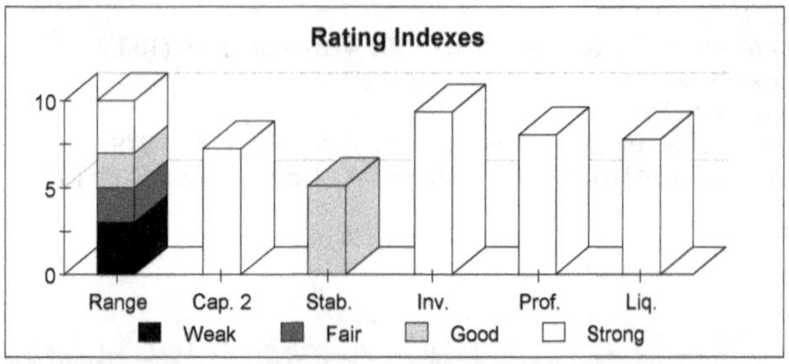

LIBERTY ADVANTAGE LLC D Weak

Major Rating Factors: Weak profitability index (0.7 on a scale of 0 to 10). Fair capitalization (3.3) based on weak current risk-adjusted capital (moderate loss scenario). High quality investment portfolio (9.3).
Other Rating Factors: Excellent liquidity (7.0) with sufficient resources (cash flows and marketable investments) to handle a spike in claims.
Principal Business: Medicare (100%)
Mem Phys: 18: 10,722 **17:** N/A **18 MLR** 87.3% **/ 18 Admin Exp** N/A
Enroll(000): Q1 19: 1 **18:** 1 **17:** N/A **Med Exp PMPM:** $1,788
Principal Investments: Cash and equiv (100%)
Provider Compensation ($000): Contr fee ($7,104), capitation ($4,217), bonus arrang ($52)
Total Member Encounters: Phys (6,850), non-phys (9,964)
Group Affiliation: Liberty Healthcare Insurance LLC
Licensed in: NC
Address: , Wilmington, NC 28403
Phone: (804) 396-6412 **Dom State:** NC **Commenced Bus:** N/A

Data Date	Rating	RACR #1	RACR #2	Total Assets ($mil)	Capital ($mil)	Net Premium ($mil)	Net Income ($mil)
3-19	D	0.67	0.56	5.5	1.8	4.2	-0.3
3-18	N/A	N/A	N/A	5.2	2.0	3.5	-0.2
2018	D	0.82	0.68	4.9	2.2	15.4	-0.5
2017	N/A	N/A	N/A	2.2	2.2	N/A	-0.5
2016	N/A	N/A	N/A	N/A	N/A	N/A	N/A
2015	N/A	N/A	N/A	N/A	N/A	N/A	N/A
2014	N/A	N/A	N/A	N/A	N/A	N/A	N/A

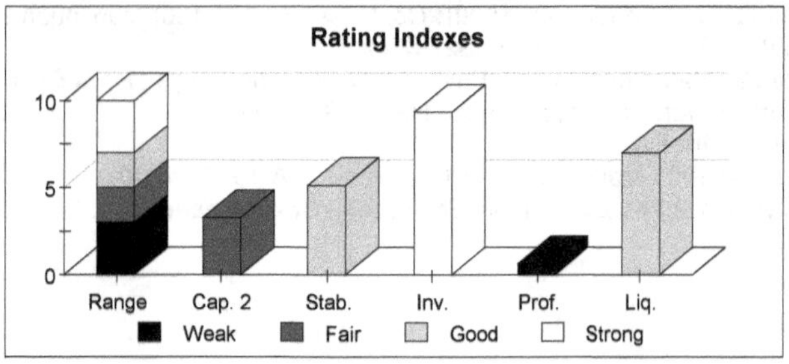

LIBERTY LIFE ASSURANCE COMPANY OF BOSTON B- Good

Major Rating Factors: Fair overall capitalization (4.0 on a scale of 0 to 10) based on mixed results -- excessive policy leverage mitigated by excellent risk adjusted capital (severe loss scenario). Nevertheless, capital levels have fluctuated during prior years. Fair overall results on stability tests (4.0) including negative cash flow from operations for 2018. Good quality investment portfolio (6.2).

Other Rating Factors: Good liquidity (6.9). Weak profitability (2.9) with investment income below regulatory standards in relation to interest assumptions of reserves.

Principal Business: Group health insurance (47%), group life insurance (23%), individual life insurance (16%), and individual annuities (14%).

Principal Investments: NonCMO investment grade bonds (69%), mortgages in good standing (20%), CMOs and structured securities (8%), cash (2%), and noninv. grade bonds (1%).

Investments in Affiliates: 1%

Group Affiliation: Liberty Mutual Group

Licensed in: All states except PR

Commenced Business: January 1964

Address: 175 Berkeley Street, Radnor, PA 19087

Phone: (484) 583-1400 **Domicile State:** NH **NAIC Code:** 65315

Data Date	Rating	RACR #1	RACR #2	Total Assets ($mil)	Capital ($mil)	Net Premium ($mil)	Net Income ($mil)
3-19	B-	4.92	2.25	4,142.3	537.5	0.3	4.8
3-18	B	2.00	1.16	19,145.9	1,369.1	708.8	33.5
2018	B-	4.68	2.16	4,021.9	531.0	-14,181.3	142.8
2017	B	1.96	1.14	19,045.9	1,336.7	2,929.6	50.6
2016	B	1.90	1.11	17,479.3	1,161.0	2,714.5	5.3
2015	B	1.77	1.04	16,054.1	966.4	2,501.1	69.9
2014	B	1.88	1.09	14,628.8	902.4	2,410.6	37.0

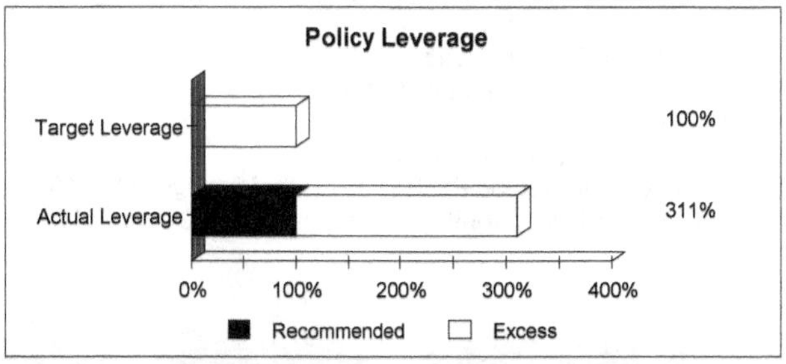

LIBERTY UNION LIFE ASR CO C+ Fair

Major Rating Factors: Excellent profitability (7.8 on a scale of 0 to 10). Strong capitalization (10.0) based on excellent current risk-adjusted capital (severe loss scenario). High quality investment portfolio (9.0).

Other Rating Factors: Excellent liquidity (7.2) with ample operational cash flow and liquid investments.

Principal Business: Dental (9%), other (91%)

Mem Phys: 18: N/A **17:** N/A **18 MLR** 15.5% **/ 18 Admin Exp** N/A

Enroll(000): Q1 19: 8 **18:** 9 **17:** 9 **Med Exp PMPM:** $24

Principal Investments: Long-term bonds (85%), cash and equiv (10%), nonaffiliate common stock (4%), other (1%)

Provider Compensation ($000): Contr fee ($8,611), FFS ($117)

Total Member Encounters: Phys (37,496), non-phys (19,232)

Group Affiliation: None

Licensed in: AL, AZ, DE, GA, IN, MI, MS, MO, MT, NE, NM, NC, ND, WV

Address: 560 Kirts Blvd Ste 125, Troy, MI 48084-4133

Phone: (248) 583-7123 **Dom State:** MI **Commenced Bus:** N/A

Data Date	Rating	RACR #1	RACR #2	Total Assets ($mil)	Capital ($mil)	Net Premium ($mil)	Net Income ($mil)
3-19	C+	9.58	7.99	14.2	8.3	4.1	0.1
3-18	C	N/A	N/A	15.9	8.6	4.2	4.8
2018	C+	9.46	7.88	14.4	8.1	16.4	5.0
2017	C	N/A	N/A	15.8	3.8	18.5	-0.1
2016	C-	3.76	3.13	14.0	4.2	22.2	0.2
2015	C-	3.24	2.70	14.5	4.0	24.8	0.0
2014	C-	2.15	1.79	14.1	4.7	21.5	0.6

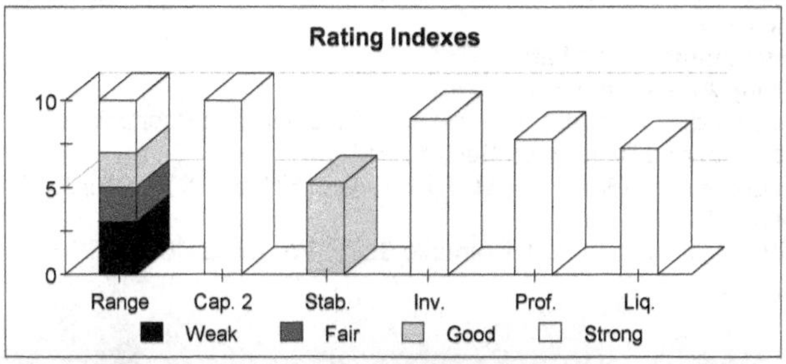

LIFE INSURANCE COMPANY OF ALABAMA B Good

Major Rating Factors: Good quality investment portfolio (6.4 on a scale of 0 to 10) despite mixed results such as: no exposure to mortgages and large holdings of BBB rated bonds but no exposure to junk bonds. Good overall profitability (6.0) despite operating losses during the first three months of 2019. Good liquidity (6.4) with sufficient resources to handle a spike in claims.

Other Rating Factors: Good overall results on stability tests (5.7) excellent operational trends and good risk diversification. Strong capitalization (9.4) based on excellent risk adjusted capital (severe loss scenario).

Principal Business: Individual health insurance (71%), individual life insurance (21%), and group health insurance (8%).

Principal Investments: NonCMO investment grade bonds (69%), CMOs and structured securities (21%), policy loans (3%), cash (1%), and real estate (1%).

Investments in Affiliates: None

Group Affiliation: None

Licensed in: AL, AR, FL, GA, KY, LA, MS, NC, OK, SC, TN

Commenced Business: August 1952

Address: 302 Broad Street, Gadsden, AL 35901

Phone: (256) 543-2022 **Domicile State:** AL **NAIC Code:** 65412

Data Date	Rating	RACR #1	RACR #2	Total Assets ($mil)	Capital ($mil)	Net Premium ($mil)	Net Income ($mil)
3-19	B	3.94	2.63	124.6	40.4	9.5	-0.4
3-18	B	3.61	2.37	124.0	41.7	9.5	-1.9
2018	B	4.03	2.69	123.9	41.4	37.2	-0.3
2017	B	3.52	2.17	124.8	42.5	36.7	2.2
2016	B	3.39	2.03	120.8	40.6	36.0	2.2
2015	A-	3.37	2.10	116.6	38.7	36.3	2.8
2014	A-	3.33	2.22	113.5	37.3	37.4	7.0

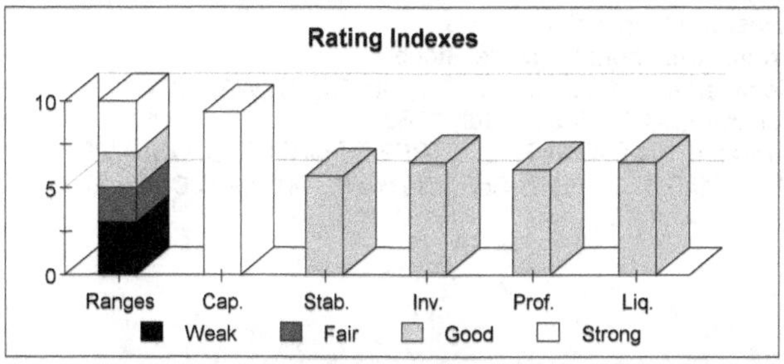

LIFE INSURANCE COMPANY OF BOSTON & NEW YORK * A- Excellent

Major Rating Factors: Good quality investment portfolio (6.6 on a scale of 0 to 10) despite mixed results such as: no exposure to mortgages and large holdings of BBB rated bonds but minimal holdings in junk bonds. Good overall profitability (6.3). Good liquidity (6.6) with sufficient resources to handle a spike in claims as well as a significant increase in policy surrenders.

Other Rating Factors: Excellent overall results on stability tests (7.0) excellent operational trends and good risk diversification. Strong capitalization (8.8) based on excellent risk adjusted capital (severe loss scenario).

Principal Business: Individual life insurance (62%), individual health insurance (19%), and group health insurance (18%).

Principal Investments: NonCMO investment grade bonds (63%), policy loans (20%), CMOs and structured securities (7%), common & preferred stock (5%), and misc. investments (4%).

Investments in Affiliates: None

Group Affiliation: Boston Mutual Group

Licensed in: NY

Commenced Business: March 1990

Address: 4300 Camp Road PO Box 331, Athol Springs, NY 14010

Phone: (212) 684-2000 **Domicile State:** NY **NAIC Code:** 78140

Data Date	Rating	RACR #1	RACR #2	Total Assets ($mil)	Capital ($mil)	Net Premium ($mil)	Net Income ($mil)
3-19	A-	3.64	2.18	163.1	33.2	5.6	0.7
3-18	A-	3.42	2.42	152.9	31.3	5.3	1.1
2018	A-	3.48	2.14	160.1	32.3	23.5	2.7
2017	A-	3.30	2.36	150.4	30.1	22.6	1.5
2016	A-	3.15	2.49	141.4	28.9	22.0	1.5
2015	A-	2.91	2.40	130.4	26.6	21.5	3.3
2014	A-	2.64	2.07	124.1	23.9	24.8	1.8

Rating Indexes

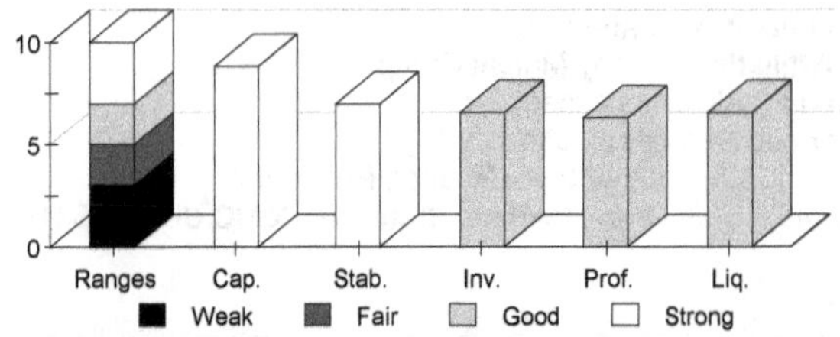

LIFE INSURANCE COMPANY OF NORTH AMERICA B Good

Major Rating Factors: Good overall results on stability tests (5.8 on a scale of 0 to 10). Stability strengths include excellent operational trends and excellent risk diversification. Good quality investment portfolio (5.4) despite large holdings of BBB rated bonds in addition to moderate junk bond exposure. Exposure to mortgages is significant, but the mortgage default rate has been low. Good liquidity (6.7).

Other Rating Factors: Strong capitalization (8.0) based on excellent risk adjusted capital (severe loss scenario). Excellent profitability (8.0).

Principal Business: Group health insurance (58%), group life insurance (38%), and reinsurance (3%).

Principal Investments: NonCMO investment grade bonds (71%), mortgages in good standing (12%), noninv. grade bonds (8%), and CMOs and structured securities (2%).

Investments in Affiliates: 9%

Group Affiliation: CIGNA Corp

Licensed in: All states, the District of Columbia and Puerto Rico

Commenced Business: September 1957

Address: 2 LIBERTY PLC 1601 CHESTNUT ST, PHILADELPHIA, PA 19192-2362

Phone: (215) 761-1000 **Domicile State:** PA **NAIC Code:** 65498

Data Date	Rating	RACR #1	RACR #2	Total Assets ($mil)	Capital ($mil)	Net Premium ($mil)	Net Income ($mil)
3-19	B	2.57	1.66	8,795.5	1,761.5	981.7	30.6
3-18	B	2.70	1.74	8,938.2	1,882.6	940.0	67.2
2018	B	2.62	1.69	8,667.9	1,776.2	3,730.7	299.0
2017	B	2.62	1.69	8,900.7	1,798.2	3,730.5	334.4
2016	B	2.20	1.41	8,604.4	1,477.8	3,751.3	111.9
2015	B	2.34	1.51	8,141.6	1,495.3	3,674.5	236.6
2014	B	2.42	1.54	7,562.6	1,346.0	3,192.3	287.8

Adverse Trends in Operations

Decrease in asset base during 2018 (3%)
Decrease in capital during 2018 (1%)
Increase in policy surrenders from 2015 to 2016 (392%)
Increase in policy surrenders from 2014 to 2015 (994%)
Change in premium mix from 2014 to 2015 (5.6%)

LIFEMAP ASSURANCE COMPANY B- Good

Major Rating Factors: Good liquidity (6.6 on a scale of 0 to 10) with sufficient resources to handle a spike in claims. Good overall results on stability tests (5.3) despite negative cash flow from operations for 2018. Strengths include good financial support from affiliation with Regence Group, excellent operational trends and excellent risk diversification. Fair quality investment portfolio (4.9).

Other Rating Factors: Weak profitability (2.9). Strong capitalization (7.7) based on excellent risk adjusted capital (severe loss scenario).

Principal Business: Group health insurance (66%), group life insurance (28%), and individual health insurance (6%).

Principal Investments: CMOs and structured securities (49%), nonCMO investment grade bonds (24%), common & preferred stock (21%), and cash (1%).

Investments in Affiliates: 2%

Group Affiliation: Regence Group

Licensed in: AK, AZ, CA, ID, MT, OR, RI, UT, WA, WY

Commenced Business: July 1966

Address: 100 SW MARKET STREET, PORTLAND, OR 97201

Phone: (503) 225-6069 **Domicile State:** OR **NAIC Code:** 97985

Data Date	Rating	RACR #1	RACR #2	Total Assets ($mil)	Capital ($mil)	Net Premium ($mil)	Net Income ($mil)
3-19	B-	2.02	1.47	95.8	50.9	19.3	1.6
3-18	B-	1.88	1.38	99.4	46.0	20.0	-1.4
2018	B-	1.96	1.44	94.2	48.0	80.1	-0.6
2017	B-	1.92	1.40	97.2	47.6	84.3	-0.2
2016	B-	1.50	1.11	84.0	38.4	81.0	-0.3
2015	B-	1.55	1.14	83.1	39.4	76.4	-1.4
2014	B	1.80	1.32	85.1	43.1	68.9	-0.1

Regence Group
Composite Group Rating: B

Largest Group Members	Assets ($mil)	Rating
REGENCE BLUESHIELD	1731	B
REGENCE BL CROSS BL SHIELD OREGON	1195	B+
REGENCE BLUE CROSS BLUE SHIELD OF UT	646	B
REGENCE BLUESHIELD OF IDAHO INC	302	B
ASURIS NORTHWEST HEALTH	99	B-

LIFESECURE INSURANCE COMPANY D Weak

Major Rating Factors: Weak profitability (1.9 on a scale of 0 to 10) with operating losses during the first three months of 2019. Weak overall results on stability tests (2.0). Good liquidity (6.8) with sufficient resources to cover a large increase in policy surrenders.
Other Rating Factors: Strong capitalization (7.9) based on excellent risk adjusted capital (severe loss scenario). High quality investment portfolio (7.3).
Principal Business: Individual health insurance (63%), reinsurance (31%), and individual life insurance (6%).
Principal Investments: NonCMO investment grade bonds (79%) and CMOs and structured securities (20%).
Investments in Affiliates: None
Group Affiliation: Blue Cross Blue Shield of Michigan
Licensed in: All states except ME, MA, NY, PR
Commenced Business: July 1954
Address: 10559 CItation Drive Suite 300, Brighton, MI 48116
Phone: (810) 220-7700 **Domicile State:** MI **NAIC Code:** 77720

Data Date	Rating	RACR #1	RACR #2	Total Assets ($mil)	Capital ($mil)	Net Premium ($mil)	Net Income ($mil)
3-19	D	2.42	1.57	429.5	46.3	20.4	-0.6
3-18	D	2.64	1.73	378.8	47.0	19.5	0.8
2018	D	2.47	1.60	416.0	46.9	81.5	0.9
2017	D	2.66	1.75	366.3	46.3	72.5	-3.4
2016	D	2.05	1.33	309.2	32.5	61.9	-0.5
2015	D	1.32	0.85	262.3	18.0	50.4	-10.3
2014	D-	1.76	1.16	226.9	20.4	42.5	-13.0

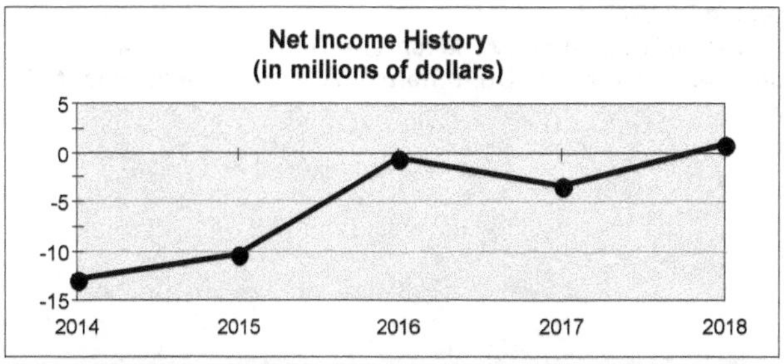

LIFESHIELD NATIONAL INSURANCE COMPANY B- Good

Major Rating Factors: Good liquidity (6.7 on a scale of 0 to 10) with sufficient resources to handle a spike in claims. Good overall results on stability tests (5.0) despite excessive premium growth. Other stability subfactors include excellent operational trends and good risk diversification. Fair quality investment portfolio (3.9).
Other Rating Factors: Strong capitalization (7.6) based on excellent risk adjusted capital (severe loss scenario). Excellent profitability (7.6).
Principal Business: Group health insurance (69%), reinsurance (23%), individual life insurance (6%), and group life insurance (1%).
Principal Investments: CMOs and structured securities (51%), common & preferred stock (20%), noninv. grade bonds (4%), nonCMO investment grade bonds (3%), and misc. investments (5%).
Investments in Affiliates: 1%
Group Affiliation: Homeshield Capital Group
Licensed in: All states except AK, HI, ME, NH, NY, RI, VT, WI, PR
Commenced Business: May 1982
Address: 5701 N Shartel 1st Floor, Oklahoma City, OK 73118
Phone: (405) 236-2640 **Domicile State:** OK **NAIC Code:** 99724

Data Date	Rating	RACR #1	RACR #2	Total Assets ($mil)	Capital ($mil)	Net Premium ($mil)	Net Income ($mil)
3-19	B-	2.04	1.43	92.3	31.8	17.6	0.7
3-18	B-	2.03	1.28	80.1	26.9	13.6	0.3
2018	B-	2.01	1.41	92.4	30.6	64.5	3.6
2017	B-	2.03	1.23	78.7	26.2	36.8	1.4
2016	B-	2.30	1.34	69.8	24.5	24.4	1.3
2015	B-	2.17	1.26	69.4	23.8	21.6	0.6
2014	B-	2.13	1.23	67.8	23.3	20.0	0.5

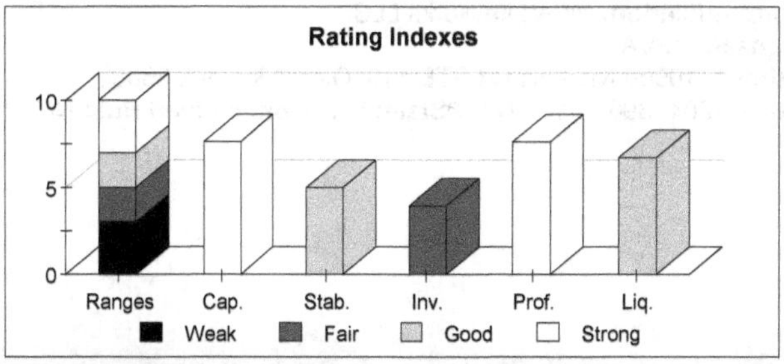

LIFEWISE ASSURANCE COMPANY * A Excellent

Major Rating Factors: Excellent overall results on stability tests (7.1 on a scale of 0 to 10). Strengths that enhance stability include excellent operational trends and excellent risk diversification. Strong capitalization (10.0) based on excellent risk adjusted capital (severe loss scenario). Furthermore, this high level of risk adjusted capital has been consistently maintained over the last five years. High quality investment portfolio (8.0).
Other Rating Factors: Excellent profitability (9.3). Excellent liquidity (7.0).
Principal Business: Group health insurance (100%).
Principal Investments: NonCMO investment grade bonds (49%), CMOs and structured securities (45%), noninv. grade bonds (1%), and cash (1%).
Investments in Affiliates: None
Group Affiliation: PREMERA
Licensed in: AK, CA, ID, IL, OR, WA
Commenced Business: November 1981
Address: 7001 220th Street SW, Mountlake Terrace, WA 98043
Phone: (425) 918-4575 **Domicile State:** WA **NAIC Code:** 94188

Data Date	Rating	RACR #1	RACR #2	Total Assets ($mil)	Capital ($mil)	Net Premium ($mil)	Net Income ($mil)
3-19	A	7.73	5.69	215.9	162.1	42.4	8.5
3-18	A	7.34	5.45	181.2	134.7	36.7	6.5
2018	A	7.62	5.63	194.7	153.6	146.3	25.4
2017	A	7.25	5.38	168.2	128.2	130.0	20.4
2016	A	6.77	5.05	142.7	108.1	118.3	11.6
2015	A	6.80	5.11	133.5	96.5	105.7	6.7
2014	A	7.38	5.56	127.0	89.9	90.9	9.3

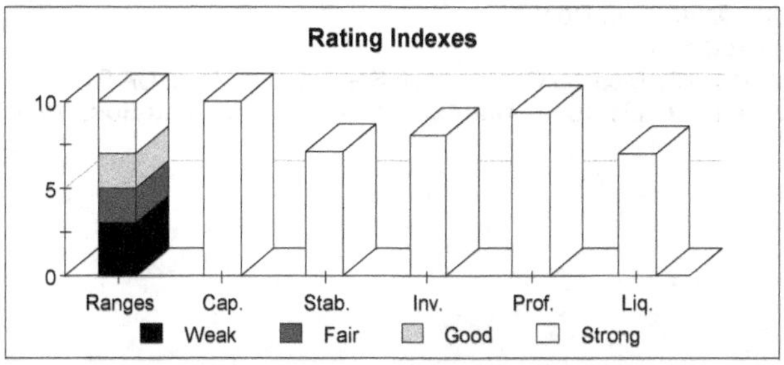

LIFEWISE HEALTH PLAN OF WASHINGTON B- Good

Major Rating Factors: Good overall profitability index (5.3 on a scale of 0 to 10). Strong capitalization (10.0) based on excellent current risk-adjusted capital (severe loss scenario). High quality investment portfolio (7.5).
Other Rating Factors: Excellent liquidity (7.0) with sufficient resources (cash flows and marketable investments) to handle a spike in claims.
Principal Business: Comp med (100%)
Mem Phys: 18: 49,633 **17:** 48,032 **18 MLR** 72.3% **/ 18 Admin Exp** N/A
Enroll(000): Q1 19: 20 **18:** 21 **17:** 38 **Med Exp PMPM:** $370
Principal Investments: Long-term bonds (88%), cash and equiv (11%)
Provider Compensation ($000): Contr fee ($104,247), FFS ($1,867)
Total Member Encounters: Phys (175,061), non-phys (62,041)
Group Affiliation: None
Licensed in: WA
Address: 7001 220th St SW, Mountlake Terrace, WA 98043
Phone: (425) 918-4000 **Dom State:** WA **Commenced Bus:** N/A

Data Date	Rating	RACR #1	RACR #2	Total Assets ($mil)	Capital ($mil)	Net Premium ($mil)	Net Income ($mil)
3-19	B-	11.75	9.79	115.7	87.6	30.8	4.5
3-18	B	6.46	5.39	115.2	69.0	35.8	-0.9
2018	B-	11.19	9.32	108.3	83.2	139.8	13.2
2017	B	4.23	3.53	115.7	70.0	183.0	-0.7
2016	B	6.84	5.70	121.1	71.2	176.0	-3.1
2015	B+	6.08	5.07	147.6	75.4	243.2	4.9
2014	B+	5.08	4.23	171.0	70.8	285.4	7.1

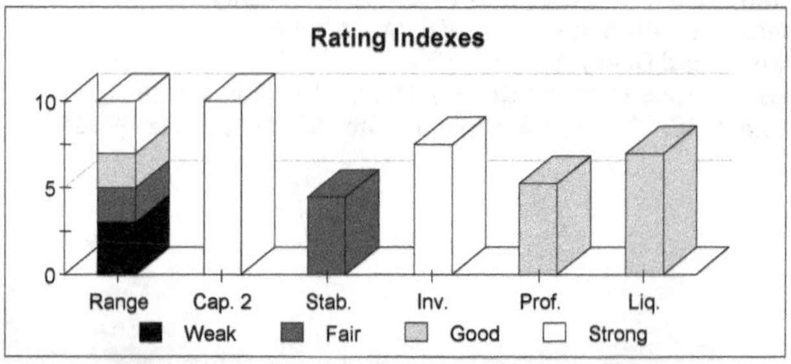

LIFEWORKS ADVANTAGE, LLC D+ Weak

Major Rating Factors: Weak profitability index (0.9 on a scale of 0 to 10). Poor capitalization (2.6) based on weak current risk-adjusted capital (moderate loss scenario). Good liquidity (6.3) with sufficient resources (cash flows and marketable investments) to handle a spike in claims.
Other Rating Factors: High quality investment portfolio (9.9).
Principal Business: Medicare (100%)
Mem Phys: 18: 3,359 **17:** 991 **18 MLR** 86.1% **/ 18 Admin Exp** N/A
Enroll(000): Q1 19: 1 **18:** 1 **17:** 1 **Med Exp PMPM:** $1,781
Principal Investments: Cash and equiv (52%), long-term bonds (48%)
Provider Compensation ($000): Contr fee ($9,499), capitation ($5,223), bonus arrang ($131)
Total Member Encounters: Phys (14,122), non-phys (23,187)
Group Affiliation: MFA LifeWorks LLC
Licensed in: VA
Address: 10900 Nuckols Rd STE 110, Glen Allen, VA 23060
Phone: (804) 396-6412 **Dom State:** VA **Commenced Bus:** N/A

Data Date	Rating	RACR #1	RACR #2	Total Assets ($mil)	Capital ($mil)	Net Premium ($mil)	Net Income ($mil)
3-19	D+	0.56	0.47	4.6	1.9	5.0	0.1
3-18	N/A	N/A	N/A	5.2	1.5	4.1	N/A
2018	U	0.56	0.47	3.9	1.9	17.8	-0.4
2017	N/A	N/A	N/A	3.1	1.5	13.9	-0.3
2016	N/A	N/A	N/A	1.9	1.9	N/A	-0.9
2015	N/A	N/A	N/A	N/A	N/A	N/A	N/A
2014	N/A	N/A	N/A	N/A	N/A	N/A	N/A

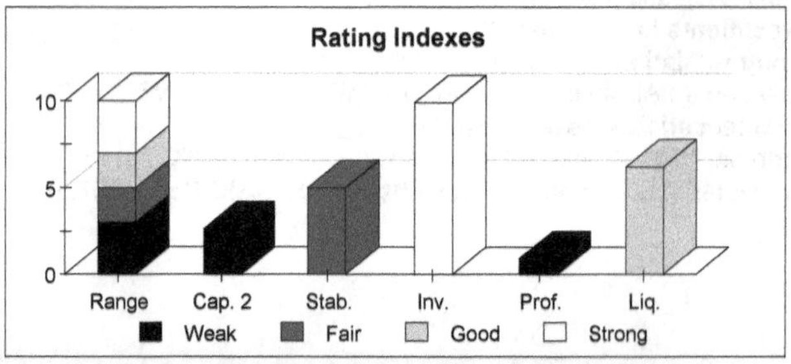

LOCAL INITIATIVE HEALTH AUTH LA C Fair

Major Rating Factors: Weak liquidity (0.0 on a scale of 0 to 10) as a spike in claims may stretch capacity. Good overall results on stability tests (5.8) based on steady enrollment growth, averaging 9% over the past five years. Excellent profitability (8.8).
Other Rating Factors: Strong capitalization index (7.0) based on excellent current risk-adjusted capital (severe loss scenario).
Principal Business: Medicaid (91%), Medicare (3%)
Mem Phys: 18: N/A **17:** N/A **18 MLR** 92.5% **/ 18 Admin Exp** N/A
Enroll(000): Q1 19: 2,158 **18:** 2,170 **17:** 2,135 **Med Exp PMPM:** $265
Principal Investments ($000): Cash and equiv ($1,225,780)
Provider Compensation ($000): None
Total Member Encounters: N/A
Group Affiliation: None
Licensed in: CA
Address: 750 Medical Center Court Ste 2, Chula Vista, CA 91911
Phone: (619) 421-1659 **Dom State:** CA **Commenced Bus:** April 1997

Data Date	Rating	RACR #1	RACR #2	Total Assets ($mil)	Capital ($mil)	Net Premium ($mil)	Net Income ($mil)
3-19	C	1.82	1.11	4,858.2	1,017.0	2,046.8	141.2
3-18	C	1.22	0.74	4,519.9	805.6	1,955.8	109.9
2018	C	1.27	0.78	3,938.1	875.8	7,595.6	180.1
2017	C	0.90	0.55	4,623.3	695.7	8,999.0	150.6
2016	C	0.69	0.42	4,136.1	523.8	7,755.3	30.9
2015	C	1.20	0.73	2,857.7	492.9	6,366.0	272.9
2014	C	0.64	0.39	1,354.7	220.1	4,137.2	44.1

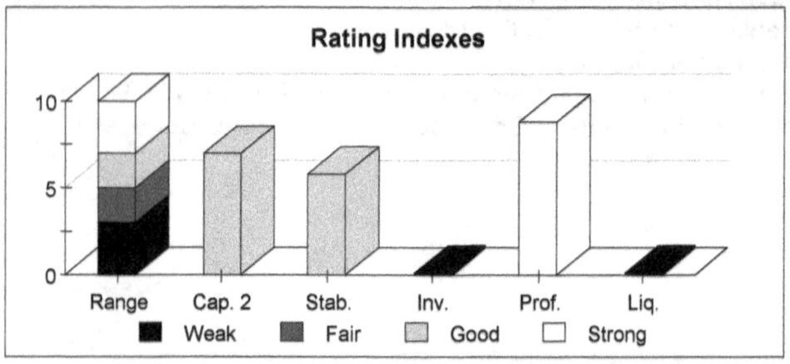

LONDON LIFE REINSURANCE COMPANY C+ Fair

Major Rating Factors: Fair overall capitalization (4.0 on a scale of 0 to 10) based on mixed results -- excessive policy leverage mitigated by excellent risk adjusted capital (severe loss scenario). Capital levels have been relatively consistent over the last five years. Fair overall results on stability tests (4.0) including negative cash flow from operations for 2018. High quality investment portfolio (7.6).
Other Rating Factors: Excellent profitability (9.0). Excellent liquidity (8.5).
Principal Business: N/A
Principal Investments: NonCMO investment grade bonds (83%), CMOs and structured securities (7%), cash (4%), and noninv. grade bonds (3%).
Investments in Affiliates: None
Group Affiliation: Great West Life Asr
Licensed in: All states, the District of Columbia and Puerto Rico
Commenced Business: December 1969
Address: 1787 Sentry Pkwy W Bldg 16, Blue Bell, PA 19422-2240
Phone: (215) 542-7200 **Domicile State:** PA **NAIC Code:** 76694

Data Date	Rating	RACR #1	RACR #2	Total Assets ($mil)	Capital ($mil)	Net Premium ($mil)	Net Income ($mil)
3-19	C+	6.98	6.28	154.4	63.7	0.3	0.5
3-18	C+	6.27	3.86	197.0	58.8	0.3	0.6
2018	C+	6.75	5.06	154.3	63.2	-55.6	4.7
2017	C+	5.97	3.66	204.0	58.3	1.1	0.9
2016	C+	5.58	3.21	289.3	58.5	1.5	2.3
2015	C+	5.43	2.91	301.3	57.4	1.9	2.1
2014	C+	5.29	2.81	316.2	56.6	2.2	4.2

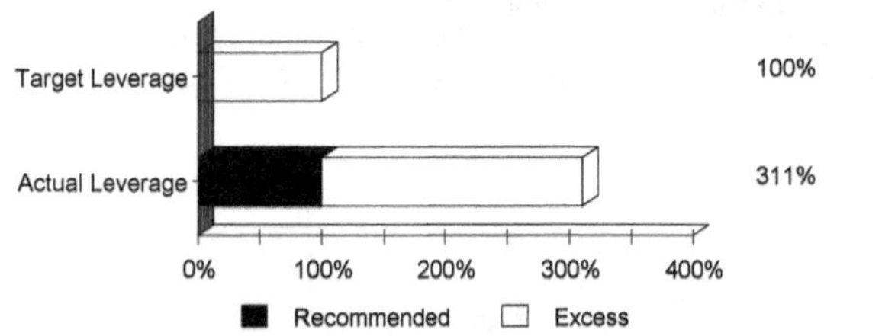

LOUISIANA HEALTHCARE CONNECTIONS INC E Very Weak

Major Rating Factors: Weak profitability index (0.9 on a scale of 0 to 10). Strong capitalization (8.4) based on excellent current risk-adjusted capital (severe loss scenario). High quality investment portfolio (8.6).
Other Rating Factors: Excellent liquidity (7.0) with ample operational cash flow and liquid investments.
Principal Business: Medicaid (100%)
Mem Phys: 18: 23,375 **17:** 21,736 **18 MLR** 85.0% **/ 18 Admin Exp** N/A
Enroll(000): Q1 19: 483 **18:** 470 **17:** 487 **Med Exp PMPM:** $337
Principal Investments: Cash and equiv (69%), long-term bonds (31%)
Provider Compensation ($000): Contr fee ($1,499,044), salary ($385,316), capitation ($38,995), bonus arrang ($13,527)
Total Member Encounters: Phys (2,298,823), non-phys (4,163,120)
Group Affiliation: None
Licensed in: LA
Address: 7700 Forsyth Blvd, Baton Rouge, LA 70809
Phone: (314) 725-4477 **Dom State:** LA **Commenced Bus:** N/A

Data Date	Rating	RACR #1	RACR #2	Total Assets ($mil)	Capital ($mil)	Net Premium ($mil)	Net Income ($mil)
3-19	E	2.47	2.06	562.2	125.1	582.7	-12.1
3-18	E	1.36	1.13	481.9	78.4	572.8	-36.9
2018	E	2.61	2.17	561.3	133.2	2,279.9	-18.0
2017	E	1.30	1.08	486.0	109.5	2,103.5	-36.0
2016	E	1.40	1.17	451.1	96.5	1,740.3	-22.9
2015	E	1.56	1.30	247.5	88.4	1,188.1	-17.1
2014	C-	2.74	2.28	117.7	64.6	451.1	-5.0

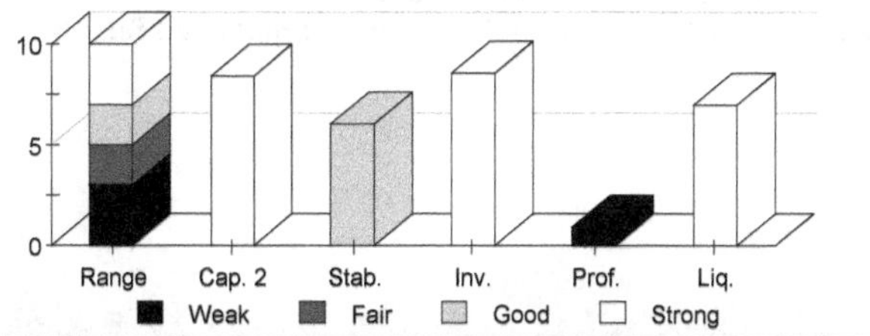

LOYAL AMERICAN LIFE INSURANCE COMPANY B- Good

Major Rating Factors: Good capitalization (6.9 on a scale of 0 to 10) based on good risk adjusted capital (severe loss scenario). Moreover, capital levels have been consistent over the last five years. Good quality investment portfolio (6.1) despite mixed results such as: no exposure to mortgages and large holdings of BBB rated bonds but minimal holdings in junk bonds. Good liquidity (6.6).
Other Rating Factors: Good overall results on stability tests (5.3) excellent operational trends and excellent risk diversification. Excellent profitability (7.0).
Principal Business: Individual health insurance (72%), reinsurance (25%), individual life insurance (2%), and group health insurance (2%).
Principal Investments: NonCMO investment grade bonds (82%), common & preferred stock (20%), and noninv. grade bonds (1%).
Investments in Affiliates: 20%
Group Affiliation: CIGNA Corp
Licensed in: All states except NY, PR
Commenced Business: July 1955
Address: 1300 East Ninth Street, Cleveland, OH 44114
Phone: (512) 451-2224 **Domicile State:** OH **NAIC Code:** 65722

Data Date	Rating	RACR #1	RACR #2	Total Assets ($mil)	Capital ($mil)	Net Premium ($mil)	Net Income ($mil)
3-19	B-	1.17	0.99	354.6	135.0	92.4	2.1
3-18	B-	1.14	0.98	331.1	120.4	84.4	1.8
2018	B-	1.07	0.92	338.7	116.8	345.3	8.5
2017	B-	0.95	0.82	310.6	96.6	311.5	9.1
2016	C+	1.08	0.91	272.9	86.3	281.7	15.6
2015	C+	1.00	0.86	266.7	85.6	278.5	16.5
2014	C	1.11	0.93	249.3	73.5	243.7	20.2

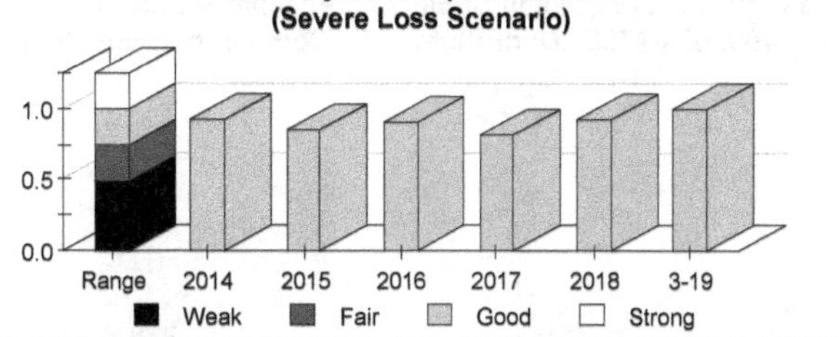

MADISON NATIONAL LIFE INSURANCE COMPANY INCORPORAT A- Excellent

Major Rating Factors: Good quality investment portfolio (5.9 on a scale of 0 to 10) with no exposure to mortgages and no exposure to junk bonds. Good overall results on stability tests (6.9). Strengths that enhance stability include excellent operational trends and excellent risk diversification. Strong capitalization (7.6) based on excellent risk adjusted capital (severe loss scenario).
Other Rating Factors: Excellent profitability (8.2). Excellent liquidity (7.2).
Principal Business: Group health insurance (64%), group life insurance (21%), individual life insurance (7%), and individual annuities (7%).
Principal Investments: NonCMO investment grade bonds (51%), common & preferred stock (44%), cash (2%), and CMOs and structured securities (1%).
Investments in Affiliates: 43%
Group Affiliation: Geneve Holdings Inc
Licensed in: All states except NY, PR
Commenced Business: March 1962
Address: 1241 John Q Hammons Drive, Madison, WI 53717-1929
Phone: (800) 356-9601 **Domicile State:** WI **NAIC Code:** 65781

Data Date	Rating	RACR #1	RACR #2	Total Assets ($mil)	Capital ($mil)	Net Premium ($mil)	Net Income ($mil)
3-19	A-	1.46	1.39	337.4	199.8	25.1	4.0
3-18	B	1.54	1.45	335.5	189.2	23.6	4.6
2018	B	1.44	1.37	337.4	196.0	93.9	16.0
2017	B-	1.48	1.41	326.3	179.6	87.9	12.8
2016	C+	1.48	1.41	329.7	179.0	86.9	-1.6
2015	B-	1.95	1.71	256.9	116.7	126.4	20.3
2014	C+	1.26	1.06	496.7	81.5	147.5	9.9

Adverse Trends in Operations

Decrease in asset base during 2017 (1%)
Decrease in premium volume from 2015 to 2016 (31%)
Change in asset mix during 2016 (4.7%)
Decrease in asset base during 2015 (48%)
Decrease in premium volume from 2014 to 2015 (14%)

MAGELLAN BEHAVIORAL HEALTH OF PA INC C+ Fair

Major Rating Factors: Excellent profitability (8.2 on a scale of 0 to 10). Strong capitalization (7.2) based on excellent current risk-adjusted capital (severe loss scenario). High quality investment portfolio (9.9).
Other Rating Factors: Excellent liquidity (7.0) with ample operational cash flow and liquid investments.
Principal Business: Medicaid (100%)
Mem Phys: 18: 728 **17:** 685 **18 MLR** 88.0% **/ 18 Admin Exp** N/A
Enroll(000): Q1 19: 450 **18:** 435 **17:** 440 **Med Exp PMPM:** $90
Principal Investments: Cash and equiv (98%), long-term bonds (2%)
Provider Compensation ($000): Contr fee ($475,818)
Total Member Encounters: Phys (642,452), non-phys (1,476,139)
Group Affiliation: Magellan Health Inc
Licensed in: PA
Address: 105 Terry Dr Ste 103, Newtown, PA 18940
Phone: (215) 504-3907 **Dom State:** PA **Commenced Bus:** N/A

Data Date	Rating	RACR #1	RACR #2	Total Assets ($mil)	Capital ($mil)	Net Premium ($mil)	Net Income ($mil)
3-19	C+	1.48	1.23	125.9	66.5	131.2	2.7
3-18	C	1.23	1.03	108.8	48.0	136.6	-5.5
2018	C+	1.42	1.19	124.3	63.9	543.4	13.3
2017	B-	1.13	0.94	103.8	53.6	489.0	5.0
2016	C+	1.37	1.14	107.9	50.6	460.3	5.7
2015	B-	1.41	1.18	92.7	44.9	395.2	5.4
2014	C+	1.52	1.26	98.1	46.5	369.3	5.2

Rating Indexes

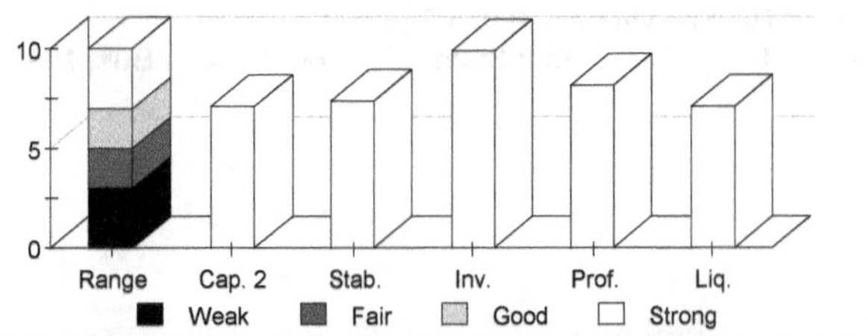

MAGELLAN COMPLETE CARE OF ARIZONA D+ Weak

Major Rating Factors: Weak profitability index (0.8 on a scale of 0 to 10). Strong capitalization (9.5) based on excellent current risk-adjusted capital (severe loss scenario). High quality investment portfolio (9.9).
Other Rating Factors: Excellent liquidity (8.0) with ample operational cash flow and liquid investments.
Principal Business: Medicaid (100%)
Mem Phys: 18: 4,822 **17:** N/A **18 MLR** 95.1% **/ 18 Admin Exp** N/A
Enroll(000): Q1 19: 9 **18:** 5 **17:** N/A **Med Exp PMPM:** $539
Principal Investments: Cash and equiv (81%), long-term bonds (19%)
Provider Compensation ($000): Contr fee ($1,439)
Total Member Encounters: Phys (1,802), non-phys (273)
Group Affiliation: Magellan Health Inc
Licensed in: AZ
Address: 4801 E Washington St Ste 100, Phoenix, AZ 85034
Phone: (480) 624-9735 **Dom State:** AZ **Commenced Bus:** N/A

Data Date	Rating	RACR #1	RACR #2	Total Assets ($mil)	Capital ($mil)	Net Premium ($mil)	Net Income ($mil)
3-19	D+	3.37	2.81	19.1	7.4	10.9	-2.3
3-18	N/A	N/A	N/A	N/A	N/A	N/A	N/A
2018	D+	4.42	3.69	17.4	9.8	5.7	-2.3
2017	N/A	N/A	N/A	1.5	1.5	N/A	N/A
2016	N/A	N/A	N/A	1.5	1.5	N/A	N/A
2015	N/A	N/A	N/A	1.5	1.5	N/A	N/A
2014	N/A	N/A	N/A	1.5	1.5	N/A	N/A

Rating Indexes

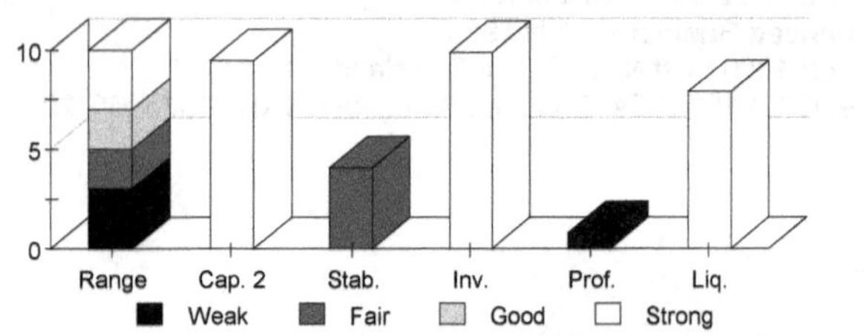

MAGELLAN COMPLETE CARE OF LOUISIANA C Fair

Major Rating Factors: Excellent profitability (7.4 on a scale of 0 to 10). Strong capitalization (8.1) based on excellent current risk-adjusted capital (severe loss scenario). High quality investment portfolio (9.9).
Other Rating Factors: Excellent liquidity (7.1) with ample operational cash flow and liquid investments.
Principal Business: Medicaid (100%)
Mem Phys: 18: 1,385 **17:** N/A **18 MLR** 75.8% **/ 18 Admin Exp** N/A
Enroll(000): Q1 19: 3 **18:** 3 **17:** N/A **Med Exp PMPM:** $1,867
Principal Investments: Long-term bonds (63%), cash and equiv (37%)
Provider Compensation ($000): Contr fee ($2,221)
Total Member Encounters: Phys (78), non-phys (203,283)
Group Affiliation: Magellan Health Inc
Licensed in: LA
Address: 10000 Perkins Rowe Ste 500, Baton Rouge, LA 70810
Phone: (314) 387-5044 **Dom State:** LA **Commenced Bus:** N/A

Data Date	Rating	RACR #1	RACR #2	Total Assets ($mil)	Capital ($mil)	Net Premium ($mil)	Net Income ($mil)
3-19	C	2.22	1.85	17.2	4.7	17.8	0.9
3-18	N/A	N/A	N/A	3.1	3.1	N/A	N/A
2018	D+	1.80	1.50	12.0	3.9	12.4	0.8
2017	N/A	N/A	N/A	3.1	3.1	N/A	N/A
2016	N/A	N/A	N/A	3.1	3.1	N/A	N/A
2015	N/A	N/A	N/A	3.1	3.1	N/A	N/A
2014	N/A	N/A	N/A	3.0	3.0	N/A	N/A

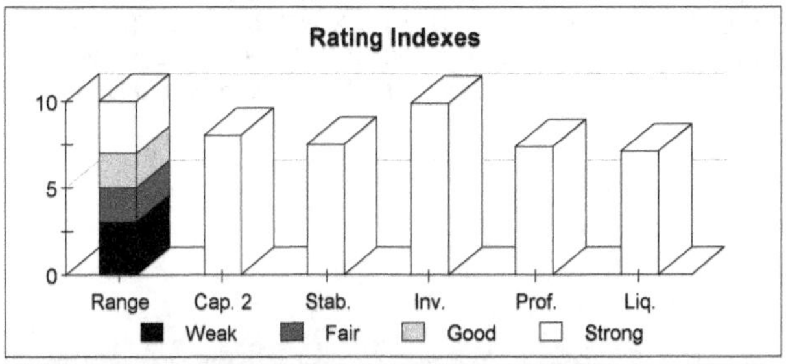

MAGELLAN COMPLETE CARE OF VA D+ Weak

Major Rating Factors: Weak profitability index (0.9 on a scale of 0 to 10). Good liquidity (6.8) with sufficient resources (cash flows and marketable investments) to handle a spike in claims. Strong capitalization (7.4) based on excellent current risk-adjusted capital (severe loss scenario).
Other Rating Factors: High quality investment portfolio (9.9).
Principal Business: Medicaid (100%)
Mem Phys: 18: 25,065 **17:** 15,805 **18 MLR** 100.8% **/ 18 Admin Exp** N/A
Enroll(000): Q1 19: 75 **18:** 54 **17:** 14 **Med Exp PMPM:** $1,321
Principal Investments: Cash and equiv (87%), long-term bonds (13%)
Provider Compensation ($000): Contr fee ($402,784), capitation ($29,211)
Total Member Encounters: Phys (380,786), non-phys (355,915)
Group Affiliation: Magellan Health Inc
Licensed in: VA
Address: , Columbia, MD 21046
Phone: (314) 387-4269 **Dom State:** VA **Commenced Bus:** N/A

Data Date	Rating	RACR #1	RACR #2	Total Assets ($mil)	Capital ($mil)	Net Premium ($mil)	Net Income ($mil)
3-19	D+	1.66	1.39	191.7	68.3	193.9	-2.8
3-18	N/A	N/A	N/A	98.1	28.9	117.3	-9.0
2018	D+	1.50	1.25	149.9	61.2	473.2	-42.4
2017	N/A	N/A	N/A	45.5	12.9	73.8	-10.1
2016	N/A	N/A	N/A	4.4	4.4	N/A	N/A
2015	N/A	N/A	N/A	N/A	N/A	N/A	N/A
2014	N/A	N/A	N/A	N/A	N/A	N/A	N/A

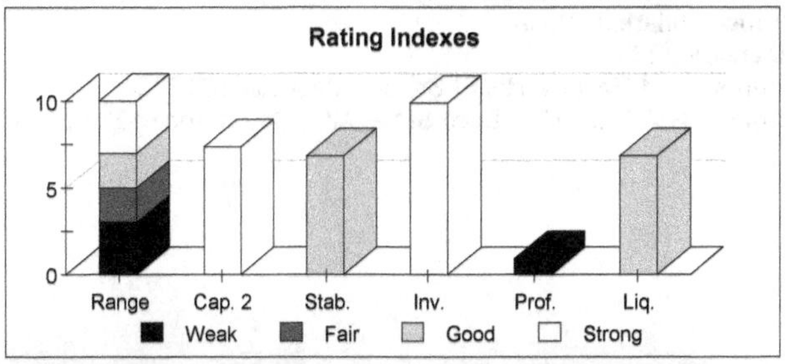

MAGELLAN LIFE INS CO B- Good

Major Rating Factors: Excellent profitability (8.5 on a scale of 0 to 10). Strong capitalization (10.0) based on excellent current risk-adjusted capital (severe loss scenario). High quality investment portfolio (9.9).
Other Rating Factors: Excellent liquidity (8.7) with ample operational cash flow and liquid investments.
Principal Business: Other (100%)
Mem Phys: 18: N/A **17:** N/A **18 MLR** 64.5% **/ 18 Admin Exp** N/A
Enroll(000): Q1 19: 171 **18:** 170 **17:** 217 **Med Exp PMPM:** $3
Principal Investments: Cash and equiv (83%), long-term bonds (17%)
Provider Compensation ($000): Other ($6,345)
Total Member Encounters: N/A
Group Affiliation: Magellan Health Inc
Licensed in: AZ, CA, DE, GA, HI, IN, KS, MS, MT, NE, NM, ND, SC, SD, TN, TX, UT, WV, WY
Address: 1209 Orange St, Wilmington, DE 19801
Phone: (619) 326-9204 **Dom State:** DE **Commenced Bus:** N/A

Data Date	Rating	RACR #1	RACR #2	Total Assets ($mil)	Capital ($mil)	Net Premium ($mil)	Net Income ($mil)
3-19	B-	6.71	5.59	11.1	10.3	2.1	0.2
3-18	B	2.10	1.75	21.3	15.3	4.5	-0.2
2018	B-	6.53	5.44	11.0	10.0	11.7	0.6
2017	B	1.57	1.31	21.8	15.2	58.2	3.8
2016	C-	1.62	1.35	16.2	11.5	61.3	7.1
2015	U	3.05	2.54	13.1	9.1	25.6	3.5
2014	N/A	N/A	N/A	6.2	3.9	14.2	0.2

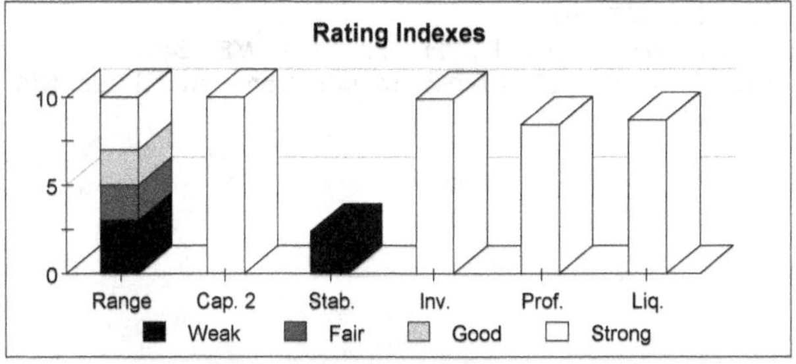

MAGNA INS CO D- Weak

Major Rating Factors: Weak profitability index (0.8 on a scale of 0 to 10). Poor capitalization (1.6) based on weak current risk-adjusted capital (moderate loss scenario). High quality investment portfolio (9.1).
Other Rating Factors: Excellent liquidity (7.5) with ample operational cash flow and liquid investments.
Principal Business: Other (100%)
Mem Phys: 18: N/A **17:** N/A **18 MLR** 0.8% **/ 18 Admin Exp** N/A
Enroll(000): Q1 19: N/A **18:** 7 **17:** 33 **Med Exp PMPM:** $14
Principal Investments: Long-term bonds (71%), cash and equiv (29%)
Provider Compensation ($000): Other ($61)
Total Member Encounters: Non-phys (7,221)
Group Affiliation: Magna Holding Company LLC
Licensed in: AL, AR, FL, IL, IN, KY, LA, MS, MO, SC, TN, TX
Address: 190 CAPITOL St Ste 800, JACKSON, MS 39201-2155
Phone: (985) 206-5113 **Dom State:** MS **Commenced Bus:** N/A

Data Date	Rating	RACR #1	RACR #2	Total Assets ($mil)	Capital ($mil)	Net Premium ($mil)	Net Income ($mil)
3-19	D-	0.46	0.38	5.1	2.5	2.3	-0.8
3-18	C-	N/A	N/A	4.2	2.3	2.6	N/A
2018	U	0.60	0.50	5.7	2.9	12.6	-0.7
2017	C-	N/A	N/A	4.1	2.3	4.4	-0.7
2016	C-	14.53	12.10	2.7	2.4	0.4	0.0
2015	N/A	N/A	N/A	3.0	2.5	2.8	N/A
2014	N/A	N/A	N/A	2.6	2.4	0.9	N/A

Rating Indexes

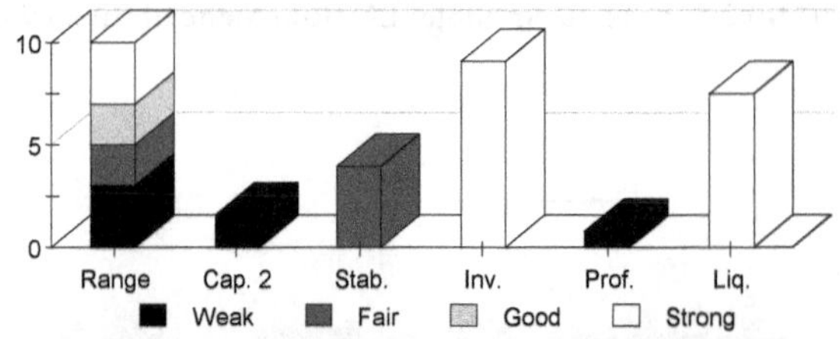

MAGNOLIA HEALTH PLAN INC D+ Weak

Major Rating Factors: Weak profitability index (0.9 on a scale of 0 to 10). Weak liquidity (1.5) as a spike in claims may stretch capacity. Good capitalization (6.8) based on excellent current risk-adjusted capital (severe loss scenario).
Other Rating Factors: High quality investment portfolio (8.4).
Principal Business: Medicaid (100%)
Mem Phys: 18: 14,527 **17:** 12,345 **18 MLR** 90.0% **/ 18 Admin Exp** N/A
Enroll(000): Q1 19: 230 **18:** 238 **17:** 264 **Med Exp PMPM:** $381
Principal Investments: Long-term bonds (71%), cash and equiv (29%)
Provider Compensation ($000): Contr fee ($1,098,327), capitation ($26,123), salary ($16,174)
Total Member Encounters: Phys (1,226,626), non-phys (1,669,930)
Group Affiliation: None
Licensed in: MS
Address: 111 East Capitol St Ste 500, Jackson, MS 39201
Phone: (314) 725-4477 **Dom State:** MS **Commenced Bus:** N/A

Data Date	Rating	RACR #1	RACR #2	Total Assets ($mil)	Capital ($mil)	Net Premium ($mil)	Net Income ($mil)
3-19	D+	1.23	1.02	222.1	90.9	303.0	-23.6
3-18	D+	1.52	1.27	228.2	105.8	317.8	-18.3
2018	D+	1.24	1.03	220.3	91.6	1,280.6	-50.1
2017	D	1.25	1.05	261.2	124.2	1,251.3	-39.2
2016	D	1.21	1.01	197.6	85.1	1,248.5	-43.3
2015	D	1.26	1.05	167.0	56.2	879.6	-28.8
2014	N/A	N/A	N/A	149.0	61.1	547.3	-14.9

Rating Indexes

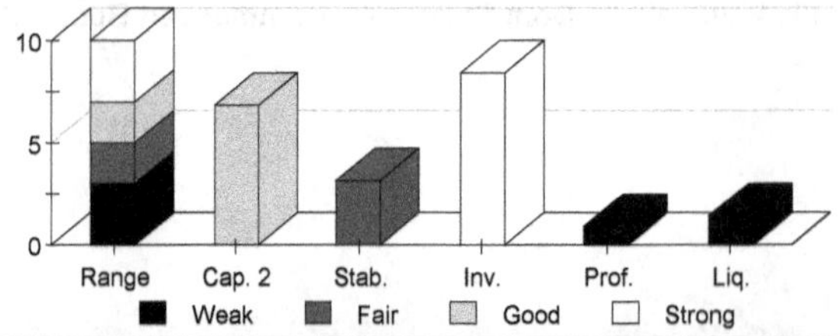

MAINE COMMUNITY HEALTH OPTIONS D+ Weak

Major Rating Factors: Weak profitability index (1.8 on a scale of 0 to 10). Fair capitalization (2.9) based on fair current risk-adjusted capital (moderate loss scenario). Fair quality investment portfolio (4.2).
Other Rating Factors: Excellent liquidity (7.3) with ample operational cash flow and liquid investments.
Principal Business: Comp med (100%)
Mem Phys: 18: 33,126 **17:** 24,173 **18 MLR** 75.0% **/ 18 Admin Exp** N/A
Enroll(000): Q1 19: 40 **18:** 50 **17:** 38 **Med Exp PMPM:** $450
Principal Investments: Cash and equiv (60%), long-term bonds (40%)
Provider Compensation ($000): FFS ($268,333), bonus arrang ($295)
Total Member Encounters: Phys (233,704), non-phys (94,774)
Group Affiliation: None
Licensed in: ME, NH
Address: 150 MILL St THIRD Fl, LEWISTON, ME 4240
Phone: (207) 402-3330 **Dom State:** ME **Commenced Bus:** N/A

Data Date	Rating	RACR #1	RACR #2	Total Assets ($mil)	Capital ($mil)	Net Premium ($mil)	Net Income ($mil)
3-19	D+	0.89	0.74	185.7	62.2	68.3	3.8
3-18	D	N/A	N/A	118.0	46.0	104.2	12.3
2018	D+	0.82	0.68	170.7	57.3	380.3	25.3
2017	D	N/A	N/A	72.9	33.7	266.2	-6.3
2016	D	0.43	0.36	102.0	38.6	377.8	-14.0
2015	N/A	N/A	N/A	167.6	49.8	287.0	-74.0
2014	D+	0.58	0.49	77.4	27.4	167.4	5.9

Rating Indexes

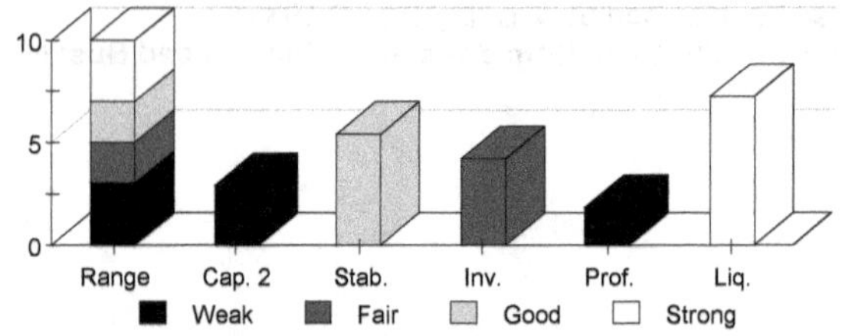

MAMSI L&H INS CO — C+ — Fair

Major Rating Factors: Low quality investment portfolio (0.5 on a scale of 0 to 10). Excellent profitability (8.4). Strong capitalization (9.1) based on excellent current risk-adjusted capital (severe loss scenario).
Other Rating Factors: Excellent liquidity (7.3) with ample operational cash flow and liquid investments.
Principal Business: Comp med (89%), Medicare (11%)
Mem Phys: **18:** 67,359 **17:** 63,577 **18 MLR** 74.1% **/ 18 Admin Exp** N/A
Enroll(000): **Q1 19:** 24 **18:** 23 **17:** 23 **Med Exp PMPM:** $346
Principal Investments: Cash and equiv (97%), long-term bonds (3%)
Provider Compensation ($000): Contr fee ($84,288), FFS ($11,908), capitation ($173), bonus arrang ($14)
Total Member Encounters: Phys (194,096), non-phys (22,887)
Group Affiliation: None
Licensed in: DC, DE, LA, MD, MO, ND, TX, VA, WV
Address: 800 KING FARM BLVD, ROCKVILLE, MD 20850
Phone: (301) 762-8205 **Dom State:** MD **Commenced Bus:** N/A

Data Date	Rating	RACR #1	RACR #2	Total Assets ($mil)	Capital ($mil)	Net Premium ($mil)	Net Income ($mil)
3-19	C+	3.03	2.53	47.9	20.8	35.4	-2.4
3-18	C+	N/A	N/A	37.4	15.1	30.8	0.9
2018	C+	3.32	2.77	40.3	23.0	131.4	8.9
2017	C+	N/A	N/A	30.9	14.1	83.0	5.4
2016	C+	2.90	2.42	21.9	8.8	61.6	4.2
2015	C+	5.42	4.52	21.1	11.7	52.6	4.9
2014	B	4.31	3.60	25.7	17.2	66.4	2.3

Rating Indexes

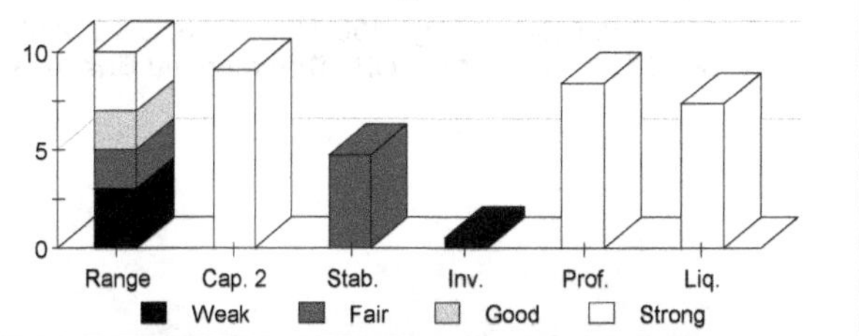

MANHATTAN LIFE INSURANCE COMPANY — B — Good

Major Rating Factors: Good overall results on stability tests (5.4 on a scale of 0 to 10) despite fair financial strength of affiliated Manhattan Life Group Inc. Other stability subfactors include good operational trends, good risk adjusted capital for prior years and good risk diversification. Good quality investment portfolio (6.1) despite mixed results such as: minimal exposure to mortgages and large holdings of BBB rated bonds but small junk bond holdings. Good overall profitability (5.7).
Other Rating Factors: Good liquidity (5.5). Strong capitalization (7.0) based on excellent risk adjusted capital (severe loss scenario).
Principal Business: Individual health insurance (70%), individual annuities (21%), individual life insurance (4%), reinsurance (3%), and group health insurance (2%).
Principal Investments: NonCMO investment grade bonds (64%), CMOs and structured securities (12%), mortgages in good standing (9%), common & preferred stock (5%), and misc. investments (5%).
Investments in Affiliates: 5%
Group Affiliation: Manhattan Life Group Inc
Licensed in: All states, the District of Columbia and Puerto Rico
Commenced Business: August 1850
Address: 225 Community Drive Suite 11, Great Neck, NY 11021
Phone: (713) 529-0045 **Domicile State:** NY **NAIC Code:** 65870

Data Date	Rating	RACR #1	RACR #2	Total Assets ($mil)	Capital ($mil)	Net Premium ($mil)	Net Income ($mil)
3-19	B	1.45	1.02	631.6	61.9	17.0	3.5
3-18	B	1.32	0.95	588.5	54.9	18.7	2.7
2018	B	1.39	0.98	633.3	59.0	79.8	12.3
2017	B	1.30	0.94	581.1	54.1	90.1	8.6
2016	B	1.26	0.94	543.1	51.1	125.6	13.9
2015	B	1.18	0.91	484.6	47.1	152.1	11.2
2014	B	1.17	0.96	362.4	41.0	71.1	2.8

Manhattan Life Group Inc
Composite Group Rating: C+

Largest Group Members	Assets ($mil)	Rating
WESTERN UNITED LIFE ASR CO	1223	B-
MANHATTANLIFE ASSR CO OF AM	700	C
MANHATTAN LIFE INS CO	633	B
FAMILY LIFE INS CO	147	C

MAPFRE LIFE INSURANCE COMPANY — C — Fair

Major Rating Factors: Fair overall results on stability tests (3.6 on a scale of 0 to 10) including negative cash flow from operations for 2018. Weak profitability (2.0). Strong capitalization (10.0) based on excellent risk adjusted capital (severe loss scenario). Capital levels have been relatively consistent over the last five years.
Other Rating Factors: High quality investment portfolio (8.6). Excellent liquidity (10.0).
Principal Business: Individual life insurance (65%), group health insurance (20%), and individual health insurance (15%).
Principal Investments: NonCMO investment grade bonds (100%).
Investments in Affiliates: None
Group Affiliation: MAPFRE Ins Group
Licensed in: All states except NY, PR
Commenced Business: October 1975
Address: 116 WEST WATER STREET, JEFFERSON CITY, MO 65101
Phone: (847) 273-1261 **Domicile State:** MO **NAIC Code:** 85561

Data Date	Rating	RACR #1	RACR #2	Total Assets ($mil)	Capital ($mil)	Net Premium ($mil)	Net Income ($mil)
3-19	C	6.06	5.45	36.3	34.6	0.0	0.3
3-18	C	5.31	4.78	27.3	20.1	0.0	-0.4
2018	C	5.99	5.39	40.5	34.3	0.1	-6.0
2017	C	5.39	4.85	22.6	20.4	-0.1	-1.7
2016	C	4.94	4.44	21.6	18.1	1.0	-1.0
2015	C-	5.30	4.77	23.5	20.6	0.0	-1.0
2014	C+	5.48	4.93	26.0	22.8	0.0	-1.3

Rating Indexes

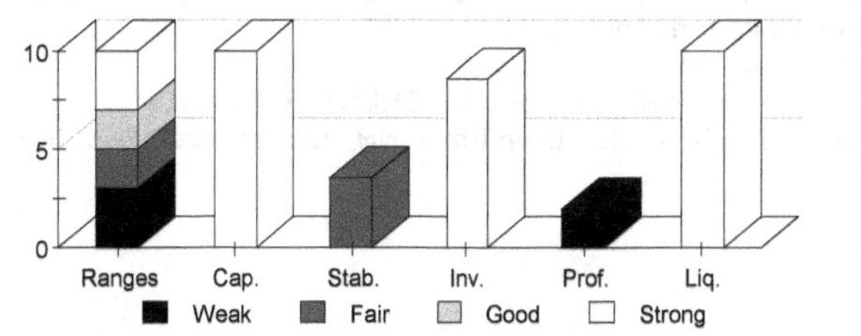

MARQUIS ADVANTAGE, INC. D+ Weak

Major Rating Factors: Weak profitability index (1.8 on a scale of 0 to 10). Fair capitalization (2.9) based on fair current risk-adjusted capital (moderate loss scenario). High quality investment portfolio (9.9).
Other Rating Factors: Excellent liquidity (7.4) with ample operational cash flow and liquid investments.
Principal Business: Medicare (100%)
Mem Phys: 18: 4,605 **17:** 1,393 **18 MLR** 82.8% **/ 18 Admin Exp** N/A
Enroll(000): Q1 19: 0 **18:** 0 **17:** 0 **Med Exp PMPM:** $1,541
Principal Investments: Cash and equiv (100%)
Provider Compensation ($000): Contr fee ($6,630), capitation ($970), bonus arrang ($139)
Total Member Encounters: Phys (2,516), non-phys (9,884)
Group Affiliation: Marquis Companies I Inc
Licensed in: OR
Address: 4560 SE International Way #100, Milwaukee, OR 97222
Phone: (804) 396-6412 **Dom State:** OR **Commenced Bus:** N/A

Data Date	Rating	RACR #1	RACR #2	Total Assets ($mil)	Capital ($mil)	Net Premium ($mil)	Net Income ($mil)
3-19	D+	0.87	0.72	5.3	2.9	2.5	-0.2
3-18	N/A	N/A	N/A	6.2	3.0	2.4	N/A
2018	U	0.93	0.78	5.2	3.1	9.5	0.0
2017	N/A	N/A	N/A	4.9	3.1	6.7	0.1
2016	N/A	N/A	N/A	3.0	3.0	N/A	-0.7
2015	N/A	N/A	N/A	N/A	N/A	N/A	N/A
2014	N/A	N/A	N/A	N/A	N/A	N/A	N/A

Rating Indexes

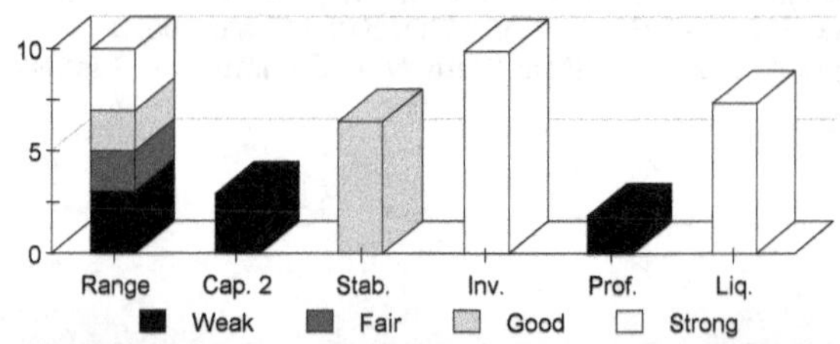

MARTINS POINT GENERATIONS ADVANTAGE B Good

Major Rating Factors: Fair profitability index (4.6 on a scale of 0 to 10). Strong capitalization (8.0) based on excellent current risk-adjusted capital (severe loss scenario). High quality investment portfolio (9.6).
Other Rating Factors: Excellent liquidity (7.0) with ample operational cash flow and liquid investments.
Principal Business: Medicare (100%)
Mem Phys: 18: 17,514 **17:** 16,124 **18 MLR** 86.3% **/ 18 Admin Exp** N/A
Enroll(000): Q1 19: 48 **18:** 45 **17:** 42 **Med Exp PMPM:** $649
Principal Investments: Long-term bonds (42%), cash and equiv (41%), nonaffiliate common stock (18%)
Provider Compensation ($000): Bonus arrang ($251,914), contr fee ($94,189), capitation ($1,426)
Total Member Encounters: Phys (703,322), non-phys (322,788)
Group Affiliation: Martins Point Health Care Inc
Licensed in: ME, NH
Address: 331 Veranda St, PORTLAND, ME 4103
Phone: (207) 774-5801 **Dom State:** ME **Commenced Bus:** N/A

Data Date	Rating	RACR #1	RACR #2	Total Assets ($mil)	Capital ($mil)	Net Premium ($mil)	Net Income ($mil)
3-19	B	2.18	1.82	131.1	77.7	116.5	8.1
3-18	C	1.80	1.50	144.0	63.3	108.4	6.3
2018	B	1.84	1.53	120.7	66.7	401.3	15.7
2017	C	1.60	1.34	99.9	56.9	391.0	11.5
2016	D+	1.28	1.07	88.4	43.3	329.3	-13.2
2015	N/A	N/A	N/A	73.6	36.9	275.1	N/A
2014	N/A	N/A	N/A	62.8	34.5	231.6	N/A

Rating Indexes

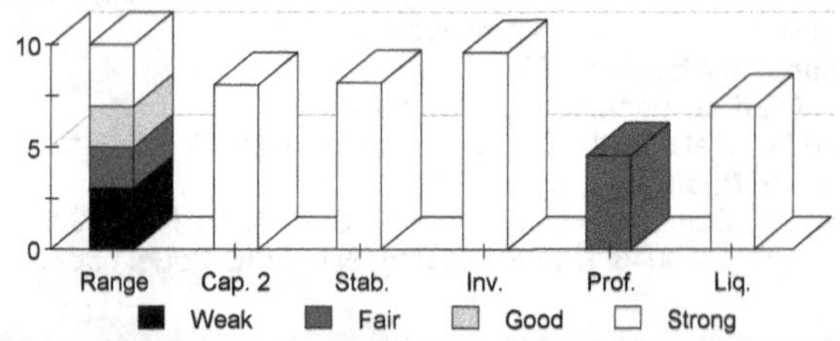

MATTHEW THORNTON HEALTH PLAN B Good

Major Rating Factors: Good overall results on stability tests (6.2 on a scale of 0 to 10). Rating is significantly influenced by the good financial results of Anthem Inc. Fair quality investment portfolio (3.6). Excellent profitability (9.3).
Other Rating Factors: Strong capitalization index (10.0) based on excellent current risk-adjusted capital (severe loss scenario). Excellent liquidity (7.2) with ample operational cash flow and liquid investments.
Principal Business: Comp med (96%), Medicare (4%)
Mem Phys: 18: 22,513 **17:** 19,919 **18 MLR** 69.8% **/ 18 Admin Exp** N/A
Enroll(000): Q1 19: 93 **18:** 107 **17:** 96 **Med Exp PMPM:** $375
Principal Investments: Long-term bonds (62%), cash and equiv (37%), other (1%)
Provider Compensation ($000): Contr fee ($221,749), bonus arrang ($181,501), FFS ($94,482), capitation ($2,128)
Total Member Encounters: Phys (704,579), non-phys (350,429)
Group Affiliation: Anthem Inc
Licensed in: NH
Address: 1155 ELM STREET, MANCHESTER, NH 3101
Phone: (603) 541-2000 **Dom State:** NH **Commenced Bus:** N/A

Data Date	Rating	RACR #1	RACR #2	Total Assets ($mil)	Capital ($mil)	Net Premium ($mil)	Net Income ($mil)
3-19	B	4.43	3.69	310.5	157.9	146.7	22.9
3-18	B	3.95	3.29	260.5	119.4	193.6	23.4
2018	B	3.84	3.20	288.2	135.5	712.8	80.4
2017	B	2.22	1.85	199.4	95.7	531.3	24.3
2016	B	3.32	2.77	202.4	94.1	508.0	13.3
2015	A-	4.17	3.47	218.8	111.3	514.6	33.9
2014	A-	3.44	2.87	230.3	106.9	585.8	36.7

Rating Indexes

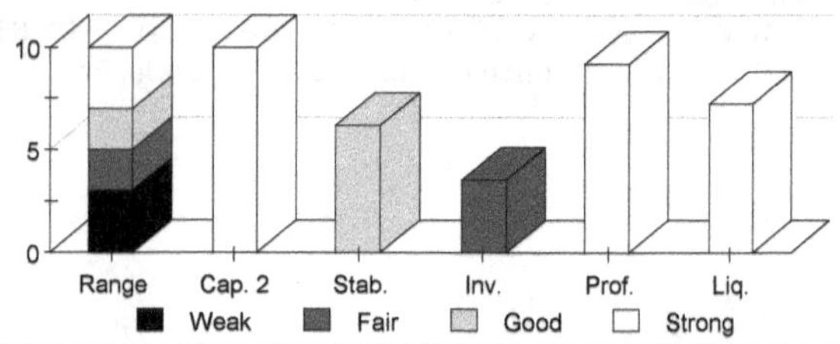

MCLAREN HEALTH PLAN COMMUNITY B- Good

Major Rating Factors: Fair profitability index (3.5 on a scale of 0 to 10). Fair quality investment portfolio (3.4). Strong capitalization (7.1) based on excellent current risk-adjusted capital (severe loss scenario).
Other Rating Factors: Excellent liquidity (7.1) with ample operational cash flow and liquid investments.
Principal Business: Comp med (100%)
Mem Phys: 18: 31,182 **17:** 29,199 **18 MLR** 88.5% **/ 18 Admin Exp** N/A
Enroll(000): Q1 19: 25 **18:** 29 **17:** 28 **Med Exp PMPM:** $358
Principal Investments: Cash and equiv (97%), long-term bonds (3%)
Provider Compensation ($000): Contr fee ($116,087), FFS ($5,750), capitation ($978)
Total Member Encounters: Phys (206,962), non-phys (35,405)
Group Affiliation: None
Licensed in: MI
Address: G3245 Beecher Rd, Flint, MI 48532
Phone: (888) 327-0671 **Dom State:** MI **Commenced Bus:** N/A

Data Date	Rating	RACR #1	RACR #2	Total Assets ($mil)	Capital ($mil)	Net Premium ($mil)	Net Income ($mil)
3-19	B-	1.43	1.19	39.1	18.0	31.1	-0.9
3-18	B-	N/A	N/A	43.0	15.9	36.3	1.4
2018	B-	1.49	1.25	40.2	18.9	143.8	4.6
2017	B-	N/A	N/A	35.7	14.6	119.4	-2.2
2016	C+	1.75	1.46	32.3	13.9	61.0	-1.0
2015	N/A	N/A	N/A	3.1	3.0	N/A	N/A
2014	N/A	N/A	N/A	3.0	3.0	N/A	N/A

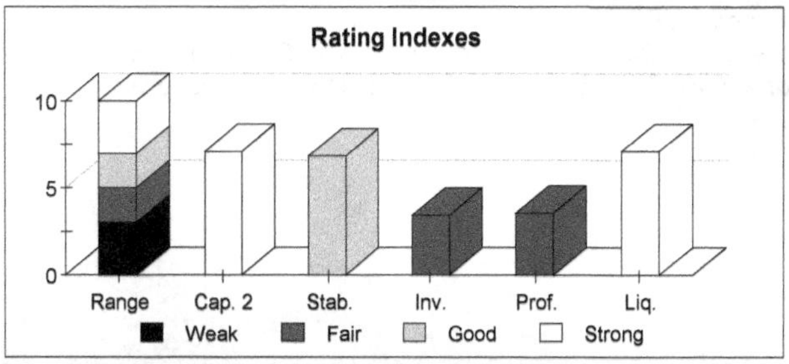

MCLAREN HEALTH PLAN INC B- Good

Major Rating Factors: Good overall results on stability tests (6.0 on a scale of 0 to 10). Excellent profitability (8.9). Strong capitalization index (7.8) based on excellent current risk-adjusted capital (severe loss scenario).
Other Rating Factors: Excellent liquidity (7.1) with ample operational cash flow and liquid investments. Low quality investment portfolio (2.7).
Principal Business: Medicaid (100%)
Mem Phys: 18: 31,182 **17:** 29,199 **18 MLR** 91.7% **/ 18 Admin Exp** N/A
Enroll(000): Q1 19: 202 **18:** 202 **17:** 195 **Med Exp PMPM:** $279
Principal Investments: Cash and equiv (76%), nonaffiliate common stock (12%), affiliate common stock (11%), real estate (1%)
Provider Compensation ($000): Contr fee ($338,629), capitation ($305,980), FFS ($24,915)
Total Member Encounters: Phys (1,521,034), non-phys (318,734)
Group Affiliation: None
Licensed in: MI
Address: G-3245 Beecher Rd, FLINT, MI 48532
Phone: (810) 733-9723 **Dom State:** MI **Commenced Bus:** N/A

Data Date	Rating	RACR #1	RACR #2	Total Assets ($mil)	Capital ($mil)	Net Premium ($mil)	Net Income ($mil)
3-19	B-	2.02	1.69	241.5	122.7	190.0	8.0
3-18	B+	1.34	1.12	255.9	103.3	264.9	2.3
2018	B	1.90	1.58	227.9	115.9	729.6	15.6
2017	B+	1.30	1.08	200.8	100.6	840.4	22.2
2016	B	1.20	1.00	207.5	83.0	929.6	20.5
2015	B	1.01	0.84	231.5	70.8	902.6	23.4
2014	B-	0.87	0.72	170.2	51.9	722.6	12.2

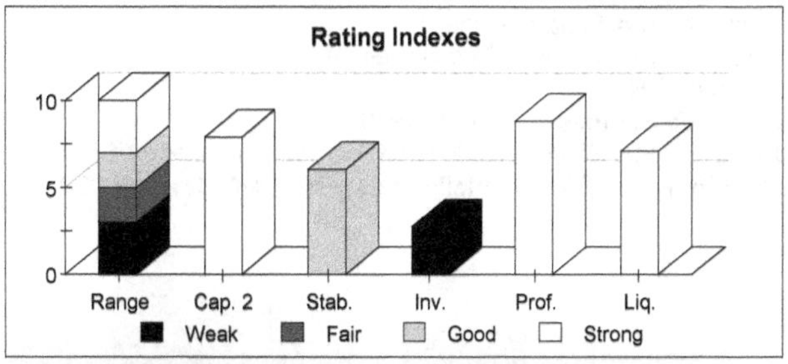

MCNA INS CO C- Fair

Major Rating Factors: Weak liquidity (2.5 on a scale of 0 to 10) as a spike in claims may stretch capacity. Excellent profitability (7.7). Strong capitalization (7.6) based on excellent current risk-adjusted capital (severe loss scenario).
Other Rating Factors: High quality investment portfolio (8.1).
Principal Business: Medicaid (100%)
Mem Phys: 18: 9,641 **17:** 8,611 **18 MLR** 108.4% **/ 18 Admin Exp** N/A
Enroll(000): Q1 19: 3,889 **18:** 3,830 **17:** 3,559 **Med Exp PMPM:** $17
Principal Investments: Long-term bonds (76%), cash and equiv (22%), pref stock (2%)
Provider Compensation ($000): FFS ($786,219), bonus arrang ($2,248)
Total Member Encounters: N/A
Group Affiliation: MCNA Health Care Holdings LLC
Licensed in: (No states)
Address: 100 Congress Ave Ste 1100, Austin, TX 78701
Phone: (800) 494-6262 **Dom State:** TX **Commenced Bus:** N/A

Data Date	Rating	RACR #1	RACR #2	Total Assets ($mil)	Capital ($mil)	Net Premium ($mil)	Net Income ($mil)
3-19	C-	1.85	1.54	194.7	125.5	175.7	3.6
3-18	N/A	N/A	N/A	198.3	131.1	195.3	11.4
2018	U	1.79	1.49	184.1	121.7	726.5	17.4
2017	N/A	N/A	N/A	175.8	125.1	594.9	17.0
2016	N/A	N/A	N/A	171.9	121.4	551.4	N/A
2015	N/A	N/A	N/A	160.0	111.8	556.6	N/A
2014	N/A	N/A	N/A	188.8	77.1	429.7	N/A

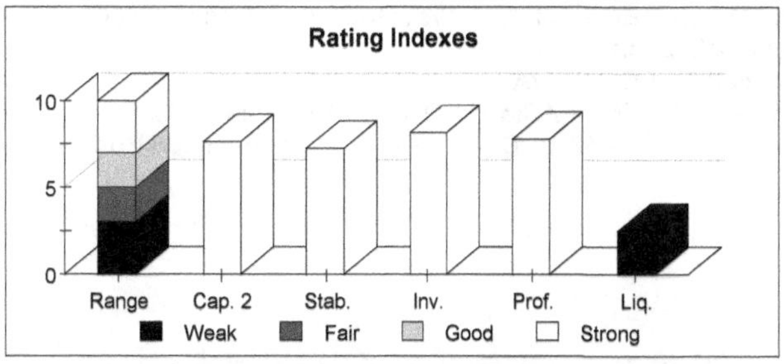

MCS ADVANTAGE INC — D — Weak

Major Rating Factors: Good overall profitability index (6.3 on a scale of 0 to 10). Strong capitalization (7.1) based on excellent current risk-adjusted capital (severe loss scenario). High quality investment portfolio (9.8).
Other Rating Factors: Excellent liquidity (6.9) with sufficient resources (cash flows and marketable investments) to handle a spike in claims.
Principal Business: Medicare (100%)
Mem Phys: 18: 11,334 **17:** 11,522 **18 MLR** 84.1% **/ 18 Admin Exp** N/A
Enroll(000): Q1 19: 177 **18:** 207 **17:** 192 **Med Exp PMPM:** $650
Principal Investments: Long-term bonds (68%), cash and equiv (32%)
Provider Compensation ($000): Contr fee ($1,204,391), capitation ($362,777)
Total Member Encounters: Phys (2,875,255), non-phys (22,646)
Group Affiliation: Medical Card System Inc
Licensed in: PR
Address: Ste 203 255 Ponce de LeÃ³n Ave, San Juan, PR 917
Phone: (787) 758-2500 **Dom State:** PR **Commenced Bus:** N/A

Data Date	Rating	RACR #1	RACR #2	Total Assets ($mil)	Capital ($mil)	Net Premium ($mil)	Net Income ($mil)
3-19	D	1.46	1.22	378.2	188.0	441.2	-7.8
3-18	E+	N/A	N/A	592.0	132.0	486.0	-21.3
2018	D-	1.52	1.27	381.4	196.0	1,907.8	42.6
2017	E+	N/A	N/A	379.7	156.1	1,690.9	51.3
2016	E	0.64	0.53	257.4	82.5	1,763.2	19.5
2015	E	0.47	0.40	287.3	55.7	1,535.4	6.3
2014	E+	0.45	0.38	217.7	51.6	1,462.8	-21.1

Rating Indexes

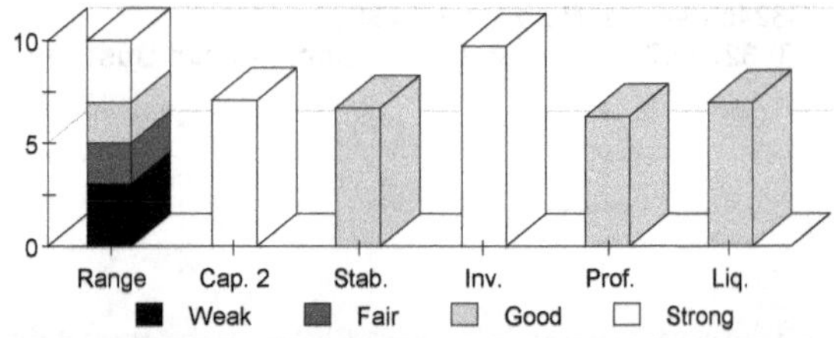

MCS LIFE INSURANCE COMPANY — D- — Weak

Major Rating Factors: Weak overall results on stability tests (1.0 on a scale of 0 to 10) including potential financial drain due to affiliation with Medical Card System Inc and weak risk adjusted capital in prior years. Fair current capitalization (4.8) based on mixed results -- excessive policy leverage mitigated by good risk adjusted capital (severe loss scenario) reflecting significant improvement over results in 2016. Fair liquidity (4.6).
Other Rating Factors: Good overall profitability (5.3). High quality investment portfolio (9.4).
Principal Business: Group health insurance (92%), individual health insurance (7%), and group life insurance (1%).
Principal Investments: Cash (57%) and nonCMO investment grade bonds (43%).
Investments in Affiliates: None
Group Affiliation: Medical Card System Inc
Licensed in: PR
Commenced Business: January 1996
Address: Ste 900 255 Ponce de Leon Ave, San Juan, PR 917
Phone: (787) 758-2500 **Domicile State:** PR **NAIC Code:** 60030

Data Date	Rating	RACR #1	RACR #2	Total Assets ($mil)	Capital ($mil)	Net Premium ($mil)	Net Income ($mil)
9-18	D-	0.96	0.79	92.7	45.0	217.1	1.5
9-17	D-	0.56	0.49	83.9	30.3	233.3	9.1
2017	D-	0.89	0.73	0.0	0.0	0.0	0.0
2016	E	0.38	0.34	0.0	0.0	0.0	0.0
2015	E	0.18	0.16	0.0	0.0	0.0	0.0
2014	E+	0.42	0.37	0.0	0.0	0.0	0.0
2013	D-	0.44	0.36	0.0	0.0	0.0	0.0

Medical Card System Inc
Composite Group Rating: E+

Largest Group Members	Assets ($mil)	Rating
MCS ADVANTAGE INC	252	E+
MCS LIFE INS CO	98	D-

MD INDIVIDUAL PRACTICE ASSOC INC — C — Fair

Major Rating Factors: Low quality investment portfolio (0.2 on a scale of 0 to 10). Good overall results on stability tests (5.0). Rating is significantly influenced by the good financial results of . Excellent profitability (8.6).
Other Rating Factors: Strong capitalization index (10.0) based on excellent current risk-adjusted capital (severe loss scenario). Excellent liquidity (7.3) with ample operational cash flow and liquid investments.
Principal Business: FEHB (100%)
Mem Phys: 18: 55,087 **17:** 52,438 **18 MLR** 81.0% **/ 18 Admin Exp** N/A
Enroll(000): Q1 19: 32 **18:** 36 **17:** 41 **Med Exp PMPM:** $522
Principal Investments: Cash and equiv (98%), long-term bonds (2%)
Provider Compensation ($000): Contr fee ($186,416), FFS ($32,795), capitation ($4,522), bonus arrang ($19)
Total Member Encounters: Phys (415,628), non-phys (32,861)
Group Affiliation: None
Licensed in: DC, MD, VA
Address: 800 KING FARM BLVD, ROCKVILLE, MD 20850
Phone: (240) 683-5250 **Dom State:** MD **Commenced Bus:** N/A

Data Date	Rating	RACR #1	RACR #2	Total Assets ($mil)	Capital ($mil)	Net Premium ($mil)	Net Income ($mil)
3-19	C	11.09	9.24	86.0	59.1	64.4	7.4
3-18	C	13.01	10.84	86.4	49.9	72.5	2.9
2018	C	9.81	8.17	81.7	51.9	281.8	24.8
2017	C	9.10	7.58	84.5	56.4	288.7	30.7
2016	B-	8.30	6.92	72.3	33.1	307.8	17.1
2015	C	5.68	4.74	76.3	32.2	350.0	16.5
2014	B-	10.88	9.07	107.9	66.3	401.5	35.6

Rating Indexes

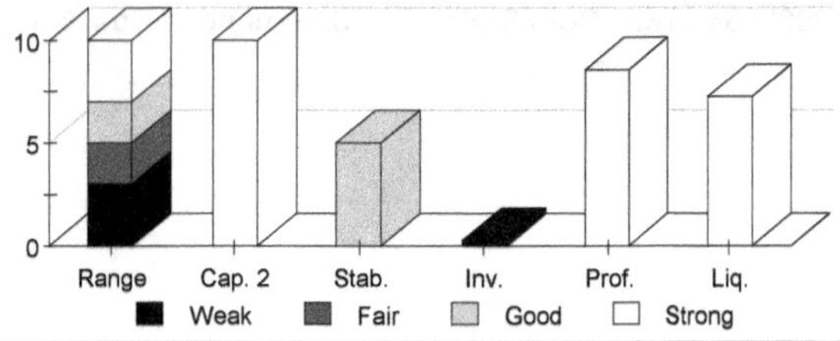

MDWISE INC * B+ Good

Major Rating Factors: Good overall results on stability tests (6.0 on a scale of 0 to 10). Excellent profitability (8.1). Strong capitalization index (7.6) based on excellent current risk-adjusted capital (severe loss scenario).
Other Rating Factors: High quality investment portfolio (9.9). Excellent liquidity (7.2) with ample operational cash flow and liquid investments.
Principal Business: Medicaid (100%)
Mem Phys: 18: 30,035 **17:** 28,242 **18 MLR** 95.1% **/ 18 Admin Exp** N/A
Enroll(000): Q1 19: 296 **18:** 302 **17:** 347 **Med Exp PMPM:** $313
Principal Investments: Cash and equiv (69%), long-term bonds (31%)
Provider Compensation ($000): Capitation ($1,202,531)
Total Member Encounters: N/A
Group Affiliation: None
Licensed in: IN
Address: 1200 Madison Avenue Suite 400, Indianapolis, IN 46225
Phone: (317) 822-7300 **Dom State:** IN **Commenced Bus:** N/A

Data Date	Rating	RACR #1	RACR #2	Total Assets ($mil)	Capital ($mil)	Net Premium ($mil)	Net Income ($mil)
3-19	B+	1.82	1.52	542.8	115.8	302.2	10.8
3-18	B	N/A	N/A	468.5	103.5	314.2	2.2
2018	B+	1.57	1.31	356.1	100.4	1,264.0	23.9
2017	B	N/A	N/A	379.3	103.0	1,513.4	11.5
2016	B	1.32	1.10	199.6	93.8	1,433.7	28.8
2015	B	1.47	1.23	144.2	69.4	1,033.2	20.3
2014	B-	1.28	1.07	76.6	39.0	583.8	3.2

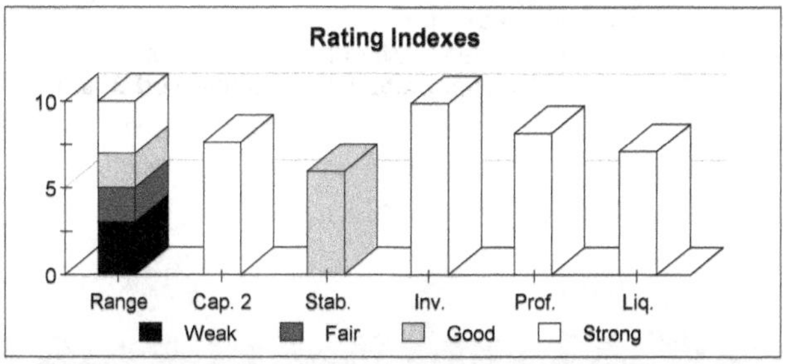

MEDAMERICA INSURANCE COMPANY C Fair

Major Rating Factors: Poor current capitalization (2.4 on a scale of 0 to 10) based on weak risk adjusted capital (moderate loss scenario), although results have slipped from the fair range during the last year. Low quality investment portfolio (0.8) containing large holdings of BBB rated bonds in addition to significant exposure to junk bonds. Weak profitability (1.0) with operating losses during the first three months of 2019.
Other Rating Factors: Weak overall results on stability tests (2.4) including weak risk adjusted capital in prior years. Excellent liquidity (8.3).
Principal Business: Individual health insurance (67%), reinsurance (24%), and group health insurance (9%).
Principal Investments: NonCMO investment grade bonds (80%), noninv. grade bonds (5%), common & preferred stock (3%), and CMOs and structured securities (3%).
Investments in Affiliates: 1%
Group Affiliation: Lifetime Healthcare Inc
Licensed in: All states except FL, NY, PR
Commenced Business: August 1966
Address: 651 Holiday Drive Foster Plaza, Pittsburgh, PA 15220-2740
Phone: (585) 238-4464 **Domicile State:** PA **NAIC Code:** 69515

Data Date	Rating	RACR #1	RACR #2	Total Assets ($mil)	Capital ($mil)	Net Premium ($mil)	Net Income ($mil)
3-19	C	0.68	0.39	1,218.5	29.6	15.8	0.0
3-18	C	0.87	0.47	964.0	27.2	11.4	-2.0
2018	C	0.85	0.47	1,199.8	31.0	57.3	-134.6
2017	C	0.99	0.54	960.2	31.2	62.2	-8.7
2016	B-	1.14	0.62	939.2	31.7	64.6	-1.2
2015	B	1.23	0.67	890.9	34.4	63.2	-45.8
2014	B	1.66	0.91	859.4	43.2	60.9	-1.9

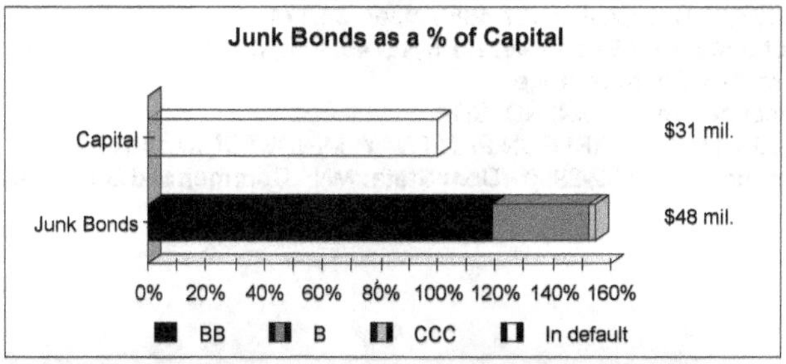

MEDCO CONTAINMENT INS CO OF NY C Fair

Major Rating Factors: Weak profitability index (2.3 on a scale of 0 to 10). Strong capitalization (10.0) based on excellent current risk-adjusted capital (severe loss scenario). High quality investment portfolio (7.0).
Other Rating Factors: Excellent liquidity (7.6) with ample operational cash flow and liquid investments.
Principal Business: Other (100%)
Mem Phys: 18: N/A **17:** N/A **18 MLR** 73.0% **/ 18 Admin Exp** N/A
Enroll(000): Q1 19: 95 **18:** 97 **17:** 96 **Med Exp PMPM:** $86
Principal Investments: Cash and equiv (97%), long-term bonds (3%)
Provider Compensation ($000): FFS ($100,133)
Total Member Encounters: N/A
Group Affiliation: Cigna Corporation
Licensed in: NY
Address: 433 River St Ste 800, Troy, NY 12180
Phone: (800) 322-5455 **Dom State:** NY **Commenced Bus:** N/A

Data Date	Rating	RACR #1	RACR #2	Total Assets ($mil)	Capital ($mil)	Net Premium ($mil)	Net Income ($mil)
3-19	C	5.68	4.73	111.2	46.8	39.8	-4.2
3-18	B-	5.23	4.36	147.0	49.8	46.8	-0.1
2018	C	6.20	5.17	70.0	51.2	138.6	0.8
2017	B-	4.07	3.39	66.1	49.9	129.9	-5.6
2016	B	5.71	4.76	67.4	55.8	123.8	5.2
2015	B-	9.27	7.72	59.4	47.6	102.3	-0.5
2014	B+	11.11	9.26	59.1	50.4	100.0	-3.3

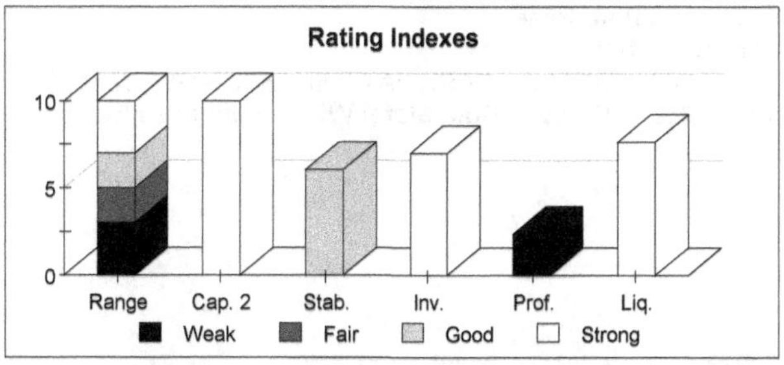

MEDCO CONTAINMENT LIFE INS CO C Fair

Major Rating Factors: Low quality investment portfolio (0.6 on a scale of 0 to 10). Excellent profitability (7.5). Strong capitalization (10.0) based on excellent current risk-adjusted capital (severe loss scenario).
Other Rating Factors: Excellent liquidity (8.9) with ample operational cash flow and liquid investments.
Principal Business: Other (100%)
Mem Phys: 18: N/A **17:** N/A **18 MLR** 80.6% **/ 18 Admin Exp** N/A
Enroll(000): Q1 19: 804 **18:** 815 **17:** 595 **Med Exp PMPM:** $77
Principal Investments: Cash and equiv (99%), long-term bonds (1%)
Provider Compensation ($000): FFS ($575,110)
Total Member Encounters: N/A
Group Affiliation: Cigna Corporation
Licensed in: All states except NY
Address: 4415 Lewis Rd Ste #1, Warrendale, PA 15086
Phone: (800) 332-5455 **Dom State:** PA **Commenced Bus:** N/A

Data Date	Rating	RACR #1	RACR #2	Total Assets ($mil)	Capital ($mil)	Net Premium ($mil)	Net Income ($mil)
3-19	C	5.33	4.44	762.4	367.8	248.8	-23.2
3-18	C	5.78	4.82	1,127.7	394.7	253.5	-23.3
2018	C	5.62	4.69	1,163.6	388.4	896.1	11.6
2017	B-	6.07	5.06	1,292.5	418.4	790.6	22.0
2016	A-	6.54	5.45	1,689.0	462.5	672.2	80.5
2015	B	6.25	5.21	1,391.5	403.5	657.7	28.5
2014	B+	8.29	6.91	1,180.8	309.6	584.0	23.6

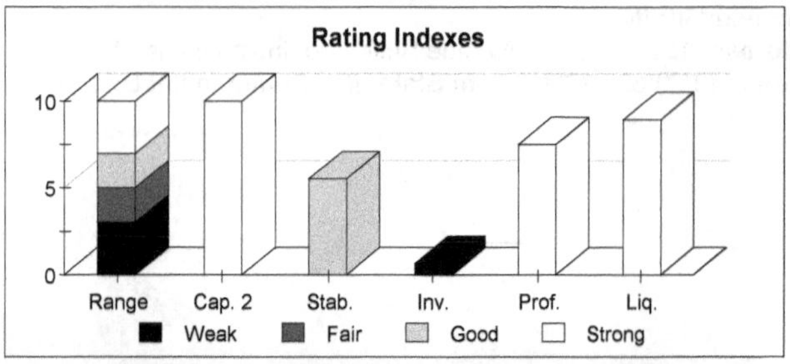

MEDICA HEALTH PLANS C+ Fair

Major Rating Factors: Fair quality investment portfolio (4.2 on a scale of 0 to 10). Fair overall results on stability tests (4.1) based on a steep decline in premium revenue in 2018. Weak profitability index (2.4).
Other Rating Factors: Strong capitalization index (10.0) based on excellent current risk-adjusted capital (severe loss scenario). Excellent liquidity (7.2) with ample operational cash flow and liquid investments.
Principal Business: Medicaid (99%)
Mem Phys: 18: 109,221 **17:** 103,390 **18 MLR** 90.2% **/ 18 Admin Exp** N/A
Enroll(000): Q1 19: 70 **18:** 30 **17:** 32 **Med Exp PMPM:** $1,860
Principal Investments: Long-term bonds (33%), cash and equiv (30%), real estate (17%), nonaffiliate common stock (13%), other (7%)
Provider Compensation ($000): Contr fee ($492,415), bonus arrang ($166,604), capitation ($7,488), other ($5,174)
Total Member Encounters: Phys (745,405), non-phys (1,026,387)
Group Affiliation: None
Licensed in: IA, MN, ND, SD
Address: 401 CARLSON PARKWAY, MINNETONKA, MN 55305
Phone: (952) 992-2900 **Dom State:** MN **Commenced Bus:** N/A

Data Date	Rating	RACR #1	RACR #2	Total Assets ($mil)	Capital ($mil)	Net Premium ($mil)	Net Income ($mil)
3-19	C+	5.95	4.96	547.8	308.9	266.5	9.6
3-18	C	3.71	3.09	488.2	302.7	184.8	15.0
2018	C+	5.67	4.72	539.7	293.1	732.6	39.6
2017	C	2.81	2.35	482.0	287.9	1,269.9	78.5
2016	C	1.80	1.50	803.3	317.4	2,327.5	-189.9
2015	B+	4.37	3.64	896.8	504.0	1,777.0	45.4
2014	B+	4.10	3.41	856.9	460.1	1,719.6	46.9

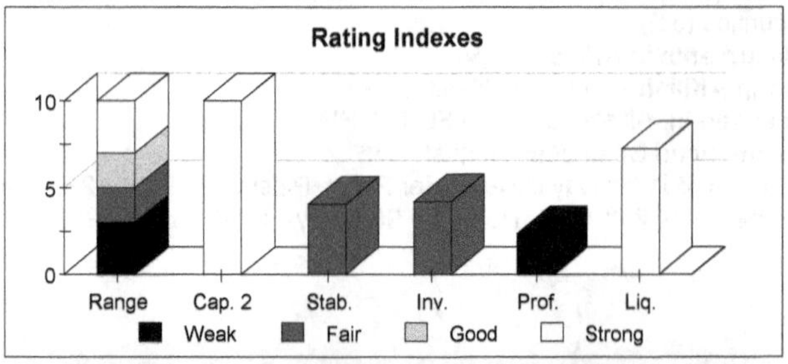

MEDICA HEALTH PLANS OF WI C+ Fair

Major Rating Factors: Fair overall results on stability tests (4.0 on a scale of 0 to 10) based on a significant 80% decrease in enrollment during the period. Good quality investment portfolio (6.7). Weak profitability index (1.6)
Other Rating Factors: Strong capitalization index (10.0) based on excellent current risk-adjusted capital (severe loss scenario). Excellent liquidity (8.9) with ample operational cash flow and liquid investments.
Principal Business: Comp med (100%)
Mem Phys: 18: 109,221 **17:** 103,390 **18 MLR** 68.9% **/ 18 Admin Exp** N/A
Enroll(000): Q1 19: 7 **18:** 7 **17:** 35 **Med Exp PMPM:** $662
Principal Investments: Cash and equiv (68%), long-term bonds (32%)
Provider Compensation ($000): Contr fee ($43,883), bonus arrang ($31,192)
Total Member Encounters: Phys (69,281), non-phys (10,915)
Group Affiliation: None
Licensed in: MN, WI
Address: 401 CARLSON PARKWAY, MINNETONKA, MN 55305
Phone: (952) 992-2900 **Dom State:** WI **Commenced Bus:** N/A

Data Date	Rating	RACR #1	RACR #2	Total Assets ($mil)	Capital ($mil)	Net Premium ($mil)	Net Income ($mil)
3-19	C+	16.92	14.10	140.6	97.3	15.8	6.1
3-18	C	N/A	N/A	101.5	80.3	20.7	7.2
2018	C+	15.66	13.05	144.1	91.3	83.0	18.0
2017	C	N/A	N/A	110.3	72.1	274.7	15.3
2016	C	0.75	0.63	98.2	27.6	221.6	-32.3
2015	B	4.32	3.60	67.8	40.1	66.5	-12.4
2014	B-	11.22	9.35	57.8	47.6	30.6	4.8

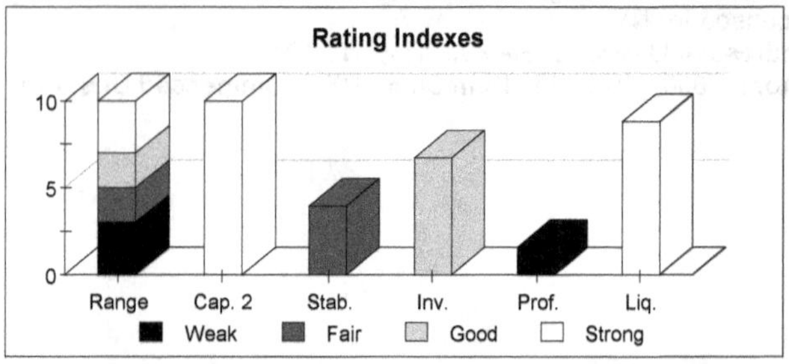

MEDICA HEALTHCARE PLANS INC B Good

Major Rating Factors: Good overall profitability index (5.8 on a scale of 0 to 10). Good liquidity (6.5) with sufficient resources (cash flows and marketable investments) to handle a spike in claims. Strong capitalization (7.3) based on excellent current risk-adjusted capital (severe loss scenario).
Other Rating Factors: High quality investment portfolio (8.9).
Principal Business: Medicare (100%)
Mem Phys: 18: 42,366 **17:** 39,639 **18 MLR** 87.7% **/ 18 Admin Exp** N/A
Enroll(000): Q1 19: 45 **18:** 46 **17:** 42 **Med Exp PMPM:** $1,076
Principal Investments: Long-term bonds (96%), cash and equiv (4%)
Provider Compensation ($000): Contr fee ($374,303), capitation ($113,558), FFS ($76,513), bonus arrang ($21,717)
Total Member Encounters: Phys (906,338), non-phys (229,122)
Group Affiliation: None
Licensed in: FL
Address: 9100 S DADELAND Blvd Ste 1250, MIAMI, FL 33156
Phone: (305) 670-8440 **Dom State:** FL **Commenced Bus:** N/A

Data Date	Rating	RACR #1	RACR #2	Total Assets ($mil)	Capital ($mil)	Net Premium ($mil)	Net Income ($mil)
3-19	B	1.63	1.36	179.8	54.8	178.7	8.5
3-18	C	1.29	1.07	214.9	36.8	162.0	-4.3
2018	B	1.33	1.10	154.2	43.3	661.7	13.3
2017	E	0.78	0.65	146.7	37.2	547.9	5.1
2016	E	2.32	1.93	139.6	61.4	533.9	24.9
2015	E-	1.82	1.52	132.9	54.1	523.1	11.6
2014	E-	0.61	0.51	118.8	20.4	486.6	-7.4

Rating Indexes

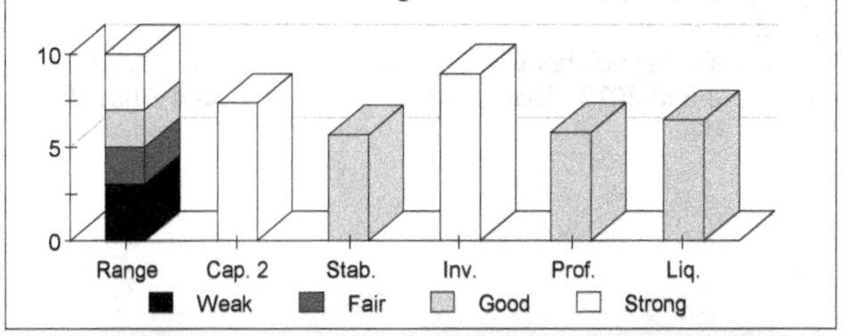

MEDICA INS CO B Good

Major Rating Factors: Good overall profitability index (6.4 on a scale of 0 to 10). Good quality investment portfolio (6.5). Good liquidity (6.3) with sufficient resources (cash flows and marketable investments) to handle a spike in claims.
Other Rating Factors: Strong capitalization (10.0) based on excellent current risk-adjusted capital (severe loss scenario).
Principal Business: Comp med (74%), Medicare (23%), other (3%)
Mem Phys: 18: 103,390 **17:** 103,390 **18 MLR** 83.7% **/ 18 Admin Exp** N/A
Enroll(000): Q1 19: 476 **18:** 532 **17:** 422 **Med Exp PMPM:** $461
Principal Investments: Long-term bonds (78%), nonaffiliate common stock (14%), cash and equiv (7%), pref stock (2%)
Provider Compensation ($000): Contr fee ($1,620,694), bonus arrang ($1,069,201), other ($87,210)
Total Member Encounters: Phys (5,958,258), non-phys (1,873,234)
Group Affiliation: None
Licensed in: IA, KS, MN, MO, NE, ND, OK, SD, WI
Address: 401 CARLSON PARKWAY, MINNETONKA, MN 55305
Phone: (952) 992-2900 **Dom State:** MN **Commenced Bus:** N/A

Data Date	Rating	RACR #1	RACR #2	Total Assets ($mil)	Capital ($mil)	Net Premium ($mil)	Net Income ($mil)
3-19	B	4.73	3.94	1,536.7	863.9	844.5	155.5
3-18	B	4.00	3.33	1,170.7	502.7	903.6	81.4
2018	B	3.83	3.19	1,397.8	695.2	3,536.4	242.4
2017	B	2.82	2.35	807.5	421.0	2,179.8	53.1
2016	B	2.29	1.91	595.0	277.2	1,967.7	-28.7
2015	A-	3.17	2.64	623.1	313.7	1,790.2	-2.3
2014	B	3.48	2.90	545.0	309.7	1,664.5	74.8

Rating Indexes

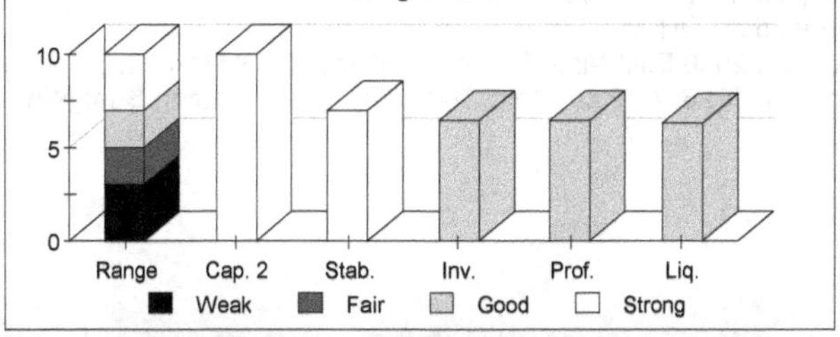

MEDICAL ASSOC CLINIC HEALTH PLAN B- Good

Major Rating Factors: Fair profitability index (3.5 on a scale of 0 to 10). Good overall results on stability tests (6.4). Strong capitalization index (7.0) based on excellent current risk-adjusted capital (severe loss scenario).
Other Rating Factors: High quality investment portfolio (7.8). Excellent liquidity (6.9) with sufficient resources (cash flows and marketable investments) to handle a spike in claims.
Principal Business: Comp med (78%), Medicare (22%)
Mem Phys: 18: 4,769 **17:** 390 **18 MLR** 88.4% **/ 18 Admin Exp** N/A
Enroll(000): Q1 19: 8 **18:** 8 **17:** 7 **Med Exp PMPM:** $248
Principal Investments: Long-term bonds (61%), cash and equiv (31%), nonaffiliate common stock (8%)
Provider Compensation ($000): Capitation ($23,086)
Total Member Encounters: Phys (113,418)
Group Affiliation: Medical Associates Clinic PC
Licensed in: WI
Address: 1605 Associates Drive Suite 10, Dubuque, IA 52002-2270
Phone: (563) 556-8070 **Dom State:** WI **Commenced Bus:** N/A

Data Date	Rating	RACR #1	RACR #2	Total Assets ($mil)	Capital ($mil)	Net Premium ($mil)	Net Income ($mil)
3-19	B-	1.35	1.13	4.2	3.2	6.1	0.0
3-18	C+	N/A	N/A	5.2	3.0	6.7	0.1
2018	B-	1.34	1.12	5.4	3.2	26.1	0.3
2017	C+	N/A	N/A	4.2	2.9	25.3	0.1
2016	C+	1.22	1.01	3.2	2.7	25.5	0.1
2015	C+	1.08	0.90	4.0	2.6	25.7	-0.7
2014	B-	1.71	1.43	4.3	3.4	22.3	0.3

Rating Indexes

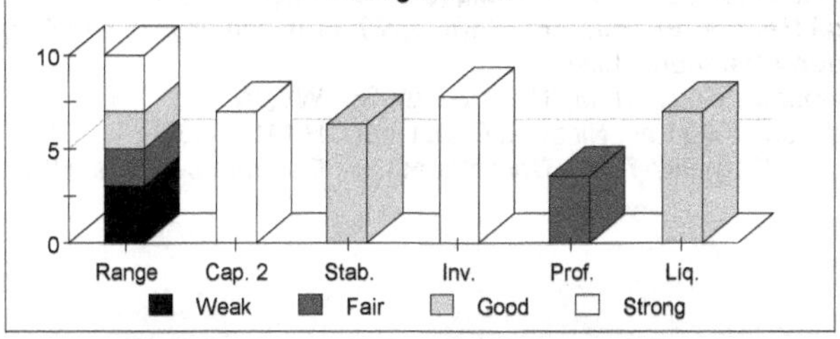

MEDICAL ASSOCIATES HEALTH PLAN INC — B- Good

Major Rating Factors: Fair profitability index (3.8 on a scale of 0 to 10). Good liquidity (6.6) with sufficient resources (cash flows and marketable investments) to handle a spike in claims. Strong capitalization index (8.6) based on excellent current risk-adjusted capital (severe loss scenario).
Other Rating Factors: High quality investment portfolio (7.2). Excellent overall results on stability tests (7.4).
Principal Business: Comp med (76%), Medicare (24%)
Mem Phys: 18: 4,769 **17:** 390 **18 MLR** 87.9% **/ 18 Admin Exp** N/A
Enroll(000): Q1 19: 25 **18:** 24 **17:** 24 **Med Exp PMPM:** $270
Principal Investments: Long-term bonds (81%), nonaffiliate common stock (9%), cash and equiv (9%)
Provider Compensation ($000): Contr fee ($49,951), capitation ($28,380)
Total Member Encounters: Phys (374,322)
Group Affiliation: Medical Associates Clinic PC
Licensed in: IL, IA
Address: 1605 Associates Drive Ste 101, Dubuque, IA 52002-2270
Phone: (563) 556-8070 **Dom State:** IA **Commenced Bus:** N/A

Data Date	Rating	RACR #1	RACR #2	Total Assets ($mil)	Capital ($mil)	Net Premium ($mil)	Net Income ($mil)
3-19	B-	2.60	2.17	40.5	21.7	23.0	0.7
3-18	B-	2.71	2.26	40.8	21.4	22.0	0.8
2018	B-	2.55	2.12	38.4	21.2	89.1	0.2
2017	B-	2.61	2.18	33.9	20.8	84.8	1.4
2016	B-	2.62	2.18	32.4	19.8	82.5	1.4
2015	B-	2.12	1.77	32.2	18.1	80.3	-1.1
2014	B	2.03	1.69	32.8	19.3	86.3	-1.2

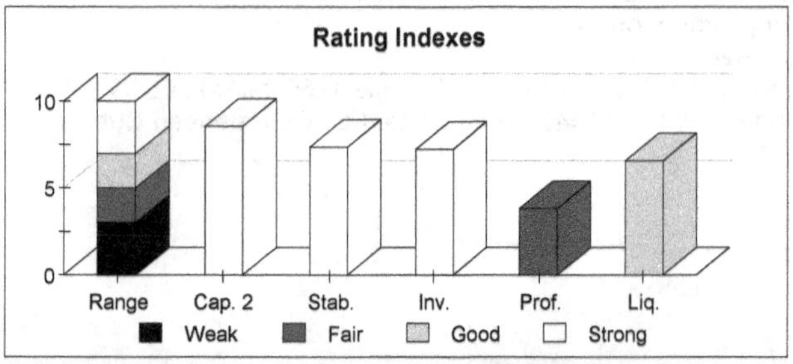

MEDICAL HEALTH INS CORP OF OHIO — B Good

Major Rating Factors: Fair quality investment portfolio (3.3 on a scale of 0 to 10). Fair overall results on stability tests (4.4) based on an excessive 47% enrollment growth during the period. Strong capitalization index (10.0) based on excellent current risk-adjusted capital (severe loss scenario).
Other Rating Factors: Excellent liquidity (7.2) with ample operational cash flow and liquid investments. Weak profitability index (1.7).
Principal Business: Comp med (83%), med supp (17%)
Mem Phys: 18: 53,140 **17:** 53,229 **18 MLR** 75.5% **/ 18 Admin Exp** N/A
Enroll(000): Q1 19: 185 **18:** 128 **17:** 87 **Med Exp PMPM:** $246
Principal Investments: Cash and equiv (64%), long-term bonds (36%)
Provider Compensation ($000): Contr fee ($360,933), FFS ($2,640), bonus arrang ($492), capitation ($126)
Total Member Encounters: Phys (1,158,555), non-phys (707,659)
Group Affiliation: None
Licensed in: OH
Address: 2060 East Ninth Street, Cleveland, OH 44115-1355
Phone: (216) 687-7000 **Dom State:** OH **Commenced Bus:** N/A

Data Date	Rating	RACR #1	RACR #2	Total Assets ($mil)	Capital ($mil)	Net Premium ($mil)	Net Income ($mil)
3-19	B	4.16	3.47	266.2	100.3	158.5	16.8
3-18	B	3.39	2.83	172.9	56.7	126.8	6.7
2018	B	3.54	2.95	230.9	84.2	497.7	24.4
2017	C+	1.73	1.44	140.5	46.3	305.9	-19.2
2016	B+	3.48	2.90	155.6	66.5	328.2	-18.1
2015	B+	3.99	3.33	123.3	59.6	252.8	-8.4
2014	B+	6.10	5.08	118.6	69.5	159.8	-20.3

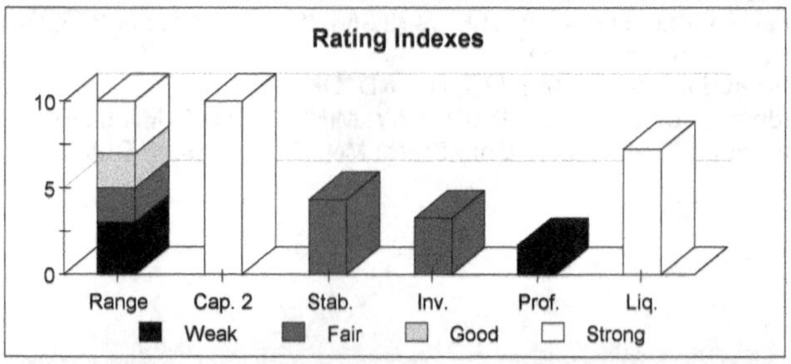

MEDICAL MUTUAL OF OHIO * — A Excellent

Major Rating Factors: Excellent profitability (7.7 on a scale of 0 to 10). Strong capitalization (10.0) based on excellent current risk-adjusted capital (severe loss scenario). Excellent liquidity (6.9) with sufficient resources (cash flows and marketable investments) to handle a spike in claims.
Other Rating Factors: Good quality investment portfolio (6.3).
Principal Business: Comp med (78%), Medicare (13%), med supp (1%), other (7%)
Mem Phys: 18: 56,424 **17:** 65,970 **18 MLR** 82.9% **/ 18 Admin Exp** N/A
Enroll(000): Q1 19: 1,061 **18:** 1,025 **17:** 991 **Med Exp PMPM:** $179
Principal Investments: Long-term bonds (56%), nonaffiliate common stock (12%), cash and equiv (12%), affiliate common stock (6%), real estate (2%), other (12%)
Provider Compensation ($000): Contr fee ($2,019,631), FFS ($9,252), capitation ($4,369), bonus arrang ($2,495), other ($140,875)
Total Member Encounters: Phys (3,287,119), non-phys (2,443,426)
Group Affiliation: None
Licensed in: GA, IN, MI, NC, OH, PA, SC, WV, WI
Address: 2060 East Ninth St, Cleveland, OH 44115-1355
Phone: (216) 687-7000 **Dom State:** OH **Commenced Bus:** N/A

Data Date	Rating	RACR #1	RACR #2	Total Assets ($mil)	Capital ($mil)	Net Premium ($mil)	Net Income ($mil)
3-19	A	7.42	6.18	2,490.1	1,879.3	677.8	72.7
3-18	A	7.26	6.05	2,296.9	1,659.1	642.7	36.3
2018	A	7.08	5.90	2,453.9	1,793.1	2,636.1	128.0
2017	A	7.05	5.88	2,233.7	1,610.5	2,470.3	22.4
2016	A	6.47	5.39	1,991.5	1,395.8	2,368.3	57.9
2015	A-	7.18	5.99	1,853.2	1,352.8	2,146.9	126.7
2014	A-	6.64	5.53	1,766.9	1,279.9	2,238.2	97.3

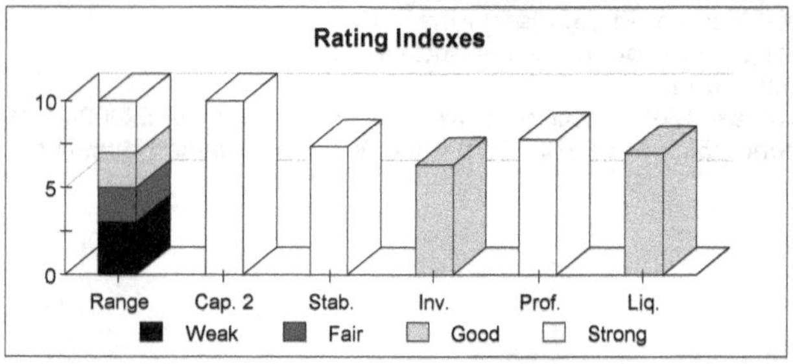

MEDICO INSURANCE COMPANY B- Good

Major Rating Factors: Good overall profitability (6.5 on a scale of 0 to 10). Good liquidity (6.8) with sufficient resources to handle a spike in claims. Fair overall results on stability tests (4.8) including fair financial strength of affiliated American Enterprise Mutual Holding and negative cash flow from operations for 2018.
Other Rating Factors: Strong capitalization (10.0) based on excellent risk adjusted capital (severe loss scenario). High quality investment portfolio (7.7).
Principal Business: Individual health insurance (82%), group health insurance (17%), and individual life insurance (1%).
Principal Investments: NonCMO investment grade bonds (68%), CMOs and structured securities (27%), and cash (4%).
Investments in Affiliates: None
Group Affiliation: American Enterprise Mutual Holding
Licensed in: All states except CT, NJ, NY, PR
Commenced Business: April 1930
Address: 1010 North 102nd St Ste 201, Des Moines, IA 50309
Phone: (800) 228-6080 **Domicile State:** NE **NAIC Code:** 31119

Data Date	Rating	RACR #1	RACR #2	Total Assets ($mil)	Capital ($mil)	Net Premium ($mil)	Net Income ($mil)
3-19	B-	4.66	4.20	83.1	38.3	0.1	0.3
3-18	B	4.58	4.12	84.0	37.3	0.1	1.6
2018	B-	4.59	4.13	83.7	37.7	0.5	7.1
2017	B	4.28	3.85	81.9	34.8	0.5	1.3
2016	B	4.63	4.16	87.3	38.8	0.6	1.8
2015	B	4.12	3.71	74.3	31.9	0.7	2.1
2014	B	4.14	3.73	69.1	30.9	0.9	-0.2

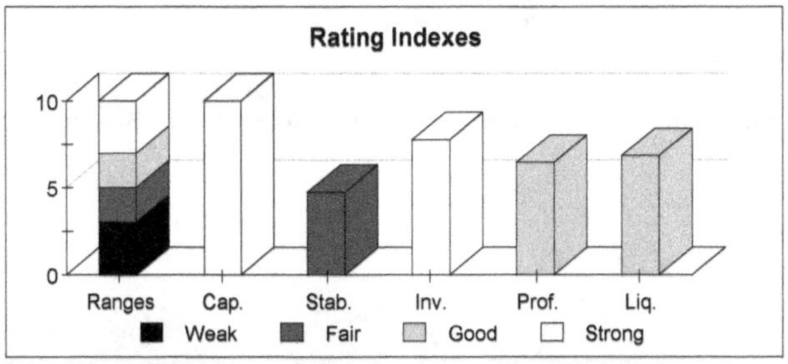

MEDIEXCEL HEALTH PLAN C- Fair

Major Rating Factors: Fair overall results on stability tests (3.5 on a scale of 0 to 10) based on an excessive 35% enrollment growth during the period. Good capitalization index (5.8) based on fair current risk-adjusted capital (moderate loss scenario). Excellent profitability (8.5).
Other Rating Factors: Excellent liquidity (6.9) with sufficient resources (cash flows and marketable investments) to handle a spike in claims.
Principal Business: Managed care (100%)
Mem Phys: 18: N/A **17:** N/A **18 MLR** 72.4% **/ 18 Admin Exp** N/A
Enroll(000): Q1 19: 14 **18:** 13 **17:** 10 **Med Exp PMPM:** $89
Principal Investments ($000): Cash and equiv ($944)
Provider Compensation ($000): None
Total Member Encounters: N/A
Group Affiliation: None
Licensed in: (No states)
Address: 750 Medical Cntr Court Ste 2, Chula Vista, CA 91911-6634
Phone: (855) 633-4392 **Dom State:** CA **Commenced Bus:** N/A

Data Date	Rating	RACR #1	RACR #2	Total Assets ($mil)	Capital ($mil)	Net Premium ($mil)	Net Income ($mil)
3-19	C-	0.87	0.58	4.8	1.8	5.2	0.4
3-18	C-	1.06	0.72	4.4	1.6	4.3	0.3
2018	C-	0.67	0.45	4.4	1.4	17.6	0.1
2017	C-	0.83	0.56	3.8	1.3	12.9	0.1
2016	N/A	N/A	N/A	N/A	N/A	N/A	N/A
2015	N/A	N/A	N/A	N/A	N/A	N/A	N/A
2014	N/A	N/A	N/A	N/A	N/A	N/A	N/A

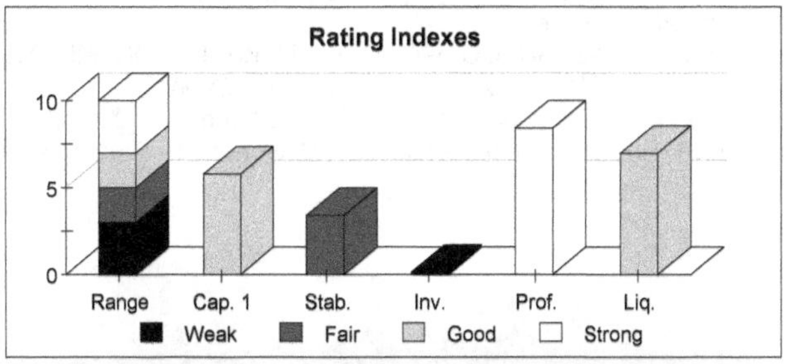

MEDISUN INC B Good

Major Rating Factors: Good overall profitability index (6.4 on a scale of 0 to 10). Fair overall results on stability tests (4.7) based on a significant 19% decrease in enrollment during the period, a decline in the number of member physicians during 2019. Strong capitalization index (7.3) based on excellent current risk-adjusted capital (severe loss scenario).
Other Rating Factors: High quality investment portfolio (9.4). Excellent liquidity (7.1) with ample operational cash flow and liquid investments.
Principal Business: Medicare (98%)
Mem Phys: 18: 5,830 **17:** 6,577 **18 MLR** 84.5% **/ 18 Admin Exp** N/A
Enroll(000): Q1 19: 44 **18:** 53 **17:** 66 **Med Exp PMPM:** $727
Principal Investments: Cash and equiv (86%), long-term bonds (14%)
Provider Compensation ($000): Capitation ($434,128), FFS ($57,416)
Total Member Encounters: Phys (1,211,911), non-phys (331,802)
Group Affiliation: Veritage LLC
Licensed in: AZ
Address: 2901 N Central Ave Suite 160, Phoenix, AZ 85012
Phone: (602) 864-4100 **Dom State:** AZ **Commenced Bus:** N/A

Data Date	Rating	RACR #1	RACR #2	Total Assets ($mil)	Capital ($mil)	Net Premium ($mil)	Net Income ($mil)
3-19	B	1.57	1.31	102.4	60.5	119.1	0.4
3-18	B-	0.97	0.81	147.4	49.6	139.6	0.2
2018	B	1.52	1.27	102.0	58.7	562.4	5.3
2017	B-	1.01	0.84	94.5	51.2	658.9	13.0
2016	C+	0.76	0.63	72.4	39.8	590.9	4.3
2015	B-	0.83	0.69	69.3	35.0	467.6	-3.7
2014	B	0.97	0.81	38.9	24.0	229.2	-0.5

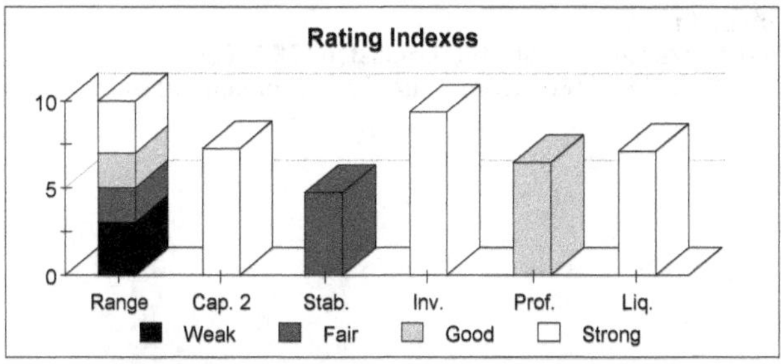

MEDSTAR FAMILY CHOICE INC C- Fair

Major Rating Factors: Weak profitability index (0.9 on a scale of 0 to 10). Strong capitalization (7.1) based on excellent current risk-adjusted capital (severe loss scenario). High quality investment portfolio (9.9).
Other Rating Factors: Excellent liquidity (7.2) with ample operational cash flow and liquid investments.
Principal Business: Medicaid (87%), Medicare (13%)
Mem Phys: 18: N/A **17:** N/A **18 MLR** 89.7% **/ 18 Admin Exp** N/A
Enroll(000): Q1 19: 93 **18:** 96 **17:** 100 **Med Exp PMPM:** $425
Principal Investments: Cash and equiv (100%)
Provider Compensation ($000): FFS ($329,053), contr fee ($182,650), capitation ($4,176)
Total Member Encounters: N/A
Group Affiliation: MedStar Health Inc
Licensed in: DC, MD
Address: 5233 King Ave Ste 400, Baltimore, MD 21237
Phone: (410) 933-2200 **Dom State:** MD **Commenced Bus:** N/A

Data Date	Rating	RACR #1	RACR #2	Total Assets ($mil)	Capital ($mil)	Net Premium ($mil)	Net Income ($mil)
3-19	C-	1.44	1.20	188.5	76.3	117.7	3.7
3-18	C-	0.98	0.81	234.4	74.1	139.0	-9.3
2018	C-	1.36	1.13	199.8	72.4	555.0	-11.6
2017	C-	1.10	0.92	230.7	82.8	786.5	-23.1
2016	C-	1.17	0.97	244.5	84.5	749.3	-16.2
2015	N/A	N/A	N/A	219.7	84.2	599.6	N/A
2014	C-	0.51	0.42	131.1	27.1	478.2	4.6

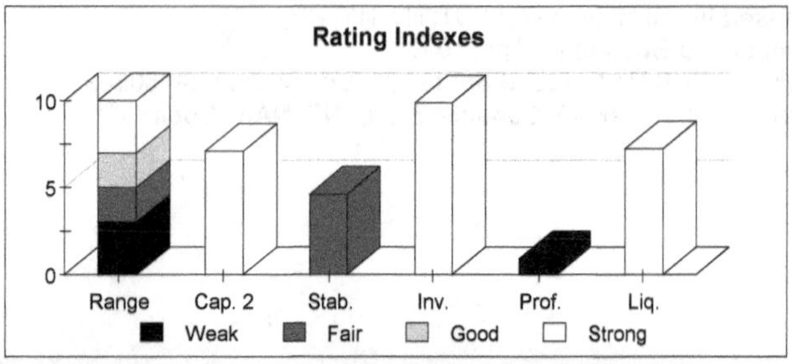

MEMBERS HEALTH INS CO C- Fair

Major Rating Factors: Weak profitability index (0.9 on a scale of 0 to 10). Strong capitalization (10.0) based on excellent current risk-adjusted capital (severe loss scenario). High quality investment portfolio (9.1).
Other Rating Factors: Excellent liquidity (7.2) with ample operational cash flow and liquid investments.
Principal Business: Med supp (28%), other (72%)
Mem Phys: 18: N/A **17:** N/A **18 MLR** 108.7% **/ 18 Admin Exp** N/A
Enroll(000): Q1 19: 7 **18:** 8 **17:** 5 **Med Exp PMPM:** $132
Principal Investments: Long-term bonds (75%), nonaffiliate common stock (14%), cash and equiv (11%)
Provider Compensation ($000): FFS ($2,481), other ($13,860)
Total Member Encounters: Phys (28,961), non-phys (549,647)
Group Affiliation: None
Licensed in: AL, AZ, AR, CO, GA, ID, IL, IN, KS, KY, MD, MN, MS, MO, MT, NE, NM, ND, OK, OR, PA, SC, SD, TN, TX, UT, WA, WV
Address: 24 West Camelback Ave Ste A546, Phoenix, AZ 85013
Phone: (931) 560-0041 **Dom State:** AZ **Commenced Bus:** N/A

Data Date	Rating	RACR #1	RACR #2	Total Assets ($mil)	Capital ($mil)	Net Premium ($mil)	Net Income ($mil)
3-19	C-	15.26	12.72	38.8	32.8	2.5	-1.2
3-18	C-	14.24	11.87	36.1	28.5	2.6	-1.8
2018	C-	14.87	12.39	37.9	32.2	10.9	-3.7
2017	C-	12.12	10.10	34.4	28.3	6.6	-5.2
2016	C	17.30	14.42	32.8	30.9	2.5	-1.1
2015	C	18.55	15.46	33.4	31.9	2.0	-0.1
2014	C	17.19	14.32	33.1	31.9	1.5	0.8

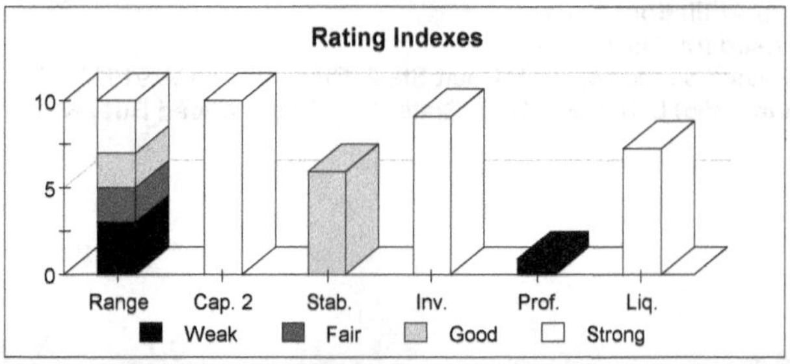

MEMORIAL HERMANN HEALTH INS CO C- Fair

Major Rating Factors: Weak profitability index (1.2 on a scale of 0 to 10). Strong capitalization (9.4) based on excellent current risk-adjusted capital (severe loss scenario). High quality investment portfolio (9.9).
Other Rating Factors: Excellent liquidity (8.0) with ample operational cash flow and liquid investments.
Principal Business: Comp med (58%), Medicare (42%)
Mem Phys: 18: 66,924 **17:** 54,130 **18 MLR** 83.0% **/ 18 Admin Exp** N/A
Enroll(000): Q1 19: 2 **18:** 4 **17:** 11 **Med Exp PMPM:** $492
Principal Investments: Cash and equiv (100%)
Provider Compensation ($000): FFS ($36,172)
Total Member Encounters: Phys (41,146), non-phys (47,674)
Group Affiliation: None
Licensed in: TX
Address: 929 Gessner Ste 1500, Houston, TX 77024
Phone: (713) 338-6480 **Dom State:** TX **Commenced Bus:** N/A

Data Date	Rating	RACR #1	RACR #2	Total Assets ($mil)	Capital ($mil)	Net Premium ($mil)	Net Income ($mil)
3-19	C-	3.28	2.73	26.1	19.0	3.0	-0.5
3-18	C-	1.89	1.58	34.1	20.3	10.4	-1.7
2018	C-	3.12	2.60	27.3	18.1	38.5	3.3
2017	C-	2.06	1.72	38.1	22.6	70.9	-5.1
2016	C-	1.74	1.45	53.3	25.0	92.8	-15.0
2015	C-	1.87	1.55	31.0	16.2	50.2	-9.7
2014	C-	2.36	1.96	27.9	18.1	42.6	-4.9

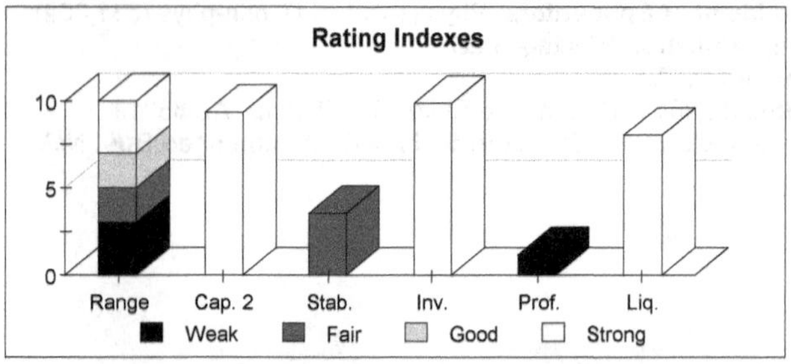

MEMORIAL HERMANN HEALTH PLAN INC C- Fair

Major Rating Factors: Weak profitability index (1.6 on a scale of 0 to 10). Strong capitalization (7.4) based on excellent current risk-adjusted capital (severe loss scenario). High quality investment portfolio (9.9).
Other Rating Factors: Excellent liquidity (7.4) with ample operational cash flow and liquid investments.
Principal Business: Medicare (53%), comp med (47%)
Mem Phys: 18: 33,005 **17:** 26,125 **18 MLR** 85.4% **/ 18 Admin Exp** N/A
Enroll(000): Q1 19: 10 **18:** 14 **17:** 20 **Med Exp PMPM:** $392
Principal Investments: Cash and equiv (100%)
Provider Compensation ($000): FFS ($70,661)
Total Member Encounters: Phys (91,465), non-phys (103,294)
Group Affiliation: None
Licensed in: TX
Address: 929 Gessner Ste 1500, Houston, TX 77024
Phone: (713) 338-6480 **Dom State:** TX **Commenced Bus:** N/A

Data Date	Rating	RACR #1	RACR #2	Total Assets ($mil)	Capital ($mil)	Net Premium ($mil)	Net Income ($mil)
3-19	C-	1.65	1.38	47.8	15.8	11.0	-0.2
3-18	D+	N/A	N/A	47.1	17.2	19.3	-1.0
2018	C-	1.74	1.45	40.5	16.7	78.9	-1.4
2017	D+	N/A	N/A	41.7	16.3	98.4	-7.3
2016	D+	1.10	0.92	26.7	10.5	55.7	-10.9
2015	D+	1.50	1.25	11.9	7.5	18.0	-8.3
2014	N/A	N/A	N/A	7.3	6.5	N/A	-4.8

Rating Indexes

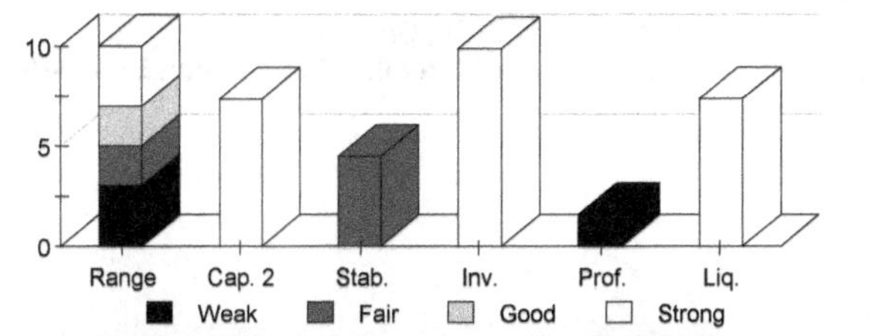

MERCYCARE HMO C Fair

Major Rating Factors: Fair liquidity (4.3 on a scale of 0 to 10) as cash resources may not be adequate to cover a spike in claims. Weak profitability index (1.3). Good capitalization (6.4) based on good current risk-adjusted capital (severe loss scenario).
Other Rating Factors: Good quality investment portfolio (5.0).
Principal Business: Comp med (73%), Medicaid (23%), med supp (3%), FEHB (1%)
Mem Phys: 18: 483 **17:** 819 **18 MLR** 94.6% **/ 18 Admin Exp** N/A
Enroll(000): Q1 19: 29 **18:** 29 **17:** 30 **Med Exp PMPM:** $277
Principal Investments: Nonaffiliate common stock (55%), long-term bonds (28%), cash and equiv (17%)
Provider Compensation ($000): Contr fee ($70,226), capitation ($30,629), FFS ($4,937)
Total Member Encounters: N/A
Group Affiliation: None
Licensed in: IL, WI
Address: 580 N Washington, Janesville, WI 53545
Phone: (608) 752-3431 **Dom State:** WI **Commenced Bus:** N/A

Data Date	Rating	RACR #1	RACR #2	Total Assets ($mil)	Capital ($mil)	Net Premium ($mil)	Net Income ($mil)
3-19	C	1.14	0.95	42.9	14.3	27.0	-0.5
3-18	C	1.77	1.47	48.9	18.5	27.4	0.9
2018	C	0.85	0.71	35.7	10.8	106.8	-2.4
2017	C	1.56	1.30	43.9	17.0	93.0	-1.9
2016	C	1.54	1.29	31.0	15.8	82.0	1.5
2015	C	1.47	1.23	27.3	14.2	79.5	0.0
2014	C	1.34	1.12	28.9	15.1	98.6	-1.9

Rating Indexes

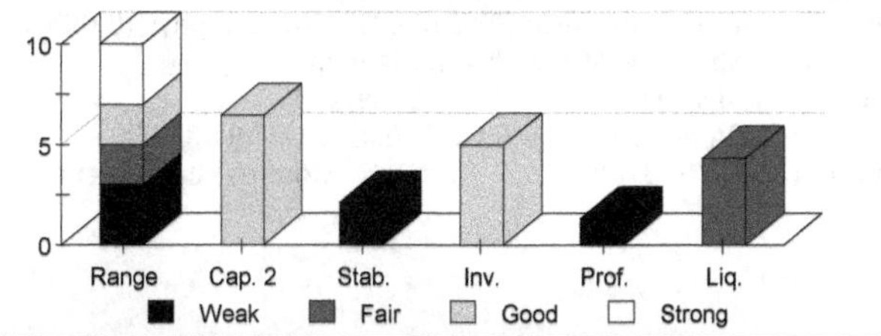

MERCYCARE INS CO D+ Weak

Major Rating Factors: Weak profitability index (0.9 on a scale of 0 to 10). Low quality investment portfolio (2.7). Good liquidity (6.7) with sufficient resources (cash flows and marketable investments) to handle a spike in claims.
Other Rating Factors: Strong capitalization (7.1) based on excellent current risk-adjusted capital (severe loss scenario).
Principal Business: Comp med (100%)
Mem Phys: 18: 483 **17:** 819 **18 MLR** 111.3% **/ 18 Admin Exp** N/A
Enroll(000): Q1 19: 1 **18:** 1 **17:** 1 **Med Exp PMPM:** $41
Principal Investments: Affiliate common stock (88%), long-term bonds (18%)
Provider Compensation ($000): FFS ($443), contr fee ($156), capitation ($70)
Total Member Encounters: N/A
Group Affiliation: None
Licensed in: IL, WI
Address: 580 N Washington, Janesville, WI 53545
Phone: (608) 752-3431 **Dom State:** WI **Commenced Bus:** N/A

Data Date	Rating	RACR #1	RACR #2	Total Assets ($mil)	Capital ($mil)	Net Premium ($mil)	Net Income ($mil)
3-19	D+	1.47	1.22	12.8	12.4	0.1	0.0
3-18	D+	N/A	N/A	17.2	16.2	0.2	-0.1
2018	D+	1.21	1.01	12.3	10.3	0.4	0.3
2017	D+	N/A	N/A	18.8	16.4	0.6	-0.1
2016	D+	1.29	1.08	17.4	15.4	0.6	-1.4
2015	C-	1.33	1.11	16.1	15.2	2.2	-1.0
2014	N/A	N/A	N/A	17.2	16.9	1.2	-0.1

Rating Indexes

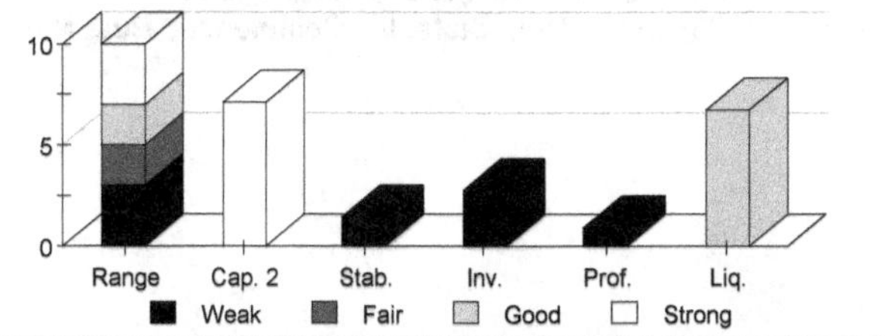

MERIDIAN HEALTH PLAN OF ILLINOIS INC — C — Fair

Major Rating Factors: Fair liquidity (3.5 on a scale of 0 to 10) as cash resources may not be adequate to cover a spike in claims. Weak profitability index (0.9). Strong capitalization (7.6) based on excellent current risk-adjusted capital (severe loss scenario).
Other Rating Factors: High quality investment portfolio (9.9).
Principal Business: Medicaid (92%), Medicare (8%)
Mem Phys: 18: 42,324 **17:** 33,756 **18 MLR** 96.7% **/ 18 Admin Exp** N/A
Enroll(000): Q1 19: 804 **18:** 622 **17:** 388 **Med Exp PMPM:** $346
Principal Investments: Cash and equiv (100%)
Provider Compensation ($000): Contr fee ($1,927,344), FFS ($192,162), capitation ($73,073), bonus arrang ($9,275)
Total Member Encounters: Phys (4,101,176), non-phys (3,060,376)
Group Affiliation: WellCare Health Plans Inc
Licensed in: IL
Address: 333 S Wabash Ste 2900, Chicago, IL 60604
Phone: (313) 324-3700 **Dom State:** IL **Commenced Bus:** N/A

Data Date	Rating	RACR #1	RACR #2	Total Assets ($mil)	Capital ($mil)	Net Premium ($mil)	Net Income ($mil)
3-19	C	1.84	1.53	804.7	315.9	856.1	-17.2
3-18	C	0.79	0.66	549.8	116.4	490.5	-8.4
2018	C	1.02	0.85	685.5	231.8	2,421.4	-179.4
2017	C	0.84	0.70	478.1	128.8	1,436.3	-14.2
2016	B-	0.93	0.78	405.5	96.5	1,125.7	-30.4
2015	B	1.11	0.92	282.6	87.3	1,017.2	7.2
2014	B	1.02	0.85	130.5	31.6	320.5	-0.2

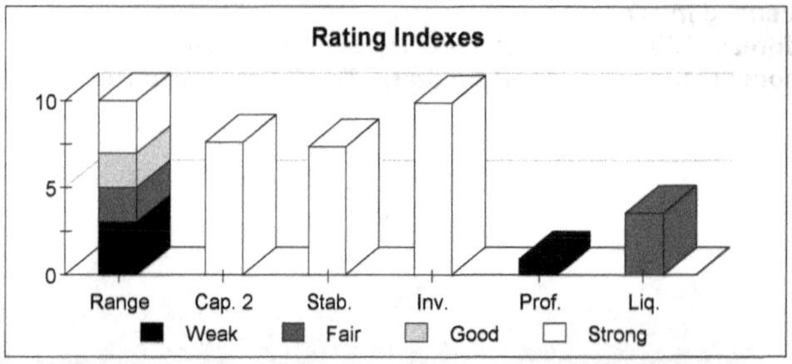

MERIDIAN HEALTH PLAN OF MICHIGAN INC — C — Fair

Major Rating Factors: Fair liquidity (3.8 on a scale of 0 to 10) as cash resources may not be adequate to cover a spike in claims. Weak profitability index (0.9). Good capitalization index (6.6) based on good current risk-adjusted capital (severe loss scenario).
Other Rating Factors: Good overall results on stability tests (5.2) based on steady enrollment growth, averaging 9% over the past five years. Potentially strong support from affiliation with WellCare Health Plans Inc. High quality investment portfolio (9.9).
Principal Business: Medicaid (86%), Medicare (13%)
Mem Phys: 18: 40,971 **17:** 37,693 **18 MLR** 90.2% **/ 18 Admin Exp** N/A
Enroll(000): Q1 19: 527 **18:** 519 **17:** 517 **Med Exp PMPM:** $285
Principal Investments: Cash and equiv (100%)
Provider Compensation ($000): Contr fee ($1,559,770), FFS ($174,206), capitation ($45,681), bonus arrang ($10,839)
Total Member Encounters: Phys (5,847,600), non-phys (6,093,195)
Group Affiliation: WellCare Health Plans Inc
Licensed in: DC, DE, IL, IN, KY, ME, MI, OH
Address: 1 Campus Martius Suite 700, Detroit, MI 48226
Phone: (313) 324-3700 **Dom State:** MI **Commenced Bus:** N/A

Data Date	Rating	RACR #1	RACR #2	Total Assets ($mil)	Capital ($mil)	Net Premium ($mil)	Net Income ($mil)
3-19	C	1.16	0.97	383.1	143.2	482.2	-25.7
3-18	B	1.19	0.99	529.9	183.3	542.7	-3.2
2018	C	1.07	0.89	423.2	169.9	1,988.4	-88.0
2017	B	1.17	0.97	451.8	186.8	2,201.8	0.5
2016	B+	1.16	0.97	537.4	185.3	2,420.8	3.9
2015	B+	1.09	0.91	477.6	153.4	2,113.2	6.8
2014	B+	1.09	0.91	324.5	107.4	1,443.3	3.4

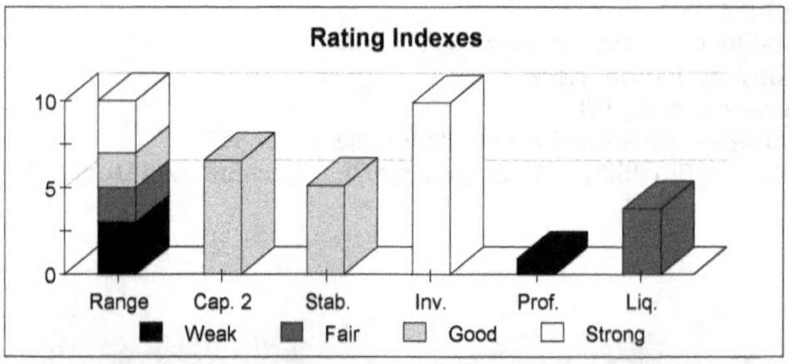

MERIT HEALTH INS CO — C+ — Fair

Major Rating Factors: Good overall profitability index (5.6 on a scale of 0 to 10). Strong capitalization (10.0) based on excellent current risk-adjusted capital (severe loss scenario). High quality investment portfolio (9.9).
Other Rating Factors: Excellent liquidity (8.0) with ample operational cash flow and liquid investments.
Principal Business: Other (100%)
Mem Phys: 18: N/A **17:** N/A **18 MLR** 86.5% **/ 18 Admin Exp** N/A
Enroll(000): Q1 19: 60 **18:** 88 **17:** 109 **Med Exp PMPM:** $87
Principal Investments: Long-term bonds (66%), cash and equiv (34%)
Provider Compensation ($000): Other ($89,679)
Total Member Encounters: N/A
Group Affiliation: Magellan Health Inc
Licensed in: All states except FL, NV, NJ, PR
Address: 5215 Old Orchard Rd Ste 600, Skokie, IL 60077
Phone: (224) 935-9809 **Dom State:** IL **Commenced Bus:** N/A

Data Date	Rating	RACR #1	RACR #2	Total Assets ($mil)	Capital ($mil)	Net Premium ($mil)	Net Income ($mil)
3-19	C+	9.74	8.11	129.9	52.0	17.5	-1.7
3-18	C	N/A	N/A	125.6	48.9	30.7	-3.6
2018	C+	9.98	8.31	127.6	53.5	103.7	-1.9
2017	C	N/A	N/A	131.0	51.9	113.3	9.1
2016	C+	5.46	4.55	147.0	58.3	59.8	8.8
2015	B-	3.57	2.98	65.0	47.9	118.5	10.4
2014	C+	5.84	4.87	67.2	27.0	128.8	7.5

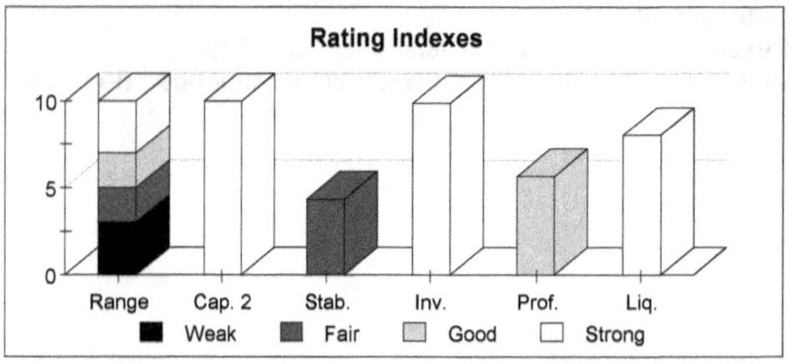

MG INSURANCE CO — C- — Fair

Major Rating Factors: Excellent profitability (7.5 on a scale of 0 to 10). Strong capitalization index (10.0) based on weak current risk-adjusted capital (severe loss scenario). High quality investment portfolio (9.8).
Other Rating Factors: Excellent liquidity (9.0) with ample operational cash flow and liquid investments.
Principal Business: Other (100%)
Mem Phys: 18: N/A **17:** N/A **18 MLR** 60.3% **/ 18 Admin Exp** N/A
Enroll(000): Q1 19: N/A **18:** 65 **17:** N/A **Med Exp PMPM:** $152
Principal Investments: Cash and equiv (100%)
Provider Compensation ($000): Other ($9,885)
Total Member Encounters: Non-phys (65,030)
Group Affiliation: HFT Equity Holdings LLC
Licensed in: (No states)
Address: , Scottsdale, AZ 85253
Phone: (858) 566-2727 **Dom State:** AZ **Commenced Bus:** N/A

Data Date	Rating	RACR #1	RACR #2	Total Assets ($mil)	Capital ($mil)	Net Premium ($mil)	Net Income ($mil)
3-19	C-	N/A	N/A	29.9	29.4	N/A	0.6
3-18	N/A	N/A	N/A	34.7	33.0	4.1	-0.2
2018	C-	N/A	N/A	29.5	28.8	16.4	1.5
2017	N/A	N/A	N/A	N/A	N/A	N/A	N/A
2016	N/A	N/A	N/A	N/A	N/A	N/A	N/A
2015	N/A	N/A	N/A	N/A	N/A	N/A	N/A
2014	N/A	N/A	N/A	N/A	N/A	N/A	N/A

Rating Indexes

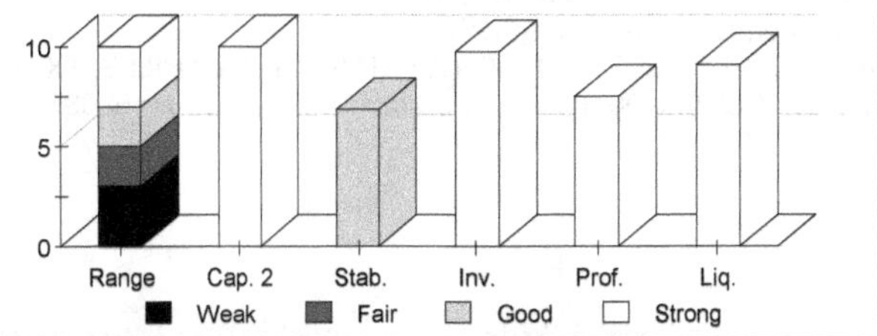

MHS HEALTH WISCONSIN — B- — Good

Major Rating Factors: Good quality investment portfolio (6.6 on a scale of 0 to 10). Good overall results on stability tests (6.4). Rating is significantly influenced by the fair financial results of . Excellent profitability (9.0).
Other Rating Factors: Strong capitalization index (10.0) based on excellent current risk-adjusted capital (severe loss scenario). Excellent liquidity (6.9) with sufficient resources (cash flows and marketable investments) to handle a spike in claims.
Principal Business: Medicaid (93%), Medicare (7%)
Mem Phys: 18: 22,918 **17:** 24,523 **18 MLR** 83.9% **/ 18 Admin Exp** N/A
Enroll(000): Q1 19: 41 **18:** 40 **17:** 36 **Med Exp PMPM:** $375
Principal Investments: Long-term bonds (73%), cash and equiv (24%), affiliate common stock (1%), other (2%)
Provider Compensation ($000): Contr fee ($126,833), bonus arrang ($25,511), salary ($10,979), capitation ($3,302)
Total Member Encounters: Phys (204,092), non-phys (366,601)
Group Affiliation: None
Licensed in: WI
Address: 10700 W Research Drive Suite 3, Milwaukee, WI 53226
Phone: (314) 725-4477 **Dom State:** WI **Commenced Bus:** N/A

Data Date	Rating	RACR #1	RACR #2	Total Assets ($mil)	Capital ($mil)	Net Premium ($mil)	Net Income ($mil)
3-19	B-	4.67	3.89	89.2	56.3	57.0	5.3
3-18	C+	N/A	N/A	78.2	52.3	44.9	1.0
2018	B-	4.29	3.57	86.2	51.2	210.3	12.9
2017	C+	N/A	N/A	69.6	50.7	163.3	9.2
2016	C+	4.92	4.10	72.3	51.5	183.6	9.5
2015	C+	4.59	3.83	75.7	46.6	196.8	15.8
2014	C+	3.51	2.93	69.0	30.9	174.6	6.7

Rating Indexes

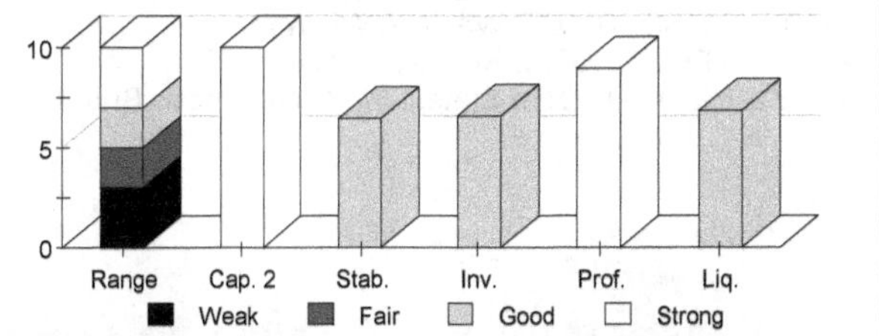

MICHIGAN COMPLETE HEALTH INC — C- — Fair

Major Rating Factors: Weak profitability index (0.9 on a scale of 0 to 10). Good liquidity (6.9) with sufficient resources (cash flows and marketable investments) to handle a spike in claims. Strong capitalization (8.0) based on excellent current risk-adjusted capital (severe loss scenario).
Other Rating Factors: High quality investment portfolio (9.9).
Principal Business: Medicare (100%)
Mem Phys: 18: 8,113 **17:** 7,125 **18 MLR** 86.2% **/ 18 Admin Exp** N/A
Enroll(000): Q1 19: 2 **18:** 2 **17:** 2 **Med Exp PMPM:** $1,735
Principal Investments: Long-term bonds (273%)
Provider Compensation ($000): Capitation ($54,750), salary ($556), contr fee ($151), bonus arrang ($15)
Total Member Encounters: Phys (73,544), non-phys (166,576)
Group Affiliation: None
Licensed in: MI
Address: 800 Tower Rd Ste 200, Troy, MI 48098
Phone: (314) 725-4477 **Dom State:** MO **Commenced Bus:** N/A

Data Date	Rating	RACR #1	RACR #2	Total Assets ($mil)	Capital ($mil)	Net Premium ($mil)	Net Income ($mil)
3-19	C-	2.16	1.80	15.8	7.4	15.3	-6.2
3-18	C-	2.06	1.71	13.6	6.3	17.2	-0.9
2018	C-	1.91	1.59	11.0	6.5	63.7	-5.0
2017	C-	1.22	1.02	12.0	7.1	54.3	0.6
2016	C-	2.34	1.95	10.6	6.5	46.9	-0.6
2015	C	1.77	1.47	11.3	5.0	60.5	-3.4
2014	C	1.32	1.10	8.8	4.9	30.7	N/A

Rating Indexes

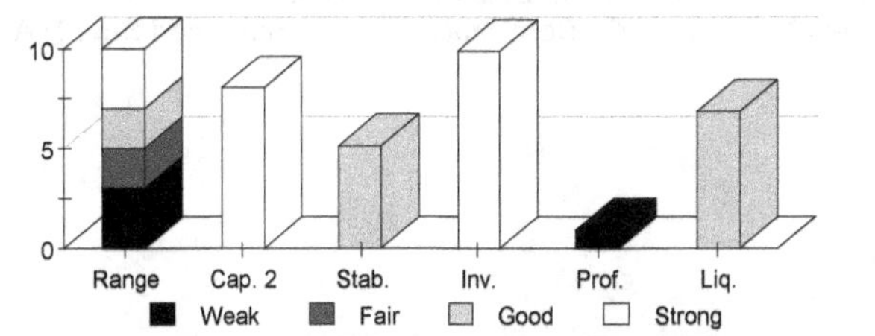

MID-WEST NATIONAL LIFE INSURANCE COMPANY OF TENNESS B Good

Major Rating Factors: Good overall profitability (6.5 on a scale of 0 to 10). Good overall results on stability tests (5.0). Stability strengths include good operational trends and excellent risk diversification. Strong capitalization (10.0) based on excellent risk adjusted capital (severe loss scenario).
Other Rating Factors: High quality investment portfolio (8.0). Excellent liquidity (8.1).
Principal Business: Individual life insurance (51%), group health insurance (28%), individual health insurance (12%), individual annuities (5%), and group life insurance (4%).
Principal Investments: Cash (9%), nonCMO investment grade bonds (7%), and CMOs and structured securities (3%).
Investments in Affiliates: 4%
Group Affiliation: Blackstone Investor Group
Licensed in: All states except NY, VT, PR
Commenced Business: May 1965
Address: 9151 BOULEVARD 26, NORTH RICHLAND HILLS, TX 76180
Phone: (817) 255-3100 **Domicile State:** TX **NAIC Code:** 66087

Data Date	Rating	RACR #1	RACR #2	Total Assets ($mil)	Capital ($mil)	Net Premium ($mil)	Net Income ($mil)
3-19	B	4.00	3.60	62.2	28.9	1.5	0.4
3-18	C	3.79	3.41	61.5	27.3	1.7	0.7
2018	B-	3.99	3.59	62.5	28.9	6.4	3.2
2017	C	3.74	3.36	63.8	26.9	7.3	9.4
2016	C-	2.17	1.95	86.1	17.1	8.8	-18.0
2015	C+	7.62	6.21	166.2	71.5	32.2	17.8
2014	B-	2.91	2.07	291.8	90.6	194.1	19.0

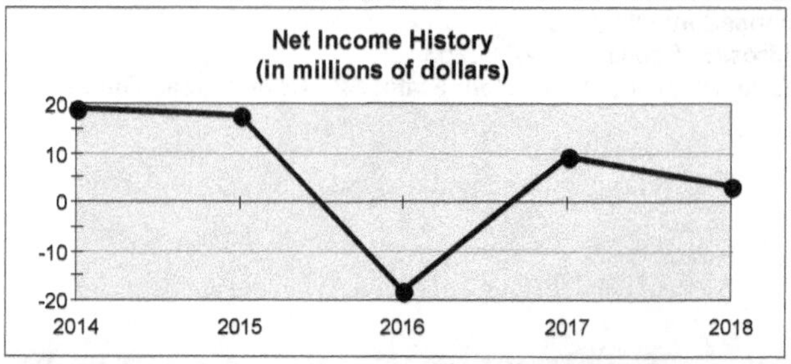

MII LIFE INSURANCE INC C Fair

Major Rating Factors: Fair profitability index (4.1 on a scale of 0 to 10). Low quality investment portfolio (1.5). Strong capitalization (8.4) based on excellent current risk-adjusted capital (severe loss scenario).
Other Rating Factors: Excellent liquidity (8.4) with ample operational cash flow and liquid investments.
Principal Business: Other (39%)
Mem Phys: 18: N/A **17:** N/A **18 MLR** 81.2% **/ 18 Admin Exp** N/A
Enroll(000): Q1 19: 56 **18:** 44 **17:** 34 **Med Exp PMPM:** $61
Principal Investments: Long-term bonds (88%), cash and equiv (7%), nonaffiliate common stock (5%)
Provider Compensation ($000): Other ($27,853)
Total Member Encounters: N/A
Group Affiliation: Aware Integrated Inc
Licensed in: AL, AR, CA, DC, DE, FL, GA, IA, KS, LA, MD, MI, MN, MT, NE, NC, ND, OR, PA, SD, TN, UT, WA, WV, WI, WY
Address: 3535 BLUE CROSS Rd, Eagan, MN 55122
Phone: (651) 662-8000 **Dom State:** MN **Commenced Bus:** N/A

Data Date	Rating	RACR #1	RACR #2	Total Assets ($mil)	Capital ($mil)	Net Premium ($mil)	Net Income ($mil)
3-19	C	2.43	2.03	1,321.8	41.0	7.3	0.1
3-18	B-	N/A	N/A	1,068.2	44.9	2.4	0.1
2018	C	2.14	1.78	1,196.5	36.0	35.0	0.4
2017	B-	N/A	N/A	985.5	45.0	23.5	2.8
2016	B-	2.91	2.43	813.0	39.9	17.2	9.5
2015	B	2.66	2.21	596.6	27.7	16.2	3.2
2014	B	2.68	2.24	511.4	27.4	15.6	1.9

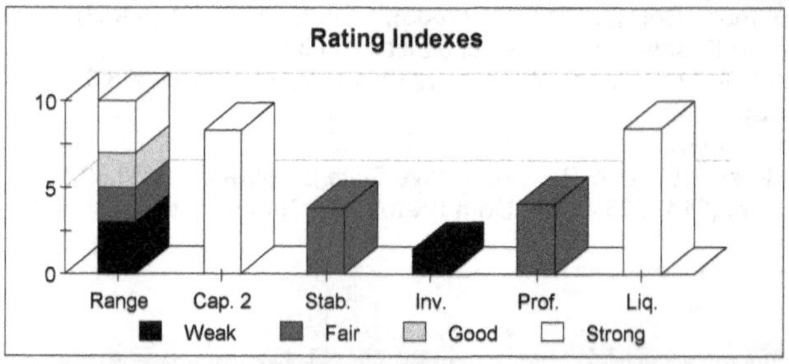

MISSOURI CARE INC C- Fair

Major Rating Factors: Fair quality investment portfolio (4.8 on a scale of 0 to 10). Excellent profitability (7.4). Strong capitalization (8.6) based on excellent current risk-adjusted capital (severe loss scenario).
Other Rating Factors: Excellent liquidity (7.1) with ample operational cash flow and liquid investments.
Principal Business: Medicaid (97%), comp med (3%)
Mem Phys: 18: 36,400 **17:** 30,800 **18 MLR** 85.9% **/ 18 Admin Exp** N/A
Enroll(000): Q1 19: 242 **18:** 251 **17:** 286 **Med Exp PMPM:** $201
Principal Investments: Cash and equiv (99%), long-term bonds (1%)
Provider Compensation ($000): Contr fee ($574,514), capitation ($86,919)
Total Member Encounters: Phys (855,630), non-phys (492,596)
Group Affiliation: WellCare Health Plans Inc
Licensed in: MO
Address: 2404 Forum Blvd, Columbia, MO 65203
Phone: (813) 206-6200 **Dom State:** MO **Commenced Bus:** N/A

Data Date	Rating	RACR #1	RACR #2	Total Assets ($mil)	Capital ($mil)	Net Premium ($mil)	Net Income ($mil)
3-19	C-	2.62	2.19	221.9	102.3	184.6	1.8
3-18	D	2.62	2.18	223.4	81.5	193.4	-13.3
2018	D+	2.58	2.15	218.6	100.3	767.3	7.8
2017	E	2.05	1.71	207.6	94.1	651.1	15.4
2016	E	2.73	2.27	87.6	42.6	349.5	3.5
2015	E	2.35	1.96	74.1	34.5	308.9	-0.7
2014	E	3.47	2.90	79.9	47.1	275.2	4.0

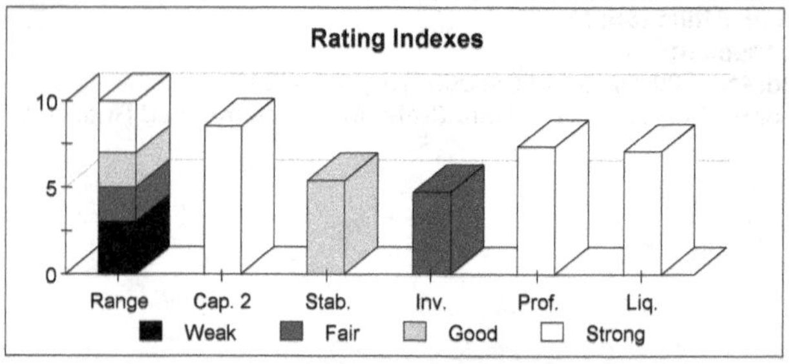

MISSOURI CHAMBER FEDN BENEFIT C Fair

Major Rating Factors: Weak liquidity (2.8 on a scale of 0 to 10) as a spike in claims may stretch capacity. Excellent profitability (10.0). Strong capitalization (9.2) based on excellent current risk-adjusted capital (severe loss scenario).
Other Rating Factors: High quality investment portfolio (9.4).
Principal Business: Comp med (100%)
Mem Phys: 18: N/A **17:** N/A **18 MLR** 747.7% **/ 18 Admin Exp** N/A
Enroll(000): Q1 19: 17 **18:** 10 **17:** 1 **Med Exp PMPM:** $217
Principal Investments: Cash and equiv (100%)
Provider Compensation ($000): Contr fee ($9,450), FFS ($6,300)
Total Member Encounters: N/A
Group Affiliation: Missouri Chamber Federation Benefit
Licensed in: MO
Address: , Jefferson City, MO 65101
Phone: (573) 634-3511 **Dom State:** MO **Commenced Bus:** November 2017

Data Date	Rating	RACR #1	RACR #2	Total Assets ($mil)	Capital ($mil)	Net Premium ($mil)	Net Income ($mil)
3-19	C	3.10	2.58	18.6	1.5	1.5	0.3
3-18	N/A	N/A	N/A	3.1	0.8	0.4	0.2
2018	C-	2.43	2.03	11.9	1.2	2.5	0.6
2017	N/A	N/A	N/A	1.0	0.7	N/A	N/A
2016	N/A	N/A	N/A	N/A	N/A	N/A	N/A
2015	N/A	N/A	N/A	N/A	N/A	N/A	N/A
2014	N/A	N/A	N/A	N/A	N/A	N/A	N/A

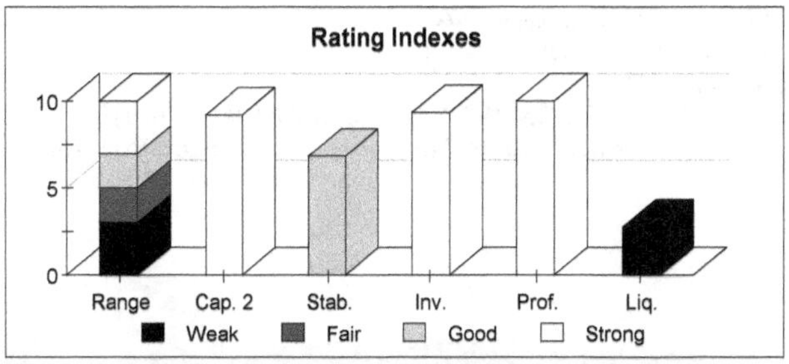

MISSOURI MEDICARE SELECT LLC D+ Weak

Major Rating Factors: Weak profitability index (0.9 on a scale of 0 to 10). Good capitalization (6.5) based on good current risk-adjusted capital (severe loss scenario). Good liquidity (5.3) with sufficient resources (cash flows and marketable investments) to handle a spike in claims.
Other Rating Factors: High quality investment portfolio (9.9).
Principal Business: Medicare (100%)
Mem Phys: 18: 1,533 **17:** 935 **18 MLR** 104.2% **/ 18 Admin Exp** N/A
Enroll(000): Q1 19: N/A **18:** N/A **17:** 0 **Med Exp PMPM:** N/A
Principal Investments: Long-term bonds (57%), cash and equiv (43%)
Provider Compensation ($000): Contr fee ($2,174), capitation ($435)
Total Member Encounters: Phys (1,041), non-phys (2,703)
Group Affiliation: American Health Companies Inc
Licensed in: MO
Address: 10954 Kennerly Rd, Clayton, MO 63105
Phone: (615) 565-3654 **Dom State:** MO **Commenced Bus:** N/A

Data Date	Rating	RACR #1	RACR #2	Total Assets ($mil)	Capital ($mil)	Net Premium ($mil)	Net Income ($mil)
3-19	D+	1.15	0.96	2.1	1.5	0.0	-0.3
3-18	C-	N/A	N/A	1.9	0.4	1.0	-0.4
2018	D+	0.47	0.40	1.1	0.7	2.0	-0.5
2017	C-	N/A	N/A	1.6	0.8	4.5	-1.0
2016	C-	1.11	0.93	1.7	0.9	4.9	0.2
2015	N/A	N/A	N/A	1.2	1.2	N/A	-0.2
2014	N/A	N/A	N/A	N/A	N/A	N/A	N/A

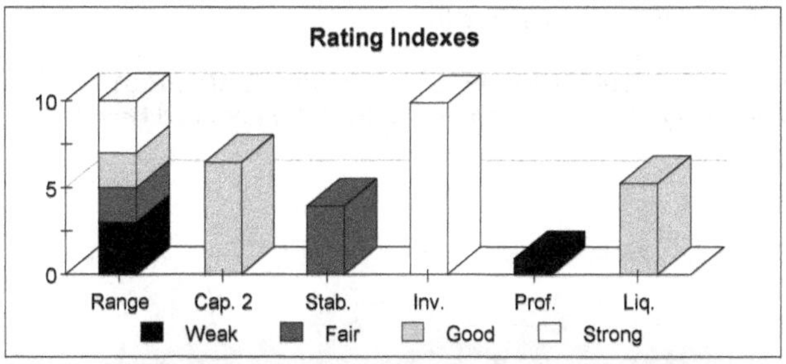

MISSOURI VALLEY L&H INS CO C- Fair

Major Rating Factors: Good overall profitability index (6.6 on a scale of 0 to 10). Good capitalization (5.3) based on good current risk-adjusted capital (severe loss scenario). High quality investment portfolio (7.4).
Other Rating Factors: Excellent liquidity (7.1) with ample operational cash flow and liquid investments.
Principal Business: Medicare (25%), other (75%)
Mem Phys: 18: 4,041 **17:** N/A **18 MLR** 81.4% **/ 18 Admin Exp** N/A
Enroll(000): Q1 19: 2 **18:** 1 **17:** N/A **Med Exp PMPM:** $2,898
Principal Investments: Long-term bonds (87%), cash and equiv (13%)
Provider Compensation ($000): Contr fee ($31,440), FFS ($6,260), capitation ($142)
Total Member Encounters: Phys (9,553), non-phys (3,865)
Group Affiliation: None
Licensed in: KS, MO
Address: , Kansas City, MO 64108-2428
Phone: (816) 395-3355 **Dom State:** MO **Commenced Bus:** N/A

Data Date	Rating	RACR #1	RACR #2	Total Assets ($mil)	Capital ($mil)	Net Premium ($mil)	Net Income ($mil)
3-19	C-	0.97	0.81	36.4	19.8	17.1	-4.1
3-18	N/A	N/A	N/A	22.8	13.3	10.9	-0.3
2018	U	1.27	1.05	33.8	25.6	47.8	5.3
2017	N/A	N/A	N/A	18.1	13.8	26.1	N/A
2016	N/A	N/A	N/A	15.7	10.9	16.0	N/A
2015	N/A	N/A	N/A	16.7	16.1	0.8	N/A
2014	N/A	N/A	N/A	16.2	15.5	1.1	N/A

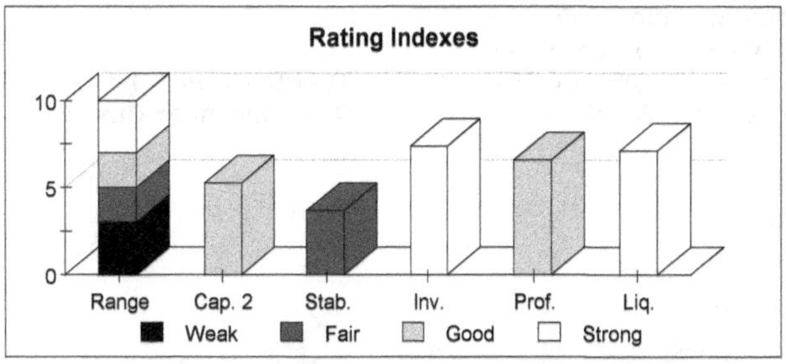

MMM HEALTHCARE LLC — E- Very Weak

Major Rating Factors: Good overall profitability index (6.1 on a scale of 0 to 10). Good capitalization (5.6) based on good current risk-adjusted capital (severe loss scenario). Good liquidity (6.8) with sufficient resources (cash flows and marketable investments) to handle a spike in claims.
Other Rating Factors: High quality investment portfolio (9.9).
Principal Business: Medicare (100%)
Mem Phys: 18: N/A **17:** N/A **18 MLR** 83.7% **/ 18 Admin Exp** N/A
Enroll(000): Q1 19: 240 **18:** 215 **17:** 202 **Med Exp PMPM:** $692
Principal Investments: Long-term bonds (52%), cash and equiv (34%), other (14%)
Provider Compensation ($000): FFS ($795,212), capitation ($399,337), bonus arrang ($69,245), other ($511,422)
Total Member Encounters: N/A
Group Affiliation: InnovaCare Inc
Licensed in: PR
Address: 350 CHARDON AVE STE 500, SAN JUAN, PR 918
Phone: (787) 622-3000 **Dom State:** PR **Commenced Bus:** N/A

Data Date	Rating	RACR #1	RACR #2	Total Assets ($mil)	Capital ($mil)	Net Premium ($mil)	Net Income ($mil)
3-19	E-	1.02	0.85	493.5	147.8	655.1	15.9
3-18	E-	1.06	0.89	586.8	128.3	500.3	-22.2
2018	E-	0.92	0.76	377.2	132.1	2,039.8	24.0
2017	E-	1.14	0.95	395.9	141.9	1,806.3	35.4
2016	E-	1.01	0.85	310.7	117.0	1,593.6	37.3
2015	E-	0.99	0.82	272.5	120.8	1,531.9	11.2
2014	C	0.71	0.60	272.3	104.1	1,463.7	-28.9

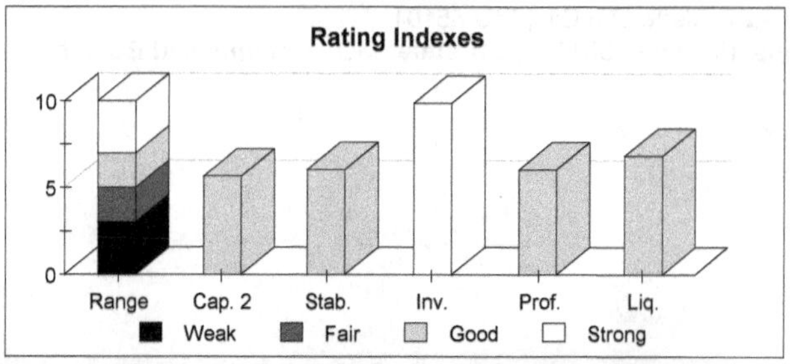

MMM MULTI HEALTH LLC — D Weak

Major Rating Factors: Weak profitability index (2.9 on a scale of 0 to 10). Fair capitalization (4.4) based on fair current risk-adjusted capital (moderate loss scenario). Good liquidity (5.6) with sufficient resources (cash flows and marketable investments) to handle a spike in claims.
Other Rating Factors: High quality investment portfolio (9.9).
Principal Business: Medicaid (100%)
Mem Phys: 18: N/A **17:** N/A **18 MLR** 87.6% **/ 18 Admin Exp** N/A
Enroll(000): Q1 19: 282 **18:** 276 **17:** 258 **Med Exp PMPM:** $156
Principal Investments: Cash and equiv (59%), long-term bonds (41%)
Provider Compensation ($000): FFS ($248,992), capitation ($83,048), bonus arrang ($36,968), other ($136,683)
Total Member Encounters: N/A
Group Affiliation: InnovaCare Inc
Licensed in: PR
Address: 350 CHARDON AVE STE 350, SAN JUAN, PR 918
Phone: (787) 724-7504 **Dom State:** PR **Commenced Bus:** N/A

Data Date	Rating	RACR #1	RACR #2	Total Assets ($mil)	Capital ($mil)	Net Premium ($mil)	Net Income ($mil)
3-19	D	0.84	0.70	136.1	51.9	141.9	2.2
3-18	D	N/A	N/A	162.8	57.8	137.7	1.9
2018	D	0.79	0.66	140.2	49.6	570.7	12.0
2017	D	N/A	N/A	171.7	55.8	541.7	4.2
2016	D	1.10	0.92	63.5	18.8	249.6	-1.3
2015	N/A	N/A	N/A	67.5	15.6	193.4	-2.3
2014	N/A	N/A	N/A	0.6	N/A	N/A	N/A

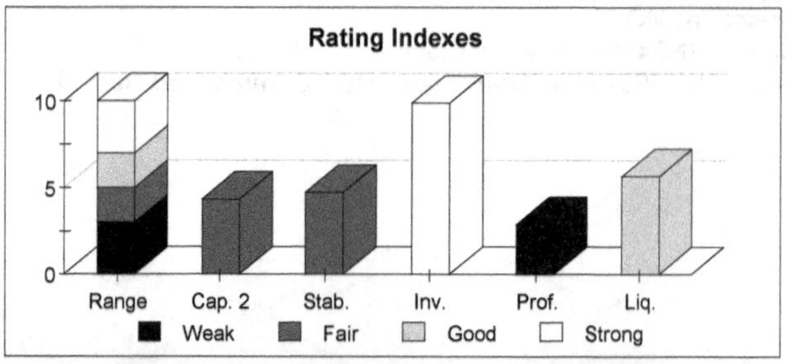

MODA HEALTH PLAN INC — E Very Weak

Major Rating Factors: Weak profitability index (0.9 on a scale of 0 to 10). Weak liquidity (0.0) as a spike in claims may stretch capacity. Fair quality investment portfolio (4.8).
Other Rating Factors: Strong capitalization (7.0) based on excellent current risk-adjusted capital (severe loss scenario).
Principal Business: Comp med (56%), Medicare (43%), other (1%)
Mem Phys: 18: 33,515 **17:** 31,724 **18 MLR** 146.8% **/ 18 Admin Exp** N/A
Enroll(000): Q1 19: 126 **18:** 90 **17:** 73 **Med Exp PMPM:** $592
Principal Investments: Cash and equiv (52%), affiliate common stock (44%), long-term bonds (4%)
Provider Compensation ($000): Contr fee ($595,366), FFS ($36,906)
Total Member Encounters: Phys (74,029), non-phys (62,086)
Group Affiliation: None
Licensed in: AK, CA, ID, OR, TX, WA
Address: 601 SW SECOND AVE, PORTLAND, OR 97204-3156
Phone: (503) 228-6554 **Dom State:** OR **Commenced Bus:** N/A

Data Date	Rating	RACR #1	RACR #2	Total Assets ($mil)	Capital ($mil)	Net Premium ($mil)	Net Income ($mil)
3-19	E	1.36	1.13	310.0	126.2	175.3	-6.3
3-18	E	0.75	0.63	278.2	75.9	168.4	-15.7
2018	E	1.43	1.19	317.0	130.8	437.4	-227.1
2017	E	1.04	0.87	251.8	90.2	561.1	44.2
2016	E	0.45	0.38	366.4	77.6	903.9	-12.9
2015	E-	0.42	0.35	558.7	67.0	777.1	-49.5
2014	C	1.41	1.17	353.7	121.1	749.5	-5.2

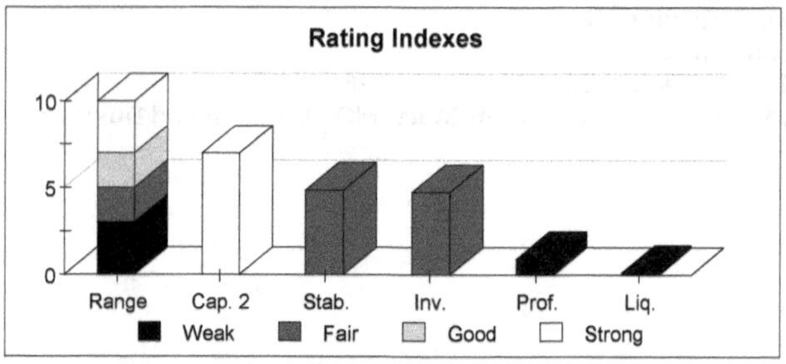

MOLINA HEALTHCARE OF CALIFORNIA C- Fair

Major Rating Factors: Weak overall results on stability tests (1.6 on a scale of 0 to 10) based on a significant 19% decrease in enrollment during the period. Potentially strong support from affiliation with Molina Healthcare Inc. Good overall profitability index (6.2). Good capitalization index (6.6) based on fair current risk-adjusted capital (moderate loss scenario).
Other Rating Factors: Excellent liquidity (7.1) with ample operational cash flow and liquid investments.
Principal Business: Medicaid (71%), Medicare (8%)
Mem Phys: 18: N/A **17:** N/A **18 MLR** 81.3% **/ 18 Admin Exp** N/A
Enroll(000): Q1 19: 606 **18:** 615 **17:** 754 **Med Exp PMPM:** $240
Principal Investments ($000): Cash and equiv ($361,717)
Provider Compensation ($000): None
Total Member Encounters: N/A
Group Affiliation: Molina Healthcare Inc
Licensed in: CA
Address: 200 Oceangate Ste 100, Long Beach, CA 90802
Phone: (800) 562-5442 **Dom State:** CA **Commenced Bus:** April 1989

Data Date	Rating	RACR #1	RACR #2	Total Assets ($mil)	Capital ($mil)	Net Premium ($mil)	Net Income ($mil)
3-19	C-	0.98	0.61	924.0	110.6	589.1	14.7
3-18	C-	1.16	0.72	975.8	167.6	574.2	34.5
2018	C-	1.46	0.91	802.7	169.9	2,280.8	85.8
2017	C-	0.94	0.58	878.9	134.7	2,829.7	57.0
2016	C-	1.63	1.01	973.4	208.6	2,470.4	82.3
2015	C-	1.40	0.86	683.8	175.7	2,272.2	65.2
2014	C-	1.18	0.77	566.4	124.7	1,566.2	67.9

Rating Indexes

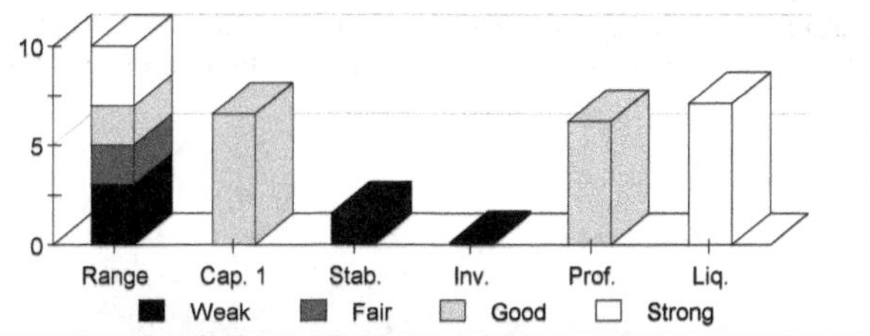

MOLINA HEALTHCARE OF FLORIDA INC C Fair

Major Rating Factors: Weak profitability index (0.9 on a scale of 0 to 10). Strong capitalization (10.0) based on excellent current risk-adjusted capital (severe loss scenario). High quality investment portfolio (9.0).
Other Rating Factors: Excellent liquidity (7.1) with ample operational cash flow and liquid investments.
Principal Business: Medicaid (70%), comp med (15%), Medicare (2%), other (13%)
Mem Phys: 18: 46,361 **17:** 39,132 **18 MLR** 80.5% **/ 18 Admin Exp** N/A
Enroll(000): Q1 19: 144 **18:** 313 **17:** 625 **Med Exp PMPM:** $313
Principal Investments: Cash and equiv (53%), long-term bonds (47%)
Provider Compensation ($000): Contr fee ($1,383,373), capitation ($161,388), FFS ($107,491)
Total Member Encounters: Phys (2,599,566), non-phys (3,650,834)
Group Affiliation: Molina Healthcare Inc
Licensed in: FL
Address: 8300 NW 33rd St Ste 400, Doral, FL 33122
Phone: (866) 422-2541 **Dom State:** FL **Commenced Bus:** N/A

Data Date	Rating	RACR #1	RACR #2	Total Assets ($mil)	Capital ($mil)	Net Premium ($mil)	Net Income ($mil)
3-19	C	4.07	3.39	552.3	373.3	223.0	39.2
3-18	C-	1.71	1.43	1,121.8	263.4	455.6	28.5
2018	C	3.68	3.07	662.0	334.7	1,845.7	93.8
2017	E	1.11	0.93	1,155.3	233.0	2,578.0	-259.7
2016	E	1.83	1.53	802.9	200.0	1,961.9	-62.0
2015	E	1.94	1.62	632.8	137.0	1,217.3	-38.7
2014	E	0.20	0.17	113.8	8.1	454.3	-20.2

Rating Indexes

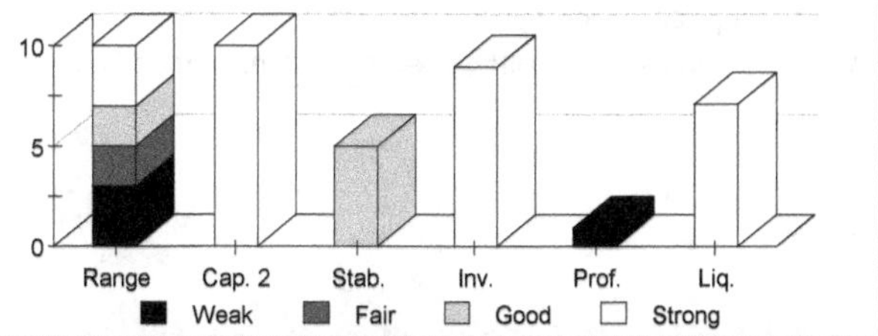

MOLINA HEALTHCARE OF ILLINOIS INC C Fair

Major Rating Factors: Weak profitability index (0.9 on a scale of 0 to 10). Strong capitalization (9.2) based on excellent current risk-adjusted capital (severe loss scenario). High quality investment portfolio (9.9).
Other Rating Factors: Excellent liquidity (7.0) with ample operational cash flow and liquid investments.
Principal Business: Medicaid (94%), Medicare (6%)
Mem Phys: 18: 26,111 **17:** 14,875 **18 MLR** 83.0% **/ 18 Admin Exp** N/A
Enroll(000): Q1 19: 219 **18:** 224 **17:** 165 **Med Exp PMPM:** $341
Principal Investments: Cash and equiv (100%)
Provider Compensation ($000): Contr fee ($513,163), capitation ($234,673), FFS ($116,639)
Total Member Encounters: Phys (1,108,914), non-phys (1,449,430)
Group Affiliation: Molina Healthcare Inc
Licensed in: IL
Address: 1520 Kensington Rd # 212, Oakbrook, IL 60523
Phone: (888) 858-2156 **Dom State:** IL **Commenced Bus:** N/A

Data Date	Rating	RACR #1	RACR #2	Total Assets ($mil)	Capital ($mil)	Net Premium ($mil)	Net Income ($mil)
3-19	C	3.10	2.58	269.9	131.5	281.8	18.5
3-18	C-	1.83	1.52	242.0	75.7	202.9	1.4
2018	C	2.69	2.24	242.3	113.7	1,009.0	38.7
2017	E	1.15	0.96	230.9	73.4	752.5	-90.7
2016	E	1.40	1.16	152.2	35.8	796.9	-20.6
2015	N/A	N/A	N/A	125.0	46.4	467.4	-5.9
2014	E	1.81	1.51	80.6	18.5	170.7	-3.8

Rating Indexes

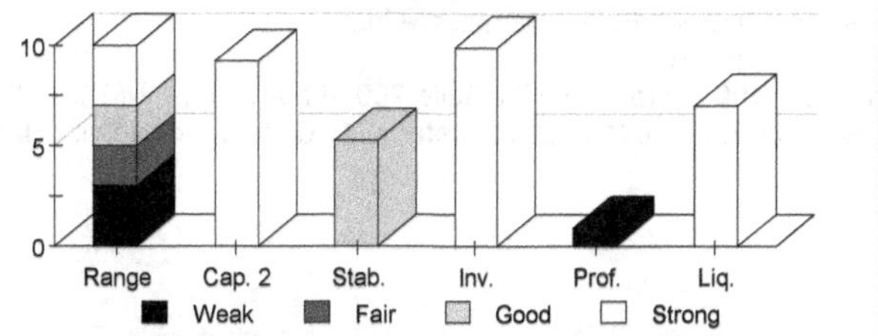

MOLINA HEALTHCARE OF MICHIGAN INC — B — Good

Major Rating Factors: Good overall results on stability tests (5.4 on a scale of 0 to 10). Excellent profitability (8.2). Strong capitalization index (8.3) based on excellent current risk-adjusted capital (severe loss scenario).
Other Rating Factors: High quality investment portfolio (9.9). Excellent liquidity (7.1) with ample operational cash flow and liquid investments.
Principal Business: Medicaid (74%), Medicare (23%), comp med (3%)
Mem Phys: 18: 35,274 **17:** 33,044 **18 MLR** 77.6% **/ 18 Admin Exp** N/A
Enroll(000): Q1 19: 369 **18:** 383 **17:** 398 **Med Exp PMPM:** $295
Principal Investments: Cash and equiv (76%), long-term bonds (24%)
Provider Compensation ($000): Contr fee ($1,197,651), capitation ($142,766), FFS ($64,894)
Total Member Encounters: Phys (2,387,090), non-phys (3,645,252)
Group Affiliation: Molina Healthcare Inc
Licensed in: MI
Address: 880 W Long Lake Rd Suite 600, Troy, MI 48098-4504
Phone: (248) 925-1700 **Dom State:** MI **Commenced Bus:** N/A

Data Date	Rating	RACR #1	RACR #2	Total Assets ($mil)	Capital ($mil)	Net Premium ($mil)	Net Income ($mil)
3-19	B	2.39	2.00	466.0	202.5	421.8	32.7
3-18	B-	N/A	N/A	537.7	170.2	450.2	2.7
2018	B	2.79	2.32	498.5	237.2	1,789.7	97.5
2017	B-	N/A	N/A	422.5	160.3	1,949.3	33.0
2016	B-	2.01	1.68	476.9	172.3	2,104.8	30.9
2015	B-	2.40	2.00	376.0	138.7	1,467.9	53.8
2014	B	2.71	2.26	254.5	125.1	1,059.7	26.7

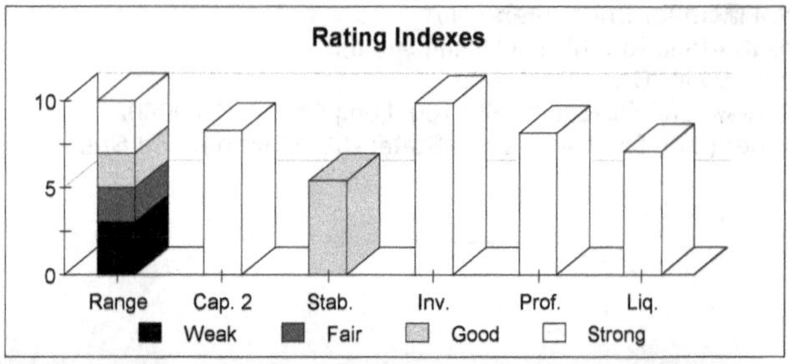

MOLINA HEALTHCARE OF MS INC — D — Weak

Major Rating Factors: Weak profitability index (0.9 on a scale of 0 to 10). Low quality investment portfolio (0.0). Strong capitalization (10.0) based on excellent current risk-adjusted capital (severe loss scenario).
Other Rating Factors: Excellent liquidity (8.2) with ample operational cash flow and liquid investments.
Principal Business: Medicaid (100%)
Mem Phys: 18: 5,680 **17:** N/A **18 MLR** 84.5% **/ 18 Admin Exp** N/A
Enroll(000): Q1 19: 44 **18:** 26 **17:** N/A **Med Exp PMPM:** $373
Principal Investments: Cash and equiv (99%), long-term bonds (1%)
Provider Compensation ($000): Contr fee ($8,222), FFS ($637), capitation ($406)
Total Member Encounters: Phys (16,704), non-phys (26,889)
Group Affiliation: Molina Healthcare Inc
Licensed in: (No states)
Address: , Jackson, MS 39201
Phone: (844) 826-4333 **Dom State:** MS **Commenced Bus:** January 2018

Data Date	Rating	RACR #1	RACR #2	Total Assets ($mil)	Capital ($mil)	Net Premium ($mil)	Net Income ($mil)
3-19	D	6.90	5.75	55.9	18.4	56.5	-10.5
3-18	N/A	N/A	N/A	4.8	4.8	N/A	N/A
2018	C	10.82	9.02	40.9	28.9	22.8	-3.0
2017	N/A	N/A	N/A	5.0	5.0	N/A	N/A
2016	N/A	N/A	N/A	N/A	N/A	N/A	N/A
2015	N/A	N/A	N/A	N/A	N/A	N/A	N/A
2014	N/A	N/A	N/A	N/A	N/A	N/A	N/A

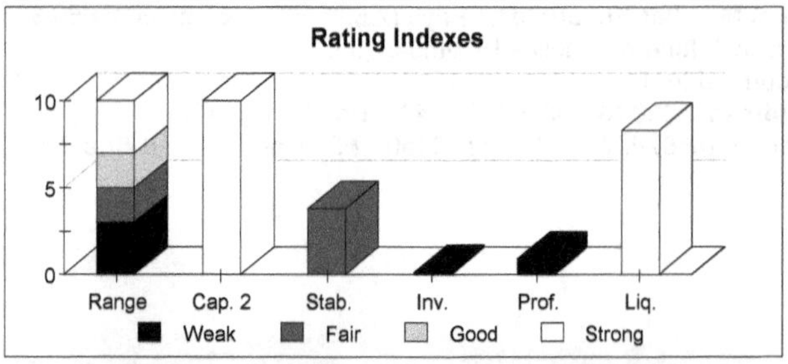

MOLINA HEALTHCARE OF NEW MEXICO — C — Fair

Major Rating Factors: Weak profitability index (0.9 on a scale of 0 to 10). Good overall results on stability tests (6.6) despite a decline in enrollment during 2018. Potentially strong support from affiliation with Molina Healthcare Inc. Strong capitalization index (8.4) based on excellent current risk-adjusted capital (severe loss scenario).
Other Rating Factors: High quality investment portfolio (9.3). Excellent liquidity (7.0) with ample operational cash flow and liquid investments.
Principal Business: Medicaid (87%), comp med (8%), Medicare (4%)
Mem Phys: 18: 16,939 **17:** 16,699 **18 MLR** 81.9% **/ 18 Admin Exp** N/A
Enroll(000): Q1 19: 27 **18:** 222 **17:** 253 **Med Exp PMPM:** $403
Principal Investments: Cash and equiv (79%), long-term bonds (21%)
Provider Compensation ($000): Contr fee ($1,088,668), FFS ($61,850), capitation ($33,611)
Total Member Encounters: Phys (905,521), non-phys (3,833,334)
Group Affiliation: Molina Healthcare Inc
Licensed in: NM
Address: 400 Tijeras Ave NW Suite 200, Albuquerque, NM 87102-3234
Phone: (505) 348-0410 **Dom State:** NM **Commenced Bus:** N/A

Data Date	Rating	RACR #1	RACR #2	Total Assets ($mil)	Capital ($mil)	Net Premium ($mil)	Net Income ($mil)
3-19	C	2.51	2.09	332.8	197.6	40.5	25.2
3-18	C	1.64	1.37	438.2	122.5	363.9	-34.0
2018	C	2.24	1.86	423.6	174.8	1,428.8	14.8
2017	C	1.12	0.94	421.3	118.7	1,414.1	-43.6
2016	C	1.68	1.40	468.3	122.7	1,386.6	-28.5
2015	C	1.61	1.34	409.1	109.7	1,318.0	-1.6
2014	C+	1.33	1.10	304.3	86.1	1,121.2	-24.9

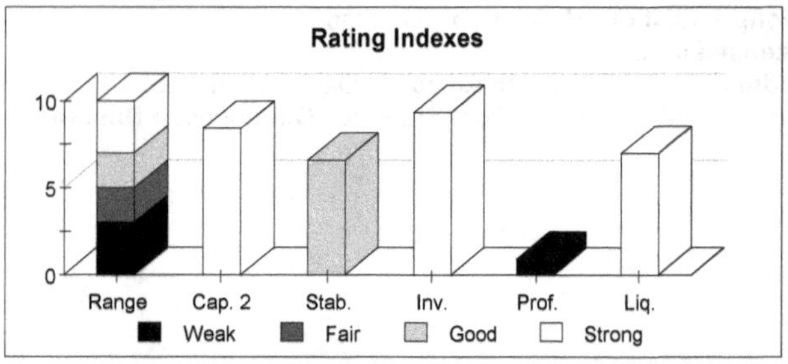

MOLINA HEALTHCARE OF OHIO INC B Good

Major Rating Factors: Fair quality investment portfolio (4.4 on a scale of 0 to 10). Excellent profitability (8.6). Strong capitalization (7.9) based on excellent current risk-adjusted capital (severe loss scenario).
Other Rating Factors: Excellent liquidity (7.0) with ample operational cash flow and liquid investments.
Principal Business: Medicaid (85%), Medicare (11%), comp med (4%)
Mem Phys: 18: 52,032 **17:** 47,392 **18 MLR** 78.7% **/ 18 Admin Exp** N/A
Enroll(000): Q1 19: 295 **18:** 302 **17:** 327 **Med Exp PMPM:** $513
Principal Investments: Cash and equiv (80%), long-term bonds (20%)
Provider Compensation ($000): Contr fee ($1,537,976), capitation ($375,708), FFS ($87,791)
Total Member Encounters: Phys (1,644,131), non-phys (5,481,503)
Group Affiliation: Molina Healthcare Inc
Licensed in: OH
Address: 3000 Corporate Exchange Dr, Columbus, OH 43231
Phone: (888) 562-5442 **Dom State:** OH **Commenced Bus:** N/A

Data Date	Rating	RACR #1	RACR #2	Total Assets ($mil)	Capital ($mil)	Net Premium ($mil)	Net Income ($mil)
3-19	B	2.09	1.74	585.3	252.8	663.3	30.5
3-18	B-	2.43	2.03	650.2	275.4	651.9	42.1
2018	B	2.28	1.90	609.1	277.9	2,593.0	120.3
2017	B-	1.50	1.25	485.3	229.5	2,398.7	44.7
2016	B-	2.29	1.91	507.2	234.9	2,198.5	45.9
2015	B-	1.92	1.60	440.4	190.7	2,270.8	110.0
2014	B	2.25	1.87	464.1	182.7	1,781.8	55.9

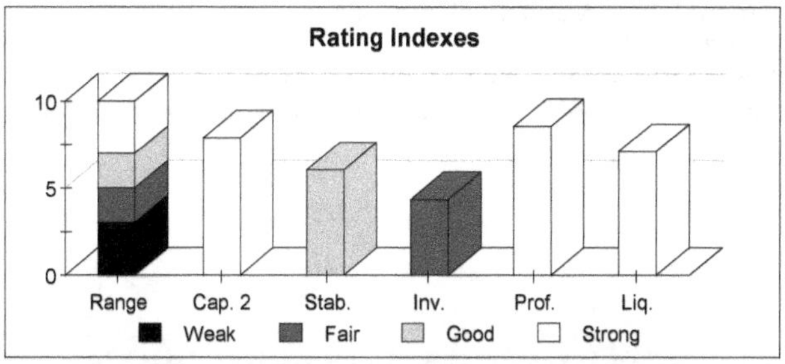

MOLINA HEALTHCARE OF PUERTO RICO INC C+ Fair

Major Rating Factors: Fair profitability index (3.5 on a scale of 0 to 10). Good quality investment portfolio (5.5). Strong capitalization (8.8) based on excellent current risk-adjusted capital (severe loss scenario).
Other Rating Factors: Excellent liquidity (7.0) with ample operational cash flow and liquid investments.
Principal Business: Medicaid (100%)
Mem Phys: 18: 5,203 **17:** 3,411 **18 MLR** 86.4% **/ 18 Admin Exp** N/A
Enroll(000): Q1 19: 208 **18:** 252 **17:** 314 **Med Exp PMPM:** $164
Principal Investments: Cash and equiv (100%)
Provider Compensation ($000): Contr fee ($481,235), capitation ($96,279), FFS ($27,255)
Total Member Encounters: Phys (1,936,445), non-phys (1,837,333)
Group Affiliation: Molina Healthcare Inc
Licensed in: PR
Address: 654 Plaza 654 Munoz Rivera Ave, San Juan, PR 00918-4123
Phone: (787) 200-3300 **Dom State:** PR **Commenced Bus:** N/A

Data Date	Rating	RACR #1	RACR #2	Total Assets ($mil)	Capital ($mil)	Net Premium ($mil)	Net Income ($mil)
3-19	C+	2.82	2.35	198.5	112.6	102.1	6.5
3-18	C-	N/A	N/A	216.7	71.1	185.6	-11.8
2018	C	2.67	2.23	217.5	106.5	710.8	17.5
2017	C-	N/A	N/A	184.4	78.9	731.6	-5.4
2016	C-	1.79	1.49	158.8	66.4	746.3	-9.9
2015	U	1.56	1.30	130.6	49.1	556.6	-5.3
2014	N/A	N/A	N/A	5.1	5.0	N/A	N/A

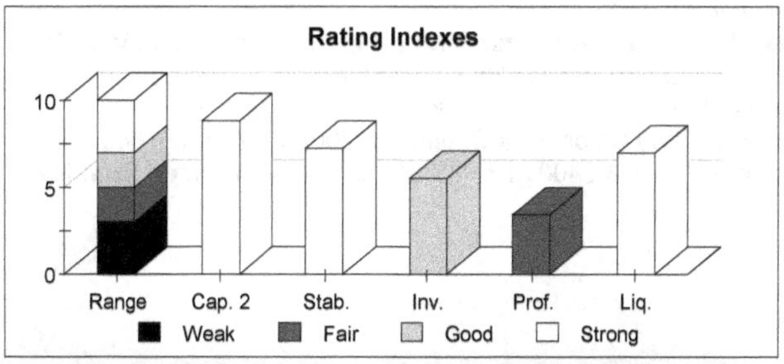

MOLINA HEALTHCARE OF SOUTH CAROLINA B Good

Major Rating Factors: Good overall profitability index (5.2 on a scale of 0 to 10). Strong capitalization (9.0) based on excellent current risk-adjusted capital (severe loss scenario). High quality investment portfolio (9.0).
Other Rating Factors: Excellent liquidity (7.0) with ample operational cash flow and liquid investments.
Principal Business: Medicaid (92%), Medicare (8%)
Mem Phys: 18: 17,007 **17:** 16,039 **18 MLR** 82.7% **/ 18 Admin Exp** N/A
Enroll(000): Q1 19: 126 **18:** 120 **17:** 116 **Med Exp PMPM:** $308
Principal Investments: Cash and equiv (73%), long-term bonds (27%)
Provider Compensation ($000): Contr fee ($383,677), FFS ($27,156), capitation ($25,258)
Total Member Encounters: Phys (798,901), non-phys (1,006,560)
Group Affiliation: Molina Healthcare Inc
Licensed in: OH, SC
Address: 4105 Faber Place Dr Ste 120, North Charleston, SC 29405
Phone: (843) 740-1780 **Dom State:** SC **Commenced Bus:** N/A

Data Date	Rating	RACR #1	RACR #2	Total Assets ($mil)	Capital ($mil)	Net Premium ($mil)	Net Income ($mil)
3-19	B	2.98	2.49	166.1	79.6	140.5	6.9
3-18	C	N/A	N/A	146.6	51.0	136.7	4.9
2018	C+	2.69	2.24	144.7	70.9	525.2	17.1
2017	C	N/A	N/A	116.3	44.1	463.7	-8.3
2016	C	2.51	2.09	102.3	49.0	411.8	13.4
2015	B-	4.79	3.99	125.5	83.0	369.3	17.3
2014	C	2.06	1.72	120.4	59.2	398.2	14.9

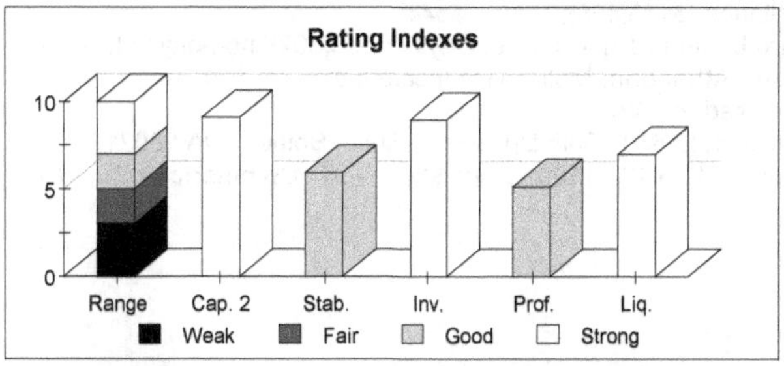

MOLINA HEALTHCARE OF TEXAS INC B Good

Major Rating Factors: Good overall profitability index (6.6 on a scale of 0 to 10). Strong capitalization (7.8) based on excellent current risk-adjusted capital (severe loss scenario). High quality investment portfolio (7.2).
Other Rating Factors: Excellent liquidity (7.3) with ample operational cash flow and liquid investments.
Principal Business: Medicaid (62%), comp med (31%), Medicare (7%)
Mem Phys: 18: 69,925 **17:** 66,760 **18 MLR** 76.9% **/ 18 Admin Exp** N/A
Enroll(000): Q1 19: 357 **18:** 402 **17:** 406 **Med Exp PMPM:** $499
Principal Investments: Cash and equiv (88%), long-term bonds (12%)
Provider Compensation ($000): Contr fee ($2,262,487), FFS ($213,423), capitation ($3,438)
Total Member Encounters: Phys (2,070,673), non-phys (7,180,716)
Group Affiliation: Molina Healthcare Inc
Licensed in: TX
Address: 5605 N MacArthur Blvd Ste 400, Irving, TX 75038
Phone: (877) 665-4622 **Dom State:** TX **Commenced Bus:** N/A

Data Date	Rating	RACR #1	RACR #2	Total Assets ($mil)	Capital ($mil)	Net Premium ($mil)	Net Income ($mil)
3-19	B	1.97	1.64	1,007.6	346.4	760.1	38.3
3-18	B	1.67	1.39	1,080.2	265.8	823.3	16.4
2018	B	2.31	1.93	1,094.2	408.1	3,325.0	187.0
2017	B	1.16	0.97	893.1	250.6	2,864.5	16.8
2016	B-	1.75	1.46	696.6	237.5	2,606.1	82.4
2015	C	1.26	1.05	477.2	148.7	2,056.4	-12.3
2014	C	1.70	1.41	301.0	141.7	1,359.4	-7.3

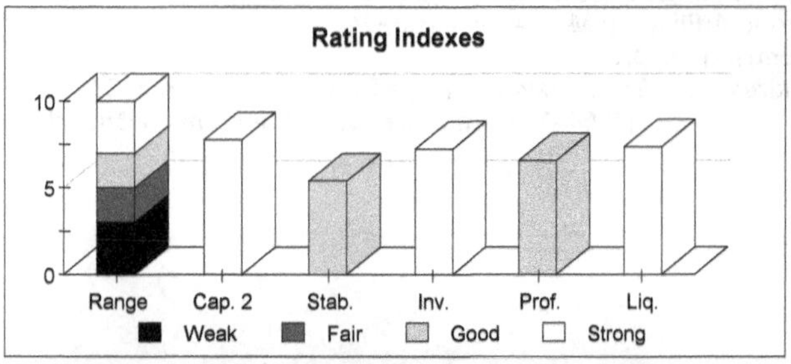

MOLINA HEALTHCARE OF UTAH INC C+ Fair

Major Rating Factors: Fair quality investment portfolio (3.6 on a scale of 0 to 10). Good profitability index (5.0). Good overall results on stability tests (5.8). Rating is significantly influenced by the good financial results of Molina Healthcare Inc.
Other Rating Factors: Strong capitalization index (10.0) based on excellent current risk-adjusted capital (severe loss scenario). Excellent liquidity (7.2) with ample operational cash flow and liquid investments.
Principal Business: Medicaid (56%), Medicare (40%), comp med (5%)
Mem Phys: 18: 19,632 **17:** 11,640 **18 MLR** 70.5% **/ 18 Admin Exp** N/A
Enroll(000): Q1 19: 74 **18:** 77 **17:** 152 **Med Exp PMPM:** $262
Principal Investments: Cash and equiv (64%), long-term bonds (36%)
Provider Compensation ($000): Contr fee ($281,006), FFS ($13,170), capitation ($2,201)
Total Member Encounters: Phys (511,855), non-phys (534,779)
Group Affiliation: Molina Healthcare Inc
Licensed in: UT
Address: 7050 Union Park Center Ste 200, Midvale, UT 84047
Phone: (801) 858-0400 **Dom State:** UT **Commenced Bus:** N/A

Data Date	Rating	RACR #1	RACR #2	Total Assets ($mil)	Capital ($mil)	Net Premium ($mil)	Net Income ($mil)
3-19	C+	3.95	3.29	171.2	74.9	82.5	5.3
3-18	C-	2.52	2.10	235.7	76.1	98.4	3.5
2018	C+	3.71	3.09	151.4	70.1	384.1	37.6
2017	C-	1.50	1.25	245.8	70.0	534.9	-2.5
2016	C	1.84	1.53	191.3	50.7	453.9	-19.1
2015	B-	2.58	2.15	122.7	50.8	343.7	0.6
2014	B	2.53	2.10	107.4	51.2	320.4	-4.3

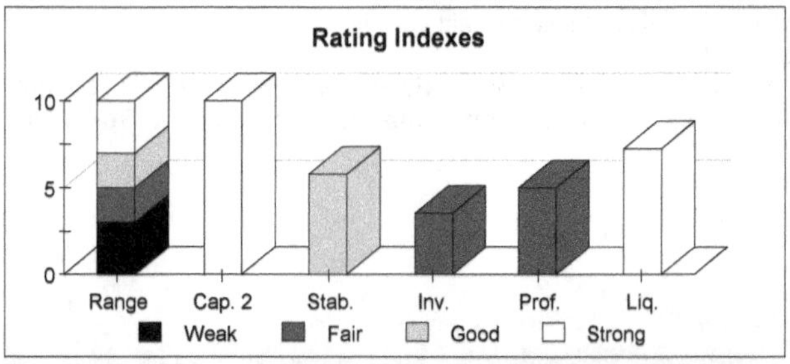

MOLINA HEALTHCARE OF WASHINGTON INC B Good

Major Rating Factors: Good overall profitability index (5.5 on a scale of 0 to 10). Good overall results on stability tests (6.8). Good financial strength from affiliates. Strong capitalization index (8.2) based on excellent current risk-adjusted capital (severe loss scenario).
Other Rating Factors: High quality investment portfolio (9.9). Excellent liquidity (7.0) with sufficient resources (cash flows and marketable investments) to handle a spike in claims.
Principal Business: Medicaid (85%), comp med (9%), Medicare (6%)
Mem Phys: 18: 37,348 **17:** 35,896 **18 MLR** 84.8% **/ 18 Admin Exp** N/A
Enroll(000): Q1 19: 815 **18:** 781 **17:** 777 **Med Exp PMPM:** $224
Principal Investments: Cash and equiv (75%), long-term bonds (25%)
Provider Compensation ($000): Contr fee ($1,305,097), FFS ($631,757), capitation ($115,495), salary ($544)
Total Member Encounters: Phys (3,555,362), non-phys (4,771,437)
Group Affiliation: Molina Healthcare Inc
Licensed in: WA
Address: 21540 - 30th Drive SE Suite, Bothell, WA 98021
Phone: (425) 424-1100 **Dom State:** WA **Commenced Bus:** N/A

Data Date	Rating	RACR #1	RACR #2	Total Assets ($mil)	Capital ($mil)	Net Premium ($mil)	Net Income ($mil)
3-19	B	2.27	1.90	920.4	333.4	673.7	-8.1
3-18	B-	1.89	1.58	839.6	283.7	686.5	-26.8
2018	B	2.31	1.93	855.1	339.0	2,466.1	53.3
2017	B	1.52	1.27	793.8	304.9	2,657.5	69.5
2016	B	1.78	1.48	685.6	235.9	2,307.8	8.2
2015	B	1.99	1.66	589.8	190.8	1,671.7	-3.4
2014	B	1.69	1.41	669.2	145.8	1,357.0	-24.6

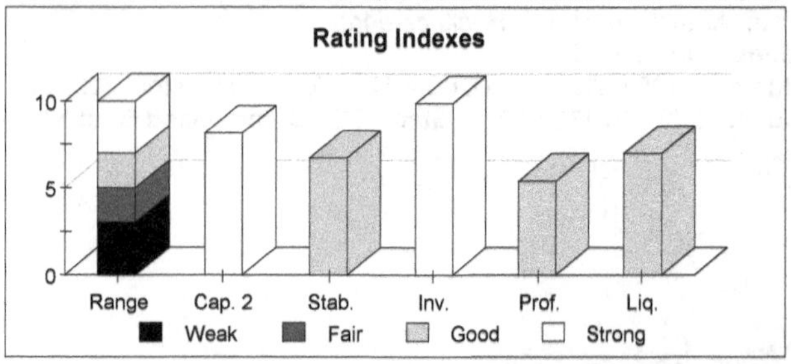

MOLINA HEALTHCARE OF WISCONSIN INC — C — Fair

Major Rating Factors: Weak profitability index (1.2 on a scale of 0 to 10). Strong capitalization (10.0) based on excellent current risk-adjusted capital (severe loss scenario). High quality investment portfolio (9.9).
Other Rating Factors: Excellent liquidity (7.4) with ample operational cash flow and liquid investments.
Principal Business: Medicaid (87%), Medicare (9%), comp med (5%)
Mem Phys: 18: 20,773 **17:** 19,243 **18 MLR** 66.6% **/ 18 Admin Exp** N/A
Enroll(000): Q1 19: 65 **18:** 59 **17:** 118 **Med Exp PMPM:** $143
Principal Investments: Cash and equiv (97%), long-term bonds (3%)
Provider Compensation ($000): Contr fee ($122,738), FFS ($9,636), capitation ($1,157)
Total Member Encounters: Phys (266,670), non-phys (519,457)
Group Affiliation: Molina Healthcare Inc
Licensed in: WI
Address: 11200 W Parkland Ave, Milwaukee, WI 53224-3615
Phone: (888) 999-2404 **Dom State:** WI **Commenced Bus:** N/A

Data Date	Rating	RACR #1	RACR #2	Total Assets ($mil)	Capital ($mil)	Net Premium ($mil)	Net Income ($mil)
3-19	C	5.27	4.39	65.8	35.2	52.5	4.5
3-18	C-	2.63	2.19	123.9	70.4	34.6	0.5
2018	C	4.75	3.96	58.9	30.9	157.4	8.8
2017	E+	1.64	1.37	154.9	68.1	491.3	-12.2
2016	E+	1.86	1.55	141.0	47.2	403.1	-34.2
2015	D	2.04	1.70	69.7	29.9	266.0	4.2
2014	D	2.22	1.85	53.3	22.4	161.0	-0.9

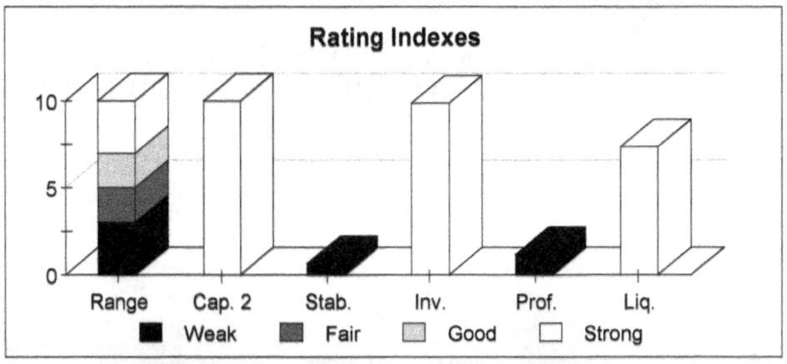

MONARCH HEALTH PLAN — E+ — Very Weak

Major Rating Factors: Weak liquidity (0.0 on a scale of 0 to 10) as a spike in claims may stretch capacity. Good overall results on stability tests (6.3) despite a decline in enrollment during 2018. Excellent profitability (9.0).
Other Rating Factors: Strong capitalization index (7.0) based on good current risk-adjusted capital (moderate loss scenario).
Principal Business: Managed care (100%)
Mem Phys: 18: N/A **17:** N/A **18 MLR** 93.6% **/ 18 Admin Exp** N/A
Enroll(000): Q1 19: 143 **18:** 143 **17:** 154 **Med Exp PMPM:** $371
Principal Investments ($000): Cash and equiv ($159,560)
Provider Compensation ($000): None
Total Member Encounters: N/A
Group Affiliation: None
Licensed in: CA
Address: 11 Technology Drive, Irvine, CA 92618
Phone: (949) 923-3350 **Dom State:** CA **Commenced Bus:** January 2008

Data Date	Rating	RACR #1	RACR #2	Total Assets ($mil)	Capital ($mil)	Net Premium ($mil)	Net Income ($mil)
3-19	E+	1.12	0.67	186.4	83.8	183.9	9.0
3-18	E-	0.17	0.10	145.4	50.3	173.3	6.6
2018	E	0.90	0.54	169.0	73.8	692.1	29.6
2017	E-	0.05	0.03	133.9	44.0	669.4	26.3
2016	E-	N/A	N/A	72.9	17.7	359.8	5.5
2015	E-	N/A	N/A	75.0	12.5	359.9	10.8
2014	E-	N/A	N/A	35.2	1.7	181.9	0.5

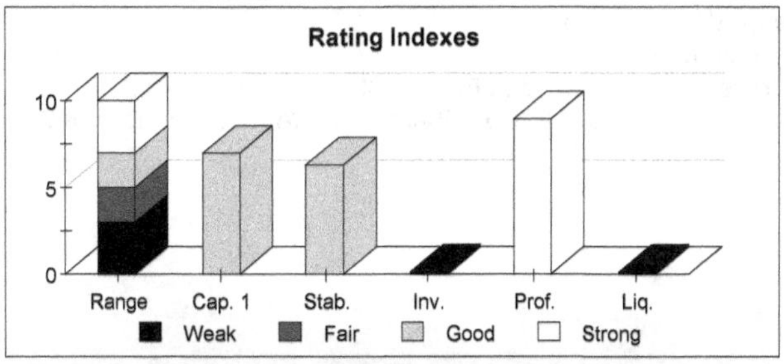

MONTANA HEALTH COOPERATIVE — D — Weak

Major Rating Factors: Weak profitability index (0.9 on a scale of 0 to 10). Fair capitalization (2.9) based on good current risk-adjusted capital (moderate loss scenario). High quality investment portfolio (7.0).
Other Rating Factors: Excellent liquidity (7.0) with ample operational cash flow and liquid investments.
Principal Business: Comp med (100%)
Mem Phys: 18: N/A **17:** N/A **18 MLR** 82.0% **/ 18 Admin Exp** N/A
Enroll(000): Q1 19: 35 **18:** 45 **17:** 30 **Med Exp PMPM:** $368
Principal Investments: Cash and equiv (68%), nonaffiliate common stock (16%), long-term bonds (15%)
Provider Compensation ($000): FFS ($98,011), capitation ($75,944), contr fee ($15,494)
Total Member Encounters: N/A
Group Affiliation: None
Licensed in: ID, MT
Address: 1005 PARTRIDGE PLACE, HELENA, MT 59601
Phone: (406) 447-9510 **Dom State:** MT **Commenced Bus:** N/A

Data Date	Rating	RACR #1	RACR #2	Total Assets ($mil)	Capital ($mil)	Net Premium ($mil)	Net Income ($mil)
3-19	D	1.07	0.89	135.3	52.1	56.3	7.0
3-18	D	N/A	N/A	116.0	43.6	61.1	12.4
2018	D	0.83	0.69	125.5	41.9	258.0	13.4
2017	D	N/A	N/A	86.0	39.1	156.6	15.1
2016	D	0.62	0.51	51.8	24.0	123.0	-19.7
2015	D+	0.77	0.64	67.2	33.0	135.3	-40.7
2014	D+	1.27	1.06	54.4	25.9	50.8	-3.5

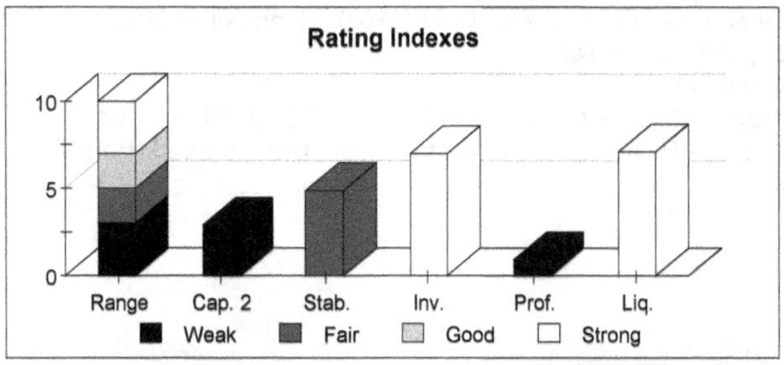

MOTIVHEALTH INSURANCE CO — D — Weak

Major Rating Factors: Weak profitability index (0.9 on a scale of 0 to 10). Good capitalization (6.0) based on good current risk-adjusted capital (severe loss scenario). High quality investment portfolio (9.9).
Other Rating Factors: Excellent liquidity (7.1) with ample operational cash flow and liquid investments.
Principal Business: Comp med (58%), other (42%)
Mem Phys: 18: 15,766 **17:** 27,314 **18 MLR** 82.9% **/ 18 Admin Exp** N/A
Enroll(000): Q1 19: 23 **18:** 18 **17:** 10 **Med Exp PMPM:** $46
Principal Investments: Long-term bonds (54%), cash and equiv (46%)
Provider Compensation ($000): Contr fee ($9,442)
Total Member Encounters: Phys (8,781), non-phys (65,854)
Group Affiliation: None
Licensed in: UT
Address: 10437 S Jordan Gateway, SOUTH JORDAN, UT 84095
Phone: (844) 234-4472 **Dom State:** UT **Commenced Bus:** N/A

Data Date	Rating	RACR #1	RACR #2	Total Assets ($mil)	Capital ($mil)	Net Premium ($mil)	Net Income ($mil)
3-19	D	1.08	0.90	9.5	1.8	3.7	0.0
3-18	D	N/A	N/A	8.5	2.3	2.4	0.4
2018	D	1.19	0.99	7.2	2.0	10.4	0.8
2017	D	N/A	N/A	6.8	1.6	12.0	1.0
2016	D	0.78	0.65	4.6	1.0	4.8	-3.2
2015	N/A	N/A	N/A	2.4	2.2	N/A	-0.9
2014	N/A	N/A	N/A	N/A	N/A	N/A	N/A

Rating Indexes

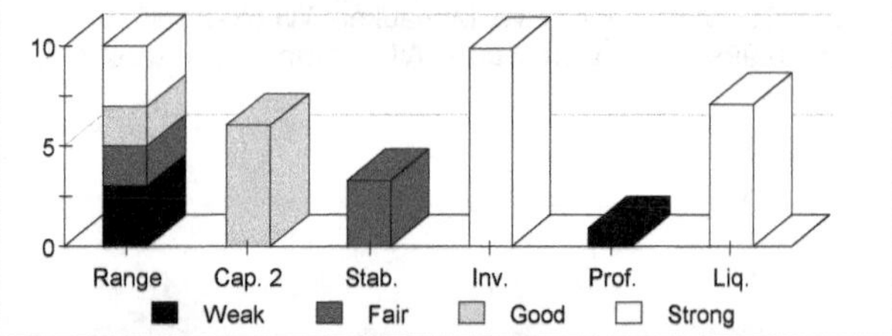

MOUNT CARMEL HEALTH INS CO — B- — Good

Major Rating Factors: Strong capitalization (10.0 on a scale of 0 to 10) based on excellent current risk-adjusted capital (severe loss scenario). High quality investment portfolio (9.9). Excellent liquidity (7.0) with ample operational cash flow and liquid investments.
Other Rating Factors: Weak profitability index (1.9).
Principal Business: Medicare (100%)
Mem Phys: 18: 8,801 **17:** 7,938 **18 MLR** 87.7% **/ 18 Admin Exp** N/A
Enroll(000): Q1 19: 1 **18:** 1 **17:** 1 **Med Exp PMPM:** $806
Principal Investments: Long-term bonds (62%), cash and equiv (38%)
Provider Compensation ($000): Contr fee ($6,419), FFS ($1,101), capitation ($35)
Total Member Encounters: Phys (22,711), non-phys (7,574)
Group Affiliation: None
Licensed in: OH
Address: 6150 East BRd St EE320, COLUMBUS, OH 43213
Phone: (614) 546-3211 **Dom State:** OH **Commenced Bus:** N/A

Data Date	Rating	RACR #1	RACR #2	Total Assets ($mil)	Capital ($mil)	Net Premium ($mil)	Net Income ($mil)
3-19	B-	4.98	4.15	7.4	6.0	2.2	-0.3
3-18	C	4.84	4.03	7.9	5.8	2.1	-0.5
2018	B-	5.22	4.35	7.3	6.3	8.7	0.1
2017	D	3.73	3.10	7.7	6.3	8.1	0.0
2016	D	1.40	1.17	9.0	5.4	24.8	-1.3
2015	D	1.67	1.39	6.6	3.6	14.2	-1.1
2014	D	2.75	2.29	7.3	5.9	12.5	-1.0

Rating Indexes

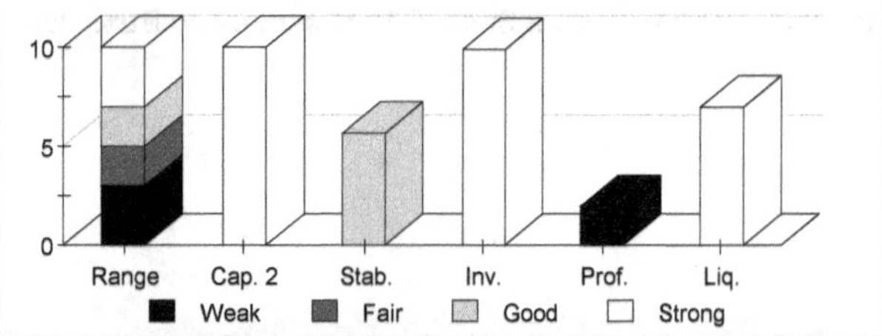

MOUNT CARMEL HEALTH PLAN INC — B — Good

Major Rating Factors: Good overall results on stability tests (5.9 on a scale of 0 to 10). Fair profitability index (4.9). Strong capitalization index (10.0) based on excellent current risk-adjusted capital (severe loss scenario).
Other Rating Factors: High quality investment portfolio (9.9). Excellent liquidity (7.3) with ample operational cash flow and liquid investments.
Principal Business: Medicare (100%)
Mem Phys: 18: 8,801 **17:** 7,938 **18 MLR** 84.3% **/ 18 Admin Exp** N/A
Enroll(000): Q1 19: 46 **18:** 49 **17:** 54 **Med Exp PMPM:** $830
Principal Investments: Cash and equiv (44%), long-term bonds (40%), nonaffiliate common stock (15%), affiliate common stock (1%)
Provider Compensation ($000): Contr fee ($421,744), FFS ($51,765), capitation ($8,668), bonus arrang ($8,221)
Total Member Encounters: Phys (479,933), non-phys (75,252)
Group Affiliation: None
Licensed in: OH
Address: 6150 East Broad Street EE320, COLUMBUS, OH 43213
Phone: (614) 546-3211 **Dom State:** OH **Commenced Bus:** N/A

Data Date	Rating	RACR #1	RACR #2	Total Assets ($mil)	Capital ($mil)	Net Premium ($mil)	Net Income ($mil)
3-19	B	5.17	4.31	347.1	252.7	138.3	8.1
3-18	B-	4.10	3.42	357.2	208.5	144.2	9.5
2018	B	4.85	4.05	335.5	238.4	582.5	45.2
2017	B-	3.92	3.26	305.0	200.1	607.2	33.9
2016	C	2.75	2.29	277.9	148.8	566.2	-9.6
2015	C	3.33	2.78	275.3	155.1	509.8	-1.2
2014	B-	4.19	3.50	251.3	210.6	473.1	6.8

Rating Indexes

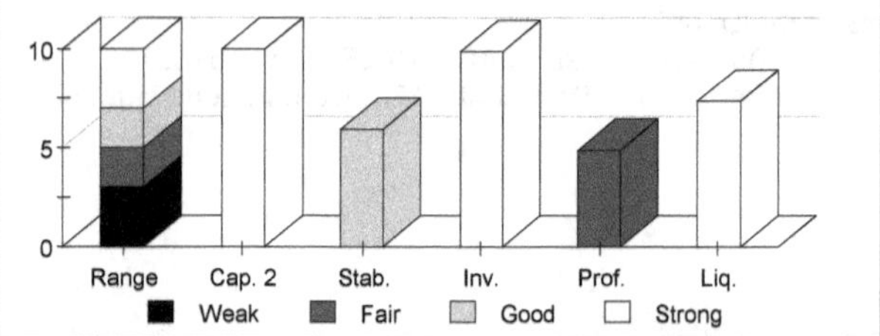

MUTUAL OF OMAHA INSURANCE COMPANY B- Good

Major Rating Factors: Good capitalization (6.3 on a scale of 0 to 10) based on good risk adjusted capital (severe loss scenario). Capital levels have been relatively consistent over the last five years. Good quality investment portfolio (6.1) despite mixed results such as: minimal exposure to mortgages and large holdings of BBB rated bonds but minimal holdings in junk bonds. Good liquidity (6.9).
Other Rating Factors: Good overall results on stability tests (5.2) excellent operational trends and excellent risk diversification. Fair profitability (3.1) with operating losses during the first three months of 2019.
Principal Business: Reinsurance (57%), individual health insurance (38%), and group health insurance (6%).
Principal Investments: NonCMO investment grade bonds (42%), common & preferred stock (38%), CMOs and structured securities (9%), mortgages in good standing (4%), and noninv. grade bonds (1%).
Investments in Affiliates: 39%
Group Affiliation: Mutual Of Omaha Group
Licensed in: All states, the District of Columbia and Puerto Rico
Commenced Business: January 1910
Address: MUTUAL OF OMAHA PLAZA, OMAHA, NE 68175
Phone: (402) 342-7600 **Domicile State:** NE **NAIC Code:** 71412

Data Date	Rating	RACR #1	RACR #2	Total Assets ($mil)	Capital ($mil)	Net Premium ($mil)	Net Income ($mil)
3-19	B-	0.98	0.91	8,332.2	3,209.7	867.9	-9.6
3-18	B	1.01	0.94	7,813.6	3,153.5	806.1	-15.7
2018	B-	0.98	0.92	8,084.0	3,172.7	3,282.6	-157.4
2017	B+	1.03	0.96	7,824.4	3,189.6	3,036.5	-7.1
2016	B+	1.07	0.99	7,278.9	3,048.3	2,726.5	103.4
2015	B+	1.02	0.95	6,945.1	2,862.8	2,411.8	11.2
2014	B+	1.02	0.96	6,426.8	2,795.7	2,186.3	30.4

Risk-Adjusted Capital Ratio #2
(Severe Loss Scenario)

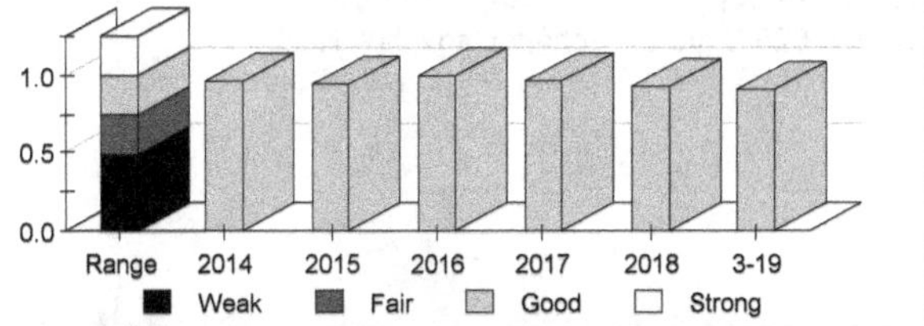

MVP HEALTH INS CO D- Weak

Major Rating Factors: Weak profitability index (1.1 on a scale of 0 to 10). Strong capitalization (8.1) based on excellent current risk-adjusted capital (severe loss scenario). High quality investment portfolio (9.4).
Other Rating Factors: Excellent liquidity (7.1) with ample operational cash flow and liquid investments.
Principal Business: Comp med (100%)
Mem Phys: 18: 50,439 **17:** 50,238 **18 MLR** 91.5% **/ 18 Admin Exp** N/A
Enroll(000): Q1 19: 0 **18:** 3 **17:** 4 **Med Exp PMPM:** $434
Principal Investments: Cash and equiv (96%), long-term bonds (4%)
Provider Compensation ($000): Contr fee ($19,030), FFS ($501), capitation ($9), other ($324)
Total Member Encounters: Phys (35,250), non-phys (27,375)
Group Affiliation: MVP Health Care Inc
Licensed in: NY, VT
Address: 625 State St, Schenectady, NY 12305
Phone: (518) 370-4793 **Dom State:** NY **Commenced Bus:** N/A

Data Date	Rating	RACR #1	RACR #2	Total Assets ($mil)	Capital ($mil)	Net Premium ($mil)	Net Income ($mil)
3-19	D-	2.24	1.87	5.4	3.9	0.3	-0.3
3-18	E+	N/A	N/A	8.3	3.3	5.3	-1.3
2018	D-	2.37	1.97	7.3	4.3	19.8	-0.7
2017	E+	N/A	N/A	7.0	3.0	20.9	-1.0
2016	E+	4.98	4.15	31.9	25.0	69.4	10.5
2015	E	2.54	2.12	112.0	64.1	251.3	-9.8
2014	E	2.30	1.92	117.8	77.4	351.5	5.2

Rating Indexes

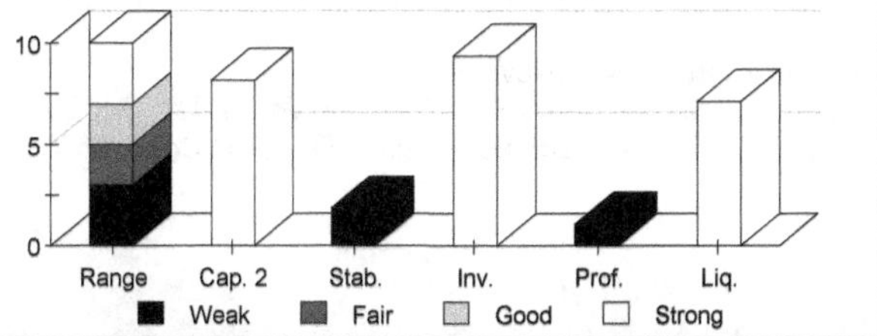

MVP HEALTH PLAN INC B Good

Major Rating Factors: Good quality investment portfolio (4.9 on a scale of 0 to 10). Good overall results on stability tests (6.4). Fair profitability index (4.2).
Other Rating Factors: Strong capitalization index (8.0) based on excellent current risk-adjusted capital (severe loss scenario). Excellent liquidity (6.9) with sufficient resources (cash flows and marketable investments) to handle a spike in claims.
Principal Business: Medicaid (46%), Medicare (27%), comp med (23%), FEHB (4%)
Mem Phys: 18: 47,465 **17:** 46,940 **18 MLR** 90.8% **/ 18 Admin Exp** N/A
Enroll(000): Q1 19: 379 **18:** 371 **17:** 364 **Med Exp PMPM:** $541
Principal Investments: Long-term bonds (40%), cash and equiv (26%), nonaffiliate common stock (11%), other (23%)
Provider Compensation ($000): Contr fee ($2,017,907), capitation ($125,551), FFS ($77,317), bonus arrang ($65,358), other ($54,895)
Total Member Encounters: Phys (6,138,880), non-phys (2,822,815)
Group Affiliation: MVP Health Care Inc
Licensed in: NY, VT
Address: 625 State Street, Schenectady, NY 12305
Phone: (518) 370-4793 **Dom State:** NY **Commenced Bus:** N/A

Data Date	Rating	RACR #1	RACR #2	Total Assets ($mil)	Capital ($mil)	Net Premium ($mil)	Net Income ($mil)
3-19	B	2.13	1.78	711.3	406.6	666.7	2.3
3-18	B	1.97	1.64	734.6	353.8	653.4	-17.9
2018	B	2.12	1.77	736.7	404.7	2,649.0	24.5
2017	B	2.12	1.77	696.1	388.7	2,516.4	43.7
2016	B-	2.30	1.92	736.0	343.5	2,501.8	9.7
2015	B-	3.63	3.02	570.7	389.9	1,560.1	5.8
2014	B-	3.42	2.85	485.7	328.0	1,656.7	-23.7

Rating Indexes

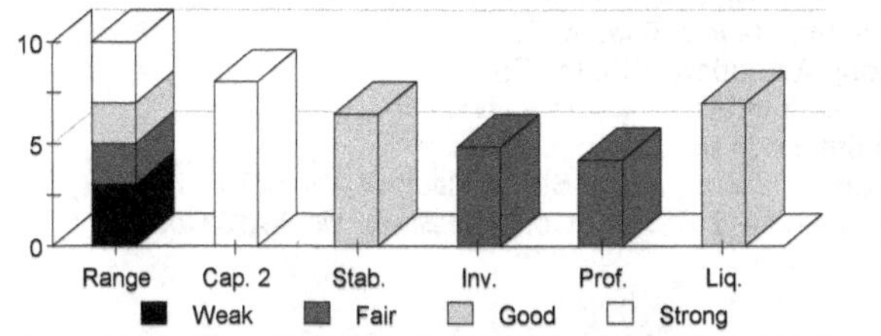

MVP HEALTH SERVICES CORP C Fair

Major Rating Factors: Fair capitalization (4.8 on a scale of 0 to 10) based on good current risk-adjusted capital (severe loss scenario). Weak profitability index (1.6). Good liquidity (6.7) with sufficient resources (cash flows and marketable investments) to handle a spike in claims.
Other Rating Factors: High quality investment portfolio (9.3).
Principal Business: Comp med (99%)
Mem Phys: 18: 37,556 **17:** 35,856 **18 MLR** 84.9% **/ 18 Admin Exp** N/A
Enroll(000): Q1 19: 118 **18:** 130 **17:** 145 **Med Exp PMPM:** $395
Principal Investments: Long-term bonds (81%), nonaffiliate common stock (10%), cash and equiv (9%)
Provider Compensation ($000): Contr fee ($462,079), FFS ($122,991), bonus arrang ($7,997), capitation ($4,127), other ($34,646)
Total Member Encounters: Phys (1,453,921), non-phys (495,756)
Group Affiliation: MVP Health Care Inc
Licensed in: NY
Address: 625 State St, Schenectady, NY 12305
Phone: (518) 370-4793 **Dom State:** NY **Commenced Bus:** N/A

Data Date	Rating	RACR #1	RACR #2	Total Assets ($mil)	Capital ($mil)	Net Premium ($mil)	Net Income ($mil)
3-19	C	0.90	0.75	166.5	88.9	182.5	3.0
3-18	C	0.54	0.45	152.7	59.1	180.8	-10.6
2018	C	0.84	0.70	167.2	85.7	734.1	15.9
2017	C-	0.52	0.44	164.7	70.3	670.6	-20.6
2016	C	0.92	0.77	135.1	69.6	491.4	6.4
2015	C-	0.93	0.78	64.6	28.0	187.6	0.3
2014	N/A	N/A	N/A	65.2	27.4	101.3	-25.1

Rating Indexes

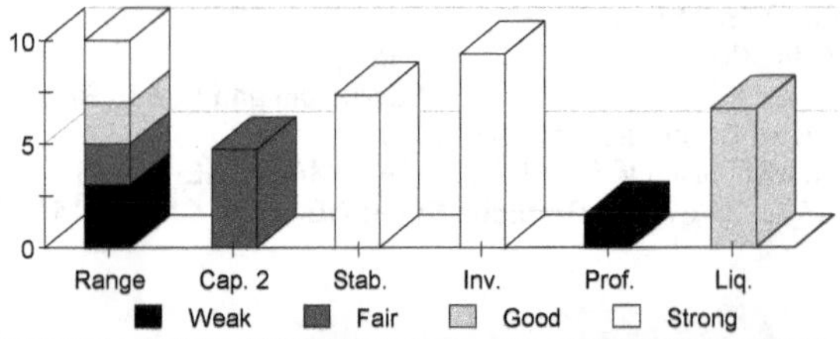

NATIONAL FOUNDATION LIFE INSURANCE COMPANY * B+ Good

Major Rating Factors: Good overall results on stability tests (6.3 on a scale of 0 to 10). Stability strengths include excellent operational trends and good risk diversification. Strong capitalization (7.6) based on excellent risk adjusted capital (severe loss scenario). Moreover, capital has steadily grown over the last five years. High quality investment portfolio (8.0).
Other Rating Factors: Excellent profitability (9.2). Excellent liquidity (7.4).
Principal Business: Individual health insurance (55%), group health insurance (34%), individual life insurance (7%), and reinsurance (4%).
Principal Investments: NonCMO investment grade bonds (57%), CMOs and structured securities (26%), cash (13%), and noninv. grade bonds (1%).
Investments in Affiliates: None
Group Affiliation: Credit Suisse Group
Licensed in: AL, AK, AZ, AR, CA, CO, DC, DE, GA, ID, IN, IA, KS, KY, LA, ME, MS, MO, MT, NE, NV, NM, NC, ND, OH, OK, OR, PA, SC, SD, TN, TX, UT, VA, WA, WY
Commenced Business: November 1983
Address: 300 Burnett Street Suite 200, Fort Worth, TX 76102-2734
Phone: (817) 878-3300 **Domicile State:** TX **NAIC Code:** 98205

Data Date	Rating	RACR #1	RACR #2	Total Assets ($mil)	Capital ($mil)	Net Premium ($mil)	Net Income ($mil)
3-19	B+	1.76	1.37	59.6	36.3	22.6	3.4
3-18	B	1.67	1.30	43.6	24.4	18.2	2.6
2018	B+	1.66	1.28	53.8	33.0	78.6	10.7
2017	B	1.61	1.25	38.9	21.7	53.7	5.4
2016	B	2.10	1.63	33.8	19.9	40.1	5.4
2015	B-	2.08	1.61	29.9	16.5	34.9	6.0
2014	C	1.38	1.06	25.1	11.5	37.3	2.3

Adverse Trends in Operations

Change in asset mix during 2018 (4%)
Change in asset mix during 2016 (4.5%)
Decrease in premium volume from 2014 to 2015 (6%)

NATIONAL GUARDIAN LIFE INSURANCE COMPANY B- Good

Major Rating Factors: Good quality investment portfolio (5.9 on a scale of 0 to 10) despite mixed results such as: minimal exposure to mortgages and large holdings of BBB rated bonds but small junk bond holdings. Good overall profitability (5.8) although investment income, in comparison to reserve requirements, is below regulatory standards. Good liquidity (6.0).
Other Rating Factors: Good overall results on stability tests (5.3) excellent operational trends, good risk adjusted capital for prior years and excellent risk diversification. Strong capitalization (7.0) based on excellent risk adjusted capital (severe loss scenario).
Principal Business: Group health insurance (38%), group life insurance (34%), individual life insurance (18%), reinsurance (5%), and other lines (4%).
Principal Investments: NonCMO investment grade bonds (81%), CMOs and structured securities (5%), common & preferred stock (4%), mortgages in good standing (3%), and misc. investments (5%).
Investments in Affiliates: 2%
Group Affiliation: NGL Ins Group
Licensed in: All states except NY, PR
Commenced Business: October 1910
Address: 2 East Gilman Street, Madison, WI 53703-1494
Phone: (608) 257-5611 **Domicile State:** WI **NAIC Code:** 66583

Data Date	Rating	RACR #1	RACR #2	Total Assets ($mil)	Capital ($mil)	Net Premium ($mil)	Net Income ($mil)
3-19	B-	1.59	1.02	4,139.1	353.4	161.1	6.5
3-18	B-	1.59	1.01	3,928.8	336.3	163.0	6.3
2018	B-	1.52	0.98	4,080.0	333.2	653.9	30.0
2017	B-	1.53	0.98	3,884.4	322.6	603.4	28.8
2016	B-	1.52	0.95	3,657.9	293.3	553.0	18.1
2015	B-	1.45	0.91	3,422.2	271.1	790.0	-4.5
2014	B	1.47	0.96	2,948.3	250.1	476.1	24.4

Rating Indexes

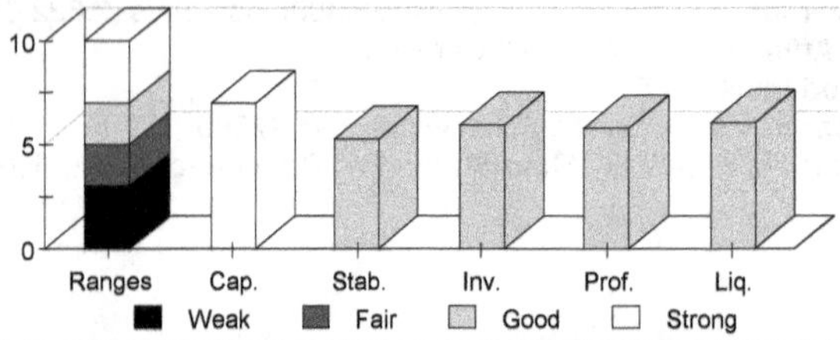

NATIONAL TEACHERS ASSOCIATES LIFE INSURANCE COMPAN — B — Good

Major Rating Factors: Good quality investment portfolio (6.8 on a scale of 0 to 10) despite mixed results such as: minimal exposure to mortgages and large holdings of BBB rated bonds but small junk bond holdings. Good overall results on stability tests (6.0). Stability strengths include excellent operational trends and excellent risk diversification. Fair profitability (4.5) with investment income below regulatory standards in relation to interest assumptions of reserves.
Other Rating Factors: Strong capitalization (9.0) based on excellent risk adjusted capital (severe loss scenario). Excellent liquidity (8.6).
Principal Business: Individual health insurance (98%) and individual life insurance (2%).
Principal Investments: NonCMO investment grade bonds (53%), CMOs and structured securities (32%), noninv. grade bonds (5%), common & preferred stock (4%), and misc. investments (6%).
Investments in Affiliates: 2%
Group Affiliation: Ellard Family Holdings Inc
Licensed in: All states except NY, PR
Commenced Business: July 1938
Address: 4949 Keller Springs Rd, Addison, TX 75001
Phone: (972) 532-2100 **Domicile State:** TX **NAIC Code:** 87963

Data Date	Rating	RACR #1	RACR #2	Total Assets ($mil)	Capital ($mil)	Net Premium ($mil)	Net Income ($mil)
3-19	B	3.56	2.33	596.1	146.7	32.4	7.0
3-18	B	3.04	2.04	557.1	122.7	32.4	7.6
2018	B	3.46	2.29	583.6	138.7	130.2	28.9
2017	B	2.89	1.95	544.9	115.9	130.7	20.3
2016	B	2.86	1.94	510.5	102.4	129.2	11.2
2015	B	N/A	N/A	464.1	92.1	123.6	11.1
2014	B	2.47	1.73	422.9	80.9	117.5	7.8

Adverse Trends in Operations

Increase in policy surrenders from 2017 to 2018 (109%)

NEBRASKA TOTAL CARE INC — C- — Fair

Major Rating Factors: Weak profitability index (0.9 on a scale of 0 to 10). Weak liquidity (2.1) as a spike in claims may stretch capacity. Strong capitalization (7.4) based on excellent current risk-adjusted capital (severe loss scenario).
Other Rating Factors: High quality investment portfolio (9.0).
Principal Business: Medicaid (100%)
Mem Phys: 18: 21,798 **17:** 13,794 **18 MLR** 94.5% **/ 18 Admin Exp** N/A
Enroll(000): Q1 19: 83 **18:** 83 **17:** 82 **Med Exp PMPM:** $421
Principal Investments: Long-term bonds (71%), cash and equiv (29%)
Provider Compensation ($000): Contr fee ($295,365), bonus arrang ($102,003), salary ($6,518), capitation ($3,309), other ($7,654)
Total Member Encounters: Phys (517,258), non-phys (1,207,627)
Group Affiliation: None
Licensed in: NE
Address: 2525 N 117th Ave Ste 100, Omaha, NE 68164
Phone: (314) 725-4477 **Dom State:** NE **Commenced Bus:** N/A

Data Date	Rating	RACR #1	RACR #2	Total Assets ($mil)	Capital ($mil)	Net Premium ($mil)	Net Income ($mil)
3-19	C-	1.67	1.39	101.8	36.9	117.5	2.4
3-18	N/A	N/A	N/A	116.0	37.6	116.7	-12.5
2018	C-	1.60	1.33	98.2	34.9	444.8	-16.3
2017	N/A	N/A	N/A	112.6	45.7	426.8	-26.8
2016	N/A	N/A	N/A	1.5	1.5	N/A	N/A
2015	N/A	N/A	N/A	N/A	N/A	N/A	N/A
2014	N/A	N/A	N/A	N/A	N/A	N/A	N/A

Rating Indexes

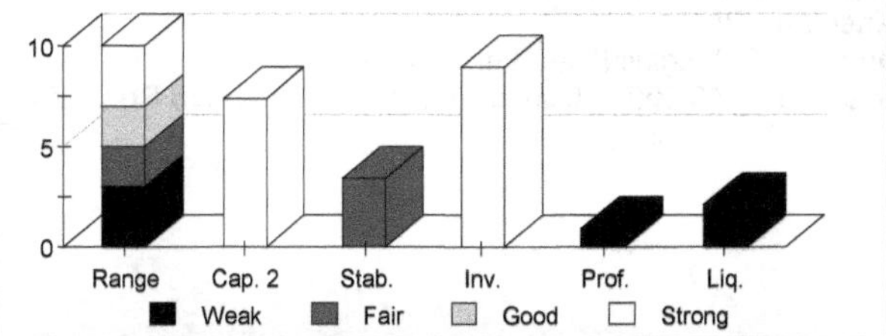

NEIGHBORHOOD HEALTH PARTNERSHIP INC — C — Fair

Major Rating Factors: Fair liquidity (3.1 on a scale of 0 to 10) as cash resources may not be adequate to cover a spike in claims. Weak overall results on stability tests (1.8). Rating is significantly influenced by the good financial results of . Good capitalization index (6.8) based on excellent current risk-adjusted capital (severe loss scenario).
Other Rating Factors: Excellent profitability (8.3). High quality investment portfolio (9.3).
Principal Business: Comp med (100%)
Mem Phys: 18: 60,867 **17:** 21,245 **18 MLR** 83.6% **/ 18 Admin Exp** N/A
Enroll(000): Q1 19: 170 **18:** 159 **17:** 130 **Med Exp PMPM:** $345
Principal Investments: Long-term bonds (98%), cash and equiv (2%)
Provider Compensation ($000): Contr fee ($524,870), FFS ($45,328), capitation ($13,160)
Total Member Encounters: Phys (1,068,234), non-phys (36,842)
Group Affiliation: None
Licensed in: FL
Address: 7600 CORPORATE CENTER DRIVE, MIRAMAR, FL 33027
Phone: (800) 825-8792 **Dom State:** FL **Commenced Bus:** N/A

Data Date	Rating	RACR #1	RACR #2	Total Assets ($mil)	Capital ($mil)	Net Premium ($mil)	Net Income ($mil)
3-19	C	1.22	1.01	184.9	52.6	209.4	20.1
3-18	B	2.05	1.70	177.3	64.8	168.2	-0.3
2018	C	0.86	0.72	156.2	37.5	714.4	17.8
2017	B	1.25	1.04	150.6	62.6	622.5	46.0
2016	B	2.11	1.76	149.0	60.2	578.0	41.4
2015	B	1.48	1.24	121.7	39.9	528.5	26.1
2014	B-	1.18	0.99	93.4	28.4	485.6	21.9

Rating Indexes

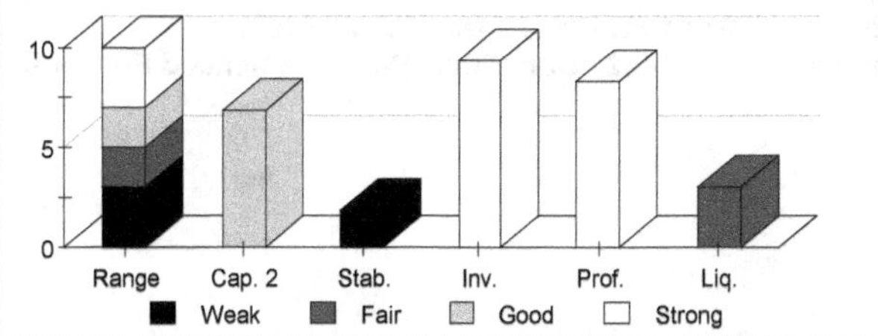

NEIGHBORHOOD HEALTH PLAN D Weak

Major Rating Factors: Weak profitability index (0.9 on a scale of 0 to 10). Low quality investment portfolio (0.4). Fair overall results on stability tests (3.9) based on a significant 66% decrease in enrollment during the period, a steep decline in premium revenue in 2018.
Other Rating Factors: Strong capitalization index (9.3) based on excellent current risk-adjusted capital (severe loss scenario). Excellent liquidity (7.0) with sufficient resources (cash flows and marketable investments) to handle a spike in claims.
Principal Business: Comp med (65%), Medicaid (35%)
Mem Phys: 18: 37,912 **17:** 35,060 **18 MLR** 87.5% **/ 18 Admin Exp** N/A
Enroll(000): Q1 19: 115 **18:** 121 **17:** 350 **Med Exp PMPM:** $475
Principal Investments: Nonaffiliate common stock (67%), cash and equiv (32%)
Provider Compensation ($000): Contr fee ($620,605), capitation ($357,784), FFS ($12,645), other ($33,039)
Total Member Encounters: Phys (1,145,120), non-phys (1,283,712)
Group Affiliation: Partners HealthCare System Inc
Licensed in: MA
Address: 253 Summer St, Somerville, MA 02145-1446
Phone: (857) 282-3374 **Dom State:** MA **Commenced Bus:** N/A

Data Date	Rating	RACR #1	RACR #2	Total Assets ($mil)	Capital ($mil)	Net Premium ($mil)	Net Income ($mil)
3-19	D	3.17	2.64	393.9	279.9	196.3	-0.2
3-18	D	2.21	1.84	506.4	347.2	415.1	10.2
2018	D	3.07	2.56	413.0	271.4	1,047.4	0.8
2017	D	2.14	1.78	562.8	337.1	2,422.0	104.5
2016	D	0.99	0.83	531.0	192.4	2,560.0	-130.9
2015	D	1.09	0.91	450.2	186.9	2,163.0	-25.5
2014	D	0.89	0.74	420.4	128.7	1,717.8	-101.3

Rating Indexes

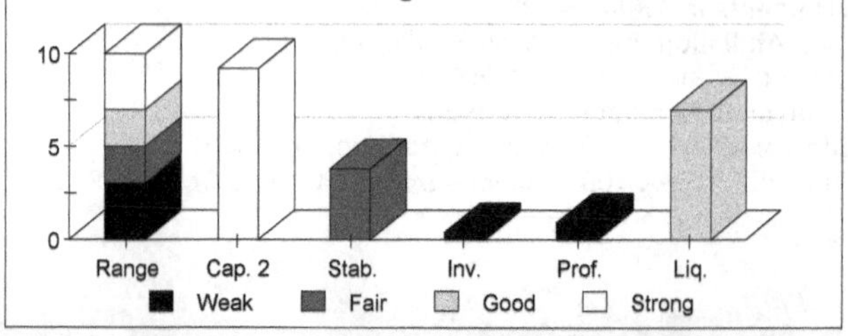

NEIGHBORHOOD HEALTH PLAN OF RI INC C+ Fair

Major Rating Factors: Fair capitalization index (4.8 on a scale of 0 to 10) based on good current risk-adjusted capital (severe loss scenario). Good liquidity (6.9) with sufficient resources (cash flows and marketable investments) to handle a spike in claims. Excellent profitability (7.2).
Other Rating Factors: High quality investment portfolio (9.9). Excellent overall results on stability tests (7.3).
Principal Business: Medicaid (93%), comp med (7%)
Mem Phys: 18: 6,740 **17:** 6,799 **18 MLR** 90.3% **/ 18 Admin Exp** N/A
Enroll(000): Q1 19: 196 **18:** 194 **17:** 200 **Med Exp PMPM:** $509
Principal Investments: Cash and equiv (58%), long-term bonds (42%)
Provider Compensation ($000): Contr fee ($1,262,523), capitation ($15,166), bonus arrang ($1,335)
Total Member Encounters: Phys (7,754,601), non-phys (1,061,119)
Group Affiliation: None
Licensed in: RI
Address: 910 Douglas Pike, Smithfield, RI 2917
Phone: (401) 459-6000 **Dom State:** RI **Commenced Bus:** N/A

Data Date	Rating	RACR #1	RACR #2	Total Assets ($mil)	Capital ($mil)	Net Premium ($mil)	Net Income ($mil)
3-19	C+	0.89	0.75	329.5	103.5	316.8	4.0
3-18	B-	0.85	0.71	415.7	100.2	356.1	1.4
2018	C+	0.88	0.73	333.9	101.6	1,377.7	6.1
2017	B-	0.85	0.71	382.6	100.3	1,365.9	-1.7
2016	B	1.09	0.91	348.8	102.7	1,121.9	19.7
2015	B-	1.00	0.83	369.5	85.6	1,011.4	28.6
2014	C	0.68	0.57	252.0	58.1	894.4	21.1

Rating Indexes

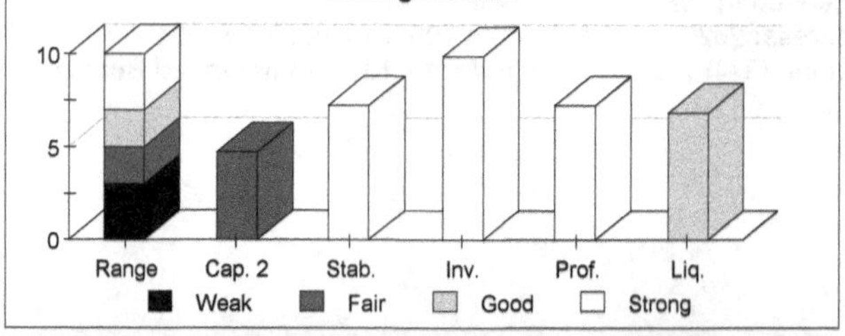

NETWORK HEALTH INS CORP C Fair

Major Rating Factors: Weak profitability index (0.9 on a scale of 0 to 10). Good liquidity (4.9) as cash resources may not be adequate to cover a spike in claims. Strong capitalization (7.1) based on excellent current risk-adjusted capital (severe loss scenario).
Other Rating Factors: High quality investment portfolio (9.9).
Principal Business: Medicare (99%)
Mem Phys: 18: 14,795 **17:** 13,490 **18 MLR** 91.6% **/ 18 Admin Exp** N/A
Enroll(000): Q1 19: 70 **18:** 70 **17:** 67 **Med Exp PMPM:** $656
Principal Investments: Long-term bonds (102%)
Provider Compensation ($000): Contr fee ($372,136), FFS ($179,781), capitation ($923)
Total Member Encounters: Phys (421,824), non-phys (172,728)
Group Affiliation: Network Health Inc
Licensed in: WI
Address: 1570 Midway Place, Menasha, WI 54952
Phone: (920) 720-1452 **Dom State:** WI **Commenced Bus:** N/A

Data Date	Rating	RACR #1	RACR #2	Total Assets ($mil)	Capital ($mil)	Net Premium ($mil)	Net Income ($mil)
3-19	C	1.46	1.22	185.3	79.0	168.7	5.0
3-18	C	1.24	1.03	214.0	61.6	145.8	-2.4
2018	C	1.38	1.15	161.3	74.6	590.1	-2.3
2017	C	1.17	0.97	172.2	64.5	561.6	-16.6
2016	C	1.65	1.37	185.0	81.5	550.6	-3.3
2015	C	1.65	1.37	176.0	81.7	556.5	-5.7
2014	C-	1.44	1.20	155.2	64.7	499.1	-33.2

Rating Indexes

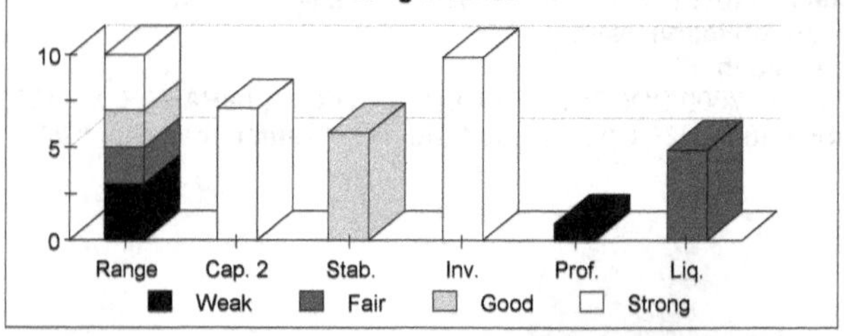

NETWORK HEALTH PLAN B- Good

Major Rating Factors: Good overall results on stability tests (5.6 on a scale of 0 to 10). Fair financial strength from affiliates. Good liquidity (6.8) with sufficient resources (cash flows and marketable investments) to handle a spike in claims. Excellent profitability (7.9).
Other Rating Factors: Strong capitalization index (8.1) based on excellent current risk-adjusted capital (severe loss scenario). High quality investment portfolio (7.9).
Principal Business: Comp med (78%), Medicaid (22%)
Mem Phys: 18: 14,795 **17:** 13,490 **18 MLR** 85.5% **/ 18 Admin Exp** N/A
Enroll(000): Q1 19: 85 **18:** 88 **17:** 75 **Med Exp PMPM:** $324
Principal Investments: Long-term bonds (59%), cash and equiv (38%), real estate (3%)
Provider Compensation ($000): Contr fee ($233,004), capitation ($78,725), FFS ($18,946), bonus arrang ($116)
Total Member Encounters: Phys (195,376), non-phys (321,578)
Group Affiliation: Network Health Inc
Licensed in: WI
Address: 1570 Midway Place, Menasha, WI 54952
Phone: (920) 720-1200 **Dom State:** WI **Commenced Bus:** N/A

Data Date	Rating	RACR #1	RACR #2	Total Assets ($mil)	Capital ($mil)	Net Premium ($mil)	Net Income ($mil)
3-19	B-	2.20	1.84	111.7	65.2	95.4	6.7
3-18	B-	3.17	2.64	121.1	65.3	100.2	6.6
2018	B-	1.97	1.64	106.5	58.3	401.0	10.2
2017	B-	2.28	1.90	92.7	53.0	298.9	11.7
2016	B-	1.52	1.27	102.6	41.4	370.9	0.6
2015	B-	1.60	1.34	103.2	45.3	403.4	6.0
2014	C-	1.33	1.11	83.8	39.3	402.6	2.5

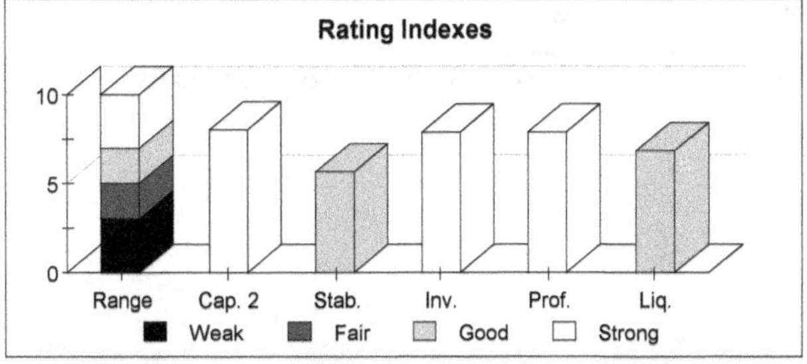

NEW ERA LIFE INSURANCE COMPANY C Fair

Major Rating Factors: Fair overall results on stability tests (4.2 on a scale of 0 to 10) including negative cash flow from operations for 2018, fair risk adjusted capital in prior years. Good current capitalization (5.2) based on good risk adjusted capital (severe loss scenario) reflecting some improvement over results in 2017. Good quality investment portfolio (5.3).
Other Rating Factors: Good liquidity (6.3). Excellent profitability (8.3).
Principal Business: Individual health insurance (64%), individual annuities (34%), and individual life insurance (2%).
Principal Investments: NonCMO investment grade bonds (48%), mortgages in good standing (25%), common & preferred stock (12%), noninv. grade bonds (7%), and misc. investments (6%).
Investments in Affiliates: 11%
Group Affiliation: New Era Life Group
Licensed in: AL, AZ, AR, CA, CO, DE, FL, GA, IN, KS, KY, LA, MI, MS, MO, MT, NE, NM, NC, ND, OH, OK, PA, SC, SD, TN, TX, UT, WA, WV
Commenced Business: June 1924
Address: 11720 Katy Freeway Suite 1700, Houston, TX 77079
Phone: (281) 368-7200 **Domicile State:** TX **NAIC Code:** 78743

Data Date	Rating	RACR #1	RACR #2	Total Assets ($mil)	Capital ($mil)	Net Premium ($mil)	Net Income ($mil)
3-19	C	0.99	0.78	546.2	93.8	41.7	0.2
3-18	C	0.96	0.73	541.8	81.6	39.1	0.3
2018	C	0.97	0.77	543.1	90.2	152.3	2.8
2017	C	0.94	0.73	538.3	79.3	181.4	3.5
2016	C	0.94	0.72	504.2	75.1	190.3	4.5
2015	C	0.95	0.73	463.5	70.7	111.2	5.1
2014	C	0.95	0.73	402.5	66.2	99.3	4.3

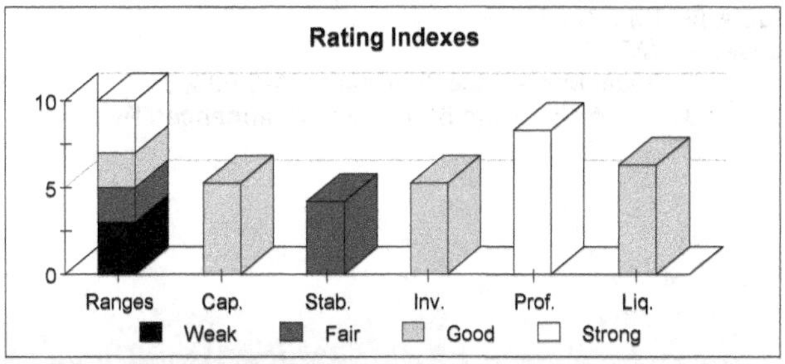

NEW MEXICO HEALTH CONNECTIONS E- Very Weak

Major Rating Factors: Weak profitability index (0.7 on a scale of 0 to 10). Poor capitalization (0.0) based on weak current risk-adjusted capital (severe loss scenario). Weak liquidity (1.5) as a spike in claims may stretch capacity.
Other Rating Factors: High quality investment portfolio (9.9).
Principal Business: Comp med (99%)
Mem Phys: 18: 10,259 **17:** N/A **18 MLR** 185.8% **/ 18 Admin Exp** N/A
Enroll(000): Q1 19: 19 **18:** 17 **17:** 39 **Med Exp PMPM:** $402
Principal Investments: Long-term bonds (66%), cash and equiv (34%)
Provider Compensation ($000): Contr fee ($89,376), FFS ($12,114)
Total Member Encounters: Phys (136,765), non-phys (28,220)
Group Affiliation: None
Licensed in: NM
Address: 2440 LOUISIANA BLVD NE Ste 601, ALBUQUERQUE, NM 87110
Phone: (505) 633-8023 **Dom State:** NM **Commenced Bus:** N/A

Data Date	Rating	RACR #1	RACR #2	Total Assets ($mil)	Capital ($mil)	Net Premium ($mil)	Net Income ($mil)
3-19	E-	0.06	0.05	49.8	1.5	3.7	0.0
3-18	E-	N/A	N/A	36.3	9.2	31.5	0.6
2018	E-	0.06	0.05	45.2	1.5	46.3	6.3
2017	N/A	N/A	N/A	34.2	-4.9	158.6	N/A
2016	E-	0.43	0.36	36.8	10.8	152.5	-17.9
2015	D	1.39	1.16	61.0	31.4	96.2	-23.0
2014	D	1.89	1.57	58.1	23.2	29.9	-4.3

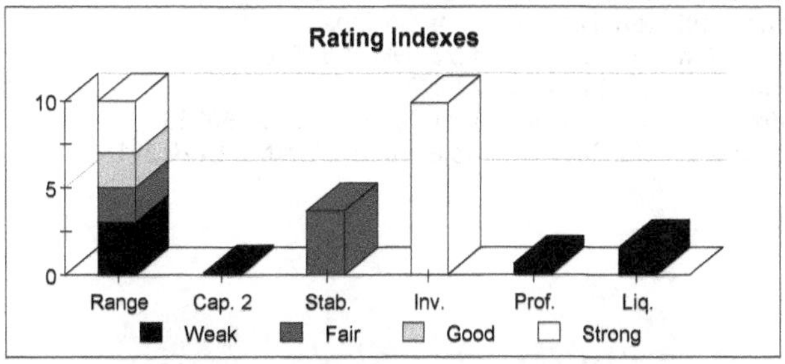

NEXTLEVEL HEALTH PARTNERS INC — C — Fair

Major Rating Factors: Fair capitalization (4.6 on a scale of 0 to 10) based on fair current risk-adjusted capital (moderate loss scenario). Excellent profitability (9.1). High quality investment portfolio (9.9).
Other Rating Factors: Excellent liquidity (7.1) with ample operational cash flow and liquid investments.
Principal Business: Medicaid (100%)
Mem Phys: 18: 3,875 **17:** N/A **18 MLR** 80.7% **/ 18 Admin Exp** N/A
Enroll(000): Q1 19: 44 **18:** 48 **17:** N/A **Med Exp PMPM:** $296
Principal Investments: Cash and equiv (99%), long-term bonds (1%)
Provider Compensation ($000): Contr fee ($222,931)
Total Member Encounters: Phys (283,741), non-phys (126,854)
Group Affiliation: NextLevel Health Innovations Inc
Licensed in: (No states)
Address: , Chicago, IL 60606
Phone: (844) 807-9734 **Dom State:** IL **Commenced Bus:** January 2016

Data Date	Rating	RACR #1	RACR #2	Total Assets ($mil)	Capital ($mil)	Net Premium ($mil)	Net Income ($mil)
3-19	C	0.88	0.73	77.4	23.8	59.0	1.7
3-18	N/A	N/A	N/A	65.3	13.6	72.0	-1.1
2018	C-	0.81	0.68	72.9	22.2	261.5	6.6
2017	N/A	N/A	N/A	N/A	16.8	N/A	N/A
2016	N/A	N/A	N/A	N/A	N/A	N/A	N/A
2015	N/A	N/A	N/A	N/A	N/A	N/A	N/A
2014	N/A	N/A	N/A	N/A	N/A	N/A	N/A

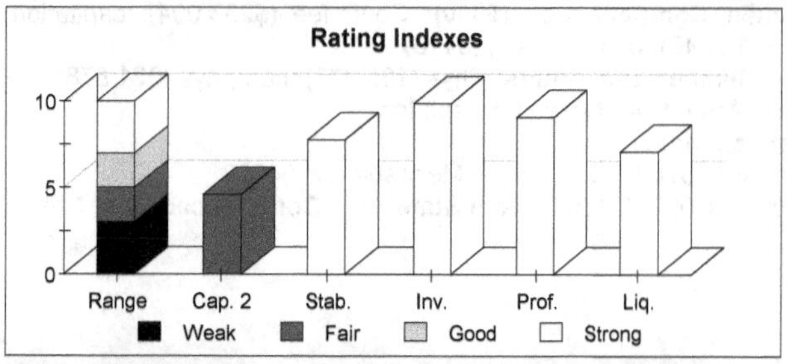

NHC ADVANTAGE LLC — C- — Fair

Major Rating Factors: Weak profitability index (0.9 on a scale of 0 to 10). Good liquidity (6.2) with sufficient resources (cash flows and marketable investments) to handle a spike in claims. Strong capitalization (7.7) based on excellent current risk-adjusted capital (severe loss scenario).
Other Rating Factors: High quality investment portfolio (9.9).
Principal Business: Medicare (100%)
Mem Phys: 18: 8,429 **17:** 1,358 **18 MLR** 91.9% **/ 18 Admin Exp** N/A
Enroll(000): Q1 19: 1 **18:** 0 **17:** 0 **Med Exp PMPM:** $1,664
Principal Investments: Long-term bonds (70%), cash and equiv (30%)
Provider Compensation ($000): Contr fee ($1,788), capitation ($669), bonus arrang ($105)
Total Member Encounters: Phys (1,115), non-phys (2,406)
Group Affiliation: None
Licensed in: MO, TN
Address: 39 Sugar Maple Lane, St. Charles, MO 63303
Phone: (804) 396-6412 **Dom State:** MO **Commenced Bus:** N/A

Data Date	Rating	RACR #1	RACR #2	Total Assets ($mil)	Capital ($mil)	Net Premium ($mil)	Net Income ($mil)
3-19	C-	1.91	1.60	6.4	1.7	7.0	-0.2
3-18	N/A	N/A	N/A	3.1	2.0	0.7	-0.3
2018	C-	2.10	1.75	2.5	1.8	2.7	-1.0
2017	N/A	N/A	N/A	2.0	1.3	2.6	-0.2
2016	N/A	N/A	N/A	1.6	1.6	N/A	-0.6
2015	N/A	N/A	N/A	N/A	N/A	N/A	N/A
2014	N/A	N/A	N/A	N/A	N/A	N/A	N/A

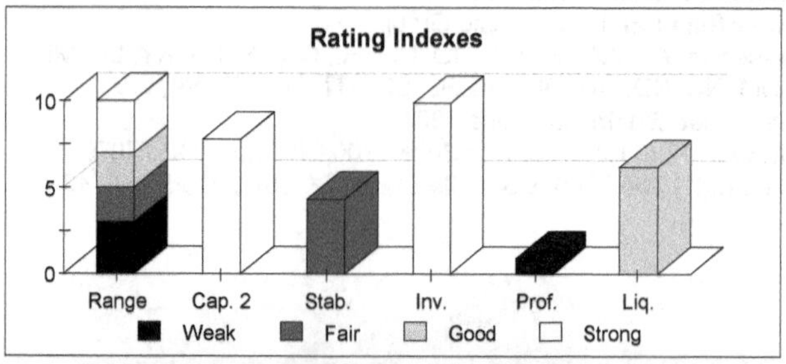

NIPPON LIFE INSURANCE COMPANY OF AMERICA * — A- — Excellent

Major Rating Factors: Good liquidity (6.5 on a scale of 0 to 10) with sufficient resources to handle a spike in claims. Strong capitalization (9.4) based on excellent risk adjusted capital (severe loss scenario). Furthermore, this high level of risk adjusted capital has been consistently maintained over the last five years. High quality investment portfolio (8.1).
Other Rating Factors: Excellent profitability (7.0). Excellent overall results on stability tests (7.0) excellent operational trends and excellent risk diversification.
Principal Business: Group health insurance (99%) and group life insurance (1%).
Principal Investments: NonCMO investment grade bonds (70%), CMOs and structured securities (13%), cash (4%), and common & preferred stock (2%).
Investments in Affiliates: None
Group Affiliation: Nippon Life Ins Co Japan
Licensed in: All states except ME, NH, WY, PR
Commenced Business: July 1973
Address: 7115 Vista Drive, West Des Moines, IA 50266
Phone: (212) 682-3000 **Domicile State:** IA **NAIC Code:** 81264

Data Date	Rating	RACR #1	RACR #2	Total Assets ($mil)	Capital ($mil)	Net Premium ($mil)	Net Income ($mil)
3-19	A-	3.25	2.57	229.2	142.7	88.6	1.7
3-18	B	3.58	2.84	229.8	135.0	82.9	-3.8
2018	A-	3.13	2.48	224.1	143.3	350.0	4.5
2017	A-	3.42	2.71	220.7	139.7	311.5	1.5
2016	A-	3.73	2.96	212.3	139.6	285.7	0.5
2015	A-	3.92	3.11	212.6	140.8	277.0	4.6
2014	A-	3.39	2.71	216.4	141.1	315.7	8.2

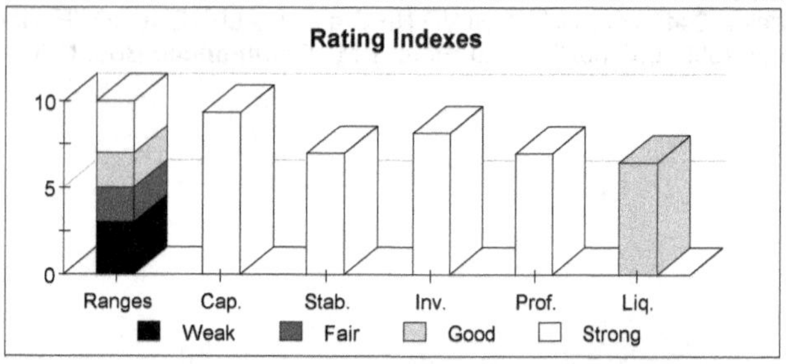

NORTHWESTERN LONG TERM CARE INSURANCE COMPANY B Good

Major Rating Factors: Good liquidity (6.6 on a scale of 0 to 10) with sufficient resources to handle a spike in claims. Good overall results on stability tests (6.3). Stability strengths include good operational trends and excellent risk diversification. Strong capitalization (8.0) based on excellent risk adjusted capital (severe loss scenario). Moreover, capital levels have been consistently high over the last five years.
Other Rating Factors: High quality investment portfolio (8.4). Excellent profitability (7.7).
Principal Business: Individual health insurance (100%).
Principal Investments: NonCMO investment grade bonds (100%).
Investments in Affiliates: None
Group Affiliation: Northwestern Mutual Group
Licensed in: All states except PR
Commenced Business: October 1953
Address: 720 EAST WISCONSIN AVENUE, MILWAUKEE, WI 53202
Phone: (414) 271-1444 **Domicile State:** WI **NAIC Code:** 69000

Data Date	Rating	RACR #1	RACR #2	Total Assets ($mil)	Capital ($mil)	Net Premium ($mil)	Net Income ($mil)
3-19	B	9.08	3.66	245.4	143.5	0.0	1.8
3-18	B	7.92	3.18	205.3	104.9	0.0	0.8
2018	B	9.04	3.65	240.4	141.8	0.0	2.9
2017	B	8.03	3.23	200.6	104.1	-0.1	7.5
2016	B	6.46	2.60	172.7	82.2	0.2	2.6
2015	B	6.57	2.65	166.0	79.5	0.3	2.5
2014	B	8.08	7.27	161.4	77.2	-1,548.3	403.6

Adverse Trends in Operations

Decrease in premium volume from 2016 to 2017 (145%)
Decrease in premium volume from 2015 to 2016 (45%)

OKLAHOMA SUPERIOR SELECT INC E+ Very Weak

Major Rating Factors: Weak profitability index (1.3 on a scale of 0 to 10). Good liquidity (6.7) with sufficient resources (cash flows and marketable investments) to handle a spike in claims. Strong capitalization (7.0) based on excellent current risk-adjusted capital (severe loss scenario).
Other Rating Factors: High quality investment portfolio (9.9).
Principal Business: Medicare (100%)
Mem Phys: 18: 1,160 **17:** 1,890 **18 MLR** 87.2% **/ 18 Admin Exp** N/A
Enroll(000): Q1 19: 0 **18:** 0 **17:** 0 **Med Exp PMPM:** $1,722
Principal Investments: Cash and equiv (82%), long-term bonds (18%)
Provider Compensation ($000): Contr fee ($3,139), capitation ($988)
Total Member Encounters: Phys (8,693), non-phys (2,744)
Group Affiliation: American Health Companies Inc
Licensed in: OK
Address: 909 S Meridian Ave Ste 425, Oklahoma City, OK 73108
Phone: (405) 602-5488 **Dom State:** OK **Commenced Bus:** N/A

Data Date	Rating	RACR #1	RACR #2	Total Assets ($mil)	Capital ($mil)	Net Premium ($mil)	Net Income ($mil)
3-19	E+	1.40	1.16	3.2	1.8	1.6	-0.3
3-18	E+	1.06	0.89	3.2	1.5	1.2	-0.1
2018	E+	1.41	1.18	3.6	1.8	5.4	0.1
2017	E+	1.21	1.01	2.8	1.7	4.6	-0.7
2016	E	1.40	1.16	3.7	1.6	4.0	-1.9
2015	E-	0.50	0.42	2.3	0.6	2.9	-3.1
2014	B-	3.13	2.61	2.3	2.1	3.1	0.3

Rating Indexes

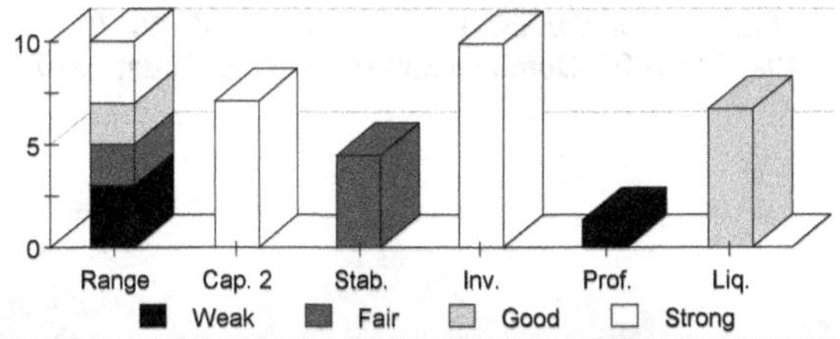

OLD REPUBLIC LIFE INSURANCE COMPANY B- Good

Major Rating Factors: Good quality investment portfolio (5.5 on a scale of 0 to 10) despite mixed results such as: no exposure to mortgages and substantial holdings of BBB bonds but minimal holdings in junk bonds. Good liquidity (6.7) with sufficient resources to handle a spike in claims. Good overall results on stability tests (5.1) despite negative cash flow from operations for 2018 good operational trends and excellent risk diversification.
Other Rating Factors: Fair profitability (3.2) with investment income below regulatory standards in relation to interest assumptions of reserves. Strong capitalization (9.3) based on excellent risk adjusted capital (severe loss scenario).
Principal Business: Group health insurance (53%), individual life insurance (30%), and reinsurance (17%).
Principal Investments: NonCMO investment grade bonds (77%), common & preferred stock (16%), noninv. grade bonds (2%), policy loans (1%), and cash (1%).
Investments in Affiliates: None
Group Affiliation: Old Republic Group
Licensed in: All states except NY
Commenced Business: April 1923
Address: 307 NORTH MICHIGAN AVENUE, CHICAGO, IL 60601
Phone: (312) 346-8100 **Domicile State:** IL **NAIC Code:** 67261

Data Date	Rating	RACR #1	RACR #2	Total Assets ($mil)	Capital ($mil)	Net Premium ($mil)	Net Income ($mil)
3-19	B-	4.09	2.50	109.4	35.1	3.0	0.3
3-18	B-	3.51	2.19	118.9	33.7	3.9	-0.6
2018	B-	4.05	2.48	109.0	33.6	14.3	0.8
2017	B-	3.66	2.28	122.7	34.8	18.2	1.7
2016	B-	3.43	2.12	125.0	31.4	19.4	2.3
2015	B-	2.84	1.77	126.9	27.0	18.1	-0.3
2014	B-	3.22	2.02	125.1	30.6	20.1	0.8

Adverse Trends in Operations

Decrease in premium volume from 2017 to 2018 (21%)
Decrease in asset base during 2018 (11%)
Increase in policy surrenders from 2015 to 2016 (64%)
Decrease in premium volume from 2014 to 2015 (10%)
Decrease in capital during 2015 (12%)

OLD UNITED LIFE INSURANCE COMPANY B Good

Major Rating Factors: Good overall results on stability tests (5.0 on a scale of 0 to 10). Stability strengths include good operational trends and excellent risk diversification. Good quality investment portfolio (5.2) despite mixed results such as: no exposure to mortgages and substantial holdings of BBB bonds but minimal holdings in junk bonds. Strong capitalization (10.0) based on excellent risk adjusted capital (severe loss scenario).
Other Rating Factors: Excellent profitability (8.6). Excellent liquidity (10.0).
Principal Business: Credit health insurance (51%) and credit life insurance (49%).
Principal Investments: NonCMO investment grade bonds (65%), common & preferred stock (23%), CMOs and structured securities (5%), noninv. grade bonds (2%), and cash (1%).
Investments in Affiliates: None
Group Affiliation: Berkshire Hathaway Inc
Licensed in: All states except ME, NH, NY, PR
Commenced Business: January 1964
Address: 3800 N Central Ave Ste 460, Phoenix, AZ 85012
Phone: (913) 895-0200 **Domicile State:** AZ **NAIC Code:** 76007

Data Date	Rating	RACR #1	RACR #2	Total Assets ($mil)	Capital ($mil)	Net Premium ($mil)	Net Income ($mil)
3-19	B	6.88	4.17	85.7	55.8	1.2	1.7
3-18	B	6.56	4.67	84.2	48.6	1.2	0.8
2018	B	6.96	4.21	88.8	52.5	5.6	7.6
2017	B	6.47	4.50	84.7	47.8	6.1	2.9
2016	B	5.88	4.49	81.6	43.9	7.9	1.8
2015	B	5.56	5.01	82.5	42.0	6.2	4.2
2014	B	6.13	3.70	91.4	46.3	8.2	2.4

Adverse Trends in Operations

Increase in policy surrenders from 2016 to 2017 (120%)
Decrease in premium volume from 2016 to 2017 (22%)
Change in asset mix during 2016 (5.7%)
Increase in policy surrenders from 2015 to 2016 (152%)
Decrease in premium volume from 2014 to 2015 (24%)

OMAHA INS CO B- Good

Major Rating Factors: Good overall capitalization (6.4 on a scale of 0 to 10) based on good risk adjusted capital (severe loss scenario). However, capital levels have fluctuated somewhat during past years. Good liquidity (5.5) with sufficient resources to handle a spike in claims. Fair overall results on stability tests (4.8) including negative cash flow from operations for 2018.
Other Rating Factors: Weak profitability (1.9) with operating losses during the first three months of 2019. High quality investment portfolio (7.7).
Principal Business: Individual health insurance (100%).
Principal Investments: NonCMO investment grade bonds (57%), CMOs and structured securities (34%), and noninv. grade bonds (1%).
Investments in Affiliates: None
Group Affiliation: Mutual Of Omaha Group
Licensed in: All states except CA, FL, NV, NH, NY, WI, PR
Commenced Business: November 2006
Address: MUTUAL OF OMAHA PLAZA, OMAHA, NE 68175
Phone: (402) 342-7600 **Domicile State:** NE **NAIC Code:** 13100

Data Date	Rating	RACR #1	RACR #2	Total Assets ($mil)	Capital ($mil)	Net Premium ($mil)	Net Income ($mil)
3-19	B-	1.76	0.92	95.8	48.6	18.0	-1.1
3-18	B-	1.78	0.94	101.5	44.9	15.9	-0.6
2018	B-	1.81	0.95	98.9	49.3	65.5	-6.7
2017	B-	1.84	0.97	98.3	45.2	56.2	-5.3
2016	C+	2.48	1.31	99.2	49.2	44.4	-5.4
2015	C+	3.70	1.97	88.2	54.1	29.3	-5.4
2014	B-	2.47	1.33	43.8	21.1	14.3	-3.9

Risk-Adjusted Capital Ratio #2 (Severe Loss Scenario)

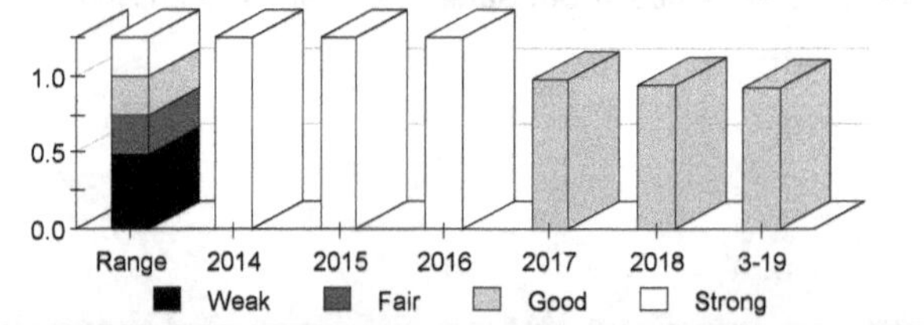

ON LOK SENIOR HEALTH SERVICES B Good

Major Rating Factors: Good overall profitability index (5.7 on a scale of 0 to 10). Good liquidity (6.8) with sufficient resources (cash flows and marketable investments) to handle a spike in claims. Fair overall results on stability tests (4.9).
Other Rating Factors: Strong capitalization index (9.6) based on excellent current risk-adjusted capital (severe loss scenario).
Principal Business: Medicaid (71%), Medicare (28%)
Mem Phys: 18: N/A **17:** N/A **18 MLR** 92.4% **/ 18 Admin Exp** N/A
Enroll(000): Q1 19: 2 **18:** 2 **17:** 1 **Med Exp PMPM:** $8,002
Principal Investments ($000): Cash and equiv ($3,825)
Provider Compensation ($000): None
Total Member Encounters: N/A
Group Affiliation: None
Licensed in: CA
Address: 1333 Bush Street, San Francisco, CA 94109
Phone: (415) 292-8722 **Dom State:** CA **Commenced Bus:** September 1971

Data Date	Rating	RACR #1	RACR #2	Total Assets ($mil)	Capital ($mil)	Net Premium ($mil)	Net Income ($mil)
3-19	B	3.91	2.85	170.3	132.9	42.8	10.0
3-18	B	4.07	2.97	170.2	130.8	36.9	-2.0
2018	B	3.72	2.70	160.6	122.9	157.5	-7.0
2017	B	4.10	3.00	167.8	132.9	149.0	21.1
2016	B	3.94	2.85	141.6	106.0	133.2	11.0
2015	B	3.79	2.75	133.7	98.0	115.6	8.5
2014	B+	3.90	2.84	129.0	99.5	105.9	10.1

Rating Indexes

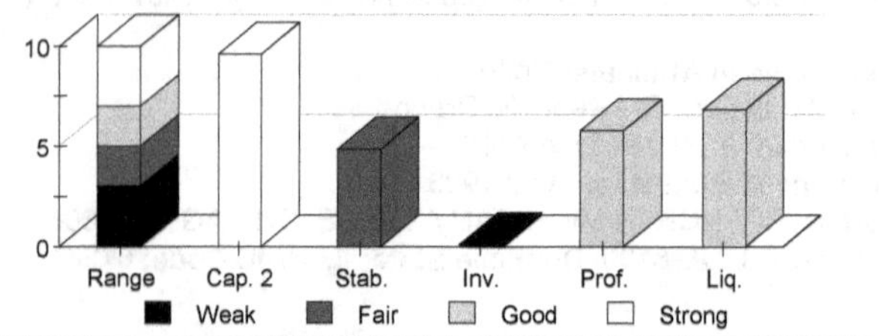

OPTIMA HEALTH INS CO — C — Fair

Major Rating Factors: Weak profitability index (0.7 on a scale of 0 to 10). Good liquidity (6.9) with sufficient resources (cash flows and marketable investments) to handle a spike in claims. Strong capitalization (9.0) based on excellent current risk-adjusted capital (severe loss scenario).
Other Rating Factors: High quality investment portfolio (9.5).
Principal Business: Comp med (100%)
Mem Phys: 18: 9,222 **17:** 8,578 **18 MLR** 87.8% **/ 18 Admin Exp** N/A
Enroll(000): Q1 19: 6 **18:** 7 **17:** 7 **Med Exp PMPM:** $455
Principal Investments: Long-term bonds (61%), cash and equiv (33%), nonaffiliate common stock (6%)
Provider Compensation ($000): Contr fee ($36,046), capitation ($577), bonus arrang ($383)
Total Member Encounters: Phys (1,173), non-phys (12,338)
Group Affiliation: None
Licensed in: VA
Address: 4417 Corporation Lane, Virginia Beach, VA 23462
Phone: (757) 552-7401 **Dom State:** VA **Commenced Bus:** N/A

Data Date	Rating	RACR #1	RACR #2	Total Assets ($mil)	Capital ($mil)	Net Premium ($mil)	Net Income ($mil)
3-19	C	2.96	2.47	29.5	13.7	14.2	-1.1
3-18	C-	2.09	1.75	29.5	10.1	12.3	-1.8
2018	C	3.06	2.55	30.1	14.3	44.3	0.3
2017	C-	2.24	1.86	27.9	14.6	47.3	-1.8
2016	C	3.15	2.62	28.8	16.1	51.6	-1.5
2015	C	2.75	2.29	28.7	17.4	71.0	-1.5
2014	C	1.39	1.16	31.4	15.0	110.5	-14.5

Rating Indexes

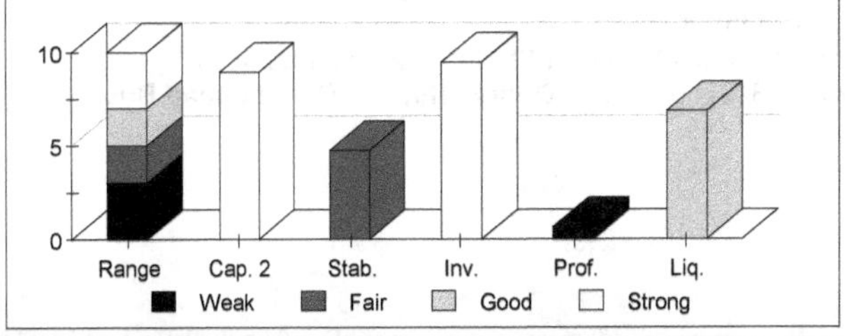

OPTIMA HEALTH PLAN * — A — Excellent

Major Rating Factors: Excellent profitability (8.7 on a scale of 0 to 10). Strong capitalization index (7.8) based on excellent current risk-adjusted capital (severe loss scenario). High quality investment portfolio (9.8).
Other Rating Factors: Excellent overall results on stability tests (8.3) based on healthy premium and capital growth during 2018. Excellent liquidity (7.0) with sufficient resources (cash flows and marketable investments) to handle a spike in claims.
Principal Business: Medicaid (52%), comp med (46%), Medicare (2%)
Mem Phys: 18: 17,219 **17:** 16,458 **18 MLR** 85.0% **/ 18 Admin Exp** N/A
Enroll(000): Q1 19: 342 **18:** 347 **17:** 304 **Med Exp PMPM:** $479
Principal Investments: Long-term bonds (61%), cash and equiv (32%), nonaffiliate common stock (7%)
Provider Compensation ($000): Contr fee ($1,835,314), capitation ($37,845), bonus arrang ($21,516)
Total Member Encounters: Phys (1,899,498), non-phys (1,284,054)
Group Affiliation: None
Licensed in: VA
Address: 4417 Corporation Lane, Virginia Beach, VA 23462
Phone: (757) 552-7401 **Dom State:** VA **Commenced Bus:** N/A

Data Date	Rating	RACR #1	RACR #2	Total Assets ($mil)	Capital ($mil)	Net Premium ($mil)	Net Income ($mil)
3-19	A	1.99	1.66	795.0	352.8	599.9	33.6
3-18	A-	2.14	1.79	610.6	256.3	605.8	22.5
2018	A	1.76	1.47	791.9	315.6	2,376.0	139.3
2017	A-	2.03	1.69	476.7	244.2	1,502.6	15.7
2016	B+	1.92	1.60	372.9	222.6	1,423.6	9.6
2015	B+	1.96	1.63	352.3	212.4	1,357.3	15.5
2014	B+	1.96	1.64	329.6	197.7	1,382.1	51.5

Rating Indexes

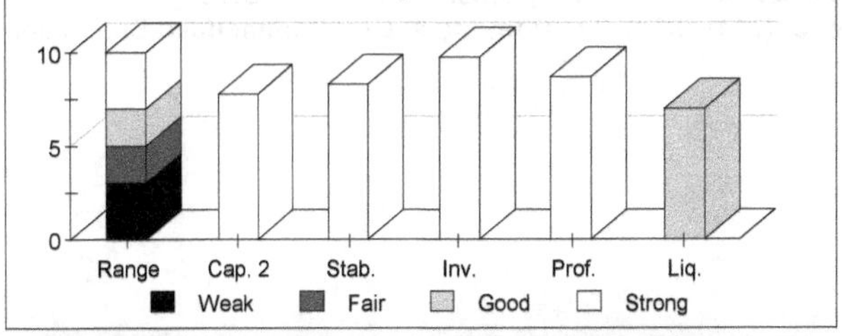

OPTIMUM CHOICE INC — B — Good

Major Rating Factors: Good overall results on stability tests (5.7 on a scale of 0 to 10). Rating is significantly influenced by the good financial results of . Good liquidity (6.9) with sufficient resources (cash flows and marketable investments) to handle a spike in claims. Excellent profitability (8.5).
Other Rating Factors: Strong capitalization index (10.0) based on excellent current risk-adjusted capital (severe loss scenario). High quality investment portfolio (9.5).
Principal Business: Comp med (100%)
Mem Phys: 18: 67,323 **17:** 63,577 **18 MLR** 73.0% **/ 18 Admin Exp** N/A
Enroll(000): Q1 19: 57 **18:** 59 **17:** 58 **Med Exp PMPM:** $282
Principal Investments: Long-term bonds (91%), cash and equiv (9%)
Provider Compensation ($000): Contr fee ($188,621), capitation ($9,497), bonus arrang ($17)
Total Member Encounters: Phys (348,194), non-phys (15,849)
Group Affiliation: None
Licensed in: DC, DE, MD, VA, WV
Address: 800 KING FARM BLVD, ROCKVILLE, MD 20850
Phone: (240) 632-8109 **Dom State:** MD **Commenced Bus:** N/A

Data Date	Rating	RACR #1	RACR #2	Total Assets ($mil)	Capital ($mil)	Net Premium ($mil)	Net Income ($mil)
3-19	B	6.31	5.25	114.2	37.8	71.1	4.1
3-18	B	3.76	3.14	95.7	25.4	66.2	2.8
2018	B	5.69	4.75	99.0	33.9	272.3	21.1
2017	B	1.92	1.60	79.0	22.4	221.6	10.8
2016	C+	4.40	3.67	58.2	19.9	182.8	15.4
2015	C	4.71	3.93	60.6	22.8	197.2	15.9
2014	B-	7.39	6.16	83.7	54.1	219.9	25.6

Rating Indexes

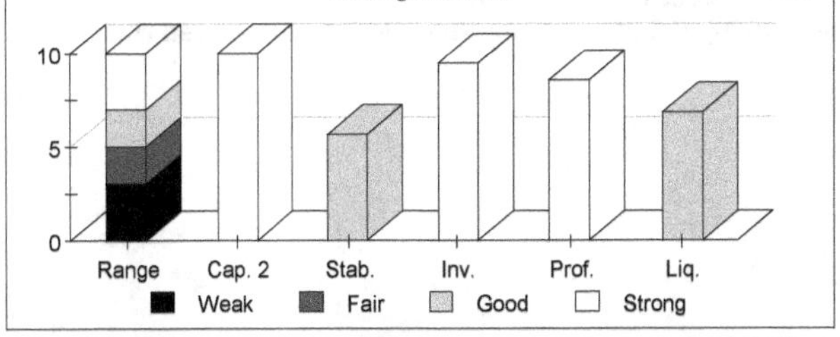

OPTIMUM HEALTHCARE INC — B — Good

Major Rating Factors: Good liquidity (6.8 on a scale of 0 to 10) with sufficient resources (cash flows and marketable investments) to handle a spike in claims. Excellent profitability (9.1). Strong capitalization (8.0) based on excellent current risk-adjusted capital (severe loss scenario).
Other Rating Factors: High quality investment portfolio (9.0).
Principal Business: Medicare (100%)
Mem Phys: 18: 16,489 **17:** 17,760 **18 MLR** 83.0% **/ 18 Admin Exp** N/A
Enroll(000): Q1 19: 57 **18:** 60 **17:** 54 **Med Exp PMPM:** $858
Principal Investments: Long-term bonds (61%), cash and equiv (38%), other (1%)
Provider Compensation ($000): Capitation ($450,430), contr fee ($135,511), FFS ($2,476)
Total Member Encounters: Phys (15,228), non-phys (77,829)
Group Affiliation: Anthem Inc
Licensed in: FL
Address: 5600 Mariner St Ste 227, Tampa, FL 33609
Phone: (813) 506-6000 **Dom State:** FL **Commenced Bus:** N/A

Data Date	Rating	RACR #1	RACR #2	Total Assets ($mil)	Capital ($mil)	Net Premium ($mil)	Net Income ($mil)
3-19	B	2.19	1.82	189.0	66.1	187.9	17.0
3-18	D-	1.38	1.15	202.0	47.8	176.1	4.5
2018	B-	1.65	1.38	144.9	49.9	722.1	12.8
2017	E	0.87	0.72	125.6	35.7	611.6	12.0
2016	E-	0.75	0.62	112.5	30.5	529.9	6.7
2015	E-	0.67	0.56	73.7	25.9	415.7	2.6
2014	D+	0.57	0.48	77.7	23.2	440.7	5.5

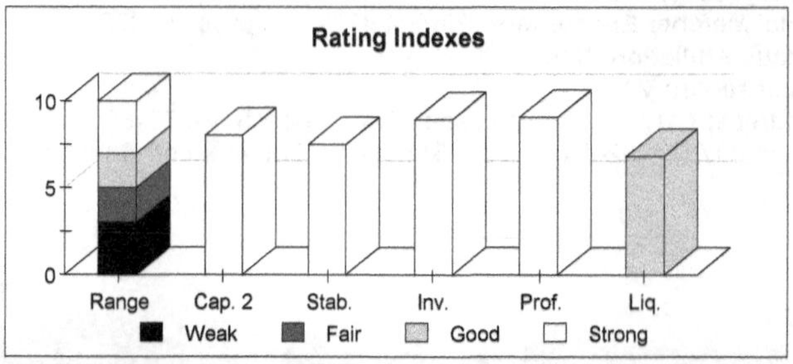

ORANGE PREVENTION & TREATMENT INTEGR * — A- — Excellent

Major Rating Factors: Excellent profitability (8.7 on a scale of 0 to 10). Strong capitalization index (8.0) based on excellent current risk-adjusted capital (severe loss scenario). Excellent overall results on stability tests (7.5).
Other Rating Factors: Good liquidity (6.5) with sufficient resources (cash flows and marketable investments) to handle a spike in claims.
Principal Business: Medicaid (93%), Medicare (7%)
Mem Phys: 17: N/A **16:** N/A **17 MLR** 95.4% **/ 17 Admin Exp** N/A
Enroll(000): Q3 18: 774 **17:** 791 **16:** 807 **Med Exp PMPM:** $359
Principal Investments ($000): Cash and equiv ($1,312,255)
Provider Compensation ($000): None
Total Member Encounters: N/A
Group Affiliation: None
Licensed in: CA
Address: 505 City Parkway West, Orange, CA 92868
Phone: (714) 796-6122 **Dom State:** CA **Commenced Bus:** June 2000

Data Date	Rating	RACR #1	RACR #2	Total Assets ($mil)	Capital ($mil)	Net Premium ($mil)	Net Income ($mil)
9-18	A-	2.77	1.81	1,882.3	785.2	2,564.0	45.0
9-17	A-	2.77	1.82	2,819.9	724.8	2,728.4	60.2
2017	A-	2.53	1.65	2,321.3	736.5	3,577.2	71.9
2016	A-	2.54	1.66	2,304.9	659.6	3,163.8	32.5
2015	A-	2.75	1.81	1,866.5	627.0	3,236.6	231.1
2014	A-	2.77	1.77	1,007.5	400.3	2,002.0	188.4
2013	B	1.58	1.01	690.4	211.9	1,743.2	55.1

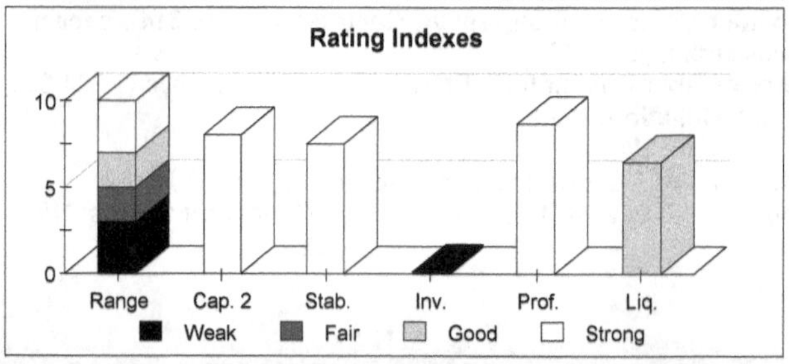

OSCAR GARDEN STATE INSURANCE — D — Weak

Major Rating Factors: Weak profitability index (0.9 on a scale of 0 to 10). Low quality investment portfolio (1.6). Strong capitalization (7.5) based on excellent current risk-adjusted capital (severe loss scenario).
Other Rating Factors: Excellent liquidity (7.4) with ample operational cash flow and liquid investments.
Principal Business: Comp med (100%)
Mem Phys: 18: 5,613 **17:** N/A **18 MLR** 152.3% **/ 18 Admin Exp** N/A
Enroll(000): Q1 19: 14 **18:** 11 **17:** N/A **Med Exp PMPM:** $250
Principal Investments: Cash and equiv (100%)
Provider Compensation ($000): FFS ($25,843), capitation ($3)
Total Member Encounters: Phys (37,687), non-phys (13,070)
Group Affiliation: None
Licensed in: NJ
Address: , West Trenton, NJ 8628
Phone: (646) 403-3677 **Dom State:** NJ **Commenced Bus:** N/A

Data Date	Rating	RACR #1	RACR #2	Total Assets ($mil)	Capital ($mil)	Net Premium ($mil)	Net Income ($mil)
3-19	D	1.74	1.45	49.6	7.3	9.7	-0.6
3-18	N/A	N/A	N/A	N/A	N/A	N/A	N/A
2018	D	2.06	1.72	43.3	8.7	20.9	-9.1
2017	N/A	N/A	N/A	6.3	3.2	N/A	-2.6
2016	N/A	N/A	N/A	N/A	N/A	N/A	N/A
2015	N/A	N/A	N/A	N/A	N/A	N/A	N/A
2014	N/A	N/A	N/A	N/A	N/A	N/A	N/A

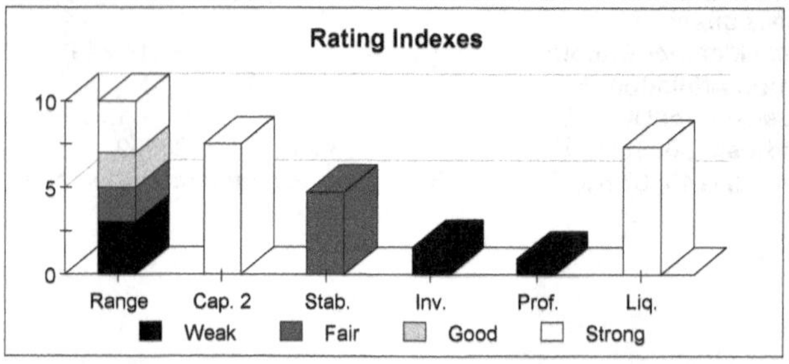

OSCAR HEALTH PLAN OF CALIFORNIA E- Very Weak

Major Rating Factors: Weak profitability index (0.0 on a scale of 0 to 10). Poor capitalization index (0.0) based on weak current risk-adjusted capital (severe loss scenario). Weak overall results on stability tests (1.5) based on a steep decline in capital during 2018, an excessive 299% enrollment growth during the period.
Other Rating Factors: Excellent liquidity (8.4) with ample operational cash flow and liquid investments.
Principal Business: Managed care (100%)
Mem Phys: 18: N/A **17:** N/A **18 MLR** 75.4% **/ 18 Admin Exp** N/A
Enroll(000): Q1 19: 59 **18:** 40 **17:** 10 **Med Exp PMPM:** $118
Principal Investments ($000): Cash and equiv ($62,851)
Provider Compensation ($000): None
Total Member Encounters: N/A
Group Affiliation: None
Licensed in: CA
Address: 3535 Hayden Avenue Suite 230, Culver City, CA 90232
Phone: (424) 261-4363 **Dom State:** CA **Commenced Bus:** N/A

Data Date	Rating	RACR #1	RACR #2	Total Assets ($mil)	Capital ($mil)	Net Premium ($mil)	Net Income ($mil)
3-19	E-	N/A	N/A	157.0	-67.7	26.1	-3.0
3-18	E-	N/A	N/A	67.1	-50.8	15.0	-3.6
2018	E-	N/A	N/A	114.9	-64.7	76.4	-17.5
2017	E-	N/A	N/A	35.0	-47.2	26.3	-20.2
2016	E-	N/A	N/A	16.4	-27.0	9.1	-20.8
2015	N/A	N/A	N/A	N/A	N/A	N/A	N/A
2014	N/A	N/A	N/A	N/A	N/A	N/A	N/A

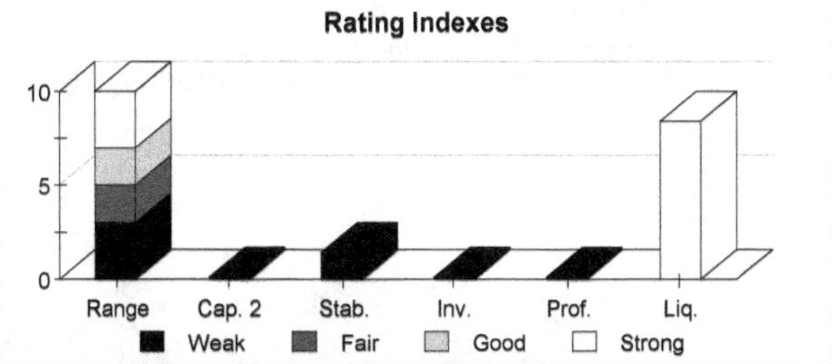

OSCAR INS CORP E- Very Weak

Major Rating Factors: Weak profitability index (0.3 on a scale of 0 to 10). Good liquidity (6.9) with sufficient resources (cash flows and marketable investments) to handle a spike in claims. Strong capitalization (8.9) based on excellent current risk-adjusted capital (severe loss scenario).
Other Rating Factors: High quality investment portfolio (9.9).
Principal Business: Comp med (100%)
Mem Phys: 18: 20,295 **17:** 7,750 **18 MLR** 134.8% **/ 18 Admin Exp** N/A
Enroll(000): Q1 19: 54 **18:** 57 **17:** 43 **Med Exp PMPM:** $351
Principal Investments: Cash and equiv (92%), long-term bonds (8%)
Provider Compensation ($000): FFS ($228,666), capitation ($4,046)
Total Member Encounters: Phys (235,182), non-phys (157,543)
Group Affiliation: None
Licensed in: NY
Address: 295 Lafayette St, New York, NY 10011
Phone: (646) 403-3677 **Dom State:** NY **Commenced Bus:** N/A

Data Date	Rating	RACR #1	RACR #2	Total Assets ($mil)	Capital ($mil)	Net Premium ($mil)	Net Income ($mil)
3-19	E-	2.86	2.39	225.8	32.8	40.5	6.4
3-18	E-	N/A	N/A	207.5	42.0	50.4	3.1
2018	E-	2.59	2.16	187.5	28.0	180.4	-5.2
2017	E-	N/A	N/A	178.2	39.3	126.3	-62.8
2016	E-	1.42	1.18	148.8	45.2	246.3	-123.7
2015	D	1.10	0.92	118.6	21.3	117.4	-92.4
2014	D	2.32	1.93	60.0	27.3	56.9	-27.6

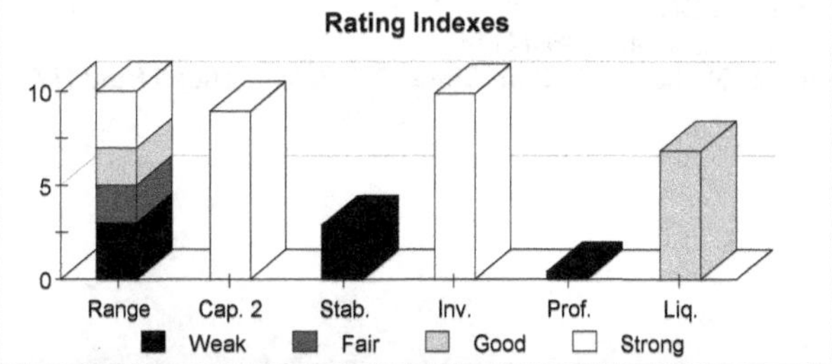

OSCAR INS CORP OF NEW JERSEY D Weak

Major Rating Factors: Weak profitability index (0.9 on a scale of 0 to 10). Strong capitalization (10.0) based on excellent current risk-adjusted capital (severe loss scenario). High quality investment portfolio (9.9).
Other Rating Factors: Excellent liquidity (10.0) with ample operational cash flow and liquid investments.
Principal Business: Comp med (100%)
Mem Phys: 18: N/A **17:** N/A **18 MLR** 46.9% **/ 18 Admin Exp** N/A
Enroll(000): 18: N/A **17:** N/A **Med Exp PMPM:** N/A
Principal Investments: Cash and equiv (100%)
Provider Compensation ($000): FFS ($119)
Total Member Encounters: N/A
Group Affiliation: None
Licensed in: NJ
Address: 295 Lafayette St, West Trenton, NJ 8628
Phone: (646) 403-3677 **Dom State:** NJ **Commenced Bus:** N/A

Data Date	Rating	RACR #1	RACR #2	Total Assets ($mil)	Capital ($mil)	Net Premium ($mil)	Net Income ($mil)
2018	D	3.79	3.15	5.4	5.4	0.3	0.1
2017	D	22.88	19.07	13.1	11.7	1.6	2.4
2016	D	1.09	0.91	70.4	10.2	82.1	-15.0
2015	N/A	N/A	N/A	14.9	4.6	9.0	-12.8
2014	N/A	N/A	N/A	4.4	3.6	N/A	-3.4

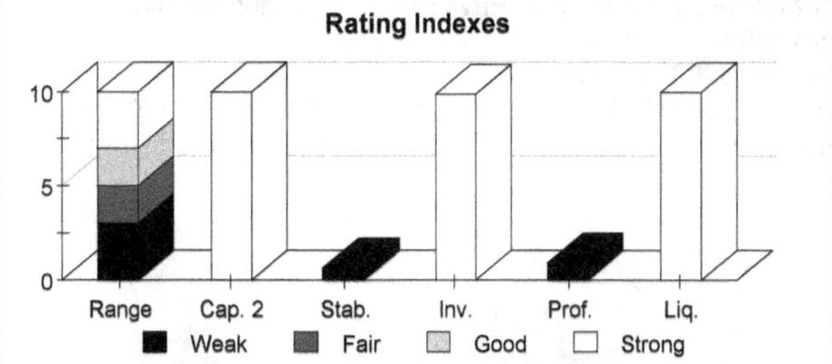

OSCAR INSURANCE COMPANY D- Weak

Major Rating Factors: Weak profitability index (0.5 on a scale of 0 to 10). Strong capitalization (7.2) based on excellent current risk-adjusted capital (severe loss scenario). High quality investment portfolio (9.2).
Other Rating Factors: Excellent liquidity (7.2) with ample operational cash flow and liquid investments.
Principal Business: Comp med (100%)
Mem Phys: 18: 8,677 **17:** 2,539 **18 MLR** 108.2% **/ 18 Admin Exp** N/A
Enroll(000): Q1 19: 69 **18:** 102 **17:** 28 **Med Exp PMPM:** $298
Principal Investments: Cash and equiv (96%), long-term bonds (4%)
Provider Compensation ($000): FFS ($347,138), capitation ($1,854)
Total Member Encounters: Phys (505,421), non-phys (168,326)
Group Affiliation: None
Licensed in: MI, TN, TX
Address: 3102 Oak Lawn Ste 602, Dallas, TX 75201
Phone: (646) 403-3677 **Dom State:** TX **Commenced Bus:** N/A

Data Date	Rating	RACR #1	RACR #2	Total Assets ($mil)	Capital ($mil)	Net Premium ($mil)	Net Income ($mil)
3-19	D-	1.48	1.23	333.4	49.8	46.8	2.8
3-18	D-	N/A	N/A	196.0	46.5	89.2	6.6
2018	D-	1.72	1.44	301.1	58.4	359.8	-15.9
2017	D-	N/A	N/A	87.7	13.0	75.6	-46.7
2016	D	1.80	1.50	88.1	29.5	88.6	-45.2
2015	N/A	N/A	N/A	17.9	11.6	N/A	-9.1
2014	N/A	N/A	N/A	N/A	N/A	N/A	N/A

Rating Indexes

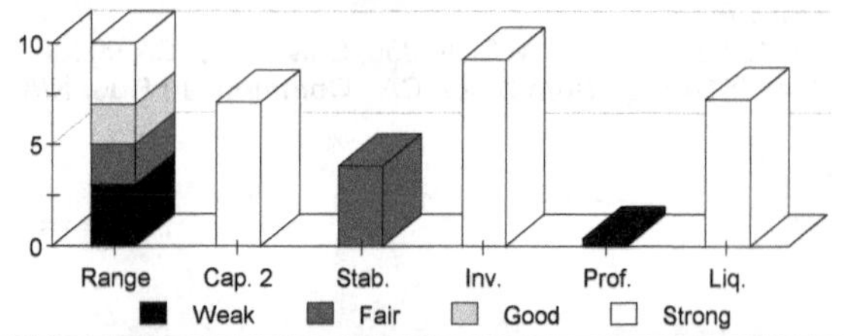

OSCAR INSURANCE CORP OF OHIO D Weak

Major Rating Factors: Weak profitability index (0.9 on a scale of 0 to 10). Strong capitalization (8.3) based on excellent current risk-adjusted capital (severe loss scenario). High quality investment portfolio (9.9).
Other Rating Factors: Excellent liquidity (7.3) with ample operational cash flow and liquid investments.
Principal Business: Comp med (100%)
Mem Phys: 18: 1,756 **17:** N/A **18 MLR** 86.7% **/ 18 Admin Exp** N/A
Enroll(000): Q1 19: 11 **18:** 10 **17:** N/A **Med Exp PMPM:** $587
Principal Investments: Cash and equiv (97%), long-term bonds (3%)
Provider Compensation ($000): FFS ($65,386), capitation ($160)
Total Member Encounters: Phys (62,121), non-phys (11,633)
Group Affiliation: None
Licensed in: OH
Address: , Cleveland, OH 44114
Phone: (646) 403-3677 **Dom State:** OH **Commenced Bus:** N/A

Data Date	Rating	RACR #1	RACR #2	Total Assets ($mil)	Capital ($mil)	Net Premium ($mil)	Net Income ($mil)
3-19	D	2.36	1.97	41.0	27.8	25.2	6.5
3-18	N/A	N/A	N/A	17.0	8.9	17.4	2.3
2018	D	1.81	1.51	36.8	21.4	86.3	-2.0
2017	N/A	N/A	N/A	7.5	2.5	N/A	-1.4
2016	N/A	N/A	N/A	N/A	N/A	N/A	N/A
2015	N/A	N/A	N/A	N/A	N/A	N/A	N/A
2014	N/A	N/A	N/A	N/A	N/A	N/A	N/A

Rating Indexes

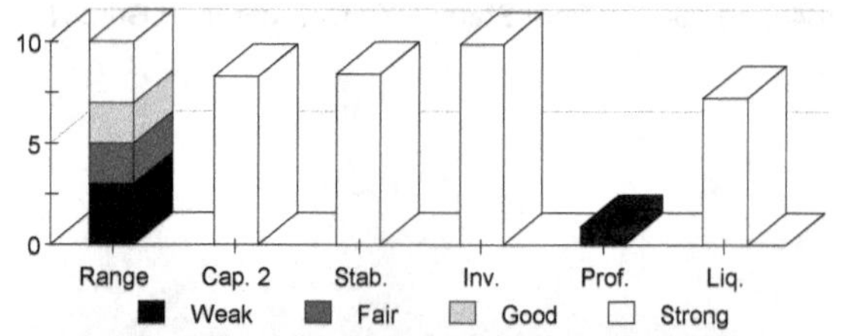

OXFORD HEALTH INS INC B Good

Major Rating Factors: Good liquidity (6.8 on a scale of 0 to 10) with sufficient resources (cash flows and marketable investments) to handle a spike in claims. Excellent profitability (9.2). Strong capitalization (9.5) based on excellent current risk-adjusted capital (severe loss scenario).
Other Rating Factors: High quality investment portfolio (9.4).
Principal Business: Comp med (100%)
Mem Phys: 18: 149,439 **17:** 114,415 **18 MLR** 79.7% **/ 18 Admin Exp** N/A
Enroll(000): Q1 19: 1,023 **18:** 1,029 **17:** 1,006 **Med Exp PMPM:** $534
Principal Investments: Long-term bonds (86%), cash and equiv (12%), other (2%)
Provider Compensation ($000): Contr fee ($4,614,671), FFS ($1,362,807), capitation ($409,104), bonus arrang ($37,495)
Total Member Encounters: Phys (9,476,039), non-phys (346,296)
Group Affiliation: None
Licensed in: CT, NJ, NY, PA
Address: ONE PENN PLAZA Fl 8, NEW YORK, NY 10119
Phone: (203) 447-4500 **Dom State:** NY **Commenced Bus:** N/A

Data Date	Rating	RACR #1	RACR #2	Total Assets ($mil)	Capital ($mil)	Net Premium ($mil)	Net Income ($mil)
3-19	B	3.35	2.79	2,945.6	1,477.0	2,148.5	133.2
3-18	B	3.54	2.95	2,754.9	1,328.4	1,980.1	-14.1
2018	B	3.03	2.52	2,624.1	1,334.3	8,182.0	410.7
2017	B+	3.55	2.96	2,570.1	1,331.0	7,217.1	365.4
2016	B	3.86	3.21	2,210.8	1,192.6	6,431.1	363.6
2015	B	4.35	3.62	2,195.0	1,257.2	5,819.0	418.5
2014	B	3.52	2.93	1,946.6	917.3	4,922.3	237.0

Rating Indexes

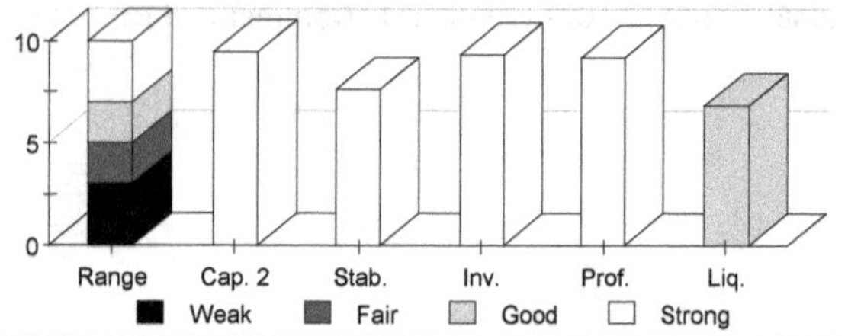

OXFORD HEALTH PLANS (CT) INC B Good

Major Rating Factors: Good overall results on stability tests (5.1 on a scale of 0 to 10). Rating is significantly influenced by the good financial results of . Good liquidity (6.8) with sufficient resources (cash flows and marketable investments) to handle a spike in claims. Excellent profitability (9.3).
Other Rating Factors: Strong capitalization index (8.6) based on excellent current risk-adjusted capital (severe loss scenario). High quality investment portfolio (9.2).
Principal Business: Medicare (97%), comp med (3%)
Mem Phys: 18: 58,410 **17:** 56,501 **18 MLR** 79.7% **/ 18 Admin Exp** N/A
Enroll(000): Q1 19: 157 **18:** 157 **17:** 142 **Med Exp PMPM:** $724
Principal Investments: Long-term bonds (96%), cash and equiv (4%)
Provider Compensation ($000): Contr fee ($1,083,632), FFS ($203,574), capitation ($40,391)
Total Member Encounters: Phys (3,021,383), non-phys (1,030,994)
Group Affiliation: None
Licensed in: CT, NJ
Address: 4 RESEARCH DRIVE, SHELTON, CT 6484
Phone: (203) 447-4500 **Dom State:** CT **Commenced Bus:** N/A

Data Date	Rating	RACR #1	RACR #2	Total Assets ($mil)	Capital ($mil)	Net Premium ($mil)	Net Income ($mil)
3-19	B	2.61	2.17	584.4	219.3	451.3	33.0
3-18	B-	2.30	1.92	660.9	165.0	416.8	9.3
2018	B	2.20	1.84	554.6	183.8	1,661.7	80.9
2017	B-	1.55	1.29	485.6	155.5	1,450.1	78.4
2016	B-	3.61	3.01	220.1	88.7	476.1	8.2
2015	C	3.73	3.11	178.7	79.7	456.1	32.2
2014	B-	3.96	3.30	240.3	102.6	499.5	19.6

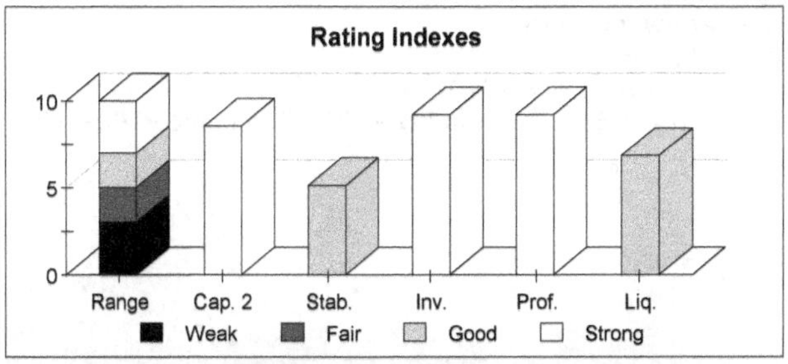

OXFORD HEALTH PLANS (NJ) INC B Good

Major Rating Factors: Good overall results on stability tests (5.4 on a scale of 0 to 10). Rating is significantly influenced by the good financial results of . Excellent profitability (9.1). Strong capitalization index (10.0) based on excellent current risk-adjusted capital (severe loss scenario).
Other Rating Factors: High quality investment portfolio (9.7). Excellent liquidity (7.0) with ample operational cash flow and liquid investments.
Principal Business: Medicare (96%), comp med (4%)
Mem Phys: 18: 166,357 **17:** 125,270 **18 MLR** 79.4% **/ 18 Admin Exp** N/A
Enroll(000): Q1 19: 45 **18:** 44 **17:** 33 **Med Exp PMPM:** $952
Principal Investments: Long-term bonds (85%), cash and equiv (15%)
Provider Compensation ($000): Contr fee ($361,209), FFS ($58,029), capitation ($29,743), bonus arrang ($1,468)
Total Member Encounters: Phys (925,597), non-phys (398,920)
Group Affiliation: None
Licensed in: DE, MO, NJ, OR, PA, RI
Address: 170 WOOD AVENUE FLOOR 3, ISELIN, NJ 8830
Phone: (203) 447-4500 **Dom State:** NJ **Commenced Bus:** N/A

Data Date	Rating	RACR #1	RACR #2	Total Assets ($mil)	Capital ($mil)	Net Premium ($mil)	Net Income ($mil)
3-19	B	7.55	6.29	279.6	166.7	192.3	15.1
3-18	B	6.20	5.17	318.7	130.0	117.1	4.2
2018	B	6.71	5.60	269.5	147.2	576.3	40.9
2017	B	4.91	4.09	268.8	146.1	412.7	38.2
2016	B	2.21	1.84	302.8	117.2	1,057.0	48.9
2015	B	2.35	1.96	289.5	121.0	970.1	14.6
2014	B	2.34	1.95	284.6	126.6	1,018.8	22.5

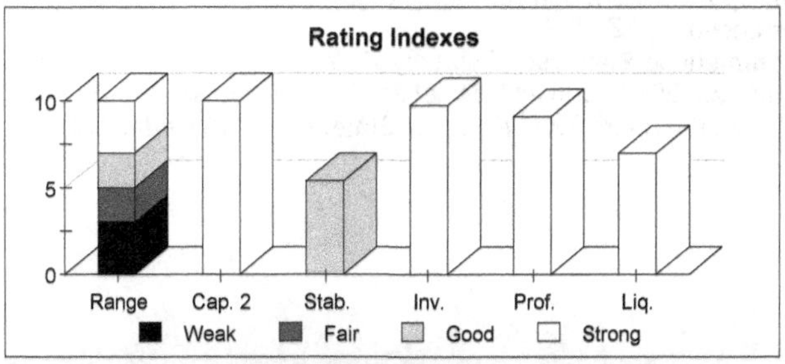

OXFORD HEALTH PLANS (NY) INC B Good

Major Rating Factors: Good liquidity (6.3 on a scale of 0 to 10) with sufficient resources (cash flows and marketable investments) to handle a spike in claims. Fair profitability index (3.3). Fair overall results on stability tests (4.1) based on a steep decline in premium revenue in 2018. Rating is significantly influenced by the good financial results of .
Other Rating Factors: Strong capitalization index (10.0) based on excellent current risk-adjusted capital (severe loss scenario). High quality investment portfolio (8.2).
Principal Business: Medicare (101%)
Mem Phys: 18: 77,487 **17:** 73,990 **18 MLR** 88.8% **/ 18 Admin Exp** N/A
Enroll(000): Q1 19: 74 **18:** 85 **17:** 88 **Med Exp PMPM:** $747
Principal Investments: Long-term bonds (106%)
Provider Compensation ($000): Contr fee ($676,169), FFS ($101,090), bonus arrang ($7,527), capitation ($933)
Total Member Encounters: Phys (1,905,408), non-phys (412,419)
Group Affiliation: None
Licensed in: NY
Address: ONE PENN PLAZA FLOOR 8, NEW YORK, NY 10119
Phone: (203) 447-4500 **Dom State:** NY **Commenced Bus:** N/A

Data Date	Rating	RACR #1	RACR #2	Total Assets ($mil)	Capital ($mil)	Net Premium ($mil)	Net Income ($mil)
3-19	B	4.76	3.97	449.9	253.9	201.4	11.9
3-18	B+	4.27	3.55	615.4	268.5	227.8	3.4
2018	B	4.54	3.78	471.6	240.9	871.1	-0.7
2017	B+	3.15	2.62	546.7	267.2	1,105.0	-14.2
2016	B+	3.01	2.51	614.8	282.4	1,707.7	22.4
2015	A	5.32	4.43	821.9	474.7	1,793.4	110.0
2014	A	3.60	3.00	750.1	406.6	2,028.4	4.9

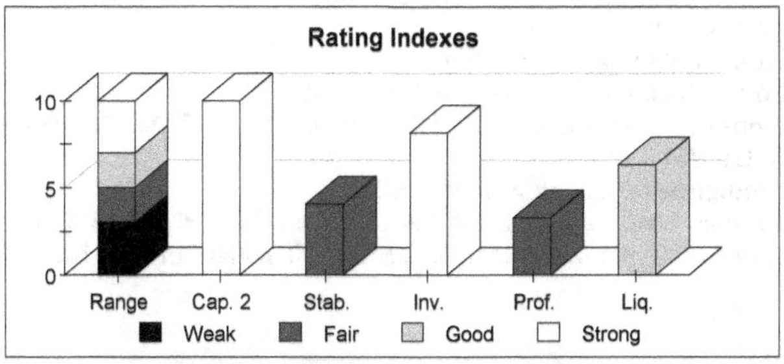

PA HEALTH & WELLNESS INC C Fair

Major Rating Factors: Fair quality investment portfolio (4.0 on a scale of 0 to 10). Excellent profitability (7.5). Strong capitalization (9.0) based on excellent current risk-adjusted capital (severe loss scenario).
Other Rating Factors: Excellent liquidity (7.1) with ample operational cash flow and liquid investments.
Principal Business: Medicaid (99%), Medicare (1%)
Mem Phys: 18: 26,855 **17:** N/A **18 MLR** 96.1% **/ 18 Admin Exp** N/A
Enroll(000): Q1 19: 55 **18:** 23 **17:** N/A **Med Exp PMPM:** $1,739
Principal Investments: Cash and equiv (77%), long-term bonds (23%)
Provider Compensation ($000): Contr fee ($412,112), salary ($14,447), capitation ($972)
Total Member Encounters: Phys (135,603), non-phys (833,991)
Group Affiliation: None
Licensed in: PA
Address: , Camp Hill, PA 17011
Phone: (314) 725-4477 **Dom State:** PA **Commenced Bus:** N/A

Data Date	Rating	RACR #1	RACR #2	Total Assets ($mil)	Capital ($mil)	Net Premium ($mil)	Net Income ($mil)
3-19	C	2.91	2.43	267.5	95.3	384.4	-8.0
3-18	N/A	N/A	N/A	80.0	26.4	112.5	-1.1
2018	C-	2.10	1.75	126.3	68.7	483.4	1.5
2017	N/A	N/A	N/A	1.6	1.6	N/A	N/A
2016	N/A	N/A	N/A	1.5	1.5	N/A	N/A
2015	N/A	N/A	N/A	N/A	N/A	N/A	N/A
2014	N/A	N/A	N/A	N/A	N/A	N/A	N/A

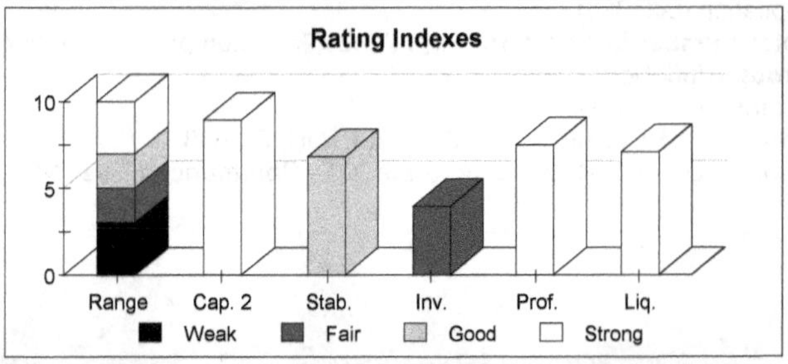

PACIFIC CENTURY LIFE INSURANCE CORPORATION C- Fair

Major Rating Factors: Fair overall results on stability tests (3.0 on a scale of 0 to 10). Good overall profitability (6.3). Strong overall capitalization (10.0) based on excellent risk adjusted capital (severe loss scenario). However, capital levels have fluctuated somewhat during past years.
Other Rating Factors: High quality investment portfolio (7.4). Excellent liquidity (10.0).
Principal Business: Reinsurance (92%), credit life insurance (5%), and credit health insurance (3%).
Principal Investments: Mortgages in good standing (95%), cash (4%), and nonCMO investment grade bonds (2%).
Investments in Affiliates: None
Group Affiliation: Bank of Hawaii Corp
Licensed in: AZ, HI
Commenced Business: February 1982
Address: 2910 North 44th Street 2nd Fl, Phoenix, AZ 85018-7269
Phone: (602) 200-6900 **Domicile State:** AZ **NAIC Code:** 93815

Data Date	Rating	RACR #1	RACR #2	Total Assets ($mil)	Capital ($mil)	Net Premium ($mil)	Net Income ($mil)
3-19	C-	32.29	19.54	368.7	366.5	0.0	2.4
3-18	U	N/A	N/A	366.8	364.7	0.0	2.2
2018	C-	32.08	21.00	365.7	364.1	0.1	8.8
2017	U	31.97	22.03	364.0	362.4	0.1	7.1
2016	B	31.49	22.90	357.6	355.2	0.2	7.3
2015	B	31.00	21.87	351.3	347.9	0.4	7.7
2014	B	30.50	21.00	344.3	340.2	0.8	7.5

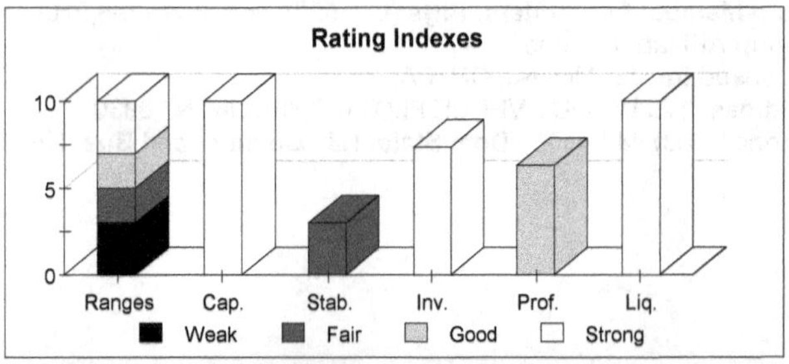

PACIFIC GUARDIAN LIFE INSURANCE COMPANY LIMITED * A- Excellent

Major Rating Factors: Good quality investment portfolio (6.6 on a scale of 0 to 10) despite large exposure to mortgages . Mortgage default rate has been low. substantial holdings of BBB bonds in addition to minimal holdings in junk bonds. Good overall profitability (5.1) although investment income, in comparison to reserve requirements, is below regulatory standards. Good liquidity (5.9).
Other Rating Factors: Excellent overall results on stability tests (7.0) excellent operational trends and excellent risk diversification. Strong capitalization (8.2) based on excellent risk adjusted capital (severe loss scenario).
Principal Business: Group health insurance (52%), individual life insurance (37%), and group life insurance (11%).
Principal Investments: Mortgages in good standing (37%), nonCMO investment grade bonds (36%), CMOs and structured securities (17%), policy loans (6%), and misc. investments (3%).
Investments in Affiliates: None
Group Affiliation: Meiji Yasuda Life Ins Co
Licensed in: AK, AZ, CA, CO, HI, ID, IA, LA, MO, MT, NE, NV, NM, OK, OR, SD, TX, UT, WA, WY
Commenced Business: June 1962
Address: 1440 Kapiolani Blvd Ste 1600, Honolulu, HI 96814-3698
Phone: (808) 955-2236 **Domicile State:** HI **NAIC Code:** 64343

Data Date	Rating	RACR #1	RACR #2	Total Assets ($mil)	Capital ($mil)	Net Premium ($mil)	Net Income ($mil)
3-19	A-	3.06	1.78	568.1	86.7	28.5	0.2
3-18	A-	3.56	2.08	562.2	96.6	28.1	0.7
2018	A-	3.47	2.03	556.9	94.0	77.7	4.8
2017	A-	3.96	2.31	553.9	102.4	74.4	4.0
2016	A-	4.30	2.51	543.1	107.1	74.3	5.2
2015	A-	4.52	2.62	528.4	108.5	70.2	6.7
2014	A-	4.72	2.73	515.6	108.8	68.4	8.1

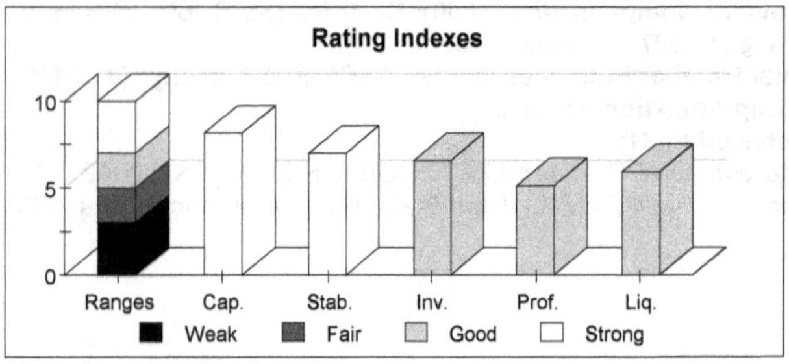

PACIFICARE LIFE & HEALTH INSURANCE COMPANY B Good

Major Rating Factors: Good overall results on stability tests (5.9 on a scale of 0 to 10) despite fair financial strength of affiliated UnitedHealth Group Inc. Other stability subfactors include good operational trends and excellent risk diversification. Strong capitalization (10.0) based on excellent risk adjusted capital (severe loss scenario). High quality investment portfolio (8.2).
Other Rating Factors: Excellent profitability (7.0). Excellent liquidity (9.7).
Principal Business: Individual health insurance (73%) and group health insurance (27%).
Principal Investments: NonCMO investment grade bonds (78%) and CMOs and structured securities (20%).
Investments in Affiliates: None
Group Affiliation: UnitedHealth Group Inc
Licensed in: All states except NY, PR
Commenced Business: September 1967
Address: 7440 WOODLAND DRIVE, INDIANAPOLIS, IN 46278
Phone: (952) 979-7959 **Domicile State:** IN **NAIC Code:** 70785

Data Date	Rating	RACR #1	RACR #2	Total Assets ($mil)	Capital ($mil)	Net Premium ($mil)	Net Income ($mil)
3-19	B	18.81	16.93	188.5	183.5	3.1	1.1
3-18	B-	18.71	16.84	188.2	182.5	3.3	1.0
2018	B	18.71	16.84	187.5	182.4	12.8	4.3
2017	B	18.62	16.75	187.3	181.5	13.6	3.4
2016	C+	18.52	16.67	189.2	180.8	14.3	3.2
2015	C+	19.90	17.91	205.7	197.4	15.8	4.1
2014	C+	19.49	17.54	204.8	193.3	36.3	7.9

UnitedHealth Group Inc Composite Group Rating: C+ Largest Group Members	Assets ($mil)	Rating
UNITED HEALTHCARE INS CO	20752	C
SIERRA HEALTH AND LIFE INS CO INC	3270	B
OXFORD HEALTH INS INC	2570	B
UNITED HEALTHCARE OF WISCONSIN INC	1760	B+
UNITED HEALTHCARE INS CO OF NY	1262	B-

PACIFICARE OF ARIZONA INC E Very Weak

Major Rating Factors: Low quality investment portfolio (0.7 on a scale of 0 to 10). Fair overall results on stability tests (3.8). Rating is significantly influenced by the good financial results of . Good overall profitability index (5.0).
Other Rating Factors: Strong capitalization index (10.0) based on excellent current risk-adjusted capital (severe loss scenario). Excellent liquidity (7.9) with ample operational cash flow and liquid investments.
Principal Business: Medicare (100%)
Mem Phys: 18: N/A **17:** N/A **18 MLR** -66.0% **/ 18 Admin Exp** N/A
Enroll(000): Q1 19: N/A **18:** N/A **17:** N/A **Med Exp PMPM:** N/A
Principal Investments: Cash and equiv (95%), long-term bonds (5%)
Provider Compensation ($000): Bonus arrang ($1,651)
Total Member Encounters: N/A
Group Affiliation: None
Licensed in: AZ
Address: 1 EAST WASHINGTON STREET # 170, PHOENIX, AZ 85004
Phone: (952) 936-1300 **Dom State:** AZ **Commenced Bus:** N/A

Data Date	Rating	RACR #1	RACR #2	Total Assets ($mil)	Capital ($mil)	Net Premium ($mil)	Net Income ($mil)
3-19	E	8.49	7.07	33.2	12.9	0.0	1.0
3-18	E	8.31	6.93	41.9	12.6	0.0	0.8
2018	E	8.17	6.81	35.3	12.5	2.8	4.1
2017	E	4.52	3.77	41.0	12.3	0.6	1.5
2016	U	332.10	276.70	105.2	71.8	0.1	1.6
2015	B	2.35	1.96	189.6	94.3	964.6	30.2
2014	B	3.26	2.71	206.2	125.9	987.5	45.3

Rating Indexes

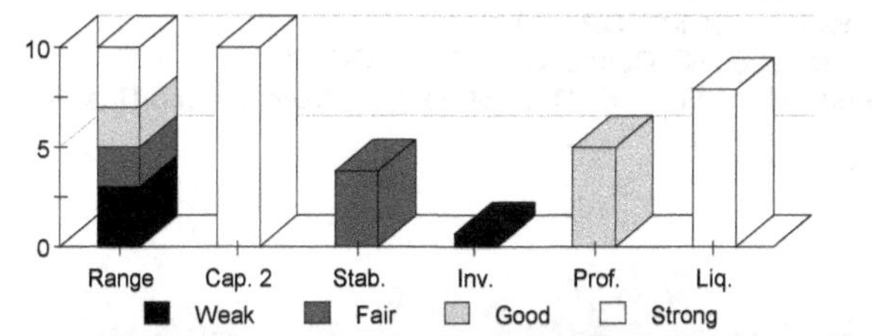

PACIFICARE OF COLORADO INC B Good

Major Rating Factors: Good overall results on stability tests (6.1 on a scale of 0 to 10). Rating is significantly influenced by the good financial results of . Good liquidity (6.9) with sufficient resources (cash flows and marketable investments) to handle a spike in claims. Excellent profitability (9.1).
Other Rating Factors: Strong capitalization index (9.2) based on excellent current risk-adjusted capital (severe loss scenario). High quality investment portfolio (8.9).
Principal Business: Medicare (100%)
Mem Phys: 18: 46,288 **17:** 42,249 **18 MLR** 82.6% **/ 18 Admin Exp** N/A
Enroll(000): Q1 19: 334 **18:** 295 **17:** 276 **Med Exp PMPM:** $766
Principal Investments: Long-term bonds (100%)
Provider Compensation ($000): Capitation ($1,276,851), contr fee ($1,259,581), FFS ($97,490), bonus arrang ($40,221)
Total Member Encounters: Phys (2,193,350), non-phys (584,989)
Group Affiliation: None
Licensed in: AZ, CO, NV
Address: 6465 GREENWOOD PLAZA BLVD SUIT, CENTENNIAL, CO 80111
Phone: (952) 979-7959 **Dom State:** CO **Commenced Bus:** N/A

Data Date	Rating	RACR #1	RACR #2	Total Assets ($mil)	Capital ($mil)	Net Premium ($mil)	Net Income ($mil)
3-19	B	3.10	2.58	827.7	450.9	1,071.8	63.4
3-18	B	2.04	1.70	955.8	251.0	806.6	-28.0
2018	B	2.66	2.22	664.6	387.2	3,243.6	137.6
2017	B	1.69	1.41	601.9	279.0	2,839.8	97.0
2016	B	1.75	1.46	412.6	182.6	2,469.4	73.4
2015	B	2.78	2.32	209.8	109.3	973.1	43.1
2014	B	3.21	2.68	211.4	128.6	929.4	45.0

Rating Indexes

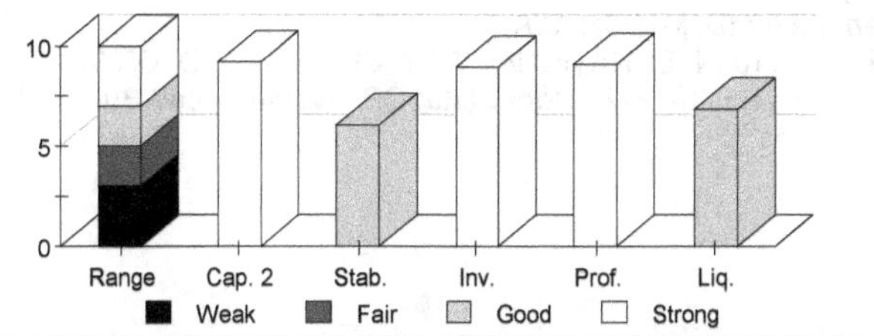

PACIFICARE OF NEVADA INC C Fair

Major Rating Factors: Fair profitability index (4.2 on a scale of 0 to 10). Weak overall results on stability tests (2.3). Rating is significantly influenced by the good financial results of . Strong capitalization index (10.0) based on excellent current risk-adjusted capital (severe loss scenario).
Other Rating Factors: High quality investment portfolio (9.8). Excellent liquidity (7.2) with ample operational cash flow and liquid investments.
Principal Business: Medicare (100%)
Mem Phys: 18: N/A **17:** N/A **18 MLR** -6.2% **/ 18 Admin Exp** N/A
Enroll(000): Q1 19: N/A **18:** N/A **17:** N/A **Med Exp PMPM:** N/A
Principal Investments: Cash and equiv (66%), long-term bonds (34%)
Provider Compensation ($000): FFS ($13)
Total Member Encounters: N/A
Group Affiliation: None
Licensed in: NV
Address: 2720 N TENAYA WAY, LAS VEGAS, NV 89128
Phone: (702) 242-7000 **Dom State:** NV **Commenced Bus:** N/A

Data Date	Rating	RACR #1	RACR #2	Total Assets ($mil)	Capital ($mil)	Net Premium ($mil)	Net Income ($mil)
3-19	C	3.99	3.32	6.5	5.4	-0.1	0.3
3-18	U	3.41	2.84	6.6	4.5	0.0	0.0
2018	C	3.93	3.27	6.8	5.3	0.7	0.6
2017	U	1.70	1.42	6.6	4.5	-0.2	0.0
2016	E	1.95	1.62	12.4	8.5	-1.3	-0.5
2015	E	4.00	3.33	29.8	16.6	128.6	6.1
2014	E	4.34	3.62	30.9	18.7	113.1	-1.1

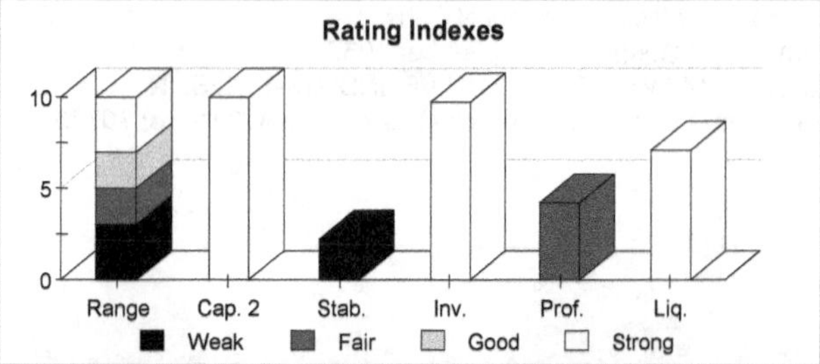

PACIFICSOURCE COMMUNITY HEALTH PLANS B Good

Major Rating Factors: Good overall profitability index (5.0 on a scale of 0 to 10). Good liquidity (6.7) with sufficient resources (cash flows and marketable investments) to handle a spike in claims. Fair quality investment portfolio (4.7).
Other Rating Factors: Strong capitalization (8.9) based on excellent current risk-adjusted capital (severe loss scenario).
Principal Business: Medicare (100%)
Mem Phys: 18: 20,700 **17:** 16,900 **18 MLR** 86.9% **/ 18 Admin Exp** N/A
Enroll(000): Q1 19: 33 **18:** 30 **17:** 35 **Med Exp PMPM:** $742
Principal Investments: Affiliate common stock (41%), long-term bonds (28%), cash and equiv (20%), nonaffiliate common stock (11%)
Provider Compensation ($000): Contr fee ($185,270), bonus arrang ($81,343), FFS ($4,497), capitation ($934)
Total Member Encounters: Phys (249,111), non-phys (71,848)
Group Affiliation: None
Licensed in: ID, MT, OR, WA
Address: 2965 NE Conners Ave, Bend, OR 97701
Phone: (541) 385-5315 **Dom State:** OR **Commenced Bus:** N/A

Data Date	Rating	RACR #1	RACR #2	Total Assets ($mil)	Capital ($mil)	Net Premium ($mil)	Net Income ($mil)
3-19	B	2.89	2.41	139.6	93.4	85.6	2.1
3-18	B	2.37	1.97	152.8	79.3	81.7	-0.6
2018	B	2.64	2.20	127.9	86.4	309.2	-2.4
2017	B-	1.86	1.55	123.4	71.4	357.2	27.0
2016	C	1.92	1.60	123.1	66.4	345.1	5.5
2015	C	1.86	1.55	101.6	59.3	301.1	4.2
2014	C	1.48	1.24	100.8	51.0	328.2	-5.6

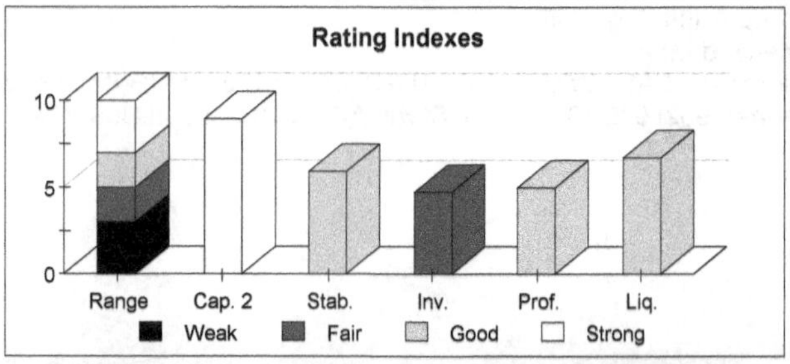

PACIFICSOURCE HEALTH PLANS C+ Fair

Major Rating Factors: Fair profitability index (3.9 on a scale of 0 to 10). Good quality investment portfolio (5.4). Good liquidity (6.7) with sufficient resources (cash flows and marketable investments) to handle a spike in claims.
Other Rating Factors: Strong capitalization (8.3) based on excellent current risk-adjusted capital (severe loss scenario).
Principal Business: Comp med (97%), dental (2%)
Mem Phys: 18: 51,200 **17:** 47,359 **18 MLR** 81.5% **/ 18 Admin Exp** N/A
Enroll(000): Q1 19: 247 **18:** 229 **17:** 210 **Med Exp PMPM:** $244
Principal Investments: Long-term bonds (38%), affiliate common stock (32%), cash and equiv (17%), nonaffiliate common stock (12%)
Provider Compensation ($000): Contr fee ($371,487), FFS ($254,811), bonus arrang ($32,760), capitation ($368)
Total Member Encounters: Phys (424,719), non-phys (418,849)
Group Affiliation: None
Licensed in: ID, MT, OR, WA
Address: 110 INTERNATIONAL WAY, SPRINGFIELD, OR 97477
Phone: (541) 686-1242 **Dom State:** OR **Commenced Bus:** N/A

Data Date	Rating	RACR #1	RACR #2	Total Assets ($mil)	Capital ($mil)	Net Premium ($mil)	Net Income ($mil)
3-19	C+	2.41	2.01	355.1	237.7	236.9	18.0
3-18	C	2.00	1.67	326.5	186.1	200.8	-6.2
2018	C+	2.09	1.74	319.9	209.0	800.7	13.9
2017	C	1.73	1.44	275.2	165.9	698.9	20.2
2016	C	1.84	1.54	238.1	157.4	547.9	-21.1
2015	C	1.72	1.43	228.9	144.4	564.8	-10.2
2014	C+	1.62	1.35	235.1	148.2	610.6	-16.9

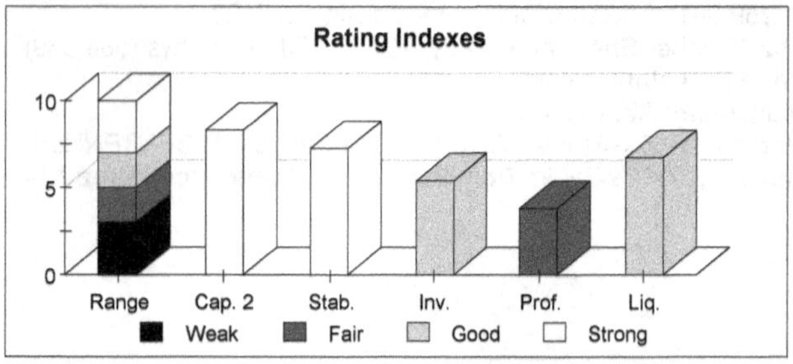

PAN-AMERICAN LIFE INSURANCE COMPANY B Good

Major Rating Factors: Good overall results on stability tests (6.0 on a scale of 0 to 10) despite negative cash flow from operations for 2018. Other stability subfactors include excellent operational trends and excellent risk diversification. Good quality investment portfolio (5.4) despite mixed results such as: minimal exposure to mortgages and large holdings of BBB rated bonds but small junk bond holdings. Good overall profitability (6.3).
Other Rating Factors: Good liquidity (6.6). Strong capitalization (7.8) based on excellent risk adjusted capital (severe loss scenario).
Principal Business: Group health insurance (72%), reinsurance (10%), individual life insurance (9%), individual health insurance (5%), and group life insurance (4%).
Principal Investments: NonCMO investment grade bonds (55%), CMOs and structured securities (19%), common & preferred stock (6%), policy loans (5%), and misc. investments (10%).
Investments in Affiliates: 2%
Group Affiliation: Pan-American Life
Licensed in: All states except ME, NY, VT
Commenced Business: March 1912
Address: PAN-AMERICAN LIFE CENTER, NEW ORLEANS, LA 70130-6060
Phone: (504) 566-1300 **Domicile State:** LA **NAIC Code:** 67539

Data Date	Rating	RACR #1	RACR #2	Total Assets ($mil)	Capital ($mil)	Net Premium ($mil)	Net Income ($mil)
3-19	B	2.29	1.52	1,280.0	247.7	156.7	4.3
3-18	B	2.46	1.57	1,219.7	238.3	54.5	6.4
2018	B	2.48	1.61	1,205.2	243.6	217.1	15.5
2017	B	2.41	1.53	1,221.1	234.1	212.9	14.5
2016	B	2.53	1.60	1,260.9	244.6	226.5	21.3
2015	B	2.52	1.62	1,293.7	244.9	237.9	22.0
2014	B	2.20	1.40	1,345.4	237.5	238.9	23.8

Adverse Trends in Operations

Decrease in asset base during 2018 (1%)
Decrease in asset base during 2017 (3%)
Decrease in capital during 2017 (4%)
Decrease in premium volume from 2015 to 2016 (5%)
Decrease in asset base during 2015 (4%)

PARAMOUNT ADVANTAGE B Good

Major Rating Factors: Good capitalization (5.8 on a scale of 0 to 10) based on good current risk-adjusted capital (severe loss scenario). Good liquidity (5.3) with sufficient resources (cash flows and marketable investments) to handle a spike in claims. High quality investment portfolio (8.5).
Other Rating Factors: Weak profitability index (2.9).
Principal Business: Medicaid (100%)
Mem Phys: 18: 24,310 **17:** 24,120 **18 MLR** 89.2% **/ 18 Admin Exp** N/A
Enroll(000): Q1 19: 241 **18:** 238 **17:** 238 **Med Exp PMPM:** $409
Principal Investments: Long-term bonds (73%), nonaffiliate common stock (17%), cash and equiv (10%)
Provider Compensation ($000): Contr fee ($734,597), FFS ($376,449), capitation ($72,657)
Total Member Encounters: Phys (423,157), non-phys (56,267)
Group Affiliation: ProMedica Health System Inc
Licensed in: OH
Address: 1901 Indian Wood Circle, Maumee, OH 43537
Phone: (419) 887-2500 **Dom State:** OH **Commenced Bus:** N/A

Data Date	Rating	RACR #1	RACR #2	Total Assets ($mil)	Capital ($mil)	Net Premium ($mil)	Net Income ($mil)
3-19	B	1.05	0.88	258.9	106.6	341.3	-36.1
3-18	A-	2.13	1.78	307.2	168.1	307.2	-0.5
2018	B	1.35	1.13	289.6	140.2	1,341.1	-23.5
2017	A-	2.06	1.72	303.4	169.4	1,144.9	27.6
2016	A-	1.81	1.51	290.4	135.3	1,000.4	-12.8
2015	A-	2.13	1.78	269.5	146.2	1,004.2	47.2
2014	A-	1.84	1.53	256.0	100.9	727.1	10.5

Rating Indexes

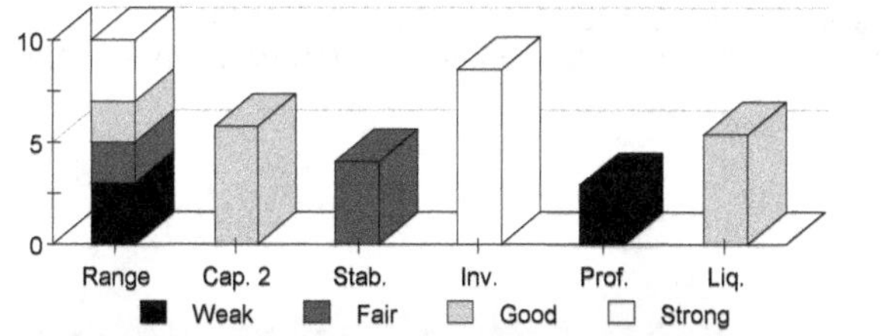

PARAMOUNT CARE OF MI INC B Good

Major Rating Factors: Excellent overall profitability index (6.9 on a scale of 0 to 10). Strong capitalization index (10.0) based on excellent current risk-adjusted capital (severe loss scenario). High quality investment portfolio (9.9).
Other Rating Factors: Excellent overall results on stability tests (7.6) based on steady enrollment growth, averaging 5% over the past five years. Rating is significantly influenced by the good financial results of ProMedica Health System Inc. Excellent liquidity (7.6) with ample operational cash flow and liquid investments.
Principal Business: Medicare (100%)
Mem Phys: 18: 2,182 **17:** 1,798 **18 MLR** 83.9% **/ 18 Admin Exp** N/A
Enroll(000): Q1 19: 2 **18:** 2 **17:** 2 **Med Exp PMPM:** $787
Principal Investments: Cash and equiv (66%), long-term bonds (34%)
Provider Compensation ($000): Contr fee ($16,530), FFS ($2,932)
Total Member Encounters: Phys (4,680), non-phys (379)
Group Affiliation: ProMedica Health System Inc
Licensed in: MI
Address: 106 Park Place, Dundee, MI 48131
Phone: (734) 529-7800 **Dom State:** MI **Commenced Bus:** N/A

Data Date	Rating	RACR #1	RACR #2	Total Assets ($mil)	Capital ($mil)	Net Premium ($mil)	Net Income ($mil)
3-19	B	4.26	3.55	15.9	13.2	5.8	1.0
3-18	B	3.97	3.31	15.0	11.6	5.5	0.4
2018	B	3.98	3.32	15.3	12.2	22.9	1.5
2017	B	2.88	2.40	15.2	11.2	21.7	2.0
2016	B	4.46	3.72	14.9	11.7	22.3	2.8
2015	B-	3.17	2.64	11.1	8.5	18.7	1.2
2014	B-	2.82	2.35	10.5	7.2	16.8	-0.3

Rating Indexes

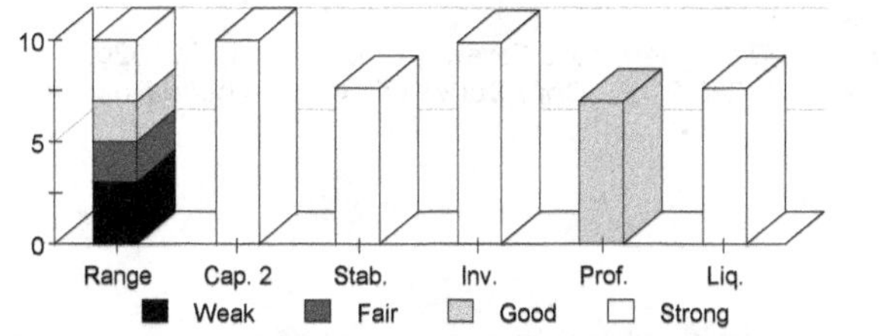

PARAMOUNT HEALTH CARE B Good

Major Rating Factors: Fair profitability index (3.5 on a scale of 0 to 10). Fair overall results on stability tests (4.7). Strong capitalization index (10.0) based on excellent current risk-adjusted capital (severe loss scenario).
Other Rating Factors: High quality investment portfolio (9.8). Excellent liquidity (7.1) with ample operational cash flow and liquid investments.
Principal Business: Medicare (100%)
Mem Phys: 18: 3,081 **17:** 2,770 **18 MLR** 89.9% **/ 18 Admin Exp** N/A
Enroll(000): Q1 19: 14 **18:** 14 **17:** 14 **Med Exp PMPM:** $921
Principal Investments: Long-term bonds (56%), cash and equiv (44%)
Provider Compensation ($000): Contr fee ($134,502), FFS ($20,353)
Total Member Encounters: Phys (36,319), non-phys (3,306)
Group Affiliation: ProMedica Health System Inc
Licensed in: OH
Address: 1901 Indian Wood Circle, Maumee, OH 43537
Phone: (419) 887-2500 **Dom State:** OH **Commenced Bus:** N/A

Data Date	Rating	RACR #1	RACR #2	Total Assets ($mil)	Capital ($mil)	Net Premium ($mil)	Net Income ($mil)
3-19	B	4.15	3.46	98.9	66.3	44.3	3.2
3-18	B	4.92	4.10	124.5	71.3	40.6	0.1
2018	B	3.97	3.31	92.4	62.9	170.9	0.5
2017	C+	4.23	3.52	106.3	70.7	169.9	12.6
2016	C	4.79	3.99	105.3	74.2	176.5	10.4
2015	C	4.10	3.42	91.6	64.5	150.8	-6.5
2014	C	3.80	3.17	105.1	55.8	143.0	0.9

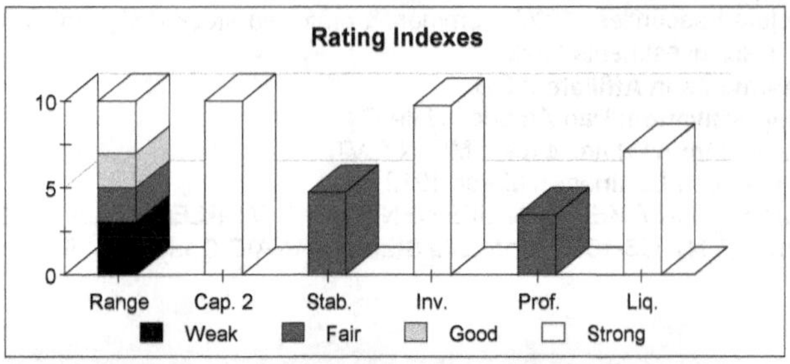

PARAMOUNT INS CO (OH) * A- Excellent

Major Rating Factors: Excellent profitability (9.6 on a scale of 0 to 10). Strong capitalization (8.8) based on excellent current risk-adjusted capital (severe loss scenario). High quality investment portfolio (9.1).
Other Rating Factors: Excellent liquidity (7.3) with ample operational cash flow and liquid investments.
Principal Business: Comp med (98%), med supp (2%)
Mem Phys: 18: 3,081 **17:** 2,770 **18 MLR** 77.6% **/ 18 Admin Exp** N/A
Enroll(000): Q1 19: 28 **18:** 31 **17:** 36 **Med Exp PMPM:** $352
Principal Investments: Cash and equiv (47%), long-term bonds (38%), nonaffiliate common stock (15%)
Provider Compensation ($000): FFS ($91,527), contr fee ($53,429)
Total Member Encounters: Phys (35,866), non-phys (3,765)
Group Affiliation: ProMedica Health System Inc
Licensed in: MI, OH
Address: 1901 Indian Wood Circle, Maumee, OH 43537
Phone: (419) 887-2500 **Dom State:** OH **Commenced Bus:** N/A

Data Date	Rating	RACR #1	RACR #2	Total Assets ($mil)	Capital ($mil)	Net Premium ($mil)	Net Income ($mil)
3-19	A-	2.80	2.33	87.0	45.2	38.2	2.2
3-18	A	2.60	2.17	98.1	38.8	48.1	4.5
2018	A-	2.63	2.19	86.2	41.9	184.1	13.5
2017	A-	1.87	1.56	89.3	35.0	160.9	9.8
2016	B+	2.10	1.75	87.5	30.7	158.0	5.3
2015	B	1.94	1.62	68.8	25.1	146.9	4.6
2014	B	1.52	1.27	44.6	20.6	151.6	6.3

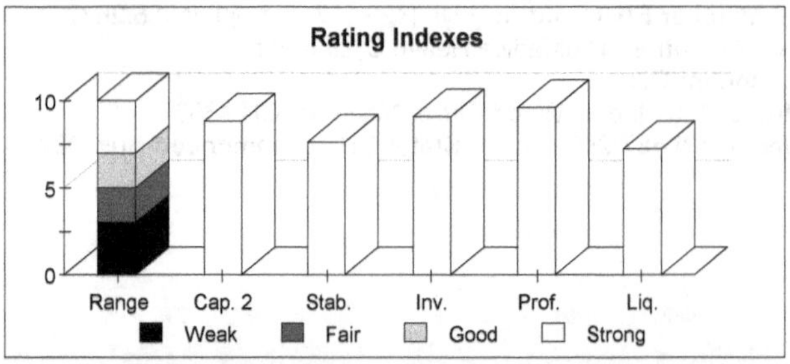

PARKLAND COMMUNITY HEALTH PLAN INC B- Good

Major Rating Factors: Fair overall results on stability tests (4.5 on a scale of 0 to 10). Good liquidity (6.5) with sufficient resources (cash flows and marketable investments) to handle a spike in claims. Strong capitalization index (7.2) based on excellent current risk-adjusted capital (severe loss scenario).
Other Rating Factors: High quality investment portfolio (7.3). Weak profitability index (2.5).
Principal Business: Medicaid (91%), comp med (9%)
Mem Phys: 18: 7,258 **17:** 6,933 **18 MLR** 85.1% **/ 18 Admin Exp** N/A
Enroll(000): Q1 19: 179 **18:** 183 **17:** 200 **Med Exp PMPM:** $211
Principal Investments: Long-term bonds (75%), cash and equiv (25%)
Provider Compensation ($000): Contr fee ($476,109), capitation ($2,346), bonus arrang ($571)
Total Member Encounters: Phys (1,434,637), non-phys (459,136)
Group Affiliation: Parkland Community Health Plan Inc
Licensed in: TX
Address: 2777 N Stemmons Freeway Suite, Dallas, TX 75207
Phone: (214) 266-2100 **Dom State:** TX **Commenced Bus:** N/A

Data Date	Rating	RACR #1	RACR #2	Total Assets ($mil)	Capital ($mil)	Net Premium ($mil)	Net Income ($mil)
3-19	B-	1.49	1.24	131.2	73.2	144.0	-17.8
3-18	B-	1.90	1.58	131.3	80.4	137.7	-16.7
2018	B-	1.98	1.65	150.0	93.7	574.7	-5.9
2017	B-	2.43	2.03	144.7	99.6	539.7	17.8
2016	B-	2.45	2.04	144.4	81.6	520.7	3.2
2015	B	2.85	2.38	168.8	98.3	525.7	-13.5
2014	B+	3.36	2.80	175.0	130.3	500.6	23.6

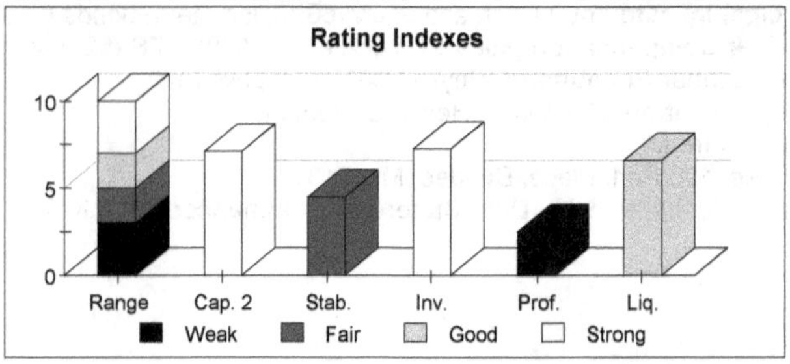

PARTNERRE AMERICA INS CO C+ Fair

Major Rating Factors: Fair long-term capitalization (3.7 on a scale of 0 to 10) based on fair current risk adjusted capital (moderate loss scenario), although results have slipped from the good range over the last two years. Fair reserve development (4.9) as reserves have generally been sufficient to cover claims.

Other Rating Factors: Fair profitability index (3.1) with operating losses during 2017. Return on equity has been low, averaging 1.5% over the past five years. Fair overall results on stability tests (3.3) including fair risk adjusted capital in prior years. Good liquidity (6.4) with sufficient resources (cash flows and marketable investments) to handle a spike in claims.

Principal Business: Other accident & health (50%), other liability (45%), and aircraft (5%).

Principal Investments: Investment grade bonds (82%), misc. investments (11%), and cash (7%).

Investments in Affiliates: None

Group Affiliation: Giovanni Agnelli e C Sapaz

Licensed in: All states, the District of Columbia and Puerto Rico

Commenced Business: August 1919

Address: 1209 ORANGE STREET, Wilmington, DE 19801

Phone: (203) 485-4287 **Domicile State:** DE **NAIC Code:** 11835

Data Date	Rating	RACR #1	RACR #2	Loss Ratio %	Total Assets ($mil)	Capital ($mil)	Net Premium ($mil)	Net Income ($mil)
3-19	C+	0.89	0.66	N/A	353.7	109.2	29.5	0.1
3-18	C+	3.26	2.14	N/A	339.8	110.5	55.2	-1.2
2018	C+	0.77	0.57	89.9	380.9	108.3	272.5	0.4
2017	C+	5.89	3.93	126.0	393.0	110.1	38.4	-4.5
2016	C+	10.77	6.63	85.8	370.9	116.0	32.1	0.8
2015	C+	11.97	7.29	90.3	375.8	128.4	32.2	5.6
2014	C	14.47	10.40	75.4	298.4	133.6	25.7	8.2

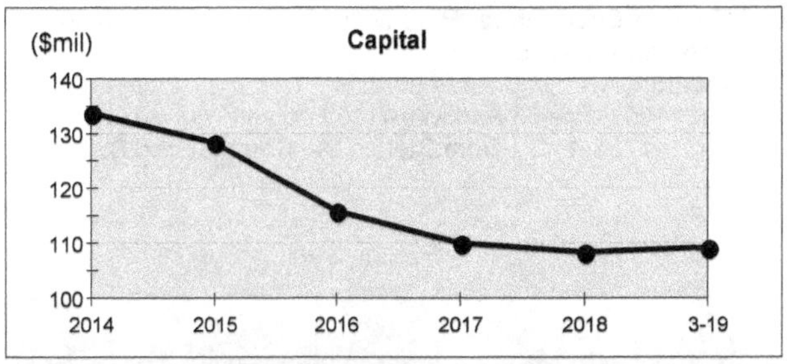

PARTNERSHIP HEALTHPLAN OF CALIFORNIA C+ Fair

Major Rating Factors: Fair profitability index (3.4 on a scale of 0 to 10). Fair overall results on stability tests (3.7) based on a steep decline in capital during 2018. Strong capitalization index (10.0) based on excellent current risk-adjusted capital (severe loss scenario).

Other Rating Factors: Excellent liquidity (7.2) with ample operational cash flow and liquid investments.

Principal Business: Medicaid (100%)

Mem Phys: 18: N/A **17:** N/A **18 MLR** 96.8% **/ 18 Admin Exp** N/A

Enroll(000): Q1 19: 549 **18:** 551 **17:** 567 **Med Exp PMPM:** $375

Principal Investments ($000): Cash and equiv ($651,851)

Provider Compensation ($000): None

Total Member Encounters: N/A

Group Affiliation: None

Licensed in: CA

Address: 4665 Business Center Drive, Fairfield, CA 94534

Phone: (707) 863-4218 **Dom State:** CA **Commenced Bus:** November 2005

Data Date	Rating	RACR #1	RACR #2	Total Assets ($mil)	Capital ($mil)	Net Premium ($mil)	Net Income ($mil)
3-19	C+	5.10	3.12	1,412.7	585.2	695.5	-27.8
3-18	B	7.04	4.31	1,466.6	731.4	633.7	-41.1
2018	C+	5.39	3.29	1,082.1	613.0	2,595.1	-144.8
2017	B+	7.59	4.64	1,527.5	772.4	2,491.5	-84.6
2016	A	9.68	5.92	1,717.6	848.1	2,436.1	166.7
2015	A-	8.79	5.36	1,483.2	681.5	2,251.2	267.4
2014	A-	6.72	4.10	727.2	414.1	1,614.5	178.0

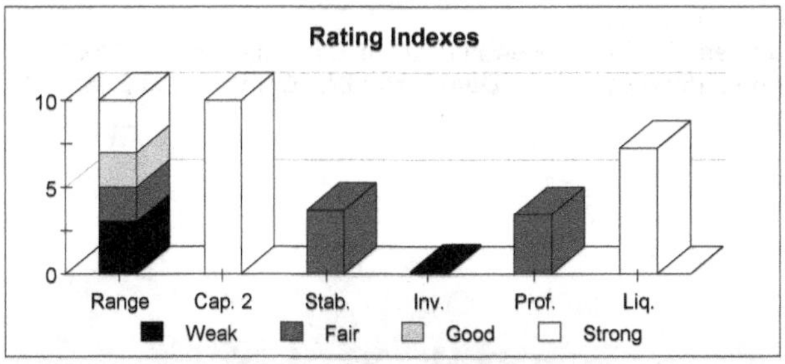

PAUL REVERE LIFE INSURANCE COMPANY C+ Fair

Major Rating Factors: Fair overall results on stability tests (4.8 on a scale of 0 to 10) including fair financial strength of affiliated Unum Group and negative cash flow from operations for 2018. Fair quality investment portfolio (3.9) with large holdings of BBB rated bonds in addition to junk bond exposure equal to 84% of capital. Good capitalization (6.6) based on good risk adjusted capital (severe loss scenario).

Other Rating Factors: Good overall profitability (6.3). Excellent liquidity (7.4).

Principal Business: Individual health insurance (67%), reinsurance (24%), group health insurance (5%), individual life insurance (4%), and group life insurance (1%).

Principal Investments: NonCMO investment grade bonds (85%), noninv. grade bonds (5%), common & preferred stock (4%), CMOs and structured securities (3%), and mortgages in good standing (2%).

Investments in Affiliates: 2%

Group Affiliation: Unum Group

Licensed in: All states except PR

Commenced Business: July 1930

Address: 1 MERCANTILE STREET, WORCESTER, MA 1608

Phone: (423) 294-1011 **Domicile State:** MA **NAIC Code:** 67598

Data Date	Rating	RACR #1	RACR #2	Total Assets ($mil)	Capital ($mil)	Net Premium ($mil)	Net Income ($mil)
3-19	C+	1.56	0.95	3,369.3	194.1	21.0	12.8
3-18	C+	1.57	0.92	3,567.4	206.1	25.5	18.2
2018	C+	1.55	0.94	3,410.2	191.1	93.2	70.4
2017	C+	1.40	0.82	3,570.6	177.3	93.8	55.4
2016	C+	1.71	1.01	3,790.4	251.4	95.2	65.6
2015	C+	1.72	1.02	3,977.0	257.7	96.8	63.1
2014	C+	1.85	1.09	4,145.1	278.0	91.0	76.5

Unum Group
Composite Group Rating: C+

Largest Group Members	Assets ($mil)	Rating
UNUM LIFE INS CO OF AMERICA	22022	C+
PROVIDENT LIFE ACCIDENT INS CO	7994	C+
FIRST UNUM LIFE INS CO	3761	C+
COLONIAL LIFE ACCIDENT INS CO	3422	C+
PAUL REVERE LIFE INS CO	3410	C+

PEACH STATE HEALTH PLAN INC B- Good

Major Rating Factors: Excellent profitability (9.3 on a scale of 0 to 10). Strong capitalization (10.0) based on excellent current risk-adjusted capital (severe loss scenario). High quality investment portfolio (8.0).

Other Rating Factors: Excellent liquidity (7.0) with sufficient resources (cash flows and marketable investments) to handle a spike in claims.

Principal Business: Medicaid (99%), Medicare (1%)

Mem Phys: 18: 39,679 **17:** 25,882 **18 MLR** 80.5% **/ 18 Admin Exp** N/A

Enroll(000): Q1 19: 374 **18:** 369 **17:** 368 **Med Exp PMPM:** $200

Principal Investments: Long-term bonds (66%), cash and equiv (30%), affiliate common stock (4%)

Provider Compensation ($000): Contr fee ($767,840), capitation ($75,871), salary ($19,920), bonus arrang ($6,156)

Total Member Encounters: Phys (286,365), non-phys (253,560)

Group Affiliation: None

Licensed in: GA

Address: 1100 Circle 75 Parkway #1100, Atlanta, GA 30339

Phone: (314) 725-4477 **Dom State:** GA **Commenced Bus:** N/A

Data Date	Rating	RACR #1	RACR #2	Total Assets ($mil)	Capital ($mil)	Net Premium ($mil)	Net Income ($mil)
3-19	B-	4.39	3.66	360.0	236.0	264.0	3.4
3-18	C+	N/A	N/A	319.5	186.9	262.5	-15.5
2018	B-	4.33	3.61	357.8	232.3	1,090.1	50.0
2017	C+	N/A	N/A	301.9	201.8	1,133.6	34.2
2016	C+	3.17	2.64	286.7	186.4	1,207.0	69.1
2015	C+	2.77	2.31	314.6	145.6	1,101.6	39.1
2014	C+	2.10	1.75	244.4	107.2	1,041.9	12.4

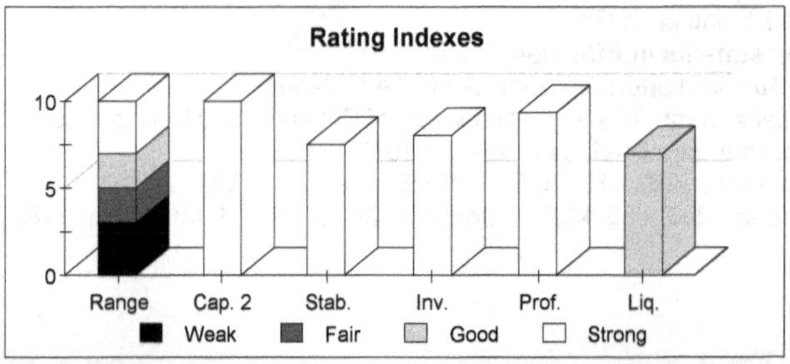

PEOPLES HEALTH INC C Fair

Major Rating Factors: Low quality investment portfolio (0.2 on a scale of 0 to 10). Excellent profitability (7.3). Strong capitalization (6.9) based on excellent current risk-adjusted capital (severe loss scenario).

Other Rating Factors: Excellent liquidity (7.0) with sufficient resources (cash flows and marketable investments) to handle a spike in claims.

Principal Business: Medicare (100%)

Mem Phys: 18: 5,786 **17:** 5,234 **18 MLR** 85.0% **/ 18 Admin Exp** N/A

Enroll(000): Q1 19: 76 **18:** 64 **17:** 61 **Med Exp PMPM:** $947

Principal Investments: Cash and equiv (99%), long-term bonds (1%)

Provider Compensation ($000): Capitation ($717,115)

Total Member Encounters: Phys (1,252,235), non-phys (634,281)

Group Affiliation: None

Licensed in: LA

Address: 3838 N Causeway Blvd Ste 2200, Metairie, LA 70002

Phone: (504) 849-4500 **Dom State:** LA **Commenced Bus:** N/A

Data Date	Rating	RACR #1	RACR #2	Total Assets ($mil)	Capital ($mil)	Net Premium ($mil)	Net Income ($mil)
3-19	C	1.30	1.08	73.3	45.7	262.6	1.0
3-18	D	N/A	N/A	157.1	43.6	213.4	0.5
2018	D	0.77	0.64	63.0	44.7	843.7	1.6
2017	D	N/A	N/A	69.3	43.1	768.3	0.8
2016	D	0.73	0.61	65.6	34.9	736.6	1.3
2015	D	0.71	0.59	55.3	33.6	710.4	1.3
2014	D	0.72	0.60	52.4	32.3	696.2	1.2

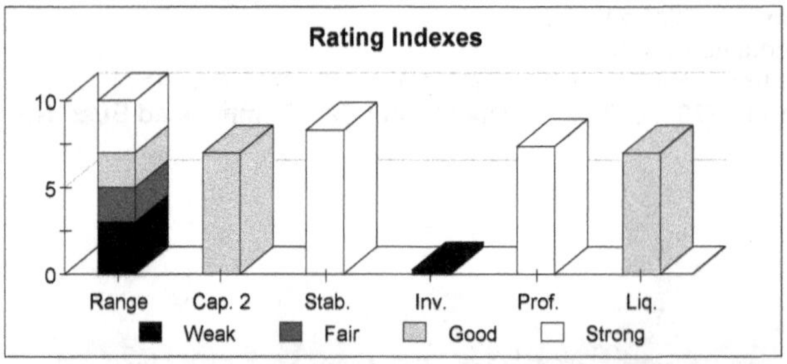

PHILADELPHIA AMERICAN LIFE INSURANCE COMPANY B Good

Major Rating Factors: Good overall results on stability tests (5.7 on a scale of 0 to 10) despite fair financial strength of affiliated New Era Life Group. Other stability subfactors include excellent operational trends, good risk adjusted capital for prior years and good risk diversification. Fair quality investment portfolio (4.8) with large holdings of BBB rated bonds in addition to junk bond exposure equal to 52% of capital. Strong capitalization (7.2) based on excellent risk adjusted capital (severe loss scenario).

Other Rating Factors: Excellent profitability (9.0). Excellent liquidity (7.1).

Principal Business: Individual health insurance (91%), individual annuities (6%), group health insurance (2%), and individual life insurance (1%).

Principal Investments: NonCMO investment grade bonds (73%), noninv. grade bonds (9%), CMOs and structured securities (7%), cash (5%), and misc. investments (5%).

Investments in Affiliates: None

Group Affiliation: New Era Life Group

Licensed in: All states except NY, RI, PR

Commenced Business: March 1978

Address: 11720 Katy Freeway Suite 1700, Houston, TX 77079

Phone: (281) 368-7200 **Domicile State:** TX **NAIC Code:** 67784

Data Date	Rating	RACR #1	RACR #2	Total Assets ($mil)	Capital ($mil)	Net Premium ($mil)	Net Income ($mil)
3-19	B	1.66	1.13	304.4	49.2	55.4	4.6
3-18	B	1.53	0.98	287.9	37.5	46.1	2.9
2018	B	1.56	1.06	303.3	44.3	190.3	8.1
2017	B	1.51	0.97	284.8	35.5	157.2	3.9
2016	B	1.62	1.03	263.3	34.2	141.1	1.4
2015	B	1.46	0.95	235.2	33.9	160.1	1.1
2014	B-	1.50	0.96	220.2	33.2	144.1	5.9

New Era Life Group
Composite Group Rating: C+

Largest Group Members	Assets ($mil)	Rating
NEW ERA LIFE INS CO	543	C
PHILADELPHIA AMERICAN LIFE INS CO	303	B
NEW ERA LIFE INS CO OF THE MIDWEST	140	C+
LIFE OF AMERICA INS CO	12	C

PHP INS CO — C — Fair

Major Rating Factors: Fair profitability index (4.8 on a scale of 0 to 10). Low quality investment portfolio (0.0). Strong capitalization (9.4) based on excellent current risk-adjusted capital (severe loss scenario).
Other Rating Factors: Excellent liquidity (7.8) with ample operational cash flow and liquid investments.
Principal Business: Comp med (100%)
Mem Phys: 18: 4,381 **17:** 3,641 **18 MLR** 81.4% **/ 18 Admin Exp** N/A
Enroll(000): Q1 19: 4 **18:** 5 **17:** 6 **Med Exp PMPM:** $367
Principal Investments: Cash and equiv (100%)
Provider Compensation ($000): Contr fee ($15,914), FFS ($6,672)
Total Member Encounters: Phys (53,011), non-phys (29,017)
Group Affiliation: None
Licensed in: MI
Address: 1400 EAST MICHIGAN Ave, LANSING, MI 48912
Phone: (517) 364-8400 **Dom State:** MI **Commenced Bus:** N/A

Data Date	Rating	RACR #1	RACR #2	Total Assets ($mil)	Capital ($mil)	Net Premium ($mil)	Net Income ($mil)
3-19	C	3.29	2.74	16.5	13.0	5.0	0.2
3-18	C	3.31	2.76	17.1	12.7	6.6	0.3
2018	C	3.26	2.71	17.4	12.9	26.9	0.6
2017	C	2.96	2.47	16.4	12.7	29.7	1.2
2016	C+	3.08	2.57	16.2	11.6	35.7	2.9
2015	C	1.59	1.33	14.0	8.4	42.9	-2.4
2014	C	1.55	1.29	16.3	8.6	46.0	-0.2

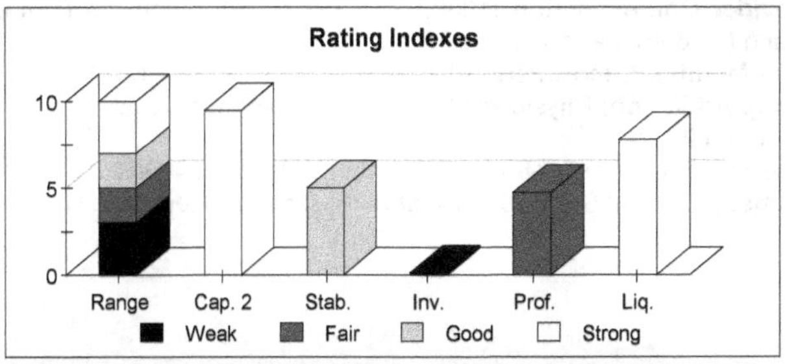

PHP INS CO OF IN INC — C+ — Fair

Major Rating Factors: Weak profitability index (1.5 on a scale of 0 to 10). Strong capitalization (10.0) based on excellent current risk-adjusted capital (severe loss scenario). High quality investment portfolio (8.5).
Other Rating Factors: Excellent liquidity (9.0) with ample operational cash flow and liquid investments.
Principal Business: Other (92%)
Mem Phys: 18: N/A **17:** N/A **18 MLR** 85.4% **/ 18 Admin Exp** N/A
Enroll(000): Q1 19: 0 **18:** 0 **17:** 0 **Med Exp PMPM:** $140
Principal Investments: Cash and equiv (52%), long-term bonds (31%), nonaffiliate common stock (17%)
Provider Compensation ($000): Other ($419)
Total Member Encounters: N/A
Group Affiliation: Physicians Health Plan of Northern I
Licensed in: IN
Address: 8101 W Jefferson Blvd, Ft. Wayne, IN 46804
Phone: (260) 432-6690 **Dom State:** IN **Commenced Bus:** N/A

Data Date	Rating	RACR #1	RACR #2	Total Assets ($mil)	Capital ($mil)	Net Premium ($mil)	Net Income ($mil)
3-19	C+	7.69	6.41	3.4	2.4	0.2	0.1
3-18	U	17.06	14.21	2.8	2.3	0.1	0.0
2018	C+	7.28	6.06	3.0	2.3	0.6	0.0
2017	U	12.84	10.70	2.6	2.3	0.1	-0.1
2016	U	20.54	17.12	2.5	2.4	0.0	0.0
2015	N/A	N/A	N/A	2.4	2.4	0.1	N/A
2014	N/A	N/A	N/A	2.5	2.4	0.8	N/A

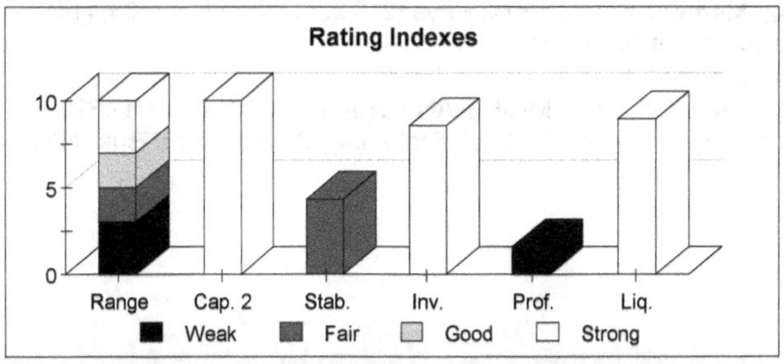

PHYSICIANS HEALTH CHOICE OF TEXAS — C — Fair

Major Rating Factors: Fair quality investment portfolio (3.3 on a scale of 0 to 10). Weak profitability index (0.9). Good liquidity (6.8) with sufficient resources (cash flows and marketable investments) to handle a spike in claims.
Other Rating Factors: Strong capitalization (7.3) based on excellent current risk-adjusted capital (severe loss scenario).
Principal Business: Medicare (100%)
Mem Phys: 18: 78,116 **17:** 58,440 **18 MLR** 89.7% **/ 18 Admin Exp** N/A
Enroll(000): Q1 19: 86 **18:** 77 **17:** 69 **Med Exp PMPM:** $977
Principal Investments: Cash and equiv (56%), long-term bonds (44%)
Provider Compensation ($000): Capitation ($489,579), contr fee ($320,931), FFS ($68,068), bonus arrang ($3,744)
Total Member Encounters: Phys (1,082,789), non-phys (497,430)
Group Affiliation: None
Licensed in: TX
Address: 1311 W PRESIDENT GEORGE BUSH, RICHARDSON, TX 75080
Phone: (952) 936-1300 **Dom State:** TX **Commenced Bus:** N/A

Data Date	Rating	RACR #1	RACR #2	Total Assets ($mil)	Capital ($mil)	Net Premium ($mil)	Net Income ($mil)
3-19	C	1.58	1.32	188.6	70.9	315.5	6.4
3-18	C	N/A	N/A	250.7	39.0	244.5	-11.2
2018	C	1.23	1.03	137.4	54.8	983.0	-6.1
2017	C	N/A	N/A	161.7	50.4	765.2	-6.9
2016	C+	2.32	1.93	64.0	33.5	417.5	-5.5
2015	C+	3.46	2.88	67.7	38.6	372.6	4.4
2014	B-	4.17	3.48	80.2	54.0	338.9	-2.2

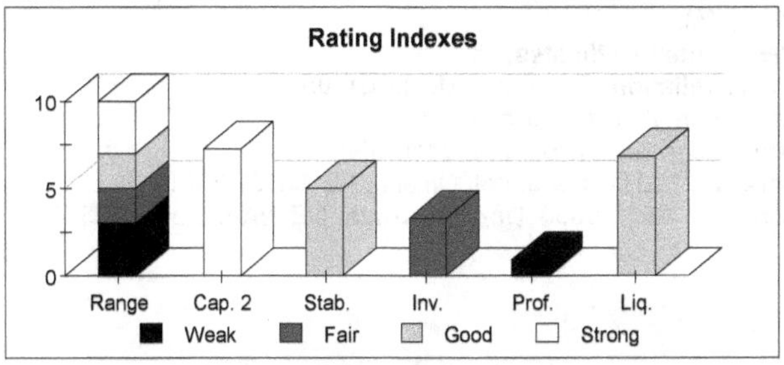

PHYSICIANS HEALTH PLAN OF NO IN — B — Good

Major Rating Factors: Good overall profitability index (6.2 on a scale of 0 to 10). Good quality investment portfolio (6.3). Good overall results on stability tests (6.3).

Other Rating Factors: Good liquidity (6.7) with sufficient resources (cash flows and marketable investments) to handle a spike in claims. Strong capitalization index (9.3) based on excellent current risk-adjusted capital (severe loss scenario).

Principal Business: Comp med (100%)

Mem Phys: 18: 16,043 **17:** 11,981 **18 MLR** 82.8% **/ 18 Admin Exp** N/A

Enroll(000): Q1 19: 35 **18:** 34 **17:** 33 **Med Exp PMPM:** $351

Principal Investments: Long-term bonds (69%), nonaffiliate common stock (19%), cash and equiv (7%), affiliate common stock (3%), real estate (2%)

Provider Compensation ($000): FFS ($119,038), contr fee ($14,972), bonus arrang ($5,658), capitation ($1,681)

Total Member Encounters: Phys (161,423), non-phys (120,150)

Group Affiliation: Physicians Health Plan of Northern I

Licensed in: IN

Address: 8101 West Jefferson Blvd, Fort Wayne, IN 46804

Phone: (260) 432-6690 **Dom State:** IN **Commenced Bus:** N/A

Data Date	Rating	RACR #1	RACR #2	Total Assets ($mil)	Capital ($mil)	Net Premium ($mil)	Net Income ($mil)
3-19	B	3.17	2.65	101.2	63.7	45.7	3.5
3-18	B	3.30	2.75	91.1	59.7	43.7	5.9
2018	B	2.85	2.37	94.9	57.9	173.0	7.2
2017	B	3.06	2.55	86.5	56.1	157.1	4.3
2016	B	2.32	1.94	82.3	49.1	180.1	-0.2
2015	B	1.97	1.64	84.6	43.9	192.5	2.7
2014	B	1.80	1.50	87.6	44.8	212.8	1.8

Rating Indexes

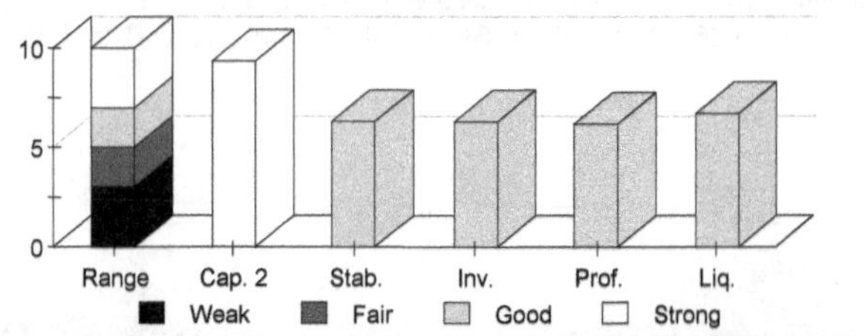

PHYSICIANS HP OF MID-MICHIGAN — C — Fair

Major Rating Factors: Fair profitability index (4.4 on a scale of 0 to 10). Low quality investment portfolio (0.0). Good overall results on stability tests (5.5).

Other Rating Factors: Strong capitalization index (7.7) based on excellent current risk-adjusted capital (severe loss scenario). Excellent liquidity (7.1) with ample operational cash flow and liquid investments.

Principal Business: Comp med (100%)

Mem Phys: 18: 5,143 **17:** 4,344 **18 MLR** 85.8% **/ 18 Admin Exp** N/A

Enroll(000): Q1 19: 35 **18:** 34 **17:** 35 **Med Exp PMPM:** $399

Principal Investments: Cash and equiv (48%), nonaffiliate common stock (30%), affiliate common stock (18%), real estate (4%)

Provider Compensation ($000): Contr fee ($124,998), FFS ($52,395), bonus arrang ($1,250)

Total Member Encounters: Phys (235,237), non-phys (124,414)

Group Affiliation: None

Licensed in: MI

Address: 1400 EAST MICHIGAN AVENUE, LANSING, MI 48912

Phone: (517) 364-8400 **Dom State:** MI **Commenced Bus:** N/A

Data Date	Rating	RACR #1	RACR #2	Total Assets ($mil)	Capital ($mil)	Net Premium ($mil)	Net Income ($mil)
3-19	C	1.93	1.61	88.3	51.9	43.5	0.0
3-18	C	1.95	1.63	89.4	48.7	47.3	-0.5
2018	C	1.83	1.53	83.1	49.5	199.6	6.0
2017	C	1.96	1.63	83.5	50.3	182.4	9.3
2016	B	2.22	1.85	91.9	62.1	178.6	-1.2
2015	B	2.07	1.72	96.5	60.8	251.8	0.5
2014	B	1.96	1.63	86.3	59.8	157.9	2.9

Rating Indexes

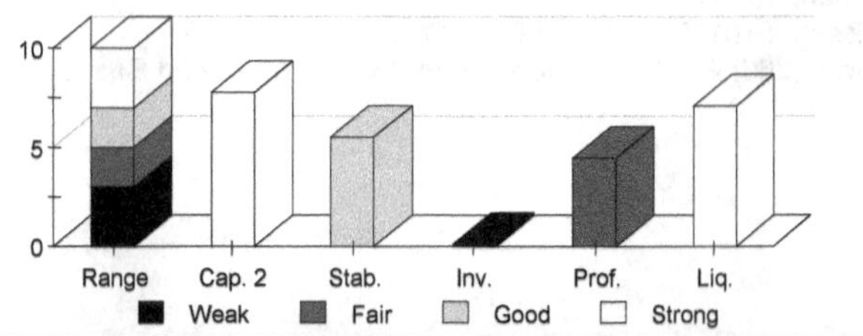

PHYSICIANS MUTUAL INSURANCE COMPANY * — A+ — Excellent

Major Rating Factors: Good quality investment portfolio (6.1 on a scale of 0 to 10) despite mixed results such as: no exposure to mortgages and large holdings of BBB rated bonds but small junk bond holdings. Strong capitalization (9.4) based on excellent risk adjusted capital (severe loss scenario). Furthermore, this high level of risk adjusted capital has been consistently maintained over the last five years. Excellent profitability (8.8).

Other Rating Factors: Excellent liquidity (7.2). Excellent overall results on stability tests (7.9) excellent operational trends and excellent risk diversification.

Principal Business: Individual health insurance (73%), reinsurance (15%), and group health insurance (13%).

Principal Investments: NonCMO investment grade bonds (49%), CMOs and structured securities (26%), common & preferred stock (16%), and noninv. grade bonds (7%).

Investments in Affiliates: 7%

Group Affiliation: Physicians Mutual Group

Licensed in: All states except PR

Commenced Business: February 1902

Address: 2600 Dodge Street, Omaha, NE 68131-2671

Phone: (402) 633-1000 **Domicile State:** NE **NAIC Code:** 80578

Data Date	Rating	RACR #1	RACR #2	Total Assets ($mil)	Capital ($mil)	Net Premium ($mil)	Net Income ($mil)
3-19	A+	3.49	2.61	2,391.2	1,015.5	120.9	11.4
3-18	A+	3.43	2.55	2,305.5	962.2	114.8	17.7
2018	A+	3.40	2.56	2,356.3	993.4	463.5	52.1
2017	A+	3.43	2.56	2,291.9	951.2	436.2	39.8
2016	A+	3.41	2.58	2,208.6	919.2	454.5	29.1
2015	A+	3.51	2.65	2,106.2	885.5	454.2	39.6
2014	A+	3.67	2.78	2,026.2	845.5	424.5	42.8

Rating Indexes

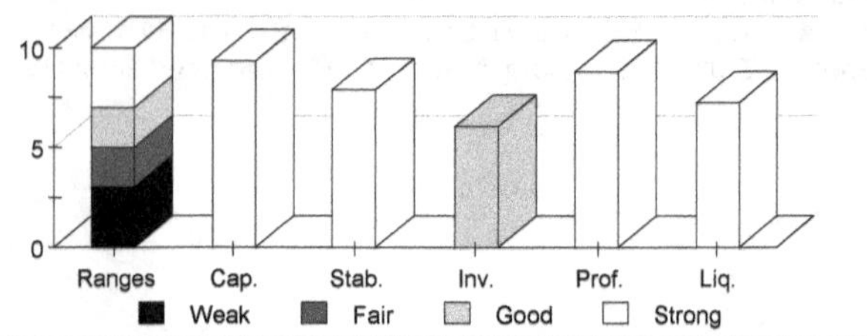

PHYSICIANS PLUS INS CORP — C- — Fair

Major Rating Factors: Fair quality investment portfolio (3.9 on a scale of 0 to 10). Fair overall results on stability tests (4.6) based on a significant 42% decrease in enrollment during the period. Weak profitability index (1.8).
Other Rating Factors: Strong capitalization index (7.2) based on excellent current risk-adjusted capital (severe loss scenario). Excellent liquidity (6.9) with sufficient resources (cash flows and marketable investments) to handle a spike in claims.
Principal Business: Comp med (82%), Medicaid (10%), FEHB (6%), med supp (2%)
Mem Phys: 18: 9,567 **17:** 5,468 **18 MLR** 88.1% **/ 18 Admin Exp** N/A
Enroll(000): Q1 19: 1 **18:** 35 **17:** 61 **Med Exp PMPM:** $348
Principal Investments: Affiliate common stock (64%), cash and equiv (34%), long-term bonds (1%)
Provider Compensation ($000): Capitation ($172,773)
Total Member Encounters: Phys (181,122), non-phys (194,799)
Group Affiliation: University Health Care Inc
Licensed in: IL, WI
Address: 2650 Novation Parkway, Madison, WI 53713
Phone: (608) 643-2491 **Dom State:** WI **Commenced Bus:** N/A

Data Date	Rating	RACR #1	RACR #2	Total Assets ($mil)	Capital ($mil)	Net Premium ($mil)	Net Income ($mil)
3-19	C-	1.47	1.23	127.1	106.3	1.2	0.5
3-18	D+	0.88	0.74	96.4	61.5	55.0	-0.4
2018	C-	1.38	1.15	133.1	100.1	193.0	2.8
2017	D+	1.03	0.86	121.8	77.4	240.7	-10.0
2016	D+	0.84	0.70	75.4	33.4	244.1	1.9
2015	D+	0.75	0.62	64.6	29.9	252.0	-9.2
2014	D+	1.18	0.98	74.5	39.2	232.3	2.8

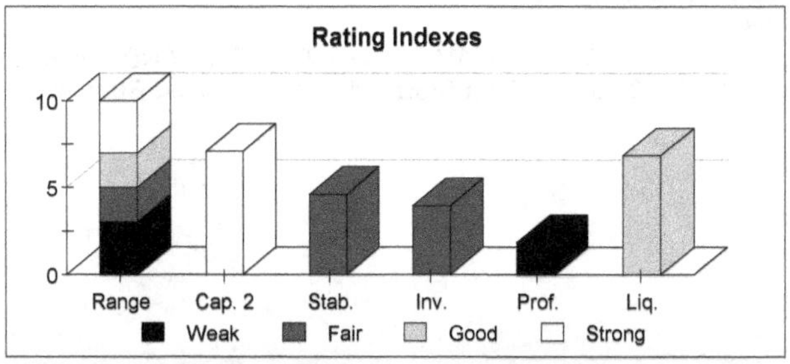

PIEDMONT COMMUNITY HEALTHCARE — D+ — Weak

Major Rating Factors: Weak profitability index (0.9 on a scale of 0 to 10). Weak liquidity (0.0) as a spike in claims may stretch capacity. Fair capitalization index (4.9) based on good current risk-adjusted capital (severe loss scenario).
Other Rating Factors: Fair overall results on stability tests (4.6) based on a significant 27% decrease in enrollment during the period. High quality investment portfolio (9.9).
Principal Business: Medicare (71%), comp med (29%)
Mem Phys: 18: 1,302 **17:** 927 **18 MLR** 99.5% **/ 18 Admin Exp** N/A
Enroll(000): Q1 19: 8 **18:** 9 **17:** 12 **Med Exp PMPM:** $655
Principal Investments: Cash and equiv (100%)
Provider Compensation ($000): Contr fee ($76,157), FFS ($3,747)
Total Member Encounters: Phys (101,481), non-phys (86,448)
Group Affiliation: Centra Health Inc
Licensed in: VA
Address: 2316 Atherholt Road, Lynchburg, VA 24501
Phone: (434) 947-4463 **Dom State:** VA **Commenced Bus:** N/A

Data Date	Rating	RACR #1	RACR #2	Total Assets ($mil)	Capital ($mil)	Net Premium ($mil)	Net Income ($mil)
3-19	D+	0.91	0.76	26.0	11.0	17.3	-3.1
3-18	D+	0.87	0.72	28.4	11.9	20.0	-0.8
2018	D+	0.92	0.77	24.8	11.1	77.5	-8.1
2017	D+	0.92	0.77	25.1	12.6	94.4	-6.2
2016	D+	0.88	0.73	24.1	11.5	94.3	-2.5
2015	B-	0.96	0.80	26.7	10.7	84.7	-0.8
2014	B-	0.89	0.74	18.7	7.8	64.7	0.4

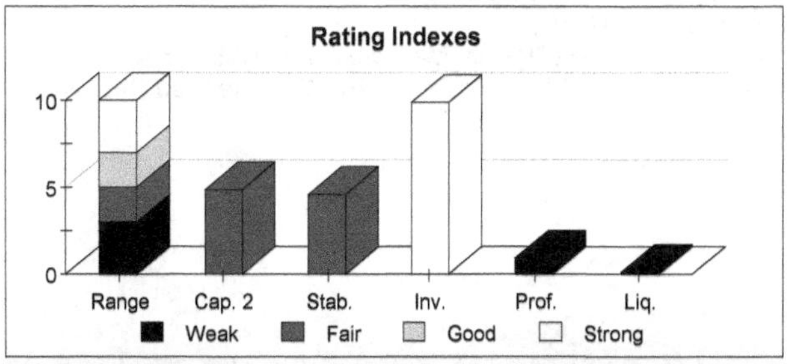

PIEDMONT COMMUNITY HEALTHCARE HMO — C- — Fair

Major Rating Factors: Fair capitalization (3.8 on a scale of 0 to 10) based on fair current risk-adjusted capital (moderate loss scenario). Weak profitability index (0.9). Good liquidity (6.8) with sufficient resources (cash flows and marketable investments) to handle a spike in claims.
Other Rating Factors: High quality investment portfolio (9.9).
Principal Business: Comp med (100%)
Mem Phys: 18: 1,732 **17:** 1,014 **18 MLR** 85.6% **/ 18 Admin Exp** N/A
Enroll(000): Q1 19: 9 **18:** 20 **17:** 4 **Med Exp PMPM:** $604
Principal Investments: Cash and equiv (100%)
Provider Compensation ($000): Contr fee ($137,794), FFS ($2,661)
Total Member Encounters: Phys (130,836), non-phys (92,361)
Group Affiliation: Centra Health Inc
Licensed in: VA
Address: 2316 Atherholt Rd, Lynchburg, VA 24501
Phone: (434) 947-4463 **Dom State:** VA **Commenced Bus:** N/A

Data Date	Rating	RACR #1	RACR #2	Total Assets ($mil)	Capital ($mil)	Net Premium ($mil)	Net Income ($mil)
3-19	C-	0.75	0.63	25.0	15.0	19.0	0.4
3-18	C-	N/A	N/A	34.4	17.5	45.6	4.4
2018	C-	0.73	0.61	31.6	14.6	176.2	2.3
2017	C-	N/A	N/A	8.8	3.7	17.7	-1.9
2016	D	1.29	1.08	4.6	3.2	10.7	-1.6
2015	N/A	N/A	N/A	4.6	4.5	N/A	N/A
2014	N/A	N/A	N/A	N/A	N/A	N/A	N/A

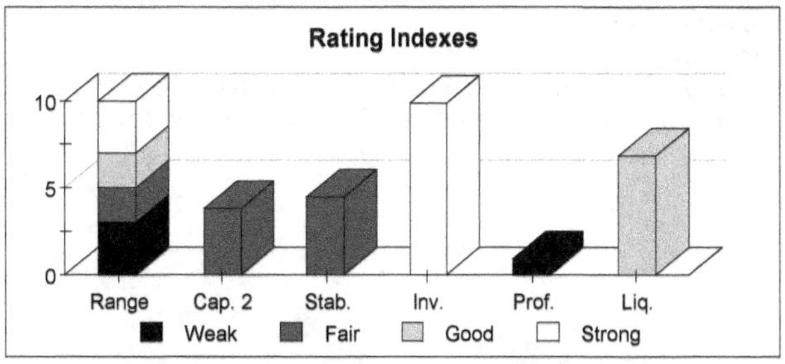

PIONEER EDUCATORS HEALTH TRUST E+ Very Weak

Major Rating Factors: Weak profitability index (0.9 on a scale of 0 to 10). Low quality investment portfolio (0.0). Strong capitalization index (10.0) based on weak current risk-adjusted capital (severe loss scenario).
Other Rating Factors: Excellent liquidity (7.1) with ample operational cash flow and liquid investments.
Principal Business: Comp med (89%), dental (11%)
Mem Phys: 18: N/A **17:** N/A **18 MLR** 108.1% **/ 18 Admin Exp** N/A
Enroll(000): Q1 19: 4 **18:** 4 **17:** 4 **Med Exp PMPM:** $285
Principal Investments: Cash and equiv (100%)
Provider Compensation ($000): FFS ($13,959)
Total Member Encounters: Phys (42,144), non-phys (25,455)
Group Affiliation: None
Licensed in: OR
Address: 700 NE MULTNOMAH ST Ste 1300, PORTLAND, OR 97232
Phone: (503) 299-3401 **Dom State:** OR **Commenced Bus:** N/A

Data Date	Rating	RACR #1	RACR #2	Total Assets ($mil)	Capital ($mil)	Net Premium ($mil)	Net Income ($mil)
3-19	E+	N/A	N/A	2.8	1.8	2.8	-0.3
3-18	E	N/A	N/A	3.3	0.9	3.5	N/A
2018	E+	N/A	N/A	3.9	2.1	12.5	N/A
2017	E	N/A	N/A	3.3	0.9	14.7	-0.6
2016	E	0.34	0.28	4.5	1.5	17.4	-0.4
2015	N/A	N/A	N/A	3.3	1.9	21.0	-1.8
2014	N/A	N/A	N/A	4.3	2.6	16.7	-4.8

Rating Indexes

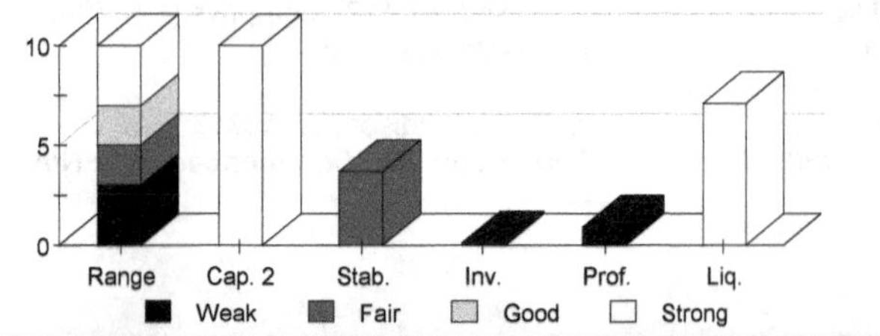

PL MEDICO SERV DE SALUD BELLA VISTA C+ Fair

Major Rating Factors: Good overall profitability index (5.2 on a scale of 0 to 10). Good capitalization index (5.2) based on good current risk-adjusted capital (severe loss scenario). Good quality investment portfolio (5.7).
Other Rating Factors: Good overall results on stability tests (5.0). Excellent liquidity (7.4) with ample operational cash flow and liquid investments.
Principal Business: Comp med (97%)
Mem Phys: 18: N/A **17:** 1,000 **18 MLR** 80.9% **/ 18 Admin Exp** N/A
Enroll(000): Q1 19: 18 **18:** 18 **17:** 19 **Med Exp PMPM:** $74
Principal Investments: Cash and equiv (98%), long-term bonds (2%)
Provider Compensation ($000): None
Total Member Encounters: N/A
Group Affiliation: Plan Medico Servicios de Salud Bella
Licensed in: (No states)
Address: 770 Avenida Hostos, Mayaguez, PR 00683-1538
Phone: (787) 833-8070 **Dom State:** PR **Commenced Bus:** N/A

Data Date	Rating	RACR #1	RACR #2	Total Assets ($mil)	Capital ($mil)	Net Premium ($mil)	Net Income ($mil)
3-19	C+	0.96	0.80	3.3	1.4	1.7	0.2
3-18	C-	N/A	N/A	2.8	1.0	1.5	0.1
2018	C	0.85	0.71	3.1	1.2	6.6	0.4
2017	C-	N/A	N/A	2.9	0.9	6.3	0.1
2016	D	0.50	0.42	2.6	0.8	6.1	-0.2
2015	U	0.73	0.61	2.7	1.0	5.6	0.2
2014	N/A	N/A	N/A	2.5	0.7	5.3	0.1

Rating Indexes

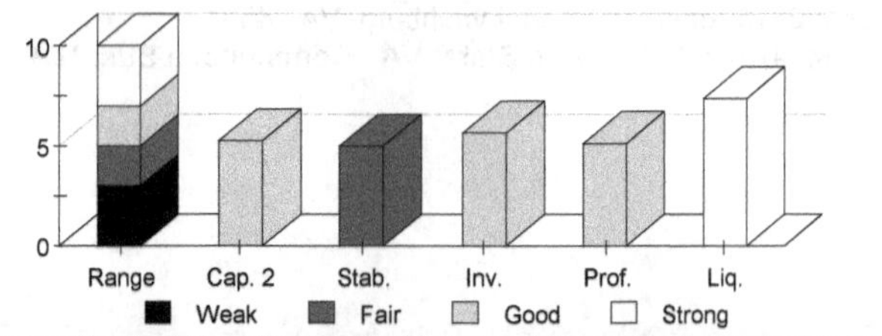

PREFERRED CARE PARTNERS INC B Good

Major Rating Factors: Good liquidity (6.3 on a scale of 0 to 10) with sufficient resources (cash flows and marketable investments) to handle a spike in claims. Excellent profitability (8.2). Strong capitalization (7.4) based on excellent current risk-adjusted capital (severe loss scenario).
Other Rating Factors: High quality investment portfolio (8.8).
Principal Business: Medicare (100%)
Mem Phys: 18: 42,617 **17:** 39,639 **18 MLR** 84.7% **/ 18 Admin Exp** N/A
Enroll(000): Q1 19: 191 **18:** 187 **17:** 165 **Med Exp PMPM:** $882
Principal Investments: Long-term bonds (97%), cash and equiv (3%)
Provider Compensation ($000): Contr fee ($976,769), capitation ($595,809), FFS ($282,024), bonus arrang ($42,600)
Total Member Encounters: Phys (2,857,034), non-phys (920,412)
Group Affiliation: None
Licensed in: FL
Address: 9100 S DADELAND Blvd Ste 1250, MIAMI, FL 33156
Phone: (305) 670-8438 **Dom State:** FL **Commenced Bus:** N/A

Data Date	Rating	RACR #1	RACR #2	Total Assets ($mil)	Capital ($mil)	Net Premium ($mil)	Net Income ($mil)
3-19	B	1.64	1.37	559.2	169.9	651.8	25.8
3-18	C	0.90	0.75	642.5	61.9	560.0	-22.7
2018	B	1.38	1.15	451.7	139.6	2,261.0	66.6
2017	E	0.76	0.63	411.1	82.0	1,751.8	23.8
2016	E	1.34	1.11	325.0	82.7	1,484.4	13.8
2015	E-	1.76	1.47	169.4	54.9	732.4	24.2
2014	E-	3.51	2.92	196.9	109.6	585.1	19.9

Rating Indexes

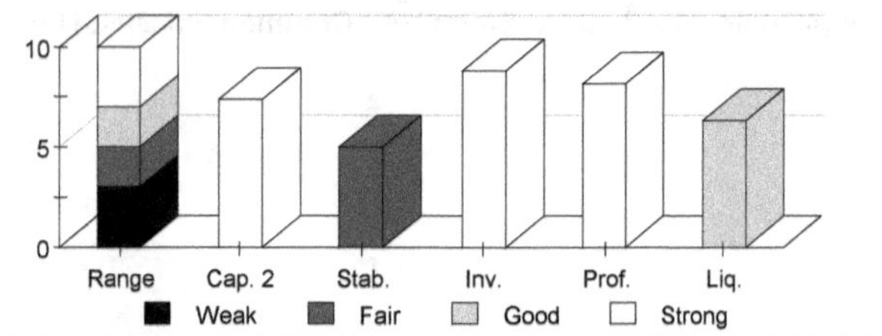

PREFERREDONE COMMUNITY HEALTH PLAN — D+ — Weak

Major Rating Factors: Weak profitability index (0.8 on a scale of 0 to 10). Weak overall results on stability tests (2.1) based on a significant 34% decrease in enrollment during the period. Rating is significantly influenced by the fair financial results of . Good liquidity (6.6) with sufficient resources (cash flows and marketable investments) to handle a spike in claims.
Other Rating Factors: Strong capitalization index (9.7) based on excellent current risk-adjusted capital (severe loss scenario). High quality investment portfolio (8.8).
Principal Business: Comp med (100%)
Mem Phys: 18: 43,290 **17:** 42,108 **18 MLR** 107.6% **/ 18 Admin Exp** N/A
Enroll(000): Q1 19: 0 **18:** 0 **17:** 1 **Med Exp PMPM:** $417
Principal Investments: Long-term bonds (83%), cash and equiv (17%)
Provider Compensation ($000): Contr fee ($2,300), FFS ($362), bonus arrang ($166)
Total Member Encounters: N/A
Group Affiliation: None
Licensed in: MN
Address: 6105 Golden Hills Drive, Golden Valley, MN 55416-1023
Phone: (763) 847-4000 **Dom State:** MN **Commenced Bus:** N/A

Data Date	Rating	RACR #1	RACR #2	Total Assets ($mil)	Capital ($mil)	Net Premium ($mil)	Net Income ($mil)
3-19	D+	3.48	2.90	3.8	2.7	0.5	0.0
3-18	D	3.96	3.30	3.4	2.8	0.7	-0.1
2018	D+	3.41	2.84	3.5	2.7	2.6	-0.3
2017	D	3.29	2.75	3.7	3.0	3.5	-0.5
2016	D	2.26	1.88	5.7	3.5	10.3	0.1
2015	D	0.75	0.63	7.6	3.4	26.1	-0.9
2014	D	0.68	0.57	11.8	4.8	57.4	-2.8

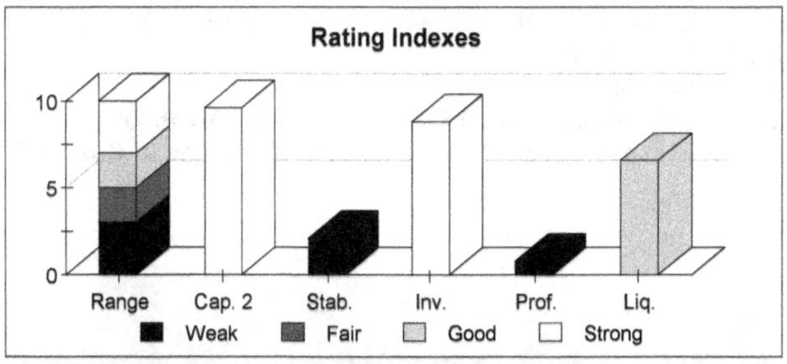

PREFERREDONE INS CO — C- — Fair

Major Rating Factors: Weak profitability index (0.9 on a scale of 0 to 10). Good capitalization (6.7) based on good current risk-adjusted capital (severe loss scenario). Good liquidity (5.5) with sufficient resources (cash flows and marketable investments) to handle a spike in claims.
Other Rating Factors: High quality investment portfolio (7.3).
Principal Business: Comp med (82%), other (18%)
Mem Phys: 18: 43,290 **17:** 42,108 **18 MLR** 95.6% **/ 18 Admin Exp** N/A
Enroll(000): Q1 19: 147 **18:** 135 **17:** 145 **Med Exp PMPM:** $134
Principal Investments: Long-term bonds (74%), nonaffiliate common stock (17%), cash and equiv (9%)
Provider Compensation ($000): Contr fee ($132,685), FFS ($34,792), bonus arrang ($8,542), other ($42,225)
Total Member Encounters: N/A
Group Affiliation: None
Licensed in: IA, MN, NE, ND, SD, WI
Address: 6105 Golden Hills Dr, Golden Valley, MN 55416-1023
Phone: (763) 847-4000 **Dom State:** MN **Commenced Bus:** N/A

Data Date	Rating	RACR #1	RACR #2	Total Assets ($mil)	Capital ($mil)	Net Premium ($mil)	Net Income ($mil)
3-19	C-	1.19	0.99	95.6	42.3	66.2	0.9
3-18	C-	1.08	0.90	88.1	41.3	55.3	-1.0
2018	C-	1.09	0.91	80.9	38.7	230.3	-11.4
2017	C-	1.15	0.96	87.2	44.1	256.0	-2.0
2016	D+	1.40	1.17	78.3	38.9	178.2	-5.8
2015	D+	0.76	0.63	62.9	30.8	153.3	-43.6
2014	C+	0.68	0.57	146.8	47.9	430.2	-20.9

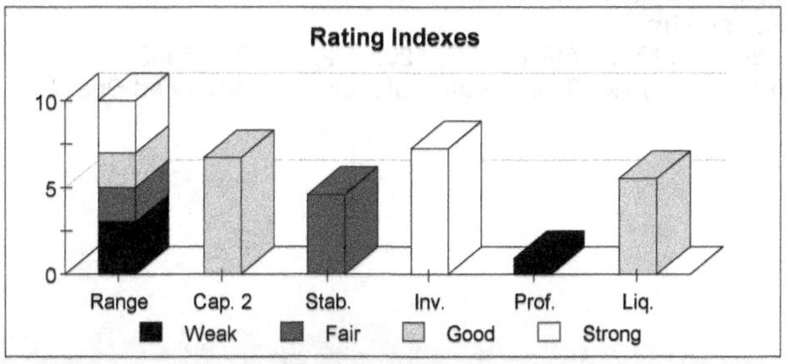

PREMERA BLUE CROSS — B — Good

Major Rating Factors: Good overall profitability index (6.5 on a scale of 0 to 10). Fair quality investment portfolio (4.4). Strong capitalization (10.0) based on excellent current risk-adjusted capital (severe loss scenario).
Other Rating Factors: Excellent liquidity (6.9) with sufficient resources (cash flows and marketable investments) to handle a spike in claims.
Principal Business: Comp med (67%), FEHB (24%), Medicare (4%), med supp (3%), dental (1%)
Mem Phys: 18: 55,256 **17:** 53,308 **18 MLR** 83.8% **/ 18 Admin Exp** N/A
Enroll(000): Q1 19: 730 **18:** 695 **17:** 631 **Med Exp PMPM:** $374
Principal Investments: Long-term bonds (41%), nonaffiliate common stock (21%), affiliate common stock (11%), cash and equiv (4%), pref stock (2%), real estate (1%), other (20%)
Provider Compensation ($000): Contr fee ($2,800,635), FFS ($162,351)
Total Member Encounters: Phys (4,221,995), non-phys (1,473,060)
Group Affiliation: None
Licensed in: AK, WA
Address: 7001 220th St SW, Mountlake Terrace, WA 98043
Phone: (425) 918-4000 **Dom State:** WA **Commenced Bus:** N/A

Data Date	Rating	RACR #1	RACR #2	Total Assets ($mil)	Capital ($mil)	Net Premium ($mil)	Net Income ($mil)
3-19	B	8.11	6.76	3,465.4	2,289.7	908.8	41.0
3-18	B	6.14	5.12	2,649.6	1,678.7	861.9	-21.2
2018	B	7.77	6.48	3,133.8	2,193.0	3,571.1	400.9
2017	B+	7.04	5.87	2,801.4	1,931.3	3,361.9	115.0
2016	B+	5.17	4.31	2,428.9	1,476.2	3,780.1	45.2
2015	B+	5.27	4.39	2,276.0	1,388.4	3,489.4	12.9
2014	A-	5.80	4.83	2,211.0	1,415.3	3,072.7	65.9

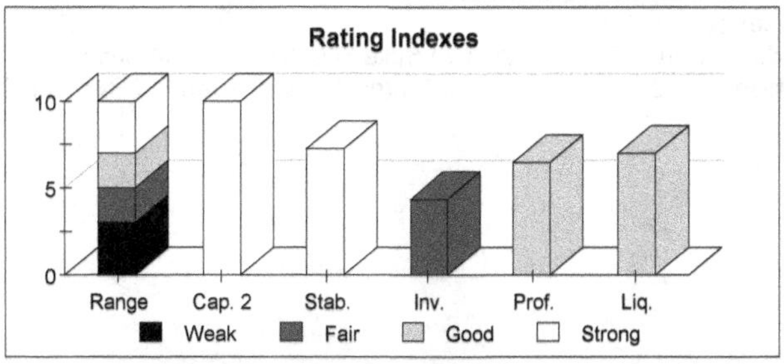

PREMIER HEALTH INSURING CORP E Very Weak

Major Rating Factors: Weak profitability index (0.2 on a scale of 0 to 10). Good quality investment portfolio (6.1). Good liquidity (5.1) with sufficient resources (cash flows and marketable investments) to handle a spike in claims.
Other Rating Factors: Strong capitalization (7.8) based on excellent current risk-adjusted capital (severe loss scenario).
Principal Business: Medicare (100%)
Mem Phys: 18: N/A **17:** 6,508 **18 MLR** 93.1% **/ 18 Admin Exp** N/A
Enroll(000): Q1 19: N/A **18:** N/A **17:** 10 **Med Exp PMPM:** N/A
Principal Investments: Affiliate common stock (58%), cash and equiv (38%), long-term bonds (4%)
Provider Compensation ($000): Contr fee ($24,960), FFS ($2,597), other ($2,303)
Total Member Encounters: Phys (12,972), non-phys (2,747)
Group Affiliation: None
Licensed in: OH
Address: 110 N MAIN ST STE 1200, DAYTON, OH 45402
Phone: (937) 499-9588 **Dom State:** OH **Commenced Bus:** N/A

Data Date	Rating	RACR #1	RACR #2	Total Assets ($mil)	Capital ($mil)	Net Premium ($mil)	Net Income ($mil)
3-19	E	2.00	1.67	10.2	7.7	-0.3	-0.3
3-18	E	N/A	N/A	28.1	10.9	22.7	-3.1
2018	E	2.19	1.82	11.5	8.5	21.7	-5.2
2017	E	N/A	N/A	30.5	15.0	90.5	-12.9
2016	E	1.41	1.18	30.0	15.2	77.0	-21.3
2015	E	1.25	1.04	25.3	14.8	59.5	-14.4
2014	N/A	N/A	N/A	32.8	32.5	N/A	-3.2

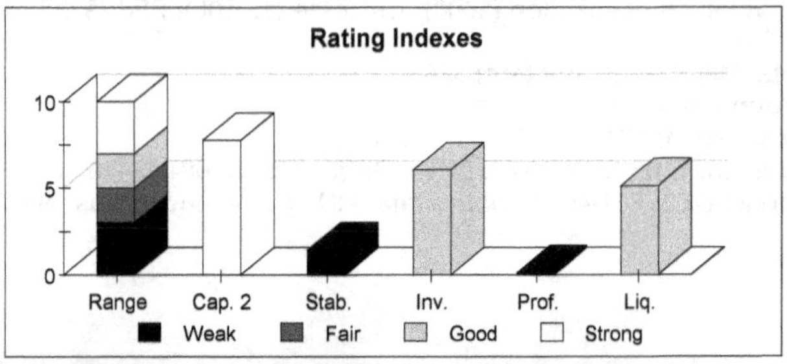

PREMIER HEALTH PLAN INC D- Weak

Major Rating Factors: Weak profitability index (0.0 on a scale of 0 to 10). Strong capitalization (8.5) based on excellent current risk-adjusted capital (severe loss scenario). High quality investment portfolio (9.9).
Other Rating Factors: Excellent liquidity (7.3) with ample operational cash flow and liquid investments.
Principal Business: Comp med (99%)
Mem Phys: 18: 5,468 **17:** 5,147 **18 MLR** 107.4% **/ 18 Admin Exp** N/A
Enroll(000): Q1 19: N/A **18:** 1 **17:** 5 **Med Exp PMPM:** $453
Principal Investments: Cash and equiv (94%), long-term bonds (6%)
Provider Compensation ($000): Contr fee ($6,679), FFS ($329), other ($605)
Total Member Encounters: Phys (3,133), non-phys (995)
Group Affiliation: None
Licensed in: OH
Address: 110 N MAIN ST STE 1200, Dayton, OH 45402
Phone: (937) 499-9588 **Dom State:** OH **Commenced Bus:** N/A

Data Date	Rating	RACR #1	RACR #2	Total Assets ($mil)	Capital ($mil)	Net Premium ($mil)	Net Income ($mil)
3-19	D-	2.54	2.12	6.4	5.9	0.0	-0.1
3-18	D-	N/A	N/A	10.6	6.9	1.3	-0.6
2018	D-	2.59	2.15	7.3	5.9	3.9	-1.7
2017	D-	N/A	N/A	14.3	7.6	30.3	-0.9
2016	D-	1.44	1.20	16.9	6.5	20.7	-9.9
2015	E+	2.29	1.91	11.7	5.8	8.2	-3.2
2014	N/A	N/A	N/A	22.7	22.5	N/A	-7.9

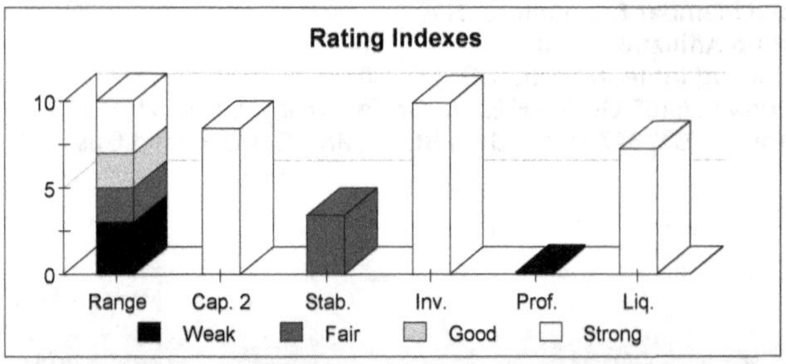

PREMIER HEALTH PLAN SERVICES INC D Weak

Major Rating Factors: Weak profitability index (0.9 on a scale of 0 to 10). Weak overall results on stability tests (2.2). Good liquidity (6.9) with sufficient resources (cash flows and marketable investments) to handle a spike in claims.
Other Rating Factors: Strong capitalization index (7.2) based on excellent current risk-adjusted capital (severe loss scenario).
Principal Business: Managed care (100%)
Mem Phys: 18: N/A **17:** N/A **18 MLR** 99.2% **/ 18 Admin Exp** N/A
Enroll(000): Q1 19: 30 **18:** 37 **17:** 36 **Med Exp PMPM:** $203
Principal Investments ($000): Cash and equiv ($24,711)
Provider Compensation ($000): None
Total Member Encounters: N/A
Group Affiliation: Lakewood IPA
Licensed in: CA
Address: 10833 Valley View St Suite 300, Cypress, CA 90630
Phone: (310) 277-9003 **Dom State:** CA **Commenced Bus:** June 2009

Data Date	Rating	RACR #1	RACR #2	Total Assets ($mil)	Capital ($mil)	Net Premium ($mil)	Net Income ($mil)
3-19	D	1.93	1.24	32.7	15.9	23.3	-3.1
3-18	D	0.69	0.43	27.7	5.7	21.6	1.2
2018	D	2.66	1.70	38.8	21.6	87.0	-10.1
2017	D	0.52	0.33	25.2	4.5	89.9	-1.9
2016	C-	0.79	0.49	29.2	6.6	99.6	0.5
2015	U	-262.00	-8.66	27.0	9.2	0.0	1.8
2014	C	1.29	0.82	24.5	8.2	77.4	3.0

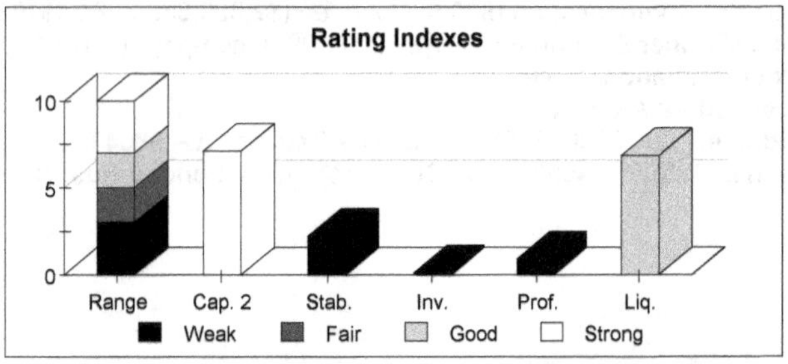

PRESBYTERIAN HEALTH PLAN INC B Good

Major Rating Factors: Good liquidity (6.9 on a scale of 0 to 10) with sufficient resources (cash flows and marketable investments) to handle a spike in claims. Fair overall results on stability tests (3.6) based on a steep decline in capital during 2018, a decline in the number of member physicians during 2019. Excellent overall profitability index (7.0)

Other Rating Factors: Strong capitalization index (7.0) based on excellent current risk-adjusted capital (severe loss scenario). High quality investment portfolio (8.5).

Principal Business: Medicaid (68%), Medicare (18%), comp med (10%), FEHB (4%)

Mem Phys: 18: 14,729 **17:** 18,949 **18 MLR** 84.9% **/ 18 Admin Exp** N/A

Enroll(000): Q1 19: 468 **18:** 404 **17:** 317 **Med Exp PMPM:** $437

Principal Investments: Long-term bonds (44%), cash and equiv (39%), nonaffiliate common stock (17%), other (1%)

Provider Compensation ($000): Contr fee ($1,239,210), capitation ($434,041), FFS ($95,134)

Total Member Encounters: Phys (2,422,862), non-phys (1,689,155)

Group Affiliation: None

Licensed in: AZ, NM

Address: 9521 SAN MATEO BLVD NE, ALBUQUERQUE, NM 87113

Phone: (505) 923-6107 **Dom State:** NM **Commenced Bus:** N/A

Data Date	Rating	RACR #1	RACR #2	Total Assets ($mil)	Capital ($mil)	Net Premium ($mil)	Net Income ($mil)
3-19	B	1.34	1.12	633.7	192.4	747.4	-1.6
3-18	B	1.65	1.37	531.5	198.3	467.8	6.5
2018	B	1.29	1.07	578.5	185.3	2,149.4	37.6
2017	B	1.89	1.58	488.5	236.3	1,832.5	58.0
2016	B	1.95	1.62	664.9	238.2	1,838.9	31.8
2015	B	1.96	1.63	606.0	209.9	1,658.6	29.8
2014	A-	2.78	2.31	506.8	246.1	1,447.8	71.0

Rating Indexes

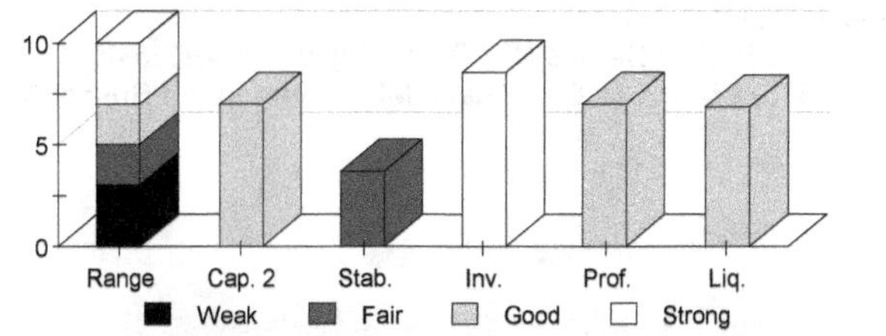

PRESBYTERIAN INS CO C+ Fair

Major Rating Factors: Good liquidity (6.5 on a scale of 0 to 10) with sufficient resources (cash flows and marketable investments) to handle a spike in claims. Weak profitability index (1.4). Strong capitalization (7.5) based on excellent current risk-adjusted capital (severe loss scenario).

Other Rating Factors: High quality investment portfolio (9.0).

Principal Business: Comp med (63%), Medicare (24%), other (13%)

Mem Phys: 18: 14,729 **17:** 18,742 **18 MLR** 87.4% **/ 18 Admin Exp** N/A

Enroll(000): Q1 19: 22 **18:** 24 **17:** 27 **Med Exp PMPM:** $397

Principal Investments: Long-term bonds (53%), cash and equiv (24%), nonaffiliate common stock (24%)

Provider Compensation ($000): Contr fee ($92,071), FFS ($25,621), capitation ($1,756)

Total Member Encounters: Phys (138,919), non-phys (56,735)

Group Affiliation: None

Licensed in: NM

Address: 9521 SAN MATEO BLVD NE, ALBUQUERQUE, NM 87113

Phone: (505) 923-6107 **Dom State:** NM **Commenced Bus:** N/A

Data Date	Rating	RACR #1	RACR #2	Total Assets ($mil)	Capital ($mil)	Net Premium ($mil)	Net Income ($mil)
3-19	C+	1.78	1.48	48.9	32.3	32.3	2.4
3-18	B-	N/A	N/A	52.6	32.4	34.0	N/A
2018	B-	1.59	1.32	46.6	28.8	136.3	-2.7
2017	B-	N/A	N/A	50.1	30.5	142.9	-7.3
2016	B-	1.22	1.02	46.5	22.8	176.8	-9.1
2015	B	2.19	1.82	53.3	31.6	168.0	1.8
2014	B+	2.22	1.85	61.9	35.9	202.1	6.8

Rating Indexes

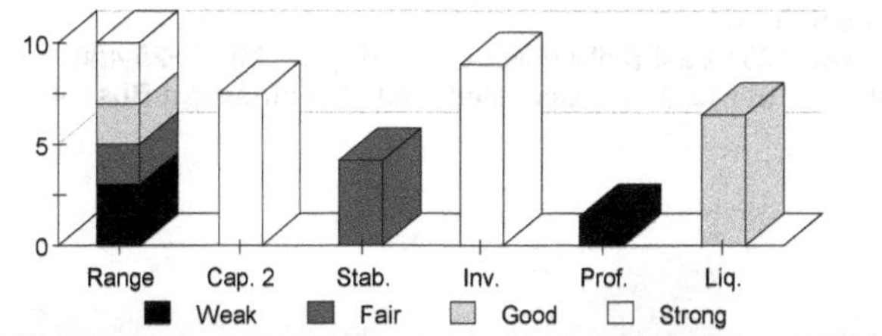

PRIMECARE MEDICAL NETWORK INC B- Good

Major Rating Factors: Fair overall results on stability tests (2.9 on a scale of 0 to 10) based on inconsistent enrollment growth in the past five years due to declines in 2016 and 2017. Rating is significantly influenced by the good financial results of UnitedHealth Group Inc. Good overall profitability index (6.5). Strong capitalization index (7.3) based on excellent current risk-adjusted capital (severe loss scenario).

Other Rating Factors: Excellent liquidity (7.1) with ample operational cash flow and liquid investments.

Principal Business: Managed care (100%)

Mem Phys: 18: N/A **17:** N/A **18 MLR** 83.9% **/ 18 Admin Exp** N/A

Enroll(000): Q1 19: 211 **18:** 209 **17:** 194 **Med Exp PMPM:** $334

Principal Investments ($000): Cash and equiv ($244,654)

Provider Compensation ($000): None

Total Member Encounters: N/A

Group Affiliation: UnitedHealth Group Inc

Licensed in: CA

Address: 3990 Concours Street 5th Floor, Ontario, CA 91764

Phone: (909) 605-8000 **Dom State:** CA **Commenced Bus:** October 1998

Data Date	Rating	RACR #1	RACR #2	Total Assets ($mil)	Capital ($mil)	Net Premium ($mil)	Net Income ($mil)
3-19	B-	2.16	1.34	277.5	78.7	272.2	20.0
3-18	C+	1.71	1.06	212.7	54.6	245.9	6.9
2018	B-	1.54	0.95	251.7	56.1	1,005.4	43.1
2017	B	2.47	1.53	236.6	78.6	894.4	35.9
2016	B	1.98	1.23	214.0	62.5	846.4	18.3
2015	B-	1.53	0.95	192.9	44.4	809.8	26.4
2014	B	2.56	1.59	178.6	62.7	674.7	19.5

Rating Indexes

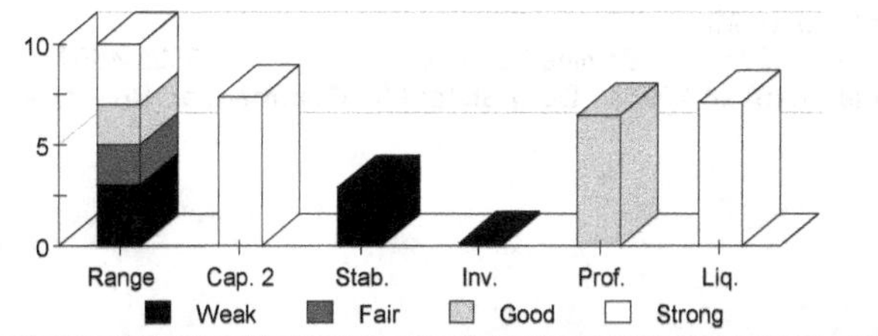

PRIORITY HEALTH * A Excellent

Major Rating Factors: Excellent profitability (8.5 on a scale of 0 to 10). Strong capitalization index (10.0) based on excellent current risk-adjusted capital (severe loss scenario). High quality investment portfolio (8.6).
Other Rating Factors: Excellent overall results on stability tests (8.1). Excellent liquidity (7.0) with ample operational cash flow and liquid investments
Principal Business: Comp med (53%), Medicare (45%), med supp (1%)
Mem Phys: 18: 19,911 **17:** 18,845 **18 MLR** 85.1% **/ 18 Admin Exp** N/A
Enroll(000): Q1 19: 541 **18:** 514 **17:** 522 **Med Exp PMPM:** $441
Principal Investments: Cash and equiv (40%), long-term bonds (38%), affiliate common stock (12%), nonaffiliate common stock (11%)
Provider Compensation ($000): Contr fee ($1,719,644), bonus arrang ($847,888), FFS ($143,977), capitation ($2,660)
Total Member Encounters: Phys (6,647,978), non-phys (747,215)
Group Affiliation: None
Licensed in: MI
Address: 1231 East Beltline NE, Grand Rapids, MI 49525-4501
Phone: (616) 942-0954 **Dom State:** MI **Commenced Bus:** N/A

Data Date	Rating	RACR #1	RACR #2	Total Assets ($mil)	Capital ($mil)	Net Premium ($mil)	Net Income ($mil)
3-19	A	3.74	3.11	1,388.7	843.4	841.4	44.9
3-18	A	2.88	2.40	1,422.0	692.3	783.1	36.3
2018	A	3.21	2.67	1,253.8	759.8	3,180.0	123.8
2017	A	2.61	2.18	1,166.5	669.0	3,015.1	78.7
2016	A-	2.49	2.07	1,000.4	574.5	2,663.2	51.1
2015	A-	2.71	2.26	910.2	529.8	2,187.7	91.1
2014	B+	2.63	2.19	746.6	470.6	1,984.6	91.4

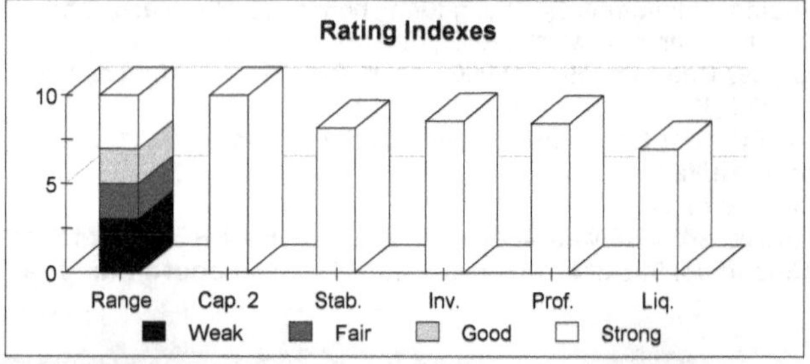

PRIORITY HEALTH CHOICE INC * A- Excellent

Major Rating Factors: Excellent profitability (7.6 on a scale of 0 to 10). Strong capitalization (10.0) based on excellent current risk-adjusted capital (severe loss scenario). High quality investment portfolio (7.9).
Other Rating Factors: Excellent liquidity (7.0) with ample operational cash flow and liquid investments.
Principal Business: Medicaid (99%), Medicare (1%)
Mem Phys: 18: 8,687 **17:** 8,259 **18 MLR** 91.1% **/ 18 Admin Exp** N/A
Enroll(000): Q1 19: 124 **18:** 126 **17:** 124 **Med Exp PMPM:** $238
Principal Investments: Cash and equiv (62%), nonaffiliate common stock (38%), long-term bonds (1%)
Provider Compensation ($000): Contr fee ($189,637), bonus arrang ($82,185), capitation ($72,171), FFS ($15,624)
Total Member Encounters: Phys (1,387,695), non-phys (299,519)
Group Affiliation: None
Licensed in: MI
Address: 1231 East Beltline NE, Grand Rapids, MI 49525-4501
Phone: (616) 942-0954 **Dom State:** MI **Commenced Bus:** N/A

Data Date	Rating	RACR #1	RACR #2	Total Assets ($mil)	Capital ($mil)	Net Premium ($mil)	Net Income ($mil)
3-19	A-	3.74	3.12	143.1	86.3	103.6	8.3
3-18	B+	2.45	2.05	139.3	65.4	127.4	-3.4
2018	A-	3.18	2.65	129.3	76.2	396.5	8.7
2017	B+	1.81	1.51	125.1	68.8	517.5	12.8
2016	B+	2.18	1.82	132.3	55.3	484.5	10.5
2015	B+	1.82	1.51	122.8	44.9	452.0	15.2
2014	B+	1.47	1.23	85.4	29.8	341.1	0.2

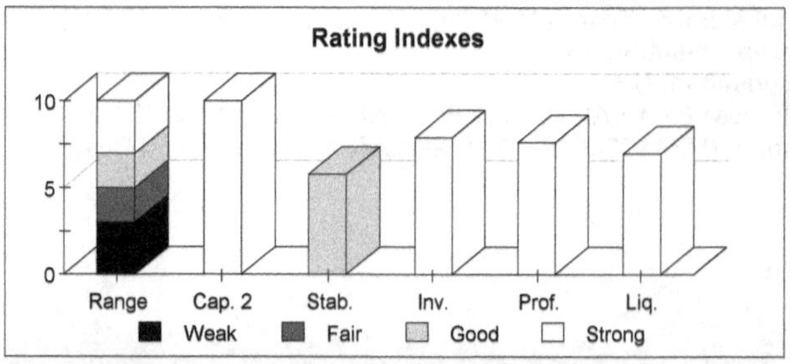

PRIORITY HEALTH INS CO B Good

Major Rating Factors: Fair quality investment portfolio (4.8 on a scale of 0 to 10). Excellent profitability (7.5). Strong capitalization (9.7) based on excellent current risk-adjusted capital (severe loss scenario).
Other Rating Factors: Excellent liquidity (7.1) with ample operational cash flow and liquid investments.
Principal Business: Comp med (88%), other (12%)
Mem Phys: 18: 20,026 **17:** 18,964 **18 MLR** 75.2% **/ 18 Admin Exp** N/A
Enroll(000): Q1 19: 63 **18:** 57 **17:** 54 **Med Exp PMPM:** $284
Principal Investments: Nonaffiliate common stock (53%), cash and equiv (47%)
Provider Compensation ($000): Contr fee ($101,996), FFS ($38,601), bonus arrang ($36,777)
Total Member Encounters: Phys (387,758), non-phys (19,735)
Group Affiliation: None
Licensed in: MI
Address: 1231 East Beltline NE, Grand Rapids, MI 49525-4501
Phone: (616) 942-0954 **Dom State:** MI **Commenced Bus:** N/A

Data Date	Rating	RACR #1	RACR #2	Total Assets ($mil)	Capital ($mil)	Net Premium ($mil)	Net Income ($mil)
3-19	B	3.52	2.93	135.2	62.2	69.2	4.8
3-18	B	2.59	2.16	122.0	51.3	59.1	-1.0
2018	B	3.01	2.51	119.7	55.6	245.3	4.7
2017	B	1.81	1.51	113.5	53.1	238.5	4.6
2016	B-	2.31	1.93	110.9	47.7	259.2	5.8
2015	B-	2.54	2.11	107.0	44.6	218.7	9.3
2014	C+	3.55	2.96	120.3	59.5	216.9	5.5

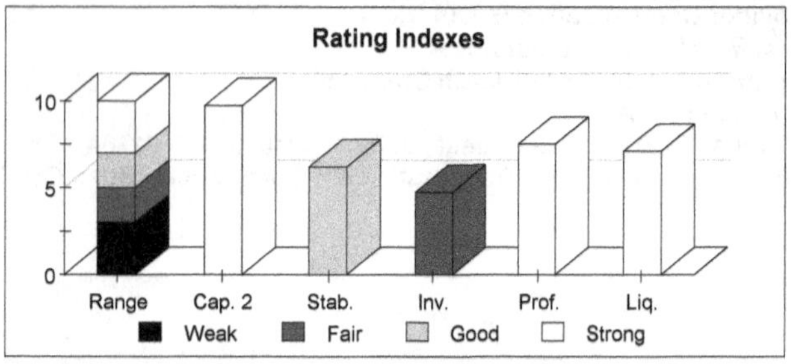

PROFESSIONAL INSURANCE COMPANY D+ Weak

Major Rating Factors: Weak overall results on stability tests (2.9 on a scale of 0 to 10) including potential financial drain due to affiliation with Sun Life Assurance Group. Good quality investment portfolio (6.7) despite mixed results such as: no exposure to mortgages and large holdings of BBB rated bonds but no exposure to junk bonds. Strong capitalization (10.0) based on excellent risk adjusted capital (severe loss scenario).
Other Rating Factors: Excellent profitability (8.9). Excellent liquidity (7.3).
Principal Business: Individual health insurance (93%) and individual life insurance (7%).
Principal Investments: NonCMO investment grade bonds (78%), CMOs and structured securities (16%), policy loans (3%), and cash (1%).
Investments in Affiliates: None
Group Affiliation: Sun Life Assurance Group
Licensed in: All states except AK, DE, ME, NH, NJ, NY, RI, VT, PR
Commenced Business: September 1937
Address: 350 North St Paul Street, Dallas, TX 75201
Phone: (781) 237-6030 **Domicile State:** TX **NAIC Code:** 68047

Data Date	Rating	RACR #1	RACR #2	Total Assets ($mil)	Capital ($mil)	Net Premium ($mil)	Net Income ($mil)
3-19	D+	5.73	5.16	111.9	51.5	4.4	1.3
3-18	D	5.13	4.61	108.9	46.0	4.9	1.3
2018	D+	5.59	5.03	111.2	50.2	19.2	5.1
2017	D	5.02	4.51	109.6	45.0	21.6	4.4
2016	D-	4.68	4.11	110.0	42.0	24.5	4.5
2015	C	4.32	3.34	109.2	38.6	27.7	2.7
2014	C	4.02	2.88	108.9	35.9	31.6	1.8

Sun Life Assurance Group
Composite Group Rating: D

Largest Group Members	Assets ($mil)	Rating
SUN LIFE ASR CO OF CANADA	18836	D
INDEPENDENCE LIFE ANNUITY CO	3170	D+
SUN LIFE HEALTH INS CO	931	D
PROFESSIONAL INS CO	111	D+

PROMINENCE HEALTHFIRST D Weak

Major Rating Factors: Weak profitability index (1.9 on a scale of 0 to 10). Low quality investment portfolio (0.2). Good overall results on stability tests (5.4).
Other Rating Factors: Good liquidity (6.9) with sufficient resources (cash flows and marketable investments) to handle a spike in claims. Strong capitalization index (10.0) based on excellent current risk-adjusted capital (severe loss scenario).
Principal Business: Comp med (60%), Medicare (40%)
Mem Phys: 18: 5,693 **17:** 5,654 **18 MLR** 89.8% **/ 18 Admin Exp** N/A
Enroll(000): Q1 19: 21 **18:** 18 **17:** 28 **Med Exp PMPM:** $440
Principal Investments: Cash and equiv (44%), affiliate common stock (41%), nonaffiliate common stock (14%), real estate (2%)
Provider Compensation ($000): Contr fee ($103,360), capitation ($9,429)
Total Member Encounters: Phys (90,047), non-phys (24,420)
Group Affiliation: Universal Health Services Inc
Licensed in: NV
Address: 1510 Meadow Wood Lane, Reno, NV 89502
Phone: (775) 770-9300 **Dom State:** NV **Commenced Bus:** N/A

Data Date	Rating	RACR #1	RACR #2	Total Assets ($mil)	Capital ($mil)	Net Premium ($mil)	Net Income ($mil)
3-19	D	4.66	3.88	100.6	61.9	36.0	-1.5
3-18	D-	2.46	2.05	102.4	50.6	30.2	-8.3
2018	D	4.77	3.97	95.9	63.3	116.8	-9.7
2017	E	2.29	1.91	99.2	53.0	178.9	-15.4
2016	E	1.41	1.17	91.9	34.3	169.5	-29.7
2015	E	1.22	1.01	55.5	25.8	89.2	-15.8
2014	E	1.15	0.96	52.7	26.1	105.4	-10.0

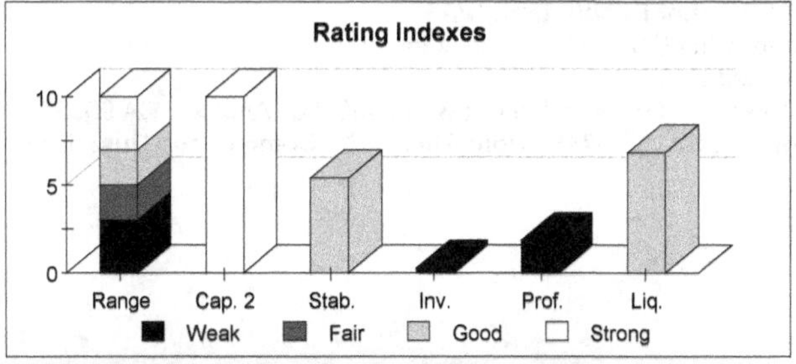

PROMINENCE HEALTHFIRST OF TEXAS INC D+ Weak

Major Rating Factors: Weak profitability index (1.8 on a scale of 0 to 10). Low quality investment portfolio (1.0). Strong capitalization (10.0) based on excellent current risk-adjusted capital (severe loss scenario).
Other Rating Factors: Excellent liquidity (9.0) with ample operational cash flow and liquid investments.
Principal Business: Medicare (98%), comp med (2%)
Mem Phys: 18: 2,089 **17:** 1,951 **18 MLR** 59.2% **/ 18 Admin Exp** N/A
Enroll(000): Q1 19: 1 **18:** 1 **17:** 7 **Med Exp PMPM:** $432
Principal Investments: Cash and equiv (100%)
Provider Compensation ($000): Contr fee ($12,102), capitation ($101)
Total Member Encounters: Phys (185), non-phys (68)
Group Affiliation: Universal Health Services Inc
Licensed in: TX
Address: 367 S Gulph Rd, Reno, NV 89502
Phone: (775) 770-9300 **Dom State:** TX **Commenced Bus:** N/A

Data Date	Rating	RACR #1	RACR #2	Total Assets ($mil)	Capital ($mil)	Net Premium ($mil)	Net Income ($mil)
3-19	D+	17.00	14.17	22.3	19.4	3.0	0.2
3-18	D+	N/A	N/A	25.5	17.5	3.3	1.4
2018	D+	16.39	13.66	21.6	18.6	12.7	1.7
2017	D+	N/A	N/A	24.3	13.1	39.1	-6.9
2016	D+	1.66	1.38	14.7	6.9	23.2	-6.4
2015	D	9.14	7.61	8.9	7.4	3.6	-2.6
2014	N/A	N/A	N/A	5.4	5.4	N/A	-0.1

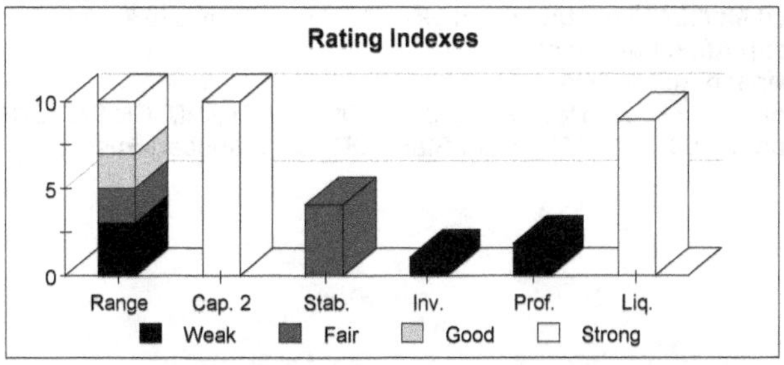

PROMINENCE PREFERRED HEALTH INS CO D- Weak

Major Rating Factors: Weak profitability index (0.9 on a scale of 0 to 10). Low quality investment portfolio (0.3). Strong capitalization (10.0) based on excellent current risk-adjusted capital (severe loss scenario).
Other Rating Factors: Excellent liquidity (9.3) with ample operational cash flow and liquid investments.
Principal Business: Comp med (100%)
Mem Phys: 18: 11,081 **17:** 11,168 **18 MLR** 78.0% **/ 18 Admin Exp** N/A
Enroll(000): Q1 19: 3 **18:** 2 **17:** 3 **Med Exp PMPM:** $360
Principal Investments: Cash and equiv (96%), real estate (4%)
Provider Compensation ($000): Contr fee ($8,956), capitation ($1,476)
Total Member Encounters: Phys (15,631), non-phys (4,037)
Group Affiliation: Universal Health Services Inc
Licensed in: NV
Address: 1510 Meadow Wood Lane, Reno, NV 89502
Phone: (775) 770-9300 **Dom State:** NV **Commenced Bus:** N/A

Data Date	Rating	RACR #1	RACR #2	Total Assets ($mil)	Capital ($mil)	Net Premium ($mil)	Net Income ($mil)
3-19	D-	21.39	17.83	38.2	33.9	3.2	-0.3
3-18	D-	24.00	20.00	38.8	35.9	3.1	-0.2
2018	D-	22.01	18.34	38.0	34.9	12.5	0.7
2017	E	19.62	16.35	37.5	34.4	14.2	4.0
2016	E	4.88	4.06	37.0	28.7	44.4	-4.7
2015	E	2.80	2.33	40.0	24.3	63.1	-11.4
2014	E	2.05	1.71	36.2	19.7	74.2	-11.1

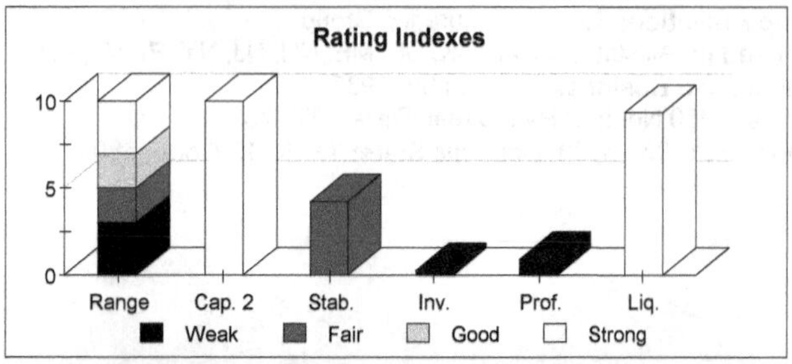

PROSPECT HEALTH PLAN E+ Very Weak

Major Rating Factors: Poor capitalization index (0.0 on a scale of 0 to 10) based on weak current risk-adjusted capital (severe loss scenario). Good overall results on stability tests (5.7) despite poor risk diversification due to the company's size but healthy premium and capital growth during 2018. Excellent profitability (8.4).
Other Rating Factors: Excellent liquidity (6.9) with sufficient resources (cash flows and marketable investments) to handle a spike in claims.
Principal Business: Managed care (105%)
Mem Phys: 18: N/A **17:** N/A **18 MLR** 97.5% **/ 18 Admin Exp** N/A
Enroll(000): Q1 19: 52 **18:** 51 **17:** 51 **Med Exp PMPM:** $408
Principal Investments ($000): Cash and equiv ($2,401)
Provider Compensation ($000): None
Total Member Encounters: N/A
Group Affiliation: PHP Holdings Inc
Licensed in: CA
Address: 10780 Santa Monica Blvd #400, Los Angeles, CA 90025
Phone: (310) 228-3745 **Dom State:** CA **Commenced Bus:** November 2014

Data Date	Rating	RACR #1	RACR #2	Total Assets ($mil)	Capital ($mil)	Net Premium ($mil)	Net Income ($mil)
3-19	E+	0.36	0.22	22.6	7.5	62.9	0.8
3-18	E+	0.42	0.26	19.3	5.2	57.6	0.7
2018	E+	0.28	0.17	22.4	6.0	243.0	2.1
2017	E+	0.31	0.19	10.3	3.9	133.2	0.9
2016	E	0.31	0.20	21.4	2.6	58.1	0.3
2015	U	2.34	1.42	6.0	2.3	7.1	0.0
2014	N/A	N/A	N/A	N/A	N/A	N/A	N/A

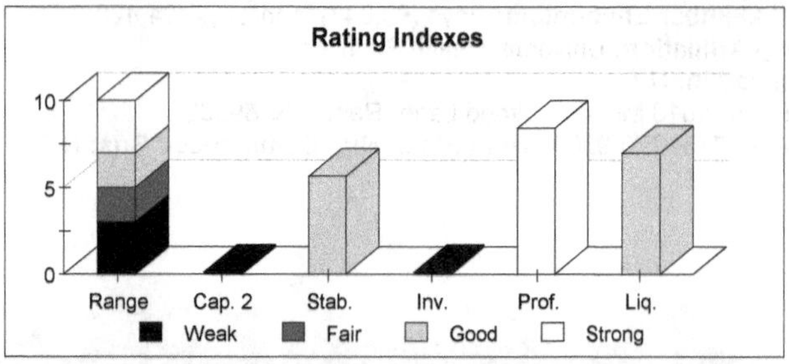

PROVIDENCE HEALTH ASR * A- Excellent

Major Rating Factors: Excellent profitability (7.9 on a scale of 0 to 10). Strong capitalization (10.0) based on excellent current risk-adjusted capital (severe loss scenario). High quality investment portfolio (9.6).
Other Rating Factors: Excellent liquidity (7.0) with ample operational cash flow and liquid investments.
Principal Business: Medicare (78%), Medicaid (22%)
Mem Phys: 18: 18,160 **17:** 12,717 **18 MLR** 89.1% **/ 18 Admin Exp** N/A
Enroll(000): Q1 19: 113 **18:** 112 **17:** 89 **Med Exp PMPM:** $557
Principal Investments: Long-term bonds (78%), cash and equiv (20%), nonaffiliate common stock (2%)
Provider Compensation ($000): Contr fee ($453,316), FFS ($184,059), bonus arrang ($145,397), capitation ($17,658), other ($7,692)
Total Member Encounters: Phys (781,993), non-phys (936,411)
Group Affiliation: None
Licensed in: OR, WA
Address: 4400 NE Halsey Bldg 2 Ste 690, PORTLAND, OR 97213-1545
Phone: (503) 574-7500 **Dom State:** OR **Commenced Bus:** N/A

Data Date	Rating	RACR #1	RACR #2	Total Assets ($mil)	Capital ($mil)	Net Premium ($mil)	Net Income ($mil)
3-19	A-	5.00	4.17	457.3	288.7	214.4	11.2
3-18	B+	4.83	4.03	453.8	251.9	195.7	2.1
2018	A-	4.87	4.06	416.7	284.4	824.8	37.1
2017	B	3.96	3.30	394.0	250.0	719.2	37.8
2016	B+	5.18	4.32	376.5	262.4	670.1	24.5
2015	B-	1.91	1.59	40.2	21.3	130.6	4.5
2014	N/A	N/A	N/A	29.0	17.1	117.6	7.6

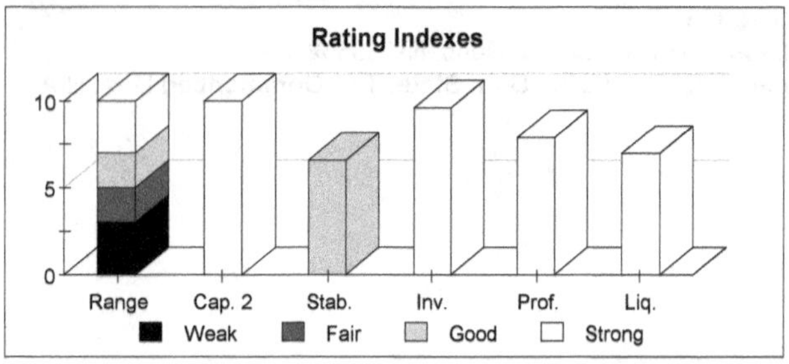

PROVIDENCE HEALTH NETWORK E- Very Weak

Major Rating Factors: Weak profitability index (0.9 on a scale of 0 to 10). Poor capitalization index (0.0) based on weak current risk-adjusted capital (severe loss scenario). Weak overall results on stability tests (0.0).
Other Rating Factors: Good liquidity (6.8) with sufficient resources (cash flows and marketable investments) to handle a spike in claims.
Principal Business: Managed care (99%)
Mem Phys: 18: N/A **17:** N/A **18 MLR** 99.6% **/ 18 Admin Exp** N/A
Enroll(000): Q1 19: 74 **18:** 54 **17:** 24 **Med Exp PMPM:** $206
Principal Investments ($000): Cash and equiv ($12,278)
Provider Compensation ($000): None
Total Member Encounters: N/A
Group Affiliation: None
Licensed in: CA
Address: 20555 Earl Street, Torrance, CA 90503
Phone: (805) 705-4451 **Dom State:** CA **Commenced Bus:** November 2013

Data Date	Rating	RACR #1	RACR #2	Total Assets ($mil)	Capital ($mil)	Net Premium ($mil)	Net Income ($mil)
3-19	E-	0.13	0.08	13.2	0.1	37.0	-0.5
3-18	E-	0.36	0.22	12.7	2.6	33.2	0.4
2018	E-	0.18	0.11	13.6	0.0	135.9	-2.0
2017	E-	0.31	0.19	14.3	2.0	108.7	-2.9
2016	E-	N/A	N/A	11.7	-10.1	89.7	-13.7
2015	E+	0.30	0.18	7.1	1.6	38.6	-2.1
2014	U	0.40	0.24	5.4	1.7	33.8	-0.6

Rating Indexes

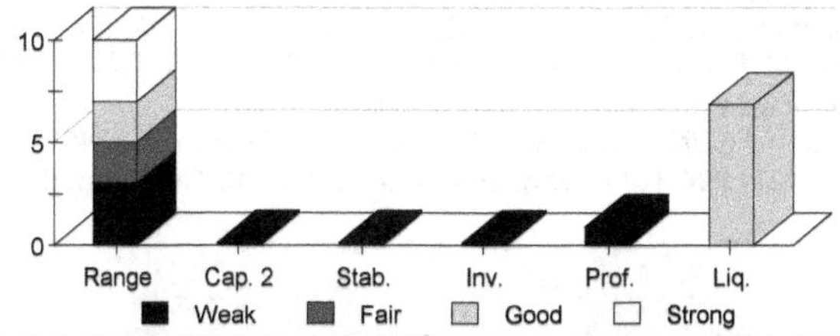

PROVIDENCE HEALTH PLAN B Good

Major Rating Factors: Good quality investment portfolio (6.4 on a scale of 0 to 10). Good liquidity (6.7) with sufficient resources (cash flows and marketable investments) to handle a spike in claims. Fair profitability index (3.3).
Other Rating Factors: Strong capitalization index (10.0) based on excellent current risk-adjusted capital (severe loss scenario). Excellent overall results on stability tests (7.1).
Principal Business: Comp med (100%)
Mem Phys: 18: 16,567 **17:** 16,090 **18 MLR** 89.3% **/ 18 Admin Exp** N/A
Enroll(000): Q1 19: 221 **18:** 241 **17:** 270 **Med Exp PMPM:** $405
Principal Investments: Long-term bonds (43%), affiliate common stock (36%), nonaffiliate common stock (8%), real estate (7%), cash and equiv (6%)
Provider Compensation ($000): Contr fee ($853,366), FFS ($315,358), capitation ($74,984), bonus arrang ($19,490), other ($5,868)
Total Member Encounters: Phys (823,916), non-phys (1,564,828)
Group Affiliation: None
Licensed in: OR, WA
Address: 4400 NE Halsey Bldg # 2 Ste #, PORTLAND, OR 97213-1545
Phone: (503) 574-7500 **Dom State:** OR **Commenced Bus:** N/A

Data Date	Rating	RACR #1	RACR #2	Total Assets ($mil)	Capital ($mil)	Net Premium ($mil)	Net Income ($mil)
3-19	B	4.05	3.37	933.4	575.9	312.6	10.8
3-18	B	3.62	3.02	865.3	492.2	347.8	-4.9
2018	B	3.87	3.22	863.9	555.5	1,377.6	39.1
2017	B	3.32	2.77	812.4	499.2	1,294.6	16.5
2016	A+	3.65	3.05	750.7	466.2	1,107.6	-28.1
2015	A+	4.31	3.59	799.3	464.6	1,193.2	-63.0
2014	A+	5.73	4.77	762.1	530.4	1,102.1	22.3

Rating Indexes

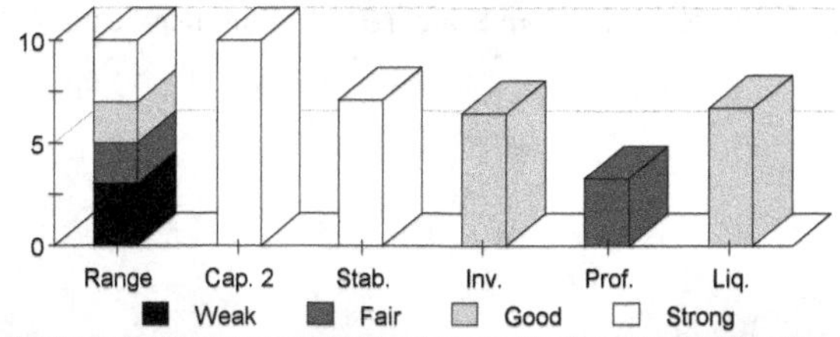

PROVIDENT LIFE & ACCIDENT INSURANCE COMPANY C+ Fair

Major Rating Factors: Fair overall results on stability tests (4.8 on a scale of 0 to 10) including fair financial strength of affiliated Unum Group. Fair quality investment portfolio (4.7) with large holdings of BBB rated bonds in addition to junk bond exposure equal to 73% of capital. Good overall profitability (6.5). Excellent expense controls.
Other Rating Factors: Strong capitalization (7.4) based on excellent risk adjusted capital (severe loss scenario). Excellent liquidity (7.1).
Principal Business: Individual health insurance (68%), individual life insurance (30%), and reinsurance (1%).
Principal Investments: NonCMO investment grade bonds (78%), mortgages in good standing (6%), noninv. grade bonds (6%), CMOs and structured securities (4%), and misc. investments (6%).
Investments in Affiliates: None
Group Affiliation: Unum Group
Licensed in: All states except NY
Commenced Business: May 1887
Address: 1 FOUNTAIN SQUARE, CHATTANOOGA, TN 37402-1330
Phone: (423) 294-1011 **Domicile State:** TN **NAIC Code:** 68195

Data Date	Rating	RACR #1	RACR #2	Total Assets ($mil)	Capital ($mil)	Net Premium ($mil)	Net Income ($mil)
3-19	C+	2.49	1.26	7,975.2	627.6	275.2	62.4
3-18	C+	2.51	1.27	8,105.0	643.5	270.5	54.2
2018	C+	2.50	1.26	7,994.0	607.3	771.0	204.8
2017	C+	2.44	1.22	8,034.0	605.0	769.3	163.5
2016	C+	2.76	1.38	8,272.6	728.2	840.8	191.7
2015	C+	2.74	1.38	8,325.3	727.5	869.4	178.9
2014	C+	2.72	1.37	8,297.3	720.0	889.8	187.1

Unum Group Composite Group Rating: C+ Largest Group Members	Assets ($mil)	Rating
UNUM LIFE INS CO OF AMERICA	22022	C+
PROVIDENT LIFE ACCIDENT INS CO	7994	C+
FIRST UNUM LIFE INS CO	3761	C+
COLONIAL LIFE ACCIDENT INS CO	3422	C+
PAUL REVERE LIFE INS CO	3410	C+

PROVIDENT LIFE & CASUALTY INSURANCE COMPANY B- Good

Major Rating Factors: Good overall results on stability tests (5.0 on a scale of 0 to 10) despite fair financial strength of affiliated Unum Group. Other stability subfactors include excellent operational trends and excellent risk diversification. Good overall profitability (5.5) despite operating losses during the first three months of 2019. Fair quality investment portfolio (4.8).
Other Rating Factors: Strong capitalization (9.1) based on excellent risk adjusted capital (severe loss scenario). Excellent liquidity (7.0).
Principal Business: Individual health insurance (94%), reinsurance (4%), and individual life insurance (2%).
Principal Investments: NonCMO investment grade bonds (85%), mortgages in good standing (5%), noninv. grade bonds (5%), and CMOs and structured securities (4%).
Investments in Affiliates: None
Group Affiliation: Unum Group
Licensed in: AK, AR, CO, CT, DC, DE, GA, HI, ID, IL, IA, KY, LA, MA, MS, MO, NE, NH, NJ, NM, NY, NC, ND, OH, OK, PA, RI, SC, SD, TN, VA, WA
Commenced Business: January 1952
Address: 1 FOUNTAIN SQUARE, CHATTANOOGA, TN 37402-1330
Phone: (423) 294-1011 **Domicile State:** TN **NAIC Code:** 68209

Data Date	Rating	RACR #1	RACR #2	Total Assets ($mil)	Capital ($mil)	Net Premium ($mil)	Net Income ($mil)
3-19	B-	4.10	2.37	734.2	128.4	25.2	-3.1
3-18	B-	4.57	2.55	749.6	147.9	24.0	-2.6
2018	B-	4.30	2.47	736.0	131.2	94.8	6.1
2017	B-	4.75	2.63	746.7	150.2	92.2	26.0
2016	B-	4.43	2.38	753.2	141.7	90.3	13.7
2015	B-	4.65	2.50	755.8	147.2	87.0	21.3
2014	B-	4.38	2.32	767.2	139.4	84.5	6.8

Unum Group Composite Group Rating: C+ Largest Group Members	Assets ($mil)	Rating
UNUM LIFE INS CO OF AMERICA	22022	C+
PROVIDENT LIFE ACCIDENT INS CO	7994	C+
FIRST UNUM LIFE INS CO	3761	C+
COLONIAL LIFE ACCIDENT INS CO	3422	C+
PAUL REVERE LIFE INS CO	3410	C+

PROVIDER PARTNERS HEALTH PLAN INC E Very Weak

Major Rating Factors: Weak profitability index (0.2 on a scale of 0 to 10). Poor capitalization (2.9) based on weak current risk-adjusted capital (moderate loss scenario). Good liquidity (5.6) with sufficient resources (cash flows and marketable investments) to handle a spike in claims.
Other Rating Factors: High quality investment portfolio (9.9).
Principal Business: Medicare (100%)
Mem Phys: 18: N/A **17:** 2,338 **18 MLR** 66.5% **/ 18 Admin Exp** N/A
Enroll(000): Q1 19: 0 **18:** 0 **17:** 0 **Med Exp PMPM:** $1,397
Principal Investments: Cash and equiv (76%), long-term bonds (24%)
Provider Compensation ($000): Contr fee ($4,242), capitation ($1,955)
Total Member Encounters: N/A
Group Affiliation: None
Licensed in: IL, MD
Address: 1922 GREENSPRING DR STE 6, LINTHICUM HEIGHTS, MD 21090
Phone: (410) 308-2300 **Dom State:** MD **Commenced Bus:** N/A

Data Date	Rating	RACR #1	RACR #2	Total Assets ($mil)	Capital ($mil)	Net Premium ($mil)	Net Income ($mil)
3-19	E	0.59	0.49	3.9	1.5	3.1	-0.9
3-18	E-	N/A	N/A	4.5	2.0	1.7	-0.8
2018	E-	0.68	0.56	3.3	1.7	8.0	-2.1
2017	E-	N/A	N/A	2.4	1.1	6.6	-1.7
2016	E-	0.31	0.26	1.8	0.8	0.7	-1.8
2015	N/A	N/A	N/A	1.8	1.5	N/A	-0.9
2014	N/A	N/A	N/A	N/A	N/A	N/A	N/A

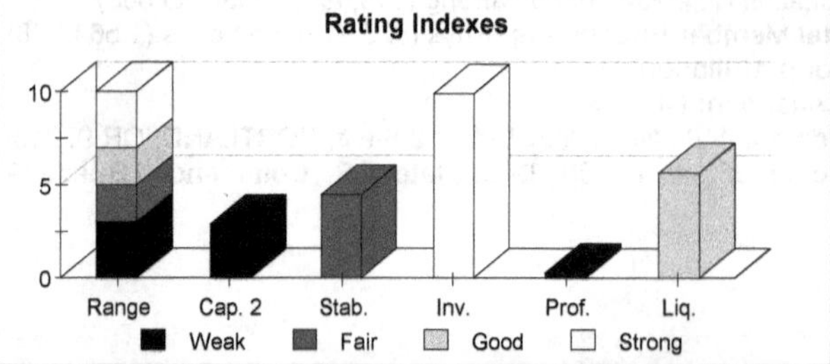

PROVIDER PARTNERS HEALTH PLAN OF PA E- Very Weak

Major Rating Factors: Weak profitability index (0.5 on a scale of 0 to 10). Poor capitalization (0.0) based on weak current risk-adjusted capital (severe loss scenario). Weak liquidity (1.8) as a spike in claims may stretch capacity.
Other Rating Factors: High quality investment portfolio (9.9).
Principal Business: Medicare (100%)
Mem Phys: 18: N/A **17:** 4,018 **18 MLR** 74.1% **/ 18 Admin Exp** N/A
Enroll(000): Q1 19: 1 **18:** 1 **17:** 0 **Med Exp PMPM:** $1,377
Principal Investments: Cash and equiv (100%)
Provider Compensation ($000): Contr fee ($6,404), capitation ($3,535)
Total Member Encounters: N/A
Group Affiliation: None
Licensed in: PA
Address: 2595 INTERSTATE DR STE 103, HARRISBURG, PA 17110
Phone: (410) 308-2300 **Dom State:** PA **Commenced Bus:** N/A

Data Date	Rating	RACR #1	RACR #2	Total Assets ($mil)	Capital ($mil)	Net Premium ($mil)	Net Income ($mil)
3-19	E-	0.19	0.16	3.6	0.7	4.1	-0.5
3-18	N/A	N/A	N/A	4.2	0.4	3.1	-0.7
2018	U	0.40	0.33	3.4	1.2	12.9	-1.9
2017	N/A	N/A	N/A	3.0	1.4	4.0	-2.4
2016	N/A	N/A	N/A	1.8	1.3	N/A	-1.1
2015	N/A	N/A	N/A	1.7	1.3	N/A	-0.4
2014	N/A	N/A	N/A	1.5	1.5	N/A	N/A

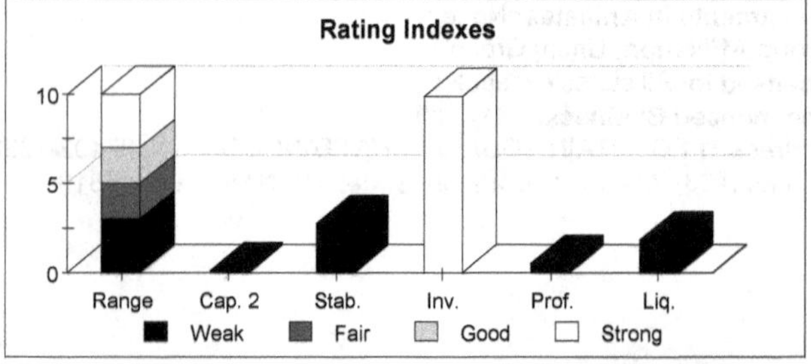

PRUITTHEALTH PREMIER INC D+ Weak

Major Rating Factors: Weak profitability index (0.9 on a scale of 0 to 10). Poor capitalization (2.9) based on weak current risk-adjusted capital (moderate loss scenario). High quality investment portfolio (9.9).
Other Rating Factors: Excellent liquidity (6.9) with sufficient resources (cash flows and marketable investments) to handle a spike in claims.
Principal Business: Medicare (100%)
Mem Phys: 18: 2,405 **17:** 1,219 **18 MLR** 89.2% **/ 18 Admin Exp** N/A
Enroll(000): Q1 19: 2 **18:** 2 **17:** 0 **Med Exp PMPM:** $1,775
Principal Investments: Cash and equiv (99%), long-term bonds (1%)
Provider Compensation ($000): Contr fee ($19,462), capitation ($12,219), bonus arrang ($264)
Total Member Encounters: Phys (22,370), non-phys (58,029)
Group Affiliation: UNICO Services Inc
Licensed in: GA
Address: 1626 Jeurgens Court, Norcross, GA 30393
Phone: (804) 396-6412 **Dom State:** GA **Commenced Bus:** N/A

Data Date	Rating	RACR #1	RACR #2	Total Assets ($mil)	Capital ($mil)	Net Premium ($mil)	Net Income ($mil)
3-19	D+	0.59	0.49	10.3	3.3	9.9	0.0
3-18	N/A	N/A	N/A	12.6	3.1	10.2	0.1
2018	U	0.63	0.53	10.7	3.5	39.9	-0.5
2017	N/A	N/A	N/A	4.2	3.0	8.5	-2.0
2016	N/A	N/A	N/A	4.3	3.1	7.1	N/A
2015	N/A	N/A	N/A	3.2	3.0	N/A	-1.2
2014	N/A	N/A	N/A	N/A	N/A	N/A	N/A

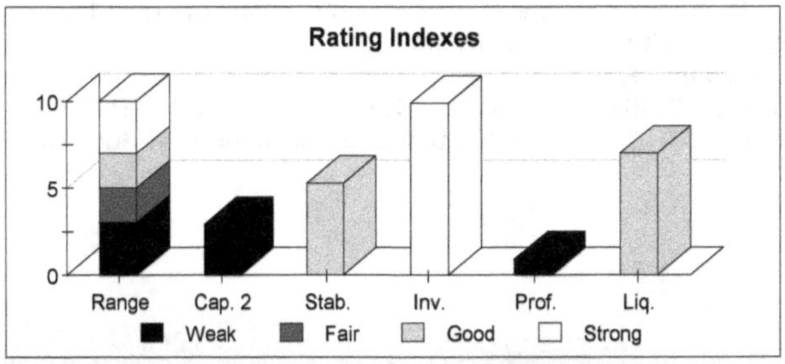

PUPIL BENEFITS PLAN INC C- Fair

Major Rating Factors: Good quality investment portfolio (6.6 on a scale of 0 to 10). Excellent profitability (8.5). Strong capitalization (10.0) based on excellent current risk-adjusted capital (severe loss scenario).
Other Rating Factors: Excellent liquidity (8.4) with ample operational cash flow and liquid investments.
Principal Business: Other (100%)
Mem Phys: 18: N/A **17:** N/A **18 MLR** 56.7% **/ 18 Admin Exp** N/A
Enroll(000): Q1 19: 622 **18:** 622 **17:** 674 **Med Exp PMPM:** $0
Principal Investments: Cash and equiv (65%), long-term bonds (27%), nonaffiliate common stock (7%), real estate (1%)
Provider Compensation ($000): FFS ($5,075)
Total Member Encounters: N/A
Group Affiliation: Pupil Benefits Plan Inc
Licensed in: NY
Address: 101 DUTCH MEADOWS LANE, GLENVILLE, NY 12302
Phone: (518) 377-5144 **Dom State:** NY **Commenced Bus:** N/A

Data Date	Rating	RACR #1	RACR #2	Total Assets ($mil)	Capital ($mil)	Net Premium ($mil)	Net Income ($mil)
3-19	C-	6.26	5.22	13.4	8.1	2.1	0.7
3-18	C-	5.19	4.33	12.5	6.6	2.2	0.6
2018	C-	5.51	4.59	15.3	7.2	8.5	1.5
2017	C-	4.69	3.91	14.5	6.0	8.8	1.1
2016	C-	3.48	2.90	14.3	4.7	9.6	1.6
2015	C-	1.88	1.56	14.3	3.1	9.8	1.2
2014	C-	0.98	0.82	12.4	1.9	9.0	-0.1

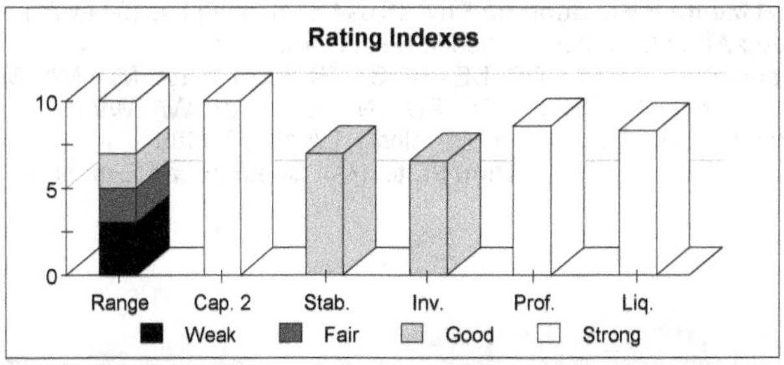

QBE INS CORP B Good

Major Rating Factors: Good liquidity (5.0 on a scale of 0 to 10) with sufficient resources (cash flows and marketable investments) to handle a spike in claims. Fair profitability index (4.9) with operating losses during 2017. Return on equity has been low, averaging 2.7% over the past five years.
Other Rating Factors: Fair overall results on stability tests (4.5). Strong long-term capitalization index (7.4) based on excellent current risk adjusted capital (severe and moderate loss scenarios), despite some fluctuation in capital levels. Ample reserve history (7.0) that can protect against increases in claims costs.
Principal Business: Group accident & health (28%), other liability (24%), homeowners multiple peril (16%), workers compensation (8%), aircraft (7%), allied lines (6%), and other lines (12%).
Principal Investments: Investment grade bonds (56%), misc. investments (43%), and cash (1%).
Investments in Affiliates: 9%
Group Affiliation: QBE Ins Group Ltd
Licensed in: All states except PR
Commenced Business: October 1980
Address: 600 N 2ND STE 401, Harrisburg, PA 17101
Phone: (800) 362-5448 **Domicile State:** PA **NAIC Code:** 39217

Data Date	Rating	RACR #1	RACR #2	Loss Ratio %	Total Assets ($mil)	Capital ($mil)	Net Premium ($mil)	Net Income ($mil)
3-19	B	2.00	1.34	N/A	2,551.2	785.6	214.0	23.6
3-18	B	2.21	1.46	N/A	2,502.2	696.1	179.3	4.8
2018	B	1.87	1.26	67.4	2,182.1	740.7	1,048.9	47.2
2017	B	2.16	1.43	75.6	2,054.3	678.0	890.9	-23.7
2016	B	2.48	1.70	58.8	2,325.0	748.9	846.9	27.7
2015	B-	2.46	1.81	63.9	2,134.5	735.7	597.0	28.8
2014	C+	2.08	1.58	69.2	2,113.3	681.2	742.1	4.2

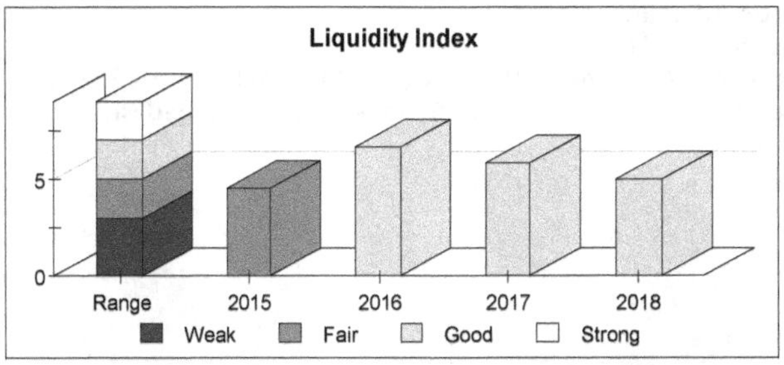

QCA HEALTH PLAN INC C Fair

Major Rating Factors: Good profitability index (4.9 on a scale of 0 to 10). Good overall results on stability tests (5.7). Fair financial strength from affiliates. Strong capitalization index (10.0) based on excellent current risk-adjusted capital (severe loss scenario).
Other Rating Factors: High quality investment portfolio (9.9). Excellent liquidity (7.1) with ample operational cash flow and liquid investments.
Principal Business: Comp med (98%), FEHB (2%)
Mem Phys: 18: 20,660 **17:** 19,232 **18 MLR** 74.9% **/ 18 Admin Exp** N/A
Enroll(000): Q1 19: 48 **18:** 46 **17:** 46 **Med Exp PMPM:** $274
Principal Investments: Cash and equiv (52%), long-term bonds (46%), other (2%)
Provider Compensation ($000): Contr fee ($131,731), FFS ($13,654)
Total Member Encounters: Phys (344,091), non-phys (502,132)
Group Affiliation: Centene Corporation
Licensed in: AR
Address: 12615 Chenal Parkway Suite 300, Little Rock, AR 72211
Phone: (501) 228-7111 **Dom State:** AR **Commenced Bus:** N/A

Data Date	Rating	RACR #1	RACR #2	Total Assets ($mil)	Capital ($mil)	Net Premium ($mil)	Net Income ($mil)
3-19	C	3.91	3.26	103.9	61.7	53.5	6.3
3-18	C-	N/A	N/A	91.8	48.8	50.0	2.1
2018	C	3.81	3.17	112.7	60.0	206.4	16.7
2017	C-	N/A	N/A	75.4	43.6	197.6	11.1
2016	D+	1.46	1.22	75.2	31.9	214.8	-18.3
2015	C-	2.21	1.84	81.3	39.6	205.8	9.3
2014	C-	1.05	0.87	64.0	20.3	159.8	-5.2

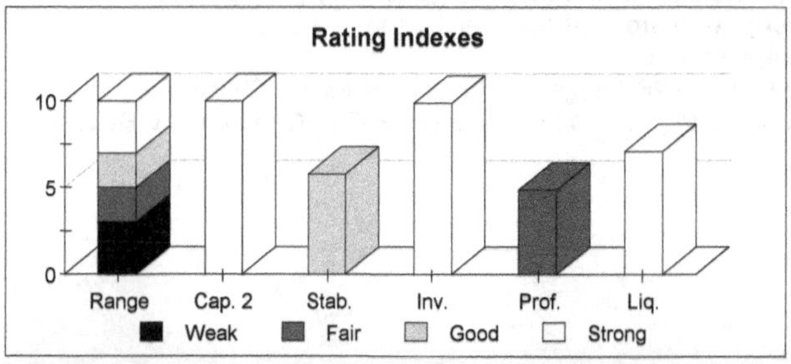

QCC INS CO B- Good

Major Rating Factors: Fair quality investment portfolio (3.8 on a scale of 0 to 10). Good overall profitability index (5.8). Strong capitalization (10.0) based on excellent current risk-adjusted capital (severe loss scenario).
Other Rating Factors: Excellent liquidity (7.1) with ample operational cash flow and liquid investments.
Principal Business: Comp med (89%), Medicare (6%), dental (2%), other (3%)
Mem Phys: 18: 62,480 **17:** 60,575 **18 MLR** 71.3% **/ 18 Admin Exp** N/A
Enroll(000): Q1 19: 297 **18:** 282 **17:** 308 **Med Exp PMPM:** $442
Principal Investments: Long-term bonds (61%), nonaffiliate common stock (26%), cash and equiv (11%), other (3%)
Provider Compensation ($000): Contr fee ($1,468,040), FFS ($21,705), capitation ($15,665), bonus arrang ($9,973)
Total Member Encounters: Phys (5,694,834), non-phys (984,670)
Group Affiliation: Independence Health Group Inc
Licensed in: AZ, CO, DC, DE, FL, GA, IN, KS, KY, LA, MD, MA, MS, MT, NE, NV, NM, ND, OH, OK, PA, SC, SD, TN, TX, UT, VT, WA, WV
Address: 1901 Market St, Philadelphia, PA 19103-1480
Phone: (215) 241-2400 **Dom State:** PA **Commenced Bus:** N/A

Data Date	Rating	RACR #1	RACR #2	Total Assets ($mil)	Capital ($mil)	Net Premium ($mil)	Net Income ($mil)
3-19	B-	4.63	3.86	1,265.6	608.3	520.7	42.5
3-18	C	3.30	2.75	1,176.5	449.3	512.0	-14.9
2018	B-	4.18	3.48	1,194.9	544.6	2,106.6	193.2
2017	C	2.75	2.29	1,105.6	470.0	2,216.6	83.2
2016	C	2.96	2.46	1,157.6	401.0	2,248.6	-10.6
2015	C	3.13	2.61	1,161.6	408.5	2,246.3	-57.6
2014	C+	3.68	3.07	1,100.8	496.0	2,309.2	5.5

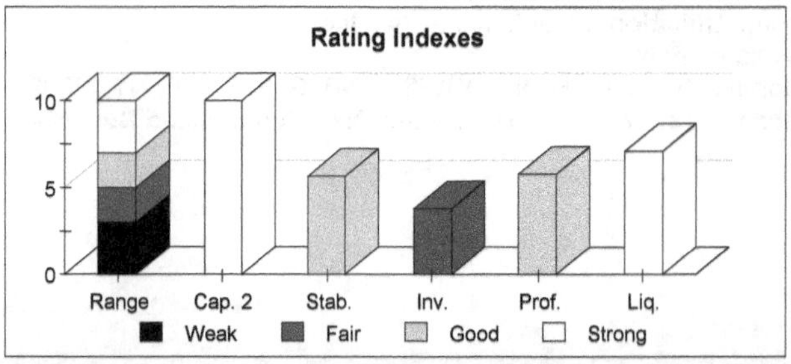

QUALCHOICE ADVANTAGE INC C- Fair

Major Rating Factors: Weak profitability index (0.8 on a scale of 0 to 10). Good liquidity (5.7) with sufficient resources (cash flows and marketable investments) to handle a spike in claims. Strong capitalization (7.6) based on excellent current risk-adjusted capital (severe loss scenario).
Other Rating Factors: High quality investment portfolio (9.6).
Principal Business: Medicare (100%)
Mem Phys: 18: 2,626 **17:** 2,876 **18 MLR** 97.6% **/ 18 Admin Exp** N/A
Enroll(000): Q1 19: N/A **18:** 1 **17:** 1 **Med Exp PMPM:** $703
Principal Investments: Long-term bonds (93%), cash and equiv (7%)
Provider Compensation ($000): Contr fee ($8,544), capitation ($212), other ($385)
Total Member Encounters: Phys (10,284), non-phys (9,662)
Group Affiliation: None
Licensed in: AR
Address: 12615 Chenal Parkway Ste 300, Little Rock, AR 72211
Phone: (866) 789-7747 **Dom State:** AR **Commenced Bus:** N/A

Data Date	Rating	RACR #1	RACR #2	Total Assets ($mil)	Capital ($mil)	Net Premium ($mil)	Net Income ($mil)
3-19	C-	1.80	1.50	4.7	2.7	0.0	0.1
3-18	C-	N/A	N/A	7.1	3.9	2.3	0.3
2018	C-	1.77	1.48	5.6	2.6	9.4	-0.9
2017	C-	N/A	N/A	6.4	3.6	11.8	0.3
2016	C-	1.74	1.45	5.1	3.3	12.0	-0.2
2015	N/A	N/A	N/A	3.5	3.5	N/A	N/A
2014	N/A	N/A	N/A	N/A	N/A	N/A	N/A

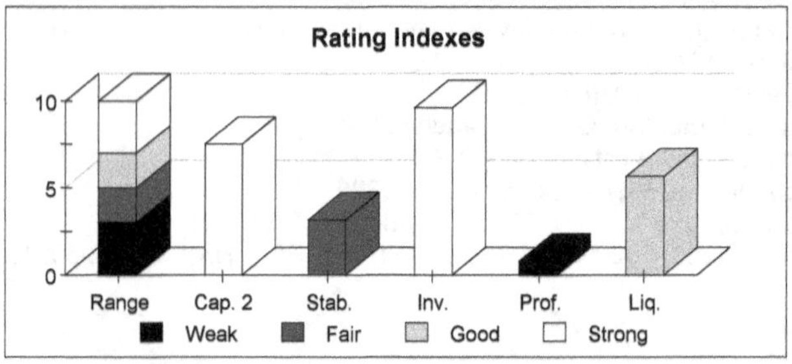

QUALCHOICE L&H INS CO — C — Fair

Major Rating Factors: Fair profitability index (3.1 on a scale of 0 to 10). Strong capitalization (10.0) based on excellent current risk-adjusted capital (severe loss scenario). High quality investment portfolio (9.9).
Other Rating Factors: Excellent liquidity (7.6) with ample operational cash flow and liquid investments.
Principal Business: Comp med (95%), med supp (4%)
Mem Phys: 18: 20,660 **17:** 19,232 **18 MLR** 65.5% **/ 18 Admin Exp** N/A
Enroll(000): Q1 19: 30 **18:** 28 **17:** 29 **Med Exp PMPM:** $239
Principal Investments: Cash and equiv (61%), long-term bonds (39%)
Provider Compensation ($000): Contr fee ($73,484), FFS ($5,913)
Total Member Encounters: Phys (228,887), non-phys (218,903)
Group Affiliation: Centene Corporation
Licensed in: AR, NE
Address: 12615 Chenal Parkway Ste 300, Little Rock, AR 72211
Phone: (501) 219-5109 **Dom State:** AR **Commenced Bus:** N/A

Data Date	Rating	RACR #1	RACR #2	Total Assets ($mil)	Capital ($mil)	Net Premium ($mil)	Net Income ($mil)
3-19	C	5.38	4.49	75.4	49.8	32.9	-1.1
3-18	D	2.18	1.81	60.3	26.5	31.1	-1.4
2018	C	5.51	4.59	74.8	50.9	126.7	23.1
2017	D	1.87	1.56	54.5	27.6	114.3	-2.4
2016	D-	1.97	1.64	51.1	29.9	129.2	-15.5
2015	C	2.57	2.15	44.7	21.3	61.9	-5.1
2014	C	1.82	1.52	7.5	6.3	6.1	-0.9

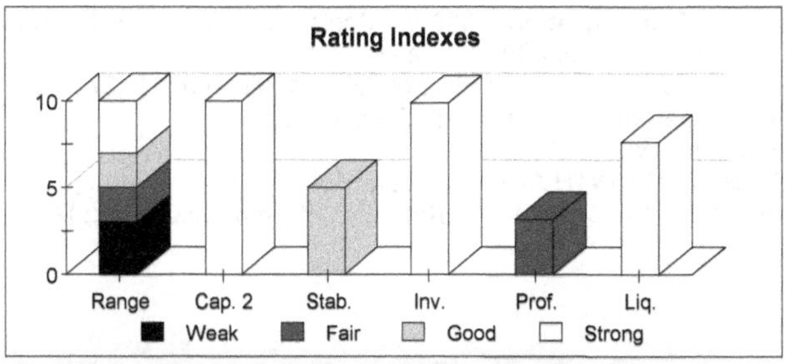

REGENCE BL CROSS BL SHIELD OREGON * — A- — Excellent

Major Rating Factors: Strong capitalization (10.0 on a scale of 0 to 10) based on excellent current risk-adjusted capital (severe loss scenario). Good overall profitability index (6.8). Good quality investment portfolio (6.4).
Other Rating Factors: Good liquidity (6.9) with sufficient resources (cash flows and marketable investments) to handle a spike in claims.
Principal Business: Comp med (44%), Medicare (30%), FEHB (20%), med supp (1%), other (3%)
Mem Phys: 18: 27,948 **17:** 26,798 **18 MLR** 81.8% **/ 18 Admin Exp** N/A
Enroll(000): Q1 19: 429 **18:** 530 **17:** 521 **Med Exp PMPM:** $257
Principal Investments: Long-term bonds (73%), nonaffiliate common stock (25%), affiliate common stock (1%), real estate (1%)
Provider Compensation ($000): Contr fee ($1,336,752), bonus arrang ($135,740), FFS ($97,986), capitation ($188), other ($22,232)
Total Member Encounters: Phys (5,041,701), non-phys (6,211,930)
Group Affiliation: Cambia Health Solutions Inc
Licensed in: OR, WA
Address: 100 SW MARKET St, PORTLAND, OR 97201
Phone: (503) 225-5221 **Dom State:** OR **Commenced Bus:** N/A

Data Date	Rating	RACR #1	RACR #2	Total Assets ($mil)	Capital ($mil)	Net Premium ($mil)	Net Income ($mil)
3-19	A-	7.27	6.06	1,319.0	835.2	523.8	36.8
3-18	B+	6.26	5.22	1,258.5	717.7	487.8	-6.0
2018	A-	6.77	5.65	1,255.6	776.6	1,965.5	62.2
2017	B+	5.65	4.71	1,194.8	730.9	1,913.4	78.8
2016	B+	6.57	5.48	1,092.9	661.0	1,780.8	30.2
2015	B+	5.99	4.99	1,045.8	639.2	1,877.6	25.8
2014	B+	5.91	4.93	1,039.7	635.3	1,871.4	35.9

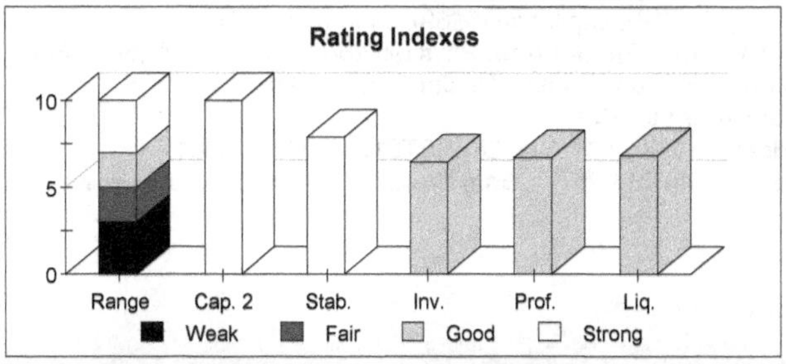

REGENCE BLUE CROSS BLUE SHIELD OF UT * — B+ — Good

Major Rating Factors: Good overall profitability index (6.3 on a scale of 0 to 10). Good quality investment portfolio (6.5). Strong capitalization (10.0) based on excellent current risk-adjusted capital (severe loss scenario).
Other Rating Factors: Excellent liquidity (7.2) with ample operational cash flow and liquid investments.
Principal Business: Comp med (42%), FEHB (41%), Medicare (10%), med supp (4%), other (2%)
Mem Phys: 18: 14,688 **17:** 14,083 **18 MLR** 81.3% **/ 18 Admin Exp** N/A
Enroll(000): Q1 19: 281 **18:** 307 **17:** 217 **Med Exp PMPM:** $222
Principal Investments: Long-term bonds (69%), nonaffiliate common stock (13%), cash and equiv (12%), affiliate common stock (5%), real estate (1%)
Provider Compensation ($000): Contr fee ($671,203), FFS ($124,262), bonus arrang ($40,088), capitation ($212), other ($10,972)
Total Member Encounters: Phys (2,003,202), non-phys (2,023,453)
Group Affiliation: Cambia Health Solutions Inc
Licensed in: UT
Address: 2890 EAST COTTONWOOD PARKWAY, SALT LAKE CITY, UT 84121-7035
Phone: (801) 333-2000 **Dom State:** UT **Commenced Bus:** N/A

Data Date	Rating	RACR #1	RACR #2	Total Assets ($mil)	Capital ($mil)	Net Premium ($mil)	Net Income ($mil)
3-19	B+	9.33	7.77	739.4	443.0	255.2	9.9
3-18	B	6.92	5.77	686.3	355.7	254.8	4.1
2018	B+	8.97	7.47	715.9	425.4	1,030.5	77.2
2017	B	5.26	4.38	645.7	353.5	1,036.0	67.5
2016	B-	5.59	4.66	564.0	271.2	1,020.1	8.6
2015	B-	4.97	4.14	529.7	261.8	1,084.9	3.1
2014	B	5.11	4.26	524.1	269.8	1,120.7	-3.3

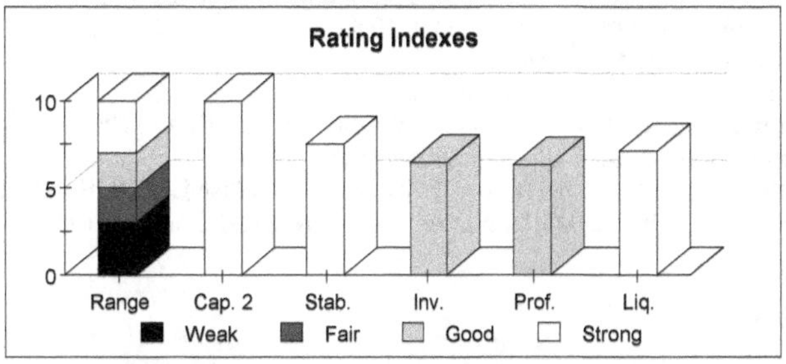

REGENCE BLUESHIELD — B Good

Major Rating Factors: Good overall profitability index (5.9 on a scale of 0 to 10). Good quality investment portfolio (5.2). Good liquidity (6.9) with sufficient resources (cash flows and marketable investments) to handle a spike in claims.
Other Rating Factors: Strong capitalization (10.0) based on excellent current risk-adjusted capital (severe loss scenario).
Principal Business: Comp med (65%), FEHB (15%), Medicare (14%), med supp (5%)
Mem Phys: 18: 38,152 **17:** 37,277 **18 MLR** 77.6% **/ 18 Admin Exp** N/A
Enroll(000): Q1 19: 429 **18:** 434 **17:** 428 **Med Exp PMPM:** $257
Principal Investments: Long-term bonds (59%), nonaffiliate common stock (22%), affiliate common stock (14%), pref stock (2%), real estate (1%), cash and equiv (1%), other (2%)
Provider Compensation ($000): Contr fee ($1,145,224), bonus arrang ($118,130), FFS ($105,489), capitation ($341)
Total Member Encounters: Phys (4,653,764), non-phys (5,279,463)
Group Affiliation: Cambia Health Solutions Inc
Licensed in: WA
Address: 1800 NINTH Ave, SEATTLE, WA 98101
Phone: (206) 464-3600 **Dom State:** WA **Commenced Bus:** N/A

Data Date	Rating	RACR #1	RACR #2	Total Assets ($mil)	Capital ($mil)	Net Premium ($mil)	Net Income ($mil)
3-19	B	9.42	7.85	1,694.5	1,254.3	422.8	24.7
3-18	B	7.60	6.33	1,805.4	1,196.8	439.7	2.1
2018	B	8.98	7.49	1,634.2	1,195.2	1,755.0	75.9
2017	B	7.71	6.42	1,731.0	1,213.9	1,979.6	85.2
2016	B	8.78	7.31	1,652.3	1,150.7	1,673.9	53.7
2015	B	8.18	6.81	1,611.9	1,114.6	1,784.1	11.8
2014	B	8.12	6.77	1,640.5	1,145.6	1,826.3	17.1

Rating Indexes

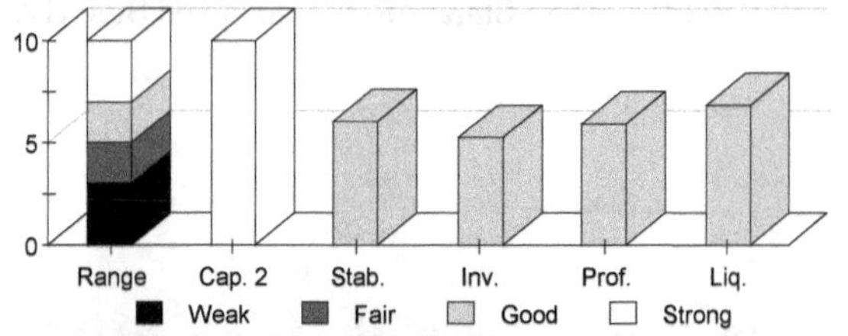

REGENCE BLUESHIELD OF IDAHO INC * — B+ Good

Major Rating Factors: Good overall profitability index (5.9 on a scale of 0 to 10). Good quality investment portfolio (6.5). Good liquidity (6.8) with sufficient resources (cash flows and marketable investments) to handle a spike in claims.
Other Rating Factors: Strong capitalization (10.0) based on excellent current risk-adjusted capital (severe loss scenario).
Principal Business: Comp med (71%), Medicare (17%), FEHB (4%), med supp (3%), other (4%)
Mem Phys: 18: 10,004 **17:** 9,529 **18 MLR** 77.7% **/ 18 Admin Exp** N/A
Enroll(000): Q1 19: 168 **18:** 172 **17:** 106 **Med Exp PMPM:** $168
Principal Investments: Long-term bonds (69%), nonaffiliate common stock (13%), cash and equiv (9%), real estate (6%), affiliate common stock (2%)
Provider Compensation ($000): Contr fee ($309,873), FFS ($16,247), bonus arrang ($10,556), capitation ($269), other ($10,177)
Total Member Encounters: Phys (963,687), non-phys (1,688,122)
Group Affiliation: Cambia Health Solutions Inc
Licensed in: ID, WA
Address: 1602 21ST Ave, LEWISTON, ID 83501-4061
Phone: (208) 746-2671 **Dom State:** ID **Commenced Bus:** N/A

Data Date	Rating	RACR #1	RACR #2	Total Assets ($mil)	Capital ($mil)	Net Premium ($mil)	Net Income ($mil)
3-19	B+	8.48	7.07	340.7	223.8	103.8	6.9
3-18	B	6.17	5.14	311.7	179.1	112.1	-2.0
2018	B+	8.13	6.77	356.4	214.4	448.2	33.0
2017	B	4.50	3.75	302.4	181.5	467.1	27.4
2016	C+	6.30	5.25	265.4	152.1	418.7	15.6
2015	B-	4.92	4.10	237.7	135.3	433.4	-10.2
2014	B	5.73	4.77	248.1	149.9	441.2	-5.6

Rating Indexes

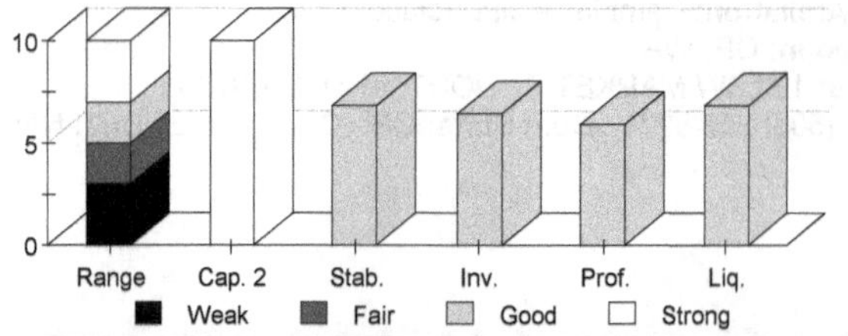

RELIASTAR LIFE INSURANCE COMPANY — B- Good

Major Rating Factors: Good quality investment portfolio (6.0 on a scale of 0 to 10) despite large holdings of BBB rated bonds in addition to moderate junk bond exposure. Exposure to mortgages is significant, but the mortgage default rate has been low. Fair profitability (3.5) with operating losses during the first three months of 2019. Fair liquidity (4.2).
Other Rating Factors: Fair overall results on stability tests (4.1) including negative cash flow from operations for 2018. Strong capitalization (7.3) based on excellent risk adjusted capital (severe loss scenario).
Principal Business: Group health insurance (29%), reinsurance (29%), individual life insurance (24%), group life insurance (12%), and other lines (6%).
Principal Investments: NonCMO investment grade bonds (60%), mortgages in good standing (12%), CMOs and structured securities (11%), noninv. grade bonds (4%), and misc. investments (10%).
Investments in Affiliates: 2%
Group Affiliation: Voya Financial Inc
Licensed in: All states, the District of Columbia and Puerto Rico
Commenced Business: September 1885
Address: 20 WASHINGTON AVENUE SOUTH, MINNEAPOLIS, MN 55401
Phone: (770) 980-5100 **Domicile State:** MN **NAIC Code:** 67105

Data Date	Rating	RACR #1	RACR #2	Total Assets ($mil)	Capital ($mil)	Net Premium ($mil)	Net Income ($mil)
3-19	B-	2.08	1.23	20,397.1	1,694.2	223.2	-86.8
3-18	C+	2.05	1.21	19,823.7	1,555.5	204.6	38.6
2018	B-	2.05	1.21	20,238.5	1,632.9	1,122.5	100.6
2017	C+	1.98	1.18	19,910.1	1,483.1	633.1	234.3
2016	C+	2.09	1.26	19,828.5	1,662.0	777.1	-506.6
2015	C+	2.03	1.23	19,805.1	1,609.2	740.9	74.2
2014	C+	2.40	1.42	21,468.7	1,944.7	-149.0	103.9

Rating Indexes

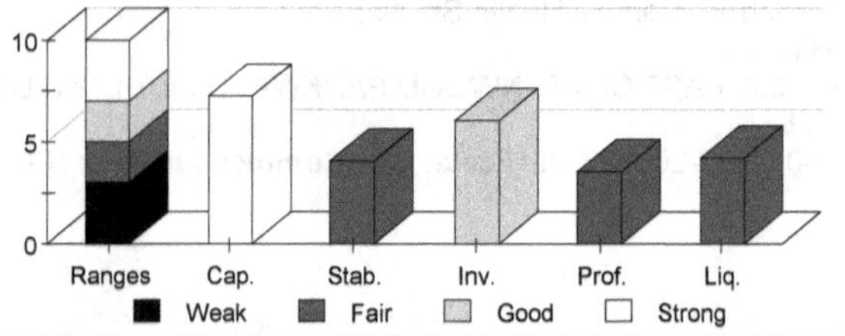

RESERVE NATIONAL INSURANCE COMPANY B- Good

Major Rating Factors: Good overall capitalization (5.6 on a scale of 0 to 10) based on mixed results -- excessive policy leverage mitigated by good risk adjusted capital (severe loss scenario). Nevertheless, capital levels have fluctuated during prior years. Good liquidity (5.2) with sufficient resources to handle a spike in claims. Fair overall results on stability tests (4.7) including fair financial strength of affiliated Kemper Corporation and negative cash flow from operations for 2018.

Other Rating Factors: Weak profitability (1.8) with operating losses during the first three months of 2019. High quality investment portfolio (7.5).

Principal Business: Individual health insurance (85%), individual life insurance (8%), group health insurance (3%), reinsurance (3%), and group life insurance (1%).

Principal Investments: NonCMO investment grade bonds (88%), CMOs and structured securities (6%), and noninv. grade bonds (1%).

Investments in Affiliates: None

Group Affiliation: Kemper Corporation

Licensed in: All states except NY, PR

Commenced Business: September 1956

Address: 601 EAST BRITTON ROAD, OKLAHOMA CITY, OK 73114

Phone: (405) 848-7931 **Domicile State:** OK **NAIC Code:** 68462

Data Date	Rating	RACR #1	RACR #2	Total Assets ($mil)	Capital ($mil)	Net Premium ($mil)	Net Income ($mil)
3-19	B-	1.28	0.97	142.2	33.5	44.5	-1.3
3-18	B-	0.93	0.71	119.5	21.4	41.7	-3.3
2018	B-	1.17	0.89	136.0	30.9	162.6	-9.7
2017	B-	1.03	0.79	121.5	24.8	152.5	-9.3
2016	B+	1.77	1.34	126.9	40.2	143.6	-2.0
2015	A	2.18	1.66	122.8	45.1	132.7	-0.5
2014	A	2.44	1.88	118.2	51.0	131.8	1.7

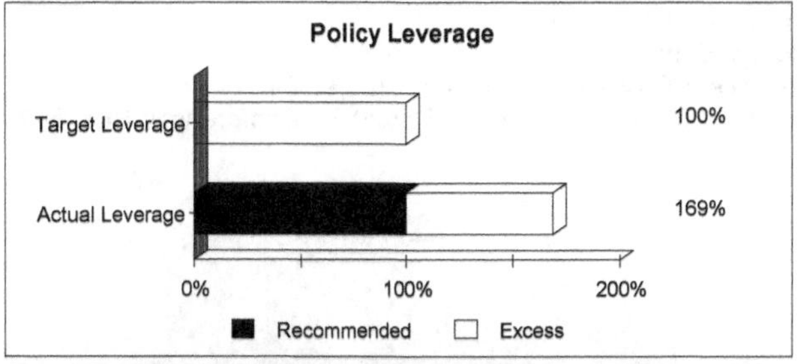

RGA REINSURANCE COMPANY B- Good

Major Rating Factors: Good capitalization (6.8 on a scale of 0 to 10) based on good risk adjusted capital (severe loss scenario). Capital levels have been relatively consistent over the last five years. Good quality investment portfolio (5.0) despite large holdings of BBB rated bonds in addition to junk bond exposure equal to 71% of capital. Exposure to mortgages is significant, but the mortgage default rate has been low. Good liquidity (5.9).

Other Rating Factors: Fair overall results on stability tests (4.5) including negative cash flow from operations for 2018. Excellent profitability (9.0).

Principal Business: Reinsurance (100%).

Principal Investments: NonCMO investment grade bonds (49%), mortgages in good standing (17%), CMOs and structured securities (16%), noninv. grade bonds (6%), and misc. investments (12%).

Investments in Affiliates: 3%

Group Affiliation: Reinsurance Group of America Inc

Licensed in: All states, the District of Columbia and Puerto Rico

Commenced Business: October 1982

Address: 16600 Swingley Ridge Road, Chesterfield, MO 63017-1706

Phone: (636) 736-7000 **Domicile State:** MO **NAIC Code:** 93572

Data Date	Rating	RACR #1	RACR #2	Total Assets ($mil)	Capital ($mil)	Net Premium ($mil)	Net Income ($mil)
3-19	B-	1.80	0.97	36,492.4	2,131.1	725.4	67.2
3-18	B-	1.63	0.86	33,882.7	1,537.4	1,907.6	-28.0
2018	B-	1.70	0.93	36,983.5	2,078.7	4,488.1	659.9
2017	B-	1.63	0.87	33,356.1	1,584.0	4,286.4	138.4
2016	B-	1.61	0.87	25,432.8	1,521.6	2,636.1	148.6
2015	B-	1.42	0.81	24,593.0	1,503.4	3,364.2	-23.6
2014	B	1.69	0.88	24,178.4	1,528.3	3,494.2	17.1

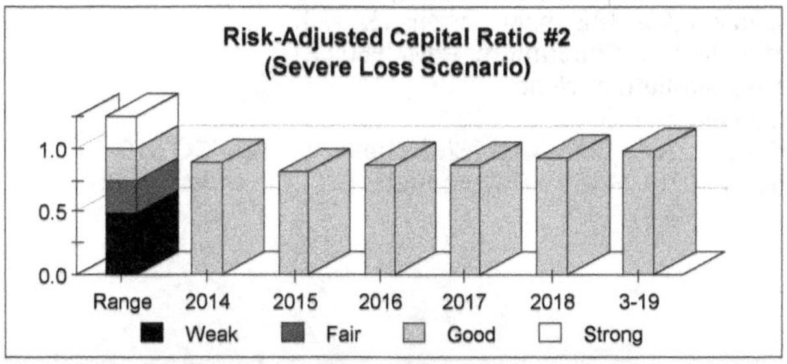

RIVERLINK HEALTH D Weak

Major Rating Factors: Weak profitability index (1.4 on a scale of 0 to 10). Strong capitalization (10.0) based on excellent current risk-adjusted capital (severe loss scenario). High quality investment portfolio (9.9).

Other Rating Factors: Excellent liquidity (7.4) with ample operational cash flow and liquid investments.

Principal Business: Medicare (100%)

Mem Phys: 18: 7,181 **17:** 7,000 **18 MLR** 82.5% **/ 18 Admin Exp** N/A

Enroll(000): Q1 19: N/A **18:** 1 **17:** 1 **Med Exp PMPM:** $671

Principal Investments: Long-term bonds (65%), cash and equiv (35%)

Provider Compensation ($000): Contr fee ($7,474), capitation ($369)

Total Member Encounters: Phys (10,081), non-phys (8,963)

Group Affiliation: None

Licensed in: OH

Address: PO Box 8849, Cincinnati, OH 45242

Phone: (866) 789-7747 **Dom State:** OH **Commenced Bus:** N/A

Data Date	Rating	RACR #1	RACR #2	Total Assets ($mil)	Capital ($mil)	Net Premium ($mil)	Net Income ($mil)
3-19	D	5.12	4.27	6.0	5.4	0.0	-0.4
3-18	E+	N/A	N/A	7.6	5.0	2.2	0.3
2018	D	5.50	4.58	7.0	5.8	8.8	1.2
2017	E+	N/A	N/A	6.7	4.7	9.1	-0.1
2016	E+	1.30	1.08	5.4	1.8	9.3	-2.6
2015	D+	4.37	3.64	5.0	3.5	4.1	-1.2
2014	N/A	N/A	N/A	3.4	3.4	N/A	N/A

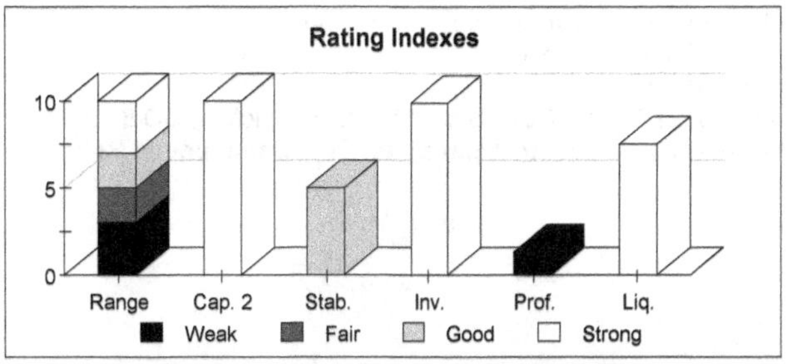

RIVERLINK HEALTH OF KENTUCKY INC D+ Weak

Major Rating Factors: Weak profitability index (1.2 on a scale of 0 to 10). Strong capitalization (10.0) based on excellent current risk-adjusted capital (severe loss scenario). High quality investment portfolio (9.9).
Other Rating Factors: Excellent liquidity (7.2) with ample operational cash flow and liquid investments.
Principal Business: Medicare (100%)
Mem Phys: 18: 7,181 **17:** 7,000 **18 MLR** 90.6% **/ 18 Admin Exp** N/A
Enroll(000): Q1 19: N/A **18:** 1 **17:** 1 **Med Exp PMPM:** $809
Principal Investments: Long-term bonds (58%), cash and equiv (42%)
Provider Compensation ($000): Contr fee ($7,665), capitation ($119), other ($88)
Total Member Encounters: Phys (8,981), non-phys (7,264)
Group Affiliation: None
Licensed in: KY
Address: PO Box 1109, Lexington, KY 40504
Phone: (866) 789-7747 **Dom State:** KY **Commenced Bus:** N/A

Data Date	Rating	RACR #1	RACR #2	Total Assets ($mil)	Capital ($mil)	Net Premium ($mil)	Net Income ($mil)
3-19	D+	3.98	3.32	5.4	5.0	0.0	0.0
3-18	D-	N/A	N/A	7.1	5.2	2.0	0.2
2018	D	4.21	3.51	6.6	5.3	8.7	0.3
2017	D-	N/A	N/A	6.9	5.0	8.6	-0.4
2016	D-	3.18	2.65	6.5	4.5	8.5	-1.8
2015	C-	9.29	7.74	6.0	5.2	3.1	-0.4
2014	N/A	N/A	N/A	5.5	5.5	N/A	N/A

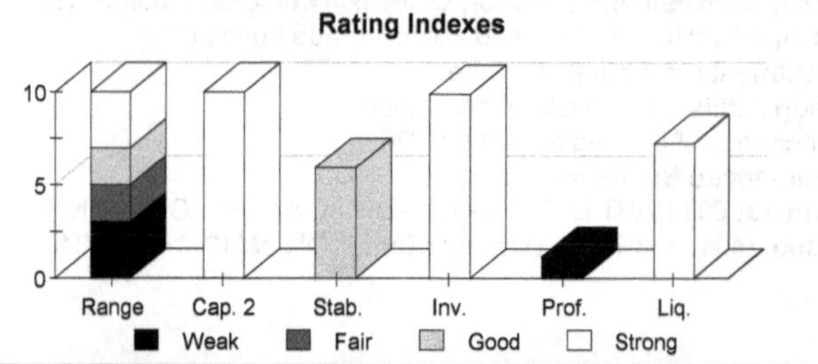

ROCKY MOUNTAIN HEALTH MAINT ORG B- Good

Major Rating Factors: Fair profitability index (3.8 on a scale of 0 to 10). Good quality investment portfolio (5.2). Good overall results on stability tests (5.5). Rating is significantly influenced by the good financial results of .
Other Rating Factors: Strong capitalization index (9.7) based on excellent current risk-adjusted capital (severe loss scenario). Excellent liquidity (7.1) with ample operational cash flow and liquid investments.
Principal Business: Medicaid (60%), comp med (35%), Medicare (4%)
Mem Phys: 18: 20,862 **17:** 20,776 **18 MLR** 77.6% **/ 18 Admin Exp** N/A
Enroll(000): Q1 19: 217 **18:** 223 **17:** 218 **Med Exp PMPM:** $117
Principal Investments: Cash and equiv (60%), long-term bonds (31%), real estate (6%), affiliate common stock (3%), other (1%)
Provider Compensation ($000): Contr fee ($199,675), FFS ($75,065), capitation ($39,182), bonus arrang ($2,223)
Total Member Encounters: Phys (960,621)
Group Affiliation: None
Licensed in: CO
Address: 2775 Crossroads Blvd, Grand Junction, CO 81506
Phone: (970) 244-7760 **Dom State:** CO **Commenced Bus:** N/A

Data Date	Rating	RACR #1	RACR #2	Total Assets ($mil)	Capital ($mil)	Net Premium ($mil)	Net Income ($mil)
3-19	B-	3.55	2.96	156.7	75.3	107.0	1.5
3-18	C	2.11	1.76	142.0	44.3	88.6	-1.4
2018	B-	3.51	2.92	161.9	74.2	404.2	21.8
2017	C	1.46	1.22	121.4	50.4	376.0	2.6
2016	C	1.09	0.91	152.3	46.9	449.2	-6.8
2015	C	0.75	0.62	186.5	39.6	481.0	-21.8
2014	B	1.62	1.35	164.1	63.2	332.4	-13.6

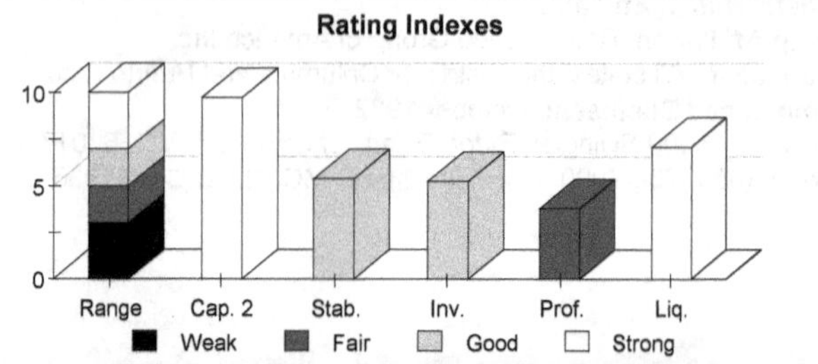

ROCKY MOUNTAIN HEALTHCARE OPTIONS D Weak

Major Rating Factors: Weak profitability index (0.7 on a scale of 0 to 10). Fair capitalization (2.9) based on fair current risk-adjusted capital (moderate loss scenario). Good liquidity (6.4) with sufficient resources (cash flows and marketable investments) to handle a spike in claims.
Other Rating Factors: High quality investment portfolio (9.4).
Principal Business: Comp med (100%)
Mem Phys: 17: 20,772 **16:** 20,354 **17 MLR** 100.7% **/ 17 Admin Exp** N/A
Enroll(000): Q1 18: 2 **17:** 5 **16:** 10 **Med Exp PMPM:** $516
Principal Investments: Long-term bonds (55%), cash and equiv (37%), affiliate common stock (8%)
Provider Compensation ($000): Contr fee ($37,986), bonus arrang ($7,620), FFS ($4,043), capitation ($640), other ($1,125)
Total Member Encounters: Phys (56,395)
Group Affiliation: None
Licensed in: CO
Address: 2775 CROSSRdS BLVD, Grand Junction, CO 81506
Phone: (970) 244-7760 **Dom State:** CO **Commenced Bus:** N/A

Data Date	Rating	RACR #1	RACR #2	Total Assets ($mil)	Capital ($mil)	Net Premium ($mil)	Net Income ($mil)
3-18	D	0.99	0.82	14.2	8.4	2.9	-1.0
3-17	D	1.00	0.83	23.4	11.0	13.7	-1.0
2017	D	0.72	0.60	19.6	10.9	46.8	-4.2
2016	E+	0.72	0.60	27.6	12.7	73.7	-4.6
2015	E	0.53	0.44	28.4	10.9	85.3	-4.2
2014	E	0.39	0.33	34.8	10.7	106.1	-5.3
2013	E	0.50	0.41	40.8	13.6	170.4	-4.2

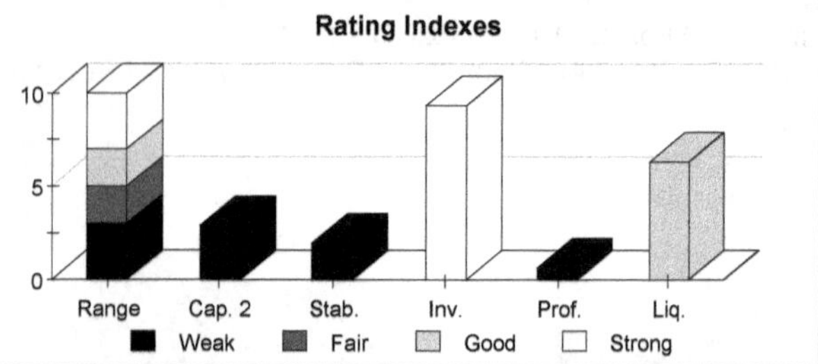

ROCKY MOUNTAIN HOSPITAL & MEDICAL B Good

Major Rating Factors: Good liquidity (5.9 on a scale of 0 to 10) with sufficient resources (cash flows and marketable investments) to handle a spike in claims. Fair quality investment portfolio (3.7). Excellent profitability (8.2).
Other Rating Factors: Strong capitalization (9.2) based on excellent current risk-adjusted capital (severe loss scenario).
Principal Business: Comp med (52%), FEHB (38%), med supp (5%), dental (2%), other (3%)
Mem Phys: 18: 22,058 **17:** 21,099 **18 MLR** 95.4% **/ 18 Admin Exp** N/A
Enroll(000): Q1 19: 646 **18:** 609 **17:** 639 **Med Exp PMPM:** $229
Principal Investments: Affiliate common stock (63%), long-term bonds (52%), other (3%)
Provider Compensation ($000): Bonus arrang ($1,065,551), contr fee ($315,386), FFS ($242,825), capitation ($115), other ($36,930)
Total Member Encounters: Phys (2,164,135), non-phys (1,553,360)
Group Affiliation: Anthem Inc
Licensed in: CO, NV
Address: 700 Broadway, DENVER, CO 80273
Phone: (303) 831-2131 **Dom State:** CO **Commenced Bus:** N/A

Data Date	Rating	RACR #1	RACR #2	Total Assets ($mil)	Capital ($mil)	Net Premium ($mil)	Net Income ($mil)
3-19	B	3.11	2.59	1,046.8	537.6	431.5	42.0
3-18	B	2.75	2.29	956.7	432.9	439.0	6.8
2018	B	2.61	2.18	964.1	449.8	1,748.7	91.5
2017	B	1.98	1.65	930.1	399.0	1,942.0	71.8
2016	B	2.50	2.09	1,007.6	374.9	2,337.6	87.7
2015	B	3.71	3.09	907.0	387.1	1,907.8	89.7
2014	B+	3.53	2.94	861.7	440.9	1,960.5	108.4

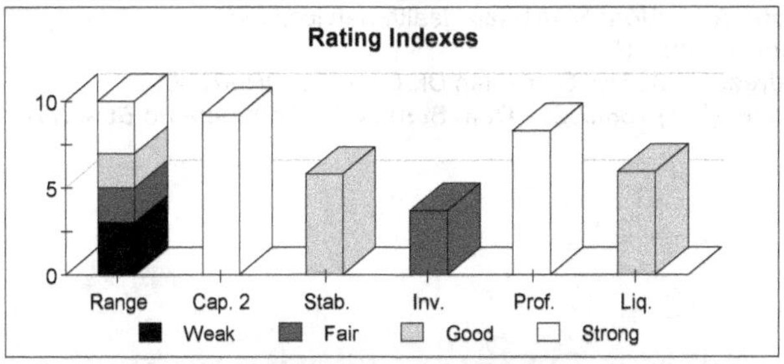

ROYAL STATE NATIONAL INSURANCE COMPANY LIMITED C Fair

Major Rating Factors: Fair profitability (4.0 on a scale of 0 to 10). Fair overall results on stability tests (4.2). Good quality investment portfolio (5.6) despite mixed results such as: no exposure to mortgages and large holdings of BBB rated bonds but no exposure to junk bonds.
Other Rating Factors: Strong capitalization (10.0) based on excellent risk adjusted capital (severe loss scenario). Excellent liquidity (7.1).
Principal Business: Group health insurance (54%), group life insurance (35%), individual life insurance (10%), and reinsurance (1%).
Principal Investments: NonCMO investment grade bonds (64%), common & preferred stock (17%), CMOs and structured securities (14%), cash (3%), and policy loans (1%).
Investments in Affiliates: None
Group Affiliation: Royal State Group
Licensed in: HI
Commenced Business: August 1961
Address: 819 SOUTH BERETANIA STREET, HONOLULU, HI 96813
Phone: (808) 539-1600 **Domicile State:** HI **NAIC Code:** 68551

Data Date	Rating	RACR #1	RACR #2	Total Assets ($mil)	Capital ($mil)	Net Premium ($mil)	Net Income ($mil)
3-18	C	5.02	3.72	39.7	30.3	1.2	0.4
3-17	C	4.90	3.27	46.2	29.3	1.3	0.0
2017	C	5.14	3.70	0.0	0.0	0.0	0.0
2016	C	5.11	3.41	0.0	0.0	0.0	0.0
2015	C	4.91	3.29	0.0	0.0	0.0	0.0
2014	B-	3.27	2.29	0.0	0.0	0.0	0.0
2013	B-	3.29	2.33	0.0	0.0	0.0	0.0

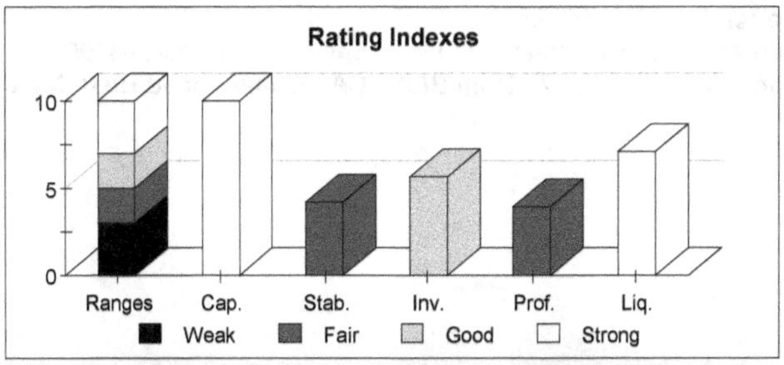

RYDER HEALTH PLAN INC B Good

Major Rating Factors: Fair profitability index (3.8 on a scale of 0 to 10). Fair overall results on stability tests (4.5) based on a significant 25% decrease in enrollment during the period. Strong capitalization index (7.1) based on excellent current risk-adjusted capital (severe loss scenario).
Other Rating Factors: High quality investment portfolio (9.7). Excellent liquidity (7.8) with ample operational cash flow and liquid investments.
Principal Business: Comp med (99%), med supp (1%)
Mem Phys: 18: N/A **17:** N/A **18 MLR** 75.3% **/ 18 Admin Exp** N/A
Enroll(000): Q1 19: 3 **18:** 2 **17:** 3 **Med Exp PMPM:** $50
Principal Investments: Cash and equiv (78%), long-term bonds (22%)
Provider Compensation ($000): Capitation ($1,357), other ($199)
Total Member Encounters: N/A
Group Affiliation: Ryder Health Plan Inc
Licensed in: PR
Address: 353 FONT MARTELO AVE SUITE 1, HUMACAO, PR 791
Phone: (787) 852-0846 **Dom State:** PR **Commenced Bus:** N/A

Data Date	Rating	RACR #1	RACR #2	Total Assets ($mil)	Capital ($mil)	Net Premium ($mil)	Net Income ($mil)
3-19	B	1.44	1.20	1.4	0.6	0.5	0.0
3-18	C+	1.66	1.39	1.7	0.7	0.5	0.0
2018	B	1.41	1.18	1.5	0.6	2.0	0.1
2017	C+	1.64	1.37	1.6	0.7	2.5	0.2
2016	C-	1.24	1.03	1.5	0.5	2.6	0.0
2015	C-	1.28	1.07	1.3	0.5	1.9	-0.2
2014	C-	1.61	1.34	1.5	0.7	2.5	0.0

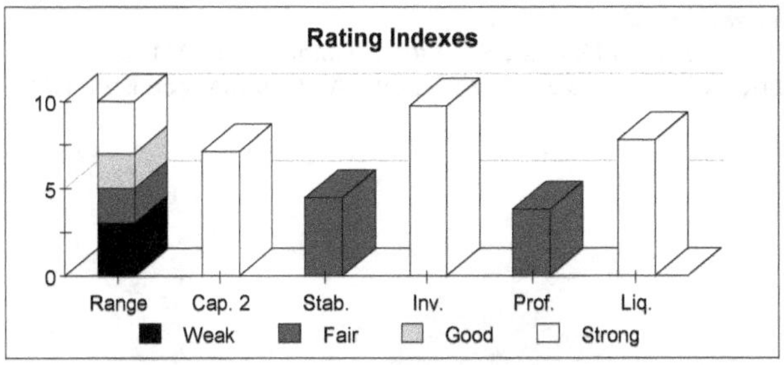

SAMARITAN HEALTH PLANS INC — C+ — Fair

Major Rating Factors: Fair profitability index (4.1 on a scale of 0 to 10). Fair capitalization (4.5) based on fair current risk-adjusted capital (moderate loss scenario). Good liquidity (6.3) with sufficient resources (cash flows and marketable investments) to handle a spike in claims.
Other Rating Factors: High quality investment portfolio (9.9).
Principal Business: Medicare (69%), comp med (31%)
Mem Phys: 18: 9,960 **17:** 8,142 **18 MLR** 91.6% **/ 18 Admin Exp** N/A
Enroll(000): Q1 19: 10 **18:** 11 **17:** 10 **Med Exp PMPM:** $633
Principal Investments: Cash and equiv (53%), long-term bonds (41%), nonaffiliate common stock (6%), other (1%)
Provider Compensation ($000): Contr fee ($81,512)
Total Member Encounters: Phys (118,487), non-phys (67,607)
Group Affiliation: Samaritan Health Services Inc
Licensed in: OR
Address: 3600 NW Samaritan Dr, Corvallis, OR 97330
Phone: (541) 768-5328 **Dom State:** OR **Commenced Bus:** N/A

Data Date	Rating	RACR #1	RACR #2	Total Assets ($mil)	Capital ($mil)	Net Premium ($mil)	Net Income ($mil)
3-19	C+	0.85	0.71	24.6	11.0	22.7	-0.8
3-18	B	1.28	1.06	33.7	14.2	21.6	-0.6
2018	B-	0.90	0.75	25.5	11.5	89.1	-3.1
2017	B	1.39	1.16	30.8	15.3	92.2	5.1
2016	C+	0.94	0.79	20.7	9.5	73.4	2.8
2015	C	0.85	0.71	17.4	8.1	61.1	-0.9
2014	B	1.08	0.90	19.1	9.1	57.8	0.8

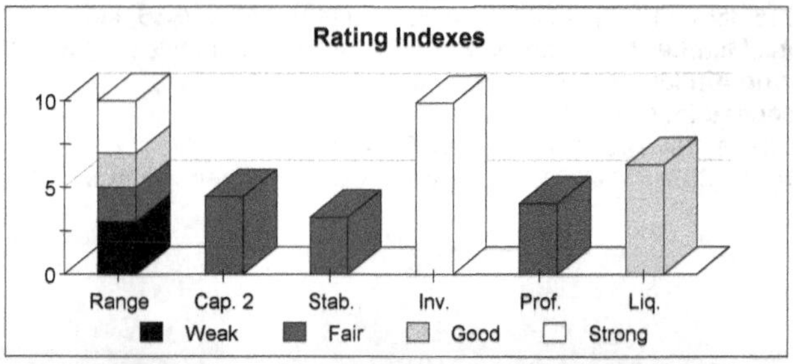

SAN FRANCISCO HEALTH AUTHORITY — B- — Good

Major Rating Factors: Fair overall results on stability tests (4.5 on a scale of 0 to 10). Good overall profitability index (5.1). Strong capitalization index (7.8) based on excellent current risk-adjusted capital (severe loss scenario).
Other Rating Factors: Excellent liquidity (8.2) with ample operational cash flow and liquid investments.
Principal Business: Medicaid (90%)
Mem Phys: 18: N/A **17:** N/A **18 MLR** 96.2% **/ 18 Admin Exp** N/A
Enroll(000): Q1 19: 141 **18:** 141 **17:** 146 **Med Exp PMPM:** $334
Principal Investments ($000): Cash and equiv ($100,014)
Provider Compensation ($000): None
Total Member Encounters: N/A
Group Affiliation: None
Licensed in: (No states)
Address: 50 Beale Street 12th Floor, San Francisco, CA 94105
Phone: (415) 615-4217 **Dom State:** CA **Commenced Bus:** March 1996

Data Date	Rating	RACR #1	RACR #2	Total Assets ($mil)	Capital ($mil)	Net Premium ($mil)	Net Income ($mil)
3-19	B-	2.67	1.69	662.6	108.9	140.4	-0.1
3-18	B	2.86	1.79	632.6	120.1	135.4	-5.8
2018	B-	2.66	1.68	624.8	109.0	600.1	-16.9
2017	B	3.01	1.88	632.5	125.8	618.5	12.2
2016	B	2.91	1.83	484.8	112.6	572.8	29.9
2015	B	2.20	1.39	346.1	82.7	545.1	37.8
2014	B	1.75	1.13	217.4	47.4	311.9	11.2

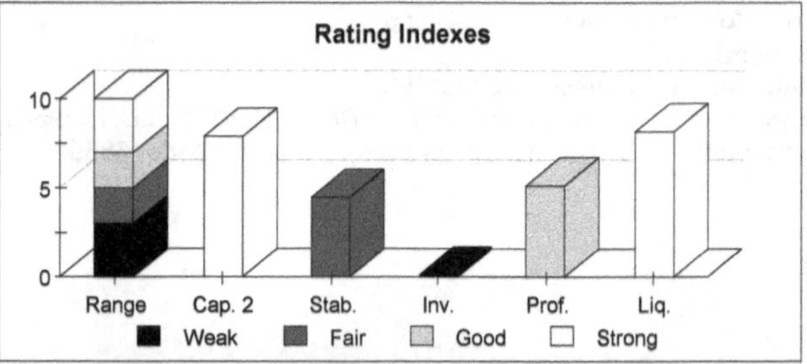

SAN JOAQUIN CNTY HEALTH * — B+ — Good

Major Rating Factors: Good overall results on stability tests (6.5 on a scale of 0 to 10). Excellent profitability (8.1). Strong capitalization index (10.0) based on excellent current risk-adjusted capital (severe loss scenario).
Other Rating Factors: Excellent liquidity (7.5) with ample operational cash flow and liquid investments.
Principal Business: Medicaid (100%)
Mem Phys: 18: N/A **17:** N/A **18 MLR** 94.1% **/ 18 Admin Exp** N/A
Enroll(000): Q1 19: 341 **18:** 343 **17:** 350 **Med Exp PMPM:** $237
Principal Investments ($000): Cash and equiv ($344,474)
Provider Compensation ($000): None
Total Member Encounters: N/A
Group Affiliation: None
Licensed in: CA
Address: 7751 S Manthey Rd, French Camp, CA 95231-9802
Phone: (888) 936-7526 **Dom State:** CA **Commenced Bus:** N/A

Data Date	Rating	RACR #1	RACR #2	Total Assets ($mil)	Capital ($mil)	Net Premium ($mil)	Net Income ($mil)
3-19	B+	5.63	3.42	660.0	344.7	263.6	22.8
3-18	B	4.12	2.51	604.0	303.2	252.3	13.1
2018	B+	5.21	3.17	523.8	321.9	1,050.0	31.8
2017	B	3.87	2.35	601.2	290.1	1,036.4	78.1
2016	C+	1.89	1.15	561.1	140.8	920.6	26.7
2015	C+	2.18	1.33	455.2	114.2	729.1	79.9
2014	C+	1.22	0.75	169.0	39.4	446.4	-14.0

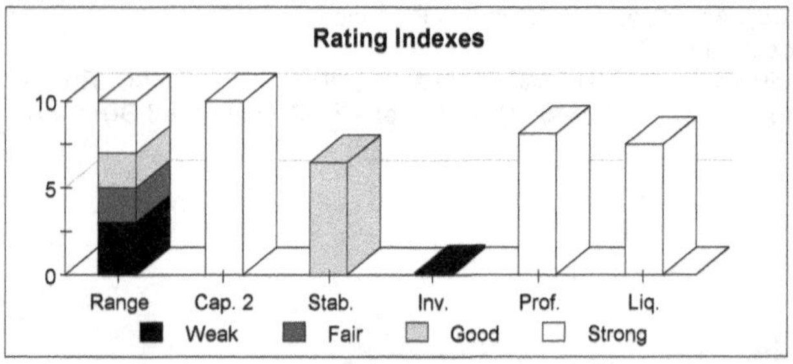

SAN MATEO HEALTH COMMISSION B Good

Major Rating Factors: Good overall profitability index (5.8 on a scale of 0 to 10). Fair overall results on stability tests (4.2). Strong capitalization index (10.0) based on excellent current risk-adjusted capital (severe loss scenario).
Other Rating Factors: Excellent liquidity (7.7) with ample operational cash flow and liquid investments.
Principal Business: Medicaid (77%), Medicare (23%)
Mem Phys: 18: N/A **17:** N/A **18 MLR** 87.3% **/ 18 Admin Exp** N/A
Enroll(000): Q1 19: 113 **18:** 115 **17:** 131 **Med Exp PMPM:** $468
Principal Investments ($000): Cash and equiv ($403,719)
Provider Compensation ($000): None
Total Member Encounters: N/A
Group Affiliation: None
Licensed in: CA
Address: 7751 S Manthey Road, French Camp, CA 95231
Phone: (209) 461-2211 **Dom State:** CA **Commenced Bus:** December 1987

Data Date	Rating	RACR #1	RACR #2	Total Assets ($mil)	Capital ($mil)	Net Premium ($mil)	Net Income ($mil)
3-19	B	6.39	3.93	628.3	343.0	203.1	3.5
3-18	B+	6.96	4.29	615.9	351.5	197.7	12.2
2018	B	6.31	3.89	574.4	339.5	770.9	0.3
2017	B+	6.67	4.11	745.3	339.2	906.4	41.8
2016	B+	5.55	3.41	800.6	297.4	792.3	-20.3
2015	A-	6.65	4.08	641.5	317.8	911.0	103.4
2014	A-	5.38	3.31	408.4	214.3	728.9	69.2

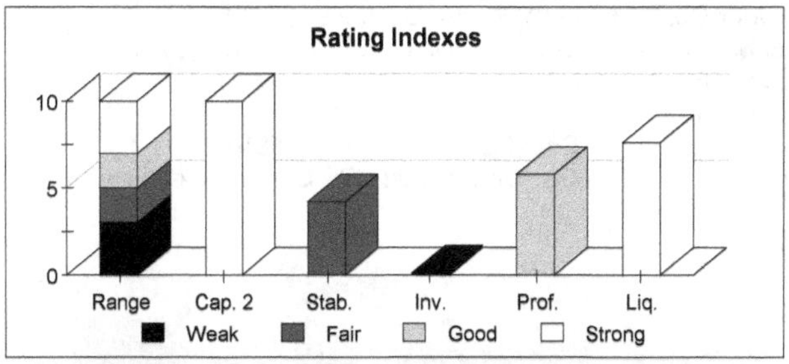

SANFORD HEALTH PLAN C Fair

Major Rating Factors: Weak profitability index (0.9 on a scale of 0 to 10). Good quality investment portfolio (5.7). Good liquidity (6.7) with sufficient resources (cash flows and marketable investments) to handle a spike in claims.
Other Rating Factors: Strong capitalization index (7.3) based on excellent current risk-adjusted capital (severe loss scenario). Excellent overall results on stability tests (7.5).
Principal Business: Comp med (67%), Medicaid (33%)
Mem Phys: 18: 59,836 **17:** 53,371 **18 MLR** 93.2% **/ 18 Admin Exp** N/A
Enroll(000): Q1 19: 142 **18:** 139 **17:** 129 **Med Exp PMPM:** $507
Principal Investments: Long-term bonds (51%), cash and equiv (34%), nonaffiliate common stock (13%), other (1%)
Provider Compensation ($000): Contr fee ($844,106)
Total Member Encounters: Phys (587,609), non-phys (647,475)
Group Affiliation: None
Licensed in: IA, ND, SD
Address: 300 Cherapa Place Suite 201, Sioux Falls, SD 57103
Phone: (605) 328-6868 **Dom State:** SD **Commenced Bus:** N/A

Data Date	Rating	RACR #1	RACR #2	Total Assets ($mil)	Capital ($mil)	Net Premium ($mil)	Net Income ($mil)
3-19	C	1.60	1.33	285.2	141.3	230.8	16.1
3-18	C	1.50	1.25	290.4	123.2	229.4	7.1
2018	C	1.49	1.24	270.8	131.4	908.5	9.7
2017	C	1.43	1.19	268.2	117.7	839.5	11.2
2016	C	0.96	0.80	230.5	86.4	823.7	-8.9
2015	C	0.74	0.62	223.0	55.1	613.2	-73.2
2014	C+	0.70	0.58	78.1	24.1	295.6	-1.6

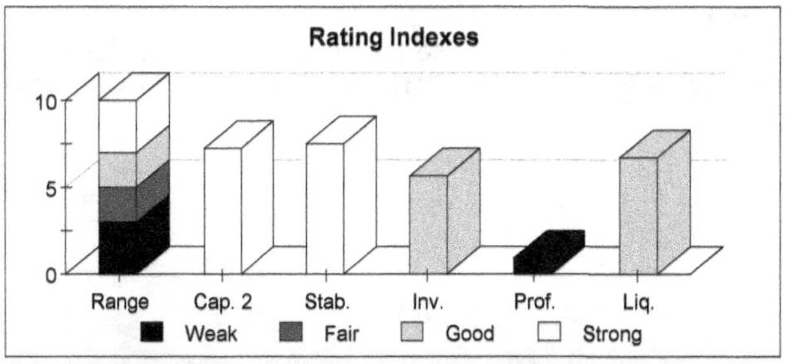

SANFORD HEALTH PLAN OF MINNESOTA D+ Weak

Major Rating Factors: Weak profitability index (0.9 on a scale of 0 to 10). Fair quality investment portfolio (3.1). Fair overall results on stability tests (4.0) based on an excessive 85% enrollment growth during the period. Rating is significantly influenced by the fair financial results of .
Other Rating Factors: Strong capitalization index (7.5) based on excellent current risk-adjusted capital (severe loss scenario). Excellent liquidity (7.6) with ample operational cash flow and liquid investments.
Principal Business: Comp med (93%), med supp (7%)
Mem Phys: 18: 59,836 **17:** 53,371 **18 MLR** 101.7% **/ 18 Admin Exp** N/A
Enroll(000): Q1 19: 1 **18:** 1 **17:** 0 **Med Exp PMPM:** $393
Principal Investments: Cash and equiv (100%)
Provider Compensation ($000): Contr fee ($3,122)
Total Member Encounters: Phys (2,575), non-phys (3,381)
Group Affiliation: None
Licensed in: MN
Address: 300 Cherapa Place Suite 201, Sioux Falls, SD 57109-1110
Phone: (605) 328-6868 **Dom State:** MN **Commenced Bus:** N/A

Data Date	Rating	RACR #1	RACR #2	Total Assets ($mil)	Capital ($mil)	Net Premium ($mil)	Net Income ($mil)
3-19	D+	1.76	1.47	3.2	1.3	1.4	-0.4
3-18	D	1.85	1.54	2.1	1.4	0.8	0.0
2018	D+	2.35	1.96	3.1	1.8	3.6	-0.9
2017	E+	1.27	1.06	2.3	1.4	1.8	-0.1
2016	E+	1.88	1.57	2.2	1.5	2.4	-0.2
2015	E	2.00	1.67	2.5	1.7	2.6	-0.4
2014	E	1.34	1.12	1.8	1.2	2.2	0.0

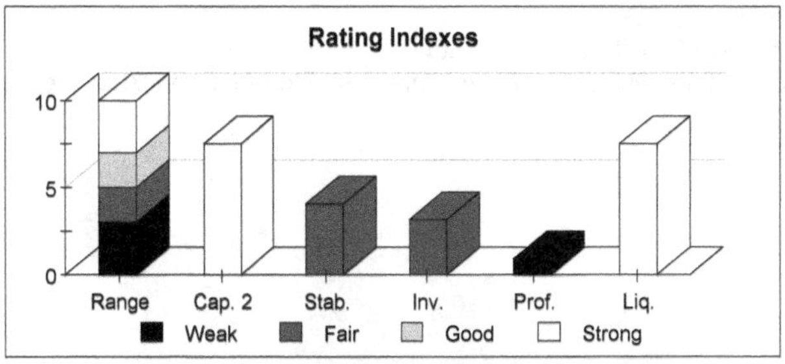

SANFORD HEART OF AMERICA HEALTH PLAN C- Fair

Major Rating Factors: Fair overall results on stability tests (3.7 on a scale of 0 to 10) based on a steep decline in capital during 2018. Rating is significantly influenced by the fair financial results of . Weak profitability index (0.9). Good liquidity (6.4) with sufficient resources (cash flows and marketable investments) to handle a spike in claims.
Other Rating Factors: Strong capitalization index (8.0) based on excellent current risk-adjusted capital (severe loss scenario). High quality investment portfolio (9.7).
Principal Business: Comp med (51%), other (49%)
Mem Phys: 18: 36,569 **17:** 22,180 **18 MLR** 109.6% **/ 18 Admin Exp** N/A
Enroll(000): Q1 19: 0 **18:** 1 **17:** 1 **Med Exp PMPM:** $464
Principal Investments: Long-term bonds (78%), cash and equiv (22%)
Provider Compensation ($000): Contr fee ($3,225)
Total Member Encounters: Phys (2,087), non-phys (2,248)
Group Affiliation: None
Licensed in: ND
Address: 1749 38th Street South, Fargo, ND 58104
Phone: (605) 328-6868 **Dom State:** ND **Commenced Bus:** N/A

Data Date	Rating	RACR #1	RACR #2	Total Assets ($mil)	Capital ($mil)	Net Premium ($mil)	Net Income ($mil)
3-19	C-	2.14	1.78	2.4	2.1	0.4	-0.2
3-18	C-	2.71	2.26	3.3	2.5	0.8	-0.3
2018	C-	2.28	1.90	2.9	2.3	3.0	-0.6
2017	C-	2.10	1.75	3.5	2.9	3.3	0.7
2016	D+	2.22	1.85	3.1	2.2	3.4	0.2
2015	D+	1.67	1.39	3.1	1.9	3.5	-0.6
2014	E	0.34	0.29	1.5	0.5	3.7	-0.7

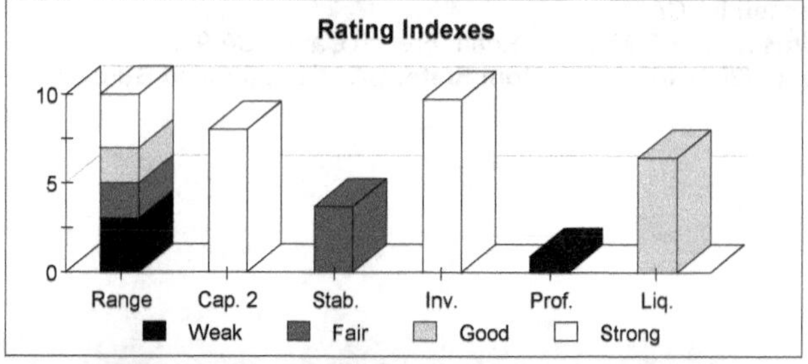

SANTA BARBARA SAN LUIS OBISPO REGION B- Good

Major Rating Factors: Good liquidity (5.1 on a scale of 0 to 10) with sufficient resources (cash flows and marketable investments) to handle a spike in claims. Excellent profitability (10.0). Strong capitalization index (9.0) based on excellent current risk-adjusted capital (severe loss scenario).
Other Rating Factors: Excellent overall results on stability tests (7.5).
Principal Business: Medicaid (100%)
Mem Phys: 18: N/A **17:** N/A **18 MLR** 83.7% **/ 18 Admin Exp** N/A
Enroll(000): Q1 19: 176 **18:** 176 **17:** 180 **Med Exp PMPM:** $301
Principal Investments ($000): Cash and equiv ($313,759)
Provider Compensation ($000): None
Total Member Encounters: N/A
Group Affiliation: None
Licensed in: CA
Address: 801 Gateway Blvd Suite 100, So. San Francisco, CA 94080
Phone: (650) 616-2151 **Dom State:** CA **Commenced Bus:** September 1983

Data Date	Rating	RACR #1	RACR #2	Total Assets ($mil)	Capital ($mil)	Net Premium ($mil)	Net Income ($mil)
3-19	B-	4.04	2.47	529.0	232.7	235.4	4.8
3-18	B	4.41	2.66	451.9	217.1	183.3	-1.4
2018	C	4.19	2.55	394.7	227.9	770.0	9.3
2017	B	4.44	2.68	471.6	218.5	716.3	36.2
2016	C	2.97	1.79	359.9	150.6	658.3	61.2
2015	D-	1.58	0.96	250.1	89.4	597.5	58.9
2014	E+	0.14	0.09	135.4	37.8	383.7	2.8

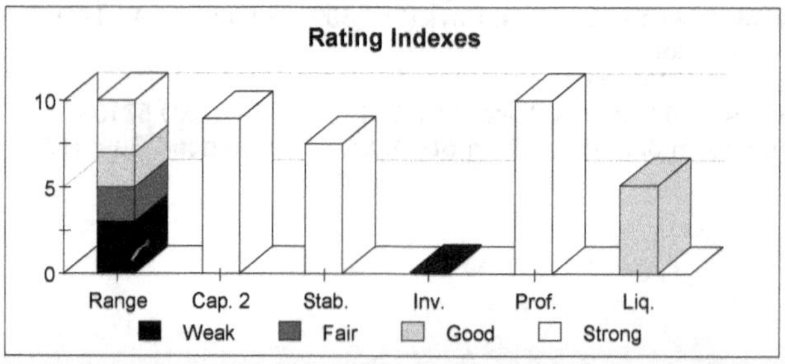

SANTA CLARA COUNTY HEALTH AUTHORITY C Fair

Major Rating Factors: Good overall results on stability tests (5.7 on a scale of 0 to 10). Excellent profitability (10.0). Strong capitalization index (8.0) based on excellent current risk-adjusted capital (severe loss scenario).
Other Rating Factors: Excellent liquidity (8.0) with ample operational cash flow and liquid investments.
Principal Business: Medicaid (91%), Medicare (9%)
Mem Phys: 18: N/A **17:** N/A **18 MLR** 81.6% **/ 18 Admin Exp** N/A
Enroll(000): Q1 19: 251 **18:** 254 **17:** 268 **Med Exp PMPM:** $349
Principal Investments ($000): Cash and equiv ($207,721)
Provider Compensation ($000): None
Total Member Encounters: N/A
Group Affiliation: None
Licensed in: CA
Address: 4050 Calle Real, Santa Barbara, CA 93110
Phone: (805) 685-9525 **Dom State:** CA **Commenced Bus:** February 1997

Data Date	Rating	RACR #1	RACR #2	Total Assets ($mil)	Capital ($mil)	Net Premium ($mil)	Net Income ($mil)
3-19	C	2.90	1.77	920.5	190.5	382.8	4.4
3-18	C	2.76	1.68	780.9	175.9	283.3	1.9
2018	C	2.82	1.72	793.2	186.1	1,332.5	12.1
2017	C	2.72	1.65	821.3	173.9	1,524.6	62.8
2016	C	1.67	1.01	576.5	100.3	1,259.2	27.7
2015	C	1.43	0.86	295.9	72.6	959.7	37.4
2014	C	1.39	0.85	114.5	40.9	452.2	8.3

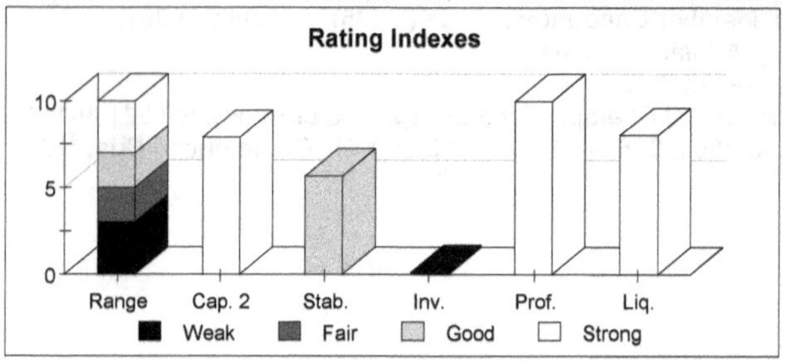

SANTA CLARA VALLEY D+ Weak

Major Rating Factors: Fair capitalization index (4.8 on a scale of 0 to 10) based on fair current risk-adjusted capital (moderate loss scenario). Good overall results on stability tests (5.9). Good liquidity (6.6) with sufficient resources (cash flows and marketable investments) to handle a spike in claims.
Other Rating Factors: Excellent profitability (7.5).
Principal Business: Managed care (99%)
Mem Phys: 18: N/A **17:** N/A **18 MLR** 89.7% **/ 18 Admin Exp** N/A
Enroll(000): Q1 19: 161 **18:** 157 **17:** 161 **Med Exp PMPM:** $253
Principal Investments ($000): Cash and equiv ($122,107)
Provider Compensation ($000): None
Total Member Encounters: N/A
Group Affiliation: None
Licensed in: CA
Address: 2480 North 1st St Suite 200, San Jose, CA 95131
Phone: (408) 885-5606 **Dom State:** CA **Commenced Bus:** September 1985

Data Date	Rating	RACR #1	RACR #2	Total Assets ($mil)	Capital ($mil)	Net Premium ($mil)	Net Income ($mil)
3-19	D+	0.75	0.47	192.6	36.8	137.9	1.7
3-18	D	0.76	0.47	163.3	31.0	137.7	1.8
2018	D+	0.71	0.44	203.3	35.1	544.4	5.9
2017	D	0.71	0.44	169.1	29.1	518.2	3.0
2016	D	0.62	0.38	130.8	25.3	514.9	9.8
2015	C	0.78	0.48	96.0	29.4	487.9	8.4
2014	C	0.99	0.61	56.8	21.1	281.6	5.7

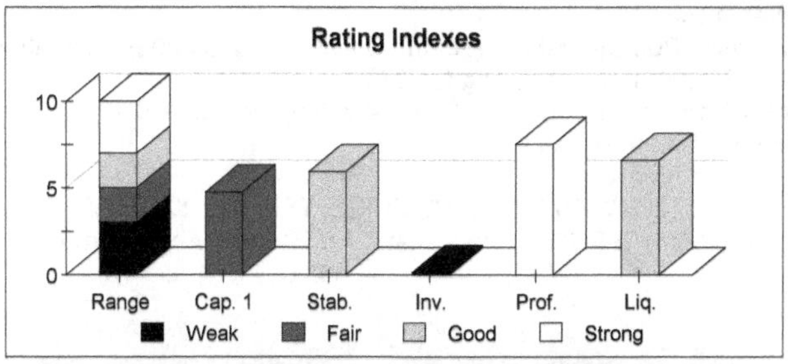

SANTA CRUZ-MONTEREY-MERCED MGD MED B- Good

Major Rating Factors: Fair profitability index (3.0 on a scale of 0 to 10). Fair overall results on stability tests (4.2). Good liquidity (6.8) with sufficient resources (cash flows and marketable investments) to handle a spike in claims.
Other Rating Factors: Strong capitalization index (10.0) based on excellent current risk-adjusted capital (severe loss scenario).
Principal Business: Medicaid (100%)
Mem Phys: 18: N/A **17:** N/A **18 MLR** 100.4% **/ 18 Admin Exp** N/A
Enroll(000): Q1 19: 343 **18:** 342 **17:** 352 **Med Exp PMPM:** $1,115
Principal Investments ($000): Cash and equiv ($276,442)
Provider Compensation ($000): None
Total Member Encounters: N/A
Group Affiliation: None
Licensed in: CA
Address: 210 East Hacienda Avenue, Campbell, CA 95008
Phone: (408) 874-1701 **Dom State:** CA **Commenced Bus:** N/A

Data Date	Rating	RACR #1	RACR #2	Total Assets ($mil)	Capital ($mil)	Net Premium ($mil)	Net Income ($mil)
3-19	B-	8.24	5.11	851.6	501.9	296.2	-17.9
3-18	B-	11.14	6.86	1,104.8	597.1	266.5	-18.7
2018	B-	8.60	5.34	753.4	519.8	1,145.9	-96.0
2017	B-	11.59	7.13	1,195.0	615.8	1,129.9	23.4
2016	B-	11.77	7.21	1,393.4	592.4	1,075.9	73.1
2015	B-	12.48	7.62	1,097.2	519.2	985.4	118.4
2014	B-	11.20	6.92	714.0	400.9	789.8	87.7

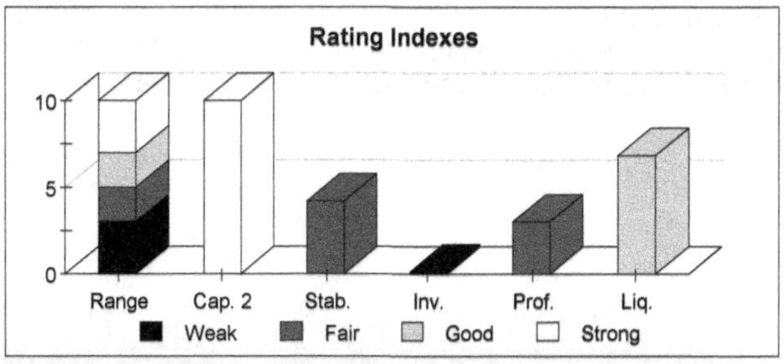

SCAN HEALTH PLAN B Good

Major Rating Factors: Good overall results on stability tests (6.5 on a scale of 0 to 10) based on steady enrollment growth, averaging 6% over the past five years. Fair profitability index (4.5). Strong capitalization index (8.2) based on excellent current risk-adjusted capital (severe loss scenario).
Other Rating Factors: Excellent liquidity (7.2) with ample operational cash flow and liquid investments.
Principal Business: Medicare (98%), Medicaid (2%)
Mem Phys: 18: N/A **17:** N/A **18 MLR** 89.8% **/ 18 Admin Exp** N/A
Enroll(000): Q1 19: 203 **18:** 198 **17:** 188 **Med Exp PMPM:** $1,040
Principal Investments ($000): Cash and equiv ($479,805)
Provider Compensation ($000): None
Total Member Encounters: N/A
Group Affiliation: SCAN Group
Licensed in: CA
Address: 300 Santana Row Suite 300, San Jose, CA 95128
Phone: (650) 404-3798 **Dom State:** CA **Commenced Bus:** March 1985

Data Date	Rating	RACR #1	RACR #2	Total Assets ($mil)	Capital ($mil)	Net Premium ($mil)	Net Income ($mil)
3-19	B	3.14	1.94	691.6	409.4	767.9	-0.1
3-18	C+	3.04	1.89	832.3	377.4	679.3	1.3
2018	B	3.03	1.88	621.9	396.9	2,717.8	32.6
2017	C+	3.06	1.90	563.5	379.0	2,563.2	32.6
2016	C-	2.96	1.84	571.9	332.1	2,251.5	41.2
2015	C	3.10	1.93	569.8	352.2	2,165.1	24.8
2014	C	3.83	2.38	575.5	402.4	2,013.4	-59.1

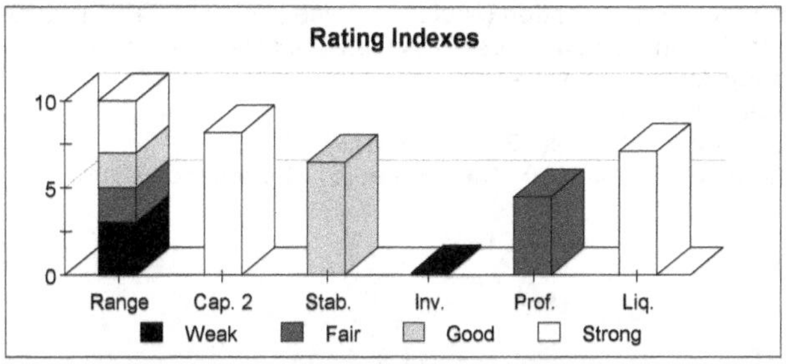

SCOTT & WHITE HEALTH PLAN C Fair

Major Rating Factors: Weak profitability index (2.8 on a scale of 0 to 10). Good quality investment portfolio (5.8). Strong capitalization index (8.4) based on excellent current risk-adjusted capital (severe loss scenario).
Other Rating Factors: Excellent overall results on stability tests (7.5) despite a decline in enrollment during 2018. Excellent liquidity (7.0) with sufficient resources (cash flows and marketable investments) to handle a spike in claims.
Principal Business: Comp med (57%), Medicare (22%), Medicaid (19%), FEHB (1%)
Mem Phys: 18: 16,648 **17:** 14,772 **18 MLR** 82.8% **/ 18 Admin Exp** N/A
Enroll(000): Q1 19: 85 **18:** 142 **17:** 157 **Med Exp PMPM:** $334
Principal Investments: Cash and equiv (24%), long-term bonds (18%), nonaffiliate common stock (5%), affiliate common stock (5%), real estate (5%), other (43%)
Provider Compensation ($000): Contr fee ($490,208), capitation ($60,053), FFS ($37,007), bonus arrang ($1,328)
Total Member Encounters: Phys (468,890), non-phys (217,790)
Group Affiliation: None
Licensed in: TX
Address: 1206 WEST CAMPUS DRIVE, TEMPLE, TX 76502
Phone: (254) 298-3000 **Dom State:** TX **Commenced Bus:** N/A

Data Date	Rating	RACR #1	RACR #2	Total Assets ($mil)	Capital ($mil)	Net Premium ($mil)	Net Income ($mil)
3-19	C	2.49	2.07	434.5	223.6	142.6	5.4
3-18	C-	0.91	0.76	289.4	97.2	178.5	0.3
2018	C	2.29	1.91	381.2	213.3	716.1	27.7
2017	C-	0.93	0.77	267.2	99.0	704.9	12.3
2016	C-	0.66	0.55	270.8	97.1	670.1	-59.1
2015	B	1.28	1.07	218.5	83.3	688.9	-12.2
2014	B	1.79	1.49	174.3	84.8	662.4	24.2

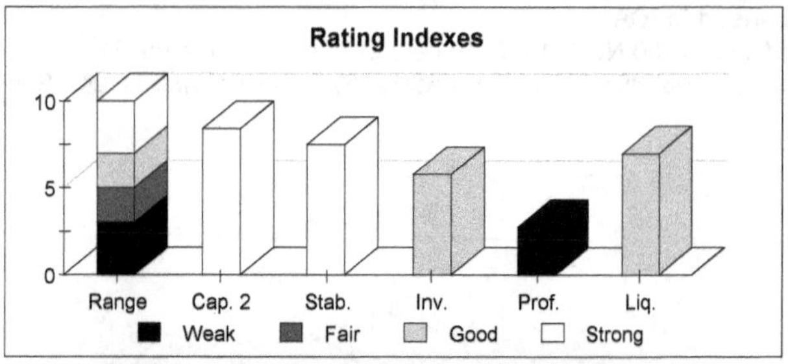

SCRIPPS HEALTH PLAN SERVICES INC C- Fair

Major Rating Factors: Good capitalization index (5.7 on a scale of 0 to 10) based on fair current risk-adjusted capital (moderate loss scenario). Good overall results on stability tests (6.6). Excellent profitability (7.9).
Other Rating Factors: Excellent liquidity (6.9) with sufficient resources (cash flows and marketable investments) to handle a spike in claims.
Principal Business: Managed care (100%)
Mem Phys: 18: N/A **17:** N/A **18 MLR** 99.6% **/ 18 Admin Exp** N/A
Enroll(000): Q1 19: 147 **18:** 144 **17:** 118 **Med Exp PMPM:** $399
Principal Investments ($000): Cash and equiv ($109,812)
Provider Compensation ($000): None
Total Member Encounters: N/A
Group Affiliation: Scripps Health
Licensed in: CA
Address: 3800 Kilroy Airport Way #100, Long Beach, CA 90801-5616
Phone: (562) 989-8320 **Dom State:** CA **Commenced Bus:** October 1997

Data Date	Rating	RACR #1	RACR #2	Total Assets ($mil)	Capital ($mil)	Net Premium ($mil)	Net Income ($mil)
3-19	C-	0.86	0.52	130.9	41.1	176.9	1.7
3-18	C-	0.83	0.51	115.0	36.8	162.9	-0.4
2018	D+	0.82	0.50	115.1	39.4	674.1	2.2
2017	C-	0.78	0.47	119.3	34.7	604.8	3.5
2016	D+	0.77	0.46	90.7	29.1	515.3	2.1
2015	D+	0.64	0.39	85.1	22.3	475.0	0.2
2014	D	0.73	0.44	78.8	18.7	338.1	0.2

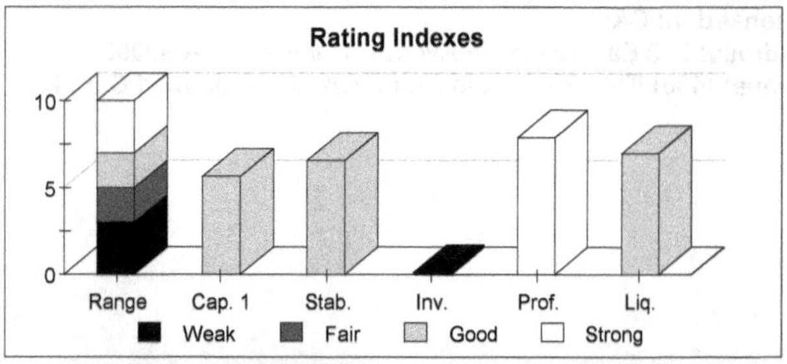

SD STATE MEDICAL HOLDING CO D Weak

Major Rating Factors: Weak profitability index (1.5 on a scale of 0 to 10). Weak overall results on stability tests (1.9) based on a significant 34% decrease in enrollment during the period, a steep decline in capital during 2018. Fair capitalization index (2.9) based on good current risk-adjusted capital (moderate loss scenario
Other Rating Factors: High quality investment portfolio (7.7). Excellent liquidity (7.2) with ample operational cash flow and liquid investments.
Principal Business: Comp med (100%)
Mem Phys: 18: 2,143 **17:** 2,081 **18 MLR** 68.7% **/ 18 Admin Exp** N/A
Enroll(000): Q1 19: 6 **18:** 7 **17:** 10 **Med Exp PMPM:** $271
Principal Investments: Cash and equiv (46%), long-term bonds (29%), affiliate common stock (28%)
Provider Compensation ($000): Contr fee ($26,159), FFS ($2,239)
Total Member Encounters: Phys (63,287), non-phys (7,836)
Group Affiliation: None
Licensed in: SD
Address: 2600 W 49th St, Sioux Falls, SD 57105
Phone: (605) 334-4000 **Dom State:** SD **Commenced Bus:** N/A

Data Date	Rating	RACR #1	RACR #2	Total Assets ($mil)	Capital ($mil)	Net Premium ($mil)	Net Income ($mil)
3-19	D	1.40	1.16	21.5	8.2	7.5	-0.7
3-18	D	1.12	0.93	25.5	15.1	12.0	0.4
2018	D	1.55	1.29	22.9	9.0	36.6	1.4
2017	D	1.10	0.92	26.5	14.8	57.4	6.7
2016	D	0.46	0.39	26.8	9.3	79.2	-4.5
2015	N/A	N/A	N/A	50.3	11.5	107.9	-19.7
2014	B	1.47	1.23	40.2	20.5	111.8	0.4

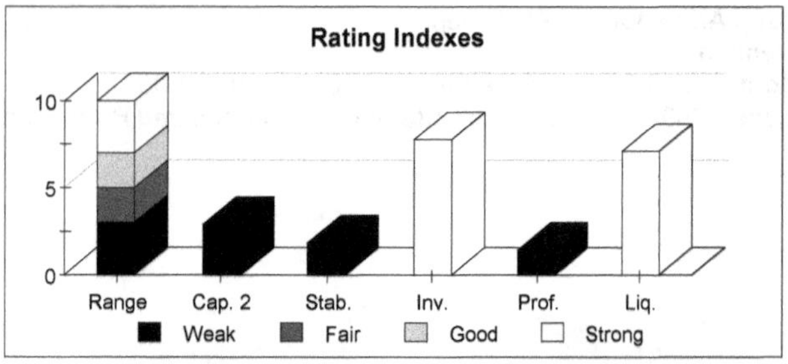

SEASIDE HEALTH PLAN D- Weak

Major Rating Factors: Weak profitability index (0.9 on a scale of 0 to 10). Poor capitalization index (0.0) based on weak current risk-adjusted capital (severe loss scenario). Weak liquidity (0.0) as a spike in claims may stretch capacity.
Other Rating Factors: Fair overall results on stability tests (3.9).
Principal Business: Managed care (100%)
Mem Phys: 18: N/A **17:** N/A **18 MLR** 113.2% **/ 18 Admin Exp** N/A
Enroll(000): Q1 19: 42 **18:** 42 **17:** 40 **Med Exp PMPM:** $95
Principal Investments ($000): Cash and equiv ($5,622)
Provider Compensation ($000): None
Total Member Encounters: N/A
Group Affiliation: None
Licensed in: CA
Address: 10790 Rancho Bernardo Road, San Diego, CA 92127
Phone: (858) 927-5360 **Dom State:** CA **Commenced Bus:** May 2013

Data Date	Rating	RACR #1	RACR #2	Total Assets ($mil)	Capital ($mil)	Net Premium ($mil)	Net Income ($mil)
3-19	D-	0.29	0.19	13.0	8.3	10.5	-3.8
3-18	D-	0.35	0.22	14.3	8.3	10.4	-2.8
2018	D-	0.26	0.16	12.4	8.1	42.7	-13.3
2017	D-	0.31	0.20	14.0	8.1	40.8	-7.9
2016	D	0.59	0.38	15.1	9.1	31.4	-9.8
2015	D	0.55	0.38	11.2	5.9	21.5	-9.7
2014	U	2.22	1.53	11.0	7.6	10.1	-5.1

Rating Indexes

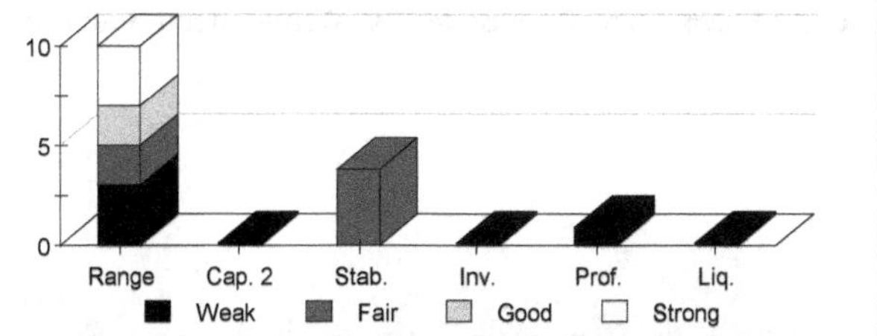

SECURITY HEALTH PLAN OF WI INC * B+ Good

Major Rating Factors: Good overall profitability index (6.1 on a scale of 0 to 10). Good overall results on stability tests (5.2). Good liquidity (6.0) with sufficient resources (cash flows and marketable investments) to handle a spike in claims.
Other Rating Factors: Strong capitalization index (7.6) based on excellent current risk-adjusted capital (severe loss scenario). High quality investment portfolio (7.4).
Principal Business: Comp med (51%), Medicare (39%), Medicaid (9%)
Mem Phys: 18: 9,708 **17:** 10,659 **18 MLR** 89.8% **/ 18 Admin Exp** N/A
Enroll(000): Q1 19: 202 **18:** 205 **17:** 204 **Med Exp PMPM:** $479
Principal Investments: Long-term bonds (59%), nonaffiliate common stock (14%), cash and equiv (9%), real estate (3%), other (15%)
Provider Compensation ($000): Capitation ($466,553), contr fee ($423,504), FFS ($280,117)
Total Member Encounters: N/A
Group Affiliation: Marshfield Clinic Health System Inc
Licensed in: WI
Address: 1515 St Joseph Ave, Marshfield, WI 54449
Phone: (715) 221-9555 **Dom State:** WI **Commenced Bus:** N/A

Data Date	Rating	RACR #1	RACR #2	Total Assets ($mil)	Capital ($mil)	Net Premium ($mil)	Net Income ($mil)
3-19	B+	1.82	1.52	445.1	183.0	339.8	35.1
3-18	B+	1.94	1.62	451.7	192.8	362.8	34.7
2018	B+	1.69	1.41	420.4	170.6	1,340.1	28.0
2017	B+	1.72	1.43	351.3	172.0	1,222.3	9.8
2016	A-	2.25	1.88	384.0	225.1	1,178.1	11.4
2015	A-	2.06	1.72	350.6	202.4	1,158.3	18.6
2014	A-	1.95	1.62	320.2	187.9	1,098.0	28.3

Rating Indexes

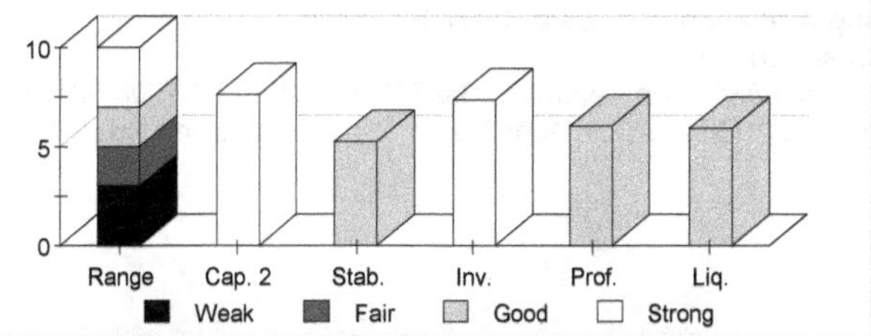

SELECT HEALTH OF SOUTH CAROLINA INC B Good

Major Rating Factors: Good overall results on stability tests (5.6 on a scale of 0 to 10). Good liquidity (6.8) with sufficient resources (cash flows and marketable investments) to handle a spike in claims. Excellent profitability (7.7).
Other Rating Factors: Strong capitalization index (7.8) based on excellent current risk-adjusted capital (severe loss scenario). High quality investment portfolio (8.8).
Principal Business: Medicaid (93%), Medicare (7%)
Mem Phys: 18: 22,330 **17:** 20,075 **18 MLR** 87.7% **/ 18 Admin Exp** N/A
Enroll(000): Q1 19: 371 **18:** 382 **17:** 370 **Med Exp PMPM:** $287
Principal Investments: Cash and equiv (47%), long-term bonds (45%), nonaffiliate common stock (8%)
Provider Compensation ($000): Contr fee ($1,221,808), capitation ($60,033)
Total Member Encounters: Phys (2,713,607), non-phys (961,396)
Group Affiliation: Independence Health Group Inc
Licensed in: KY, MS, RI, SC
Address: 4390 Belle Oaks Drive Suite 40, North Charleston, SC 29405
Phone: (843) 569-1759 **Dom State:** SC **Commenced Bus:** N/A

Data Date	Rating	RACR #1	RACR #2	Total Assets ($mil)	Capital ($mil)	Net Premium ($mil)	Net Income ($mil)
3-19	B	2.00	1.67	332.4	151.7	366.9	-4.3
3-18	B-	1.58	1.31	324.0	113.1	360.3	-24.7
2018	B	2.01	1.68	336.7	152.6	1,465.7	19.6
2017	B-	1.60	1.33	353.5	166.0	1,364.2	29.9
2016	B-	2.37	1.97	354.0	169.7	1,337.3	46.8
2015	B-	2.12	1.77	271.5	133.3	1,175.8	32.2
2014	B	1.89	1.58	277.7	119.3	1,135.5	36.1

Rating Indexes

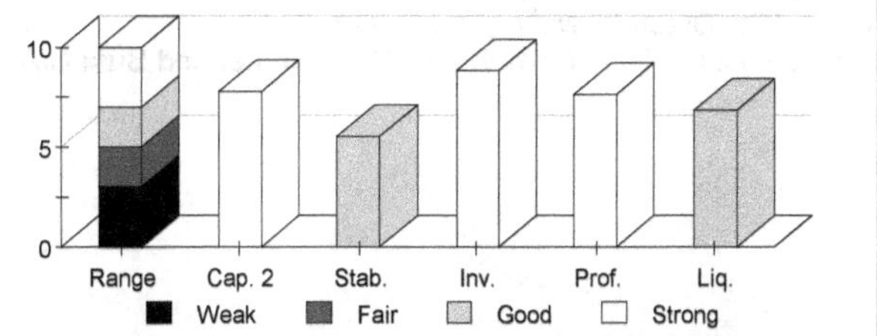

SELECTCARE HEALTH PLANS INC — B- Good

Major Rating Factors: Fair profitability index (4.9 on a scale of 0 to 10). Strong capitalization (9.8) based on excellent current risk-adjusted capital (severe loss scenario). High quality investment portfolio (7.8).
Other Rating Factors: Excellent liquidity (6.9) with sufficient resources (cash flows and marketable investments) to handle a spike in claims.
Principal Business: Medicare (100%)
Mem Phys: 18: 8,800 **17:** 461 **18 MLR** 80.2% **/ 18 Admin Exp** N/A
Enroll(000): Q1 19: 2 **18:** 2 **17:** 2 **Med Exp PMPM:** $748
Principal Investments: Long-term bonds (95%), cash and equiv (5%)
Provider Compensation ($000): Contr fee ($18,225), capitation ($553)
Total Member Encounters: Phys (28,577), non-phys (7,754)
Group Affiliation: WellCare Health Plans Inc
Licensed in: TX
Address: 4888 Loop Central Dr Ste 700, Houston, TX 77081-2181
Phone: (813) 206-2725 **Dom State:** TX **Commenced Bus:** N/A

Data Date	Rating	RACR #1	RACR #2	Total Assets ($mil)	Capital ($mil)	Net Premium ($mil)	Net Income ($mil)
3-19	B-	3.57	2.97	12.4	7.2	5.8	0.6
3-18	C-	2.52	2.10	11.5	5.6	5.8	-0.2
2018	C+	3.33	2.78	10.2	6.8	22.8	1.0
2017	C-	1.32	1.10	10.0	5.7	24.3	1.0
2016	C+	3.90	3.25	18.9	14.7	33.7	0.7
2015	C+	3.30	2.75	19.0	14.0	42.7	0.7
2014	C	2.70	2.25	20.4	13.5	51.4	-0.4

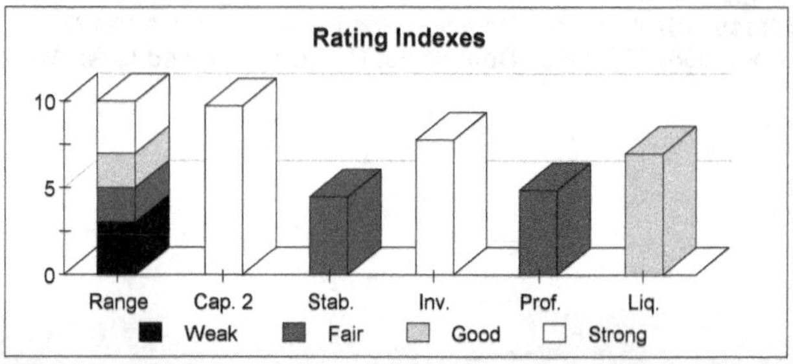

SELECTCARE OF TEXAS INC — B Good

Major Rating Factors: Good quality investment portfolio (6.0 on a scale of 0 to 10). Good liquidity (6.9) with sufficient resources (cash flows and marketable investments) to handle a spike in claims. Excellent profitability (8.1).
Other Rating Factors: Strong capitalization index (7.9) based on excellent current risk-adjusted capital (severe loss scenario). Excellent overall results on stability tests (7.8). Rating is significantly influenced by the fair financial results of WellCare Health Plans Inc.
Principal Business: Medicare (100%)
Mem Phys: 18: 11,500 **17:** 9,357 **18 MLR** 84.2% **/ 18 Admin Exp** N/A
Enroll(000): Q1 19: 66 **18:** 65 **17:** 67 **Med Exp PMPM:** $929
Principal Investments: Long-term bonds (99%), cash and equiv (1%)
Provider Compensation ($000): Capitation ($363,538), contr fee ($361,237), bonus arrang ($10,736)
Total Member Encounters: Phys (925,017), non-phys (143,468)
Group Affiliation: WellCare Health Plans Inc
Licensed in: TX
Address: 4888 Loop Central Dr Ste 700, Houston, TX 77081-2181
Phone: (813) 290-6200 **Dom State:** TX **Commenced Bus:** N/A

Data Date	Rating	RACR #1	RACR #2	Total Assets ($mil)	Capital ($mil)	Net Premium ($mil)	Net Income ($mil)
3-19	B	2.10	1.75	240.2	80.9	239.6	6.7
3-18	B	N/A	N/A	233.0	56.4	224.3	-18.3
2018	B	1.97	1.64	179.7	75.4	870.9	14.4
2017	B	N/A	N/A	190.0	71.6	842.1	8.2
2016	B	1.27	1.06	160.6	62.6	833.8	10.3
2015	B	1.37	1.14	146.4	61.5	799.0	9.6
2014	C	1.60	1.34	138.8	62.9	728.5	9.0

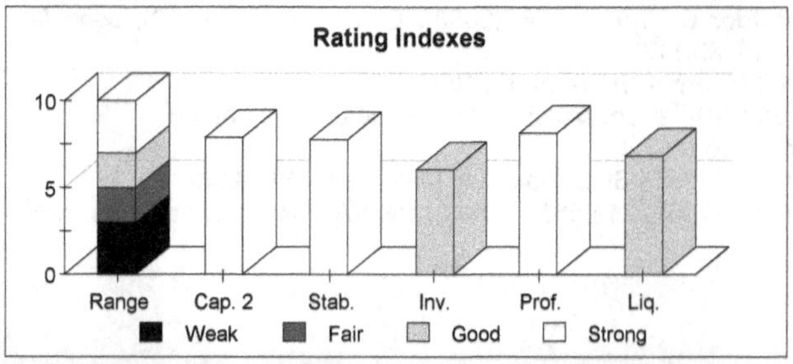

SELECTHEALTH BENEFIT ASR CO INC — C+ Fair

Major Rating Factors: Excellent profitability (7.9 on a scale of 0 to 10). Strong capitalization (9.8) based on excellent current risk-adjusted capital (severe loss scenario). High quality investment portfolio (9.2).
Other Rating Factors: Excellent liquidity (8.3) with ample operational cash flow and liquid investments.
Principal Business: Other (100%)
Mem Phys: 18: N/A **17:** N/A **18 MLR** 13.8% **/ 18 Admin Exp** N/A
Enroll(000): Q1 19: 0 **18:** 0 **17:** 0 **Med Exp PMPM:** $1,259
Principal Investments: Long-term bonds (74%), cash and equiv (24%), other (2%)
Provider Compensation ($000): FFS ($3,834)
Total Member Encounters: Phys (47), non-phys (43)
Group Affiliation: Intermountain Health Care Inc
Licensed in: ID, UT
Address: 5381Green St, Murray, UT 84123
Phone: (801) 442-5000 **Dom State:** UT **Commenced Bus:** N/A

Data Date	Rating	RACR #1	RACR #2	Total Assets ($mil)	Capital ($mil)	Net Premium ($mil)	Net Income ($mil)
3-19	C+	3.60	3.00	26.7	18.5	7.8	0.8
3-18	C+	3.14	2.61	29.0	17.8	8.0	1.0
2018	C+	3.31	2.76	29.2	17.5	31.9	1.3
2017	C	2.11	1.76	29.1	17.1	38.6	1.5
2016	C	3.35	2.79	25.1	16.0	34.4	1.2
2015	B-	2.80	2.33	23.1	15.0	30.7	2.2
2014	B	5.02	4.18	21.1	14.0	14.1	0.8

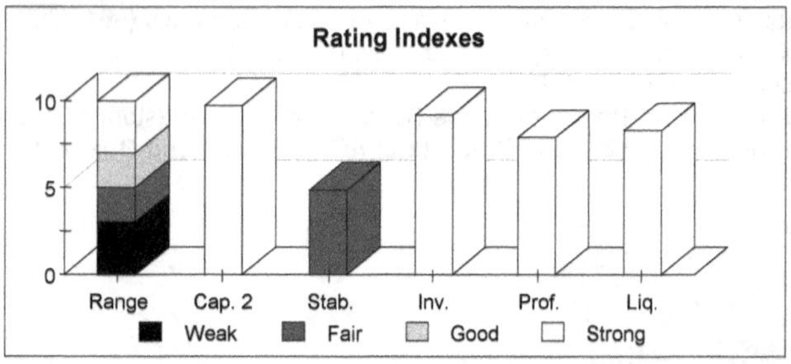

SELECTHEALTH INC C Fair

Major Rating Factors: Weak profitability index (2.3 on a scale of 0 to 10). Good overall results on stability tests (6.0). Good liquidity (6.8) with sufficient resources (cash flows and marketable investments) to handle a spike in claims.
Other Rating Factors: Strong capitalization index (8.8) based on excellent current risk-adjusted capital (severe loss scenario). High quality investment portfolio (7.3).
Principal Business: Comp med (77%), Medicaid (11%), Medicare (10%), FEHB (2%)
Mem Phys: 18: 9,342 **17:** 9,308 **18 MLR** 86.8% **/ 18 Admin Exp** N/A
Enroll(000): Q1 19: 724 **18:** 691 **17:** 647 **Med Exp PMPM:** $323
Principal Investments: Long-term bonds (53%), nonaffiliate common stock (33%), cash and equiv (8%), other (6%)
Provider Compensation ($000): Bonus arrang ($1,495,641), contr fee ($1,041,228), FFS ($185,031), capitation ($8,103)
Total Member Encounters: Phys (3,344,552), non-phys (1,623,269)
Group Affiliation: Intermountain Health Care Inc
Licensed in: ID, UT
Address: 5381 Green Street, Murray, UT 84123
Phone: (801) 442-5000 **Dom State:** UT **Commenced Bus:** N/A

Data Date	Rating	RACR #1	RACR #2	Total Assets ($mil)	Capital ($mil)	Net Premium ($mil)	Net Income ($mil)
3-19	C	2.76	2.30	1,428.1	613.9	836.4	41.7
3-18	C	2.36	1.96	1,072.9	496.1	793.7	23.1
2018	C	2.37	1.98	1,123.0	540.0	3,113.3	141.8
2017	C	2.27	1.89	1,090.1	482.3	2,641.9	88.0
2016	C	1.49	1.24	1,085.9	332.0	2,611.6	-136.6
2015	C	1.61	1.35	912.5	298.8	2,029.2	-374.0
2014	A	2.94	2.45	848.5	444.8	1,891.4	26.9

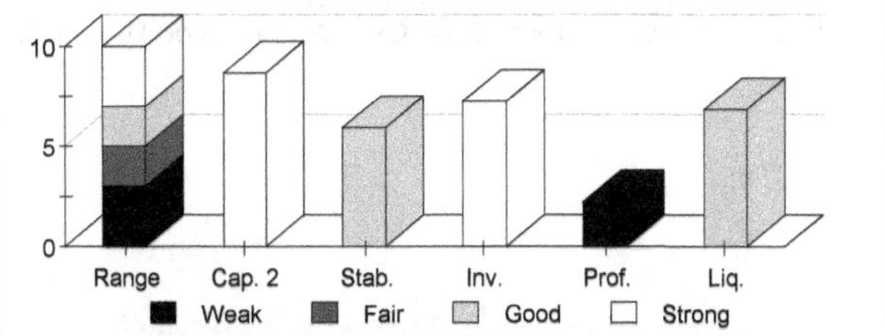

SENDERO HEALTH PLANS INC E Very Weak

Major Rating Factors: Weak profitability index (0.9 on a scale of 0 to 10). Poor capitalization (1.7) based on weak current risk-adjusted capital (moderate loss scenario). High quality investment portfolio (9.9).
Other Rating Factors: Excellent liquidity (7.1) with ample operational cash flow and liquid investments.
Principal Business: Comp med (87%), Medicaid (13%)
Mem Phys: 18: N/A **17:** N/A **18 MLR** 93.5% **/ 18 Admin Exp** N/A
Enroll(000): Q1 19: 14 **18:** 23 **17:** 49 **Med Exp PMPM:** $305
Principal Investments: Cash and equiv (100%)
Provider Compensation ($000): FFS ($98,343), capitation ($27,441)
Total Member Encounters: Phys (201,168), non-phys (51,035)
Group Affiliation: None
Licensed in: TX
Address: 2028 E Ben White Blvd Ste 400, Austin, TX 78741
Phone: (512) 978-8454 **Dom State:** TX **Commenced Bus:** N/A

Data Date	Rating	RACR #1	RACR #2	Total Assets ($mil)	Capital ($mil)	Net Premium ($mil)	Net Income ($mil)
3-19	E	0.47	0.39	57.3	13.0	19.2	0.0
3-18	E-	0.43	0.36	88.2	12.8	45.4	0.9
2018	E	0.47	0.39	56.6	13.1	124.3	-18.9
2017	E-	0.41	0.34	90.4	12.0	145.8	-32.9
2016	E-	0.74	0.62	56.9	11.5	85.1	4.5
2015	E-	0.79	0.66	31.8	11.0	58.6	-4.8
2014	D+	0.89	0.74	30.4	8.7	49.0	-17.7

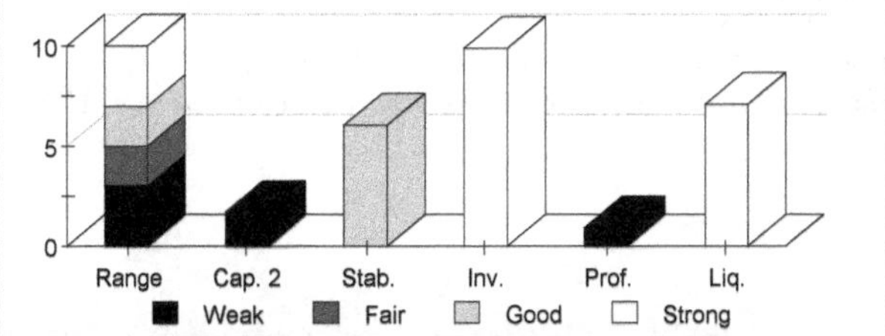

SENIOR WHOLE HEALTH OF NEW YORK INC C- Fair

Major Rating Factors: Fair capitalization (3.0 on a scale of 0 to 10) based on weak current risk-adjusted capital (moderate loss scenario). Weak profitability index (0.8). High quality investment portfolio (9.9).
Other Rating Factors: Excellent liquidity (6.9) with sufficient resources (cash flows and marketable investments) to handle a spike in claims.
Principal Business: Medicaid (97%), Medicare (1%), other (2%)
Mem Phys: 18: 16,663 **17:** 23,718 **18 MLR** 97.1% **/ 18 Admin Exp** N/A
Enroll(000): Q1 19: 15 **18:** 15 **17:** 14 **Med Exp PMPM:** $3,934
Principal Investments: Cash and equiv (89%), long-term bonds (11%)
Provider Compensation ($000): Contr fee ($625,981), FFS ($21,433)
Total Member Encounters: Non-phys (856,563)
Group Affiliation: Magellan Health Inc
Licensed in: NY
Address: 111 Broadway Ste 1505, New York, NY 10006
Phone: (314) 387-5631 **Dom State:** NY **Commenced Bus:** N/A

Data Date	Rating	RACR #1	RACR #2	Total Assets ($mil)	Capital ($mil)	Net Premium ($mil)	Net Income ($mil)
3-19	C-	0.63	0.53	178.6	42.8	196.8	4.5
3-18	D	1.98	1.65	183.2	68.5	181.4	6.3
2018	C-	0.57	0.48	176.2	38.4	688.2	-24.6
2017	E	0.82	0.68	153.0	61.4	598.8	7.4
2016	E	0.93	0.78	78.0	26.8	245.7	9.5
2015	E	1.10	0.92	53.6	17.5	133.1	10.6
2014	E	0.63	0.53	23.1	5.6	53.2	-2.1

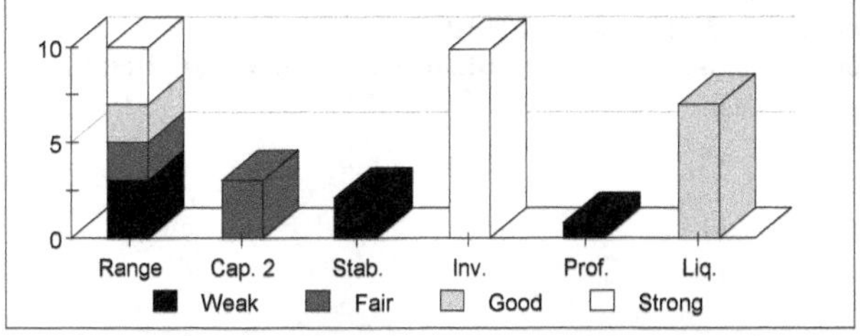

SEQUOIA HEALTH PLAN INC — E+ Very Weak

Major Rating Factors: Poor capitalization index (0.0 on a scale of 0 to 10) based on weak current risk-adjusted capital (severe loss scenario). Fair overall results on stability tests (3.4). Good liquidity (6.9) with sufficient resources (cash flows and marketable investments) to handle a spike in claims.
Other Rating Factors: Excellent profitability (8.0).
Principal Business: Managed care (100%)
Mem Phys: 18: N/A **17:** N/A **18 MLR** 96.7% **/ 18 Admin Exp** N/A
Enroll(000): Q1 19: 9 **18:** 8 **17:** 8 **Med Exp PMPM:** $679
Principal Investments ($000): Cash and equiv ($2,497)
Provider Compensation ($000): None
Total Member Encounters: N/A
Group Affiliation: None
Licensed in: (No states)
Address: 3350 S Fairway Ave, Visalia, CA 93277-8109
Phone: (Phone number **Dom State:** CA **Commenced Bus:** N/A

Data Date	Rating	RACR #1	RACR #2	Total Assets ($mil)	Capital ($mil)	Net Premium ($mil)	Net Income ($mil)
3-19	E+	0.35	0.21	2.9	2.4	20.8	0.2
3-18	D-	0.58	0.35	2.5	2.0	16.5	0.1
2018	E+	0.32	0.19	2.9	2.2	68.9	0.2
2017	D-	0.56	0.34	2.4	2.0	32.9	0.1
2016	N/A	N/A	N/A	N/A	N/A	N/A	N/A
2015	N/A	N/A	N/A	N/A	N/A	N/A	N/A
2014	N/A	N/A	N/A	N/A	N/A	N/A	N/A

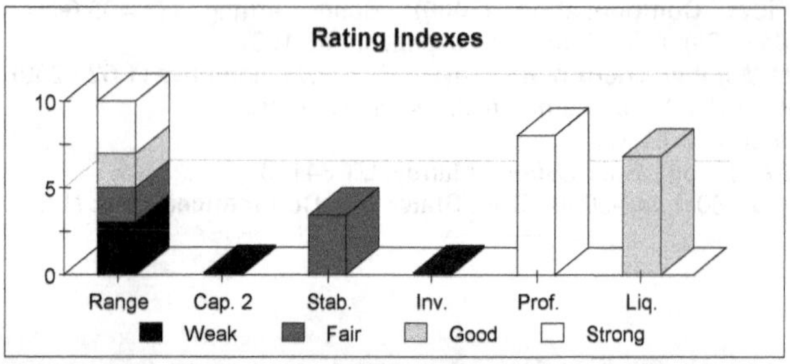

SETON HEALTH PLAN INC — B Good

Major Rating Factors: Good quality investment portfolio (5.7 on a scale of 0 to 10). Good overall results on stability tests (5.7). Excellent profitability (7.0).
Other Rating Factors: Strong capitalization index (10.0) based on excellent current risk-adjusted capital (severe loss scenario). Excellent liquidity (7.3) with ample operational cash flow and liquid investments.
Principal Business: Medicaid (77%), comp med (23%)
Mem Phys: 18: 5,318 **17:** 4,661 **18 MLR** 155.2% **/ 18 Admin Exp** N/A
Enroll(000): Q1 19: 31 **18:** 31 **17:** 25 **Med Exp PMPM:** $127
Principal Investments: Cash and equiv (57%), nonaffiliate common stock (39%), long-term bonds (4%)
Provider Compensation ($000): Contr fee ($34,299), FFS ($10,894), capitation ($235), other ($2)
Total Member Encounters: Phys (115,523), non-phys (103,716)
Group Affiliation: None
Licensed in: TX
Address: 1345 Philomena Strret, Austin, TX 78723
Phone: (512) 324-3350 **Dom State:** TX **Commenced Bus:** N/A

Data Date	Rating	RACR #1	RACR #2	Total Assets ($mil)	Capital ($mil)	Net Premium ($mil)	Net Income ($mil)
3-19	B	3.94	3.28	49.0	30.8	7.9	0.1
3-18	B-	3.55	2.96	38.6	26.6	6.6	2.0
2018	B	3.79	3.16	49.5	29.6	28.9	6.1
2017	B-	3.35	2.79	40.6	25.1	29.1	7.0
2016	C+	1.84	1.53	28.0	17.4	58.3	1.9
2015	C	1.73	1.45	32.6	15.1	53.5	1.5
2014	B-	1.97	1.64	35.7	23.5	50.0	-0.3

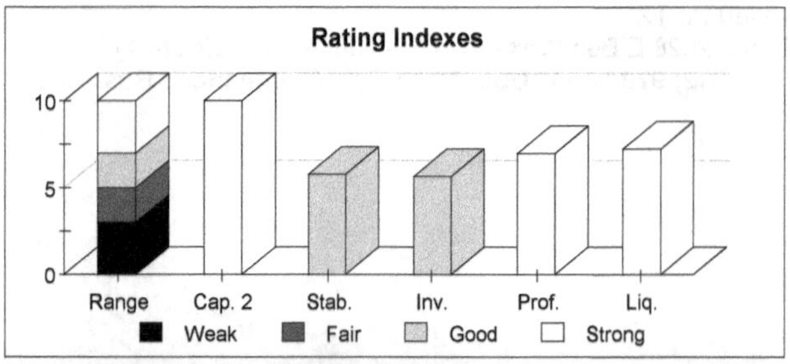

SETON INSURANCE COMPANY — C+ Fair

Major Rating Factors: Fair quality investment portfolio (2.9 on a scale of 0 to 10). Weak profitability index (0.4). Strong capitalization (9.3) based on excellent current risk-adjusted capital (severe loss scenario).
Other Rating Factors: Excellent liquidity (10.0) with ample operational cash flow and liquid investments.
Principal Business: Comp med (91%)
Mem Phys: 18: 5,318 **17:** 4,661 **18 MLR** -27.9% **/ 18 Admin Exp** N/A
Enroll(000): Q1 19: N/A **18:** N/A **17:** 0 **Med Exp PMPM:** N/A
Principal Investments: Cash and equiv (73%), nonaffiliate common stock (27%)
Provider Compensation ($000): Contr fee ($111), FFS ($51)
Total Member Encounters: Phys (284), non-phys (202)
Group Affiliation: None
Licensed in: TX
Address: 1345 Philomena St, Austin, TX 78723
Phone: (512) 324-3350 **Dom State:** TX **Commenced Bus:** N/A

Data Date	Rating	RACR #1	RACR #2	Total Assets ($mil)	Capital ($mil)	Net Premium ($mil)	Net Income ($mil)
3-19	C+	3.18	2.65	8.2	7.8	0.0	-0.1
3-18	N/A	N/A	N/A	8.8	8.2	0.1	-0.1
2018	C	3.15	2.62	8.3	7.7	0.2	-0.4
2017	N/A	N/A	N/A	9.3	8.3	0.4	-0.5
2016	N/A	N/A	N/A	9.2	8.7	N/A	-1.3
2015	N/A	N/A	N/A	N/A	N/A	N/A	N/A
2014	N/A	N/A	N/A	N/A	N/A	N/A	N/A

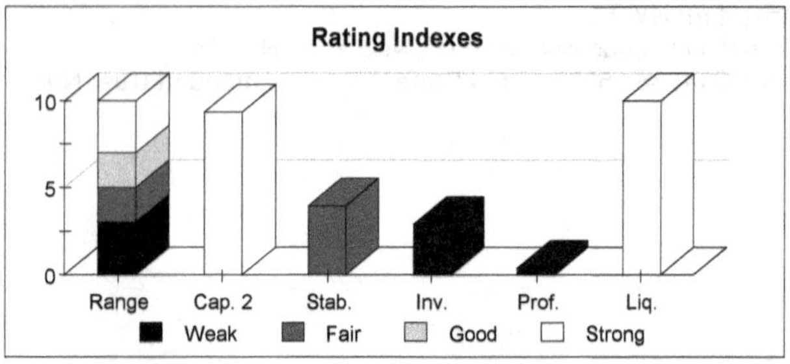

SHA LLC D Weak

Major Rating Factors: Weak profitability index (0.8 on a scale of 0 to 10). Fair overall results on stability tests (4.2) based on a decline in the number of member physicians during 2019. Fair liquidity (4.6) as cash resources may not be adequate to cover a spike in claims.
Other Rating Factors: Good capitalization index (6.0) based on good current risk-adjusted capital (severe loss scenario). High quality investment portfolio (8.3).
Principal Business: Comp med (54%), Medicaid (46%)
Mem Phys: 18: 13,065 **17:** 15,063 **18 MLR** 93.1% **/ 18 Admin Exp** N/A
Enroll(000): Q1 19: 145 **18:** 154 **17:** 169 **Med Exp PMPM:** $273
Principal Investments: Cash and equiv (55%), long-term bonds (19%), nonaffiliate common stock (12%), affiliate common stock (10%), real estate (3%)
Provider Compensation ($000): Contr fee ($533,815), FFS ($5,836), capitation ($38)
Total Member Encounters: Phys (785,406), non-phys (706,480)
Group Affiliation: None
Licensed in: TX
Address: 12940 N Hwy 183, Austin, TX 78750-3203
Phone: (254) 298-3000 **Dom State:** TX **Commenced Bus:** N/A

Data Date	Rating	RACR #1	RACR #2	Total Assets ($mil)	Capital ($mil)	Net Premium ($mil)	Net Income ($mil)
3-19	D	1.08	0.90	142.8	56.5	136.2	2.5
3-18	E	0.78	0.65	104.2	48.0	145.6	-5.3
2018	E	0.87	0.73	141.4	54.0	568.5	-80.6
2017	E	1.07	0.89	107.2	64.1	563.2	-22.9
2016	E	1.11	0.92	131.5	66.4	614.6	-18.2
2015	E	1.51	1.26	136.3	72.2	510.0	-1.2
2014	E	1.09	0.90	121.1	56.4	490.6	-31.9

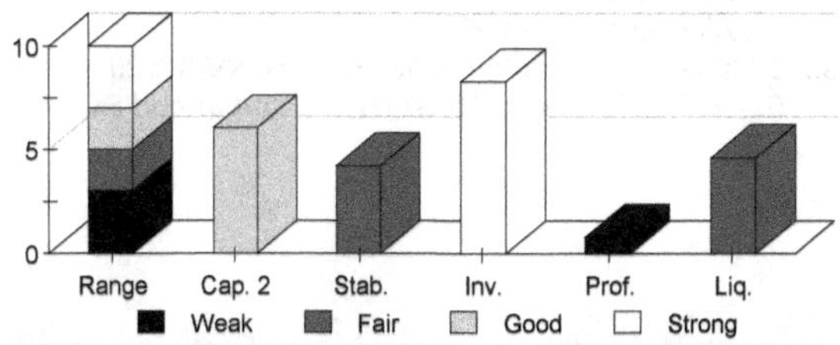

SHARP HEALTH PLAN * B+ Good

Major Rating Factors: Good capitalization index (6.7 on a scale of 0 to 10) based on good current risk-adjusted capital (severe loss scenario). Excellent profitability (8.0). Excellent overall results on stability tests (7.1).
Other Rating Factors: Excellent liquidity (7.1) with ample operational cash flow and liquid investments.
Principal Business: Medicare (3%)
Mem Phys: 18: N/A **17:** N/A **18 MLR** 88.1% **/ 18 Admin Exp** N/A
Enroll(000): Q1 19: 136 **18:** 143 **17:** 137 **Med Exp PMPM:** $378
Principal Investments ($000): Cash and equiv ($82,852)
Provider Compensation ($000): None
Total Member Encounters: N/A
Group Affiliation: San Diego Hospital Assoc
Licensed in: CA
Address: 2801 Atlantic Avenue, Long Beach, CA 90806
Phone: (714) 377-3215 **Dom State:** CA **Commenced Bus:** November 1992

Data Date	Rating	RACR #1	RACR #2	Total Assets ($mil)	Capital ($mil)	Net Premium ($mil)	Net Income ($mil)
3-19	B+	1.52	0.99	177.2	92.9	194.9	7.2
3-18	B	1.57	1.02	152.3	88.4	190.3	2.9
2018	B	1.43	0.93	165.8	85.7	744.8	0.0
2017	B	1.51	0.98	135.2	85.5	691.5	15.2
2016	B	1.38	0.89	115.3	70.4	612.1	6.7
2015	B	1.43	0.93	103.4	64.1	498.5	7.9
2014	B	1.55	1.01	86.7	56.4	382.6	9.4

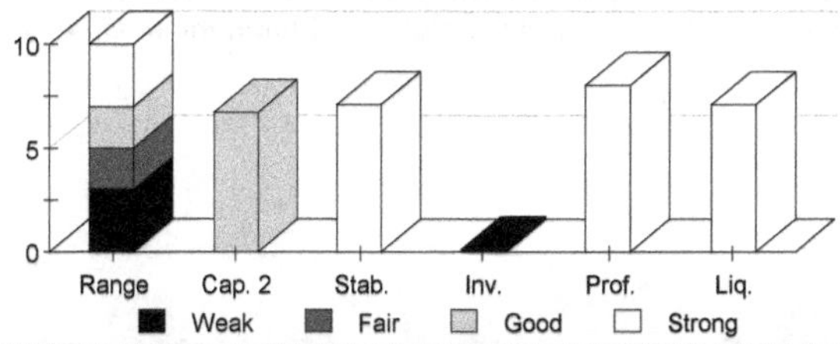

SHELTERPOINT LIFE INSURANCE COMPANY * A Excellent

Major Rating Factors: Good overall profitability (6.7 on a scale of 0 to 10) despite operating losses during the first three months of 2019. Good overall results on stability tests (6.8). Strengths that enhance stability include excellent operational trends and good risk diversification. Strong capitalization (7.8) based on excellent risk adjusted capital (severe loss scenario).
Other Rating Factors: High quality investment portfolio (7.5). Excellent liquidity (7.2).
Principal Business: Group health insurance (98%), reinsurance (1%), and group life insurance (1%).
Principal Investments: NonCMO investment grade bonds (49%), CMOs and structured securities (20%), common & preferred stock (7%), and cash (3%).
Investments in Affiliates: 7%
Group Affiliation: ShelterPoint Group Inc
Licensed in: CA, CO, CT, DC, DE, FL, IL, MD, MA, MI, MN, NJ, NY, NC, PA, RI, SC, TN
Commenced Business: November 1972
Address: 600 NORTHERN BLVD, GREAT NECK, NY 11530
Phone: (516) 829-8100 **Domicile State:** NY **NAIC Code:** 81434

Data Date	Rating	RACR #1	RACR #2	Total Assets ($mil)	Capital ($mil)	Net Premium ($mil)	Net Income ($mil)
3-19	A	1.85	1.56	183.5	65.3	66.4	-3.5
3-18	A	2.25	1.90	139.1	61.7	62.6	0.5
2018	A	2.08	1.75	156.0	68.4	187.6	8.8
2017	A	2.63	2.23	114.9	61.0	97.2	3.5
2016	A	2.47	2.09	106.5	58.8	91.8	5.5
2015	A	2.38	2.01	107.5	54.9	88.6	5.6
2014	A	2.40	2.03	104.4	54.9	86.7	10.0

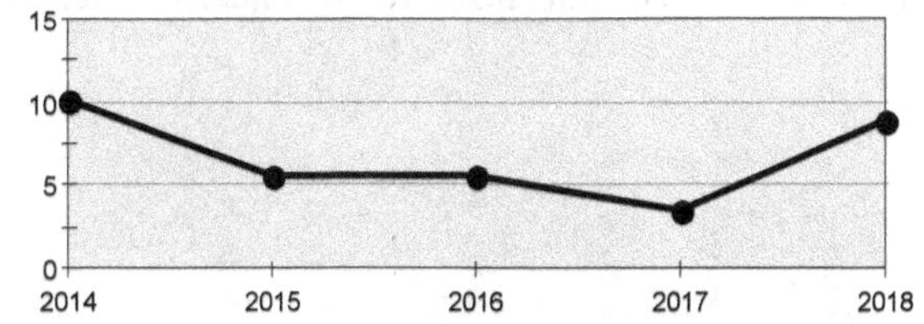

SIERRA HEALTH AND LIFE INS CO INC B Good

Major Rating Factors: Good liquidity (6.9 on a scale of 0 to 10) with sufficient resources (cash flows and marketable investments) to handle a spike in claims. Excellent profitability (9.7). Strong capitalization (8.6) based on excellent current risk-adjusted capital (severe loss scenario).
Other Rating Factors: High quality investment portfolio (9.2).
Principal Business: Medicare (98%), comp med (2%)
Mem Phys: 18: 1,334,335 **17:** 1,272,638 **18 MLR** 84.3% **/ 18 Admin Exp** N/A
Enroll(000): Q1 19: 1,499 **18:** 1,394 **17:** 1,236 **Med Exp PMPM:** $818
Principal Investments: Long-term bonds (87%), cash and equiv (13%)
Provider Compensation ($000): Contr fee ($9,452,215), FFS ($3,908,172), capitation ($97,816), bonus arrang ($58,763)
Total Member Encounters: Phys (15,254,236), non-phys (6,108,416)
Group Affiliation: None
Licensed in: All states except PR
Address: 2720 N TENAYA WAY, LAS VEGAS, NV 89128
Phone: (702) 242-7732 **Dom State:** NV **Commenced Bus:** N/A

Data Date	Rating	RACR #1	RACR #2	Total Assets ($mil)	Capital ($mil)	Net Premium ($mil)	Net Income ($mil)
3-19	B	2.66	2.21	4,933.9	2,593.1	4,845.4	524.2
3-18	B	2.14	1.78	5,080.7	1,690.0	4,125.9	175.5
2018	B	2.17	1.81	4,126.5	2,116.5	16,213.6	762.8
2017	B+	1.91	1.60	3,270.0	1,511.8	13,316.8	482.6
2016	B	2.46	2.05	2,396.9	1,177.4	8,918.3	438.3
2015	B	2.03	1.69	1,676.6	779.0	6,732.9	96.0
2014	B	3.71	3.09	170.1	75.6	426.9	15.8

Rating Indexes

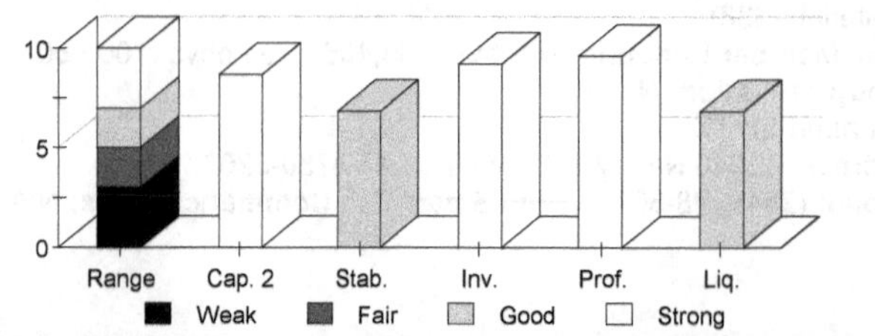

SIGNATURE ADVANTAGE LLC D Weak

Major Rating Factors: Weak profitability index (0.7 on a scale of 0 to 10). Poor capitalization (1.2) based on weak current risk-adjusted capital (moderate loss scenario). Fair liquidity (4.9) as cash resources may not be adequate to cover a spike in claims.
Other Rating Factors: High quality investment portfolio (9.9).
Principal Business: Medicare (100%)
Mem Phys: 18: 5,714 **17:** 1,054 **18 MLR** 94.3% **/ 18 Admin Exp** N/A
Enroll(000): Q1 19: 0 **18:** 0 **17:** 0 **Med Exp PMPM:** $2,238
Principal Investments: Cash and equiv (84%), long-term bonds (16%)
Provider Compensation ($000): Capitation ($236), other ($4,452)
Total Member Encounters: Phys (1,676), non-phys (19,930)
Group Affiliation: Las Palmas I-SNP LLC
Licensed in: KY
Address: 12201 Bluegrass Parkway, Louisville, KY 40299
Phone: (502) 568-7359 **Dom State:** KY **Commenced Bus:** N/A

Data Date	Rating	RACR #1	RACR #2	Total Assets ($mil)	Capital ($mil)	Net Premium ($mil)	Net Income ($mil)
3-19	D	0.42	0.35	2.9	1.0	1.3	-0.3
3-18	D+	N/A	N/A	2.1	-0.4	1.2	N/A
2018	D+	0.55	0.46	2.5	1.3	4.7	-0.1
2017	D+	N/A	N/A	1.7	-0.3	4.8	-0.5
2016	D+	1.36	1.13	2.2	1.5	4.1	0.1
2015	N/A	N/A	N/A	1.5	1.5	N/A	-1.0
2014	N/A	N/A	N/A	N/A	N/A	N/A	N/A

Rating Indexes

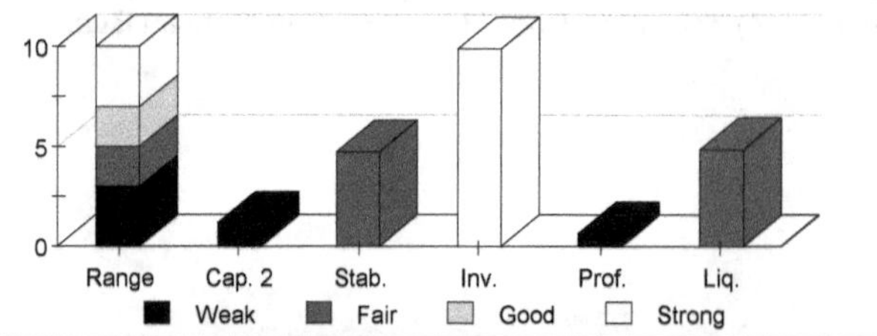

SILVERSCRIPT INS CO D Weak

Major Rating Factors: Low quality investment portfolio (0.0 on a scale of 0 to 10). Excellent profitability (8.8). Strong capitalization (10.0) based on excellent current risk-adjusted capital (severe loss scenario).
Other Rating Factors: Excellent liquidity (7.4) with ample operational cash flow and liquid investments.
Principal Business: Other (100%)
Mem Phys: 18: 68,000 **17:** 68,000 **18 MLR** 103.1% **/ 18 Admin Exp** N/A
Enroll(000): Q1 19: 4,767 **18:** 4,868 **17:** 4,520 **Med Exp PMPM:** $48
Principal Investments: Cash and equiv (98%), long-term bonds (2%)
Provider Compensation ($000): Other ($2,703,244)
Total Member Encounters: N/A
Group Affiliation: None
Licensed in: All states, the District of Columbia and Puerto Rico
Address: 445 GREAT CIRCLE RD, NASHVILLE, TN 37228
Phone: (615) 743-6600 **Dom State:** TN **Commenced Bus:** N/A

Data Date	Rating	RACR #1	RACR #2	Total Assets ($mil)	Capital ($mil)	Net Premium ($mil)	Net Income ($mil)
3-19	D	5.68	4.74	2,971.8	865.4	1,024.5	-74.4
3-18	D	6.36	5.30	3,765.1	793.4	1,057.2	-123.0
2018	D	6.93	5.78	2,371.8	998.8	2,720.5	28.3
2017	D	8.22	6.85	2,075.4	965.6	2,880.3	214.3
2016	D	6.84	5.70	2,823.6	799.2	2,483.6	206.1
2015	D	7.54	6.29	2,385.7	613.7	2,337.3	38.0
2014	D	3.99	3.32	2,764.2	448.1	2,516.2	124.6

Rating Indexes

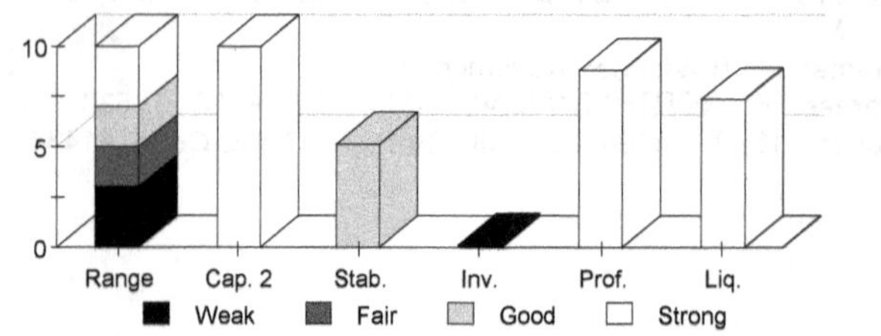

SILVERSUMMIT HEALTHPLAN INC C- Fair

Major Rating Factors: Weak profitability index (0.9 on a scale of 0 to 10). Strong capitalization (10.0) based on excellent current risk-adjusted capital (severe loss scenario). High quality investment portfolio (9.1).
Other Rating Factors: Excellent liquidity (7.0) with ample operational cash flow and liquid investments.
Principal Business: Medicaid (55%), comp med (45%)
Mem Phys: 18: 5,808 **17:** 9,234 **18 MLR** 84.0% **/ 18 Admin Exp** N/A
Enroll(000): Q1 19: 84 **18:** 76 **17:** 35 **Med Exp PMPM:** $345
Principal Investments: Cash and equiv (62%), long-term bonds (38%)
Provider Compensation ($000): Contr fee ($267,355), salary ($11,491), capitation ($2,917)
Total Member Encounters: Phys (342,226), non-phys (445,444)
Group Affiliation: None
Licensed in: NV
Address: , Las Vegas, NV 89128
Phone: (314) 725-4477 **Dom State:** NV **Commenced Bus:** N/A

Data Date	Rating	RACR #1	RACR #2	Total Assets ($mil)	Capital ($mil)	Net Premium ($mil)	Net Income ($mil)
3-19	C-	5.87	4.89	154.6	83.5	127.0	8.2
3-18	N/A	N/A	N/A	77.1	16.6	82.2	-5.1
2018	C-	5.24	4.36	146.4	74.5	372.0	-2.8
2017	N/A	N/A	N/A	27.7	7.7	34.5	-7.6
2016	N/A	N/A	N/A	1.8	0.8	N/A	N/A
2015	N/A	N/A	N/A	N/A	N/A	N/A	N/A
2014	N/A	N/A	N/A	N/A	N/A	N/A	N/A

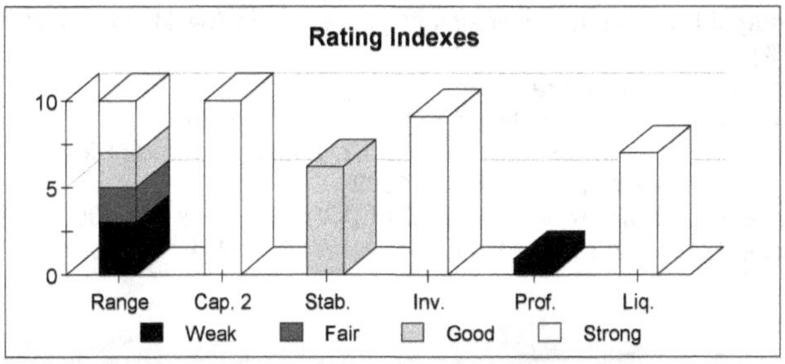

SIMPLY HEALTHCARE PLANS INC B- Good

Major Rating Factors: Good liquidity (5.9 on a scale of 0 to 10) with sufficient resources (cash flows and marketable investments) to handle a spike in claims. Excellent profitability (7.2). Strong capitalization (7.0) based on excellent current risk-adjusted capital (severe loss scenario).
Other Rating Factors: High quality investment portfolio (7.4).
Principal Business: Medicaid (63%), Medicare (28%), comp med (3%), other (6%)
Mem Phys: 18: 41,161 **17:** 43,120 **18 MLR** 85.8% **/ 18 Admin Exp** N/A
Enroll(000): Q1 19: 587 **18:** 582 **17:** 607 **Med Exp PMPM:** $385
Principal Investments: Long-term bonds (85%), cash and equiv (8%), other (7%)
Provider Compensation ($000): Bonus arrang ($1,406,584), contr fee ($677,060), FFS ($380,406), capitation ($258,733)
Total Member Encounters: Phys (5,044,429), non-phys (3,272,903)
Group Affiliation: Anthem Inc
Licensed in: FL
Address: 9250 W FLAGLER St Ste 600, MIAMI, FL 33174
Phone: (757) 490-6900 **Dom State:** FL **Commenced Bus:** N/A

Data Date	Rating	RACR #1	RACR #2	Total Assets ($mil)	Capital ($mil)	Net Premium ($mil)	Net Income ($mil)
3-19	B-	1.39	1.16	654.2	248.9	804.8	8.3
3-18	B	1.54	1.28	781.2	269.9	782.8	-35.3
2018	B-	1.38	1.15	599.8	245.9	3,171.7	46.6
2017	B+	1.37	1.14	684.8	319.2	3,092.1	115.4
2016	B	1.73	1.44	596.2	214.7	2,965.6	55.6
2015	B-	0.60	0.50	442.4	137.0	2,563.4	21.8
2014	N/A	N/A	N/A	481.2	126.7	1,931.5	11.9

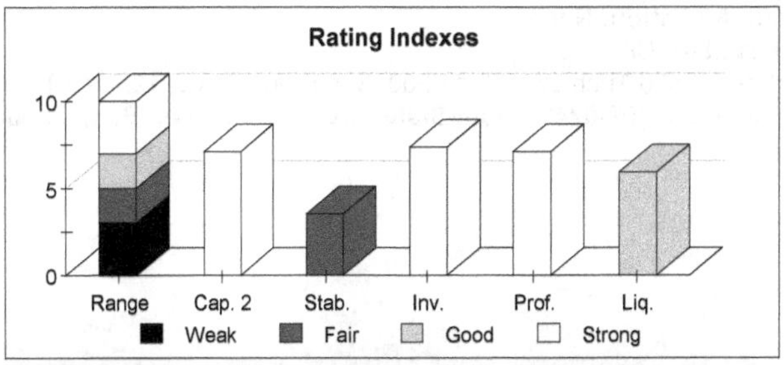

SIMPRA ADVANTAGE INC D+ Weak

Major Rating Factors: Weak profitability index (1.2 on a scale of 0 to 10). Good capitalization (6.6) based on good current risk-adjusted capital (severe loss scenario). High quality investment portfolio (9.9).
Other Rating Factors: Excellent liquidity (6.9) with sufficient resources (cash flows and marketable investments) to handle a spike in claims.
Principal Business: Medicare (100%)
Mem Phys: 18: 12,650 **17:** N/A **18 MLR** 88.3% **/ 18 Admin Exp** N/A
Enroll(000): Q1 19: 3 **18:** 2 **17:** N/A **Med Exp PMPM:** $1,600
Principal Investments: Cash and equiv (99%), long-term bonds (1%)
Provider Compensation ($000): Contr fee ($28,204)
Total Member Encounters: Phys (7,326), non-phys (33,529)
Group Affiliation: SeniorSelect Partners LLC
Licensed in: AL
Address: , Birmingham, AL 35203
Phone: (205) 320-7527 **Dom State:** AL **Commenced Bus:** N/A

Data Date	Rating	RACR #1	RACR #2	Total Assets ($mil)	Capital ($mil)	Net Premium ($mil)	Net Income ($mil)
3-19	D+	1.18	0.98	19.4	7.7	14.7	0.5
3-18	N/A	N/A	N/A	11.9	2.2	8.1	-1.2
2018	D+	1.00	0.84	16.2	6.7	40.7	-0.6
2017	N/A	N/A	N/A	1.4	1.4	N/A	N/A
2016	N/A	N/A	N/A	N/A	N/A	N/A	N/A
2015	N/A	N/A	N/A	N/A	N/A	N/A	N/A
2014	N/A	N/A	N/A	N/A	N/A	N/A	N/A

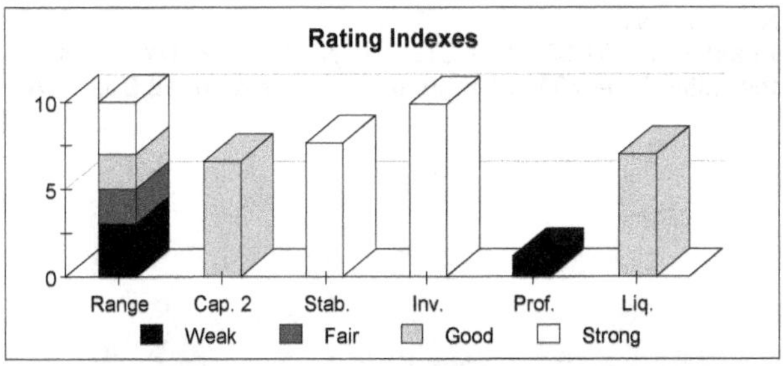

SIRIUS AMERICA INS CO C Fair

Major Rating Factors: Fair long-term capitalization index (3.6 on a scale of 0 to 10) based on fair current risk adjusted capital (severe loss scenario), although results have slipped from the excellent range over the last two years. Fair reserve development (4.7) as reserves have generally been sufficient to cover claims.

Other Rating Factors: Fair profitability index (3.5) with operating losses during 2017 and the first three months of 2019. Return on equity has been fair, averaging 6.6% over the past five years. Weak overall results on stability tests (2.5) including excessive premium growth. The largest net exposure for one risk is excessive at 7.8% of capital. Excellent liquidity (7.3) with ample operational cash flow and liquid investments.

Principal Business: Group accident & health (94%), surety (2%), workers compensation (2%), and commercial multiple peril (1%).

Principal Investments: Investment grade bonds (64%) and misc. investments (36%).

Investments in Affiliates: 7%

Group Affiliation: China Minsheng Investment Co Ltd

Licensed in: All states, the District of Columbia and Puerto Rico

Commenced Business: January 1980

Address: 140 BROADWAY - 32ND FLOOR, New York, NY 10005-1108

Phone: (212) 312-2500 **Domicile State:** NY **NAIC Code:** 38776

Data Date	Rating	RACR #1	RACR #2	Loss Ratio %	Total Assets ($mil)	Capital ($mil)	Net Premium ($mil)	Net Income ($mil)
3-19	C	0.91	0.57	N/A	1,257.7	519.8	44.2	-4.7
3-18	B-	1.67	1.05	N/A	1,348.6	523.7	24.1	1.6
2018	B-	0.93	0.57	74.0	1,228.0	522.2	182.0	-9.9
2017	B-	1.60	1.01	107.6	1,337.5	521.8	101.2	-6.4
2016	B-	0.96	0.69	73.8	1,395.1	544.3	217.3	82.7
2015	C+	1.42	0.87	53.7	1,387.6	517.6	283.9	74.7
2014	C+	1.58	0.94	45.1	1,550.5	620.6	267.2	56.1

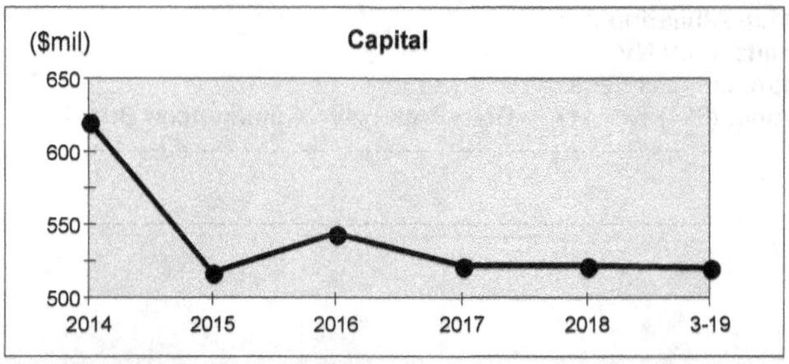

SISTEMAS MEDICOS NACIONALES SA DE CV B- Good

Major Rating Factors: Good overall results on stability tests (6.2 on a scale of 0 to 10) based on steady enrollment growth, averaging 8% over the past five years. Excellent profitability (10.0). Strong capitalization index (8.5) based on excellent current risk-adjusted capital (severe loss scenario).

Other Rating Factors: Excellent liquidity (7.1) with ample operational cash flow and liquid investments.

Principal Business: Managed care (94%), indemnity (6%)

Mem Phys: 18: N/A **17:** N/A **18 MLR** 57.9% **/ 18 Admin Exp** N/A

Enroll(000): Q1 19: 53 **18:** 52 **17:** 47 **Med Exp PMPM:** $92

Principal Investments ($000): Cash and equiv ($15,821)

Provider Compensation ($000): None

Total Member Encounters: N/A

Group Affiliation: None

Licensed in: CA

Address: 8520 Tech Way Suite 200, San Diego, CA 92123-1450

Phone: (858) 499-8240 **Dom State:** CA **Commenced Bus:** January 2000

Data Date	Rating	RACR #1	RACR #2	Total Assets ($mil)	Capital ($mil)	Net Premium ($mil)	Net Income ($mil)
3-19	B-	3.16	2.10	66.9	38.2	26.0	3.9
3-18	C+	3.52	2.35	56.3	33.2	24.6	5.0
2018	B-	2.91	1.93	64.7	34.3	95.5	6.4
2017	C+	2.96	1.97	47.6	28.2	88.0	6.3
2016	C+	3.05	2.02	37.8	22.7	78.6	7.1
2015	C+	2.69	1.79	28.6	17.6	69.1	6.8
2014	C+	1.62	1.08	19.1	10.8	64.7	3.7

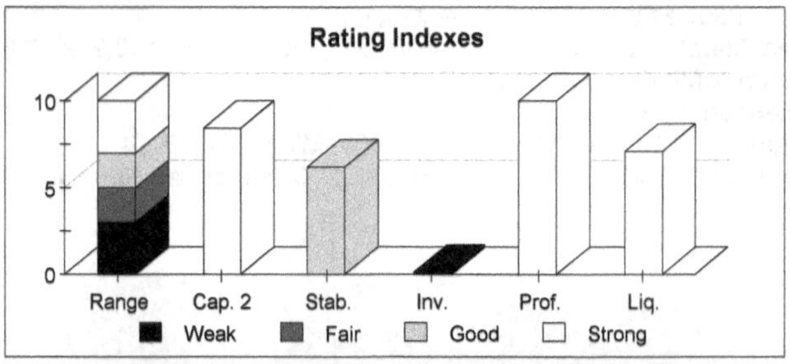

SOLSTICE HEALTH INS CO C+ Fair

Major Rating Factors: Good overall profitability index (6.8 on a scale of 0 to 10). Strong capitalization (8.4) based on excellent current risk-adjusted capital (severe loss scenario). High quality investment portfolio (9.9).

Other Rating Factors: Excellent liquidity (7.4) with ample operational cash flow and liquid investments.

Principal Business: Dental (20%), vision (6%), other (74%)

Mem Phys: 18: 14,341 **17:** 9,532 **18 MLR** 48.6% **/ 18 Admin Exp** N/A

Enroll(000): Q1 19: 104 **18:** 102 **17:** 60 **Med Exp PMPM:** $7

Principal Investments: Cash and equiv (100%)

Provider Compensation ($000): FFS ($2,823)

Total Member Encounters: N/A

Group Affiliation: None

Licensed in: NY

Address: 42 WEST 38TH ST STE 700, NEW YORK, NY 10018

Phone: (954) 370-1700 **Dom State:** NY **Commenced Bus:** N/A

Data Date	Rating	RACR #1	RACR #2	Total Assets ($mil)	Capital ($mil)	Net Premium ($mil)	Net Income ($mil)
3-19	C+	2.50	2.08	19.2	3.2	5.2	0.2
3-18	C-	2.30	1.92	8.9	2.9	3.7	1.1
2018	C+	2.34	1.95	17.2	3.0	16.7	0.9
2017	U	1.37	1.14	5.5	1.7	8.9	0.9
2016	N/A	N/A	N/A	1.4	0.6	2.4	N/A
2015	N/A	N/A	N/A	5.4	2.1	6.4	N/A
2014	N/A	N/A	N/A	1.7	0.6	2.7	N/A

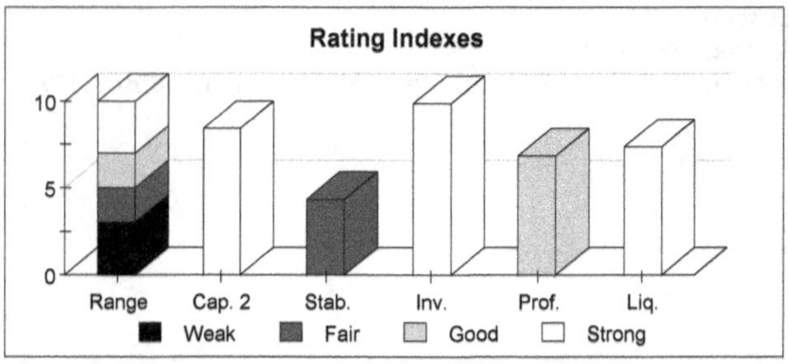

SOUNDPATH HEALTH D Weak

Major Rating Factors: Weak profitability index (0.9 on a scale of 0 to 10). Strong capitalization (7.8) based on excellent current risk-adjusted capital (severe loss scenario). High quality investment portfolio (9.9).
Other Rating Factors: Excellent liquidity (7.1) with ample operational cash flow and liquid investments.
Principal Business: Medicare (100%)
Mem Phys: 18: 13,540 **17:** 12,980 **18 MLR** 90.3% **/ 18 Admin Exp** N/A
Enroll(000): Q1 19: N/A **18:** 23 **17:** 24 **Med Exp PMPM:** $625
Principal Investments: Cash and equiv (73%), long-term bonds (27%)
Provider Compensation ($000): Contr fee ($140,728), capitation ($28,902), bonus arrang ($511)
Total Member Encounters: Phys (193,010), non-phys (205,579)
Group Affiliation: None
Licensed in: WA
Address: 33820 Weyerhaeuser Way S, Federal Way, WA 98001
Phone: (866) 789-7747 **Dom State:** WA **Commenced Bus:** N/A

Data Date	Rating	RACR #1	RACR #2	Total Assets ($mil)	Capital ($mil)	Net Premium ($mil)	Net Income ($mil)
3-19	D	2.03	1.69	51.7	41.8	0.4	-3.8
3-18	E	2.10	1.75	85.9	43.7	46.1	4.8
2018	D-	2.25	1.88	71.5	45.5	188.4	6.1
2017	F	1.50	1.25	66.8	38.5	181.2	-8.8
2016	E	1.55	1.29	55.6	34.8	198.1	-0.9
2015	E	0.38	0.32	50.6	10.6	155.2	-17.3
2014	C	0.80	0.67	32.8	15.6	137.9	-3.3

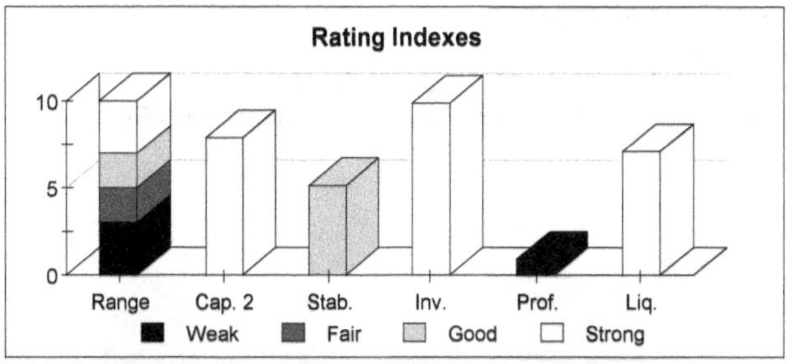

SOUTHEASTERN INDIANA HEALTH ORG INC C+ Fair

Major Rating Factors: Fair profitability index (3.5 on a scale of 0 to 10). Good overall results on stability tests (5.2). Strong capitalization index (7.6) based on excellent current risk-adjusted capital (severe loss scenario).
Other Rating Factors: High quality investment portfolio (9.4). Excellent liquidity (7.2) with ample operational cash flow and liquid investments.
Principal Business: Comp med (99%)
Mem Phys: 18: 30,346 **17:** 22,043 **18 MLR** 88.6% **/ 18 Admin Exp** N/A
Enroll(000): Q1 19: 6 **18:** 6 **17:** 6 **Med Exp PMPM:** $425
Principal Investments: Cash and equiv (83%), real estate (17%)
Provider Compensation ($000): Contr fee ($24,691), bonus arrang ($5,393), FFS ($515), capitation ($462)
Total Member Encounters: Phys (24,887), non-phys (11,278)
Group Affiliation: SIHO Holding Inc
Licensed in: IN
Address: 417 WASHINGTON STREET, COLUMBUS, IN 47201
Phone: (812) 378-7000 **Dom State:** IN **Commenced Bus:** N/A

Data Date	Rating	RACR #1	RACR #2	Total Assets ($mil)	Capital ($mil)	Net Premium ($mil)	Net Income ($mil)
3-19	C+	1.80	1.50	15.2	9.4	8.3	0.4
3-18	C+	2.10	1.75	15.6	9.8	8.6	0.7
2018	C+	1.72	1.43	13.5	9.0	34.1	0.7
2017	C	1.89	1.57	14.0	9.1	29.9	0.4
2016	C	1.21	1.01	13.0	6.1	33.5	0.6
2015	B	1.75	1.46	16.4	9.1	36.4	-1.6
2014	B	1.74	1.45	18.8	10.3	47.4	0.7

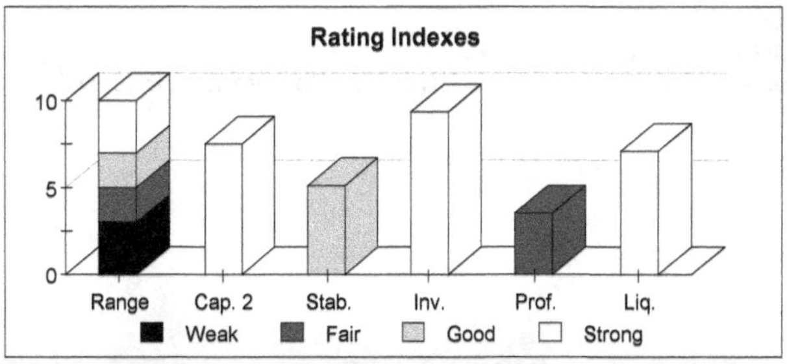

SOUTHERN GUARANTY INS CO C+ Fair

Major Rating Factors: Fair profitability index (3.2) with operating losses during 2014, 2017 and 2018. Return on equity has been fair, averaging 10.1% over the past five years.
Other Rating Factors: Fair overall results on stability tests (3.1) including negative cash flow from operations for 2018. The largest net exposure for one risk is conservative at 1.1% of capital. Strong long-term capitalization index (8.8) based on excellent current risk adjusted capital (severe and moderate loss scenarios), despite some fluctuation in capital levels. Excellent liquidity (8.5) with ample operational cash flow and liquid investments.
Principal Business: Other accident & health (100%).
Principal Investments: Misc. investments (69%), investment grade bonds (29%), and cash (2%).
Investments in Affiliates: None
Group Affiliation: QBE Ins Group Ltd
Licensed in: AL, AZ, AR, GA, IL, IN, IA, KS, KY, LA, MD, MI, MS, NE, NV, NM, NC, OH, OK, OR, PA, SC, TN, TX, UT, WA, WI
Commenced Business: July 1963
Address: 13600 ICOT BLVD BLDG A, Clearwater, FL 33760-3703
Phone: (727) 565-1485 **Domicile State:** WI **NAIC Code:** 19178

Data Date	Rating	RACR #1	RACR #2	Loss Ratio %	Total Assets ($mil)	Capital ($mil)	Net Premium ($mil)	Net Income ($mil)
3-19	C+	4.86	3.09	N/A	30.2	29.0	0.5	0.0
3-18	U	5.67	3.27	N/A	30.1	29.3	0.0	-0.1
2018	B-	4.49	2.69	78.3	26.8	25.7	0.5	-0.7
2017	U	23.76	12.19	0.0	30.3	29.7	0.0	-0.4
2016	C	1.76	1.59	0.0	13.2	4.5	-11.0	2.2
2015	C-	1.47	0.97	63.9	90.3	22.8	30.3	1.7
2014	D+	1.53	1.04	69.2	90.0	23.9	32.1	0.0

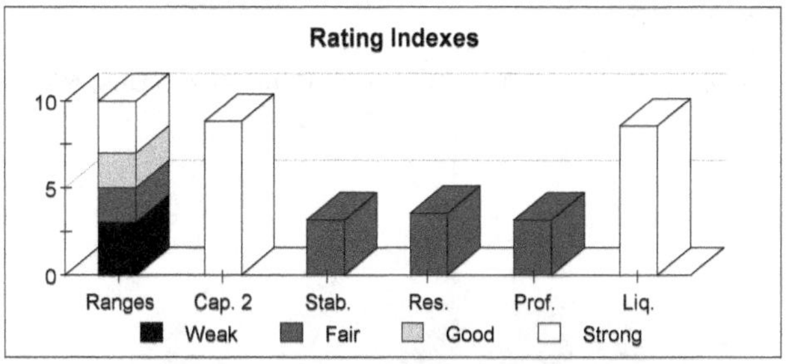

SOUTHWEST L&H INS CO D Weak

Major Rating Factors: Weak profitability index (1.1 on a scale of 0 to 10). Strong capitalization (10.0) based on excellent current risk-adjusted capital (severe loss scenario). High quality investment portfolio (9.3).
Other Rating Factors: Excellent liquidity (7.4) with ample operational cash flow and liquid investments.
Principal Business: Comp med (99%)
Mem Phys: 18: 13,065 **17:** 15,063 **18 MLR** 89.1% **/ 18 Admin Exp** N/A
Enroll(000): Q1 19: 2 **18:** 2 **17:** 2 **Med Exp PMPM:** $345
Principal Investments: Cash and equiv (50%), long-term bonds (33%), nonaffiliate common stock (17%)
Provider Compensation ($000): Contr fee ($8,629), FFS ($15)
Total Member Encounters: Phys (12,769), non-phys (8,205)
Group Affiliation: None
Licensed in: LA, NM, TX
Address: 12940 N Hwy 183, TEMPLE, TX 76502
Phone: (254) 298-3000 **Dom State:** TX **Commenced Bus:** N/A

Data Date	Rating	RACR #1	RACR #2	Total Assets ($mil)	Capital ($mil)	Net Premium ($mil)	Net Income ($mil)
3-19	D	3.88	3.23	9.8	7.6	1.8	-1.2
3-18	D	4.19	3.49	11.2	9.5	2.7	-0.1
2018	D	3.76	3.13	10.8	8.7	9.5	-0.7
2017	C-	3.74	3.12	11.4	9.6	8.0	-1.9
2016	C-	3.33	2.77	11.0	7.5	11.1	-2.9
2015	C	1.91	1.59	10.4	5.7	14.6	-5.1
2014	C	2.29	1.91	11.3	7.8	20.4	-2.7

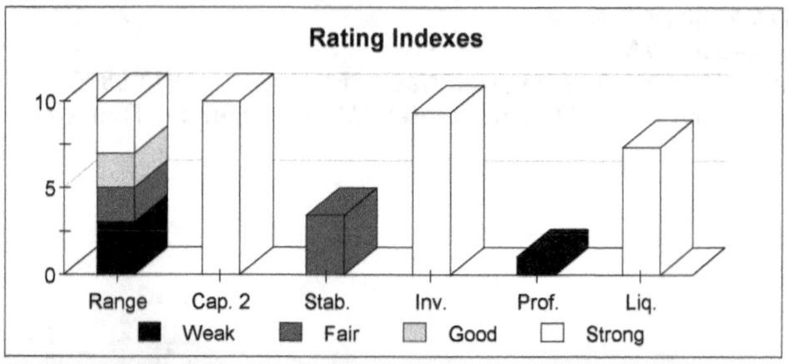

SPARTAN PLAN IL INC D+ Weak

Major Rating Factors: Weak profitability index (0.8 on a scale of 0 to 10). Good liquidity (6.6) with sufficient resources (cash flows and marketable investments) to handle a spike in claims. Strong capitalization (7.2) based on excellent current risk-adjusted capital (severe loss scenario).
Other Rating Factors: High quality investment portfolio (9.0).
Principal Business: Medicare (100%)
Mem Phys: 18: 5,270 **17:** N/A **18 MLR** 354.7% **/ 18 Admin Exp** N/A
Enroll(000): Q1 19: 0 **18:** 0 **17:** N/A **Med Exp PMPM:** $1,721
Principal Investments: Cash and equiv (56%), affiliate common stock (44%)
Provider Compensation ($000): Contr fee ($1,388), bonus arrang ($6)
Total Member Encounters: Phys (853)
Group Affiliation: Public Sector Pension Investment Boa
Licensed in: IL
Address: , Lombard, IL 60148
Phone: (804) 396-6412 **Dom State:** IL **Commenced Bus:** N/A

Data Date	Rating	RACR #1	RACR #2	Total Assets ($mil)	Capital ($mil)	Net Premium ($mil)	Net Income ($mil)
3-19	D+	1.50	1.25	2.9	2.1	0.8	-0.4
3-18	N/A	N/A	N/A	2.2	1.8	0.3	-0.2
2018	D+	1.86	1.55	2.9	2.5	0.6	-0.9
2017	N/A	N/A	N/A	2.0	2.0	N/A	N/A
2016	N/A	N/A	N/A	N/A	N/A	N/A	N/A
2015	N/A	N/A	N/A	N/A	N/A	N/A	N/A
2014	N/A	N/A	N/A	N/A	N/A	N/A	N/A

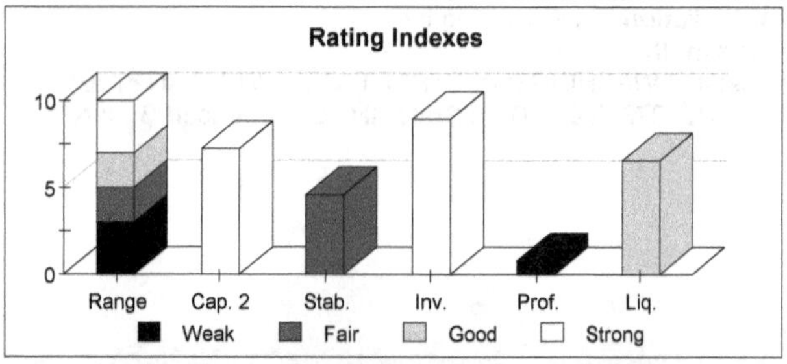

SPARTAN PLAN NY INC D Weak

Major Rating Factors: Weak profitability index (0.1 on a scale of 0 to 10). Strong capitalization (8.2) based on excellent current risk-adjusted capital (severe loss scenario). High quality investment portfolio (9.9).
Other Rating Factors: Excellent liquidity (7.5) with ample operational cash flow and liquid investments.
Principal Business: Medicare (100%)
Mem Phys: 18: 7,152 **17:** N/A **18 MLR** 413.3% **/ 18 Admin Exp** N/A
Enroll(000): Q1 19: 0 **18:** 0 **17:** N/A **Med Exp PMPM:** $2,433
Principal Investments: Cash and equiv (100%)
Provider Compensation ($000): Contr fee ($1,240), bonus arrang ($242)
Total Member Encounters: Phys (4,225), non-phys (15,064)
Group Affiliation: Public Sector Pension Investment Boa
Licensed in: NY
Address: , Lynbrook, NY 11563
Phone: (804) 396-6412 **Dom State:** NY **Commenced Bus:** N/A

Data Date	Rating	RACR #1	RACR #2	Total Assets ($mil)	Capital ($mil)	Net Premium ($mil)	Net Income ($mil)
3-19	D	2.33	1.95	2.3	1.6	0.6	-0.4
3-18	N/A	N/A	N/A	3.0	2.6	0.2	-0.2
2018	D	3.05	2.54	2.3	2.1	0.5	-0.7
2017	N/A	N/A	N/A	2.8	2.8	N/A	-0.2
2016	N/A	N/A	N/A	N/A	N/A	N/A	N/A
2015	N/A	N/A	N/A	N/A	N/A	N/A	N/A
2014	N/A	N/A	N/A	N/A	N/A	N/A	N/A

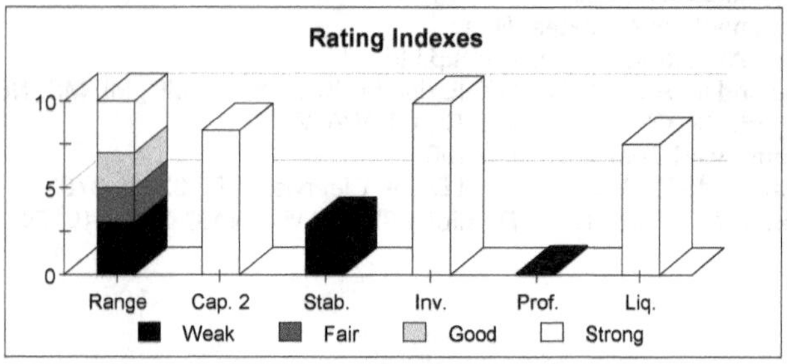

SPARTAN PLAN PA INC — D — Weak

Major Rating Factors: Weak profitability index (0.0 on a scale of 0 to 10). Weak liquidity (1.8) as a spike in claims may stretch capacity. Strong capitalization (7.5) based on excellent current risk-adjusted capital (severe loss scenario).
Other Rating Factors: High quality investment portfolio (9.9).
Principal Business: Medicare (100%)
Mem Phys: 18: 2,316 **17:** N/A **18 MLR** 496.7% **/ 18 Admin Exp** N/A
Enroll(000): Q1 19: 0 **18:** 0 **17:** N/A **Med Exp PMPM:** $2,635
Principal Investments: Cash and equiv (100%)
Provider Compensation ($000): Contr fee ($2,416), capitation ($362), bonus arrang ($10)
Total Member Encounters: Phys (1,520), non-phys (2,914)
Group Affiliation: Public Sector Pension Investment Boa
Licensed in: PA
Address: , Haverford, PA 19041
Phone: (804) 396-6412 **Dom State:** PA **Commenced Bus:** N/A

Data Date	Rating	RACR #1	RACR #2	Total Assets ($mil)	Capital ($mil)	Net Premium ($mil)	Net Income ($mil)
3-19	D	1.74	1.45	2.4	1.2	0.8	-0.8
3-18	N/A	N/A	N/A	1.8	1.3	0.4	-0.2
2018	D	1.84	1.54	1.7	1.2	0.7	-1.2
2017	N/A	N/A	N/A	1.5	1.5	N/A	N/A
2016	N/A	N/A	N/A	N/A	N/A	N/A	N/A
2015	N/A	N/A	N/A	N/A	N/A	N/A	N/A
2014	N/A	N/A	N/A	N/A	N/A	N/A	N/A

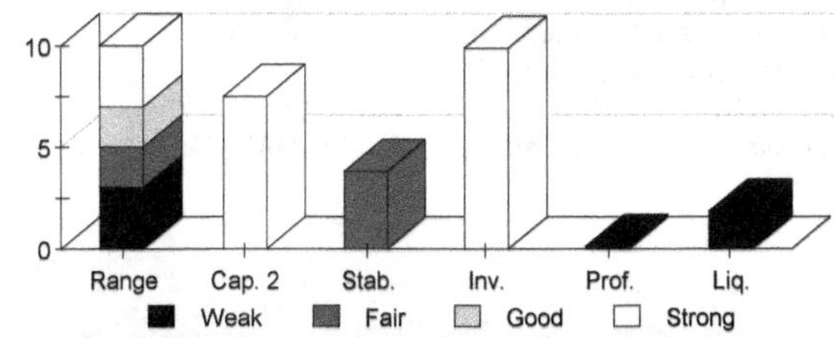

SPARTAN PLAN VA INC — D+ — Weak

Major Rating Factors: Weak profitability index (0.8 on a scale of 0 to 10). Fair quality investment portfolio (4.2). Good capitalization (6.9) based on excellent current risk-adjusted capital (severe loss scenario).
Other Rating Factors: Good liquidity (6.6) with sufficient resources (cash flows and marketable investments) to handle a spike in claims.
Principal Business: Medicare (100%)
Mem Phys: 18: 2,852 **17:** N/A **18 MLR** 358.1% **/ 18 Admin Exp** N/A
Enroll(000): Q1 19: 0 **18:** 0 **17:** N/A **Med Exp PMPM:** $1,787
Principal Investments: Affiliate common stock (70%), cash and equiv (30%)
Provider Compensation ($000): Contr fee ($895), bonus arrang ($244)
Total Member Encounters: Phys (865), non-phys (959)
Group Affiliation: Public Sector Pension Investment Boa
Licensed in: VA
Address: , McLean, VA 22102
Phone: (804) 396-6412 **Dom State:** VA **Commenced Bus:** N/A

Data Date	Rating	RACR #1	RACR #2	Total Assets ($mil)	Capital ($mil)	Net Premium ($mil)	Net Income ($mil)
3-19	D+	1.24	1.03	3.2	2.6	0.5	-0.3
3-18	N/A	N/A	N/A	1.7	1.4	0.2	-0.1
2018	D+	1.65	1.38	3.6	3.4	0.4	-0.6
2017	N/A	N/A	N/A	1.5	1.5	N/A	-0.7
2016	N/A	N/A	N/A	N/A	N/A	N/A	N/A
2015	N/A	N/A	N/A	N/A	N/A	N/A	N/A
2014	N/A	N/A	N/A	N/A	N/A	N/A	N/A

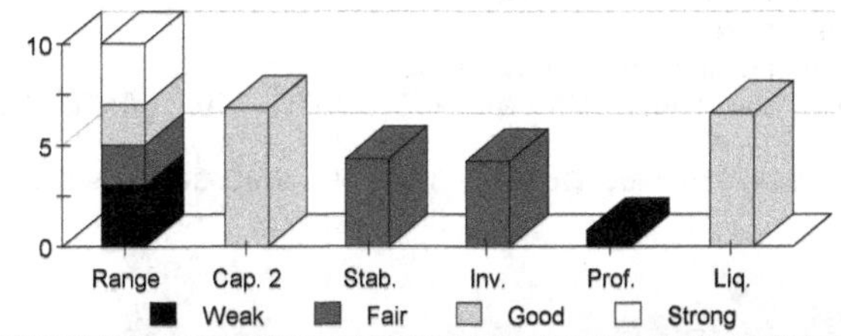

STANDARD INSURANCE COMPANY * — B+ — Good

Major Rating Factors: Good quality investment portfolio (5.1 on a scale of 0 to 10) despite substantial holdings of BBB bonds in addition to moderate junk bond exposure. Exposure to mortgages is large, but the mortgage default rate has been low. Good liquidity (6.7) with sufficient resources to cover a large increase in policy surrenders. Good overall results on stability tests (6.5) despite excessive premium growth excellent operational trends and excellent risk diversification.
Other Rating Factors: Strong capitalization (7.3) based on excellent risk adjusted capital (severe loss scenario). Excellent profitability (7.5).
Principal Business: Group retirement contracts (44%), group health insurance (23%), group life insurance (15%), individual annuities (11%), and other lines (6%).
Principal Investments: NonCMO investment grade bonds (45%), mortgages in good standing (41%), CMOs and structured securities (8%), and noninv. grade bonds (3%).
Investments in Affiliates: None
Group Affiliation: Meiji Yasuda Life Ins Company
Licensed in: All states except NY
Commenced Business: April 1906
Address: 1100 SOUTHWEST SIXTH AVENUE, PORTLAND, OR 97204-1093
Phone: (503) 321-7000 **Domicile State:** OR **NAIC Code:** 69019

Data Date	Rating	RACR #1	RACR #2	Total Assets ($mil)	Capital ($mil)	Net Premium ($mil)	Net Income ($mil)
3-19	B+	2.32	1.21	25,172.5	1,342.9	1,337.1	48.8
3-18	B+	2.14	1.11	23,669.3	1,154.4	805.6	51.4
2018	B+	2.32	1.21	23,862.6	1,294.0	4,459.1	201.6
2017	B+	2.02	1.06	23,952.0	1,108.4	4,300.3	178.2
2016	B+	2.04	1.06	21,792.1	1,040.4	4,075.8	144.8
2015	B+	2.21	1.16	20,781.6	1,085.0	3,528.4	160.1
2014	B+	2.38	1.26	20,361.1	1,151.8	4,019.8	209.4

Adverse Trends in Operations

Decrease in capital during 2016 (4%)
Increase in policy surrenders from 2015 to 2016 (26%)
Decrease in capital during 2015 (6%)
Decrease in premium volume from 2014 to 2015 (12%)

STANDARD LIFE & ACCIDENT INSURANCE COMPANY * A- Excellent

Major Rating Factors: Good overall results on stability tests (6.7 on a scale of 0 to 10). Strengths that enhance stability include good operational trends and excellent risk diversification. Good liquidity (6.8) with sufficient resources to handle a spike in claims as well as a significant increase in policy surrenders. Fair quality investment portfolio (4.9).

Other Rating Factors: Strong capitalization (10.0) based on excellent risk adjusted capital (severe loss scenario). Excellent profitability (7.2).

Principal Business: Reinsurance (40%), individual health insurance (32%), group health insurance (21%), and individual life insurance (7%).

Principal Investments: NonCMO investment grade bonds (77%), common & preferred stock (15%), mortgages in good standing (4%), noninv. grade bonds (2%), and misc. investments (2%).

Investments in Affiliates: None

Group Affiliation: American National Group Inc

Licensed in: All states except ME, NH, NJ, NY, PR

Commenced Business: June 1976

Address: ONE MOODY PLAZA, GALVESTON, TX 77550

Phone: (409) 763-4661 **Domicile State:** TX **NAIC Code:** 86355

Data Date	Rating	RACR #1	RACR #2	Total Assets ($mil)	Capital ($mil)	Net Premium ($mil)	Net Income ($mil)
3-19	A-	6.09	3.81	511.2	296.4	20.7	3.5
3-18	A-	5.70	3.55	517.4	289.2	25.0	2.3
2018	A-	6.05	3.79	516.9	291.9	107.6	10.9
2017	A-	5.78	3.59	521.6	289.5	98.3	10.7
2016	A-	6.21	3.82	518.8	287.1	95.1	13.6
2015	A-	5.93	3.68	514.5	278.1	105.2	8.6
2014	A-	5.09	3.17	530.2	259.1	120.7	20.6

Adverse Trends in Operations

Decrease in premium volume from 2015 to 2016 (10%)
Decrease in asset base during 2015 (3%)
Decrease in premium volume from 2014 to 2015 (13%)

STANDARD LIFE INSURANCE COMPANY OF NEW YORK * A- Excellent

Major Rating Factors: Good liquidity (6.9 on a scale of 0 to 10) with sufficient resources to handle a spike in claims. Excellent overall results on stability tests (7.2). Strengths that enhance stability include excellent operational trends and excellent risk diversification. Strong capitalization (10.0) based on excellent risk adjusted capital (severe loss scenario). Furthermore, this high level of risk adjusted capital has been consistently maintained over the last five years.

Other Rating Factors: High quality investment portfolio (7.4). Excellent profitability (7.9).

Principal Business: Group health insurance (63%), group life insurance (32%), and individual health insurance (5%).

Principal Investments: NonCMO investment grade bonds (47%), mortgages in good standing (46%), cash (6%), and noninv. grade bonds (1%).

Investments in Affiliates: None

Group Affiliation: Meiji Yasuda Life Ins Company

Licensed in: NY

Commenced Business: January 2001

Address: 360 HAMILTON AVENUE SUITE 210, WHITE PLAINS, NY 10601-1871

Phone: (914) 989-4400 **Domicile State:** NY **NAIC Code:** 89009

Data Date	Rating	RACR #1	RACR #2	Total Assets ($mil)	Capital ($mil)	Net Premium ($mil)	Net Income ($mil)
3-19	A-	4.73	3.11	304.9	104.7	25.8	7.4
3-18	A-	4.80	3.11	295.5	96.5	25.9	0.3
2018	A-	4.56	3.05	303.0	99.0	104.0	1.2
2017	A-	4.90	3.20	292.2	96.2	90.0	11.9
2016	A-	4.25	2.80	286.6	85.9	89.1	3.6
2015	A-	4.14	2.73	282.7	80.9	89.4	6.3
2014	A-	3.57	2.37	275.3	76.6	95.2	4.0

Adverse Trends in Operations

Increase in policy surrenders from 2016 to 2017 (375%)
Increase in policy surrenders from 2015 to 2016 (415%)
Decrease in premium volume from 2014 to 2015 (6%)

STANDARD SECURITY LIFE INSURANCE CO OF NEW YORK * B+ Good

Major Rating Factors: Good overall results on stability tests (6.6 on a scale of 0 to 10). Stability strengths include good operational trends and excellent risk diversification. Good overall profitability (5.6) despite operating losses during the first three months of 2019. Good liquidity (6.9) with sufficient resources to handle a spike in claims.

Other Rating Factors: Strong capitalization (10.0) based on excellent risk adjusted capital (severe loss scenario). High quality investment portfolio (8.2).

Principal Business: Group health insurance (90%), individual health insurance (8%), and group life insurance (2%).

Principal Investments: NonCMO investment grade bonds (80%), common & preferred stock (13%), noninv. grade bonds (3%), and CMOs and structured securities (1%).

Investments in Affiliates: 10%

Group Affiliation: Geneve Holdings Inc

Licensed in: All states, the District of Columbia and Puerto Rico

Commenced Business: December 1958

Address: 485 Madison Avenue 14th Floor, New York, NY 10022-5872

Phone: (212) 355-4141 **Domicile State:** NY **NAIC Code:** 69078

Data Date	Rating	RACR #1	RACR #2	Total Assets ($mil)	Capital ($mil)	Net Premium ($mil)	Net Income ($mil)
3-19	B+	6.86	5.26	139.6	70.8	30.3	-0.9
3-18	B	6.00	4.67	139.9	66.7	33.9	1.3
2018	B+	6.86	5.24	129.1	70.8	89.0	8.3
2017	B	6.77	5.23	131.5	65.6	80.3	3.6
2016	B+	6.84	5.28	154.9	70.6	84.7	-10.5
2015	A-	3.95	3.20	269.9	125.1	211.0	13.2
2014	B	3.55	2.81	252.4	116.5	207.3	12.1

Adverse Trends in Operations

Increase in policy surrenders from 2017 to 2018 (1284%)
Decrease in asset base during 2017 (15%)
Decrease in asset base during 2016 (43%)
Decrease in capital during 2016 (44%)
Decrease in premium volume from 2015 to 2016 (60%)

STANFORD HEALTH CARE ADVANTAGE E Very Weak

Major Rating Factors: Weak profitability index (0.9 on a scale of 0 to 10). Weak overall results on stability tests (2.5) based on an excessive 52% enrollment growth during the period. Weak liquidity (0.5) as a spike in claims may stretch capacity.
Other Rating Factors: Good capitalization index (6.9) based on good current risk-adjusted capital (moderate loss scenario).
Principal Business: Medicare (100%)
Mem Phys: 18: N/A **17:** N/A **18 MLR** 123.4% **/ 18 Admin Exp** N/A
Enroll(000): Q1 19: 4 **18:** 3 **17:** 2 **Med Exp PMPM:** $1,013
Principal Investments ($000): Cash and equiv ($14,039)
Provider Compensation ($000): None
Total Member Encounters: N/A
Group Affiliation: None
Licensed in: CA
Address: 4365 Executive Drive Suite 500, San Diego, CA 92121
Phone: (858) 658-8662 **Dom State:** CA **Commenced Bus:** August 2013

Data Date	Rating	RACR #1	RACR #2	Total Assets ($mil)	Capital ($mil)	Net Premium ($mil)	Net Income ($mil)
3-19	E	1.03	0.65	17.1	5.5	9.2	-1.7
3-18	E-	0.48	0.31	10.4	1.8	6.2	-3.7
2018	E-	0.47	0.30	15.0	2.7	27.5	-14.3
2017	E-	0.95	0.61	9.3	3.5	16.5	-10.7
2016	D	1.82	1.25	5.1	3.0	6.7	-5.7
2015	U	5.31	4.78	3.2	2.6	0.5	-4.2
2014	N/A	N/A	N/A	1.3	1.3	N/A	N/A

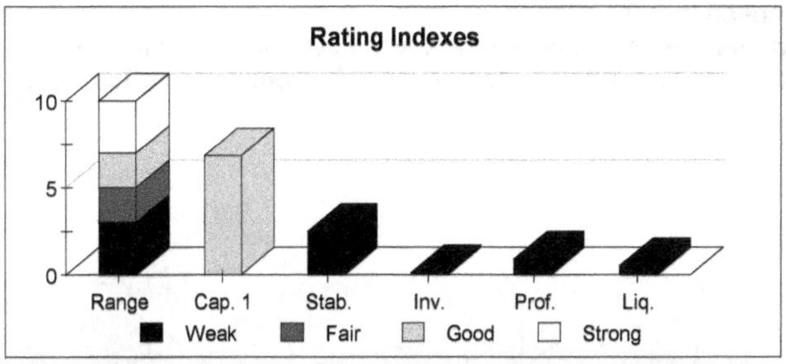

STARMOUNT LIFE INSURANCE COMPANY C Fair

Major Rating Factors: Fair liquidity (3.4 on a scale of 0 to 10) as cash from operations and sale of marketable assets may not be adequate to cover a spike in claims. Fair overall results on stability tests (3.9). Good overall capitalization (5.8) based on mixed results -- excessive policy leverage mitigated by excellent risk adjusted capital (severe loss scenario).
Other Rating Factors: Weak profitability (2.0) with operating losses during the first three months of 2019. High quality investment portfolio (7.3).
Principal Business: Group health insurance (85%), individual health insurance (11%), individual life insurance (3%), and reinsurance (1%).
Principal Investments: NonCMO investment grade bonds (55%), cash (34%), real estate (7%), and policy loans (1%).
Investments in Affiliates: None
Group Affiliation: Unum Group
Licensed in: All states except NY, PR
Commenced Business: August 1983
Address: 8485 Goodwood Blvd, PORTLAND, ME 4122
Phone: (225) 926-2888 **Domicile State:** ME **NAIC Code:** 68985

Data Date	Rating	RACR #1	RACR #2	Total Assets ($mil)	Capital ($mil)	Net Premium ($mil)	Net Income ($mil)
3-19	C	1.36	1.06	103.0	47.9	61.4	-0.5
3-18	C+	0.98	0.76	74.9	32.1	51.0	-5.3
2018	C	1.37	1.08	94.0	45.3	209.9	-9.5
2017	B	1.18	0.92	79.9	37.4	179.7	-2.8
2016	B	1.20	0.94	76.2	32.3	144.3	-0.4
2015	B	N/A	N/A	65.9	28.3	121.0	4.0
2014	B	1.35	1.02	59.1	25.0	95.2	3.8

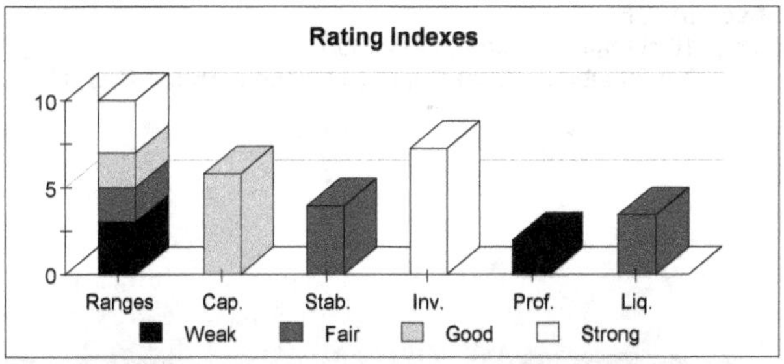

STATE MUTUAL INSURANCE COMPANY D Weak

Major Rating Factors: Weak profitability (1.3 on a scale of 0 to 10) with operating losses during the first three months of 2019. Weak overall results on stability tests (1.9) including negative cash flow from operations for 2018. Fair quality investment portfolio (3.4) with substantial holdings of BBB bonds in addition to moderate junk bond exposure.
Other Rating Factors: Good capitalization (5.1) based on good risk adjusted capital (moderate loss scenario). Good liquidity (6.1).
Principal Business: Individual health insurance (65%), individual life insurance (25%), and reinsurance (10%).
Principal Investments: NonCMO investment grade bonds (34%), CMOs and structured securities (12%), real estate (12%), common & preferred stock (9%), and misc. investments (32%).
Investments in Affiliates: 8%
Group Affiliation: None
Licensed in: All states except CA, CT, ME, NH, NJ, NY, PR
Commenced Business: October 1890
Address: 210 E Second Avenue Suite 301, Rome, GA 30161
Phone: (706) 291-1054 **Domicile State:** GA **NAIC Code:** 69132

Data Date	Rating	RACR #1	RACR #2	Total Assets ($mil)	Capital ($mil)	Net Premium ($mil)	Net Income ($mil)
3-19	D	1.07	0.69	187.8	25.4	10.2	-1.3
3-18	C-	1.09	0.70	264.9	26.8	4.4	-0.3
2018	D	1.14	0.73	189.5	26.3	25.5	-15.4
2017	C-	1.19	0.77	267.3	29.1	-33.1	-7.8
2016	C-	1.05	0.73	279.4	26.1	22.8	-9.0
2015	D+	2.31	1.27	286.7	33.7	18.7	1.0
2014	C	1.64	1.02	292.5	33.9	0.4	0.2

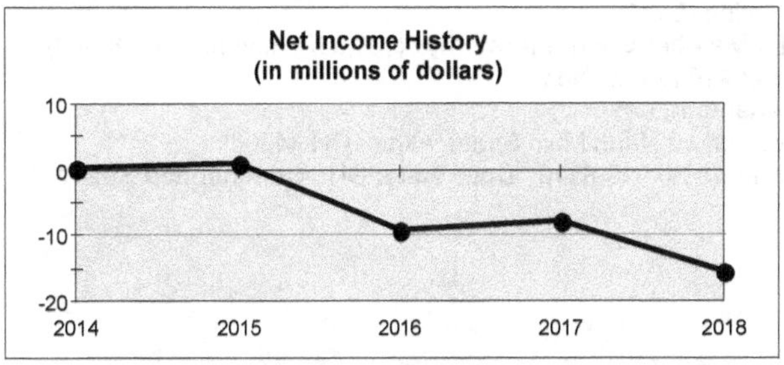

STEWARD HEALTH CHOICE UTAH INC — E- Very Weak

Major Rating Factors: Good overall profitability index (6.6 on a scale of 0 to 10). Strong capitalization (8.2) based on excellent current risk-adjusted capital (severe loss scenario). High quality investment portfolio (9.9).
Other Rating Factors: Excellent liquidity (7.3) with ample operational cash flow and liquid investments.
Principal Business: Medicaid (100%)
Mem Phys: 18: 2,576 **17:** 2,777 **18 MLR** 79.7% **/ 18 Admin Exp** N/A
Enroll(000): Q1 19: 19 **18:** 19 **17:** 18 **Med Exp PMPM:** $214
Principal Investments: Cash and equiv (100%)
Provider Compensation ($000): Contr fee ($46,357), FFS ($2,617)
Total Member Encounters: Phys (68,303), non-phys (75,651)
Group Affiliation: Craig Court Inc
Licensed in: UT
Address: 406 W S Jordan Parkway Ste 500, South Jordan, UT 84095
Phone: (801) 984-3388 **Dom State:** UT **Commenced Bus:** N/A

Data Date	Rating	RACR #1	RACR #2	Total Assets ($mil)	Capital ($mil)	Net Premium ($mil)	Net Income ($mil)
3-19	E-	2.34	1.95	32.2	16.4	16.5	0.6
3-18	E-	2.28	1.90	26.9	15.7	14.3	2.1
2018	E-	2.27	1.90	31.2	16.0	59.3	5.2
2017	E-	1.95	1.62	32.4	13.5	53.5	2.8
2016	E-	1.13	0.94	34.2	10.2	55.6	-1.2
2015	E-	1.30	1.08	20.5	8.4	32.9	0.8
2014	D+	0.49	0.41	7.3	1.8	13.5	-0.6

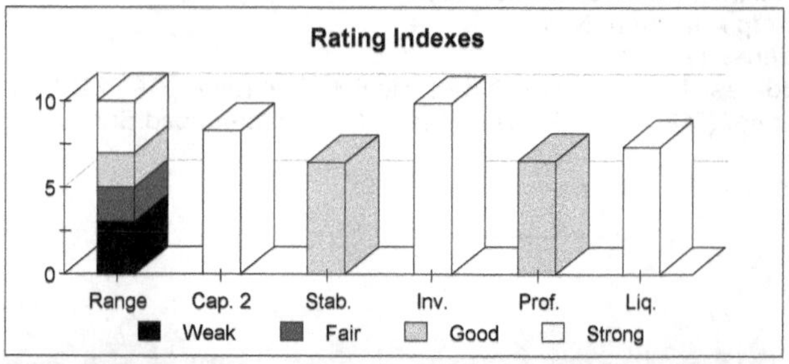

SUMMA INS CO — C- Fair

Major Rating Factors: Weak profitability index (0.9 on a scale of 0 to 10). Good liquidity (6.7) with sufficient resources (cash flows and marketable investments) to handle a spike in claims. Strong capitalization (7.1) based on excellent current risk-adjusted capital (severe loss scenario).
Other Rating Factors: High quality investment portfolio (9.9).
Principal Business: Comp med (100%)
Mem Phys: 18: N/A **17:** 10,000 **18 MLR** 91.2% **/ 18 Admin Exp** N/A
Enroll(000): Q1 19: 23 **18:** 31 **17:** 31 **Med Exp PMPM:** $414
Principal Investments: Cash and equiv (54%), long-term bonds (46%)
Provider Compensation ($000): Contr fee ($154,935), capitation ($445)
Total Member Encounters: Phys (47,490), non-phys (71,623)
Group Affiliation: None
Licensed in: OH
Address: 10 N Main St, Akron, OH 44305
Phone: (330) 996-8410 **Dom State:** OH **Commenced Bus:** N/A

Data Date	Rating	RACR #1	RACR #2	Total Assets ($mil)	Capital ($mil)	Net Premium ($mil)	Net Income ($mil)
3-19	C-	1.40	1.17	51.4	24.6	33.3	1.4
3-18	C-	1.03	0.85	44.8	16.2	42.7	-4.5
2018	C-	1.36	1.13	50.0	24.0	170.8	-11.9
2017	C-	1.22	1.02	48.3	21.4	170.2	-5.0
2016	C-	1.73	1.44	54.9	28.4	190.6	4.0
2015	C-	1.25	1.04	59.7	24.4	214.9	-7.6
2014	D	1.41	1.17	71.5	31.5	234.6	-13.5

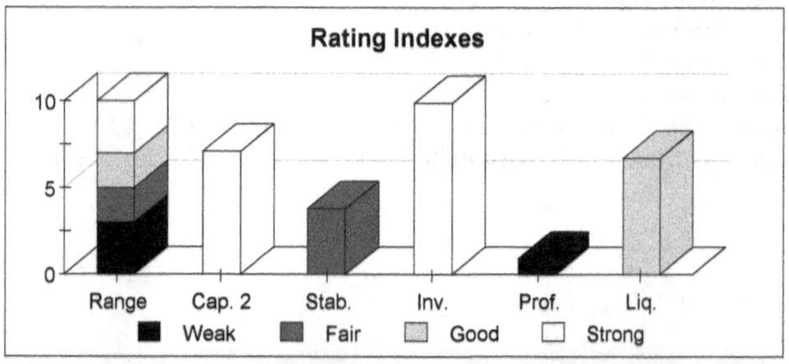

SUMMACARE INC — C Fair

Major Rating Factors: Fair overall results on stability tests (4.3 on a scale of 0 to 10). Weak profitability index (1.2). Good capitalization index (6.9) based on excellent current risk-adjusted capital (severe loss scenario).
Other Rating Factors: Good liquidity (6.8) with sufficient resources (cash flows and marketable investments) to handle a spike in claims. High quality investment portfolio (9.9).
Principal Business: Medicare (100%)
Mem Phys: 18: N/A **17:** 10,000 **18 MLR** 87.2% **/ 18 Admin Exp** N/A
Enroll(000): Q1 19: 23 **18:** 23 **17:** 24 **Med Exp PMPM:** $795
Principal Investments: Long-term bonds (44%), affiliate common stock (36%), cash and equiv (20%)
Provider Compensation ($000): Contr fee ($222,684), bonus arrang ($2,625), capitation ($525)
Total Member Encounters: Phys (106,332), non-phys (148,529)
Group Affiliation: None
Licensed in: OH
Address: 10 North Main Street, Akron, OH 44308
Phone: (330) 996-8410 **Dom State:** OH **Commenced Bus:** N/A

Data Date	Rating	RACR #1	RACR #2	Total Assets ($mil)	Capital ($mil)	Net Premium ($mil)	Net Income ($mil)
3-19	C	1.26	1.05	86.1	42.1	64.9	1.4
3-18	C	1.15	0.95	95.2	36.6	62.9	2.8
2018	C	1.19	0.99	78.2	40.0	258.8	-0.3
2017	C	1.09	0.91	75.3	36.4	245.9	-10.9
2016	B-	1.85	1.54	91.4	55.5	252.6	-0.5
2015	B-	1.49	1.24	90.6	51.6	271.4	-5.2
2014	C	1.09	0.91	85.2	42.8	315.7	2.0

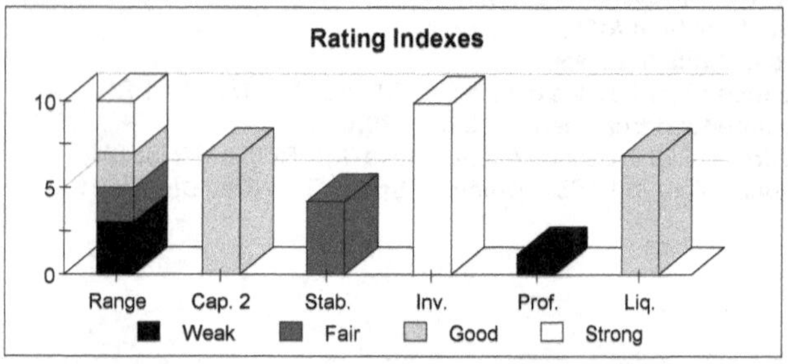

SUN LIFE & HEALTH INSURANCE COMPANY D Weak

Major Rating Factors: Weak overall results on stability tests (2.0 on a scale of 0 to 10) including weak financial strength of affiliated Sun Life Assurance Group and weak results on operational trends. Weak profitability (0.9) with operating losses during the first three months of 2019. Good quality investment portfolio (6.9).

Other Rating Factors: Good liquidity (5.8). Strong capitalization (7.5) based on excellent risk adjusted capital (severe loss scenario).

Principal Business: Group health insurance (58%), group life insurance (27%), and reinsurance (14%).

Principal Investments: NonCMO investment grade bonds (69%), CMOs and structured securities (20%), mortgages in good standing (7%), noninv. grade bonds (1%), and common & preferred stock (1%).

Investments in Affiliates: None

Group Affiliation: Sun Life Assurance Group

Licensed in: All states, the District of Columbia and Puerto Rico

Commenced Business: January 1975

Address: 201 Townsend Street Ste 900, Lansing, MI 48933

Phone: (781) 237-6030 **Domicile State:** MI **NAIC Code:** 80926

Data Date	Rating	RACR #1	RACR #2	Total Assets ($mil)	Capital ($mil)	Net Premium ($mil)	Net Income ($mil)
3-19	D	2.22	1.32	932.6	99.0	28.5	-6.0
3-18	D	3.14	1.82	946.5	135.0	28.3	5.1
2018	D	2.34	1.39	930.6	105.4	116.9	7.2
2017	D	2.95	1.74	943.2	129.9	644.6	-68.3
2016	D-	4.36	2.91	485.3	198.5	248.1	-44.8
2015	C	6.46	4.17	447.7	241.5	173.5	17.2
2014	C-	4.77	3.13	371.8	175.5	168.0	-1.4

Sun Life Assurance Group
Composite Group Rating: D

Largest Group Members	Assets ($mil)	Rating
SUN LIFE ASR CO OF CANADA	18836	D
INDEPENDENCE LIFE ANNUITY CO	3170	D+
SUN LIFE HEALTH INS CO	931	D
PROFESSIONAL INS CO	111	D+

SUN LIFE ASSURANCE COMPANY OF CANADA D+ Weak

Major Rating Factors: Low quality investment portfolio (2.8 on a scale of 0 to 10) containing significant exposure to mortgages . Mortgage default rate has been low. Weak overall results on stability tests (2.5) including weak risk adjusted capital in prior years. Fair capitalization (3.3) based on fair risk adjusted capital (moderate loss scenario).

Other Rating Factors: Fair profitability (3.8). Fair liquidity (3.8).

Principal Business: Group health insurance (53%), reinsurance (19%), group life insurance (14%), and individual life insurance (13%).

Principal Investments: NonCMO investment grade bonds (57%), mortgages in good standing (19%), CMOs and structured securities (10%), real estate (5%), and misc. investments (8%).

Investments in Affiliates: 1%

Group Affiliation: Sun Life Assurance Group

Licensed in: All states except NY

Commenced Business: May 1871

Address: 150 King Street West, Toronto, Ontario, MI 2481

Phone: (781) 237-6030 **Domicile State:** MI **NAIC Code:** 80802

Data Date	Rating	RACR #1	RACR #2	Total Assets ($mil)	Capital ($mil)	Net Premium ($mil)	Net Income ($mil)
3-19	D+	0.79	0.46	18,892.8	1,374.7	911.4	84.5
3-18	D-	0.61	0.35	18,862.7	976.6	930.3	99.2
2018	D	0.72	0.42	18,836.1	1,323.9	3,434.0	581.8
2017	D-	0.62	0.35	19,086.1	916.9	1,789.4	259.6
2016	E	0.53	0.32	19,562.8	1,019.0	3,803.2	-535.1
2015	D	1.27	0.74	18,222.4	1,925.8	2,207.2	86.4
2014	D	0.75	0.43	17,090.5	940.3	2,349.1	-64.3

Rating Indexes

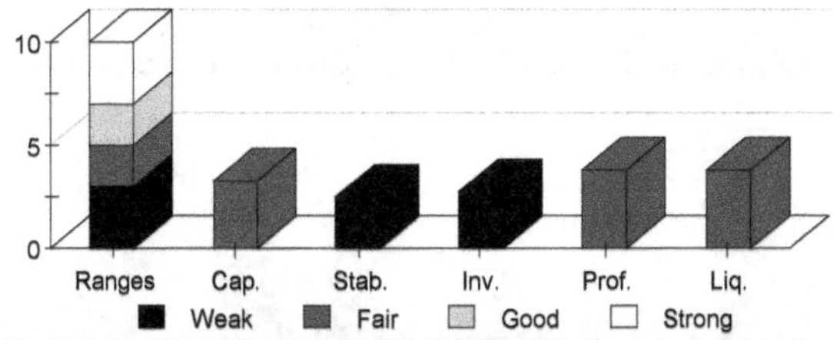

SUNFLOWER STATE HEALTH PLAN INC C Fair

Major Rating Factors: Fair profitability index (3.6 on a scale of 0 to 10). Good quality investment portfolio (6.0). Strong capitalization (8.0) based on excellent current risk-adjusted capital (severe loss scenario).

Other Rating Factors: Excellent liquidity (6.9) with sufficient resources (cash flows and marketable investments) to handle a spike in claims.

Principal Business: Medicaid (89%), comp med (10%)

Mem Phys: 18: 6,095 **17:** 6,900 **18 MLR** 82.7% **/ 18 Admin Exp** N/A

Enroll(000): Q1 19: 159 **18:** 152 **17:** 129 **Med Exp PMPM:** $616

Principal Investments: Long-term bonds (57%), cash and equiv (43%)

Provider Compensation ($000): Contr fee ($984,079), bonus arrang ($91,590), capitation ($12,472)

Total Member Encounters: Phys (728,682), non-phys (2,279,771)

Group Affiliation: None

Licensed in: KS

Address: 8325 Lenexa Dr, Lenexa, KS 66214

Phone: (314) 725-4477 **Dom State:** KS **Commenced Bus:** N/A

Data Date	Rating	RACR #1	RACR #2	Total Assets ($mil)	Capital ($mil)	Net Premium ($mil)	Net Income ($mil)
3-19	C	2.17	1.81	306.3	133.6	381.6	4.0
3-18	C-	N/A	N/A	254.3	114.2	329.7	-7.1
2018	C	2.32	1.93	284.5	143.8	1,355.5	9.8
2017	C-	N/A	N/A	257.4	134.7	1,114.1	12.1
2016	C-	2.36	1.96	254.0	133.3	1,106.7	9.7
2015	C-	2.21	1.84	265.6	134.8	1,115.0	20.8
2014	D+	1.98	1.65	273.0	112.8	1,039.9	-39.3

Rating Indexes

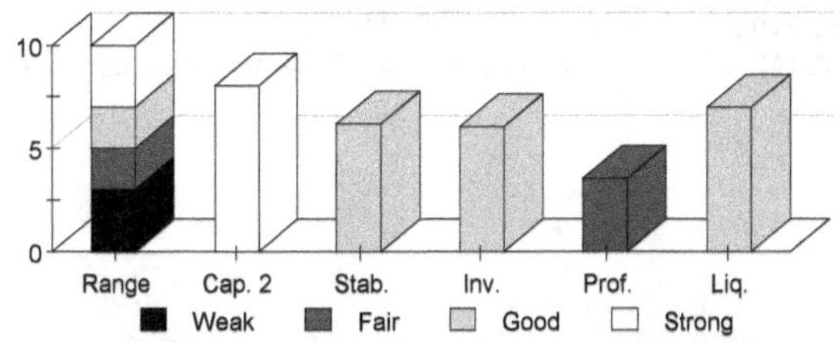

SUNSHINE HEALTH D+ Weak

Major Rating Factors: Weak profitability index (1.4 on a scale of 0 to 10). Good liquidity (6.4) with sufficient resources (cash flows and marketable investments) to handle a spike in claims. Strong capitalization (7.2) based on excellent current risk-adjusted capital (severe loss scenario).
Other Rating Factors: High quality investment portfolio (8.3).
Principal Business: Comp med (51%), Medicaid (48%)
Mem Phys: 18: 35,884 **17:** 30,304 **18 MLR** 93.5% **/ 18 Admin Exp** N/A
Enroll(000): Q1 19: 628 **18:** 593 **17:** 577 **Med Exp PMPM:** $537
Principal Investments: Long-term bonds (65%), cash and equiv (35%)
Provider Compensation ($000): Contr fee ($3,346,037), capitation ($128,135), bonus arrang ($100,153), salary ($96,509)
Total Member Encounters: Phys (3,403,233), non-phys (7,964,537)
Group Affiliation: None
Licensed in: FL
Address: 1301 International Parkway, Sunrise, FL 33323
Phone: (314) 725-4477 **Dom State:** FL **Commenced Bus:** N/A

Data Date	Rating	RACR #1	RACR #2	Total Assets ($mil)	Capital ($mil)	Net Premium ($mil)	Net Income ($mil)
3-19	D+	1.53	1.27	794.0	351.5	1,098.9	8.7
3-18	D+	1.61	1.34	767.4	334.8	956.3	-31.4
2018	D+	1.54	1.28	752.5	353.2	3,945.8	-15.5
2017	E	1.35	1.13	735.6	368.5	3,761.9	5.9
2016	E	1.81	1.51	676.5	357.9	3,627.5	23.0
2015	E	1.88	1.57	692.8	330.9	3,125.4	27.1
2014	E	0.84	0.70	541.5	116.2	2,268.5	-119.3

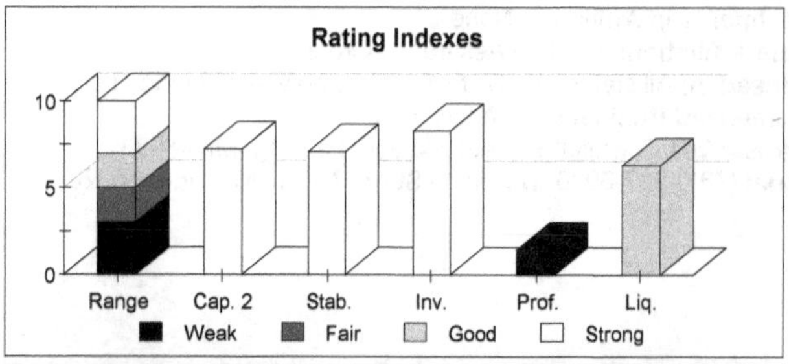

SUNSHINE HEALTH COMMUNITY SOLUTIONS C- Fair

Major Rating Factors: Weak profitability index (0.0 on a scale of 0 to 10). Good liquidity (6.7) with sufficient resources (cash flows and marketable investments) to handle a spike in claims. Strong capitalization (9.0) based on excellent current risk-adjusted capital (severe loss scenario).
Other Rating Factors: High quality investment portfolio (9.9).
Principal Business: Medicare (100%)
Mem Phys: 18: 26,920 **17:** 19,040 **18 MLR** 118.1% **/ 18 Admin Exp** N/A
Enroll(000): Q1 19: 1 **18:** 3 **17:** 0 **Med Exp PMPM:** $842
Principal Investments: Cash and equiv (58%), long-term bonds (42%)
Provider Compensation ($000): Contr fee ($19,037), capitation ($1,028), salary ($551), bonus arrang ($98)
Total Member Encounters: Phys (42,767), non-phys (7,634)
Group Affiliation: None
Licensed in: FL
Address: 1301 International Parkway, Sunrise, FL 33323
Phone: (314) 725-4477 **Dom State:** FL **Commenced Bus:** N/A

Data Date	Rating	RACR #1	RACR #2	Total Assets ($mil)	Capital ($mil)	Net Premium ($mil)	Net Income ($mil)
3-19	C-	2.93	2.44	15.9	8.1	2.9	0.1
3-18	N/A	N/A	N/A	21.9	11.5	5.1	0.5
2018	C-	2.96	2.47	18.7	8.2	21.7	-2.5
2017	N/A	N/A	N/A	18.0	11.1	1.4	-7.2
2016	N/A	N/A	N/A	19.1	18.3	N/A	-1.6
2015	N/A	N/A	N/A	0.3	-0.1	N/A	N/A
2014	N/A	N/A	N/A	N/A	N/A	N/A	N/A

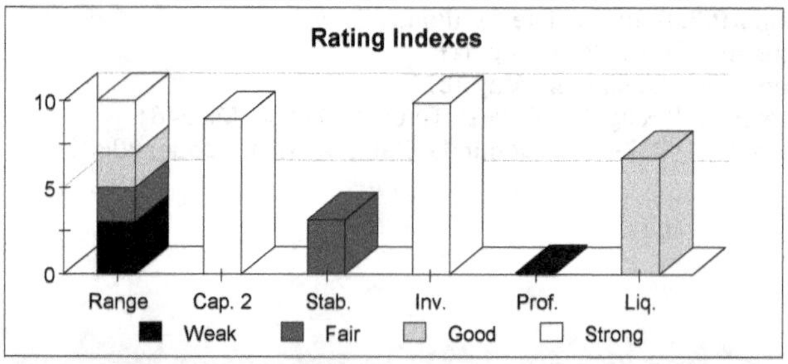

SUPERIOR HEALTHPLAN COMMUNITY SOLUTI C- Fair

Major Rating Factors: Weak profitability index (0.8 on a scale of 0 to 10). Strong capitalization (8.8) based on excellent current risk-adjusted capital (severe loss scenario). High quality investment portfolio (9.9).
Other Rating Factors: Excellent liquidity (7.4) with ample operational cash flow and liquid investments.
Principal Business: Medicare (100%)
Mem Phys: 18: 33,870 **17:** 22,932 **18 MLR** 99.6% **/ 18 Admin Exp** N/A
Enroll(000): Q1 19: 2 **18:** 1 **17:** 0 **Med Exp PMPM:** $829
Principal Investments: Cash and equiv (84%), long-term bonds (16%)
Provider Compensation ($000): Contr fee ($7,569), salary ($321), capitation ($7), bonus arrang ($3)
Total Member Encounters: Phys (19,690), non-phys (3,683)
Group Affiliation: None
Licensed in: TX
Address: 2100 S IH 35, Austin, TX 78704
Phone: (314) 725-4477 **Dom State:** TX **Commenced Bus:** N/A

Data Date	Rating	RACR #1	RACR #2	Total Assets ($mil)	Capital ($mil)	Net Premium ($mil)	Net Income ($mil)
3-19	C-	2.77	2.31	12.9	3.8	4.2	-0.9
3-18	N/A	N/A	N/A	10.1	6.0	2.4	-1.0
2018	C-	3.49	2.91	10.9	4.8	10.3	-2.1
2017	N/A	N/A	N/A	8.2	6.9	2.8	-0.1
2016	N/A	N/A	N/A	7.7	7.1	N/A	-1.5
2015	N/A	N/A	N/A	N/A	N/A	N/A	N/A
2014	N/A	N/A	N/A	N/A	N/A	N/A	N/A

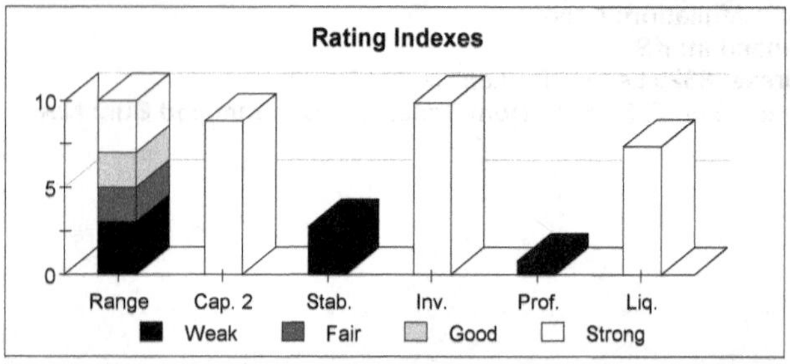

SUPERIOR HEALTHPLAN INC C+ Fair

Major Rating Factors: Good liquidity (6.8 on a scale of 0 to 10) with sufficient resources (cash flows and marketable investments) to handle a spike in claims. Excellent profitability (8.8). Strong capitalization index (7.6) based on excellent current risk-adjusted capital (severe loss scenario).
Other Rating Factors: High quality investment portfolio (7.4). Excellent overall results on stability tests (8.5).
Principal Business: Medicaid (86%), comp med (10%), Medicare (4%)
Mem Phys: 18: 59,918 **17:** 55,538 **18 MLR** 89.0% **/ 18 Admin Exp** N/A
Enroll(000): Q1 19: 529 **18:** 534 **17:** 538 **Med Exp PMPM:** $596
Principal Investments: Long-term bonds (61%), cash and equiv (35%), affiliate common stock (2%), other (2%)
Provider Compensation ($000): Contr fee ($2,684,142), bonus arrang ($953,857), salary ($130,572), capitation ($49,943), FFS ($19,533)
Total Member Encounters: Phys (3,491,117), non-phys (12,916,390)
Group Affiliation: None
Licensed in: TX
Address: 2100 South IH 35 Suite 202, Austin, TX 78741
Phone: (314) 725-4477 **Dom State:** TX **Commenced Bus:** N/A

Data Date	Rating	RACR #1	RACR #2	Total Assets ($mil)	Capital ($mil)	Net Premium ($mil)	Net Income ($mil)
3-19	C+	1.84	1.53	862.6	442.5	1,098.1	7.0
3-18	C+	1.64	1.37	784.5	343.9	1,063.6	-29.1
2018	C+	1.81	1.51	839.7	437.1	4,327.9	63.0
2017	B	1.35	1.12	753.9	369.5	3,957.4	63.8
2016	C+	1.64	1.37	664.3	308.4	3,522.0	52.2
2015	C+	1.68	1.40	620.4	260.9	2,882.1	13.6
2014	C+	2.12	1.77	384.7	208.8	1,856.8	32.1

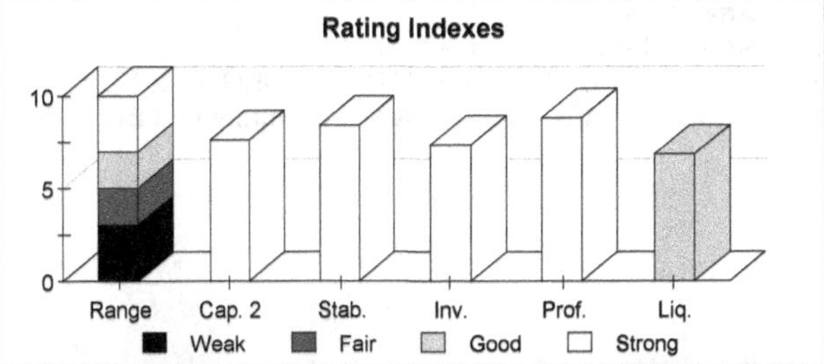

SUTTER HEALTH PLAN D Weak

Major Rating Factors: Weak profitability index (0.7 on a scale of 0 to 10). Weak overall results on stability tests (2.5). Fair capitalization index (3.3) based on weak current risk-adjusted capital (moderate loss scenario).
Other Rating Factors: Excellent liquidity (7.1) with ample operational cash flow and liquid investments.
Principal Business: Managed care (100%)
Mem Phys: 18: N/A **17:** N/A **18 MLR** 90.6% **/ 18 Admin Exp** N/A
Enroll(000): Q1 19: 88 **18:** 84 **17:** 69 **Med Exp PMPM:** $399
Principal Investments ($000): Cash and equiv ($58,157)
Provider Compensation ($000): None
Total Member Encounters: N/A
Group Affiliation: None
Licensed in: CA
Address: 2088 OtayLakesRd #102, Chula Vista, CA 91915
Phone: (619) 407-4082 **Dom State:** CA **Commenced Bus:** April 2013

Data Date	Rating	RACR #1	RACR #2	Total Assets ($mil)	Capital ($mil)	Net Premium ($mil)	Net Income ($mil)
3-19	D	0.56	0.35	106.1	19.8	123.9	2.5
3-18	D	0.82	0.52	100.6	22.6	104.1	-2.8
2018	D	0.48	0.30	95.2	16.9	428.8	-16.1
2017	D	0.92	0.58	98.0	25.2	319.8	-23.9
2016	E+	0.72	0.46	76.2	13.1	188.2	-40.6
2015	E	1.11	0.74	41.4	10.2	77.1	-27.5
2014	U	5.04	3.53	41.2	23.7	30.9	-19.0

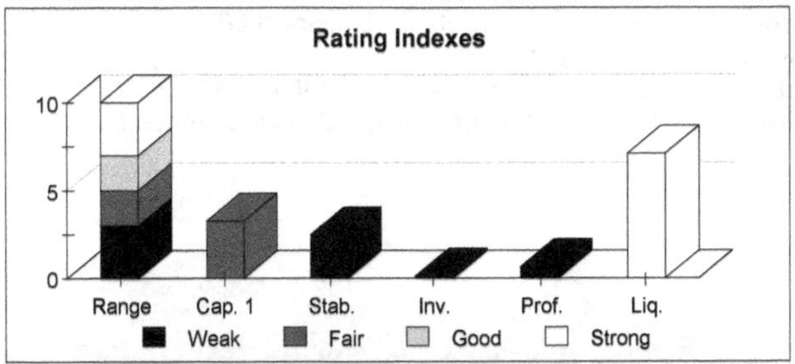

SWISS RE LIFE & HEALTH AMERICA INCORPORATED C Fair

Major Rating Factors: Fair profitability (4.8 on a scale of 0 to 10). Excellent expense controls. Fair overall results on stability tests (3.8). Good liquidity (6.1) with sufficient resources to handle a spike in claims as well as a significant increase in policy surrenders.
Other Rating Factors: Strong capitalization (8.1) based on excellent risk adjusted capital (severe loss scenario). High quality investment portfolio (7.2).
Principal Business: Reinsurance (100%).
Principal Investments: NonCMO investment grade bonds (71%), CMOs and structured securities (13%), mortgages in good standing (7%), noninv. grade bonds (3%), and common & preferred stock (1%).
Investments in Affiliates: 13%
Group Affiliation: Swiss Reinsurance Group
Licensed in: All states, the District of Columbia and Puerto Rico
Commenced Business: September 1967
Address: 237 EAST HIGH STREET, JEFFERSON CITY, MO 65101
Phone: (877) 794-7773 **Domicile State:** MO **NAIC Code:** 82627

Data Date	Rating	RACR #1	RACR #2	Total Assets ($mil)	Capital ($mil)	Net Premium ($mil)	Net Income ($mil)
3-19	C	2.70	1.72	14,338.0	2,720.9	-982.3	1,828.8
3-18	C	1.48	0.93	15,421.7	1,260.1	3,220.9	-1,839.8
2018	C	2.00	1.28	15,932.4	2,035.8	6,288.5	-1,164.9
2017	C	1.36	0.86	14,134.1	1,157.4	2,548.5	139.9
2016	C	1.57	0.99	14,226.8	1,380.9	2,289.7	-5.8
2015	C	1.83	1.08	12,264.0	1,318.3	2,983.5	85.8
2014	C	1.69	1.12	11,247.5	1,461.0	2,107.9	-924.1

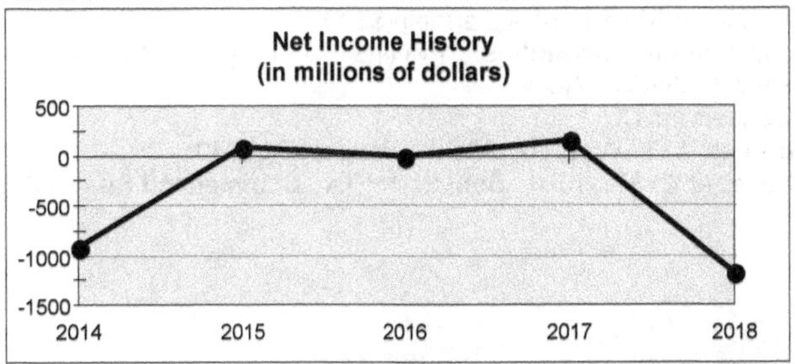

SYMPHONIX HEALTH INS INC E+ Very Weak

Major Rating Factors: Weak profitability index (1.4 on a scale of 0 to 10). Strong capitalization (10.0) based on excellent current risk-adjusted capital (severe loss scenario). High quality investment portfolio (9.9).
Other Rating Factors: Excellent liquidity (7.5) with ample operational cash flow and liquid investments.
Principal Business: Other (100%)
Mem Phys: 18: 32,252 **17:** 42,219 **18 MLR** 80.9% **/ 18 Admin Exp** N/A
Enroll(000): Q1 19: 24 **18:** 740 **17:** 834 **Med Exp PMPM:** $51
Principal Investments: Cash and equiv (63%), long-term bonds (37%)
Provider Compensation ($000): FFS ($460,213), contr fee ($81,193), bonus arrang ($8,923)
Total Member Encounters: N/A
Group Affiliation: None
Licensed in: All states except NY, PR
Address: 1900 EAST GOLF RD, SCHAUMBURG, IL 60173
Phone: (224) 231-1451 **Dom State:** IL **Commenced Bus:** N/A

Data Date	Rating	RACR #1	RACR #2	Total Assets ($mil)	Capital ($mil)	Net Premium ($mil)	Net Income ($mil)
3-19	E+	5.48	4.56	203.8	115.9	84.0	8.6
3-18	E+	N/A	N/A	560.8	73.0	167.7	-49.8
2018	E+	4.95	4.13	338.0	104.9	541.5	-17.7
2017	E+	N/A	N/A	357.7	67.0	474.2	-54.3
2016	C	4.96	4.13	531.6	59.1	357.9	-38.8
2015	D-	1.23	1.03	228.3	22.6	173.0	-1.8
2014	N/A	N/A	N/A	64.9	7.6	80.1	N/A

Rating Indexes

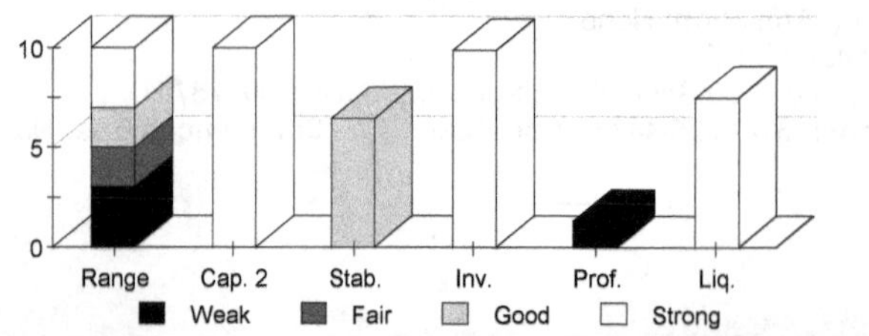

TAKECARE INS CO C Fair

Major Rating Factors: Fair profitability index (4.6 on a scale of 0 to 10). Fair capitalization (4.6) based on fair current risk-adjusted capital (moderate loss scenario). Fair quality investment portfolio (4.1).
Other Rating Factors: Good liquidity (6.5) with sufficient resources (cash flows and marketable investments) to handle a spike in claims.
Principal Business: Comp med (63%), FEHB (35%), other (3%)
Mem Phys: 18: 375 **17:** 419 **18 MLR** 89.2% **/ 18 Admin Exp** N/A
Enroll(000): Q1 19: 29 **18:** 28 **17:** 28 **Med Exp PMPM:** $255
Principal Investments: Affiliate common stock (62%), cash and equiv (28%), real estate (9%), other (2%)
Provider Compensation ($000): Contr fee ($44,055), capitation ($36,544)
Total Member Encounters: N/A
Group Affiliation: TakeCare Health Systems LLP
Licensed in: (No states)
Address: STE 308 415 CHN SAN ANTONIO, TAMUNING, GU 96913
Phone: (671) 300-7142 **Dom State:** GU **Commenced Bus:** N/A

Data Date	Rating	RACR #1	RACR #2	Total Assets ($mil)	Capital ($mil)	Net Premium ($mil)	Net Income ($mil)
3-19	C	0.88	0.73	35.4	13.1	23.8	0.6
3-18	D+	N/A	N/A	33.2	12.5	22.9	0.4
2018	C	1.06	0.89	36.4	15.2	90.7	3.1
2017	D+	N/A	N/A	36.2	15.7	97.7	2.2
2016	C	1.06	0.89	32.1	14.0	101.0	-0.7
2015	C+	1.25	1.04	38.5	18.0	106.3	5.0
2014	U	1.07	0.89	34.1	14.8	100.7	4.7

Rating Indexes

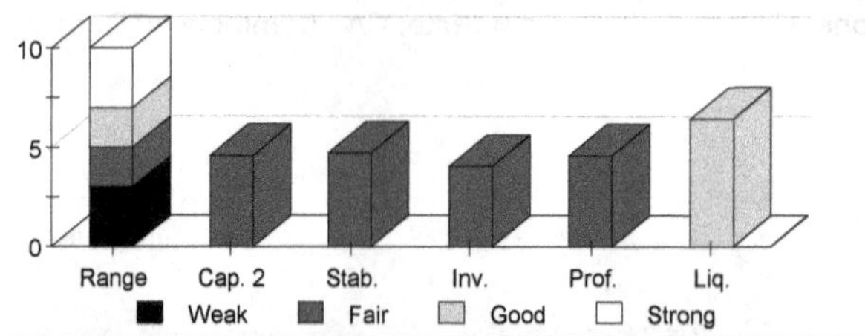

TEXAS CHILDRENS HEALTH PLAN INC D+ Weak

Major Rating Factors: Weak profitability index (0.9 on a scale of 0 to 10). Low quality investment portfolio (2.7). Fair capitalization index (4.1) based on fair current risk-adjusted capital (moderate loss scenario).
Other Rating Factors: Good overall results on stability tests (6.0). Good liquidity (6.5) with sufficient resources (cash flows and marketable investments) to handle a spike in claims.
Principal Business: Medicaid (91%), comp med (9%)
Mem Phys: 18: 22,790 **17:** 18,241 **18 MLR** 92.3% **/ 18 Admin Exp** N/A
Enroll(000): Q1 19: 425 **18:** 440 **17:** 465 **Med Exp PMPM:** $290
Principal Investments: Cash and equiv (48%), long-term bonds (43%), affiliate common stock (9%)
Provider Compensation ($000): Contr fee ($766,052), FFS ($717,423), capitation ($51,084), bonus arrang ($2,177)
Total Member Encounters: Phys (1,914,714), non-phys (1,726,201)
Group Affiliation: None
Licensed in: TX
Address: 6330 West Loop South, Bellaire, TX 77401
Phone: (832) 828-1020 **Dom State:** TX **Commenced Bus:** N/A

Data Date	Rating	RACR #1	RACR #2	Total Assets ($mil)	Capital ($mil)	Net Premium ($mil)	Net Income ($mil)
3-19	D+	0.79	0.66	328.5	132.3	427.1	-9.8
3-18	D+	0.93	0.77	292.8	136.7	415.8	-3.5
2018	D+	0.84	0.70	348.6	141.0	1,677.5	-63.2
2017	D+	0.94	0.78	297.1	138.0	1,562.7	-40.6
2016	B-	1.08	0.90	226.3	104.9	1,067.6	-17.7
2015	B	1.49	1.24	210.4	125.1	958.4	15.7
2014	B-	1.01	0.84	167.7	86.4	918.4	2.2

Rating Indexes

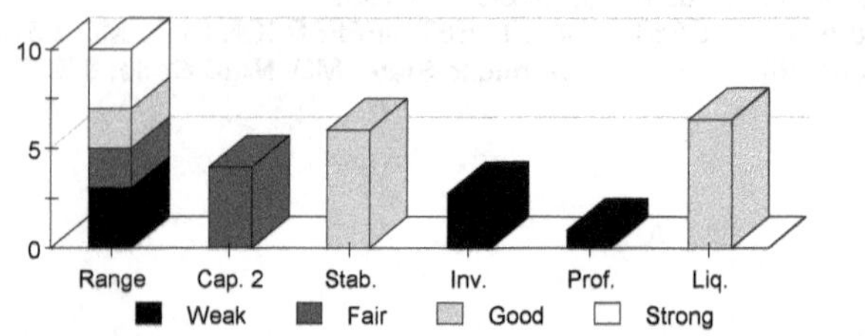

TEXAS HLTH + AETNA HLTH INS CO C Fair

Major Rating Factors: Weak profitability index (1.5 on a scale of 0 to 10). Strong capitalization (10.0) based on excellent current risk-adjusted capital (severe loss scenario). High quality investment portfolio (8.4).
Other Rating Factors: Excellent liquidity (8.5) with ample operational cash flow and liquid investments.
Principal Business: Comp med (100%)
Mem Phys: 18: 20,738 **17:** 20,281 **18 MLR** 7.3% **/ 18 Admin Exp** N/A
Enroll(000): Q1 19: 16 **18:** 8 **17:** 4 **Med Exp PMPM:** $285
Principal Investments: Long-term bonds (70%), cash and equiv (16%), affiliate common stock (10%), nonaffiliate common stock (3%)
Provider Compensation ($000): Contr fee ($15,076), FFS ($3,854), bonus arrang ($302)
Total Member Encounters: Phys (58,381), non-phys (63,277)
Group Affiliation: None
Licensed in: TX
Address: , ARLINGTON, TX 76011
Phone: (800) 872-3862 **Dom State:** TX **Commenced Bus:** N/A

Data Date	Rating	RACR #1	RACR #2	Total Assets ($mil)	Capital ($mil)	Net Premium ($mil)	Net Income ($mil)
3-19	C	4.67	3.89	157.3	88.1	63.4	2.9
3-18	N/A	N/A	N/A	167.7	54.9	76.7	3.3
2018	C	4.30	3.58	164.2	80.7	278.7	-3.7
2017	N/A	N/A	N/A	151.0	46.5	328.1	-3.8
2016	N/A	N/A	N/A	N/A	N/A	N/A	N/A
2015	N/A	N/A	N/A	N/A	N/A	N/A	N/A
2014	N/A	N/A	N/A	N/A	N/A	N/A	N/A

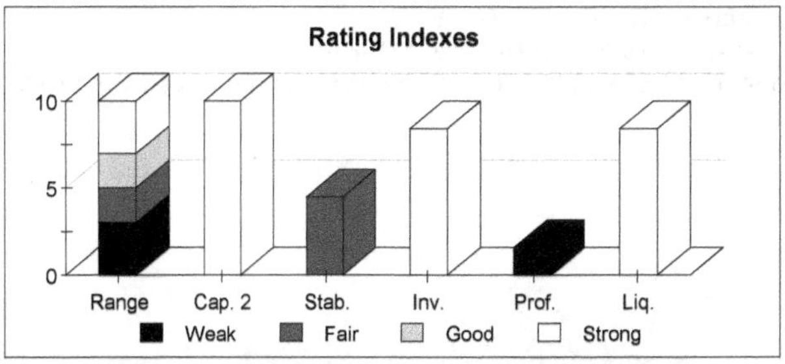

TEXAS HLTH + AETNA HLTH PLAN C Fair

Major Rating Factors: Weak profitability index (0.9 on a scale of 0 to 10). Strong capitalization (9.6) based on excellent current risk-adjusted capital (severe loss scenario). High quality investment portfolio (8.0).
Other Rating Factors: Excellent liquidity (7.2) with ample operational cash flow and liquid investments.
Principal Business: Comp med (100%)
Mem Phys: 18: 20,313 **17:** 18,309 **18 MLR** 60.8% **/ 18 Admin Exp** N/A
Enroll(000): Q1 19: 3 **18:** 2 **17:** N/A **Med Exp PMPM:** $441
Principal Investments: Cash and equiv (60%), long-term bonds (35%), nonaffiliate common stock (6%)
Provider Compensation ($000): Contr fee ($8,196), FFS ($2,591), bonus arrang ($92)
Total Member Encounters: Phys (20,931), non-phys (25,062)
Group Affiliation: None
Licensed in: TX
Address: , ARLINGTON, TX 76011
Phone: (800) 872-3862 **Dom State:** TX **Commenced Bus:** N/A

Data Date	Rating	RACR #1	RACR #2	Total Assets ($mil)	Capital ($mil)	Net Premium ($mil)	Net Income ($mil)
3-19	C	3.43	2.86	15.4	9.4	4.7	0.4
3-18	N/A	N/A	N/A	10.2	4.8	6.4	1.0
2018	C	3.16	2.63	18.6	8.7	20.9	-3.2
2017	N/A	N/A	N/A	7.5	3.5	14.0	-0.5
2016	N/A	N/A	N/A	N/A	N/A	N/A	N/A
2015	N/A	N/A	N/A	N/A	N/A	N/A	N/A
2014	N/A	N/A	N/A	N/A	N/A	N/A	N/A

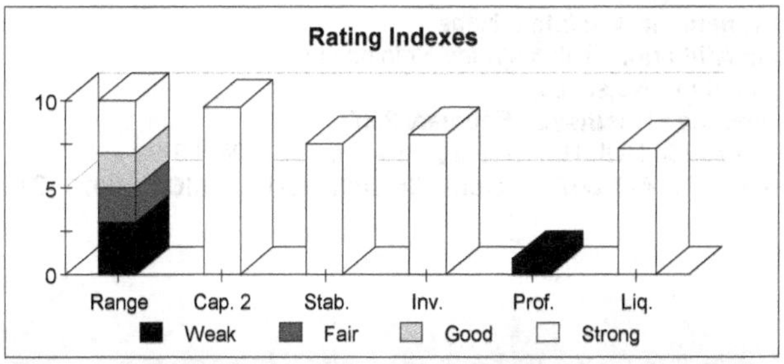

THP INS CO D+ Weak

Major Rating Factors: Weak profitability index (0.9 on a scale of 0 to 10). Low quality investment portfolio (1.2). Good liquidity (6.4) with sufficient resources (cash flows and marketable investments) to handle a spike in claims.
Other Rating Factors: Strong capitalization (7.1) based on excellent current risk-adjusted capital (severe loss scenario).
Principal Business: Comp med (53%), Medicare (19%), med supp (16%), other (11%)
Mem Phys: 18: 22,982 **17:** 19,746 **18 MLR** 101.1% **/ 18 Admin Exp** N/A
Enroll(000): Q1 19: 19 **18:** 21 **17:** 20 **Med Exp PMPM:** $462
Principal Investments: Nonaffiliate common stock (69%), cash and equiv (31%)
Provider Compensation ($000): Contr fee ($104,561), capitation ($93)
Total Member Encounters: Phys (348,855), non-phys (83,024)
Group Affiliation: Health Plan of West Virginia Inc
Licensed in: OH, PA, WV
Address: 52160 National Rd East E, Wheeling, WV 26003
Phone: (740) 695-3585 **Dom State:** WV **Commenced Bus:** N/A

Data Date	Rating	RACR #1	RACR #2	Total Assets ($mil)	Capital ($mil)	Net Premium ($mil)	Net Income ($mil)
3-19	D+	1.44	1.20	59.7	21.7	29.9	0.8
3-18	D+	2.91	2.43	57.1	29.4	27.8	1.2
2018	D+	1.29	1.07	61.0	19.4	112.1	-7.4
2017	D	2.31	1.93	53.1	28.8	92.0	2.5
2016	D	3.00	2.50	43.0	24.1	71.7	2.3
2015	D	3.58	2.99	38.8	24.7	52.8	-1.8
2014	D	2.45	2.04	34.8	18.9	52.0	-13.1

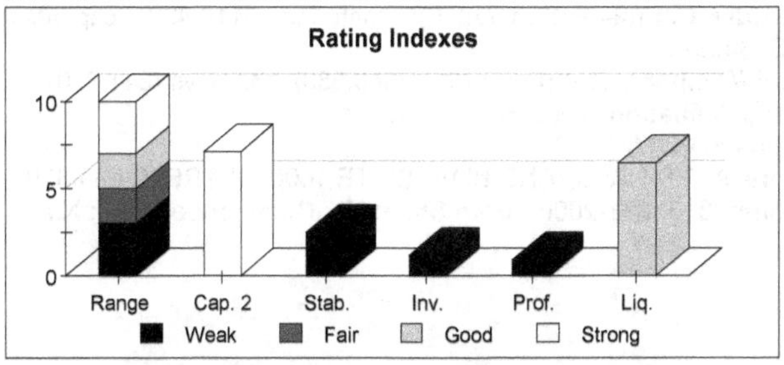

TIMBER PRODUCTS MANUFACTURERS TRUST C+ Fair

Major Rating Factors: Good overall profitability index (5.8 on a scale of 0 to 10). Strong capitalization (9.0) based on excellent current risk-adjusted capital (severe loss scenario). High quality investment portfolio (9.9).
Other Rating Factors: Excellent liquidity (7.6) with ample operational cash flow and liquid investments.
Principal Business: Comp med (97%), dental (3%)
Mem Phys: 18: N/A **17:** N/A **18 MLR** 73.4% **/ 18 Admin Exp** N/A
Enroll(000): Q1 19: 12 **18:** 12 **17:** 13 **Med Exp PMPM:** $202
Principal Investments: Cash and equiv (53%), long-term bonds (47%)
Provider Compensation ($000): Contr fee ($31,114)
Total Member Encounters: Phys (46,874), non-phys (8,126)
Group Affiliation: None
Licensed in: ID, MT, OR, WA, WY
Address: 951 EAST THIRD Ave, SPOKANE, WA 99202
Phone: (509) 535-4646 **Dom State:** WA **Commenced Bus:** N/A

Data Date	Rating	RACR #1	RACR #2	Total Assets ($mil)	Capital ($mil)	Net Premium ($mil)	Net Income ($mil)
3-19	C+	2.98	2.49	18.2	14.9	9.6	1.0
3-18	D+	1.31	1.09	12.5	8.5	10.1	2.2
2018	C+	2.79	2.33	17.4	14.0	40.7	7.7
2017	D	0.95	0.79	10.7	6.3	47.6	3.4
2016	E+	0.32	0.26	10.0	2.9	57.7	-4.3
2015	C	0.71	0.59	14.2	5.4	54.6	-2.5
2014	C+	1.30	1.08	14.3	8.1	43.7	1.1

Rating Indexes

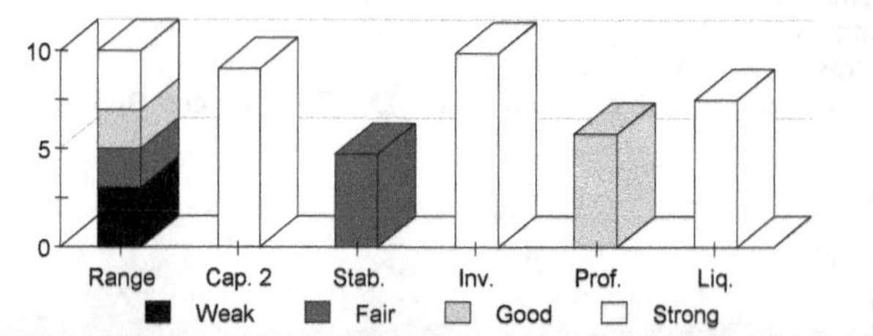

TOKIO MARINE PACIFIC INS LTD C Fair

Major Rating Factors: Fair overall results on stability tests (3.2 on a scale of 0 to 10). Vulnerable liquidity (1.4) as a spike in claims may stretch capacity.
Other Rating Factors: Strong long-term capitalization index (9.5) based on excellent current risk adjusted capital (severe and moderate loss scenarios), despite some fluctuation in capital levels. Ample reserve history (9.3) that helps to protect the company against sharp claims increases. Excellent profitability (8.4) with operating gains in each of the last five years.
Principal Business: Group accident & health (91%), auto physical damage (2%), commercial multiple peril (2%), auto liability (1%), other liability (1%), homeowners multiple peril (1%), and other lines (2%).
Principal Investments: Investment grade bonds (77%), cash (22%), and misc. investments (1%).
Investments in Affiliates: None
Group Affiliation: Tokio Marine Holdings Inc
Licensed in: (No states)
Commenced Business: February 2002
Address: 250 ROUTE 4 STE 202, Hagatna, GU 96910
Phone: (671) 475-8671 **Domicile State:** GU **NAIC Code:** 11216

Data Date	Rating	RACR #1	RACR #2	Loss Ratio %	Total Assets ($mil)	Capital ($mil)	Net Premium ($mil)	Net Income ($mil)
3-19	C	4.92	2.68	N/A	128.7	87.5	43.4	2.1
3-18	C	4.83	2.62	N/A	124.1	80.8	40.6	-1.8
2018	C	4.95	2.70	88.4	128.6	85.5	164.7	2.3
2017	C	5.41	2.91	82.5	121.0	82.7	149.4	8.0
2016	C	3.82	2.05	82.5	105.0	62.8	143.9	7.5
2015	C	4.01	2.18	81.1	109.3	67.0	135.2	5.3
2014	C	3.31	1.87	81.5	98.5	61.0	121.8	4.3

Tokio Marine Holdings Inc
Composite Group Rating: C+

Largest Group Members	Assets ($mil)	Rating
RELIANCE STANDARD LIFE INS CO	13875	C+
PHILADELPHIA INDEMNITY INS CO	9058	B-
SAFETY NATIONAL CASUALTY CORP	8028	C+
HOUSTON CASUALTY CO	3437	B-
US SPECIALTY INS CO	2042	C

TOTAL HEALTH CARE INC C+ Fair

Major Rating Factors: Fair quality investment portfolio (4.3 on a scale of 0 to 10). Fair overall results on stability tests (4.6) based on a decline in the number of member physicians during 2019. Good liquidity (6.9) with sufficient resources (cash flows and marketable investments) to handle a spike in claims.
Other Rating Factors: Weak profitability index (2.6). Strong capitalization index (7.6) based on excellent current risk-adjusted capital (severe loss scenario).
Principal Business: Medicaid (100%)
Mem Phys: 18: 5,751 **17:** 6,674 **18 MLR** 92.5% **/ 18 Admin Exp** N/A
Enroll(000): Q1 19: 52 **18:** 51 **17:** 52 **Med Exp PMPM:** $273
Principal Investments: Affiliate common stock (62%), cash and equiv (37%), long-term bonds (1%)
Provider Compensation ($000): Contr fee ($118,433), capitation ($46,111), FFS ($406)
Total Member Encounters: Phys (348,589), non-phys (241,070)
Group Affiliation: Total Health Care Inc
Licensed in: MI
Address: 3011 W GRAND BLVD SUITE 1600, DETROIT, MI 48202
Phone: (313) 871-2000 **Dom State:** MI **Commenced Bus:** N/A

Data Date	Rating	RACR #1	RACR #2	Total Assets ($mil)	Capital ($mil)	Net Premium ($mil)	Net Income ($mil)
3-19	C+	1.81	1.51	98.7	53.0	46.2	0.0
3-18	C+	1.63	1.36	90.8	47.7	60.7	0.1
2018	C+	1.70	1.41	107.9	50.4	183.4	6.7
2017	C	1.43	1.19	95.2	47.2	261.2	-15.4
2016	B-	1.48	1.23	83.2	46.5	284.1	-1.8
2015	B-	1.14	0.95	84.2	41.7	322.4	5.9
2014	C	0.82	0.69	60.5	29.9	272.3	5.0

Rating Indexes

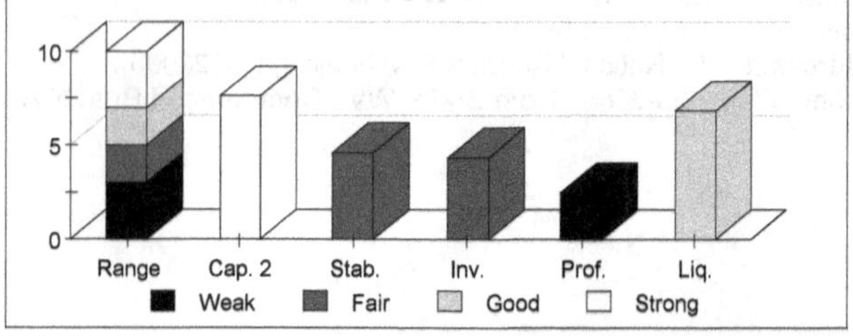

TOTAL HEALTH CARE USA INC * B+ Good

Major Rating Factors: Excellent profitability (8.6 on a scale of 0 to 10). Strong capitalization (9.2) based on excellent current risk-adjusted capital (severe loss scenario). High quality investment portfolio (9.9).
Other Rating Factors: Excellent liquidity (7.6) with ample operational cash flow and liquid investments.
Principal Business: Comp med (100%)
Mem Phys: 18: 6,201 **17:** 6,674 **18 MLR** 76.5% **/ 18 Admin Exp** N/A
Enroll(000): Q1 19: 45 **18:** 42 **17:** 34 **Med Exp PMPM:** $262
Principal Investments: Cash and equiv (99%), long-term bonds (1%)
Provider Compensation ($000): Contr fee ($131,375), capitation ($5,971), FFS ($871)
Total Member Encounters: Phys (276,778), non-phys (100,465)
Group Affiliation: Total Health Care Inc
Licensed in: MI
Address: 3011 W GRAND BLVD Ste 1600, DETROIT, MI 48202
Phone: (313) 871-2000 **Dom State:** MI **Commenced Bus:** N/A

Data Date	Rating	RACR #1	RACR #2	Total Assets ($mil)	Capital ($mil)	Net Premium ($mil)	Net Income ($mil)
3-19	B+	3.12	2.60	95.2	44.9	49.5	2.3
3-18	B+	4.14	3.45	82.5	46.4	49.9	1.8
2018	B+	2.92	2.43	76.8	42.6	182.2	10.6
2017	B+	3.61	3.01	67.5	45.8	148.0	15.5
2016	B+	2.54	2.12	55.4	29.9	139.3	6.7
2015	B	1.80	1.50	53.5	23.4	154.9	5.5
2014	C+	1.20	1.00	45.0	17.6	160.5	2.3

Rating Indexes

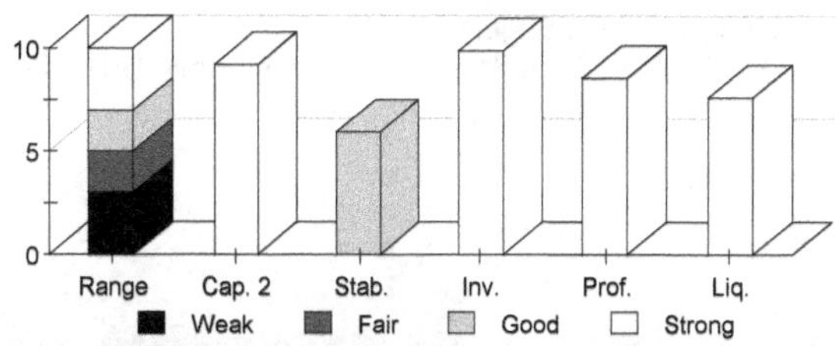

TRANS OCEANIC LIFE INSURANCE COMPANY * A- Excellent

Major Rating Factors: Good overall results on stability tests (6.4 on a scale of 0 to 10). Strengths that enhance stability include excellent operational trends and good risk diversification. Fair quality investment portfolio (4.9). Strong capitalization (7.9) based on excellent risk adjusted capital (severe loss scenario).
Other Rating Factors: Excellent profitability (7.3). Excellent liquidity (7.7).
Principal Business: Individual health insurance (93%) and individual life insurance (7%).
Principal Investments: NonCMO investment grade bonds (48%), CMOs and structured securities (13%), common & preferred stock (12%), real estate (10%), and cash (8%).
Investments in Affiliates: None
Group Affiliation: Trans-Oceanic Group Inc
Licensed in: FL, PR
Commenced Business: December 1959
Address: # 121 ONEILL, SAN JUAN, PR 00918-2404
Phone: (787) 620-2680 **Domicile State:** PR **NAIC Code:** 69523

Data Date	Rating	RACR #1	RACR #2	Total Assets ($mil)	Capital ($mil)	Net Premium ($mil)	Net Income ($mil)
3-19	A-	2.57	1.63	76.6	34.6	7.6	0.4
3-18	A-	2.58	1.65	72.9	33.4	7.4	0.3
2018	A-	2.54	1.61	74.4	32.9	29.5	2.1
2017	A-	2.59	1.65	72.5	33.3	30.1	1.9
2016	A-	2.54	1.61	70.6	32.8	30.7	1.2
2015	A	3.12	1.95	67.4	35.2	30.4	4.7
2014	A	3.09	2.06	65.1	33.7	29.8	4.6

Adverse Trends in Operations

Increase in policy surrenders from 2017 to 2018 (3207%)
Decrease in capital during 2018 (1%)
Change in asset mix during 2016 (4.2%)
Decrease in capital during 2016 (9%)
Increase in policy surrenders from 2015 to 2016 (8879%)

TRH HEALTH INS CO C+ Fair

Major Rating Factors: Fair profitability index (3.3 on a scale of 0 to 10). Good liquidity (6.5) with sufficient resources (cash flows and marketable investments) to handle a spike in claims. Strong capitalization (9.5) based on excellent current risk-adjusted capital (severe loss scenario).
Other Rating Factors: High quality investment portfolio (9.5).
Principal Business: Comp med (50%), med supp (50%)
Mem Phys: 18: 710,100 **17:** 710,100 **18 MLR** 79.4% **/ 18 Admin Exp** N/A
Enroll(000): Q1 19: 101 **18:** 104 **17:** 132 **Med Exp PMPM:** $182
Principal Investments: Long-term bonds (79%), cash and equiv (16%), nonaffiliate common stock (5%)
Provider Compensation ($000): FFS ($262,713)
Total Member Encounters: Phys (4,655,485), non-phys (636,149)
Group Affiliation: None
Licensed in: TN
Address: 147 Bear Creek Pike, Columbia, TN 38401-2266
Phone: (931) 560-0041 **Dom State:** TN **Commenced Bus:** N/A

Data Date	Rating	RACR #1	RACR #2	Total Assets ($mil)	Capital ($mil)	Net Premium ($mil)	Net Income ($mil)
3-19	C+	3.36	2.80	118.8	85.3	71.9	8.5
3-18	C	1.28	1.07	112.0	60.6	74.7	1.0
2018	C	2.61	2.18	104.7	66.7	290.4	19.7
2017	C	1.23	1.02	126.4	62.2	414.9	-11.9
2016	C+	2.41	2.01	127.5	71.1	296.7	-12.3
2015	B-	3.06	2.55	120.7	79.3	287.6	9.8
2014	C+	2.98	2.49	82.9	53.3	159.7	-0.7

Rating Indexes

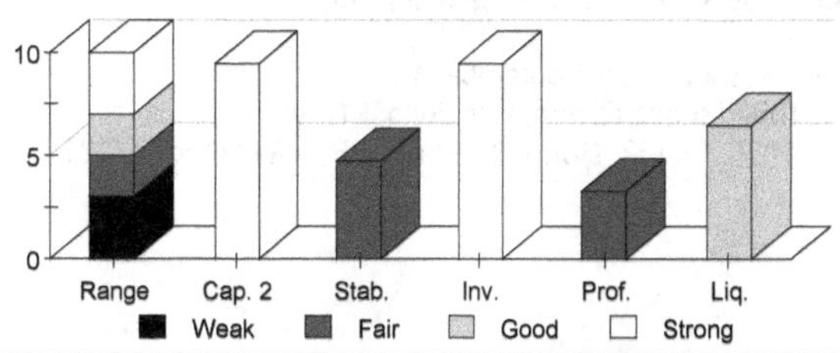

TRILLIUM COMMUNITY HEALTH PLAN INC C+ Fair

Major Rating Factors: Fair profitability index (4.4 on a scale of 0 to 10). Good liquidity (5.0) with sufficient resources (cash flows and marketable investments) to handle a spike in claims. Strong capitalization (7.8) based on excellent current risk-adjusted capital (severe loss scenario).
Other Rating Factors: High quality investment portfolio (8.5).
Principal Business: Medicaid (93%), Medicare (7%)
Mem Phys: 18: 4,377 **17:** 3,769 **18 MLR** 91.5% **/ 18 Admin Exp** N/A
Enroll(000): Q1 19: 95 **18:** 94 **17:** 93 **Med Exp PMPM:** $438
Principal Investments: Long-term bonds (89%), cash and equiv (11%)
Provider Compensation ($000): Contr fee ($422,755), capitation ($50,287), bonus arrang ($12,311), salary ($10,337)
Total Member Encounters: Phys (564,103), non-phys (1,325,117)
Group Affiliation: None
Licensed in: OR
Address: 1800 Millrace Dr, Eugene, OR 97403
Phone: (314) 725-4477 **Dom State:** OR **Commenced Bus:** N/A

Data Date	Rating	RACR #1	RACR #2	Total Assets ($mil)	Capital ($mil)	Net Premium ($mil)	Net Income ($mil)
3-19	C+	1.97	1.64	150.1	55.0	139.4	1.5
3-18	C+	N/A	N/A	159.0	56.5	129.0	-8.9
2018	C+	2.03	1.70	153.2	57.1	536.1	-13.6
2017	C+	N/A	N/A	156.8	65.5	492.0	7.2
2016	C+	2.49	2.08	174.7	64.5	519.7	5.0
2015	C+	1.61	1.34	154.8	41.3	522.9	14.1
2014	B	1.20	1.00	118.8	43.5	407.5	22.2

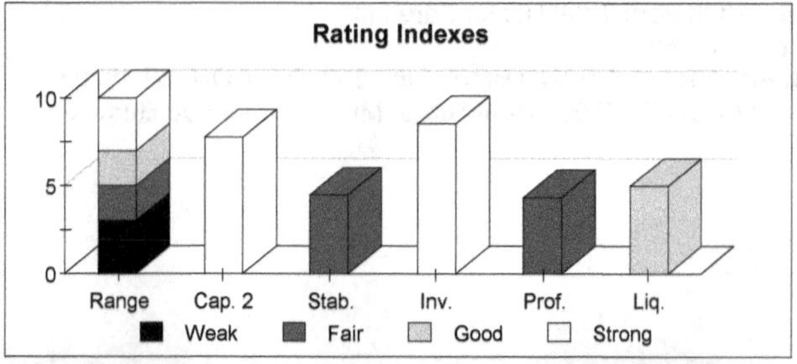

TRILOGY HEALTH INS INC C Fair

Major Rating Factors: Fair profitability index (4.2 on a scale of 0 to 10). Fair capitalization (4.5) based on fair current risk-adjusted capital (moderate loss scenario). High quality investment portfolio (9.9).
Other Rating Factors: Excellent liquidity (7.2) with ample operational cash flow and liquid investments.
Principal Business: Medicaid (100%)
Mem Phys: 18: 18,856 **17:** 16,769 **18 MLR** 86.1% **/ 18 Admin Exp** N/A
Enroll(000): Q1 19: 12 **18:** 11 **17:** 10 **Med Exp PMPM:** $187
Principal Investments: Cash and equiv (100%)
Provider Compensation ($000): Contr fee ($23,502), capitation ($242)
Total Member Encounters: Phys (64,115), non-phys (21,261)
Group Affiliation: Trilogy Health Holdings LLC
Licensed in: WI
Address: 18000 West Sarah Lane Ste 310, Brookfield, WI 53045-5842
Phone: (262) 432-9145 **Dom State:** WI **Commenced Bus:** N/A

Data Date	Rating	RACR #1	RACR #2	Total Assets ($mil)	Capital ($mil)	Net Premium ($mil)	Net Income ($mil)
3-19	C	0.86	0.71	7.5	3.9	7.5	0.2
3-18	C	0.88	0.73	6.1	3.2	6.8	0.0
2018	C	0.83	0.69	10.5	3.8	28.3	0.5
2017	C	0.88	0.73	6.2	3.2	22.1	-0.6
2016	C	1.05	0.87	7.3	3.8	20.4	0.1
2015	C	1.61	1.34	7.3	4.7	17.7	3.1
2014	E+	0.68	0.57	3.1	1.2	5.1	-1.7

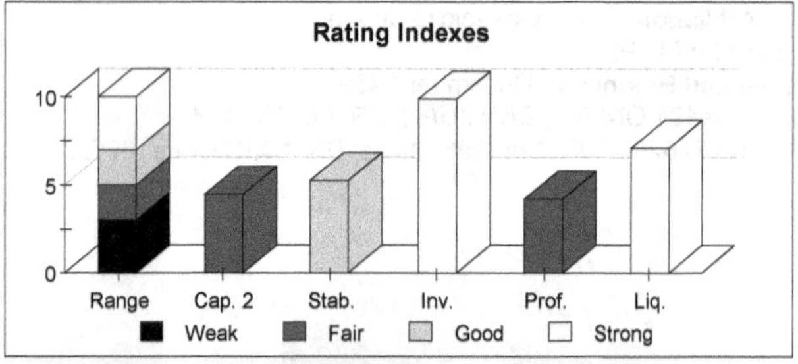

TRIPLE S VIDA INCORPORATED B- Good

Major Rating Factors: Good overall capitalization (5.7 on a scale of 0 to 10) based on good risk adjusted capital (severe loss scenario). Nevertheless, capital levels have fluctuated during prior years. Good overall profitability (6.1). Excellent expense controls. Good liquidity (5.8).
Other Rating Factors: Good overall results on stability tests (5.3) excellent operational trends and good risk diversification. Fair quality investment portfolio (4.8).
Principal Business: Individual life insurance (54%), individual health insurance (32%), group life insurance (5%), individual annuities (4%), and other lines (5%).
Principal Investments: NonCMO investment grade bonds (70%), common & preferred stock (12%), CMOs and structured securities (11%), policy loans (2%), and cash (2%).
Investments in Affiliates: 1%
Group Affiliation: Triple-S Management Corp
Licensed in: PR
Commenced Business: September 1964
Address: 1052 Munoz Rivera, San Juan, PR 927
Phone: (787) 777-8432 **Domicile State:** PR **NAIC Code:** 73814

Data Date	Rating	RACR #1	RACR #2	Total Assets ($mil)	Capital ($mil)	Net Premium ($mil)	Net Income ($mil)
3-19	B-	1.28	0.84	679.7	63.8	45.6	3.9
3-18	B-	1.26	0.82	649.0	68.2	45.2	5.8
2018	B-	1.18	0.77	655.1	60.3	182.4	6.4
2017	B-	1.27	0.83	637.9	67.1	169.6	10.9
2016	B-	1.16	0.75	601.8	62.0	170.9	9.5
2015	B-	N/A	N/A	572.2	59.1	161.0	5.3
2014	B-	1.19	0.81	550.3	64.8	158.3	12.3

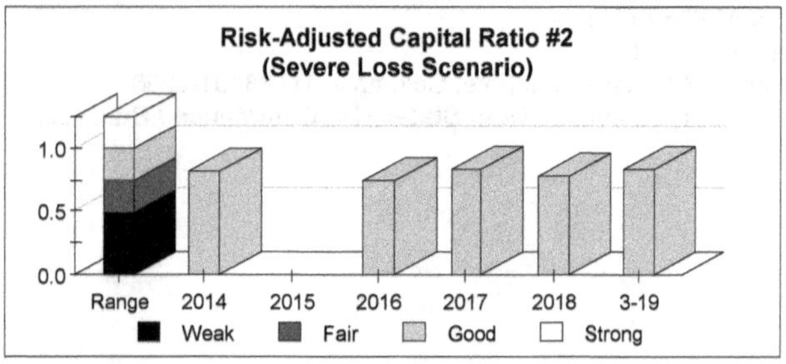

TRIPLE-S ADVANTAGE INC C+ Fair

Major Rating Factors: Fair liquidity (4.7 on a scale of 0 to 10) as cash resources may not be adequate to cover a spike in claims. Good capitalization (5.0) based on good current risk-adjusted capital (severe loss scenario). Weak profitability index (2.4).
Other Rating Factors: High quality investment portfolio (9.5).
Principal Business: Medicare (100%)
Mem Phys: 18: N/A **17:** N/A **18 MLR** 83.3% **/ 18 Admin Exp** N/A
Enroll(000): Q1 19: 128 **18:** 109 **17:** 118 **Med Exp PMPM:** $704
Principal Investments: Long-term bonds (82%), nonaffiliate common stock (10%), cash and equiv (4%), other (3%)
Provider Compensation ($000): FFS ($748,243), capitation ($101,600)
Total Member Encounters: Phys (5,320,331), non-phys (3,907,022)
Group Affiliation: None
Licensed in: PR
Address: FD ROOSEVELT AVE 1441, SAN JUAN, PR 920
Phone: (787) 620-1919 **Dom State:** PR **Commenced Bus:** N/A

Data Date	Rating	RACR #1	RACR #2	Total Assets ($mil)	Capital ($mil)	Net Premium ($mil)	Net Income ($mil)
3-19	C+	0.92	0.77	365.6	109.6	332.6	23.4
3-18	C	0.51	0.42	397.8	73.3	287.9	-6.5
2018	C+	0.95	0.79	396.1	112.6	1,130.3	14.8
2017	C	0.64	0.54	273.5	93.1	1,035.6	3.9
2016	C	0.44	0.36	265.8	67.1	1,024.0	-40.2
2015	N/A	N/A	N/A	286.8	87.0	1,097.3	N/A
2014	B	1.08	0.90	227.7	45.4	539.8	10.4

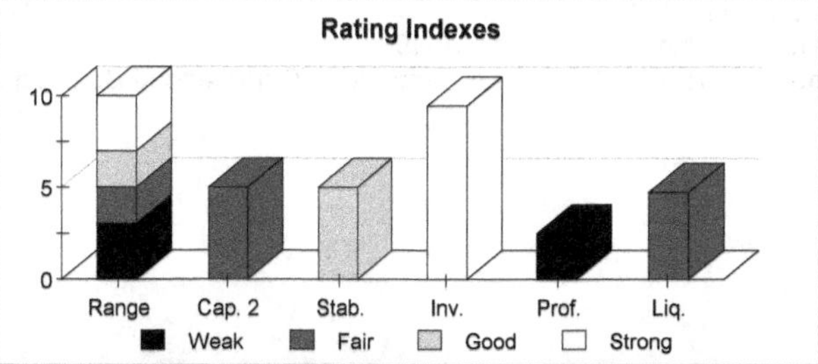

TRIPLE-S SALUD INC * B+ Good

Major Rating Factors: Good overall profitability index (6.3 on a scale of 0 to 10). Good liquidity (6.8) with sufficient resources (cash flows and marketable investments) to handle a spike in claims. Strong capitalization (7.9) based on excellent current risk-adjusted capital (severe loss scenario).
Other Rating Factors: High quality investment portfolio (7.8).
Principal Business: Medicaid (50%), comp med (38%), FEHB (10%), med supp (1%)
Mem Phys: 18: N/A **17:** N/A **18 MLR** 85.0% **/ 18 Admin Exp** N/A
Enroll(000): Q1 19: 811 **18:** 784 **17:** 876 **Med Exp PMPM:** $129
Principal Investments: Long-term bonds (49%), nonaffiliate common stock (21%), affiliate common stock (13%), cash and equiv (11%), other (6%)
Provider Compensation ($000): Contr fee ($1,233,911), capitation ($72,605)
Total Member Encounters: Phys (3,019,123), non-phys (1,435,439)
Group Affiliation: None
Licensed in: PR
Address: FD Roosevelt Ave 1441, San Juan, PR 920
Phone: (787) 749-4949 **Dom State:** PR **Commenced Bus:** N/A

Data Date	Rating	RACR #1	RACR #2	Total Assets ($mil)	Capital ($mil)	Net Premium ($mil)	Net Income ($mil)
3-19	B+	2.06	1.72	827.7	366.7	374.1	4.5
3-18	B	1.78	1.48	765.2	290.7	400.0	-15.0
2018	B+	2.04	1.70	795.2	362.8	1,565.7	27.7
2017	B	2.11	1.76	761.8	354.6	1,558.0	66.7
2016	B	3.10	2.58	701.1	371.2	1,626.3	38.4
2015	N/A	N/A	N/A	734.6	404.8	1,453.6	N/A
2014	B+	3.31	2.76	653.6	395.1	1,355.7	39.9

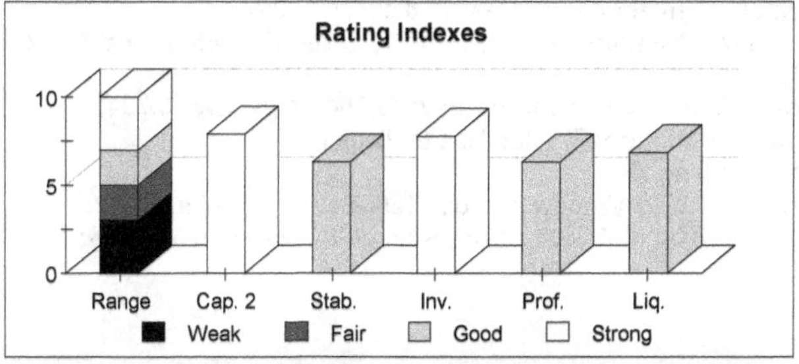

TRITON INS CO C+ Fair

Major Rating Factors: Fair profitability index (3.1 on a scale of 0 to 10). Weak expense controls. Return on equity has been fair, averaging 18.6% over the past five years. Fair overall results on stability tests (3.4) including excessive premium growth.
Other Rating Factors: Strong long-term capitalization index (9.4) based on excellent current risk adjusted capital (severe and moderate loss scenarios), despite some fluctuation in capital levels. Ample reserve history (7.5) that can protect against increases in claims costs. Excellent liquidity (7.0) with ample operational cash flow and liquid investments.
Principal Business: Aggregate write-ins for other lines of business (65%), credit accident & health (27%), and credit (8%).
Principal Investments: Investment grade bonds (84%), misc. investments (11%), cash (3%), and non investment grade bonds (2%).
Investments in Affiliates: None
Group Affiliation: Citigroup Inc
Licensed in: All states except PR
Commenced Business: July 1982
Address: 3001 Meacham Boulevard Ste 100, Fort Worth, TX 76137
Phone: (800) 307-0048 **Domicile State:** TX **NAIC Code:** 41211

Data Date	Rating	RACR #1	RACR #2	Loss Ratio %	Total Assets ($mil)	Capital ($mil)	Net Premium ($mil)	Net Income ($mil)
3-19	C+	4.81	2.82	N/A	463.0	123.4	31.8	7.0
3-18	B-	7.62	4.60	N/A	462.0	171.9	24.3	4.4
2018	C+	4.20	2.51	37.3	447.3	113.2	172.0	17.9
2017	B-	7.69	4.71	35.1	453.9	169.9	105.8	31.0
2016	C+	4.76	3.33	41.3	426.1	139.5	101.5	13.9
2015	B-	8.82	5.08	39.7	482.4	180.8	117.8	34.0
2014	C+	9.84	5.43	31.2	492.8	190.4	115.1	55.0

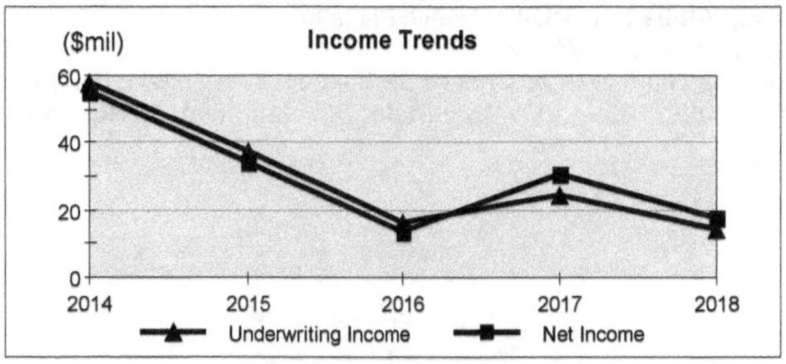

TRUE HEALTH NEW MEXICO INC — C — Fair

Major Rating Factors: Excellent profitability (7.7 on a scale of 0 to 10). Strong capitalization (7.0) based on excellent current risk-adjusted capital (severe loss scenario). High quality investment portfolio (9.2).
Other Rating Factors: Excellent liquidity (7.7) with ample operational cash flow and liquid investments.
Principal Business: Comp med (100%)
Mem Phys: 18: 10,259 **17:** N/A **18 MLR** 42.2% **/ 18 Admin Exp** N/A
Enroll(000): Q1 19: 17 **18:** 17 **17:** N/A **Med Exp PMPM:** $291
Principal Investments: Cash and equiv (73%), long-term bonds (27%)
Provider Compensation ($000): Contr fee ($48,990), FFS ($10,021)
Total Member Encounters: Phys (115,339), non-phys (25,491)
Group Affiliation: Evolent Health Inc
Licensed in: NM
Address: , Albuquerque, NM 87110
Phone: (505) 633-8020 **Dom State:** NM **Commenced Bus:** January 2018

Data Date	Rating	RACR #1	RACR #2	Total Assets ($mil)	Capital ($mil)	Net Premium ($mil)	Net Income ($mil)
3-19	C	1.34	1.12	66.3	23.0	47.0	0.4
3-18	N/A	N/A	N/A	38.8	21.5	23.1	0.7
2018	C-	1.30	1.08	65.8	22.3	159.7	1.5
2017	N/A	N/A	N/A	19.6	11.8	9.7	0.1
2016	N/A	N/A	N/A	N/A	N/A	N/A	N/A
2015	N/A	N/A	N/A	N/A	N/A	N/A	N/A
2014	N/A	N/A	N/A	N/A	N/A	N/A	N/A

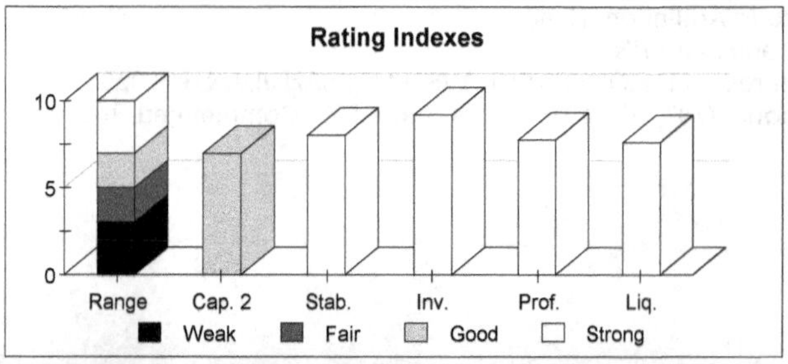

TRUSTED HEALTH PLAN (MI) INC — C — Fair

Major Rating Factors: Weak profitability index (1.5 on a scale of 0 to 10). Weak overall results on stability tests (1.8) based on a steep decline in capital during 2018, inconsistent enrollment growth in the past five years due to declines in 2017 and 2018. Potentially strong support from affiliation with Trusted Health Plans Inc. Good liquidity (6.9) with sufficient resources (cash flows and marketable investments) to handle a spike in claims.
Other Rating Factors: Strong capitalization index (7.5) based on excellent current risk-adjusted capital (severe loss scenario). High quality investment portfolio (9.4).
Principal Business: Medicaid (100%)
Mem Phys: 18: 15,027 **17:** 3,445 **18 MLR** 71.8% **/ 18 Admin Exp** N/A
Enroll(000): Q1 19: 9 **18:** 8 **17:** 9 **Med Exp PMPM:** $200
Principal Investments: Cash and equiv (100%)
Provider Compensation ($000): Contr fee ($11,430), FFS ($8,228), capitation ($2,952)
Total Member Encounters: Phys (8,654), non-phys (6,724)
Group Affiliation: Trusted Health Plans Inc
Licensed in: MI
Address: 3663 Woodward Suite 120, Detroit, MI 48201
Phone: (844) 427-2671 **Dom State:** MI **Commenced Bus:** N/A

Data Date	Rating	RACR #1	RACR #2	Total Assets ($mil)	Capital ($mil)	Net Premium ($mil)	Net Income ($mil)
3-19	C	1.74	1.45	16.7	6.3	8.4	0.1
3-18	C-	1.61	1.35	18.2	8.3	9.5	0.4
2018	C-	1.34	1.12	12.8	4.8	26.9	-3.6
2017	E	1.44	1.20	17.9	8.0	44.5	-0.1
2016	E	1.70	1.42	31.0	7.9	51.8	2.5
2015	E-	3.56	2.97	17.8	10.0	36.6	4.3
2014	E-	2.22	1.85	14.5	7.0	21.9	0.4

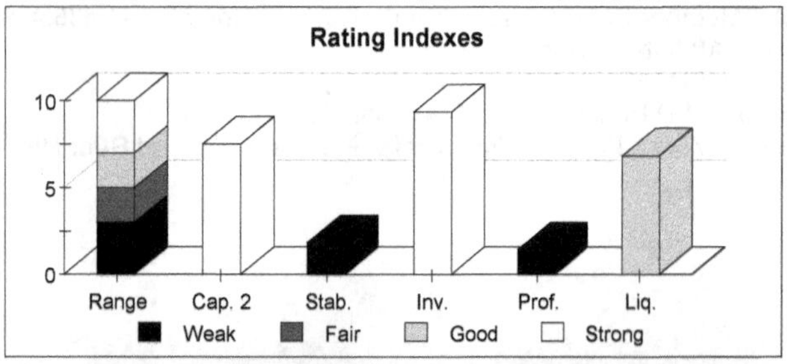

TRUSTED HEALTH PLAN INC — B — Good

Major Rating Factors: Fair liquidity (4.7 on a scale of 0 to 10) as cash resources may not be adequate to cover a spike in claims. Excellent profitability (10.0). Strong capitalization (7.3) based on excellent current risk-adjusted capital (severe loss scenario).
Other Rating Factors: High quality investment portfolio (8.4).
Principal Business: Medicaid (91%), comp med (9%)
Mem Phys: 18: 17,741 **17:** 6,839 **18 MLR** 69.0% **/ 18 Admin Exp** N/A
Enroll(000): Q1 19: 34 **18:** 34 **17:** 38 **Med Exp PMPM:** $261
Principal Investments: Long-term bonds (78%), cash and equiv (21%)
Provider Compensation ($000): Contr fee ($93,317), FFS ($14,816), capitation ($10,542)
Total Member Encounters: Phys (320,956), non-phys (125,602)
Group Affiliation: Trusted Health Plans Inc
Licensed in: DC, VA, WV
Address: 1100 New Jersey Ave SE Ste 840, Washington, DC 20003
Phone: (202) 821-1100 **Dom State:** DC **Commenced Bus:** N/A

Data Date	Rating	RACR #1	RACR #2	Total Assets ($mil)	Capital ($mil)	Net Premium ($mil)	Net Income ($mil)
3-19	B	1.60	1.33	60.9	21.8	36.0	2.6
3-18	C+	N/A	N/A	61.5	17.1	44.0	1.5
2018	B-	1.41	1.18	58.6	19.4	160.0	7.2
2017	C+	N/A	N/A	65.2	16.1	160.3	4.6
2016	C	0.83	0.70	45.0	14.8	147.4	4.2
2015	D+	0.66	0.55	39.8	12.3	131.6	4.3
2014	D	0.34	0.28	26.0	8.7	119.1	3.0

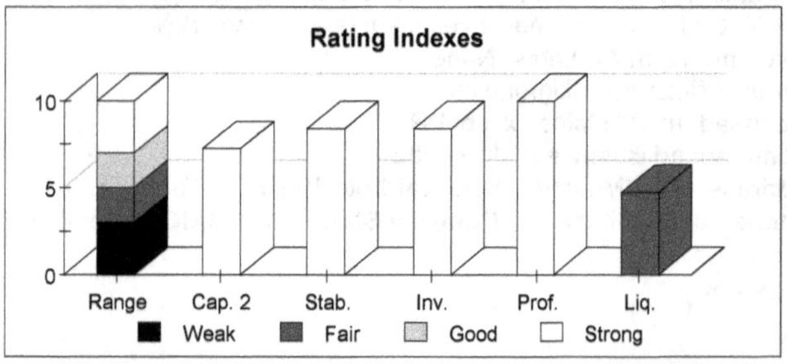

TRUSTMARK INSURANCE COMPANY * B+ Good

Major Rating Factors: Good overall profitability (6.6 on a scale of 0 to 10). Good overall results on stability tests (6.8). Stability strengths include excellent operational trends and excellent risk diversification. Fair quality investment portfolio (4.8).
Other Rating Factors: Strong capitalization (8.0) based on excellent risk adjusted capital (severe loss scenario). Excellent liquidity (7.0).
Principal Business: Group life insurance (47%), group health insurance (28%), individual health insurance (16%), individual life insurance (8%), and reinsurance (1%).
Principal Investments: NonCMO investment grade bonds (41%), CMOs and structured securities (26%), common & preferred stock (9%), mortgages in good standing (5%), and misc. investments (13%).
Investments in Affiliates: None
Group Affiliation: Trustmark Group Inc
Licensed in: All states, the District of Columbia and Puerto Rico
Commenced Business: January 1913
Address: 400 FIELD DRIVE, LAKE FOREST, IL 60045-2581
Phone: (847) 615-1500 **Domicile State:** IL **NAIC Code:** 61425

Data Date	Rating	RACR #1	RACR #2	Total Assets ($mil)	Capital ($mil)	Net Premium ($mil)	Net Income ($mil)
3-19	B+	2.88	1.66	1,625.3	342.8	90.9	3.1
3-18	B+	2.76	1.56	1,565.9	322.9	90.9	0.2
2018	B+	3.12	1.80	1,585.5	335.0	366.5	13.8
2017	B+	3.12	1.77	1,548.0	323.8	343.3	22.6
2016	B+	3.12	1.77	1,460.2	294.8	322.0	21.0
2015	B+	3.15	1.77	1,406.8	286.7	293.6	16.3
2014	B+	3.02	1.75	1,393.5	287.7	312.2	18.9

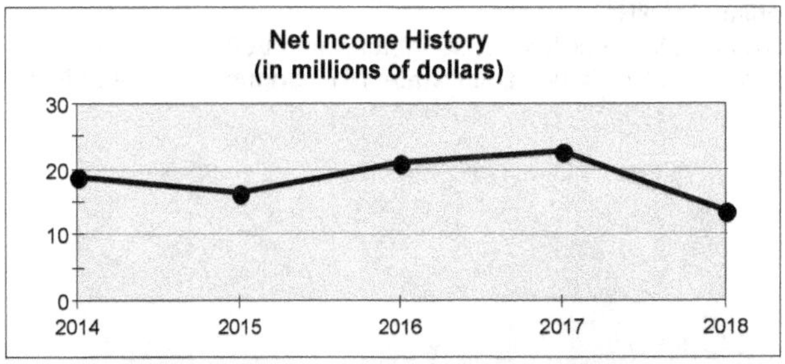

TRUSTMARK LIFE INSURANCE COMPANY * B+ Good

Major Rating Factors: Good overall results on stability tests (6.6 on a scale of 0 to 10). Stability strengths include excellent operational trends and excellent risk diversification. Strong capitalization (10.0) based on excellent risk adjusted capital (severe loss scenario). Capital levels have been relatively consistent over the last five years. High quality investment portfolio (8.0).
Other Rating Factors: Excellent profitability (8.4). Excellent liquidity (7.4).
Principal Business: Group health insurance (95%) and group life insurance (5%).
Principal Investments: NonCMO investment grade bonds (77%), CMOs and structured securities (13%), common & preferred stock (2%), and , and misc. investments (2%).
Investments in Affiliates: None
Group Affiliation: Trustmark Group Inc
Licensed in: All states except PR
Commenced Business: February 1925
Address: 400 FIELD DRIVE, LAKE FOREST, IL 60045-2581
Phone: (847) 615-1500 **Domicile State:** IL **NAIC Code:** 62863

Data Date	Rating	RACR #1	RACR #2	Total Assets ($mil)	Capital ($mil)	Net Premium ($mil)	Net Income ($mil)
3-19	B+	8.84	6.20	330.1	184.3	32.2	8.0
3-18	B+	7.62	4.78	321.8	169.3	31.4	3.5
2018	B+	8.38	5.94	319.9	175.5	124.6	25.7
2017	B+	7.49	4.70	303.0	164.4	112.6	17.4
2016	B+	6.63	4.33	308.6	162.7	137.4	16.7
2015	B+	5.62	3.77	321.3	159.8	163.7	8.4
2014	B+	4.41	3.01	353.2	162.6	206.9	14.0

Adverse Trends in Operations

Decrease in premium volume from 2016 to 2017 (18%)
Decrease in asset base during 2017 (2%)
Decrease in premium volume from 2015 to 2016 (16%)
Decrease in asset base during 2015 (9%)
Decrease in premium volume from 2014 to 2015 (21%)

TUFTS ASSOCIATED HEALTH MAINT ORG C Fair

Major Rating Factors: Fair quality investment portfolio (3.6 on a scale of 0 to 10). Good overall profitability index (6.2). Good overall results on stability tests (5.7).
Other Rating Factors: Good liquidity (6.7) with sufficient resources (cash flows and marketable investments) to handle a spike in claims. Strong capitalization index (10.0) based on excellent current risk-adjusted capital (severe loss scenario).
Principal Business: Medicare (50%), comp med (45%), Medicaid (5%)
Mem Phys: 18: 62,944 **17:** 57,744 **18 MLR** 85.0% **/ 18 Admin Exp** N/A
Enroll(000): Q1 19: 287 **18:** 289 **17:** 298 **Med Exp PMPM:** $637
Principal Investments: Nonaffiliate common stock (34%), long-term bonds (30%), affiliate common stock (18%), real estate (10%), cash and equiv (1%), other (7%)
Provider Compensation ($000): Contr fee ($908,694), capitation ($833,633), FFS ($250,165), bonus arrang ($226,731)
Total Member Encounters: Phys (1,889,461), non-phys (616,689)
Group Affiliation: Tufts Health Plan Inc
Licensed in: MA, RI
Address: 705 Mount Auburn Street, Watertown, MA 02472-1508
Phone: (617) 972-9400 **Dom State:** MA **Commenced Bus:** N/A

Data Date	Rating	RACR #1	RACR #2	Total Assets ($mil)	Capital ($mil)	Net Premium ($mil)	Net Income ($mil)
3-19	C	3.90	3.25	1,112.4	668.7	653.5	8.2
3-18	C	3.63	3.02	1,190.0	599.2	636.7	-19.9
2018	C	3.75	3.12	1,085.1	642.5	2,582.0	89.1
2017	C+	3.50	2.92	1,086.8	644.3	2,555.3	85.0
2016	B	2.95	2.45	1,245.3	786.5	2,553.4	-3.2
2015	B	3.12	2.60	1,126.6	745.4	2,519.1	54.6
2014	B	3.44	2.86	1,112.2	765.0	2,641.8	65.8

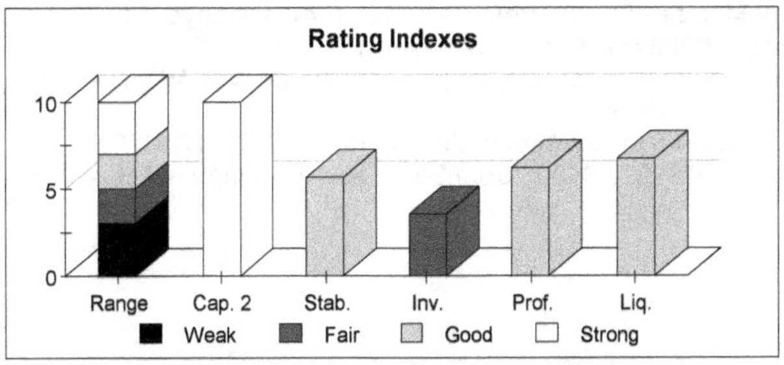

TUFTS HEALTH FREEDOM INS CO C- Fair

Major Rating Factors: Weak profitability index (0.9 on a scale of 0 to 10). Strong capitalization (8.9) based on excellent current risk-adjusted capital (severe loss scenario). High quality investment portfolio (7.7).
Other Rating Factors: Excellent liquidity (7.0) with sufficient resources (cash flows and marketable investments) to handle a spike in claims.
Principal Business: Comp med (100%)
Mem Phys: 18: 62,944 **17:** 52,724 **18 MLR** 85.2% **/ 18 Admin Exp** N/A
Enroll(000): Q1 19: 20 **18:** 19 **17:** 12 **Med Exp PMPM:** $398
Principal Investments: Long-term bonds (64%), cash and equiv (36%)
Provider Compensation ($000): Contr fee ($67,921), FFS ($12,853)
Total Member Encounters: Phys (55,246), non-phys (25,880)
Group Affiliation: Tufts Health Plan Inc
Licensed in: NH
Address: 705 Mount Auburn St, Watertown, MA 02472-1508
Phone: (617) 972-9400 **Dom State:** NH **Commenced Bus:** N/A

Data Date	Rating	RACR #1	RACR #2	Total Assets ($mil)	Capital ($mil)	Net Premium ($mil)	Net Income ($mil)
3-19	C-	2.90	2.42	47.2	19.0	29.2	0.7
3-18	C	N/A	N/A	34.4	12.4	23.2	N/A
2018	C-	2.81	2.35	44.6	18.4	95.5	-1.3
2017	C	N/A	N/A	27.4	10.5	42.9	-2.7
2016	C	8.60	7.17	20.3	13.3	5.3	-2.2
2015	N/A	N/A	N/A	15.7	12.5	N/A	-6.5
2014	N/A	N/A	N/A	N/A	N/A	N/A	N/A

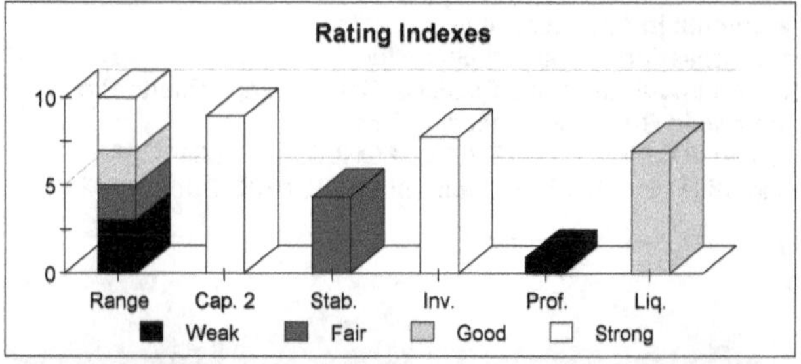

TUFTS HEALTH PUBLIC PLANS INC C Fair

Major Rating Factors: Fair profitability index (4.6 on a scale of 0 to 10). Low quality investment portfolio (2.3). Good liquidity (6.6) with sufficient resources (cash flows and marketable investments) to handle a spike in claims.
Other Rating Factors: Strong capitalization (8.4) based on excellent current risk-adjusted capital (severe loss scenario).
Principal Business: Medicaid (75%), comp med (25%)
Mem Phys: 18: 33,941 **17:** 29,113 **18 MLR** 89.5% **/ 18 Admin Exp** N/A
Enroll(000): Q1 19: 454 **18:** 439 **17:** 357 **Med Exp PMPM:** $369
Principal Investments: Nonaffiliate common stock (57%), long-term bonds (28%), cash and equiv (14%)
Provider Compensation ($000): Contr fee ($1,317,910), bonus arrang ($553,147), FFS ($66,601)
Total Member Encounters: Phys (5,623,834), non-phys (1,507,344)
Group Affiliation: Tufts Health Plan Inc
Licensed in: MA, RI
Address: 705 Mount Auburn St, Watertown, MA 02472-1508
Phone: (617) 972-9400 **Dom State:** MA **Commenced Bus:** N/A

Data Date	Rating	RACR #1	RACR #2	Total Assets ($mil)	Capital ($mil)	Net Premium ($mil)	Net Income ($mil)
3-19	C	2.47	2.06	715.6	330.3	523.4	29.4
3-18	C	1.91	1.59	652.3	229.3	526.8	-6.4
2018	C	2.11	1.76	654.0	278.7	2,151.8	54.0
2017	C	1.59	1.33	581.8	247.3	1,792.5	-6.1
2016	C+	1.98	1.65	529.7	193.5	1,528.3	-9.6
2015	C+	2.39	1.99	490.6	202.2	1,326.7	34.0
2014	C+	2.37	1.98	358.6	179.9	1,245.8	33.1

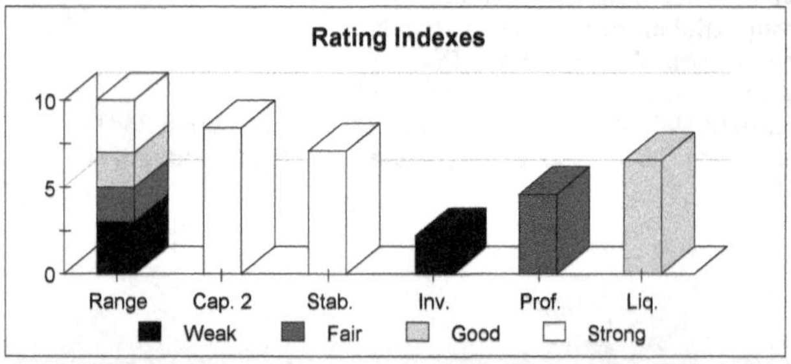

TUFTS INS CO C Fair

Major Rating Factors: Weak profitability index (1.9 on a scale of 0 to 10). Good liquidity (6.9) with sufficient resources (cash flows and marketable investments) to handle a spike in claims. Strong capitalization (10.0) based on excellent current risk-adjusted capital (severe loss scenario).
Other Rating Factors: High quality investment portfolio (9.9).
Principal Business: Comp med (75%), med supp (12%), other (13%)
Mem Phys: 18: 62,944 **17:** 57,744 **18 MLR** 83.6% **/ 18 Admin Exp** N/A
Enroll(000): Q1 19: 64 **18:** 60 **17:** 64 **Med Exp PMPM:** $337
Principal Investments: Long-term bonds (74%), cash and equiv (17%), nonaffiliate common stock (9%)
Provider Compensation ($000): Contr fee ($185,878), FFS ($54,304), other ($10,840)
Total Member Encounters: Phys (325,774), non-phys (132,341)
Group Affiliation: Tufts Health Plan Inc
Licensed in: AZ, CA, CT, DC, FL, GA, IL, IN, ME, MD, MA, MI, NH, NY, NC, OH, PA, RI, TX, VT, VA
Address: 705 Mount Auburn St, Watertown, MA 02472-1508
Phone: (617) 972-9400 **Dom State:** MA **Commenced Bus:** N/A

Data Date	Rating	RACR #1	RACR #2	Total Assets ($mil)	Capital ($mil)	Net Premium ($mil)	Net Income ($mil)
3-19	C	3.93	3.27	114.9	71.7	76.9	1.0
3-18	C-	2.50	2.08	102.6	47.5	73.5	-4.5
2018	C	3.88	3.23	113.5	70.8	294.4	9.4
2017	C-	1.79	1.49	98.9	52.6	278.8	-9.7
2016	C-	3.01	2.51	101.6	50.7	258.4	-21.9
2015	D+	3.32	2.77	97.8	53.4	263.1	-5.9
2014	D+	3.16	2.63	97.5	50.5	248.2	-17.8

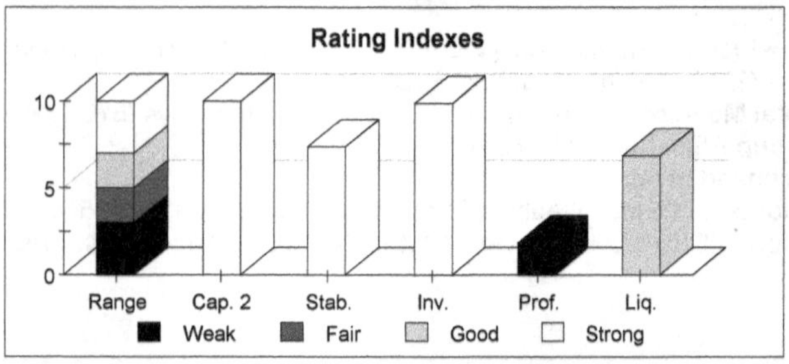

U S HEALTH & LIFE INS CO B Good

Major Rating Factors: Fair profitability index (4.4 on a scale of 0 to 10). Strong capitalization (10.0) based on excellent current risk-adjusted capital (severe loss scenario). High quality investment portfolio (9.9).
Other Rating Factors: Excellent liquidity (7.4) with ample operational cash flow and liquid investments.
Principal Business: Comp med (52%), other (46%)
Mem Phys: 18: N/A **17:** N/A **18 MLR** 83.5% **/ 18 Admin Exp** N/A
Enroll(000): Q1 19: 7 **18:** 9 **17:** 11 **Med Exp PMPM:** $217
Principal Investments: Cash and equiv (68%), long-term bonds (27%), real estate (5%)
Provider Compensation ($000): Contr fee ($27,638)
Total Member Encounters: Phys (41,984), non-phys (20,921)
Group Affiliation: None
Licensed in: AK, AZ, DC, DE, ID, IL, IN, KS, LA, MI, NE, NM, ND, OH, OR, SC, SD, TN, TX, UT, VA, WI
Address: 8220 Irving Rd, Sterling Heights, MI 48312
Phone: (586) 693-4300 **Dom State:** MI **Commenced Bus:** N/A

Data Date	Rating	RACR #1	RACR #2	Total Assets ($mil)	Capital ($mil)	Net Premium ($mil)	Net Income ($mil)
3-19	B	4.68	3.90	28.6	14.4	6.7	0.7
3-18	B	3.03	2.53	28.9	14.4	8.1	0.2
2018	B	4.46	3.71	28.4	13.7	32.7	-0.5
2017	B	2.99	2.49	26.4	14.2	31.8	0.3
2016	B	2.94	2.45	31.2	14.0	33.7	2.6
2015	B	2.60	2.16	29.5	11.3	38.4	3.0
2014	C-	1.49	1.25	26.8	8.3	56.9	-1.0

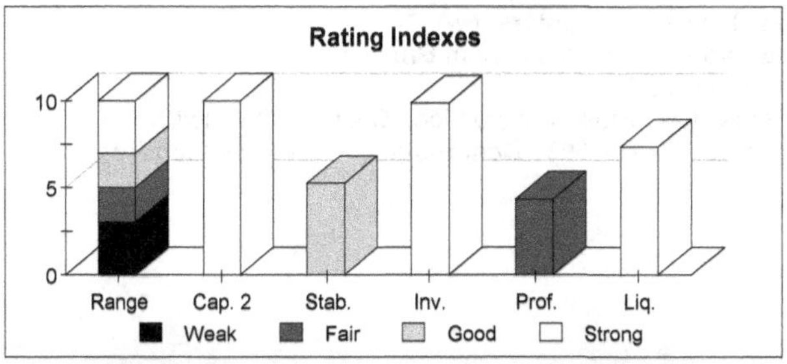

UCARE HEALTH INC C+ Fair

Major Rating Factors: Weak profitability index (0.9 on a scale of 0 to 10). Low quality investment portfolio (0.0). Strong capitalization (10.0) based on excellent current risk-adjusted capital (severe loss scenario).
Other Rating Factors: Excellent liquidity (10.0) with ample operational cash flow and liquid investments.
Principal Business: Comp med (96%), Medicare (4%)
Mem Phys: 18: N/A **17:** N/A **18 MLR** 94.9% **/ 18 Admin Exp** N/A
Enroll(000): Q1 19: 2 **18:** N/A **17:** N/A **Med Exp PMPM:** N/A
Principal Investments: Cash and equiv (100%)
Provider Compensation ($000): FFS ($6,367)
Total Member Encounters: Phys (3,702), non-phys (2,372)
Group Affiliation: None
Licensed in: MN, WI
Address: 500 Stinson Blvd NE, Minneapolis, MN 55413-2615
Phone: (612) 676-6500 **Dom State:** WI **Commenced Bus:** N/A

Data Date	Rating	RACR #1	RACR #2	Total Assets ($mil)	Capital ($mil)	Net Premium ($mil)	Net Income ($mil)
3-19	C+	15.49	12.91	37.2	35.1	5.7	-0.1
3-18	C	6.82	5.68	19.6	19.6	1.1	0.0
2018	C+	15.45	12.87	35.3	35.3	6.7	0.7
2017	E	4.58	3.82	19.7	19.6	8.9	5.0
2016	E	6.24	5.20	15.7	14.5	1.6	4.7
2015	E	0.77	0.64	22.9	9.7	55.8	-9.1
2014	E	0.30	0.25	23.5	3.6	73.9	-10.7

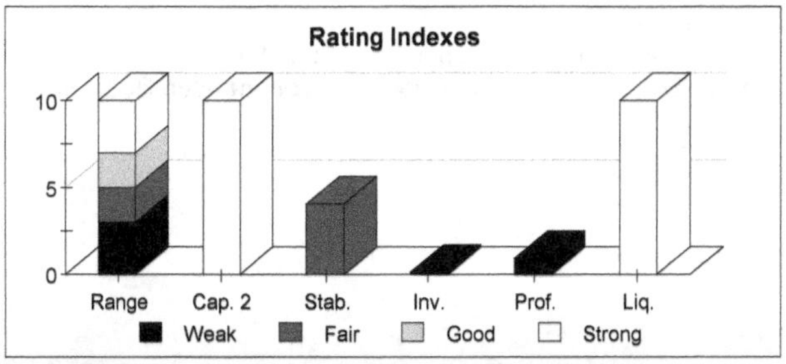

UCARE MINNESOTA B Good

Major Rating Factors: Good overall profitability index (5.0 on a scale of 0 to 10). Good liquidity (6.8) with sufficient resources (cash flows and marketable investments) to handle a spike in claims. Fair overall results on stability tests (4.8).
Other Rating Factors: Strong capitalization index (8.9) based on excellent current risk-adjusted capital (severe loss scenario). High quality investment portfolio (6.9).
Principal Business: Medicaid (70%), Medicare (25%), comp med (5%)
Mem Phys: 18: 38,194 **17:** 39,739 **18 MLR** 92.0% **/ 18 Admin Exp** N/A
Enroll(000): Q1 19: 422 **18:** 402 **17:** 381 **Med Exp PMPM:** $648
Principal Investments: Long-term bonds (55%), cash and equiv (29%), nonaffiliate common stock (11%), real estate (2%), affiliate common stock (1%), other (2%)
Provider Compensation ($000): Contr fee ($2,929,887), FFS ($141,084), capitation ($6,657)
Total Member Encounters: Phys (1,779,308), non-phys (2,377,368)
Group Affiliation: None
Licensed in: MN
Address: 500 Stinson Boulevard NE, Minneapolis, MN 55413
Phone: (612) 676-6500 **Dom State:** MN **Commenced Bus:** N/A

Data Date	Rating	RACR #1	RACR #2	Total Assets ($mil)	Capital ($mil)	Net Premium ($mil)	Net Income ($mil)
3-19	B	2.88	2.40	1,263.2	686.6	911.5	9.4
3-18	B	3.23	2.69	1,228.8	616.0	837.9	3.2
2018	B	2.76	2.30	1,340.5	662.8	3,419.1	39.8
2017	B	3.22	2.69	1,251.2	619.4	2,726.2	86.7
2016	B+	4.14	3.45	938.5	516.2	1,686.7	-25.0
2015	A	2.16	1.80	1,233.9	546.4	3,513.9	27.7
2014	A-	2.49	2.07	1,314.9	536.4	3,053.3	107.8

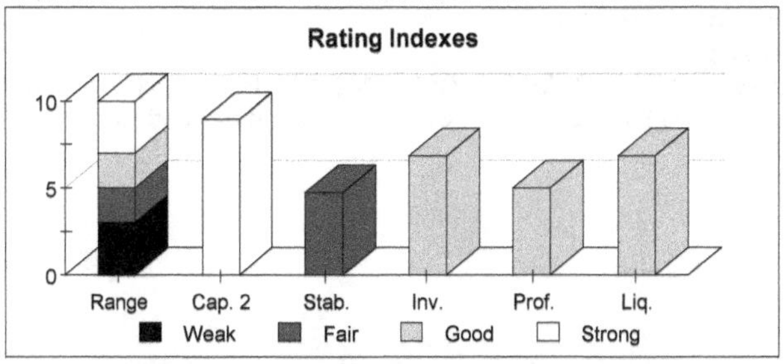

UHC OF CALIFORNIA INC — B- Good

Major Rating Factors: Good overall profitability index (6.7 on a scale of 0 to 10). Good overall results on stability tests (5.7). Rating is significantly influenced by the good financial results of UnitedHealth Group Inc. Strong capitalization index (7.1) based on good current risk-adjusted capital (moderate loss scenario).
Other Rating Factors: Excellent liquidity (6.9) with sufficient resources (cash flows and marketable investments) to handle a spike in claims.
Principal Business: Medicare (66%)
Mem Phys: 18: N/A **17:** N/A **18 MLR** 84.9% **/ 18 Admin Exp** N/A
Enroll(000): Q1 19: 783 **18:** 829 **17:** 869 **Med Exp PMPM:** $559
Principal Investments ($000): Cash and equiv ($298,275)
Provider Compensation ($000): None
Total Member Encounters: N/A
Group Affiliation: UnitedHealth Group Inc
Licensed in: CA
Address: 1221 Broadway 3rd Floor, Oakland, CA 94612
Phone: (510) 470-0590 **Dom State:** CA **Commenced Bus:** March 1975

Data Date	Rating	RACR #1	RACR #2	Total Assets ($mil)	Capital ($mil)	Net Premium ($mil)	Net Income ($mil)
3-19	B-	1.20	0.75	988.2	361.8	1,757.9	64.0
3-18	C	0.79	0.49	1,443.7	255.9	1,698.4	22.9
2018	B-	1.33	0.83	885.7	393.7	6,693.4	211.3
2017	C	0.73	0.45	865.6	238.3	6,605.9	91.2
2016	C+	0.98	0.61	837.4	293.1	6,668.2	114.0
2015	C+	1.18	0.73	778.4	314.4	6,267.3	143.7
2014	C+	1.45	0.90	824.7	354.2	6,195.4	209.1

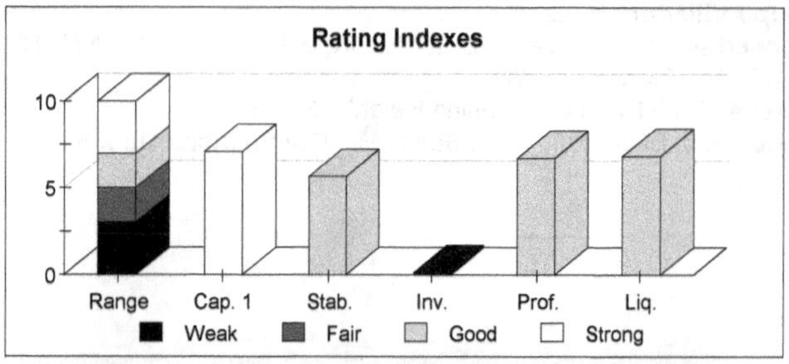

ULTIMATE HEALTH PLANS INC — E- Very Weak

Major Rating Factors: Weak profitability index (0.6 on a scale of 0 to 10). Poor capitalization (0.0) based on weak current risk-adjusted capital (severe loss scenario). Weak liquidity (0.1) as a spike in claims may stretch capacity.
Other Rating Factors: High quality investment portfolio (9.9).
Principal Business: Medicare (100%)
Mem Phys: 18: 935 **17:** 819 **18 MLR** 89.9% **/ 18 Admin Exp** N/A
Enroll(000): Q1 19: 8 **18:** 7 **17:** 7 **Med Exp PMPM:** $685
Principal Investments: Cash and equiv (98%), other (2%)
Provider Compensation ($000): FFS ($47,748), capitation ($4,115), contr fee ($1,895), bonus arrang ($227)
Total Member Encounters: Phys (211,135), non-phys (10,110)
Group Affiliation: Ultimate Healthcare Holdings LLC
Licensed in: FL
Address: 1244 Mariner Blvd, Spring Hill, FL 33609
Phone: (352) 835-7151 **Dom State:** FL **Commenced Bus:** N/A

Data Date	Rating	RACR #1	RACR #2	Total Assets ($mil)	Capital ($mil)	Net Premium ($mil)	Net Income ($mil)
3-19	E-	0.22	0.19	16.6	2.6	16.6	-1.2
3-18	E	N/A	N/A	20.8	6.1	15.8	-0.1
2018	E	0.35	0.29	17.6	3.9	62.2	-8.0
2017	E	N/A	N/A	15.0	6.2	56.5	-1.6
2016	E	0.83	0.69	12.8	6.5	52.0	0.4
2015	E	0.77	0.64	9.9	5.1	39.2	-0.5
2014	E	0.75	0.62	8.8	4.8	26.7	-1.9

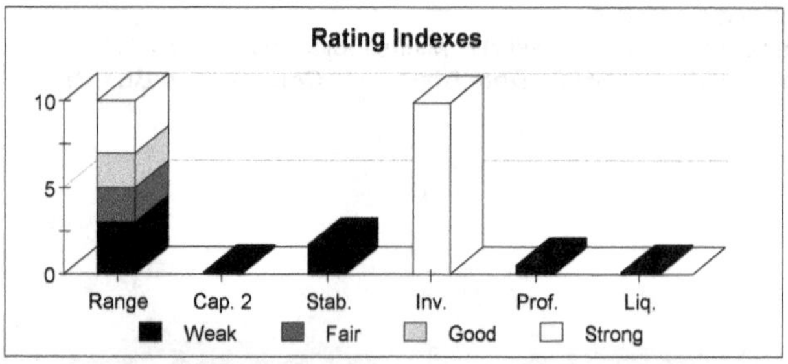

UNICARE HEALTH PLAN OF WEST VIRGINIA * — B+ Good

Major Rating Factors: Excellent profitability (8.6 on a scale of 0 to 10). Strong capitalization (10.0) based on excellent current risk-adjusted capital (severe loss scenario). High quality investment portfolio (7.7).
Other Rating Factors: Excellent liquidity (7.0) with ample operational cash flow and liquid investments.
Principal Business: Medicaid (100%)
Mem Phys: 18: 1,486 **17:** 1,444 **18 MLR** 81.8% **/ 18 Admin Exp** N/A
Enroll(000): Q1 19: 135 **18:** 137 **17:** 141 **Med Exp PMPM:** $219
Principal Investments: Long-term bonds (68%), cash and equiv (32%)
Provider Compensation ($000): Contr fee ($207,145), bonus arrang ($138,429), FFS ($27,971), capitation ($4,030)
Total Member Encounters: Phys (1,001,745), non-phys (890,900)
Group Affiliation: Anthem Inc
Licensed in: WV
Address: 200 ASSOCIATION Dr Ste 200, CHARLESTON, WV 25311
Phone: (877) 864-2273 **Dom State:** WV **Commenced Bus:** N/A

Data Date	Rating	RACR #1	RACR #2	Total Assets ($mil)	Capital ($mil)	Net Premium ($mil)	Net Income ($mil)
3-19	B+	3.73	3.11	150.9	93.7	110.6	8.3
3-18	A-	2.24	1.86	117.1	68.4	110.3	-2.2
2018	B+	3.41	2.84	150.9	85.3	449.0	21.4
2017	A-	1.50	1.25	116.5	71.1	503.0	1.9
2016	B+	2.52	2.10	120.0	71.7	484.5	15.7
2015	A-	3.20	2.67	100.9	58.8	314.7	2.0
2014	A-	4.16	3.47	83.0	59.9	275.5	24.5

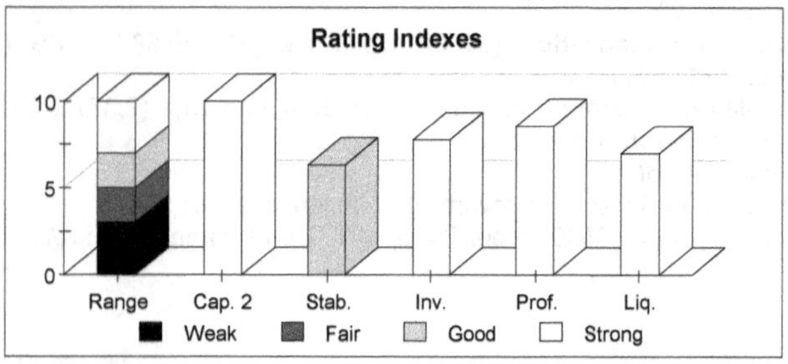

UNICARE LIFE & HEALTH INSURANCE COMPANY B- Good

Major Rating Factors: Good overall capitalization (5.4 on a scale of 0 to 10) based on mixed results -- excessive policy leverage mitigated by excellent risk adjusted capital (severe loss scenario). Nevertheless, capital levels have fluctuated during prior years. Fair quality investment portfolio (4.7). Fair profitability (3.3) with operating losses during the first three months of 2019.
Other Rating Factors: Fair overall results on stability tests (4.4). Weak liquidity (2.4).
Principal Business: Reinsurance (56%), group life insurance (33%), group health insurance (8%), and individual health insurance (4%).
Principal Investments: NonCMO investment grade bonds (76%) and noninv. grade bonds (12%).
Investments in Affiliates: None
Group Affiliation: Anthem Inc
Licensed in: All states, the District of Columbia and Puerto Rico
Commenced Business: December 1980
Address: 120 MONUMENT CIRCLE, INDIANAPOLIS, IN 46204
Phone: (877) 864-2273 **Domicile State:** IN **NAIC Code:** 80314

Data Date	Rating	RACR #1	RACR #2	Total Assets ($mil)	Capital ($mil)	Net Premium ($mil)	Net Income ($mil)
3-19	B-	1.75	1.35	540.8	93.7	160.1	-15.4
3-18	B-	1.79	1.36	272.3	69.6	74.6	0.3
2018	B-	1.71	1.31	310.6	60.5	353.9	-7.2
2017	B-	2.12	1.60	283.9	70.1	312.7	8.8
2016	B-	2.81	2.12	306.0	88.1	275.2	28.3
2015	B-	3.06	2.27	373.8	108.4	291.9	21.5
2014	B-	1.77	1.32	413.3	63.8	329.6	25.0

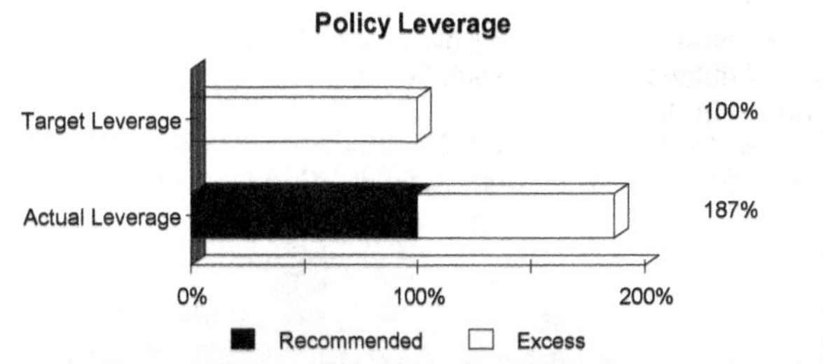

UNIMERICA INSURANCE COMPANY B Good

Major Rating Factors: Fair overall results on stability tests (4.5 on a scale of 0 to 10) including fair financial strength of affiliated UnitedHealth Group Inc and negative cash flow from operations for 2018. Strong capitalization (10.0) based on excellent risk adjusted capital (severe loss scenario). Capital levels have been relatively consistent over the last five years. High quality investment portfolio (8.5).
Other Rating Factors: Excellent profitability (8.8). Excellent liquidity (7.2).
Principal Business: Group health insurance (94%), reinsurance (4%), and group life insurance (2%).
Principal Investments: NonCMO investment grade bonds (82%) and CMOs and structured securities (15%).
Investments in Affiliates: None
Group Affiliation: UnitedHealth Group Inc
Licensed in: All states except NY, PR
Commenced Business: December 1980
Address: 10701 WEST RESEARCH DRIVE, MILWAUKEE, WI 53226-0649
Phone: (952) 979-6128 **Domicile State:** WI **NAIC Code:** 91529

Data Date	Rating	RACR #1	RACR #2	Total Assets ($mil)	Capital ($mil)	Net Premium ($mil)	Net Income ($mil)
3-19	B	4.63	3.63	431.4	241.1	101.0	8.3
3-18	B-	2.30	1.85	421.6	206.2	107.8	20.2
2018	B	4.14	3.24	436.7	230.7	431.8	62.5
2017	B	1.73	1.39	502.5	186.1	874.3	31.4
2016	B	1.43	1.15	476.4	154.7	877.0	21.1
2015	B	1.99	1.59	435.9	167.7	669.4	65.7
2014	B	2.54	2.02	415.0	187.8	582.4	76.9

UnitedHealth Group Inc
Composite Group Rating: C+

Largest Group Members	Assets ($mil)	Rating
UNITED HEALTHCARE INS CO	20752	C
SIERRA HEALTH AND LIFE INS CO INC	3270	B
OXFORD HEALTH INS INC	2570	B
UNITED HEALTHCARE OF WISCONSIN INC	1760	B+
UNITED HEALTHCARE INS CO OF NY	1262	B-

UNION FIDELITY LIFE INSURANCE COMPANY E Very Weak

Major Rating Factors: Weak profitability (1.4 on a scale of 0 to 10) with operating losses during the first three months of 2019. Weak overall results on stability tests (0.1) including weak risk adjusted capital in prior years, negative cash flow from operations for 2018. Fair quality investment portfolio (3.5) with large holdings of BBB rated bonds in addition to junk bond exposure equal to 64% of capital.
Other Rating Factors: Good capitalization (5.5) based on good risk adjusted capital (moderate loss scenario). Excellent liquidity (7.9).
Principal Business: Reinsurance (91%), group health insurance (5%), group life insurance (3%), individual life insurance (1%), and individual health insurance (1%).
Principal Investments: NonCMO investment grade bonds (78%), CMOs and structured securities (12%), mortgages in good standing (5%), and noninv. grade bonds (2%).
Investments in Affiliates: 1%
Group Affiliation: General Electric Corp Group
Licensed in: All states except NY, PR
Commenced Business: February 1926
Address: 7101 College Blvd Ste 1400, Overland Park, KS 66210
Phone: (913) 982-3700 **Domicile State:** KS **NAIC Code:** 62596

Data Date	Rating	RACR #1	RACR #2	Total Assets ($mil)	Capital ($mil)	Net Premium ($mil)	Net Income ($mil)
3-19	E	1.36	0.69	20,654.0	658.3	57.0	-20.9
3-18	E	1.10	0.55	20,368.8	527.5	60.8	4.1
2018	E	1.44	0.73	20,505.2	667.8	253.5	-298.8
2017	E	1.14	0.57	20,435.4	536.6	263.9	-1,210.0
2016	D+	1.53	0.76	19,644.5	765.8	266.4	-65.0
2015	D+	0.89	0.46	19,365.0	428.3	276.3	-60.9
2014	D+	1.04	0.54	19,673.7	518.4	285.9	-280.8

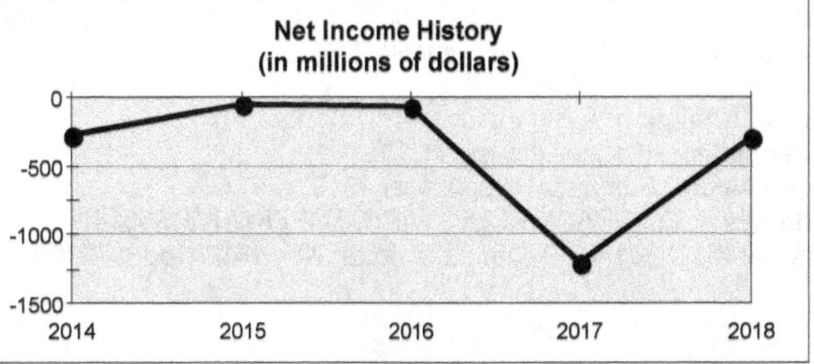

UNION HEALTH SERVICE INC — C+ Fair

Major Rating Factors: Fair profitability index (3.0 on a scale of 0 to 10). Good capitalization index (5.9) based on good current risk-adjusted capital (severe loss scenario). Good liquidity (6.9) with sufficient resources (cash flows and marketable investments) to handle a spike in claims.
Other Rating Factors: High quality investment portfolio (7.9). Excellent overall results on stability tests (7.1).
Principal Business: FEHB (7%), Medicare (3%), other (90%)
Mem Phys: 18: 290 **17:** 290 **18 MLR** 98.2% **/ 18 Admin Exp** N/A
Enroll(000): Q1 19: 48 **18:** 48 **17:** 46 **Med Exp PMPM:** $141
Principal Investments: Long-term bonds (42%), cash and equiv (34%), nonaffiliate common stock (24%)
Provider Compensation ($000): FFS ($23,753), contr fee ($1,902), other ($52,481)
Total Member Encounters: Phys (184,840), non-phys (62,522)
Group Affiliation: Union Health Service Inc
Licensed in: IL
Address: 1634 W POLK STREET, CHICAGO, IL 60612
Phone: (312) 423-4200 **Dom State:** IL **Commenced Bus:** N/A

Data Date	Rating	RACR #1	RACR #2	Total Assets ($mil)	Capital ($mil)	Net Premium ($mil)	Net Income ($mil)
3-19	C+	1.06	0.89	29.7	16.6	21.0	0.9
3-18	B	1.12	0.93	28.6	15.4	20.0	-0.2
2018	C+	0.91	0.76	27.4	14.3	80.8	-0.7
2017	B	1.01	0.85	28.3	14.0	73.5	-0.5
2016	B	1.00	0.83	25.6	14.8	73.7	1.0
2015	B	1.02	0.85	23.7	14.9	70.0	0.5
2014	B	1.21	1.01	23.5	14.8	68.2	0.3

Rating Indexes

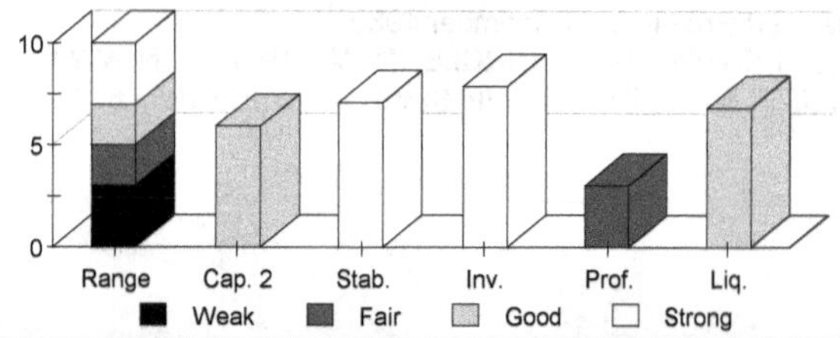

UNION LABOR LIFE INSURANCE COMPANY — B Good

Major Rating Factors: Good overall results on stability tests (6.3 on a scale of 0 to 10). Stability strengths include excellent operational trends and excellent risk diversification. Strong capitalization (7.6) based on excellent risk adjusted capital (severe loss scenario). Moreover, capital levels have been consistently high over the last five years. High quality investment portfolio (7.3).
Other Rating Factors: Excellent profitability (7.9). Excellent liquidity (7.7).
Principal Business: Group health insurance (61%), group life insurance (27%), reinsurance (9%), and group retirement contracts (2%).
Principal Investments: NonCMO investment grade bonds (53%), CMOs and structured securities (26%), common & preferred stock (6%), mortgages in good standing (6%), and noninv. grade bonds (1%).
Investments in Affiliates: 4%
Group Affiliation: ULLICO Inc
Licensed in: All states except PR
Commenced Business: May 1927
Address: 8403 COLESVILLE ROAD, SILVER SPRING, MD 20910
Phone: (202) 682-0900 **Domicile State:** MD **NAIC Code:** 69744

Data Date	Rating	RACR #1	RACR #2	Total Assets ($mil)	Capital ($mil)	Net Premium ($mil)	Net Income ($mil)
3-19	B	2.12	1.38	3,999.1	112.0	40.7	2.2
3-18	B	2.01	1.29	3,740.7	95.4	36.2	1.6
2018	B	2.11	1.37	3,892.6	108.7	150.2	13.3
2017	B	2.03	1.31	3,614.2	94.2	138.1	9.3
2016	B-	2.04	1.32	3,354.7	89.2	124.2	10.2
2015	B-	1.52	1.07	3,238.8	79.6	138.3	3.5
2014	B-	1.42	1.00	3,337.5	76.4	142.1	1.4

Adverse Trends in Operations

Decrease in premium volume from 2015 to 2016 (10%)
Decrease in premium volume from 2014 to 2015 (3%)
Decrease in asset base during 2015 (3%)

UNION SECURITY INSURANCE COMPANY — B Good

Major Rating Factors: Good quality investment portfolio (5.4 on a scale of 0 to 10) despite mixed results such as: minimal exposure to mortgages and large holdings of BBB rated bonds but small junk bond holdings. Good overall profitability (5.5). Good liquidity (5.1) with sufficient resources to handle a spike in claims.
Other Rating Factors: Fair overall results on stability tests (4.3) including negative cash flow from operations for 2018. Strong capitalization (7.8) based on excellent risk adjusted capital (severe loss scenario).
Principal Business: Group health insurance (64%), group life insurance (16%), individual health insurance (10%), individual life insurance (7%), and individual annuities (1%).
Principal Investments: NonCMO investment grade bonds (63%), CMOs and structured securities (14%), common & preferred stock (7%), mortgages in good standing (6%), and misc. investments (8%).
Investments in Affiliates: 1%
Group Affiliation: Assurant Inc
Licensed in: All states except NY, PR
Commenced Business: September 1910
Address: 2323 GRAND BOULEVARD, TOPEKA, KS 66614
Phone: (651) 361-4000 **Domicile State:** KS **NAIC Code:** 70408

Data Date	Rating	RACR #1	RACR #2	Total Assets ($mil)	Capital ($mil)	Net Premium ($mil)	Net Income ($mil)
3-19	B	2.91	1.50	2,637.1	131.1	1.0	16.9
3-18	B	2.58	1.34	2,693.0	121.6	1.0	29.3
2018	B	2.86	1.48	2,448.4	126.3	3.8	90.0
2017	B	2.37	1.23	2,698.7	113.9	4.1	106.2
2016	B	3.14	1.62	2,690.3	158.5	-1,468.9	481.7
2015	B	1.91	1.26	4,711.8	428.4	1,028.4	71.5
2014	B	1.82	1.18	4,937.1	415.7	1,016.0	67.3

Rating Indexes

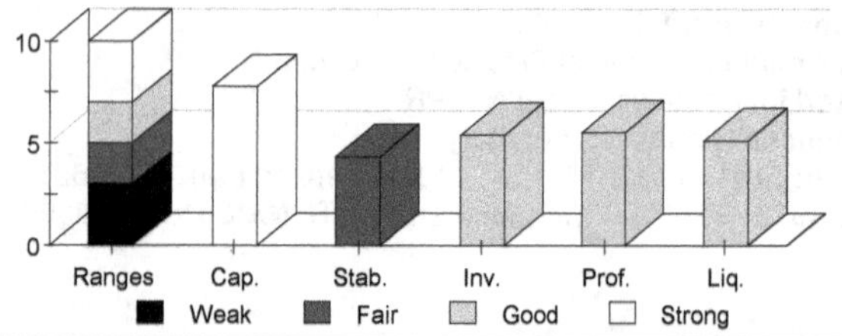

UNION SECURITY LIFE INSURANCE COMPANY OF NEW YORK C+ Fair

Major Rating Factors: Fair overall results on stability tests (3.0 on a scale of 0 to 10) including weak results on operational trends. Good overall profitability (5.9). Strong capitalization (10.0) based on excellent risk adjusted capital (severe loss scenario).
Other Rating Factors: High quality investment portfolio (8.1). Excellent liquidity (9.5).
Principal Business: N/A
Principal Investments: NonCMO investment grade bonds (74%), CMOs and structured securities (23%), and cash (1%).
Investments in Affiliates: None
Group Affiliation: Assurant Inc
Licensed in: NY
Commenced Business: April 1974
Address: 212 HIGHBRIDGE STREET SUITE D, FAYETTEVILLE, NY 13066
Phone: (315) 637-4232 **Domicile State:** NY **NAIC Code:** 81477

Data Date	Rating	RACR #1	RACR #2	Total Assets ($mil)	Capital ($mil)	Net Premium ($mil)	Net Income ($mil)
3-19	C+	6.77	6.09	60.6	48.5	0.2	0.9
3-18	C+	7.09	6.39	66.0	53.0	0.2	1.3
2018	C+	6.72	6.05	59.9	48.2	0.8	5.0
2017	C+	7.06	6.36	66.7	52.7	1.0	6.3
2016	B-	8.30	7.47	81.0	67.4	-72.0	22.0
2015	B+	4.34	3.91	128.3	39.5	21.6	3.3
2014	B+	4.66	4.19	138.7	42.8	23.8	5.6

Adverse Trends in Operations

Decrease in asset base during 2018 (10%)
Decrease in capital during 2017 (22%)
Decrease in asset base during 2017 (18%)
Change in asset mix during 2017 (11%)
Decrease in premium volume from 2015 to 2016 (433%)

UNITED AMERICAN INSURANCE COMPANY B- Good

Major Rating Factors: Good quality investment portfolio (6.2 on a scale of 0 to 10) despite mixed results such as: no exposure to mortgages and large holdings of BBB rated bonds but small junk bond holdings. Good overall profitability (6.8). Excellent expense controls. Good overall results on stability tests (5.2) good operational trends, good risk adjusted capital for prior years and excellent risk diversification.
Other Rating Factors: Fair liquidity (4.3). Strong capitalization (7.1) based on excellent risk adjusted capital (severe loss scenario).
Principal Business: Individual health insurance (53%), group health insurance (36%), reinsurance (5%), individual annuities (3%), and individual life insurance (3%).
Principal Investments: NonCMO investment grade bonds (76%), common & preferred stock (8%), noninv. grade bonds (4%), CMOs and structured securities (4%), and policy loans (1%).
Investments in Affiliates: 13%
Group Affiliation: Torchmark Corp
Licensed in: All states except NY, PR
Commenced Business: August 1981
Address: 10306 REGENCY PARKWAY DR, OMAHA, NE 68114
Phone: (972) 529-5085 **Domicile State:** NE **NAIC Code:** 92916

Data Date	Rating	RACR #1	RACR #2	Total Assets ($mil)	Capital ($mil)	Net Premium ($mil)	Net Income ($mil)
3-19	B-	1.44	1.08	760.7	145.5	128.7	3.8
3-18	B-	1.32	0.99	775.4	132.1	123.6	15.2
2018	B-	1.52	1.14	743.3	158.3	488.5	30.4
2017	B-	1.56	1.17	766.7	162.0	481.4	88.1
2016	B-	1.07	0.78	1,563.3	157.7	706.0	37.1
2015	B-	1.24	0.90	1,559.7	192.7	815.3	80.1
2014	B-	1.01	0.74	1,694.9	178.4	870.9	29.5

Adverse Trends in Operations

Decrease in asset base during 2017 (51%)
Decrease in premium volume from 2016 to 2017 (32%)
Decrease in capital during 2016 (18%)
Decrease in premium volume from 2015 to 2016 (13%)
Decrease in premium volume from 2014 to 2015 (6%)

UNITED HEALTHCARE INS CO OF IL * B+ Good

Major Rating Factors: Good liquidity (6.8 on a scale of 0 to 10) with sufficient resources (cash flows and marketable investments) to handle a spike in claims. Excellent profitability (9.1). Strong capitalization (8.9) based on excellent current risk-adjusted capital (severe loss scenario).
Other Rating Factors: High quality investment portfolio (9.0).
Principal Business: Comp med (100%)
Mem Phys: 18: 54,728 **17:** 51,172 **18 MLR** 79.6% **/ 18 Admin Exp** N/A
Enroll(000): Q1 19: 208 **18:** 217 **17:** 238 **Med Exp PMPM:** $372
Principal Investments: Long-term bonds (85%), cash and equiv (13%), other (2%)
Provider Compensation ($000): Contr fee ($923,013), FFS ($68,771), capitation ($1,369), bonus arrang ($237)
Total Member Encounters: Phys (2,613,992), non-phys (95,088)
Group Affiliation: None
Licensed in: IL
Address: 200 EAST RANDOLPH St Ste 5300, CHICAGO, IL 60601
Phone: (312) 424-4460 **Dom State:** IL **Commenced Bus:** N/A

Data Date	Rating	RACR #1	RACR #2	Total Assets ($mil)	Capital ($mil)	Net Premium ($mil)	Net Income ($mil)
3-19	B+	2.86	2.38	546.3	193.0	295.8	31.4
3-18	B+	2.61	2.18	396.1	165.3	313.2	9.5
2018	B+	2.41	2.01	361.6	162.5	1,249.1	71.4
2017	B+	1.73	1.44	350.1	153.1	1,211.2	87.8
2016	B	1.95	1.63	302.3	109.9	1,065.1	44.0
2015	B	2.47	2.06	266.0	117.3	939.9	60.5
2014	B	2.09	1.74	246.7	106.3	932.7	24.7

Rating Indexes

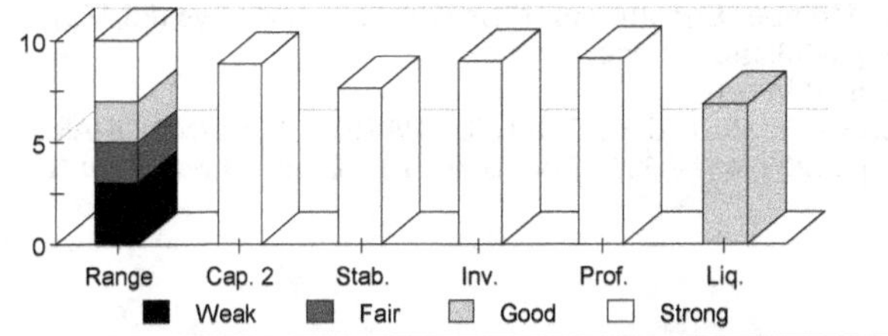

UNITED HEALTHCARE INS CO OF NY — B — Good

Major Rating Factors: Fair liquidity (4.1 on a scale of 0 to 10) as cash resources may not be adequate to cover a spike in claims. Excellent profitability (8.4). Strong capitalization (10.0) based on excellent current risk-adjusted capital (severe loss scenario).
Other Rating Factors: High quality investment portfolio (9.2).
Principal Business: Medicare (49%), med supp (25%), comp med (16%), dental (1%), other (8%)
Mem Phys: 18: 91,159 **17:** 95,998 **18 MLR** 118.3% **/ 18 Admin Exp** N/A
Enroll(000): Q1 19: 1,403 **18:** 1,400 **17:** 1,407 **Med Exp PMPM:** $159
Principal Investments: Long-term bonds (93%), cash and equiv (7%)
Provider Compensation ($000): Contr fee ($1,996,075), FFS ($583,461), capitation ($42,054), bonus arrang ($11,919), other ($16,942)
Total Member Encounters: Phys (10,627,568), non-phys (1,374,390)
Group Affiliation: None
Licensed in: DC, NY
Address: 2950 EXPRESSWAY Dr S Ste 240, ISLANDIA, NY 11749-1412
Phone: (877) 832-7734 **Dom State:** NY **Commenced Bus:** N/A

Data Date	Rating	RACR #1	RACR #2	Total Assets ($mil)	Capital ($mil)	Net Premium ($mil)	Net Income ($mil)
3-19	B	7.70	6.42	1,381.2	642.1	568.0	32.9
3-18	B-	10.19	8.49	1,510.4	504.2	582.0	-10.5
2018	B-	7.22	6.01	1,350.4	601.4	2,257.0	102.2
2017	B-	8.28	6.90	1,261.8	506.3	1,774.5	52.2
2016	B-	19.57	16.30	1,228.8	462.9	1,664.4	61.4
2015	B-	36.40	30.33	1,223.3	474.4	1,448.9	48.2
2014	B-	38.77	32.31	1,180.3	475.1	1,386.3	55.5

Rating Indexes

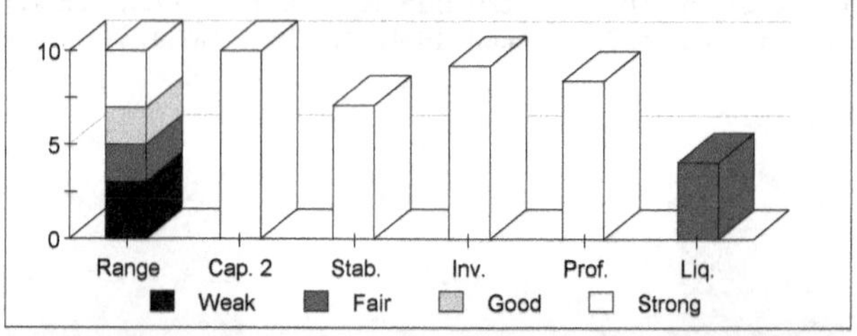

UNITED HEALTHCARE INSURANCE COMPANY — C — Fair

Major Rating Factors: Fair overall results on stability tests (3.9 on a scale of 0 to 10) including fair risk adjusted capital in prior years. Good current capitalization (5.0) based on mixed results -- excessive policy leverage mitigated by good risk adjusted capital (severe loss scenario) reflecting some improvement over results in 2016. Good quality investment portfolio (6.4).
Other Rating Factors: Weak liquidity (1.9). Excellent profitability (9.1).
Principal Business: Group health insurance (86%), individual health insurance (9%), and reinsurance (4%).
Principal Investments: NonCMO investment grade bonds (56%), common & preferred stock (19%), CMOs and structured securities (18%), noninv. grade bonds (4%), and misc. investments (2%).
Investments in Affiliates: 16%
Group Affiliation: UnitedHealth Group Inc
Licensed in: All states except NY
Commenced Business: April 1972
Address: 185 ASYLUM STREET, HARTFORD, CT 06103-3408
Phone: (877) 832-7734 **Domicile State:** CT **NAIC Code:** 79413

Data Date	Rating	RACR #1	RACR #2	Total Assets ($mil)	Capital ($mil)	Net Premium ($mil)	Net Income ($mil)
3-19	C	1.02	0.85	19,982.2	7,133.9	14,148.8	562.0
3-18	C	0.81	0.68	20,336.6	4,933.1	13,793.3	-186.8
2018	C	1.05	0.88	20,752.5	8,128.2	54,442.0	3,080.5
2017	C	0.89	0.75	19,617.5	6,355.2	50,538.6	2,599.6
2016	C	0.79	0.67	17,922.6	5,250.4	44,379.2	1,924.6
2015	C	0.89	0.75	15,791.2	5,589.7	41,950.2	1,930.3
2014	C	0.82	0.69	15,113.4	5,595.8	43,936.4	2,658.1

Rating Indexes

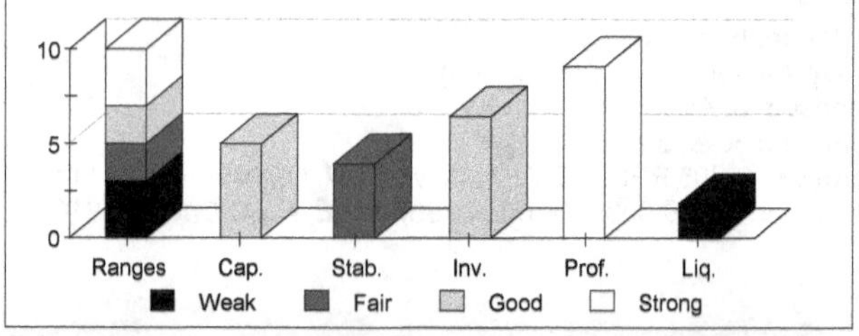

UNITED HEALTHCARE OF ALABAMA INC — C — Fair

Major Rating Factors: Fair overall results on stability tests (4.2 on a scale of 0 to 10) based on an excessive 237% enrollment growth during the period. Rating is significantly influenced by the good financial results of . Excellent profitability (7.7). Strong capitalization index (10.0) based on excellent current risk-adjusted capital (severe loss scenario).
Other Rating Factors: High quality investment portfolio (9.0). Excellent liquidity (7.4) with ample operational cash flow and liquid investments.
Principal Business: Medicare (82%), comp med (14%), Medicaid (3%), med supp (1%)
Mem Phys: 18: 14,988 **17:** 13,943 **18 MLR** 85.3% **/ 18 Admin Exp** N/A
Enroll(000): Q1 19: 13 **18:** 11 **17:** 3 **Med Exp PMPM:** $642
Principal Investments: Long-term bonds (58%), cash and equiv (42%)
Provider Compensation ($000): Contr fee ($58,152), FFS ($11,953), capitation ($3,092), bonus arrang ($39)
Total Member Encounters: Phys (201,884), non-phys (85,182)
Group Affiliation: None
Licensed in: AL
Address: 33 INVERNESS CENTER PARKWAY, BIRMINGHAM, AL 35242
Phone: (205) 437-8500 **Dom State:** AL **Commenced Bus:** N/A

Data Date	Rating	RACR #1	RACR #2	Total Assets ($mil)	Capital ($mil)	Net Premium ($mil)	Net Income ($mil)
3-19	C	72.65	60.54	61.6	38.7	35.3	2.5
3-18	C	213.60	178.00	82.1	38.9	17.9	0.0
2018	C	68.18	56.81	78.7	36.0	93.9	2.1
2017	C	125.90	104.90	74.9	38.3	2.8	4.3
2016	B	2.46	2.05	176.2	56.4	559.7	10.2
2015	B	3.66	3.05	142.7	51.2	455.7	20.6
2014	B	3.40	2.83	121.1	61.3	426.0	29.9

Rating Indexes

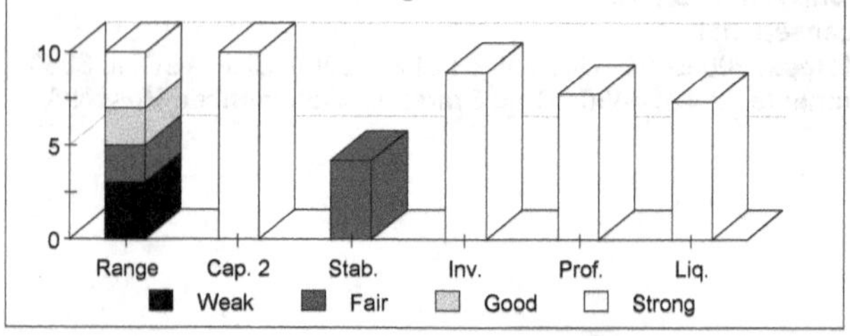

UNITED HEALTHCARE OF ARIZONA INC C Fair

Major Rating Factors: Fair overall results on stability tests (4.6 on a scale of 0 to 10) based on a significant 36% decrease in enrollment during the period. Rating is significantly influenced by the good financial results of . Low quality investment portfolio (0.5). Excellent profitability (8.2).
Other Rating Factors: Strong capitalization index (10.0) based on excellent current risk-adjusted capital (severe loss scenario). Excellent liquidity (7.5) with ample operational cash flow and liquid investments.
Principal Business: Comp med (100%)
Mem Phys: 18: 28,509 **17:** 26,598 **18 MLR** 78.6% **/ 18 Admin Exp** N/A
Enroll(000): Q1 19: 16 **18:** 16 **17:** 24 **Med Exp PMPM:** $420
Principal Investments: Cash and equiv (96%), long-term bonds (4%)
Provider Compensation ($000): Contr fee ($90,969), FFS ($6,869), capitation ($1,861)
Total Member Encounters: Phys (212,047), non-phys (9,702)
Group Affiliation: None
Licensed in: AZ
Address: 1 EAST WASHINGTON STREET, PHOENIX, AZ 85004
Phone: (952) 979-6171 **Dom State:** AZ **Commenced Bus:** N/A

Data Date	Rating	RACR #1	RACR #2	Total Assets ($mil)	Capital ($mil)	Net Premium ($mil)	Net Income ($mil)
3-19	C	5.35	4.46	52.8	26.6	27.7	2.6
3-18	C	4.87	4.06	59.9	23.0	34.4	0.0
2018	C	4.83	4.03	49.1	23.8	125.2	9.1
2017	C-	2.76	2.30	53.5	22.5	127.3	6.1
2016	C	4.41	3.67	39.4	17.4	111.4	0.6
2015	C	2.85	2.38	64.9	32.3	256.3	14.0
2014	B	3.14	2.62	89.9	53.5	325.3	16.6

Rating Indexes

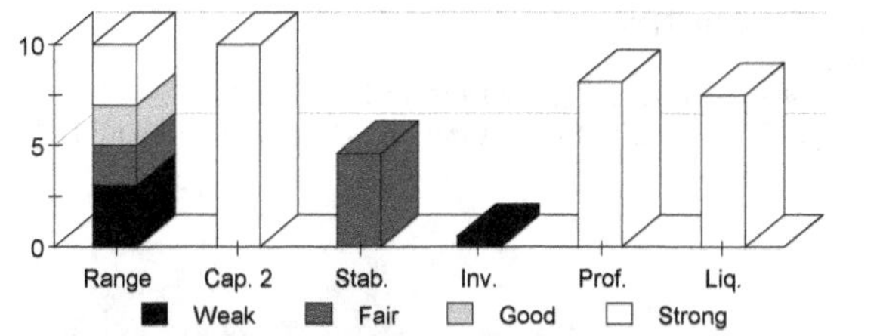

UNITED HEALTHCARE OF ARKANSAS INC B- Good

Major Rating Factors: Fair profitability index (4.4 on a scale of 0 to 10). Fair overall results on stability tests (4.4) based on an excessive 80% enrollment growth during the period. Rating is significantly influenced by the good financial results of . Strong capitalization index (10.0) based on excellent current risk-adjusted capital (severe loss scenario).
Other Rating Factors: High quality investment portfolio (9.9). Excellent liquidity (7.5) with ample operational cash flow and liquid investments.
Principal Business: Medicare (63%), comp med (37%)
Mem Phys: 18: 10,794 **17:** 10,248 **18 MLR** 75.2% **/ 18 Admin Exp** N/A
Enroll(000): Q1 19: 13 **18:** 9 **17:** 5 **Med Exp PMPM:** $466
Principal Investments: Cash and equiv (99%), long-term bonds (1%)
Provider Compensation ($000): Contr fee ($39,222), FFS ($5,713), capitation ($967), bonus arrang ($14)
Total Member Encounters: Phys (123,641), non-phys (33,485)
Group Affiliation: None
Licensed in: AR
Address: 1401 CAPITOL AVE 3RD FLOOR STE, LITTLE ROCK, AR 72201-2994
Phone: (501) 664-7700 **Dom State:** AR **Commenced Bus:** N/A

Data Date	Rating	RACR #1	RACR #2	Total Assets ($mil)	Capital ($mil)	Net Premium ($mil)	Net Income ($mil)
3-19	B-	4.89	4.08	37.7	20.3	30.0	1.4
3-18	C	11.28	9.40	29.5	17.8	14.7	0.4
2018	B-	4.55	3.79	28.9	18.8	65.2	4.9
2017	D-	6.14	5.12	21.7	17.0	22.1	4.4
2016	D-	2.49	2.08	43.1	16.7	41.7	-9.7
2015	B	6.74	5.61	10.0	7.1	10.2	0.9
2014	B	9.23	7.69	10.0	7.8	8.2	0.6

Rating Indexes

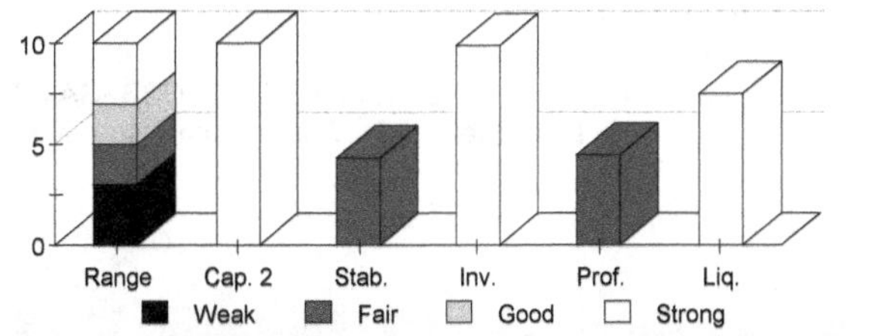

UNITED HEALTHCARE OF COLORADO INC C Fair

Major Rating Factors: Low quality investment portfolio (0.5 on a scale of 0 to 10). Good overall profitability index (5.7). Good overall results on stability tests (5.0). Rating is significantly influenced by the good financial results of .
Other Rating Factors: Strong capitalization index (9.5) based on excellent current risk-adjusted capital (severe loss scenario). Excellent liquidity (7.5) with ample operational cash flow and liquid investments.
Principal Business: Comp med (100%)
Mem Phys: 18: 25,905 **17:** 24,285 **18 MLR** 75.6% **/ 18 Admin Exp** N/A
Enroll(000): Q1 19: 24 **18:** 24 **17:** 22 **Med Exp PMPM:** $249
Principal Investments: Cash and equiv (99%), long-term bonds (1%)
Provider Compensation ($000): Contr fee ($59,314), capitation ($4,136), FFS ($3,708), bonus arrang ($23)
Total Member Encounters: Phys (131,569), non-phys (4,341)
Group Affiliation: None
Licensed in: CO
Address: 6465 SOUTH GREENWOOD PLAZA BLV, CENTENNIAL, CO 80111
Phone: (952) 936-1300 **Dom State:** CO **Commenced Bus:** N/A

Data Date	Rating	RACR #1	RACR #2	Total Assets ($mil)	Capital ($mil)	Net Premium ($mil)	Net Income ($mil)
3-19	C	3.32	2.77	48.3	16.3	24.4	0.7
3-18	C	3.01	2.51	41.2	12.6	22.5	2.1
2018	C	3.15	2.63	43.1	15.4	92.3	4.9
2017	D-	1.46	1.22	35.8	10.9	73.2	0.8
2016	D-	1.74	1.45	31.8	9.8	87.9	0.0
2015	C	3.12	2.60	18.4	5.9	36.4	-0.9
2014	B	5.38	4.48	16.0	10.9	32.1	2.3

Rating Indexes

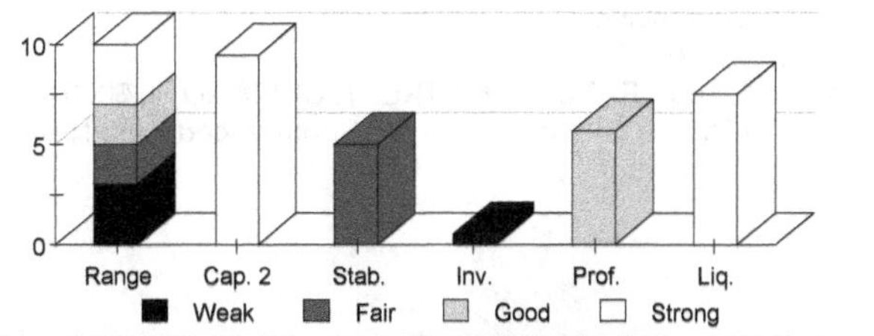

UNITED HEALTHCARE OF FLORIDA INC C+ Fair

Major Rating Factors: Fair profitability index (3.4 on a scale of 0 to 10). Fair overall results on stability tests (4.4). Rating is significantly influenced by the good financial results of . Good liquidity (6.7) with sufficient resources (cash flows and marketable investments) to handle a spike in claims.

Other Rating Factors: Strong capitalization index (7.6) based on excellent current risk-adjusted capital (severe loss scenario). High quality investment portfolio (9.8).

Principal Business: Medicaid (74%), comp med (26%)

Mem Phys: 18: 62,780 **17:** 58,410 **18 MLR** 86.2% **/ 18 Admin Exp** N/A

Enroll(000): Q1 19: 370 **18:** 395 **17:** 395 **Med Exp PMPM:** $449

Principal Investments: Long-term bonds (69%), cash and equiv (31%)

Provider Compensation ($000): Contr fee ($1,708,972), FFS ($318,900), capitation ($126,289), bonus arrang ($10,632)

Total Member Encounters: Phys (2,882,412), non-phys (2,069,583)

Group Affiliation: None

Licensed in: FL

Address: 495 NORTH KELLER ROAD SUITE 20, MAITLAND, FL 32751

Phone: (407) 659-6900 **Dom State:** FL **Commenced Bus:** N/A

Data Date	Rating	RACR #1	RACR #2	Total Assets ($mil)	Capital ($mil)	Net Premium ($mil)	Net Income ($mil)
3-19	C+	1.85	1.54	521.9	251.3	516.1	11.8
3-18	C	2.09	1.74	629.4	267.1	618.7	-0.6
2018	C+	1.72	1.43	534.9	231.1	2,493.0	32.9
2017	D+	1.56	1.30	598.7	269.3	2,454.9	91.2
2016	D+	2.15	1.79	792.7	348.7	3,000.4	84.7
2015	C	1.48	1.23	808.6	274.5	3,248.8	-12.9
2014	C	0.78	0.65	651.3	105.0	2,349.5	-165.1

Rating Indexes

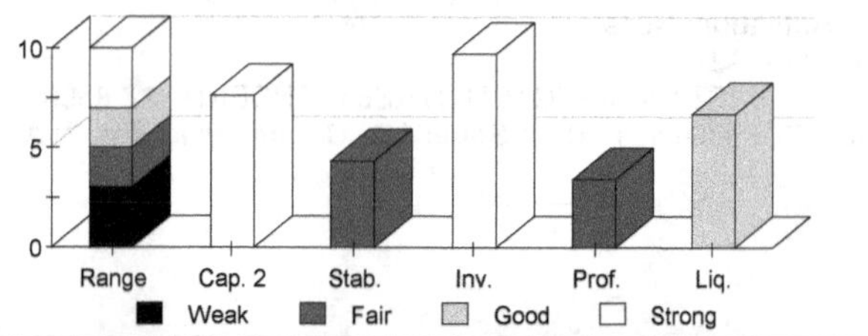

UNITED HEALTHCARE OF GEORGIA INC C+ Fair

Major Rating Factors: Fair overall results on stability tests (3.9 on a scale of 0 to 10). Rating is significantly influenced by the good financial results of . Good liquidity (5.5) with sufficient resources (cash flows and marketable investments) to handle a spike in claims. Weak profitability index (2.6).

Other Rating Factors: Strong capitalization index (7.6) based on excellent current risk-adjusted capital (severe loss scenario). High quality investment portfolio (9.6).

Principal Business: Comp med (64%), Medicare (36%)

Mem Phys: 18: 30,341 **17:** 29,493 **18 MLR** 89.4% **/ 18 Admin Exp** N/A

Enroll(000): Q1 19: 53 **18:** 60 **17:** 55 **Med Exp PMPM:** $449

Principal Investments: Long-term bonds (94%), cash and equiv (6%)

Provider Compensation ($000): Contr fee ($270,262), FFS ($41,348), capitation ($6,239), bonus arrang ($1,369)

Total Member Encounters: Phys (697,449), non-phys (136,205)

Group Affiliation: None

Licensed in: GA

Address: 3720 DAVINCI COURT SUITE 300, NORCROSS, GA 30092

Phone: (770) 300-3501 **Dom State:** GA **Commenced Bus:** N/A

Data Date	Rating	RACR #1	RACR #2	Total Assets ($mil)	Capital ($mil)	Net Premium ($mil)	Net Income ($mil)
3-19	C+	1.86	1.55	96.0	39.0	89.5	8.2
3-18	B	2.50	2.09	110.6	35.6	90.1	-3.5
2018	C+	1.54	1.28	95.5	31.5	363.7	-8.3
2017	B	1.64	1.36	89.5	39.1	281.5	14.0
2016	C+	2.54	2.12	105.0	45.2	287.3	21.9
2015	C	2.72	2.27	91.5	28.0	174.0	-35.2
2014	B-	4.45	3.71	45.5	30.2	123.6	8.4

Rating Indexes

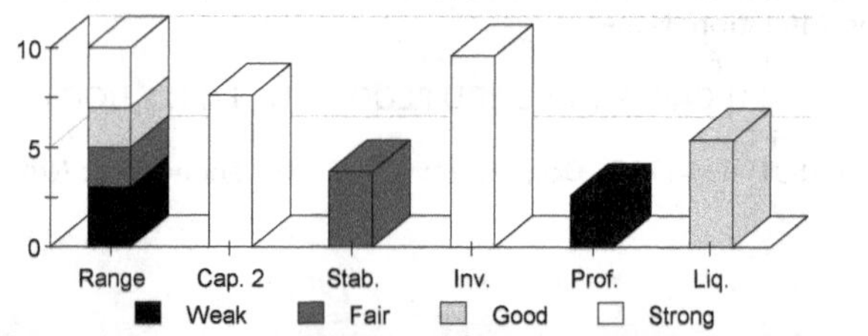

UNITED HEALTHCARE OF ILLINOIS INC B Good

Major Rating Factors: Good overall results on stability tests (6.1 on a scale of 0 to 10). Rating is significantly influenced by the good financial results of . Good liquidity (6.9) with sufficient resources (cash flows and marketable investments) to handle a spike in claims. Excellent profitability (9.3).

Other Rating Factors: Strong capitalization index (10.0) based on excellent current risk-adjusted capital (severe loss scenario). High quality investment portfolio (8.1).

Principal Business: Comp med (100%)

Mem Phys: 18: 54,760 **17:** 51,172 **18 MLR** 75.7% **/ 18 Admin Exp** N/A

Enroll(000): Q1 19: 34 **18:** 34 **17:** 36 **Med Exp PMPM:** $311

Principal Investments: Long-term bonds (87%), cash and equiv (13%)

Provider Compensation ($000): Contr fee ($124,442), FFS ($8,671), capitation ($3,422), bonus arrang ($3)

Total Member Encounters: Phys (304,261), non-phys (10,570)

Group Affiliation: None

Licensed in: IL, IN

Address: 200 EAST RANDOLPH STREET, CHICAGO, IL 60601

Phone: (312) 803-5900 **Dom State:** IL **Commenced Bus:** N/A

Data Date	Rating	RACR #1	RACR #2	Total Assets ($mil)	Capital ($mil)	Net Premium ($mil)	Net Income ($mil)
3-19	B	4.41	3.67	67.6	34.1	41.0	5.9
3-18	B-	3.46	2.88	64.2	26.9	46.7	3.0
2018	B	3.71	3.09	58.8	28.5	178.6	10.1
2017	B-	1.77	1.48	53.2	23.7	173.0	9.3
2016	B-	2.56	2.13	38.5	17.5	135.1	10.2
2015	C	2.89	2.41	32.1	16.0	108.0	7.2
2014	C	3.35	2.79	35.4	20.4	105.9	5.1

Rating Indexes

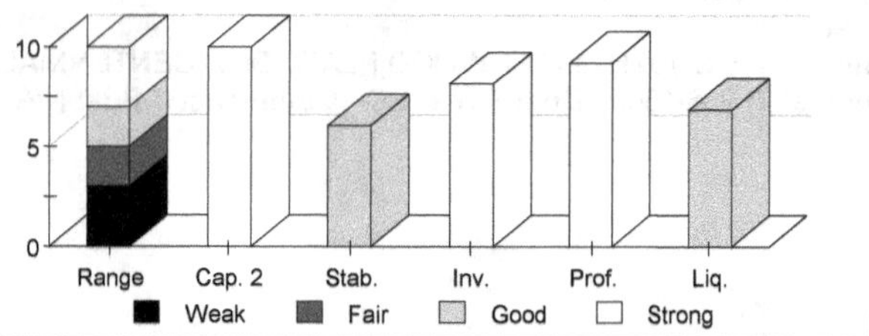

UNITED HEALTHCARE OF KENTUCKY LTD B- Good

Major Rating Factors: Fair quality investment portfolio (3.3 on a scale of 0 to 10). Good overall profitability index (5.4). Good overall results on stability tests (5.3). Rating is significantly influenced by the good financial results of .
Other Rating Factors: Strong capitalization index (8.2) based on excellent current risk-adjusted capital (severe loss scenario). Excellent liquidity (7.0) with sufficient resources (cash flows and marketable investments) to handle a spike in claims.
Principal Business: Comp med (100%)
Mem Phys: 18: 19,818 **17:** 19,412 **18 MLR** 80.9% **/ 18 Admin Exp** N/A
Enroll(000): Q1 19: 31 **18:** 33 **17:** 24 **Med Exp PMPM:** $351
Principal Investments: Cash and equiv (58%), long-term bonds (42%)
Provider Compensation ($000): Contr fee ($108,708), FFS ($12,103), capitation ($2,725), bonus arrang ($4)
Total Member Encounters: Phys (236,103), non-phys (10,909)
Group Affiliation: None
Licensed in: IN, KY
Address: 230 LEXINGTON GREEN CIRCLE, LEXINGTON, KY 40503
Phone: (859) 825-6132 **Dom State:** KY **Commenced Bus:** N/A

Data Date	Rating	RACR #1	RACR #2	Total Assets ($mil)	Capital ($mil)	Net Premium ($mil)	Net Income ($mil)
3-19	B-	2.30	1.91	47.4	21.4	41.7	2.6
3-18	C+	2.27	1.89	41.5	14.5	35.8	-0.2
2018	B-	2.04	1.70	44.2	18.9	158.6	4.2
2017	C+	1.28	1.06	33.8	14.4	113.4	4.8
2016	C	1.53	1.28	31.7	9.9	105.1	-2.5
2015	B	2.85	2.38	29.8	14.7	90.1	3.4
2014	B	2.13	1.78	26.1	11.6	86.9	-4.2

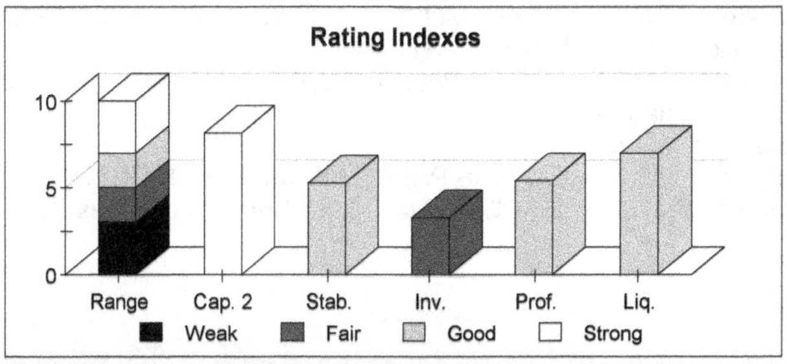

UNITED HEALTHCARE OF LOUISIANA INC B Good

Major Rating Factors: Good quality investment portfolio (5.8 on a scale of 0 to 10). Good overall results on stability tests (5.3). Rating is significantly influenced by the good financial results of . Good liquidity (6.8) with sufficient resources (cash flows and marketable investments) to handle a spike in claims.
Other Rating Factors: Excellent profitability (7.7). Strong capitalization index (7.3) based on excellent current risk-adjusted capital (severe loss scenario).
Principal Business: Medicaid (98%), comp med (2%)
Mem Phys: 18: 23,066 **17:** 18,795 **18 MLR** 83.8% **/ 18 Admin Exp** N/A
Enroll(000): Q1 19: 452 **18:** 449 **17:** 444 **Med Exp PMPM:** $348
Principal Investments: Long-term bonds (65%), cash and equiv (35%)
Provider Compensation ($000): Contr fee ($1,138,284), FFS ($398,619), capitation ($356,021), bonus arrang ($12,158)
Total Member Encounters: Phys (4,191,916), non-phys (2,198,529)
Group Affiliation: None
Licensed in: LA
Address: 3838 N CAUSEWAY BLVD SUITE 260, METAIRIE, LA 70002
Phone: (504) 849-1603 **Dom State:** LA **Commenced Bus:** N/A

Data Date	Rating	RACR #1	RACR #2	Total Assets ($mil)	Capital ($mil)	Net Premium ($mil)	Net Income ($mil)
3-19	B	1.58	1.32	560.0	158.2	581.9	-12.3
3-18	C	1.66	1.38	565.9	141.5	548.5	-24.0
2018	B	1.67	1.39	562.2	168.3	2,252.3	-3.6
2017	D	1.44	1.20	550.2	171.7	1,998.6	55.6
2016	D	1.56	1.30	479.2	126.5	1,644.8	43.9
2015	D	1.45	1.21	275.9	84.5	1,069.8	29.5
2014	D	17.39	14.50	37.1	18.9	7.5	-2.2

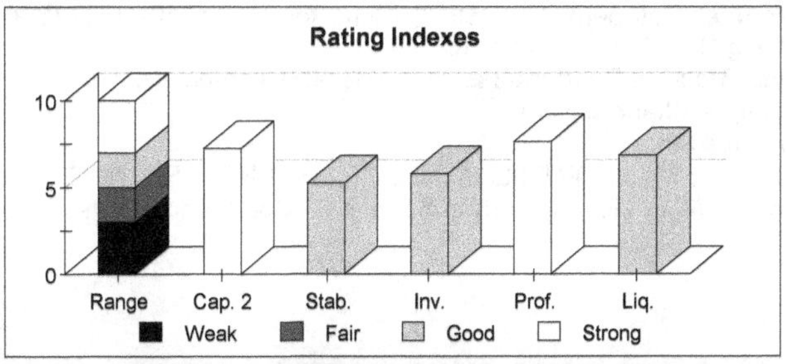

UNITED HEALTHCARE OF MID-ATLANTIC B- Good

Major Rating Factors: Fair overall results on stability tests (3.9 on a scale of 0 to 10) based on a decline in the number of member physicians during 2019. Rating is significantly influenced by the good financial results of . Good overall profitability index (5.7). Strong capitalization index (8.3) based on excellent current risk-adjusted capital (severe loss scenario).
Other Rating Factors: High quality investment portfolio (7.9). Excellent liquidity (7.0) with sufficient resources (cash flows and marketable investments) to handle a spike in claims.
Principal Business: Medicaid (88%), comp med (10%), Medicare (2%)
Mem Phys: 18: 58,540 **17:** 68,443 **18 MLR** 78.2% **/ 18 Admin Exp** N/A
Enroll(000): Q1 19: 297 **18:** 245 **17:** 244 **Med Exp PMPM:** $271
Principal Investments: Long-term bonds (70%), cash and equiv (30%)
Provider Compensation ($000): Contr fee ($630,970), FFS ($130,055), capitation ($6,686), bonus arrang ($117)
Total Member Encounters: Phys (1,527,296), non-phys (704,645)
Group Affiliation: None
Licensed in: DC, MD, VA
Address: 800 KING FARM BOULEVARD, ROCKVILLE, MD 20850
Phone: (866) 297-9264 **Dom State:** MD **Commenced Bus:** N/A

Data Date	Rating	RACR #1	RACR #2	Total Assets ($mil)	Capital ($mil)	Net Premium ($mil)	Net Income ($mil)
3-19	B-	2.43	2.02	421.3	121.0	427.9	-42.6
3-18	B-	2.23	1.86	315.7	100.2	240.5	-4.2
2018	B	3.09	2.58	338.3	155.7	980.8	47.2
2017	B-	1.62	1.35	300.4	104.5	861.5	39.2
2016	B	3.02	2.51	321.2	139.8	896.7	62.4
2015	C+	2.33	1.94	350.5	138.5	894.5	-64.2
2014	B	2.20	1.84	368.0	141.0	1,159.7	12.6

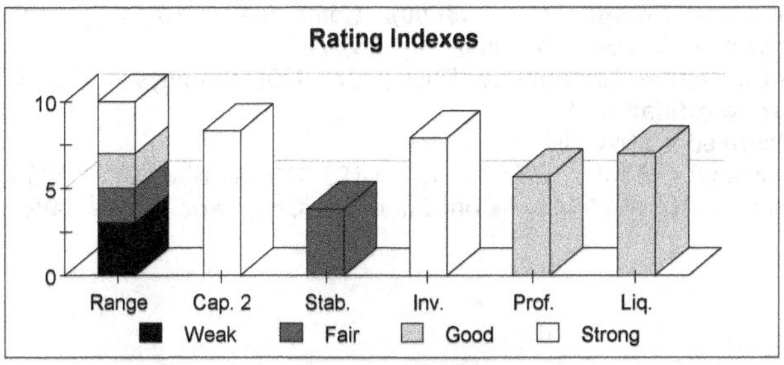

UNITED HEALTHCARE OF MISSISSIPPI INC — B- Good

Major Rating Factors: Fair profitability index (4.0 on a scale of 0 to 10). Good quality investment portfolio (5.7). Good overall results on stability tests (6.7) despite a decline in enrollment during 2018. Rating is significantly influenced by the good financial results of .

Other Rating Factors: Good liquidity (6.9) with sufficient resources (cash flows and marketable investments) to handle a spike in claims. Strong capitalization index (8.3) based on excellent current risk-adjusted capital (severe loss scenario).

Principal Business: Medicaid (90%), comp med (10%)

Mem Phys: 18: 11,220 **17:** 10,565 **18 MLR** 86.3% **/ 18 Admin Exp** N/A

Enroll(000): Q1 19: 210 **18:** 225 **17:** 262 **Med Exp PMPM:** $342

Principal Investments: Long-term bonds (68%), cash and equiv (32%)

Provider Compensation ($000): Contr fee ($763,806), FFS ($229,770), capitation ($4,735), bonus arrang ($94)

Total Member Encounters: Phys (2,029,130), non-phys (1,314,698)

Group Affiliation: None

Licensed in: MS

Address: 795 WOODLANDS PARKWAY SUITE 30, RIDGELAND, MS 39157

Phone: (504) 849-1603 **Dom State:** MS **Commenced Bus:** N/A

Data Date	Rating	RACR #1	RACR #2	Total Assets ($mil)	Capital ($mil)	Net Premium ($mil)	Net Income ($mil)
3-19	B-	2.36	1.97	269.4	166.7	258.7	-0.1
3-18	C	N/A	N/A	280.8	129.1	290.3	-5.3
2018	C+	2.33	1.95	277.0	164.8	1,144.6	32.6
2017	C	N/A	N/A	286.6	140.6	1,106.6	-30.2
2016	B-	1.33	1.11	223.4	96.8	1,233.0	8.9
2015	B-	1.32	1.10	220.6	66.8	897.1	-14.6
2014	C+	2.31	1.92	113.9	54.7	400.3	13.4

Rating Indexes

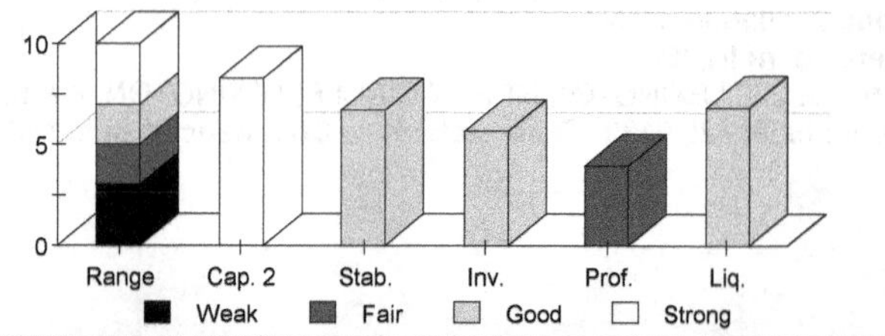

UNITED HEALTHCARE OF NC INC — C Fair

Major Rating Factors: Fair overall results on stability tests (3.3 on a scale of 0 to 10) based on a steep decline in capital during 2018. Rating is significantly influenced by the good financial results of . Good overall profitability index (5.5). Good liquidity (6.7) with sufficient resources (cash flows and marketable investments) to handle a spike in claims.

Other Rating Factors: Strong capitalization index (9.6) based on excellent current risk-adjusted capital (severe loss scenario). High quality investment portfolio (7.1).

Principal Business: Comp med (100%)

Mem Phys: 18: 39,218 **17:** 36,145 **18 MLR** 83.7% **/ 18 Admin Exp** N/A

Enroll(000): Q1 19: 94 **18:** 94 **17:** 94 **Med Exp PMPM:** $364

Principal Investments: Long-term bonds (75%), cash and equiv (25%)

Provider Compensation ($000): Contr fee ($360,010), FFS ($24,367), bonus arrang ($10,730), capitation ($7,271)

Total Member Encounters: Phys (862,006), non-phys (24,372)

Group Affiliation: None

Licensed in: NC

Address: 3803 NORTH ELM STREET, GREENSBORO, NC 27455

Phone: (336) 282-0900 **Dom State:** NC **Commenced Bus:** N/A

Data Date	Rating	RACR #1	RACR #2	Total Assets ($mil)	Capital ($mil)	Net Premium ($mil)	Net Income ($mil)
3-19	C	3.46	2.88	192.5	95.5	125.3	14.5
3-18	C+	5.78	4.81	193.2	108.6	124.9	-1.8
2018	C	3.00	2.50	180.7	81.8	496.9	-1.2
2017	C+	4.08	3.40	181.3	109.4	397.6	31.6
2016	B	3.24	2.70	403.7	148.4	931.0	26.4
2015	B	2.00	1.67	375.5	126.9	1,280.4	6.5
2014	B	2.53	2.11	263.6	130.8	1,013.8	39.6

Rating Indexes

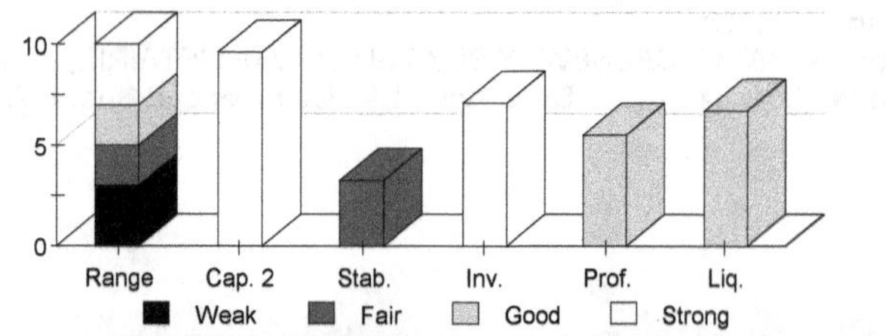

UNITED HEALTHCARE OF NEW ENGLAND INC — B Good

Major Rating Factors: Good overall results on stability tests (5.5 on a scale of 0 to 10). Rating is significantly influenced by the good financial results of . Good liquidity (6.6) with sufficient resources (cash flows and marketable investments) to handle a spike in claims. Excellent profitability (7.8).

Other Rating Factors: Strong capitalization index (8.3) based on excellent current risk-adjusted capital (severe loss scenario). High quality investment portfolio (9.4).

Principal Business: Medicare (54%), Medicaid (45%)

Mem Phys: 18: 134,473 **17:** 130,815 **18 MLR** 84.6% **/ 18 Admin Exp** N/A

Enroll(000): Q1 19: 159 **18:** 154 **17:** 144 **Med Exp PMPM:** $532

Principal Investments: Long-term bonds (93%), nonaffiliate common stock (5%), cash and equiv (2%)

Provider Compensation ($000): Contr fee ($667,525), FFS ($199,747), capitation ($99,543), bonus arrang ($5,522)

Total Member Encounters: Phys (2,073,320), non-phys (1,039,265)

Group Affiliation: None

Licensed in: MA, NH, PA, RI, VT

Address: 475 KILVERT STREET SUITE 310, WARWICK, RI 02886-1392

Phone: (203) 447-4444 **Dom State:** RI **Commenced Bus:** N/A

Data Date	Rating	RACR #1	RACR #2	Total Assets ($mil)	Capital ($mil)	Net Premium ($mil)	Net Income ($mil)
3-19	B	2.40	2.00	358.8	142.4	322.9	10.5
3-18	B-	2.30	1.92	406.6	102.0	285.6	-11.6
2018	B	2.25	1.87	331.0	132.6	1,160.8	18.4
2017	B-	1.79	1.49	326.4	113.9	974.5	23.6
2016	B-	2.76	2.30	313.5	119.0	866.6	12.7
2015	B	3.53	2.94	363.9	147.2	768.5	27.5
2014	B	4.37	3.64	314.9	160.7	691.5	36.7

Rating Indexes

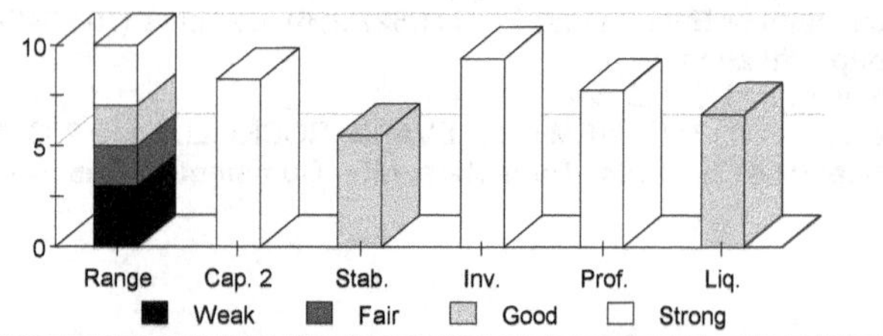

UNITED HEALTHCARE OF NY INC * B+ Good

Major Rating Factors: Good liquidity (6.5 on a scale of 0 to 10) with sufficient resources (cash flows and marketable investments) to handle a spike in claims. Excellent profitability (8.3). Strong capitalization index (7.7) based on excellent current risk-adjusted capital (severe loss scenario).

Other Rating Factors: High quality investment portfolio (9.3). Excellent overall results on stability tests (7.4). Rating is significantly influenced by the good financial results of .

Principal Business: Medicaid (53%), Medicare (32%), comp med (4%), other (11%)

Mem Phys: 18: 97,444 **17:** 93,552 **18 MLR** 84.5% **/ 18 Admin Exp** N/A

Enroll(000): Q1 19: 794 **18:** 794 **17:** 728 **Med Exp PMPM:** $485

Principal Investments: Long-term bonds (86%), cash and equiv (14%)

Provider Compensation ($000): Contr fee ($4,182,391), FFS ($136,279), capitation ($28,016), bonus arrang ($15,562), other ($111,874)

Total Member Encounters: Phys (8,323,944), non-phys (4,741,675)

Group Affiliation: None

Licensed in: NY

Address: 77 WATER STREET 14TH / 15TH FL, NEW YORK, NY 10005

Phone: (203) 447-4439 **Dom State:** NY **Commenced Bus:** N/A

Data Date	Rating	RACR #1	RACR #2	Total Assets ($mil)	Capital ($mil)	Net Premium ($mil)	Net Income ($mil)
3-19	B+	1.91	1.60	1,443.0	597.1	1,372.7	-21.1
3-18	B+	N/A	N/A	1,401.8	541.3	1,288.6	-29.4
2018	B+	1.96	1.64	1,295.8	613.0	5,344.2	46.6
2017	B+	N/A	N/A	1,195.0	570.8	4,412.6	107.1
2016	B+	2.55	2.12	1,096.2	568.0	3,870.2	115.2
2015	B+	2.77	2.31	846.1	455.9	3,025.2	106.0
2014	B+	2.82	2.35	648.2	363.0	2,481.1	112.3

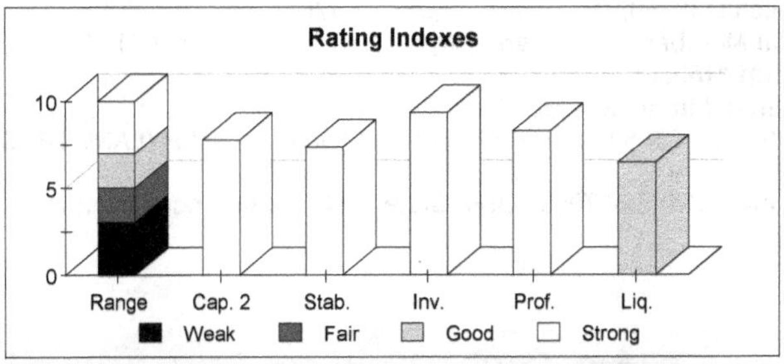

UNITED HEALTHCARE OF OHIO INC C Fair

Major Rating Factors: Weak overall results on stability tests (2.4 on a scale of 0 to 10) based on a steep decline in capital during 2018. Rating is significantly influenced by the good financial results of . Excellent profitability (7.4). Strong capitalization index (10.0) based on excellent current risk-adjusted capital (severe loss scenario).

Other Rating Factors: High quality investment portfolio (9.9). Excellent liquidity (8.7) with ample operational cash flow and liquid investments.

Principal Business: Comp med (102%)

Mem Phys: 18: 76,285 **17:** 52,364 **18 MLR** 72.4% **/ 18 Admin Exp** N/A

Enroll(000): Q1 19: 10 **18:** 11 **17:** 9 **Med Exp PMPM:** $336

Principal Investments: Cash and equiv (98%), long-term bonds (2%)

Provider Compensation ($000): Contr fee ($39,970), capitation ($977), bonus arrang ($19)

Total Member Encounters: Phys (73,620), non-phys (3,532)

Group Affiliation: None

Licensed in: KY, OH

Address: OH020-3010 9200 WORTHINGTON RO, WESTERVILLE, OH 43082-8823

Phone: (614) 595-3774 **Dom State:** OH **Commenced Bus:** N/A

Data Date	Rating	RACR #1	RACR #2	Total Assets ($mil)	Capital ($mil)	Net Premium ($mil)	Net Income ($mil)
3-19	C	15.62	13.02	59.7	50.0	14.5	1.8
3-18	C	27.39	22.83	81.6	70.5	13.3	0.7
2018	C	14.90	12.42	58.2	47.5	57.7	6.3
2017	D+	17.30	14.42	79.2	69.0	41.6	4.2
2016	C	18.09	15.07	88.6	64.1	81.6	5.4
2015	C	2.43	2.02	177.5	78.5	682.6	37.7
2014	B	2.82	2.35	257.9	134.9	879.6	21.6

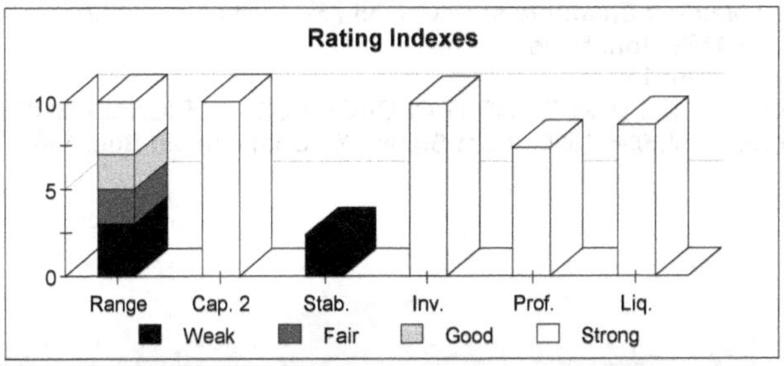

UNITED HEALTHCARE OF THE MIDLANDS B Good

Major Rating Factors: Good overall profitability index (6.6 on a scale of 0 to 10). Good overall results on stability tests (5.2) based on healthy premium and capital growth during 2018. Rating is significantly influenced by the good financial results of . Good liquidity (6.8) with sufficient resources (cash flows and marketable investments) to handle a spike in claims.

Other Rating Factors: Strong capitalization index (8.1) based on excellent current risk-adjusted capital (severe loss scenario). High quality investment portfolio (9.1).

Principal Business: Medicare (86%), Medicaid (14%)

Mem Phys: 18: 140,626 **17:** 136,309 **18 MLR** 81.5% **/ 18 Admin Exp** N/A

Enroll(000): Q1 19: 336 **18:** 325 **17:** 278 **Med Exp PMPM:** $664

Principal Investments: Long-term bonds (93%), cash and equiv (7%)

Provider Compensation ($000): Contr fee ($1,903,491), FFS ($346,203), capitation ($212,245), bonus arrang ($55,455)

Total Member Encounters: Phys (5,285,882), non-phys (2,370,405)

Group Affiliation: None

Licensed in: AL, AR, IL, IN, IA, KS, MO, NE

Address: 2717 NORTH 118TH STREET, OMAHA, NE 68164-9672

Phone: (402) 445-5600 **Dom State:** NE **Commenced Bus:** N/A

Data Date	Rating	RACR #1	RACR #2	Total Assets ($mil)	Capital ($mil)	Net Premium ($mil)	Net Income ($mil)
3-19	B	2.27	1.89	845.2	349.3	897.1	47.0
3-18	B	1.54	1.28	947.9	183.0	774.4	-9.2
2018	B	1.97	1.64	729.7	302.7	3,102.5	124.3
2017	B	1.17	0.98	645.5	193.3	2,542.9	126.3
2016	B	2.21	1.84	207.3	72.2	573.2	-8.4
2015	B+	1.75	1.46	90.9	26.0	286.4	-11.6
2014	B+	2.53	2.11	69.9	32.6	261.8	12.1

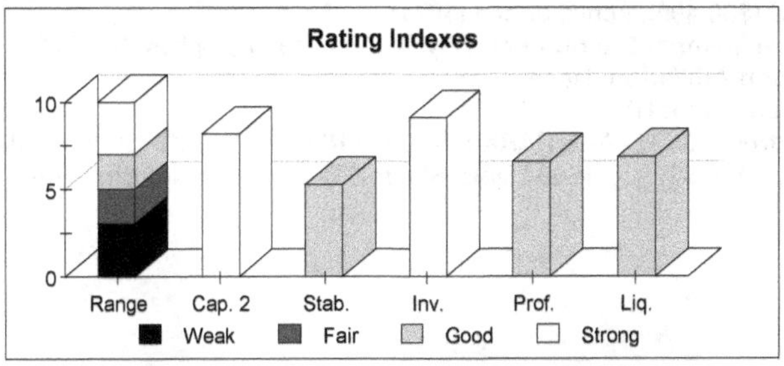

UNITED HEALTHCARE OF THE MIDWEST INC C+ Fair

Major Rating Factors: Good overall results on stability tests (5.4 on a scale of 0 to 10). Rating is significantly influenced by the good financial results of . Weak liquidity (2.2) as a spike in claims may stretch capacity. Excellent profitability (8.6).
Other Rating Factors: Strong capitalization index (10.0) based on excellent current risk-adjusted capital (severe loss scenario). High quality investment portfolio (8.2).
Principal Business: Medicaid (74%), Medicare (24%), comp med (2%)
Mem Phys: 18: 126,438 **17:** 98,944 **18 MLR** 176.8% **/ 18 Admin Exp** N/A
Enroll(000): Q1 19: 329 **18:** 318 **17:** 296 **Med Exp PMPM:** $399
Principal Investments: Long-term bonds (90%), cash and equiv (10%)
Provider Compensation ($000): Contr fee ($1,202,377), FFS ($177,923), capitation ($159,946), bonus arrang ($3,476)
Total Member Encounters: Phys (1,935,515), non-phys (1,731,544)
Group Affiliation: None
Licensed in: IL, KS, MO
Address: 13655 RIVERPORT DRIVE MO050-10, MARYLAND HEIGHTS, MO 63043
Phone: (314) 592-7000 **Dom State:** MO **Commenced Bus:** N/A

Data Date	Rating	RACR #1	RACR #2	Total Assets ($mil)	Capital ($mil)	Net Premium ($mil)	Net Income ($mil)
3-19	C+	4.84	4.03	587.4	195.3	302.6	17.4
3-18	C+	6.01	5.01	460.8	163.9	191.2	-5.2
2018	C+	4.72	3.94	451.1	190.3	860.4	40.3
2017	C+	4.70	3.92	422.4	179.2	528.7	5.2
2016	C+	2.82	2.35	490.5	179.6	1,275.7	56.5
2015	C+	2.67	2.22	408.7	144.1	1,025.2	14.0
2014	C+	3.42	2.85	344.3	155.0	911.6	47.1

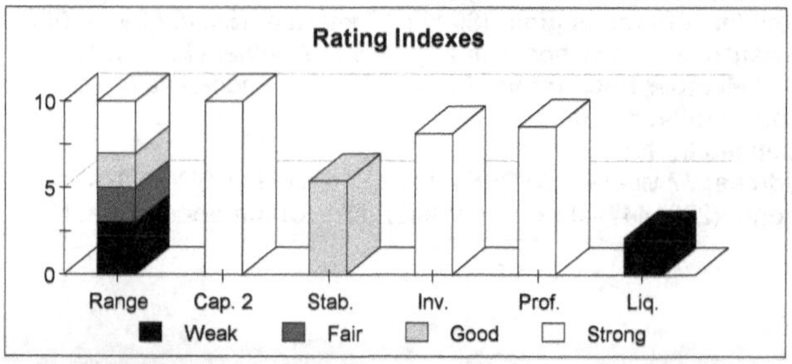

UNITED HEALTHCARE OF TX INC B Good

Major Rating Factors: Good overall results on stability tests (6.0 on a scale of 0 to 10). Rating is significantly influenced by the good financial results of . Excellent profitability (7.3). Strong capitalization index (10.0) based on excellent current risk-adjusted capital (severe loss scenario).
Other Rating Factors: High quality investment portfolio (9.9). Excellent liquidity (7.7) with ample operational cash flow and liquid investments.
Principal Business: Comp med (100%)
Mem Phys: 18: 84,979 **17:** 78,666 **18 MLR** 71.4% **/ 18 Admin Exp** N/A
Enroll(000): Q1 19: 31 **18:** 27 **17:** 27 **Med Exp PMPM:** $265
Principal Investments: Cash and equiv (100%)
Provider Compensation ($000): Contr fee ($76,903), FFS ($6,041), bonus arrang ($2,744), capitation ($84)
Total Member Encounters: Phys (165,757), non-phys (5,442)
Group Affiliation: None
Licensed in: TX
Address: 1311 W PRESIDENT GEORGE BUSH H, RICHARDSON, TX 75080
Phone: (952) 936-1300 **Dom State:** TX **Commenced Bus:** N/A

Data Date	Rating	RACR #1	RACR #2	Total Assets ($mil)	Capital ($mil)	Net Premium ($mil)	Net Income ($mil)
3-19	B	12.37	10.31	65.4	26.5	34.6	4.2
3-18	B	4.99	4.16	57.3	22.0	29.3	3.1
2018	B	10.48	8.73	55.2	22.3	122.1	11.4
2017	B	2.44	2.03	47.7	18.7	112.1	12.6
2016	B-	2.18	1.82	30.9	7.7	80.2	5.4
2015	C	2.17	1.81	14.4	5.5	27.9	-1.1
2014	C	4.92	4.10	6.5	6.1	0.8	0.1

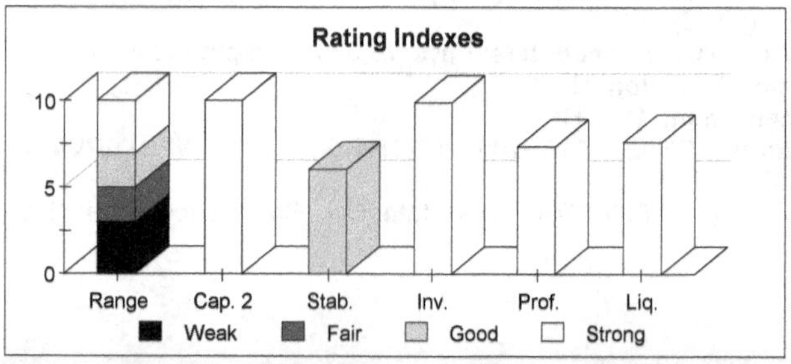

UNITED HEALTHCARE OF UTAH B Good

Major Rating Factors: Good overall profitability index (5.5 on a scale of 0 to 10). Good liquidity (6.6) with sufficient resources (cash flows and marketable investments) to handle a spike in claims. Strong capitalization index (8.1) based on excellent current risk-adjusted capital (severe loss scenario).
Other Rating Factors: High quality investment portfolio (9.9). Excellent overall results on stability tests (7.0) based on healthy premium and capital growth during 2018. Rating is significantly influenced by the good financial results of .
Principal Business: Medicare (99%), comp med (1%)
Mem Phys: 18: 17,905 **17:** 11,207 **18 MLR** 87.4% **/ 18 Admin Exp** N/A
Enroll(000): Q1 19: 79 **18:** 80 **17:** 69 **Med Exp PMPM:** $753
Principal Investments: Long-term bonds (94%), cash and equiv (6%)
Provider Compensation ($000): Capitation ($616,255), contr fee ($66,211), FFS ($30,496), bonus arrang ($671)
Total Member Encounters: Phys (1,269,216), non-phys (613,528)
Group Affiliation: None
Licensed in: UT
Address: 2525 LAKE PARK BOULEVARD, SALT LAKE CITY, UT 84120
Phone: (952) 936-1300 **Dom State:** UT **Commenced Bus:** N/A

Data Date	Rating	RACR #1	RACR #2	Total Assets ($mil)	Capital ($mil)	Net Premium ($mil)	Net Income ($mil)
3-19	B	2.27	1.89	210.5	86.3	229.9	8.1
3-18	B	1.65	1.37	221.5	47.5	199.7	-14.1
2018	B	2.04	1.70	181.8	78.1	810.8	15.4
2017	B	1.34	1.12	180.2	60.7	668.1	6.0
2016	B	2.68	2.24	121.8	55.0	514.7	3.5
2015	B-	3.55	2.96	110.1	59.9	443.6	31.4
2014	C	2.07	1.73	110.5	38.3	343.1	-21.6

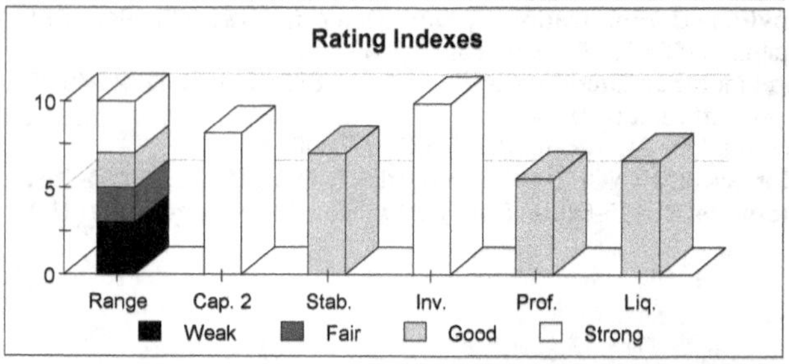

UNITED HEALTHCARE OF WISCONSIN INC * B+ Good

Major Rating Factors: Good liquidity (6.8 on a scale of 0 to 10) with sufficient resources (cash flows and marketable investments) to handle a spike in claims. Excellent profitability (10.0). Strong capitalization index (9.1) based on excellent current risk-adjusted capital (severe loss scenario).
Other Rating Factors: High quality investment portfolio (9.4). Excellent overall results on stability tests (7.5) based on healthy premium and capital growth during 2018. Rating is significantly influenced by the good financial results of .
Principal Business: Medicare (91%), Medicaid (7%), comp med (2%)
Mem Phys: 18: 240,865 **17:** 41,457 **18 MLR** 79.4% **/ 18 Admin Exp** N/A
Enroll(000): Q1 19: 701 **18:** 678 **17:** 620 **Med Exp PMPM:** $640
Principal Investments: Long-term bonds (92%), cash and equiv (8%)
Provider Compensation ($000): Contr fee ($4,174,256), FFS ($544,603), capitation ($272,840), bonus arrang ($128,541)
Total Member Encounters: Phys (11,936,070), non-phys (5,437,842)
Group Affiliation: None
Licensed in: AZ, IL, IA, KY, NC, OH, TN, VA, WI
Address: WI030-1000 10701 WEST RESEARCH, WAUWATOSA, WI 53226-0649
Phone: (414) 443-4000 **Dom State:** WI **Commenced Bus:** N/A

Data Date	Rating	RACR #1	RACR #2	Total Assets ($mil)	Capital ($mil)	Net Premium ($mil)	Net Income ($mil)
3-19	B+	3.06	2.55	2,025.5	1,006.8	1,844.4	147.5
3-18	B+	2.86	2.38	2,361.2	674.1	1,609.8	9.8
2018	B+	2.54	2.11	1,705.5	833.4	6,426.8	383.8
2017	B+	2.44	2.03	1,760.0	665.9	5,491.3	358.4
2016	B	2.26	1.89	1,223.8	452.6	4,484.3	199.9
2015	B	3.76	3.13	489.4	270.3	1,502.6	53.6
2014	B	2.62	2.19	373.2	171.1	1,433.4	31.0

Rating Indexes

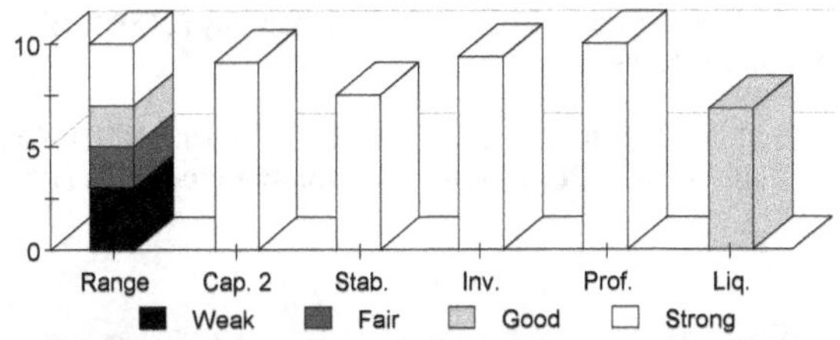

UNITED OF OMAHA LIFE INSURANCE COMPANY B Good

Major Rating Factors: Good quality investment portfolio (5.1 on a scale of 0 to 10) despite large holdings of BBB rated bonds in addition to moderate junk bond exposure. Exposure to mortgages is significant, but the mortgage default rate has been low. Good liquidity (6.5) with sufficient resources to cover a large increase in policy surrenders. Fair overall results on stability tests (4.9).
Other Rating Factors: Strong capitalization (7.3) based on excellent risk adjusted capital (severe loss scenario). Excellent profitability (7.1).
Principal Business: Individual life insurance (33%), individual health insurance (19%), group retirement contracts (19%), group health insurance (14%), and other lines (15%).
Principal Investments: NonCMO investment grade bonds (59%), CMOs and structured securities (19%), mortgages in good standing (12%), noninv. grade bonds (3%), and misc. investments (4%).
Investments in Affiliates: 2%
Group Affiliation: Mutual Of Omaha Group
Licensed in: All states except NY
Commenced Business: November 1926
Address: MUTUAL OF OMAHA PLAZA, OMAHA, NE 68175
Phone: (402) 342-7600 **Domicile State:** NE **NAIC Code:** 69868

Data Date	Rating	RACR #1	RACR #2	Total Assets ($mil)	Capital ($mil)	Net Premium ($mil)	Net Income ($mil)
3-19	B	2.04	1.17	24,356.1	1,657.3	1,012.3	26.2
3-18	B	1.97	1.12	23,007.1	1,588.2	961.2	-5.3
2018	B	2.06	1.18	23,038.8	1,639.4	3,263.6	55.4
2017	B	2.00	1.14	22,803.2	1,605.7	4,024.6	61.7
2016	B	1.89	1.06	20,698.2	1,429.5	3,692.0	9.0
2015	B	1.90	1.11	19,622.5	1,441.7	3,572.3	153.6
2014	B	1.95	1.15	18,786.7	1,422.7	2,712.4	164.4

Rating Indexes

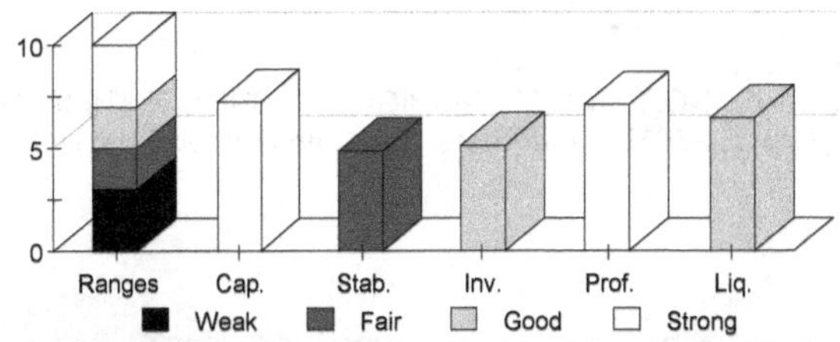

UNITED WORLD LIFE INSURANCE COMPANY * B+ Good

Major Rating Factors: Good overall results on stability tests (6.7 on a scale of 0 to 10) despite negative cash flow from operations for 2018. Other stability subfactors include excellent operational trends and excellent risk diversification. Good liquidity (6.4) with sufficient resources to handle a spike in claims. Fair profitability (4.8).
Other Rating Factors: Strong capitalization (7.9) based on excellent risk adjusted capital (severe loss scenario). High quality investment portfolio (7.6).
Principal Business: Individual health insurance (100%).
Principal Investments: NonCMO investment grade bonds (56%), CMOs and structured securities (28%), policy loans (1%), and noninv. grade bonds (1%).
Investments in Affiliates: None
Group Affiliation: Mutual Of Omaha Group
Licensed in: All states except CT, NY, PR
Commenced Business: April 1970
Address: MUTUAL OF OMAHA PLAZA, OMAHA, NE 68175
Phone: (402) 342-7600 **Domicile State:** NE **NAIC Code:** 72850

Data Date	Rating	RACR #1	RACR #2	Total Assets ($mil)	Capital ($mil)	Net Premium ($mil)	Net Income ($mil)
3-19	B+	3.82	1.60	132.1	45.0	0.2	0.6
3-18	B+	4.75	2.01	118.9	47.9	0.3	0.5
2018	B+	3.95	1.66	128.5	44.6	1.2	2.8
2017	B+	4.96	2.11	122.8	48.7	1.3	1.9
2016	B+	5.42	2.30	119.8	51.4	1.3	4.8
2015	B+	4.92	2.09	123.7	48.9	1.4	-0.5
2014	B+	4.62	1.95	119.4	49.4	1.5	1.6

Adverse Trends in Operations

Decrease in capital during 2018 (9%)
Decrease in capital during 2017 (5%)
Decrease in asset base during 2016 (3%)
Increase in policy surrenders from 2014 to 2015 (38%)
Decrease in premium volume from 2014 to 2015 (5%)

UNITEDHEALTHCARE BENEFITS OF TEXAS B Good

Major Rating Factors: Good overall results on stability tests (6.2 on a scale of 0 to 10) based on steady enrollment growth, averaging 7% over the past five years. Rating is significantly influenced by the good financial results of . Good liquidity (6.8) with sufficient resources (cash flows and marketable investments) to handle a spike in claims. Excellent profitability (8.3).
Other Rating Factors: Strong capitalization index (8.2) based on excellent current risk-adjusted capital (severe loss scenario). High quality investment portfolio (7.4).
Principal Business: Medicare (100%)
Mem Phys: 18: 90,503 **17:** 82,146 **18 MLR** 87.5% **/ 18 Admin Exp** N/A
Enroll(000): Q1 19: 256 **18:** 248 **17:** 231 **Med Exp PMPM:** $1,063
Principal Investments: Long-term bonds (76%), cash and equiv (24%)
Provider Compensation ($000): Capitation ($2,607,571), contr fee ($381,670), FFS ($60,299), bonus arrang ($25,594)
Total Member Encounters: Phys (572,971), non-phys (158,928)
Group Affiliation: None
Licensed in: TX
Address: 1311 W PRESIDENT GEORGE BUSH H, RICHARDSON, TX 75080
Phone: (952) 936-1300 **Dom State:** TX **Commenced Bus:** N/A

Data Date	Rating	RACR #1	RACR #2	Total Assets ($mil)	Capital ($mil)	Net Premium ($mil)	Net Income ($mil)
3-19	B	2.27	1.90	622.5	304.4	1,058.9	16.3
3-18	B-	1.75	1.46	901.4	195.1	910.5	-60.8
2018	B	2.19	1.82	504.3	292.5	3,566.8	49.5
2017	B-	1.70	1.42	503.2	257.8	3,115.7	66.8
2016	B	2.28	1.90	403.3	226.9	2,727.3	35.8
2015	B	2.51	2.09	459.2	241.3	2,609.2	84.5
2014	B+	3.06	2.55	530.8	309.5	2,482.3	144.1

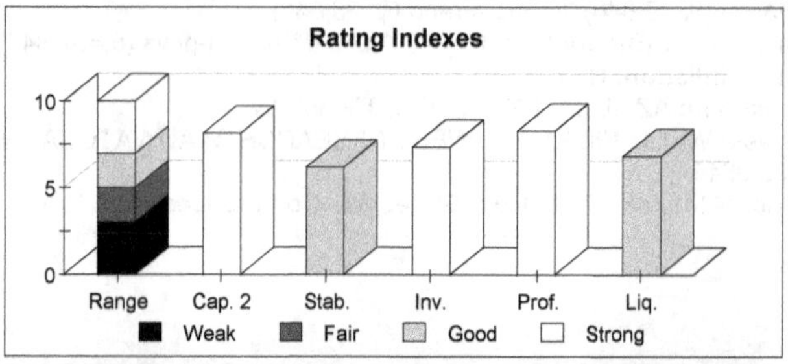

UNITEDHEALTHCARE COMMUNITY PLAN INC B Good

Major Rating Factors: Good overall results on stability tests (5.6 on a scale of 0 to 10). Rating is significantly influenced by the good financial results of . Excellent profitability (8.4). Strong capitalization index (9.1) based on excellent current risk-adjusted capital (severe loss scenario).
Other Rating Factors: High quality investment portfolio (9.5). Excellent liquidity (7.0) with ample operational cash flow and liquid investments.
Principal Business: Medicaid (99%)
Mem Phys: 18: 41,468 **17:** 25,296 **18 MLR** 79.7% **/ 18 Admin Exp** N/A
Enroll(000): Q1 19: 252 **18:** 249 **17:** 255 **Med Exp PMPM:** $229
Principal Investments: Cash and equiv (54%), long-term bonds (38%), other (7%)
Provider Compensation ($000): Contr fee ($487,158), FFS ($204,473), capitation ($26,004), bonus arrang ($5,943)
Total Member Encounters: Phys (1,960,745), non-phys (1,277,713)
Group Affiliation: None
Licensed in: MI
Address: 26957 NORTHWESTERN HIGHWAY SUI, SOUTHFIELD, MI 48033
Phone: (248) 559-5656 **Dom State:** MI **Commenced Bus:** N/A

Data Date	Rating	RACR #1	RACR #2	Total Assets ($mil)	Capital ($mil)	Net Premium ($mil)	Net Income ($mil)
3-19	B	3.05	2.54	272.1	146.2	230.5	14.9
3-18	B	2.01	1.68	266.6	111.5	282.9	-13.0
2018	B	2.75	2.30	260.9	131.3	872.2	25.1
2017	B	1.58	1.32	257.2	124.8	1,064.1	18.5
2016	B	2.38	1.98	289.8	122.2	1,242.1	26.8
2015	B	1.89	1.58	282.9	95.8	1,232.2	44.2
2014	B	2.10	1.75	250.8	104.6	1,090.8	30.4

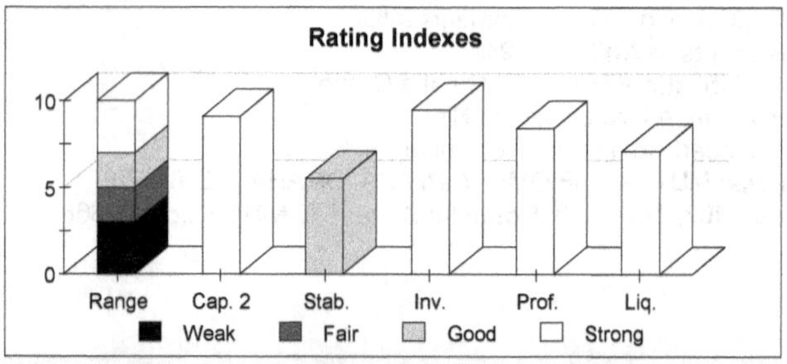

UNITEDHEALTHCARE COMMUNITY PLAN TX B- Good

Major Rating Factors: Fair profitability index (2.9 on a scale of 0 to 10). Fair liquidity (4.7) as cash resources may not be adequate to cover a spike in claims. Good capitalization index (6.9) based on excellent current risk-adjusted capital (severe loss scenario).
Other Rating Factors: Good overall results on stability tests (6.2) based on steady enrollment growth, averaging 4% over the past five years. Rating is significantly influenced by the good financial results of . High quality investment portfolio (9.3).
Principal Business: Medicaid (74%), Medicare (25%), comp med (1%)
Mem Phys: 18: 78,116 **17:** 61,157 **18 MLR** 90.4% **/ 18 Admin Exp** N/A
Enroll(000): Q1 19: 270 **18:** 270 **17:** 270 **Med Exp PMPM:** $722
Principal Investments: Long-term bonds (96%), cash and equiv (4%)
Provider Compensation ($000): Contr fee ($2,128,313), FFS ($140,432), capitation ($25,286), bonus arrang ($2,698)
Total Member Encounters: Phys (3,202,661), non-phys (3,200,649)
Group Affiliation: None
Licensed in: TX
Address: 14141 S W FREEWAY, SUGAR LAND, TX 77478
Phone: (832) 500-6437 **Dom State:** TX **Commenced Bus:** N/A

Data Date	Rating	RACR #1	RACR #2	Total Assets ($mil)	Capital ($mil)	Net Premium ($mil)	Net Income ($mil)
3-19	B-	1.24	1.04	586.7	200.7	692.4	5.3
3-18	B	1.39	1.16	592.3	188.3	646.6	-18.8
2018	B-	1.21	1.01	559.0	194.6	2,567.2	-18.2
2017	B	1.00	0.83	558.6	186.8	2,303.2	-39.7
2016	B+	1.72	1.43	549.9	220.1	2,369.4	33.8
2015	B+	2.25	1.88	571.4	229.7	2,072.5	73.4
2014	B+	2.40	2.00	411.3	187.5	1,546.0	43.5

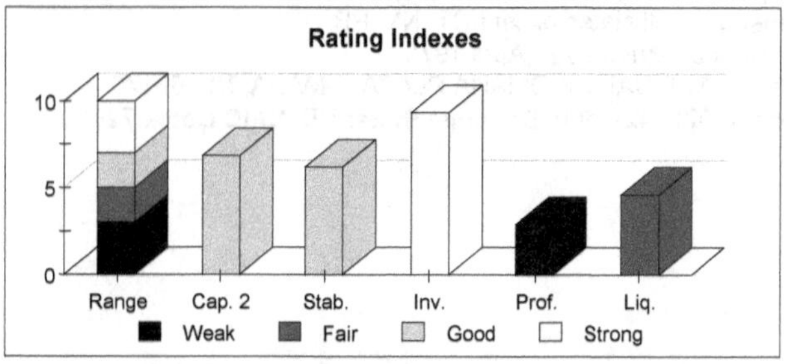

UNITEDHEALTHCARE COMMUNITYPLAN OHIO B Good

Major Rating Factors: Excellent profitability (9.0 on a scale of 0 to 10). Strong capitalization (8.7) based on excellent current risk-adjusted capital (severe loss scenario). High quality investment portfolio (7.5).
Other Rating Factors: Excellent liquidity (6.9) with sufficient resources (cash flows and marketable investments) to handle a spike in claims.
Principal Business: Medicaid (100%)
Mem Phys: 18: 64,894 **17:** 50,309 **18 MLR** 81.3% **/ 18 Admin Exp** N/A
Enroll(000): Q1 19: 304 **18:** 304 **17:** 313 **Med Exp PMPM:** $532
Principal Investments: Long-term bonds (79%), cash and equiv (21%)
Provider Compensation ($000): Contr fee ($1,399,691), FFS ($406,643), capitation ($228,982), bonus arrang ($624)
Total Member Encounters: Phys (3,166,585), non-phys (2,225,915)
Group Affiliation: None
Licensed in: OH
Address: 9200 WORTHINGTON Rd OH020-1000, DUBLIN, OH 43016
Phone: (952) 931-4014 **Dom State:** OH **Commenced Bus:** N/A

Data Date	Rating	RACR #1	RACR #2	Total Assets ($mil)	Capital ($mil)	Net Premium ($mil)	Net Income ($mil)
3-19	B	2.74	2.28	577.2	358.6	608.5	-4.5
3-18	B	N/A	N/A	559.6	277.4	607.6	3.7
2018	B	2.77	2.31	576.7	362.8	2,510.5	124.7
2017	B	N/A	N/A	494.6	273.1	2,231.8	78.8
2016	B	2.14	1.78	449.4	219.7	2,059.4	22.9
2015	B	2.27	1.89	430.3	226.9	2,145.2	120.5
2014	B	3.45	2.88	409.0	154.2	1,363.9	47.8

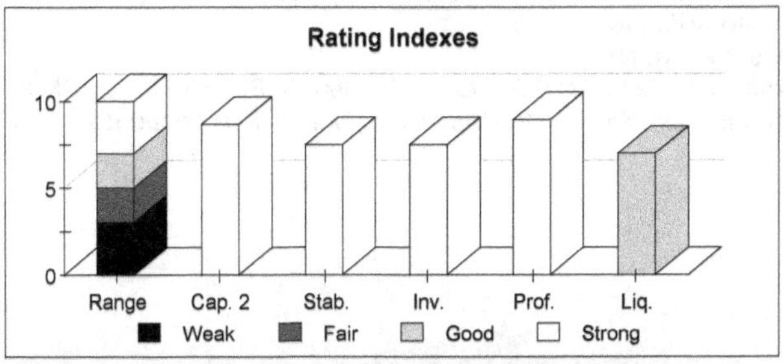

UNITEDHEALTHCARE INS CO RIVER VALLEY B Good

Major Rating Factors: Good overall profitability index (5.5 on a scale of 0 to 10). Good liquidity (6.8) with sufficient resources (cash flows and marketable investments) to handle a spike in claims. Strong capitalization (8.3) based on excellent current risk-adjusted capital (severe loss scenario).
Other Rating Factors: High quality investment portfolio (9.5).
Principal Business: Comp med (74%), Medicare (26%)
Mem Phys: 18: 364,451 **17:** 241,927 **18 MLR** 81.5% **/ 18 Admin Exp** N/A
Enroll(000): Q1 19: 252 **18:** 238 **17:** 195 **Med Exp PMPM:** $424
Principal Investments: Long-term bonds (80%), cash and equiv (20%)
Provider Compensation ($000): Contr fee ($936,488), FFS ($156,669), capitation ($22,519), bonus arrang ($306)
Total Member Encounters: Phys (2,455,659), non-phys (450,507)
Group Affiliation: None
Licensed in: AR, GA, IL, IA, KY, LA, NC, OH, OK, SC, TN, TX, VA
Address: 1300 RIVER Dr Ste 200, MOLINE, IL 61265
Phone: (309) 736-4600 **Dom State:** IL **Commenced Bus:** N/A

Data Date	Rating	RACR #1	RACR #2	Total Assets ($mil)	Capital ($mil)	Net Premium ($mil)	Net Income ($mil)
3-19	B	2.38	1.98	426.7	185.4	451.9	41.2
3-18	B	2.11	1.75	340.1	109.4	309.5	-1.2
2018	B	1.85	1.54	395.1	142.5	1,395.6	35.2
2017	B	1.47	1.22	276.3	108.7	974.5	14.2
2016	B	1.97	1.64	261.9	92.1	896.7	0.8
2015	B	2.36	1.97	219.5	93.1	722.6	-12.2
2014	B	1.96	1.63	154.7	60.7	594.7	10.7

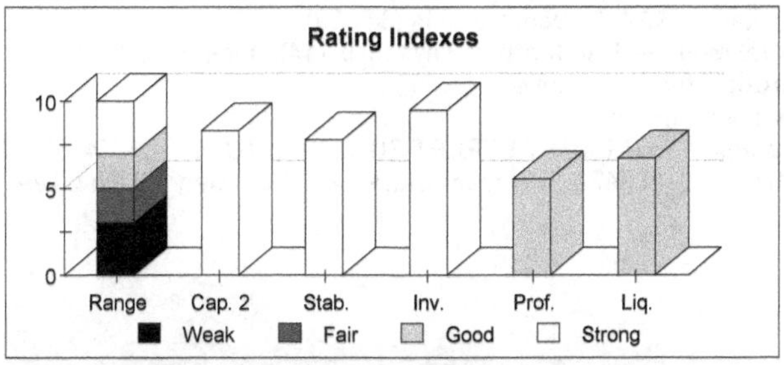

UNITEDHEALTHCARE LIFE INSURANCE COMPANY C Fair

Major Rating Factors: Fair overall results on stability tests (3.9 on a scale of 0 to 10). Good liquidity (6.4) with sufficient resources to handle a spike in claims. Weak profitability (2.3). Excellent expense controls.
Other Rating Factors: Strong capitalization (8.9) based on excellent risk adjusted capital (severe loss scenario). High quality investment portfolio (8.0).
Principal Business: Group health insurance (96%) and individual health insurance (4%).
Principal Investments: NonCMO investment grade bonds (65%) and CMOs and structured securities (35%).
Investments in Affiliates: None
Group Affiliation: UnitedHealth Group Inc
Licensed in: All states except MA, NY, PR
Commenced Business: December 1982
Address: 3100 AMS BOULEVARD, GREEN BAY, WI 54313
Phone: (800) 232-5432 **Domicile State:** WI **NAIC Code:** 97179

Data Date	Rating	RACR #1	RACR #2	Total Assets ($mil)	Capital ($mil)	Net Premium ($mil)	Net Income ($mil)
3-19	C	2.89	2.28	253.1	170.1	118.7	12.3
3-18	C	2.58	2.04	232.2	142.2	115.0	-1.5
2018	C	2.76	2.18	241.2	158.9	471.7	15.6
2017	C	2.68	2.12	224.2	142.9	435.6	32.1
2016	C	1.44	1.14	508.1	167.5	960.8	-9.0
2015	C	1.61	1.28	488.4	137.1	700.9	-143.0
2014	B	1.51	1.23	132.6	41.4	245.0	-15.4

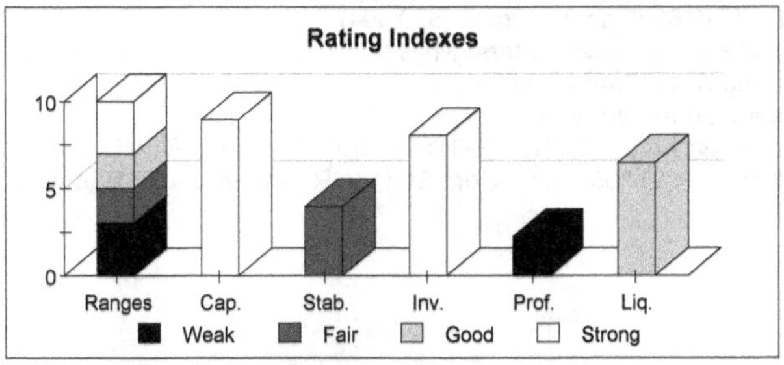

UNITEDHEALTHCARE OF NEW MEXICO INC B- Good

Major Rating Factors: Excellent profitability (8.9 on a scale of 0 to 10). Strong capitalization (10.0) based on excellent current risk-adjusted capital (severe loss scenario). High quality investment portfolio (8.1).
Other Rating Factors: Excellent liquidity (7.1) with ample operational cash flow and liquid investments.
Principal Business: Medicaid (98%), Medicare (2%)
Mem Phys: 18: 12,227 **17:** 11,787 **18 MLR** 75.4% **/ 18 Admin Exp** N/A
Enroll(000): Q1 19: 4 **18:** 2 **17:** 88 **Med Exp PMPM:** $567
Principal Investments: Long-term bonds (54%), cash and equiv (46%)
Provider Compensation ($000): Contr fee ($366,581), FFS ($79,966), capitation ($10,793), bonus arrang ($403)
Total Member Encounters: Phys (530,908), non-phys (808,198)
Group Affiliation: None
Licensed in: NM
Address: 8220 SAN PEDRO NE Ste 300, ALBUQUERQUE, NM 87113
Phone: (505) 449-4131 **Dom State:** NM **Commenced Bus:** N/A

Data Date	Rating	RACR #1	RACR #2	Total Assets ($mil)	Capital ($mil)	Net Premium ($mil)	Net Income ($mil)
3-19	B-	10.51	8.75	225.5	174.3	8.2	3.5
3-18	C	3.61	3.01	267.6	108.7	207.5	-9.0
2018	C+	9.76	8.13	238.0	161.0	543.6	52.9
2017	E	2.82	2.35	263.8	121.3	790.0	11.0
2016	E	20.02	16.69	355.2	136.0	865.4	34.4
2015	E	9.31	7.75	362.6	126.2	918.9	14.9
2014	E	9.24	7.70	312.4	130.2	812.4	34.2

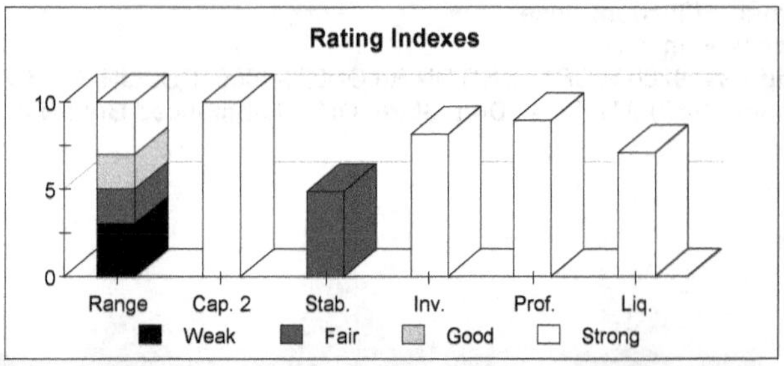

UNITEDHEALTHCARE OF OKLAHOMA INC B Good

Major Rating Factors: Good overall results on stability tests (6.3 on a scale of 0 to 10). Rating is significantly influenced by the good financial results of . Good liquidity (6.8) with sufficient resources (cash flows and marketable investments) to handle a spike in claims. Excellent profitability (9.2).
Other Rating Factors: Strong capitalization index (8.8) based on excellent current risk-adjusted capital (severe loss scenario). High quality investment portfolio (9.2).
Principal Business: Medicare (77%), comp med (23%)
Mem Phys: 18: 14,041 **17:** 13,202 **18 MLR** 81.7% **/ 18 Admin Exp** N/A
Enroll(000): Q1 19: 51 **18:** 52 **17:** 47 **Med Exp PMPM:** $653
Principal Investments: Long-term bonds (99%), cash and equiv (1%)
Provider Compensation ($000): Contr fee ($369,147), FFS ($19,341), capitation ($7,418), bonus arrang ($4,009)
Total Member Encounters: Phys (819,114), non-phys (166,169)
Group Affiliation: None
Licensed in: OK
Address: 7666 E 61ST STREET SUITE 500, TULSA, OK 74133
Phone: (512) 347-2600 **Dom State:** OK **Commenced Bus:** N/A

Data Date	Rating	RACR #1	RACR #2	Total Assets ($mil)	Capital ($mil)	Net Premium ($mil)	Net Income ($mil)
3-19	B	2.82	2.35	138.5	77.0	136.6	14.3
3-18	B	2.58	2.15	171.6	57.8	125.2	-0.6
2018	B	2.32	1.93	117.0	62.7	490.1	26.9
2017	B	1.63	1.36	122.3	58.3	425.3	32.9
2016	B	1.91	1.59	106.7	42.9	401.5	6.6
2015	B-	2.21	1.84	106.5	41.2	353.5	2.1
2014	B	2.72	2.27	94.4	53.5	371.5	16.5

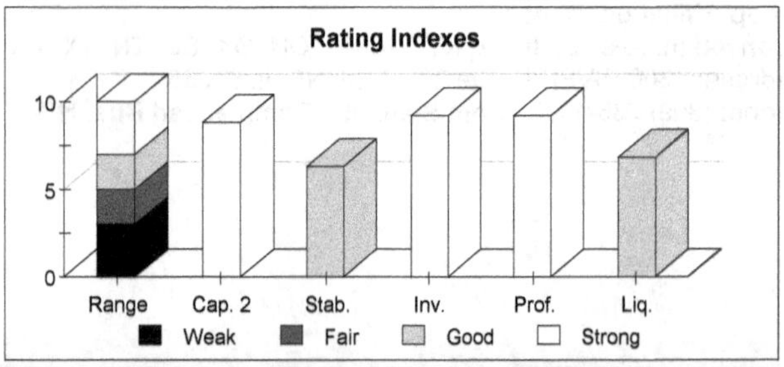

UNITEDHEALTHCARE OF OREGON * B+ Good

Major Rating Factors: Good overall results on stability tests (6.5 on a scale of 0 to 10). Rating is significantly influenced by the good financial results of . Good liquidity (6.7) with sufficient resources (cash flows and marketable investments) to handle a spike in claims. Excellent profitability (9.1).
Other Rating Factors: Strong capitalization index (9.2) based on excellent current risk-adjusted capital (severe loss scenario). High quality investment portfolio (9.3).
Principal Business: Medicare (100%)
Mem Phys: 18: 57,039 **17:** 62,705 **18 MLR** 82.8% **/ 18 Admin Exp** N/A
Enroll(000): Q1 19: 139 **18:** 133 **17:** 122 **Med Exp PMPM:** $742
Principal Investments: Long-term bonds (100%)
Provider Compensation ($000): Contr fee ($949,718), capitation ($144,867), FFS ($40,592), bonus arrang ($20,404)
Total Member Encounters: Phys (2,173,914), non-phys (428,188)
Group Affiliation: None
Licensed in: OR, WA
Address: FIVE CENTERPOINTE DRIVE, LAKE OSWEGO, OR 97035
Phone: (952) 936-1300 **Dom State:** OR **Commenced Bus:** N/A

Data Date	Rating	RACR #1	RACR #2	Total Assets ($mil)	Capital ($mil)	Net Premium ($mil)	Net Income ($mil)
3-19	B+	3.08	2.57	462.8	228.8	400.7	27.6
3-18	B+	2.45	2.04	528.3	151.9	357.4	6.1
2018	B+	2.73	2.28	402.3	202.4	1,410.5	56.2
2017	B+	1.71	1.43	371.7	149.2	1,233.7	19.9
2016	B	2.22	1.85	260.1	107.4	975.1	4.1
2015	B-	7.21	6.01	126.9	89.1	256.0	8.4
2014	B-	3.51	2.93	64.2	38.6	229.1	12.6

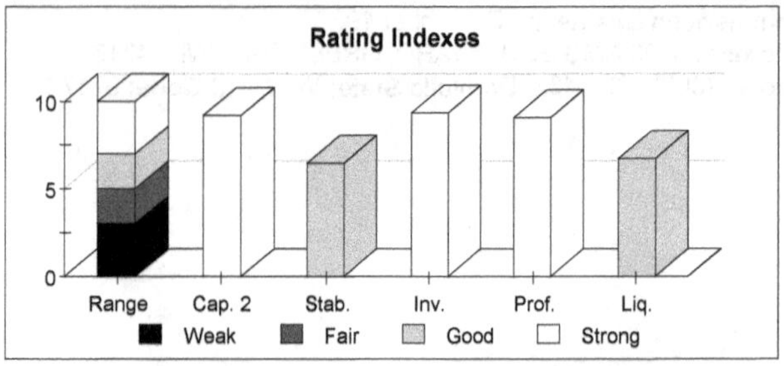

UNITEDHEALTHCARE OF PENNSYLVANIA INC B Good

Major Rating Factors: Good overall results on stability tests (6.6 on a scale of 0 to 10). Rating is significantly influenced by the good financial results of . Excellent profitability (8.4). Strong capitalization index (10.0) based on excellent current risk-adjusted capital (severe loss scenario).
Other Rating Factors: High quality investment portfolio (9.1). Excellent liquidity (7.0) with ample operational cash flow and liquid investments.
Principal Business: Medicaid (94%), comp med (6%)
Mem Phys: 18: 47,685 **17:** 47,959 **18 MLR** 79.1% **/ 18 Admin Exp** N/A
Enroll(000): Q1 19: 261 **18:** 258 **17:** 264 **Med Exp PMPM:** $313
Principal Investments: Long-term bonds (81%), cash and equiv (19%)
Provider Compensation ($000): Contr fee ($710,791), FFS ($279,086), capitation ($17,848), bonus arrang ($1,300)
Total Member Encounters: Phys (1,786,973), non-phys (977,737)
Group Affiliation: None
Licensed in: PA
Address: 1001 BRINTON ROAD, PITTSBURGH, PA 15212
Phone: (412) 858-4000 **Dom State:** PA **Commenced Bus:** N/A

Data Date	Rating	RACR #1	RACR #2	Total Assets ($mil)	Capital ($mil)	Net Premium ($mil)	Net Income ($mil)
3-19	B	4.49	3.74	411.0	198.3	296.6	7.7
3-18	B	4.10	3.41	422.5	172.4	242.2	-2.4
2018	B	4.33	3.61	400.6	190.6	1,241.1	45.2
2017	B	3.41	2.84	411.9	199.6	1,239.9	57.4
2016	B	7.66	6.39	525.8	173.0	1,347.1	30.5
2015	B	2.51	2.09	428.2	143.0	1,123.0	8.8
2014	B	2.95	2.46	278.4	145.0	919.9	10.1

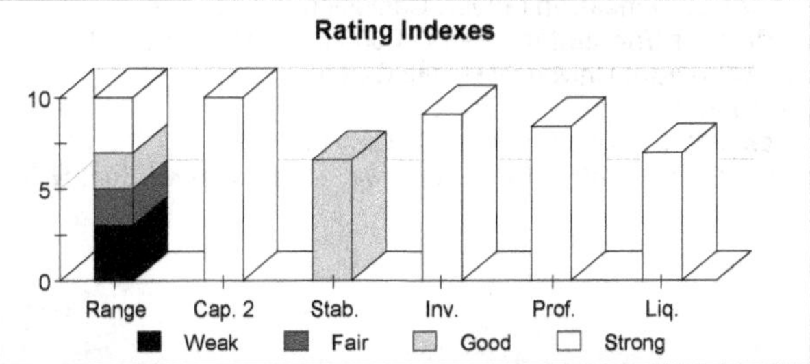

UNITEDHEALTHCARE OF WASHINGTON INC B Good

Major Rating Factors: Good liquidity (6.5 on a scale of 0 to 10) with sufficient resources (cash flows and marketable investments) to handle a spike in claims. Excellent profitability (7.1). Strong capitalization (9.7) based on excellent current risk-adjusted capital (severe loss scenario).
Other Rating Factors: High quality investment portfolio (8.6).
Principal Business: Medicaid (74%), comp med (26%)
Mem Phys: 18: 41,364 **17:** 39,750 **18 MLR** 81.4% **/ 18 Admin Exp** N/A
Enroll(000): Q1 19: 229 **18:** 252 **17:** 268 **Med Exp PMPM:** $240
Principal Investments: Long-term bonds (92%), cash and equiv (8%)
Provider Compensation ($000): Contr fee ($655,109), FFS ($67,976), capitation ($47,384), bonus arrang ($1,054)
Total Member Encounters: Phys (1,817,544), non-phys (657,557)
Group Affiliation: None
Licensed in: WA
Address: 7525 SE 24TH Ste 200, SEATTLE, WA 98101
Phone: (952) 936-1300 **Dom State:** WA **Commenced Bus:** N/A

Data Date	Rating	RACR #1	RACR #2	Total Assets ($mil)	Capital ($mil)	Net Premium ($mil)	Net Income ($mil)
3-19	B	3.48	2.90	352.7	173.5	214.5	22.1
3-18	C	N/A	N/A	363.9	136.6	251.3	-9.2
2018	C+	3.07	2.56	287.2	152.1	923.2	17.2
2017	C	N/A	N/A	358.3	144.1	1,076.8	10.8
2016	C	2.68	2.23	358.1	140.7	1,027.2	16.3
2015	B	3.14	2.62	480.4	222.4	1,428.2	15.0
2014	B	24.37	20.31	638.8	212.3	1,334.4	22.5

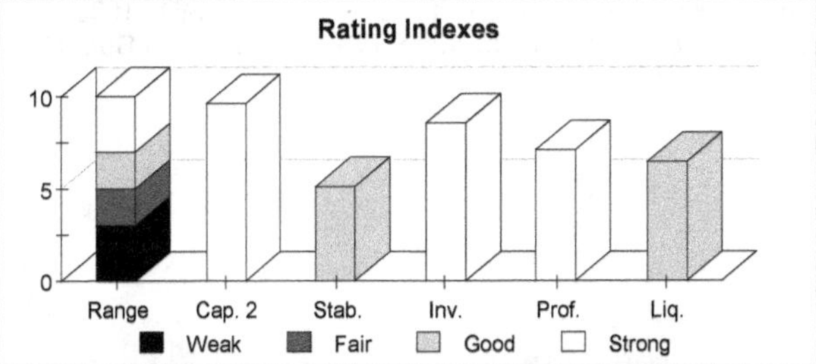

UNITEDHEALTHCARE PLAN RIVER VALLEY B Good

Major Rating Factors: Good capitalization index (6.9 on a scale of 0 to 10) based on excellent current risk-adjusted capital (severe loss scenario). Good overall results on stability tests (5.8). Rating is significantly influenced by the good financial results of . Good liquidity (6.6) with sufficient resources (cash flows and marketable investments) to handle a spike in claims.
Other Rating Factors: Fair profitability index (4.4). High quality investment portfolio (6.9).
Principal Business: Medicaid (82%), Medicare (15%), comp med (3%)
Mem Phys: 18: 135,644 **17:** 126,348 **18 MLR** 89.0% **/ 18 Admin Exp** N/A
Enroll(000): Q1 19: 931 **18:** 937 **17:** 935 **Med Exp PMPM:** $481
Principal Investments: Long-term bonds (59%), cash and equiv (40%), other (1%)
Provider Compensation ($000): Contr fee ($4,709,615), FFS ($529,674), capitation ($108,777), bonus arrang ($16,325)
Total Member Encounters: Phys (9,685,597), non-phys (6,660,426)
Group Affiliation: None
Licensed in: IL, IA, TN, VA
Address: 1300 RIVER DRIVE SUITE 200, MOLINE, IL 61265
Phone: (309) 736-4600 **Dom State:** IL **Commenced Bus:** N/A

Data Date	Rating	RACR #1	RACR #2	Total Assets ($mil)	Capital ($mil)	Net Premium ($mil)	Net Income ($mil)
3-19	B	1.23	1.03	1,413.7	410.7	1,560.7	-62.9
3-18	B	2.20	1.83	1,323.8	402.2	1,476.7	-38.4
2018	B	1.38	1.15	1,274.7	463.0	6,121.5	-30.0
2017	B	1.92	1.60	1,243.6	446.3	4,007.7	66.1
2016	B	2.61	2.17	1,063.1	434.3	3,591.4	126.0
2015	B-	2.79	2.33	1,131.1	423.3	3,404.1	62.5
2014	B+	2.98	2.48	1,342.9	600.3	4,245.8	237.0

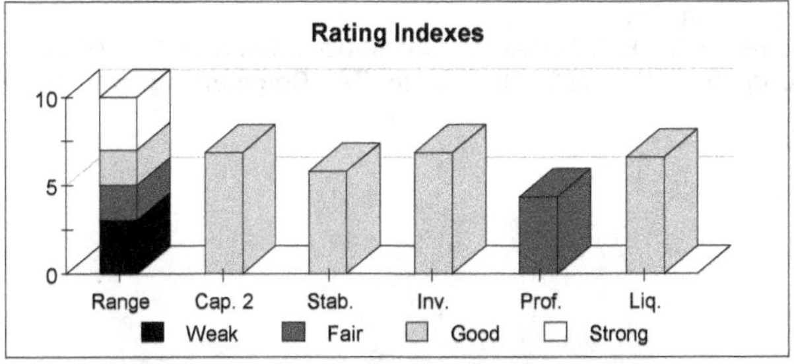

UNITY HEALTH PLANS INS CORP C Fair

Major Rating Factors: Fair profitability index (3.7 on a scale of 0 to 10). Fair quality investment portfolio (4.4). Good liquidity (6.8) with sufficient resources (cash flows and marketable investments) to handle a spike in claims.
Other Rating Factors: Strong capitalization index (7.3) based on excellent current risk-adjusted capital (severe loss scenario). Excellent overall results on stability tests (7.2) based on healthy premium and capital growth during 2018, steady enrollment growth, averaging 9% over the past five years.
Principal Business: Comp med (100%)
Mem Phys: 18: 9,567 **17:** 6,272 **18 MLR** 89.3% **/ 18 Admin Exp** N/A
Enroll(000): Q1 19: 255 **18:** 237 **17:** 204 **Med Exp PMPM:** $410
Principal Investments: Cash and equiv (55%), long-term bonds (41%), nonaffiliate common stock (4%)
Provider Compensation ($000): Capitation ($1,132,644)
Total Member Encounters: Phys (1,003,014), non-phys (1,026,764)
Group Affiliation: University Health Care Inc
Licensed in: WI
Address: 840 Carolina Street, Sauk City, WI 53583
Phone: (608) 643-2491 **Dom State:** WI **Commenced Bus:** N/A

Data Date	Rating	RACR #1	RACR #2	Total Assets ($mil)	Capital ($mil)	Net Premium ($mil)	Net Income ($mil)
3-19	C	1.62	1.35	283.4	100.3	359.3	0.3
3-18	C	1.09	0.90	199.1	48.1	313.6	-13.4
2018	C	1.33	1.11	241.0	82.6	1,276.8	5.8
2017	C	1.18	0.98	170.2	59.7	960.8	0.7
2016	C	1.38	1.15	167.4	61.3	863.5	-8.0
2015	B-	1.23	1.03	148.2	54.1	829.9	-2.7
2014	B-	1.47	1.22	143.1	59.1	755.1	4.6

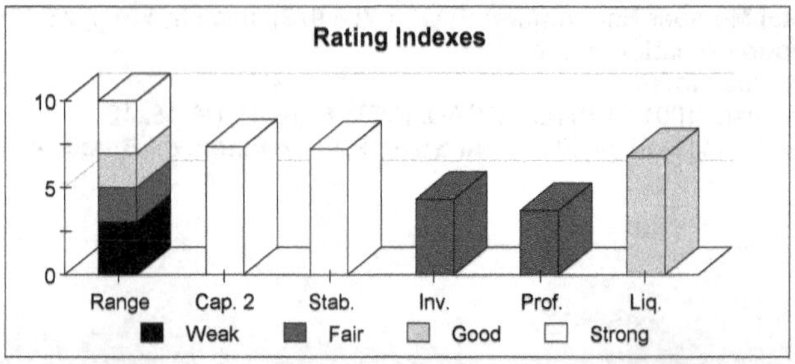

UNIV OF MD HEALTH ADVANTAGE INC E- Very Weak

Major Rating Factors: Weak profitability index (0.4 on a scale of 0 to 10). Poor capitalization (0.0) based on weak current risk-adjusted capital (severe loss scenario). Weak liquidity (0.0) as a spike in claims may stretch capacity.
Other Rating Factors: High quality investment portfolio (9.9).
Principal Business: Medicare (100%)
Mem Phys: 18: N/A **17:** 10,100 **18 MLR** 103.8% **/ 18 Admin Exp** N/A
Enroll(000): Q1 19: 5 **18:** 11 **17:** 7 **Med Exp PMPM:** $1,292
Principal Investments: Cash and equiv (99%), long-term bonds (1%)
Provider Compensation ($000): Contr fee ($172,897), FFS ($15,908)
Total Member Encounters: Phys (222,720), non-phys (8,155)
Group Affiliation: University of Maryland Health Ventur
Licensed in: MD
Address: 1966 Greenspring Dr Ste 600, Timonium, MD 21093
Phone: (410) 878-7709 **Dom State:** MD **Commenced Bus:** N/A

Data Date	Rating	RACR #1	RACR #2	Total Assets ($mil)	Capital ($mil)	Net Premium ($mil)	Net Income ($mil)
3-19	E-	0.25	0.21	23.9	5.8	20.7	-1.6
3-18	E-	N/A	N/A	38.6	4.9	37.7	-4.0
2018	E-	0.13	0.11	28.7	3.1	154.3	-32.4
2017	E-	N/A	N/A	23.4	8.4	91.0	-20.4
2016	D	0.49	0.41	15.9	5.1	41.6	-18.0
2015	N/A	N/A	N/A	N/A	N/A	N/A	N/A
2014	N/A	N/A	N/A	N/A	N/A	N/A	N/A

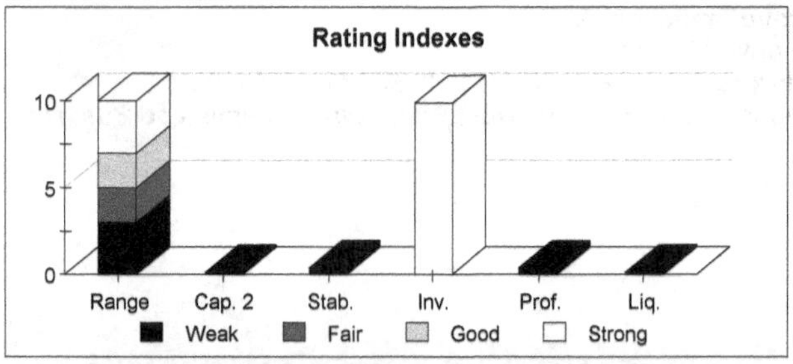

UNIVERSAL CARE E- Very Weak

Major Rating Factors: Weak profitability index (0.8 on a scale of 0 to 10). Poor capitalization index (0.0) based on weak current risk-adjusted capital (severe loss scenario). Weak overall results on stability tests (0.0).
Other Rating Factors: Good liquidity (6.8) with sufficient resources (cash flows and marketable investments) to handle a spike in claims.
Principal Business: Medicare (97%), Medicaid (3%)
Mem Phys: 18: N/A **17:** N/A **18 MLR** 90.1% **/ 18 Admin Exp** N/A
Enroll(000): Q1 19: 39 **18:** 36 **17:** 19 **Med Exp PMPM:** $767
Principal Investments ($000): Cash and equiv ($28,806)
Provider Compensation ($000): None
Total Member Encounters: N/A
Group Affiliation: None
Licensed in: CA
Address: 5701 Katella Ave MS CA120-0368, Cypress, CA 90630
Phone: (916) 451-1592 **Dom State:** CA **Commenced Bus:** November 1985

Data Date	Rating	RACR #1	RACR #2	Total Assets ($mil)	Capital ($mil)	Net Premium ($mil)	Net Income ($mil)
3-19	E-	N/A	N/A	114.9	-15.1	113.3	2.1
3-18	E-	N/A	N/A	69.4	-5.7	72.7	N/A
2018	E-	N/A	N/A	97.8	-17.2	327.6	-11.5
2017	E-	N/A	N/A	58.8	-5.6	188.4	-4.8
2016	E-	N/A	N/A	52.9	-4.6	142.0	-1.6
2015	E-	N/A	N/A	30.4	-13.7	95.3	-3.2
2014	E-	N/A	N/A	23.6	-4.5	65.5	0.4

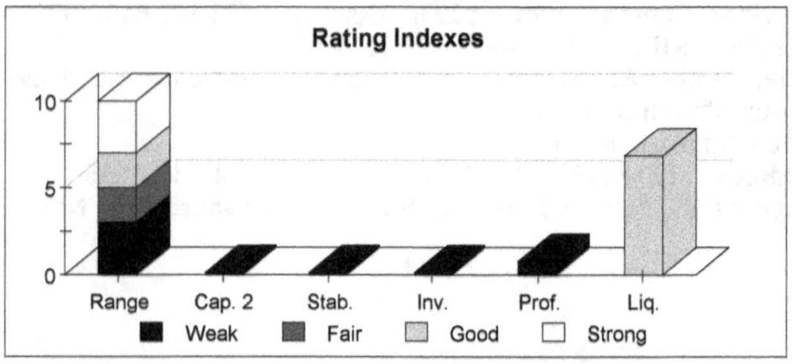

UNIVERSITY HEALTH ALLIANCE C+ Fair

Major Rating Factors: Good liquidity (6.9 on a scale of 0 to 10) with sufficient resources (cash flows and marketable investments) to handle a spike in claims. Low quality investment portfolio (2.2). Excellent profitability (7.5).
Other Rating Factors: Strong capitalization (8.7) based on excellent current risk-adjusted capital (severe loss scenario).
Principal Business: Comp med (80%), dental (2%), other (18%)
Mem Phys: 18: 3,900 **17:** 6,554 **18 MLR** 80.0% **/ 18 Admin Exp** N/A
Enroll(000): Q1 19: 62 **18:** 62 **17:** 56 **Med Exp PMPM:** $356
Principal Investments: Nonaffiliate common stock (76%), cash and equiv (17%), long-term bonds (7%)
Provider Compensation ($000): FFS ($188,110), contr fee ($58,961), capitation ($5,304), bonus arrang ($867)
Total Member Encounters: Phys (358,676), non-phys (172,850)
Group Affiliation: None
Licensed in: HI
Address: 700 BISHOP ST Ste 300, HONOLULU, HI 96813
Phone: (808) 532-2019 **Dom State:** HI **Commenced Bus:** N/A

Data Date	Rating	RACR #1	RACR #2	Total Assets ($mil)	Capital ($mil)	Net Premium ($mil)	Net Income ($mil)
3-19	C+	2.69	2.24	151.8	99.8	82.8	7.5
3-18	C+	2.10	1.75	129.1	72.6	77.5	6.3
2018	C+	2.27	1.89	137.8	87.0	327.9	28.7
2017	C+	1.94	1.62	115.8	67.8	287.0	18.6
2016	C+	1.40	1.17	96.5	50.1	272.7	3.6
2015	C+	1.43	1.19	83.6	46.3	240.8	-0.9
2014	C+	1.65	1.38	81.0	48.6	227.9	2.3

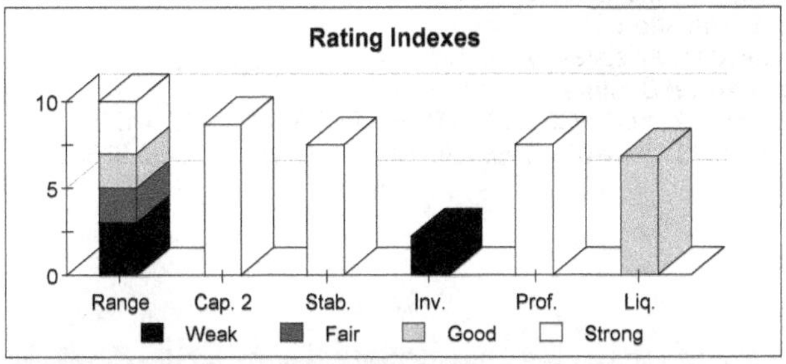

UNIVERSITY HEALTH CARE INC D Weak

Major Rating Factors: Weak profitability index (0.8 on a scale of 0 to 10). Poor capitalization index (1.8) based on weak current risk-adjusted capital (moderate loss scenario). Weak overall results on stability tests (0.6) based on a steep decline in capital during 2018 but steady enrollment growth, averaging 8% over the past five years.
Other Rating Factors: Weak liquidity (0.6) as a spike in claims may stretch capacity. High quality investment portfolio (7.2).
Principal Business: Medicaid (98%), Medicare (2%)
Mem Phys: 18: 27,234 **17:** 26,748 **18 MLR** 94.8% **/ 18 Admin Exp** N/A
Enroll(000): Q1 19: 319 **18:** 320 **17:** 318 **Med Exp PMPM:** $477
Principal Investments: Long-term bonds (40%), nonaffiliate common stock (32%), cash and equiv (29%)
Provider Compensation ($000): Contr fee ($1,642,676), capitation ($193,055), FFS ($45,894)
Total Member Encounters: Phys (2,450,742), non-phys (2,459,054)
Group Affiliation: University of Louisville Physicians
Licensed in: KY
Address: 5100 Commerce Crossings Drive, Louisville, KY 40229
Phone: (502) 585-7900 **Dom State:** KY **Commenced Bus:** N/A

Data Date	Rating	RACR #1	RACR #2	Total Assets ($mil)	Capital ($mil)	Net Premium ($mil)	Net Income ($mil)
3-19	D	0.48	0.40	252.2	62.7	468.3	-3.8
3-18	B	1.31	1.09	407.7	192.5	491.8	-27.3
2018	D+	0.72	0.60	387.0	92.1	1,945.9	-122.6
2017	B	1.46	1.22	454.4	213.4	1,925.0	17.1
2016	B	1.37	1.15	414.6	196.8	1,747.8	-57.9
2015	B+	1.94	1.62	444.2	249.9	1,653.1	39.1
2014	B+	2.30	1.92	357.2	214.9	1,290.3	115.0

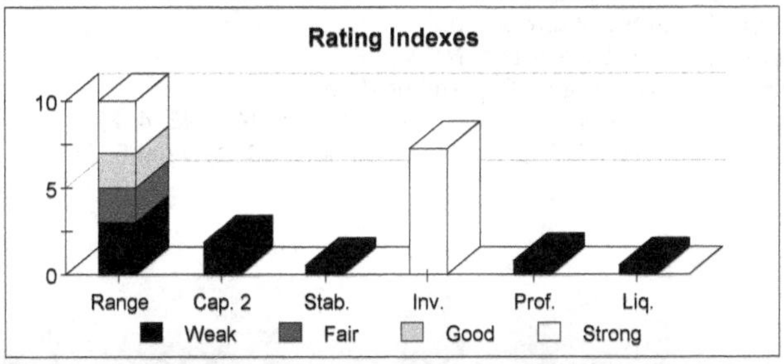

UNIVERSITY OF UTAH HEALTH INS PLANS C+ Fair

Major Rating Factors: Fair quality investment portfolio (4.8 on a scale of 0 to 10). Good overall profitability index (5.8). Strong capitalization (9.7) based on excellent current risk-adjusted capital (severe loss scenario).
Other Rating Factors: Excellent liquidity (7.6) with ample operational cash flow and liquid investments.
Principal Business: Comp med (100%)
Mem Phys: 18: 37,492 **17:** 16,463 **18 MLR** 74.5% **/ 18 Admin Exp** N/A
Enroll(000): Q1 19: 32 **18:** 30 **17:** 10 **Med Exp PMPM:** $385
Principal Investments: Long-term bonds (50%), cash and equiv (39%), pref stock (10%)
Provider Compensation ($000): Contr fee ($121,012), FFS ($3,904)
Total Member Encounters: Phys (134,159), non-phys (127,376)
Group Affiliation: None
Licensed in: UT
Address: 6053 Fashion Square Dr Ste 110, Murray, UT 84107
Phone: (801) 587-6480 **Dom State:** UT **Commenced Bus:** N/A

Data Date	Rating	RACR #1	RACR #2	Total Assets ($mil)	Capital ($mil)	Net Premium ($mil)	Net Income ($mil)
3-19	C+	3.50	2.92	122.0	56.1	48.5	11.5
3-18	D+	N/A	N/A	72.3	16.7	37.0	-3.7
2018	C	2.69	2.24	110.6	44.1	181.1	24.3
2017	D+	N/A	N/A	35.8	20.5	51.1	1.8
2016	D+	2.22	1.85	17.1	10.6	19.1	-4.2
2015	N/A	N/A	N/A	4.8	3.8	N/A	-1.2
2014	N/A	N/A	N/A	2.0	2.0	N/A	N/A

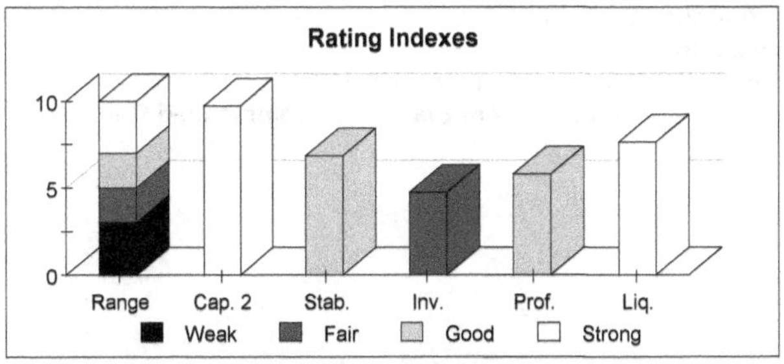

UNUM INSURANCE COMPANY C Fair

Major Rating Factors: Fair overall results on stability tests (3.8 on a scale of 0 to 10). Weak profitability (2.1) with investment income below regulatory standards in relation to interest assumptions of reserves. Strong overall capitalization (10.0) based on excellent risk adjusted capital (severe loss scenario). However, capital levels have fluctuated somewhat during past years.
Other Rating Factors: High quality investment portfolio (7.1). Excellent liquidity (7.0).
Principal Business: Group health insurance (67%) and individual life insurance (33%).
Principal Investments: NonCMO investment grade bonds (78%) and CMOs and structured securities (19%).
Investments in Affiliates: None
Group Affiliation: Unum Group
Licensed in: All states except NY, PR
Commenced Business: February 1966
Address: 2211 CONGRESS STREET, PORTLAND, ME 4122
Phone: (423) 294-1011 **Domicile State:** ME **NAIC Code:** 67601

Data Date	Rating	RACR #1	RACR #2	Total Assets ($mil)	Capital ($mil)	Net Premium ($mil)	Net Income ($mil)
3-19	C	6.89	4.10	65.3	46.7	4.8	0.2
3-18	C	7.00	4.49	61.3	46.6	1.1	0.6
2018	C	6.92	4.51	62.8	46.9	4.8	1.2
2017	C	6.93	4.58	60.0	46.1	0.0	1.9
2016	C	6.79	4.45	59.5	45.0	0.0	1.8
2015	C	6.71	4.19	57.0	43.7	0.0	2.5
2014	C	6.46	3.96	56.2	41.6	0.0	2.3

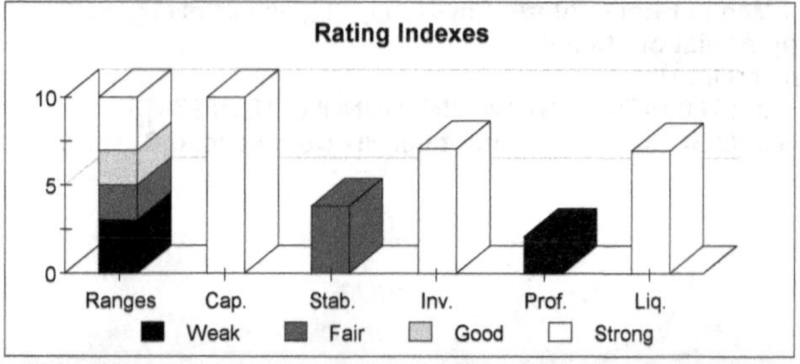

UNUM LIFE INSURANCE COMPANY OF AMERICA C+ Fair

Major Rating Factors: Fair quality investment portfolio (3.7 on a scale of 0 to 10) with large holdings of BBB rated bonds in addition to significant exposure to junk bonds. Fair overall results on stability tests (4.8). Strong capitalization (7.3) based on excellent risk adjusted capital (severe loss scenario). Capital levels have been relatively consistent over the last five years.
Other Rating Factors: Excellent profitability (8.0). Excellent liquidity (7.2).
Principal Business: Group health insurance (63%), group life insurance (30%), individual health insurance (6%), and reinsurance (1%).
Principal Investments: NonCMO investment grade bonds (75%), noninv. grade bonds (11%), mortgages in good standing (6%), and CMOs and structured securities (5%).
Investments in Affiliates: None
Group Affiliation: Unum Group
Licensed in: All states except NY
Commenced Business: September 1966
Address: 2211 CONGRESS STREET, PORTLAND, ME 4122
Phone: (207) 575-2211 **Domicile State:** ME **NAIC Code:** 62235

Data Date	Rating	RACR #1	RACR #2	Total Assets ($mil)	Capital ($mil)	Net Premium ($mil)	Net Income ($mil)
3-19	C+	2.25	1.19	21,897.0	1,705.7	929.9	111.9
3-18	C+	2.24	1.19	21,596.2	1,660.0	895.3	140.2
2018	C+	2.41	1.28	22,022.4	1,834.2	3,616.2	493.2
2017	C+	2.35	1.24	21,455.0	1,728.0	3,486.2	378.2
2016	C+	2.33	1.23	21,077.8	1,686.5	3,348.0	349.3
2015	C+	2.28	1.22	20,552.3	1,567.3	3,168.1	203.5
2014	C+	2.42	1.29	19,701.4	1,546.1	2,914.6	195.0

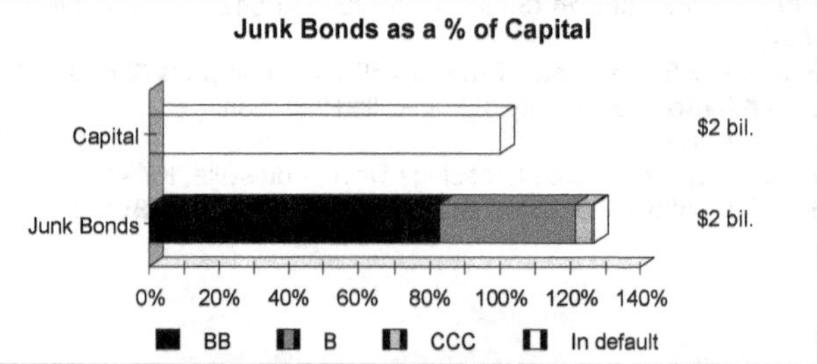

UPMC FOR YOU INC * B+ Good

Major Rating Factors: Good quality investment portfolio (6.8 on a scale of 0 to 10). Excellent profitability (7.9). Strong capitalization (7.8) based on excellent current risk-adjusted capital (severe loss scenario).
Other Rating Factors: Excellent liquidity (6.9) with sufficient resources (cash flows and marketable investments) to handle a spike in claims.
Principal Business: Medicaid (87%), Medicare (13%)
Mem Phys: 18: 33,093 **17:** 25,665 **18 MLR** 88.2% **/ 18 Admin Exp** N/A
Enroll(000): Q1 19: 524 **18:** 491 **17:** 445 **Med Exp PMPM:** $538
Principal Investments: Long-term bonds (68%), cash and equiv (29%), other (3%)
Provider Compensation ($000): Contr fee ($3,114,270), capitation ($1,636)
Total Member Encounters: Phys (4,069,308), non-phys (4,967,454)
Group Affiliation: None
Licensed in: PA
Address: 600 Grant St, Pittsburgh, PA 15219
Phone: (412) 434-1200 **Dom State:** PA **Commenced Bus:** N/A

Data Date	Rating	RACR #1	RACR #2	Total Assets ($mil)	Capital ($mil)	Net Premium ($mil)	Net Income ($mil)
3-19	B+	2.03	1.69	991.0	445.1	1,162.9	28.5
3-18	A-	2.80	2.34	867.9	441.6	879.8	14.7
2018	B+	1.89	1.57	810.4	413.9	3,603.0	36.8
2017	B+	2.12	1.77	668.5	425.4	2,650.0	72.7
2016	B+	2.49	2.07	750.6	351.4	2,383.2	105.6
2015	B	1.64	1.37	527.8	247.6	2,061.8	66.4
2014	B+	2.12	1.76	428.1	228.2	1,687.5	59.0

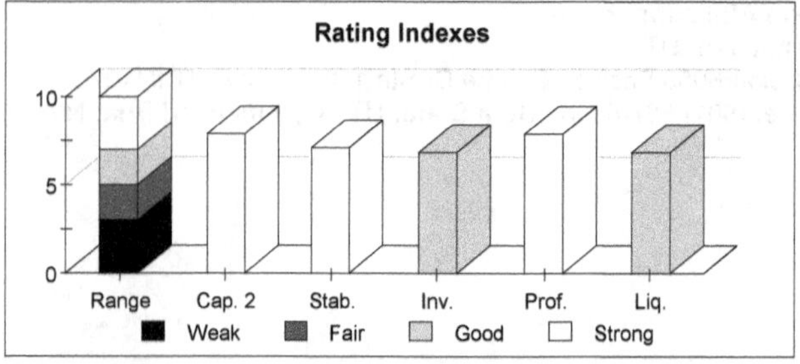

UPMC HEALTH BENEFITS INC — C — Fair

Major Rating Factors: Fair reserve development (3.8 on a scale of 0 to 10) as the level of reserves has at times been insufficient to cover claims. In four of the last five years reserves (two year development) were between 17% and 42% deficient. Poor long-term capitalization index (2.9) based on fair current risk adjusted capital (severe loss scenario).
Other Rating Factors: Weak overall results on stability tests (2.8). Good liquidity (6.4) with sufficient resources (cash flows and marketable investments) to handle a spike in claims. Excellent profitability (8.5) with operating gains in each of the last five years.
Principal Business: Workers compensation (71%) and other accident & health (29%).
Principal Investments: Investment grade bonds (58%), misc. investments (23%), cash (18%), and non investment grade bonds (1%).
Investments in Affiliates: None
Group Affiliation: UPMC Health System
Licensed in: DE, MD, OH, PA, WV
Commenced Business: February 2000
Address: 600 Grant Street, Pittsburgh, PA 15219
Phone: (412) 434-1200 **Domicile State:** PA **NAIC Code:** 11018

Data Date	Rating	RACR #1	RACR #2	Loss Ratio %	Total Assets ($mil)	Capital ($mil)	Net Premium ($mil)	Net Income ($mil)
3-19	C	0.87	0.54	N/A	286.6	128.0	37.8	1.4
3-18	D+	0.92	0.58	N/A	241.3	110.7	30.9	1.2
2018	C	0.85	0.53	72.3	274.5	120.0	140.2	11.4
2017	D+	1.01	0.62	81.5	237.5	110.6	117.7	3.4
2016	D+	0.58	0.36	74.5	170.5	56.4	101.0	0.1
2015	D+	0.96	0.59	76.9	147.9	45.3	91.2	1.1
2014	C	0.27	0.17	73.9	85.4	17.9	88.6	2.6

Reserve Deficiency (as % of capital)

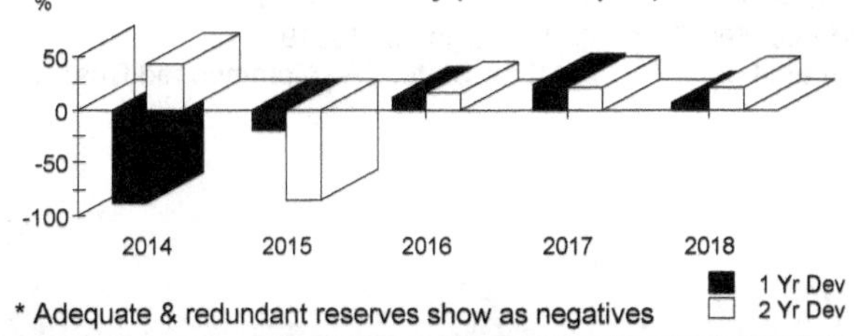

UPMC HEALTH COVERAGE INC — B- — Good

Major Rating Factors: Excellent profitability (9.2 on a scale of 0 to 10). Strong capitalization (10.0) based on excellent current risk-adjusted capital (severe loss scenario). Excellent liquidity (8.1) with ample operational cash flow and liquid investments.
Other Rating Factors: Low quality investment portfolio (0.7).
Principal Business: Comp med (100%)
Mem Phys: 18: 17,047 **17:** 13,089 **18 MLR** 78.2% **/ 18 Admin Exp** N/A
Enroll(000): Q1 19: 6 **18:** 5 **17:** 5 **Med Exp PMPM:** $362
Principal Investments: Cash and equiv (99%), long-term bonds (1%)
Provider Compensation ($000): Contr fee ($21,781)
Total Member Encounters: Phys (34,971), non-phys (23,825)
Group Affiliation: None
Licensed in: PA
Address: 600 Grant St, Pittsburgh, PA 15219
Phone: (412) 434-1200 **Dom State:** PA **Commenced Bus:** N/A

Data Date	Rating	RACR #1	RACR #2	Total Assets ($mil)	Capital ($mil)	Net Premium ($mil)	Net Income ($mil)
3-19	B-	7.00	5.84	20.2	16.4	8.0	0.6
3-18	B	N/A	N/A	18.8	15.4	7.2	1.0
2018	B-	6.78	5.65	19.1	15.8	27.5	1.0
2017	B	N/A	N/A	17.4	14.9	32.8	3.9
2016	B	5.27	4.39	15.7	10.9	27.7	1.8
2015	B	6.57	5.48	14.7	9.8	27.5	7.7
2014	U	1.59	1.33	7.1	2.1	5.2	-0.6

Rating Indexes

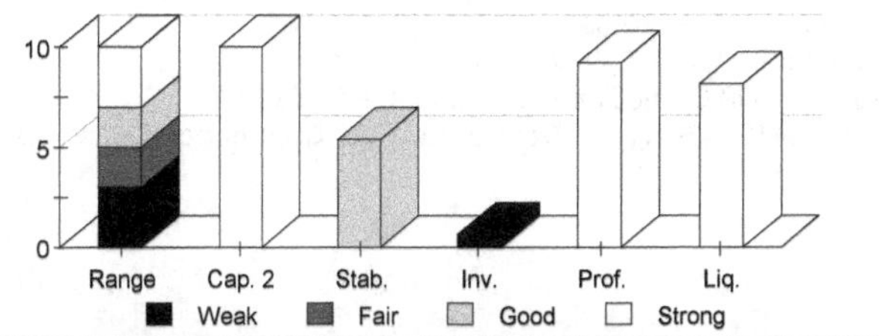

UPMC HEALTH NETWORK INC — C+ — Fair

Major Rating Factors: Fair capitalization (2.9 on a scale of 0 to 10) based on good current risk-adjusted capital (moderate loss scenario). Low quality investment portfolio (1.4). Excellent profitability (7.2).
Other Rating Factors: Excellent liquidity (7.5) with ample operational cash flow and liquid investments.
Principal Business: Medicare (100%)
Mem Phys: 18: 32,531 **17:** 25,147 **18 MLR** 84.4% **/ 18 Admin Exp** N/A
Enroll(000): Q1 19: 10 **18:** 9 **17:** 9 **Med Exp PMPM:** $745
Principal Investments: Cash and equiv (85%), nonaffiliate common stock (2%), other (13%)
Provider Compensation ($000): Contr fee ($82,628)
Total Member Encounters: Phys (135,404), non-phys (139,686)
Group Affiliation: None
Licensed in: PA
Address: 600 Grant St, Pittsburgh, PA 15219
Phone: (412) 434-1200 **Dom State:** PA **Commenced Bus:** N/A

Data Date	Rating	RACR #1	RACR #2	Total Assets ($mil)	Capital ($mil)	Net Premium ($mil)	Net Income ($mil)
3-19	C+	3.78	3.15	48.7	37.6	28.3	2.8
3-18	B-	3.58	2.98	51.4	30.7	24.4	2.5
2018	C+	3.32	2.77	41.7	33.4	97.8	7.0
2017	C	1.97	1.64	36.3	28.2	84.3	9.1
2016	C	3.00	2.50	38.1	19.3	82.2	8.5
2015	D+	2.68	2.23	40.9	25.6	92.2	2.6
2014	D+	3.12	2.60	57.3	40.9	104.1	-1.9

Rating Indexes

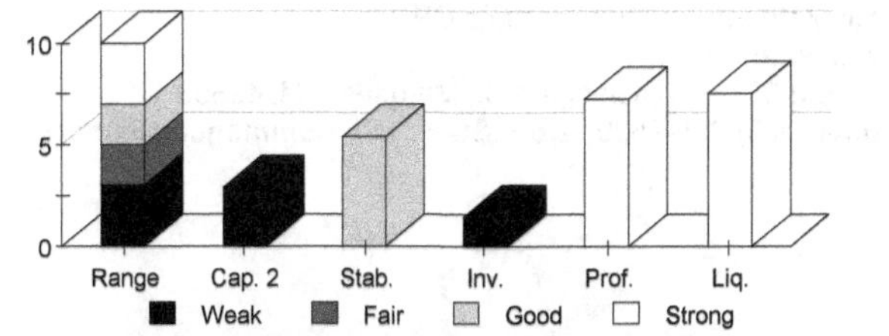

UPMC HEALTH OPTIONS INC — C+ Fair

Major Rating Factors: Good quality investment portfolio (6.8 on a scale of 0 to 10). Good liquidity (6.8) with sufficient resources (cash flows and marketable investments) to handle a spike in claims. Weak profitability index (1.9).
Other Rating Factors: Strong capitalization (8.0) based on excellent current risk-adjusted capital (severe loss scenario).
Principal Business: Comp med (100%)
Mem Phys: 18: 28,556 **17:** 21,311 **18 MLR** 89.5% **/ 18 Admin Exp** N/A
Enroll(000): Q1 19: 442 **18:** 424 **17:** 416 **Med Exp PMPM:** $385
Principal Investments: Long-term bonds (76%), nonaffiliate common stock (22%), cash and equiv (2%)
Provider Compensation ($000): Contr fee ($1,998,260)
Total Member Encounters: Phys (3,231,153), non-phys (2,056,350)
Group Affiliation: None
Licensed in: PA
Address: 600 Grant St, Pittsburgh, PA 15219
Phone: (412) 434-1200 **Dom State:** PA **Commenced Bus:** N/A

Data Date	Rating	RACR #1	RACR #2	Total Assets ($mil)	Capital ($mil)	Net Premium ($mil)	Net Income ($mil)
3-19	C+	2.13	1.78	520.9	300.1	620.7	50.6
3-18	C+	N/A	N/A	525.9	250.1	574.6	58.9
2018	C+	1.70	1.42	461.8	240.0	2,212.4	19.4
2017	C+	N/A	N/A	461.7	222.0	1,984.7	5.0
2016	C+	1.88	1.57	358.2	191.3	1,551.5	-49.6
2015	C	0.89	0.74	344.0	167.7	1,312.9	-76.3
2014	C	0.77	0.64	257.2	132.2	1,046.5	-37.8

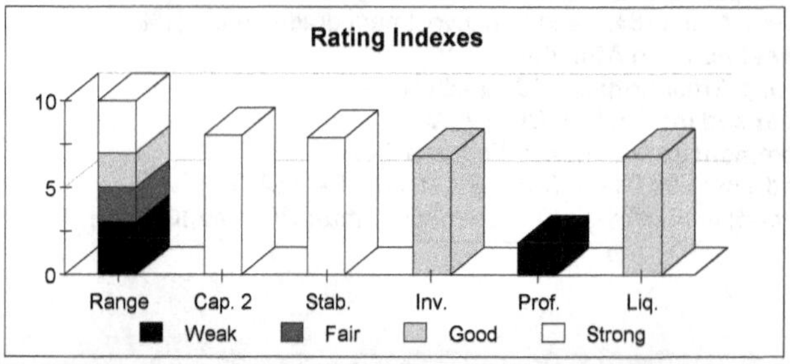

UPMC HEALTH PLAN INC — C+ Fair

Major Rating Factors: Fair overall results on stability tests (3.1 on a scale of 0 to 10) in spite of steady enrollment growth, averaging 8% over the past five years. Good overall profitability index (6.8). Strong capitalization index (7.4) based on excellent current risk-adjusted capital (severe loss scenario).
Other Rating Factors: High quality investment portfolio (7.1). Excellent liquidity (7.0) with sufficient resources (cash flows and marketable investments) to handle a spike in claims.
Principal Business: Medicare (91%), comp med (5%), FEHB (4%)
Mem Phys: 18: 34,738 **17:** 27,635 **18 MLR** 87.0% **/ 18 Admin Exp** N/A
Enroll(000): Q1 19: 161 **18:** 191 **17:** 183 **Med Exp PMPM:** $665
Principal Investments: Long-term bonds (76%), nonaffiliate common stock (23%), other (4%)
Provider Compensation ($000): Contr fee ($1,521,395), capitation ($45)
Total Member Encounters: Phys (2,440,507), non-phys (2,438,959)
Group Affiliation: None
Licensed in: OH, PA, WV
Address: 600 Grant Street, Pittsburgh, PA 15219
Phone: (412) 434-1200 **Dom State:** PA **Commenced Bus:** N/A

Data Date	Rating	RACR #1	RACR #2	Total Assets ($mil)	Capital ($mil)	Net Premium ($mil)	Net Income ($mil)
3-19	C+	1.65	1.37	607.0	186.4	464.0	4.7
3-18	A-	2.15	1.79	744.3	250.4	439.5	25.5
2018	B-	1.68	1.40	566.6	190.2	1,736.2	52.9
2017	A-	1.67	1.39	551.8	260.5	1,605.0	54.1
2016	B+	1.92	1.60	454.5	211.7	1,490.4	27.1
2015	B	1.21	1.00	350.9	185.8	1,371.4	3.3
2014	B	1.16	0.97	376.2	149.7	1,193.0	12.6

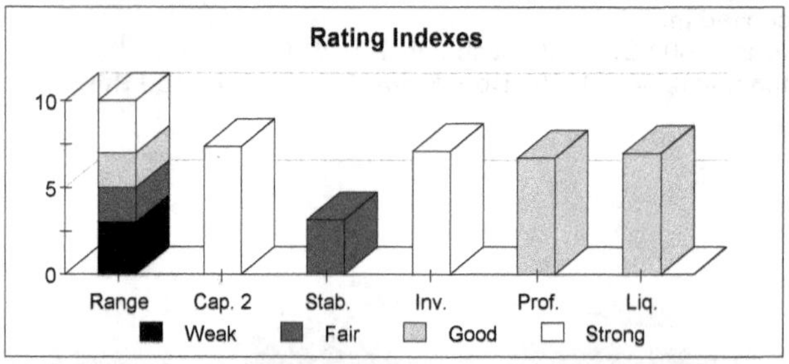

UPPER PENINSULA HEALTH PLAN INC * — B+ Good

Major Rating Factors: Good overall results on stability tests (6.5 on a scale of 0 to 10) based on steady enrollment growth, averaging 5% over the past five years. Rating is significantly influenced by the fair financial results of BRH Holdings GP Ltd. Excellent profitability (9.0). Strong capitalization index (10.0) based on excellent current risk-adjusted capital (severe loss scenario).
Other Rating Factors: High quality investment portfolio (7.8). Excellent liquidity (7.1) with ample operational cash flow and liquid investments.
Principal Business: Medicaid (61%), Medicare (39%)
Mem Phys: 18: 1,731 **17:** 1,558 **18 MLR** 87.8% **/ 18 Admin Exp** N/A
Enroll(000): Q1 19: 50 **18:** 49 **17:** 49 **Med Exp PMPM:** $378
Principal Investments: Cash and equiv (55%), long-term bonds (29%), real estate (16%)
Provider Compensation ($000): Contr fee ($236,056)
Total Member Encounters: Phys (332,562), non-phys (285,546)
Group Affiliation: BRH Holdings GP Ltd
Licensed in: MI
Address: 853 W Washington St, Marquette, MI 49855
Phone: (906) 225-7500 **Dom State:** MI **Commenced Bus:** N/A

Data Date	Rating	RACR #1	RACR #2	Total Assets ($mil)	Capital ($mil)	Net Premium ($mil)	Net Income ($mil)
3-19	B+	3.82	3.19	110.1	56.8	62.0	3.3
3-18	A	2.26	1.88	99.3	57.5	64.4	0.7
2018	B+	3.76	3.13	97.6	55.7	254.4	10.9
2017	A	2.16	1.80	94.5	55.2	292.8	12.0
2016	B	1.80	1.50	82.6	44.7	283.6	8.9
2015	B-	1.68	1.40	77.4	36.3	248.1	13.1
2014	B-	1.73	1.44	46.2	23.5	150.4	4.6

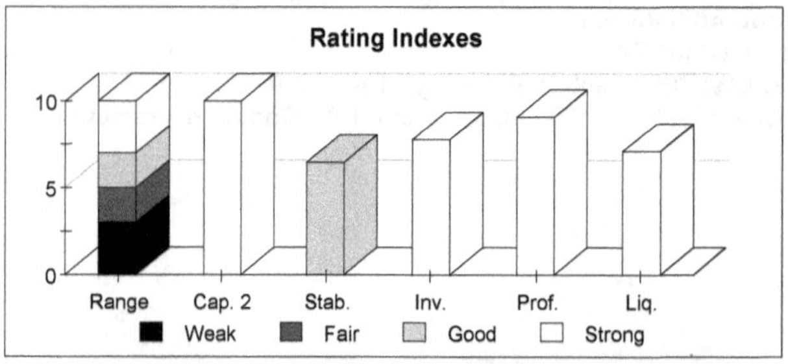

US FIRE INS CO C Fair

Major Rating Factors: Fair overall results on stability tests (3.7 on a scale of 0 to 10) including potential drain of affiliation with Fairfax Financial. Fair profitability index (4.9) with operating losses during 2017. Return on equity has been fair, averaging 5.5% over the past five years.
Other Rating Factors: Good long-term capitalization index (6.9) based on good current risk adjusted capital (moderate loss scenario). Moreover, capital levels have been consistent over the last several years. History of adequate reserve strength (6.4) as reserves have been consistently at an acceptable level. Good liquidity (6.8) with sufficient resources (cash flows and marketable investments) to handle a spike in claims.
Principal Business: Group accident & health (31%), inland marine (26%), other liability (11%), auto liability (9%), workers compensation (8%), commercial multiple peril (5%), and other lines (10%).
Principal Investments: Investment grade bonds (49%), misc. investments (44%), cash (3%), real estate (3%), and non investment grade bonds (1%).
Investments in Affiliates: 28%
Group Affiliation: Fairfax Financial
Licensed in: All states, the District of Columbia and Puerto Rico
Commenced Business: April 1824
Address: 1209 ORANGE STREET, Wilmington, DE 19801
Phone: (973) 490-6600 **Domicile State:** DE **NAIC Code:** 21113

Data Date	Rating	RACR #1	RACR #2	Loss Ratio %	Total Assets ($mil)	Capital ($mil)	Net Premium ($mil)	Net Income ($mil)
3-19	C	1.23	0.99	N/A	4,122.9	1,366.6	379.2	9.6
3-18	C	1.19	0.96	N/A	4,102.4	1,363.2	355.3	25.9
2018	C	1.22	0.99	63.3	4,085.8	1,317.6	1,505.0	80.0
2017	C	1.15	0.94	64.7	4,094.3	1,302.3	1,418.1	-132.0
2016	C	1.35	1.04	63.7	3,949.6	1,218.9	1,370.7	32.3
2015	C	1.45	1.14	64.1	3,736.1	1,178.0	1,262.9	94.5
2014	C	1.62	1.14	67.5	3,248.6	898.6	1,025.1	195.7

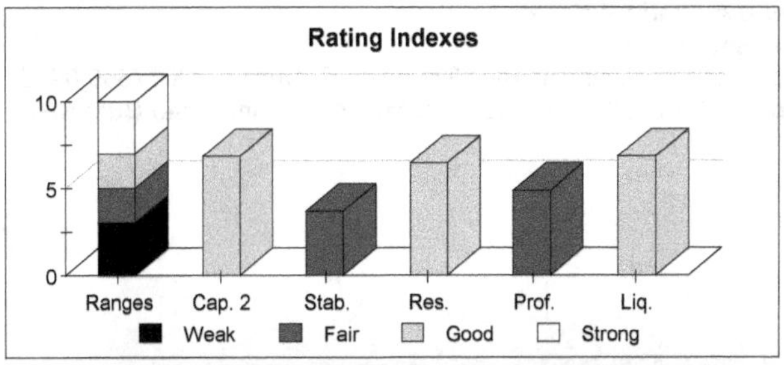

USABLE LIFE * A- Excellent

Major Rating Factors: Good overall results on stability tests (5.9 on a scale of 0 to 10). Strengths that enhance stability include good operational trends and excellent risk diversification. Good liquidity (6.8) with sufficient resources to handle a spike in claims. Strong capitalization (8.6) based on excellent risk adjusted capital (severe loss scenario).
Other Rating Factors: High quality investment portfolio (7.1). Excellent profitability (8.5).
Principal Business: Reinsurance (60%), group life insurance (19%), group health insurance (16%), individual health insurance (5%), and individual life insurance (1%).
Principal Investments: NonCMO investment grade bonds (73%), CMOs and structured securities (14%), common & preferred stock (5%), cash (2%), and misc. investments (3%).
Investments in Affiliates: None
Group Affiliation: Arkansas Bl Cross Bl Shield Group
Licensed in: All states except NY, PR
Commenced Business: December 1980
Address: 320 W Capitol Suite 700, Little Rock, AR 72201
Phone: (501) 375-7200 **Domicile State:** AR **NAIC Code:** 94358

Data Date	Rating	RACR #1	RACR #2	Total Assets ($mil)	Capital ($mil)	Net Premium ($mil)	Net Income ($mil)
3-19	A-	2.76	2.05	497.8	259.2	116.7	4.5
3-18	A-	2.85	2.13	543.3	286.4	154.5	9.0
2018	A-	2.84	2.13	514.7	273.8	572.6	142.5
2017	A-	2.80	2.10	535.3	278.1	586.1	37.8
2016	B+	2.41	1.80	498.2	241.6	587.8	24.3
2015	B+	2.07	1.52	467.9	215.3	580.2	27.3
2014	B+	1.83	1.34	446.0	194.3	591.7	24.6

Adverse Trends in Operations

Decrease in asset base during 2018 (4%)
Decrease in capital during 2018 (2%)
Decrease in premium volume from 2017 to 2018 (2%)
Decrease in premium volume from 2014 to 2015 (2%)

USABLE MUTUAL INS CO B Good

Major Rating Factors: Fair profitability index (3.5 on a scale of 0 to 10). Strong capitalization (10.0) based on excellent current risk-adjusted capital (severe loss scenario). High quality investment portfolio (8.7).
Other Rating Factors: Excellent liquidity (6.9) with sufficient resources (cash flows and marketable investments) to handle a spike in claims.
Principal Business: Comp med (70%), FEHB (11%), med supp (11%), Medicare (7%), other (1%)
Mem Phys: 18: 18,605 **17:** 17,077 **18 MLR** 78.8% **/ 18 Admin Exp** N/A
Enroll(000): Q1 19: 616 **18:** 619 **17:** 665 **Med Exp PMPM:** $252
Principal Investments: Long-term bonds (50%), cash and equiv (14%), affiliate common stock (12%), real estate (4%), nonaffiliate common stock (4%), other (15%)
Provider Compensation ($000): Contr fee ($1,955,055), bonus arrang ($12,857)
Total Member Encounters: Phys (3,836,445), non-phys (4,751,789)
Group Affiliation: None
Licensed in: AR, TX
Address: 601 S Gaines, Little Rock, AR 72201
Phone: (501) 378-2000 **Dom State:** AR **Commenced Bus:** N/A

Data Date	Rating	RACR #1	RACR #2	Total Assets ($mil)	Capital ($mil)	Net Premium ($mil)	Net Income ($mil)
3-19	B	5.02	4.19	1,801.4	872.7	609.3	28.0
3-18	A	5.05	4.21	1,709.2	873.4	636.8	42.5
2018	B	4.79	3.99	1,747.3	830.5	2,480.2	-21.3
2017	A	4.71	3.92	1,664.5	866.3	2,523.7	30.7
2016	A+	4.98	4.15	1,623.7	842.8	2,466.7	9.8
2015	A+	5.52	4.60	1,579.9	817.8	2,239.7	4.3
2014	A+	5.86	4.88	1,580.8	820.0	1,983.6	46.0

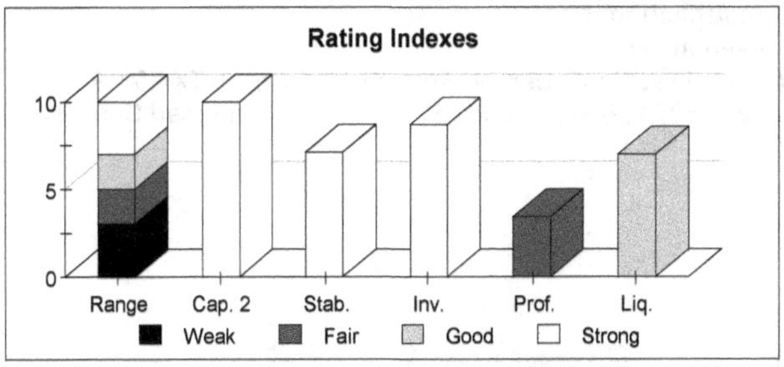

UTMB HEALTH PLANS INC B- Good

Major Rating Factors: Fair overall results on stability tests (4.3 on a scale of 0 to 10) based on a significant 17% decrease in enrollment during the period. Excellent profitability (7.2). Strong capitalization index (10.0) based on excellent current risk-adjusted capital (severe loss scenario)
Other Rating Factors: High quality investment portfolio (8.7). Excellent liquidity (10.0) with ample operational cash flow and liquid investments.
Principal Business: Med supp (100%)
Mem Phys: 18: 26 **17:** 26 **18 MLR** 53.2% **/ 18 Admin Exp** N/A
Enroll(000): Q1 19: 0 **18:** 0 **17:** 0 **Med Exp PMPM:** $122
Principal Investments: Cash and equiv (100%)
Provider Compensation ($000): Capitation ($184), FFS ($113)
Total Member Encounters: Phys (520), non-phys (899)
Group Affiliation: None
Licensed in: TX
Address: 301 University Blvd Rte 0985, Galveston, TX 77555-0985
Phone: (409) 766-4000 **Dom State:** TX **Commenced Bus:** N/A

Data Date	Rating	RACR #1	RACR #2	Total Assets ($mil)	Capital ($mil)	Net Premium ($mil)	Net Income ($mil)
3-19	B-	58.67	48.89	5.8	5.7	0.1	0.0
3-18	B-	N/A	N/A	5.7	5.6	0.1	0.1
2018	B-	55.33	46.11	5.5	5.4	0.6	0.2
2017	B-	N/A	N/A	5.6	5.5	1.2	0.7
2016	B-	49.96	41.63	5.7	5.1	0.7	0.3
2015	B-	51.16	42.63	6.3	5.6	0.7	0.3
2014	N/A	N/A	N/A	7.2	6.6	1.8	1.3

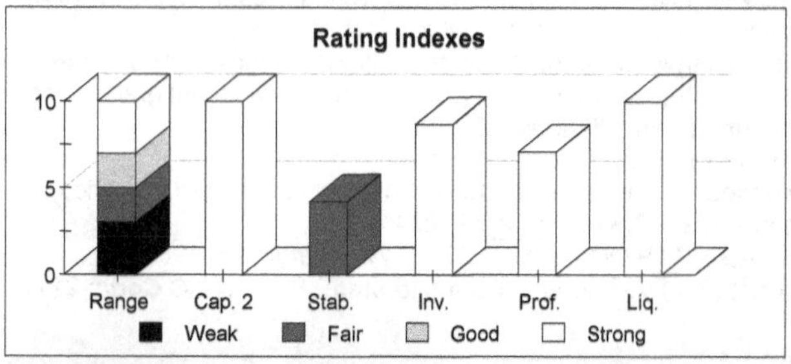

VALUEOPTIONS OF NEW JERSEY INC E Very Weak

Major Rating Factors: Poor capitalization index (0.0 on a scale of 0 to 10) based on weak current risk-adjusted capital (severe loss scenario). Good liquidity (6.6) with sufficient resources (cash flows and marketable investments) to handle a spike in claims. Excellent profitability (7.3).
Other Rating Factors: High quality investment portfolio (9.9).
Principal Business: Other (99%)
Mem Phys: 18: 16,460 **17:** 18,479 **18 MLR** 74.9% **/ 18 Admin Exp** N/A
Enroll(000): 18: 881 **17:** 961 **Med Exp PMPM:** $12
Principal Investments: Cash and equiv (100%)
Provider Compensation ($000): Contr fee ($137,130)
Total Member Encounters: Phys (105,585), non-phys (548,275)
Group Affiliation: DCP 2014 GP-GP LLC
Licensed in: NJ
Address: 103 Eisenhower Pkwy, Parkway, NJ 7068
Phone: (757) 459-5418 **Dom State:** NJ **Commenced Bus:** N/A

Data Date	Rating	RACR #1	RACR #2	Total Assets ($mil)	Capital ($mil)	Net Premium ($mil)	Net Income ($mil)
2018	E	N/A	N/A	19.0	9.2	181.4	8.2
2017	E	N/A	N/A	16.9	7.0	177.6	0.1
2016	E	N/A	N/A	16.1	5.4	203.9	-0.1
2015	U	N/A	N/A	12.0	3.0	111.3	0.1
2014	N/A	N/A	N/A	10.2	1.7	65.0	-0.4

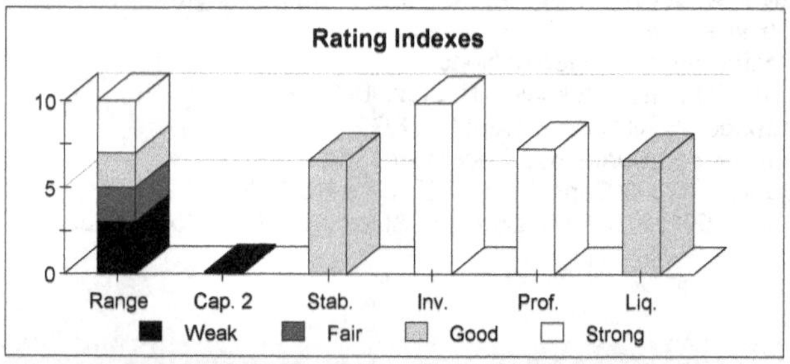

VALUEOPTIONS OF TEXAS INC D Weak

Major Rating Factors: Fair overall results on stability tests (3.5 on a scale of 0 to 10) based on a significant 100% decrease in enrollment during the period. Excellent profitability (8.3). Strong capitalization index (9.6) based on excellent current risk-adjusted capital (severe loss scenario)
Other Rating Factors: High quality investment portfolio (9.9). Excellent liquidity (10.0) with ample operational cash flow and liquid investments.
Principal Business: Medicaid (65%), other (35%)
Mem Phys: 17: N/A **16:** 248 **17 MLR** 3.1% **/ 17 Admin Exp** N/A
Enroll(000): Q1 18: N/A **17:** N/A **16:** 493 **Med Exp PMPM:** N/A
Principal Investments: Cash and equiv (100%)
Provider Compensation ($000): Contr fee ($5,441)
Total Member Encounters: N/A
Group Affiliation: None
Licensed in: TX
Address: 1199 South Beltline Road Suite, Coppell, TX 75019
Phone: (757) 459-5418 **Dom State:** TX **Commenced Bus:** N/A

Data Date	Rating	RACR #1	RACR #2	Total Assets ($mil)	Capital ($mil)	Net Premium ($mil)	Net Income ($mil)
3-18	D	3.46	2.88	6.2	6.2	N/A	0.2
3-17	E+	0.94	0.78	14.9	5.5	0.1	0.1
2017	D+	2.94	2.45	13.8	6.0	0.3	0.6
2016	E	0.92	0.77	20.3	5.4	146.3	0.3
2015	N/A	N/A	N/A	20.1	5.6	164.7	1.7
2014	N/A	N/A	N/A	17.3	5.6	168.8	N/A
2013	N/A	N/A	N/A	15.5	4.7	161.9	-0.1

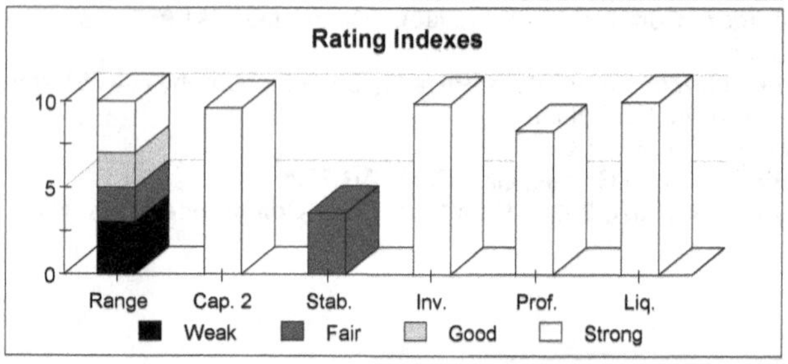

VANTAGE HEALTH PLAN INC D+ Weak

Major Rating Factors: Weak liquidity (2.3 on a scale of 0 to 10) as a spike in claims may stretch capacity. Fair capitalization index (3.3) based on weak current risk-adjusted capital (moderate loss scenario). Fair quality investment portfolio (3.9).
Other Rating Factors: Good overall profitability index (6.1). Good overall results on stability tests (6.0).
Principal Business: Medicare (58%), comp med (42%)
Mem Phys: 18: 14,205 **17:** 13,310 **18 MLR** 82.4% **/ 18 Admin Exp** N/A
Enroll(000): Q1 19: 40 **18:** 43 **17:** 47 **Med Exp PMPM:** $635
Principal Investments: Real estate (60%), cash and equiv (14%), other (26%)
Provider Compensation ($000): Contr fee ($290,126), FFS ($25,600), capitation ($5,075)
Total Member Encounters: Phys (703,788), non-phys (101,534)
Group Affiliation: Vantage Holdings Inc
Licensed in: LA
Address: 130 DeSiard Street Suite 300, Monroe, LA 71201
Phone: (318) 361-0900 **Dom State:** LA **Commenced Bus:** N/A

Data Date	Rating	RACR #1	RACR #2	Total Assets ($mil)	Capital ($mil)	Net Premium ($mil)	Net Income ($mil)
3-19	D+	0.67	0.56	90.4	34.8	98.0	0.9
3-18	D+	0.47	0.39	96.2	17.6	102.1	-3.0
2018	D+	0.75	0.62	98.3	37.9	402.9	3.0
2017	C-	0.62	0.52	76.8	24.2	408.0	2.6
2016	C-	0.75	0.63	93.8	28.2	368.6	17.3
2015	C	0.85	0.70	64.1	24.0	270.0	1.2
2014	B-	0.91	0.76	53.4	21.2	227.7	5.5

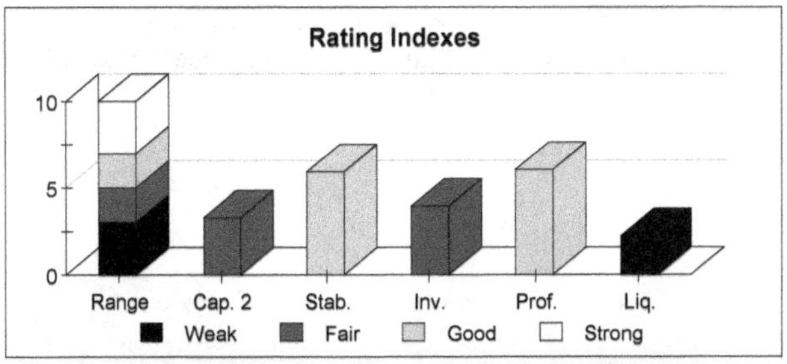

VENTURA COUNTY HEALTH CARE PLAN E- Very Weak

Major Rating Factors: Poor capitalization index (2.5 on a scale of 0 to 10) based on weak current risk-adjusted capital (moderate loss scenario). Weak overall results on stability tests (1.9) based on an excessive 99547% enrollment growth during the period. Fair profitability index (3.8).
Other Rating Factors: Excellent liquidity (7.0) with sufficient resources (cash flows and marketable investments) to handle a spike in claims.
Principal Business: Managed care (100%)
Mem Phys: 18: N/A **17:** N/A **18 MLR** 87.7% **/ 18 Admin Exp** N/A
Enroll(000): Q1 19: 14 **18:** 15 **17:** 0 **Med Exp PMPM:** $388
Principal Investments ($000): Cash and equiv ($7,210)
Provider Compensation ($000): None
Total Member Encounters: N/A
Group Affiliation: None
Licensed in: CA
Address: 5455 Garden Grove Blvd Ste 500, Westminster, CA 92683
Phone: (562) 981-4004 **Dom State:** CA **Commenced Bus:** June 1996

Data Date	Rating	RACR #1	RACR #2	Total Assets ($mil)	Capital ($mil)	Net Premium ($mil)	Net Income ($mil)
3-19	E-	0.46	0.29	18.1	4.6	20.4	0.7
3-18	E-	0.29	0.19	18.7	2.3	20.0	0.8
2018	E-	0.39	0.25	18.6	3.9	79.9	2.4
2017	E-	0.22	0.14	18.5	1.5	75.1	0.6
2016	E-	0.19	0.12	17.9	1.3	63.5	-5.0
2015	B-	1.31	0.82	17.4	8.7	57.6	-1.6
2014	B	1.87	1.18	23.5	10.4	53.9	0.1

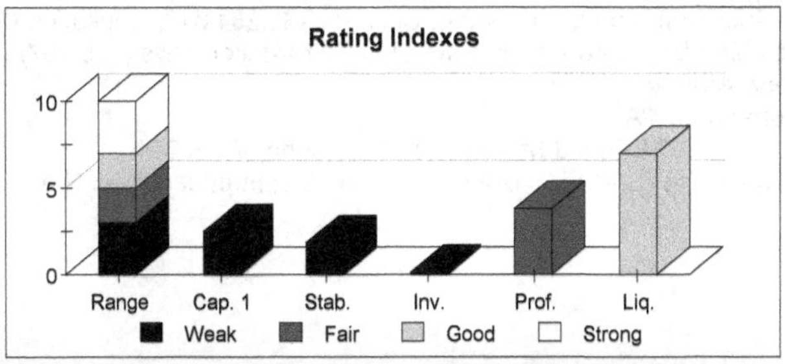

VERMONT HEALTH PLAN LLC C+ Fair

Major Rating Factors: Good overall results on stability tests (5.2 on a scale of 0 to 10). Weak profitability index (2.0). Strong capitalization index (10.0) based on excellent current risk-adjusted capital (severe loss scenario).
Other Rating Factors: High quality investment portfolio (8.2). Excellent liquidity (7.3) with ample operational cash flow and liquid investments.
Principal Business: Comp med (51%), med supp (49%)
Mem Phys: 18: 8,200 **17:** 8,096 **18 MLR** 85.7% **/ 18 Admin Exp** N/A
Enroll(000): Q1 19: 11 **18:** 11 **17:** 10 **Med Exp PMPM:** $216
Principal Investments: Long-term bonds (63%), cash and equiv (37%)
Provider Compensation ($000): FFS ($19,638), contr fee ($7,673)
Total Member Encounters: Phys (10,987), non-phys (15,924)
Group Affiliation: None
Licensed in: VT
Address: 445 Industrial Lane, Berlin, VT 5602
Phone: (802) 223-6131 **Dom State:** VT **Commenced Bus:** N/A

Data Date	Rating	RACR #1	RACR #2	Total Assets ($mil)	Capital ($mil)	Net Premium ($mil)	Net Income ($mil)
3-19	C+	8.21	6.84	40.3	31.4	8.4	-0.2
3-18	C+	8.39	6.99	38.4	31.7	7.9	-0.7
2018	C+	8.30	6.92	38.3	31.8	31.9	-0.7
2017	C+	7.10	5.91	38.5	32.5	28.5	-1.9
2016	B-	9.12	7.60	40.1	34.4	30.6	1.1
2015	B-	5.53	4.61	43.1	33.2	50.9	-0.7
2014	B	4.47	3.73	47.8	33.7	69.6	0.7

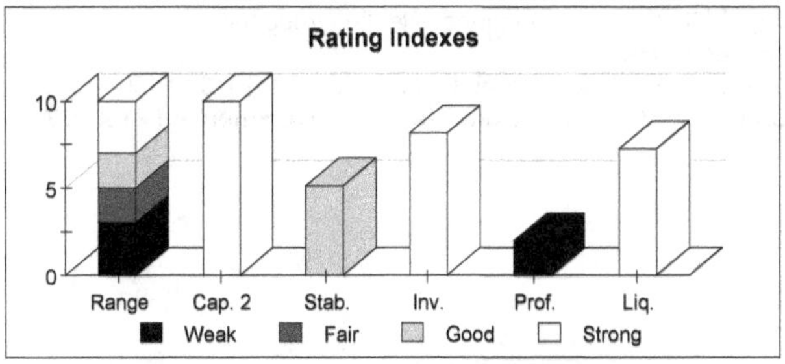

VIBRA HEALTH PLAN INC — E+ Very Weak

Major Rating Factors: Weak profitability index (0.0 on a scale of 0 to 10). Weak liquidity (0.0) as a spike in claims may stretch capacity. Fair capitalization (3.3) based on weak current risk-adjusted capital (moderate loss scenario).
Other Rating Factors: High quality investment portfolio (9.9).
Principal Business: Medicare (100%)
Mem Phys: 18: 10,794 **17:** 10,794 **18 MLR** 99.8% **/ 18 Admin Exp** N/A
Enroll(000): Q1 19: 1 **18:** 1 **17:** 1 **Med Exp PMPM:** $804
Principal Investments: Cash and equiv (100%)
Provider Compensation ($000): Contr fee ($12,713)
Total Member Encounters: Phys (13,290), non-phys (2,203)
Group Affiliation: None
Licensed in: PA
Address: 4000 CRUMS MILL Rd Ste 201, Harrisburg, PA 17112
Phone: (717) 510-6200 **Dom State:** PA **Commenced Bus:** N/A

Data Date	Rating	RACR #1	RACR #2	Total Assets ($mil)	Capital ($mil)	Net Premium ($mil)	Net Income ($mil)
3-19	E+	0.67	0.56	4.1	0.8	3.4	-2.8
3-18	N/A	N/A	N/A	8.0	3.2	3.1	-2.3
2018	C-	2.11	1.76	7.8	3.6	12.6	-10.3
2017	N/A	N/A	N/A	8.1	5.4	8.3	-12.3
2016	N/A	N/A	N/A	4.4	3.2	N/A	-8.7
2015	N/A	N/A	N/A	2.6	2.1	N/A	-0.9
2014	N/A	N/A	N/A	N/A	N/A	N/A	N/A

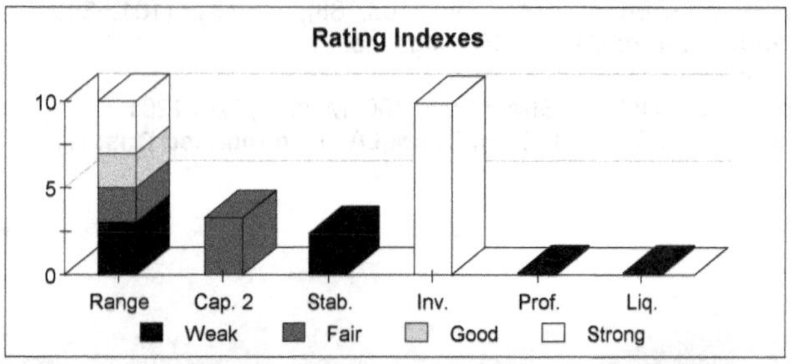

VIRGINIA PREMIER HEALTH PLAN INC — C+ Fair

Major Rating Factors: Fair capitalization index (4.9 on a scale of 0 to 10) based on good current risk-adjusted capital (severe loss scenario). Fair overall results on stability tests (3.6) based on an excessive 194% enrollment growth during the period. Good liquidity (5.4) with sufficient resources (cash flows and marketable investments) to handle a spike in claims.
Other Rating Factors: Weak profitability index (1.4). Low quality investment portfolio (1.6).
Principal Business: Medicaid (96%), Medicare (4%)
Mem Phys: 18: 21,840 **17:** 20 **18 MLR** 94.0% **/ 18 Admin Exp** N/A
Enroll(000): Q1 19: 791 **18:** 643 **17:** 218 **Med Exp PMPM:** $529
Principal Investments: Cash and equiv (38%), nonaffiliate common stock (26%), long-term bonds (8%), other (28%)
Provider Compensation ($000): Contr fee ($1,254,840), capitation ($120,657)
Total Member Encounters: Phys (11,872,744), non-phys (185,107)
Group Affiliation: None
Licensed in: VA
Address: 600 E Broad St Suite 400, Richmond, VA 23219
Phone: (804) 819-5151 **Dom State:** VA **Commenced Bus:** N/A

Data Date	Rating	RACR #1	RACR #2	Total Assets ($mil)	Capital ($mil)	Net Premium ($mil)	Net Income ($mil)
3-19	C+	0.91	0.76	384.4	165.0	482.3	-4.5
3-18	B+	N/A	N/A	382.1	180.5	351.3	-26.1
2018	C+	0.88	0.74	355.7	161.4	1,462.7	-82.8
2017	B+	N/A	N/A	366.4	206.1	1,206.9	25.8
2016	B+	1.85	1.54	302.8	199.8	1,070.4	30.7
2015	B+	1.51	1.26	281.9	168.3	1,024.6	16.3
2014	A-	1.79	1.49	282.3	157.7	825.1	7.6

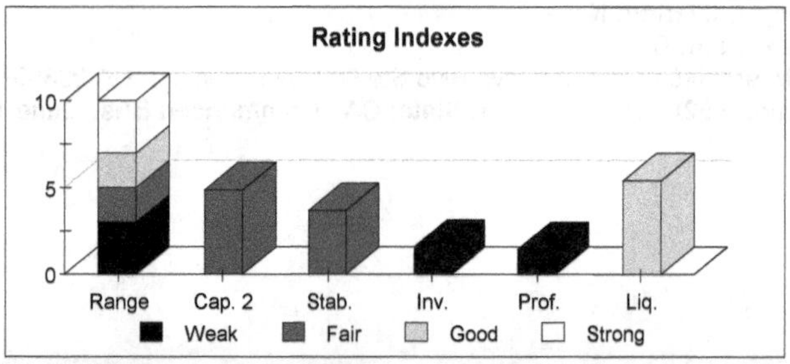

VISTA HEALTH PLAN INC * — B+ Good

Major Rating Factors: Good overall profitability index (6.7 on a scale of 0 to 10). Strong capitalization index (7.8) based on excellent current risk-adjusted capital (severe loss scenario). High quality investment portfolio (7.4).
Other Rating Factors: Excellent overall results on stability tests (7.7). Good financial strength from affiliates. Excellent liquidity (7.1) with ample operational cash flow and liquid investments.
Principal Business: Medicaid (98%), Medicare (2%)
Mem Phys: 18: 56,902 **17:** 49 **18 MLR** 94.1% **/ 18 Admin Exp** N/A
Enroll(000): Q1 19: 806 **18:** 735 **17:** 713 **Med Exp PMPM:** $531
Principal Investments: Long-term bonds (62%), cash and equiv (38%)
Provider Compensation ($000): Capitation ($4,718,714)
Total Member Encounters: Phys (4,915,214), non-phys (1,253,728)
Group Affiliation: Independence Health Group Inc
Licensed in: PA
Address: 1901 Market Street, Philadelphia, PA 19103-1480
Phone: (215) 241-2400 **Dom State:** PA **Commenced Bus:** N/A

Data Date	Rating	RACR #1	RACR #2	Total Assets ($mil)	Capital ($mil)	Net Premium ($mil)	Net Income ($mil)
3-19	B+	2.01	1.68	1,254.9	329.2	1,820.7	1.8
3-18	B-	N/A	N/A	1,066.4	263.6	1,254.0	-59.4
2018	B	2.00	1.67	982.8	327.7	5,009.8	3.6
2017	B-	N/A	N/A	880.4	282.7	4,379.1	3.5
2016	B-	2.14	1.78	1,158.0	278.5	4,574.3	3.2
2015	B-	1.75	1.46	453.3	227.9	3,750.6	3.0
2014	B	2.04	1.70	546.1	188.0	3,079.1	2.2

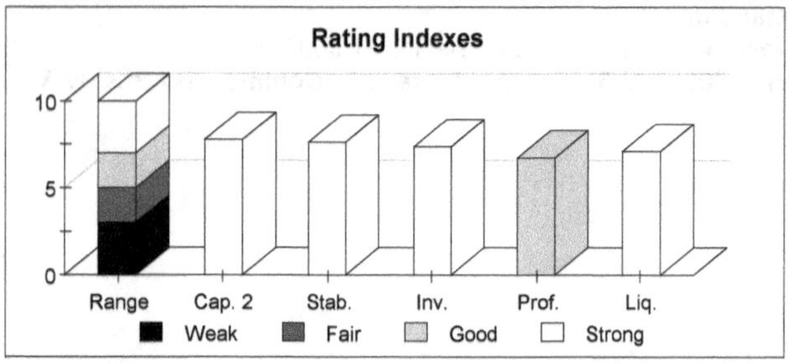

VIVA HEALTH INC * B+ Good

Major Rating Factors: Good overall profitability index (5.9 on a scale of 0 to 10). Strong capitalization index (8.2) based on excellent current risk-adjusted capital (severe loss scenario). High quality investment portfolio (9.9).
Other Rating Factors: Excellent overall results on stability tests (7.0). Excellent liquidity (6.9) with sufficient resources (cash flows and marketable investments) to handle a spike in claims
Principal Business: Medicare (85%), comp med (15%)
Mem Phys: 18: 13,618 **17:** 12 **18 MLR** 85.3% **/ 18 Admin Exp** N/A
Enroll(000): Q1 19: 75 **18:** 73 **17:** 75 **Med Exp PMPM:** $701
Principal Investments: Long-term bonds (60%), cash and equiv (40%)
Provider Compensation ($000): Contr fee ($462,535), capitation ($155,099), FFS ($14,305)
Total Member Encounters: Phys (1,491,185), non-phys (1,598,168)
Group Affiliation: None
Licensed in: AL
Address: 417 20TH STREET NORTH SUITE 11, BIRMINGHAM, AL 35203
Phone: (205) 939-1718 **Dom State:** AL **Commenced Bus:** N/A

Data Date	Rating	RACR #1	RACR #2	Total Assets ($mil)	Capital ($mil)	Net Premium ($mil)	Net Income ($mil)
3-19	B+	2.31	1.92	214.0	120.4	191.8	-2.2
3-18	B+	2.34	1.95	274.8	112.3	184.2	3.4
2018	B+	2.36	1.97	207.2	123.2	735.3	12.3
2017	B+	2.31	1.93	208.2	110.9	710.6	13.5
2016	B+	2.23	1.86	181.0	97.2	625.2	10.6
2015	B	1.74	1.45	161.1	83.1	610.4	-3.6
2014	B+	2.11	1.76	153.8	94.2	603.3	6.4

Rating Indexes

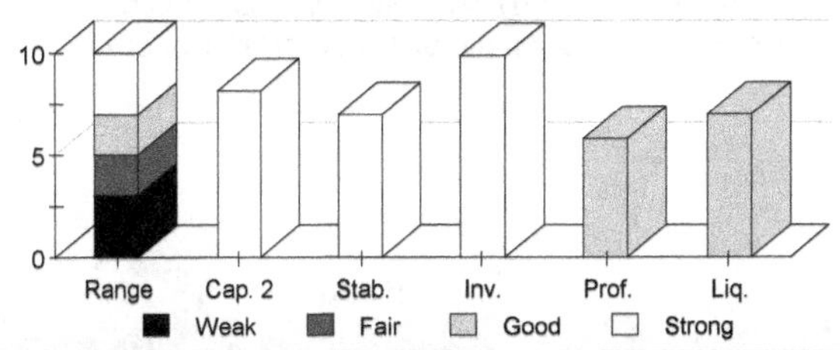

VOLUNTEER STATE HEALTH PLAN INC * A+ Excellent

Major Rating Factors: Strong capitalization index (9.1 on a scale of 0 to 10) based on excellent current risk-adjusted capital (severe loss scenario). Good overall profitability index (6.1). Good quality investment portfolio (6.6).
Other Rating Factors: Good liquidity (6.8) with sufficient resources (cash flows and marketable investments) to handle a spike in claims. Fair overall results on stability tests (4.4).
Principal Business: Medicaid (91%), Medicare (9%)
Mem Phys: 18: 28,338 **17:** 28 **18 MLR** 84.5% **/ 18 Admin Exp** N/A
Enroll(000): Q1 19: 529 **18:** 520 **17:** 544 **Med Exp PMPM:** $346
Principal Investments: Long-term bonds (62%), cash and equiv (18%), nonaffiliate common stock (16%), pref stock (3%)
Provider Compensation ($000): Contr fee ($2,130,369), capitation ($43,273), bonus arrang ($2,947)
Total Member Encounters: Phys (5,578,558), non-phys (485,092)
Group Affiliation: BlueCross BlueShield of Tennessee In
Licensed in: (No states)
Address: 1 Cameron Hill Circle, Chattanooga, TN 37402-0001
Phone: (423) 535-5600 **Dom State:** TN **Commenced Bus:** N/A

Data Date	Rating	RACR #1	RACR #2	Total Assets ($mil)	Capital ($mil)	Net Premium ($mil)	Net Income ($mil)
3-19	A+	3.00	2.50	889.1	407.8	650.0	-15.0
3-18	A+	3.62	3.01	959.2	496.6	688.4	18.9
2018	A+	3.02	2.52	860.0	410.9	2,576.0	-12.2
2017	A+	2.80	2.34	803.5	479.8	2,484.1	48.3
2016	A+	3.36	2.80	737.6	420.8	2,440.8	109.6
2015	A+	3.00	2.50	805.5	330.8	2,196.7	75.2
2014	A+	3.58	2.99	729.4	330.1	1,815.8	60.3

Rating Indexes

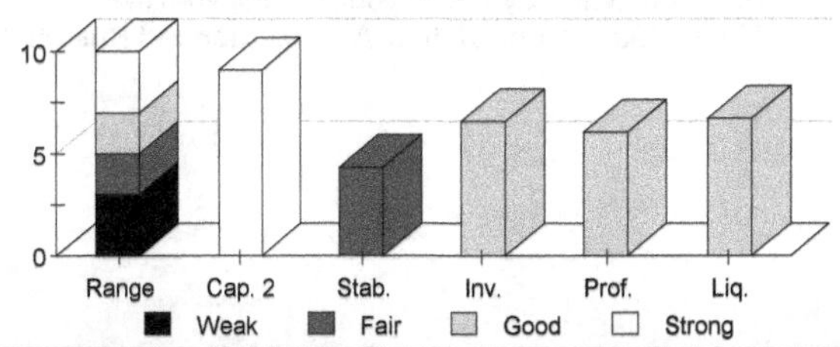

WASHINGTON NATIONAL INSURANCE COMPANY D+ Weak

Major Rating Factors: Weak overall results on stability tests (2.7 on a scale of 0 to 10) including potential financial drain due to affiliation with CNO Financial Group Inc. Fair quality investment portfolio (4.7) with large holdings of BBB rated bonds in addition to moderate junk bond exposure. Good capitalization (6.3) based on good risk adjusted capital (severe loss scenario).
Other Rating Factors: Good profitability (5.0). Good liquidity (6.6).
Principal Business: Individual health insurance (58%), group health insurance (31%), individual life insurance (7%), reinsurance (4%), and individual annuities (1%).
Principal Investments: NonCMO investment grade bonds (64%), CMOs and structured securities (19%), common & preferred stock (4%), mortgages in good standing (4%), and misc. investments (9%).
Investments in Affiliates: 1%
Group Affiliation: CNO Financial Group Inc
Licensed in: All states except NY
Commenced Business: September 1923
Address: 11825 NORTH PENNSYLVANIA STREE, CARMEL, IN 46032
Phone: (317) 817-6100 **Domicile State:** IN **NAIC Code:** 70319

Data Date	Rating	RACR #1	RACR #2	Total Assets ($mil)	Capital ($mil)	Net Premium ($mil)	Net Income ($mil)
3-19	D+	1.55	0.91	5,491.6	365.2	179.1	10.9
3-18	D+	1.64	0.91	5,430.9	366.8	176.3	19.8
2018	D+	1.52	0.89	5,466.1	365.8	703.3	61.2
2017	D+	1.71	0.95	5,418.5	373.2	688.9	26.7
2016	D+	2.09	1.09	5,397.6	431.1	663.1	-53.0
2015	D+	1.70	0.93	4,807.8	333.1	649.7	60.9
2014	D+	1.67	0.90	4,775.3	327.0	610.0	50.8

CNO Financial Group Inc
Composite Group Rating: D+

Largest Group Members	Assets ($mil)	Rating
BANKERS LIFE CAS CO	15515	D+
WASHINGTON NATIONAL INS CO	5466	D+
COLONIAL PENN LIFE INS CO	870	D+
BANKERS CONSECO LIFE INS CO	496	D

WEA INSURANCE CORPORATION C Fair

Major Rating Factors: Fair quality investment portfolio (4.4 on a scale of 0 to 10). Fair profitability (3.4). Excellent expense controls. Fair overall results on stability tests (3.7).
Other Rating Factors: Good liquidity (6.4) with sufficient resources to handle a spike in claims. Strong capitalization (7.3) based on excellent risk adjusted capital (severe loss scenario).
Principal Business: Group health insurance (100%).
Principal Investments: NonCMO investment grade bonds (49%), common & preferred stock (22%), CMOs and structured securities (22%), and cash (3%).
Investments in Affiliates: 2%
Group Affiliation: Wisconsin Education Assn Ins Trust
Licensed in: WI
Commenced Business: July 1985
Address: 45 NOB HILL ROAD, MADISON, WI 53713-0000
Phone: (608) 276-4000 **Domicile State:** WI **NAIC Code:** 72273

Data Date	Rating	RACR #1	RACR #2	Total Assets ($mil)	Capital ($mil)	Net Premium ($mil)	Net Income ($mil)
3-19	C	1.69	1.22	698.8	192.1	152.6	6.2
3-18	C	1.83	1.27	679.2	173.3	156.6	6.3
2018	C	1.52	1.10	661.5	170.7	603.8	20.2
2017	C	1.85	1.27	661.0	167.0	466.6	1.4
2016	C	1.57	1.09	644.9	140.9	496.6	1.1
2015	C	1.70	1.20	644.2	160.7	550.6	-34.2
2014	C	1.97	1.40	683.9	200.2	593.3	-28.0

Rating Indexes

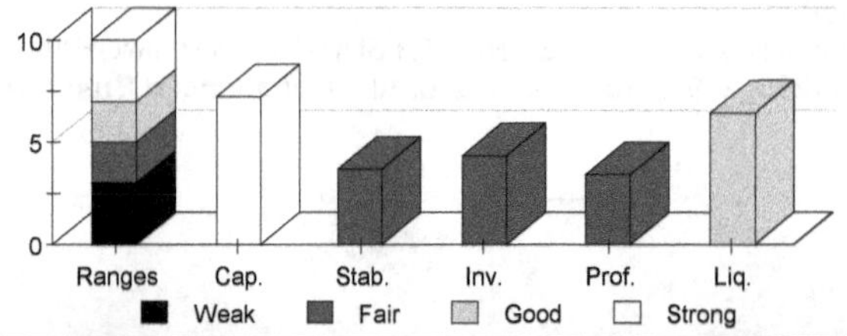

WELLCALL INC C- Fair

Major Rating Factors: Fair profitability index (4.6 on a scale of 0 to 10). Fair overall results on stability tests (3.2). Strong capitalization index (7.3) based on excellent current risk-adjusted capital (severe loss scenario).
Other Rating Factors: Excellent liquidity (7.3) with ample operational cash flow and liquid investments.
Principal Business: Managed care (100%)
Mem Phys: 18: N/A **17:** N/A **18 MLR** 939.0% **/ 18 Admin Exp** N/A
Enroll(000): Q1 19: 64 **18:** 63 **17:** 53 **Med Exp PMPM:** $11
Principal Investments ($000): Cash and equiv ($764)
Provider Compensation ($000): None
Total Member Encounters: N/A
Group Affiliation: None
Licensed in: (No states)
Address: 1004 Industrial Way Ste A, Lodi, CA 95240-3142
Phone: (415) 621-1606 **Dom State:** CA **Commenced Bus:** N/A

Data Date	Rating	RACR #1	RACR #2	Total Assets ($mil)	Capital ($mil)	Net Premium ($mil)	Net Income ($mil)
3-19	C-	2.06	1.35	3.6	2.7	0.3	0.3
3-18	C-	2.56	1.69	4.1	3.4	0.1	0.1
2018	C-	1.74	1.14	3.2	2.3	1.0	1.2
2017	C-	2.35	1.55	3.9	3.1	0.8	0.6
2016	N/A	N/A	N/A	N/A	N/A	N/A	N/A
2015	N/A	N/A	N/A	N/A	N/A	N/A	N/A
2014	N/A	N/A	N/A	N/A	N/A	N/A	N/A

Rating Indexes

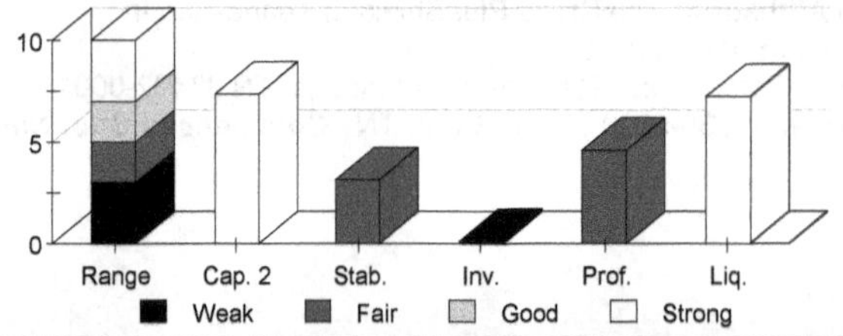

WELLCARE HEALTH INS OF ARIZONA INC C Fair

Major Rating Factors: Fair profitability index (3.3 on a scale of 0 to 10). Good liquidity (6.9) with sufficient resources (cash flows and marketable investments) to handle a spike in claims. Strong capitalization (7.7) based on excellent current risk-adjusted capital (severe loss scenario).
Other Rating Factors: High quality investment portfolio (9.5).
Principal Business: Medicaid (65%), Medicare (35%)
Mem Phys: 18: 20,300 **17:** 18 **18 MLR** 84.6% **/ 18 Admin Exp** N/A
Enroll(000): Q1 19: 63 **18:** 64 **17:** 66 **Med Exp PMPM:** $790
Principal Investments: Cash and equiv (71%), long-term bonds (30%)
Provider Compensation ($000): Contr fee ($545,048), capitation ($48,602)
Total Member Encounters: Phys (368,369), non-phys (370,926)
Group Affiliation: WellCare Health Plans Inc
Licensed in: AL, AK, AZ, AR, CO, DC, DE, FL, GA, HI, ID, IL, IN, IA, KS, KY, LA, MD, MI, MN, MS, MO, MT, NE, NV, NM, NC, ND, OK, OR, SC, SD, TN, TX, UT, VA, WA, WY
Address: 3800 N Central Ave Ste 460, Kapolei, HI 96707
Phone: (813) 206-6200 **Dom State:** AZ **Commenced Bus:** N/A

Data Date	Rating	RACR #1	RACR #2	Total Assets ($mil)	Capital ($mil)	Net Premium ($mil)	Net Income ($mil)
3-19	C	1.90	1.58	224.3	70.5	180.7	6.2
3-18	C	1.80	1.50	235.8	60.6	180.0	-8.8
2018	C	1.76	1.47	201.7	64.6	711.8	-3.8
2017	C	1.30	1.08	206.0	68.9	706.3	12.0
2016	C	2.63	2.19	223.9	97.4	731.0	10.4
2015	C	2.28	1.90	217.6	86.1	739.3	1.0
2014	B-	2.26	1.89	192.8	82.0	701.8	-2.4

Rating Indexes

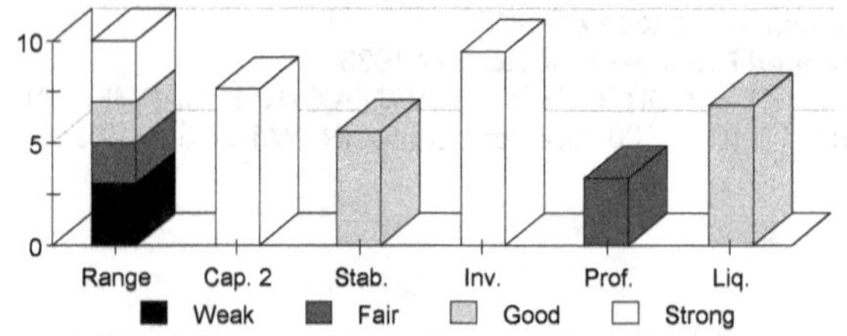

WELLCARE HEALTH INS OF KENTUCKY INC B- Good

Major Rating Factors: Excellent profitability (8.4 on a scale of 0 to 10). Strong capitalization (8.6) based on excellent current risk-adjusted capital (severe loss scenario). High quality investment portfolio (9.5).
Other Rating Factors: Excellent liquidity (7.0) with sufficient resources (cash flows and marketable investments) to handle a spike in claims.
Principal Business: Medicaid (92%), Medicare (6%), other (2%)
Mem Phys: 18: 47,400 **17:** 38 **18 MLR** 83.9% **/ 18 Admin Exp** N/A
Enroll(000): Q1 19: 778 **18:** 552 **17:** 559 **Med Exp PMPM:** $378
Principal Investments: Cash and equiv (62%), long-term bonds (38%)
Provider Compensation ($000): Contr fee ($2,432,745), capitation ($113,022)
Total Member Encounters: Phys (2,878,612), non-phys (2,993,558)
Group Affiliation: WellCare Health Plans Inc
Licensed in: All states except FL, ME, MI, NH, NY, NC, TX, VT, PR
Address: 13551Triton Park Blvd Ste 1800, Louisville, KY 40223
Phone: (813) 206-6200 **Dom State:** KY **Commenced Bus:** N/A

Data Date	Rating	RACR #1	RACR #2	Total Assets ($mil)	Capital ($mil)	Net Premium ($mil)	Net Income ($mil)
3-19	B-	2.66	2.22	846.5	393.0	755.6	31.1
3-18	C	1.95	1.63	872.9	292.8	747.9	-20.4
2018	C+	2.48	2.07	811.5	362.9	3,023.4	126.7
2017	B-	1.56	1.30	908.1	313.7	2,815.2	80.2
2016	C	1.97	1.64	682.9	283.2	2,753.4	42.2
2015	C+	2.10	1.75	691.8	301.3	2,763.2	119.0
2014	B-	1.65	1.37	522.6	211.7	2,419.4	89.0

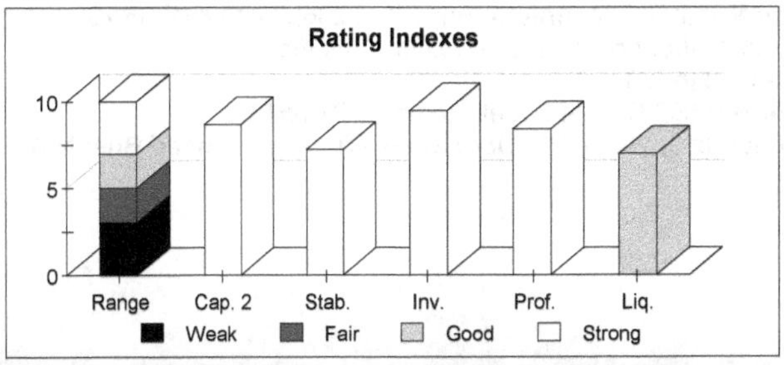

WELLCARE HEALTH INS OF NEW YORK INC C Fair

Major Rating Factors: Weak profitability index (2.8 on a scale of 0 to 10). Strong capitalization (10.0) based on excellent current risk-adjusted capital (severe loss scenario). High quality investment portfolio (9.9).
Other Rating Factors: Excellent liquidity (10.0) with ample operational cash flow and liquid investments.
Principal Business: Medicare (100%)
Mem Phys: 18: 3,100 **17:** N/A **18 MLR** 101.5% **/ 18 Admin Exp** N/A
Enroll(000): Q1 19: 0 **18:** 0 **17:** N/A **Med Exp PMPM:** $642
Principal Investments: Cash and equiv (92%), long-term bonds (8%)
Provider Compensation ($000): Contr fee ($460)
Total Member Encounters: Phys (433), non-phys (165)
Group Affiliation: WellCare Health Plans Inc
Licensed in: NY
Address: One New York Plaza 15th Fl, New York, NY 10004
Phone: (813) 206-6200 **Dom State:** NY **Commenced Bus:** N/A

Data Date	Rating	RACR #1	RACR #2	Total Assets ($mil)	Capital ($mil)	Net Premium ($mil)	Net Income ($mil)
3-19	C	4.02	3.35	6.4	6.1	0.3	0.0
3-18	N/A	N/A	N/A	6.2	6.1	0.1	N/A
2018	C-	4.01	3.34	6.1	6.1	0.5	0.0
2017	N/A	N/A	N/A	6.1	6.1	N/A	N/A
2016	N/A	N/A	N/A	6.1	6.1	N/A	N/A
2015	N/A	N/A	N/A	6.1	6.1	N/A	N/A
2014	N/A	N/A	N/A	12.1	12.1	N/A	N/A

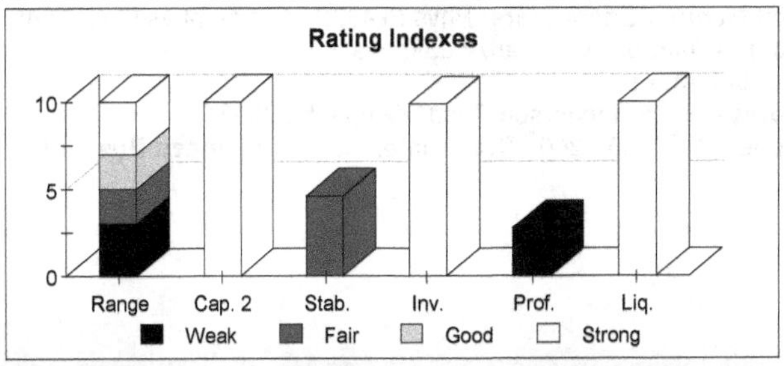

WELLCARE HEALTH PLANS OF NEW JERSEY C+ Fair

Major Rating Factors: Fair profitability index (3.5 on a scale of 0 to 10). Good liquidity (6.8) with sufficient resources (cash flows and marketable investments) to handle a spike in claims. Strong capitalization (8.4) based on excellent current risk-adjusted capital (severe loss scenario).
Other Rating Factors: High quality investment portfolio (9.9).
Principal Business: Medicaid (90%), Medicare (10%)
Mem Phys: 18: 29,700 **17:** 21 **18 MLR** 84.5% **/ 18 Admin Exp** N/A
Enroll(000): Q1 19: 79 **18:** 76 **17:** 69 **Med Exp PMPM:** $676
Principal Investments: Cash and equiv (53%), long-term bonds (47%)
Provider Compensation ($000): Contr fee ($581,595), capitation ($12,671)
Total Member Encounters: Phys (603,848), non-phys (762,261)
Group Affiliation: WellCare Health Plans Inc
Licensed in: NJ
Address: 550 BRd St Ste 1200, Newark, NJ 7102
Phone: (813) 206-6200 **Dom State:** NJ **Commenced Bus:** N/A

Data Date	Rating	RACR #1	RACR #2	Total Assets ($mil)	Capital ($mil)	Net Premium ($mil)	Net Income ($mil)
3-19	C+	2.48	2.07	198.7	89.0	200.6	4.7
3-18	C	2.24	1.87	175.1	64.9	170.1	-4.8
2018	C+	2.33	1.94	184.3	82.5	717.0	4.5
2017	C	1.52	1.27	157.9	69.1	589.4	-2.1
2016	C-	3.34	2.79	159.5	73.1	454.6	10.0
2015	C-	2.46	2.05	140.4	46.5	350.0	1.3
2014	C-	1.46	1.22	70.4	15.8	179.2	-6.5

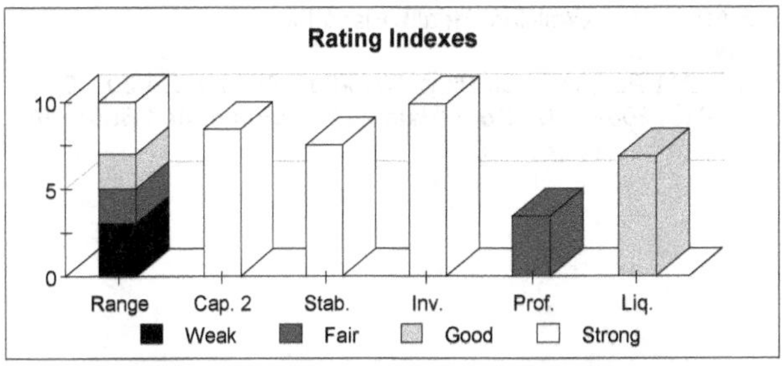

WELLCARE OF CONNECTICUT INC C Fair

Major Rating Factors: Weak profitability index (1.4 on a scale of 0 to 10). Good overall results on stability tests (5.7). Rating is significantly influenced by the fair financial results of WellCare Health Plans Inc. Strong capitalization index (10.0) based on excellent current risk-adjusted capital (severe loss scenario).
Other Rating Factors: High quality investment portfolio (8.4). Excellent liquidity (7.1) with ample operational cash flow and liquid investments.
Principal Business: Medicare (100%)
Mem Phys: 18: 29,000 **17:** 21 **18 MLR** 87.7% **/ 18 Admin Exp** N/A
Enroll(000): Q1 19: 9 **18:** 9 **17:** 8 **Med Exp PMPM:** $865
Principal Investments: Cash and equiv (98%), long-term bonds (2%)
Provider Compensation ($000): Contr fee ($83,529), capitation ($1,630)
Total Member Encounters: Phys (110,236), non-phys (65,756)
Group Affiliation: WellCare Health Plans Inc
Licensed in: CT
Address: 902 Chapel Street, Hamden, CT 6518
Phone: (813) 206-6200 **Dom State:** CT **Commenced Bus:** N/A

Data Date	Rating	RACR #1	RACR #2	Total Assets ($mil)	Capital ($mil)	Net Premium ($mil)	Net Income ($mil)
3-19	C	3.88	3.23	46.3	25.6	28.9	0.2
3-18	C-	3.53	2.94	45.5	19.0	24.2	-3.3
2018	C	3.92	3.27	42.1	25.9	99.8	-4.6
2017	C	2.37	1.98	35.7	22.4	86.5	-1.9
2016	C+	4.55	3.79	39.1	24.2	81.2	-3.4
2015	C+	3.07	2.56	45.0	27.5	146.5	6.1
2014	C	2.67	2.23	37.4	20.7	115.1	0.9

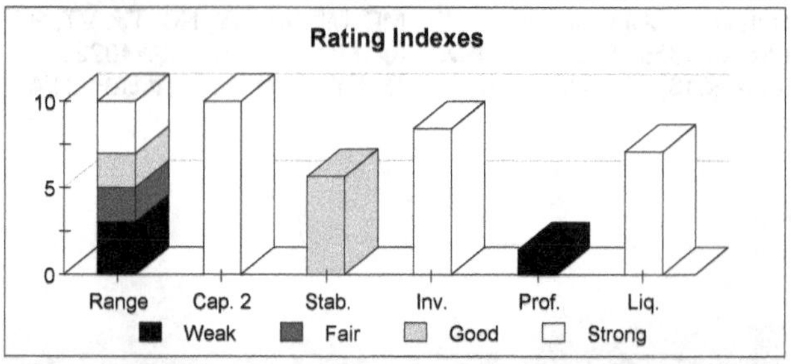

WELLCARE OF FLORIDA INC B Good

Major Rating Factors: Good liquidity (6.9 on a scale of 0 to 10) with sufficient resources (cash flows and marketable investments) to handle a spike in claims. Excellent profitability (7.3). Strong capitalization index (7.5) based on excellent current risk-adjusted capital (severe loss scenario).
Other Rating Factors: High quality investment portfolio (8.3). Excellent overall results on stability tests (7.9). Fair financial strength from affiliates.
Principal Business: Medicaid (64%), Medicare (33%), comp med (3%)
Mem Phys: 18: 53,300 **17:** 45 **18 MLR** 82.6% **/ 18 Admin Exp** N/A
Enroll(000): Q1 19: 1,111 **18:** 873 **17:** 852 **Med Exp PMPM:** $308
Principal Investments: Cash and equiv (56%), long-term bonds (44%)
Provider Compensation ($000): Contr fee ($2,893,019), capitation ($246,762), bonus arrang ($25,029)
Total Member Encounters: Phys (5,437,191), non-phys (2,625,545)
Group Affiliation: WellCare Health Plans Inc
Licensed in: FL
Address: 8735 Henderson Road, Tampa, FL 33634
Phone: (813) 206-6200 **Dom State:** FL **Commenced Bus:** N/A

Data Date	Rating	RACR #1	RACR #2	Total Assets ($mil)	Capital ($mil)	Net Premium ($mil)	Net Income ($mil)
3-19	B	1.71	1.43	1,091.0	300.4	1,510.8	26.0
3-18	D	0.81	0.68	946.8	136.1	921.4	-30.2
2018	B-	1.59	1.32	749.1	274.4	3,757.4	138.1
2017	E	0.75	0.62	761.8	182.4	3,835.7	137.5
2016	E	1.02	0.85	688.9	170.8	3,679.1	128.0
2015	E-	1.03	0.86	568.1	167.1	3,554.9	49.6
2014	C-	0.65	0.55	537.4	76.5	2,812.0	-55.3

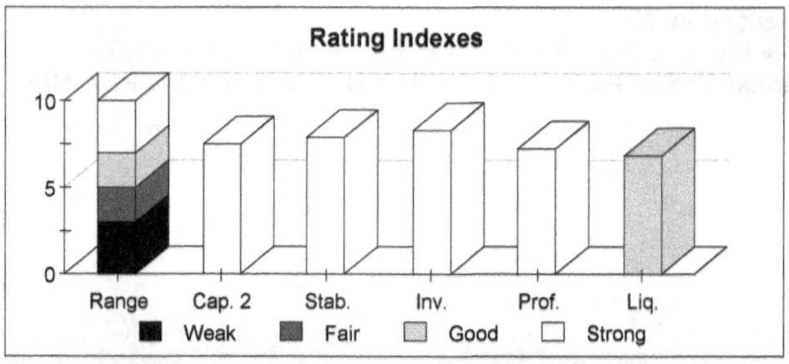

WELLCARE OF GEORGIA INC B Good

Major Rating Factors: Excellent profitability (8.1 on a scale of 0 to 10). Strong capitalization (8.0) based on excellent current risk-adjusted capital (severe loss scenario). High quality investment portfolio (9.3).
Other Rating Factors: Excellent liquidity (7.0) with ample operational cash flow and liquid investments.
Principal Business: Medicaid (67%), Medicare (27%), comp med (5%)
Mem Phys: 18: 49,600 **17:** 40 **18 MLR** 82.6% **/ 18 Admin Exp** N/A
Enroll(000): Q1 19: 544 **18:** 544 **17:** 560 **Med Exp PMPM:** $256
Principal Investments: Cash and equiv (93%), long-term bonds (7%)
Provider Compensation ($000): Contr fee ($1,550,717), capitation ($136,397), bonus arrang ($6,503)
Total Member Encounters: Phys (2,778,491), non-phys (1,457,492)
Group Affiliation: WellCare Health Plans Inc
Licensed in: GA
Address: 211 Perimeter Ctr Pkwy NW #800, Atlanta, GA 30346
Phone: (813) 206-6200 **Dom State:** GA **Commenced Bus:** N/A

Data Date	Rating	RACR #1	RACR #2	Total Assets ($mil)	Capital ($mil)	Net Premium ($mil)	Net Income ($mil)
3-19	B	2.15	1.79	531.8	219.1	513.4	14.2
3-18	C	2.33	1.94	604.9	233.1	575.5	6.8
2018	B-	2.04	1.70	494.8	206.7	2,078.6	39.0
2017	B-	1.63	1.36	496.4	222.2	2,100.1	87.2
2016	C	1.96	1.63	493.6	195.2	2,041.1	16.7
2015	C	1.83	1.52	374.6	175.4	1,991.3	1.2
2014	B-	1.58	1.31	355.4	154.0	1,972.6	0.4

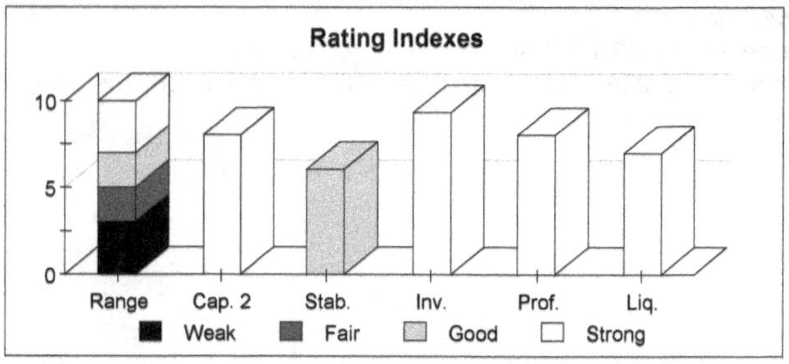

WELLCARE OF NEBRASKA INC C Fair

Major Rating Factors: Excellent profitability (7.6 on a scale of 0 to 10). Strong capitalization (9.8) based on excellent current risk-adjusted capital (severe loss scenario). High quality investment portfolio (9.1).
Other Rating Factors: Excellent liquidity (7.2) with ample operational cash flow and liquid investments.
Principal Business: Medicaid (100%)
Mem Phys: 18: 27,000 **17:** 16 **18 MLR** 83.9% **/ 18 Admin Exp** N/A
Enroll(000): Q1 19: 80 **18:** 80 **17:** 80 **Med Exp PMPM:** $298
Principal Investments: Cash and equiv (71%), long-term bonds (29%)
Provider Compensation ($000): Contr fee ($297,916)
Total Member Encounters: Phys (364,549), non-phys (270,957)
Group Affiliation: WellCare Health Plans Inc
Licensed in: NE
Address: 8055 O St Ste 300, Lincoln, NE 68510
Phone: (813) 206-6200 **Dom State:** NE **Commenced Bus:** N/A

Data Date	Rating	RACR #1	RACR #2	Total Assets ($mil)	Capital ($mil)	Net Premium ($mil)	Net Income ($mil)
3-19	C	3.56	2.97	170.9	51.1	84.6	4.3
3-18	N/A	N/A	N/A	151.1	40.3	80.3	-2.7
2018	C-	3.35	2.80	168.4	46.8	341.3	14.0
2017	N/A	N/A	N/A	142.5	43.0	348.1	0.8
2016	N/A	N/A	N/A	26.9	26.8	N/A	-0.1
2015	N/A	N/A	N/A	N/A	N/A	N/A	N/A
2014	N/A	N/A	N/A	N/A	N/A	N/A	N/A

Rating Indexes

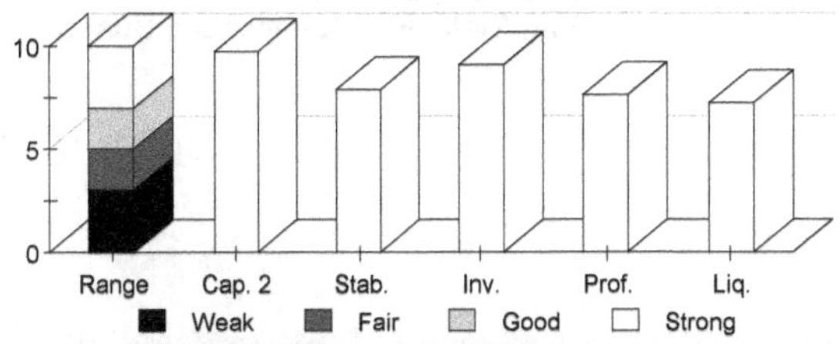

WELLCARE OF SOUTH CAROLINA INC B- Good

Major Rating Factors: Excellent profitability (8.3 on a scale of 0 to 10). Strong capitalization (10.0) based on excellent current risk-adjusted capital (severe loss scenario). High quality investment portfolio (7.7).
Other Rating Factors: Excellent liquidity (7.3) with ample operational cash flow and liquid investments.
Principal Business: Medicaid (95%), Medicare (5%)
Mem Phys: 18: 32,200 **17:** 21 **18 MLR** 81.7% **/ 18 Admin Exp** N/A
Enroll(000): Q1 19: 84 **18:** 79 **17:** 82 **Med Exp PMPM:** $259
Principal Investments: Cash and equiv (100%)
Provider Compensation ($000): Contr fee ($250,242), capitation ($1,719)
Total Member Encounters: Phys (399,244), non-phys (191,024)
Group Affiliation: WellCare Health Plans Inc
Licensed in: SC
Address: 200 Center Point Circle #180, Columbia, SC 29210
Phone: (813) 206-6200 **Dom State:** SC **Commenced Bus:** N/A

Data Date	Rating	RACR #1	RACR #2	Total Assets ($mil)	Capital ($mil)	Net Premium ($mil)	Net Income ($mil)
3-19	B-	3.78	3.15	107.3	61.2	79.6	-0.2
3-18	C	4.19	3.49	119.6	64.7	76.6	-2.6
2018	B-	3.77	3.14	104.9	61.0	304.2	7.6
2017	B-	2.76	2.30	114.1	66.6	297.1	16.2
2016	C	3.64	3.03	110.1	53.4	277.6	4.9
2015	C	3.85	3.21	78.7	43.2	222.7	12.5
2014	B-	3.78	3.15	75.5	43.7	217.3	10.4

Rating Indexes

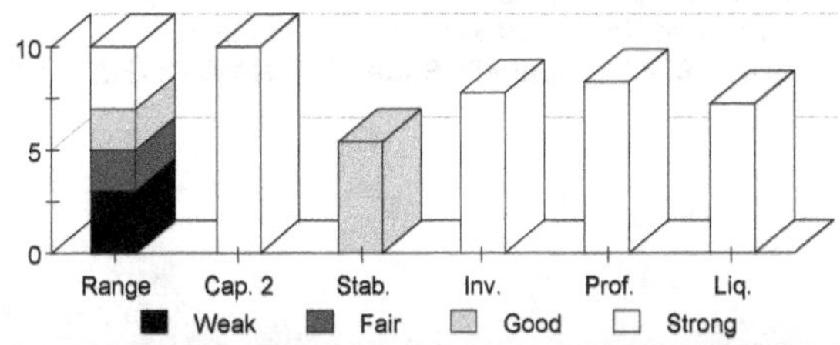

WELLCARE OF TEXAS INC B Good

Major Rating Factors: Good overall profitability index (5.5 on a scale of 0 to 10). Strong capitalization (9.2) based on excellent current risk-adjusted capital (severe loss scenario). High quality investment portfolio (8.8).
Other Rating Factors: Excellent liquidity (7.1) with ample operational cash flow and liquid investments.
Principal Business: Medicare (100%)
Mem Phys: 18: 24,900 **17:** 25 **18 MLR** 80.9% **/ 18 Admin Exp** N/A
Enroll(000): Q1 19: 46 **18:** 49 **17:** 50 **Med Exp PMPM:** $577
Principal Investments: Cash and equiv (77%), long-term bonds (23%)
Provider Compensation ($000): Contr fee ($331,876), capitation ($16,793)
Total Member Encounters: Phys (565,317), non-phys (234,803)
Group Affiliation: WellCare Health Plans Inc
Licensed in: AZ, TX
Address: 11200 Richmond Ave Ste 450, Houston, TX 77081
Phone: (813) 206-6200 **Dom State:** TX **Commenced Bus:** N/A

Data Date	Rating	RACR #1	RACR #2	Total Assets ($mil)	Capital ($mil)	Net Premium ($mil)	Net Income ($mil)
3-19	B	3.09	2.57	149.2	67.5	106.8	9.7
3-18	C	2.44	2.03	164.9	52.3	106.9	-7.0
2018	B-	2.78	2.31	132.3	60.0	423.2	11.7
2017	C	1.70	1.41	121.7	58.4	409.7	10.7
2016	C	2.51	2.09	130.1	58.0	387.8	1.1
2015	C	2.57	2.14	105.2	55.4	366.8	2.1
2014	C+	1.56	1.30	77.0	28.1	299.5	-13.8

Rating Indexes

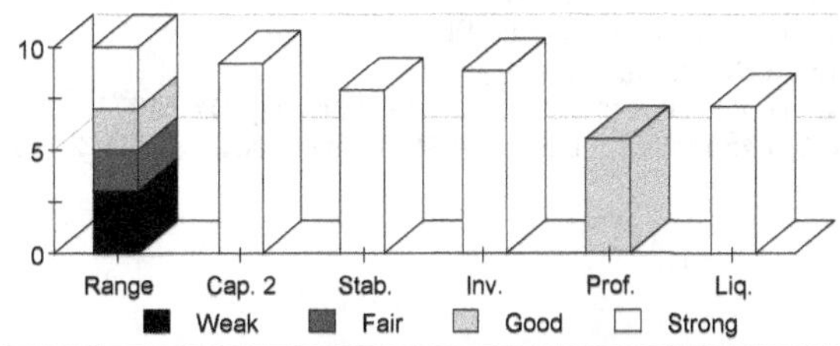

WELLCARE PRESCRIPTION INS INC C Fair

Major Rating Factors: Good overall profitability index (6.6 on a scale of 0 to 10). Strong capitalization (10.0) based on excellent current risk-adjusted capital (severe loss scenario). High quality investment portfolio (7.3).
Other Rating Factors: Excellent liquidity (8.9) with ample operational cash flow and liquid investments.
Principal Business: Other (100%)
Mem Phys: 18: N/A **17:** N/A **18 MLR** 70.9% **/ 18 Admin Exp** N/A
Enroll(000): Q1 19: 3,648 **18:** 963 **17:** 1,051 **Med Exp PMPM:** $46
Principal Investments: Cash and equiv (99%), long-term bonds (1%)
Provider Compensation ($000): Contr fee ($589,215)
Total Member Encounters: N/A
Group Affiliation: None
Licensed in: All states except AL, AR, CO, CT, MN, MT, RI, PR
Address: 8735 Henderson Rd, Tampa, FL 33634
Phone: (813) 206-6200 **Dom State:** FL **Commenced Bus:** N/A

Data Date	Rating	RACR #1	RACR #2	Total Assets ($mil)	Capital ($mil)	Net Premium ($mil)	Net Income ($mil)
3-19	C	7.12	5.93	1,378.7	161.6	264.2	1.4
3-18	D	9.24	7.70	1,887.1	230.1	237.4	-16.4
2018	C	8.41	7.01	1,136.5	191.6	762.4	91.9
2017	E	7.23	6.03	1,491.3	245.2	834.5	38.0
2016	E	10.83	9.02	852.9	209.5	755.6	68.4
2015	E-	6.07	5.06	721.2	141.3	814.8	23.6
2014	D	3.81	3.18	822.2	109.0	986.8	-14.8

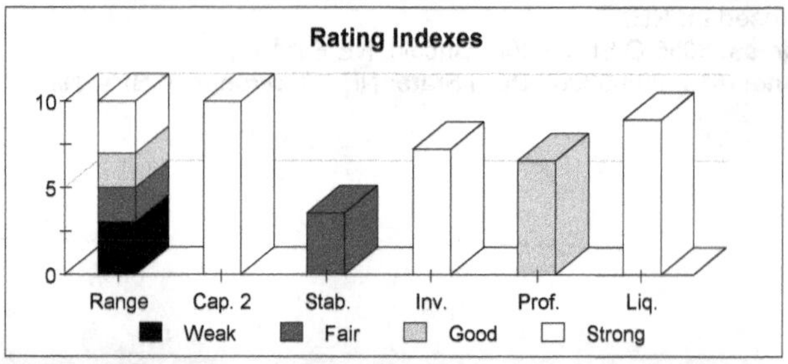

WELLFLEET INS CO C- Fair

Major Rating Factors: Fair profitability index (4.2 on a scale of 0 to 10) with operating losses during 2015. Average return on equity over the last five years has been poor at 0.0%. Fair overall results on stability tests (3.0).
Other Rating Factors: Strong long-term capitalization index (10.0) based on excellent current risk adjusted capital (severe and moderate loss scenarios), despite some fluctuation in capital levels. Superior liquidity (9.3) with ample operational cash flow and liquid investments.
Principal Business: Group accident & health (99%) and workers compensation (1%).
Principal Investments: Cash (92%) and investment grade bonds (8%).
Investments in Affiliates: None
Group Affiliation: Berkshire-Hathaway
Licensed in: All states except NY, PR
Commenced Business: August 1987
Address: 5814 Reed Road, Fort Wayne, IN 46835-3568
Phone: (260) 485-9622 **Domicile State:** IN **NAIC Code:** 32280

Data Date	Rating	RACR #1	RACR #2	Loss Ratio %	Total Assets ($mil)	Capital ($mil)	Net Premium ($mil)	Net Income ($mil)
3-19	C-	13.16	11.84	N/A	105.0	63.8	0.0	0.3
3-18	U	198.91	179.00	N/A	64.6	63.8	0.0	0.2
2018	C-	13.10	11.79	84.2	104.5	63.3	0.0	0.9
2017	U	131.24	118.10	0.0	65.1	63.7	0.0	0.7
2016	U	41.53	21.05	104.7	67.6	62.6	-55.0	2.2
2015	U	4.87	1.44	N/A	116.1	59.0	0.0	-4.3
2014	U	4.34	2.66	N/A	117.2	54.3	N/A	0.4

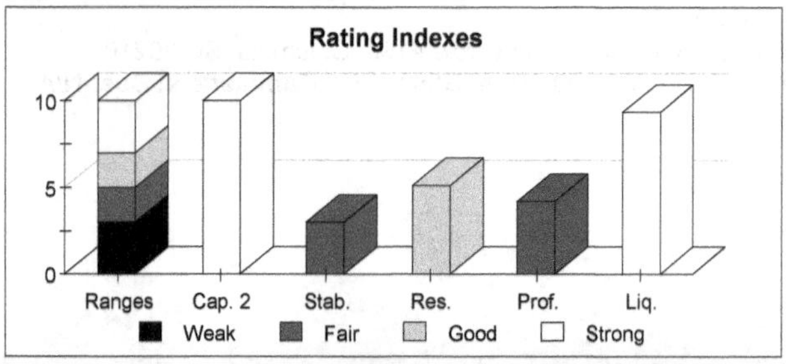

WELLFLEET NEW YORK INS CO C Fair

Major Rating Factors: Weak overall results on stability tests (2.9 on a scale of 0 to 10) including negative cash flow from operations for 2018.
Other Rating Factors: Strong long-term capitalization index (8.7) based on excellent current risk adjusted capital (severe and moderate loss scenarios), despite some fluctuation in capital levels. Excellent profitability (8.5) with operating gains in each of the last five years. Return on equity has been good over the last five years, averaging 10.0%. Excellent liquidity (7.7) with ample operational cash flow and liquid investments.
Principal Business: Group accident & health (98%) and workers compensation (2%).
Principal Investments: Cash (78%), misc. investments (14%), and investment grade bonds (8%).
Investments in Affiliates: None
Group Affiliation: Berkshire-Hathaway
Licensed in: All states except IL, PR
Commenced Business: January 1929
Address: Marine Air Terminal LaGuardia, Flushing, NY 11371
Phone: (260) 485-9622 **Domicile State:** NY **NAIC Code:** 20931

Data Date	Rating	RACR #1	RACR #2	Loss Ratio %	Total Assets ($mil)	Capital ($mil)	Net Premium ($mil)	Net Income ($mil)
3-19	C	3.10	2.24	N/A	107.5	27.9	5.5	0.3
3-18	C	1.56	1.31	N/A	133.7	25.9	6.1	-0.1
2018	C	2.97	2.13	86.2	86.8	28.9	22.8	1.3
2017	C	2.17	1.79	78.3	96.2	27.0	14.3	9.0
2016	U	6.97	6.28	111.0	42.2	22.3	-17.5	2.3
2015	U	2.05	1.00	0.0	43.3	20.2	0.0	0.4
2014	U	1.71	0.84	N/A	44.6	19.9	0.0	0.3

Berkshire-Hathaway Composite Group Rating: C+ Largest Group Members	Assets ($mil)	Rating
NATIONAL INDEMNITY CO	228202	C+
GOVERNMENT EMPLOYEES INS CO	32565	B
COLUMBIA INS CO	24011	C+
BERKSHIRE HATHAWAY LIFE INS CO OF NE	18412	C+
GENERAL REINS CORP	16067	C+

WELLMARK HEALTH PLAN OF IOWA B Good

Major Rating Factors: Good overall profitability index (5.6 on a scale of 0 to 10). Good quality investment portfolio (4.9). Good liquidity (6.8) with sufficient resources (cash flows and marketable investments) to handle a spike in claims.
Other Rating Factors: Strong capitalization index (10.0) based on excellent current risk-adjusted capital (severe loss scenario). Excellent overall results on stability tests (7.1).
Principal Business: Comp med (100%)
Mem Phys: 18: 10,982 **17:** 10 **18 MLR** 76.0% **/ 18 Admin Exp** N/A
Enroll(000): Q1 19: 95 **18:** 90 **17:** 82 **Med Exp PMPM:** $317
Principal Investments: Long-term bonds (67%), nonaffiliate common stock (29%), cash and equiv (2%), other (3%)
Provider Compensation ($000): Bonus arrang ($159,421), contr fee ($133,170), FFS ($20,949), capitation ($2,226)
Total Member Encounters: Phys (376,439), non-phys (273,033)
Group Affiliation: Wellmark Inc
Licensed in: IA
Address: 1331 Grand Avenue, Des Moines, IA 50309-2901
Phone: (515) 376-4500 **Dom State:** IA **Commenced Bus:** N/A

Data Date	Rating	RACR #1	RACR #2	Total Assets ($mil)	Capital ($mil)	Net Premium ($mil)	Net Income ($mil)
3-19	B	7.78	6.48	330.3	218.1	125.9	22.8
3-18	B	8.19	6.82	303.5	198.9	99.4	8.9
2018	B	6.82	5.69	286.1	191.2	419.9	35.1
2017	B	5.63	4.70	283.1	189.6	384.0	28.1
2016	B	7.23	6.03	232.7	153.6	316.0	5.5
2015	B+	6.08	5.07	227.6	148.2	358.7	-9.4
2014	B+	7.14	5.95	218.0	159.3	342.4	10.7

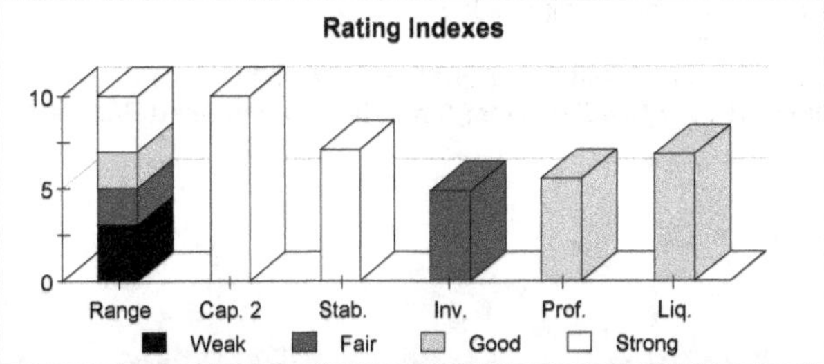

WELLMARK INC B- Good

Major Rating Factors: Fair quality investment portfolio (4.1 on a scale of 0 to 10). Good profitability index (5.0). Good liquidity (6.8) with sufficient resources (cash flows and marketable investments) to handle a spike in claims.
Other Rating Factors: Strong capitalization (10.0) based on excellent current risk-adjusted capital (severe loss scenario).
Principal Business: Comp med (63%), med supp (16%), FEHB (10%), dental (1%), other (10%)
Mem Phys: 18: 9,204 **17:** 8 **18 MLR** 86.2% **/ 18 Admin Exp** N/A
Enroll(000): Q1 19: 1,232 **18:** 1,224 **17:** 1,255 **Med Exp PMPM:** $152
Principal Investments: Long-term bonds (42%), affiliate common stock (24%), nonaffiliate common stock (17%), cash and equiv (8%), real estate (7%), other (2%)
Provider Compensation ($000): Contr fee ($1,318,916), bonus arrang ($561,359), FFS ($180,184), other ($197,986)
Total Member Encounters: Phys (3,556,247), non-phys (2,276,090)
Group Affiliation: Wellmark Inc
Licensed in: IA, SD
Address: 1331 Grand Ave, Des Moines, IA 50309-2901
Phone: (515) 376-4500 **Dom State:** IA **Commenced Bus:** N/A

Data Date	Rating	RACR #1	RACR #2	Total Assets ($mil)	Capital ($mil)	Net Premium ($mil)	Net Income ($mil)
3-19	B-	6.35	5.30	2,611.4	1,722.3	645.0	63.1
3-18	B-	N/A	N/A	2,476.1	1,528.7	670.1	20.8
2018	B-	5.78	4.82	2,438.7	1,567.3	2,625.9	127.5
2017	B-	N/A	N/A	2,423.5	1,524.1	2,646.9	43.1
2016	B-	5.36	4.47	2,129.5	1,330.3	2,656.3	-26.5
2015	B	5.40	4.50	2,043.9	1,322.0	2,535.8	-1.8
2014	B	5.86	4.88	2,018.0	1,359.7	2,409.4	15.4

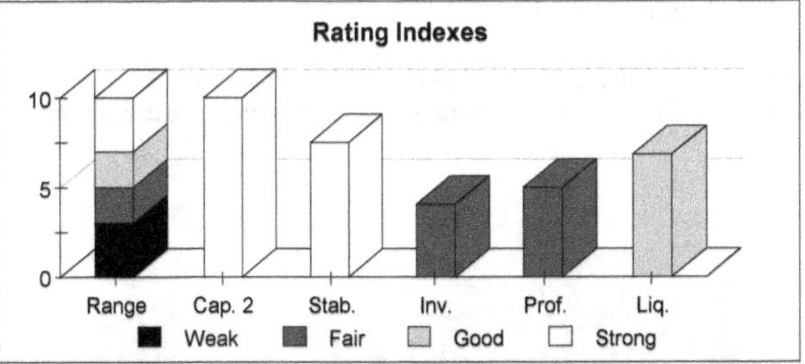

WELLMARK OF SOUTH DAKOTA INC * B+ Good

Major Rating Factors: Good overall profitability index (5.4 on a scale of 0 to 10). Strong capitalization (10.0) based on excellent current risk-adjusted capital (severe loss scenario). Excellent liquidity (7.0) with sufficient resources (cash flows and marketable investments) to handle a spike in claims.
Other Rating Factors: Fair quality investment portfolio (4.8).
Principal Business: Comp med (69%), FEHB (22%), med supp (7%), other (2%)
Mem Phys: 18: 2,793 **17:** 2 **18 MLR** 83.7% **/ 18 Admin Exp** N/A
Enroll(000): Q1 19: 164 **18:** 166 **17:** 175 **Med Exp PMPM:** $322
Principal Investments: Long-term bonds (65%), nonaffiliate common stock (30%), cash and equiv (4%), real estate (1%)
Provider Compensation ($000): Contr fee ($433,143), bonus arrang ($105,895), FFS ($104,515)
Total Member Encounters: Phys (870,073), non-phys (464,420)
Group Affiliation: Wellmark Inc
Licensed in: SD
Address: 1601 West Madison St, Sioux Falls, SD 57104-5710
Phone: (605) 373-7200 **Dom State:** SD **Commenced Bus:** N/A

Data Date	Rating	RACR #1	RACR #2	Total Assets ($mil)	Capital ($mil)	Net Premium ($mil)	Net Income ($mil)
3-19	B+	7.31	6.10	508.1	313.1	192.7	24.3
3-18	B+	N/A	N/A	506.6	297.7	194.0	12.4
2018	B+	6.61	5.51	472.7	283.1	779.3	48.7
2017	B+	N/A	N/A	476.0	291.1	742.1	41.0
2016	B+	6.17	5.14	414.4	238.6	696.1	4.5
2015	B+	6.02	5.01	407.3	232.7	694.8	27.7
2014	B+	6.22	5.18	420.4	228.0	670.1	-9.4

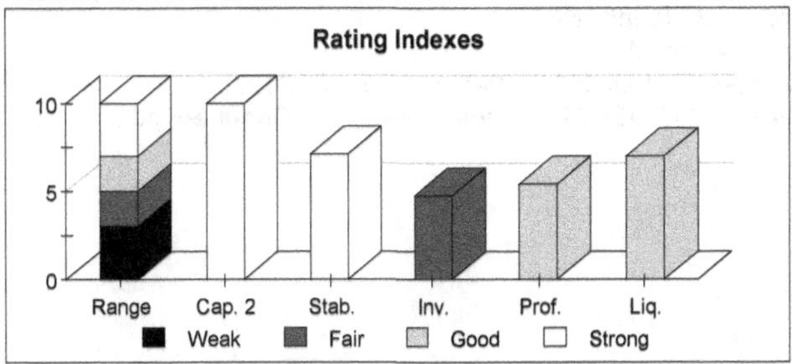

WELLMARK SYNERGY HEALTH INC C+ Fair

Major Rating Factors: Good overall profitability index (6.3 on a scale of 0 to 10). Strong capitalization (10.0) based on excellent current risk-adjusted capital (severe loss scenario). High quality investment portfolio (9.9).
Other Rating Factors: Excellent liquidity (10.0) with ample operational cash flow and liquid investments.
Principal Business: Comp med (100%)
Mem Phys: 18: 4,906 **17:** 2 **18 MLR** 55.4% **/ 18 Admin Exp** N/A
Enroll(000): Q1 19: N/A **18:** 0 **17:** 2 **Med Exp PMPM:** $114
Principal Investments: Cash and equiv (100%)
Provider Compensation ($000): Bonus arrang ($753), contr fee ($423), FFS ($245), capitation ($7)
Total Member Encounters: Phys (1,477), non-phys (740)
Group Affiliation: Wellmark Inc
Licensed in: IA
Address: 1331 Grand Ave, Des Moines, IA 50309-2901
Phone: (515) 376-4500 **Dom State:** IA **Commenced Bus:** N/A

Data Date	Rating	RACR #1	RACR #2	Total Assets ($mil)	Capital ($mil)	Net Premium ($mil)	Net Income ($mil)
3-19	C+	10.49	8.74	14.9	13.6	0.0	0.0
3-18	N/A	N/A	N/A	16.5	12.9	0.7	-0.3
2018	C+	10.48	8.74	15.0	13.6	1.2	0.4
2017	N/A	N/A	N/A	17.3	13.2	9.2	1.4
2016	N/A	N/A	N/A	12.1	11.9	N/A	-0.1
2015	N/A	N/A	N/A	N/A	N/A	N/A	N/A
2014	N/A	N/A	N/A	N/A	N/A	N/A	N/A

Rating Indexes

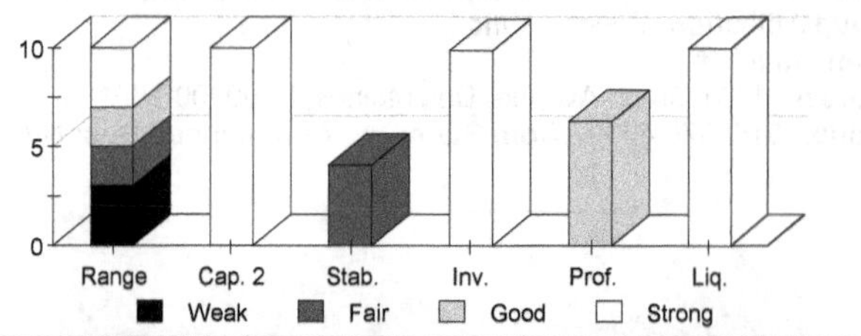

WELLMARK VALUE HEALTH PLAN INC C+ Fair

Major Rating Factors: Excellent overall profitability index (6.9 on a scale of 0 to 10). Strong capitalization (10.0) based on excellent current risk-adjusted capital (severe loss scenario). High quality investment portfolio (9.9).
Other Rating Factors: Excellent liquidity (10.0) with ample operational cash flow and liquid investments.
Principal Business: Comp med (100%)
Mem Phys: 18: 5,490 **17:** 4 **18 MLR** 56.4% **/ 18 Admin Exp** N/A
Enroll(000): Q1 19: 4 **18:** 1 **17:** 2 **Med Exp PMPM:** $100
Principal Investments: Cash and equiv (100%)
Provider Compensation ($000): FFS ($625), bonus arrang ($618), contr fee ($11), capitation ($8)
Total Member Encounters: Phys (1,648), non-phys (1,116)
Group Affiliation: Wellmark Inc
Licensed in: IA
Address: 1331 Grand Ave, Des Moines, IA 50309-2901
Phone: (515) 376-4500 **Dom State:** IA **Commenced Bus:** N/A

Data Date	Rating	RACR #1	RACR #2	Total Assets ($mil)	Capital ($mil)	Net Premium ($mil)	Net Income ($mil)
3-19	C+	6.68	5.57	15.1	8.6	9.1	2.0
3-18	N/A	N/A	N/A	10.4	6.6	0.5	0.1
2018	C+	5.22	4.35	8.6	6.7	1.2	0.2
2017	N/A	N/A	N/A	10.5	6.5	11.2	1.7
2016	N/A	N/A	N/A	5.0	4.8	N/A	-0.2
2015	N/A	N/A	N/A	N/A	N/A	N/A	N/A
2014	N/A	N/A	N/A	N/A	N/A	N/A	N/A

Rating Indexes

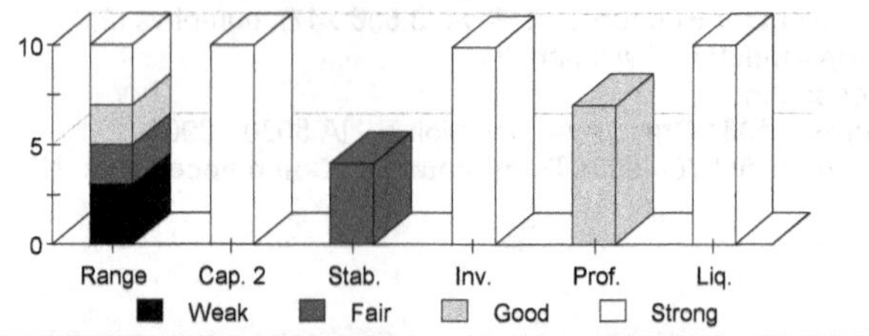

WEST VIRGINIA FAMILY HEALTH PLAN INC B- Good

Major Rating Factors: Good overall profitability index (6.7 on a scale of 0 to 10). Good liquidity (6.7) with sufficient resources (cash flows and marketable investments) to handle a spike in claims. Strong capitalization (8.5) based on excellent current risk-adjusted capital (severe loss scenario).
Other Rating Factors: High quality investment portfolio (8.3).
Principal Business: Medicaid (100%)
Mem Phys: 18: 9,803 **17:** 8 **18 MLR** 88.3% **/ 18 Admin Exp** N/A
Enroll(000): Q1 19: 62 **18:** 63 **17:** 66 **Med Exp PMPM:** $384
Principal Investments: Long-term bonds (64%), cash and equiv (36%)
Provider Compensation ($000): Contr fee ($291,333), capitation ($2,898), bonus arrang ($258)
Total Member Encounters: Phys (461,519), non-phys (415,052)
Group Affiliation: None
Licensed in: WV
Address: 614 Market St, Parkersburg, WV 26101
Phone: (304) 424-7700 **Dom State:** WV **Commenced Bus:** N/A

Data Date	Rating	RACR #1	RACR #2	Total Assets ($mil)	Capital ($mil)	Net Premium ($mil)	Net Income ($mil)
3-19	B-	2.55	2.12	82.8	36.6	77.8	0.9
3-18	C-	N/A	N/A	87.6	28.6	83.3	2.2
2018	C	2.51	2.09	79.1	35.9	337.7	1.8
2017	C-	N/A	N/A	67.1	25.0	324.1	18.6
2016	C-	0.28	0.23	60.7	8.3	299.6	4.9
2015	C	1.36	1.14	51.0	4.9	102.6	0.8
2014	U	1.19	0.99	5.4	3.6	1.7	-2.8

Rating Indexes

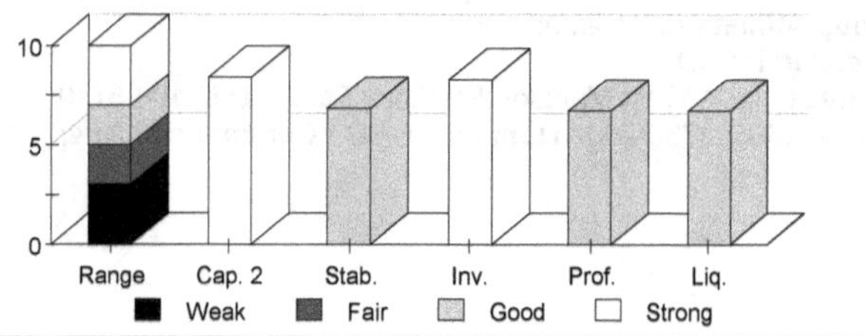

WESTERN GROCERS EMPLOYEE BENEFITS E+ Very Weak

Major Rating Factors: Weak profitability index (1.2 on a scale of 0 to 10). Good liquidity (5.6) with sufficient resources (cash flows and marketable investments) to handle a spike in claims. Strong capitalization index (10.0) based on weak current risk-adjusted capital (severe loss scenario).
Other Rating Factors: High quality investment portfolio (9.4).
Principal Business: Comp med (93%), dental (7%)
Mem Phys: 18: N/A **17:** N/A **18 MLR** 97.2% **/ 18 Admin Exp** N/A
Enroll(000): Q1 19: 7 **18:** 7 **17:** 6 **Med Exp PMPM:** $260
Principal Investments: Long-term bonds (69%), cash and equiv (31%)
Provider Compensation ($000): FFS ($20,566)
Total Member Encounters: Phys (43,047), non-phys (77,231)
Group Affiliation: None
Licensed in: AK, OR, WA
Address: 12901 SE 97TH AVE #200, CLACKAMAS, OR 97015
Phone: (503) 968-2360 **Dom State:** OR **Commenced Bus:** N/A

Data Date	Rating	RACR #1	RACR #2	Total Assets ($mil)	Capital ($mil)	Net Premium ($mil)	Net Income ($mil)
3-19	E+	N/A	N/A	8.0	3.1	5.7	-0.2
3-18	E	N/A	N/A	7.8	4.2	5.4	0.7
2018	E+	N/A	N/A	6.6	3.3	21.2	-0.2
2017	E	N/A	N/A	7.1	3.5	19.3	0.6
2016	E	-0.77	-0.64	6.0	2.9	16.4	-1.7
2015	N/A	N/A	N/A	7.6	4.6	15.6	-1.3
2014	N/A	N/A	N/A	8.3	5.9	15.8	1.1

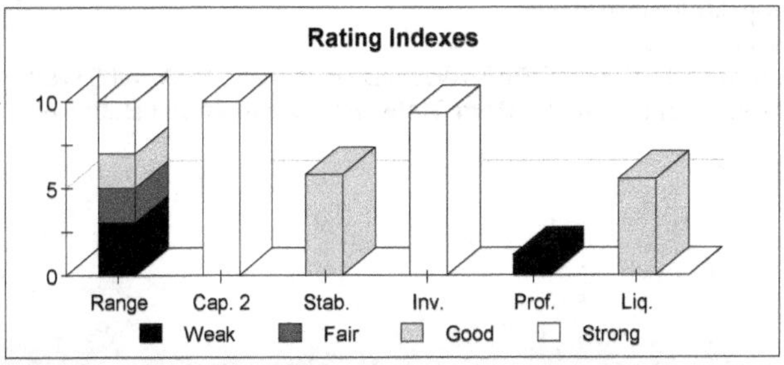

WESTERN HEALTH ADVANTAGE E Very Weak

Major Rating Factors: Poor capitalization index (0.0 on a scale of 0 to 10) based on weak current risk-adjusted capital (severe loss scenario). Weak overall results on stability tests (2.4) based on an excessive 95993% enrollment growth during the period. Fair profitability index (3.6).
Other Rating Factors: Good liquidity (6.9) with sufficient resources (cash flows and marketable investments) to handle a spike in claims.
Principal Business: Managed care (100%)
Mem Phys: 18: N/A **17:** N/A **18 MLR** 89.7% **/ 18 Admin Exp** N/A
Enroll(000): Q1 19: 130 **18:** 126 **17:** 0 **Med Exp PMPM:** $445
Principal Investments ($000): Cash and equiv ($31,422)
Provider Compensation ($000): None
Total Member Encounters: N/A
Group Affiliation: None
Licensed in: CA
Address: 2349 Gateway Oaks Suite 100, Sacramento, CA 95833
Phone: (916) 563-3183 **Dom State:** CA **Commenced Bus:** May 1997

Data Date	Rating	RACR #1	RACR #2	Total Assets ($mil)	Capital ($mil)	Net Premium ($mil)	Net Income ($mil)
3-19	E	0.24	0.15	74.5	11.0	201.1	0.8
3-18	E	0.20	0.13	85.8	11.0	191.3	0.7
2018	E	0.22	0.14	63.0	10.2	760.7	0.0
2017	E	0.19	0.12	60.0	10.3	758.7	4.6
2016	E	0.18	0.11	83.5	8.8	664.4	1.5
2015	E	0.15	0.09	93.9	7.3	594.9	-13.2
2014	D	0.55	0.34	68.0	20.6	515.5	0.9

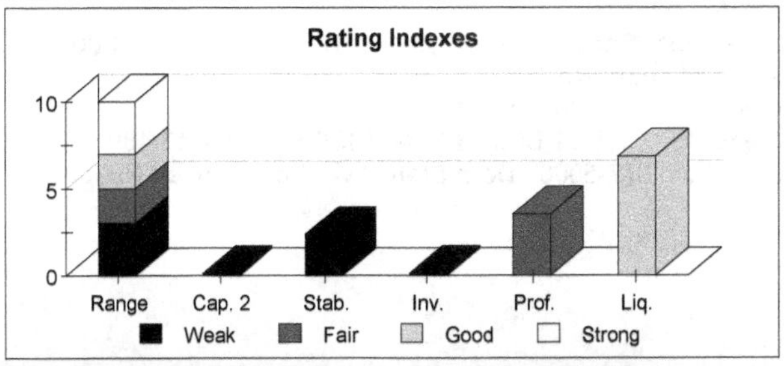

WESTPORT INS CORP C Fair

Major Rating Factors: Weak overall results on stability tests (2.6 on a scale of 0 to 10). The largest net exposure for one risk is excessive at 6.9% of capital. Strengths include potentially strong support from affiliation with Swiss Reinsurance. Good overall long-term capitalization (5.5) based on good current risk adjusted capital (moderate loss scenario). However, capital levels have fluctuated somewhat during past years.
Other Rating Factors: History of adequate reserve strength (6.2) as reserves have been consistently at an acceptable level. Good profitability index (5.0) despite operating losses during 2018. Return on equity has been fair, averaging 6.7% over the past five years. Excellent liquidity (7.0) with ample operational cash flow and liquid investments.
Principal Business: Group accident & health (41%), other liability (23%), allied lines (14%), fire (10%), earthquake (4%), inland marine (2%), and other lines (6%).
Principal Investments: Investment grade bonds (84%), misc. investments (15%), and cash (1%).
Investments in Affiliates: 11%
Group Affiliation: Swiss Reinsurance
Licensed in: All states, the District of Columbia and Puerto Rico
Commenced Business: September 1981
Address: 237 EAST HIGH STREET, Jefferson City, MO 65101-3206
Phone: (816) 235-3700 **Domicile State:** MO **NAIC Code:** 39845

Data Date	Rating	RACR #1	RACR #2	Loss Ratio %	Total Assets ($mil)	Capital ($mil)	Net Premium ($mil)	Net Income ($mil)
3-19	C	1.52	0.91	N/A	5,367.9	1,809.0	223.8	181.2
3-18	B	1.57	0.98	N/A	5,418.5	1,734.7	363.4	-140.5
2018	B-	1.31	0.78	74.4	5,450.1	1,634.1	2,292.9	-245.2
2017	B	1.61	1.04	77.1	5,517.6	1,535.5	321.9	93.8
2016	B	1.78	1.23	80.1	4,730.1	1,558.6	287.1	189.7
2015	B-	1.48	1.03	61.5	4,693.0	1,505.3	281.6	177.3
2014	C+	1.56	1.08	67.9	5,215.7	1,630.5	135.9	160.8

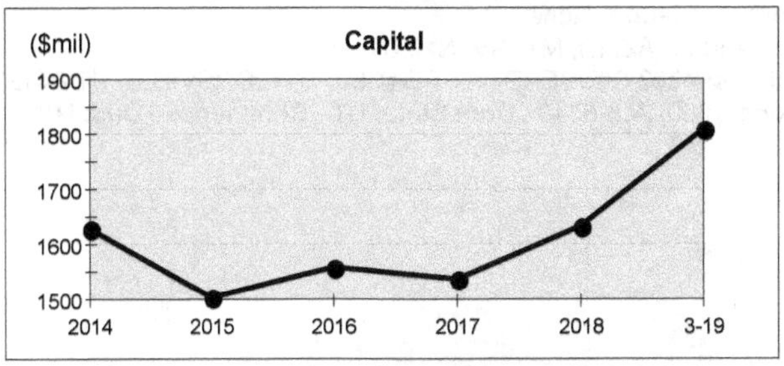

WISCONSIN COLLABORATIVE INSURANCE CO — B- Good

Major Rating Factors: Strong capitalization (10.0 on a scale of 0 to 10) based on excellent current risk-adjusted capital (severe loss scenario). High quality investment portfolio (9.9). Excellent liquidity (7.2) with ample operational cash flow and liquid investments.
Other Rating Factors: Weak profitability index (1.9).
Principal Business: Comp med (100%)
Mem Phys: 18: 8,924 **17:** 8 **18 MLR** 95.3% **/ 18 Admin Exp** N/A
Enroll(000): Q1 19: 13 **18:** 13 **17:** N/A **Med Exp PMPM:** $344
Principal Investments: Cash and equiv (100%)
Provider Compensation ($000): Bonus arrang ($23,434), contr fee ($7,239), FFS ($5,545)
Total Member Encounters: Phys (41,767), non-phys (30,522)
Group Affiliation: None
Licensed in: WI
Address: N17 W24340 RIVERWOOD Dr, WAUKESHA, WI 53188
Phone: (262) 523-4020 **Dom State:** WI **Commenced Bus:** N/A

Data Date	Rating	RACR #1	RACR #2	Total Assets ($mil)	Capital ($mil)	Net Premium ($mil)	Net Income ($mil)
3-19	B-	3.93	3.27	34.5	21.2	14.5	4.5
3-18	N/A	N/A	N/A	12.9	8.7	9.6	1.4
2018	B-	3.03	2.52	26.4	16.3	43.7	0.1
2017	N/A	N/A	N/A	18.1	9.3	N/A	-1.9
2016	N/A	N/A	N/A	4.1	3.6	N/A	-6.4
2015	N/A	N/A	N/A	N/A	N/A	N/A	N/A
2014	N/A	N/A	N/A	N/A	N/A	N/A	N/A

Rating Indexes

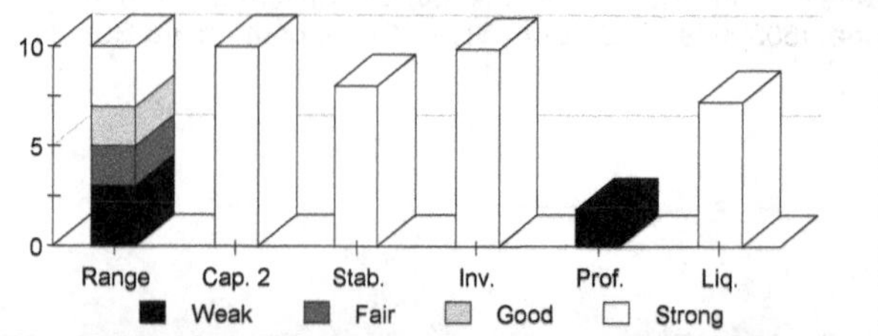

WISCONSIN PHYSICIANS SERVICE INS — C Fair

Major Rating Factors: Fair profitability index (4.0 on a scale of 0 to 10). Fair quality investment portfolio (2.9). Good liquidity (6.8) with sufficient resources (cash flows and marketable investments) to handle a spike in claims.
Other Rating Factors: Strong capitalization (8.3) based on excellent current risk-adjusted capital (severe loss scenario).
Principal Business: Comp med (53%), med supp (35%), dental (2%), other (10%)
Mem Phys: 18: N/A **17:** N/A **18 MLR** 78.0% **/ 18 Admin Exp** N/A
Enroll(000): Q1 19: 96 **18:** 102 **17:** 110 **Med Exp PMPM:** $245
Principal Investments: Long-term bonds (33%), affiliate common stock (22%), real estate (19%), nonaffiliate common stock (13%), cash and equiv (12%)
Provider Compensation ($000): Contr fee ($187,948), FFS ($101,436), other ($18,945)
Total Member Encounters: Phys (855,123), non-phys (311,802)
Group Affiliation: None
Licensed in: IL, IN, MI, OH, WI
Address: 1717 WEST BRdWAY, MADISON, WI 53713-1895
Phone: (608) 977-5000 **Dom State:** WI **Commenced Bus:** N/A

Data Date	Rating	RACR #1	RACR #2	Total Assets ($mil)	Capital ($mil)	Net Premium ($mil)	Net Income ($mil)
3-19	C	2.39	1.99	279.6	122.4	86.9	-7.6
3-18	C	N/A	N/A	274.0	121.6	101.0	-0.9
2018	C	2.49	2.08	289.3	127.7	396.0	-1.3
2017	C	N/A	N/A	277.1	122.2	417.1	11.8
2016	C	1.83	1.53	267.8	109.8	435.4	8.8
2015	C-	1.35	1.12	265.5	93.9	547.5	-7.1
2014	C	1.91	1.59	315.6	145.4	560.9	3.6

Rating Indexes

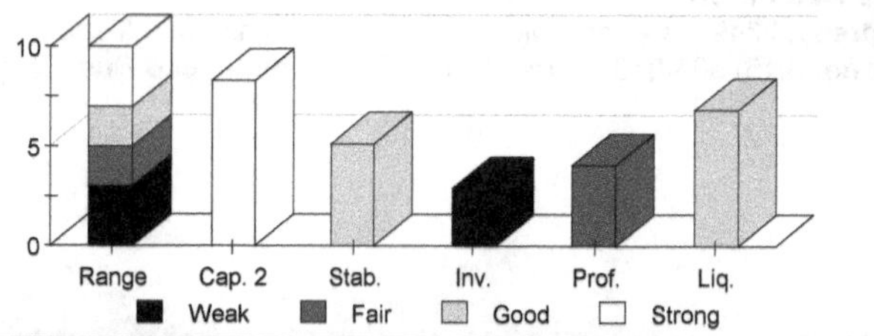

WMI MUTUAL INS CO — B- Good

Major Rating Factors: Fair profitability index (4.0 on a scale of 0 to 10). Good liquidity (6.5) with sufficient resources (cash flows and marketable investments) to handle a spike in claims. Strong capitalization (9.8) based on excellent current risk-adjusted capital (severe loss scenario).
Other Rating Factors: High quality investment portfolio (7.9).
Principal Business: Comp med (93%), dental (3%), med supp (2%)
Mem Phys: 18: N/A **17:** N/A **18 MLR** 80.0% **/ 18 Admin Exp** N/A
Enroll(000): Q1 19: 5 **18:** 5 **17:** 6 **Med Exp PMPM:** $216
Principal Investments: Long-term bonds (71%), nonaffiliate common stock (21%), cash and equiv (5%), affiliate common stock (3%)
Provider Compensation ($000): Other ($14,276)
Total Member Encounters: N/A
Group Affiliation: None
Licensed in: AZ, ID, MT, NV, NM, UT, WA
Address: 4393 S RIVERBOAT RD #380, TAYLORSVILLE, UT 84123
Phone: (800) 748-5340 **Dom State:** UT **Commenced Bus:** N/A

Data Date	Rating	RACR #1	RACR #2	Total Assets ($mil)	Capital ($mil)	Net Premium ($mil)	Net Income ($mil)
3-19	B-	3.57	2.98	15.9	11.3	4.4	0.3
3-18	C	3.91	3.26	15.1	10.5	4.5	0.4
2018	B-	3.39	2.83	14.8	10.7	18.1	0.7
2017	C	3.85	3.21	14.6	10.3	17.9	1.5
2016	C	2.40	2.00	13.8	8.4	18.0	-1.1
2015	N/A	N/A	N/A	14.7	9.3	18.4	N/A
2014	N/A	N/A	N/A	13.5	709.8	19.8	N/A

Rating Indexes

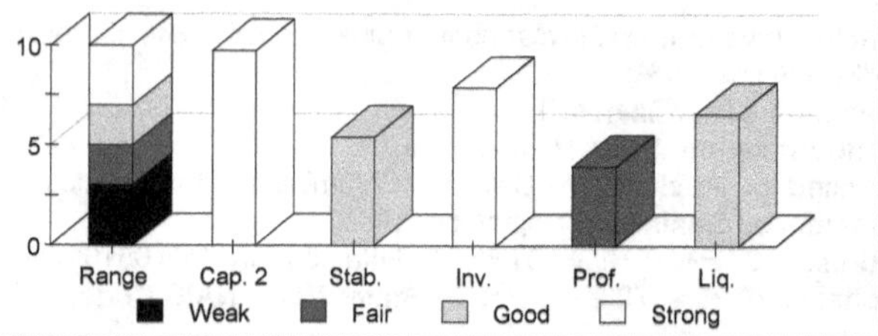

WPS HEALTH PLAN INC C- Fair

Major Rating Factors: Weak profitability index (0.9 on a scale of 0 to 10). Good liquidity (5.7) with sufficient resources (cash flows and marketable investments) to handle a spike in claims. Strong capitalization (7.5) based on excellent current risk-adjusted capital (severe loss scenario).
Other Rating Factors: High quality investment portfolio (8.4).
Principal Business: Comp med (100%)
Mem Phys: 18: 11,046 **17:** 9 **18 MLR** 87.7% **/ 18 Admin Exp** N/A
Enroll(000): Q1 19: 12 **18:** 14 **17:** 22 **Med Exp PMPM:** $402
Principal Investments: Long-term bonds (82%), cash and equiv (18%)
Provider Compensation ($000): Contr fee ($60,906), FFS ($18,623)
Total Member Encounters: Phys (105,334), non-phys (37,979)
Group Affiliation: None
Licensed in: WI
Address: 421 LAWRENCE Dr STE 100, DEPERE, WI 54115
Phone: (920) 490-6900 **Dom State:** WI **Commenced Bus:** N/A

Data Date	Rating	RACR #1	RACR #2	Total Assets ($mil)	Capital ($mil)	Net Premium ($mil)	Net Income ($mil)
3-19	C-	1.75	1.46	26.3	12.7	17.5	-0.4
3-18	C-	1.57	1.31	33.3	14.3	24.9	-2.4
2018	C-	1.80	1.50	28.4	13.1	89.1	-3.5
2017	C-	1.37	1.14	34.0	16.1	106.0	-6.7
2016	C-	1.40	1.17	50.4	23.1	185.8	-6.0
2015	C-	1.36	1.13	50.2	20.2	150.2	-22.4
2014	C	1.12	0.93	28.4	14.6	140.0	-7.4

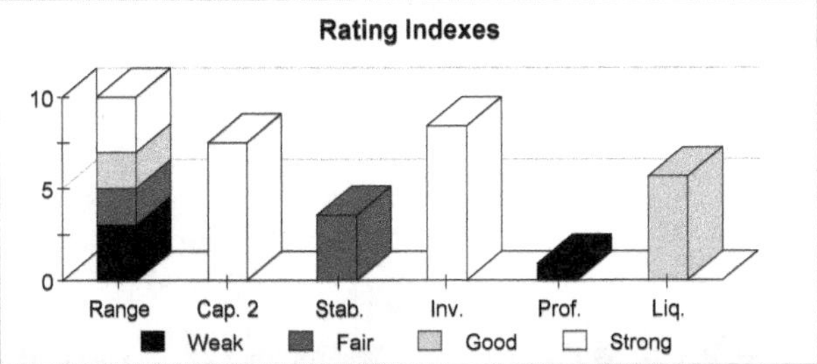

WV SENIOR ADVANTAGE INC C- Fair

Major Rating Factors: Weak profitability index (1.9 on a scale of 0 to 10). Strong capitalization (7.4) based on excellent current risk-adjusted capital (severe loss scenario). High quality investment portfolio (9.9).
Other Rating Factors: Excellent liquidity (7.4) with ample operational cash flow and liquid investments.
Principal Business: Medicare (100%)
Mem Phys: 18: 3,071 **17:** 598 **18 MLR** 84.9% **/ 18 Admin Exp** N/A
Enroll(000): Q1 19: 1 **18:** 1 **17:** 1 **Med Exp PMPM:** $1,463
Principal Investments: Cash and equiv (100%)
Provider Compensation ($000): Contr fee ($5,560), capitation ($3,193), bonus arrang ($359)
Total Member Encounters: Phys (13,372), non-phys (17,346)
Group Affiliation: Stonerise Senior Advantage Holdings
Licensed in: WV
Address: 700 Chappell Rd, Charleston, WV 25034
Phone: (804) 396-6412 **Dom State:** WV **Commenced Bus:** N/A

Data Date	Rating	RACR #1	RACR #2	Total Assets ($mil)	Capital ($mil)	Net Premium ($mil)	Net Income ($mil)
3-19	C-	1.66	1.38	6.0	2.8	3.4	0.1
3-18	N/A	N/A	N/A	6.4	2.3	3.1	0.1
2018	U	1.63	1.35	5.0	2.7	10.3	0.3
2017	N/A	N/A	N/A	4.8	2.2	11.9	-0.5
2016	N/A	N/A	N/A	2.1	2.1	N/A	-1.2
2015	N/A	N/A	N/A	N/A	N/A	N/A	N/A
2014	N/A	N/A	N/A	N/A	N/A	N/A	N/A

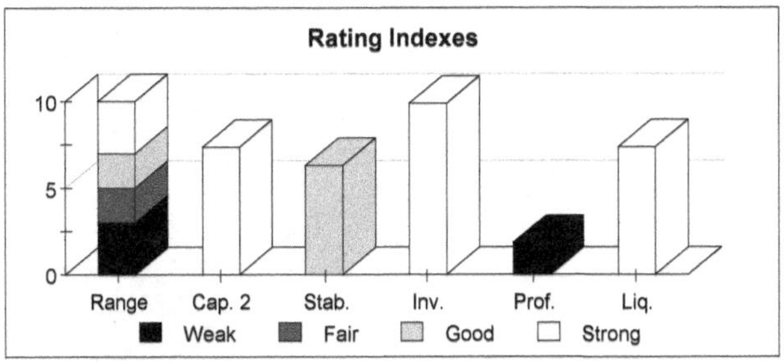

Section III

Weiss Recommended Companies

A compilation of those

U.S. Health Insurers

receiving a Weiss Safety Rating of A+, A, A-, or B+.

Companies are listed in alphabetical order.

Section III Contents

This section provides contact addresses and phone numbers for all recommended carriers analyzed by Weiss Ratings. It contains all insurers receiving a Safety Rating of A+, A, A-, or B+. If an insurer is not on this list, it should not automatically be assumed that the firm is weak. Indeed, there are many firms that have not achieved a B+ or better rating but are in relatively good condition with adequate resources to cover their risk during an average recession. Not being included in this list should not be construed as a recommendation to cancel policies.

1. **Safety Rating** — Our rating is measured on a scale from A to F and considers a wide range of factors. Highly-rated companies are, in our opinion, less likely to experience financial difficulties than lower-rated firms. See *About Weiss Safety Ratings* for more information.

2. **Insurance Company Name** — The legally-registered name, which can sometimes differ from the name that the company uses for advertising. An insurer's name can be very similar to the name of other companies, so make sure you note the exact name before contacting your agent.

3. **Address** — The address of the main office where you can contact the firm for additional financial data or for the location of local branches and/or registered agents.

4. **Telephone Number** — The number to call for additional financial data or for the phone numbers of local branches and/or registered agents.

Weiss Safety Ratings are not deemed to be a recommendation concerning the purchase or sale of the securities of any insurance company that is publicly owned

RATING	INSURANCE COMPANY NAME	ADDRESS	CITY	STATE	ZIP	PHONE
B+	ADVANCE INS CO OF KANSAS	1133 SW TOPEKA BLVD	TOPEKA	KS	66629	(785) 273-98
B+	AETNA BETTER HLTH OF KY INS CO	9900 CORPORATE CAMPUS DR SUITE	LOUISVILLE	KY	40202	(800) 627-47
B+	ALLIANZ LIFE INS CO OF NY	28 LIBERTY STREET 38TH FLOOR	NEW YORK	NY	10005	(763) 765-29
A	AMALGAMATED LIFE INS CO	333 WESTCHESTER AVENUE	WHITE PLAINS	NY	10604	(914) 367-50
A-	AMERICAN FAMILY LIFE ASR CO OF NY	22 CORPORATE WOODS BLVD STE 2	ALBANY	NY	12211	(518) 438-07
B+	AMERICAN FAMILY MUTL INS CO SI	6000 AMERICAN PARKWAY	MADISON	WI	53783	(608) 249-21
B+	AMERICAN FIDELITY ASR CO	9000 CAMERON PARKWAY	OKLAHOMA CITY	OK	73114	(405) 523-20
A-	AMERICAN HEALTH & LIFE INS CO	3001 MEACHAM BLVD STE 100	FORT WORTH	TX	76137	(800) 307-00
B+	AMERICAN UNITED LIFE INS CO	ONE AMERICAN SQUARE	INDIANAPOLIS	IN	46282	(317) 285-18
A-	AMERIGROUP NEW JERSEY INC	101 WOOD AVENUE SOUTH 8TH FLO	ISELIN	NJ	8830	(757) 490-69
A-	AMERIGROUP TEXAS INC	3800 BUFFALO SPEEDWAY SUITE 4	HOUSTON	TX	77098	(757) 490-69
A-	AMERIGROUP WASHINGTON INC	705 FIFTH AVENUE SOUTH SUITE	SEATTLE	WA	98104	(757) 490-69
A-	AMGP GEORGIA MANAGED CARE CO INC	4170 ASHFORD DUNWOODY ROAD	ATLANTA	GA	30319	(678) 587-48
A-	ANTHEM KENTUCKY MANAGED CARE PLAN	13550 TRITON PARK BLVD	LOUISVILLE	KY	40223	(800) 331-14
B+	ANTHEM LIFE INS CO	220 VIRGINIA AVENUE	INDIANAPOLIS	IN	46204	(614) 433-88
B+	ASSURITY LIFE INS CO	2000 Q STREET	LINCOLN	NE	68503	(402) 476-65
B+	AXA EQUITABLE LIFE INS CO	1290 AVENUE OF THE AMERICAS	NEW YORK	NY	10104	(212) 554-12
A	BERKLEY LIFE & HEALTH INS CO	11201 DOUGLAS AVE	URBANDALE	IA	50322	(609) 584-69
B+	BEST LIFE & HEALTH INS CO	AUSTIN	AUSTIN	TX	78752	(949) 253-40
B+	BLUE CROSS & BLUE SHIELD MA HMO BLUE	101 HUNTINGTON AVENUE SUITE 1	BOSTON	MA	2199	(617) 246-50
A-	BLUE CROSS BLUE SHIELD HEALTHCARE GA	3350 PEACHTREE ROAD NE	ATLANTA	GA	30326	(404) 842-80
B+	BLUE CROSS BLUE SHIELD OF ALABAMA	450 RIVERCHASE PARKWAY EAST	BIRMINGHAM	AL	35244	(205) 220-21
A+	BLUE CROSS BLUE SHIELD OF ARIZONA	2444 W LAS PALMARITAS DRIVE	PHOENIX	AZ	85021	(602) 864-41
A	BLUE CROSS BLUE SHIELD OF MS, MUTUAL	3545 LAKELAND DRIVE	FLOWOOD	MS	39232	(601) 664-45
B+	BLUE CROSS BLUE SHIELD OF NC	4705 UNIVERSITY DRIVE BUILDIN	DURHAM	NC	27707	(919) 489-74
B+	BLUE CROSS BLUE SHIELD OF SC INC	2501 FARAWAY DRIVE	COLUMBIA	SC	29219	(803) 788-38
A+	BLUE CROSS OF CALIFORNIA	1 WELLPOINT WAY	THOUSAND OAKS	CA	91362	(916) 403-05
A-	BLUEBONNET LIFE INS CO	3545 LAKELAND DR	FLOWOOD	MS	39232	(601) 664-42
B+	BLUECROSS BLUESHIELD OF TENNESSEE	1 CAMERON HILL CIRCLE	CHATTANOOGA	TN	37402	(423) 535-56
B+	BOSTON MUTUAL LIFE INS CO	120 ROYALL STREET	CANTON	MA	02021	(781) 828-70
A+	CALIFORNIA PHYSICIANS SERVICE	50 BEALE STREET 22ND FLOOR	SAN FRANCISCO	CA	94105	(415) 229-51
A	CAPITAL DISTRICT PHYSICIANS HEALTH P	500 PATROON CREEK BOULEVARD	ALBANY	NY	12206	(518) 641-30
B+	CAPITAL HEALTH PLAN INC	2140 CENTERVILLE PLACE	TALLAHASSEE	FL	32308	(850) 383-33
A+	CARE 1ST HEALTH PLAN INC	601 POTRERO GRANDE DR	MONTEREY PARK	CA	91755	(323) 889-66
B+	CARE WISCONSIN HEALTH PLAN INC	1617 SHERMAN AVENUE	MADISON	WI	53704	(608) 240-00
A+	CHESAPEAKE LIFE INS CO	1833 SOUTH MORGAN ROAD	OKLAHOMA CITY	OK	73128	(817) 255-31
B+	CHILDRENS COMMUNITY HEALTH PLAN INC	9000 W WISCONSIN AVE	MILWAUKEE	WI	53226	(800) 482-80
A-	CHRISTIAN FIDELITY LIFE INS CO	1999 BRYAN STREET SUITE 900	DALLAS	TX	75201	(602) 263-66
A-	CIGNA LIFE INS CO OF NEW YORK	140 EAST 45TH STREET	NEW YORK	NY	10017	(215) 761-10
B+	COMMUNITY CARE BEHAVIORAL HEALTH	339 SIXTH AVENUE SUITE 1300	PITTSBURGH	PA	15222	(412) 454-21
B+	COMPANION LIFE INS CO	2501 FARAWAY DRIVE	COLUMBIA	SC	29219	(803) 735-12
A-	COMPCARE HEALTH SERVICES INS CORP	N17 W24340 RIVERWOOD DRIVE	WAUKESHA	WI	53188	(262) 523-40
A+	COUNTRY LIFE INS CO	1701 N TOWANDA AVENUE	BLOOMINGTON	IL	61701	(309) 821-30
A	DEAN HEALTH PLAN INC	1277 DEMING WAY	MADISON	WI	53717	(608) 836-14
B+	DEARBORN NATIONAL LIFE INS CO	300 EAST RANDOLPH STREET	CHICAGO	IL	60601	(800) 348-45
B+	DEARBORN NATIONAL LIFE INS CO OF NY	1250 PITTSFORD VICTOR ROAD	PITTSFORD	NY	14534	(800) 348-45
B+	DELAWARE AMERICAN LIFE INS CO	1209 ORANGE STREET	WILMINGTON	DE	19801	(302) 594-20
B+	EL PASO FIRST HEALTH PLANS INC	1145 WESTMORELAND DRIVE	EL PASO	TX	79925	(915) 298-71

RATING	INSURANCE COMPANY NAME	ADDRESS	CITY	STATE	ZIP	PHONE
A	EMI HEALTH	5101 S COMMERCE DR	MURRAY	UT	84107	(801) 262-7476
A-	ESSENCE HEALTHCARE INC	13900 RIVERPORT DRIVE	ST. LOUIS	MO	63043	(314) 209-2780
B+	FARM BUREAU LIFE INS CO	5400 UNIVERSITY AVENUE	WEST DES MOINES	IA	50266	(515) 225-5400
A-	FARM BUREAU LIFE INS CO OF MISSOURI	701 SOUTH COUNTRY CLUB DRIVE	JEFFERSON CITY	MO	65109	(573) 893-1400
A	FEDERATED LIFE INS CO	121 EAST PARK SQUARE	OWATONNA	MN	55060	(507) 455-5200
A-	FIDELITY SECURITY LIFE INS CO	3130 BROADWAY	KANSAS CITY	MO	64111	(816) 756-1060
B+	FIDELITY SECURITY LIFE INS CO OF NY	162 PROSPECT HILL RD STE 101A	BREWSTER	NY	10509	(800) 821-7303
A-	FIRST RELIANCE STANDARD LIFE INS CO	590 MADISON AVENUE 29TH FLOOR	NEW YORK	NY	10022	(212) 303-8400
A-	FLORIDA HEALTH CARE PLAN INC	1340 RIDGEWOOD AVENUE	HOLLY HILL	FL	32117	(386) 676-7100
B+	FREEDOM LIFE INS CO OF AMERICA	300 BURNETT STREET SUITE 200	FORT WORTH	TX	76102	(817) 878-3300
A	GARDEN STATE LIFE INS CO	ONE MOODY PLAZA	GALVESTON	TX	77550	(409) 763-4661
B+	GEISINGER HEALTH PLAN	100 NORTH ACADEMY AVENUE	DANVILLE	PA	17822	(570) 271-8777
B+	GERBER LIFE INS CO	1311 MAMARONECK AVENUE	WHITE PLAINS	NY	10605	(914) 272-4000
A-	GREAT SOUTHERN LIFE INS CO	PO BOX 139061	DALLAS	TX	75313	(816) 391-2000
A	GUARDIAN LIFE INS CO OF AMERICA	7 HANOVER SQUARE	NEW YORK	NY	10004	(212) 598-8000
A-	HEALTH OPTIONS INC	4800 DEERWOOD CAMPUS	JACKSONVILLE	FL	32246	(904) 791-6111
B+	HEALTH PLAN OF NEVADA INC	2720 NORTH TENAYA WAY	LAS VEGAS	NV	89128	(702) 242-7732
B+	HEALTHPARTNERS	8170 33RD AVENUE SOUTH P O BO	MINNEAPOLIS	MN	55440	(952) 883-6000
B+	HEALTHPARTNERS INS CO	8170 33RD AVENUE SOUTH	MINNEAPOLIS	MN	55440	(952) 883-6000
A+	HMO LOUISIANA INC	5525 REITZ AVENUE	BATON ROUGE	LA	70809	(225) 295-3307
A+	HMO PARTNERS INC	320 WEST CAPITOL	LITTLE ROCK	AR	72203	(501) 221-1800
B+	HUMANA BENEFIT PLAN OF ILLINOIS	4501 NORTH STERLING AVE 2ND	PEORIA	IL	61615	(502) 580-1000
B+	HUMANA INS CO OF KENTUCKY	500 WEST MAIN STREET	LOUISVILLE	KY	40202	(502) 580-1000
A-	HUMANA MEDICAL PLAN INC	3501 SW 160TH AVENUE	MIRAMAR	FL	33027	(305) 626-5616
B+	ILLINOIS MUTUAL LIFE INS CO	300 SW ADAMS STREET	PEORIA	IL	61634	(309) 674-8255
B+	INDEPENDENT CARE HEALTH PLAN	1555 N RIVERCENTER DRIVE SUI	MILWAUKEE	WI	53212	(414) 223-4847
A	INLAND EMPIRE HEALTH PLAN	300 S PARK AVENUE	POMONA	CA	91769	(909) 623-6333
B+	K S PLAN ADMINISTRATORS LLC	2727 WEST HOLCOMBE BLVD	HOUSTON	TX	77025	(713) 442-0757
A	KAISER FOUNDATION HEALTH PLAN INC	9700 STOCKDALE HIGHWAY	BAKERSFIELD	CA	93311	(661) 664-5016
A-	KAISER PERMANENTE INS CO	300 LAKESIDE DRIVE 13TH FLOOR	OAKLAND	CA	94612	(877) 847-7572
B+	KERN HEALTH SYSTEMS	1055 WEST 7TH STREET	LOS ANGELES	CA	90017	(213) 694-1250
A-	LIFE INS CO OF BOSTON & NEW YORK	4300 CAMP ROAD PO BOX 331	ATHOL SPRINGS	NY	14010	(800) 645-2317
A	LIFEWISE ASR CO	7001 220TH STREET SW	MOUNTLAKE TERRACE	WA	98043	(425) 918-4575
A-	MADISON NATIONAL LIFE INS CO INC	1241 JOHN Q HAMMONS DRIVE	MADISON	WI	53717	(800) 356-9601
A-	MASSACHUSETTS MUTUAL LIFE INS CO	1295 STATE STREET	SPRINGFIELD	MA	1111	(413) 788-8411
B+	MDWISE INC	1200 MADISON AVENUE SUITE 400	INDIANAPOLIS	IN	46225	(317) 822-7300
A	MEDICAL MUTUAL OF OHIO	2060 EAST NINTH STREET	CLEVELAND	OH	44115	(216) 687-7000
B+	MIDLAND NATIONAL LIFE INS CO	4350 WESTOWN PARKWAY	WEST DES MOINES	IA	50266	(515) 273-0874
B+	MINNESOTA LIFE INS CO	400 ROBERT STREET NORTH	ST. PAUL	MN	55101	(651) 665-3500
B+	MUTUAL OF AMERICA LIFE INS CO	320 PARK AVENUE	NEW YORK	NY	10022	(212) 224-1600
A-	NATIONAL BENEFIT LIFE INS CO	ONE COURT SQUARE	LONG ISLAND CITY	NY	11120	(718) 361-3636
B+	NATIONAL CASUALTY CO	ONE W NATIONWIDE BLVD 1-04-701	COLUMBUS	OH	43215	(480) 365-4000
B+	NATIONAL FOUNDATION LIFE INS CO	300 BURNETT STREET SUITE 200	FORT WORTH	TX	76102	(817) 878-3300
B+	NATIONAL INCOME LIFE INS CO	301 PLAINFIELD RD STE 150	SYRACUSE	NY	13212	(315) 451-8180
A-	NEW YORK LIFE INS CO	51 MADISON AVENUE	NEW YORK	NY	10010	(212) 576-7000
A-	NIPPON LIFE INS CO OF AMERICA	7115 VISTA DRIVE	WEST DES MOINES	IA	50266	(212) 682-3000
B+	NORTH AMERICAN INS CO	575 DONOFRIO DRIVE SUITE 100	MADISON	WI	53719	(877) 667-9368
B+	NORTHWESTERN MUTUAL LIFE INS CO	720 EAST WISCONSIN AVENUE	MILWAUKEE	WI	53202	(414) 271-1444

RATING	INSURANCE COMPANY NAME	ADDRESS	CITY	STATE	ZIP	PHONE
A	OPTIMA HEALTH PLAN	4417 CORPORATION LANE	VIRGINIA BEACH	VA	23462	(757) 552-74
B+	OXFORD LIFE INS CO	2721 NORTH CENTRAL AVENUE	PHOENIX	AZ	85004	(602) 263-66
A-	PACIFIC GUARDIAN LIFE INS CO LTD	1440 KAPIOLANI BLVD STE 1600	HONOLULU	HI	96814	(808) 955-22
A-	PARAMOUNT INS CO (OH)	1901 INDIAN WOOD CIRCLE	MAUMEE	OH	43537	(419) 887-25
A-	PHYSICIANS LIFE INS CO	2600 DODGE STREET	OMAHA	NE	68131	(402) 633-10
A+	PHYSICIANS MUTUAL INS CO	2600 DODGE STREET	OMAHA	NE	68131	(402) 633-10
B+	PRINCIPAL LIFE INS CO	711 HIGH STREET	DES MOINES	IA	50392	(515) 247-51
A	PRIORITY HEALTH	1231 EAST BELTLINE NE	GRAND RAPIDS	MI	49525	(616) 942-09
A-	PRIORITY HEALTH CHOICE INC	1231 EAST BELTLINE NE	GRAND RAPIDS	MI	49525	(616) 942-09
A-	PROVIDENCE HEALTH ASR	4400 N E HALSEY BLDG # 2 STE	PORTLAND	OR	97213	(503) 574-75
A-	REGENCE BL CROSS BL SHIELD OREGON	100 SW MARKET STREET	PORTLAND	OR	97201	(503) 225-52
B+	REGENCE BLUE CROSS BLUE SHIELD OF UT	2890 EAST COTTONWOOD PARKWAY	SALT LAKE CITY	UT	84121	(801) 333-20
B+	REGENCE BLUESHIELD OF IDAHO INC	1602 21ST AVENUE	LEWISTON	ID	83501	(208) 746-26
B+	SAN JOAQUIN CNTY HEALTH	7751 S MANTHEY RD	FRENCH CAMP	CA	95231	(888) 936-75
B+	SECURITY HEALTH PLAN OF WI INC	1515 NORTH SAINT JOSEPH AVENUE	MARSHFIELD	WI	54449	(715) 221-95
A	SENTRY LIFE INS CO	1800 NORTH POINT DRIVE	STEVENS POINT	WI	54481	(715) 346-60
B+	SHARP HEALTH PLAN	2801 ATLANTIC AVENUE	LONG BEACH	CA	90806	(714) 377-32
A	SHELTERPOINT LIFE INS CO	1225 FRANKLIN AVE STE 475	GARDEN CITY	NY	11530	(516) 829-81
A	SOUTHERN FARM BUREAU LIFE INS CO	1401 LIVINGSTON LANE	JACKSON	MS	39213	(601) 981-74
B+	STANDARD INS CO	1100 SOUTHWEST SIXTH AVENUE	PORTLAND	OR	97204	(971) 321-70
A-	STANDARD LIFE & ACCIDENT INS CO	ONE MOODY PLAZA	GALVESTON	TX	77550	(409) 763-46
A-	STANDARD LIFE INS CO OF NY	360 HAMILTON AVENUE SUITE 210	WHITE PLAINS	NY	10601	(914) 989-44
B+	STANDARD SECURITY LIFE INS CO OF NY	485 MADISON AVENUE 14TH FLOOR	NEW YORK	NY	10022	(212) 355-41
A-	SWBC LIFE INS CO	9311 SAN PEDRO STE 600	SAN ANTONIO	TX	78216	(210) 321-73
A+	TEACHERS INS & ANNUITY ASN OF AM	730 THIRD AVENUE	NEW YORK	NY	10017	(212) 490-90
B+	TOTAL HEALTH CARE USA INC	3011 W GRAND BLVD SUITE 160	DETROIT	MI	48202	(313) 871-20
A-	TRANS OCEANIC LIFE INS CO	#121 ONEILL	SAN JUAN	PR	00918	(787) 620-26
B+	TRIPLE-S SALUD INC	FD ROOSEVELT AVE 1441	SAN JUAN	PR	920	(787) 749-49
B+	TRUSTMARK INS CO	400 FIELD DRIVE	LAKE FOREST	IL	60045	(847) 615-15
B+	TRUSTMARK LIFE INS CO	400 FIELD DRIVE	LAKE FOREST	IL	60045	(847) 615-15
B+	UNICARE HEALTH PLAN OF WEST VIRGINIA	200 ASSOCIATION DRIVE SUITE 2	CHARLESTON	WV	25311	(877) 864-22
A	UNITED FARM FAMILY LIFE INS CO	225 SOUTH EAST STREET	INDIANAPOLIS	IN	46202	(317) 692-72
B+	UNITED HEALTHCARE INS CO OF IL	200 EAST RANDOLPH STREET SUIT	CHICAGO	IL	60601	(312) 424-44
B+	UNITED HEALTHCARE OF NY INC	77 WATER STREET 14TH / 15TH F	NEW YORK	NY	10005	(203) 447-44
B+	UNITED HEALTHCARE OF WISCONSIN INC	WI030-1000 10701 WEST RESEARC	WAUWATOSA	WI	53226	(414) 443-40
B+	UNITED WORLD LIFE INS CO	MUTUAL OF OMAHA PLAZA	OMAHA	NE	68175	(402) 342-76
B+	UNITEDHEALTHCARE OF OREGON	FIVE CENTERPOINTE DRIVE SUITE	LAKE OSWEGO	OR	97035	(952) 936-13
B+	UNIVERSAL LIFE INS CO	CALLE BOLIVIA #33 6TO PISO	SAN JUAN	PR	917	(787) 706-73
B+	UPMC FOR YOU INC	600 GRANT STREET	PITTSBURGH	PA	15219	(412) 434-12
B+	UPPER PENINSULA HEALTH PLAN INC	853 W WASHINGTON ST	MARQUETTE	MI	49855	(906) 225-75
A	USAA LIFE INS CO	9800 FREDERICKSBURG RD	SAN ANTONIO	TX	78288	(210) 531-87
A-	USABLE LIFE	320 W CAPITOL SUITE 700	LITTLE ROCK	AR	72201	(501) 375-72
B+	UTIC INS CO	450 RIVERCHASE PARKWAY EAST	BIRMINGHAM	AL	35244	(205) 220-21
B+	VISTA HEALTH PLAN INC	1901 MARKET STREET	PHILADELPHIA	PA	19103	(215) 241-24
B+	VIVA HEALTH INC	417 20TH STREET NORTH SUITE 1	BIRMINGHAM	AL	35203	(205) 939-17
A+	VOLUNTEER STATE HEALTH PLAN INC	1 CAMERON HILL CIRCLE	CHATTANOOGA	TN	37402	(423) 535-56
B+	VOYA RETIREMENT INS & ANNUITY CO	ONE ORANGE WAY	WINDSOR	CT	06095	(860) 580-46
B+	WELLMARK OF SOUTH DAKOTA INC	1601 WEST MADISON STREET	SIOUX FALLS	SD	57104	(605) 373-72

Section IV

Weiss Recommended Companies by State

A summary analysis of those

U.S. Health Insurers

receiving a Weiss Safety Rating of A+, A, A-, or B+.

Companies are ranked by Safety Rating in each state where they are licensed to do business.

Section IV Contents

This section provides a list of the recommended carriers licensed to do business in each state. It contains all insurers receiving a Safety Rating of A+, A, A-, or B+. If an insurer is not on this list, it should not automatically be assumed that the firm is weak. Indeed, there are many firms that have not achieved a B+ or better rating but are in relatively good condition with adequate resources to cover their risk during an average recession. Not being included in this list should not be construed as a recommendation to cancel policies.

Companies are ranked within each state by their Safety Rating, and are listed alphabetically within each rating category. Companies with the same rating should be viewed as having the same relative strength regardless of their ranking in this table.

1. **Insurance Company Name** — The legally-registered name, which can sometimes differ from the name that the company uses for advertising. An insurer's name can be very similar to the name of other companies which may not be on our Recommended List, so make sure you note the exact name before contacting your agent.

2. **Domicile State** — The state which has primary regulatory responsibility for the company. It may differ from the location of the company's corporate headquarters. You do not have to be living in the domicile state to purchase insurance from this firm, provided it is licensed to do business in your state.

3. **Total Assets** — All assets admitted by state insurance regulators in millions of dollars as of the most recent year end. This includes investments and current business assets such as receivables from agents, reinsurers and subscribers.

Weiss Safety Ratings are not deemed to be a recommendation concerning the purchase or sale of the securities of any insurance company that is publicly owned.

Alabama

INSURANCE COMPANY NAME	DOM. STATE	TOTAL ASSETS ($MIL)
Rating: A+		
CHESAPEAKE LIFE INS CO	OK	213.1
COUNTRY LIFE INS CO	IL	9,777.7
PHYSICIANS MUTUAL INS CO	NE	2,391.2
TEACHERS INS & ANNUITY ASN OF AM	NY	307,655.9
Rating: A		
AMALGAMATED LIFE INS CO	NY	148.4
BERKLEY LIFE & HEALTH INS CO	IA	336.2
FEDERATED LIFE INS CO	MN	2,039.8
GARDEN STATE LIFE INS CO	TX	138.9
GUARDIAN LIFE INS CO OF AMERICA	NY	59,690.7
SENTRY LIFE INS CO	WI	7,524.4
SOUTHERN FARM BUREAU LIFE INS CO	MS	14,368.9
USAA LIFE INS CO	TX	25,796.7
Rating: A-		
AMERICAN HEALTH & LIFE INS CO	TX	1,083.3
BLUEBONNET LIFE INS CO	MS	65.0
CHRISTIAN FIDELITY LIFE INS CO	TX	59.8
CIGNA LIFE INS CO OF NEW YORK	NY	419.6
FIDELITY SECURITY LIFE INS CO	MO	970.0
GREAT SOUTHERN LIFE INS CO	TX	209.9
MADISON NATIONAL LIFE INS CO INC	WI	337.4
MASSACHUSETTS MUTUAL LIFE INS CO	MA	249,945.6
NATIONAL BENEFIT LIFE INS CO	NY	585.5
NEW YORK LIFE INS CO	NY	181,647.2
NIPPON LIFE INS CO OF AMERICA	IA	229.2
PHYSICIANS LIFE INS CO	NE	1,685.6
STANDARD LIFE & ACCIDENT INS CO	TX	511.2
USABLE LIFE	AR	497.8
Rating: B+		
AMERICAN FIDELITY ASR CO	OK	6,256.2
AMERICAN UNITED LIFE INS CO	IN	29,538.7
ANTHEM LIFE INS CO	IN	759.7
ASSURITY LIFE INS CO	NE	2,750.1
AXA EQUITABLE LIFE INS CO	NY	201,023.4
BLUE CROSS BLUE SHIELD OF ALABAMA	AL	4,116.3
BOSTON MUTUAL LIFE INS CO	MA	1,484.3
COMPANION LIFE INS CO	SC	420.6
DEARBORN NATIONAL LIFE INS CO	IL	1,669.0
DELAWARE AMERICAN LIFE INS CO	DE	119.0
FREEDOM LIFE INS CO OF AMERICA	TX	247.5
GERBER LIFE INS CO	NY	4,180.6
HUMANA BENEFIT PLAN OF ILLINOIS	IL	693.4
ILLINOIS MUTUAL LIFE INS CO	IL	1,507.2
MIDLAND NATIONAL LIFE INS CO	IA	58,679.0
MINNESOTA LIFE INS CO	MN	50,012.0
MUTUAL OF AMERICA LIFE INS CO	NY	21,688.9
NATIONAL CASUALTY CO	OH	493.4
NATIONAL FOUNDATION LIFE INS CO	TX	59.6
NORTH AMERICAN INS CO	WI	18.5
NORTHWESTERN MUTUAL LIFE INS CO	WI	278,047.4
OXFORD LIFE INS CO	AZ	2,251.8
PRINCIPAL LIFE INS CO	IA	196,332.3
STANDARD INS CO	OR	25,172.5
STANDARD SECURITY LIFE INS CO OF NY	NY	139.6
TRUSTMARK INS CO	IL	1,625.3
TRUSTMARK LIFE INS CO	IL	330.1
UNITED WORLD LIFE INS CO	NE	132.1
UTIC INS CO	AL	106.7
VIVA HEALTH INC	AL	214.0
VOYA RETIREMENT INS & ANNUITY CO	CT	106,305.7

Alaska

INSURANCE COMPANY NAME	DOM. STATE	TOTAL ASSETS ($MIL)
Rating: A+		
CHESAPEAKE LIFE INS CO	OK	213.1
COUNTRY LIFE INS CO	IL	9,777.7
PHYSICIANS MUTUAL INS CO	NE	2,391.2
TEACHERS INS & ANNUITY ASN OF AM	NY	307,655.9
Rating: A		
AMALGAMATED LIFE INS CO	NY	148.4
BERKLEY LIFE & HEALTH INS CO	IA	336.2
GARDEN STATE LIFE INS CO	TX	138.9
GUARDIAN LIFE INS CO OF AMERICA	NY	59,690.7
LIFEWISE ASR CO	WA	215.9
SENTRY LIFE INS CO	WI	7,524.4
USAA LIFE INS CO	TX	25,796.7
Rating: A-		
AMERICAN HEALTH & LIFE INS CO	TX	1,083.3
FIDELITY SECURITY LIFE INS CO	MO	970.0
GREAT SOUTHERN LIFE INS CO	TX	209.9
MADISON NATIONAL LIFE INS CO INC	WI	337.4
MASSACHUSETTS MUTUAL LIFE INS CO	MA	249,945.6
NATIONAL BENEFIT LIFE INS CO	NY	585.5
NEW YORK LIFE INS CO	NY	181,647.2
NIPPON LIFE INS CO OF AMERICA	IA	229.2
PACIFIC GUARDIAN LIFE INS CO LTD	HI	568.1
PHYSICIANS LIFE INS CO	NE	1,685.6
STANDARD LIFE & ACCIDENT INS CO	TX	511.2
USABLE LIFE	AR	497.8
Rating: B+		
AMERICAN FIDELITY ASR CO	OK	6,256.2
AMERICAN UNITED LIFE INS CO	IN	29,538.7
ANTHEM LIFE INS CO	IN	759.7
ASSURITY LIFE INS CO	NE	2,750.1
AXA EQUITABLE LIFE INS CO	NY	201,023.4
BOSTON MUTUAL LIFE INS CO	MA	1,484.3
COMPANION LIFE INS CO	SC	420.6
DEARBORN NATIONAL LIFE INS CO	IL	1,669.0
DELAWARE AMERICAN LIFE INS CO	DE	119.0
GERBER LIFE INS CO	NY	4,180.6
HUMANA BENEFIT PLAN OF ILLINOIS	IL	693.4
MIDLAND NATIONAL LIFE INS CO	IA	58,679.0
MINNESOTA LIFE INS CO	MN	50,012.0
MUTUAL OF AMERICA LIFE INS CO	NY	21,688.9
NATIONAL CASUALTY CO	OH	493.4
NATIONAL FOUNDATION LIFE INS CO	TX	59.6
NORTHWESTERN MUTUAL LIFE INS CO	WI	278,047.4
OXFORD LIFE INS CO	AZ	2,251.8
PRINCIPAL LIFE INS CO	IA	196,332.3
STANDARD INS CO	OR	25,172.5
STANDARD SECURITY LIFE INS CO OF NY	NY	139.6
TRUSTMARK INS CO	IL	1,625.3
TRUSTMARK LIFE INS CO	IL	330.1
UNITED WORLD LIFE INS CO	NE	132.1
VOYA RETIREMENT INS & ANNUITY CO	CT	106,305.7

Arizona

INSURANCE COMPANY NAME	DOM. STATE	TOTAL ASSETS ($MIL)
Rating: A+		
BLUE CROSS BLUE SHIELD OF ARIZONA	AZ	2,403.3
CHESAPEAKE LIFE INS CO	OK	213.1
COUNTRY LIFE INS CO	IL	9,777.7
PHYSICIANS MUTUAL INS CO	NE	2,391.2
TEACHERS INS & ANNUITY ASN OF AM	NY	307,655.9
Rating: A		
AMALGAMATED LIFE INS CO	NY	148.4
BERKLEY LIFE & HEALTH INS CO	IA	336.2
FEDERATED LIFE INS CO	MN	2,039.8
GARDEN STATE LIFE INS CO	TX	138.9
GUARDIAN LIFE INS CO OF AMERICA	NY	59,690.7
SENTRY LIFE INS CO	WI	7,524.4
UNITED FARM FAMILY LIFE INS CO	IN	2,373.1
USAA LIFE INS CO	TX	25,796.7
Rating: A-		
AMERICAN HEALTH & LIFE INS CO	TX	1,083.3
CHRISTIAN FIDELITY LIFE INS CO	TX	59.8
FIDELITY SECURITY LIFE INS CO	MO	970.0
GREAT SOUTHERN LIFE INS CO	TX	209.9
MADISON NATIONAL LIFE INS CO INC	WI	337.4
MASSACHUSETTS MUTUAL LIFE INS CO	MA	249,945.6
NATIONAL BENEFIT LIFE INS CO	NY	585.5
NEW YORK LIFE INS CO	NY	181,647.2
NIPPON LIFE INS CO OF AMERICA	IA	229.2
PACIFIC GUARDIAN LIFE INS CO LTD	HI	568.1
PHYSICIANS LIFE INS CO	NE	1,685.6
STANDARD LIFE & ACCIDENT INS CO	TX	511.2
USABLE LIFE	AR	497.8
Rating: B+		
AMERICAN FAMILY MUTL INS CO SI	WI	18,119.9
AMERICAN FIDELITY ASR CO	OK	6,256.2
AMERICAN UNITED LIFE INS CO	IN	29,538.7
ANTHEM LIFE INS CO	IN	759.7
ASSURITY LIFE INS CO	NE	2,750.1
AXA EQUITABLE LIFE INS CO	NY	201,023.4
BOSTON MUTUAL LIFE INS CO	MA	1,484.3
COMPANION LIFE INS CO	SC	420.6
DEARBORN NATIONAL LIFE INS CO	IL	1,669.0
DELAWARE AMERICAN LIFE INS CO	DE	119.0
FARM BUREAU LIFE INS CO	IA	9,174.1
FREEDOM LIFE INS CO OF AMERICA	TX	247.5
GERBER LIFE INS CO	NY	4,180.6
HUMANA BENEFIT PLAN OF ILLINOIS	IL	693.4
ILLINOIS MUTUAL LIFE INS CO	IL	1,507.2
MIDLAND NATIONAL LIFE INS CO	IA	58,679.0
MINNESOTA LIFE INS CO	MN	50,012.0
MUTUAL OF AMERICA LIFE INS CO	NY	21,688.9
NATIONAL CASUALTY CO	OH	493.4
NATIONAL FOUNDATION LIFE INS CO	TX	59.6
NORTHWESTERN MUTUAL LIFE INS CO	WI	278,047.4
OXFORD LIFE INS CO	AZ	2,251.8
PRINCIPAL LIFE INS CO	IA	196,332.3
STANDARD INS CO	OR	25,172.5
STANDARD SECURITY LIFE INS CO OF NY	NY	139.6
TRUSTMARK INS CO	IL	1,625.3
TRUSTMARK LIFE INS CO	IL	330.1
UNITED HEALTHCARE OF WISCONSIN INC	WI	2,025.5
UNITED WORLD LIFE INS CO	NE	132.1
VOYA RETIREMENT INS & ANNUITY CO	CT	106,305.7

Arkansas

INSURANCE COMPANY NAME	DOM. STATE	TOTAL ASSETS ($MIL)
Rating: A+		
CHESAPEAKE LIFE INS CO	OK	213.1
COUNTRY LIFE INS CO	IL	9,777.7
HMO PARTNERS INC	AR	127.5
PHYSICIANS MUTUAL INS CO	NE	2,391.2
TEACHERS INS & ANNUITY ASN OF AM	NY	307,655.9
Rating: A		
AMALGAMATED LIFE INS CO	NY	148.4
BERKLEY LIFE & HEALTH INS CO	IA	336.2
FEDERATED LIFE INS CO	MN	2,039.8
GARDEN STATE LIFE INS CO	TX	138.9
GUARDIAN LIFE INS CO OF AMERICA	NY	59,690.7
SENTRY LIFE INS CO	WI	7,524.4
SOUTHERN FARM BUREAU LIFE INS CO	MS	14,368.9
USAA LIFE INS CO	TX	25,796.7
Rating: A-		
AMERICAN HEALTH & LIFE INS CO	TX	1,083.3
BLUEBONNET LIFE INS CO	MS	65.0
CHRISTIAN FIDELITY LIFE INS CO	TX	59.8
FIDELITY SECURITY LIFE INS CO	MO	970.0
GREAT SOUTHERN LIFE INS CO	TX	209.9
MADISON NATIONAL LIFE INS CO INC	WI	337.4
MASSACHUSETTS MUTUAL LIFE INS CO	MA	249,945.6
NATIONAL BENEFIT LIFE INS CO	NY	585.5
NEW YORK LIFE INS CO	NY	181,647.2
NIPPON LIFE INS CO OF AMERICA	IA	229.2
PHYSICIANS LIFE INS CO	NE	1,685.6
STANDARD LIFE & ACCIDENT INS CO	TX	511.2
USABLE LIFE	AR	497.8
Rating: B+		
AMERICAN FIDELITY ASR CO	OK	6,256.2
AMERICAN UNITED LIFE INS CO	IN	29,538.7
ANTHEM LIFE INS CO	IN	759.7
ASSURITY LIFE INS CO	NE	2,750.1
AXA EQUITABLE LIFE INS CO	NY	201,023.4
BOSTON MUTUAL LIFE INS CO	MA	1,484.3
COMPANION LIFE INS CO	SC	420.6
DEARBORN NATIONAL LIFE INS CO	IL	1,669.0
DELAWARE AMERICAN LIFE INS CO	DE	119.0
FREEDOM LIFE INS CO OF AMERICA	TX	247.5
GERBER LIFE INS CO	NY	4,180.6
HUMANA BENEFIT PLAN OF ILLINOIS	IL	693.4
ILLINOIS MUTUAL LIFE INS CO	IL	1,507.2
MIDLAND NATIONAL LIFE INS CO	IA	58,679.0
MINNESOTA LIFE INS CO	MN	50,012.0
MUTUAL OF AMERICA LIFE INS CO	NY	21,688.9
NATIONAL CASUALTY CO	OH	493.4
NATIONAL FOUNDATION LIFE INS CO	TX	59.6
NORTHWESTERN MUTUAL LIFE INS CO	WI	278,047.4
OXFORD LIFE INS CO	AZ	2,251.8
PRINCIPAL LIFE INS CO	IA	196,332.3
STANDARD INS CO	OR	25,172.5
STANDARD SECURITY LIFE INS CO OF NY	NY	139.6
TRUSTMARK INS CO	IL	1,625.3
TRUSTMARK LIFE INS CO	IL	330.1
UNITED WORLD LIFE INS CO	NE	132.1
VOYA RETIREMENT INS & ANNUITY CO	CT	106,305.7

California

INSURANCE COMPANY NAME	DOM. STATE	TOTAL ASSETS ($MIL)
Rating: A+		
BLUE CROSS OF CALIFORNIA	CA	7,997.8
CALIFORNIA PHYSICIANS SERVICE	CA	9,021.3
CARE 1ST HEALTH PLAN INC	CA	1,214.3
CHESAPEAKE LIFE INS CO	OK	213.1
PHYSICIANS MUTUAL INS CO	NE	2,391.2
TEACHERS INS & ANNUITY ASN OF AM	NY	307,655.9
Rating: A		
AMALGAMATED LIFE INS CO	NY	148.4
BERKLEY LIFE & HEALTH INS CO	IA	336.2
CAPITAL DISTRICT PHYSICIANS HEALTH P	NY	621.6
FEDERATED LIFE INS CO	MN	2,039.8
GARDEN STATE LIFE INS CO	TX	138.9
GUARDIAN LIFE INS CO OF AMERICA	NY	59,690.7
INLAND EMPIRE HEALTH PLAN	CA	1,855.4
KAISER FOUNDATION HEALTH PLAN INC	CA	80,034.0
LIFEWISE ASR CO	WA	215.9
SENTRY LIFE INS CO	WI	7,524.4
SHELTERPOINT LIFE INS CO	NY	183.5
UNITED FARM FAMILY LIFE INS CO	IN	2,373.1
USAA LIFE INS CO	TX	25,796.7
Rating: A-		
AMERICAN HEALTH & LIFE INS CO	TX	1,083.3
FIDELITY SECURITY LIFE INS CO	MO	970.0
GREAT SOUTHERN LIFE INS CO	TX	209.9
KAISER PERMANENTE INS CO	CA	197.7
MADISON NATIONAL LIFE INS CO INC	WI	337.4
MASSACHUSETTS MUTUAL LIFE INS CO	MA	249,945.6
NATIONAL BENEFIT LIFE INS CO	NY	585.5
NEW YORK LIFE INS CO	NY	181,647.2
NIPPON LIFE INS CO OF AMERICA	IA	229.2
PACIFIC GUARDIAN LIFE INS CO LTD	HI	568.1
PHYSICIANS LIFE INS CO	NE	1,685.6
STANDARD LIFE & ACCIDENT INS CO	TX	511.2
USABLE LIFE	AR	497.8
Rating: B+		
AMERICAN FIDELITY ASR CO	OK	6,256.2
AMERICAN UNITED LIFE INS CO	IN	29,538.7
ANTHEM LIFE INS CO	IN	759.7
ASSURITY LIFE INS CO	NE	2,750.1
AXA EQUITABLE LIFE INS CO	NY	201,023.4
BOSTON MUTUAL LIFE INS CO	MA	1,484.3
DEARBORN NATIONAL LIFE INS CO	IL	1,669.0
DELAWARE AMERICAN LIFE INS CO	DE	119.0
GERBER LIFE INS CO	NY	4,180.6
HUMANA BENEFIT PLAN OF ILLINOIS	IL	693.4
HUMANA INS CO OF KENTUCKY	KY	222.0
ILLINOIS MUTUAL LIFE INS CO	IL	1,507.2
KERN HEALTH SYSTEMS	CA	467.7
MIDLAND NATIONAL LIFE INS CO	IA	58,679.0
MINNESOTA LIFE INS CO	MN	50,012.0
MUTUAL OF AMERICA LIFE INS CO	NY	21,688.9
NATIONAL CASUALTY CO	OH	493.4
NATIONAL FOUNDATION LIFE INS CO	TX	59.6
NORTHWESTERN MUTUAL LIFE INS CO	WI	278,047.4
OXFORD LIFE INS CO	AZ	2,251.8
PRINCIPAL LIFE INS CO	IA	196,332.3
SAN JOAQUIN CNTY HEALTH	CA	660.0
SHARP HEALTH PLAN	CA	177.2
STANDARD INS CO	OR	25,172.5
STANDARD SECURITY LIFE INS CO OF NY	NY	139.6
TRUSTMARK INS CO	IL	1,625.3
TRUSTMARK LIFE INS CO	IL	330.1
UNITED WORLD LIFE INS CO	NE	132.1
VOYA RETIREMENT INS & ANNUITY CO	CT	106,305.7

Colorado

INSURANCE COMPANY NAME	DOM. STATE	TOTAL ASSETS ($MIL)
Rating: A+		
CHESAPEAKE LIFE INS CO	OK	213.1
COUNTRY LIFE INS CO	IL	9,777.7
PHYSICIANS MUTUAL INS CO	NE	2,391.2
TEACHERS INS & ANNUITY ASN OF AM	NY	307,655.9
Rating: A		
AMALGAMATED LIFE INS CO	NY	148.4
BERKLEY LIFE & HEALTH INS CO	IA	336.2
FEDERATED LIFE INS CO	MN	2,039.8
GARDEN STATE LIFE INS CO	TX	138.9
GUARDIAN LIFE INS CO OF AMERICA	NY	59,690.7
SENTRY LIFE INS CO	WI	7,524.4
SHELTERPOINT LIFE INS CO	NY	183.5
SOUTHERN FARM BUREAU LIFE INS CO	MS	14,368.9
USAA LIFE INS CO	TX	25,796.7
Rating: A-		
AMERICAN HEALTH & LIFE INS CO	TX	1,083.3
CHRISTIAN FIDELITY LIFE INS CO	TX	59.8
FIDELITY SECURITY LIFE INS CO	MO	970.0
GREAT SOUTHERN LIFE INS CO	TX	209.9
KAISER PERMANENTE INS CO	CA	197.7
MADISON NATIONAL LIFE INS CO INC	WI	337.4
MASSACHUSETTS MUTUAL LIFE INS CO	MA	249,945.6
NATIONAL BENEFIT LIFE INS CO	NY	585.5
NEW YORK LIFE INS CO	NY	181,647.2
NIPPON LIFE INS CO OF AMERICA	IA	229.2
PACIFIC GUARDIAN LIFE INS CO LTD	HI	568.1
PHYSICIANS LIFE INS CO	NE	1,685.6
STANDARD LIFE & ACCIDENT INS CO	TX	511.2
USABLE LIFE	AR	497.8
Rating: B+		
AMERICAN FAMILY MUTL INS CO SI	WI	18,119.9
AMERICAN FIDELITY ASR CO	OK	6,256.2
AMERICAN UNITED LIFE INS CO	IN	29,538.7
ANTHEM LIFE INS CO	IN	759.7
ASSURITY LIFE INS CO	NE	2,750.1
AXA EQUITABLE LIFE INS CO	NY	201,023.4
BOSTON MUTUAL LIFE INS CO	MA	1,484.3
COMPANION LIFE INS CO	SC	420.6
DEARBORN NATIONAL LIFE INS CO	IL	1,669.0
DELAWARE AMERICAN LIFE INS CO	DE	119.0
FARM BUREAU LIFE INS CO	IA	9,174.1
FREEDOM LIFE INS CO OF AMERICA	TX	247.5
GERBER LIFE INS CO	NY	4,180.6
HUMANA BENEFIT PLAN OF ILLINOIS	IL	693.4
HUMANA INS CO OF KENTUCKY	KY	222.0
ILLINOIS MUTUAL LIFE INS CO	IL	1,507.2
MIDLAND NATIONAL LIFE INS CO	IA	58,679.0
MINNESOTA LIFE INS CO	MN	50,012.0
MUTUAL OF AMERICA LIFE INS CO	NY	21,688.9
NATIONAL CASUALTY CO	OH	493.4
NATIONAL FOUNDATION LIFE INS CO	TX	59.6
NORTH AMERICAN INS CO	WI	18.5
NORTHWESTERN MUTUAL LIFE INS CO	WI	278,047.4
OXFORD LIFE INS CO	AZ	2,251.8
PRINCIPAL LIFE INS CO	IA	196,332.3
STANDARD INS CO	OR	25,172.5
STANDARD SECURITY LIFE INS CO OF NY	NY	139.6
TRUSTMARK INS CO	IL	1,625.3
TRUSTMARK LIFE INS CO	IL	330.1
UNITED WORLD LIFE INS CO	NE	132.1
VOYA RETIREMENT INS & ANNUITY CO	CT	106,305.7

Connecticut

INSURANCE COMPANY NAME	DOM. STATE	TOTAL ASSETS ($MIL)
Rating: A+		
CHESAPEAKE LIFE INS CO	OK	213.1
COUNTRY LIFE INS CO	IL	9,777.7
PHYSICIANS MUTUAL INS CO	NE	2,391.2
TEACHERS INS & ANNUITY ASN OF AM	NY	307,655.9
Rating: A		
AMALGAMATED LIFE INS CO	NY	148.4
BERKLEY LIFE & HEALTH INS CO	IA	336.2
FEDERATED LIFE INS CO	MN	2,039.8
GARDEN STATE LIFE INS CO	TX	138.9
GUARDIAN LIFE INS CO OF AMERICA	NY	59,690.7
SENTRY LIFE INS CO	WI	7,524.4
SHELTERPOINT LIFE INS CO	NY	183.5
USAA LIFE INS CO	TX	25,796.7
Rating: A-		
AMERICAN FAMILY LIFE ASR CO OF NY	NY	978.2
AMERICAN HEALTH & LIFE INS CO	TX	1,083.3
FIDELITY SECURITY LIFE INS CO	MO	970.0
GREAT SOUTHERN LIFE INS CO	TX	209.9
MADISON NATIONAL LIFE INS CO INC	WI	337.4
MASSACHUSETTS MUTUAL LIFE INS CO	MA	249,945.6
NATIONAL BENEFIT LIFE INS CO	NY	585.5
NEW YORK LIFE INS CO	NY	181,647.2
NIPPON LIFE INS CO OF AMERICA	IA	229.2
PHYSICIANS LIFE INS CO	NE	1,685.6
STANDARD LIFE & ACCIDENT INS CO	TX	511.2
USABLE LIFE	AR	497.8
Rating: B+		
ALLIANZ LIFE INS CO OF NY	NY	3,530.0
AMERICAN FIDELITY ASR CO	OK	6,256.2
AMERICAN UNITED LIFE INS CO	IN	29,538.7
ANTHEM LIFE INS CO	IN	759.7
ASSURITY LIFE INS CO	NE	2,750.1
AXA EQUITABLE LIFE INS CO	NY	201,023.4
BOSTON MUTUAL LIFE INS CO	MA	1,484.3
DEARBORN NATIONAL LIFE INS CO	IL	1,669.0
DELAWARE AMERICAN LIFE INS CO	DE	119.0
GERBER LIFE INS CO	NY	4,180.6
HUMANA BENEFIT PLAN OF ILLINOIS	IL	693.4
ILLINOIS MUTUAL LIFE INS CO	IL	1,507.2
MIDLAND NATIONAL LIFE INS CO	IA	58,679.0
MINNESOTA LIFE INS CO	MN	50,012.0
MUTUAL OF AMERICA LIFE INS CO	NY	21,688.9
NATIONAL CASUALTY CO	OH	493.4
NORTHWESTERN MUTUAL LIFE INS CO	WI	278,047.4
OXFORD LIFE INS CO	AZ	2,251.8
PRINCIPAL LIFE INS CO	IA	196,332.3
STANDARD INS CO	OR	25,172.5
STANDARD SECURITY LIFE INS CO OF NY	NY	139.6
TRUSTMARK INS CO	IL	1,625.3
TRUSTMARK LIFE INS CO	IL	330.1
VOYA RETIREMENT INS & ANNUITY CO	CT	106,305.7

Delaware

INSURANCE COMPANY NAME	DOM. STATE	TOTAL ASSETS ($MIL)
Rating: A+		
CHESAPEAKE LIFE INS CO	OK	213.1
COUNTRY LIFE INS CO	IL	9,777.7
PHYSICIANS MUTUAL INS CO	NE	2,391.2
TEACHERS INS & ANNUITY ASN OF AM	NY	307,655.9
Rating: A		
AMALGAMATED LIFE INS CO	NY	148.4
BERKLEY LIFE & HEALTH INS CO	IA	336.2
FEDERATED LIFE INS CO	MN	2,039.8
GARDEN STATE LIFE INS CO	TX	138.9
GUARDIAN LIFE INS CO OF AMERICA	NY	59,690.7
SENTRY LIFE INS CO	WI	7,524.4
SHELTERPOINT LIFE INS CO	NY	183.5
USAA LIFE INS CO	TX	25,796.7
Rating: A-		
AMERICAN HEALTH & LIFE INS CO	TX	1,083.3
FIDELITY SECURITY LIFE INS CO	MO	970.0
FIRST RELIANCE STANDARD LIFE INS CO	NY	218.0
GREAT SOUTHERN LIFE INS CO	TX	209.9
MADISON NATIONAL LIFE INS CO INC	WI	337.4
MASSACHUSETTS MUTUAL LIFE INS CO	MA	249,945.6
NATIONAL BENEFIT LIFE INS CO	NY	585.5
NEW YORK LIFE INS CO	NY	181,647.2
NIPPON LIFE INS CO OF AMERICA	IA	229.2
PHYSICIANS LIFE INS CO	NE	1,685.6
STANDARD LIFE & ACCIDENT INS CO	TX	511.2
USABLE LIFE	AR	497.8
Rating: B+		
AMERICAN FIDELITY ASR CO	OK	6,256.2
AMERICAN UNITED LIFE INS CO	IN	29,538.7
ANTHEM LIFE INS CO	IN	759.7
ASSURITY LIFE INS CO	NE	2,750.1
AXA EQUITABLE LIFE INS CO	NY	201,023.4
BOSTON MUTUAL LIFE INS CO	MA	1,484.3
COMPANION LIFE INS CO	SC	420.6
DEARBORN NATIONAL LIFE INS CO	IL	1,669.0
DELAWARE AMERICAN LIFE INS CO	DE	119.0
FREEDOM LIFE INS CO OF AMERICA	TX	247.5
GERBER LIFE INS CO	NY	4,180.6
HUMANA BENEFIT PLAN OF ILLINOIS	IL	693.4
ILLINOIS MUTUAL LIFE INS CO	IL	1,507.2
MIDLAND NATIONAL LIFE INS CO	IA	58,679.0
MINNESOTA LIFE INS CO	MN	50,012.0
MUTUAL OF AMERICA LIFE INS CO	NY	21,688.9
NATIONAL CASUALTY CO	OH	493.4
NATIONAL FOUNDATION LIFE INS CO	TX	59.6
NORTHWESTERN MUTUAL LIFE INS CO	WI	278,047.4
OXFORD LIFE INS CO	AZ	2,251.8
PRINCIPAL LIFE INS CO	IA	196,332.3
STANDARD INS CO	OR	25,172.5
STANDARD SECURITY LIFE INS CO OF NY	NY	139.6
TRUSTMARK INS CO	IL	1,625.3
TRUSTMARK LIFE INS CO	IL	330.1
UNITED WORLD LIFE INS CO	NE	132.1
VOYA RETIREMENT INS & ANNUITY CO	CT	106,305.7

District of Columbia

INSURANCE COMPANY NAME	DOM. STATE	TOTAL ASSETS ($MIL)
Rating: A+		
CHESAPEAKE LIFE INS CO	OK	213.1
PHYSICIANS MUTUAL INS CO	NE	2,391.2
TEACHERS INS & ANNUITY ASN OF AM	NY	307,655.9
Rating: A		
AMALGAMATED LIFE INS CO	NY	148.4
BERKLEY LIFE & HEALTH INS CO	IA	336.2
GARDEN STATE LIFE INS CO	TX	138.9
GUARDIAN LIFE INS CO OF AMERICA	NY	59,690.7
SENTRY LIFE INS CO	WI	7,524.4
SHELTERPOINT LIFE INS CO	NY	183.5
USAA LIFE INS CO	TX	25,796.7
Rating: A-		
AMERICAN HEALTH & LIFE INS CO	TX	1,083.3
CIGNA LIFE INS CO OF NEW YORK	NY	419.6
FIDELITY SECURITY LIFE INS CO	MO	970.0
FIRST RELIANCE STANDARD LIFE INS CO	NY	218.0
GREAT SOUTHERN LIFE INS CO	TX	209.9
KAISER PERMANENTE INS CO	CA	197.7
MADISON NATIONAL LIFE INS CO INC	WI	337.4
MASSACHUSETTS MUTUAL LIFE INS CO	MA	249,945.6
NATIONAL BENEFIT LIFE INS CO	NY	585.5
NEW YORK LIFE INS CO	NY	181,647.2
NIPPON LIFE INS CO OF AMERICA	IA	229.2
PHYSICIANS LIFE INS CO	NE	1,685.6
STANDARD LIFE & ACCIDENT INS CO	TX	511.2
USABLE LIFE	AR	497.8
Rating: B+		
ALLIANZ LIFE INS CO OF NY	NY	3,530.0
AMERICAN FIDELITY ASR CO	OK	6,256.2
AMERICAN UNITED LIFE INS CO	IN	29,538.7
ANTHEM LIFE INS CO	IN	759.7
ASSURITY LIFE INS CO	NE	2,750.1
AXA EQUITABLE LIFE INS CO	NY	201,023.4
BOSTON MUTUAL LIFE INS CO	MA	1,484.3
COMPANION LIFE INS CO	SC	420.6
DEARBORN NATIONAL LIFE INS CO	IL	1,669.0
DELAWARE AMERICAN LIFE INS CO	DE	119.0
GERBER LIFE INS CO	NY	4,180.6
HUMANA BENEFIT PLAN OF ILLINOIS	IL	693.4
MIDLAND NATIONAL LIFE INS CO	IA	58,679.0
MINNESOTA LIFE INS CO	MN	50,012.0
MUTUAL OF AMERICA LIFE INS CO	NY	21,688.9
NATIONAL CASUALTY CO	OH	493.4
NATIONAL FOUNDATION LIFE INS CO	TX	59.6
NORTH AMERICAN INS CO	WI	18.5
NORTHWESTERN MUTUAL LIFE INS CO	WI	278,047.4
OXFORD LIFE INS CO	AZ	2,251.8
PRINCIPAL LIFE INS CO	IA	196,332.3
STANDARD INS CO	OR	25,172.5
STANDARD SECURITY LIFE INS CO OF NY	NY	139.6
TRUSTMARK INS CO	IL	1,625.3
TRUSTMARK LIFE INS CO	IL	330.1
UNITED WORLD LIFE INS CO	NE	132.1
VOYA RETIREMENT INS & ANNUITY CO	CT	106,305.7

Florida

INSURANCE COMPANY NAME	DOM. STATE	TOTAL ASSETS ($MIL)
Rating: A+		
CHESAPEAKE LIFE INS CO	OK	213.1
COUNTRY LIFE INS CO	IL	9,777.7
PHYSICIANS MUTUAL INS CO	NE	2,391.2
TEACHERS INS & ANNUITY ASN OF AM	NY	307,655.9
Rating: A		
AMALGAMATED LIFE INS CO	NY	148.4
BERKLEY LIFE & HEALTH INS CO	IA	336.2
FEDERATED LIFE INS CO	MN	2,039.8
GARDEN STATE LIFE INS CO	TX	138.9
GUARDIAN LIFE INS CO OF AMERICA	NY	59,690.7
SENTRY LIFE INS CO	WI	7,524.4
SHELTERPOINT LIFE INS CO	NY	183.5
SOUTHERN FARM BUREAU LIFE INS CO	MS	14,368.9
USAA LIFE INS CO	TX	25,796.7
Rating: A-		
AMERICAN HEALTH & LIFE INS CO	TX	1,083.3
CHRISTIAN FIDELITY LIFE INS CO	TX	59.8
FIDELITY SECURITY LIFE INS CO	MO	970.0
FLORIDA HEALTH CARE PLAN INC	FL	213.3
GREAT SOUTHERN LIFE INS CO	TX	209.9
HEALTH OPTIONS INC	FL	2,415.5
HUMANA MEDICAL PLAN INC	FL	2,319.2
MADISON NATIONAL LIFE INS CO INC	WI	337.4
MASSACHUSETTS MUTUAL LIFE INS CO	MA	249,945.6
NATIONAL BENEFIT LIFE INS CO	NY	585.5
NEW YORK LIFE INS CO	NY	181,647.2
NIPPON LIFE INS CO OF AMERICA	IA	229.2
PHYSICIANS LIFE INS CO	NE	1,685.6
STANDARD LIFE & ACCIDENT INS CO	TX	511.2
TRANS OCEANIC LIFE INS CO	PR	76.6
USABLE LIFE	AR	497.8
Rating: B+		
AMERICAN FAMILY MUTL INS CO SI	WI	18,119.9
AMERICAN FIDELITY ASR CO	OK	6,256.2
AMERICAN UNITED LIFE INS CO	IN	29,538.7
ANTHEM LIFE INS CO	IN	759.7
ASSURITY LIFE INS CO	NE	2,750.1
AXA EQUITABLE LIFE INS CO	NY	201,023.4
BOSTON MUTUAL LIFE INS CO	MA	1,484.3
CAPITAL HEALTH PLAN INC	FL	575.1
COMPANION LIFE INS CO	SC	420.6
DEARBORN NATIONAL LIFE INS CO	IL	1,669.0
DELAWARE AMERICAN LIFE INS CO	DE	119.0
FREEDOM LIFE INS CO OF AMERICA	TX	247.5
GERBER LIFE INS CO	NY	4,180.6
ILLINOIS MUTUAL LIFE INS CO	IL	1,507.2
MIDLAND NATIONAL LIFE INS CO	IA	58,679.0
MINNESOTA LIFE INS CO	MN	50,012.0
MUTUAL OF AMERICA LIFE INS CO	NY	21,688.9
NATIONAL CASUALTY CO	OH	493.4
NORTHWESTERN MUTUAL LIFE INS CO	WI	278,047.4
OXFORD LIFE INS CO	AZ	2,251.8
PRINCIPAL LIFE INS CO	IA	196,332.3
STANDARD INS CO	OR	25,172.5
STANDARD SECURITY LIFE INS CO OF NY	NY	139.6
TRUSTMARK INS CO	IL	1,625.3
TRUSTMARK LIFE INS CO	IL	330.1
UNITED WORLD LIFE INS CO	NE	132.1
VOYA RETIREMENT INS & ANNUITY CO	CT	106,305.7

Georgia

INSURANCE COMPANY NAME	DOM. STATE	TOTAL ASSETS ($MIL)
Rating: A+		
CHESAPEAKE LIFE INS CO	OK	213.1
COUNTRY LIFE INS CO	IL	9,777.7
PHYSICIANS MUTUAL INS CO	NE	2,391.2
TEACHERS INS & ANNUITY ASN OF AM	NY	307,655.9
Rating: A		
AMALGAMATED LIFE INS CO	NY	148.4
BERKLEY LIFE & HEALTH INS CO	IA	336.2
FEDERATED LIFE INS CO	MN	2,039.8
GARDEN STATE LIFE INS CO	TX	138.9
GUARDIAN LIFE INS CO OF AMERICA	NY	59,690.7
MEDICAL MUTUAL OF OHIO	OH	2,490.1
SENTRY LIFE INS CO	WI	7,524.4
SOUTHERN FARM BUREAU LIFE INS CO	MS	14,368.9
USAA LIFE INS CO	TX	25,796.7
Rating: A-		
AMERICAN HEALTH & LIFE INS CO	TX	1,083.3
AMGP GEORGIA MANAGED CARE CO INC	GA	310.5
BLUE CROSS BLUE SHIELD HEALTHCARE GA	GA	2,584.7
CHRISTIAN FIDELITY LIFE INS CO	TX	59.8
FIDELITY SECURITY LIFE INS CO	MO	970.0
GREAT SOUTHERN LIFE INS CO	TX	209.9
KAISER PERMANENTE INS CO	CA	197.7
MADISON NATIONAL LIFE INS CO INC	WI	337.4
MASSACHUSETTS MUTUAL LIFE INS CO	MA	249,945.6
NATIONAL BENEFIT LIFE INS CO	NY	585.5
NEW YORK LIFE INS CO	NY	181,647.2
NIPPON LIFE INS CO OF AMERICA	IA	229.2
PHYSICIANS LIFE INS CO	NE	1,685.6
STANDARD LIFE & ACCIDENT INS CO	TX	511.2
SWBC LIFE INS CO	TX	33.5
USABLE LIFE	AR	497.8
Rating: B+		
AMERICAN FAMILY MUTL INS CO SI	WI	18,119.9
AMERICAN FIDELITY ASR CO	OK	6,256.2
AMERICAN UNITED LIFE INS CO	IN	29,538.7
ANTHEM LIFE INS CO	IN	759.7
ASSURITY LIFE INS CO	NE	2,750.1
AXA EQUITABLE LIFE INS CO	NY	201,023.4
BOSTON MUTUAL LIFE INS CO	MA	1,484.3
COMPANION LIFE INS CO	SC	420.6
DEARBORN NATIONAL LIFE INS CO	IL	1,669.0
DELAWARE AMERICAN LIFE INS CO	DE	119.0
FREEDOM LIFE INS CO OF AMERICA	TX	247.5
GERBER LIFE INS CO	NY	4,180.6
HUMANA BENEFIT PLAN OF ILLINOIS	IL	693.4
ILLINOIS MUTUAL LIFE INS CO	IL	1,507.2
MIDLAND NATIONAL LIFE INS CO	IA	58,679.0
MINNESOTA LIFE INS CO	MN	50,012.0
MUTUAL OF AMERICA LIFE INS CO	NY	21,688.9
NATIONAL CASUALTY CO	OH	493.4
NATIONAL FOUNDATION LIFE INS CO	TX	59.6
NORTHWESTERN MUTUAL LIFE INS CO	WI	278,047.4
OXFORD LIFE INS CO	AZ	2,251.8
PRINCIPAL LIFE INS CO	IA	196,332.3
STANDARD INS CO	OR	25,172.5
STANDARD SECURITY LIFE INS CO OF NY	NY	139.6
TRUSTMARK INS CO	IL	1,625.3
TRUSTMARK LIFE INS CO	IL	330.1
UNITED WORLD LIFE INS CO	NE	132.1
VOYA RETIREMENT INS & ANNUITY CO	CT	106,305.7

Hawaii

INSURANCE COMPANY NAME	DOM. STATE	TOTAL ASSETS ($MIL)
Rating: A+		
CHESAPEAKE LIFE INS CO	OK	213.1
PHYSICIANS MUTUAL INS CO	NE	2,391.2
TEACHERS INS & ANNUITY ASN OF AM	NY	307,655.9
Rating: A		
AMALGAMATED LIFE INS CO	NY	148.4
BERKLEY LIFE & HEALTH INS CO	IA	336.2
GARDEN STATE LIFE INS CO	TX	138.9
GUARDIAN LIFE INS CO OF AMERICA	NY	59,690.7
SENTRY LIFE INS CO	WI	7,524.4
USAA LIFE INS CO	TX	25,796.7
Rating: A-		
AMERICAN HEALTH & LIFE INS CO	TX	1,083.3
FIDELITY SECURITY LIFE INS CO	MO	970.0
GREAT SOUTHERN LIFE INS CO	TX	209.9
KAISER PERMANENTE INS CO	CA	197.7
MADISON NATIONAL LIFE INS CO INC	WI	337.4
MASSACHUSETTS MUTUAL LIFE INS CO	MA	249,945.6
NATIONAL BENEFIT LIFE INS CO	NY	585.5
NEW YORK LIFE INS CO	NY	181,647.2
NIPPON LIFE INS CO OF AMERICA	IA	229.2
PACIFIC GUARDIAN LIFE INS CO LTD	HI	568.1
PHYSICIANS LIFE INS CO	NE	1,685.6
STANDARD LIFE & ACCIDENT INS CO	TX	511.2
USABLE LIFE	AR	497.8
Rating: B+		
AMERICAN FIDELITY ASR CO	OK	6,256.2
AMERICAN UNITED LIFE INS CO	IN	29,538.7
ANTHEM LIFE INS CO	IN	759.7
ASSURITY LIFE INS CO	NE	2,750.1
AXA EQUITABLE LIFE INS CO	NY	201,023.4
BOSTON MUTUAL LIFE INS CO	MA	1,484.3
DEARBORN NATIONAL LIFE INS CO	IL	1,669.0
DELAWARE AMERICAN LIFE INS CO	DE	119.0
GERBER LIFE INS CO	NY	4,180.6
HUMANA BENEFIT PLAN OF ILLINOIS	IL	693.4
MIDLAND NATIONAL LIFE INS CO	IA	58,679.0
MINNESOTA LIFE INS CO	MN	50,012.0
MUTUAL OF AMERICA LIFE INS CO	NY	21,688.9
NATIONAL CASUALTY CO	OH	493.4
NORTHWESTERN MUTUAL LIFE INS CO	WI	278,047.4
OXFORD LIFE INS CO	AZ	2,251.8
PRINCIPAL LIFE INS CO	IA	196,332.3
STANDARD INS CO	OR	25,172.5
STANDARD SECURITY LIFE INS CO OF NY	NY	139.6
TRUSTMARK INS CO	IL	1,625.3
TRUSTMARK LIFE INS CO	IL	330.1
UNITED WORLD LIFE INS CO	NE	132.1
VOYA RETIREMENT INS & ANNUITY CO	CT	106,305.7

Idaho

INSURANCE COMPANY NAME	DOM. STATE	TOTAL ASSETS ($MIL)
Rating: A+		
CHESAPEAKE LIFE INS CO	OK	213.1
COUNTRY LIFE INS CO	IL	9,777.7
PHYSICIANS MUTUAL INS CO	NE	2,391.2
TEACHERS INS & ANNUITY ASN OF AM	NY	307,655.9
Rating: A		
AMALGAMATED LIFE INS CO	NY	148.4
BERKLEY LIFE & HEALTH INS CO	IA	336.2
EMI HEALTH	UT	158.9
FEDERATED LIFE INS CO	MN	2,039.8
GARDEN STATE LIFE INS CO	TX	138.9
GUARDIAN LIFE INS CO OF AMERICA	NY	59,690.7
LIFEWISE ASR CO	WA	215.9
SENTRY LIFE INS CO	WI	7,524.4
USAA LIFE INS CO	TX	25,796.7
Rating: A-		
AMERICAN HEALTH & LIFE INS CO	TX	1,083.3
CHRISTIAN FIDELITY LIFE INS CO	TX	59.8
FIDELITY SECURITY LIFE INS CO	MO	970.0
GREAT SOUTHERN LIFE INS CO	TX	209.9
MADISON NATIONAL LIFE INS CO INC	WI	337.4
MASSACHUSETTS MUTUAL LIFE INS CO	MA	249,945.6
NATIONAL BENEFIT LIFE INS CO	NY	585.5
NEW YORK LIFE INS CO	NY	181,647.2
NIPPON LIFE INS CO OF AMERICA	IA	229.2
PACIFIC GUARDIAN LIFE INS CO LTD	HI	568.1
PHYSICIANS LIFE INS CO	NE	1,685.6
STANDARD LIFE & ACCIDENT INS CO	TX	511.2
USABLE LIFE	AR	497.8
Rating: B+		
AMERICAN FAMILY MUTL INS CO SI	WI	18,119.9
AMERICAN FIDELITY ASR CO	OK	6,256.2
AMERICAN UNITED LIFE INS CO	IN	29,538.7
ANTHEM LIFE INS CO	IN	759.7
ASSURITY LIFE INS CO	NE	2,750.1
AXA EQUITABLE LIFE INS CO	NY	201,023.4
BOSTON MUTUAL LIFE INS CO	MA	1,484.3
COMPANION LIFE INS CO	SC	420.6
DEARBORN NATIONAL LIFE INS CO	IL	1,669.0
DELAWARE AMERICAN LIFE INS CO	DE	119.0
FARM BUREAU LIFE INS CO	IA	9,174.1
GERBER LIFE INS CO	NY	4,180.6
HUMANA BENEFIT PLAN OF ILLINOIS	IL	693.4
ILLINOIS MUTUAL LIFE INS CO	IL	1,507.2
MIDLAND NATIONAL LIFE INS CO	IA	58,679.0
MINNESOTA LIFE INS CO	MN	50,012.0
MUTUAL OF AMERICA LIFE INS CO	NY	21,688.9
NATIONAL CASUALTY CO	OH	493.4
NATIONAL FOUNDATION LIFE INS CO	TX	59.6
NORTHWESTERN MUTUAL LIFE INS CO	WI	278,047.4
OXFORD LIFE INS CO	AZ	2,251.8
PRINCIPAL LIFE INS CO	IA	196,332.3
REGENCE BLUESHIELD OF IDAHO INC	ID	340.7
STANDARD INS CO	OR	25,172.5
STANDARD SECURITY LIFE INS CO OF NY	NY	139.6
TRUSTMARK INS CO	IL	1,625.3
TRUSTMARK LIFE INS CO	IL	330.1
UNITED WORLD LIFE INS CO	NE	132.1
VOYA RETIREMENT INS & ANNUITY CO	CT	106,305.7

Illinois

INSURANCE COMPANY NAME	DOM. STATE	TOTAL ASSETS ($MIL)
Rating: A+		
CHESAPEAKE LIFE INS CO	OK	213.1
COUNTRY LIFE INS CO	IL	9,777.7
PHYSICIANS MUTUAL INS CO	NE	2,391.2
TEACHERS INS & ANNUITY ASN OF AM	NY	307,655.9
Rating: A		
AMALGAMATED LIFE INS CO	NY	148.4
BERKLEY LIFE & HEALTH INS CO	IA	336.2
FEDERATED LIFE INS CO	MN	2,039.8
GARDEN STATE LIFE INS CO	TX	138.9
GUARDIAN LIFE INS CO OF AMERICA	NY	59,690.7
LIFEWISE ASR CO	WA	215.9
SENTRY LIFE INS CO	WI	7,524.4
SHELTERPOINT LIFE INS CO	NY	183.5
UNITED FARM FAMILY LIFE INS CO	IN	2,373.1
USAA LIFE INS CO	TX	25,796.7
Rating: A-		
AMERICAN HEALTH & LIFE INS CO	TX	1,083.3
CHRISTIAN FIDELITY LIFE INS CO	TX	59.8
ESSENCE HEALTHCARE INC	MO	223.8
FIDELITY SECURITY LIFE INS CO	MO	970.0
GREAT SOUTHERN LIFE INS CO	TX	209.9
MADISON NATIONAL LIFE INS CO INC	WI	337.4
MASSACHUSETTS MUTUAL LIFE INS CO	MA	249,945.6
NATIONAL BENEFIT LIFE INS CO	NY	585.5
NEW YORK LIFE INS CO	NY	181,647.2
NIPPON LIFE INS CO OF AMERICA	IA	229.2
PHYSICIANS LIFE INS CO	NE	1,685.6
STANDARD LIFE & ACCIDENT INS CO	TX	511.2
USABLE LIFE	AR	497.8
Rating: B+		
ALLIANZ LIFE INS CO OF NY	NY	3,530.0
AMERICAN FAMILY MUTL INS CO SI	WI	18,119.9
AMERICAN FIDELITY ASR CO	OK	6,256.2
AMERICAN UNITED LIFE INS CO	IN	29,538.7
ANTHEM LIFE INS CO	IN	759.7
ASSURITY LIFE INS CO	NE	2,750.1
AXA EQUITABLE LIFE INS CO	NY	201,023.4
BOSTON MUTUAL LIFE INS CO	MA	1,484.3
COMPANION LIFE INS CO	SC	420.6
DEARBORN NATIONAL LIFE INS CO	IL	1,669.0
DELAWARE AMERICAN LIFE INS CO	DE	119.0
FREEDOM LIFE INS CO OF AMERICA	TX	247.5
GERBER LIFE INS CO	NY	4,180.6
HUMANA BENEFIT PLAN OF ILLINOIS	IL	693.4
ILLINOIS MUTUAL LIFE INS CO	IL	1,507.2
INDEPENDENT CARE HEALTH PLAN	WI	86.5
MIDLAND NATIONAL LIFE INS CO	IA	58,679.0
MINNESOTA LIFE INS CO	MN	50,012.0
MUTUAL OF AMERICA LIFE INS CO	NY	21,688.9
NATIONAL CASUALTY CO	OH	493.4
NORTH AMERICAN INS CO	WI	18.5
NORTHWESTERN MUTUAL LIFE INS CO	WI	278,047.4
OXFORD LIFE INS CO	AZ	2,251.8
PRINCIPAL LIFE INS CO	IA	196,332.3
STANDARD INS CO	OR	25,172.5
STANDARD SECURITY LIFE INS CO OF NY	NY	139.6
TRUSTMARK INS CO	IL	1,625.3
TRUSTMARK LIFE INS CO	IL	330.1
UNITED HEALTHCARE INS CO OF IL	IL	546.3
UNITED HEALTHCARE OF WISCONSIN INC	WI	2,025.5
UNITED WORLD LIFE INS CO	NE	132.1
VOYA RETIREMENT INS & ANNUITY CO	CT	106,305.7

Indiana

INSURANCE COMPANY NAME	DOM. STATE	TOTAL ASSETS ($MIL)
Rating: A+		
CHESAPEAKE LIFE INS CO	OK	213.1
COUNTRY LIFE INS CO	IL	9,777.7
PHYSICIANS MUTUAL INS CO	NE	2,391.2
TEACHERS INS & ANNUITY ASN OF AM	NY	307,655.9
Rating: A		
AMALGAMATED LIFE INS CO	NY	148.4
BERKLEY LIFE & HEALTH INS CO	IA	336.2
FEDERATED LIFE INS CO	MN	2,039.8
GARDEN STATE LIFE INS CO	TX	138.9
GUARDIAN LIFE INS CO OF AMERICA	NY	59,690.7
MEDICAL MUTUAL OF OHIO	OH	2,490.1
SENTRY LIFE INS CO	WI	7,524.4
UNITED FARM FAMILY LIFE INS CO	IN	2,373.1
USAA LIFE INS CO	TX	25,796.7
Rating: A-		
AMERICAN HEALTH & LIFE INS CO	TX	1,083.3
CHRISTIAN FIDELITY LIFE INS CO	TX	59.8
FIDELITY SECURITY LIFE INS CO	MO	970.0
GREAT SOUTHERN LIFE INS CO	TX	209.9
MADISON NATIONAL LIFE INS CO INC	WI	337.4
MASSACHUSETTS MUTUAL LIFE INS CO	MA	249,945.6
NATIONAL BENEFIT LIFE INS CO	NY	585.5
NEW YORK LIFE INS CO	NY	181,647.2
NIPPON LIFE INS CO OF AMERICA	IA	229.2
PHYSICIANS LIFE INS CO	NE	1,685.6
STANDARD LIFE & ACCIDENT INS CO	TX	511.2
USABLE LIFE	AR	497.8
Rating: B+		
AMERICAN FAMILY MUTL INS CO SI	WI	18,119.9
AMERICAN FIDELITY ASR CO	OK	6,256.2
AMERICAN UNITED LIFE INS CO	IN	29,538.7
ANTHEM LIFE INS CO	IN	759.7
ASSURITY LIFE INS CO	NE	2,750.1
AXA EQUITABLE LIFE INS CO	NY	201,023.4
BOSTON MUTUAL LIFE INS CO	MA	1,484.3
COMPANION LIFE INS CO	SC	420.6
DEARBORN NATIONAL LIFE INS CO	IL	1,669.0
DELAWARE AMERICAN LIFE INS CO	DE	119.0
FREEDOM LIFE INS CO OF AMERICA	TX	247.5
GERBER LIFE INS CO	NY	4,180.6
HUMANA BENEFIT PLAN OF ILLINOIS	IL	693.4
ILLINOIS MUTUAL LIFE INS CO	IL	1,507.2
MDWISE INC	IN	542.8
MIDLAND NATIONAL LIFE INS CO	IA	58,679.0
MINNESOTA LIFE INS CO	MN	50,012.0
MUTUAL OF AMERICA LIFE INS CO	NY	21,688.9
NATIONAL CASUALTY CO	OH	493.4
NATIONAL FOUNDATION LIFE INS CO	TX	59.6
NORTH AMERICAN INS CO	WI	18.5
NORTHWESTERN MUTUAL LIFE INS CO	WI	278,047.4
OXFORD LIFE INS CO	AZ	2,251.8
PRINCIPAL LIFE INS CO	IA	196,332.3
STANDARD INS CO	OR	25,172.5
STANDARD SECURITY LIFE INS CO OF NY	NY	139.6
TRUSTMARK INS CO	IL	1,625.3
TRUSTMARK LIFE INS CO	IL	330.1
UNITED WORLD LIFE INS CO	NE	132.1
VOYA RETIREMENT INS & ANNUITY CO	CT	106,305.7

Iowa

INSURANCE COMPANY NAME	DOM. STATE	TOTAL ASSETS ($MIL)
Rating: A+		
CHESAPEAKE LIFE INS CO	OK	213.1
COUNTRY LIFE INS CO	IL	9,777.7
PHYSICIANS MUTUAL INS CO	NE	2,391.2
TEACHERS INS & ANNUITY ASN OF AM	NY	307,655.9
Rating: A		
AMALGAMATED LIFE INS CO	NY	148.4
BERKLEY LIFE & HEALTH INS CO	IA	336.2
FEDERATED LIFE INS CO	MN	2,039.8
GARDEN STATE LIFE INS CO	TX	138.9
GUARDIAN LIFE INS CO OF AMERICA	NY	59,690.7
SENTRY LIFE INS CO	WI	7,524.4
UNITED FARM FAMILY LIFE INS CO	IN	2,373.1
USAA LIFE INS CO	TX	25,796.7
Rating: A-		
AMERICAN HEALTH & LIFE INS CO	TX	1,083.3
FIDELITY SECURITY LIFE INS CO	MO	970.0
GREAT SOUTHERN LIFE INS CO	TX	209.9
MADISON NATIONAL LIFE INS CO INC	WI	337.4
MASSACHUSETTS MUTUAL LIFE INS CO	MA	249,945.6
NATIONAL BENEFIT LIFE INS CO	NY	585.5
NEW YORK LIFE INS CO	NY	181,647.2
NIPPON LIFE INS CO OF AMERICA	IA	229.2
PACIFIC GUARDIAN LIFE INS CO LTD	HI	568.1
PHYSICIANS LIFE INS CO	NE	1,685.6
STANDARD LIFE & ACCIDENT INS CO	TX	511.2
USABLE LIFE	AR	497.8
Rating: B+		
AMERICAN FAMILY MUTL INS CO SI	WI	18,119.9
AMERICAN FIDELITY ASR CO	OK	6,256.2
AMERICAN UNITED LIFE INS CO	IN	29,538.7
ANTHEM LIFE INS CO	IN	759.7
ASSURITY LIFE INS CO	NE	2,750.1
AXA EQUITABLE LIFE INS CO	NY	201,023.4
BOSTON MUTUAL LIFE INS CO	MA	1,484.3
COMPANION LIFE INS CO	SC	420.6
DEARBORN NATIONAL LIFE INS CO	IL	1,669.0
DELAWARE AMERICAN LIFE INS CO	DE	119.0
FARM BUREAU LIFE INS CO	IA	9,174.1
FREEDOM LIFE INS CO OF AMERICA	TX	247.5
GERBER LIFE INS CO	NY	4,180.6
HEALTHPARTNERS INS CO	MN	416.8
HUMANA BENEFIT PLAN OF ILLINOIS	IL	693.4
ILLINOIS MUTUAL LIFE INS CO	IL	1,507.2
MIDLAND NATIONAL LIFE INS CO	IA	58,679.0
MINNESOTA LIFE INS CO	MN	50,012.0
MUTUAL OF AMERICA LIFE INS CO	NY	21,688.9
NATIONAL CASUALTY CO	OH	493.4
NATIONAL FOUNDATION LIFE INS CO	TX	59.6
NORTHWESTERN MUTUAL LIFE INS CO	WI	278,047.4
OXFORD LIFE INS CO	AZ	2,251.8
PRINCIPAL LIFE INS CO	IA	196,332.3
STANDARD INS CO	OR	25,172.5
STANDARD SECURITY LIFE INS CO OF NY	NY	139.6
TRUSTMARK INS CO	IL	1,625.3
TRUSTMARK LIFE INS CO	IL	330.1
UNITED HEALTHCARE OF WISCONSIN INC	WI	2,025.5
UNITED WORLD LIFE INS CO	NE	132.1
VOYA RETIREMENT INS & ANNUITY CO	CT	106,305.7

Kansas

INSURANCE COMPANY NAME	DOM. STATE	TOTAL ASSETS ($MIL)
Rating: A+		
CHESAPEAKE LIFE INS CO	OK	213.1
COUNTRY LIFE INS CO	IL	9,777.7
PHYSICIANS MUTUAL INS CO	NE	2,391.2
TEACHERS INS & ANNUITY ASN OF AM	NY	307,655.9
Rating: A		
AMALGAMATED LIFE INS CO	NY	148.4
BERKLEY LIFE & HEALTH INS CO	IA	336.2
FEDERATED LIFE INS CO	MN	2,039.8
GARDEN STATE LIFE INS CO	TX	138.9
GUARDIAN LIFE INS CO OF AMERICA	NY	59,690.7
SENTRY LIFE INS CO	WI	7,524.4
USAA LIFE INS CO	TX	25,796.7
Rating: A-		
AMERICAN HEALTH & LIFE INS CO	TX	1,083.3
CHRISTIAN FIDELITY LIFE INS CO	TX	59.8
FIDELITY SECURITY LIFE INS CO	MO	970.0
GREAT SOUTHERN LIFE INS CO	TX	209.9
KAISER PERMANENTE INS CO	CA	197.7
MADISON NATIONAL LIFE INS CO INC	WI	337.4
MASSACHUSETTS MUTUAL LIFE INS CO	MA	249,945.6
NATIONAL BENEFIT LIFE INS CO	NY	585.5
NEW YORK LIFE INS CO	NY	181,647.2
NIPPON LIFE INS CO OF AMERICA	IA	229.2
PHYSICIANS LIFE INS CO	NE	1,685.6
STANDARD LIFE & ACCIDENT INS CO	TX	511.2
USABLE LIFE	AR	497.8
Rating: B+		
ADVANCE INS CO OF KANSAS	KS	61.2
AMERICAN FAMILY MUTL INS CO SI	WI	18,119.9
AMERICAN FIDELITY ASR CO	OK	6,256.2
AMERICAN UNITED LIFE INS CO	IN	29,538.7
ANTHEM LIFE INS CO	IN	759.7
ASSURITY LIFE INS CO	NE	2,750.1
AXA EQUITABLE LIFE INS CO	NY	201,023.4
BOSTON MUTUAL LIFE INS CO	MA	1,484.3
COMPANION LIFE INS CO	SC	420.6
DEARBORN NATIONAL LIFE INS CO	IL	1,669.0
DELAWARE AMERICAN LIFE INS CO	DE	119.0
FARM BUREAU LIFE INS CO	IA	9,174.1
FREEDOM LIFE INS CO OF AMERICA	TX	247.5
GERBER LIFE INS CO	NY	4,180.6
HUMANA BENEFIT PLAN OF ILLINOIS	IL	693.4
ILLINOIS MUTUAL LIFE INS CO	IL	1,507.2
MIDLAND NATIONAL LIFE INS CO	IA	58,679.0
MINNESOTA LIFE INS CO	MN	50,012.0
MUTUAL OF AMERICA LIFE INS CO	NY	21,688.9
NATIONAL CASUALTY CO	OH	493.4
NATIONAL FOUNDATION LIFE INS CO	TX	59.6
NORTH AMERICAN INS CO	WI	18.5
NORTHWESTERN MUTUAL LIFE INS CO	WI	278,047.4
OXFORD LIFE INS CO	AZ	2,251.8
PRINCIPAL LIFE INS CO	IA	196,332.3
STANDARD INS CO	OR	25,172.5
STANDARD SECURITY LIFE INS CO OF NY	NY	139.6

INSURANCE COMPANY NAME	DOM. STATE	TOTAL ASSETS ($MIL)
TRUSTMARK INS CO	IL	1,625.3
TRUSTMARK LIFE INS CO	IL	330.1
UNITED WORLD LIFE INS CO	NE	132.1
VOYA RETIREMENT INS & ANNUITY CO	CT	106,305.7

Kentucky

INSURANCE COMPANY NAME	DOM. STATE	TOTAL ASSETS ($MIL)
Rating: A+		
CHESAPEAKE LIFE INS CO	OK	213.1
COUNTRY LIFE INS CO	IL	9,777.7
PHYSICIANS MUTUAL INS CO	NE	2,391.2
TEACHERS INS & ANNUITY ASN OF AM	NY	307,655.9
Rating: A		
AMALGAMATED LIFE INS CO	NY	148.4
BERKLEY LIFE & HEALTH INS CO	IA	336.2
FEDERATED LIFE INS CO	MN	2,039.8
GARDEN STATE LIFE INS CO	TX	138.9
GUARDIAN LIFE INS CO OF AMERICA	NY	59,690.7
SENTRY LIFE INS CO	WI	7,524.4
SOUTHERN FARM BUREAU LIFE INS CO	MS	14,368.9
USAA LIFE INS CO	TX	25,796.7
Rating: A-		
AMERICAN HEALTH & LIFE INS CO	TX	1,083.3
ANTHEM KENTUCKY MANAGED CARE PLAN	KY	243.4
CHRISTIAN FIDELITY LIFE INS CO	TX	59.8
FIDELITY SECURITY LIFE INS CO	MO	970.0
GREAT SOUTHERN LIFE INS CO	TX	209.9
HUMANA MEDICAL PLAN INC	FL	2,319.2
MADISON NATIONAL LIFE INS CO INC	WI	337.4
MASSACHUSETTS MUTUAL LIFE INS CO	MA	249,945.6
NATIONAL BENEFIT LIFE INS CO	NY	585.5
NEW YORK LIFE INS CO	NY	181,647.2
NIPPON LIFE INS CO OF AMERICA	IA	229.2
PHYSICIANS LIFE INS CO	NE	1,685.6
STANDARD LIFE & ACCIDENT INS CO	TX	511.2
USABLE LIFE	AR	497.8
Rating: B+		
AETNA BETTER HLTH OF KY INS CO	KY	524.3
AMERICAN FIDELITY ASR CO	OK	6,256.2
AMERICAN UNITED LIFE INS CO	IN	29,538.7
ANTHEM LIFE INS CO	IN	759.7
ASSURITY LIFE INS CO	NE	2,750.1
AXA EQUITABLE LIFE INS CO	NY	201,023.4
BOSTON MUTUAL LIFE INS CO	MA	1,484.3
COMPANION LIFE INS CO	SC	420.6
DEARBORN NATIONAL LIFE INS CO	IL	1,669.0
DELAWARE AMERICAN LIFE INS CO	DE	119.0
FREEDOM LIFE INS CO OF AMERICA	TX	247.5
GERBER LIFE INS CO	NY	4,180.6
HUMANA BENEFIT PLAN OF ILLINOIS	IL	693.4
HUMANA INS CO OF KENTUCKY	KY	222.0
ILLINOIS MUTUAL LIFE INS CO	IL	1,507.2
MIDLAND NATIONAL LIFE INS CO	IA	58,679.0
MINNESOTA LIFE INS CO	MN	50,012.0
MUTUAL OF AMERICA LIFE INS CO	NY	21,688.9
NATIONAL CASUALTY CO	OH	493.4
NATIONAL FOUNDATION LIFE INS CO	TX	59.6
NORTHWESTERN MUTUAL LIFE INS CO	WI	278,047.4
OXFORD LIFE INS CO	AZ	2,251.8
PRINCIPAL LIFE INS CO	IA	196,332.3
STANDARD INS CO	OR	25,172.5
STANDARD SECURITY LIFE INS CO OF NY	NY	139.6
TRUSTMARK INS CO	IL	1,625.3
TRUSTMARK LIFE INS CO	IL	330.1
UNITED HEALTHCARE OF WISCONSIN INC	WI	2,025.5
UNITED WORLD LIFE INS CO	NE	132.1
VOYA RETIREMENT INS & ANNUITY CO	CT	106,305.7

Louisiana

INSURANCE COMPANY NAME	DOM. STATE	TOTAL ASSETS ($MIL)
Rating: A+		
CHESAPEAKE LIFE INS CO	OK	213.1
COUNTRY LIFE INS CO	IL	9,777.7
HMO LOUISIANA INC	LA	801.6
PHYSICIANS MUTUAL INS CO	NE	2,391.2
TEACHERS INS & ANNUITY ASN OF AM	NY	307,655.9
Rating: A		
AMALGAMATED LIFE INS CO	NY	148.4
BERKLEY LIFE & HEALTH INS CO	IA	336.2
FEDERATED LIFE INS CO	MN	2,039.8
GARDEN STATE LIFE INS CO	TX	138.9
GUARDIAN LIFE INS CO OF AMERICA	NY	59,690.7
SENTRY LIFE INS CO	WI	7,524.4
SOUTHERN FARM BUREAU LIFE INS CO	MS	14,368.9
USAA LIFE INS CO	TX	25,796.7
Rating: A-		
AMERICAN HEALTH & LIFE INS CO	TX	1,083.3
BLUEBONNET LIFE INS CO	MS	65.0
CHRISTIAN FIDELITY LIFE INS CO	TX	59.8
FIDELITY SECURITY LIFE INS CO	MO	970.0
GREAT SOUTHERN LIFE INS CO	TX	209.9
MADISON NATIONAL LIFE INS CO INC	WI	337.4
MASSACHUSETTS MUTUAL LIFE INS CO	MA	249,945.6
NATIONAL BENEFIT LIFE INS CO	NY	585.5
NEW YORK LIFE INS CO	NY	181,647.2
NIPPON LIFE INS CO OF AMERICA	IA	229.2
PACIFIC GUARDIAN LIFE INS CO LTD	HI	568.1
PHYSICIANS LIFE INS CO	NE	1,685.6
STANDARD LIFE & ACCIDENT INS CO	TX	511.2
SWBC LIFE INS CO	TX	33.5
USABLE LIFE	AR	497.8
Rating: B+		
AMERICAN FIDELITY ASR CO	OK	6,256.2
AMERICAN UNITED LIFE INS CO	IN	29,538.7
ANTHEM LIFE INS CO	IN	759.7
ASSURITY LIFE INS CO	NE	2,750.1
AXA EQUITABLE LIFE INS CO	NY	201,023.4
BOSTON MUTUAL LIFE INS CO	MA	1,484.3
COMPANION LIFE INS CO	SC	420.6
DEARBORN NATIONAL LIFE INS CO	IL	1,669.0
DELAWARE AMERICAN LIFE INS CO	DE	119.0
FREEDOM LIFE INS CO OF AMERICA	TX	247.5
GERBER LIFE INS CO	NY	4,180.6
HUMANA BENEFIT PLAN OF ILLINOIS	IL	693.4
ILLINOIS MUTUAL LIFE INS CO	IL	1,507.2
MIDLAND NATIONAL LIFE INS CO	IA	58,679.0
MINNESOTA LIFE INS CO	MN	50,012.0
MUTUAL OF AMERICA LIFE INS CO	NY	21,688.9
NATIONAL CASUALTY CO	OH	493.4
NATIONAL FOUNDATION LIFE INS CO	TX	59.6
NORTH AMERICAN INS CO	WI	18.5
NORTHWESTERN MUTUAL LIFE INS CO	WI	278,047.4
OXFORD LIFE INS CO	AZ	2,251.8
PRINCIPAL LIFE INS CO	IA	196,332.3
STANDARD INS CO	OR	25,172.5
STANDARD SECURITY LIFE INS CO OF NY	NY	139.6
TRUSTMARK INS CO	IL	1,625.3
TRUSTMARK LIFE INS CO	IL	330.1
UNITED WORLD LIFE INS CO	NE	132.1
VOYA RETIREMENT INS & ANNUITY CO	CT	106,305.7

Maine

INSURANCE COMPANY NAME	DOM. STATE	TOTAL ASSETS ($MIL)
Rating: A+		
CHESAPEAKE LIFE INS CO	OK	213.1
COUNTRY LIFE INS CO	IL	9,777.7
PHYSICIANS MUTUAL INS CO	NE	2,391.2
TEACHERS INS & ANNUITY ASN OF AM	NY	307,655.9
Rating: A		
AMALGAMATED LIFE INS CO	NY	148.4
BERKLEY LIFE & HEALTH INS CO	IA	336.2
FEDERATED LIFE INS CO	MN	2,039.8
GARDEN STATE LIFE INS CO	TX	138.9
GUARDIAN LIFE INS CO OF AMERICA	NY	59,690.7
SENTRY LIFE INS CO	WI	7,524.4
USAA LIFE INS CO	TX	25,796.7
Rating: A-		
AMERICAN HEALTH & LIFE INS CO	TX	1,083.3
FIDELITY SECURITY LIFE INS CO	MO	970.0
GREAT SOUTHERN LIFE INS CO	TX	209.9
MADISON NATIONAL LIFE INS CO INC	WI	337.4
MASSACHUSETTS MUTUAL LIFE INS CO	MA	249,945.6
NATIONAL BENEFIT LIFE INS CO	NY	585.5
NEW YORK LIFE INS CO	NY	181,647.2
PHYSICIANS LIFE INS CO	NE	1,685.6
USABLE LIFE	AR	497.8
Rating: B+		
AMERICAN FIDELITY ASR CO	OK	6,256.2
AMERICAN UNITED LIFE INS CO	IN	29,538.7
ANTHEM LIFE INS CO	IN	759.7
ASSURITY LIFE INS CO	NE	2,750.1
AXA EQUITABLE LIFE INS CO	NY	201,023.4
BOSTON MUTUAL LIFE INS CO	MA	1,484.3
COMPANION LIFE INS CO	SC	420.6
DEARBORN NATIONAL LIFE INS CO	IL	1,669.0
DELAWARE AMERICAN LIFE INS CO	DE	119.0
GERBER LIFE INS CO	NY	4,180.6
HUMANA BENEFIT PLAN OF ILLINOIS	IL	693.4
ILLINOIS MUTUAL LIFE INS CO	IL	1,507.2
MIDLAND NATIONAL LIFE INS CO	IA	58,679.0
MINNESOTA LIFE INS CO	MN	50,012.0
MUTUAL OF AMERICA LIFE INS CO	NY	21,688.9
NATIONAL CASUALTY CO	OH	493.4
NATIONAL FOUNDATION LIFE INS CO	TX	59.6
NORTHWESTERN MUTUAL LIFE INS CO	WI	278,047.4
OXFORD LIFE INS CO	AZ	2,251.8
PRINCIPAL LIFE INS CO	IA	196,332.3
STANDARD INS CO	OR	25,172.5
STANDARD SECURITY LIFE INS CO OF NY	NY	139.6
TRUSTMARK INS CO	IL	1,625.3
TRUSTMARK LIFE INS CO	IL	330.1
UNITED WORLD LIFE INS CO	NE	132.1
VOYA RETIREMENT INS & ANNUITY CO	CT	106,305.7

Maryland

INSURANCE COMPANY NAME	DOM. STATE	TOTAL ASSETS ($MIL)
Rating: A+		
CHESAPEAKE LIFE INS CO	OK	213.1
COUNTRY LIFE INS CO	IL	9,777.7
PHYSICIANS MUTUAL INS CO	NE	2,391.2
TEACHERS INS & ANNUITY ASN OF AM	NY	307,655.9
Rating: A		
AMALGAMATED LIFE INS CO	NY	148.4
BERKLEY LIFE & HEALTH INS CO	IA	336.2
FEDERATED LIFE INS CO	MN	2,039.8
GARDEN STATE LIFE INS CO	TX	138.9
GUARDIAN LIFE INS CO OF AMERICA	NY	59,690.7
SENTRY LIFE INS CO	WI	7,524.4
SHELTERPOINT LIFE INS CO	NY	183.5
UNITED FARM FAMILY LIFE INS CO	IN	2,373.1
USAA LIFE INS CO	TX	25,796.7
Rating: A-		
AMERICAN HEALTH & LIFE INS CO	TX	1,083.3
FIDELITY SECURITY LIFE INS CO	MO	970.0
GREAT SOUTHERN LIFE INS CO	TX	209.9
KAISER PERMANENTE INS CO	CA	197.7
MADISON NATIONAL LIFE INS CO INC	WI	337.4
MASSACHUSETTS MUTUAL LIFE INS CO	MA	249,945.6
NATIONAL BENEFIT LIFE INS CO	NY	585.5
NEW YORK LIFE INS CO	NY	181,647.2
NIPPON LIFE INS CO OF AMERICA	IA	229.2
PHYSICIANS LIFE INS CO	NE	1,685.6
STANDARD LIFE & ACCIDENT INS CO	TX	511.2
USABLE LIFE	AR	497.8
Rating: B+		
AMERICAN FIDELITY ASR CO	OK	6,256.2
AMERICAN UNITED LIFE INS CO	IN	29,538.7
ANTHEM LIFE INS CO	IN	759.7
ASSURITY LIFE INS CO	NE	2,750.1
AXA EQUITABLE LIFE INS CO	NY	201,023.4
BOSTON MUTUAL LIFE INS CO	MA	1,484.3
COMPANION LIFE INS CO	SC	420.6
DEARBORN NATIONAL LIFE INS CO	IL	1,669.0
DELAWARE AMERICAN LIFE INS CO	DE	119.0
FREEDOM LIFE INS CO OF AMERICA	TX	247.5
GERBER LIFE INS CO	NY	4,180.6
HUMANA BENEFIT PLAN OF ILLINOIS	IL	693.4
ILLINOIS MUTUAL LIFE INS CO	IL	1,507.2
MIDLAND NATIONAL LIFE INS CO	IA	58,679.0
MINNESOTA LIFE INS CO	MN	50,012.0
MUTUAL OF AMERICA LIFE INS CO	NY	21,688.9
NATIONAL CASUALTY CO	OH	493.4
NORTH AMERICAN INS CO	WI	18.5
NORTHWESTERN MUTUAL LIFE INS CO	WI	278,047.4
OXFORD LIFE INS CO	AZ	2,251.8
PRINCIPAL LIFE INS CO	IA	196,332.3
STANDARD INS CO	OR	25,172.5
STANDARD SECURITY LIFE INS CO OF NY	NY	139.6
TRUSTMARK INS CO	IL	1,625.3
TRUSTMARK LIFE INS CO	IL	330.1
UNITED WORLD LIFE INS CO	NE	132.1
VOYA RETIREMENT INS & ANNUITY CO	CT	106,305.7

Massachusetts

INSURANCE COMPANY NAME	DOM. STATE	TOTAL ASSETS ($MIL)
Rating: A+		
CHESAPEAKE LIFE INS CO	OK	213.1
COUNTRY LIFE INS CO	IL	9,777.7
PHYSICIANS MUTUAL INS CO	NE	2,391.2
TEACHERS INS & ANNUITY ASN OF AM	NY	307,655.9
Rating: A		
AMALGAMATED LIFE INS CO	NY	148.4
BERKLEY LIFE & HEALTH INS CO	IA	336.2
FEDERATED LIFE INS CO	MN	2,039.8
GARDEN STATE LIFE INS CO	TX	138.9
GUARDIAN LIFE INS CO OF AMERICA	NY	59,690.7
SENTRY LIFE INS CO	WI	7,524.4
SHELTERPOINT LIFE INS CO	NY	183.5
UNITED FARM FAMILY LIFE INS CO	IN	2,373.1
USAA LIFE INS CO	TX	25,796.7
Rating: A-		
AMERICAN FAMILY LIFE ASR CO OF NY	NY	978.2
AMERICAN HEALTH & LIFE INS CO	TX	1,083.3
FIDELITY SECURITY LIFE INS CO	MO	970.0
GREAT SOUTHERN LIFE INS CO	TX	209.9
MADISON NATIONAL LIFE INS CO INC	WI	337.4
MASSACHUSETTS MUTUAL LIFE INS CO	MA	249,945.6
NATIONAL BENEFIT LIFE INS CO	NY	585.5
NEW YORK LIFE INS CO	NY	181,647.2
NIPPON LIFE INS CO OF AMERICA	IA	229.2
PHYSICIANS LIFE INS CO	NE	1,685.6
STANDARD LIFE & ACCIDENT INS CO	TX	511.2
USABLE LIFE	AR	497.8
Rating: B+		
AMERICAN FIDELITY ASR CO	OK	6,256.2
AMERICAN UNITED LIFE INS CO	IN	29,538.7
ANTHEM LIFE INS CO	IN	759.7
ASSURITY LIFE INS CO	NE	2,750.1
AXA EQUITABLE LIFE INS CO	NY	201,023.4
BLUE CROSS & BLUE SHIELD MA HMO BLUE	MA	2,326.3
BOSTON MUTUAL LIFE INS CO	MA	1,484.3
COMPANION LIFE INS CO	SC	420.6
DEARBORN NATIONAL LIFE INS CO	IL	1,669.0
DELAWARE AMERICAN LIFE INS CO	DE	119.0
GERBER LIFE INS CO	NY	4,180.6
HUMANA BENEFIT PLAN OF ILLINOIS	IL	693.4
ILLINOIS MUTUAL LIFE INS CO	IL	1,507.2
MIDLAND NATIONAL LIFE INS CO	IA	58,679.0
MINNESOTA LIFE INS CO	MN	50,012.0
MUTUAL OF AMERICA LIFE INS CO	NY	21,688.9
NATIONAL CASUALTY CO	OH	493.4
NORTHWESTERN MUTUAL LIFE INS CO	WI	278,047.4
OXFORD LIFE INS CO	AZ	2,251.8
PRINCIPAL LIFE INS CO	IA	196,332.3
STANDARD INS CO	OR	25,172.5
STANDARD SECURITY LIFE INS CO OF NY	NY	139.6
TRUSTMARK INS CO	IL	1,625.3
TRUSTMARK LIFE INS CO	IL	330.1
UNITED WORLD LIFE INS CO	NE	132.1
VOYA RETIREMENT INS & ANNUITY CO	CT	106,305.7

Michigan

INSURANCE COMPANY NAME	DOM. STATE	TOTAL ASSETS ($MIL)
Rating: A+		
CHESAPEAKE LIFE INS CO	OK	213.1
COUNTRY LIFE INS CO	IL	9,777.7
PHYSICIANS MUTUAL INS CO	NE	2,391.2
TEACHERS INS & ANNUITY ASN OF AM	NY	307,655.9
Rating: A		
AMALGAMATED LIFE INS CO	NY	148.4
BERKLEY LIFE & HEALTH INS CO	IA	336.2
FEDERATED LIFE INS CO	MN	2,039.8
GARDEN STATE LIFE INS CO	TX	138.9
GUARDIAN LIFE INS CO OF AMERICA	NY	59,690.7
MEDICAL MUTUAL OF OHIO	OH	2,490.1
PRIORITY HEALTH	MI	1,388.7
SENTRY LIFE INS CO	WI	7,524.4
SHELTERPOINT LIFE INS CO	NY	183.5
USAA LIFE INS CO	TX	25,796.7
Rating: A-		
AMERICAN HEALTH & LIFE INS CO	TX	1,083.3
FIDELITY SECURITY LIFE INS CO	MO	970.0
GREAT SOUTHERN LIFE INS CO	TX	209.9
MADISON NATIONAL LIFE INS CO INC	WI	337.4
MASSACHUSETTS MUTUAL LIFE INS CO	MA	249,945.6
NATIONAL BENEFIT LIFE INS CO	NY	585.5
NEW YORK LIFE INS CO	NY	181,647.2
NIPPON LIFE INS CO OF AMERICA	IA	229.2
PARAMOUNT INS CO (OH)	OH	87.0
PHYSICIANS LIFE INS CO	NE	1,685.6
PRIORITY HEALTH CHOICE INC	MI	143.1
STANDARD LIFE & ACCIDENT INS CO	TX	511.2
SWBC LIFE INS CO	TX	33.5
USABLE LIFE	AR	497.8
Rating: B+		
AMERICAN FIDELITY ASR CO	OK	6,256.2
AMERICAN UNITED LIFE INS CO	IN	29,538.7
ANTHEM LIFE INS CO	IN	759.7
ASSURITY LIFE INS CO	NE	2,750.1
AXA EQUITABLE LIFE INS CO	NY	201,023.4
BOSTON MUTUAL LIFE INS CO	MA	1,484.3
COMPANION LIFE INS CO	SC	420.6
DEARBORN NATIONAL LIFE INS CO	IL	1,669.0
DELAWARE AMERICAN LIFE INS CO	DE	119.0
FREEDOM LIFE INS CO OF AMERICA	TX	247.5
GERBER LIFE INS CO	NY	4,180.6
HUMANA BENEFIT PLAN OF ILLINOIS	IL	693.4
ILLINOIS MUTUAL LIFE INS CO	IL	1,507.2
MIDLAND NATIONAL LIFE INS CO	IA	58,679.0
MINNESOTA LIFE INS CO	MN	50,012.0
MUTUAL OF AMERICA LIFE INS CO	NY	21,688.9
NATIONAL CASUALTY CO	OH	493.4
NORTH AMERICAN INS CO	WI	18.5
NORTHWESTERN MUTUAL LIFE INS CO	WI	278,047.4
OXFORD LIFE INS CO	AZ	2,251.8
PRINCIPAL LIFE INS CO	IA	196,332.3
STANDARD INS CO	OR	25,172.5
STANDARD SECURITY LIFE INS CO OF NY	NY	139.6
TOTAL HEALTH CARE USA INC	MI	95.2
TRUSTMARK INS CO	IL	1,625.3
TRUSTMARK LIFE INS CO	IL	330.1
UNITED WORLD LIFE INS CO	NE	132.1
UPPER PENINSULA HEALTH PLAN INC	MI	110.1
VOYA RETIREMENT INS & ANNUITY CO	CT	106,305.7

Minnesota

INSURANCE COMPANY NAME	DOM. STATE	TOTAL ASSETS ($MIL)
Rating: A+		
CHESAPEAKE LIFE INS CO	OK	213.1
COUNTRY LIFE INS CO	IL	9,777.7
PHYSICIANS MUTUAL INS CO	NE	2,391.2
TEACHERS INS & ANNUITY ASN OF AM	NY	307,655.9
Rating: A		
AMALGAMATED LIFE INS CO	NY	148.4
BERKLEY LIFE & HEALTH INS CO	IA	336.2
FEDERATED LIFE INS CO	MN	2,039.8
GARDEN STATE LIFE INS CO	TX	138.9
GUARDIAN LIFE INS CO OF AMERICA	NY	59,690.7
SENTRY LIFE INS CO	WI	7,524.4
SHELTERPOINT LIFE INS CO	NY	183.5
USAA LIFE INS CO	TX	25,796.7
Rating: A-		
AMERICAN HEALTH & LIFE INS CO	TX	1,083.3
FIDELITY SECURITY LIFE INS CO	MO	970.0
GREAT SOUTHERN LIFE INS CO	TX	209.9
MADISON NATIONAL LIFE INS CO INC	WI	337.4
MASSACHUSETTS MUTUAL LIFE INS CO	MA	249,945.6
NATIONAL BENEFIT LIFE INS CO	NY	585.5
NEW YORK LIFE INS CO	NY	181,647.2
NIPPON LIFE INS CO OF AMERICA	IA	229.2
PHYSICIANS LIFE INS CO	NE	1,685.6
STANDARD LIFE & ACCIDENT INS CO	TX	511.2
USABLE LIFE	AR	497.8
Rating: B+		
ALLIANZ LIFE INS CO OF NY	NY	3,530.0
AMERICAN FAMILY MUTL INS CO SI	WI	18,119.9
AMERICAN FIDELITY ASR CO	OK	6,256.2
AMERICAN UNITED LIFE INS CO	IN	29,538.7
ANTHEM LIFE INS CO	IN	759.7
ASSURITY LIFE INS CO	NE	2,750.1
AXA EQUITABLE LIFE INS CO	NY	201,023.4
BOSTON MUTUAL LIFE INS CO	MA	1,484.3
COMPANION LIFE INS CO	SC	420.6
DEARBORN NATIONAL LIFE INS CO	IL	1,669.0
DELAWARE AMERICAN LIFE INS CO	DE	119.0
FARM BUREAU LIFE INS CO	IA	9,174.1
FREEDOM LIFE INS CO OF AMERICA	TX	247.5
GERBER LIFE INS CO	NY	4,180.6
HEALTHPARTNERS	MN	1,327.1
HEALTHPARTNERS INS CO	MN	416.8
HUMANA BENEFIT PLAN OF ILLINOIS	IL	693.4
ILLINOIS MUTUAL LIFE INS CO	IL	1,507.2
MIDLAND NATIONAL LIFE INS CO	IA	58,679.0
MINNESOTA LIFE INS CO	MN	50,012.0
MUTUAL OF AMERICA LIFE INS CO	NY	21,688.9
NATIONAL CASUALTY CO	OH	493.4
NORTH AMERICAN INS CO	WI	18.5
NORTHWESTERN MUTUAL LIFE INS CO	WI	278,047.4
OXFORD LIFE INS CO	AZ	2,251.8
PRINCIPAL LIFE INS CO	IA	196,332.3
STANDARD INS CO	OR	25,172.5
STANDARD SECURITY LIFE INS CO OF NY	NY	139.6
TRUSTMARK INS CO	IL	1,625.3
TRUSTMARK LIFE INS CO	IL	330.1
UNITED WORLD LIFE INS CO	NE	132.1
VOYA RETIREMENT INS & ANNUITY CO	CT	106,305.7

Mississippi

INSURANCE COMPANY NAME	DOM. STATE	TOTAL ASSETS ($MIL)
Rating: A+		
CHESAPEAKE LIFE INS CO	OK	213.1
COUNTRY LIFE INS CO	IL	9,777.7
PHYSICIANS MUTUAL INS CO	NE	2,391.2
TEACHERS INS & ANNUITY ASN OF AM	NY	307,655.9
Rating: A		
AMALGAMATED LIFE INS CO	NY	148.4
BERKLEY LIFE & HEALTH INS CO	IA	336.2
BLUE CROSS BLUE SHIELD OF MS, MUTUAL	MS	1,042.9
FEDERATED LIFE INS CO	MN	2,039.8
GARDEN STATE LIFE INS CO	TX	138.9
GUARDIAN LIFE INS CO OF AMERICA	NY	59,690.7
SENTRY LIFE INS CO	WI	7,524.4
SOUTHERN FARM BUREAU LIFE INS CO	MS	14,368.9
USAA LIFE INS CO	TX	25,796.7
Rating: A-		
AMERICAN HEALTH & LIFE INS CO	TX	1,083.3
BLUEBONNET LIFE INS CO	MS	65.0
CHRISTIAN FIDELITY LIFE INS CO	TX	59.8
FIDELITY SECURITY LIFE INS CO	MO	970.0
GREAT SOUTHERN LIFE INS CO	TX	209.9
HUMANA MEDICAL PLAN INC	FL	2,319.2
MADISON NATIONAL LIFE INS CO INC	WI	337.4
MASSACHUSETTS MUTUAL LIFE INS CO	MA	249,945.6
NATIONAL BENEFIT LIFE INS CO	NY	585.5
NEW YORK LIFE INS CO	NY	181,647.2
NIPPON LIFE INS CO OF AMERICA	IA	229.2
PHYSICIANS LIFE INS CO	NE	1,685.6
STANDARD LIFE & ACCIDENT INS CO	TX	511.2
USABLE LIFE	AR	497.8
Rating: B+		
AMERICAN FIDELITY ASR CO	OK	6,256.2
AMERICAN UNITED LIFE INS CO	IN	29,538.7
ANTHEM LIFE INS CO	IN	759.7
ASSURITY LIFE INS CO	NE	2,750.1
AXA EQUITABLE LIFE INS CO	NY	201,023.4
BOSTON MUTUAL LIFE INS CO	MA	1,484.3
COMPANION LIFE INS CO	SC	420.6
DEARBORN NATIONAL LIFE INS CO	IL	1,669.0
DELAWARE AMERICAN LIFE INS CO	DE	119.0
FIDELITY SECURITY LIFE INS CO OF NY	NY	39.6
FREEDOM LIFE INS CO OF AMERICA	TX	247.5
GERBER LIFE INS CO	NY	4,180.6
HUMANA BENEFIT PLAN OF ILLINOIS	IL	693.4
ILLINOIS MUTUAL LIFE INS CO	IL	1,507.2
MIDLAND NATIONAL LIFE INS CO	IA	58,679.0
MINNESOTA LIFE INS CO	MN	50,012.0
MUTUAL OF AMERICA LIFE INS CO	NY	21,688.9
NATIONAL CASUALTY CO	OH	493.4
NATIONAL FOUNDATION LIFE INS CO	TX	59.6
NORTHWESTERN MUTUAL LIFE INS CO	WI	278,047.4
OXFORD LIFE INS CO	AZ	2,251.8
PRINCIPAL LIFE INS CO	IA	196,332.3
STANDARD INS CO	OR	25,172.5
STANDARD SECURITY LIFE INS CO OF NY	NY	139.6
TRUSTMARK INS CO	IL	1,625.3
TRUSTMARK LIFE INS CO	IL	330.1
UNITED WORLD LIFE INS CO	NE	132.1
VOYA RETIREMENT INS & ANNUITY CO	CT	106,305.7

Missouri

INSURANCE COMPANY NAME	DOM. STATE	TOTAL ASSETS ($MIL)
Rating: A+		
CHESAPEAKE LIFE INS CO	OK	213.1
COUNTRY LIFE INS CO	IL	9,777.7
PHYSICIANS MUTUAL INS CO	NE	2,391.2
TEACHERS INS & ANNUITY ASN OF AM	NY	307,655.9
Rating: A		
AMALGAMATED LIFE INS CO	NY	148.4
BERKLEY LIFE & HEALTH INS CO	IA	336.2
FEDERATED LIFE INS CO	MN	2,039.8
GARDEN STATE LIFE INS CO	TX	138.9
GUARDIAN LIFE INS CO OF AMERICA	NY	59,690.7
SENTRY LIFE INS CO	WI	7,524.4
USAA LIFE INS CO	TX	25,796.7
Rating: A-		
AMERICAN HEALTH & LIFE INS CO	TX	1,083.3
CHRISTIAN FIDELITY LIFE INS CO	TX	59.8
CIGNA LIFE INS CO OF NEW YORK	NY	419.6
ESSENCE HEALTHCARE INC	MO	223.8
FARM BUREAU LIFE INS CO OF MISSOURI	MO	615.1
FIDELITY SECURITY LIFE INS CO	MO	970.0
GREAT SOUTHERN LIFE INS CO	TX	209.9
KAISER PERMANENTE INS CO	CA	197.7
MADISON NATIONAL LIFE INS CO INC	WI	337.4
MASSACHUSETTS MUTUAL LIFE INS CO	MA	249,945.6
NATIONAL BENEFIT LIFE INS CO	NY	585.5
NEW YORK LIFE INS CO	NY	181,647.2
NIPPON LIFE INS CO OF AMERICA	IA	229.2
PACIFIC GUARDIAN LIFE INS CO LTD	HI	568.1
PHYSICIANS LIFE INS CO	NE	1,685.6
STANDARD LIFE & ACCIDENT INS CO	TX	511.2
USABLE LIFE	AR	497.8
Rating: B+		
ALLIANZ LIFE INS CO OF NY	NY	3,530.0
AMERICAN FAMILY MUTL INS CO SI	WI	18,119.9
AMERICAN FIDELITY ASR CO	OK	6,256.2
AMERICAN UNITED LIFE INS CO	IN	29,538.7
ANTHEM LIFE INS CO	IN	759.7
ASSURITY LIFE INS CO	NE	2,750.1
AXA EQUITABLE LIFE INS CO	NY	201,023.4
BOSTON MUTUAL LIFE INS CO	MA	1,484.3
COMPANION LIFE INS CO	SC	420.6
DEARBORN NATIONAL LIFE INS CO	IL	1,669.0
DELAWARE AMERICAN LIFE INS CO	DE	119.0
FREEDOM LIFE INS CO OF AMERICA	TX	247.5
GERBER LIFE INS CO	NY	4,180.6
HUMANA BENEFIT PLAN OF ILLINOIS	IL	693.4
ILLINOIS MUTUAL LIFE INS CO	IL	1,507.2
MIDLAND NATIONAL LIFE INS CO	IA	58,679.0
MINNESOTA LIFE INS CO	MN	50,012.0
MUTUAL OF AMERICA LIFE INS CO	NY	21,688.9
NATIONAL CASUALTY CO	OH	493.4
NATIONAL FOUNDATION LIFE INS CO	TX	59.6
NORTH AMERICAN INS CO	WI	18.5
NORTHWESTERN MUTUAL LIFE INS CO	WI	278,047.4
OXFORD LIFE INS CO	AZ	2,251.8
PRINCIPAL LIFE INS CO	IA	196,332.3
STANDARD INS CO	OR	25,172.5
STANDARD SECURITY LIFE INS CO OF NY	NY	139.6
TRUSTMARK INS CO	IL	1,625.3
TRUSTMARK LIFE INS CO	IL	330.1
UNITED WORLD LIFE INS CO	NE	132.1
VOYA RETIREMENT INS & ANNUITY CO	CT	106,305.7

Montana

INSURANCE COMPANY NAME	DOM. STATE	TOTAL ASSETS ($MIL)
Rating: A+		
CHESAPEAKE LIFE INS CO	OK	213.1
COUNTRY LIFE INS CO	IL	9,777.7
PHYSICIANS MUTUAL INS CO	NE	2,391.2
TEACHERS INS & ANNUITY ASN OF AM	NY	307,655.9
Rating: A		
AMALGAMATED LIFE INS CO	NY	148.4
BERKLEY LIFE & HEALTH INS CO	IA	336.2
FEDERATED LIFE INS CO	MN	2,039.8
GARDEN STATE LIFE INS CO	TX	138.9
GUARDIAN LIFE INS CO OF AMERICA	NY	59,690.7
SENTRY LIFE INS CO	WI	7,524.4
USAA LIFE INS CO	TX	25,796.7
Rating: A-		
AMERICAN HEALTH & LIFE INS CO	TX	1,083.3
CHRISTIAN FIDELITY LIFE INS CO	TX	59.8
FIDELITY SECURITY LIFE INS CO	MO	970.0
GREAT SOUTHERN LIFE INS CO	TX	209.9
MADISON NATIONAL LIFE INS CO INC	WI	337.4
MASSACHUSETTS MUTUAL LIFE INS CO	MA	249,945.6
NATIONAL BENEFIT LIFE INS CO	NY	585.5
NEW YORK LIFE INS CO	NY	181,647.2
NIPPON LIFE INS CO OF AMERICA	IA	229.2
PACIFIC GUARDIAN LIFE INS CO LTD	HI	568.1
PHYSICIANS LIFE INS CO	NE	1,685.6
STANDARD LIFE & ACCIDENT INS CO	TX	511.2
USABLE LIFE	AR	497.8
Rating: B+		
AMERICAN FAMILY MUTL INS CO SI	WI	18,119.9
AMERICAN FIDELITY ASR CO	OK	6,256.2
AMERICAN UNITED LIFE INS CO	IN	29,538.7
ANTHEM LIFE INS CO	IN	759.7
ASSURITY LIFE INS CO	NE	2,750.1
AXA EQUITABLE LIFE INS CO	NY	201,023.4
BOSTON MUTUAL LIFE INS CO	MA	1,484.3
COMPANION LIFE INS CO	SC	420.6
DEARBORN NATIONAL LIFE INS CO	IL	1,669.0
DELAWARE AMERICAN LIFE INS CO	DE	119.0
FARM BUREAU LIFE INS CO	IA	9,174.1
GERBER LIFE INS CO	NY	4,180.6
HUMANA BENEFIT PLAN OF ILLINOIS	IL	693.4
ILLINOIS MUTUAL LIFE INS CO	IL	1,507.2
MIDLAND NATIONAL LIFE INS CO	IA	58,679.0
MINNESOTA LIFE INS CO	MN	50,012.0
MUTUAL OF AMERICA LIFE INS CO	NY	21,688.9
NATIONAL CASUALTY CO	OH	493.4
NATIONAL FOUNDATION LIFE INS CO	TX	59.6
NORTHWESTERN MUTUAL LIFE INS CO	WI	278,047.4
OXFORD LIFE INS CO	AZ	2,251.8
PRINCIPAL LIFE INS CO	IA	196,332.3
STANDARD INS CO	OR	25,172.5
STANDARD SECURITY LIFE INS CO OF NY	NY	139.6
TRUSTMARK INS CO	IL	1,625.3
TRUSTMARK LIFE INS CO	IL	330.1
UNITED WORLD LIFE INS CO	NE	132.1
VOYA RETIREMENT INS & ANNUITY CO	CT	106,305.7

Nebraska

INSURANCE COMPANY NAME	DOM. STATE	TOTAL ASSETS ($MIL)
Rating: A+		
CHESAPEAKE LIFE INS CO	OK	213.1
COUNTRY LIFE INS CO	IL	9,777.7
PHYSICIANS MUTUAL INS CO	NE	2,391.2
TEACHERS INS & ANNUITY ASN OF AM	NY	307,655.9
Rating: A		
AMALGAMATED LIFE INS CO	NY	148.4
BERKLEY LIFE & HEALTH INS CO	IA	336.2
FEDERATED LIFE INS CO	MN	2,039.8
GARDEN STATE LIFE INS CO	TX	138.9
GUARDIAN LIFE INS CO OF AMERICA	NY	59,690.7
SENTRY LIFE INS CO	WI	7,524.4
USAA LIFE INS CO	TX	25,796.7
Rating: A-		
AMERICAN HEALTH & LIFE INS CO	TX	1,083.3
CHRISTIAN FIDELITY LIFE INS CO	TX	59.8
FIDELITY SECURITY LIFE INS CO	MO	970.0
GREAT SOUTHERN LIFE INS CO	TX	209.9
MADISON NATIONAL LIFE INS CO INC	WI	337.4
MASSACHUSETTS MUTUAL LIFE INS CO	MA	249,945.6
NATIONAL BENEFIT LIFE INS CO	NY	585.5
NEW YORK LIFE INS CO	NY	181,647.2
NIPPON LIFE INS CO OF AMERICA	IA	229.2
PACIFIC GUARDIAN LIFE INS CO LTD	HI	568.1
PHYSICIANS LIFE INS CO	NE	1,685.6
STANDARD LIFE & ACCIDENT INS CO	TX	511.2
USABLE LIFE	AR	497.8
Rating: B+		
AMERICAN FAMILY MUTL INS CO SI	WI	18,119.9
AMERICAN FIDELITY ASR CO	OK	6,256.2
AMERICAN UNITED LIFE INS CO	IN	29,538.7
ANTHEM LIFE INS CO	IN	759.7
ASSURITY LIFE INS CO	NE	2,750.1
AXA EQUITABLE LIFE INS CO	NY	201,023.4
BOSTON MUTUAL LIFE INS CO	MA	1,484.3
COMPANION LIFE INS CO	SC	420.6
DEARBORN NATIONAL LIFE INS CO	IL	1,669.0
DELAWARE AMERICAN LIFE INS CO	DE	119.0
FARM BUREAU LIFE INS CO	IA	9,174.1
FREEDOM LIFE INS CO OF AMERICA	TX	247.5
GERBER LIFE INS CO	NY	4,180.6
HEALTHPARTNERS INS CO	MN	416.8
HUMANA BENEFIT PLAN OF ILLINOIS	IL	693.4
ILLINOIS MUTUAL LIFE INS CO	IL	1,507.2
MIDLAND NATIONAL LIFE INS CO	IA	58,679.0
MINNESOTA LIFE INS CO	MN	50,012.0
MUTUAL OF AMERICA LIFE INS CO	NY	21,688.9
NATIONAL CASUALTY CO	OH	493.4
NATIONAL FOUNDATION LIFE INS CO	TX	59.6
NORTHWESTERN MUTUAL LIFE INS CO	WI	278,047.4
OXFORD LIFE INS CO	AZ	2,251.8
PRINCIPAL LIFE INS CO	IA	196,332.3
STANDARD INS CO	OR	25,172.5
STANDARD SECURITY LIFE INS CO OF NY	NY	139.6
TRUSTMARK INS CO	IL	1,625.3
TRUSTMARK LIFE INS CO	IL	330.1
UNITED WORLD LIFE INS CO	NE	132.1
VOYA RETIREMENT INS & ANNUITY CO	CT	106,305.7

Nevada

INSURANCE COMPANY NAME	DOM. STATE	TOTAL ASSETS ($MIL)
Rating: A+		
CHESAPEAKE LIFE INS CO	OK	213.1
COUNTRY LIFE INS CO	IL	9,777.7
PHYSICIANS MUTUAL INS CO	NE	2,391.2
TEACHERS INS & ANNUITY ASN OF AM	NY	307,655.9
Rating: A		
AMALGAMATED LIFE INS CO	NY	148.4
BERKLEY LIFE & HEALTH INS CO	IA	336.2
FEDERATED LIFE INS CO	MN	2,039.8
GARDEN STATE LIFE INS CO	TX	138.9
GUARDIAN LIFE INS CO OF AMERICA	NY	59,690.7
SENTRY LIFE INS CO	WI	7,524.4
USAA LIFE INS CO	TX	25,796.7
Rating: A-		
AMERICAN HEALTH & LIFE INS CO	TX	1,083.3
CHRISTIAN FIDELITY LIFE INS CO	TX	59.8
FIDELITY SECURITY LIFE INS CO	MO	970.0
GREAT SOUTHERN LIFE INS CO	TX	209.9
MADISON NATIONAL LIFE INS CO INC	WI	337.4
MASSACHUSETTS MUTUAL LIFE INS CO	MA	249,945.6
NATIONAL BENEFIT LIFE INS CO	NY	585.5
NEW YORK LIFE INS CO	NY	181,647.2
NIPPON LIFE INS CO OF AMERICA	IA	229.2
PACIFIC GUARDIAN LIFE INS CO LTD	HI	568.1
PHYSICIANS LIFE INS CO	NE	1,685.6
STANDARD LIFE & ACCIDENT INS CO	TX	511.2
USABLE LIFE	AR	497.8
Rating: B+		
AMERICAN FAMILY MUTL INS CO SI	WI	18,119.9
AMERICAN FIDELITY ASR CO	OK	6,256.2
AMERICAN UNITED LIFE INS CO	IN	29,538.7
ANTHEM LIFE INS CO	IN	759.7
ASSURITY LIFE INS CO	NE	2,750.1
AXA EQUITABLE LIFE INS CO	NY	201,023.4
BOSTON MUTUAL LIFE INS CO	MA	1,484.3
COMPANION LIFE INS CO	SC	420.6
DEARBORN NATIONAL LIFE INS CO	IL	1,669.0
DELAWARE AMERICAN LIFE INS CO	DE	119.0
FARM BUREAU LIFE INS CO	IA	9,174.1
FREEDOM LIFE INS CO OF AMERICA	TX	247.5
GERBER LIFE INS CO	NY	4,180.6
HEALTH PLAN OF NEVADA INC	NV	708.2
HUMANA BENEFIT PLAN OF ILLINOIS	IL	693.4
ILLINOIS MUTUAL LIFE INS CO	IL	1,507.2
MIDLAND NATIONAL LIFE INS CO	IA	58,679.0
MINNESOTA LIFE INS CO	MN	50,012.0
MUTUAL OF AMERICA LIFE INS CO	NY	21,688.9
NATIONAL CASUALTY CO	OH	493.4
NATIONAL FOUNDATION LIFE INS CO	TX	59.6
NORTHWESTERN MUTUAL LIFE INS CO	WI	278,047.4
OXFORD LIFE INS CO	AZ	2,251.8
PRINCIPAL LIFE INS CO	IA	196,332.3
STANDARD INS CO	OR	25,172.5
STANDARD SECURITY LIFE INS CO OF NY	NY	139.6
TRUSTMARK INS CO	IL	1,625.3
TRUSTMARK LIFE INS CO	IL	330.1
UNITED WORLD LIFE INS CO	NE	132.1
VOYA RETIREMENT INS & ANNUITY CO	CT	106,305.7

New Hampshire

INSURANCE COMPANY NAME	DOM. STATE	TOTAL ASSETS ($MIL)
Rating: A+		
CHESAPEAKE LIFE INS CO	OK	213.1
PHYSICIANS MUTUAL INS CO	NE	2,391.2
TEACHERS INS & ANNUITY ASN OF AM	NY	307,655.9
Rating: A		
AMALGAMATED LIFE INS CO	NY	148.4
BERKLEY LIFE & HEALTH INS CO	IA	336.2
FEDERATED LIFE INS CO	MN	2,039.8
GARDEN STATE LIFE INS CO	TX	138.9
GUARDIAN LIFE INS CO OF AMERICA	NY	59,690.7
SENTRY LIFE INS CO	WI	7,524.4
UNITED FARM FAMILY LIFE INS CO	IN	2,373.1
USAA LIFE INS CO	TX	25,796.7
Rating: A-		
AMERICAN HEALTH & LIFE INS CO	TX	1,083.3
FIDELITY SECURITY LIFE INS CO	MO	970.0
MADISON NATIONAL LIFE INS CO INC	WI	337.4
MASSACHUSETTS MUTUAL LIFE INS CO	MA	249,945.6
NATIONAL BENEFIT LIFE INS CO	NY	585.5
NEW YORK LIFE INS CO	NY	181,647.2
PHYSICIANS LIFE INS CO	NE	1,685.6
USABLE LIFE	AR	497.8
Rating: B+		
AMERICAN FIDELITY ASR CO	OK	6,256.2
AMERICAN UNITED LIFE INS CO	IN	29,538.7
ANTHEM LIFE INS CO	IN	759.7
ASSURITY LIFE INS CO	NE	2,750.1
AXA EQUITABLE LIFE INS CO	NY	201,023.4
BOSTON MUTUAL LIFE INS CO	MA	1,484.3
COMPANION LIFE INS CO	SC	420.6
DEARBORN NATIONAL LIFE INS CO	IL	1,669.0
DELAWARE AMERICAN LIFE INS CO	DE	119.0
GERBER LIFE INS CO	NY	4,180.6
HUMANA BENEFIT PLAN OF ILLINOIS	IL	693.4
ILLINOIS MUTUAL LIFE INS CO	IL	1,507.2
MIDLAND NATIONAL LIFE INS CO	IA	58,679.0
MINNESOTA LIFE INS CO	MN	50,012.0
MUTUAL OF AMERICA LIFE INS CO	NY	21,688.9
NATIONAL CASUALTY CO	OH	493.4
NORTHWESTERN MUTUAL LIFE INS CO	WI	278,047.4
OXFORD LIFE INS CO	AZ	2,251.8
PRINCIPAL LIFE INS CO	IA	196,332.3
STANDARD INS CO	OR	25,172.5
STANDARD SECURITY LIFE INS CO OF NY	NY	139.6
TRUSTMARK INS CO	IL	1,625.3
TRUSTMARK LIFE INS CO	IL	330.1
UNITED WORLD LIFE INS CO	NE	132.1
VOYA RETIREMENT INS & ANNUITY CO	CT	106,305.7

New Jersey

INSURANCE COMPANY NAME	DOM. STATE	TOTAL ASSETS ($MIL)
Rating: A+		
PHYSICIANS MUTUAL INS CO	NE	2,391.2
TEACHERS INS & ANNUITY ASN OF AM	NY	307,655.9
Rating: A		
AMALGAMATED LIFE INS CO	NY	148.4
BERKLEY LIFE & HEALTH INS CO	IA	336.2
FEDERATED LIFE INS CO	MN	2,039.8
GARDEN STATE LIFE INS CO	TX	138.9
GUARDIAN LIFE INS CO OF AMERICA	NY	59,690.7
SENTRY LIFE INS CO	WI	7,524.4
SHELTERPOINT LIFE INS CO	NY	183.5
UNITED FARM FAMILY LIFE INS CO	IN	2,373.1
USAA LIFE INS CO	TX	25,796.7
Rating: A-		
AMERICAN FAMILY LIFE ASR CO OF NY	NY	978.2
AMERICAN HEALTH & LIFE INS CO	TX	1,083.3
AMERIGROUP NEW JERSEY INC	NJ	324.9
FIDELITY SECURITY LIFE INS CO	MO	970.0
GREAT SOUTHERN LIFE INS CO	TX	209.9
MADISON NATIONAL LIFE INS CO INC	WI	337.4
MASSACHUSETTS MUTUAL LIFE INS CO	MA	249,945.6
NATIONAL BENEFIT LIFE INS CO	NY	585.5
NEW YORK LIFE INS CO	NY	181,647.2
NIPPON LIFE INS CO OF AMERICA	IA	229.2
PHYSICIANS LIFE INS CO	NE	1,685.6
USABLE LIFE	AR	497.8
Rating: B+		
AMERICAN FIDELITY ASR CO	OK	6,256.2
AMERICAN UNITED LIFE INS CO	IN	29,538.7
ANTHEM LIFE INS CO	IN	759.7
ASSURITY LIFE INS CO	NE	2,750.1
AXA EQUITABLE LIFE INS CO	NY	201,023.4
BOSTON MUTUAL LIFE INS CO	MA	1,484.3
DEARBORN NATIONAL LIFE INS CO	IL	1,669.0
DELAWARE AMERICAN LIFE INS CO	DE	119.0
GEISINGER HEALTH PLAN	PA	663.7
GERBER LIFE INS CO	NY	4,180.6
HUMANA BENEFIT PLAN OF ILLINOIS	IL	693.4
ILLINOIS MUTUAL LIFE INS CO	IL	1,507.2
MIDLAND NATIONAL LIFE INS CO	IA	58,679.0
MINNESOTA LIFE INS CO	MN	50,012.0
MUTUAL OF AMERICA LIFE INS CO	NY	21,688.9
NATIONAL CASUALTY CO	OH	493.4
NORTHWESTERN MUTUAL LIFE INS CO	WI	278,047.4
OXFORD LIFE INS CO	AZ	2,251.8
PRINCIPAL LIFE INS CO	IA	196,332.3
STANDARD INS CO	OR	25,172.5
STANDARD SECURITY LIFE INS CO OF NY	NY	139.6
TRUSTMARK INS CO	IL	1,625.3
TRUSTMARK LIFE INS CO	IL	330.1
UNITED WORLD LIFE INS CO	NE	132.1
VOYA RETIREMENT INS & ANNUITY CO	CT	106,305.7

New Mexico

INSURANCE COMPANY NAME	DOM. STATE	TOTAL ASSETS ($MIL)
Rating: A+		
CHESAPEAKE LIFE INS CO	OK	213.1
COUNTRY LIFE INS CO	IL	9,777.7
PHYSICIANS MUTUAL INS CO	NE	2,391.2
TEACHERS INS & ANNUITY ASN OF AM	NY	307,655.9
Rating: A		
AMALGAMATED LIFE INS CO	NY	148.4
BERKLEY LIFE & HEALTH INS CO	IA	336.2
FEDERATED LIFE INS CO	MN	2,039.8
GARDEN STATE LIFE INS CO	TX	138.9
GUARDIAN LIFE INS CO OF AMERICA	NY	59,690.7
SENTRY LIFE INS CO	WI	7,524.4
USAA LIFE INS CO	TX	25,796.7
Rating: A-		
AMERICAN HEALTH & LIFE INS CO	TX	1,083.3
CHRISTIAN FIDELITY LIFE INS CO	TX	59.8
FIDELITY SECURITY LIFE INS CO	MO	970.0
GREAT SOUTHERN LIFE INS CO	TX	209.9
MADISON NATIONAL LIFE INS CO INC	WI	337.4
MASSACHUSETTS MUTUAL LIFE INS CO	MA	249,945.6
NATIONAL BENEFIT LIFE INS CO	NY	585.5
NEW YORK LIFE INS CO	NY	181,647.2
NIPPON LIFE INS CO OF AMERICA	IA	229.2
PACIFIC GUARDIAN LIFE INS CO LTD	HI	568.1
PHYSICIANS LIFE INS CO	NE	1,685.6
STANDARD LIFE & ACCIDENT INS CO	TX	511.2
USABLE LIFE	AR	497.8
Rating: B+		
AMERICAN FAMILY MUTL INS CO SI	WI	18,119.9
AMERICAN FIDELITY ASR CO	OK	6,256.2
AMERICAN UNITED LIFE INS CO	IN	29,538.7
ANTHEM LIFE INS CO	IN	759.7
ASSURITY LIFE INS CO	NE	2,750.1
AXA EQUITABLE LIFE INS CO	NY	201,023.4
BOSTON MUTUAL LIFE INS CO	MA	1,484.3
COMPANION LIFE INS CO	SC	420.6
DEARBORN NATIONAL LIFE INS CO	IL	1,669.0
DELAWARE AMERICAN LIFE INS CO	DE	119.0
FARM BUREAU LIFE INS CO	IA	9,174.1
FREEDOM LIFE INS CO OF AMERICA	TX	247.5
GERBER LIFE INS CO	NY	4,180.6
HUMANA BENEFIT PLAN OF ILLINOIS	IL	693.4
ILLINOIS MUTUAL LIFE INS CO	IL	1,507.2
MIDLAND NATIONAL LIFE INS CO	IA	58,679.0
MINNESOTA LIFE INS CO	MN	50,012.0
MUTUAL OF AMERICA LIFE INS CO	NY	21,688.9
NATIONAL CASUALTY CO	OH	493.4
NATIONAL FOUNDATION LIFE INS CO	TX	59.6
NORTH AMERICAN INS CO	WI	18.5
NORTHWESTERN MUTUAL LIFE INS CO	WI	278,047.4
OXFORD LIFE INS CO	AZ	2,251.8
PRINCIPAL LIFE INS CO	IA	196,332.3
STANDARD INS CO	OR	25,172.5
STANDARD SECURITY LIFE INS CO OF NY	NY	139.6
TRUSTMARK INS CO	IL	1,625.3
TRUSTMARK LIFE INS CO	IL	330.1
UNITED WORLD LIFE INS CO	NE	132.1
VOYA RETIREMENT INS & ANNUITY CO	CT	106,305.7

New York

INSURANCE COMPANY NAME	DOM. STATE	TOTAL ASSETS ($MIL)
Rating: A+		
PHYSICIANS MUTUAL INS CO	NE	2,391.2
TEACHERS INS & ANNUITY ASN OF AM	NY	307,655.9
Rating: A		
AMALGAMATED LIFE INS CO	NY	148.4
BERKLEY LIFE & HEALTH INS CO	IA	336.2
CAPITAL DISTRICT PHYSICIANS HEALTH P	NY	621.6
FEDERATED LIFE INS CO	MN	2,039.8
GARDEN STATE LIFE INS CO	TX	138.9
GUARDIAN LIFE INS CO OF AMERICA	NY	59,690.7
SHELTERPOINT LIFE INS CO	NY	183.5
Rating: A-		
AMERICAN FAMILY LIFE ASR CO OF NY	NY	978.2
CIGNA LIFE INS CO OF NEW YORK	NY	419.6
FIDELITY SECURITY LIFE INS CO	MO	970.0
FIRST RELIANCE STANDARD LIFE INS CO	NY	218.0
LIFE INS CO OF BOSTON & NEW YORK	NY	163.1
MASSACHUSETTS MUTUAL LIFE INS CO	MA	249,945.6
NATIONAL BENEFIT LIFE INS CO	NY	585.5
NEW YORK LIFE INS CO	NY	181,647.2
NIPPON LIFE INS CO OF AMERICA	IA	229.2
STANDARD LIFE INS CO OF NY	NY	304.9
Rating: B+		
ALLIANZ LIFE INS CO OF NY	NY	3,530.0
AMERICAN UNITED LIFE INS CO	IN	29,538.7
AXA EQUITABLE LIFE INS CO	NY	201,023.4
BOSTON MUTUAL LIFE INS CO	MA	1,484.3
DEARBORN NATIONAL LIFE INS CO OF NY	NY	21.1
DELAWARE AMERICAN LIFE INS CO	DE	119.0
FIDELITY SECURITY LIFE INS CO OF NY	NY	39.6
GERBER LIFE INS CO	NY	4,180.6
MUTUAL OF AMERICA LIFE INS CO	NY	21,688.9
NATIONAL CASUALTY CO	OH	493.4
NATIONAL INCOME LIFE INS CO	NY	280.7
NORTHWESTERN MUTUAL LIFE INS CO	WI	278,047.4
PRINCIPAL LIFE INS CO	IA	196,332.3
STANDARD SECURITY LIFE INS CO OF NY	NY	139.6
TRUSTMARK INS CO	IL	1,625.3
TRUSTMARK LIFE INS CO	IL	330.1
UNITED HEALTHCARE OF NY INC	NY	1,443.0
VOYA RETIREMENT INS & ANNUITY CO	CT	106,305.7

North Carolina

INSURANCE COMPANY NAME	DOM. STATE	TOTAL ASSETS ($MIL)
Rating: A+		
CHESAPEAKE LIFE INS CO	OK	213.1
COUNTRY LIFE INS CO	IL	9,777.7
PHYSICIANS MUTUAL INS CO	NE	2,391.2
TEACHERS INS & ANNUITY ASN OF AM	NY	307,655.9
Rating: A		
AMALGAMATED LIFE INS CO	NY	148.4
BERKLEY LIFE & HEALTH INS CO	IA	336.2
FEDERATED LIFE INS CO	MN	2,039.8
GARDEN STATE LIFE INS CO	TX	138.9
GUARDIAN LIFE INS CO OF AMERICA	NY	59,690.7
MEDICAL MUTUAL OF OHIO	OH	2,490.1
SENTRY LIFE INS CO	WI	7,524.4
SHELTERPOINT LIFE INS CO	NY	183.5
SOUTHERN FARM BUREAU LIFE INS CO	MS	14,368.9
UNITED FARM FAMILY LIFE INS CO	IN	2,373.1
USAA LIFE INS CO	TX	25,796.7
Rating: A-		
AMERICAN HEALTH & LIFE INS CO	TX	1,083.3
FIDELITY SECURITY LIFE INS CO	MO	970.0
GREAT SOUTHERN LIFE INS CO	TX	209.9
HUMANA MEDICAL PLAN INC	FL	2,319.2
MADISON NATIONAL LIFE INS CO INC	WI	337.4
MASSACHUSETTS MUTUAL LIFE INS CO	MA	249,945.6
NATIONAL BENEFIT LIFE INS CO	NY	585.5
NEW YORK LIFE INS CO	NY	181,647.2
NIPPON LIFE INS CO OF AMERICA	IA	229.2
PHYSICIANS LIFE INS CO	NE	1,685.6
STANDARD LIFE & ACCIDENT INS CO	TX	511.2
USABLE LIFE	AR	497.8
Rating: B+		
AMERICAN FAMILY MUTL INS CO SI	WI	18,119.9
AMERICAN FIDELITY ASR CO	OK	6,256.2
AMERICAN UNITED LIFE INS CO	IN	29,538.7
ANTHEM LIFE INS CO	IN	759.7
ASSURITY LIFE INS CO	NE	2,750.1
AXA EQUITABLE LIFE INS CO	NY	201,023.4
BLUE CROSS BLUE SHIELD OF NC	NC	6,006.9
BOSTON MUTUAL LIFE INS CO	MA	1,484.3
COMPANION LIFE INS CO	SC	420.6
DEARBORN NATIONAL LIFE INS CO	IL	1,669.0
DELAWARE AMERICAN LIFE INS CO	DE	119.0
FREEDOM LIFE INS CO OF AMERICA	TX	247.5
GERBER LIFE INS CO	NY	4,180.6
HUMANA BENEFIT PLAN OF ILLINOIS	IL	693.4
ILLINOIS MUTUAL LIFE INS CO	IL	1,507.2
MIDLAND NATIONAL LIFE INS CO	IA	58,679.0
MINNESOTA LIFE INS CO	MN	50,012.0
MUTUAL OF AMERICA LIFE INS CO	NY	21,688.9
NATIONAL CASUALTY CO	OH	493.4
NATIONAL FOUNDATION LIFE INS CO	TX	59.6
NORTHWESTERN MUTUAL LIFE INS CO	WI	278,047.4
OXFORD LIFE INS CO	AZ	2,251.8
PRINCIPAL LIFE INS CO	IA	196,332.3
STANDARD INS CO	OR	25,172.5
STANDARD SECURITY LIFE INS CO OF NY	NY	139.6
TRUSTMARK INS CO	IL	1,625.3
TRUSTMARK LIFE INS CO	IL	330.1
UNITED HEALTHCARE OF WISCONSIN INC	WI	2,025.5
UNITED WORLD LIFE INS CO	NE	132.1
VOYA RETIREMENT INS & ANNUITY CO	CT	106,305.7

North Dakota

INSURANCE COMPANY NAME	DOM. STATE	TOTAL ASSETS ($MIL)
Rating: A+		
CHESAPEAKE LIFE INS CO	OK	213.1
COUNTRY LIFE INS CO	IL	9,777.7
PHYSICIANS MUTUAL INS CO	NE	2,391.2
TEACHERS INS & ANNUITY ASN OF AM	NY	307,655.9
Rating: A		
AMALGAMATED LIFE INS CO	NY	148.4
BERKLEY LIFE & HEALTH INS CO	IA	336.2
FEDERATED LIFE INS CO	MN	2,039.8
GARDEN STATE LIFE INS CO	TX	138.9
GUARDIAN LIFE INS CO OF AMERICA	NY	59,690.7
SENTRY LIFE INS CO	WI	7,524.4
UNITED FARM FAMILY LIFE INS CO	IN	2,373.1
USAA LIFE INS CO	TX	25,796.7
Rating: A-		
AMERICAN FAMILY LIFE ASR CO OF NY	NY	978.2
AMERICAN HEALTH & LIFE INS CO	TX	1,083.3
CHRISTIAN FIDELITY LIFE INS CO	TX	59.8
FIDELITY SECURITY LIFE INS CO	MO	970.0
GREAT SOUTHERN LIFE INS CO	TX	209.9
MADISON NATIONAL LIFE INS CO INC	WI	337.4
MASSACHUSETTS MUTUAL LIFE INS CO	MA	249,945.6
NATIONAL BENEFIT LIFE INS CO	NY	585.5
NEW YORK LIFE INS CO	NY	181,647.2
NIPPON LIFE INS CO OF AMERICA	IA	229.2
PHYSICIANS LIFE INS CO	NE	1,685.6
STANDARD LIFE & ACCIDENT INS CO	TX	511.2
USABLE LIFE	AR	497.8
Rating: B+		
ALLIANZ LIFE INS CO OF NY	NY	3,530.0
AMERICAN FAMILY MUTL INS CO SI	WI	18,119.9
AMERICAN FIDELITY ASR CO	OK	6,256.2
AMERICAN UNITED LIFE INS CO	IN	29,538.7
ANTHEM LIFE INS CO	IN	759.7
ASSURITY LIFE INS CO	NE	2,750.1
AXA EQUITABLE LIFE INS CO	NY	201,023.4
BOSTON MUTUAL LIFE INS CO	MA	1,484.3
COMPANION LIFE INS CO	SC	420.6
DEARBORN NATIONAL LIFE INS CO	IL	1,669.0
DELAWARE AMERICAN LIFE INS CO	DE	119.0
FARM BUREAU LIFE INS CO	IA	9,174.1
GERBER LIFE INS CO	NY	4,180.6
HEALTHPARTNERS INS CO	MN	416.8
HUMANA BENEFIT PLAN OF ILLINOIS	IL	693.4
ILLINOIS MUTUAL LIFE INS CO	IL	1,507.2
MIDLAND NATIONAL LIFE INS CO	IA	58,679.0
MINNESOTA LIFE INS CO	MN	50,012.0
MUTUAL OF AMERICA LIFE INS CO	NY	21,688.9
NATIONAL CASUALTY CO	OH	493.4
NATIONAL FOUNDATION LIFE INS CO	TX	59.6
NORTH AMERICAN INS CO	WI	18.5
NORTHWESTERN MUTUAL LIFE INS CO	WI	278,047.4
OXFORD LIFE INS CO	AZ	2,251.8
PRINCIPAL LIFE INS CO	IA	196,332.3
STANDARD INS CO	OR	25,172.5
STANDARD SECURITY LIFE INS CO OF NY	NY	139.6
TRUSTMARK INS CO	IL	1,625.3
TRUSTMARK LIFE INS CO	IL	330.1
UNITED WORLD LIFE INS CO	NE	132.1
VOYA RETIREMENT INS & ANNUITY CO	CT	106,305.7

Ohio

INSURANCE COMPANY NAME	DOM. STATE	TOTAL ASSETS ($MIL)
Rating: A+		
CHESAPEAKE LIFE INS CO	OK	213.1
COUNTRY LIFE INS CO	IL	9,777.7
PHYSICIANS MUTUAL INS CO	NE	2,391.2
TEACHERS INS & ANNUITY ASN OF AM	NY	307,655.9
Rating: A		
AMALGAMATED LIFE INS CO	NY	148.4
BERKLEY LIFE & HEALTH INS CO	IA	336.2
FEDERATED LIFE INS CO	MN	2,039.8
GARDEN STATE LIFE INS CO	TX	138.9
GUARDIAN LIFE INS CO OF AMERICA	NY	59,690.7
MEDICAL MUTUAL OF OHIO	OH	2,490.1
SENTRY LIFE INS CO	WI	7,524.4
UNITED FARM FAMILY LIFE INS CO	IN	2,373.1
USAA LIFE INS CO	TX	25,796.7
Rating: A-		
AMERICAN HEALTH & LIFE INS CO	TX	1,083.3
CHRISTIAN FIDELITY LIFE INS CO	TX	59.8
FIDELITY SECURITY LIFE INS CO	MO	970.0
GREAT SOUTHERN LIFE INS CO	TX	209.9
KAISER PERMANENTE INS CO	CA	197.7
MADISON NATIONAL LIFE INS CO INC	WI	337.4
MASSACHUSETTS MUTUAL LIFE INS CO	MA	249,945.6
NATIONAL BENEFIT LIFE INS CO	NY	585.5
NEW YORK LIFE INS CO	NY	181,647.2
NIPPON LIFE INS CO OF AMERICA	IA	229.2
PARAMOUNT INS CO (OH)	OH	87.0
PHYSICIANS LIFE INS CO	NE	1,685.6
STANDARD LIFE & ACCIDENT INS CO	TX	511.2
USABLE LIFE	AR	497.8
Rating: B+		
AMERICAN FAMILY MUTL INS CO SI	WI	18,119.9
AMERICAN FIDELITY ASR CO	OK	6,256.2
AMERICAN UNITED LIFE INS CO	IN	29,538.7
ANTHEM LIFE INS CO	IN	759.7
ASSURITY LIFE INS CO	NE	2,750.1
AXA EQUITABLE LIFE INS CO	NY	201,023.4
BOSTON MUTUAL LIFE INS CO	MA	1,484.3
COMPANION LIFE INS CO	SC	420.6
DEARBORN NATIONAL LIFE INS CO	IL	1,669.0
DELAWARE AMERICAN LIFE INS CO	DE	119.0
FREEDOM LIFE INS CO OF AMERICA	TX	247.5
GERBER LIFE INS CO	NY	4,180.6
HUMANA BENEFIT PLAN OF ILLINOIS	IL	693.4
ILLINOIS MUTUAL LIFE INS CO	IL	1,507.2
MIDLAND NATIONAL LIFE INS CO	IA	58,679.0
MINNESOTA LIFE INS CO	MN	50,012.0
MUTUAL OF AMERICA LIFE INS CO	NY	21,688.9
NATIONAL CASUALTY CO	OH	493.4
NATIONAL FOUNDATION LIFE INS CO	TX	59.6
NORTH AMERICAN INS CO	WI	18.5
NORTHWESTERN MUTUAL LIFE INS CO	WI	278,047.4
OXFORD LIFE INS CO	AZ	2,251.8
PRINCIPAL LIFE INS CO	IA	196,332.3
STANDARD INS CO	OR	25,172.5
STANDARD SECURITY LIFE INS CO OF NY	NY	139.6
TRUSTMARK INS CO	IL	1,625.3
TRUSTMARK LIFE INS CO	IL	330.1
UNITED HEALTHCARE OF WISCONSIN INC	WI	2,025.5
UNITED WORLD LIFE INS CO	NE	132.1
VOYA RETIREMENT INS & ANNUITY CO	CT	106,305.7

Oklahoma

INSURANCE COMPANY NAME	DOM. STATE	TOTAL ASSETS ($MIL)
Rating: A+		
CHESAPEAKE LIFE INS CO	OK	213.1
COUNTRY LIFE INS CO	IL	9,777.7
PHYSICIANS MUTUAL INS CO	NE	2,391.2
TEACHERS INS & ANNUITY ASN OF AM	NY	307,655.9
Rating: A		
AMALGAMATED LIFE INS CO	NY	148.4
BERKLEY LIFE & HEALTH INS CO	IA	336.2
FEDERATED LIFE INS CO	MN	2,039.8
GARDEN STATE LIFE INS CO	TX	138.9
GUARDIAN LIFE INS CO OF AMERICA	NY	59,690.7
SENTRY LIFE INS CO	WI	7,524.4
USAA LIFE INS CO	TX	25,796.7
Rating: A-		
AMERICAN HEALTH & LIFE INS CO	TX	1,083.3
CHRISTIAN FIDELITY LIFE INS CO	TX	59.8
FIDELITY SECURITY LIFE INS CO	MO	970.0
GREAT SOUTHERN LIFE INS CO	TX	209.9
MADISON NATIONAL LIFE INS CO INC	WI	337.4
MASSACHUSETTS MUTUAL LIFE INS CO	MA	249,945.6
NATIONAL BENEFIT LIFE INS CO	NY	585.5
NEW YORK LIFE INS CO	NY	181,647.2
NIPPON LIFE INS CO OF AMERICA	IA	229.2
PACIFIC GUARDIAN LIFE INS CO LTD	HI	568.1
PHYSICIANS LIFE INS CO	NE	1,685.6
STANDARD LIFE & ACCIDENT INS CO	TX	511.2
SWBC LIFE INS CO	TX	33.5
USABLE LIFE	AR	497.8
Rating: B+		
AMERICAN FIDELITY ASR CO	OK	6,256.2
AMERICAN UNITED LIFE INS CO	IN	29,538.7
ANTHEM LIFE INS CO	IN	759.7
ASSURITY LIFE INS CO	NE	2,750.1
AXA EQUITABLE LIFE INS CO	NY	201,023.4
BOSTON MUTUAL LIFE INS CO	MA	1,484.3
COMPANION LIFE INS CO	SC	420.6
DEARBORN NATIONAL LIFE INS CO	IL	1,669.0
DELAWARE AMERICAN LIFE INS CO	DE	119.0
FARM BUREAU LIFE INS CO	IA	9,174.1
FREEDOM LIFE INS CO OF AMERICA	TX	247.5
GERBER LIFE INS CO	NY	4,180.6
HUMANA BENEFIT PLAN OF ILLINOIS	IL	693.4
ILLINOIS MUTUAL LIFE INS CO	IL	1,507.2
MIDLAND NATIONAL LIFE INS CO	IA	58,679.0
MINNESOTA LIFE INS CO	MN	50,012.0
MUTUAL OF AMERICA LIFE INS CO	NY	21,688.9
NATIONAL CASUALTY CO	OH	493.4
NATIONAL FOUNDATION LIFE INS CO	TX	59.6
NORTH AMERICAN INS CO	WI	18.5
NORTHWESTERN MUTUAL LIFE INS CO	WI	278,047.4
OXFORD LIFE INS CO	AZ	2,251.8
PRINCIPAL LIFE INS CO	IA	196,332.3
STANDARD INS CO	OR	25,172.5
STANDARD SECURITY LIFE INS CO OF NY	NY	139.6
TRUSTMARK INS CO	IL	1,625.3
TRUSTMARK LIFE INS CO	IL	330.1
UNITED WORLD LIFE INS CO	NE	132.1
VOYA RETIREMENT INS & ANNUITY CO	CT	106,305.7

Oregon

INSURANCE COMPANY NAME	DOM. STATE	TOTAL ASSETS ($MIL)
Rating: A+		
CHESAPEAKE LIFE INS CO	OK	213.1
COUNTRY LIFE INS CO	IL	9,777.7
PHYSICIANS MUTUAL INS CO	NE	2,391.2
TEACHERS INS & ANNUITY ASN OF AM	NY	307,655.9
Rating: A		
AMALGAMATED LIFE INS CO	NY	148.4
BERKLEY LIFE & HEALTH INS CO	IA	336.2
FEDERATED LIFE INS CO	MN	2,039.8
GARDEN STATE LIFE INS CO	TX	138.9
GUARDIAN LIFE INS CO OF AMERICA	NY	59,690.7
LIFEWISE ASR CO	WA	215.9
SENTRY LIFE INS CO	WI	7,524.4
USAA LIFE INS CO	TX	25,796.7
Rating: A-		
AMERICAN HEALTH & LIFE INS CO	TX	1,083.3
CHRISTIAN FIDELITY LIFE INS CO	TX	59.8
FIDELITY SECURITY LIFE INS CO	MO	970.0
GREAT SOUTHERN LIFE INS CO	TX	209.9
HUMANA MEDICAL PLAN INC	FL	2,319.2
KAISER PERMANENTE INS CO	CA	197.7
MADISON NATIONAL LIFE INS CO INC	WI	337.4
MASSACHUSETTS MUTUAL LIFE INS CO	MA	249,945.6
NATIONAL BENEFIT LIFE INS CO	NY	585.5
NEW YORK LIFE INS CO	NY	181,647.2
NIPPON LIFE INS CO OF AMERICA	IA	229.2
PACIFIC GUARDIAN LIFE INS CO LTD	HI	568.1
PHYSICIANS LIFE INS CO	NE	1,685.6
PROVIDENCE HEALTH ASR	OR	457.3
REGENCE BL CROSS BL SHIELD OREGON	OR	1,319.0
STANDARD LIFE & ACCIDENT INS CO	TX	511.2
USABLE LIFE	AR	497.8
Rating: B+		
AMERICAN FAMILY MUTL INS CO SI	WI	18,119.9
AMERICAN FIDELITY ASR CO	OK	6,256.2
AMERICAN UNITED LIFE INS CO	IN	29,538.7
ANTHEM LIFE INS CO	IN	759.7
ASSURITY LIFE INS CO	NE	2,750.1
AXA EQUITABLE LIFE INS CO	NY	201,023.4
BOSTON MUTUAL LIFE INS CO	MA	1,484.3
COMPANION LIFE INS CO	SC	420.6
DEARBORN NATIONAL LIFE INS CO	IL	1,669.0
DELAWARE AMERICAN LIFE INS CO	DE	119.0
FARM BUREAU LIFE INS CO	IA	9,174.1
FREEDOM LIFE INS CO OF AMERICA	TX	247.5
GERBER LIFE INS CO	NY	4,180.6
HUMANA BENEFIT PLAN OF ILLINOIS	IL	693.4
ILLINOIS MUTUAL LIFE INS CO	IL	1,507.2
MIDLAND NATIONAL LIFE INS CO	IA	58,679.0
MINNESOTA LIFE INS CO	MN	50,012.0
MUTUAL OF AMERICA LIFE INS CO	NY	21,688.9
NATIONAL CASUALTY CO	OH	493.4
NATIONAL FOUNDATION LIFE INS CO	TX	59.6
NORTH AMERICAN INS CO	WI	18.5
NORTHWESTERN MUTUAL LIFE INS CO	WI	278,047.4
OXFORD LIFE INS CO	AZ	2,251.8
PRINCIPAL LIFE INS CO	IA	196,332.3
STANDARD INS CO	OR	25,172.5
STANDARD SECURITY LIFE INS CO OF NY	NY	139.6
TRUSTMARK INS CO	IL	1,625.3
TRUSTMARK LIFE INS CO	IL	330.1
UNITED WORLD LIFE INS CO	NE	132.1
UNITEDHEALTHCARE OF OREGON	OR	462.8
VOYA RETIREMENT INS & ANNUITY CO	CT	106,305.7

Pennsylvania

INSURANCE COMPANY NAME	DOM. STATE	TOTAL ASSETS ($MIL)
Rating: A+		
CHESAPEAKE LIFE INS CO	OK	213.1
COUNTRY LIFE INS CO	IL	9,777.7
PHYSICIANS MUTUAL INS CO	NE	2,391.2
TEACHERS INS & ANNUITY ASN OF AM	NY	307,655.9
Rating: A		
AMALGAMATED LIFE INS CO	NY	148.4
BERKLEY LIFE & HEALTH INS CO	IA	336.2
FEDERATED LIFE INS CO	MN	2,039.8
GARDEN STATE LIFE INS CO	TX	138.9
GUARDIAN LIFE INS CO OF AMERICA	NY	59,690.7
MEDICAL MUTUAL OF OHIO	OH	2,490.1
SENTRY LIFE INS CO	WI	7,524.4
SHELTERPOINT LIFE INS CO	NY	183.5
UNITED FARM FAMILY LIFE INS CO	IN	2,373.1
USAA LIFE INS CO	TX	25,796.7
Rating: A-		
AMERICAN HEALTH & LIFE INS CO	TX	1,083.3
CIGNA LIFE INS CO OF NEW YORK	NY	419.6
FIDELITY SECURITY LIFE INS CO	MO	970.0
GREAT SOUTHERN LIFE INS CO	TX	209.9
MADISON NATIONAL LIFE INS CO INC	WI	337.4
MASSACHUSETTS MUTUAL LIFE INS CO	MA	249,945.6
NATIONAL BENEFIT LIFE INS CO	NY	585.5
NEW YORK LIFE INS CO	NY	181,647.2
NIPPON LIFE INS CO OF AMERICA	IA	229.2
PHYSICIANS LIFE INS CO	NE	1,685.6
STANDARD LIFE & ACCIDENT INS CO	TX	511.2
USABLE LIFE	AR	497.8
Rating: B+		
AMERICAN FIDELITY ASR CO	OK	6,256.2
AMERICAN UNITED LIFE INS CO	IN	29,538.7
ANTHEM LIFE INS CO	IN	759.7
ASSURITY LIFE INS CO	NE	2,750.1
AXA EQUITABLE LIFE INS CO	NY	201,023.4
BOSTON MUTUAL LIFE INS CO	MA	1,484.3
COMMUNITY CARE BEHAVIORAL HEALTH	PA	386.8
COMPANION LIFE INS CO	SC	420.6
DEARBORN NATIONAL LIFE INS CO	IL	1,669.0
DELAWARE AMERICAN LIFE INS CO	DE	119.0
FREEDOM LIFE INS CO OF AMERICA	TX	247.5
GEISINGER HEALTH PLAN	PA	663.7
GERBER LIFE INS CO	NY	4,180.6
HUMANA BENEFIT PLAN OF ILLINOIS	IL	693.4
ILLINOIS MUTUAL LIFE INS CO	IL	1,507.2
MIDLAND NATIONAL LIFE INS CO	IA	58,679.0
MINNESOTA LIFE INS CO	MN	50,012.0
MUTUAL OF AMERICA LIFE INS CO	NY	21,688.9
NATIONAL CASUALTY CO	OH	493.4
NATIONAL FOUNDATION LIFE INS CO	TX	59.6
NORTH AMERICAN INS CO	WI	18.5
NORTHWESTERN MUTUAL LIFE INS CO	WI	278,047.4
OXFORD LIFE INS CO	AZ	2,251.8
PRINCIPAL LIFE INS CO	IA	196,332.3
STANDARD INS CO	OR	25,172.5
STANDARD SECURITY LIFE INS CO OF NY	NY	139.6
TRUSTMARK INS CO	IL	1,625.3
TRUSTMARK LIFE INS CO	IL	330.1
UNITED WORLD LIFE INS CO	NE	132.1
UPMC FOR YOU INC	PA	991.0
VISTA HEALTH PLAN INC	PA	1,254.9
VOYA RETIREMENT INS & ANNUITY CO	CT	106,305.7

Puerto Rico

INSURANCE COMPANY NAME	DOM. STATE	TOTAL ASSETS ($MIL)
Rating: A+		
TEACHERS INS & ANNUITY ASN OF AM	NY	307,655.9
Rating: A		
SOUTHERN FARM BUREAU LIFE INS CO	MS	14,368.9
Rating: A-		
MASSACHUSETTS MUTUAL LIFE INS CO	MA	249,945.6
NEW YORK LIFE INS CO	NY	181,647.2
TRANS OCEANIC LIFE INS CO	PR	76.6
Rating: B+		
AMERICAN FIDELITY ASR CO	OK	6,256.2
AXA EQUITABLE LIFE INS CO	NY	201,023.4
BOSTON MUTUAL LIFE INS CO	MA	1,484.3
DEARBORN NATIONAL LIFE INS CO	IL	1,669.0
GERBER LIFE INS CO	NY	4,180.6
MIDLAND NATIONAL LIFE INS CO	IA	58,679.0
MINNESOTA LIFE INS CO	MN	50,012.0
PRINCIPAL LIFE INS CO	IA	196,332.3
STANDARD INS CO	OR	25,172.5
STANDARD SECURITY LIFE INS CO OF NY	NY	139.6
TRIPLE-S SALUD INC	PR	827.7
TRUSTMARK INS CO	IL	1,625.3
UNIVERSAL LIFE INS CO	PR	1,757.3
VOYA RETIREMENT INS & ANNUITY CO	CT	106,305.7

Rhode Island

INSURANCE COMPANY NAME	DOM. STATE	TOTAL ASSETS ($MIL)
Rating: A+		
CHESAPEAKE LIFE INS CO	OK	213.1
COUNTRY LIFE INS CO	IL	9,777.7
PHYSICIANS MUTUAL INS CO	NE	2,391.2
TEACHERS INS & ANNUITY ASN OF AM	NY	307,655.9
Rating: A		
AMALGAMATED LIFE INS CO	NY	148.4
BERKLEY LIFE & HEALTH INS CO	IA	336.2
FEDERATED LIFE INS CO	MN	2,039.8
GARDEN STATE LIFE INS CO	TX	138.9
GUARDIAN LIFE INS CO OF AMERICA	NY	59,690.7
SENTRY LIFE INS CO	WI	7,524.4
SHELTERPOINT LIFE INS CO	NY	183.5
USAA LIFE INS CO	TX	25,796.7
Rating: A-		
AMERICAN HEALTH & LIFE INS CO	TX	1,083.3
FIDELITY SECURITY LIFE INS CO	MO	970.0
MADISON NATIONAL LIFE INS CO INC	WI	337.4
MASSACHUSETTS MUTUAL LIFE INS CO	MA	249,945.6
NATIONAL BENEFIT LIFE INS CO	NY	585.5
NEW YORK LIFE INS CO	NY	181,647.2
NIPPON LIFE INS CO OF AMERICA	IA	229.2
PHYSICIANS LIFE INS CO	NE	1,685.6
STANDARD LIFE & ACCIDENT INS CO	TX	511.2
USABLE LIFE	AR	497.8
Rating: B+		
AMERICAN FIDELITY ASR CO	OK	6,256.2
AMERICAN UNITED LIFE INS CO	IN	29,538.7
ASSURITY LIFE INS CO	NE	2,750.1
AXA EQUITABLE LIFE INS CO	NY	201,023.4
BOSTON MUTUAL LIFE INS CO	MA	1,484.3
COMPANION LIFE INS CO	SC	420.6
DEARBORN NATIONAL LIFE INS CO	IL	1,669.0
DELAWARE AMERICAN LIFE INS CO	DE	119.0
GERBER LIFE INS CO	NY	4,180.6
HUMANA BENEFIT PLAN OF ILLINOIS	IL	693.4
ILLINOIS MUTUAL LIFE INS CO	IL	1,507.2
MIDLAND NATIONAL LIFE INS CO	IA	58,679.0
MINNESOTA LIFE INS CO	MN	50,012.0
MUTUAL OF AMERICA LIFE INS CO	NY	21,688.9
NATIONAL CASUALTY CO	OH	493.4
NORTHWESTERN MUTUAL LIFE INS CO	WI	278,047.4
OXFORD LIFE INS CO	AZ	2,251.8
PRINCIPAL LIFE INS CO	IA	196,332.3
STANDARD INS CO	OR	25,172.5
STANDARD SECURITY LIFE INS CO OF NY	NY	139.6
TRUSTMARK INS CO	IL	1,625.3
TRUSTMARK LIFE INS CO	IL	330.1
UNITED WORLD LIFE INS CO	NE	132.1
VOYA RETIREMENT INS & ANNUITY CO	CT	106,305.7

South Carolina

INSURANCE COMPANY NAME	DOM. STATE	TOTAL ASSETS ($MIL)
Rating: A+		
CHESAPEAKE LIFE INS CO	OK	213.1
COUNTRY LIFE INS CO	IL	9,777.7
PHYSICIANS MUTUAL INS CO	NE	2,391.2
TEACHERS INS & ANNUITY ASN OF AM	NY	307,655.9
Rating: A		
AMALGAMATED LIFE INS CO	NY	148.4
BERKLEY LIFE & HEALTH INS CO	IA	336.2
FEDERATED LIFE INS CO	MN	2,039.8
GARDEN STATE LIFE INS CO	TX	138.9
GUARDIAN LIFE INS CO OF AMERICA	NY	59,690.7
MEDICAL MUTUAL OF OHIO	OH	2,490.1
SENTRY LIFE INS CO	WI	7,524.4
SHELTERPOINT LIFE INS CO	NY	183.5
SOUTHERN FARM BUREAU LIFE INS CO	MS	14,368.9
USAA LIFE INS CO	TX	25,796.7
Rating: A-		
AMERICAN HEALTH & LIFE INS CO	TX	1,083.3
CHRISTIAN FIDELITY LIFE INS CO	TX	59.8
FIDELITY SECURITY LIFE INS CO	MO	970.0
GREAT SOUTHERN LIFE INS CO	TX	209.9
KAISER PERMANENTE INS CO	CA	197.7
MADISON NATIONAL LIFE INS CO INC	WI	337.4
MASSACHUSETTS MUTUAL LIFE INS CO	MA	249,945.6
NATIONAL BENEFIT LIFE INS CO	NY	585.5
NEW YORK LIFE INS CO	NY	181,647.2
NIPPON LIFE INS CO OF AMERICA	IA	229.2
PHYSICIANS LIFE INS CO	NE	1,685.6
STANDARD LIFE & ACCIDENT INS CO	TX	511.2
USABLE LIFE	AR	497.8
Rating: B+		
AMERICAN FAMILY MUTL INS CO SI	WI	18,119.9
AMERICAN FIDELITY ASR CO	OK	6,256.2
AMERICAN UNITED LIFE INS CO	IN	29,538.7
ANTHEM LIFE INS CO	IN	759.7
ASSURITY LIFE INS CO	NE	2,750.1
AXA EQUITABLE LIFE INS CO	NY	201,023.4
BLUE CROSS BLUE SHIELD OF SC INC	SC	4,742.7
BOSTON MUTUAL LIFE INS CO	MA	1,484.3
COMPANION LIFE INS CO	SC	420.6
DEARBORN NATIONAL LIFE INS CO	IL	1,669.0
DELAWARE AMERICAN LIFE INS CO	DE	119.0
FREEDOM LIFE INS CO OF AMERICA	TX	247.5
GERBER LIFE INS CO	NY	4,180.6
HUMANA BENEFIT PLAN OF ILLINOIS	IL	693.4
ILLINOIS MUTUAL LIFE INS CO	IL	1,507.2
MIDLAND NATIONAL LIFE INS CO	IA	58,679.0
MINNESOTA LIFE INS CO	MN	50,012.0
MUTUAL OF AMERICA LIFE INS CO	NY	21,688.9
NATIONAL CASUALTY CO	OH	493.4
NATIONAL FOUNDATION LIFE INS CO	TX	59.6
NORTH AMERICAN INS CO	WI	18.5
NORTHWESTERN MUTUAL LIFE INS CO	WI	278,047.4
OXFORD LIFE INS CO	AZ	2,251.8
PRINCIPAL LIFE INS CO	IA	196,332.3
STANDARD INS CO	OR	25,172.5
STANDARD SECURITY LIFE INS CO OF NY	NY	139.6
TRUSTMARK INS CO	IL	1,625.3
TRUSTMARK LIFE INS CO	IL	330.1
UNITED WORLD LIFE INS CO	NE	132.1
VOYA RETIREMENT INS & ANNUITY CO	CT	106,305.7

South Dakota

INSURANCE COMPANY NAME	DOM. STATE	TOTAL ASSETS ($MIL)
Rating: A+		
CHESAPEAKE LIFE INS CO	OK	213.1
COUNTRY LIFE INS CO	IL	9,777.7
PHYSICIANS MUTUAL INS CO	NE	2,391.2
TEACHERS INS & ANNUITY ASN OF AM	NY	307,655.9
Rating: A		
AMALGAMATED LIFE INS CO	NY	148.4
BERKLEY LIFE & HEALTH INS CO	IA	336.2
FEDERATED LIFE INS CO	MN	2,039.8
GARDEN STATE LIFE INS CO	TX	138.9
GUARDIAN LIFE INS CO OF AMERICA	NY	59,690.7
SENTRY LIFE INS CO	WI	7,524.4
USAA LIFE INS CO	TX	25,796.7
Rating: A-		
AMERICAN HEALTH & LIFE INS CO	TX	1,083.3
CHRISTIAN FIDELITY LIFE INS CO	TX	59.8
FIDELITY SECURITY LIFE INS CO	MO	970.0
GREAT SOUTHERN LIFE INS CO	TX	209.9
MADISON NATIONAL LIFE INS CO INC	WI	337.4
MASSACHUSETTS MUTUAL LIFE INS CO	MA	249,945.6
NATIONAL BENEFIT LIFE INS CO	NY	585.5
NEW YORK LIFE INS CO	NY	181,647.2
NIPPON LIFE INS CO OF AMERICA	IA	229.2
PACIFIC GUARDIAN LIFE INS CO LTD	HI	568.1
PHYSICIANS LIFE INS CO	NE	1,685.6
STANDARD LIFE & ACCIDENT INS CO	TX	511.2
USABLE LIFE	AR	497.8
Rating: B+		
AMERICAN FAMILY MUTL INS CO SI	WI	18,119.9
AMERICAN FIDELITY ASR CO	OK	6,256.2
AMERICAN UNITED LIFE INS CO	IN	29,538.7
ANTHEM LIFE INS CO	IN	759.7
ASSURITY LIFE INS CO	NE	2,750.1
AXA EQUITABLE LIFE INS CO	NY	201,023.4
BOSTON MUTUAL LIFE INS CO	MA	1,484.3
COMPANION LIFE INS CO	SC	420.6
DEARBORN NATIONAL LIFE INS CO	IL	1,669.0
DELAWARE AMERICAN LIFE INS CO	DE	119.0
FARM BUREAU LIFE INS CO	IA	9,174.1
FREEDOM LIFE INS CO OF AMERICA	TX	247.5
GERBER LIFE INS CO	NY	4,180.6
HEALTHPARTNERS INS CO	MN	416.8
HUMANA BENEFIT PLAN OF ILLINOIS	IL	693.4
ILLINOIS MUTUAL LIFE INS CO	IL	1,507.2
MIDLAND NATIONAL LIFE INS CO	IA	58,679.0
MINNESOTA LIFE INS CO	MN	50,012.0
MUTUAL OF AMERICA LIFE INS CO	NY	21,688.9
NATIONAL CASUALTY CO	OH	493.4
NATIONAL FOUNDATION LIFE INS CO	TX	59.6
NORTHWESTERN MUTUAL LIFE INS CO	WI	278,047.4
OXFORD LIFE INS CO	AZ	2,251.8
PRINCIPAL LIFE INS CO	IA	196,332.3
STANDARD INS CO	OR	25,172.5
STANDARD SECURITY LIFE INS CO OF NY	NY	139.6
TRUSTMARK INS CO	IL	1,625.3
TRUSTMARK LIFE INS CO	IL	330.1
UNITED WORLD LIFE INS CO	NE	132.1
VOYA RETIREMENT INS & ANNUITY CO	CT	106,305.7
WELLMARK OF SOUTH DAKOTA INC	SD	508.1

Tennessee

INSURANCE COMPANY NAME	DOM. STATE	TOTAL ASSETS ($MIL)
Rating: A+		
CHESAPEAKE LIFE INS CO	OK	213.1
COUNTRY LIFE INS CO	IL	9,777.7
PHYSICIANS MUTUAL INS CO	NE	2,391.2
TEACHERS INS & ANNUITY ASN OF AM	NY	307,655.9
Rating: A		
AMALGAMATED LIFE INS CO	NY	148.4
BERKLEY LIFE & HEALTH INS CO	IA	336.2
FEDERATED LIFE INS CO	MN	2,039.8
GARDEN STATE LIFE INS CO	TX	138.9
GUARDIAN LIFE INS CO OF AMERICA	NY	59,690.7
SENTRY LIFE INS CO	WI	7,524.4
SHELTERPOINT LIFE INS CO	NY	183.5
SOUTHERN FARM BUREAU LIFE INS CO	MS	14,368.9
USAA LIFE INS CO	TX	25,796.7
Rating: A-		
AMERICAN HEALTH & LIFE INS CO	TX	1,083.3
BLUEBONNET LIFE INS CO	MS	65.0
CHRISTIAN FIDELITY LIFE INS CO	TX	59.8
CIGNA LIFE INS CO OF NEW YORK	NY	419.6
FIDELITY SECURITY LIFE INS CO	MO	970.0
GREAT SOUTHERN LIFE INS CO	TX	209.9
MADISON NATIONAL LIFE INS CO INC	WI	337.4
MASSACHUSETTS MUTUAL LIFE INS CO	MA	249,945.6
NATIONAL BENEFIT LIFE INS CO	NY	585.5
NEW YORK LIFE INS CO	NY	181,647.2
NIPPON LIFE INS CO OF AMERICA	IA	229.2
PHYSICIANS LIFE INS CO	NE	1,685.6
STANDARD LIFE & ACCIDENT INS CO	TX	511.2
SWBC LIFE INS CO	TX	33.5
USABLE LIFE	AR	497.8
Rating: B+		
AMERICAN FAMILY MUTL INS CO SI	WI	18,119.9
AMERICAN FIDELITY ASR CO	OK	6,256.2
AMERICAN UNITED LIFE INS CO	IN	29,538.7
ANTHEM LIFE INS CO	IN	759.7
ASSURITY LIFE INS CO	NE	2,750.1
AXA EQUITABLE LIFE INS CO	NY	201,023.4
BLUECROSS BLUESHIELD OF TENNESSEE	TN	4,339.8
BOSTON MUTUAL LIFE INS CO	MA	1,484.3
COMPANION LIFE INS CO	SC	420.6
DEARBORN NATIONAL LIFE INS CO	IL	1,669.0
DELAWARE AMERICAN LIFE INS CO	DE	119.0
FREEDOM LIFE INS CO OF AMERICA	TX	247.5
GERBER LIFE INS CO	NY	4,180.6
HUMANA BENEFIT PLAN OF ILLINOIS	IL	693.4
ILLINOIS MUTUAL LIFE INS CO	IL	1,507.2
MIDLAND NATIONAL LIFE INS CO	IA	58,679.0
MINNESOTA LIFE INS CO	MN	50,012.0
MUTUAL OF AMERICA LIFE INS CO	NY	21,688.9
NATIONAL CASUALTY CO	OH	493.4
NATIONAL FOUNDATION LIFE INS CO	TX	59.6
NORTHWESTERN MUTUAL LIFE INS CO	WI	278,047.4
OXFORD LIFE INS CO	AZ	2,251.8
PRINCIPAL LIFE INS CO	IA	196,332.3
STANDARD INS CO	OR	25,172.5
STANDARD SECURITY LIFE INS CO OF NY	NY	139.6
TRUSTMARK INS CO	IL	1,625.3
TRUSTMARK LIFE INS CO	IL	330.1
UNITED HEALTHCARE OF WISCONSIN INC	WI	2,025.5
UNITED WORLD LIFE INS CO	NE	132.1
UTIC INS CO	AL	106.7
VOYA RETIREMENT INS & ANNUITY CO	CT	106,305.7

Texas

INSURANCE COMPANY NAME	DOM. STATE	TOTAL ASSETS ($MIL)
Rating: A+		
CARE 1ST HEALTH PLAN INC	CA	1,214.3
CHESAPEAKE LIFE INS CO	OK	213.1
COUNTRY LIFE INS CO	IL	9,777.7
PHYSICIANS MUTUAL INS CO	NE	2,391.2
TEACHERS INS & ANNUITY ASN OF AM	NY	307,655.9
Rating: A		
AMALGAMATED LIFE INS CO	NY	148.4
BERKLEY LIFE & HEALTH INS CO	IA	336.2
FEDERATED LIFE INS CO	MN	2,039.8
GARDEN STATE LIFE INS CO	TX	138.9
GUARDIAN LIFE INS CO OF AMERICA	NY	59,690.7
SENTRY LIFE INS CO	WI	7,524.4
SOUTHERN FARM BUREAU LIFE INS CO	MS	14,368.9
USAA LIFE INS CO	TX	25,796.7
Rating: A-		
AMERICAN HEALTH & LIFE INS CO	TX	1,083.3
AMERIGROUP TEXAS INC	TX	1,025.7
CHRISTIAN FIDELITY LIFE INS CO	TX	59.8
ESSENCE HEALTHCARE INC	MO	223.8
FIDELITY SECURITY LIFE INS CO	MO	970.0
GREAT SOUTHERN LIFE INS CO	TX	209.9
MADISON NATIONAL LIFE INS CO INC	WI	337.4
MASSACHUSETTS MUTUAL LIFE INS CO	MA	249,945.6
NATIONAL BENEFIT LIFE INS CO	NY	585.5
NEW YORK LIFE INS CO	NY	181,647.2
NIPPON LIFE INS CO OF AMERICA	IA	229.2
PACIFIC GUARDIAN LIFE INS CO LTD	HI	568.1
PHYSICIANS LIFE INS CO	NE	1,685.6
STANDARD LIFE & ACCIDENT INS CO	TX	511.2
SWBC LIFE INS CO	TX	33.5
USABLE LIFE	AR	497.8
Rating: B+		
AMERICAN FAMILY MUTL INS CO SI	WI	18,119.9
AMERICAN FIDELITY ASR CO	OK	6,256.2
AMERICAN UNITED LIFE INS CO	IN	29,538.7
ANTHEM LIFE INS CO	IN	759.7
ASSURITY LIFE INS CO	NE	2,750.1
AXA EQUITABLE LIFE INS CO	NY	201,023.4
BOSTON MUTUAL LIFE INS CO	MA	1,484.3
COMPANION LIFE INS CO	SC	420.6
DEARBORN NATIONAL LIFE INS CO	IL	1,669.0
DELAWARE AMERICAN LIFE INS CO	DE	119.0
EL PASO FIRST HEALTH PLANS INC	TX	58.8
FREEDOM LIFE INS CO OF AMERICA	TX	247.5
GERBER LIFE INS CO	NY	4,180.6
HUMANA BENEFIT PLAN OF ILLINOIS	IL	693.4
HUMANA INS CO OF KENTUCKY	KY	222.0
ILLINOIS MUTUAL LIFE INS CO	IL	1,507.2
K S PLAN ADMINISTRATORS LLC	TX	113.3
MIDLAND NATIONAL LIFE INS CO	IA	58,679.0
MINNESOTA LIFE INS CO	MN	50,012.0
MUTUAL OF AMERICA LIFE INS CO	NY	21,688.9
NATIONAL CASUALTY CO	OH	493.4
NATIONAL FOUNDATION LIFE INS CO	TX	59.6
NORTH AMERICAN INS CO	WI	18.5
NORTHWESTERN MUTUAL LIFE INS CO	WI	278,047.4
OXFORD LIFE INS CO	AZ	2,251.8
PRINCIPAL LIFE INS CO	IA	196,332.3
STANDARD INS CO	OR	25,172.5
STANDARD SECURITY LIFE INS CO OF NY	NY	139.6
TRUSTMARK INS CO	IL	1,625.3
TRUSTMARK LIFE INS CO	IL	330.1
UNITED WORLD LIFE INS CO	NE	132.1
VOYA RETIREMENT INS & ANNUITY CO	CT	106,305.7

Utah

INSURANCE COMPANY NAME	DOM. STATE	TOTAL ASSETS ($MIL)
Rating: A+		
CHESAPEAKE LIFE INS CO	OK	213.1
COUNTRY LIFE INS CO	IL	9,777.7
PHYSICIANS MUTUAL INS CO	NE	2,391.2
TEACHERS INS & ANNUITY ASN OF AM	NY	307,655.9
Rating: A		
AMALGAMATED LIFE INS CO	NY	148.4
BERKLEY LIFE & HEALTH INS CO	IA	336.2
EMI HEALTH	UT	158.9
FEDERATED LIFE INS CO	MN	2,039.8
GARDEN STATE LIFE INS CO	TX	138.9
GUARDIAN LIFE INS CO OF AMERICA	NY	59,690.7
SENTRY LIFE INS CO	WI	7,524.4
USAA LIFE INS CO	TX	25,796.7
Rating: A-		
AMERICAN HEALTH & LIFE INS CO	TX	1,083.3
CHRISTIAN FIDELITY LIFE INS CO	TX	59.8
FIDELITY SECURITY LIFE INS CO	MO	970.0
GREAT SOUTHERN LIFE INS CO	TX	209.9
MADISON NATIONAL LIFE INS CO INC	WI	337.4
MASSACHUSETTS MUTUAL LIFE INS CO	MA	249,945.6
NATIONAL BENEFIT LIFE INS CO	NY	585.5
NEW YORK LIFE INS CO	NY	181,647.2
NIPPON LIFE INS CO OF AMERICA	IA	229.2
PACIFIC GUARDIAN LIFE INS CO LTD	HI	568.1
PHYSICIANS LIFE INS CO	NE	1,685.6
STANDARD LIFE & ACCIDENT INS CO	TX	511.2
SWBC LIFE INS CO	TX	33.5
USABLE LIFE	AR	497.8
Rating: B+		
AMERICAN FAMILY MUTL INS CO SI	WI	18,119.9
AMERICAN FIDELITY ASR CO	OK	6,256.2
AMERICAN UNITED LIFE INS CO	IN	29,538.7
ANTHEM LIFE INS CO	IN	759.7
ASSURITY LIFE INS CO	NE	2,750.1
AXA EQUITABLE LIFE INS CO	NY	201,023.4
BOSTON MUTUAL LIFE INS CO	MA	1,484.3
COMPANION LIFE INS CO	SC	420.6
DEARBORN NATIONAL LIFE INS CO	IL	1,669.0
DELAWARE AMERICAN LIFE INS CO	DE	119.0
FARM BUREAU LIFE INS CO	IA	9,174.1
FREEDOM LIFE INS CO OF AMERICA	TX	247.5
GERBER LIFE INS CO	NY	4,180.6
ILLINOIS MUTUAL LIFE INS CO	IL	1,507.2
MIDLAND NATIONAL LIFE INS CO	IA	58,679.0
MINNESOTA LIFE INS CO	MN	50,012.0
MUTUAL OF AMERICA LIFE INS CO	NY	21,688.9
NATIONAL CASUALTY CO	OH	493.4
NATIONAL FOUNDATION LIFE INS CO	TX	59.6
NORTHWESTERN MUTUAL LIFE INS CO	WI	278,047.4
OXFORD LIFE INS CO	AZ	2,251.8
PRINCIPAL LIFE INS CO	IA	196,332.3
REGENCE BLUE CROSS BLUE SHIELD OF UT	UT	739.4
STANDARD INS CO	OR	25,172.5
STANDARD SECURITY LIFE INS CO OF NY	NY	139.6
TRUSTMARK INS CO	IL	1,625.3
TRUSTMARK LIFE INS CO	IL	330.1
UNITED WORLD LIFE INS CO	NE	132.1
VOYA RETIREMENT INS & ANNUITY CO	CT	106,305.7

Vermont

INSURANCE COMPANY NAME	DOM. STATE	TOTAL ASSETS ($MIL)
Rating: A+		
PHYSICIANS MUTUAL INS CO	NE	2,391.2
TEACHERS INS & ANNUITY ASN OF AM	NY	307,655.9
Rating: A		
AMALGAMATED LIFE INS CO	NY	148.4
BERKLEY LIFE & HEALTH INS CO	IA	336.2
FEDERATED LIFE INS CO	MN	2,039.8
GARDEN STATE LIFE INS CO	TX	138.9
GUARDIAN LIFE INS CO OF AMERICA	NY	59,690.7
SENTRY LIFE INS CO	WI	7,524.4
USAA LIFE INS CO	TX	25,796.7
Rating: A-		
AMERICAN FAMILY LIFE ASR CO OF NY	NY	978.2
AMERICAN HEALTH & LIFE INS CO	TX	1,083.3
FIDELITY SECURITY LIFE INS CO	MO	970.0
MADISON NATIONAL LIFE INS CO INC	WI	337.4
MASSACHUSETTS MUTUAL LIFE INS CO	MA	249,945.6
NATIONAL BENEFIT LIFE INS CO	NY	585.5
NEW YORK LIFE INS CO	NY	181,647.2
NIPPON LIFE INS CO OF AMERICA	IA	229.2
PHYSICIANS LIFE INS CO	NE	1,685.6
STANDARD LIFE & ACCIDENT INS CO	TX	511.2
USABLE LIFE	AR	497.8
Rating: B+		
AMERICAN FIDELITY ASR CO	OK	6,256.2
AMERICAN UNITED LIFE INS CO	IN	29,538.7
ASSURITY LIFE INS CO	NE	2,750.1
AXA EQUITABLE LIFE INS CO	NY	201,023.4
BOSTON MUTUAL LIFE INS CO	MA	1,484.3
COMPANION LIFE INS CO	SC	420.6
DEARBORN NATIONAL LIFE INS CO	IL	1,669.0
DELAWARE AMERICAN LIFE INS CO	DE	119.0
GERBER LIFE INS CO	NY	4,180.6
HUMANA BENEFIT PLAN OF ILLINOIS	IL	693.4
ILLINOIS MUTUAL LIFE INS CO	IL	1,507.2
MIDLAND NATIONAL LIFE INS CO	IA	58,679.0
MINNESOTA LIFE INS CO	MN	50,012.0
MUTUAL OF AMERICA LIFE INS CO	NY	21,688.9
NATIONAL CASUALTY CO	OH	493.4
NORTHWESTERN MUTUAL LIFE INS CO	WI	278,047.4
PRINCIPAL LIFE INS CO	IA	196,332.3
STANDARD INS CO	OR	25,172.5
STANDARD SECURITY LIFE INS CO OF NY	NY	139.6
TRUSTMARK INS CO	IL	1,625.3
TRUSTMARK LIFE INS CO	IL	330.1
UNITED WORLD LIFE INS CO	NE	132.1
VOYA RETIREMENT INS & ANNUITY CO	CT	106,305.7

Virginia

INSURANCE COMPANY NAME	DOM. STATE	TOTAL ASSETS ($MIL)
Rating: A+		
CHESAPEAKE LIFE INS CO	OK	213.1
COUNTRY LIFE INS CO	IL	9,777.7
PHYSICIANS MUTUAL INS CO	NE	2,391.2
TEACHERS INS & ANNUITY ASN OF AM	NY	307,655.9
Rating: A		
AMALGAMATED LIFE INS CO	NY	148.4
BERKLEY LIFE & HEALTH INS CO	IA	336.2
FEDERATED LIFE INS CO	MN	2,039.8
GARDEN STATE LIFE INS CO	TX	138.9
GUARDIAN LIFE INS CO OF AMERICA	NY	59,690.7
OPTIMA HEALTH PLAN	VA	795.0
SENTRY LIFE INS CO	WI	7,524.4
SOUTHERN FARM BUREAU LIFE INS CO	MS	14,368.9
USAA LIFE INS CO	TX	25,796.7
Rating: A-		
AMERICAN HEALTH & LIFE INS CO	TX	1,083.3
CHRISTIAN FIDELITY LIFE INS CO	TX	59.8
FIDELITY SECURITY LIFE INS CO	MO	970.0
GREAT SOUTHERN LIFE INS CO	TX	209.9
HUMANA MEDICAL PLAN INC	FL	2,319.2
KAISER PERMANENTE INS CO	CA	197.7
MADISON NATIONAL LIFE INS CO INC	WI	337.4
MASSACHUSETTS MUTUAL LIFE INS CO	MA	249,945.6
NATIONAL BENEFIT LIFE INS CO	NY	585.5
NEW YORK LIFE INS CO	NY	181,647.2
NIPPON LIFE INS CO OF AMERICA	IA	229.2
PHYSICIANS LIFE INS CO	NE	1,685.6
STANDARD LIFE & ACCIDENT INS CO	TX	511.2
SWBC LIFE INS CO	TX	33.5
USABLE LIFE	AR	497.8
Rating: B+		
AMERICAN FAMILY MUTL INS CO SI	WI	18,119.9
AMERICAN FIDELITY ASR CO	OK	6,256.2
AMERICAN UNITED LIFE INS CO	IN	29,538.7
ANTHEM LIFE INS CO	IN	759.7
ASSURITY LIFE INS CO	NE	2,750.1
AXA EQUITABLE LIFE INS CO	NY	201,023.4
BOSTON MUTUAL LIFE INS CO	MA	1,484.3
COMPANION LIFE INS CO	SC	420.6
DEARBORN NATIONAL LIFE INS CO	IL	1,669.0
DELAWARE AMERICAN LIFE INS CO	DE	119.0
FREEDOM LIFE INS CO OF AMERICA	TX	247.5
GERBER LIFE INS CO	NY	4,180.6
HUMANA BENEFIT PLAN OF ILLINOIS	IL	693.4
ILLINOIS MUTUAL LIFE INS CO	IL	1,507.2
MIDLAND NATIONAL LIFE INS CO	IA	58,679.0
MINNESOTA LIFE INS CO	MN	50,012.0
MUTUAL OF AMERICA LIFE INS CO	NY	21,688.9
NATIONAL CASUALTY CO	OH	493.4
NATIONAL FOUNDATION LIFE INS CO	TX	59.6
NORTHWESTERN MUTUAL LIFE INS CO	WI	278,047.4
OXFORD LIFE INS CO	AZ	2,251.8
PRINCIPAL LIFE INS CO	IA	196,332.3
STANDARD INS CO	OR	25,172.5
STANDARD SECURITY LIFE INS CO OF NY	NY	139.6
TRUSTMARK INS CO	IL	1,625.3
TRUSTMARK LIFE INS CO	IL	330.1
UNITED HEALTHCARE OF WISCONSIN INC	WI	2,025.5
UNITED WORLD LIFE INS CO	NE	132.1
VOYA RETIREMENT INS & ANNUITY CO	CT	106,305.7

Washington

INSURANCE COMPANY NAME	DOM. STATE	TOTAL ASSETS ($MIL)
Rating: A+		
CHESAPEAKE LIFE INS CO	OK	213.1
COUNTRY LIFE INS CO	IL	9,777.7
PHYSICIANS MUTUAL INS CO	NE	2,391.2
TEACHERS INS & ANNUITY ASN OF AM	NY	307,655.9
Rating: A		
AMALGAMATED LIFE INS CO	NY	148.4
BERKLEY LIFE & HEALTH INS CO	IA	336.2
FEDERATED LIFE INS CO	MN	2,039.8
GARDEN STATE LIFE INS CO	TX	138.9
GUARDIAN LIFE INS CO OF AMERICA	NY	59,690.7
LIFEWISE ASR CO	WA	215.9
SENTRY LIFE INS CO	WI	7,524.4
USAA LIFE INS CO	TX	25,796.7
Rating: A-		
AMERICAN HEALTH & LIFE INS CO	TX	1,083.3
AMERIGROUP WASHINGTON INC	WA	302.8
CHRISTIAN FIDELITY LIFE INS CO	TX	59.8
ESSENCE HEALTHCARE INC	MO	223.8
FIDELITY SECURITY LIFE INS CO	MO	970.0
GREAT SOUTHERN LIFE INS CO	TX	209.9
KAISER PERMANENTE INS CO	CA	197.7
MADISON NATIONAL LIFE INS CO INC	WI	337.4
MASSACHUSETTS MUTUAL LIFE INS CO	MA	249,945.6
NATIONAL BENEFIT LIFE INS CO	NY	585.5
NEW YORK LIFE INS CO	NY	181,647.2
NIPPON LIFE INS CO OF AMERICA	IA	229.2
PACIFIC GUARDIAN LIFE INS CO LTD	HI	568.1
PHYSICIANS LIFE INS CO	NE	1,685.6
PROVIDENCE HEALTH ASR	OR	457.3
REGENCE BL CROSS BL SHIELD OREGON	OR	1,319.0
STANDARD LIFE & ACCIDENT INS CO	TX	511.2
USABLE LIFE	AR	497.8
Rating: B+		
AMERICAN FAMILY MUTL INS CO SI	WI	18,119.9
AMERICAN FIDELITY ASR CO	OK	6,256.2
AMERICAN UNITED LIFE INS CO	IN	29,538.7
ANTHEM LIFE INS CO	IN	759.7
ASSURITY LIFE INS CO	NE	2,750.1
AXA EQUITABLE LIFE INS CO	NY	201,023.4
BOSTON MUTUAL LIFE INS CO	MA	1,484.3
COMPANION LIFE INS CO	SC	420.6
DEARBORN NATIONAL LIFE INS CO	IL	1,669.0
DELAWARE AMERICAN LIFE INS CO	DE	119.0
FARM BUREAU LIFE INS CO	IA	9,174.1
FREEDOM LIFE INS CO OF AMERICA	TX	247.5
GERBER LIFE INS CO	NY	4,180.6
HUMANA BENEFIT PLAN OF ILLINOIS	IL	693.4
ILLINOIS MUTUAL LIFE INS CO	IL	1,507.2
MIDLAND NATIONAL LIFE INS CO	IA	58,679.0
MINNESOTA LIFE INS CO	MN	50,012.0
MUTUAL OF AMERICA LIFE INS CO	NY	21,688.9
NATIONAL CASUALTY CO	OH	493.4
NATIONAL FOUNDATION LIFE INS CO	TX	59.6
NORTHWESTERN MUTUAL LIFE INS CO	WI	278,047.4
OXFORD LIFE INS CO	AZ	2,251.8
PRINCIPAL LIFE INS CO	IA	196,332.3
REGENCE BLUESHIELD OF IDAHO INC	ID	340.7
STANDARD INS CO	OR	25,172.5
STANDARD SECURITY LIFE INS CO OF NY	NY	139.6
TRUSTMARK INS CO	IL	1,625.3
TRUSTMARK LIFE INS CO	IL	330.1
UNITED WORLD LIFE INS CO	NE	132.1
UNITEDHEALTHCARE OF OREGON	OR	462.8
VOYA RETIREMENT INS & ANNUITY CO	CT	106,305.7

West Virginia

INSURANCE COMPANY NAME	DOM. STATE	TOTAL ASSETS ($MIL)
Rating: A+		
CHESAPEAKE LIFE INS CO	OK	213.1
COUNTRY LIFE INS CO	IL	9,777.7
PHYSICIANS MUTUAL INS CO	NE	2,391.2
TEACHERS INS & ANNUITY ASN OF AM	NY	307,655.9
Rating: A		
AMALGAMATED LIFE INS CO	NY	148.4
BERKLEY LIFE & HEALTH INS CO	IA	336.2
FEDERATED LIFE INS CO	MN	2,039.8
GARDEN STATE LIFE INS CO	TX	138.9
GUARDIAN LIFE INS CO OF AMERICA	NY	59,690.7
MEDICAL MUTUAL OF OHIO	OH	2,490.1
SENTRY LIFE INS CO	WI	7,524.4
USAA LIFE INS CO	TX	25,796.7
Rating: A-		
AMERICAN HEALTH & LIFE INS CO	TX	1,083.3
CHRISTIAN FIDELITY LIFE INS CO	TX	59.8
FIDELITY SECURITY LIFE INS CO	MO	970.0
GREAT SOUTHERN LIFE INS CO	TX	209.9
MADISON NATIONAL LIFE INS CO INC	WI	337.4
MASSACHUSETTS MUTUAL LIFE INS CO	MA	249,945.6
NATIONAL BENEFIT LIFE INS CO	NY	585.5
NEW YORK LIFE INS CO	NY	181,647.2
NIPPON LIFE INS CO OF AMERICA	IA	229.2
PHYSICIANS LIFE INS CO	NE	1,685.6
STANDARD LIFE & ACCIDENT INS CO	TX	511.2
USABLE LIFE	AR	497.8
Rating: B+		
AMERICAN FIDELITY ASR CO	OK	6,256.2
AMERICAN UNITED LIFE INS CO	IN	29,538.7
ANTHEM LIFE INS CO	IN	759.7
ASSURITY LIFE INS CO	NE	2,750.1
AXA EQUITABLE LIFE INS CO	NY	201,023.4
BOSTON MUTUAL LIFE INS CO	MA	1,484.3
COMPANION LIFE INS CO	SC	420.6
DEARBORN NATIONAL LIFE INS CO	IL	1,669.0
DELAWARE AMERICAN LIFE INS CO	DE	119.0
FREEDOM LIFE INS CO OF AMERICA	TX	247.5
GERBER LIFE INS CO	NY	4,180.6
HUMANA BENEFIT PLAN OF ILLINOIS	IL	693.4
ILLINOIS MUTUAL LIFE INS CO	IL	1,507.2
MIDLAND NATIONAL LIFE INS CO	IA	58,679.0
MINNESOTA LIFE INS CO	MN	50,012.0
MUTUAL OF AMERICA LIFE INS CO	NY	21,688.9
NATIONAL CASUALTY CO	OH	493.4
NORTHWESTERN MUTUAL LIFE INS CO	WI	278,047.4
OXFORD LIFE INS CO	AZ	2,251.8
PRINCIPAL LIFE INS CO	IA	196,332.3
STANDARD INS CO	OR	25,172.5
STANDARD SECURITY LIFE INS CO OF NY	NY	139.6
TRUSTMARK INS CO	IL	1,625.3
TRUSTMARK LIFE INS CO	IL	330.1
UNICARE HEALTH PLAN OF WEST VIRGINIA	WV	150.9
UNITED WORLD LIFE INS CO	NE	132.1
VOYA RETIREMENT INS & ANNUITY CO	CT	106,305.7

Wisconsin

INSURANCE COMPANY NAME	DOM. STATE	TOTAL ASSETS ($MIL)
Rating: A+		
CHESAPEAKE LIFE INS CO	OK	213.1
COUNTRY LIFE INS CO	IL	9,777.7
PHYSICIANS MUTUAL INS CO	NE	2,391.2
TEACHERS INS & ANNUITY ASN OF AM	NY	307,655.9
Rating: A		
AMALGAMATED LIFE INS CO	NY	148.4
BERKLEY LIFE & HEALTH INS CO	IA	336.2
DEAN HEALTH PLAN INC	WI	305.3
FEDERATED LIFE INS CO	MN	2,039.8
GARDEN STATE LIFE INS CO	TX	138.9
GUARDIAN LIFE INS CO OF AMERICA	NY	59,690.7
MEDICAL MUTUAL OF OHIO	OH	2,490.1
SENTRY LIFE INS CO	WI	7,524.4
USAA LIFE INS CO	TX	25,796.7
Rating: A-		
AMERICAN HEALTH & LIFE INS CO	TX	1,083.3
COMPCARE HEALTH SERVICES INS CORP	WI	376.3
FIDELITY SECURITY LIFE INS CO	MO	970.0
GREAT SOUTHERN LIFE INS CO	TX	209.9
MADISON NATIONAL LIFE INS CO INC	WI	337.4
MASSACHUSETTS MUTUAL LIFE INS CO	MA	249,945.6
NATIONAL BENEFIT LIFE INS CO	NY	585.5
NEW YORK LIFE INS CO	NY	181,647.2
NIPPON LIFE INS CO OF AMERICA	IA	229.2
PHYSICIANS LIFE INS CO	NE	1,685.6
STANDARD LIFE & ACCIDENT INS CO	TX	511.2
USABLE LIFE	AR	497.8
Rating: B+		
AMERICAN FAMILY MUTL INS CO SI	WI	18,119.9
AMERICAN FIDELITY ASR CO	OK	6,256.2
AMERICAN UNITED LIFE INS CO	IN	29,538.7
ANTHEM LIFE INS CO	IN	759.7
ASSURITY LIFE INS CO	NE	2,750.1
AXA EQUITABLE LIFE INS CO	NY	201,023.4
BOSTON MUTUAL LIFE INS CO	MA	1,484.3
CARE WISCONSIN HEALTH PLAN INC	WI	61.5
CHILDRENS COMMUNITY HEALTH PLAN INC	WI	161.7
COMPANION LIFE INS CO	SC	420.6
DEARBORN NATIONAL LIFE INS CO	IL	1,669.0
DELAWARE AMERICAN LIFE INS CO	DE	119.0
FARM BUREAU LIFE INS CO	IA	9,174.1
GERBER LIFE INS CO	NY	4,180.6
HEALTHPARTNERS INS CO	MN	416.8
HUMANA BENEFIT PLAN OF ILLINOIS	IL	693.4
ILLINOIS MUTUAL LIFE INS CO	IL	1,507.2
INDEPENDENT CARE HEALTH PLAN	WI	86.5
MIDLAND NATIONAL LIFE INS CO	IA	58,679.0
MINNESOTA LIFE INS CO	MN	50,012.0
MUTUAL OF AMERICA LIFE INS CO	NY	21,688.9
NATIONAL CASUALTY CO	OH	493.4
NORTH AMERICAN INS CO	WI	18.5
NORTHWESTERN MUTUAL LIFE INS CO	WI	278,047.4
OXFORD LIFE INS CO	AZ	2,251.8
PRINCIPAL LIFE INS CO	IA	196,332.3
SECURITY HEALTH PLAN OF WI INC	WI	445.1
STANDARD INS CO	OR	25,172.5
STANDARD SECURITY LIFE INS CO OF NY	NY	139.6
TRUSTMARK INS CO	IL	1,625.3
TRUSTMARK LIFE INS CO	IL	330.1
UNITED HEALTHCARE OF WISCONSIN INC	WI	2,025.5
UNITED WORLD LIFE INS CO	NE	132.1
VOYA RETIREMENT INS & ANNUITY CO	CT	106,305.7

Wyoming

INSURANCE COMPANY NAME	DOM. STATE	TOTAL ASSETS ($MIL)
Rating: A+		
CHESAPEAKE LIFE INS CO	OK	213.1
COUNTRY LIFE INS CO	IL	9,777.7
PHYSICIANS MUTUAL INS CO	NE	2,391.2
TEACHERS INS & ANNUITY ASN OF AM	NY	307,655.9
Rating: A		
AMALGAMATED LIFE INS CO	NY	148.4
BERKLEY LIFE & HEALTH INS CO	IA	336.2
FEDERATED LIFE INS CO	MN	2,039.8
GARDEN STATE LIFE INS CO	TX	138.9
GUARDIAN LIFE INS CO OF AMERICA	NY	59,690.7
SENTRY LIFE INS CO	WI	7,524.4
USAA LIFE INS CO	TX	25,796.7
Rating: A-		
AMERICAN HEALTH & LIFE INS CO	TX	1,083.3
CHRISTIAN FIDELITY LIFE INS CO	TX	59.8
FIDELITY SECURITY LIFE INS CO	MO	970.0
GREAT SOUTHERN LIFE INS CO	TX	209.9
MADISON NATIONAL LIFE INS CO INC	WI	337.4
MASSACHUSETTS MUTUAL LIFE INS CO	MA	249,945.6
NATIONAL BENEFIT LIFE INS CO	NY	585.5
NEW YORK LIFE INS CO	NY	181,647.2
PACIFIC GUARDIAN LIFE INS CO LTD	HI	568.1
PHYSICIANS LIFE INS CO	NE	1,685.6
STANDARD LIFE & ACCIDENT INS CO	TX	511.2
USABLE LIFE	AR	497.8
Rating: B+		
AMERICAN FAMILY MUTL INS CO SI	WI	18,119.9
AMERICAN FIDELITY ASR CO	OK	6,256.2
AMERICAN UNITED LIFE INS CO	IN	29,538.7
ANTHEM LIFE INS CO	IN	759.7
ASSURITY LIFE INS CO	NE	2,750.1
AXA EQUITABLE LIFE INS CO	NY	201,023.4
BOSTON MUTUAL LIFE INS CO	MA	1,484.3
COMPANION LIFE INS CO	SC	420.6
DEARBORN NATIONAL LIFE INS CO	IL	1,669.0
DELAWARE AMERICAN LIFE INS CO	DE	119.0
FARM BUREAU LIFE INS CO	IA	9,174.1
FREEDOM LIFE INS CO OF AMERICA	TX	247.5
GERBER LIFE INS CO	NY	4,180.6
HUMANA BENEFIT PLAN OF ILLINOIS	IL	693.4
ILLINOIS MUTUAL LIFE INS CO	IL	1,507.2
MIDLAND NATIONAL LIFE INS CO	IA	58,679.0
MINNESOTA LIFE INS CO	MN	50,012.0
MUTUAL OF AMERICA LIFE INS CO	NY	21,688.9
NATIONAL CASUALTY CO	OH	493.4
NATIONAL FOUNDATION LIFE INS CO	TX	59.6
NORTHWESTERN MUTUAL LIFE INS CO	WI	278,047.4
OXFORD LIFE INS CO	AZ	2,251.8
PRINCIPAL LIFE INS CO	IA	196,332.3
STANDARD INS CO	OR	25,172.5
STANDARD SECURITY LIFE INS CO OF NY	NY	139.6
TRUSTMARK INS CO	IL	1,625.3
TRUSTMARK LIFE INS CO	IL	330.1
UNITED WORLD LIFE INS CO	NE	132.1
VOYA RETIREMENT INS & ANNUITY CO	CT	106,305.7

Section V

Long-Term Care Insurers

A list of rated companies providing

Long-Term Care Insurance

Companies are listed in alphabetical order.

Section V Contents

This section provides contact addresses and phone numbers for all companies who sell long-term care insurance. The long-term care insurers in this section are listed in alphabetical order.

1. Safety Rating	Our rating is measured on a scale from A to F and considers a wide range of factors. Highly-rated companies are, in our opinion, less likely to experience financial difficulties than lower-rated firms. See *About Weiss Safety Ratings* for more information.
2. Insurance Company Name	The legally registered name, which can sometimes differ from the name that the company uses for advertising. An insurer's name can be very similar to the name of other companies, so make sure you note the exact name before contacting your agent.
3. Address	The address of the main office where you can contact the firm for additional financial data or for the location of local branches and/or registered agents.
4. Telephone Number	The number to call for additional financial data or for the phone numbers of local branches and/or registered agents.

To compare long-term care insurance policies and to walk through the maze of options, prices, and insurers, see the *Long-Term Care Insurance Planner*. It helps narrow down the choices available by addressing questions such as:

- What can you afford to pay for insurance?
- What type of care and living arrangement will suit your needs?
- When will you most likely need to utilize the insurance benefits?
- How much can you afford to pay from your own savings?
- Do you want a tax-qualified or non-qualified policy?
- What kind of insurance agent are you working with?

The planner offers an easy-to-use analysis tool to help identify the policy that best meets your needs. Based on information provided by insurance agents and literature from the provider, it addresses questions such as:

- How safe is the insurer?
- How are the coverage and facility options defined?
- What are the terms of coverage and reimbursement?
- How will the benefits be triggered?
- What other features are included in the policy?

RATING	INSURANCE COMPANY NAME	ADDRESS	CITY	STATE	ZIP	PHONE
B	AUTO-OWNERS LIFE INS CO	6101 ANACAPRI BOULEVARD	LANSING	MI	48917	(517) 323-1200
D	BANKERS CONSECO LIFE INS CO	350 JERICHO TURNPIKE SUITE 304	JERICHO	NY	11753	(317) 817-6100
D+	BANKERS LIFE & CAS CO	111 EAST WACKER DRIVE STE 2100	CHICAGO	IL	60601	(312) 396-6000
B	BLUE CROSS BLUE SHIELD OF KANSAS INC	1133 SW TOPEKA BOULEVARD	TOPEKA	KS	66629	(785) 291-7000
A+	COUNTRY LIFE INS CO	1701 N TOWANDA AVENUE	BLOOMINGTON	IL	61701	(309) 821-3000
C	EQUITABLE LIFE & CASUALTY INS CO	299 S MAIN ST #1100	SALT LAKE CITY	UT	84111	(801) 579-3400
B	FORETHOUGHT LIFE INS CO	10 W MARKET ST STE 2300	INDIANAPOLIS	IN	46204	(317) 223-2700
C	GENWORTH LIFE INS CO	251 LITTLE FALLS DR	WILMINGTON	DE	19808	(804) 662-2400
C	GENWORTH LIFE INS CO OF NEW YORK	600 THIRD AVENUE SUITE 2400	NEW YORK	NY	10016	(212) 895-4137
B	JOHN HANCOCK LIFE & HEALTH INS CO	197 CLARENDON STREET	BOSTON	MA	02116	(617) 572-6000
B-	JOHN HANCOCK LIFE INS CO (USA)	201 TOWNSEND STREET SUITE 900	LANSING	MI	48933	(617) 572-6000
D	LIFESECURE INS CO	10559 CITATION DRIVE SUITE 300	BRIGHTON	MI	48116	(810) 220-7700
A-	MADISON NATIONAL LIFE INS CO INC	1241 JOHN Q HAMMONS DRIVE	MADISON	WI	53717	(800) 356-9601
A-	MASSACHUSETTS MUTUAL LIFE INS CO	1295 STATE STREET	SPRINGFIELD	MA	1111	(413) 788-8411
C	MEDAMERICA INS CO	651 HOLIDAY DRIVE FOSTER PLAZA	PITTSBURGH	PA	15220	(585) 238-4464
C	MEDAMERICA INS CO OF NEW YORK	165 COURT STREET	ROCHESTER	NY	14647	(585) 238-4464
B-	MUTUAL OF OMAHA INS CO	MUTUAL OF OMAHA PLAZA	OMAHA	NE	68175	(402) 342-7600
C	NATIONAL INS CO OF WI INC	250 S EXECUTIVE DR	BROOKFIELD	WI	53005	(262) 785-9995
A-	NEW YORK LIFE INS CO	51 MADISON AVENUE	NEW YORK	NY	10010	(212) 576-7000
B	NORTHWESTERN LONG TERM CARE INS CO	720 EAST WISCONSIN AVENUE	MILWAUKEE	WI	53202	(414) 271-1444
B-	RESERVE NATIONAL INS CO	601 EAST BRITTON ROAD	OKLAHOMA CITY	OK	73114	(405) 848-7931
B	STATE FARM MUTUAL AUTOMOBILE INS CO	ONE STATE FARM PLAZA	BLOOMINGTON	IL	61710	(309) 766-2311
B	TRANSAMERICA FINANCIAL LIFE INS CO	440 MAMARONECK AVENUE	HARRISON	NY	10528	(914) 627-3630
B	TRANSAMERICA LIFE INS CO	4333 EDGEWOOD RD NE	CEDAR RAPIDS	IA	52499	(319) 355-8511
B	UNITED OF OMAHA LIFE INS CO	MUTUAL OF OMAHA PLAZA	OMAHA	NE	68175	(402) 342-7600
E+	UNITED SECURITY ASR CO OF PA	673 EAST CHERRY LANE	SOUDERTON	PA	18964	(215) 723-3044

Section VI

Medicare Supplement Insurance

Section VI Contents

Section VI Contents

Part I: Answers to Your Questions about Medigap

What Does Medigap Cover?

What are the Gaps in Medicare Coverage?

Medicare Prescription Drug Bill

Medicare + Medicare Advantage [illegible] Sponsored [illegible] What Does it All Mean?

Part II: Steps to Follow When Selecting a Medigap Policy

[illegible] Medigap Policies

Part III: Medigap Premium Patterns

[illegible] outlines the typical [illegible] for Plans A through [illegible] N depending on the [illegible]

Part IV: Medicare Supplement Resources

Part I: Answers to Your Questions About Medigap

The choices you make today about your health coverage – or the coverage of someone you care for – can have a major impact on both your health and your wealth. Since you are over 65, Medicare will provide you with a basic level of coverage, but there are many gaps in Medicare coverage that you will likely need to fill with a Medicare supplement insurance (Medigap) policy if you decide not to join a Medicare Advantage plan. The purpose of this report is to help you make coverage choices based on the most objective and broadest amount of information possible.

First, you want to understand what the federal Medicare program does and does not cover. We provide you with a clear layout starting on the following page.

Second, you will need to decide whether you want to fill the gaps in coverage by joining a Medicare Advantage plan or by combining Medicare supplement insurance with Medicare benefits. In Part 1 of this guide, we explain the differences between the two approaches.

Third, if you decide to use Medigap, your next step is to find out which plan best suits your needs. To help you figure this out, review Part II of this guide.

Fourth, check out the specific benefits for each plan along with the premium rates charged for those plans in Part III.

Finally, once you've found a couple of alternatives you like the best, call the companies to find the authorized agent nearest you. Phone numbers for the companies' main offices are listed in Part IV. If you need additional information on health insurance and related topics, call the agencies listed under Reference Organizations.

What Does Medicare Cover?

Table 1
MEDICARE (PART A): HOSPITAL INSURANCE-COVERED SERVICES FOR 2019

Service	Benefit	Medicare Pays	You Pay
HOSPITAL CARE (IN PATIENT CARE)			
Semi-private rooms, meals, general nursing, and drugs as part of your inpatient treatment, and other hospital services and supplies.	First 60 days	All but $1,364	$1,364
	61st to 90th day	All but $341 a day	$341 a day
	91st to 150th day*	All but $682 a day	$682 a day
Limited to 190 days in a lifetime, inpatient psychiatric care in a freestanding psychiatric hospital.	Beyond 150 days	Nothing	All costs
SKILLED NURSING FACILITY CARE			
You must have been in a hospital for at least 3 days, enter a Medicare-approved facility generally within 30 days after hospital discharge, and meet other program requirements. **	First 20 days	100% of approved amount	Nothing
	Additional 80 days	All but $170.50 a day	Up to $170.50 a day
	Beyond 100 days	Nothing	All costs
HOME HEALTH CARE			
Part-time or intermittent skilled care, home health services, physical and occupational therapy, durable medical equipment and supplies and other services	For as long as you meet Medicare requirements for home health care benefits	100% of approved amount; 80% of approved amount for durable medical equipment	Nothing for services; 20% of approved amount for durable medical equipment
HOSPICE CARE			
Includes drugs for symptom control and pain relief, medical and support services from a Medicare-approved hospice, and other services not otherwise covered by Medicare. Hospice care is usually given in your home.	For as long as doctor certifies need	All but limited costs for outpatient drugs and inpatient respite care	Limited cost sharing for outpatient drugs and inpatient respite care
BLOOD			
When furnished by a hospital or a skilled nursing facility during a covered stay	Unlimited during a benefit period if medically necessary	80% of the Medicare-approved after the first 3 pints per calendar year	***100% of the first 3 pints then 20% of the approved cost of additional pints.

* 60 reserve days may be used only once.

** Neither Medicare nor Medicare supplement insurance will pay for most nursing home care.

*** To the extent the three pints of blood are paid for or replaced under one part of Medicare during the calendar year, they do not have to be paid for or replaced under the other part.

Table 2
MEDICARE (PART B): PREVENTIVE SERVICES FOR 2019

Service	Benefit	Medicare Pays	You Pay
"WELCOME TO MEDICARE" PHYSICAL EXAM (ONE-TIME)			
	During the first 12 months that you have Part B, you can get a "Welcome to Medicare" preventive visit.	100% if provider accepts assignment.	If health care provider performs additional test or services during the same visit, you may have to pay coinsurance, and Part B deductible may apply
YEARLY "WELLNESS" VISIT			
	This visit is covered once every 12 months. If you've had Part B for longer than 12 months, you can get a yearly "Wellness" visit.	100% if provider accepts assignment.	If health care provider performs additional test or services during the same visit, you may have to pay coinsurance, and Part B deductible may apply
ABDOMINAL AORTIC ANEURYSM SCREENING			
	A one-time screening ultrasound for people at risk. You must get a referral for it as part of your one-time "Welcome to Medicare" preventive visit.	100% if provider accepts assignment	Nothing for services
ALCOHOL MISUSE SCREENING AND COUNSELING			
	Once every 12 months for adults with Medicare (including pregnant women) who use alcohol, but don't meet the medical criteria for alcohol dependency.	100% if provider accepts assignment	Nothing for services
BONE MASS MEASUREMENT (BONE DENSITY)			
	Once every 24 months (more often if medically necessary) for people who have certain medical conditions or meet certain criteria.	100% if provider accepts assignment	Nothing for services
BREAST CANCER SCREENING (MAMMOGRAMS)			
	Once every 12 months for all women with Medicare who are 40 and older. Medicare covers one baseline mammogram for women between 35 - 39.	100% if provider accepts assignment	Nothing for services
CARDIOVASCULAR DISEASE (BEHAVIORAL THERAPY)			
	One visit per year with a primary care doctor in a primary care setting (like a doctor's office) to help lower your risk	100% if provider accepts assignment	Nothing for services
CARDIOVASCULAR DISEASE SCREENINGS			
	Once every 5 years to test your cholesterol, lipid, lipoprotein, and triglyceride levels.	100% if provider accepts assignment	Nothing for services

Table 2
MEDICARE (PART B): PREVENTIVE SERVICES FOR 2019 (cont'd.)

Service	Benefit	Medicare Pays	You Pay
CERVICAL AND VAGINAL CANCER SCREENING			
	Once every 24 months. Every 12 months if you're at high risk for cervical or vaginal cancer or child-bearing age and had an abnormal Pap test in the past 36 months	100% if the doctor or provider accepts assignment	Nothing for services
COLORECTAL CANCER SCREENING			
Multi-target stool DNA test	Once every 3 years if you meet all conditions: between ages 50-85, show no symptoms of colorectal disease, at average risk for developing colorectal cancer	100% if the doctor or other qualified health care provider accepts assignment.	Nothing for services
Screening facal occult blood test	Once every 12 months if you're 50 or older	100% if the doctor or other qualified health care provider accepts assignment.	Nothing for services
Screening flexible sigmoidoscopy	Once every 48 months if you're 50 or older, or 120 months after a previous screening colonoscopy for those not at high risk.	100% if the doctor or other qualified health care provider accepts assignment.	Nothing for services
Screening colonoscopy	Once every 120 months (high risk every 24 months) or 48 months after a previous flexible sigmoidoscopy. There's no minimum age.	100% if the doctor or other qualified health care provider accepts assignment.	If a polyp or other tissue is found and removed during the colonoscopy, you may have to pay 20% of the Medicare-approved amount for the doctor's services and a copayment in a hospital outpatient setting.
Screening barium enema	Once every 48 months if you're 50 or older (high risk every 24 months) when used instead of a sigmoidoscopy or colonoscopy.	80% of the approved amount	You pay 20% for the doctor's services. In a hospital outpatient setting, you also pay the hospital a copayment.
DERPRESSION SCREENING			
	One screening per year. The screening must be done in a primary care setting (like a doctor's office) that can provide follow-up treatment and referrals.	100% if provider accepts assignment	Nothing for services

Table 2
MEDICARE (PART B): PREVENTIVE SERVICES FOR 2019 (cont'd.)

Service	Benefit	Medicare Pays	You Pay
DIABETES SCREENING			
	Covers these screenings if your doctor determines you're at risk for diabetes. Up to 2 diabetes screenings each year.	100% if your doctor or provider accepts assignment	Nothing for services
DIABETES SELF-MANAGEMENT TRAINING			
	Covers diabetes outpatient self-management training to teach you to cope with and manage your diabetes.	80% of the approved amount	20% of the Medicare approved amount, and the Part B deductible applies
FLU SHOTS			
	Covers one flu shot per flu season	100% if the doctor or provider accepts assignment	Nothing for services
GLAUCOMA TESTING			
	Once every 12 months for those at high risk for glaucoma.	80% of approved amount	20% of the approved amount after the yearly Part B deductible. Copayment in a hospital outpatient setting
HEPATITIS B SHOTS			
	Covers these shots for people at medium or high risk for Hepatitis B	100% if the doctor or provider accepts assignment	Nothing for services
HEPATITIS C SCREENING TEST			
	Covers one Hepatitis C screening test if you meet one of these conditions: – Current or past history of illicit injection drug use – Blood transfusion before 1992 – Born between 1945-1965	100% if the doctor or other qualified health care provider accepts assignment	Nothing for services
HIV SCREENING			
	Once per year for people at increased risk for HIV screenings for pregnant women up to 3 times during a pregnancy	100% if the doctor or provider accepts assignment	Nothing for services

Table 2
MEDICARE (PART B): PREVENTIVE SERVICES FOR 2019 (cont'd.)

Service	Benefit	Medicare Pays	You Pay
LUNG CANCER SCREENING			
	Covers a lung cancer screening with Low Dose Computed Tomography (LDCT) once per year	100% if the primary care doctor or other qualified primary care practitioner accepts assignment	Nothing for services
MEDICAL NUTRITION THERAPY SERVICES			
	Covers medical nutrition therapy and certain related services if you have diabetes or kidney disease, or you have had a kidney transplant in the last 36 months	100% if the doctor or provider accepts assignment	Nothing for services
OBESITY SCREENING AND COUNSELING			
	If you have a body mass index (BMI) of 30 or more, Medicare covers face-to-face individual behavioral therapy sessions to help you lose weight.	100% if the primary care doctor or other qualified primary care practitioner accepts assignment	Nothing for services
PNEUMOCOCCAL SHOT			
	Covers pneumococcal shots to help prevent pneumococcal infections (like certain types of pneumonia). Most people only need a shot once in their lifetime.	100% if the doctor or provider accepts assignment	Nothing for services
PROSTATE CANCER SCREENING			
	Prostate Specific Antigen (PSA) and a digital rectal exam once every 12 months for men over 50 (beginning the day after your 50th birthday)	100% for the PSA test	20% of the Medicare-approved amount, and the Part B deductible applies for the digital rectal exam. In a hospital outpatient setting, you also pay the hospital a copayment.

Table 2
MEDICARE (PART B): PREVENTIVE SERVICES FOR 2019 (cont'd.)

Service	Benefit	Medicare Pays	You Pay
SEXUALLY TRANSMITTED INFECTIONS SCREENING AND COUNSELING			
	Covers screenings for Chlamydia, gonorrhea, syphilis, and Hepatitis B. Covered for people who are pregnant and for certain people who are at increased risk for an STI. Once every 12 months or at certain times during a pregnancy. Covers up to 2 individual, 20-30 minute, face-to-face, high-intensity behavioral counseling sessions each year for sexually active adults.	100% if the primary care doctor or other qualified primary care practitioner accepts assignment	Nothing for services
SMOKING AND TOBACCO-USE CESSATION			
	Includes up to 8 face-to-face visits in a 12-month period	100% if the doctor or other qualified health care provider accepts assignment	Nothing for services

Table 3
MEDICARE (PART B): MEDICAL INSURANCE-COVERED SERVICES FOR 2019

Service	Benefit	Medicare Pays	You Pay
AMBULANCE SERVICES			
	Covers ground ambulance transportation when you need to be transported to a hospital, critical access hospital, or skilled nursing facility for medically necessary services, and transportation in any other vehicle could endanger your health	80% of approved amount (after deductible)	20% of the Medicare-approved amount, and the Part B deductible applies
AMBULATORY SURGICAL CENTERS			
	Covers ground ambulance transportation when you need to be transported to a hospital, critical access hospital, or skilled nursing facility for medically necessary services.	100% for certain preventive services	20% of the Medicare approved amount to both the ambulatory surgical center and the doctor who treats you, and Part B deductible applies.
BLOOD			
		100% if the provider gets blood from a blood bank	A copayment for the blood processing and handling services for each unit of blood you get, and the Part B deductible applies. If the provider has to buy blood for you, you must either pay the provider costs for the first 3 units in a calendar year or have the blood donated by you or someone else.

Table 3
MEDICARE (PART B): MEDICAL INSURANCE-COVERED SERVICES FOR 2019

Service	Benefit	Medicare Pays	You Pay
CARDIAC REHABILITATION			
	Cover comprehensive programs that include exercise, education, and counseling for patients who meet certain conditions. Medicare also covers intensive cardiac rehabilitation programs that are typically more rigorous or more intense than regular cardiac rehabilitation programs.	80% of the approved amount.	20% of the Medicare-approved amount if you get the services in a doctor's office. In a hospital outpatient setting, you also pay the hospital a copayment. The Part B deductible applies.
CHEMOTHERAPY			
	Covers chemotherapy in a doctor's office, freestanding clinic, or hospital outpatient setting for people with cancer.	80% of approved amount	A copayment for chemotherapy in a hospital outpatient setting. Chemotherapy given in a doctor's office or freestanding clinic you pay 20% of the Medicare-approved amount, and the Part B deductible applies.
CHIROPRACTIC SERVICES (LIMITED COVERAGE)			
	Covers manipulation of the spine if medically necessary to correct a subluxation (when one or more of the bones of your spine move out of position)	80% of the approved amount	20% of the Medicare-approved amount, and the Part B deductible applies. **Note:** You pay all costs for any other services or tests ordered by a chiropractor (including X-rays and massage therapy)
CLINICAL RESEARCH STUDIES			
	Covers some costs, like office visits and tests, in qualifying clinical research studies.	80% of the approved amount	20% of the Medicare-approved amount, and the Part B deductible may apply

Table 3
MEDICARE (PART B): MEDICAL INSURANCE-COVERED SERVICES FOR 2019

Service	Benefit	Medicare Pays	You Pay
CONCIERGE CARE			
	When a doctor or group of doctors charges you a membership fee before they'll see you or accept you into their practice.	Not Covered	100% of the membership fees for concierge care (also called concierge medicine, retainer-based medicine, boutique medicine, platinum practice, or direct care)
CONTINUOUS POSITIVE AIRWAY PRESSURE (CPAP) THERAPY			
	A 3-month trial of CPAP therapy if you've been diagnosed with obstructive sleep apnea.	80% of the approved amount	20% of the Medicare-approved amount for rental of the machine and purchase of related supplies (like masks and tubing) and the Part B deductible applies.
DEFIBRILLATOR (IMPLANTABLE AUTOMATIC)			
	Covers these devices for some people diagnosed with heart failure.	80% of the approved amount	20% of the Medicare-approved amount, if the surgery takes place in a outpatient setting. The doctor's services. If you get the device as a hospital outpatient, you also pay the hospital a copayment. The Part B deductible applies.

Table 3
MEDICARE (PART B): MEDICAL INSURANCE-COVERED SERVICES FOR 2019

Service	Benefit	Medicare Pays	You Pay
DIABETES SUPPLIES			
	Covers blood sugar testing monitors, test strips, lancet devices and lancets, blood sugar control solutions, and therapeutic shoes (in some cases). Covers insulin if it's medically necessary to use with an external insulin pump.	80% of the approved amount.	20% of the Medicare approved amount, the Part B deductible applies
DOCTOR AND OTHER HEALTH CARE PROVIDER SERVICES			
	Covers medically necessary doctor services (including outpatient services and some doctor services you get when you're a hospital inpatient) and covered preventive services.	80% of the approved amount.	20% of the Medicare approved amount, the Part B deductible applies
DURABLE MEDICAL EQUIPMENT (LIKE WALKERS)			
	Covers items like oxygen equipment and supplies, wheelchairs, walkers, and hospital beds ordered by a doctor or other health care provider enrolled in Medicare for use in the home	80% of the approved amount.	20% of the Medicare approved amount, the Part B deductible applies
EKG OR ECG (ELECTROCARDIOGRAM) SCREENING			
	One time screening EKG/ECG if referred by your doctor or other health care provider as part of your one-time "Welcome to Medicare" preventive visit	80% of the approved amount.	20% of the Medicare approved amount, the Part B deductible applies. An EKG/ECG is also covered as a diagnostic test.

Table 3
MEDICARE (PART B): MEDICAL INSURANCE-COVERED SERVICES FOR 2019

Service	Benefit	Medicare Pays	You Pay
EMERGENCY DEPARTMENT SERVICES			
	When you have an injury, a sudden illness, or an illness that quickly gets much worse	80% of the approved amount.	A specified copayment for the hospital emergency department visit, and you pay 20% of the Medicare-approved amount for the doctor's or other health care provider's services. The Part B deductible applies. Cost may be different if you're admitted.
EYEGLASSES (LIMITED)			
	One pair of eyeglasses with standard frames (or one set of contact lenses) after cataract surgery that implants an intraocular lens.	80% of the approved amount. Medicare will only pay for contact lenses or eye glasses from a supplier enrolled in Medicare	20% of Medicare-approved amount, and the Part B deductible applies.
FEDERALLY-QUALIFIED HEALTH CENTER SERVICES			
	Covers many outpatient primary care and preventive health services.	80% of the approved amount.	No deductible, and generally, you're responsible for paying 20% of your charges or 20% of the Medicare-approved amount.
FOOT EXAMS AND TREATMENT			
	Covers foot exams and treatment if you have diabetes-related nerve damage and/or meet certain conditions	80% of the approved amount.	20% of the Medicare-approved amount, and the Part B deductible applies. In a hospital outpatient setting, you also pay the hospital copayment.
HEARING AND BALANCE EXAMS			
	Covers these exams if your doctor or other health care provider orders them to see if your need medical treatment.	80% of the approved amount.	20% of the Medicare-approved amount, and the Part B deductible applies. In a hospital outpatient setting, you also pay the hospital a copayment.

Table 3
MEDICARE (PART B): MEDICAL INSURANCE-COVERED SERVICES FOR 2019

Service	Benefit	Medicare Pays	You Pay
HOME HEALTH SERVICES			
	Covers medically necessary part-time or intermittent skilled nursing care, and/or physical therapy, speech-language pathology services, and/or services if you have a continuing need for occupation therapy.	100% for health services.	Nothing for services
KIDNEY DIALYSIS SERVICES AND SUPPLIES			
	Covers 3 dialysis treatments per week if you have End-Stage Renal Disease (ESRD). This includes all ESRD-related drugs and biological, laboratory tests, home dialysis training, support services, equipment, and supplies	80% of the approved amount.	20% of approved Medicare-approved amount, and the Part B applies.
KIDNEY DISEASE EDUCATION SERVICES			
	Covers up to 6 sessions of kidney disease education services if you have Stage IV chronic kidney disease, and your doctor or other health care provider refers you for the service.	80% of the approved amount.	20% of approved Medicare-approved amount, and the Part B applies
LABORATORY SERVICES			
	Covers laboratory services including certain blood tests, urinalysis, certain tests on tissue specimens, and some screening tests.	Generally 100% of approved amount	Nothing for services

Table 3
MEDICARE (PART B): MEDICAL INSURANCE-COVERED SERVICES FOR 2019

Service	Benefit	Medicare Pays	You Pay
MENTAL HEALTH CARE (OUTPATIENT)			
	Covers mental health care services to help with conditions like depression or anxiety. Includes services generally provided in an outpatient setting (like a doctor's or other health care provider's office or hospital outpatient department).	100% of lab tests. 80% of the approved amount. **Note:** Inpatient mental health care is covered under Part A	20% of the Medicare-approved amount and the Part B deductible applies for: • Visits to a doctor or other health care provider to diagnose your condition or monitor or change your prescriptions • Outpatient treatment of your condition (like counseling or psychotherapy)
OCCUPATIONAL THERAPY			
	Covers evaluation and treatment to help you perform activities of daily living (like dressing or bathing) when your doctor or other health care provider certifies you need it.	80% of the approved amount.	20% of the Medicare-approved amount and the Part B deductible applies.
OUTPATIENT HOSPITAL SERVICES			
	Covers many diagnostic and treatment services in hospital outpatient departments.	80% of the approved amount.	20% of the Medicare-approved amount and the Part B deductible applies.
OUTPATIENT MEDICAL AND SURGICAL SERVICES AND SUPPLIES			
	Covers approved procedures like X-rays, casts, stitches, or outpatient surgeries.	80% of the approved amount.	20% of the Medicare-approved amount, and the Part B deductible applies. In a hospital outpatient setting, you also pay the hospital a copayment.
PHYSICAL THERAPY			
	Covers evaluation and treatment for injuries and diseases that change your ability to function when your doctor or other health care provider certifies your need for it.	80% of the approved amount.	20% of the Medicare-approved amount, and the Part B deductible applies.

Table 3
MEDICARE (PART B): MEDICAL INSURANCE-COVERED SERVICES FOR 2019

Service	Benefit	Medicare Pays	You Pay
PRESCRIPTION DRUGS (LIMITED)			
	Covers a limited number of drugs like injections you get in a doctor's office, certain oral anti-cancer drugs, drugs used with some types of durable medical equipment (like a nebulizer or external infusion pump), immunosuppressant drugs and under very limited circumstances.	80% of the approved amount.	20% of the Medicare-approved amount, and the Part B deductible applies.
PROSTHETIC/ORTHOTIC ITEMS			
	Covers arm, leg, back, and neck braces; artificial eyes; artificial limbs (and their replacement parts); some types of breast prostheses (after mastectomy); and prosthetic devices needed to replace an internal body part or function.	80% of the approved amount.	20% of the Medicare-approved amount, and the Part B deductible applies.
PULMONARY REHABILITATION			
	Covers a comprehensive pulmonary rehabilitation program if you have moderate to very severe chronic obstructive pulmonary disease (COPD) and have a referral from the doctor treating this chronic respiratory disease.	80% of the approved amount.	20% of the Medicare-approved amount, and the Part B deductible applies. In a hospital outpatient setting, you also pay the hospital a copayment.
RURAL HEALTH CLINIC SERVICES			
	Covers many outpatient primary care and preventive services in rural health clinics.	80% of the approved amount. 100% for most preventive services.	20% of the Medicare-approved amount, and the Part B deductible applies.

Table 3

MEDICARE (PART B): MEDICAL INSURANCE-COVERED SERVICES FOR 2019

Service	Benefit	Medicare Pays	You Pay
SECOND SURGICAL OPINIONS			
	Covers second surgical opinions for surgery that isn't an emergency.	80% of the approved amount.	20% of the Medicare-approved amount, and the Part B deductible applies.
SPEECH-LANGUAGE PATHOLOGY SERVICES			
	Covers evaluation and treatment to regain and strengthen speech and language skills, including cognitive and swallowing skills, when your doctor or other health care provider certifies you need it.	80% of the approved amount.	20% of the Medicare-approved amount, and the Part B deductible applies.
SURGICAL DRESSING SERVICES			
	Covers medically necessary treatment of a surgical or surgically treated wound.	80% of the approved amount.	20% of the Medicare-approved amount for the doctor's or other health care provider's services
TELEHEALTH			
	Covers limited medical or other health services, like office visits and consultations provided using an interactive, two-way telecommunications system (like real-time audio and video) by an eligible provider who isn't at your location.	80% of the approved amount.	20% of the Medicare-approved amount, and the Part B deductible applies.
TESTS (OTHER THAN LAB TEST)			
	Covers X-rays, MRIs, CT scans, ECG/EKGs, and some other diagnostic tests.	80% of the approved amount.	20% of the Medicare-approved amount, and the Part B deductible applies. You also pay the hospital a copayment that may be more than 20% of the Medicare-approved amount, but in most cases this amount can't be more than the Part A hospital stay deductible.

Table 3
MEDICARE (PART B): MEDICAL INSURANCE-COVERED SERVICES FOR 2019

Service	Benefit	Medicare Pays	You Pay
TRANSPLANTS AND IMMUNOSUPPRESSIVE DRUGS			
	Covers doctor services for heart, lung, kidney, pancreas, intestine, and liver transplants under certain conditions and only in a Medicare-certified facility. Covers bone marrow and cornea transplants under certain conditions.	80% of the approved amount.	20% of the Medicare-approved amount for the drugs, and the Part B deductible applies.
TRAVEL (HEALTH CARE NEEDED WHEN TRAVELING OUTSIDE THE U.S.)			
	Generally doesn't cover health care while you're traveling outside the U.S., there are some exceptions, including cases where Medicare may pay for services that you get while on board a ship within the territorial waters adjoining the land areas of the U.S.	80% of the approved amount.	20% of the Medicare-approved amount, and the Part B deductible applies.
URGENTLY NEEDED CARE			
	Covers urgently needed care to treat a sudden illness or injury that isn't a medical emergency.	80% of the approved amount.	20% of the Medicare-approved amount for the doctor's or other health care provider's services and the Part B deductible applies. In a hospital outpatient setting, you also pay the hospital a copayment

In addition to the services listed, Medicare also helps cover the following: ambulance services, artificial eyes, artificial limbs (prosthetic devices and replacement parts), braces (arm, leg, back, and neck), chiropractic services (limited), eyeglasses (one pair of standard frames after cataract surgery with an intraocular lens), hearing and balance exams ordered by your doctor, kidney dialysis and prosthetic/orthodontic devices (including breast prosthesis after mastectomy).

In some cases and under certain conditions, Medicare may also cover these services: a second surgical opinion by a doctor, telemedicine services (in rural areas), and therapeutic shoes for people with diabetes, and transplants (heart, lung, kidney, pancreas, intestine, bone marrow, cornea, and liver).

Table 4
MEDICARE (PART D): PRESCRIPTION DRUG COVERAGE FOR 2019
Coverage is provided by private companies that have been approved by Medicare

Service	Costs	Medicare Provider Pays	You Pay
Medicare approved drug plans will cover generic and brand-name drugs. Most plans will have a formulary, which is a list of drugs covered by the plan. This list must always meet Medicare's requirements, including: - Inclusion of at least two drugs in every drug category. - Access to retail pharmacies. - For drugs not covered, a procedure must be in place to obtain, if medically necessary.	Premium	---	On average, $36.53 per month for basic coverage, and $52.28 per month for enhanced coverage
	First $415 in costs	Nothing	Up to $415 (this is the deductible)
	Costs between $415 and $3,820	$2,455	$851 (30% for branded companies, 37% for generic)
	Next $1,280 drug costs	Nothing	Until out of pocket spending, including drug company discount total $5,100
	All additional drug costs	All but co-pay	Co-pay $3.40 generic $8.50 all other drugs

Your plan must, at a minimum, offer this standard level of service and cost coverage outlined here, however, some plans may offer more coverage. Premiums will vary depending on any additional coverage provided by the plan.

What are the Gaps in Medicare Coverage?

Medicare has never covered all medical expenses and never will. The gap between what the doctors charge and the government pays is big and getting bigger. In fact, Medicare was never designed to cover chronic conditions or prolonged medical treatments. It was directed toward Americans age 65 or older who need minor or short-term care – little more. Be sure to understand where Medicare falls short. We can't list all the possible gaps, but here are the ones that affect almost everyone (see the tables on the previous pages for more details):

Gap #1: Deductibles

Medicare has two parts: **Part A** *acts as hospital insurance* and **Part B** *acts as medical insurance.* You are responsible for deductibles under both parts. Under Part A, for instance, you would be responsible for the $1,364 deductible for the first 60 days of a hospital stay. Plus, this $1,364 deductible applies each time you re-enter the hospital after a greater than 60-day span between admissions.

Under Part B, Medicare will pick up 80% of approved medical expenses after you pay a $185 deductible.

Gap #2: Co-Payments

You are responsible for a share of the daily costs if your hospital stay lasts more than 60 days. In 2019, you would be responsible for paying a $341 daily "coinsurance" fee if you stay in the hospital longer than 60 days but less than 90 days. Worse yet, Medicare Part A pays nothing after 90 days – unless you take advantage of the 60 "lifetime reserve days." The 60 reserve days can be used only once, and even then, you would still pay $682 daily for those 60 days.

Gap #3: Shortfalls

A national fee schedule established what physicians on Medicare assignment can charge for their services; Medicare will generally pay 80% of that amount. However, not all physicians are on Medicare assignment. Those who are not on assignment may charge more than the approved amount, leaving you responsible for the shortfall.

Gap #4: Nonpayment

The Original Medicare program does not directly provide any coverage whatsoever for certain services and expenses such as prescription drugs, hearing aids, treatment in foreign countries, and much more.

The bottom line: When all is said and done, the federal Medicare program will cover no more than half to three quarters of your medical expenses. That's why private Medicare supplement insurance, or Medigap, makes sense; its goal is to cover a portion of what Medicare doesn't. But in order for Medigap to make sense for you, you need to find the right policy, from the right company, for a reasonable price.

What about Medicare Prescription Drug Coverage?

The Medicare Prescription Drug, Improvement and Modernization (MMA) Act was passed in 2003. This legislation created Medicare Part D: Prescription Drug Coverage effective January 2006. Coverage is only available by private companies that have been approved by Medicare, not through the Medicare program directly. You can obtain coverage by either directly purchasing Part D coverage through a plan sponsor or in combination with enrollment in a Medicare Advantage health plan offering drug coverage. These drug plans are standardized across providers but they are required to offer a minimum level of coverage. Plans may vary in co-pays, premiums, deductibles, and drug coverage and pharmacy networks. (See Table 4 for an outline of the required coverage.)

To assist you in the selection of a health benefit package complete with prescription drug coverage refer to our *Consumer Guide to Medicare Prescription Drug Coverage* that includes:

- Information on the Medicare prescription drug benefit.
- Help in making a choice about prescription drug coverage.
- What to consider once you enroll.
- An index of Medicare approved prescription drug plans.

Medicare, Medicare Advantage, Part D Sponsors, Medigap – What Does It All Mean?

The various terms used regarding coverage of health benefits for seniors is downright confusing. Let us take a moment here to review some of the terminology. The health insurance program for seniors managed by the federal government consists of the Original Medicare, Medicare Advantage, and Part D Prescription Drug Sponsors. Tables 1 through 3 on the preceding pages outline your coverage and coverage gaps under the Original Medicare plan. With this plan you seek services from Medicare providers who then receive payment from the government for the costs they incur for your care.

The Medicare Advantage program allows you to join a private health insurance plan that has contracted with Medicare to provide Part A and B coverage. The Medicare Advantage plans in turn receive funds from the government for providing you with benefits. These plans typically provide coverage beyond what Medicare offers, making supplemental policy unnecessary.

Medicare Part D will allow you to get prescription drug benefits in two ways. One option is to enroll with a Prescription Drug Plan sponsor in combination with your Original Medicare benefits. You will receive benefits from and pay a premium to the plan sponsor who then receives funds from the government. The second option is to enroll with a Medicare Advantage plan that is offering prescription drug coverage. Here you will receive all your benefits from the plan and pay only one premium. Refer to Table 4 for an outline of the minimum coverage that a plan sponsor must offer.

Medicare Supplement insurance, or Medigap as it is commonly referred to, is available through private insurers for those enrollees of the Original Medicare plan to fill the coverage 'gaps' in the Part A and B coverage. Basically, Medigap insurance will reimburse you for the out-of-pocket costs you incur that are not covered under Medicare. This insurance is completely optional.

Of course, if you're lucky, and your employer or union is continuing to cover your health benefits when you retire you won't need any of these types of insurance. But you want to stay educated because you never know when your old employer may discontinue retirement benefits.

Now let's take a closer look at the difference between Medicare supplement insurance policies and Medicare Advantage plans.

Medigap

To make comparing policies from one insurer to another easier Congress standardized and simplified Medigap plans. This means that all Medigap insurers offer the same exact policy (though some companies may offer only a few of the plans). If you live in Wisconsin, Massachusetts, or Minnesota there are different types of Medigap plans that are sold in your state but are still standardized across insurers in each state.

Starting in 2020 Plans C and F are to be discontinued, a high deductible version of Plan G has been introduced. Only if you were first eligible for Medicare prior to January 1, 2020 will you be able to enroll in Plans C or F. Plans D and G have the same coverage as Plans C and F respectively, less the Part D deductible that was normally provided at a substantial premium by insurers. Note, not all insures will continue to offer these plans, even to those who are eligible. In Part II we provide you with a table that outlines what each of the plans cover.

You will have to pay a premium, which can vary greatly, depending on the plan you choose and from which company you buy. Coverage is more expansive than through a Medicare Advantage plan but at a higher price. With a Medigap policy you have the freedom to choose your own doctors or specialists, and you will be covered regardless of which clinic or hospital you attend. Medicare Select plans, a type of Medigap policy, are available in some areas which offer the same benefits but require you to use providers within the policy's network, similar to an HMO. These policies should be cheaper than non-Select plans since your choice of providers is restricted. Medigap plans do not cover long-term/custodial care at home or in a nursing home, hearing aids, vision care, private-duty nursing, dental care, or prescription medicine. Even if you decide that you want a Medigap policy you may find that you will not be approved depending on your health, or you may not find an insurer in your area that sells these types of policies. However, once you do purchase a policy, Medigap policies are guaranteed renewable. This means that an insurance company cannot refuse to renew your policy unless you do not pay the premiums, or you made material misrepresentations on your application. You are typically able to obtain coverage each year once you are approved; however, the premium may change.

You are eligible to purchase a Medigap policy when you have enrolled in Medicare Parts A and B. In all states, there is an open enrollment period that lasts for six months and begins on the first day of the month in which you are both age 65 or older and enrolled in Part B. During this open enrollment period, the insurer cannot deny you coverage for any reason including pre-existing conditions. The insurer can, however, charge you a higher premium for the pre-existing condition or other health and lifestyle factors.

Medicare Advantage Plans

Under Medicare Part C, Medicare Advantage plans were introduced to offer seniors choices in coverage, more benefits at minimal cost, and to reduce the burden on the Medicare program. Insurers will often offer benefits not covered by Medicare, such as dental and vision services, at a lower price than a Medigap policy.

Prior to 2006 most offered some type of prescription drug coverage, but it varied from plan to plan. With the Medicare Prescription drug bill that took effect in 2006, health insurers may still offer prescription drug coverage but the benefits must match or exceed the requirements outlined in Medicare Part D (Refer Table). The insurers will then receive funding from the government for providing the benefits. All coverage is included in one premium charge.

With a Medicare Advantage plan you will not have to file any forms for reimbursement. You may or may not have to pay a premium and/or a co-pay for doctor's visits. In most cases you are restricted to the doctors in the plan's network, and you will need a referral before you see a specialist. Several new types of Medicare Advantage plans (PPOs, Special Need plans, Private Fee-for-Service plans, Medicare Medical Savings Account Plans, and Cost plans) have been introduced recently that vary from the current HMO plans offered including, in some cases, expanded options for accessing providers. Make sure to understand how these plans work before signing on.

There may be limited insurers offering a Medicare Advantage plan in your area and your benefits can be discontinued after the contract period (usually one year). At that time you would have to either choose a new insurer/plan or join the Original Medicare Plan.

Part II: Steps to Follow When Selecting a Medigap Policy

Follow These Steps When Selecting a Medigap Policy

1. **Determine what benefits you need.** Consider the following:

- **Income.** If you are living on a **fixed income** and are able to afford only the most basic coverage, favor Plan A, the core plan. Among other things, you'll get an extra 30 days hospitalization per year beyond what Medicare pays. It also covers 100% of the Medicare Part B coinsurance for approved medical services, which is usually 20% of the approved amount.

  You may also want to consider plans, K or L, if they are available in your area. These policies help limit out-of-pocket costs for doctor's services and hospital care at a lower premium; however, you will have to pay more of Medicare's coinsurance and deductibles before the policy pays its share of the costs. These policies also do not cover 'excess' charges billed by your physician. Wisconsin, Massachusetts, and Minnesota also offer a core or basic plan to choose from.

- **Family History.** You or your family's medical history is such that you want to be prepared to pay for nursing care, consider Plan C. Your $170.50 per-day co-payment under Medicare would be covered up to 100 days for skilled nursing facility care.

- **Foreign Travel.** If you travel overseas extensively, you can get coverage for emergency care in a foreign country with Plan C through G, M and N. In Massachusetts and Minnesota foreign travel coverage can be found in the Supplement 1 and 2 Plans and to the Basic Medigap Coverage, respectively. In Wisconsin, a Foreign Travel rider can be added.
- **Plan F is the most popular one.** In 2016, 58.6% of enrollees chose this plan. The next popular, Plan G, had 18.2% of the enrollees.

The chart below shows basic information about the different benefits Medigap policies cover.

X = the plan covers 100% of this benefit

% = the plan covers the percentage of this benefit

	Medigap Plans									
Medigap Benefits	**A**	**B**	**C[1]**	**D**	**F[2]**	**G[3]**	**K**	**L**	**M**	**N**
Part A coinsurance and hospital costs up to an additional 365 days after Medicare benefits are used up	X	X	X	X	X	X	X	X	X	X
Part B coinsurance or copayment	X	X	X	X	X	X	50%	75%	X	X[4]
Blood (first 3 pints)	X	X	X	X	X	X	50%	75%	X	X
Part A hospice care coinsurance or copayment	X	X	X	X	X	X	50%	75%	X	X
Skilled nursing facility care coinsurance			X	X	X	X	50%	75%	X	X
Part A deductible		X	X	X	X	X	50%	75%	50%	X
Part B deductible			X		X					
Part B excess charges					X	X				
Foreign travel exchange (up to plan limits)			80%	80%	80%	80%			80%	80%
Out-of-pocket limit[5]							$5,560	$2,780		

1. Plan C will be discontinued in 2020. Only if you were first eligible for Medicare prior to January 1, 2020 will you be able to enroll.
2. Plan F also offers a high-deductible option. If you choose this option, this means you must pay for Medicare-covered cost up to the deductible amount of $2,300 in 2019 before your Medigap plan pays anything. In 2020 only if you were first eligible for Medicare prior to January 1, 2020 will you be able to enroll.
3. Plan G will also offer a high deductible option. If you choose this option, this means you must pay for Medicare-covered cost up to the deductible amount before your Medigap plan pays anything.
4. Plan N pays 100% of the Part B coinsurance, except for a copayment of up to $20 for some office visits and up to a $50 copayment for emergency room visits that don't result in inpatient admission.

After you meet your out-of-pocket yearly limit and your yearly Part B deductible, the Medigap plan pays 100% of covered services for the rest of the calendar year.

In Massachusetts, Minnesota, and Wisconsin medigap policies are standardized in a different way. They consist of a core plan/core plans and additional riders can be selected to provide additional coverage at a cost.

2. Find out which policies are available to you.

- Not all insurers offer all plans in all areas.

- Will you be denied coverage by some insurers due to your health? Find out which ones and eliminate them from your choices.

- Does the insurer deny coverage for pre-existing conditions? If you are past the 6-month window following enrollment in Medicare Part B, companies most often deny you coverage for a specific period of time. However, some companies do not do this so their annual premium may be higher. You need to consider whether or not the higher premium is worth the coverage.

- Are you a member of AARP? If so, you may be able to obtain a policy through its sponsored insurer. Other affinity organizations also offer coverage through a Medigap insurer. Be sure to check with any groups of which you are a member.

- Do you want a Medicare Select plan? If you buy a Medicare Select policy, you are buying one of the 10 standardized Medigap plans A through N. With a Medicare Select plan, however, you must use the network providers to get full insurance benefits (except in an emergency). For this reason, Medicare Select policies generally cost less. If you don't use a Medicare Select hospital for non-emergency services, you will have to pay what a traditional Medicare plan doesn't pay. Medicare will pay its share of the approved charges no matter what hospital you choose.

3. Compare the premiums. Not only will you want to check out the premium you would be charged for different plans, but it is important to understand that there are three ways that insurance companies set the prices for policies. In order to compare the premium charged by two insurers for the same plan you need to make sure you are comparing apples to apples. No matter which type of pricing your Medigap insurer uses, the price of your policy will likely go up each year because of inflation and rising health care costs.

- **Attained-Age Rating.** With this type of policy the premium will rise as you age. For example: if you buy at 65, you pay what the company charges 65-year-old customers. Then at 66, you will pay whatever the company is charging a 66-year-old. The Medigap policy will go up in cost due to age, in addition to the increased cost of medical care.
- **Issue-Age Rating.** With this policy, the insurance company will charge you based on the age you were when you first signed up; you will always pay the same premium that someone that age pays. Unlike attained-age policies, issue-age policies do not go up because you are another year older. For example: if you first buy at 65, you will always pay the premium the company charges 65-year-old customers—no matter what your age. If you first buy at 70, you will always pay the premium the company charges 70-year-old customers. This is not to say that your premium won't go up. It will increase as the insurer raises rates for that particular age.
- **No-Age Rating or Community Rating.** This is the least common way that policies are priced. No matter how old you are, the policy costs the same. With this structure, younger people pay more than what they would pay for other polices and older people may pay less. The premium is the same for all people who buy this plan regardless of age. For example: XYZ Company will charge a 65-year-old $140, a 75-year-old $140 and an 85-year-old $140.

4. You may only be concerned with catastrophic illness. If so, you may not need to buy a Medigap policy at all, especially if you are relatively healthy, live a healthy lifestyle, and currently only incur routine medical expenses that would cost less than the premiums for a Medigap policy. You could purchase a catastrophic or high-deductible health insurance policy that would kick in when your medical bills exceeded a predetermined level, such as $5,100.

The Medigap K and L plans may also be a good choice. They should cost less than other Medigap plans but will provide a cap on out-of-pocket expenses.

5. What is the insurer's safety rating? If you were to experience the double misfortune of becoming seriously ill and having your insurer fail, you may be responsible for much of your unpaid claims, and it would be difficult to find replacement coverage.
We recommend you choose a company with a B+ or higher Weiss Safety Rating if you can. You should also consider an insurer's level of customer service and timeliness in reimbursing claims. Ask friends about their experiences and contact your state's insurance department or counsel for aging to find out if they keep public complaint records. As an industry, Medigap insurers have a good reputation for paying claims.

How to Switch Medigap Policies

If you are currently holding a Medigap policy and become uncomfortable with your company's financial stability, or if you find a cheaper policy at a stronger company, here are some steps to take before switching policies:

Step 1: Determine if your policy was issued prior to January 1, 1992. If it was, and if it was guaranteed renewable, you did not switch to one of the standard plans. This policy should be compared carefully to the newer standardized plans before switching. Remember: once you switch to one of the new standardized plans, you can never switch back to a non-standard plan.

Furthermore, you should know that if you already have a Medigap policy, it is against federal law for a company to sell you another one. When you buy another policy, you must sign a statement indicating that you are replacing your current policy and do not intend to keep both.

Step 2: Before switching policies, compare benefits and premiums. It is important to note that some of the older non-standard policies may provide superior coverage, and your increased age may make comparable coverage more expensive.

Step 3: Determine any impact on pre-existing conditions. Any portion of a pre-existing condition satisfied under the old policy will be credited to the new policy. Example: The old policy specified that it would not cover a pre-existing condition for the first six months. You switch policies after just two months. As a result, you only have four months to wait under the new policy to be covered for your pre-existing condition.
(Exception: If your new policy has a benefit that was not included in your old policy, a new six-month waiting period may be imposed on that particular benefit.)

Step 4: Use the "free-look" provision which allows you 30 days to review a Medigap policy once you've paid the first premium. If, during the first 30 days, you decide you don't want or need the policy you can return it to the company for a full refund.

Step 5: Do not cancel your old policy until your new policy is in force.

Part III: Medigap Premium Rates

Basic Medigap Coverage
PLAN A

If you stay in the hospital for longer than 60 days, but less than 90 days, Plan A covers Medicare Part A coinsurance amount of $341 per day (in 2019) for each benefit period.

For each Medicare "hospital reserve day" you use, Plan A pays the $682 (in 2019) per day Medicare Part A coinsurance amount. "Hospital reserve days" are 60 nonrenewable hospital days that Medicare provides which can only be used once in a lifetime. After all Medicare hospital benefits are exhausted, Plan A will cover 100% of Medicare Part A eligible hospital expenses.

If the need arises, Plan A covers costs for the first three pints of blood or equivalent quantities of packed red blood cells received each year in connection with Medicare Parts A and B covered services. Once you have met this 3-pint blood deductible under Medicare Part A, it does not have to be met again under Part B.

After your $185 annual Medicare Part B deductible is met Plan A will cover the coinsurance amount for Medicare approved medical services, which is generally 20% of the approved amount.

Plan A now includes coverage of cost sharing for all Part A Medicare-eligible hospice care and respite care expenses.

If you feel that Plan A fits your needs, take a look at the two tables below to find out what price you should expect to be charged for this plan. The tables outline the typical annual premiums charged for Plan A depending on age and gender. These rates are based on our 2019 nationwide collection of insurance premiums.

PLAN A

Female

Age	Average Premium	Lowest Premium	Highest Premium	Median Premium
65	$1,638	$606	$16,740	$1,490
70	$1,829	$763	$19,046	$1,666
75	$2,091	$883	$20,538	$1,910
80	$2,317	$993	$24,163	$2,131
85	$2,518	$1,035	$26,323	$2,326
90	$2,679	$1,035	$27,940	$2,497
95	$2,802	$1,035	$27,940	$2,631

Male

Age	Average Premium	Lowest Premium	Highest Premium	Median Premium
65	$1,793	$656	$17,832	$1,656
70	$2,010	$827	$20,287	$1,845
75	$2,299	$958	$21,877	$2,123
80	$2,554	$1,076	$25,932	$2,359
85	$2,782	$1,122	$29,340	$2,593
90	$2,962	$1,122	$31,142	$2,784
95	$3,102	$1,122	$31,142	$2,940

Basic Medigap Coverage
PLAN B

If you stay in the hospital for longer than 60 days, but less than 90 days, Plan B covers Medicare Part A coinsurance amount of $341 per day (in 2019) for each benefit period.

For each Medicare "hospital reserve day" you use, Plan B pays the $682 (in 2019) per day Medicare Part A coinsurance amount. "Hospital reserve days" are 60 nonrenewable hospital days that Medicare provides which can only be used once in a lifetime. After all Medicare hospital benefits are exhausted, Plan B will cover 100% of Medicare Part A eligible hospital expenses.

If the need arises, Plan B covers costs for the first three pints of blood or equivalent quantities of packed red blood cells received each year in connection with Medicare Parts A and B covered services. Once you have met this 3-pint blood deductible under Medicare Part A, it does not have to be met again under Part B.

After your $185 annual Medicare Part B deductible is met Plan B will cover the coinsurance amount for Medicare approved medical services, which is generally 20% of the approved amount.

Plan B now includes coverage of cost sharing for all Part A Medicare-eligible hospice care and respite care expenses.

Additional Features

Plan B includes the core Medigap coverage PLUS one extra benefit:

- It will pay for the $1,364 Medicare Part A in-patient hospital deductible (per benefit period in 2019).

If you feel that Plan B fits your needs, take a look at the two tables below to find out what price you should expect to be charged for this plan. The tables outline the typical annual premiums charged for Plan B depending on age and gender. These rates are based on our 2019 nationwide collection of insurance premiums.

PLAN B

Female

Age	Average Premium	Lowest Premium	Highest Premium	Median Premium
65	$2,004	$947	$9,961	$1,843
70	$2,296	$1,041	$9,961	$2,156
75	$2,645	$1,115	$9,961	$2,534
80	$2,891	$1,323	$9,961	$2,760
85	$3,101	$1,636	$9,961	$2,964
90	$3,267	$1,640	$9,961	$3,109
95	$3,372	$1,640	$9,961	$3,204

Male

Age	Average Premium	Lowest Premium	Highest Premium	Median Premium
65	$2,175	$947	$9,961	$2,006
70	$2,498	$1,175	$9,961	$2,343
75	$2,868	$1,350	$9,961	$2,740
80	$3,145	$1,622	$9,961	$3,018
85	$3,383	$1,640	$9,961	$3,227
90	$3,567	$1,640	$10,150	$3,393
95	$3,687	$1,640	$10,509	$3,499

Basic Medigap Coverage
PLAN C

If you stay in the hospital for longer than 60 days, but less than 90 days, Plan C covers Medicare Part A coinsurance amount of $341 per day (in 2019) for each benefit period.

For each Medicare "hospital reserve day" you use, Plan C pays the $682 (in 2019) per day Medicare Part A coinsurance amount. "Hospital reserve days" are 60 nonrenewable hospital days that Medicare provides you which can only be used once in a lifetime. After all Medicare hospital benefits are exhausted, Plan C will cover 100% of Medicare Part A eligible hospital expenses.

If the need arises, Plan C covers costs for the first three pints of blood or equivalent quantities of packed red blood cells received each year in connection with Medicare Parts A and B covered services. Once you have met this 3-pint blood deductible under Medicare Part A, it does not have to be met again under Part B.

After your $185 annual Medicare Part B deductible is met, Plan C will cover the coinsurance amount of Medicare approved medical services, which is generally 20% of the approved amount

Plan C now includes coverage of cost sharing for all Part A Medicare-eligible hospice care and respite care expenses.

Additional Features

Plan C includes the core Medigap coverage, plus four extra benefits.

- Your $1,364 Medicare Part A in-patient hospital deductible (per benefit period in 2019)
- Your coinsurance amount for skilled nursing facility care for the 21st through the 100th day of your stay (the amount is $170.50 per day in 2019).
- Your Medicare Part B deductible ($185 per calendar year in 2019).
- Any emergency care you may require when you are in a foreign country after a $250 deductible. This benefit pays 80% of the cost of your care for the first 60 days of each trip, up to $50,000 in your lifetime.

Note: The only difference between Plan C and Plan D is the Part B deductible. Compare the prices between the plans before making your choice.

If you feel that Plan C fits your needs, take a look at the two tables below to find out what price you should expect to be charged for this plan. The tables outline the typical annual premiums charged for Plan C depending on age and gender. These rates are based on our 2019 nationwide collection of insurance premiums.

PLAN C

Female

Age	Average Premium	Lowest Premium	Highest Premium	Median Premium
65	$2,347	$1,103	$6,423	$2,130
70	$2,693	$1,305	$6,814	$2,488
75	$3,129	$1,567	$7,833	$2,978
80	$3,441	$1,834	$8,471	$3,292
85	$3,701	$1,834	$10,404	$3,535
90	$3,874	$1,834	$10,404	$3,713
95	$4,010	$1,834	$10,404	$3,865

Male

Age	Average Premium	Lowest Premium	Highest Premium	Median Premium
65	$2,530	$1,142	$6,704	$2,323
70	$2,911	$1,461	$7,833	$2,702
75	$3,366	$1,747	$9,010	$3,201
80	$3,714	$1,834	$10,006	$3,566
85	$4,004	$1,834	$12,588	$3,869
90	$4,197	$1,834	$12,588	$4,044
95	$4,350	$1,834	$12,588	$4,232

Basic Medigap Coverage
PLAN D

If you stay in the hospital for longer than 60 days, but less than 90 days, Plan D covers Medicare Part A coinsurance amount of $341 per day (in 2019) for each benefit period.

For each Medicare "hospital reserve day" you use, Plan D pays the $682 (in 2019) per day Medicare Part A coinsurance amount. "Hospital reserve days" are 60 nonrenewable hospital days that Medicare provides you which can only be used once in a lifetime. After all Medicare hospital benefits are exhausted, Plan D will cover 100% of Medicare Part A eligible hospital expenses.

If the need arises, Plan D covers costs for the first three pints of blood or equivalent quantities of packed red blood cells received each year in connection with Medicare Parts A and B covered services. Once you have met this 3-pint blood deductible under Medicare Part A, it does not have to be met again under Part B.

After your $185 annual Medicare Part B deductible is met, Plan D will cover the coinsurance amount of Medicare approved medical services, which is generally 20% of the approved amount

Plan D now includes coverage of cost sharing for all Part A Medicare-eligible hospice care and respite care expenses.

Additional Features

Plan D includes the core Medigap coverage, plus three extra benefits.

- Your $1,364 Medicare Part A in-patient hospital deductible (per benefit period in 2019).
- Your coinsurance amount for skilled nursing facility care for the 21st through the 100th day of your stay (the amount is $170.50 per day in 2019).
- Any emergency care you may require when you are in a foreign country after a $250 deductible. This benefit pays 80% of the cost of your care for the first 60 days of each trip, up to $50,000 in your lifetime.

Note: The only difference between Plan D and Plan C is the Part B deductible. Compare the prices between the plans before making your choice.

If you feel that Plan D fits your needs, take a look at the two tables below to find out what price you should expect to be charged for this plan. The tables outline the typical annual premiums charged for Plan D depending on age and gender. These rates are based on our 2019 nationwide collection of insurance premiums.

PLAN D

Female

Age	Average Premium	Lowest Premium	Highest Premium	Median Premium
65	$1,936	$992	$5,876	$1,848
70	$2,272	$1,104	$5,954	$2,175
75	$2,656	$1,278	$6,958	$2,569
80	$2,975	$1,481	$7,661	$2,910
85	$3,232	$1,603	$8,172	$3,169
90	$3,411	$1,670	$8,587	$3,315
95	$3,549	$1,671	$8,898	$3,436

Male

Age	Average Premium	Lowest Premium	Highest Premium	Median Premium
65	$2,146	$1,052	$5,876	$2,044
70	$2,532	$1,219	$6,847	$2,429
75	$2,968	$1,432	$7,998	$2,883
80	$3,333	$1,659	$8,809	$3,267
85	$3,622	$1,671	$9,398	$3,544
90	$3,825	$1,671	$9,876	$3,719
95	$3,981	$1,671	$10,235	$3,848

Basic Medigap Coverage
PLAN F

If you stay in the hospital for longer than 60 days, but less than 90 days, Plan F covers Medicare Part A coinsurance amount of $341 per day (in 2019) for each benefit period.

For each Medicare "hospital reserve day" you use, Plan F pays the $682 (in 2019) per day Medicare Part A coinsurance amount. "Hospital reserve days" are 60 nonrenewable hospital days that Medicare provides you which can only be used once in a lifetime. After all Medicare hospital benefits are exhausted, Plan F will cover 100% of Medicare Part A eligible hospital expenses.

If the need arises, Plan F covers costs for the first three pints of blood or equivalent quantities of packed red blood cells received each year in connection with Medicare Parts A and B covered services. Once you have met this 3-pint blood deductible under Medicare Part A, it does not have to be met again under Part B.

After your $185 annual Medicare Part B deductible is met, Plan F will cover the coinsurance amount of Medicare approved medical services, which is generally 20% of the approved amount. A high deductible option is available, requiring you to pay the first $2,300 of Medicare covered costs before your Medigap policy pays anything.

Plan F now includes coverage of cost sharing for all Part A Medicare-eligible hospice care and respite care expenses.

Additional Features

Plan F includes all of the basic Medigap coverage plus five extra benefits.

- Your $1,364 Medicare Part A in-patient hospital deductible (per benefit period in 2019).
- Your coinsurance amount for skilled nursing facility care for the 21st through the 100th day of your stay (the amount is $170.50 per day in 2019).
- Any emergency care you may require when you are in a foreign country after a $250 deductible. This benefit pays 80% of the cost of your care for the first 60 days of each trip, up to $50,000 in your lifetime.
- Your deductible for Medicare Part B ($185 in 2019).
- 100% of any excess charges under Medicare Part B. This is the difference between the approved amount for Part B services and the actual charges (up to the charge limitations set by either Medicare or state law).

Note: The only difference between Plan F and Plan G is the Part B deductible. Compare the prices between the plans before making your choice.

If you feel that Plan F fits your needs, take a look at the two tables below to find out what price you should expect to be charged for this plan. The tables outline the typical annual premiums charged for Plan F depending on age and gender. These rates are based on our 2019 nationwide collection of insurance premiums.

PLAN F

Female

Age	Average Premium	Lowest Premium	Highest Premium	Median Premium
65	$2,232	$1,178	$7,752	$2,025
70	$2,511	$1,319	$7,752	$2,318
75	$2,921	$1,584	$8,167	$2,728
80	$3,271	$1,701	$8,527	$3,077
85	$3,602	$1,701	$9,489	$3,401
90	$3,870	$1,701	$9,489	$3,667
95	$4,087	$1,701	$10,124	$3,885

Male

Age	Average Premium	Lowest Premium	Highest Premium	Median Premium
65	$2,442	$1,226	$7,752	$2,236
70	$2,750	$1,477	$7,886	$2,533
75	$3,196	$1,701	$9,071	$2,980
80	$3,589	$1,701	$9,810	$3,378
85	$3,963	$1,701	$10,414	$3,755
90	$4,262	$1,701	$10,904	$4,064
95	$4,507	$1,701	$11,255	$4,304

Basic Medigap Coverage
PLAN F with High Deductible

If you stay in the hospital for longer than 60 days, but less than 90 days, Plan F-High Deductible covers Medicare Part A coinsurance amount of $341 per day (in 2019) for each benefit period.

For each Medicare "hospital reserve day" you use, Plan F-High Deductible pays the $682 (in 2019) per day Medicare Part A coinsurance amount. "Hospital reserve days" are 60 nonrenewable hospital days that Medicare provides you which can only be used once in a lifetime. After all Medicare hospital benefits are exhausted, Plan F – High Deductible will cover 100% of Medicare Part A eligible hospital expenses.

If the need arises, Plan F-High Deductible covers costs for the first three pints of blood or equivalent quantities of packed red blood cells received each year in connection with Medicare Parts A and B covered services. Once you have met this 3-pint blood deductible under Medicare Part A, it does not have to be met again under Part B.

After your $185 annual Medicare Part B deductible is met, Plan F-High Deductible will cover the coinsurance amount of Medicare approved medical services, which is generally 20% of the approved amount.

Plan F High Deductible includes coverage of cost sharing for all Part A Medicare-eligible hospice care and respite care expenses.

Additional Features

Plan F includes all of the basic Medigap coverage plus five extra benefits.

- Your $1,364 Medicare Part A in-patient hospital deductible (per benefit period in 2019).
- Your coinsurance amount for skilled nursing facility care for the 21st through the 100th day of your stay (the amount is $170.50 per day in 2019).
- Any emergency care you may require when you are in a foreign country after a $250 deductible. This benefit pays 80% of the cost of your care for the first 60 days of each trip, up to $50,000 in your lifetime.
- Your deductible for Medicare Part B ($185 in 2019).
- 100% of any excess charges under Medicare Part B. This is the difference between the approved amount for Part B services and the actual charges (up to the charge limitations set by either Medicare or state law).

Important Notice:

You must meet a $2,300 deductible of unpaid Medicare eligible expenses before benefits are paid by this plan.

If you feel that Plan F with High Deductible fits your needs, take a look at the two tables below to find out what price you should expect to be charged for this plan. The tables outline the typical annual premiums charged for Plan F depending on age and gender. These rates are based on our 2019 nationwide collection of insurance premiums.

PLAN F: with High Deductible

Female

Age	Average Premium	Lowest Premium	Highest Premium	Median Premium
65	$634	$232	$2,008	$576
70	$726	$303	$2,292	$657
75	$854	$334	$2,679	$786
80	$973	$389	$2,976	$884
85	$1,081	$389	$3,183	$994
90	$1,165	$389	$3,908	$1,084
95	$1,231	$389	$3,908	$1,145

Male

Age	Average Premium	Lowest Premium	Highest Premium	Median Premium
65	$687	$266	$2,304	$622
70	$790	$340	$2,635	$708
75	$933	$389	$3,078	$836
80	$1,067	$389	$3,419	$966
85	$1,190	$389	$3,657	$1,089
90	$1,281	$389	$4,201	$1,200
95	$1,354	$389	$4,298	$1,276

Basic Medigap Coverage
PLAN G

If you stay in the hospital for longer than 60 days, but less than 90 days, Plan G covers Medicare Part A coinsurance amount of $341 per day (in 2019) for each benefit period.

For each Medicare "hospital reserve day" you use, Plan G pays the $682 (in 2019) per day Medicare Part A coinsurance amount. "Hospital reserve days" are 60 nonrenewable hospital days that Medicare provides you which can only be used once in a lifetime. After all Medicare hospital benefits are exhausted, Plan G will cover 100% of Medicare Part A eligible hospital expenses.

If the need arises, Plan G covers costs for the first three pints of blood or equivalent quantities of packed red blood cells received each year in connection with Medicare Parts A and B covered services. Once you have met this 3-pint blood deductible under Medicare Part A, it does not have to be met again under Part B.

After your $185 annual Medicare Part B deductible is met, Plan G will cover the coinsurance amount of Medicare approved medical services, which is generally 20% of the approved amount.

Plan G now includes coverage of cost sharing for all Part A Medicare-eligible hospice care and respite care

Additional Features

Plan G includes the core Medigap coverage plus four extra benefits.

- Your $1,364 Medicare Part A in-patient hospital deductible (per benefit period in 2019).
- Your coinsurance amount for skilled nursing care for the 21st through the 100th day of your stay (the amount is $170.50 per day in 2019).
- Any emergency care you may require when you are in a foreign country after a $250 deductible. This benefit pays 80% of the cost of your care for the first 60 days of each trip, up to $50,000 in your lifetime.
- 100% of any excess charges under Medicare Part B. Excess charges are the difference between the approved amount for Part B services and the actual charges (up to the charge limitations set by either Medicare or state law).

Note: The only difference between Plan G and Plan F is the Part B deductible.

Compare the prices between the plans before making your choice.

If you feel that Plan G fits your needs, take a look at the two tables below to find out what price you should expect to be charged for this plan. The tables outline the typical annual premiums charged for Plan G depending on age and gender. These rates are based on our 2019 nationwide collection of insurance premiums.

PLAN G

Female

Age	Average Premium	Lowest Premium	Highest Premium	Median Premium
65	$1,764	$909	$6,866	$1,593
70	$1,988	$1,021	$6,866	$1,808
75	$2,339	$1,204	$6,866	$2,144
80	$2,638	$1,343	$7,413	$2,441
85	$2,934	$1,382	$7,906	$2,729
90	$3,190	$1,382	$8,384	$2,994
95	$3,389	$1,382	$8,625	$3,217

Male

Age	Average Premium	Lowest Premium	Highest Premium	Median Premium
65	$1,944	$1,045	$6,866	$1,752
70	$2,195	$1,116	$6,866	$1,993
75	$2,578	$1,349	$7,739	$2,367
80	$2,914	$1,382	$8,524	$2,697
85	$3,247	$1,382	$9,091	$3,043
90	$3,535	$1,382	$9,553	$3,350
95	$3,762	$1,382	$9,916	$3,601

Basic Medigap Coverage
PLAN G with High Deductible

If you stay in the hospital for longer than 60 days, but less than 90 days, Plan G-High Deductible covers Medicare Part A coinsurance amount of $341 per day (in 2019) for each benefit period.

For each Medicare "hospital reserve day" you use, Plan G-High Deductible pays the $682 (in 2019) per day Medicare Part A coinsurance amount. "Hospital reserve days" are 60 nonrenewable hospital days that Medicare provides you which can only be used once in a lifetime. After all Medicare hospital benefits are exhausted, Plan G will cover 100% of Medicare Part A eligible hospital expenses.

If the need arises, Plan G-High Deductible covers costs for the first three pints of blood or equivalent quantities of packed red blood cells received each year in connection with Medicare Parts A and B covered services. Once you have met this 3-pint blood deductible under
Medicare Part A, it does not have to be met again under Part B.

After your $185 annual Medicare Part B deductible is met, Plan G will cover the coinsurance amount of Medicare approved medical services, which is generally 20% of the approved amount.

Plan G now includes coverage of cost sharing for all Part A Medicare-eligible hospice care and respite care

Additional Features

Plan G includes the core Medigap coverage plus four extra benefits.

- Your $1,364 Medicare Part A in-patient hospital deductible (per benefit period in 2019).
- Your coinsurance amount for skilled nursing care for the 21st through the 100th day of your stay (the amount is $170.50 per day in 2019).
- Any emergency care you may require when you are in a foreign country after a $250 deductible. This benefit pays 80% of the cost of your care for the first 60 days of each trip, up to $50,000 in your lifetime.
- 100% of any excess charges under Medicare Part B. Excess charges are the difference between the approved amount for Part B services and the actual charges (up to the charge limitations set by either Medicare or state law).

Important Notice:

You must meet a $2,300 deductible of unpaid Medicare eligible expenses before benefits are paid by this plan.

If you feel that Plan G with High Deductible fits your needs, take a look at the two tables below to find out what price you should expect to be charged for this plan. The tables outline the typical annual premiums charged for Plan K depending on age and gender. These rates are based on our 2019 nationwide collection of insurance premiums.

PLAN G: with High Deductible

Female

Age	Average Premium	Lowest Premium	Highest Premium	Median Premium
65	$610	$393	$988	$576
70	$675	$435	$1,101	$628
75	$808	$510	$1,316	$748
80	$924	$522	$1,450	$942
85	$1,060	$522	$1,536	$1,088
90	$1,098	$522	$1,536	$1,095
95	$1,138	$522	$1,536	$1,152

Male

Age	Average Premium	Lowest Premium	Highest Premium	Median Premium
65	$676	$448	$1,093	$642
70	$747	$495	$1,217	$695
75	$896	$564	$1,454	$858
80	$1,024	$564	$1,547	$1,022
85	$1,176	$564	$1,698	$1,210
90	$1,220	$564	$1,698	$1,239
95	$1,266	$564	$1,723	$1,273

Basic Medigap Coverage
PLAN K

If you stay in the hospital for longer than 60 days, but less than 90 days, Plan K covers Medicare Part A coinsurance amount of $341 per day (in 2019) for each benefit period.

For each Medicare "hospital reserve day" you use, Plan K pays the $682 (in 2019) per day Medicare Part A coinsurance amount. "Hospital reserve days" are 60 nonrenewable hospital days that Medicare provides you which can only be used once in a lifetime. After all Medicare hospital benefits are exhausted, Plan K will cover 100% of Medicare Part A eligible hospital expenses up to 365 days.

If the need arises, Plan K covers 50% of the costs for the first three pints of blood or equivalent quantities of packed red blood cells received each year in connection with Medicare Parts A and B covered services. Once you have met this 3-pint blood deductible under Medicare Part A, it does not have to be met again under Part B.

After your $185 annual Medicare Part B deductible is met, Plan K will cover 50% of the coinsurance amount of Medicare approved medical services, which is generally 20% of the approved amount.

Additional Features

Plan K includes four additional benefits.

- 50% of your $1,364 Medicare Part A in-patient hospital deductible (per benefit period in 2019).
- 50% of your coinsurance amount for skilled nursing facility care for the 21st through the 100th day of your stay (the amount is $170.50 per day in 2019).
- 100% coinsurance for medicare-covered preventive medical care. Preventive care would include physical examinations, flu shots, serum cholesterol screening, hearing tests, diabetes screening, and thyroid function tests.
- 50% of hospice cost-sharing for all Part A Medicare covered expenses and respite care.

Note: There is a $5,560 out-of-pocket annual limit. Once you meet the annual limit, the plans pays 100% of the Medicare Part A and Part B co-payments and coinsurance for the rest of the calendar year. "Excess charges" are not covered and do not count toward the out-of-pocket limit.

If you feel that Plan K fits your needs, take a look at the two tables below to find out what price you should expect to be charged for this plan. The tables outline the typical annual premiums charged for Plan K depending on age and gender. These rates are based on our 2019 nationwide collection of insurance premiums.

PLAN K

Female

Age	Average Premium	Lowest Premium	Highest Premium	Median Premium
65	$1,012	$376	$2,419	$944
70	$1,184	$465	$2,508	$1,141
75	$1,345	$553	$2,880	$1,332
80	$1,478	$588	$3,271	$1,462
85	$1,590	$588	$3,609	$1,588
90	$1,654	$588	$3,609	$1,642
95	$1,690	$588	$3,609	$1,654

Male

Age	Average Premium	Lowest Premium	Highest Premium	Median Premium
65	$1,063	$376	$2,515	$1,009
70	$1,253	$465	$2,679	$1,224
75	$1,424	$553	$3,117	$1,400
80	$1,576	$588	$3,680	$1,572
85	$1,708	$588	$4,263	$1,699
90	$1,775	$588	$4,263	$1,764
95	$1,814	$588	$4,263	$1,782

Basic Medigap Coverage
PLAN L

If you stay in the hospital for longer than 60 days, but less than 90 days, Plan L covers Medicare Part A coinsurance amount of $341 per day (in 2019) for each benefit period.

For each Medicare "hospital reserve day" you use, Plan L pays the $682 (in 2019) per day Medicare Part A coinsurance amount. "Hospital reserve days" are 60 nonrenewable hospital days that Medicare provides you which can only be used once in a lifetime. After all Medicare hospital benefits are exhausted, Plan L will cover 100% of Medicare Part A eligible hospital expenses up to 365 days.

If the need arises, Plan L covers 75% of the costs for the first three pints of blood or equivalent quantities of packed red blood cells received each year in connection with Medicare Parts A and B covered services. Once you have met this 3-pint blood deductible under Medicare Part A, it does not have to be met again under Part B.

After your $185 annual Medicare Part B deductible is met, Plan L will cover 75% of the coinsurance amount of Medicare approved medical services, which is generally 20% of the approved amount.

Additional Features

Plan L includes four additional benefits.

- 75% of your $1,364 Medicare Part A in-patient hospital deductible (per benefit period in 2019).
- 75% of your coinsurance amount for skilled nursing facility care for the 21st through the 100th day of your stay (the amount is $170.50 per day in 2019).
- 100% coinsurance for medicare-covered preventive medical care. Preventive care would include physical examinations, flu shots, serum cholesterol screening, hearing tests, diabetes screening, and thyroid function tests.
- 75% of hospice cost-sharing for all Part A Medicare covered expenses and respite care.

Note: There is a $2,780 out-of-pocket annual limit. Once you meet the annual limit, the plans pays 100% of the Medicare Part A and Part B co-payments and coinsurance for the rest of the calendar year. "Excess charges" are not covered and do not count toward the out-of-pocket limit.

If you feel that Plan L fits your needs, take a look at the two tables below to find out what price you should expect to be charged for this plan. The tables outline the typical annual premiums charged for Plan L depending on age and gender. These rates are based on our 2019 nationwide collection of insurance premiums.

PLAN L

Female

Age	Average Premium	Lowest Premium	Highest Premium	Median Premium
65	$1,637	$695	$4,266	$1,532
70	$1,903	$858	$4,266	$1,860
75	$2,153	$1,021	$4,266	$2,148
80	$2,350	$1,086	$4,818	$2,315
85	$2,512	$1,086	$5,248	$2,437
90	$2,622	$1,086	$5,945	$2,448
95	$2,684	$1,086	$6,453	$2,450

Male

Age	Average Premium	Lowest Premium	Highest Premium	Median Premium
65	$1,736	$695	$4,266	$1,685
70	$2,031	$858	$4,266	$2,030
75	$2,288	$1,021	$4,362	$2,277
80	$2,511	$1,086	$5,170	$2,458
85	$2,697	$1,086	$5,850	$2,617
90	$2,841	$1,086	$6,605	$2,622
95	$2,882	$1,086	$7,170	$2,622

Basic Medigap Coverage

PLAN M

If you stay in the hospital for longer than 60 days, but less than 90 days, Plan M covers the Medicare Part A coinsurance amount, $341 per day (in 2019) for each benefit period.

For each Medicare "hospital reserve day" you use, Plan M pays the Medicare Part A coinsurance amount, $682 (in 2019) per day. "Hospital reserve days" are 60 nonrenewable hospital days that Medicare provides you which can only be used once in a lifetime. After all Medicare hospital benefits are exhausted, Plan M will cover 100% of Medicare Part A eligible hospital expenses.

If the need arises, Plan M covers costs for the first three pints of blood or equivalent quantities of packed red blood cells received each year in connection with Medicare Parts A and B covered services. Once you have met this 3-pint blood deductible under Medicare Part A, it does not have to be met again under Part B.

After your $185 annual Medicare Part B deductible is met, Plan M will cover the coinsurance amount of Medicare approved medical services, which is generally 20% of the approved amount.

Coverage of cost sharing for all Part A Medicare eligible hospice care and respite care expense is included.

Additional Features

Plan M includes the core Medigap coverage, plus three extra benefits.

- 50% of your Medicare Part A in-patient hospital deductible ($1,364 per benefit period in 2019).
- Your coinsurance amount for skilled nursing facility care for the 21st through the 100th day of your stay (the amount is $170.50 per day in 2019).
- Any emergency care you may require when you are in a foreign country after a $250 deductible. This benefit pays 80% of the cost of your care for the first 60 days of each trip, up to $50,000 in your lifetime.

If you feel that Plan M fits your needs, take a look at the two tables below to find out what price you should expect to be charged for this plan. The tables outline the typical annual premiums charged for Plan M depending on age and gender. These rates are based on our 2019 nationwide collection of insurance premiums.

PLAN M

Female

Age	Average Premium	Lowest Premium	Highest Premium	Median Premium
65	$1,911	$954	$5,902	$1,812
70	$2,281	$1,048	$5,902	$2,201
75	$2,711	$1,214	$6,238	$2,636
80	$3,115	$1,407	$7,340	$3,035
85	$3,463	$1,544	$7,995	$3,384
90	$3,736	$1,609	$8,487	$3,548
95	$3,903	$1,650	$8,487	$3,600

Male

Age	Average Premium	Lowest Premium	Highest Premium	Median Premium
65	$2,101	$954	$5,902	$2,000
70	$2,515	$1,174	$6,162	$2,404
75	$3,002	$1,360	$6,702	$2,917
80	$3,455	$1,577	$7,877	$3,395
85	$3,841	$1,650	$8,912	$3,764
90	$4,144	$1,650	$9,459	$3,956
95	$4,329	$1,650	$9,459	$4,068

Basic Medigap Coverage

PLAN N

If you stay in the hospital for longer than 60 days, but less than 90 days, Plan N covers the Medicare Part A coinsurance amount, $341 per day (in 2019) for each benefit period.

For each Medicare "hospital reserve day" you use, Plan N pays the Medicare Part A coinsurance amount, $682 (in 2019) per day. "Hospital reserve days" are 60 nonrenewable hospital days that Medicare provides you which can only be used once in a lifetime. After all Medicare hospital benefits are exhausted, Plan N will cover 100% of Medicare Part A eligible hospital expenses.

If the need arises, Plan N covers costs for the first three pints of blood or equivalent quantities of packed red blood cells received each year in connection with Medicare Parts A and B covered services. Once you have met this 3-pint blood deductible under Medicare Part A, it does not have to be met again under Part B.

After your $185 annual Medicare Part B deductible is met, Plan N will cover the coinsurance amount of Medicare approved medical services, which is generally 20% of the approved amount.

Coverage of cost sharing for all Part A Medicare eligible hospice care and respite care expense is included.

Additional Features

Plan N includes the core Medigap coverage, plus four extra features and benefits.

- Your Medicare Part A in-patient hospital deductible ($1,364 per benefit period in 2019).
- You will have a co-payment of up to $20 per physician visit or $50 per Emergency Room visit under Part B. The ER co-pay will be waived if admitted.
- Your coinsurance amount for skilled nursing facility care for the 21st through the 100th day of your stay (the amount is $170.50 per day in 2019).
- Any emergency care you may require when you are in a foreign country after a $250 deductible. This benefit pays 80% of the cost of your care for the first 60 days of each trip, up to $50,000 in your lifetime.

If you feel that Plan N fits your needs, take a look at the two tables below to find out what price you should expect to be charged for this plan. The tables outline the typical annual premiums charged for Plan N depending on age and gender. These rates are based on our 2019 nationwide collection of insurance premiums.

PLAN N

Female

Age	Average Premium	Lowest Premium	Highest Premium	Median Premium
65	$1,438	$804	$4,338	$1,307
70	$1,632	$853	$4,712	$1,500
75	$1,924	$1,041	$5,417	$1,782
80	$2,178	$1,182	$5,858	$2,029
85	$2,427	$1,182	$6,251	$2,289
90	$2,644	$1,182	$6,800	$2,512
95	$2,811	$1,182	$7,107	$2,699

Male

Age	Average Premium	Lowest Premium	Highest Premium	Median Premium
65	$1,572	$888	$4,451	$1,431
70	$1,788	$955	$5,417	$1,642
75	$2,108	$1,166	$6,231	$1,949
80	$2,393	$1,182	$6,739	$2,230
85	$2,673	$1,182	$7,154	$2,526
90	$2,916	$1,182	$7,491	$2,799
95	$3,106	$1,182	$8,429	$2,994

Part IV:
Index of Medigap Insurers

Following is a reference list of Medicare supplement insurers with their Weiss Safety Rating, corporate address, phone number, and the states in which they are licensed to do business.

RATING	INSURANCE COMPANY NAME	ADDRESS	CITY	STATE	ZIP	PHONE
C	AETNA HEALTH & LIFE INS CO	151 FARMINGTON AVENUE	HARTFORD	CT	6156	(800) 872-386
C	AETNA HEALTH INS CO	1425 UNION MEETING ROAD	BLUE BELL	PA	19422	(800) 872-386
B	AETNA LIFE INS CO	151 FARMINGTON AVENUE	HARTFORD	CT	6156	(800) 872-386
C	ALLIANCE HEALTH & LIFE INS CO	2850 WEST GRAND BOULEVARD	DETROIT	MI	48202	(313) 872-810
C	AMALGAMATED LIFE & HEALTH INS CO	333 SOUTH ASHLAND AVENUE	CHICAGO	IL	60607	(914) 367-500
C	AMERICAN CONTINENTAL INS CO	800 CRESENT CENTRE DR STE 200	FRANKLIN	TN	37067	(800) 264-400
B+	AMERICAN FAMILY MUTL INS CO SI	6000 AMERICAN PARKWAY	MADISON	WI	53783	(608) 249-211
B-	AMERICAN NATIONAL LIFE INS CO OF TX	ONE MOODY PLAZA	GALVESTON	TX	77550	(409) 763-466
C	AMERICAN PROGRESSIVE L&H I C OF NY	ONE NEW YORK PLAZA, 15 FLOOR	NEW YORK	NY	10004	(813) 206-620
C	AMERICAN REPUBLIC CORP INS CO	601 SIXTH AVE	DES MOINES	IA	50309	(866) 705-910
B-	AMERICAN REPUBLIC INS CO	601 SIXTH AVENUE	DES MOINES	IA	50309	(800) 247-219
C+	AMERICAN RETIREMENT LIFE INS CO	1300 EAST NINTH STREET	CLEVELAND	OH	44114	(512) 451-222
B-	AMERICO FINANCIAL LIFE & ANNUITY INS	PO BOX 139061	DALLAS	TX	75313	(816) 391-200
C	AMERIHEALTH INSURANCE CO OF NJ	259 PROSPECT PLAINS ROAD BUIL	CRANBURY	NJ	08512	(609) 662-240
B	ANTHEM HEALTH PLANS INC	108 LEIGUS ROAD	WALLINGFORD	CT	06492	(203) 677-400
B	ANTHEM HEALTH PLANS OF KENTUCKY INC	13550 TRITON PARK BLVD	LOUISVILLE	KY	40223	(800) 331-147
B	ANTHEM HEALTH PLANS OF MAINE INC	2 GANNETT DRIVE	SOUTH PORTLAND	ME	04106	(866) 583-618
B	ANTHEM HEALTH PLANS OF NEW	1155 ELM STREET	MANCHESTER	NH	3101	(603) 541-200
B	ANTHEM HEALTH PLANS OF VIRGINIA	2015 STAPLES MILL ROAD	RICHMOND	VA	23230	(804) 354-700
B-	ANTHEM INS COMPANIES INC	220 VIRGINIA AVENUE	INDIANAPOLIS	IN	46204	(317) 488-600
B	ASURIS NORTHWEST HEALTH	1800 NINTH AVENUE	SEATTLE	WA	98101	(206) 464-360
B	AULTCARE INS CO	2600 SIXTH STREET SW	CANTON	OH	44710	(330) 363-405
D+	AVALON INS CO	2500 ELMERTON AVENUE	HARRISBURG	PA	17177	(717) 541-700
B	AVERA HEALTH PLANS INC	3816 S ELMWOOD AVE SUITE 10	SIOUX FALLS	SD	57105	(605) 322-454
D	BANKERS CONSECO LIFE INS CO	350 JERICHO TURNPIKE SUITE 304	JERICHO	NY	11753	(317) 817-610
C+	BANKERS FIDELITY ASR CO	4370 PEACHTREE RD NE	ATLANTA	GA	30319	(800) 241-143
C	BANKERS FIDELITY LIFE INS CO	4370 PEACHTREE ROAD NE	ATLANTA	GA	30319	(800) 241-143
D+	BANKERS LIFE & CAS CO	111 EAST WACKER DRIVE STE 2100	CHICAGO	IL	60601	(312) 396-600
B	BLUE CARE NETWORK OF MICHIGAN	20500 CIVIC CENTER DRIVE	SOUTHFIELD	MI	48076	(248) 799-640
B+	BLUE CROSS & BLUE SHIELD MA HMO BLUE	101 HUNTINGTON AVENUE SUITE 1	BOSTON	MA	2199	(617) 246-500
B	BLUE CROSS & BLUE SHIELD OF FLORIDA	4800 DEERWOOD CAMPUS	JACKSONVILLE	FL	32246	(904) 791-611
B+	BLUE CROSS BLUE SHIELD OF ALABAMA	450 RIVERCHASE PARKWAY EAST	BIRMINGHAM	AL	35244	(205) 220-210
A+	BLUE CROSS BLUE SHIELD OF ARIZONA	2444 W LAS PALMARITAS DRIVE	PHOENIX	AZ	85021	(602) 864-410
B	BLUE CROSS BLUE SHIELD OF KANSAS INC	1133 SW TOPEKA BOULEVARD	TOPEKA	KS	66629	(785) 291-700
C+	BLUE CROSS BLUE SHIELD OF KC	2301 MAIN STREET	KANSAS CITY	MO	64108	(816) 395-222
C+	BLUE CROSS BLUE SHIELD OF MA	101 HUNTINGTON AVENUE SUITE 1	BOSTON	MA	2199	(617) 246-500
B-	BLUE CROSS BLUE SHIELD OF MICHIGAN	600 LAFAYETTE EAST	DETROIT	MI	48226	(313) 225-900
C	BLUE CROSS BLUE SHIELD OF MINNESOTA	3535 BLUE CROSS ROAD	EAGAN	MN	55122	(651) 662-800
A	BLUE CROSS BLUE SHIELD OF MS, MUTUAL	3545 LAKELAND DRIVE	FLOWOOD	MS	39232	(601) 664-459
B+	BLUE CROSS BLUE SHIELD OF NC	4705 UNIVERSITY DRIVE BUILDIN	DURHAM	NC	27707	(919) 489-7431
B	BLUE CROSS BLUE SHIELD OF ND	4510 13TH AVE S	FARGO	ND	58121	(701) 282-152
C	BLUE CROSS BLUE SHIELD OF NEBRASKA	1919 AKSARBEN DRIVE	OMAHA	NE	68180	(402) 982-700
C	BLUE CROSS BLUE SHIELD OF RI	500 EXCHANGE STREET	PROVIDENCE	RI	2903	(401) 459-588
B+	BLUE CROSS BLUE SHIELD OF SC INC	2501 FARAWAY DRIVE	COLUMBIA	SC	29219	(803) 788-386
C+	BLUE CROSS BLUE SHIELD OF VERMONT	445 INDUSTRIAL LANE	BERLIN	VT	5602	(802) 223-6131
B-	BLUE CROSS BLUE SHIELD OF WISCONSIN	N17 W24340 RIVERWOOD DRIVE	WAUKESHA	WI	53188	(262) 523-402
B-	BLUE CROSS BLUE SHIELD OF WYOMING	4000 HOUSE AVENUE	CHEYENNE	WY	82001	(307) 634-1393
C+	BLUE CROSS OF IDAHO CARE PLUS INC	3000 E PINE AVE	MERIDIAN	ID	83642	(208) 345-455
B	BLUE CROSS OF IDAHO HEALTH SERVICE	3000 E PINE AVE	MERIDIAN	ID	83642	(208) 345-455
B+	BLUECROSS BLUESHIELD OF TENNESSEE	1 CAMERON HILL CIRCLE	CHATTANOOGA	TN	37402	(423) 535-560
C	CAPITAL ADVANTAGE INS CO	2500 ELMERTON AVENUE	HARRISBURG	PA	17177	(717) 541-700
B-	CAPITAL BLUE CROSS	2500 ELMERTON AVENUE	HARRISBURG	PA	17177	(717) 541-7000

RATING	INSURANCE COMPANY NAME	ADDRESS	CITY	STATE	ZIP	PHONE
C+	CAREFIRST OF MARYLAND INC	1501 SOUTH CLINTON STREET	BALTIMORE	MD	21224	(410) 581-3000
B	CDPHP UNIVERSAL BENEFITS INC	500 PATROON CREEK BLVD	ALBANY	NY	12206	(518) 641-3000
B-	CELTIC INS CO	200 EAST RANDOLPH STREET SUIT	CHICAGO	IL	60601	(800) 714-4658
B	CENTRAL STATES H & L CO OF OMAHA	1212 NORTH 96TH STREET	OMAHA	NE	68114	(402) 397-1111
C+	CENTRAL STATES INDEMNITY CO OF OMAHA	1212 NORTH 96TH STREET	OMAHA	NE	68114	(402) 997-8000
A-	CHRISTIAN FIDELITY LIFE INS CO	1999 BRYAN STREET SUITE 900	DALLAS	TX	75201	(602) 263-6666
B	CIGNA HEALTH & LIFE INS CO	900 COTTAGE GROVE ROAD	BLOOMFIELD	CT	6002	(860) 226-6000
B-	CIGNA NATIONAL HEALTH INS CO	1300 EAST NINTH STREET	CLEVELAND	OH	44114	(512) 451-2224
D+	COLONIAL PENN LIFE INS CO	399 MARKET STREET	PHILADELPHIA	PA	19181	(215) 928-8000
B	COLUMBIAN MUTUAL LIFE INS CO	4704 VESTAL PKWY E PO BOX 1381	BINGHAMTON	NY	13902	(607) 724-2472
C	COMBINED INS CO OF AMERICA	111 E WACKER DRIVE	CHICAGO	IL	60601	(800) 225-4500
B-	COMMUNITY INS CO	4361 IRWIN SIMPSON ROAD	MASON	OH	45040	(513) 872-8100
C	COMMUNITYCARE L&H INS CO	TWO WEST 2ND STREET SUITE 100	TULSA	OK	74103	(918) 594-5200
B+	COMPANION LIFE INS CO	2501 FARAWAY DRIVE	COLUMBIA	SC	29219	(803) 735-1251
D	CONSTITUTION LIFE INS CO	4888 LOOP CENTRAL DR STE 700	HOUSTON	TX	77081	(407) 547-3800
C+	CONTINENTAL GENERAL INS CO	11001 LAKELINE BLVD STE 120	AUSTIN	TX	78717	(866) 830-0607
C+	CONTINENTAL LIFE INS CO OF BRENTWOOD	800 CRESCENT CENTRE DR STE 200	FRANKLIN	TN	37067	(800) 264-4000
A+	COUNTRY LIFE INS CO	1701 N TOWANDA AVENUE	BLOOMINGTON	IL	61701	(309) 821-3000
B-	COVENTRY HEALTH & LIFE INS CO	1285 FERN RIDGE PARKWAY SUITE	ST. LOUIS	MO	63141	(800) 843-7421
B-	CSI LIFE INS CO	1212 NORTH 96TH STREET	OMAHA	NE	68114	(402) 997-8000
A	DEAN HEALTH PLAN INC	1277 DEMING WAY	MADISON	WI	53717	(608) 836-1400
A	EMI HEALTH	5101 S COMMERCE DR	MURRAY	UT	84107	(801) 262-7476
B-	EMPIRE HEALTHCHOICE ASSURANCE INC	9 PINE STREET 14TH FLOOR	NEW YORK	NY	10005	(212) 563-5570
C	EQUITABLE LIFE & CASUALTY INS CO	299 S MAIN ST #1100	SALT LAKE CITY	UT	84111	(801) 579-3400
C	EQUITABLE NATIONAL LIFE INS CO	299 S MAIN ST #1100	SALT LAKE CITY	UT	84111	(801) 579-3400
C	EVEREST REINS CO	251 LITTLE FALLS DRIVE	WILMINGTON	DE	19808	(908) 604-3000
B	EXCELLUS HEALTH PLAN INC	165 COURT STREET	ROCHESTER	NY	14647	(585) 453-6325
C	FALLON HEALTH & LIFE ASR CO	10 CHESTNUT STREET	WORCESTER	MA	01608	(508) 799-2100
C	FAMILY LIFE INS CO	10777 NORTHWEST FREEWAY	HOUSTON	TX	77092	(713) 529-0045
D	FIRST CARE INC	1501 SOUTH CLINTON STREET	BALTIMORE	MD	21224	(410) 581-3000
B	FIRST COMMUNITY HEALTH PLAN INC	699 GALLATIN ST SW STE A2	HUNTSVILLE	AL	35801	(256) 532-2780
C+	FIRST HEALTH LIFE & HEALTH INS CO	3200 HIGHLAND AVENUE	DOWNERS GROVE	IL	60515	(630) 737-7900
B	FORETHOUGHT LIFE INS CO	10 W MARKET ST STE 2300	INDIANAPOLIS	IN	46204	(317) 223-2700
B-	GEISINGER INDEMNITY INS CO	100 NORTH ACADEMY AVENUE MC 3	DANVILLE	PA	17822	(570) 271-8777
C-	GENWORTH LIFE & ANNUITY INS CO	6610 WEST BROAD STREET	RICHMOND	VA	23230	(804) 662-2400
C	GENWORTH LIFE INS CO	251 LITTLE FALLS DR	WILMINGTON	DE	19808	(804) 662-2400
B+	GERBER LIFE INS CO	1311 MAMARONECK AVENUE	WHITE PLAINS	NY	10605	(914) 272-4000
C+	GLOBE LIFE & ACCIDENT INS CO	10306 REGENCY PARKWAY DRIVE	OMAHA	NE	68114	(972) 569-3744
B-	GLOBE LIFE INSURANCE CO OF NY	301 PLAINFIELD RD STE 150	SYRACUSE	NY	13212	(315) 451-2544
B	GOLDEN RULE INS CO	7440 WOODLAND DRIVE	INDIANAPOLIS	IN	46278	(317) 290-8100
B	GOVERNMENT PERSONNEL MUTUAL L I C	2211 NE LOOP 410	SAN ANTONIO	TX	78217	(210) 357-2222
B	GPM HEALTH & LIFE INS CO	1124 W RIVERSIDE AVE STE 400	SPOKANE	WA	99201	(210) 357-2222
B-	GREAT AMERICAN LIFE INS CO	301 EAST FOURTH STREET	CINCINNATI	OH	45202	(513) 357-3300
C	GROUP HEALTH COOP OF S CENTRAL WI	1265 JOHN Q HAMMONS DRIVE	MADISON	WI	53717	(608) 251-4156
D+	GROUP HEALTH INCORPORATED	55 WATER STREET	NEW YORK	NY	10041	(646) 447-5000
B	GROUP HOSP & MEDICAL SERVICES INC	840 FIRST STREET NE	WASHINGTON	DC	20065	(410) 581-3000
B	GUARANTEE TRUST LIFE INS CO	1275 MILWAUKEE AVENUE	GLENVIEW	IL	60025	(847) 699-0600
C-	GUNDERSEN HEALTH PLAN INC	1836 SOUTH AVENUE	LA CROSSE	WI	54601	(608) 643-2491
C	HARTFORD LIFE & ACCIDENT INS CO	ONE HARTFORD PLAZA	HARTFORD	CT	06155	(860) 547-5000
B-	HEALTH ALLIANCE MEDICAL PLANS	3310 FIELDS SOUTH DRIVE	CHAMPAIGN	IL	61822	(800) 851-3379
B	HEALTH CARE SVC CORP A MUT LEG RES	300 EAST RANDOLPH STREET	CHICAGO	IL	60601	(312) 653-6000
D	HEALTH NET HEALTH PLAN OF OREGON INC	13221 SW 68TH PARKWAY SUITE 2	TIGARD	OR	97223	(314) 724-4477

RATING	INSURANCE COMPANY NAME	ADDRESS	CITY	STATE	ZIP	PHONE
C	HEALTH NET LIFE INS CO	21281 BURBANK BOULEVARD B3	WOODLAND HILLS	CA	91367	(314) 725-4477
C-	HEALTH TRADITION HEALTH PLAN	1808 EAST MAIN STREET	ONALASKA	WI	54650	(608) 276-4000
B	HEALTHNOW NY INC	257 WEST GENESEE STREET	BUFFALO	NY	14202	(716) 887-6900
B	HEALTHY ALLIANCE LIFE INS CO	1831 CHESTNUT STREET	ST. LOUIS	MO	63103	(314) 923-4444
C+	HEARTLAND NATIONAL LIFE INS CO	401 PENNSYLVANIA PKWY STE 300	INDIANAPOLIS	IN	46280	(816) 478-0120
B	HIGHMARK BCBSD INC	800 DELAWARE AVENUE	WILMINGTON	DE	19801	(302) 421-3000
C	HIGHMARK INC	1800 CENTER STREET	CAMP HILL	PA	17011	(412) 544-7000
B	HIGHMARK WEST VIRGINIA INC	614 MARKET STREET	PARKERSBURG	WV	26101	(304) 424-7700
B	HNE INS CO	1 MONARCH PLACE SUITE 1500	SPRINGFIELD	MA	1144	(413) 787-4000
C+	HORIZON INS CO	3 PENN PLAZA EAST PP-15D	NEWARK	NJ	07105	(973) 466-5607
D+	HPHC INS CO	93 WORCESTER STREET	WELLESLEY	MA	02481	(781) 263-6000
B+	HUMANA BENEFIT PLAN OF ILLINOIS	4501 NORTH STERLING AVE 2ND	PEORIA	IL	61615	(502) 580-1000
C+	HUMANA HEALTH BENEFIT PLAN LA	ONE GALLERIA BLVD SUITE 1200	METAIRIE	LA	70001	(504) 219-6600
B-	HUMANA HEALTH INS CO OF FL INC	3501 SW 160TH AVENUE	MIRAMAR	FL	33027	(305) 626-5616
B	HUMANA INS CO (WI)	1100 EMPLOYERS BOULEVARD	DEPERE	WI	54115	(920) 336-1100
B+	HUMANA INS CO OF KENTUCKY	500 WEST MAIN STREET	LOUISVILLE	KY	40202	(502) 580-1000
B-	HUMANA INS CO OF NY	810 SEVENTH AVENUE	NEW YORK	NY	10019	(800) 201-3687
C+	HUMANA INS CO OF PUERTO RICO INC	383 FD ROOSEVELT AVENUE	SAN JUAN	PR	00918	(787) 282-7900
C+	INDEPENDENCE BLUE CROSS	1901 MARKET STREET	PHILADELPHIA	PA	19103	(215) 241-2400
D+	INDIVIDUAL ASR CO LIFE HEALTH & ACC	930 E 2ND ST STE 100	EDMOND	OK	73034	(405) 285-0838
B	KAISER FNDTN HLTH PLAN WA OPTN	601 UNION STREET SUITE 3100	SEATTLE	WA	98101	(206) 448-5600
B	LA HEALTH SERVICE & INDEMNITY CO	5525 REITZ AVENUE	BATON ROUGE	LA	70809	(225) 295-3307
C	LIBERTY BANKERS LIFE INS CO	1605 LBJ FREEWAY SUITE 710	DALLAS	TX	75234	(469) 522-4400
B	LIBERTY NATIONAL LIFE INS CO	10306 REGENCY PARKWAY DR	OMAHA	NE	68114	(972) 569-4000
B-	LINCOLN HERITAGE LIFE INS CO	920 S SPRING ST	SPRINGFIELD	IL	62704	(602) 957-1650
B-	LOYAL AMERICAN LIFE INS CO	1300 EAST NINTH STREET	CLEVELAND	OH	44114	(512) 451-2224
B	MANHATTAN LIFE INS CO	225 COMMUNITY DRIVE SUITE 11	GREAT NECK	NY	11021	(713) 529-0045
C+	MEDICA HEALTH PLANS	401 CARLSON PARKWAY	MINNETONKA	MN	55305	(952) 992-2900
B	MEDICAL HEALTH INS CORP OF OHIO	2060 EAST NINTH STREET	CLEVELAND	OH	44115	(216) 687-7000
A	MEDICAL MUTUAL OF OHIO	2060 EAST NINTH STREET	CLEVELAND	OH	44115	(216) 687-7000
B-	MEDICO CORP LIFE INS CO	601 SIXTH AVE	DES MOINES	IA	50309	(800) 822-9993
B-	MEDICO INS CO	601 Sixth Ave	DES MOINES	IA	50309	(800) 228-6080
C	MEDICO LIFE & HEALTH INS CO	601 6TH AVENUE	DES MOINES	IA	50309	(800) 228-6080
C-	MEMBERS HEALTH INS CO	24 WEST CAMELBACK ROAD SUITE	PHOENIX	AZ	85013	(931) 560-0041
C	MERCYCARE HMO	580 N WASHINGTON	JANESVILLE	WI	53545	(608) 752-3431
B-	MUTUAL OF OMAHA INS CO	MUTUAL OF OMAHA PLAZA	OMAHA	NE	68175	(402) 342-7600
D	NASSAU LIFE INS CO OF KS	10851 MASTIN BLVD STE 1000	OVERLAND PARK	KS	66210	(407) 547-3336
B-	NATIONWIDE LIFE INS CO	ONE WEST NATIONWIDE BLVD	COLUMBUS	OH	43215	(614) 249-7111
C	NEW ERA LIFE INS CO	11720 KATY FREEWAY SUITE 1700	HOUSTON	TX	77079	(281) 368-7200
C+	NEW ERA LIFE INS CO OF THE MIDWEST	11720 KATY FREEWAY SUITE 1700	HOUSTON	TX	77079	(281) 368-7200
A-	NEW YORK LIFE INS CO	51 MADISON AVENUE	NEW YORK	NY	10010	(212) 576-7000
B+	NORTH AMERICAN INS CO	575 DONOFRIO DRIVE SUITE 100	MADISON	WI	53719	(877) 667-9368
C	OLD SURETY LIFE INS CO	5201 NORTH LINCOL BLVD	OKLAHOMA CITY	OK	73105	(405) 523-2112
B-	OMAHA INS CO	MUTUAL OF OMAHA PLAZA	OMAHA	NE	68175	(402) 342-7600
B+	OXFORD LIFE INS CO	2721 NORTH CENTRAL AVENUE	PHOENIX	AZ	85004	(602) 263-6666
B	PACIFICARE LIFE & HEALTH INS CO	C/O DANIEL KRAJNOVICH 7440 WOO	INDIANAPOLIS	IN	46278	(952) 979-7959
A-	PARAMOUNT INS CO (OH)	1901 INDIAN WOOD CIRCLE	MAUMEE	OH	43537	(419) 887-2500
B	PEKIN LIFE INS CO	2505 COURT STREET	PEKIN	IL	61558	(309) 346-1161
U	PENNSYLVANIA LIFE INS CO	27 NORTH FRONT STREET	HARRISBURG	PA	17101	(847) 559-3992
B	PHILADELPHIA AMERICAN LIFE INS CO	11720 KATY FREEWAY SUITE 1700	HOUSTON	TX	77079	(281) 368-7200
A-	PHYSICIANS LIFE INS CO	2600 DODGE STREET	OMAHA	NE	68131	(402) 633-1000
A+	PHYSICIANS MUTUAL INS CO	2600 DODGE STREET	OMAHA	NE	68131	(402) 633-1000

RATING	INSURANCE COMPANY NAME	ADDRESS	CITY	STATE	ZIP	PHONE
C-	PHYSICIANS PLUS INS CORP	2650 NOVATION PARKWAY	MADISON	WI	53713	(608) 643-2491
B	PREMERA BLUE CROSS	7001 220TH ST SW	MOUNTLAKE TERRACE	WA	98043	(425) 918-4000
B+	PRINCIPAL LIFE INS CO	711 HIGH STREET	DES MOINES	IA	50392	(515) 247-5111
A	PRIORITY HEALTH	1231 EAST BELTLINE NE	GRAND RAPIDS	MI	49525	(616) 942-0954
B	PROVIDENT AMER LIFE & HEALTH INS CO	1300 EAST NINTH STREET	CLEVELAND	OH	44114	(512) 451-2224
C	PURITAN LIFE INS CO OF AMERICA	701 BRAZOS STREET SUITE 720	AUSTIN	TX	78701	(888) 474-9519
C	QUALCHOICE L&H INS CO	12615 CHENAL PARKWAY SUITE 30	LITTLE ROCK	AR	72211	(501) 219-5109
A-	REGENCE BL CROSS BL SHIELD OREGON	100 SW MARKET STREET	PORTLAND	OR	97201	(503) 225-5221
B+	REGENCE BLUE CROSS BLUE SHIELD OF UT	2890 EAST COTTONWOOD PARKWAY	SALT LAKE CITY	UT	84121	(801) 333-2000
B	REGENCE BLUESHIELD	1800 NINTH AVENUE	SEATTLE	WA	98101	(206) 464-3600
B+	REGENCE BLUESHIELD OF IDAHO INC	1602 21ST AVENUE	LEWISTON	ID	83501	(208) 746-2671
B-	RESERVE NATIONAL INS CO	601 EAST BRITTON ROAD	OKLAHOMA CITY	OK	73114	(405) 848-7931
B	ROCKY MOUNTAIN HOSPITAL & MEDICAL	700 BROADWAY	DENVER	CO	80273	(303) 831-2131
B-	S USA LIFE INS CO INC	815 N 1ST AVE STE 4	PHOENIX	AZ	85003	(212) 356-0300
C	SANFORD HEALTH PLAN	300 CHERAPA PLACE SUITE 201	SIOUX FALLS	SD	57103	(605) 328-6868
B-	SBLI USA MUT LIFE INS CO INC	100 WEST 33RD STREET STE 1007	NEW YORK	NY	10001	(212) 356-0300
B+	SECURITY HEALTH PLAN OF WI INC	1515 NORTH SAINT JOSEPH AVENUE	MARSHFIELD	WI	54449	(715) 221-9555
D	SENTINEL SECURITY LIFE INS CO	1405 WEST 2200 SOUTH	SALT LAKE CITY	UT	84119	(801) 484-8514
B-	SHENANDOAH LIFE INS CO	4415 PHEASANT RIDGE RD STE 300	ROANOKE	VA	24014	(540) 985-4400
B	SIERRA HEALTH AND LIFE INS CO INC	2720 NORTH TENAYA WAY	LAS VEGAS	NV	89128	(702) 242-7732
A-	STANDARD LIFE & ACCIDENT INS CO	ONE MOODY PLAZA	GALVESTON	TX	77550	(409) 763-4661
D	STANDARD LIFE & CAS INS CO	4525 S WASATCH BLVD, SUITE 150	SALT LAKE CITY	UT	84124	(801) 538-0376
B	STATE FARM MUTUAL AUTOMOBILE INS CO	ONE STATE FARM PLAZA	BLOOMINGTON	IL	61710	(309) 766-2311
D	STATE MUTUAL INS CO	210 E SECOND AVENUE SUITE 301	ROME	GA	30161	(706) 291-1054
B-	STERLING INVESTORS LIFE INS CO	10201 N ILLINOIS ST SUITE 280	INDIANAPOLIS	IN	46290	(317) 208-2200
B-	STERLING LIFE INS CO	525 W MONROE ST	CHICAGO	IL	60661	(512) 451-2224
C+	TALCOTT RESOLUTION LIFE INS CO	1 GRIFFIN ROAD N	WINDSOR	CT	06095	(800) 862-6668
D+	THP INS CO	1110 MAIN STREET	WHEELING	WV	26003	(740) 695-3585
B	TRANSAMERICA FINANCIAL LIFE INS CO	440 MAMARONECK AVENUE	HARRISON	NY	10528	(914) 627-3630
B	TRANSAMERICA LIFE INS CO	4333 EDGEWOOD RD NE	CEDAR RAPIDS	IA	52499	(319) 355-8511
C+	TRANSAMERICA PREMIER LIFE INS CO	4333 EDGEWOOD RD NE	CEDAR RAPIDS	IA	52499	(319) 355-8511
C+	TRH HEALTH INS CO	147 BEAR CREEK PIKE	COLUMBIA	TN	38401	(931) 560-0041
B+	TRIPLE-S SALUD INC	FD ROOSEVELT AVE 1441	SAN JUAN	PR	920	(787) 749-4949
C	TUFTS INS CO	705 MOUNT AUBURN STREET	WATERTOWN	MA	02472	(617) 972-9400
B-	UNICARE LIFE & HEALTH INS CO	220 VIRGINIA AVENUE	INDIANAPOLIS	IN	46204	(877) 864-2273
B	UNIFIED LIFE INS CO	CT CORPORATION SYSTEM 1999 BRY	DALLAS	TX	75201	(877) 492-4678
B-	UNITED AMERICAN INS CO	10306 REGENCY PARKWAY DR	OMAHA	NE	68114	(972) 529-5085
C	UNITED HEALTHCARE INS CO	185 ASYLUM STREET	HARTFORD	CT	06103	(877) 832-7734
B	UNITED HEALTHCARE INS CO OF NY	2950 EXPRESSWAY DRIVE SOUTH S	ISLANDIA	NY	11749	(877) 832-7734
C	UNITED HEALTHCARE OF ALABAMA INC	33 INVERNESS CENTER PARKWAY	BIRMINGHAM	AL	35242	(205) 437-8500
B	UNITED NATIONAL LIFE INS CO OF AM	1275 MILWAUKEE AVENUE	GLENVIEW	IL	60025	(847) 803-5252
B	UNITED OF OMAHA LIFE INS CO	MUTUAL OF OMAHA PLAZA	OMAHA	NE	68175	(402) 342-7600
B+	UNITED WORLD LIFE INS CO	MUTUAL OF OMAHA PLAZA	OMAHA	NE	68175	(402) 342-7600
C	UNITY HEALTH PLANS INS CORP	840 CAROLINA STREET	SAUK CITY	WI	53583	(608) 643-2491
C	UNIVERSAL FIDELITY LIFE INS CO	13931 QUAIL POINTE DRIVE	OKLAHOMA CITY	OK	73134	(800) 366-8354
A	USAA LIFE INS CO	9800 FREDERICKSBURG RD	SAN ANTONIO	TX	78288	(210) 531-8722
B	USABLE MUTUAL INS CO	601 S GAINES	LITTLE ROCK	AR	72201	(501) 378-2000
C+	VERMONT HEALTH PLAN LLC	445 INDUSTRIAL LANE	BERLIN	VT	5602	(802) 223-6131
D+	WASHINGTON NATIONAL INS CO	11825 NORTH PENNSYLVANIA STREE	CARMEL	IN	46032	(317) 817-6100
B-	WELLMARK INC	1331 GRAND AVENUE	DES MOINES	IA	50309	(515) 376-4500
B+	WELLMARK OF SOUTH DAKOTA INC	1601 WEST MADISON STREET	SIOUX FALLS	SD	57104	(605) 373-7200
B-	WESTERN UNITED LIFE ASR CO	929 WEST SPRAGUE AVE	SPOKANE	WA	99201	(713) 529-0045

RATING	INSURANCE COMPANY NAME	ADDRESS	CITY	STATE	ZIP	PHONE
C	WISCONSIN PHYSICIANS SERVICE INS	1717 WEST BROADWAY	MADISON	WI	53713	(608) 977-500

Section VII

Analysis of Medicare Managed Care Complaints

An analysis of complaints filed against

U.S. Medicare Managed Care Plans

Companies are listed in alphabetical order.

Section VII Contents

As discussed in the previous section, no single measure is an end-all indicator of the quality of service provided by a health insurer. However, if you are a Medicare beneficiary, complaint information can give you a preliminary basis for informed shopping – especially for Medicare Managed Care plans. It will answer questions such as: Does the company have a high rate of enrollee complaints against it? Are most complaints upheld or overturned? Are many withdrawn before a decision is rendered?

The complaint information on the following pages will give you an indication of what beneficiaries, like yourself, have experienced with various Medicare insurers. This section is based on "reconsideration" data, reprinted from the Centers for Medicare and Medicaid Services (formerly known as Health Care Financing Administration) for providers with Medicare contracts.

"Reconsiderations" are complaints by members of Medicare Managed Care plans that have reached a federal review. Once they reach that stage, the complaints have already gone through at least two levels of internal appeals. Consequently, they are relatively serious and involve anywhere from several hundred dollars to many thousands of dollars of unpaid medical bills. In this section, all complaints cited are reconsiderations.

Complaints that were settled within the Plan's internal appeal process are not reflected. It is difficult to say what types of complaints these might be, but, in general, they are more likely to pertain to services of a lower dollar value.

We have made no attempt to render an opinion on the data contained in this section. Rather, we are reprinting the information strictly to help provide you with valuable information when shopping for a Medicare plan.

The Drawbacks of Complaint Data

One problem with the data is the time lag due to the lengthy reconsideration process. A company that has a high complaint rate in this section may have already begun to make improvements in its system to handle the types of issues that were raised in the complaints. Therefore, because it takes so long for a complaint to make it through the federal process, the company may appear to have worse service quality than it currently has.

Conversely, numerous companies that have obtained Medicare contracts very recently (within the past year), may show few or no complaints. But this may reflect merely the fact that the complaints filed against these companies have not yet reached the federal level. So before you make a final decision to select a company with a low level of complaints, find out how long it has had its Medicare contract. We estimate that the contract should be in force for about two years before these data reflect the complaints.

If you are interested in a company with a seemingly high complaint level, do take the time to ask the company what improvements, if any, it has made to correct the problems reflected in the complaint data. If a high rate of complaints against it have been upheld at the federal level, it will be far more difficult to explain away.

The plans included here are those from whom reconsiderations were received during 2018 or companies that had members enrolled in a specific Medicare contract as of July of that year. Not included are: 1) updates for later appeals of cases that have been decided and 2) companies whose contracts are so new that they don't have any current enrollment.

The plan name in this table represents one or more contracts with the Centers for Medicare and Medicaid Services (CMS). You may find some plans listed more than once; this is because they have contracts in different CMS-designated regions (see Column 3). If a plan has more than one contract in a particular region, the reconsideration data have been combined so that the company is only listed once for each region.

Three types of Medicare contracts are included here: risk, cost, and Health Care Prepayment Plans (HCPPs). A Medicare risk contract is one in which the CMS pays the plan a capitalization rate equal to a percentage of the average fee-for-service expense, in a given geographic area. A Medicare cost contract is one in which the CMS reimburses the plan for retroactively determined Part A and B costs. And an HCPP contract is similar to a cost contract but only Part B costs are paid by the CMS.

The following **BOLD** headings are the column reference guides for the tables

1. **Insurance Company Name** — The legally-registered name, which sometimes can differ from the name that the plan uses for advertising. If you cannot find the plan you are interested in, or if you have any doubts regarding the precise name, verify the information before looking it up in this Guide. Also, determine the domicile state for confirmation.

2. **Domicile State** — The state which has primary regulatory responsibility for the company. It may differ from the location of the company's corporate headquarters. You do not have to be living in the domicile state to purchase insurance from this firm, provided it is licensed to do business in your state.

   Also use this column to confirm that you have located the correct company. It is possible for two unrelated companies to have the same name if they are domiciled in different states.

3. **Safety Rating** — Our rating is measured on a scale from A to F and considers a wide range of factors. Highly-rated companies are, in our opinion, less likely to experience financial difficulties than lower rated firms. See *About Weiss Safety Ratings* for more information.

4. Region

The CMS region in which the complaint data applies for a particular company. The regions are as follows:

Boston: 1 (Connecticut, Maine, Massachusetts, New Hampshire, Rhode Island, Vermont), **New York: 2** (New Jersey, New York, Puerto Rico, Virgin Islands), **Philadelphia: 3** (Delaware, District of Columbia, Maryland, Pennsylvania, Virginia, West Virginia), **Atlanta: 4** (Alabama, Florida, Georgia, Kentucky, Mississippi, North Carolina, South Carolina, Tennessee), **Chicago: 5** (Illinois, Indiana, Michigan, Minnesota, Ohio, Wisconsin), **Dallas: 6** (Arkansas, Louisiana, Oklahoma, New Mexico, Texas), **Kansas City: 7** (Iowa, Kansas, Missouri, Nebraska), **Denver: 8** (Colorado, Montana, North Dakota, South Dakota, Utah, Wyoming), **San Francisco: 9** (Arizona, California, Guam, Hawaii, Nevada, Samoa), **Seattle: 10** (Alaska, Idaho, Oregon, Washington).

5. Rate

The rate of reconsiderations per 1,000 members and is calculated as the sum of appeals received per year. Divided by the mid-year (July) enrollment, times 1,000.

"N/R" means that there were "no reconsiderations" for that particular plan's contract in that particular region. "N/E" means there was "no enrollment" during 2017. This happens when the complaints reflect prior enrollments in specific contracts, demonstrate the lag time between enrollment, and the complaint being represented in the reconsideration system.

6. Reconsiderations Received 2016

The number of reconsiderations received by the CMS from the health plan for the Medicare contract(s) only. Regardless of the number of complaints upheld or overturned (See columns 8 and 9), if this number is high relative to other Medicare plans, it signals that the plan has trouble satisfying its policyholders.

The health plan may have other business besides treating Medicare beneficiaries but this figure only pertains to enrollees that are served under a Medicare contract.

7. Reconsiderations Not Yet Decided

The number of reconsiderations received during 2018 that have not yet been settled.

8. Reconsiderations Upheld

The number of cases in which the CMS upheld the decision of the Medicare plan. This is the number of times CMS ruled against the policyholder in favor of the plan. If the number is high relative to the total number of reconsiderations received (Column 6), it is a sign that the firm's complaint process is somewhat ironclad and appeals beyond it are often futile. This, however, does not necessarily mean that the plan was not at fault.

9. Reconsiderations Overturned

The number of cases in which the CMS completely overturned the decision of the Medicare Managed Care plan. This is the number of times the CMS ruled in favor of the policyholder. If the number of complaints overturned is high, relative to the total number of reconsiderations received (Column 6), it is a sign that either the plan is falling short in meeting the needs of its policyholders; or, its complaint process is not streamlined enough to carry complaints to the appropriate conclusion.

10. Reconsiderations Withdrawn

The number of reconsiderations that were withdrawn from review.

The Regional CMS office will investigate the case and determine if the enrolee should revert back to fee-for-service (disenroll). If the CMS does not grant disenrollment, the case re-enters the reconsideration process and follows the same course as other complaints.

A high number of disenrollments may indicate that the plan has failed to clearly identify its coverage limitations at the time the policy is sold.

11. Reconsiderations Dismissed

The number of cases in which the CMS Regional Office decided the appeal is not valid or the CMS Regional Office does not have jurisdiction over the appeal.

INSURANCE COMPANY NAME	DOM. STATE	RATING	REGION	RATE	RECONS REC'VD	RECONS NOT YET DECIDED	RECONS UPHELD	RECONS OVER-TURNED	RECONS WITH-DRAWN	RECONS DISMISSED
ABSOLUTE TOTAL CARE INC	SC	C+	4	5.46	18	0	16	0	0	2
AETNA BETTER HEALTH OF MICHIGAN INC	MI	B	5	4.94	39	0	18	7	0	14
AETNA HEALTH INC (A CT CORP)	CT	C	8	4.52	71	0	62	4	0	4
AETNA HEALTH INC (A FLORIDA CORP)	FL	B-	8	N/E	--	--	--	--	--	--
AETNA HEALTH INC (A GEORGIA CORP)	GA	C	8	9.14	14	0	13	0	0	1
AETNA HEALTH INC (A MAINE CORP)	ME	B	8	2.90	18	0	16	1	0	1
AETNA HEALTH INC (A NEW JERSEY CORP)	NJ	B	8	4.14	184	0	167	5	0	12
AETNA HEALTH INC (A NEW YORK CORP)	NY	B	8	6.28	67	0	61	2	0	2
AETNA HEALTH INC (A PA CORP)	PA	B	8	4.38	322	0	283	5	1	33
AETNA HEALTH INC (A TEXAS CORP)	TX	C	8	6.63	244	0	231	3	0	10
AETNA HEALTH OF CALIFORNIA INC	CA	B	8	2.51	36	0	30	0	1	5
AETNA HEALTH OF IOWA INC	IA	C+	8	2.30	142	0	125	10	0	6
AETNA HEALTH OF UTAH INC	UT	C	8	1.41	9	0	5	2	0	2
AETNA LIFE INS CO	CT	B	8	3.26	3387	0	3099	83	3	190
AIDS HEALTHCARE FOUNDATION MCO OF FL	FL	E+	9	N/E	--	--	--	--	--	--
ALLIANCE HEALTH & LIFE INS CO	MI	C	5	1.90	7	0	7	0	0	0
ALOHACARE	HI	B-	9	N/E	--	--	--	--	--	--
AMERIGROUP COMMUNITY CARE NM	NM	B	5	3.91	6	0	6	0	0	0
AMERIGROUP NEW JERSEY INC	NJ	A-	5	10.90	106	0	95	2	0	9
AMERIGROUP TENNESSEE INC	TN	B-	5	1.84	22	0	14	2	0	6
AMERIGROUP TEXAS INC	TX	A-	5	2.05	84	0	68	3	0	13
AMERIGROUP TEXAS INC	TX	A-	6	5.50	75	0	60	7	0	8
AMERIGROUP WASHINGTON INC	WA	A-	5	1.23	2	0	2	0	0	0
AMERIHEALTH HMO INC	PA	C+	3	N/E	--	--	--	--	--	--
AMERIHEALTH MICHIGAN INC	MI	C	5	11.10	37	0	24	8	0	5
ANTHEM BLUE CROSS LIFE & HEALTH INS	CA	B-	5	3.66	32	0	23	1	0	7
ANTHEM HEALTH PLANS INC	CT	B	5	6.85	232	0	210	8	0	14
ANTHEM HEALTH PLANS OF KENTUCKY INC	KY	B	5	N/E	--	--	--	--	--	--
ANTHEM HEALTH PLANS OF MAINE INC	ME	B	5	15.96	196	0	152	11	0	32
ANTHEM HEALTH PLANS OF NEW HAMPSHIRE	NH	B	5	1.89	38	0	28	1	0	8
ANTHEM HEALTH PLANS OF VIRGINIA	VA	B	5	0.52	21	0	15	2	0	4
ANTHEM INS COMPANIES INC	IN	B-	5	13.03	388	0	313	13	0	61
ARKANSAS SUPERIOR SELECT INC	AR	E	6	1.07	2	0	1	0	0	1
ASPIRE HEALTH PLAN	CA	E-	9	19.32	64	0	56	7	0	1
ASURIS NORTHWEST HEALTH	WA	B	10	2.10	2	0	1	0	0	0
ATRIO HEALTH PLANS INC	OR	D	10	27.79	114	0	93	14	0	7
AULTCARE INS CO	OH	B	5	2.19	44	0	43	0	1	0
AVMED INC	FL	C	4	1.87	54	0	48	2	0	4
BEHEALTHY FLORIDA INC	FL	C-	4	14.45	140	0	123	14	0	3
BLUE CROSS & BLUE SHIELD MA HMO BLUE	MA	B+	1	4.57	136	0	124	7	0	5
BLUE CROSS & BLUE SHIELD OF FLORIDA	FL	B	4	11.03	340	0	230	15	0	93
BLUE CROSS BLUE SHIELD HEALTHCARE GA	GA	A-	5	N/E	--	--	--	--	--	--
BLUE CROSS BLUE SHIELD OF ALABAMA	AL	B+	4	0.84	75	0	67	3	0	4
BLUE CROSS BLUE SHIELD OF MICHIGAN	MI	B-	5	2.31	402	0	249	17	0	133
BLUE CROSS BLUE SHIELD OF MINNESOTA	MN	C	5	0.31	81	0	73	3	0	5
BLUE CROSS BLUE SHIELD OF NC	NC	B+	4	5.20	185	0	146	19	0	19
BLUE CROSS BLUE SHIELD OF RI	RI	C	1	2.23	117	0	100	10	0	6
BLUE CROSS OF CALIFORNIA	CA	A+	5	N/E	--	--	--	--	--	--
BLUE CROSS OF IDAHO HEALTH SERVICE	ID	B	10	19.73	343	0	284	23	0	26
BLUECROSS BLUESHIELD OF TENNESSEE	TN	B+	4	5.79	712	0	645	27	7	29
BRAVO HEALTH MID-ATLANTIC INC	MD	C	6	6.21	109	0	90	13	0	5
BRAVO HEALTH PENNSYLVANIA INC	PA	C+	6	5.22	218	0	195	18	0	4

INSURANCE COMPANY NAME	DOM. STATE	RATING	REGION	RATE	RECONS REC'VD	RECONS NOT YET DECIDED	RECONS UPHELD	RECONS OVER-TURNED	RECONS WITH-DRAWN	RECONS DISMISSED
BUCKEYE COMMUNITY HEALTH PLAN INC	OH	**B**	5	1.51	19	0	15	1	0	3
BUCKEYE COMMUNITY HEALTH PLAN INC	OH	**B**	10	1.97	1	0	1	0	0	0
CALIFORNIA PHYSICIANS SERVICE	CA	**A+**	9	5.16	433	0	356	16	2	55
CAPITAL ADVANTAGE INS CO	PA	**C**	3	3.91	52	0	47	3	0	2
CAPITAL DISTRICT PHYSICIANS HEALTH P	NY	**A**	2	7.30	282	0	252	24	0	3
CAPITAL HEALTH PLAN INC	FL	**B+**	4	1.65	35	0	31	3	0	1
CARE 1ST HEALTH PLAN INC	CA	**A+**	9	6.22	389	0	296	19	0	72
CARE IMPROVEMENT PLUS OF TEXAS INS	TX	**B**	9	9.18	1118	0	873	6	0	234
CARE IMPROVEMENT PLUS SOUTH CENTRAL	AR	**B-**	9	27.10	1304	0	1112	9	0	183
CARE IMPROVEMENT PLUS WI INS	WI	**B**	9	9.41	83	0	73	0	0	10
CARE N CARE INS CO	TX	**C**	6	11.68	53	0	44	3	0	6
CARE WISCONSIN HEALTH PLAN INC	WI	**B+**	5	3.78	7	0	6	0	0	1
CAREMORE HEALTH PLAN	CA	**B-**	5	3.88	392	0	330	25	1	34
CAREMORE HEALTH PLAN OF ARIZONA INC	AZ	**B**	5	5.24	70	0	38	8	0	24
CAREMORE HEALTH PLAN OF NEVADA	NV	**B-**	5	5.61	60	0	54	1	0	5
CAREPLUS HEALTH PLANS INC	FL	**B**	7	2.91	337	0	315	4	0	17
CARESOURCE	OH	**B-**	5	16.28	306	0	137	38	0	130
CARITEN HEALTH PLAN INC	TN	**B**	7	1.71	189	0	142	8	0	38
CATHOLIC SPECIAL NEEDS PLAN LLC	NY	**C**	2	0.57	1	0	0	0	0	1
CDPHP UNIVERSAL BENEFITS INC	NY	**B**	2	3.97	16	0	13	3	0	0
CHA HMO INC	KY	**C+**	7	1.39	27	0	22	0	0	5
CHINESE COMMUNITY HEALTH PLAN	CA	**E-**	9	6.13	30	0	22	4	0	4
CHRISTUS HEALTH PLAN	TX	**C-**	6	7.43	10	0	5	0	0	5
CIGNA HEALTH & LIFE INS CO	CT	**B**	6	N/E	--	--	--	--	--	--
CIGNA HEALTHCARE OF ARIZONA INC	AZ	**C**	6	4.07	175	0	147	16	0	12
CIGNA HEALTHCARE OF GEORGIA INC	GA	**C**	6	5.10	121	0	109	6	0	3
CIGNA HEALTHCARE OF NORTH CAROLINA	NC	**D**	6	3.93	23	0	20	2	0	1
CIGNA HEALTHCARE OF SOUTH CAROLINA	SC	**C**	6	4.38	24	0	22	2	0	0
CMNTY CARE HLTH PLAN INC (WI)	WI	**B-**	5	2.10	1	0	1	0	0	0
COMMUNITY CARE ALLIANCE OF ILLINOIS	IL	**E-**	5	11.74	61	0	47	9	1	4
COMMUNITY HEALTH GROUP	CA	**B-**	9	0.51	3	0	3	0	0	0
COMMUNITY HEALTH PLAN OF WASHINGTON	WA	**B**	10	4.08	33	0	21	4	0	7
COMMUNITY INS CO	OH	**B-**	5	3.26	574	0	494	18	0	57
COMMUNITYCARE HMO INC	OK	**B**	6	2.14	52	0	44	4	0	4
COMPCARE HEALTH SERVICES INS CORP	WI	**A-**	5	3.01	63	0	57	2	0	4
CONNECTICARE INC	CT	**C-**	2	6.53	319	0	280	24	1	12
CONSTELLATION HEALTH LLC	PR	**U**	2	22.03	137	0	8	10	0	119
CONTRA COSTA HEALTH PLAN	CA	**B**	9	N/E	--	--	--	--	--	--
COVENTRY HEALTH & LIFE INS CO	MO	**B-**	8	1.59	255	0	235	5	2	12
COVENTRY HEALTH CARE OF ILLINOIS INC	IL	**C**	8	1.44	34	0	32	0	0	2
COVENTRY HEALTH CARE OF MISSOURI INC	MO	**C+**	8	1.39	117	0	106	3	0	7
COVENTRY HEALTH CARE OF NEBRASKA INC	NE	**C**	8	1.53	10	0	9	0	0	1
COVENTRY HEALTH CARE OF VIRGINIA INC	VA	**B-**	8	13.51	11	0	9	1	0	1
COVENTRY HEALTH CARE OF WEST VA INC	WV	**B**	8	2.89	19	0	18	0	0	1
DEAN HEALTH PLAN INC	WI	**A**	5	29.76	238	0	182	29	1	25
DENVER HEALTH MEDICAL PLAN INC	CO	**B-**	8	6.83	31	0	21	2	0	8
EASY CHOICE HEALTH PLAN	CA	**C**	4	3.67	109	0	97	7	0	4
ELDERPLAN INC	NY	**C**	2	7.77	84	0	71	7	0	5
EMPIRE HEALTHCHOICE ASSURANCE INC	NY	**B-**	5	3.09	9	0	7	0	0	2
EMPIRE HEALTHCHOICE HMO INC	NY	**B-**	5	N/E	--	--	--	--	--	--
ESSENCE HEALTHCARE INC	MO	**A-**	7	7.16	465	0	399	33	2	28
EXCELLUS HEALTH PLAN INC	NY	**B**	2	12.54	922	0	820	82	1	12

INSURANCE COMPANY NAME	DOM. STATE	RATING	REGION	RATE	RECONS REC'VD	RECONS NOT YET DECIDED	RECONS UPHELD	RECONS OVER-TURNED	RECONS WITH-DRAWN	RECONS DISMISSED
FALLON COMMUNITY HEALTH PLAN	MA	**B-**	1	15.19	297	0	248	35	0	12
FAMILYCARE HEALTH PLANS INC	OR	**E-**	10	N/E	--	--	--	--	--	--
FIRSTCAROLINACARE INS CO	NC	**D**	4	0.92	6	0	3	0	0	3
GATEWAY HEALTH PLAN INC	PA	**B-**	3	5.37	262	0	244	4	0	14
GATEWAY HEALTH PLAN OF OHIO INC	OH	**C**	3	12.64	134	0	109	4	0	21
GEISINGER HEALTH PLAN	PA	**B+**	3	1.94	136	0	127	4	0	2
GEISINGER INDEMNITY INS CO	PA	**B-**	3	1.56	40	0	39	1	0	0
GHS HEALTH MAINTENANCE ORGANIZATION	OK	**B-**	6	29.60	124	0	57	24	0	39
GHS INS CO	OK	**E-**	6	20.23	96	0	54	8	0	34
GHS MANAGED HEALTH CARE PLANS INC	OK	**U**	6	N/E	--	--	--	--	--	--
GLOBALHEALTH INC	OK	**D**	6	N/E	--	--	--	--	--	--
GROUP HEALTH INCORPORATED	NY	**D+**	2	20.83	1	0	0	0	0	1
GROUP HEALTH PLAN INC	MN	**B**	5	0.69	42	0	40	2	0	0
GUNDERSEN HEALTH PLAN INC	WI	**C-**	5	5.10	80	0	65	5	0	6
GUNDERSEN HLTH PLAN MN INC	MN	**C**	5	1.22	1	0	1	0	0	0
HAP MIDWEST HEALTH PLAN INC	MI	**C-**	5	1.78	10	0	2	4	0	4
HARMONY HEALTH PLAN INC	IL	**C**	4	4.56	388	0	307	3	0	77
HARVARD PILGRIM HEALTH CARE INC	MA	**C+**	1	69.16	450	0	390	32	3	22
HAWAII MEDICAL SERVICE ASSOCIATION	HI	**B**	9	0.41	15	0	10	3	0	1
HCSC INS SERVICES CO	IL	**D-**	6	25.21	345	0	165	87	1	87
HEALTH ALLIANCE MEDICAL PLANS	IL	**B-**	5	15.10	315	0	238	72	0	2
HEALTH ALLIANCE NORTHWEST HEALTH PL	WA	**B**	5	8.15	61	0	49	12	0	0
HEALTH ALLIANCE PLAN OF MICHIGAN	MI	**C-**	5	1.86	107	0	94	2	0	9
HEALTH ALLIANCE-MIDWEST INC	IL	**U**	5	18.04	9	0	9	0	0	0
HEALTH CARE SVC CORP A MUT LEG RES	IL	**B**	5	6.25	125	0	80	26	0	16
HEALTH CARE SVC CORP A MUT LEG RES	IL	**B**	6	60.88	1218	0	530	288	1	381
HEALTH INSURANCE PLAN OF GREATER NY	NY	**C-**	2	3.82	447	0	340	22	0	78
HEALTH NET COMMUNITY SOLUTIONS INC	CA	**B**	9	4.87	64	0	55	5	0	4
HEALTH NET HEALTH PLAN OF OREGON INC	OR	**D**	10	2.47	91	0	74	3	0	14
HEALTH NET LIFE INS CO	CA	**C**	10	1.58	74	0	55	7	1	10
HEALTH NET OF ARIZONA INC	AZ	**C**	10	5.37	91	0	70	7	0	13
HEALTH NET OF CALIFORNIA INC	CA	**C**	10	2.78	339	0	277	34	2	25
HEALTH NEW ENGLAND INC	MA	**B**	1	7.19	64	0	52	10	1	1
HEALTH OPTIONS INC	FL	**A-**	4	6.05	291	0	220	13	0	58
HEALTH PARTNERS PLANS INC	PA	**B**	3	8.06	166	0	137	24	0	3
HEALTH PLAN OF CAREOREGON INC	OR	**C**	10	5.72	74	0	71	1	0	1
HEALTH PLAN OF NEVADA INC	NV	**B+**	9	2.40	117	0	108	1	0	8
HEALTHASSURANCE PENNSYLVANIA INC	PA	**C**	8	1.75	123	0	103	0	0	19
HEALTHFIRST HEALTH PLAN INC	NY	**B**	2	2.79	427	0	346	3	0	74
HEALTHKEEPERS INC	VA	**B**	3	N/E	--	--	--	--	--	--
HEALTHNOW NY INC	NY	**B**	2	2.40	58	0	55	1	1	1
HEALTHPARTNERS	MN	**B+**	5	N/E	--	--	--	--	--	--
HEALTHSPRING L&H INS CO	TX	**B-**	6	12.87	483	0	447	17	0	20
HEARTLANDPLAINS HEALTH	NE	**E**	8	14.52	8	0	6	1	0	1
HIGHMARK CHOICE CO	PA	**U**	3	3.74	400	0	356	9	0	33
HIGHMARK SENIOR HEALTH CO	PA	**U**	3	2.84	423	0	368	18	0	32
HM HEALTH INS CO	PA	**U**	3	3.62	15	0	13	0	0	2
HMO MINNESOTA	MN	**C+**	5	1.04	9	0	9	0	0	0
HMO MISSOURI INC	MO	**B**	5	3.61	34	0	24	1	0	9
HMO PARTNERS INC	AR	**A+**	6	1.01	5	0	2	0	0	3
HOMETOWN HEALTH PLAN INC	NV	**D**	10	11.38	122	0	94	10	0	15
HORIZON HEALTHCARE OF NEW JERSEY INC	NJ	**C+**	2	1.79	106	0	59	5	0	42

INSURANCE COMPANY NAME	DOM. STATE	RATING	REGION	RATE	RECONS REC'VD	RECONS NOT YET DECIDED	RECONS UPHELD	RECONS OVER-TURNED	RECONS WITH-DRAWN	RECONS DISMISSED
HORIZON INS CO	NJ	**C+**	2	7.82	179	0	116	2	1	58
HUMANA BENEFIT PLAN OF ILLINOIS	IL	**B+**	7	3.78	300	0	210	18	0	71
HUMANA EMPLOYERS HEALTH PLAN OF GA	GA	**C+**	7	2.29	112	0	80	7	0	24
HUMANA HEALTH BENEFIT PLAN LA	LA	**C+**	7	2.24	319	0	248	15	1	54
HUMANA HEALTH CO OF NEW YORK INC	NY	**C+**	7	3.58	69	0	50	1	0	18
HUMANA HEALTH INS CO OF FL INC	FL	**B-**	7	N/E	--	--	--	--	--	--
HUMANA HEALTH PLAN INC	KY	**C+**	3	N/E	--	--	--	--	--	--
HUMANA HEALTH PLAN INC	KY	**C+**	5	3.00	24	0	9	2	0	13
HUMANA HEALTH PLAN INC	KY	**C+**	7	2.46	804	0	565	47	0	184
HUMANA HEALTH PLAN OF OHIO INC	OH	**C+**	7	N/E	--	--	--	--	--	--
HUMANA HEALTH PLANS OF PUERTO RICO	PR	**D**	7	0.39	13	0	4	3	0	5
HUMANA INS CO (WI)	WI	**B**	7	46.94	4710	0	3545	251	10	872
HUMANA INS CO OF NY	NY	**B-**	7	4.67	45	0	25	9	0	11
HUMANA INS CO OF PUERTO RICO INC	PR	**C+**	7	1.79	2	0	0	0	0	2
HUMANA MEDICAL PLAN INC	FL	**A-**	7	1.78	832	0	627	44	2	155
HUMANA MEDICAL PLAN OF MICHIGAN INC	MI	**C+**	7	2.88	23	0	10	3	0	10
HUMANA MEDICAL PLAN OF PENNSYLVANIA	PA	**U**	7	N/E	--	--	--	--	--	--
HUMANA MEDICAL PLAN OF UTAH INC	UT	**C+**	7	2.47	8	0	7	0	0	1
HUMANA REGIONAL HEALTH PLAN INC	AR	**U**	7	N/E	--	--	--	--	--	--
HUMANA WISCONSIN HEALTH ORGANIZATION	WI	**B**	5	18.05	102	0	81	11	0	9
HUMANA WISCONSIN HEALTH ORGANIZATION	WI	**B**	7	1.58	329	0	230	23	0	72
ILLINICARE HEALTH PLAN INC	IL	**C-**	5	1.70	13	0	10	1	0	2
INDEPENDENT CARE HEALTH PLAN	WI	**B+**	5	13.01	103	0	85	8	0	10
INDEPENDENT HEALTH ASSOC INC	NY	**B-**	2	17.73	1161	0	1083	34	1	40
INDEPENDENT HEALTH BENEFITS CORP	NY	**C**	2	14.15	66	0	63	3	0	0
INDIANA UNIVERSITY HEALTH PLANS INC	IN	**E-**	5	6.03	86	0	75	8	0	1
INS CO OF SCOTT & WHITE	TX	**D**	6	21.03	104	0	88	8	0	8
INTERVALLEY HEALTH PLAN	CA	**D**	10	1.39	31	0	25	2	0	4
K S PLAN ADMINISTRATORS LLC	TX	**B+**	6	2.32	76	0	72	1	0	3
KAISER FOUNDATION HEALTH PLAN INC	CA	**A**	9	1.08	971	0	855	28	3	84
KAISER FOUNDATION HP MID-ATL STATES	MD	**B**	9	0.90	65	0	52	7	0	5
KAISER FOUNDATION HP NORTHWEST	OR	**B**	9	1.25	115	0	106	2	0	5
KAISER FOUNDATION HP OF CO	CO	**B**	9	1.34	149	0	135	6	1	7
KAISER FOUNDATION HP OF GA	GA	**B**	9	1.00	29	0	28	1	0	0
KEYSTONE HEALTH PLAN CENTRAL INC	PA	**C-**	3	4.15	66	0	60	4	0	2
KEYSTONE HEALTH PLAN EAST INC	PA	**B**	3	8.22	747	0	661	57	2	23
LOCAL INITIATIVE HEALTH AUTH LA	CA	**C**	9	5.34	84	0	72	5	0	6
MARTINS POINT GENERATIONS LLC	ME	**U**	1	8.06	170	0	138	20	0	10
MATTHEW THORNTON HEALTH PLAN	NH	**B**	5	4.26	11	0	9	0	0	2
MCS ADVANTAGE INC	PR	**D**	2	1.65	340	0	256	4	0	78
MEDICA HEALTH PLANS	MN	**C+**	5	0.27	3	0	3	0	0	0
MEDICA HEALTHCARE PLANS INC	FL	**B**	9	4.30	193	0	154	1	0	38
MEDICAL ASSOC CLINIC HEALTH PLAN	WI	**B-**	7	N/E	--	--	--	--	--	--
MEDICAL ASSOCIATES HEALTH PLAN INC	IA	**B-**	7	0.09	1	0	1	0	0	0
MEDISUN INC	AZ	**B**	9	14.68	801	0	556	89	1	152
MEDSTAR FAMILY CHOICE INC	MD	**C-**	3	10.21	60	0	56	2	0	2
MEMORIAL HERMANN HEALTH PLAN INC	TX	**C-**	6	31.01	95	0	62	13	0	19
MERIDIAN HEALTH PLAN OF ILLINOIS INC	IL	**C**	5	56.10	351	0	320	11	0	18
MERIDIAN HEALTH PLAN OF MICHIGAN INC	MI	**C**	5	22.04	270	0	227	21	0	19
MHS HEALTH WISCONSIN	WI	**B-**	10	7.60	8	0	7	1	0	0
MICHIGAN COMPLETE HEALTH INC	MO	**C-**	5	13.83	39	0	21	4	1	13
MMM HEALTHCARE LLC	PR	**E-**	2	1.76	283	0	188	12	0	81

INSURANCE COMPANY NAME	DOM. STATE	RATING	REGION	RATE	RECONS REC'VD	RECONS NOT YET DECIDED	RECONS UPHELD	RECONS OVER-TURNED	RECONS WITH-DRAWN	RECONS DISMISSED
MODA HEALTH PLAN INC	OR	**E**	10	20.07	115	0	91	9	1	12
MOLINA HEALTHCARE OF CALIFORNIA	CA	**C-**	9	5.80	66	0	41	9	1	14
MOLINA HEALTHCARE OF CALIFORNIA	CA	**C-**	10	6.75	13	0	8	1	1	3
MOLINA HEALTHCARE OF FLORIDA INC	FL	**C**	10	6.51	17	0	10	1	0	5
MOLINA HEALTHCARE OF ILLINOIS INC	IL	**C**	5	14.10	53	0	29	14	1	9
MOLINA HEALTHCARE OF MICHIGAN INC	MI	**B**	5	5.97	66	0	50	7	0	7
MOLINA HEALTHCARE OF MICHIGAN INC	MI	**B**	10	8.52	99	0	66	9	0	24
MOLINA HEALTHCARE OF NEW MEXICO	NM	**C**	10	11.94	60	0	42	6	0	11
MOLINA HEALTHCARE OF OHIO INC	OH	**B**	5	12.51	172	0	116	10	0	43
MOLINA HEALTHCARE OF OHIO INC	OH	**B**	10	17.67	5	0	5	0	0	0
MOLINA HEALTHCARE OF SOUTH CAROLINA	SC	**B**	4	7.20	21	0	12	6	0	3
MOLINA HEALTHCARE OF TEXAS INC	TX	**B**	6	13.16	164	0	102	25	0	36
MOLINA HEALTHCARE OF TEXAS INC	TX	**B**	10	8.79	14	0	10	1	0	3
MOLINA HEALTHCARE OF UTAH INC	UT	**C+**	10	5.68	64	0	38	9	0	17
MOLINA HEALTHCARE OF WASHINGTON INC	WA	**B**	10	5.75	57	0	42	4	0	10
MOLINA HEALTHCARE OF WISCONSIN INC	WI	**C**	10	7.76	8	0	4	2	0	2
MOUNT CARMEL HEALTH INS CO	OH	**B-**	5	2.54	2	0	2	0	0	0
MOUNT CARMEL HEALTH PLAN INC	OH	**B**	5	3.35	165	0	156	4	1	4
MVP HEALTH PLAN INC	NY	**B**	2	22.40	678	0	589	63	2	16
NETWORK HEALTH INS CORP	WI	**C**	8	2.32	4	0	3	1	0	0
OKLAHOMA SUPERIOR SELECT INC	OK	**E+**	6	N/E	--	--	--	--	--	--
ON LOK SENIOR HEALTH SERVICES	CA	**B**	9	N/E	--	--	--	--	--	--
OPTIMA HEALTH PLAN	VA	**A**	3	0.68	2	0	2	0	0	0
OXFORD HEALTH PLANS (CT) INC	CT	**B**	9	5.93	854	0	714	2	0	137
OXFORD HEALTH PLANS (NJ) INC	NJ	**B**	9	3.58	148	0	70	1	0	77
OXFORD HEALTH PLANS (NY) INC	NY	**B**	9	6.05	523	0	432	0	0	89
PACIFICARE OF COLORADO INC	CO	**B**	9	2.96	8626	0	21	6	0	232
PACIFICSOURCE COMMUNITY HEALTH PLANS	OR	**B**	10	10.67	161	0	144	7	0	10
PARAMOUNT HEALTH CARE	OH	**B**	5	1.38	22	0	19	1	0	2
PEACH STATE HEALTH PLAN INC	GA	**B-**	10	4.63	6	0	6	0	0	0
PHOENIX HEALTH PLANS INC	AZ	**U**	6	N/E	--	--	--	--	--	--
PIEDMONT COMMUNITY HEALTHCARE	VA	**D+**	3	4.13	21	0	17	2	0	1
PMC MEDICARE CHOICE LLC	PR	**U**	2	0.95	40	0	35	0	0	5
PREFERRED CARE PARTNERS INC	FL	**B**	9	4.18	755	0	573	1	1	177
PREMERA BLUE CROSS	WA	**B**	10	10.36	224	0	167	6	0	50
PREMIER HEALTH INSURING CORP	OH	**E**	5	N/E	--	--	--	--	--	--
PRESBYTERIAN INS CO	NM	**C+**	6	9.94	31	0	22	7	0	1
PRIORITY HEALTH	MI	**A**	5	11.26	794	0	731	40	1	17
PROMINENCE HEALTHFIRST OF TEXAS INC	TX	**D+**	9	32.16	137	0	37	22	0	76
PROVIDENCE HEALTH PLAN	OR	**B**	10	4.77	269	0	231	25	0	13
QCC INS CO	PA	**B-**	3	7.39	65	0	56	5	0	4
REGENCE BL CROSS BL SHIELD OREGON	OR	**A-**	10	6.46	139	0	124	9	0	6
REGENCE BLUE CROSS BLUE SHIELD OF UT	UT	**B+**	10	2.80	23	0	22	1	0	0
REGENCE BLUESHIELD	WA	**B**	10	7.72	73	0	68	3	0	2
REGENCE BLUESHIELD OF IDAHO INC	ID	**B+**	10	5.83	20	0	17	1	0	2
RIVERLINK HEALTH	OH	**D**	8	13.40	23	0	19	0	0	4
SAMARITAN HEALTH PLANS INC	OR	**C+**	10	3.53	18	0	13	2	0	3
SAN MATEO HEALTH COMMISSION	CA	**B**	9	6.99	63	0	45	10	0	8
SANFORD HEART OF AMERICA HEALTH PLAN	ND	**C-**	8	N/E	--	--	--	--	--	--
SCAN HEALTH PLAN	CA	**B**	9	87.62	1143	0	1001	76	2	61
SCOTT & WHITE HEALTH PLAN	TX	**C**	6	3.58	100	0	74	13	0	13
SECURITY HEALTH PLAN OF WI INC	WI	**B+**	5	4.16	190	0	171	16	0	2

INSURANCE COMPANY NAME	DOM. STATE	RATING	REGION	RATE	RECONS REC'VD	RECONS NOT YET DECIDED	RECONS UPHELD	RECONS OVER-TURNED	RECONS WITH-DRAWN	RECONS DISMISSED
SECURITYCARE OF TENNESSEE INC	TN	**U**	4	N/E	--	--	--	--	--	--
SELECT HEALTH OF SOUTH CAROLINA INC	SC	**B**	4	7.48	38	0	24	2	0	12
SELECTHEALTH INC	UT	**C**	8	3.17	129	0	112	4	0	10
SENIOR WHOLE HEALTH OF NEW YORK INC	NY	**C-**	1	N/E	--	--	--	--	--	--
SENIOR WHOLE HEALTH OF NEW YORK INC	NY	**C-**	2	N/E	--	--	--	--	--	--
SHARP HEALTH PLAN	CA	**B+**	9	11.74	24	0	22	2	0	0
SIDNEY HILLMAN HEALTH CENTRE	IL	**U**	5	N/E	--	--	--	--	--	--
SIERRA HEALTH AND LIFE INS CO INC	NV	**B**	9	8.61	6119	0	4398	82	7	1618
SIMPLY HEALTHCARE PLANS INC	FL	**B-**	5	13.24	740	0	698	20	0	18
STANFORD HEALTH CARE ADVANTAGE	CA	**E**	9	2.08	6	0	6	0	0	0
SUMMACARE INC	OH	**C**	5	5.62	133	0	128	2	0	3
SUNSHINE HEALTH	FL	**D+**	10	2.74	6	0	5	0	0	1
SUPERIOR HEALTHPLAN INC	TX	**C+**	6	2.30	21	0	13	5	0	3
SUPERIOR HEALTHPLAN INC	TX	**C+**	10	1.76	3	0	2	0	0	1
SUTTER HEALTH PLAN	CA	**D**	9	N/E	--	--	--	--	--	--
THP INS CO	WV	**D+**	3	1.09	2	0	2	0	0	0
TRILLIUM COMMUNITY HEALTH PLAN INC	OR	**C+**	10	1.14	3	0	1	2	0	0
TRIPLE-S ADVANTAGE INC	PR	**C+**	2	0.97	95	0	81	2	0	11
TRIPLE-S SALUD INC	PR	**B+**	2	2.16	30	0	26	2	0	2
TUFTS ASSOCIATED HEALTH MAINT ORG	MA	**C**	1	8.88	902	0	858	21	0	21
TUFTS HEALTH PUBLIC PLANS INC	MA	**C**	1	8.28	22	0	14	5	0	3
UCARE MINNESOTA	MN	**B**	5	3.90	253	0	209	19	0	21
UHC OF CALIFORNIA INC	CA	**B-**	9	2.26	789	0	651	12	0	124
ULTIMATE HEALTH PLANS INC	FL	**E-**	4	9.00	61	0	54	1	0	5
UNION HEALTH SERVICE INC	IL	**C+**	5	N/E	--	--	--	--	--	--
UNITED HEALTHCARE INS CO	CT	**C**	9	82.74	6069	0	4887	59	2	1111
UNITED HEALTHCARE OF ALABAMA INC	AL	**C**	9	4.46	34	0	32	1	0	1
UNITED HEALTHCARE OF GEORGIA INC	GA	**C+**	9	5.51	80	0	62	1	0	17
UNITED HEALTHCARE OF LOUISIANA INC	LA	**B**	9	104.13	58	0	58	0	0	0
UNITED HEALTHCARE OF NC INC	NC	**C**	9	N/E	--	--	--	--	--	--
UNITED HEALTHCARE OF NEW ENGLAND INC	RI	**B**	9	3.01	177	0	152	1	0	24
UNITED HEALTHCARE OF NY INC	NY	**B+**	9	8.14	486	0	242	3	0	240
UNITED HEALTHCARE OF OHIO INC	OH	**C**	9	N/E	--	--	--	--	--	--
UNITED HEALTHCARE OF THE MIDLANDS	NE	**B**	9	3.87	901	0	738	9	0	153
UNITED HEALTHCARE OF THE MIDWEST INC	MO	**C+**	9	2.13	38	0	29	0	0	9
UNITED HEALTHCARE OF UTAH	UT	**B**	9	1.21	91	0	64	2	0	25
UNITED HEALTHCARE OF WISCONSIN INC	WI	**B+**	9	3.05	1468	0	1198	13	0	253
UNITEDHEALTHCARE BENEFITS OF TEXAS	TX	**B**	9	1.95	478	0	380	3	0	90
UNITEDHEALTHCARE COMMUNITY PLAN TX	TX	**B-**	9	9.33	281	0	250	2	0	29
UNITEDHEALTHCARE OF OKLAHOMA INC	OK	**B**	9	3.01	96	0	71	2	0	23
UNITEDHEALTHCARE OF OREGON	OR	**B+**	9	1.66	217	0	158	1	0	57
UNITEDHEALTHCARE PLAN RIVER VALLEY	IL	**B**	9	2.48	143	0	60	1	0	82
UNIVERSAL CARE	CA	**E-**	9	0.89	25	0	21	4	0	0
UPMC FOR YOU INC	PA	**B+**	3	8.28	215	0	204	6	0	4
UPMC HEALTH PLAN INC	PA	**C+**	3	8.73	1251	0	1199	18	5	23
UPPER PENINSULA HEALTH PLAN INC	MI	**B+**	5	36.07	117	0	83	31	0	3
USABLE MUTUAL INS CO	AR	**B**	6	0.39	6	0	2	1	0	3
VANTAGE HEALTH PLAN INC	LA	**D+**	6	13.28	246	0	228	3	0	14
VISTA HEALTH PLAN INC	PA	**B+**	3	9.79	61	0	46	6	0	7
VIVA HEALTH INC	AL	**B+**	4	4.10	196	0	180	5	2	9
VOLUNTEER STATE HEALTH PLAN INC	TN	**A+**	4	0.98	15	0	14	0	0	1
WELLCARE HEALTH INS OF ARIZONA INC	AZ	**C**	4	18.64	364	0	333	3	0	28

INSURANCE COMPANY NAME	DOM. STATE	RATING	REGION	RATE	RECONS REC'VD	RECONS NOT YET DECIDED	RECONS UPHELD	RECONS OVER-TURNED	RECONS WITH-DRAWN	RECONS DISMISSED
WELLCARE HEALTH PLANS OF NEW JERSEY	NJ	**C+**	4	4.10	22	0	17	1	0	4
WELLCARE OF CONNECTICUT INC	CT	**C**	4	9.14	78	0	62	12	0	4
WELLCARE OF FLORIDA INC	FL	**B**	4	2.68	258	0	222	4	0	30
WELLCARE OF GEORGIA INC	GA	**B**	4	4.62	177	0	134	4	0	37
WELLCARE OF OHIO INC	OH	**U**	4	N/E	--	--	--	--	--	--
WELLCARE OF SOUTH CAROLINA INC	SC	**B-**	4	N/E	--	--	--	--	--	--
WELLCARE OF TEXAS INC	TX	**B**	4	12.72	176	0	137	4	0	34

Section VIII

Rating Upgrades and Downgrades

A list of all

U.S. Health Insurers

receiving a rating upgrade or downgrade
during the current quarter.

Section VIII Contents

This section identifies those companies receiving a rating change since the previous edition of this publication, whether it is a new rating to this guide, withdrawn rating, rating upgrade, rating downgrade or a, newly rated company. A rating may be withdrawn due to a merger, dissolution, or liquidation. A rating upgrade or downgrade may entail a change from one letter grade to another, or it may mean the addition or deletion of a plus or minus sign within the same letter grade previously assigned to the company. Ratings are normally updated once each quarter of the year. In some instances, however, a company's rating may be downgraded outside of the normal updates due to overriding circumstances.

1. **Insurance Company Name** — The legally-registered name, which can sometimes differ from the name that the company uses for advertising. An insurer's name can be very similar to that of another, so verify the company's exact name and state of domicile to make sure you are looking at the correct company.

2. **Domicile State** — The state which has primary regulatory responsibility for the company. It may differ from the location of the company's corporate headquarters. You do not have to be living in the domicile state to purchase insurance from this firm, provided it is licensed to do business in your state.

3. **Total Assets** — All assets admitted by state insurance regulators in millions of dollars as of the most recent year end. This includes investments and current business assets such as receivables from agents, reinsurers and subscribers.

4. **New or Current Safety Rating** — The rating assigned to the company as of the date of this Guide's publication. Our rating is measured on a scale from A to F and considers a wide range of factors. Highly-rated companies are, in our opinion, less likely to experience financial difficulties than lower-rated firms. See *About Weiss Safety Ratings* for more information.

5. **Previous Safety Rating** — The rating assigned to the company prior to its most recent change.

6. **Date of Change** — The date on which the rating upgrade or downgrade officially occurred. Normally, all rating changes are put into effect on a single day each quarter of the year. In some instances, however, a rating may have been changed outside of this normal update.

Appearing in this Edition for the First Time

INSURANCE COMPANY NAME	DOM. STATE	TOTAL ASSETS ($MIL)	RATING	DATE
MCNA INS CO	TX	194.7	C-	08/15/19
MISSOURI VALLEY L&H INS CO	MO	36.4	C-	08/15/19
WV SENIOR ADVANTAGE INC	WV	6.0	C-	08/15/19
LIFEWORKS ADVANTAGE, LLC	VA	4.6	D+	08/15/19
MARQUIS ADVANTAGE, INC.	OR	5.3	D+	08/15/19
PRUITTHEALTH PREMIER INC	GA	10.3	D+	08/15/19
HEALTHPARTNERS UNITYPOINT HLTH	IA	30.2	D-	08/15/19
MAGNA INS CO	MS	5.1	D-	08/15/19
GUARANTY ASSURANCE CO	LA	2.3	E+	08/15/19
PROVIDER PARTNERS HEALTH PLAN OF PA	PA	3.6	E-	08/15/19

Rating Upgrades

AETNA HEALTH INC (A NEW YORK CORP) (NY) was upgraded to B from B- in August 2019 based on development in the stability index.

AHF MCO OF GEORGIA INC (GA) was upgraded to D+ from D in August 2019 based on development in the stability index.

ALLIANZ LIFE INS CO OF NORTH AMERICA was upgraded to B- from C in July 2019 based on a higher capitalization index, a markedly improved investment safety index and an improved five-year profitability index.

AMERICAN LIFE & SECURITY CORP was upgraded to E+ from E in July 2019 based on an improved five-year profitability index.

AMERICASHEALTH PLAN INC (CA) was upgraded to D from D- in August 2019 based on an increase in the capitalization index, progress in the liquidity index, and development in the stability index.

ANTHEM LIFE INS CO was upgraded to B+ from B in July 2019 based on a higher capitalization index and an improved five-year profitability index.

BANNER HLTH & AETNA HLTH PLAN (AZ) was upgraded to B- from C in August 2019 based on development in the stability index.

BAPTIST HEALTH PLAN INC (KY) was upgraded to D from D- in August 2019 based on progress in the liquidity index.

BAY AREA ACCOUNTABLE CARE (CA) was upgraded to D from D- in August 2019 based on a substantial increase in the capitalization index and development in the stability index.

BEACON HEALTH OPTIONS OF PA (PA) was upgraded to E+ from E in August 2019 based on expansion in the profitability index.

BLUEBONNET LIFE INS CO was upgraded to A- from B+ in July 2019 based on composite rating for affiliated Bl Cross & Bl Shield of Mississippi Group rose to A from B+.

BRIDGEWAY HEALTH SOL OF AZ (AZ) was upgraded to C from C- in August 2019 based on expansion in the profitability index.

BRIGHT HEALTH INS CO (CO) was upgraded to E+ from E in August 2019 based on an increase in the capitalization index.

BROWN & TOLAND HEALTH SERVICES (CA) was upgraded to E+ from E in August 2019 based on an increase in the capitalization index and development in the stability index.

CARESOURCE GEORGIA CO (GA) was upgraded to C from C- in August 2019 based on an increase in the capitalization index.

CHESAPEAKE LIFE INS CO was upgraded to A+ from A- in July 2019 based on a higher capitalization index and a markedly improved stability index. transfer to affiliation with Blackstone Investor Group rated B+ from Blackstone Investor Group rated B.

CHRISTIAN FIDELITY LIFE INS CO was upgraded to A- from B+ in July 2019 based on a higher capitalization index.

CICA LIFE INS CO OF AMERICA was upgraded to C from C- in July 2019 based on improved capitalization index, an improved five-year profitability index and a greatly improved stability index. composite rating for affiliated Citizens Inc Group rose to C- from D.

COMMENCEMENT BAY RISK MGMT INS was upgraded to B from B- in July 2019 based on a markedly improved five-year profitability index. enhanced financial strength of affiliates in Regence Group.

COMMUNITY CARE HEALTH PLAN (CA) was upgraded to C+ from C in August 2019 based on an increase in the capitalization index and development in the stability index.

COMMUNITY HEALTH CHOICE TX INC (TX) was upgraded to C from C- in August 2019 based on an increase in the capitalization index.

CONTINENTAL LIFE INS CO was upgraded to C from C- in July 2019 based on a markedly improved stability index. composite rating for affiliated Liberty Life Group Trust rose to C from C-.

CONTRA COSTA HEALTH PLAN (CA) was upgraded to B from B- in August 2019 based on progress in the liquidity index.

FIDELITY SECURITY LIFE INS CO OF NY was upgraded to B+ from B in July 2019 based on a higher stability index. enhanced financial strength of affiliates in Fidelity Security Group.

FIRST MEDICAL HEALTH PLAN INC (PR) was upgraded to D from D- in August 2019 based on an increase in the capitalization index.

FLORIDA COMBINED LIFE INS CO INC was upgraded to B- from C in July 2019 based on a markedly improved stability index. composite rating for affiliated Blue Cross Blue Shield of Florida Group rose to B from B-.

HAWAII MEDICAL SERVICE ASSOCIATION (HI) was upgraded to B from B- in August 2019 based on an increase in the capitalization index.

HEALTH FIRST COMM PLANS INC (FL) was upgraded to C+ from C in August 2019 based on development in the stability index and an increase in the capitalization index.

HEALTH NEW ENGLAND INC (MA) was upgraded to B from B- in August 2019 based on an increase in the capitalization index.

HEALTHNOW NY INC (NY) was upgraded to B from B- in August 2019 based on expansion in the profitability index.

HENNEPIN HEALTH - Unable to generate grade change comment, no positive index changes.

HNE INS CO - Unable to generate grade change comment, no positive index changes.

HUMANA MEDICAL PLAN INC (FL) was upgraded to A- from B+ in August 2019 based on an increase in the capitalization index.

IMPERIAL HEALTH PLAN OF CALIFORNIA (CA) was upgraded to C- from D+ in August 2019 based on a substantial increase in the capitalization index and development in the stability index.

INDEPENDENCE BLUE CROSS - Unable to generate grade change comment, no positive index changes.

JEFFERSON INS CO was upgraded to C- from D+ in August 2019 based on an increase in the stability index from a 2.40(weak) to 2.90(fair).

KERN HEALTH SYSTEMS (CA) was upgraded to B+ from B in August 2019 based on progress in the liquidity index.

MADISON NATIONAL LIFE INS CO INC was upgraded to A- from B in July 2019 based on an improved five-year profitability index.

MAGELLAN COMPLETE CARE OF LOUISIANA (LA) was upgraded to C from D+ in August 2019 based on development in the stability index and an increase in the capitalization index.

MCS ADVANTAGE INC - Unable to generate grade change comment, no positive index changes.

MEMBERS LIFE INS CO was upgraded to B from C+ in July 2019 based on a higher five-year profitability index.

MID-WEST NATIONAL LIFE INS CO OF TN was upgraded to B from B- in July 2019 based on a higher five-year profitability index. transfer to affiliation with Blackstone Investor Group rated B+ from Blackstone Investor Group rated B, notably the recent upgrade of affiliated company CHESAPEAKE LIFE INS CO to A+ from A-.

MISSOURI CARE INC - Unable to generate grade change comment, no positive index changes.

MISSOURI CHAMBER FEDN BENEFIT (MO) was upgraded to C from C- in August 2019 based on an increase in the capitalization index.

MOLINA HEALTHCARE OF PUERTO RICO INC (PR) was upgraded to C+ from C in August 2019 based on an increase in the capitalization index.

MOLINA HEALTHCARE OF SOUTH CAROLINA (SC) was upgraded to B from C+ in August 2019 based on an increase in the capitalization index.

MONARCH HEALTH PLAN (CA) was upgraded to E+ from E in August 2019 based on an increase in the capitalization index.

NATIONAL BENEFIT LIFE INS CO was upgraded to A- from B+ in July 2019 based on a markedly improved stability index.

Rating Upgrades (Continued)

NATIONAL HEALTH INS CO was upgraded to C from C- in July 2019 based on a greatly improved stability index. composite rating for affiliated AmTrust Financial Services Inc Group rose to C+ from D.

NATIONAL INTEGRITY LIFE INS CO was upgraded to B from B- in July 2019 based on an improved capitalization index, an improved five-year profitability index and a markedly improved stability index.

NEXTLEVEL HEALTH PARTNERS INC (IL) was upgraded to C from C- in August 2019 based on development in the stability index and an increase in the capitalization index.

OPTIMUM HEALTHCARE INC (FL) was upgraded to B from B- in August 2019 based on an increase in the capitalization index.

PA HEALTH & WELLNESS INC (PA) was upgraded to C from C- in August 2019 based on an increase in the capitalization index.

PEOPLES HEALTH INC (LA) was upgraded to C from D in August 2019 based on a substantial increase in the capitalization index.

PL MEDICO SERV DE SALUD BELLA VISTA (PR) was upgraded to C+ from C in August 2019 based on an increase in the capitalization index.

PROVIDER PARTNERS HEALTH PLAN INC - Unable to generate grade change comment, no positive index changes.

PURITAN LIFE INS CO OF AMERICA was upgraded to C from D+ in July 2019 based on a higher five-year profitability index.

RIVERLINK HEALTH OF KENTUCKY INC (KY) was upgraded to D+ from D in August 2019 based on development in the stability index.

SANTA BARBARA SAN LUIS OBISPO REGION (CA) was upgraded to B- from C in August 2019 based on substantial progress in the liquidity index.

SCRIPPS HEALTH PLAN SERVICES INC (CA) was upgraded to C- from D+ in August 2019 based on an increase in the capitalization index.

SELECTCARE HEALTH PLANS INC - Unable to generate grade change comment, no positive index changes.

SETON INSURANCE COMPANY - Unable to generate grade change comment, no positive index changes.

SHA LLC (TX) was upgraded to D from E in August 2019 based on an increase in the capitalization index and progress in the liquidity index.

SHARP HEALTH PLAN (CA) was upgraded to B+ from B in August 2019 based on an increase in the capitalization index.

SOUNDPATH HEALTH - Unable to generate grade change comment, no positive index changes.

STANFORD HEALTH CARE ADVANTAGE (CA) was upgraded to E from E- in August 2019 based on a substantial increase in the capitalization index and progress in the liquidity index.

SUN LIFE ASR CO OF CANADA was upgraded to D+ from D in July 2019 based on a markedly improved capitalization index, a higher investment safety index, a higher five-year profitability index and a markedly improved stability index.

TRH HEALTH INS CO (TN) was upgraded to C+ from C in August 2019 based on an increase in the capitalization index and expansion in the profitability index.

TRIPLE-S BLUE II was upgraded to D+ from D in July 2019 based on an improved five-year profitability index. composite rating for affiliated Triple-S Management Corp Group rose to B from B-.

TRUE HEALTH NEW MEXICO INC (NM) was upgraded to C from C- in August 2019 based on development in the stability index.

TRUSTED HEALTH PLAN (MI) INC (MI) was upgraded to C from C- in August 2019 based on an increase in the capitalization index.

Rating Upgrades (Continued)

TRUSTED HEALTH PLAN INC (DC) was upgraded to B from B- in August 2019 based on progress in the liquidity index and an increase in the capitalization index.

UNITED HEALTHCARE INS CO OF NY (NY) was upgraded to B from B- in August 2019 based on progress in the liquidity index.

UNITED HEALTHCARE OF MISSISSIPPI INC - Unable to generate grade change comment, no positive index changes.

UNITEDHEALTHCARE OF NEW MEXICO INC (NM) was upgraded to B- from C+ in August 2019 based on development in the stability index.

UNITEDHEALTHCARE OF WASHINGTON INC (WA) was upgraded to B from C+ in August 2019 based on expansion in the profitability index.

UNIVERSAL FIDELITY LIFE INS CO was upgraded to C from D+ in July 2019 based on a greatly improved stability index.

UNIVERSITY OF UTAH HEALTH INS PLANS (UT) was upgraded to C+ from C in August 2019 based on an increase in the capitalization index.

USIC LIFE INS CO was upgraded to B- from C+ in July 2019 based on an improved capitalization index and a higher five-year profitability index. enhanced financial strength of affiliates in MRM Group Inc.

VISTA HEALTH PLAN INC - Unable to generate grade change comment, no positive index changes.

WELLCARE HEALTH INS OF KENTUCKY INC (KY) was upgraded to B- from C+ in August 2019 based on an increase in the capitalization index.

WELLCARE HEALTH INS OF NEW YORK INC (NY) was upgraded to C from C- in August 2019 based on development in the stability index.

WELLCARE OF FLORIDA INC (FL) was upgraded to B from B- in August 2019 based on an increase in the capitalization index.

WELLCARE OF GEORGIA INC (GA) was upgraded to B from B- in August 2019 based on an increase in the capitalization index.

WELLCARE OF NEBRASKA INC - Unable to generate grade change comment, no positive index changes.

WELLCARE OF TEXAS INC (TX) was upgraded to B from B- in August 2019 based on an increase in the capitalization index.

WESCO INS CO was upgraded to C- from D+ in August 2019 based on an increase in the stability index from a 2.50(weak) to 3.00(fair) and capitalization index from a 4.90(good) to 5.00(good).

WEST VIRGINIA FAMILY HEALTH PLAN INC - Unable to generate grade change comment, no positive index changes.

Rating Downgrades

ACE AMERICAN INS CO was downgraded to C from B- in August 2019 based on a decrease in the stability index from a 3.90(fair) to 2.80(weak). Other factors: The company's net asset base decreased during the period by 5.1%, from $25135.9 million to $23923.6 million.

AMEX ASSURANCE CO was downgraded to B- from B in August 2019 based on a decrease in the stability index from a 5.40(good) to 3.50(fair).

ATLANTIC COAST LIFE INS CO was downgraded to C- from C in July 2019 due to a significant decline in its stability index. In addition, the composite rating for affiliated Advantage Capital Partners LLC Group fell to D from D+.

AVEMCO INS CO was downgraded to C from B- in August 2019 based on a decrease in the stability index from a 4.70(fair) to 2.90(fair) and capitalization index from a 10.00(excellent) to 9.80(excellent).

AXIS INS CO was downgraded to C+ from B in August 2019 based on a decrease in the stability index from a 5.20(good) to 3.20(fair) and profitability index from a 3.70(fair) to 3.50(fair).

BCS INS CO was downgraded to B- from B in August 2019 based on a decrease in the stability index from a 5.40(good) to 3.50(fair).

BENCHMARK INS CO was downgraded to C+ from B- in August 2019 based on a decrease in the stability index from a 5.00(good) to 3.40(fair).

BERKSHIRE HATHAWAY SPECIALTY INS CO was downgraded to C from C+ in August 2019 based on a decrease in the stability index from a 3.20(fair) to 2.20(weak).

CARE N CARE INS CO OF NORTH CAROLINA (NC) was downgraded to E- from D+ in August 2019 based on a substantial drop in the stability index, a substantial decline in the capitalization index, and contraction in the liquidity index.

CENTENNIAL CASUALTY CO was downgraded to C+ from B- in August 2019 based on a decrease in the stability index from a 5.10(good) to 3.00(fair).

CHEROKEE INS CO was downgraded to B- from B in August 2019 based on a decrease in the stability index from a 5.40(good) to 3.50(fair).

CRYSTAL RUN HEALTH PLAN LLC (NY) was downgraded to E- from D- in August 2019 based on a substantial decline in the capitalization index and contraction in the liquidity index.

DB INS CO LTD US GUAM BRANCH was downgraded to C from B- in August 2019 based on a decrease in the stability index from a 4.70(fair) to 2.40(weak) and profitability index from a 6.10(good) to 6.00(good). Other factors: The company's net asset base decreased during the period by 5.9%, from $79.5 million to $75.0 million. Capital and surplus decreased during the period by 13.1%, from $43.9 million to $38.9 million.

EQUITABLE NATIONAL LIFE INS CO was downgraded to C from C+ in July 2019 due to a declining stability index. In addition, the composite rating for affiliated SILAC LLC Group fell to C from C+.

ERIE FAMILY LIFE INS CO was downgraded to B from A- in July 2019 due to a substantially lower five-year profitability index.

FAMILY BENEFIT LIFE INS CO was downgraded to D+ from C in July 2019 due to a substantially lower capitalization index, a significant decline in its investment safety index and a substantially lower five-year profitability index.

FARM BUREAU MUTUAL INS CO OF AR was downgraded to B- from B in August 2019 based on a decrease in the stability index from a 5.40(good) to 3.50(fair).

FIRST CARE INC (MD) was downgraded to D from C in August 2019 based on a drop in the stability index, a diminishment in the profitability index, and contraction in the liquidity index.

FIRST SYMETRA NATL LIFE INS CO OF NY was downgraded to B from B+ in July 2019 due to a declining capitalization index, a declining investment safety index, a significant decline in its five-year profitability index and a declining stability index. In addition, the financial strength of affiliates in Sumitomo Life Ins Company is declining Group.

Rating Downgrades (Continued)

FLORIDA TRUE HEALTH INC (FL) was downgraded to D from C in August 2019 based on a decrease in the capitalization index.

GLOBE LIFE INSURANCE CO OF NY was downgraded to B- from B in July 2019 due to a substantially lower capitalization index, a substantially lower investment safety index and a substantially lower five-year profitability index.

GOOD SAMARITAN INS PLAN OF SD (SD) was downgraded to D from D+ in August 2019 based on a substantial drop in the stability index, a decrease in the capitalization index, and a diminishment in the profitability index.

GREAT AMERICAN INS CO was downgraded to B- from B in August 2019 based on a decrease in the stability index from a 5.30(good) to 3.60(fair).

GREENWICH INS CO was downgraded to C- from C in August 2019 based on a decrease in the stability index from a 3.80(fair) to 2.10(weak).

HEARTLAND NATIONAL LIFE INS CO was downgraded to C+ from B- in July 2019 due to a lower capitalization index and a substantially lower five-year profitability index.

INDIANA UNIVERSITY HEALTH PLANS NFP (IN) was downgraded to D from C- in August 2019 based on a substantial decline in the capitalization index and a drop in the stability index.

INTEGRAND ASR CO was downgraded to D+ from B- in August 2019 based on a decrease in the stability index from a 3.60(fair) to 2.30(weak), capitalization index from a 4.40(fair) to 3.90(fair), and profitability index from a 1.40(weak) to 1.20(weak). Other factors: The company's net asset base decreased during the period by 16.6%, from $109.8 million to $94.2 million. Capital and surplus decreased during the period by 40.4%, from $40.2 million to $28.6 million.

INVESTORS HERITAGE LIFE INS CO was downgraded to C- from C+ in July 2019 due to a substantially lower capitalization index, a substantially lower investment safety index and a substantially lower five-year profitability index.

LIBERTY MUTUAL INS CO was downgraded to C+ from B in August 2019 based on a decrease in the stability index from a 5.30(good) to 3.10(fair).

LOUISIANA FARM BUREAU MUTUAL INS CO was downgraded to C+ from B- in August 2019 based on a decrease in the stability index from a 5.30(good) to 3.40(fair).

LYNDON SOUTHERN INS CO was downgraded to C+ from B- in August 2019 based on a decrease in the profitability index from a 8.50(excellent) to 6.40(good) and stability index from a 5.10(good) to 3.20(fair). Other factors: Capital and surplus decreased during the peri od by 9.9%, from $61.2 million to $55.6 million.

MCLAREN HEALTH PLAN INC (MI) was downgraded to B- from B in August 2019 based on a drop in the stability index.

MOLINA HEALTHCARE OF MS INC (MS) was downgraded to D from C in August 2019 based on a substantial drop in the stability index.

MOTORISTS COMMERCIAL MUTUAL INS CO was downgraded to B- from B in August 2019 based on a decrease in the stability index from a 6.00(good) to 3.90(fair) and capitalization index from a 7.80(excellent) to 7.40(excellent).

NATIONAL INDEMNITY CO was downgraded to C+ from B in August 2019 based on a decrease in the stability index from a 5.30(good) to 3.30(fair).

OBI NATIONAL INS CO was downgraded to C from C+ in August 2019 based on a decrease in the stability index from a 3.20(fair) to 2.60(weak).

OHIO NATIONAL LIFE ASR CORP was downgraded to B from B+ in July 2019 due to a significant decline in its stability index. In addition, the financial strength of affiliates in Ohio Natonal Mutual Inc is declining Group.

OZARK NATIONAL LIFE INS CO was downgraded to D+ from B- in July 2019 due to a substantially lower capitalization index, a substantially lower investment safety index and a substantially lower stability index.

PACIFIC INDEMNITY CO was downgraded to C+ from B in August 2019 based on a decrease in the stability index from a 4.10(fair) to 3.10(fair).

Rating Downgrades (Continued)

PRESBYTERIAN INS CO (NM) was downgraded to C+ from B- in August 2019 based on a drop in the stability index.

S USA LIFE INS CO INC was downgraded to B- from B in July 2019 due to a lower investment safety index and a declining stability index.

SAMARITAN HEALTH PLANS INC (OR) was downgraded to C+ from B- in August 2019 based on a decrease in the capitalization index and a diminishment in the profitability index.

SENTRY INS A MUTUAL CO was downgraded to B from B+ in August 2019 based on a decrease in the stability index from a 6.50(good) to 4.60(fair).

SIGNATURE ADVANTAGE LLC (KY) was downgraded to D from D+ in August 2019 based on a drop in the stability index, a decrease in the capitalization index, and contraction in the liquidity index.

SIRIUS AMERICA INS CO was downgraded to C from B- in August 2019 based on a decrease in the stability index from a 3.90(fair) to 2.50(weak), capitalization index from a 3.60(fair) to 3.00(fair), and profitability index from a 3.70(fair) to 3.50(fair).

SOUTHERN GUARANTY INS CO was downgraded to C+ from B- in August 2019 based on a decrease in the capitalization index from a 9.50(excellent) to 8.80(excellent) and stability index from a 3.60(fair) to 3.10(fair).

STATE FARM FIRE & CAS CO was downgraded to B from B+ in August 2019 based on a decrease in the stability index from a 6.50(good) to 4.60(fair).

STATE FARM MUTUAL AUTOMOBILE INS CO was downgraded to B from B+ in August 2019 based on a decrease in the stability index from a 6.50(good) to 4.60(fair).

TEXAS LIFE INS CO was downgraded to C+ from B- in July 2019 due to a significant decline in its stability index. In addition, the financial strength of affiliates in Wilton Re Holdings Ltd is declining Group.

TIME INS CO was downgraded to C from C+ in July 2019 due to a substantially lower capitalization index and a significant decline in its stability index. In addition, termination of affiliation with Assurant Inc Group rated B-.

ULTIMATE HEALTH PLANS INC (FL) was downgraded to E- from E in August 2019 based on a decrease in the capitalization index, a drop in the stability index, and contraction in the liquidity index.

UNITED HEALTHCARE OF MID-ATLANTIC (MD) was downgraded to B- from B in August 2019 based on a substantial drop in the stability index, a decrease in the capitalization index, and a diminishment in the profitability index.

UNITED SURETY & INDEMNITY CO was downgraded to C from B- in August 2019 based on a decrease in the stability index from a 4.70(fair) to 2.50(weak).

UNIVERSITY HEALTH CARE INC (KY) was downgraded to D from D+ in August 2019 based on a substantial decline in the capitalization index and contraction in the liquidity index.

UPMC HEALTH PLAN INC (PA) was downgraded to C+ from B- in August 2019 based on a diminishment in the profitability index.

US SPECIALTY INS CO was downgraded to C from B in August 2019 based on a decrease in the stability index from a 5.30(good) to 2.80(weak).

VIBRA HEALTH PLAN INC (PA) was downgraded to E+ from C- in August 2019 based on a substantial decline in the capitalization index, a diminishment in the profitability index, and a drop in the stability index.

VIRGINIA FARM BUREAU MUTUAL INS CO was downgraded to C from B- in August 2019 based on a decrease in the stability index from a 4.70(fair) to 2.90(fair).

WESTPORT INS CORP was downgraded to C from B- in August 2019 based on a decrease in the stability index from a 4.00(fair) to 2.60(weak).

Rating Downgrades (Continued)

WILTON REASSURANCE LIFE CO OF NY was downgraded to C from C+ in July 2019 due to a lower capitalization index and a significant decline in its investment safety index. In addition, the financial strength of affiliates in Wilton Re Holdings Ltd is declining Group, per the recent downgrade of affiliated company TEXAS LIFE INS CO to C+ from B-.

ZURICH AMERICAN INS CO was downgraded to C from B in August 2019 based on a decrease in the stability index from a 4.50(fair) to 2.40(weak) and capitalization index from a 7.00(excellent) to 6.80(good).

Appendix

Risk-Adjusted Capital in Weiss Rating Models

There are three distinct rating models used to generate the ratings in this Guide. The first model is for companies that register with state insurance departments under the official classification of Life and Annuity Insurers. The second model is for companies that register under the official classification of Property and Casualty Insurers. The third is for health insurers that register as Health plans with the state insurance departments.

A key aspect of both models is the risk-adjusted capital calculations. Therefore, these are discussed in greater detail.

Risk-Adjusted Capital for Life and Annuity Insurers in Weiss Rating Model

Among the most important indicators used in the analysis of an individual company are our two risk-adjusted capital ratios, which are useful tools in determining exposure to investment, liquidity and insurance risk in relation to the capital the company has to cover those risks.

The first risk-adjusted capital ratio evaluates the company's ability to withstand a moderate loss scenario. The second ratio evaluates the company's ability to withstand a severe loss scenario.

In order to calculate these risk-adjusted capital ratios, we follow these steps:

1. Capital Resources First, we add up all of the company's resources which could be used to cover losses. These include capital, surplus, the Asset Valuation Reserve (AVR), and a portion of the provision for future policyholders' dividends, where appropriate. Additional credit may also be given for the use of conservative reserving assumptions and other "hidden capital" when applicable.

2. Target Capital Next, we determine the company's target capital. This answers the question: Based upon the company's level of risk in both its insurance business and its investment portfolio, how much capital would it need to cover potential losses during a moderate loss scenario? In other words, we determine how much capital we believe this company *should* have.

3. Risk-Adjusted Capital Ratio #1 We compare the results of step 1 with those of step 2. Specifically, we divide the "capital resources" by the "target capital" and express it in terms of a ratio. This ratio is called RACR #1. (See next page for more detail on methodology.)

If a company has a Risk-Adjusted Capital Ratio of 1.0 or more, it means the company has all of the capital we believe it requires to withstand potential losses which could be inflicted by a moderate loss scenario. If the company has less than 1.0, it does not currently have all of the basic capital resources we think it needs. During times of financial distress, companies often have access to additional capital through contributions from a parent company, current profits or reductions in policyholder dividends. Therefore, an allowance is made in our rating system for firms with somewhat less than 1.0 Risk-Adjusted Capital Ratios.

4. Risk-Adjusted We repeat steps 2 and 3, but now assuming a severe loss scenario. This

Capital Ratio #2 ratio is called RACR #2.

5. Capitalization Index We convert RACR #1 and #2 into an index. It is measured on a scale of zero to ten, with ten being the best and seven or better considered strong. A company whose capital, surplus and AVR equal its target capital will have a Risk-Adjusted Capital Ratio of 1.0 and a Risk-Adjusted Capital Index of 7.0.

How We Determine Target Capital

The basic procedure for determining target capital is to ask these questions:

1. What is the breakdown of the company's investment portfolio and types of business?

2. For each category, what are the potential losses which could be incurred in the loss scenario?

3. In order to cover those potential losses, how much in capital resources does the company need? It stands to reason that more capital is needed as a cushion for losses on high-risk investments, such as junk bonds, than would be necessary for low-risk investments, such as AAA-rated utility bonds.

Unfortunately, the same questions we have raised about Wall Street rating systems with respect to how they rate insurance companies can be asked about the way they rate bonds. However, we do not rate bonds ourselves. Therefore, we must rely upon the bond ratings of other rating agencies. This is another reason why we have stricter capital requirements for the insurance companies. It accounts for the fact that they may need some extra protection in case an AAA-rated bond may not be quite as good as it appears to be.

Finally, target capital is adjusted for the company's spread of risk in the diversification of its investment portfolio, the size and number of the policies it writes and the diversification of its business.

Table 1 on the next page shows target capital percentages used in Weiss Risk-Adjusted Capital Ratios #1 and #2 (RACR #1 and RACR #2).

The percentages shown in the table answer the question: How much should the firm hold in capital resources for every $100 it has committed to each category? Several of the items in Table 1 are expressed as ranges. The actual percentages used in the calculation of target capital for an individual company may vary due to the levels of risks in the operations, investments or policy obligations of that specific company.

Table 1. Target Capital Percentages

	Weiss Ratings	
Asset Risk	**RACR#1 (%)**	**RACR#2 (%)**
Bonds		
Government guaranteed bonds	0	0
Class 1	.5-.75	1-1.5
Class 2	2	5
Class 3	5	15
Class 4	10	30
Class 5	20	60
Class 6	20	60
Mortgages		
In good standing	0.5	1
90 days overdue	1.7-20	3.8-25
In process of foreclosure	25-33	33-50
Real Estate		
Class 1	20	50
Class 2	10	33
Preferred Stock		
Class 1	3	5
Class 2	4	6
Class 3	7	9
Class 4	12	15
Class 5	22	29
Class 6	30	39
Class 7	3-30	5-39
Common Stock		
Unaffiliated	25	33
Affiliated	25-100	33-100
Short-term investment	0.5	1
Premium notes	2	5
Collateral loans	2	5
Separate account equity	25	33
Other invested assets	5	10
Insurance Risk		
Individual life reserves*	.06-.15	.08-.21
Group life reserves*	.05-.12	.06-.16
Individual Health Premiums		
Class 1	12-20	15-25
Class 2	9.6	12
Class 3	6.4	8
Class 4	12-28	15-35
Class 5	12-20	15-25
Group Health Premiums		
Class 1	5.6-12	7-15
Class 2	20	25
Class 3	9.6	12
Class 4	6.4	8
Class 5	12-20	15-25
Managed care credit	5-40	6-50
Premiums subject to rate guarantees	100-209	120-250
Individual claim reserves	4	5
Group claim reserves	4	5
Reinsurance	0-2	0-5
Interest Rate Risk		
Policy loans	0-2	0-5
Life reserves	1-2	1-3
Individual annuity reserves	1-3	1-5
Group annuity reserves	1-2	1-3
Guaranteed interest contract reserves	1-2	1-3

All numbers are shown for illustrative purposes. Figures actually used in the formula vary annually based on industry experience.
*Based on net amount at risk.

Investment Class		**Descriptions**
Government guaranteed bonds		Guaranteed bonds issued by U.S. and other governments which receive the top rating of state insurance commissioners.
Bonds	Class 1	Investment grade bonds rated AAA, AA or A by Moody's or Standard & Poor's or deemed AAA - A equivalent by state insurance commissioners.
	Class 2	Investment grade bonds with some speculative elements, rated BBB or equivalent.
	Class 3	Noninvestment grade bonds, rated BB or equivalent.
	Class 4	Noninvestment grade bonds, rated B or equivalent.
	Class 5	Noninvestment grade bonds, rated CCC, CC or C or equivalent.
	Class 6	Noninvestment grade bonds, in or near default.
Mortgages		Mortgages in good standing
		Mortgages 90 days past due
		Mortgages in process of foreclosure
Real Estate	Class 1	Properties acquired in satisfaction of debt.
	Class 2	Company occupied and other investment properties.
Preferred stock	Class 1	Highest quality unaffiliated preferred stock.
	Class 2	High quality unaffiliated preferred stock.
	Class 3	Medium quality unaffiliated preferred stock.
	Class 4	Low quality unaffiliated preferred stock.
	Class 5	Lowest quality unaffiliated preferred stock.
	Class 6	Unaffiliated preferred stock, in or near default.
	Class 7	Affiliated preferred stock.
Common stock		Unaffiliated common stock.
		Affiliated common stock.
Short-term investments		All investments whose maturities at the time of acquisition were one year or less.
Premium Notes		Loans for payment of premiums.
Collateral loans		Loans made to a company or individual where the underlying security is in the form of bonds, stocks, or other marketable securities.
Separate account assets		Investments held in an account segregated from the general assets of the company, generally used to provide variable annuity benefits.
Other invested assets		Any invested assets that do not fit under the main categories above.
Individual life reserves		Funds set aside for payment of life insurance benefits under an individual contract rather than a company or group, underwriting based on individual profile.
Group life reserves		Funds set aside for payment of life insurance benefits under a contract with at least 10 people whereby all members have a common interest and are joined for a reason other than to obtain insurance.
Individual health premiums	Class 1	Usual and customary hospital and medical premiums which include traditional medical reimbursement plans that are subject to annual rate increases based on the company's claims experience.
	Class 2	Medicare supplement, dental, and other limited benefits anticipating rate increases.
	Class 3	Hospital indemnity plans, accidental death and dismemberment policies, and other limited benefits not anticipating rate increases.
	Class 4	Noncancelable disability income.
	Class 5	Guaranteed renewable disability income.

Group health premiums	Class 1	Usual and customary hospital and medical premiums which include traditional medical reimbursement plans that are subject to annual rate increases based on the company's claims experience.
	Class 2	Stop loss and minimum premium where a known claims liability is minimal or nonexistent.
	Class 3	Medicare supplement, dental, and other limited benefits anticipating rate increases.
	Class 4	Hospital indemnity plans, accidental death and dismemberment policies, and other limited benefits not anticipating rate increases.
	Class 5	Disability Income.
Managed care credit		Premiums for HMO and PPO business which carry less risk than traditional indemnity business. Included in this credit are provider compensation arrangements such as salary, capitation and fixed payment per service.
Premiums subject to rate guarantees		Health insurance premiums from policies where the rate paid by the policyholder is guaranteed for a period of time, such as one year, 15 months, 27 months or 37 months.
Individual claim reserves		Accident and health reserves for claims on individual policies.
Group claim reserves		Accident and health reserves for claims on group policies.
Reinsurance		Amounts recoverable on paid and unpaid losses for all reinsurance ceded; unearned premiums on accident and health reinsurance ceded; and funds held with unauthorized reinsurers.
Policy loans		Loans against the cash value of a life insurance policy.
Life reserves		Reserves for life insurance claims net of reinsurance and policy loans.
Individual annuity reserves		Reserves held in order to pay off maturing individual annuities or those surrendered before maturity.
Group annuity reserves		Reserves held in order to pay off maturing group annuities or those surrendered before maturity.
GIC reserves		Reserves held to pay off maturing guaranteed interest contracts.

Table 2. Bond Default Rates - potential losses as a percent of bond portfolio

Bond Rating	(1) Moody's 15 Yr Rate (%)	(2) Moody's 12 Yr Rate (%)	(3) Worst Year (%)	(4) 3 Cum. Recession Years (%)	(5) Weiss 15 Year Rate (%)	(6) Assumed Loss Rate (%)	(7) Losses as % of Holdings (%)	(8) RACR #2 Rate (%)
Aaa	0.73	0.55	0.08	0.24	0.79	50	0.95	1.00
Aa	1.39	1.04	0.13	0.39	1.43	50	1.09	1.00
A	4.05	2.96	0.35	1.05	4.02	55	2.02	1.00
Baa	7.27	5.29	0.67	2.02	7.31	60	5.15	5.00
Ba	23.93	19.57	2.04	6.11	25.68	65	23.71	15.00
B	43.37	39.30	4.99	14.96	54.26	70	43.57	30.00

Comments On Target Capital Percentages

The factors that are chiefly responsible for the conservative results of our Risk-Adjusted Capital Ratios are the investment risks of bond Classes 2 - 6, mortgages, real estate and affiliate common stock as well as the interest rate risk for annuities and GICs. Comments on the basis of these figures are found below. Additional comments address factors that vary based on particular performance or risk characteristics of the individual company.

Bonds Target capital percentages for bonds are derived from a model that factors in historical cumulative bond default rates from the last 45 years and the additional loss potential during a prolonged economic decline. **Table 2** shows how this was done for each bond rating classification. A 15-year cumulative default rate is used (column 1), due to the 15-year average maturity at issue of bonds held by life insurance companies. These are historical default rates for 1970-2015 for each bond class, taken from *Annual Default Study.*

To factor in the additional loss potential of a severe three-year-long economic decline, we reduced the base to Moody's 12-year rate (column 2), determined the worst single year experience (column 3), extended that experience over three years (column 4), and added the historical 12-year rate to the 3-year projection to derive Weiss Ratings 15-year default rate (column 5). The next step was to determine the losses that could be expected from these defaults. This would be equivalent to the capital a company should have to cover those losses. Loss rates were assigned for each bond class (column 6), based on the fact that higher-rated issues generally carry less debt and the fact that the debt is also better secured, leading to higher recovery rates upon default. Column 7 shows losses as a percent of holdings for each bond class. Column 8 shows the target capital percentages that are used in RACR #2 (Table 1, RACR #2 column, Bonds – classes 1 to 6).

Regulations limiting junk bond holdings of insurers to a set percent of assets are a tacit acknowledgement that the reserve requirements used by State Insurance Commissioners are inadequate. If the figure adequately represented full loss potential, there would be no need to limit holdings through legislation since an adequate loss reserve would provide sufficient capital to absorb potential losses.

Mortgages Mortgage default rates for the Risk-Adjusted Capital Ratios are derived from historical studies of mortgage and real estate losses in selected depressed markets. The rate for RACR #2 (Table 1, RACR #2 column, Mortgages – 90 days overdue) will vary between 3.8% and 25%, based on the performance of the company's mortgage portfolio in terms of mortgage loans 90 days or more past due, in process of foreclosure and foreclosed during the previous year.

Real Estate The 33% rate (Table 1, RACR #2 column, Real Estate - Class 2) used for potential real estate losses in Weiss Ratings ratios is based on historical losses in depressed markets.

Affiliate Common Stock The target capital rate on affiliate common stock for RACR #2 can vary between 33% and 100% (Table 1, RACR #2 column, Common stock – Affiliate), depending on the financial strength of the affiliate and the prospects for obtaining capital from the affiliate should the need arise.

Insurance Risk Calculations of target capital for insurance risk vary according to categories. For individual and group life insurance, target capital is a percentage of net amount at risk (total amount of insurance in force less reserves). Individual and group health insurance risk is calculated as a percentage of premium. Categories vary from "usual and customary hospital and medical premiums" where risk is relatively low because losses from one year are recouped by annual rate increases, to "noncancellable disability income" where the risk of loss is greater because disability benefits are paid in future years without the possibility of recovery.

Reinsurance This factor varies with the quality of the reinsuring companies and the type of reinsurance being used (e.g., co-insurance, modified co-insurance, yearly renewable term, etc.).

Interest Rate Risk On Annuities The 1 - 5% rate on individual annuities as a percentage of reserves (Table 1, RACR #2 column 3, Individual annuity reserves), and the 1 - 3% rate for group annuities as a percentage of reserves (Table 1, RACR #2 column 3, Group annuity reserves and GICs), are derived from studies of potential losses that can occur when assets and liabilities are not properly matched.

Companies are especially prone to losses in this area for one of two reasons: (1) They promise high interest rates on their annuities and have not locked in corresponding yields on their investments. If interest rates fall, the company will have difficulties earning the promised rate. (2) They lock in high returns on their investments but allow policy surrenders without market value adjustments. If market values decline and surrenders increase, liquidity problems can result in substantial losses.

The target capital figure used for each company is based on the surrender characteristics of its policies, the interest rate used in calculating reserves and the actuarial analyses found in New York Regulation 126 filing, or similar studies where applicable.

Risk-Adjusted Capital for Property and Casualty Insurers

Over 100 companies that are registered with state insurance departments as property and casualty insurers offer health insurance policies. Our ratings on these companies make use of the data in the Property and Casualty Statutory Statements that are required by state insurance departments. These financial statements employ a system of accounting that differs from that used by companies filing Life and Health Statutory Statements. Some of the chief distinguishing features of the Property and Casualty Statutory Accounting include:

- Life and health companies must hold reserves to protect specifically against investment losses. Property and casualty insurers keep no equivalent protection. One of the consequences of the lack of an investment loss reserve is that property and casualty companies, on the average, hold more nonaffiliated common stock than do life insurers. This factor is considered in our evaluation of capital adequacy.

- Policy reserves for life insurers are reduced to reflect investment income to be earned between the time premiums are received by the company, and the time when claims are to be paid. Property and casualty companies generally do not reduce or discount their reserves for the time value of money.

- Underwriting profits and losses for property and casualty insurers are calculated without reference to investment income.

Despite these factors, it is our goal to provide ratings that consumers can easily understand and to make technical differences as transparent to consumers as possible. The final ratings are intended to give the same message about our opinion of insurers financial strength.

As with the life and health companies, there are two risk-adjusted capital ratios, which measure whether the company has enough capital to cover unexpected losses.

However, unlike the life and health companies, the risks related to pricing and claims are more important, while the risks associated with investments are reduced because there is little exposure to risky investments such as junk bonds or mortgages.

Pricing Risk The risk that premium levels are not sufficient to establish adequate reserves and/or pay claims and related expenses. Individual target capital percentages are used for each line of business based on the riskiness of the line and the company's own experience with underwriting losses and reserve shortfalls. Target capital requirements are reduced to account for the time value of money.

Risky Lines of Business and Catastrophic Losses

These include fire, earthquake, multiple peril (including storm damage), and similar personal and commercial property coverage. Even excluding Hurricane Andrew, the insured losses from natural disasters since 1989 have been far greater than in previous decades. Yet, too many insurance companies are basing their risk calculations on the assumption that losses will return to more normal levels. They are not ready for the possibility that the pattern of increasing disasters might be a real, continuing trend.

Also considered high-risk lines are medical malpractice, general liability, product liability, and other similar liability coverage. Court awards for damages often run into the millions. These settlement amounts can be very difficult to predict. This uncertainty hinders an insurer's ability to accurately assess how much to charge policyholders and how much to set aside to pay claims. Of special concern are large, unexpected liabilities related to environmental damages such as asbestos. Similar risk may lie hidden in coverage for medical equipment and procedures, industrial wastes, carcinogens, and other substances found in products previously viewed as benign. Companies that offer a variety of types of insurance in addition to health coverage can get into financial difficulties due to any of their lines of business. Accordingly, it is essential that the company's whole operation be strong. If the company is overrun with claims from an earthquake of hurricane, its ability to pay health claims will also be affected.

Risk-Adjusted Capital for Health Insurers

As with the other rating systems, the health insurance system includes two risk-adjusted capital ratios to measure a company's ability to withstand unexpected losses during moderate and severe loss scenarios. Health insurers are more likely exposed to risk from pricing and claims than from investments. They have no interest rate risk, in terms of potential policy surrenders, the way life insurance companies do.

Capital resources include the company's net worth adjusted for surplus notes; credit or penalty for overstating or understating reserves; and credit or penalty for the company's ability to spread risk based on overall net worth of the company's affiliate group.

These health plans file yet another type of statutory statement, different from life and health or property and casualty insurers. Weiss Rating System for health insurers addresses the unique business and accounting factors relevant to these firms. Among the many differences are the following:

- Rather than setting up reserves as a liability the way life insurance companies do, health insurer claims reserves are part of net worth.
- Investments are carried at book value, but market value is shown on Schedule B of the statutory statement. Market values are considered in the capitalization and liquidity indexes.
- Health insurers do not hold reserves to protect specifically against investment losses. This factor is considered in our evaluation of capital adequacy.
- Health insurers do not have long-term obligations like life insurance and annuities. Accordingly, reserves are not discounted for the time value of money. Our analysis examines reserve adequacy by comparing one year's reserve estimates with claims and medical expenses actually paid during the subsequent year, without factoring in investment income.

LONG-TERM CARE INSURANCE PLANNER

This planner is designed to help you decide what kind of long-term care insurance is best for you and help you shop for the policy that meets your needs. Many insurers charge a lot more – or less – for very similar policies. So there's a great benefit to shopping around. No policy is exactly alike. However, if you follow these steps, it will be easier to compare policies side by side:

Step 1: Try to determine, ahead of time, what type of care you think you will need from others beyond the assistance your own family members may be able to provide:

	Yes	No
Custodial Care	[ ]	[ ]
Intermediate Care	[ ]	[ ]
Skilled Care	[ ]	[ ]

This isn't easy, because it's often hard to anticipate your future needs, but try your best to decide if you're going to want access to one of the following. Custodial care is provided by someone without medical training who helps you with daily activities. Intermediate care includes occasional nursing and rehabilitative care supervised by skilled medical personnel. Skilled care includes 24-hour care provided by a skilled nurse or therapist.

Step 2: Decide where you would most likely be receiving the care?

	Yes	No
In-Home Care*	[ ]	[ ]
Nursing Home*	[ ]	[ ]
Adult Day Care	[ ]	[ ]
Assisted Living Facility	[ ]	[ ]
Other ______________	[ ]	[ ]

*Typically available with all three levels of care – custodial, intermediate, and skilled.

Most people prefer in-home care. However, if you have no family members to help you at home, in-home care could be prohibitively expensive, especially if it requires skilled care. Nursing homes are designed for 24-hour care and are best utilized for short-term stays. Adult day care is an option, but will probably require someone, such as a family member, who can drop you off and pick you up daily. Assisted living facilities are increasingly popular, offering a good balance between independence and assistance. Other types of care could include hospice care (for the terminally ill) or respite care (temporary assistance to help relieve family members).

Step 3: Check out the facilities in the area in which you plan to live, make sure you're comfortable with them, and find out much how they cost:

	Estimated Costs
In-Home Care	____________________
Nursing Home	____________________
Assisted Living Facility	____________________
Adult Day Care	____________________
Other	____________________

The insurance company is going to pay you a daily benefit that will be applied toward the cost of your care. Most of the costs above that daily benefit will have to come out of your own pocket. Therefore, find a facility that you'd be comfortable with, and then try to get a general idea of how much it would cost. Each facility may offer a different rate schedule for each level of care it provides, so make sure you understand the differences. For care within your home, contact a home care agency and ask them about the going rates for home nurses and therapists. Also consider costs associated with any modifications that may be needed for your home, such as wheelchair accessibility, handicap rails, etc.

Step 4: Try to estimate how much of the long-term care expenses you will be able to pay on your own: $________ per month.

Your financial planner may be able to give you an estimate of your retirement income available for health care. However, even a good estimate can be off the mark, so make sure your policy covers enough to avoid being financially strapped by long-term care expenses. Later, make sure your agent takes this information into consideration when he works out the terms of your policy. He should limit your out-of-pocket expenses to what you have indicated here.

Step 5: Try to arrive at a reasonable guess regarding when you might start using the benefits.

____

Again, it's hard to predict. But if you're in reasonably good health and you have a family history of longevity, that's something to consider. If you're already suffering from chronic health problems, you may need the benefits sooner rather than later. If it's more than 10 years from now, you can buy a long-term care policy with an optional inflation protection feature to help protect against the rising cost of health care. This can add significantly to the cost, but you get what you pay for. Typically, the insurance company will add an extra five percent to your daily benefit, compounded annually. Thus, if the policy provides a $100 daily benefit now, it would rise to $163 in 10 years.

Step 6: Determine whether you prefer a "tax-qualified" policy or a "non-qualified" policy:

	Yes	No
Tax-Qualified Policy	[ ]	[ ]
Non-Qualified Policy	[ ]	[ ]

If you buy a tax-qualified policy, you will be able to claim the policy premiums as itemized medical expenses on your tax return. Furthermore, the benefits you receive will not be subject to federal income taxation, up to a dollar cap. If you purchase a non-qualified policy, you will not be able to itemize the premiums. As to the benefits, the IRS has yet to clarify whether or not they will be subject to federal income taxation. Do not assume that a tax-qualified policy will automatically be more beneficial. Reason: Typically, a tax-qualified policy will have stricter guidelines as to when you can access the policy benefits. You also may not be able to take advantage of the tax benefits. You may want to consult with a tax advisor on this subject.

Step 7: Find insurance agents in your area that specialize in long-term care policies:

Agent Name	Phone Number	Specialization in LTC?	Name of insurance company
________	________	(Y / N)	________
________	________	(Y / N)	________
________	________	(Y / N)	________
________	________	(Y / N)	________

Long-term care insurance is very complex. Therefore, make sure you work with an agent who specializes in long-term care policies, and don't limit your choices to someone you know or who is associated with your broker. The agent should be able to help educate you and clarify any questions you have – not only on policies he or she sells, but on others as well. Try to avoid agents that work strictly with one insurance company. Complete the remaining steps with the direct assistance of the agent you choose.

Step 8: Ask your agent for the names of at least three different policies, from different insurers, that you can compare.

	Policy A	Policy B	Policy C
Insurance Company Name	___________	_______________	_______________
Policy Name/Number	___________	_______________	_______________

Step 9: Have your agent check the safety rating for each company.

	Safety Rating
Policy A:	_________________
Policy B:	_________________
Policy C:	_________________

It may be a long time before you begin to submit claims. Therefore, you will want to make sure your insurance company will still be viable at that time. If you use the Safety Ratings, we recommend you favor companies with a rating of B+ (good) or higher, and we suggest you avoid companies with a rating of D+ (weak) or lower.

Step 10: Favor companies that have more experience with long-term care insurance.

	Years of experience with long-term care	Have they ever raised rates for existing policyholders?
Policy A:	______________________________	(Y / N)
Policy B:	______________________________	(Y / N)
Policy C:	______________________________	(Y / N)

This should not be a deal breaker. But you're better off with a company that has been offering long-term care policies for a while and has never raised rates for existing policyholders. In contrast, companies that are new in long-term care – or have a history of raising rates on existing policies – are more likely to raise your rates in the future.

Step 11: If you're considering buying a policy with your spouse, check how you qualify for a spousal discount.

Policy A: ____
Policy B: ____
Policy C: ____

In some cases, you may need to be married to qualify; in others you don't have to be formally married. Some insurers require that the policies be exactly the same, while others do not.

Step 12: Ask your agent for quotes on the monthly premiums. Make sure the quotes are based on the preferences and needs that you outlined in steps 1-6.

	Single Policy Premium	Combined Policy Premium	% Savings
Policy A:	________________	________________	______
Policy B:	________________	________________	______
Policy C:	________________	________________	______

If you can buy your long-term care policy with a spouse or significant other, make sure you take advantage of spousal discounts, which can save you up to 20% on the combined premium.

Step 13: Find out exactly what each policy covers in addition to the basics that you require:

	Policy A	Policy B	Policy C
Custodial	(Y / N)	(Y / N)	(Y / N)
Intermediate	(Y / N)	(Y / N)	(Y / N)
Skilled	(Y / N)	(Y / N)	(Y / N)

The actual policies that your agent has suggested may differ somewhat from your wish list of benefits, including some that you did not ask for, or excluding others that you wanted. This may help explain some, but not all, of the price differences.

Step 14: Ask your agent to give you a list of the types of facilities that are included and how they are defined. Facilities may include nursing home care, in-home care, adult day care, hospice care, assisted living facilities, and other options.

Policy A

____

____

____

Policy B

____

____

____

Policy C

____

____

____

Step 15: Find out the basic terms of coverage and reimbursement, as follows:

Policy A: How the company calculates elimination period: ______________________

Facility of Care	Elimination Periods	Benefit Periods	Daily Benefit
In-home care:	____________	__________	__________
Nursing home	____________	__________	__________
Assisted living:	____________	__________	__________
Adult day care:	____________	__________	__________

Policy B: How the company calculates elimination period: ____________________________

Facility of Care	Elimination Periods	Benefit Periods	Daily Benefit
In-home care:	______________	__________	__________
Nursing home	______________	__________	__________
Assisted living:	______________	__________	__________
Adult day care:	______________	__________	__________

Policy C: How the company calculates elimination period: ____________________________

Facility of Care	Elimination Periods	Benefit Periods	Daily Benefit
In-home care:	______________	__________	__________
Nursing home	______________	__________	__________
Assisted living:	______________	__________	__________
Adult day care:	______________	__________	__________

Elimination Period: This is similar to a deductible. It is the amount of time you pay for services out of your own pocket before the insurance policy takes over. Typically, you can select elimination periods of 0, 30, 60, 90, or 180 days, depending on the policy and insurance company. But you must find out exactly how the elimination period is satisfied. Let's say, for example, you need care on days 1, 4 and 10. With some policies, that would be counted as only THREE days toward your elimination period. With other policies, it would be counted as TEN days, which would mean you'd start collecting the benefits much sooner.

Benefit Period (or maximum): Some companies tell you the length of time the policy will be paid; others just tell you the maximum value of benefits to be paid. The benefit period can typically range from 2 to 5 years, and some may even have an unlimited lifetime period.

Daily Benefit: The amount the policy will pay for each day of covered services. Some plans offer a daily benefit reimbursable on a weekly or monthly basis giving you more flexibility. For example, if you selected a daily benefit of $100 reimbursable on a weekly basis you would be reimbursed for up to $700 dollars per week in expenses no matter how much you incurred on any one day.

Step 16: Determine if the policy is "a pool of money" contract.

	Pool of money?
Policy A:	(Y / N)
Policy B:	(Y / N)
Policy C:	(Y / N)

Most current policies will actually give you more time to collect the benefits than indicated by the benefit period. For example, in a four-year policy, if you need care on and off, you may not use up all your benefits in that four-year period. So you could continue to collect those unused benefits in subsequent years as well. These are called "pool of money" contracts. (To calculate your pool, just multiple the total numbers of days by the daily benefit.) Other policies will actually end at the end of the four years, no matter what.

Step 17: Check into the requirements needed to activate the policy.

Policy A: ____
____

Policy B: ____
____

Policy C: ____
____

You will need to meet what is referred to as "benefit triggers" before the policy can begin covering expenses and these can vary from policy to policy. Under most policies, you will be qualified for benefits when you meet certain conditions, such as: 1) The inability to perform activities of daily living ("ADLs"), which typically include bathing, dressing, transferring, toileting, eating, continence, and taking medication on your own; and 2) cognitive impairment. Some plans require you to satisfy <u>either</u> condition (1) or (2); some require that you satisfy <u>both</u> conditions. Still others also allow for a third trigger, often referred to as "medical necessity." This means that a doctor determines if you need care due to an injury or sickness. Make sure you find out the precise requirements of each policy.

Step 18: Find out what other features are included (or can be added by a "rider") to the policy. Your agent should explain any additional features that may be included in the policies you are comparing including the following:

	Policy A	Policy B	Policy C
Waiver of Premium	(Y / N)	(Y / N)	(Y / N)
Nonforfeiture	(Y / N)	(Y / N)	(Y / N)
Restoration of Benefits	(Y / N)	(Y / N)	(Y / N)
Alternate Care Plan	(Y / N)	(Y / N)	(Y / N)
Bed Reservation	(Y / N)	(Y / N)	(Y / N)
Guaranteed Renewable	(Y / N)	(Y / N)	(Y / N)
Inflation Protection	(Y / N)	(Y / N)	(Y / N)

Your agent will explain the details. Just make sure that you actually need these additional benefits, because they can add substantially to your total costs.

Medicare Prescription Drug Planner

This planner is designed to help you compare the annual premium costs of a senior benefit package that includes prescription drug coverage. In conjunction with the worksheet attached, follow the steps for calculating the costs of prescription drug coverage options. Upon completion, you'll be able to compare the annual cost of each option. In addition to the cost, keep other out-of-pocket expenses, benefit coverage, and provider accessibility in mind, and then select the plan best suited to meet your needs.

STEP ONE: Review the cost of your current health care coverage.

Look up your current coverage and find the premium you pay, if any, for the coverage.

Original Medicare – Part A and Part B coverage

Do you receive benefits directly through the Original Medicare program? .... Y / N

If yes, you may be paying the Part B premium (there is no premium for Part A) yourself or perhaps you have an employer plan or a Medicare Supplement insurance policy that pays the premium.

▶ Record the annual amount, if any, you pay: **Part A and B: $** ________________

Transfer this figure to the available lines under the Part A and B column on the worksheet.

Employer Retirement Plan Coverage

Do you receive benefits through an Employer plan? .... Y / N

If yes, the coverage is most likely comprehensive and includes drug coverage.

▶ Record the annual amount, if any, you pay: **Employer Plan: $** ______________

Transfer this figure to the available lines under the Employer Plan column on the worksheet.

Medicare Supplement Insurance Policy ("Medigap")

Do you own a Medigap Plan? .... Y / N

▶ If so, what do you pay in annual premiums? **Medigap Plan A thru N: $** __________

Transfer this figure to the available line under the Medigap Plan column on the worksheet.

Medicare Advantage Plan

Medicare Advantage policies are available through private insurers. You pay the insurer a premium and they provide coverage that is at least as good, if not better, than Medicare Part A and B. In turn, they receive reimbursement from the government. You are often restricted to a network of physicians with these plans.

Do you receive your benefits from a Medicare Advantage insurer? .... Y / N

▶ If so, what do you pay in annual premiums, if any? **Medicare Advantage Plan:** $ ________

Transfer this figure to the Annual Cost column in the Medicare Advantage row on the worksheet.

STEP TWO: Find the cost of your preferred Part D Prescription Drug Provider/Plan.

Part D is the new Prescription Drug component of the Medicare program. Under Part D you can obtain some coverage for your medications through a private provider. These plans will provide, at a minimum, the coverage mandated by the government. Otherwise each plan will vary depending on drugs covered, premiums, co-pays and participating pharmacies.

In this step we guide you through what you need to do in order to select a Part D provider. The average cost for Part D plans range from $36.53 to $52.28 per month. However, the range within each state can be significant. Your goal is to find the lowest cost plan that gives you the best price on the prescriptions you use and has convenient participating pharmacies.

Everything you need to do can be done on the Medicare website, however, you will need a computer and internet access. The site is loaded with information, so we recommend that you first spend a few hours browsing the site to learn more. The site and process of selecting a provider can be overwhelming so you may want to have a family member or someone else to work with you through this process.

First: Gather critical information. Make sure to have the following:

- ✓ Medicare Number...______________
- ✓ Effective Date of Medicare Part A or B coverage..................................______________
- ✓ Birth Date ....______________
- ✓ Zip Code ....______________
- ✓ List of prescription drugs you use and their dosages.

Drug	**Dosage**
______________________________	____________
______________________________	____________
______________________________	____________
______________________________	____________
______________________________	____________
______________________________	____________

- ✓ Preferred pharmacies in your area.

Pharmacy Name

____

____

____

Second: **Visit www.Medicare.gov.**

We can't list all of the website's steps here but to start out Click [*Compare Medicare Prescription Drug Plans*] and then Click [*Find a Medicare Prescription Drug Plan*]. You will then be asked to enter your personal information. The website will walk you through entering your prescription drugs and dosages so that you can get a list of Part D providers in your state that cover your drugs, the pharmacies and the contact information. You may select three plans to compare side by side at one time.

Third: **Narrow down your choices.**

Don't overburden yourself trying to compare all 40+ plans available in your state. Narrow your list down to the five or seven plans that cover your prescriptions and contract with local pharmacies. The premium cost of a plan for the minimum coverage will run you between $14.40 to $1,870.80 per year in 2019, depending on where you live.

To narrow down your list further look for plans that reduce your out-of-pocket costs by covering the $415 deductible, the 25% co-payments and/or the $5,100 gap in coverage. After that, the government limits your co-payment to $3.40 for generic drugs and $8.50 all other drugs.

Use the lines below to enter the information to help you compare your choices. Enter the annual Premium charged by the plan and then under Deductible, Co-Pay and Gap enter the dollar amount you would be responsible for under each of the plan choices. Add these across to get an estimate of your total estimated costs under each plan.

Provider/Plan Name:	Premium		Annual Deductible (max $415)		Co-Pay Max (max $851)		Cost $1,280 Gap		Total Estimate
____________	________	+	________	+	________	+	________	=	________
____________	________	+	________	+	________	+	________	=	________
____________	________	+	________	+	________	+	________	=	________
____________	________	+	________	+	________	+	________	=	________
____________	________	+	________	+	________	+	________	=	________

If you still need to narrow down your choices, then look for plans that either reduces your co-payment amount to less than $3.40 for generic drugs and $8.50 all other drugs and/or provide other benefits that you find attractive.

Final Part D Provider Selection

Provider / Plan Name	**Total Cost Estimate**
________________________	$ ____________

Transfer the total cost estimate of your final selection (above) to the available lines under the Part D column on the worksheet.

STEP THREE: Consider a Medicare Advantage Plan.

If you already have a Medicare Advantage plan that you are happy with, you may want to skip this step.

The Medicare Advantage program allows you to join a private plan that participates in the Medicare program. Medicare Advantage providers receive funds from the government for providing you benefits and often provides coverage beyond what Medicare offers.

Most of these plans provide prescription drug coverage at the same level or better than the requirements set by Medicare, either inclusive in their plan or in combination with a Medicare Part D provider. Either way you will only pay one premium to the Medicare Advantage insurer for all the coverage.

If you already belong to a Medicare Advantage plan they will send you information regarding their coverage for prescription drugs. Otherwise you can find information on the medicare.gov website or from the insurers through the mail, local kiosks or by calling their toll-free numbers. To narrow down your choices based on the prescription drug coverage use the following space to compare the different plans. Don't forget to check Weiss Safety Rating to find out if the insurer is in good financial health.

Provider/Plan Name:	**Premium**	**Annual Deductible (max $415)**	**Co-Pay Max (max $851)**	**Cost $1,280 Gap**	**Total Estimate**
________	________ +	________ +	________ +	________ =	________
________	________ +	________ +	________ +	________ =	________
________	________ +	________ +	________ +	________ =	________
________	________ +	________ +	________ +	________ =	________
________	________ +	________ +	________ +	________ =	________

Final Medicare Advantage Provider Selection

Provider Plan Name	**Total Cost Estimate**
____________________	$ ____________

Once you have narrowed down your choices you will then want to consider other benefits that the Medicare Advantage plan offers.

When you have made a selection, transfer this figure to the Annual Cost column in the Medicare Advantage row on the worksheet.

STEP FOUR: Find the cost of your preferred Medicare Supplement Insurance ("Medigap") policy.

If you have a Medigap policy you want to keep, then you may want to skip this step.

Medigap policies are available through private insurers. Prior to 2006 there were 10 standardized plans (referred to as A through J) that an insurer could offer. Starting in 2020 Plans C and F are to be discontinued and a high deductible version of Plan G will be introduced. Medigap policies help to pay the expenses not paid under Medicare Part A and B. You cannot get any prescription drug coverage from these plans as a new policyholder after 2005.

The price of Medigap policies can differ dramatically even within the same city. You can learn more about the various Medigap plans available and the premium rates you would be charged based on your age, gender, and zip code by going to our website at http://www.weissmedigap.com. Once you have educated yourself and are leaning towards the purchase of a supplemental policy, you will need to meet with an insurance agent to further refine your selection and purchase a policy.

Make sure to check the financial stability of any insurer by using Weiss Safety Rating.

Once you have selected a Medicare Supplement policy enter the annual cost under the Medigap Plan column on the worksheet. If you need an estimate to enter into the worksheet until an amount can be determined, use $2000 as a placeholder for the annual price.

STEP FIVE: Complete the worksheet.

If you haven't done so already, use the figures from Steps 1 through 4 to fill in the dollar amounts in the relevant parts of the worksheet to determine your total annual cost for every option you want to consider. Re-use the worksheet if you need to make adjustments.

STEP SIX: Narrow down your choices.

The worksheet helps you to narrow down your choices by providing a snapshot, based on cost, of the prescription drug benefit options available to you. Of course, premiums are only one of the components needed to make a final decision. You must also consider other out-of-pocket costs, completeness of coverage, accessibility, and insurer financial strength.

STEP SEVEN: More Information.

Educate yourself. The www.Medicare.gov website, Medicare & You 2019 Handbook, local workshops, and Medicare benefit agents on hand at 1-800-MEDICARE are available to assist in answering your questions. Take advantage of these resources to make sure you fully understand your options.

RECENT INDUSTRY FAILURES
2019

Company Name	Headquarters	Industry	Date of Failure	At Date of Failure	
				Total Assets ($Mil)	Safety Rating
Capson Physicians Ins Co	Texas	P&C	02/11/19	25.3	D (Weak)
Atlantis Health Plan	Florida	Health	02/27/19	3.0	U (Unrated)
Scottish Re US Inc	North Carolina	L&A	03/06/19	1,560.0	E+ (Very Weak)
Southland National Ins. Corp	North Carolina	L&A	06/27/19	354.0	D+ (Weak)
Bankers Life Ins. Co	North Carolina	L&A	06/27/19	397.4	C- (Fair)
Colorado Bankers Life Ins. Co	North Carolina	L&A	06/27/19	2,068.0	C (Fair)

2018

Company Name	Headquarters	Industry	Date of Failure	At Date of Failure	
				Total Assets ($Mil)	Safety Rating
Healthcare Providers Ins. Exch	Pennsylvania	P&C	01/12/18	32.6	E- (Very Weak)
Access Ins. Co	Texas	P&C	03/13/18	314.1	C (Fair)
Touchstone Health HMO Inc.	New York	Health	04/19/18	12.5	E+ (Very Weak)
Reliamax Surety Co	South Dakota	P&C	06/27/18	63.0	C (Fair)
Paramount Ins. Co	Maryland	P&C	09/13/18	13.2	D- (Weak)
Real Legacy Asr Co Inc	Puerto Rico	P&C	09/28/18	230.4	D+ (Weak)
Geneva Ins. Co	Indiana	P&C	10/02/18	3.7	U (Unrated)
Merced Property & Casualty Co	California	P&C	12/03/18	23.6	C (Fair)
North Carolina Mutual Life Ins. Co	North Carolina	L&A	12/03/18	26.7	E- (Very Weak)

2017

Company Name	Headquarters	Industry	Date of Failure	At Date of Failure	
				Total Assets ($Mil)	Safety Rating
IFA Insurance Co	New Jersey	P&C	03/07/17	8.4	E (Very Weak)
Public Service Ins Co	New York	P&C	03/16/17	278.5	E (Very Weak)
Zoom Health Plan Inc	Oregon	Health	04/26/17	6.	U (Unrated)
Galen Insurance Co	Missouri	P&C	05/31/17	103.0	E- (Very Weak)
Fiduciary Ins. Co of America	New York	P&C	07/25/17	90.7	E- (Very Weak)
Evergreen Health Inc.	Maryland	Health	07/27/17	37.2	E- (Very Weak)
Minuteman Health Inc	Massachusetts	Health	08/02/17	111.7	E- (Very Weak)
Sawgrass Mutual Ins. Co	Florida	P&C	08/22/17	32.3	D+ (Weak)
Guarantee Ins. Co	Florida	P&C	08/28/17	400.4	E+ (Very Weak)
Oceanus Ins. Co A RRG	South Carolina	P&C	09/04/17	52.9	D- (Weak)

2016

Company Name	Headquarters	Industry	Date of Failure	At Date of Failure	
				Total Assets ($Mil)	Safety Rating
Consumers Choice Health Ins Co	South Carolina	Health	01/06/16	92.4	D (Weak)
Moda Health Plan Inc	Oregon	Health	01/28/16	445.5	D+ (Weak)
Family Health Hawaii MBS	Hawaii	Health	04/07/16	5.5	D (Weak)
Health Republic Ins of NY Corp	New York	Health	04/22/16	525.3	D (Weak)
Coordinated Health Mutual Inc	Ohio	Health	5/26/16	94.9	E (Very Weak)
HealthyCT Inc	Connecticut	Health	07/01/16	112.3	D+ (Weak)
Oregons Health Co-Op	Oregon	Health	07/11/16	46.6	D (Weak)
Land of Lincoln Mut Health Ins Co	Illinois	Health	07/14/16	107.8	D+ (Weak)
Excalibur Reins Corp	Pennsylvania	P&C	07/18/16	9.0	U (Unrated)
Castlepoint Florida Ins	Florida	P&C	07/28/16	100.00	D (Weak)
Castlepoint Insurance Co	New York	P&C	07/28/16	178.4	E (Very Weak)
Castlepoint National Ins Co	California	P&C	07/28/16	355.1	C- (Fair)
Hermitage Insurance Co	New York	P&C	07/28/16	167.6	E+ (Very Weak)
Massachusetts Homeland Ins Co	Massachusetts	P&C	07/28/16	8.9	C (Fair)
North East Insurance Co	Maine	P&C	07/28/16	35.9	D (Weak)
York Ins Co of Maine	Maine	P&C	07/28/16	47.0	C (Fair)
Careconcepts Ins Inc A RRG	Montana	P&C	08/08/16	3.8	E+ (Very Weak)
Freelancers Consumer Operated	New Jersey	Health	09/12/16	135.3	D+ (Weak)
Doctors & Surgeons Natl RRG IC	Kentucky	P&C	10/07/16	9.1	E+ (Very Weak)
American Medical & Life Ins Co	New York	L&A	12/28/16	4.4	U (Unrated)

2015

Company Name	Headquarters	Industry	Date of Failure	At Date of Failure	
				Total Assets ($Mil)	Safety Rating
Millers Classified Ins Co	Illinois	P&C	01/20/15	2.7	E (Very Weak)
Eveready Ins Co	New York	P&C	01/29/15	10.6	E- (Very Weak)
Jordan Funeral and Ins Co, Inc	Alabama	L&H	02/17/15	1.1	U (Unrated)
Drivers Insurance Co	New York	P&C	03/12/15	3.0	E- (Very Weak)
Lumbermens U/W Alliance	Missouri	P&C	05/19/15	354.3	E- (Very Weak)
Pinelands Ins Co RRG, Inc	D.C.	P&C	08/25/15	4.9	E (Very Weak)
Louisiana Hlth Cooperative, Inc	Louisiana	Health	09/01/15	59.5	E (Very Weak)
Affirmative Ins Co	Illinois	P&C	09/16/15	181.2	E (Very Weak)
Affirmative Casualty Ins Co	Louisiana	P&C	10/05/15	32.6	D+ (Weak)
Affirmative Direct Ins Co	New York	P&C	10/05/15	5.3	U (Unrated)
Nevada Health Co-op	Nevada	Health	10/14/15	47.9	E- (Very Weak)
WINHealth Partners	Wyoming	Health	10/21/15	34.0	D (Weak)
Health Republic Ins Co	Oregon	Health	10/21/15	8.8	E (Very Weak)
Kentucky Hlth Cooperative Inc	Kentucky	Health	10/29/15	189.5	D+ (Weak)
Regis Ins Co	Pennsylvania	P&C	10/30/15	0.6	E- (Very Weak)
Meritus Health Partners	Arizona	Health	10/30/15	43.0	D+ (Weak)
Meritus Mutual Health Partners	Arizona	Health	10/30/15	45.8	D (Weak)
Arches Mutual Ins Co	Utah	Health	11/02/15	77.2	D (Weak)
Lincoln General Ins Co	Pennsylvania	P&C	11/05/15	65.6	E- (Very Weak)
Advantage Health Solutions Inc	Indiana	Health	11/06/15	64.2	E (Very Weak)
Colorado Hlth Ins Coop Inc	Colorado	Health	11/10/15	108.7	D+ (Weak)
Consumer Mut Ins of Michigan	Michigan	Health	11/13/15	60.4	E- (Very Weak)

2014

Company Name	Headquarters	Industry	Date of Failure	At Date of Failure	
				Total Assets ($Mil)	Safety Rating
Union Mutual Ins Co	Oklahoma	P&C	01/24/14	5.1	E+ (Very Weak)
Commonwealth Ins Co	Pennsylvania	P&C	03/20/14	1.1	E (Very Weak)
LEMIC Ins Co	Louisiana	P&C	03/31/14	51.6	D (Weak)
Interstate Bankers Casualty Co	Illinois	P&C	04/16/14	16.2	D+ (Weak)
Freestone Ins Co	Delaware	P&C	04/28/14	421.2	D- (Weak)
Alameda Alliance For Health	California	Health	05/05/14	176.3	D (Weak)
Sunshine State Ins Co	Florida	P&C	06/03/14	22.9	E+ (Very Weak)
Physicians United Plan Inc	Florida	Health	06/09/14	110.7	E (Very Weak)
Professional Aviation Ins Co	Nevada	P&C	07/03/14	N/A	N/A
Red Rock Ins Co	Oklahoma	P&C	08/01/14	28.5	E+ (Very Weak)
DLE Life Ins Co	Louisiana	L&H	10/02/14	39.3	D- (Weak)
Mothe Life Ins Co	Louisiana	L&H	10/02/14	15.2	E- (Very Weak)
First Keystone RRG Inc	S. Carolina	P&C	10/21/14	13.6	E+ (Very Weak)
PROAIR Risk Retention Grp Inc	Nevada	P&C	11/12/14	0.5	U (Unrated)
SeeChange Health Ins Co	California	Health	11/19/14	23.4	D- (Weak)
Florida Healthcare Plus, Inc	Florida	Health	12/10/14	11.1	U (Unrated)
CoOportunity Health, Inc	Iowa	Health	12/23/14	195.7	U (Unrated)

State Insurance Commissioners'

Website and Departmental Phone Numbers

State	Official's Title	Website Address	Phone Number
Alabama	Commissioner	www.aldoi.org	(334) 269-3550
Alaska	Director	www.dced.state.ak.us/insurance/	(907) 465-2515
Arizona	Director	www.id.state.az.us	(800) 325-2548
Arkansas	Commissioner	www.insurance.arkansas.gov	(800) 282-9134
California	Commissioner	www.insurance.ca.gov	(800) 927-4357
Colorado	Commissioner	www.dora.state.co.us/insurance/	(800) 930-3745
Connecticut	Commissioner	www.ct.gov/cid/	(860) 297-3800
Delaware	Commissioner	www.state.de.us/inscom/	(302) 674-7300
Dist. of Columbia	Commissioner	disr.dc.gov/disr/	(202) 727-8000
Florida	Commissioner	www.fldfs.com	(800) 342-2762
Georgia	Commissioner	www.gainsurance.org	(800) 656-2298
Hawaii	Commissioner	www.hawaii.gov/dcca/areas/ins/	(808) 586-2790
Idaho	Director	www.doi.idaho.gov	(800) 721-3272
Illinois	Director	www.idfpr.com/doi/	(217) 782-4515
Indiana	Commissioner	www.ia.org/idoi/	(317) 232-2385
Iowa	Commissioner	www.iid.state.ia.us	(877) 955-1212
Kansas	Commissioner	www.ksinsurance.org	(800) 432-2484
Kentucky	Executive Director	www.doi.ppr.ky.gov/kentucky/	(800) 595-6053
Louisiana	Commissioner	www.ldi.state.la.us	(800) 259-5300
Maine	Superintendent	www.maine.gov/pfr/insurance/	(800) 300-5000
Maryland	Commissioner	www.mdinsurance.state.md.us	(800) 492-6116
Massachusetts	Commissioner	www.mass.gov/doi/	(617) 521-7794
Michigan	Commissioner	www.michigan.gov/cis/	(877) 999-6442
Minnesota	Commissioner	www.commerce.state.mn.us	(651) 296-4026
Mississippi	Commissioner	www.doi.state.ms.us	(800) 562-2957
Missouri	Director	www.insurance.mo.gov/	(800) 726-7390
Montana	Commissioner	www.sao.state.mt.us	(800) 332-6148
Nebraska	Director	www.nebraska.gov	(402) 471-2306
Nevada	Commissioner	doi.state.nv.us	(775) 687-4270
New Hampshire	Commissioner	www.nh.gov/insurance/	(800) 852-3416
New Jersey	Commissioner	www.state.nj.us/dobi/	(800) 446-7467
New Mexico	Superintendent	www.nmprc.state.nm.us/id.htm	(888) 427-5772
New York	Superintendent	www.ins.state.ny.us	(800) 342-3736
North Carolina	Commissioner	www.ncdoi.com	(800) 546-5664
North Dakota	Commissioner	www.nd.gov/ndins/	(800) 247-0560
Ohio	Director	www.ohioinsurance.gov	(800) 686-1526
Oklahoma	Commissioner	www.oid.state.ok.us	(800) 522-0071
Oregon	Insurance Administrator	www.cbs.state.or.us/ins/	(503) 947-7980
Pennsylvania	Commissioner	www.ins.state.pa.us/ins/	(877) 881-6388
Puerto Rico	Commissioner	www.ocs.gobierno.pr	(787) 722-8686
Rhode Island	Superintendent	www.dbr.state.ri.us	(401) 222-2223
South Carolina	Director	www.doi..sc.gov	(800) 768-3467
South Dakota	Director	www.state.sd.us/drr2/reg/insurance/	(605) 773-3563
Tennessee	Commissioner	www.state.tn.us/commerce/insurance/	(800) 342-4029
Texas	Commissioner	www.tdi.state.tx.us	(800) 252-3439
Utah	Commissioner	www.insurance.utah.gov	(800) 439-3805
Vermont	Commissioner	www.bishca.state.vt.us	(802) 828-3301
Virgin Islands	Lieutenant Governor	www.ltg.gov.vi	(340) 774-7166
Virginia	Commissioner	www.scc.virginia.gov/division/boi/	(877) 310-6560
Washington	Commissioner	www.insurance.wa.gov	(800) 562-6900
West Virginia	Commissioner	www.wvinsurance.gov	(304) 558-3386
Wisconsin	Commissioner	oci.wi.gov	(800) 236-8517
Wyoming	Commissioner	insurance.state.wy.us	(800) 438-5768

Glossary

This glossary contains the most important terms used in this publication.

Admitted Assets The total of all investments and business interests that are acceptable under statutory accounting rules.

Asset/Liability Matching The designation of particular investments (assets) to particular policy obligations (liabilities) so that investments mature at the appropriate times and with appropriate yields to meet policy obligations as they come due.

Asset Valuation Reserve (AVR) A liability established under statutory accounting rules whose purpose is to protect the company's surplus from the effects of defaults and market value fluctuation on stocks, bonds, mortgages, and real estate. This replaces the Mandatory Securities Valuation Reserve (MSVR) and is more comprehensive in that it includes a mortgage loss reserve, whereas the MSVR did not.

Average Recession A recession involving a decline in real GDP which is approximately equivalent to the average of the postwar recessions of 1957-58, 1960, 1970, 1974-75, 1980, 1981-82, 1990-1991, 2001, and 2007-2009. It is assumed, however, that in today's market, the financial losses suffered from a recession of that magnitude would be greater than those experienced in previous decades. (See also "Severe Recession.").

Capital Strictly speaking, capital refers to funds raised through the sale of common and preferred stock. Mutual companies have capital in the form of retained earnings. In a more general sense, the term capital is commonly used to refer to a company's equity or net worth, that is, the difference between assets and liabilities (i.e., capital and surplus as shown on the balance sheet).

Capital Resources The sum of various resources which serve as a capital cushion to losses, including capital, surplus, and Asset Valuation Reserve (AVR).

Capitalization Index An index, expressed on a scale of zero to ten, with seven or higher considered excellent, that measures the adequacy of the company's capital resources to deal with a variety of business and economic scenarios. It combines Risk-Adjusted Capital Ratios #1 and #2 as well as a leverage test that examines pricing risk.

Cash and Demand Deposits — Includes cash on hand and on deposit. A negative figure indicates that the company has more checks outstanding than current funds to cover those checks. This is not an unusual situation for an insurance company.

Collateralized Mortgage Obligation (CMO) — Mortgage-backed bond that splits the payments from mortgage pools into different classes, called tranches. The investor may purchase a bond or tranche that passes through to him or her the principal and interest payments made by the mortgage holders in that specific maturity class (usually two, five, 10, or 20 years). The risk associated with a CMO is in the variation of the payment speed on the mortgage pool which, if different than originally assumed, can cause the total return to vary greatly.

Common and Preferred Stocks — See "Stocks".

Deposit Funds — Accumulated contributions of a group out of which immediate annuities are purchased as the individual members of the group retire.

Direct Premiums Written — Total gross premiums derived from policies issued directly by the company. This figure excludes the impact of reinsurance.

Safety Rating — Weiss Safety Ratings grade insurers on a scale from A (Excellent) to F (Failed). Ratings are based on five major factors: investment safety, policy leverage, capitalization, profitability, and stability of operations.

Five-Year Profitability Index — See "Profitability Index."

Government Securities — Securities issued and/or guaranteed by U.S. and foreign governments which are rated as highest quality (Class 1) by state insurance commissioners. Included in this category are bonds issued by governmental agencies and guaranteed with the full faith and credit of the government. Regardless of the issuing entity, they are viewed as being relatively safer than the other investment categories. See "Investment Grade Bonds" to determine which items are excluded from this category.

Health Claims Reserve — Funds set aside from premiums for the eventual payment of health benefits after the end of the statement year.

Insurance Risk — The risk that the level of claims and related expenses will exceed current premiums plus reserves allocated for their payment.

Interest Rate Risk — The risk that, due to changes in interest rates, investment income will not meet the needs of policy commitments. This risk can be reduced by effective asset/liability matching.

Invested Assets	The total size of the firm's investment portfolio.
Investment Grade Bonds	This covers all investment grade bonds other than those listed in "Government Securities" (above). Specifically, this includes: (1) nonguaranteed obligations of governments, (2) obligations of governments rated as Class 2 by state insurance commissioners, (3) state and municipal bonds, plus (4) investment grade corporate bonds.
Investment Safety Index	Measured on a scale of zero to ten, with ten being the best and seven or better considered strong. Each investment area is rated as to quality and vulnerability during an unfavorable economic environment (updated using quarterly data when available).
Investments in Affiliates	Includes bonds, preferred stocks, and common stocks, as well as other vehicles which many insurance companies use to invest in, and establish a corporate link with affiliated companies.
Life and Annuity Claims Reserve	Funds set aside from premiums for the eventual payment of life and annuity claims.
Liquidity Index	An index, expressed on a scale from zero to ten, with seven or higher considered excellent, which measures the company's ability to raise the necessary cash to meet policyholder obligations. This index includes a stress test which considers the consequences of a spike in claims or a run on policy surrenders. Sometimes a company may appear to have the necessary resources, but may be unable to sell its investments at the prices at which they are valued in the company's financial statements.
Mandatory Security Valuation Reserve (MSVR)	Reserve for investment losses and asset value fluctuation mandated by the state insurance commissioners for companies registered as life and health insurers. As of December 31, 1992, this was replaced by the Asset Valuation Reserve. HMDI companies are not required to establish such a reserve.
Moderate Loss Scenario	An economic decline from current levels approximately equivalent to that of the average postwar recession.
Mortgages in Good Standing	Mortgages which are current in their payments (excludes mortgage-backed securities).
Net Premiums Written	The total dollar volume of premiums retained by the company. This figure is equal to direct premiums written, plus reinsurance assumed less reinsurance ceded.
Noninvestment Grade Bonds	Low-rated issues, commonly known as "junk bonds," which carry a high risk as defined by the state insurance commissioners. These include bond Classes 3 - 6.
Nonperforming Mortgages	Mortgages which are (a) 90 days or more past due or (b) in process of foreclosure.
Other Investments	Items not included in any of the other categories such as contract loans (which include premium notes), receivables for securities, aggregate write-ins and other invested assets.

Other Structured Securities	Nonresidential-mortgage-related and other securitized loan-backed or asset-backed securities. This category also includes CMOs with noninvestment grade ratings.
Policy Leverage	A measure of insurance risk based on the relationship of net premiums to capital resources.
Policy Loans	Loans to policyholders under insurance contracts.
Profitability Index	Measured on a scale of zero to ten, with ten being the best and seven or better considered strong. A composite of five factors: (1) gain or loss on operations, (2) consistency of operating results, (3) impact of operating results on surplus, (4) adequacy of investment income as compared to the needs of policy reserves, and (5) expenses in relation to industry averages. Thus, the overall index is an indicator of the health of a company's current and past operations.
Purchase Money Mortgages	Mortgages written by an insurance company to facilitate the sale of property owned by the company.
Real Estate	Direct real estate investments including property (a) occupied by the company, (b) acquired through foreclosure and (c) purchased as an investment.
Reinsurance Assumed	Insurance risk acquired by taking on partial or full responsibility for claims on policies written by other companies. (See "Reinsurance Ceded.")
Reinsurance Ceded	Insurance risk sold to another company.
Risk-Adjusted Capital	The capital resources that would be needed in a worsening economic environment (same as "Target Capital").
Risk-Adjusted Capital Ratio #1	The capital resources which a company currently has, in relation to the resources that would be needed to deal with a moderate loss scenario. This scenario is based on historical experience during an average recession and adjusted to reflect current conditions and vulnerabilities (updated using quarterly data when available).
Risk-Adjusted Capital Ratio #2	The capital resources which a company currently has, in relation to the resources that would be needed to deal with a severe loss scenario. This scenario is based on historical experience of the postwar period and adjusted to reflect current conditions and the potential impact of a severe recession (updated using quarterly data when available).
Separate Accounts	Funds segregated from the general account and valued at market. Used to fund indexed products, such as variable life and variable annuity products.
Severe Loss Scenario	An economic decline from current levels in which the loss experience of the single worst year of the postwar period is extended for a period of three years. (See also "Moderate Loss Scenario" above.)
Severe Recession	A prolonged economic slowdown in which the single worst year of the postwar period is extended for a period of three years. (See also "Average Recession" above.)

Stability Index Measured on a scale of zero to ten. This integrates a wide variety of factors that reflects the company's financial stability and diversification of risk.

State of Domicile Although most insurance companies are licensed to do business in many states, they have only one state of domicile. This is the state that has primary regulatory responsibility for the company. Use the state of domicile to make absolutely sure that you have the correct company. Bear in mind, however, that this need not be the state where the company's main offices are located.

State Guaranty Funds Funds that are designed to raise cash from existing insurance carriers to cover policy claims of bankrupt insurance companies.

Stocks Common and preferred equities, including ownership in affiliates.

Surplus The difference between assets and liabilities, including paid-in contributed surplus, plus the statutory equivalent of "retained earnings" in noninsurance business corporations.

Target Capital See "Risk-Adjusted Capital."

Total Assets Total admitted assets, including investments and other business assets. See "Admitted Assets."